Contemporary Theatre, Film, and Television

ISSN 0749-064X

Contemporary Theatre, Film, and Television

A Biographical Guide Featuring Performers, Directors, Writers, Producers, Designers, Managers, Choreographers, Technicians, Composers, Executives, Dancers, and Critics in the United States and Great Britain

Emily J. McMurray, Editor

Volume 10

Includes Cumulative Index Containing References to *Who's Who in the Theatre* and *Who Was Who in the Theatre*

Gale Research Inc. • DETROIT • LONDON

STAFF

Emily J. McMurray, *Editor*

Elizabeth A. Des Chenes, Kevin S. Hile, James F. Kamp, Denise E. Kasinec,
Thomas Kozikowski, Susan M. Reicha, Mary K. Ruby, and Polly A. Vedder, *Associate Editors*

Carol A. Brennan, Joanna Brod, Bruce Ching, Marie Ellavich, David M. Galens,
David Johnson, Mark F. Mikula, Tom Pendergast, Pamela L. Shelton, and Deborah A. Stanley,
Assistant Editors

Arlene True, *Sketchwriter*

Marilyn K. Basel, Katherine Huebl, Janice Jorgensen, Sharon Malinowski, Edward G. Scheff,
Neil R. Schlager, and Diane Telgen, *Contributing Editors*

James G. Lesniak, *Senior Editor*

Victoria B. Cariappa, *Research Manager*
Mary Rose Bonk, *Research Supervisor*
Reginald A. Carlton, Clare Collins, Andrew Guy Malonis, and Norma Sawaya, *Editorial Associates*
Mike Avolio, Patricia Bowen, Rachel A. Dixon,
Shirley Gates, Sharon McGilvray, and Devra M. Sladics, *Editorial Assistants*

Mary Beth Trimper, *Production Manager*
Mary Winterhalter, *External Production Assistant*

Special acknowledgment is due to James F. Kamp and Kenneth R. Shepherd for their technical assistance in the preparation of this volume.

The paper used in this publication meets the minimum requirements of American National Standard for Information Sciences—Permanence Paper for Printed Library Materials, ANSI Z39.48-1984. ™

Library of Congress Catalog Card Number 62-52046
ISBN 0-8103-2073-8
ISSN 0010-7468

Printed in the United States of America.
Published simultaneously in the United Kingdom
by Gale Research International Limited
(An affiliated company of Gale Research Inc.)

Contents

Preface

Provides Broad, Single-Source Coverage in the Entertainment Field

Contemporary Theatre, Film, and Television (*CTFT*) is a biographical reference series designed to provide students, educators, researchers, librarians, and general readers with information on a wide range of entertainment figures. Unlike single-volume reference works that focus on a limited number of artists or on a specific segment of the entertainment field, *CTFT* is an ongoing publication that includes entries on individuals active in the theatre, film, *and* television industries. Before the publication of *CTFT,* information-seekers had no choice but to consult several different sources in order to locate the in-depth biographical and credit data that makes *CTFT*'s one-stop coverage the most comprehensive available on the lives and work of performing arts professionals.

Scope

CTFT covers not only performers, directors, writers, and producers, but also behind-the-scenes specialists such as designers, managers, choreographers, technicians, composers, executives, dancers, and critics from the United States and Great Britain. With more than 400 entries in *CTFT 10,* the series now provides biographies on nearly 5800 people involved in all aspects of theatre, film, and television.

CTFT gives primary emphasis to people who are currently active. New entries are prepared on major stars as well as those who are just beginning to win acclaim for their work. *CTFT* also includes entries on personalities who have died but whose work commands lasting interest.

Compilation Methods

CTFT editors identify candidates for inclusion in the series by consulting biographical dictionaries, industry directories, entertainment annuals, trade and general interest periodicals, newspapers, and on-line databases. Entries are compiled from published biographical sources and then mailed to the listees or their agents for review and verification.

Revised Entries

To ensure *CTFT*'s timeliness and comprehensiveness, entries from previous volumes, as well as from Gale Research's *Who's Who in the Theatre,* are updated for individuals who have been active enough to require revision of their earlier biographies. Such individuals will merit revised entries as often as there is substantial new information to provide. Obituary notices for deceased entertainment personalities already listed in *CTFT* are also published.

Accessible Format Makes Data Easy to Locate

CTFT entries, modeled after those in Gale's highly regarded *Contemporary Authors* series, are written in a clear, readable style designed to help users focus quickly on specific facts. The following is a summary of the information sections found in *CTFT* sketches:

- *ENTRY HEADING:* the form of the name by which the listee is best known.

- *PERSONAL:* full or original name; dates and places of birth and death; family data; colleges attended, degrees earned, and professional training; political and religious affiliations when known; avocational interests.

- *ADDRESSES:* office, agent, publicist, and/or manager addresses.

- *CAREER:* tagline indicating principal areas of entertainment work; resume of career positions and other vocational achievements; military service.

- *MEMBER:* memberships and offices held in professional, union, civic, and social organizations.

- *AWARDS, HONORS:* theatre, film, and television awards and nominations; literary and civic awards; honorary degrees.

- *CREDITS:* comprehensive title-by-title listings of theatre, film, and television appearance and work credits, including roles and production data as well as debut and genre information.

- *RECORDINGS:* album, single song, video, and taped reading releases; recording labels and dates when available.

- *WRITINGS:* title-by-title listing of plays, screenplays, scripts, and musical compositions along with production information; books, including autobiographies, and other publications.

- *ADAPTATIONS:* a list of films, plays, and other media which have been adapted from the listee's work.

- *SIDELIGHTS:* favorite roles; portions of agent-prepared biographies or personal statements from the listee when available.

- *OTHER SOURCES:* books and periodicals where interviews or feature stories can be found.

Access Thousands of Entries Using *CTFT*'s Cumulative Index

Each volume of *CTFT* contains a cumulative index to the entire series. As an added feature, this index also includes references to all seventeen editions of *Who's Who in the Theatre* and to the four-volume compilation *Who Was Who in the Theatre.*

Suggestions Are Welcome

Contemporary Theatre, Film, and Television is intended to serve as a useful reference tool for a wide audience, so comments about any aspect of this work are encouraged. Suggestions of entertainment professionals to include in future volumes are also welcome. Send comments and suggestions to: The Editor, *Contemporary Theatre, Film, and Television,* Gale Research Inc., 835 Penobscot Bldg., Detroit, MI 48226-4094; call toll-free at 1-800-347-GALE; or fax to 1-313-961-6599.

Contemporary Theatre, Film, and Television

Contemporary Theatre, Film, and Television

** Indicates that a listing has been compiled from secondary sources believed to be reliable, but has not been personally verified for this edition by the listee or his/her representative.*

ACKERMAN, Harry S. 1912-1991

OBITUARY NOTICE—See index for *CTFT* sketch: Born November 17, 1912, in Albany, NY; died of pulmonary failure, February 3, 1991, in Burbank, CA. Producer. During his career Ackerman supervised the production elements of several popular television series, including *Gunsmoke, The Jack Benny Show,* and *I Love Lucy.* He developed and produced *Leave It to Beaver,* co-created *Bewitched*—two series that remain popular in reruns—and was involved in the production of *Studio One* and *Suspense.* Ackerman held several administrative positions with the CBS network, and he also worked for Screen Gems (now Columbia Pictures Television) and Paramount. In addition, he was president of his own company, Harry Ackerman Productions.

OBITUARIES AND OTHER SOURCES:

BOOKS

Who's Who in America, 46th edition, Marquis, 1990, p. 12.

PERIODICALS

New York Times, February 6, 1991.

* * *

ADAMS, Tony 1953-

PERSONAL: Full name, Anthony Patrick Adams; born February 15, 1953, in Dublin, Ireland; son of Charles (a contractor) and Teresa (Fitzsimons) Adams; married; children: Andrew, Alister. *Education:* Attended Florida Atlantic University and Pepperdine University; received special training at Dublin Communication Centre.

ADDRESSES: Office—Blake Edwards Entertainment, 9336 West Washington Blvd., Culver City, CA 90230.

CAREER: Producer. Assistant to director John Boorman; associated with Burt Reynolds; Blake Edwards Entertainment, Culver City, CA, producer, beginning in 1971, appointed president of Blake Edwards Co., 1988. International Institute of Kidney Diseases, past chair; Operation California, member of board of trustees; Committee of Concern for Central America, member.

MEMBER: Academy of Motion Picture Arts and Sciences, American Film Institute, Producers Guild of America.

AWARDS, HONORS: Golden Globe Award nomination, 1979, for *10;* Golden Globe Award nomination, 1981, for *S.O.B.;* Golden Globe Award, Cesar Award from French Academy of Cinema Arts and Techniques, and Golden David Award from David Di Donatello, all 1982, and Premio Sant Jordi de cinematografia de R.N.E., 1983, all for *Victor/Victoria;* President's Volunteer Action Award, 1983; Golden Globe Award, 1984, for *Micki and Maude;* Jean Hersholt Humanitarian Award nomination, Academy of Motion Picture Arts and Sciences.

CREDITS:

FILM PRODUCER, EXCEPT WHERE INDICATED

Associate producer, *Return of the Pink Panther,* United Artists (UA), 1975.

Associate producer, *The Pink Panther Strikes Again,* UA, 1976.

Executive producer, *Revenge of the Pink Panther,* UA, 1978.

(With Blake Edwards) *10,* Warner Brothers, 1979.

(With Edwards) *S.O.B.,* Paramount, 1981.

(With Edwards) *Victor/Victoria,* Metro-Goldwyn-Mayer (MGM)/UA, 1982.

(With Edwards) *Trail of the Pink Panther,* MGM/UA, 1982.

(With Edwards) *Curse of the Pink Panther,* MGM, 1983.
(With Edwards) *The Man Who Loved Women,* Columbia, 1983.
Micki and Maude, Columbia, 1984.
That's Life!, Columbia, 1986.
A Fine Mess, Columbia, 1987.
Blind Date, Tri-Star, 1988.
Sunset, Tri-Star, 1988.
Skin Deep, Twentieth Century-Fox, 1989.
Switch, Warner Brothers, 1991.

TELEVISION WORK; MOVIES

Executive producer, *Peter Gunn,* ABC, 1989.

Also worked as producer of *Because We Care.*

TELEVISION WORK; EPISODIC

Producer, "Justin Case," *The Disney Sunday Movie,* ABC, 1988.

STAGE WORK

Producer of major tours, including Julie Andrews's London concert and her U.S. and Japan tours, 1972-75.

RECORDINGS:

ALBUMS

Producer of *Julie Andrews Live in Concert,* 1980.

WRITINGS:

PLAYS

The English Can't Remember . . . The Irish Can't Forget, produced at Pepperdine University, Malibu, CA, 1972.*

* * *

ALDA, Alan 1936-

PERSONAL: Original name, Alphonso Joseph D'Abruzzo; name legally changed; born January 28, 1936, in New York, NY; son of Alphonso Giovanni Giuseppe Roberto (an actor and singer under stage name Robert Alda) and Joan (Browne) D'Abruzzo; married Arlene Weiss (a teacher, photographer, and musician), March 15, 1957; children: Eve, Elizabeth, Beatrice. *Education:* Fordham University, B.S., 1956; studied at Cleveland Playhouse; attended Paul Sills's Improvisational Workshop at *Second City,* New York City, 1963.

ADDRESSES: Office—Martin Bregman Productions, 641 Lexington Avenue, New York, NY 10022. *Contact*—MCA/Universal Studios, Inc., 100 Universal City Plaza #507, Universal City, CA 91608.

CAREER: Actor, writer, and director. Performed Abbott-and-Costello-style sketches with father at the Hollywood Canteen, 1945. Appeared in the improvisational revues *Compass,* Yachtsman Hotel, Hyannis, MA, 1962, and *Second City,* Second City at Square East, New York City, 1963. Worked as a teacher at Compass School of Improvisation, New York City, 1963. Presidential appointee, National Commission on the Observance of International Women's Year, 1976, and the National ERA Countdown Campaign, 1982. Trustee of the Museum of Broadcasting, 1985, and the Rockefeller Foundation, 1989. *Military Service:* U.S. Army Reserve; became second lieutenant.

MEMBER: Screen Actors Guild, Directors Guild of America, Writers Guild of America, American Federation of Television and Radio Artists, Actors Equity Association.

AWARDS, HONORS: All for *M*A*S*H:* Emmy Award nominations, actor—comedy series, 1973, 1975, 1976, 1977, 1978, 1979, 1980, 1981, and 1983; Emmy Awards, actor—comedy series, 1974 and 1982; Emmy Award, actor of the year—series, 1974; Golden Globe Awards, best actor in a series—musical/comedy, 1975, 1976, 1980, 1981, 1982, and 1983; Emmy Award nominations, director—comedy series, 1975, for episode "Bulletin Board," 1976, for "The Kids," 1979, for "Dear Sis," 1980, for "Dreams," 1981, for "The Life You Save," 1982, for "Where There's a Will, There's a War," and 1983, for "Goodbye, Farewell and Amen"; Outstanding Directorial Achievement Awards for Television—Comedy, Directors Guild of America, 1976, for episode "Dear Sigmund," 1981, for "The Life You Save," and 1982, for "Where There's a Will, There's a War"; Emmy Awards, director—comedy series, 1977, for episode "Dear Sigmund," and 1978 (with Burt Metcalfe), for "Comrades in Arms—Part I"; Emmy Award nominations, writing—comedy series, 1977, for episode "Dear Sigmund," 1978, for "Fallen Idol," and 1982, for "Follies of the Living, Concerns of the Dead"; Writers Guild of America Award, 1977; Emmy Award, writing—comedy or comedy-variety or music series, 1979, for episode "Inga"; Humanitas Award for writing.

Ford Foundation grant; *Theatre World* award, 1963, for *Fair Game for Lovers;* Antoinette Perry Award nomination, actor (musical), 1967, for *The Apple Tree;* Emmy Award nomination, actor—drama special, 1974, for *6 Rms Riv Vu;* Golden Apple Star of the Year, Hollywood Women's Press Club, 1974 and 1979; honorary degrees, Fordham University, 1978, Drew University, 1979, Columbia University, 1979, Connecticut College, 1980, and Kenyon College, 1982; Emmy Award nomination, actor—drama or comedy special, 1978, for *Kill Me If You Can;* People's Choice Awards, television—male performer, Procter & Gamble Productions, 1979, 1980, 1981, and 1982; People's Choice Awards, all-around favorite male entertainer, 1980 and 1981; Hasty Pudding Man of the Year, Hasty Pudding Theatricals, 1980; NATO Star of the Year, 1981; D. W. Griffith Award, and New York Film Critics Association Award, best supporting actor, 1989, both for *Crimes and Misdemeanors;* Antoinette Perry Award nomination, performance by a leading actor in a play, 1992, for *Jake's Women.*

CREDITS:

TELEVISION APPEARANCES; SERIES

That Was the Week That Was, NBC, 1964.
Capt. Benjamin Franklin (Hawkeye) Pierce, *M*A*S*H* (also see below), CBS, 1972-83.
Jack Burroughs, *The Four Seasons* (based on film of same title; also see below), CBS, 1984.

TELEVISION APPEARANCES; MOVIES

Marshall Barnett, *Playmates,* ABC, 1972.
Jonathan Paige, *Truman Capote's "The Glass House,"* CBS, 1972.
Sheriff Dan Barnes, *Isn't It Shocking?,* ABC, 1973.
Caryl W. Chessman, *Kill Me If You Can,* NBC, 1977.

TELEVISION APPEARANCES; SPECIALS

Hotel 90, CBS, 1973.
Lily, CBS, 1973.
Marlo Thomas and Friends in Free to Be . . . You and Me (also see below), ABC, 1974.
Paul Friedman, *6 Rms Riv Vu* (also see below), CBS, 1974.
Annie and the Hoods, ABC, 1974.
CBS: On the Air, CBS, 1978.
58th Annual Academy Awards Presentation, ABC, 1986.
Scared Sexless (also known as *Report on America: Scared Sexless*), NBC, 1987.
The 3rd Annual American Comedy Awards, ABC, 1989.
The All-Star Salute to Our Troops, CBS, 1991.
*Memories of M*A*S*H,* CBS, 1991.

TELEVISION APPEARANCES; EPISODIC

Phil Silvers Show, CBS, 1957.
Route 66, CBS, 1962.
Naked City, ABC, 1962.
The DuPont Show of the Week, NBC, 1962.
The Nurses, CBS, 1963.
The Shari Lewis Show, NBC, 1963.
East Side, West Side, CBS, 1963.
Trials of O'Brien, CBS, 1965.
The Match Game, NBC, 1965-66.
The David Frost Revue, syndicated, 1971.
Carol Burnett Show, CBS, 1974.

Also appeared as a guest on *Coronet Blue, Memory Lane,* and the *Today Show,* NBC.

TELEVISION APPEARANCES; PILOTS

Arnold Barker, *Where's Everett?,* CBS, 1966.
Frank St. John, *Higher and Higher, Attorneys at Law,* CBS, 1968.

OTHER TELEVISION APPEARANCES

The Tree and the Cross, ABC, 1964.
Out of the Flying Pan, NET (now PBS), 1966.
It's Almost Like Being, NET, 1966.

TELEVISION DIRECTOR; SERIES

(With others) *M*A*S*H* (including the episodes "Bulletin Board," "The Kids," "Dear Sigmund," "Dear Sis," "Comrades in Arms—Part I," "Dreams," "The Life You Save," "Where There's a Will, There's a War," and "Goodbye, Farewell and Amen"; also see below), CBS, 1972-83.

TELEVISION DIRECTOR; SPECIALS

(With Clark Jones) *6 Rms Riv Vu,* CBS, 1974.
(With Bill Davis and Fred Wolf) *Marlo Thomas and Friends in Free to Be . . . You and Me* (also see below), ABC, 1974.

TELEVISION WORK; PILOTS

Director and creator, *Hickey vs. Anybody* (also see below), NBC, 1976.
Producer (with Marc Merson), *Susan and Sam* (also see below), NBC, 1977.

TELEVISION WORK; SERIES

Executive producer (with Merson), producer (with Allan Katz and Don Reo), and creator, *We'll Get By* (also see below), CBS, 1975.
Executive producer (with Martin Bregman), and creator, *The Four Seasons* (also see below), CBS, 1984.

FILM APPEARANCES

Charley Cotchipee, *Gone Are the Days* (based on play *Purlie Victorious;* also known as *The Man from C.O.T.T.O.N.* and *Purlie Victorious;* also see below), Hammer, 1963.
George Plimpton, *Paper Lion,* United Artists, 1968.
Lt. (JG) Morton Krim, *The Extraordinary Seaman,* Metro-Goldwyn-Mayer (MGM), 1969.
Delano, *Jenny* (also known as *And Jenny Makes Three*), Cinerama, 1969.
Son Martin, *The Moonshine War,* MGM, 1970.
Myles Clarkson, *The Mephisto Waltz,* Twentieth Century-Fox, 1971.
Maj. Ritchie, *To Kill a Clown,* Twentieth Century-Fox, 1972.
Bill Warren, *California Suite,* Columbia, 1978.
George Peters, *Same Time, Next Year,* Universal, 1978.

Joe Tynan, *The Seduction of Joe Tynan* (also see below), Universal, 1979.

Jack Burroughs, *The Four Seasons* (also see below), Universal, 1981.

Michael Burgess, *Sweet Liberty* (also see below), Universal, 1986.

Steve Giardino, *A New Life* (also see below), Paramount, 1988.

Lester, *Crimes and Misdemeanors,* Orion, 1989.

Eddie Hopper, *Betsy's Wedding* (also see below), Touchstone-Buena Vista, 1990.

Also appeared in *The Killing Device,* 1991.

FILM DIRECTOR

The Four Seasons (also see below), Universal, 1981.

Sweet Liberty (also see below), Universal, 1986.

A New Life (also see below), Paramount, 1988.

Betsy's Wedding (also see below), Touchstone-Buena Vista, 1990.

STAGE APPEARANCES

Leo Davis, *Room Service,* Teatro del Eliseo, Rome, 1955.

Understudy for the role of Clarence "Lefty" McShane, *The Hot Corner,* John Golden Theatre, New York City, 1956.

Billy Tuck, *Nature's Way,* Valley Playhouse, Chagrin Falls, OH, 1958.

Telephone man, *Only in America,* Cort Theatre, New York City, 1959.

Sky Masterson, *Guys and Dolls,* Grand Theatre, Sullivan, IL, 1959.

Title role, *L'il Abner,* Grand Theatre, 1960.

Darwin's Theories (also see below), Madison Avenue Playhouse, New York City, 1960.

David, *The Woman with Red Hair,* Teatro dei Servi, Rome, 1961.

Fleider, and understudy for the title role, *Anatol,* Boston Arts Center, Boston, MA, 1961.

Fergie Howard, *Golden Fleecing,* Southbury Playhouse, CT, 1961.

Charley Cotchipee, *Purlie Victorious,* Cort Theatre, 1961, then Longacre Theatre, New York City, 1961-62.

Howard Mayer, *A Whisper in God's Ear,* Cricket Theatre, New York City, 1962.

Benny Bennington, *Fair Game for Lovers,* Cort Theatre, 1963.

Dr. Gilbert, *Cafe Crown,* Martin Beck Theatre, New York City, 1964.

Mike Mitchell, *Sunday in New York,* Bucks County Playhouse, New Hope, PA, 1964.

F. Sherman, *The Owl and the Pussycat,* ANTA Theatre, New York City, 1964-65.

Adam, "The Diary of Adam and Eve," Captain Sanjar, "The Lady or the Tiger?," and Flip, The Prince, Charming, "Passionella," in *The Apple Tree* (triple-bill; also see below), Shubert Theatre, New York City, 1966-67.

There's a Girl in My Soup, Playhouse-on-the-Mall, Paramus, NJ, 1968.

Stage Manager, *Our Town,* Shaftesbury Theatre, London, 1991.

Jake, *Jake's Women,* Neil Simon Theatre, New York City, 1992.

Also appeared as Jack Chesney in *Charley's Aunt,* Barnesville, PA, 1953; as Wade in *Roger the Sixth,* Artie in *Compulsion,* Irwin Trowbridge in *Three Men on a Horse,* and Horace in *The Little Foxes,* all in stock, 1957; and in own adaptation of *The Book of Job,* as David Williams in *Who Was That Lady I Saw You With?,* in *Monique,* and as Toni in *To Dorothy, a Son,* all at the Cleveland Playhouse, Cleveland, OH, 1958-59.

MAJOR TOURS

Willie Alvarez, *Memo,* U.S. cities, 1963.

Francis X. Dignan, *King of Hearts,* U.S. cities, 1963.

Woodrow O'Malley, *Watch the Birdie!,* U.S. cities, 1964.

STAGE DIRECTOR

The Midnight Ride of Alvin Blum, Westport Country Playhouse, CT, 1966, then Playhouse-on-the-Mall, 1966.

WRITINGS:

SCREENPLAYS

The Seduction of Joe Tynan, Universal, 1979.

The Four Seasons (also see below), Universal, 1981.

Sweet Liberty, Universal, 1986.

A New Life, Paramount, 1988.

Betsy's Wedding, Touchstone-Buena Vista, 1990.

TELEVISION SERIES

(With others) *M*A*S*H* (including the episodes "Dear Sigmund," "Fallen Idol," "Follies of the Living, Concerns of the Dead," and "Inga") CBS, 1972-83.

(With Katz, Susan Silver, and Peter Meyerson) *We'll Get By* (also see below), CBS, 1975.

(With others) *The Four Seasons,* CBS, 1984.

TELEVISION PILOTS

We'll Get By, CBS, 1974.

Hickey vs. Anybody, NBC, 1976.

Susan and Sam, NBC, 1977.

STAGE SKETCHES

Darwin's Theories (musical revue), produced at Madison Avenue Playhouse, New York City, 1960.

OTHER

Co-author of dictionary *The Language of Show Biz.* Contributor to periodicals, including *Ms., TV Guide,* and *Redbook.*

RECORDINGS:

ALBUMS

(With Marlo Thomas and others) *Free to Be. . . You and Me,* Bell Records, 1973.

The Apple Tree (original cast recording), Columbia Records.

OTHER SOURCES:

BOOKS

Contemporary Authors, Volume 103, Gale, 1981.
Strait, Raymond, *Alan Alda: A Biography,* St. Martin's, 1983.

PERIODICALS

American Film, April, 1981.
New York Times, April 19, 1981.
People, June 15, 1981.

* * *

ALLEY, Kirstie 1955-

PERSONAL: Born January 12 (one source says 21), 1955, in Wichita, KS; married Parker Stevenson (an actor), early 1980s. *Education:* Attended Kansas State University and University of Kansas.

ADDRESSES: Office—NBC-TV, 30 Rockefeller Plaza, New York, NY 10112. *Agent*—Barrett/Benson/McCartt & Weston, 10390 Santa Monica Blvd., No. 310, Los Angeles, CA 90025. *Publicist*—Annett Wolf, Inc., 1033 Gavlev Ave., Suite 208, Los Angeles, CA 90024.

CAREER: Actress. Worked as interior decorator prior to early 1980s; appeared as a contestant on game shows.

AWARDS, HONORS: Emmy Award nominations, 1988 and 1990, and Emmy Award, 1991, all for outstanding lead actress in a comedy series, Golden Globe Award, best actress in a musical/comedy series, 1991, and Golden Globe Award nomination, best actress in a comedy series, 1992, all for *Cheers;* People's Choice Award, best female performer, Proctor & Gamble Productions, 1991.

CREDITS:

FILM APPEARANCES

Lieutenant Saavik, *Star Trek II: The Wrath of Kahn,* Paramount, 1982.
Claire Parker, *Blind Date,* New Line, 1984.
Barbara, *The Champions,* Embassy, 1984.
Jackie Rogers, *Runaway,* Tri-Star, 1984.
Robin Bishop, *Summer School,* Paramount, 1987.
Sarah, *Shoot to Kill,* Touchstone, 1988.
Joyce Palmer, *Loverboy,* Tri-Star, 1989.
Mollie, *Look Who's Talking,* Tri-Star, 1989.
Marjorie Turner, *Sibling Rivalry,* Columbia, 1990.
Jessie Bannister, *Madhouse,* Orion, 1990.
Mollie, *Look Who's Talking Too,* Tri-Star, 1990.

Also appeared in *Daddy's Home,* 1989; *One More Chance,* 1990; and *Mountain King,* Disney Pictures.

TELEVISION APPEARANCES; SERIES

Casey Collins, *Masquerade,* ABC, 1983-84.
Rebecca Howe, *Cheers,* NBC, 1987—.
Host, *Friday Night Videos,* NBC, 1989.

TELEVISION APPEARANCES; MOVIES

Patrice, *Sins of the Past,* ABC, 1984.
Gloria Steinham, *A Bunny's Tale,* ABC, 1985.
Maggie, *Stark: Mirror Image,* CBS, 1986.
Jamie Harris, *The Prince of Bel Air,* ABC, 1986.
Eliot Donato, *Infidelity,* ABC, 1987.

TELEVISION APPEARANCES; MINI-SERIES

Virgilia Hazard, *North and South,* ABC, 1985.
Virgilia Hazard Grady, *North and South: Book II,* ABC, 1986.

TELEVISION APPEARANCES; SPECIALS

Mickey's 60th Birthday Special (also known as *The Magical World of Disney*), NBC, 1988.
Presenter, *The 42nd Annual Primetime Emmy Awards,* Fox, 1990.
Cheers: Special 200th Episode Celebration, NBC, 1990.
Cutting Edge with Maria Shriver, NBC, 1990.
Time Warner Presents the Earth Day Special, ABC, 1990.
The Tonight Show Starring Johnny Carson: 28th Anniversary Special, NBC, 1990.
Hostess, *The Movie Awards,* CBS, 1991.
Victory and Valor: A Special Olympics All-Star Celebration (also known as *The International Special Olympics All-Star Gala*), ABC, 1991.

Also appeared in *The 5th Annual American Comedy Awards,* 1991; *Tow Heads;* and *A Midsummer Night's Dream.*

TELEVISION APPEARANCES; EPISODIC

"Don't Take My Wife, Please," *The Love Boat,* ABC, 1983.
"Out of the Night," *The Hitchhiker,* HBO, 1985.
"The Legacy of Billy B.," *The Hitchhiker,* HBO, 1987.

TELEVISION APPEARANCES; PILOTS

Draggin' Lady, *Highway Honeys,* NBC, 1983.

STAGE APPEARANCES

Margaret, *Cat on a Hot Tin Roof,* Mark Taper Forum, Los Angeles, CA, 1983.

Also appeared in *Answers.*

OTHER SOURCES:

PERIODICALS

People, July 26, 1982, p. 43; November 30, 1987, p. 122; October 29, 1990, p. 82.

Saturday Evening Post, January-February, 1990, p. 42.*

* * *

ALMENDROS, Nestor 1930-1992

OBITUARY NOTICE—See index for *CTFT* sketch: Born October 30, 1930, in Barcelona, Spain; immigrated to Cuba, 1948; died March 4, 1992, in New York, NY. Cinematographer. Almendros was an acclaimed cinematographer best known for his natural lighting techniques. In such films as *Kramer vs. Kramer, Sophie's Choice,* and *Days of Heaven,* for which he won an Academy Award, Almendros photographed oftentimes simple pictures—like an empty apartment or a close-up of a face—that seemed to express the atmosphere of the film. Almendros started his career making film shorts during the mid-1950s, then saw his cinematic career launched in the mid-1960s, when director Eric Rohmer hired him to film *Paris vu par.* Almendros followed as cinematographer on films of several noted European directors, including Francois Truffaut and Claude Chabrol. By the mid-1970s Almendros had come to the United States, where he shot such features as *Still of the Night, Places in the Heart, Goin' South,* 1991's *Billy Bathgate,* and some retakes of *The Mambo Kings.* In 1980, he saw the publication of his autobiography, *A Man with a Camera,* which recounted his career up to that point.

OBITUARIES AND OTHER SOURCES:

BOOKS

The International Dictionary of Films and Filmmakers, Volume 4: *Writers and Production Artists,* St. James Press, 1987, pp. 10-12.

Who's Who in America, Supplement to 46th edition, Marquis, 1991, p. 16.

PERIODICALS

American Cinematographer, May, 1992, p. 88.

Variety, March 9, 1992, p. 67.

ALMODOVAR, Pedro 1951-
(Patty Diphusa)

PERSONAL: Born September 25, 1951, in Calzada de Calatrava, Spain; son of Francisca Caballero. *Education:* Educated in Caceres, Spain.

ADDRESSES: Agent—Creative Artists Agency, 9830 Wilshire Blvd., Beverly Hills, CA 90212.

CAREER: Writer and director. Held a variety of jobs in Madrid, Spain, including telephone company worker, singer in rock band *Almodovar and McNamara,* actor with independent theater troupe *Los Goliardos,* and writer of comic strips and columns for underground newspapers.

AWARDS, HONORS: Glauber Rocha Award, best director, 1987, and New Generation Award, Los Angeles Film Critics Circle, both for *Law of Desire;* National Society of Film Critics Award, special citation for originality, 1988; Venice International Film Festival Prize, best screenplay award, National Board of Review of Motion Pictures Award, best foreign film, New York Film Critics Circle Award, best foreign film, and Felix Award, best young film, all 1988, and Academy Award nomination, best foreign film, and Orson Welles Award, best non-English language film, both 1989, all for *Women on the Verge of a Nervous Breakdown;* named Man of the Year by Spanish magazine *Cambio 16,* 1989.

CREDITS:

FILM DIRECTOR

Pepi, Luci, Bom y otros chicas del monton (title means "Pepi, Luci, Bom and a Whole Lot of Other Girls," other sources translate as "Pepi, Luci, Bom and Other Girls on the Heap" or "Pepi, Luci, Bom and Other Girls Like Mom"), Figaro, 1980 (also see below).

(And production designer) *Laberinto de pasiones,* Musidora S.A., 1982, released in the United States as *Labyrinth of Passion,* 1990 (also see below).

Entre tinieblas, Tesauro P.C., 1983, released in the United States as *Dark Habits* (also known as *Dark Hideout* and *Sisters of Darkness*), Cinevista, 1988 (also see below).

Que he hecho yo para merecer esto?, Tesauro S.A./Kaktus P.C., 1984, released in the United States as *What Have I Done to Deserve This?,* Cinevista, 1985 (also see below).

Matador, Iberoamericana, 1986, released in the United States under same title, Cinevista/World Artists, 1988 (also see below).

La ley del deseo, El Deseo/Lauren Films, 1986, released in the United States as *Law of Desire,* Cinevista, 1987 (also see below).

Mujeres al borde de un ataque de nervios, El Deseo/Lauren, 1988, released in the United States as *Women*

on the Verge of a Nervous Breakdown, Orion Classics, 1988 (also see below).
Atame!, 1990, released in the United States as *Tie Me Up! Tie Me Down!,* Miramax, 1990 (also see below).
High Heels, Miramax, 1991 (also see below).

Also director of *La caida de sodoma,* 1974, *Dos putas, o historia de amor que termina en boda,* 1974, *Homenaje,* 1975, *El sueno,* 1975, *El estrella,* 1976, *Complementos,* 1977, *Sexo va,* 1977, *Folle, folle, folle me, Tim,* 1978, *Salome,* 1978, and *Trayler para amantes de lo prohibido,* 1985.

FILM APPEARANCES

Performer, *Laberinto de pasiones,* Musidora S.A., 1982, released in the United States as *Labyrinth of Passion,* 1990 (also see below).

WRITINGS:

Pepi, Luci, Bom y otros chicas del monton (screenplay; title means "Pepi, Luci, Bom and a Whole Lot of Other Girls," other sources translate as "Pepi, Luci, Bom and Other Girls on the Heap" or "Pepi, Luci, Bom and Other Girls Like Mom"), Figaro, 1980.
Laberinto de pasiones (screenplay), Musidora S.A., 1982, released in the United States as *Labyrinth of Passion,* 1990.
Entre tinieblas (screenplay and song "Suck It to Me"), Tesauro P.C., 1983, released in the United States as *Dark Habits* (also known as *Dark Hideout* and *Sisters of Darkness*), Cinevista, 1988.
Que he hecho yo para merecer esto? (screenplay), Tesauro S.A./Kaktus P.C., 1984, released in the United States as *What Have I Done to Deserve This?,* Cinevista, 1985.
Matador (screenplay), Iberoamericana, 1986, released in the United States under same title, Cinevista/World Artists, 1988.
La ley del deseo (screenplay, score, and songs "Voy a ser mama" and "Susan Get Down"), El Deseo/Lauren Films, 1986, released in the United States as *Law of Desire,* Cinevista, 1987.
Mujeres al borde de un ataque de nervios (screenplay), El Deseo/Lauren, 1988, released in the United States as *Women on the Verge of a Nervous Breakdown,* Orion Classics, 1988.
Atame! (screenplay), 1990, released in the United States as *Tie Me Up! Tie Me Down!,* Miramax, 1990.
High Heels (screenplay), Miramax, 1991.

Also author of novel *Fuego en las entranas* (title means "Fire in the Guts"), 1982, and photo-novella *Todo tuya* (title means "All Yours"); author, under pseudonym Patty Diphusa, of fictional memoirs that originally appeared in *La Luna.* Also contributor of articles to periodicals, including *El Pais, Diaro,* and *16.*

OTHER SOURCES:

PERIODICALS

Film Comment, November/December, 1988, p. 13.
Film Quarterly, fall, 1987, p. 33.
New York Times, April 22, 1990.
Time, January 30, 1989, p. 68.

* * *

ALONZO, John A. 1934-

PERSONAL: Born in 1934 in Dallas, TX; married Jan Murray. *Education:* Attended public schools in Dallas, TX.

ADDRESSES: Agent—Scott Harris, Harris & Goldberg, 2121 Avenue of the Stars, No. 950, Los Angeles, CA 90067.

CAREER: Cinematographer and director. WFAA-TV, camera operator and director, in the early 1950s; worked for KHJ-TV, Hollywood, CA.

MEMBER: American Society of Cinematographers.

AWARDS, HONORS: Academy Award nomination, best cinematography, 1974, for *Chinatown.*

CREDITS:

FILM WORK; CINEMATOGRAPHER, EXCEPT AS INDICATED

Bloody Mama, American International Pictures, 1970.
Vanishing Point, Twentieth Century-Fox, 1971.
Harold and Maude, Paramount, 1971.
Sounder, Twentieth Century-Fox, 1972.
Get to Know Your Rabbit, Warner Brothers, 1972.
Pete 'n' Tillie, Universal, 1972.
Lady Sings the Blues, Paramount, 1972.
The Naked Ape, Universal, 1973.
Hit!, Paramount, 1973.
Conrack, Twentieth Century-Fox, 1974.
Chinatown, Paramount, 1974.
Once Is Not Enough, Paramount, 1975.
The Fortune, Columbia, 1975.
Farewell, My Lovely, Avco Embassy, 1975.
The Bad News Bears, Paramount, 1976.
I Will . . .I Will . . .for Now, Twentieth Century-Fox, 1976.
Black Sunday, Paramount, 1977.
Which Way Is Up?, Universal, 1977.
Director, *FM* (also known as *Citizen's Band*), Universal, 1978.
Casey's Shadow, Columbia, 1978.
The Cheap Detective, Columbia, 1978.

Norma Rae, Twentieth Century-Fox, 1979.
Tom Horn, Warner Brothers, 1980.
Back Roads, Warner Brothers, 1981.
Zorro, the Gay Blade, Twentieth Century-Fox, 1981.
Blue Thunder, Columbia, 1983.
Cross Creek, Universal, 1983.
Scarface, Universal, 1983.
Runaway, Tri-Star, 1984.
Terror in the Aisles, Universal, 1984.
Out of Control, New World, 1985.
Nothing in Common, Tri-Star, 1986.
Jo Jo Dancer, Your Life Is Calling, Columbia, 1986.
Overboard, Metro-Goldwyn-Mayer (MGM)/United Artists (UA), 1987.
Real Men, MGM/UA, 1987.
Physical Evidence, Columbia, 1988.
Steel Magnolias, Tri-Star, 1989.
Internal Affairs, Paramount, 1990.
The Guardian, Universal, 1990.
Navy Seals, Orion, 1990.

FILM APPEARANCES

Manuel Alvarez, *The Long Rope,* Twentieth Century-Fox, 1961.
Carlos, *Hand of Death* (also known as *Five Fingers of Death*), Twentieth Century-Fox, 1962.
Terror at Black Falls, Beckman, 1962.
Manuel, *Invitation to a Gunfighter,* United Artists, 1964.

Also appeared in *The Magnificent Seven.*

TELEVISION WORK; MOVIES

Director and cinematographer, *Champions: A Love Story,* CBS, 1979.
Director, *Portrait of a Stripper,* CBS, 1979.
Director and cinematographer, *Belle Starr,* CBS, 1980.
Director and cinematographer, *Blinded by the Light,* CBS, 1980.
Cinematographer, *Roots: The Gift,* ABC, 1988.

TELEVISION WORK; SPECIALS

Cinematographer, *Knightwatch* (also known as *On the Streets*), ABC, 1988.

OTHER SOURCES:

BOOKS

Schaefer, Dennis, and Larry Salvato, *Masters of Light: Conversations With Contemporary Cinematographers,* 1984.

PERIODICALS

Film Comment, April, 1984, p. 32.*

AMES, E. Preston
See AMES, Preston

* * *

AMES, Preston 1905-1983
(E. Preston Ames)

CAREER: Art director and production designer. Worked for architect Arthur Brown, Jr., San Francisco, CA, in the early 1930s; became a draftsman in the art department, Metro-Goldwyn-Mayer.

AWARDS, HONORS: Academy Award, best art direction, 1951, for *An American in Paris;* Academy Award nominations, best art direction, 1953, for *The Story of Three Loves,* 1954, for *Brigadoon,* and 1956, for *Lust for Life;* Academy Award, best art direction, 1958, for *Gigi;* Academy Award nominations, best art direction, 1964, for *The Unsinkable Molly Brown,* 1970, for *Airport,* and 1974, for *Earthquake;* Emmy Award nomination, best art direction, 1983, for *Casablanca.*

CREDITS:

FILM WORK; ART DIRECTOR, EXCEPT AS INDICATED

(With Cedric Gibbons) *She Went to the Races,* Metro-Goldwyn-Mayer (MGM), 1945.
(With Gibbons) *The Hidden Eye,* MGM, 1945.
(With Gibbons) *The Show-Off,* MGM, 1946.
(With Gibbons) *Lady in the Lake,* MGM, 1947.
(With Gibbons) *Three Daring Daughters* (also known as *The Birds and the Bees*), MGM, 1948.
(With Gibbons) *That Midnight Kiss,* MGM, 1949.
(With Gibbons) *The Doctor and the Girl,* MGM, 1949.
(With Gibbons) *Crisis,* MGM, 1950.
(With Gibbons) *Two Weeks—With Love,* Metro, 1950.
(With Gibbons) *An American in Paris,* MGM, 1951.
(With Gibbons) *The Wild North* (also known as *The Big North*), MGM, 1952.
(With Gibbons) *Torch Song,* MGM, 1953.
(With Gibbons, Edward Carfagno, and Gabriel Scognamillo) *The Story of Three Loves,* MGM, 1953.
(With Gibbons) *Brigadoon,* MGM, 1954.
(With Gibbons) *Kismet,* MGM, 1955.
(With Gibbons and Hans Peters) *Lust for Life,* MGM, 1956.
(With Gibbons) *These Wilder Years,* MGM, 1956.
(With William A. Horning) *Gigi,* MGM, 1958.
(With Horning) *Green Mansions,* MGM, 1959.
(With George W. Davis) *Bells Are Ringing,* MGM, 1960.
(With Davis) *Home From the Hill,* MGM, 1960.
(With Davis) *Where the Boys Are,* MGM, 1960.
(With Davis) *The Honeymoon Machine,* MGM, 1961.
(With Jack Martin Smith) *Wild in the Country,* Twentieth Century-Fox, 1961.

(With Davis) *All Fall Down,* MGM, 1962.
(With Davis) *Jumbo,* MGM, 1962.
(With Davis) *It Happened at the World's Fair,* MGM, 1963.
(With Davis) *A Global Affair,* MGM, 1964.
(With Davis) *The Unsinkable Molly Brown,* MGM, 1964.
(With Davis) *Quick, Before It Melts,* MGM, 1964.
(With Davis) *Made in Paris,* MGM, 1966.
(With Davis) *Penelope,* MGM, 1966.
(With Davis) *The Impossible Years,* MGM, 1968.
(With Davis) *Live a Little, Love a Little,* MGM, 1968.
(With Alexander Golitzen) *Airport,* Universal, 1970.
(With Davis) *Brewster McCloud,* MGM, 1970.
(With Davis) *The Strawberry Statement,* MGM, 1970.
(With Davis) *Pretty Maids All in a Row,* MGM, 1971.
Lost Horizon, Columbia, 1973.
The Don Is Dead (also known as *Beautiful But Deadly*), Universal, 1973.
(As E. Preston Ames; with Golitzen) *Earthquake,* Universal, 1974.
Rooster Cogburn, Universal, 1975.
The Prisoner of Second Avenue, Warner Brothers, 1975.
Production designer, *Damnation Alley,* Twentieth Century-Fox, 1977.
(With John B. Mansbridge) *The Cat From Outer Space,* Disney, 1978.
Beyond the Poseidon Adventure, Warner Brothers, 1979.
The Last Flight of Noah's Ark, Buena Vista, 1980.
Production designer, *Oh, God! Book II,* Warner Brothers, 1980.
Production designer, *The Pursuit of D. B. Cooper,* Universal, 1981.

Also art director for *No Leave, No Love,* 1946; *The Big City,* 1948; *Outriders,* 1949; *Dear Brat, Rhubarb, Submarine Command,* and *Sailor Beware,* 1951; *The Band Wagon,* 1953; *Designing Woman,* 1957; and *The Big Operator,* 1959.

TELEVISION WORK; SERIES

Art director, *Private Benjamin,* CBS, 1981.
Art director, *Bare Essence* (also see below), NBC, 1982.
Production designer, *Casablanca,* NBC, 1983.
Art director, *The Mississippi,* CBS, 1983.

TELEVISION WORK; MOVIES

Art director, *Babe,* CBS, 1975.
Art director, *The Lives of Jenny Dolan,* NBC, 1975.
Art director, *Woman of the Year,* CBS, 1976.
Art director, *A Family Upside Down,* NBC, 1978.
Art director, *Bare Essence,* NBC, 1982.

WRITINGS:

Contributor to *IATSE Official Bulletin.*

OBITUARIES AND OTHER SOURCES:

PERIODICALS

Filmmakers Monthly, June, 1979.*

* * *

ANDERSON, Judith 1898-1992

OBITUARY NOTICE—See index for *CTFT* sketch: Born Frances Margaret Anderson-Anderson, February 10, 1898, in Adelaide, South Australia; died of pneumonia, January 3, 1992, in Santa Barbara, CA. Actress. Best known for her portrayal of villains, Anderson had a long career in film, stage, and television. She received an Academy Award nomination for her role as a malignant housekeeper in director Alfred Hitchcock's 1940 film, *Rebecca.* She also appeared in *The Ten Commandments,* directed by Cecille B. DeMille, as well as film adaptations of *Macbeth* and *Cat on a Hot Tin Roof.* Anderson appeared in numerous stage productions, including *Mourning Becomes Electra,* and she was particularly acclaimed for her work in the title role of a Broadway production of the classical Greek tragedy *Medea* in 1947. She also played Gertrude in a 1937 production of *Hamlet* that starred John Gielgud, and she appeared—at seventy-two years of age—in the title role of another production of *Hamlet* in 1970. Anderson won Emmy Awards for her portrayals of Lady Macbeth in television productions of *Macbeth* in 1954 and 1960; her television credits also included appearances in *Caesar and Cleopatra, The Bridge of San Luis Rey, The Underground Man,* and the soap opera *Santa Barbara.* She made her last film appearance in 1984, in *Star Trek III: The Search for Spock.* In 1960 she received the title of Dame Commander of the Order of the British Empire.

OBITUARIES AND OTHER SOURCES:

BOOKS

International Dictionary of Films and Filmmakers, Volume 3: *Actors and Actresses,* St. James Press, 1986, pp. 15-16.

PERIODICALS

Hollywood Reporter, January 6, 1992, pp. 1, 39.
Variety, January 13, 1992, p. 82.

* * *

ANDERSON, Melissa Sue 1962-

PERSONAL: Born September 26, 1962, in Berkeley, CA; daughter of Marion Anderson. *Education:* Attended public schools in Los Angeles, CA.

ADDRESSES: Office—10 East 44th St., New York, NY 10017.

CAREER: Actress. Began her career in television commercials.

MEMBER: Screen Actors Guild.

AWARDS, HONORS: Emmy Award nomination, outstanding lead actress in a drama series, 1978, for *Little House on the Prairie;* Emmy Award, individual achievement in children's programming, 1980, for "Which Mother Is Mine?," *ABC Afterschool Special.*

CREDITS:

TELEVISION APPEARANCES; SERIES

Mary Ingalls, *Little House on the Prairie,* NBC, 1974-82.
"Chubs" Smith, *The Love Boat,* ABC, 1977.

TELEVISION APPEARANCES; MOVIES

Mary Ingalls, *Little House on the Prairie: The Lord Is My Shepherd,* NBC, 1974.
Nancy Rizzi, *The Loneliest Runner,* NBC, 1976.
Dana Lee, *The Survival of Dana,* CBS, 1979.
Vivian Sotherland, *Midnight Offerings,* ABC, 1981.
Molly Rush, *An Innocent Love,* CBS, 1982.
Toby King, *First Affair,* CBS, 1983.
Noelle Drake, *Dark Mansions,* ABC, 1986.

TELEVISION APPEARANCES; SPECIALS

NBC Team Member, *Battle of the Network Stars,* ABC, 1976.
Hostess, *Circus Lions, Tigers, and Melissas Too,* NBC, 1977.
Kate, "Very Good Friends," *ABC Afterschool Special,* ABC, 1977.
Alexandria Benton, "Which Mother Is Mine?," *ABC Afterschool Special,* ABC, 1979.
Mary Beth, *Princess,* syndicated, 1980.
The All-Star Salute to Mother's Day, NBC, 1981.
Hostess, *Sex Symbols: Past, Present, and Future,* syndicated, 1987.

TELEVISION APPEARANCES; PILOTS

Lacey Stevens, *James at Fifteen,* NBC, 1977.
Maureen Tyler, *Advice to the Lovelorn,* NBC, 1981.
That's TV, NBC, 1982.
Finder of Lost Loves, ABC, 1984.

TELEVISION APPEARANCES; EPISODIC

"Love or Lumps" (also known as "Never Too Young"), *The Brady Bunch,* ABC, 1973.
The Love Boat, ABC, 1978.
"Chubs," *The Love Boat,* ABC, 1979.
"CHiPs Goes Roller Disco," *CHiPs,* NBC, 1979.
Fantasy Island, ABC, 1980.
Host, "Treasure Island," *Special Treat,* NBC, 1980.
"Matchmaker, Matchmaker Times Two," *The Love Boat,* ABC, 1980.
"Lifelines," *Hotel,* ABC, 1984.
"Hooray for Homicide," *Murder, She Wrote,* CBS, 1984.
"Minor Miracle," *Glitter,* ABC, 1984.
"Imperfect Union," *Hotel,* ABC, 1985.
"The Matadors," *The Love Boat,* ABC, 1986.
"Memories of Manon," *The Equalizer,* CBS, 1987.
"A Very Careful Rape," *Alfred Hitchcock Presents,* USA, 1988.
"The Mystery of Manon," *The Equalizer,* CBS, 1988.
"Murder in Mind," *Alfred Hitchcock Presents,* USA, 1989.

Also appeared in *Shaft,* c. 1973.

FILM APPEARANCES

Virginia Wainwright, *Happy Birthday to Me,* Columbia, 1981.
Jenny, *Chattanooga Choo Choo,* April Fools, 1984.

OTHER SOURCES:

PERIODICALS

People, June 1, 1981, p. 93.*

* * *

ANDREWS, David 1952-

PERSONAL: Born in 1952 in Baton Rouge, LA. *Education:* Attended Louisiana State University.

ADDRESSES: Agent—United Talent Agency, 9560 Wilshire Blvd., fifth floor, Beverly Hills, CA 90212.

CAREER: Actor.

MEMBER: Screen Actors Guild.

CREDITS:

STAGE APPEARANCES

(Off-Broadway debut) Eddie, *Fool for Love,* Circle Repertory Company, Douglas Fairbanks Theatre, New York City, c. 1985.
Stephen (Red) Ryder, *The Heart Outright,* Theater for the New City company, Theater for the New City, New York City, 1989.

Also appeared in *Safe Sex* and *Friends in High Places.*

FILM APPEARANCES

Dean Moriarty, *Kerouac* (also known as *Jack Kerouac's America*), Daybreak, 1985.
Sam Treadwell, *Cherry 2000,* Orion, 1988.

John Hall, *Graveyard Shift* (also known as *Stephen King's Graveyard Shift*), Paramount, 1990.

TELEVISION APPEARANCES; SERIES

Jack Scarlett, *The Antagonists,* CBS, 1991.
Bobby Mann, *Mann and Machine,* NBC, 1991—.

TELEVISION APPEARANCES; MOVIES

Wimpy Hughes, *The Burning Bed,* NBC, 1984.
Dean Ellis, *Wild Horses,* CBS, 1985.
Midas Valley, ABC, 1985.
Wayne O'Kelley, *A Son's Promise* (also known as *The O'Kelley Brothers; Fire in the Heart;* and *The Terry O'Kelley Story*), ABC, 1990.
Blind Faith, NBC, 1990.

OTHER TELEVISION APPEARANCES

Bodie Chase, *Lime Street,* ABC, 1985.*

* * *

ANGELOU, Maya 1928-

PERSONAL: Name originally Marguerite (some sources say Marguerita) Johnson; surname is pronounced "*an-ge-lo*"; born April 4, 1928, in St. Louis, MO; daughter of Bailey (a doorkeeper and Naval dietician) and Vivian (a nurse and realtor; maiden name, Baxter) Johnson; married Tosh Angelou (divorced c. 1952); married Paul Du Feu, December, 1973; children: Guy Johnson. *Education:* Studied dance with Martha Graham, Pearl Primus, and Ann Halprin; studied drama with Frank Silvera and Gene Frankel. *Politics:* Left.

ADDRESSES: Office— Wake Forest University, Box 7314 Reynolda Station, Winston-Salem, NC, 27109. *Agent*—Gerald W. Purcell Associates Ltd., 133 Fifth Ave., New York, NY 10003.

CAREER: Author, poet, playwright, actress, singer, dancer, director, and producer. Taught modern dance at Habima Theatre, Tel Aviv, and the Rome Opera House; formerly a nightclub performer. University of Ghana, Institute of African Studies, assistant administrator of School of Music and Drama, 1963-66; associate editor, *Arab Observer,* 1961-62; feature editor, *African Review,* 1964-66; lecturer at University of California, Los Angeles, 1966; writer in residence at University of Kansas, 1970; distinguished visiting professor at Wake Forest University, Wichita State University, and California State University, Sacramento, all 1974; professor at Wake Forest University since 1981. Northern coordinator of Southern Christian Leadership Conference, 1959-60; appointed member of American Revolution Bicentennial Council by President Gerald R. Ford, 1975-76; member of National Commission on the Observance of International Women's Year.

MEMBER: Directors Guild of America, Equity, American Federation of Television and Radio Artists, Harlem Writers Guild, American Film Institute (trustee), Women's Prison Association (member of advisory board).

AWARDS, HONORS: National Book Award nomination, 1970, for *I Know Why the Caged Bird Sings;* Yale University fellow, 1970; Pulitzer Prize nomination, 1972, for *Just Give Me A Cool Drink of Water 'fore I Diiie;* Antoinette Perry Award nomination, best supporting actress, 1973, for *Look Away;* Rockefeller Foundation scholar in Italy, 1975; named woman of the year in communications by *Ladies Home Journal,* 1976; honorary degrees from Smith College, 1975, Mills College, 1975, Lawrence University, 1976, and Wake Forest College, 1977; named one of the top 100 most influential women by *Ladies Home Journal,* 1983; North Carolina Award in Literature, 1987.

CREDITS:

STAGE APPEARANCES

Cabaret for Freedom (also see below), Village Gate, New York City, 1960.
Queen, *The Blacks,* St. Marks Playhouse, New York City, 1961, then Venice, Italy, and Berlin, West Germany, both 1964.
Medea, Theatre of Being, Hollywood, CA, 1966.
(Broadway debut) Elizabeth Keckley, *Look Away,* Playhouse Theatre, 1973.

Also appeared in *Porgy and Bess* in European and African cities, 1954-55.

STAGE WORK

Producer, *Cabaret for Freedom,* Village Gate, New York City, 1960.
Director, *And Still I Rise* (also see below), Ensemble Theatre, Oakland, CA, 1976.

TELEVISION APPEARANCES; EPISODIC

Narrator, "The Slave Coast," *Black African Heritage,* CBS, 1972.

TELEVISION APPEARANCES; SPECIALS

The Richard Pryor Special, NBC, 1977.
The Richard Pryor Special, NBC, 1982.
James Baldwin: The Price of the Ticket, PBS, 1989.
The 22nd Annual NAACP Image Awards, NBC, 1990.
Jacqueline Kennedy Onassis, Arts and Entertainment, 1991.

OTHER TELEVISION APPEARANCES

Nyo Boto, *Roots* (mini-series), ABC, 1977.

Also appeared on *Assignment America,* 1975, *Moyers: Facing Evil,* 1988, and *The R.A.C.E.,* 1989.

TELEVISION WORK

Producer, *Blacks, Blues, Black* (ten one-hour programs; also see below), National Educational Television (now PBS), 1968.

FILM APPEARANCES

Herself, *Calypso Heat Wave,* Columbia, 1957.

FILM WORK

Director, *All Day Long,* American Film Institute, 1974.

RECORDINGS:

ALBUMS

Miss Calypso (songs), Liberty Records, 1957.
Women in Business, University of Wisconsin, 1981.

TAPED READINGS

The Poetry of Maya Angelou, GWP Records, 1969.
An Evening with Maya Angelou, Pacific Tape Library, 1975.

WRITINGS:

AUTOBIOGRAPHY

I Know Why the Caged Bird Sings, Random House, 1970.
Gather Together in My Name, Random House, 1974.
Singin' and Swingin' and Gettin' Merry Like Christmas, Random House, 1976.
The Heart of a Woman, Random House, 1981.
All God's Children Need Traveling Shoes, Random House, 1986.
Selections from I Know Why the Caged Bird Sings and The Heart of a Woman, Literacy Volunteers of New York City, 1989.

POETRY

Just Give Me A Cool Drink of Water 'fore I Diiie, Random House, 1971.
Oh Pray My Wings Are Gonna Fit Me Well, Random House, 1975.
And Still I Rise (also see below), Random House, 1978.
Shaker, Why Don't You Sing, Random House, 1983.
Poems: Maya Angelou, four volumes, Bantam, 1986.

Also author of *The True Believers,* with Abbey Lincoln.

OTHER

Mrs. Flowers: A Moment of Friendship (fiction), illustrations by Etienne Delessert, Redpath Press, 1986.
Now Sheba Sings the Song, illustrations by Tom Feelings, Dial Books, 1987.
I Shall Not Be Moved, Random House, 1990.

Has contributed articles, short stories, and poems to periodicals, including *New York Times, Black Scholar, Ebony, Chicago Daily News, National Geographic,* and *Life.*

PLAYS

(With Godfrey Cambridge) *Cabaret for Freedom,* first produced at Village Gate Theatre, New York City, 1960.
The Least of These (two-act), first produced in Los Angeles, 1966.
(Adapter) Sophocles, *Ajax* (two-act), first produced by Center Theatre Group at Mark Taper Forum, Los Angeles, 1973-74.
Encounters, first produced by Center Theater Group at Mark Taper Forum, 1973.
And Still I Rise (one-act; based on Angelou's book of poetry of the same title), first produced at Ensemble Theatre, Oakland, CA, 1976.

Also author of *The Clawing Within,* 1966, and *Adjoa Amissah,* 1967.

SCREENPLAYS

Georgia, Georgia, Cinerama, 1972.
All Day Long, American Film Institute, 1974.

TELEVISION

Blacks, Blues, Black (ten one-hour programs), National Educational Television (now PBS), 1968.
(With Leona Thuna and Ralph B. Woolsey) *I Know Why the Caged Bird Sings* (movie adaptation of Angelou's autobiography of the same title), CBS, 1979.
Sister, Sister (movie), NBC, 1982.
Brewster Place (series premiere), ABC, 1990.

Also author of "Assignment America" series, 1975, and two Afro-American specials, *The Inheritors,* 1976, and *The Legacy.*

FILM MUSIC

(With Quincy Jones) "You Put It on Me," *For Love of Ivy,* Cinerama, 1968.
"I Can Call Down Rain," *Georgia, Georgia,* Cinerama, 1972.

OTHER SOURCES:

BOOKS

Contemporary Literary Criticism, Gale, Volume 12, 1980, pp. 9-10; Volume 35, 1985, pp. 29-33.
Dictionary of Literary Biography, Volume 38: *Afro-American Writers after 1955: Dramatists and Prose Writers,* Gale, 1985, pp. 3-12.
Major 20th-Century Writers, Gale, 1991, pp. 100-102.

PERIODICALS

People, March 8, 1982, p. 92.
Vogue, September 1982, p. 416.*

* * *

ANHALT, Edward 1914-
(Andrew Holt, a joint pseudonym)

PERSONAL: Born March 28, 1914, in New York, NY; married, wife's name Edna (a writer), 1935 (divorced, 1956). *Education:* Columbia University, B.A.; attended Princeton University, 1935-37; studied filmmaking with Willard Van Dyke and Ralph Steiner, 1936-38.

ADDRESSES: Agent—Arthur Axelman, William Morris Agency, 151 El Camino Drive, Beverly Hills, CA 90212.

CAREER: Screenwriter. Camera operator and film editor for Willard Van Dyke, 1937-38; CBS-TV, television camera operator, 1938-40; Columbia Pictures, staff writer, 1947-50; Twentieth Century-Fox, staff writer, 1950-52. Past member of faculty, Loyola Marymount University.

MEMBER: Academy of Motion Picture Arts and Sciences, Screen Actors Guild, Directors Guild of America, Writers Guild of America West.

AWARDS, HONORS: Fellow, Rockefeller Foundation, 1936-38; Academy Award, best motion picture story (with Edna Anhalt), 1950, for *Panic in the Streets;* Academy Award nomination, best motion picture story, 1952, for *The Sniper;* Academy Award, best screenplay based on material from another medium, and Writers Guild Award, both 1964, for *Becket;* Edgar Allan Poe Award, Mystery Writers of America, 1968, for *The Boston Strangler,* and 1978, for *Contract on Cherry Street;* Emmy Award nomination, best adaptation for a mini-series, 1975, for *QB VII;* Writers Guild Laurel Award, 1977.

CREDITS:

FILM WORK

Producer (with Edna Anhalt) *My Six Convicts,* Columbia, 1952.
Associate producer (with Edna Anhalt) *Eight Iron Men,* Columbia, 1952.
Producer, *The Member of the Wedding,* Columbia, 1952.

FILM APPEARANCES

Russian grand designer, *The Right Stuff,* Warner Brothers, 1983.

TELEVISION WORK; MOVIES

Producer, *Nowhere to Hide,* NBC, 1979.

TELEVISION WORK; EPISODIC

Director, "A Time for Killing," *The Bob Hope Chrysler Theater,* NBC, 1965.

TELEVISION APPEARANCES; MOVIES

Senator Herbert Lehman, *Tail Gunner Joe,* NBC, 1977.
Alberto Amarici, *Nowhere to Hide,* NBC, 1979.
Judge, *Madame X,* NBC, 1981.

WRITINGS:

SCREENPLAYS

Problem Child (documentary), Independent, 1935.
Thunder of the Sea (documentary), Lutheran Radio Pictures, 1936.
(With Edna Anhalt, under joint pseudonym Andrew Holt) *Strange Voyage,* Monogram, 1946.
(With Edna Anhalt, under joint pseudonym Andrew Holt) *Avalanche,* Producers Releasing Corp., 1946.
(With Edna Anhalt) *Bulldog Drummond Strikes Back,* Columbia, 1947.
The Gentleman From Nowhere, Columbia, 1948.
(With Edna Anhalt, John Lucas Meredyth, George F. Slavin, and George W. George) *Red Mountain,* Paramount, 1952.
(With Edna Anhalt) *The Member of the Wedding,* Columbia, 1952.
(With Edna Anhalt) *My Six Convicts,* Columbia, 1952.
(With Edna Anhalt) *Eight Iron Men,* Columbia, 1952.
(With Edna Anhalt) *Not as a Stranger,* United Artists (UA), 1955.
(With Edna Anhalt) *The Pride and the Passion,* UA, 1957.
The Young Lions, Twentieth Century-Fox, 1958.
In Love and War, Twentieth Century-Fox, 1958.
The Restless Years (also known as *The Wonderful Years*), Universal, 1959.
The Sins of Rachel Cade, Warner Brothers, 1960.
(With J. P. Miller) *The Young Savages,* UA, 1961.
(With Allan Weiss) *Girls! Girls! Girls!* Paramount, 1962.
A Girl Named Tamiko, Paramount, 1962.
Wives and Lovers, Paramount, 1963.
Becket, Paramount, 1964.
(With James Clavell) *The Satan Bug,* UA, 1965.
Boeing, Boeing, Paramount, 1965.
Hour of the Gun, UA, 1967.
The Boston Strangler, Twentieth Century-Fox, 1968.
(With Alfred Hayes) *In Enemy Country,* Universal, 1968.
The Madwoman of Chaillot, Warner Brothers, 1969.
(With John Milius) *Jeremiah Johnson,* Warner Brothers, 1972.
Luther, American Film Theatre, 1974.
The Man in the Glass Booth, American Film Theatre, 1975.
(With Richard S. Lochte) *Escape to Athena,* I.T.C., 1979.

(With Ray Hassett, Anthony Simmons, and Robert DeLaurentiis) *Green Ice,* I.T.C., 1981.
(With George Axelrod and John Hopkins) *The Holcroft Covenant,* Universal, 1985.

Also author of *The Salzburg Connection,* 1971, and *Splendora,* with Camilla Carr.

SCREEN STORIES

(With David Dressler) *The Crime Doctor's Diary,* Columbia, 1949.
(With Edna Anhalt) *Panic in the Streets,* Twentieth Century-Fox, 1950.
(With Edna Anhalt) *The Sniper,* Columbia, 1952.

TELEVISION SCRIPTS

"A Time for Killing" (episode), *The Bob Hope Chrysler Theater,* NBC, 1965.
QB VII (mini-series), ABC, 1974.
Contract on Cherry Street (movie), NBC, 1977.
Nowhere to Hide (movie), NBC, 1979.
(With Jean Holloway) *Madame X* (movie), NBC, 1981.
(With James Lee Barrett and James Jones) *The Day Christ Died* (movie), CBS, 1982.
Peter the Great (mini-series), NBC, 1985.
The Neon Empire (movie), Showtime, 1989.
(With Handel Glassberg) *The Take* (also known as *The Mobsters*), USA, 1990.
Alexander the Great (mini-series), TBS, 1990.

OTHER

Contributor to periodicals, including *American Cinematographer* and *Screen Actor;* contributor to pulp magazines with Edna Anhalt, under joint pseudonym Andrew Holt, during the 1940s.

OTHER SOURCES:

BOOKS

Dictionary of Literary Biography, Volume 26: *American Screenwriters,* Gale, 1984.
Marshall, J. D., *Blueprint on Babylon,* Phoenix House, 1978.

PERIODICALS

Films in Review, April, 1964; November, 1968.
New York Times, August 5, 1950; December 31, 1952; March 12, 1964; April 15, 1965; October 17, 1968.
Screen Actor, summer, 1981.
Time, March, 1965.

ANSEN, David 1945-

PERSONAL: Born April 21, 1945, in Los Angeles, CA; son of Joseph and Dorothy (Blum) Ansen. *Education:* Harvard University, B.A., 1967.

ADDRESSES: Office—Newsweek, 11835 West Olympic Blvd., Los Angeles, CA 90064.

CAREER: Film critic. *Real Paper,* Cambridge, MA, film critic and editor, 1975-77; *Newsweek,* New York City, film critic and senior writer, 1977—.

MEMBER: National Society of Film Critics, New York Film Critics Circle.

AWARDS, HONORS: Page One Award, Newspaper Guild of New York, 1983, 1987, 1989; Headliner Award, 1984.

CREDITS:

TELEVISION APPEARANCES

Host of *Bravo International Film Show* (also see below), 1983-87; guest appearances on *CNN, Entertainment Tonight, Nightline, CBS Evening News,* and *ABC World News Tonight.*

WRITINGS:

The Divine Garbo (television special), TNT, 1990.
Here He Is, the One . . . the Only . . . Groucho, (television special), HBO, 1991.

Writer for *Bravo International Film Show* (cable television program), 1983—. Contributor to periodicals.

* * *

ANTHONY, Lysette

CAREER: Actress. Worked as a model. Past member of National Youth Theater.

CREDITS:

TELEVISION APPEARANCES; MOVIES

Lady Rowena, *Ivanhoe,* CBS, 1982.
Oliver's mother, *Oliver Twist,* CBS, 1982.
Lady Sarah, *Princess Daisy,* NBC, 1983.
Lady Panthea, *The Lady and the Highwayman* (also known as *Dangerous Love*), CBS, 1989.
Mary Jane Kelly, *Jack the Ripper,* CBS, 1989.
Mistral, *A Ghost in Monte Carlo,* TNT, 1990.

Also appeared as Gilda, *The Emperor's New Clothes,* 1987.

TELEVISION APPEARANCES; SERIES

Angelique, *Dark Shadows,* NBC, 1991.

Also appeared in the British series *Three Up, Two Down,* BBC.

TELEVISION APPEARANCES; EPISODIC

Amanda Fitts, "Sweet Danger," *Mystery!* (also known as *Campion Series II*), PBS, 1990.

FILM APPEARANCES

Princess Lyssa, *Krull,* Columbia, 1983.
Fake Leslie, *Without a Clue,* Orion, 1988.
Liz, *Switch,* Warner Brothers, 1991.*

* * *

ANTOON, A. J. 1944-1992

OBITUARY NOTICE—See index for *CTFT* sketch: Full name Alfred Joseph Antoon, Jr.; born December 7, 1944, in Lawrence, MA; died of complications resulting from Acquired Immune Deficiency Syndrome (AIDS), January 22, 1992, in New York. Director. Antoon was associated with the New York Shakespeare Festival during his career, directing contemporary plays as well as modern productions of Shakespeare. Among his more notable works were Broadway productions of *Much Ado about Nothing* and *That Championship Season,* for which he won an Antoinette Perry Award for best director in 1973. He also staged sundry other plays, including *A Midsummer Night's Dream, The Taming of the Shrew, The Good Doctor, The Art of Dining,* and a 1985 revival of *South Pacific.* He directed numerous well-known performers throughout his career as well, including Sam Waterston, Meryl Streep, Morgan Freeman, and Liza Minnelli.

OBITUARIES AND OTHER SOURCES:

PERIODICALS

Variety, January 27, 1992, p. 66.

* * *

APPLEGATE, Christina 1972(?)-

PERSONAL: Born in Hollywood, CA; daughter of Nancy Priddy (an actress).

ADDRESSES: Agent—Tami Lynn Management, 4527 Park Allegra, Calabasas, CA 91302.

CAREER: Actress.

CREDITS:

TELEVISION APPEARANCES; SERIES

Days of Our Lives, NBC, 1974.
Sally Forehead, *Washingtoon,* Showtime, 1985.
Robin Kennedy, *Heart of the City,* ABC, 1986.
Kelly Bundy, *Married . . . With Children,* Fox, 1987—.

TELEVISION APPEARANCES; MOVIES

Grace (as a child), *Grace Kelly,* ABC, 1983.
Patrice, *Dance 'til Dawn,* NBC, 1988.

TELEVISION APPEARANCES; SPECIALS

Host, *Rate the '80s Awards,* MTV, 1989.
MTV's 1989 Annual Emmy Awards, MTV, 1989.
Time Warner Presents the Earth Day Special, ABC, 1990.
The 4th Annual American Comedy Awards, ABC, 1990.
The 43rd Annual Primetime Emmy Awards Presentation, Fox, 1991.

Also appeared in *The 41st Annual Emmy Awards,* 1989.

TELEVISION APPEARANCES; EPISODIC

"A Horse from Heaven," *Father Murphy,* NBC, 1981.
"Suffer the Little Children," *Quincy, M. E.,* NBC, 1983.
"The Slumber Party," *Charles in Charge,* CBS, 1984.
"Snowed In," *Charles in Charge,* CBS, 1984.
Episode 5, *All Is Forgiven,* NBC, 1986.
"Farewell to Freddie," *The New Leave It to Beaver,* TBS, 1986.
"Welcome to My Nightmare," *Amazing Stories,* NBC, 1986.
"Family Affair," *Silver Spoons,* syndicated, 1986.
"Band on the Run," *Family Ties,* NBC, 1987.
"I'm O.K.—You Need Work," *21 Jump Street,* Fox, 1988.
Animal Crack-Ups, ABC, 1988.
Hour Magazine, syndicated, 1988.
Win, Lose, or Draw, NBC, 1988.
The Pat Sajak Show, CBS, 1989.
Live with Regis and Kathie Lee, syndicated, 1989.
The Arsenio Hall Show, syndicated, 1989.

FILM APPEARANCES

Kim Perry, *Jaws of Satan,* United Artists, 1980.
Dawn, *Streets,* Concorde, 1990.
Sue Ellen "Swell" Crandell, *Don't Tell Mom the Babysitter's Dead,* Warner Brothers, 1991.

OTHER SOURCES:

PERIODICALS

People, December 4, 1989.
Premiere, June, 1991.*

ARCAND, Denys 1941-

PERSONAL: Born June 25, 1941, in Deschambault, Quebec, Canada. *Education:* University of Montreal, M.A., history, 1963.

ADDRESSES: Office—4921 Coronet, Suite 12, Montreal, Quebec, Canada.

CAREER: Director and screenwriter. National Film Board of Canada, St. Laurent, Quebec, documentary filmmaker, beginning in 1963; creator of television commercials.

AWARDS, HONORS: Canadian Film Award, best children's film, 1965, for *Quebec 1603;* Canadian Film Award, best original screenplay—feature film, 1973, for *Rejeanne Padovani;* FIPRESCI (International Federation of Cinematographic Press) Prize, Cannes International Film Festival, 1986, Genie Awards, best achievement in directing, and best original screenplay, Academy of Canadian Cinema and Television, both 1987, all for *The Decline of the American Empire;* Prix Albert-Tessier, Ministere des Affaires Culturelles (Quebec), 1989; Special Jury Prize, Cannes International Film Festival, Ecumenical Prize, World Council of Churches, both 1989, Genie Awards, best achievement in direction, and best original screenplay, both 1990, all for *Jesus of Montreal.*

CREDITS:

FILM DIRECTOR, EXCEPT WHERE INDICATED

(With Denis Heroux and Stephane Venne) *Seul ou avec d'autres* (also see below), Association Generale des Etudiants de l'Universite de Montreal, 1962.
Champlain (documentary; also see below), National Film Board of Canada, 1963.
Les Montrealistes (documentary; also see below), National Film Board of Canada, 1964.
La Route de l'ouest (documentary; also see below), National Film Board of Canada, 1964.
Montreal un jour d'ete (short film; title means "Montreal on a Summer Day"), OFQ and Les Cineastes Associes, 1965.
Volley Ball (short film), National Film Board of Canada, 1966.
Parcs atlantiques (short film; title means "Atlantic Parks"), National Film Board of Canada, 1967.
La maudite galette (title means "The Damned Loot"; also see below), Cinak, 1972.
Quebec: Duplessis et apres (also see below), National Film Board of Canada, 1972.
(And editor) *Rejeanne Padovani* (also see below), Cinak, 1973.
Gina (also see below), Carle-Lamy Productions, 1974.
On est au coton (documentary; title means "We Work in Cotton"; also see below), National Film Board of Canada, c. 1976.
Le Confort et l'indifference (documentary; title means "Comfort and Indifference"; also see below), Canadian Empire Inc., 1982.
(With Gilles Carle) *The Crime of Ovide Plouffe* (originally *Le Crime d'Ovide Plouffe,* National Film Board of Canada, 1983; also see below), released in United States by International Cinema, 1985.
The Decline of the American Empire (originally *Le Declin de l'empire americain,* Corporation Image M & M Ltee/National Film Board of Canada, 1986; also see below), released in United States by Cineplex Odeon, 1986.
Jesus of Montreal (originally *Jesus de Montreal,* 1989; also see below), Orion Classics, 1990.

Also creator of *Quebec 1603,* 1965.

FILM APPEARANCES

The Judge, *Jesus of Montreal,* Orion Classics, 1990.

Also appeared as Peep Show Man in *Un Zoo la nuit,* 1987.

TELEVISION DIRECTOR; MINI-SERIES

(With Gilles Carle) *Murder in the Family,* Antenne-21 Films A2, 1985.

TELEVISION DIRECTOR; SERIES

Empire, Inc. (three episodes), CBC, 1982.

WRITINGS:

SCREENPLAYS

(With Denis Heroux and Stephane Venne) *Seul ou avec d'autres,* Association Generale des Etudiants de l'Universite de Montreal, 1962.
Champlain (documentary), National Film Board of Canada, 1963.
Les Montrealistes (documentary), National Film Board of Canada, 1964.
La Route de l'ouest (documentary), National Film Board of Canada, 1964.
La maudite galette (title means "The Damned Loot"), Cinak, 1972.
Quebec: Duplessis et apres, National Film Board of Canada, 1972.
Rejeanne Padovani, Cinak, 1973.
Gina, Carle-Lamy Productions, 1974.
On est au coton (documentary; title means "We Work in Cotton"), National Film Board of Canada, c. 1976.
Le Confort et l'indifference (documentary; title means "Comfort and Indifference"), Canadian Empire Inc., 1982.

(With Roger Lemelin) *The Crime of Ovide Plouffe* (originally *Le Crime d'Ovide Plouffe,* National Film Board of Canada, 1983; based on a novel by Lemelin), released in United States by International Cinema, 1985.
The Decline of the American Empire (originally *Le Declin de l'empire americain,* Corporation Image M & M Ltee/National Film Board of Canada, 1986), released in United States by Cineplex Odeon, 1986.
Jesus of Montreal (originally *Jesus de Montreal,* 1989), Orion Classics, 1990.

TELEVISION MINI-SERIES

Duplessis, CBC, 1976.

OTHER

Contributor to the review *Parti pris.*

OTHER SOURCES:

PERIODICALS

Cinema Canada, October, 1986, p. 15.
Hollywood Reporter, May 22, 1989, p. 14.
Maclean's, September 15, 1986, p. 48.*

* * *

ARDOLINO, Emile

ADDRESSES: Agent—Creative Artists Agency, 9830 Wilshire Blvd., Beverly Hills, CA 90212.

CAREER: Director and producer. Compton-Ardolino Films, Inc., president, 1967-74; Triad Artists, Los Angeles, CA, director, 1974—. Public Broadcasting System (PBS), coordinating producer of "Dance in America" series (also known as "Great Performances"), 1975—.

AWARDS, HONORS: Obie Award (with Gardner Compton), *Village Voice,* special citation for projected media, 1970, for *Oh! Calcutta!;* Emmy Award nomination (with Reiner E. Moritz), outstanding classical music program, 1975, for *Three by Balanchine with the New York City Ballet;* Emmy Award nomination (with Jac Venza and Merrill Brockway), outstanding classical music program, 1976, for *City Center Joffrey Ballet;* Emmy Award nomination (with Venza and Brockway), outstanding classical program in the performing arts, 1976, for *American Ballet Theatre;* Emmy Award nomination (with Venza, Brockway, and Martha Graham), outstanding classical program in the performing arts, 1976, for *Martha Graham Dance Company;* Emmy Award nomination (with Venza and Brockway), outstanding classical program in the performing arts, 1977, for *Choreography by Balanchine, Part I;* Emmy Award nomination (with John Goberman), outstanding classical program in the performing arts, 1978, for *American Ballet Theatre: Live from Lincoln Center;* Emmy Award nomination (with Venza, Brockway, and Judy Kinberg), outstanding classical program in the performing arts, 1978, for *Choreography by Balanchine, Part III;* Emmy Award (with Venza, Brockway, and Kinberg), outstanding classical program in the performing arts, 1978, for *Choreography by Balanchine, Part IV;* Emmy Award nomination (with Gerald Slater), outstanding program achievement—special events, 1978, for *Baryshnikov at the White House.*

Emmy Award nominations, outstanding classical program in the performing arts (with Venza, Kinberg, and Rudolf Nureyev), and outstanding directing in a variety, music, or comedy program, both 1980, for *Nureyev and the Joffrey Ballet: In Tribute to Nijinsky;* Outstanding Directorial Achievement Award for Television, Directors Guild of America, 1981, for *The Spellbound Child;* Emmy Award nomination, outstanding directing in a variety or music program, 1982, for *Lincoln Center Special: Stravinsky and Balanchine—Genius Has a Birthday!;* Academy Award, best feature documentary, Emmy Award nomination (with Edgar J. Scherick and Scott Rudin), outstanding children's entertainment special, and Emmy Awards, outstanding children's program (with Scherick, Rudin, and Kinberg), and outstanding individual achievement in informational programming—directing, all 1983, for *He Makes Me Feel Like Dancin';* Emmy Award nomination, outstanding individual achievement in classical music/dance programming—directing, 1983, for *A Lincoln Center Special: New York City Ballet Tribute to George Balanchine;* Emmy Award nomination, outstanding individual achievement in classical music/dance programming—directing, 1986, for *In Memory Of. . . A Ballet by Jerome Robbins;* Peabody Award, c. 1978, for twenty-eight programs in "Dance in America" series. Golden Eagle Award, Council on International Non-Theatrical Events (CINE), for *A Desert's Dream.*

CREDITS:

TELEVISION WORK; "DANCE IN AMERICA" SERIES (ALSO KNOWN AS "GREAT PERFORMANCES")

Producer (with Reiner E. Moritz), *Three by Balanchine with the New York City Ballet,* PBS, 1975.
Producer, *City Center Joffrey Ballet,* PBS, 1976.
Producer, *American Ballet Theatre,* PBS, 1976.
Producer, *Martha Graham Dance Company,* PBS, 1976.
Producer, *The Pennsylvania Ballet,* PBS, 1976.
Producer, *Dance Theatre of Harlem,* PBS, 1977.
Producer, *Merce Cunningham and Dance Company,* PBS, 1977.
Producer, *Pilobolus Dance Theatre,* PBS, 1977.
Producer, *Trailblazers of Modern Dance,* PBS, 1977.

Producer (with Merrill Brockway), *Choreography by Balanchine, Part I,* PBS, 1977.
Producer, *Choreography by Balanchine, Part II,* PBS, 1977.
Producer, *American Ballet Theatre: Live from Lincoln Center,* PBS, 1978.
Director, *Coppelia: Live from Lincoln Center,* PBS, 1978.
Producer (with Judy Kinberg), *Choreography by Balanchine, Part III,* PBS, 1978.
Producer (with Kinberg), *Choreography by Balanchine, Part IV,* PBS, 1978.
Producer, *Clytemnestra,* PBS, 1979.
Director, *The Most Happy Fella,* PBS, 1980.
Producer (with Kinberg) and director, *Nureyev and the Joffrey Ballet: In Tribute to Nijinsky,* PBS, 1980.
Director, *Choreography by Jerome Robbins, with the New York City Ballet,* PBS, 1986.
Director, *In Memory of. . . A Ballet by Jerome Robbins,* PBS, 1986.

TELEVISION WORK; SPECIALS

Producer, *Baryshnikov at the White House,* PBS, 1978.
Producer, *The San Francisco Ballet: Romeo and Juliet,* PBS, 1978.
Producer, *The Paul Taylor Dance Company,* PBS, 1978.
Director, *Lincoln Center Special: Stravinsky and Balanchine—Genius Has a Birthday!,* PBS, 1982.
Director, *A Lincoln Center Special: New York City Ballet Tribute to George Balanchine,* PBS, 1983.
Director, *The San Francisco Ballet in Cinderella,* PBS, 1985.

TELEVISION WORK; MOVIES

Producer and director, *He Makes Me Feel Like Dancin'* (documentary; also released as a film), NBC, 1983.

TELEVISION WORK; EPISODIC

Director, "The Rise and Rise of Daniel Rocket," *American Playhouse,* PBS, 1986.

OTHER TELEVISION WORK

Director, *Dirty Dancing* (series), CBS, 1988.

Also worked as producer and director of *The Joffrey Ballet: Live from Artpark,* 1977-78; *Two Duets with Choreography by Jerome Robbins and Peter Martins,* 1979-80; *The Spellbound Child,* c. 1981; *The Paul Taylor Dance Company: Three Modern Classics, Two Landmark Dances,* 1981-82. Also producer and director of *The Tempest, The Paul Taylor Company Summerfest, The Feld Ballet, Vaudeville Alive and Dancing, The Green Table with the Joffrey Ballet,* and *Balanchine Celebrates Stravinsky.* Director of *The Dance and the Railroad,* 1982; *A Midsummer Night's Dream,* 1982; *Gala of Stars,* 1984; *Good Morning, Mr. Orwell,* 1984. Also director of *When Hell Freezes Over I'll Skate, Leonard Bernstein's Mass,* and *Alice at the Palace.* Producer of *Sue's Leg/Remembering the Thirties, Astarte, The Makropoulus Affair, The Seagull,* and *Jesus Christ Superstar.*

FILM WORK

Director, *Dirty Dancing,* Vestron, 1987.
Director, *Chances Are,* Tri-Star, 1989.
Director, *Three Men and a Little Lady,* Buena Vista, 1990.

Also worked as editor for *Seafall,* 1969; *Threatened Paradise,* 1972; *On Loan from Russia,* 1973; *A Time to Live,* 1973. Editor of *A Desert's Dream, Charlie Pride, Cherry Tree Carol,* and *Luther.*

STAGE WORK

Projection media designer (with Gardner Compton), *Oh! Calcutta!,* Eden Theatre, 1969-70, then Belasco Theatre, New York City, 1971-72.

RECORDINGS:

VIDEOS

Director of "Rumpelstiltskin," *Faerie Tale Theatre,* released on videocassette, 1980.*

* * *

ARTHUR, Jean 1905(?)-1991

PERSONAL: Born Gladys Georgianna Greene, October 17, 1905 (some sources say 1908), in New York, NY; died of heart failure, June 19, 1991, in Carmel, CA; daughter of Hubert Sidney (a photographer) and Johanna Augusta (Neilson) Greene; married Julian Anker, 1928 (marriage annulled, 1928); married Frank J. Ross, Jr. (a film producer), June 11, 1932 (divorced, 1949). *Education:* Attended Fort Washington High School, New York City, Stephens College, and Bennington College. *Avocational interests:* Books, symphonic music, collecting fine china.

CAREER: Actress. Worked as illustrator's model for Howard Chandler Christy; Vassar College, Poughkeepsie, NY, instructor in drama, c. 1968-72; North Carolina School of Arts, instructor in drama and acting, 1973. *Wartime service:* Performed for U.S. Army soldiers during World War II.

MEMBER: Actor's Equity Association.

AWARDS, HONORS: Academy Award nomination, best actress, 1943, for *The More the Merrier.*

CREDITS:

FILM APPEARANCES

(Film debut) *The Temple of Venus,* Fox Film Corporation, 1923.

Mary Spengler, *Sins of the Fathers,* Paramount, 1923.
Ruth Wells, *The Fighting Cheat,* Paramount, 1924.
Loria Gatlin, *A Man of Nerve,* FBO, 1925.
Seven Chances, Metro Goldwyn, 1925.
Rose Craddock, *The Fighting Smile,* Independent Pictures, 1925.
Under Fire, Davis, 1926.
Letty Crane, *Husband Hunters,* Tiffany, 1927.
Mary Post, *Warming Up,* Paramount, 1928.
Alice LaFosse, *The Canary Murder Case,* Paramount, 1929.
Lia Eltham, *The Mysterious Dr. Fu Manchu,* Paramount, 1929.
Ada Greene, *The Greene Murder Case,* Paramount, 1929.
Greta Nelson, *Half Way to Heaven,* Paramount, 1929.
Janie, *The Saturday Night Kid,* Paramount, 1929.
Ruth Hutt, *Stairs of Sand,* Paramount, 1929.
Mary Ryan, *Danger Lights,* RKO Radio Pictures, 1930.
Lila Eltham, *The Return of Dr. Fu Manchu* (also known as *The New Adventures of Dr. Fu Manchu*), Paramount, 1930.
Mildred Wayland, *The Silver Horde,* RKO Radio Pictures, 1930.
Judith Marsden, *Street of Chance,* Paramount, 1930.
Mary Gordon, *Young Eagles,* Paramount, 1930.
Paramount on Parade, Paramount, 1930.
Ethel Simmons, *Ex-Bad Boy,* Universal, 1931.
Sylvia Martine, *The Gang Buster,* Paramount, 1931.
Beatrice Stevens, *The Lawyer's Secret,* Paramount, 1931.
Barbara Olwell, *Virtuous Husband* (also known as *What Wives Don't Want*), Universal, 1931.
Joan Hoyt, *The Past of Mary Holmes,* RKO Radio Pictures, 1933.
Sandra Morrison, *Whirlpool,* Columbia, 1934.
Joan Hayes, *The Defense Rests,* Columbia, 1934.
Most Precious Thing in Life, Columbia, 1934.
Wilhelmina "Bill" Clark, *The Whole Town's Talking,* Columbia, 1935.
Theresa O'Reilly, *Public Hero Number One,* Metro-Goldwyn-Mayer, 1935.
Jane Matthews and Emma, *Diamond Jim,* Universal, 1935.
The Public Menace, Columbia, 1935.
Marge Oliver, *Party Wire,* Columbia, 1935.
Joan Hawthorne, *If You Could Only Cook,* Columbia, 1936.
Babe Bennett, *Mr. Deeds Goes to Town,* Columbia, 1936.
Clarie Peyton, *Adventure in Manhattan* (also known as *Manhattan Madness*), Columbia, 1936.
Paula Bradford, *The Ex-Mrs. Bradford,* RKO Radio Pictures, 1936.
Carol Baldwin, *More Than a Secretary,* Columbia, 1936.
Calamity Jane, *The Plainsman,* Paramount, 1937.
Irene Vail, *History Is Made at Night,* United Artists, 1937.
Mary Smith, *Easy Living,* Paramount, 1937.
Alice Sycamore, *You Can't Take It with You,* Columbia, 1938.
Bonnie Lee, *Only Angels Have Wings,* Columbia, 1939.
Saunders, *Mr. Smith Goes to Washington,* Columbia, 1939.
Vicky Lowndes, *Too Many Husbands* (also known as *My Two Husbands*), Columbia, 1940.
Phoebe Titus, *Arizona,* Columbia, 1940.
Mary Jones, *The Devil and Miss Jones,* RKO Radio Pictures, 1941.
Nora Shelley, *Talk of the Town,* Columbia, 1942.
Connie Milligan, *The More the Merrier,* Columbia, 1943.
Mollie Truesdale, *A Lady Takes a Chance,* Frank Ross/RKO Radio Pictures, 1943.
Janie Anderson, *The Impatient Years,* Columbia, 1944.
Phoebe Frost, *A Foreign Affair,* Paramount, 1948.
Marion Starrett, *Shane,* Paramount, 1953.

Also appeared in *Cameo Kirby,* 1923; *Biff Bang Buddy,* 1924; *Bringin' Home the Bacon,* 1924; *Fast and Fearless,* 1924; *Thundering Romance,* 1924; *Travelin' Fast,* 1924; *Drug Store Cowboy,* 1925; *Hurricane Horseman,* 1925; *Tearin' Loose,* 1925; *Thundering Through,* 1925; *The Block Signal,* 1926; *Born to Battle,* 1926; *The College Boob,* 1926; *The Cowboy Cop,* 1926; *Double Daring,* 1926; *Lighting Bill,* 1926; *Twisted Triggers,* 1926; *The Broken Gate,* 1927; *Flying Luck,* 1927; *The Poor Nut,* 1927; *Horseshoes,* 1927; *The Masked Menace,* 1927; *Brotherly Love,* 1928; *Easy Come Easy Go,* 1928; *Sins of the Father,* 1928; *Wallflowers,* 1928; *Get That Venus,* 1933; *George Stevens: A Filmmaker's Journey,* 1985; and *The Making of a Legend: "Gone with the Wind,"* 1989.

STAGE APPEARANCES

(New York debut) Ann, *Foreign Affairs,* Avon Theatre, 1932.
Adele Vernin, *The Man Who Reclaimed His Head,* Broadhurst Theatre, New York City, 1932.
Lucy, *$25 an Hour,* Masque Theatre, 1933.
Elsa Karling, *The Curtain Rises,* Vanderbilt Theatre, 1933.
Klari, *The Bride of Torozko,* Henry Miller's Theatre, 1934.
Title role, *Peter Pan,* Imperial Theatre, New York City, 1950.
Title role, *Saint Joan,* National Theatre, Washington, DC, 1954.
Title role, *The Freaking Out of Stephanie Blake,* Eugene O'Neill Theatre, New York City, 1967.
First Monday in October, Cleveland Play House, Cleveland, OH, 1975.

Also appeared in summer stock productions of *Coquette, Let Us Be Gay,* and *The Road to Rome,* all Red Bank, NJ,

1932. Toured as Kalonika, *Lysistrata,* 1932; and Billie Dawn, *Born Yesterday,* 1946.

TELEVISION APPEARANCES; EPISODIC

(Television debut) "Thursday's Child," *Gunsmoke,* CBS, 1965.

TELEVISION APPEARANCES; SERIES

Patricia Marshall, *The Jean Arthur Show,* CBS, 1966.

RADIO APPEARANCES

Mr. Deeds Goes to Town, ABC, 1937.

OBITUARIES AND OTHER SOURCES:

PERIODICALS

Detroit Free Press, June 20, 1991, p. 4B.
New York Times, May 14, 1972.*

* * *

ARTHUR, Karen 1941-

PERSONAL: Born August 24, 1941, in Omaha, NE.

ADDRESSES: Agent—Ken Gross, Robinson, Weintraub, Gross, and Associates, Inc., 8428 Melrose Pl., Los Angeles, CA 90069.

CAREER: Director. Worked as a ballet dancer, choreographer, and musical comedy singer, 1950-68; dancer and actress, 1968-75.

AWARDS, HONORS: Grant from Independent Filmmaker Program, 1974; International Film Critics Award, best first film, 1975, and Josef Von Sternberg Award, both for *Legacy;* Christopher Award, for *Victims for Victims;* Emmy Award, outstanding director of a dramatic episode, 1985, for "Heat," *Cagney and Lacey;* Christopher Award, for *Evil in Clear River.*

CREDITS:

FILM WORK

Producer and director, *Legacy,* Kino International, 1976.
Executive producer and director, *The Mafu Cage* (also known as *My Sister, My Love*), Clouds Productions, 1978.
Director, *Lady Beware,* International Video Enterprises, 1987.

FILM APPEARANCES

Lady dinner partner, *A Guide for the Married Man,* Twentieth Century-Fox, 1967.
Miss Dairy Queen, *Winning,* Universal, 1969.

TELEVISION WORK; MOVIES; DIRECTOR

Charleston, NBC, 1979.
Victims for Victims: The Theresa Saldana Story, NBC, 1984.
A Bunny's Tale, ABC, 1985.
The Rape of Richard Beck, ABC, 1985.
Cracked Up, ABC, 1987.
Fall from Grace, NBC, 1990.
Bump in the Night, CBS, 1991.
The Secret, CBS, 1992.

Also directed *Evil in Clear River,* 1988, and *Bridge to Silence,* 1989.

TELEVISION WORK; MINI-SERIES; DIRECTOR

Return to Eden, syndicated, 1984.
Crossings, ABC, 1986.
American Dream, ABC, 1992.

TELEVISION WORK; EPISODIC; DIRECTOR, EXCEPT WHERE INDICATED

Rich Man, Poor Man—Book II, ABC, 1976-77.
Hart to Hart, ABC, 1979 and 1980-81.
(And producer) *Remington Steele,* NBC, 1982 and 1984.
Cagney and Lacey (includes the episode "Heat"), CBS, 1982 and 1985-86.
Boone, NBC, 1983.
Two Marriages, ABC, 1983 and 1984.
Emerald Point, N.A.S., CBS, 1983 and 1984.
"Shadow of a Doubt," *Hallmark Hall of Fame,* CBS, 1991.

OTHER TELEVISION WORK; DIRECTOR

Project: Tin Man (pilot), ABC, 1990.

Also directed *Blue Bayou* (pilot), 1990.

OTHER SOURCES:

PERIODICALS

American Film, October, 1987, pp. 10-13.

* * *

ASHCROFT, Peggy 1907-1991

OBITUARY NOTICE—See index for *CTFT* sketch: Full name, Edith Margaret Emily Ashcroft; born December 22, 1907, in Croydon, England; died after suffering a stroke, June 14, 1991, in London, England. Actress. Regarded as one of England's most venerable actresses, Ashcroft starred in stage, film, and television. In 1930, she played Desdemona in a production of *Othello* that cast Paul Robeson in the title role. Later in her career, Ashcroft often costarred with other famous actors and actresses, including John Gielgud, Laurence Olivier, Vanessa Redgrave, Alec Guiness, and Peter O'Toole. Her many stage performances included numerous appearances in Shakespearean plays, as well as roles in *Hedda Gabler* and *The Cherry Orchard.* Aschroft was a charter member of the Royal Shakespeare Company, becoming a director in 1968. One of her most acclaimed performances was her portrayal of Margaret of Anjou in the Company's 1963 production of *Wars of the Roses.* Among Ashcroft's television appearances were Emmy Award-nominated performances in *A Perfect Spy* in 1989 and *The Jewel in the Crown* in 1984. In 1984 as well she played the role of Mrs. Moore in a film version of *A Passage to India,* for which she won an Academy Award and a British Academy of Film and Television Arts Award for best actress. Ashcroft received the title of Dame Commander of the British Empire in 1956. A theater in her hometown of Croydon was named in her honor.

OBITUARIES AND OTHER SOURCES:

BOOKS

Who's Who, 143rd edition, St. Martin's, 1991, p. 55.

PERIODICALS

Hollywood Reporter, June 17, 1991, pp. 1, 54.
Variety, June 17, 1991, p. 84.

* * *

ATKINSON, Rowan 1955-

PERSONAL: Full name, Rowan Sebastian Atkinson; born January 6, 1955; son of Eric and Ella May Atkinson; married Sunetra Sastry, 1990. *Education:* Attended Newcastle University; Oxford University, B.S., M.S. *Avocational interests:* Cars, motor sports.

ADDRESSES: Contact—c/o PBJ Management, Ltd., 47 Dean St., London W1V 5HL, England.

CAREER: Actor and writer.

AWARDS, HONORS: British Academy of Film and Television Arts (BAFTA) Award, best light entertainment television performance, 1980, for *Not the Nine O'Clock News;* Laurence Olivier Award, Society of West End Theatre, comedy performance of the year, 1981, for *Rowan Atkinson in Revue;* BAFTA Award, best light entertainment television performance, 1989, for *Blackadder Goes Forth;* award for best cable television comedy, for *Blackadder;* three Montreaux Television Festival awards, including the Golden Rose, all 1990, for *Mr. Bean;* BAFTA Award nomination, best light entertainment television performance, 1992, for "The Curse of Mr. Bean," *Mr. Bean.*

CREDITS:

STAGE APPEARANCES

Rowan Atkinson in Revue (also see below), Globe Theatre, London, 1981.
The Secret Policeman's Other Ball (comedy gala; also see below), Drury Lane Theatre, London, 1981.
Not in Front of the Audience, Drury Lane Theatre, 1982.
Rick Steadman, *The Nerd,* Aldwych Theatre, London, 1984.
Rowan Atkinson: The New Revue (also see below), Shaftesbury Theatre, London, 1986.
Rowan Atkinson at the Atkinson (also see below), Brooks Atkinson Theatre, New York City, 1986.
Mime Gala, London International Mime Festival, Bloomsbury Theatre, London, 1987.
The Sneeze, Aldwych Theatre, 1988.

Also appeared in *Beyond a Joke,* Hampstead, England, 1978, and *Oxford University Revues,* Edinburgh Festival Fringe.

TELEVISION APPEARANCES

Reporter, *Not the Nine O'Clock News* (series; also see below), syndicated, 1979-82.
Blackadder (series), BBC, beginning in 1983.
Comic Relief (special), BBC1, 1986.
"Just for Laughs II," *Showtime Comedy Spotlight* (special), Showtime, 1987.
"Live from London," *HBO Comedy Hour* (special), HBO, 1988.
"Montreal International Comedy Festival," *HBO Comedy Hour* (special), HBO, 1989.
Captain Blackadder, *Blackadder IV,* Arts and Entertainment, 1989.
Ebenezer Blackadder, *Blackadder's Christmas Carol* (special), Arts and Entertainment, 1989.
Dr. Schooner, *The Appointments of Dennis Jennings,* HBO, 1989.
Mr. Bean (includes "The Curse of Mr. Bean"; also see below), ITV, 1989-91.
Mr. Bean Rides Again, ITV, 1992.
"Rowan Atkinson," *HBO Comedy Hour* (special), HBO, 1992.

Also appeared in *Blackadder II,* 1985; *Blackadder the Third,* 1987; and *Blackadder Goes Forth,* 1989.

FILM APPEARANCES

The Secret Policeman's Ball (also see below), Tigon/Amnesty International, 1979.
The Secret Policeman's Other Ball, United International Pictures, 1981.
Small-Fawcett, *Never Say Never Again,* Warner Brothers, 1983.

Ron Anderson, *The Tall Guy,* Virgin Vision, 1989.
Mr. Stringer, *The Witches,* Warner Brothers, 1990.

WRITINGS:

The Secret Policeman's Ball (screenplay), Tigon/Amnesty International, 1979.
(With others) *Not the Nine O'Clock News* (television series), syndicated, 1979-82.
(With Richard Curtis) *Rowan Atkinson in Revue* (for the stage), produced at Globe Theatre, London, 1981.
(With Curtis and Ben Elton) *Rowan Atkinson: The New Revue* (for the stage), produced at Shaftesbury Theatre, London, 1986.
(With Curtis and Elton) *Rowan Atkinson at the Atkinson* (for the stage), produced at Brooks Atkinson Theatre, New York City, 1986.
(With Robin Driscoll, Curtis, and Elton) *Mr. Bean* (television series), ITV, 1989-91.*

* * *

AVILDSEN, John G. 1935-

PERSONAL: Full name, John Guilbert Avildsen; born December 21, 1935, in Chicago, IL; son of Clarence John and Ivy (Guilbert) Avildsen; married Tracy Brooks Swope (an actress), February, 1987; children: Anthony Guilbert, Jonathan. *Education:* Attended New York University, 1955.

ADDRESSES: *Agent*—Martin Bauer, United Talent Agency, 9560 Wilshire Blvd., 5th Floor, Beverly Hills, CA 90212.

CAREER: Director, cinematographer, and editor. Vespa Motor Scooters, advertising manager, 1959; Muller, Jordan & Herrick Industrial Films, writer and producer of film commercials, 1965-67; began film career as assistant cameraman and production manager. *Military service:* U.S. Army, 1959-61.

MEMBER: Directors Guild of America, Motion Picture Photographers Union, Motion Picture Editors Union, Writers Guild of America.

AWARDS, HONORS: Academy Award, best directing, 1976, for *Rocky;* Academy Award nomination, best documentary (short subject), 1982, for *Traveling Hopefully.* Emmy nomination for *From No House to Options House.*

CREDITS:

FILM WORK

Director and photographer, *Turn on to Love,* Haven International, 1969.
Associate producer and director of photography, *Out of It,* United Artists (UA), 1969.
Director, photographer, and editor, *Guess What We Learned in School Today?* (also see below), Cannon, 1970.
Director and photographer, *Joe,* Cannon, 1970.
Director, photographer, and editor, *Cry Uncle!,* Cambist, 1971.
Director, photographer, and editor, *Okay Bill* (also see below; also known as *Sweet Dreams*), Four Star Excelsior, 1971.
Director and photographer, *The Stoolie,* Jama, 1972.
Director, *Save the Tiger,* Paramount, 1973.
Director, *W. W. and the Dixie Dance Kings,* Twentieth Century-Fox, 1975.
Director (with Bruce Malmuth and Robert J. McCarty), photographer, and editor, *Foreplay,* Cinema International, 1975.
Director and editor, *Rocky,* UA, 1976.
Director, producer, editor, and camera operator, *Slow Dancing in the Big City,* UA, 1978.
Director and editor, *The Formula,* Metro-Goldwyn-Mayer (MGM)/UA, 1980.
Director and supervising editor, *Neighbors,* Columbia, 1981.
Director and producer, *Traveling Hopefully* (documentary short subject), Arnuthfonyus Films, 1982.
Director, editor, and camera operator, *A Night in Heaven,* Twentieth Century-Fox, 1983.
Director and editor, *The Karate Kid,* Columbia, 1984.
Director and editor, *The Karate Kid, Part II,* Columbia, 1986.
Director, *Happy New Year,* Columbia, 1987.
Director and editor, *For Keeps,* Tri-Star, 1988.
Executive producer, director, and coeditor, *Lean on Me,* Warner Brothers, 1989.
Director and coeditor, *The Karate Kid, Part III,* Columbia, 1989.
Director and coeditor, *Rocky V,* MGM/UA, 1990.
Director and editor, *The Power of One,* Warner Brothers, 1992.

Also worked as assistant director of *Hurry Sundown,* 1964, and *Black Like Me;* production manager of *Mickey One,* 1964, and *Una Moglie Americana;* producer, photographer, and editor of *Light, Sound, Diffuse* (short film).

FILM APPEARANCES

Alvie, *Greenwich Village Story* (also known as *Birthplace of the Hootenanny* and *They Love as They Please*), Lion International, 1963.

TELEVISION WORK

Director, *Murder Ink* (series), CBS, 1983.

Also director of *From No House to Options House* and *2 on the Town.*

WRITINGS:

SCREENPLAYS

(With Eugene Price) *Guess What We Learned in School Today?,* Cannon, 1970.
Okay Bill (also known as *Sweet Dreams*), Four Star Excelsior, 1971.

B

BADALAMENTI, Angelo (Andy Badale)

CAREER: Composer, music director, and orchestrator. Worked previously as a junior high school teacher in Brooklyn, NY.

AWARDS, HONORS: Emmy Award nominations, outstanding achievement in music and lyrics, and outstanding achievement in music composition for a series, both 1990, both for *Twin Peaks;* Emmy Award nomination, outstanding achievement in main title theme music, 1990, for "Twin Peaks Theme"; Grammy Award, best pop instrumental performance, 1990, for "Twin Peaks Theme."

CREDITS:

TELEVISION WORK; SERIES

Music director and orchestrator, *Twin Peaks* (also see below), ABC, 1990-91.

FILM WORK; MUSIC DIRECTOR, EXCEPT WHERE INDICATED

(And conductor) *Blue Velvet* (also see below), DiLaurentiis Entertainment Group, 1986.

Orchestrator, *Tough Guys Don't Dance* (also known as *Norman Mailer's Tough Guys Don't Dance;* also see below), Cannon, 1987.

(And orchestrator) *Cousins* (also see below), Paramount, 1989.

FILM APPEARANCES

(Under name Andy Badale) Piano player, *Blue Velvet* (also see below), DiLaurentiis Entertainment Group, 1986.

WRITINGS:

TELEVISION MUSIC

Score, theme music, and songs "The Nightingale" and "Falling," *Twin Peaks,* ABC, 1990-91.

Also author of songs for *Captain Kangaroo.*

FILM MUSIC

(Under name Andy Badale) Songs, *Gordon's War,* Twentieth Century-Fox, 1973.

(Under name Andy Badale) Score, *Law and Disorder,* Columbia, 1974.

(Under name Andy Badale) Title song lyrics, *Across the Great Divide,* Pacific International Enterprises, 1976.

Score, and songs "Blue Star" and "Mysteries of Love," *Blue Velvet,* DiLaurentiis Entertainment Group, 1986.

Score, *A Nightmare on Elm Street Part III: Dream Warriors,* New Line Cinema, 1987.

Score, and songs "You'll Come Back (You Always Do)" and "Real Man," *Tough Guys Don't Dance,* Cannon, 1987.

Score, and song "Mysteries of Love," *Weeds,* DiLaurentiis Entertainment Group, 1987.

Score, and song "I Love You for Today," *Cousins,* Paramount, 1989.

(With Jonathan Elias and Sherman Foote) Score, *Parents,* Vestron, 1989.

Score, *National Lampoon's Christmas Vacation* (also known as *National Lampoon's Winter Holiday* and *Christmas Vacation*), Warner Brothers, 1989.

Score, *Wait until Spring, Bandini,* Orion, 1989.

Score, and song "Up in Flames," *Wild at Heart,* Samuel Goldwyn, 1990.

Score, *The Comfort of Strangers,* Skouras Pictures, 1990.

Score, *Other People's Money,* Warner Brothers, 1991.

Also composer of music for *Shattered.**

* * *

BADALE, Andy
See BADALAMENTI, Angelo

* * *

BALDWIN, William

PERSONAL: Born in Massapequa, NY; son of Alexander Rae (a high school teacher) and Carol Newcomb (Martineau) Baldwin. *Education:* State University of New York at Binghamton, B.S., political science.

ADDRESSES: *Agent*—J. Michael Bloom, 9200 Sunset Blvd., Suite 710, Los Angeles, CA 90069.

CAREER: Actor. Worked briefly on Capitol Hill. Appeared in national print advertising campaigns.

CREDITS:

TELEVISION APPEARANCES; MOVIES

Robert Chambers, *The Preppie Murder,* ABC, 1989.

FILM APPEARANCES

Platoon soldier, *Born on the Fourth of July,* Universal, 1989.
Van Stretch, *Internal Affairs,* Paramount, 1990.
Joe Hurley, *Flatliners,* Columbia, 1990.
Brian McCaffrey, *Backdraft,* Universal, 1991.*

* * *

BALL, William 1931-1991

OBITUARY NOTICE—See index for *CTFT* sketch: Born April 29, 1931, in Chicago (one source says Evanston), IL; died July 30, 1991, in Los Angeles, CA. Director, producer and actor. Ball is best known as the founder and general director of American Conservatory Theatre (ACT), which is credited with the revival of San Francisco theatre in the mid 1960s. Ball began his career as an actor and director in regional theatre troops and Shakespearean festivals during the 1950s, playing major roles in *Julius Caesar, The Tempest,* and *Hamlet. Ivanov,* his 1958 Off-Broadway directorial debut, received both an Obie Award and a Vernon Rice Drama Desk Award. Ball went on to direct eighty-seven productions in California, London, Texas, and New York, receiving awards in the early 1960s for Off-Broadway productions of *Under Milk Wood* and *Six Characters in Search of an Author.* He founded the American Conservatory Theater in 1965, moving it to San Francisco in 1967. In addition to producing and directing the productions, Ball raised enough funds to add a second theatre and, in 1971, a theatre arts training academy. After his resignation from ACT in 1986, Ball played British-born poet W. H. Auden in a Public Broadcasting System (PBS) production of *Voices from Sandoner* and appeared in the film *Suburban Commando.* In 1984, Ball published *A Sense of Directing: Some Observations on the Art of Directing.*

OBITUARIES AND OTHER SOURCES:

BOOKS

The International Who's Who, 1989-1990, 53rd edition, Europa, 1989, p. 89.

PERIODICALS

Variety, August 5, 1991, p. 110.

* * *

BALLHAUS, Michael 1935-

PERSONAL: Born August 5, 1935, in Berlin, Germany; immigrated to the United States, 1982; son of Oskar (an actor) and Lenna (an actress; maiden name, Huter) Ballhaus; children: Florian, Sebastian. *Education:* Studied photography for two years.

ADDRESSES: *Agent*—Lawrence A. Mirisch, Triad Artists, Inc., 10100 Santa Monica Blvd., 16th Floor, Los Angeles, CA 90067.

CAREER: Cinematographer. Directed photography for first film, 1960; worked with German filmmaker Rainer Werner Fassbinder, 1970-c.1982.

MEMBER: American Society of Cinematographers.

AWARDS, HONORS: Academy Award nomination, best achievement in cinematography, 1987, for *Broadcast News;* Academy Award nomination, best achievement in cinematography, and Achievement Award, best cinematography, Los Angeles Film Critics Association, both 1989, for *The Fabulous Baker Boys.*

CREDITS:

FILM WORK; CINEMATOGRAPHER

Whity, Atlantis Film/Antiteater-X-Film, 1970.
Warnung vor einer heiligen Nutte (released in the U.S. as *Beware of a Holy Whore,* New Yorker, 1971), Antiteater-X-Film/Nova International, 1970.
The Bitter Tears of Petra von Kant (also known as *Die bitteren Traenen der Petra von Kant,* Tango Film, 1972), New Yorker, 1972.

Faustrecht der Freiheit, Fox (also known as *Fist-Right of Freedom;* released in the U.S. as *Fox and His Friends* and *Survival of the Fittest,* New Yorker, 1976), Tango Film, 1975.
Mutter Kuesters faehrt zum Himmel (released in the U.S. as *Mother Kusters Goes to Heaven,* New Yorker, 1976), Tango Film, 1975.
Satansbraten (released in the U.S. as *Satan's Brew,* New Yorker, 1976), Albatros Productions, 1976.
Summer Guests (also known as *Sommergaeste,* 1975), Constantin, 1976.
Chinesisches Roulette (released in the U.S. as *Chinese Roulette,* New Yorker, 1977), Albatros-Film/Les Films du Losange, 1977.
Despair, Swan Diffusion, 1978.
(With Juergen Juerges, Bodo Kessler, Dietrich Lohmann, Colin Mounier, and Joerg Schmidt-Reitwein) *Germany in Autumn* (also known as *Deutschland im Herbst*), Projekt-Filmverlag der Autoren-Hallelujah-Kairos Film, 1978.
Die Ehe der Maria Braun (also see below; released in the U.S. as *The Marriage of Maria Braun,* New Yorker, 1979), Albatros-Film, 1978.
Baby, It's You, Paramount, 1983.
Dear Mr. Wonderful, Lilienthal, 1983.
The Stationmaster's Wife, Teleculture, 1983.
Malou, Quartet, 1983.
Sheer Madness, R5/S8, 1983.
Friends and Husbands, Miracle, 1983.
Reckless, Metro-Goldwyn-Mayer/United Artists, 1984.
The Autograph (also known as *Das Autogram*), Cine-International, 1984.
Old Enough, Orion Classics, 1984.
Heartbreakers, Orion, 1984.
After Hours, Geffen/Warner Brothers, 1985.
The Color of Money, Buena Vista, 1986.
Under the Cherry Moon, Warner Brothers, 1986.
The Glass Menagerie, Cineplex Odeon, 1987.
Broadcast News, Twentieth Century-Fox, 1987.
The House on Carroll Street, Orion, 1988.
The Last Temptation of Christ, Universal, 1988.
Dirty Rotten Scoundrels, Orion, 1988.
Working Girl, Twentieth Century-Fox, 1988.
The Fabulous Baker Boys, Twentieth Century-Fox, 1989.
Postcards from the Edge, Columbia, 1990.
Goodfellas, Warner Brothers, 1990.
Guilty by Suspicion, Warner Brothers, 1991.
What about Bob?, Buena Vista, 1991.
The Mambo Kings, Warner Brothers, 1992.

Also worked as cinematographer for other films, including *Sand,* 1971; *Tschetan, der Indianerjunge,* 1973; *Martha,* 1974; *Ich will doch nur, dass ihr mich liebt,* 1976; *Adolf & Marlene,* 1976; *Also es war so . . . ,* 1976; *Frauen in New York,* 1977; *Die erste Polka,* 1978; *Bolwieser,* 1978; *Kaleidoskop: Valeska Gert, nur zum Spass-nur zum Spiel* (documentary), 1979; *Deutscher Fruehling,* 1979; *Trilogie des Wiedersehens,* 1979; *Gross und klein,* 1980; *Der Aufstand,* 1980; *Looping,* 1981; *Der Zauberberg,* 1982; *Heller Wahn,* 1982; *Edith's Tagebuch,* 1983; *Aus der Familie der Panzereschen,* 1984; *Deine Zartlichkeiten;* and *Two of Us.*

FILM APPEARANCES

Anwalt, *Die Ehe der Maria Braun* (released in the U.S. as *The Marriage of Maria Braun,* New Yorker, 1979), Albatros-Film, 1978.

Also appeared as the second film director's cameraman in *Der Kleine Godard,* 1978.

TELEVISION WORK; CINEMATOGRAPHER

Death of a Salesman (movie), CBS, 1985.
Landscape with Waitress (special), PBS, 1986.
Baja Oklahoma (movie), HBO, 1988.

TELEVISION APPEARANCES; EPISODIC

"Private Conversations: On the Set of 'Death of a Salesman,' " *American Masters,* PBS, 1986.
"Martin Scorsese Directs," *American Masters,* PBS, 1990.*

* * *

BANNERMAN, Kay 1919-1991

OBITUARY NOTICE—See index for *CTFT* sketch: Born October 11, 1919, in Hove, Sussex, England; died March 31, 1991, in Marbella, Spain. Performer and playwright. Bannerman began her career as a stage actress in the late 1930s. She had major roles in London productions of *Major Barbara* and *The Gambler,* and played Portia in a British tour of *The Merchant of Venice.* In the late 1940s Bannerman left the stage to write comedies in collaboration with her husband, Harold Brooke. Many of their nineteen scripts were produced on the stage and several were filmed. Bannerman and Brooke's works include *The Iron Maiden, No, My Darling Daughter,* and their most successful piece, *Let Sleeping Wives Lie.*

OBITUARIES AND OTHER SOURCES:

PERIODICALS

Variety, April 15, 1991, p. 218.

* * *

BARISH, Keith

PERSONAL: Born in Los Angeles, CA.

CAREER: Producer. Taft Broadcasting Co., Entertainment Division, partner, beginning in 1984.

AWARDS, HONORS: Emmy Award nomination (with Craig Baumgarten and Marc Trabulus), outstanding drama or comedy special, 1984, for "A Streetcar Named Desire," *An ABC Theatre Presentation;* NATO Award, producer of the year, 1987.

CREDITS:

FILM WORK; EXECUTIVE PRODUCER, EXCEPT WHERE INDICATED

Endless Love, Barber International Films, 1981.
Producer (with Alan J. Pakula), *Sophie's Choice,* Universal, 1982.
Kiss Me Goodbye, Twentieth Century-Fox, 1982.
Misunderstood, Metro-Goldwyn-Mayer (MGM)/United Artists, 1984.
9 1/2 Weeks, MGM, 1986.
Big Trouble in Little China, Twentieth Century-Fox, 1986.
Producer (with Rob Cohen), *Light of Day,* Tri-Star, 1987.
The Running Man, Tri-Star, 1987.
The Monster Squad, Tri-Star, 1987.
Producer (with Marcia Nasatir, Gene Kirkwood, and C. O. Erickson), *Ironweed,* Tri-Star, 1987.
The Serpent and the Rainbow, Universal, 1988.
Her Alibi, Warner Brothers, 1989.
Fire Birds (also known as *Wings of the Apache*), Buena Vista, 1990.

TELEVISION WORK; MOVIES

Executive producer (with Craig Baumgarten), "A Streetcar Named Desire," *An ABC Theatre Presentation,* ABC, 1984.

OTHER SOURCES:

PERIODICALS

New York, August 10, 1981, p. 35.*

*   *   *

BARKLEY, Deanne 1931-

PERSONAL: Born March 28, 1931, in New Orleans, LA; daughter of Newton Buckner and Elodie (Marrero) Barkley; children: Melissa, Wilson, John Shirley, Margaret, Tony, and Shannon Fitzpatrick (triplets). *Education:* Attended Northwestern University, 1948-51.

ADDRESSES: Office—555 West 57th St., No. 1230, New York, NY 10019.

CAREER: Producer, writer, and studio executive. ABC-TV, vice-president for programming; Robert Stigwood Organization, vice-president for creative affairs; NBC-TV, Burbank, CA, vice-president for motion pictures and mini-series.

CREDITS:

TELEVISION WORK; MOVIES; EXECUTIVE PRODUCER, EXCEPT WHERE INDICATED

(With Howard Rosenman) *The Virginia Hill Story,* NBC, 1974.
(With Rosenman) *All Together Now,* ABC, 1975.
Producer, *Death Scream* (also known as *Homicide* and *The Woman Who Cried Murder*), ABC, 1975.
(With Paul Klein) *The Day the Women Got Even* (also known as *Every Wednesday*), NBC, 1980.
(With Renee Wayne Golden) *The Ordeal of Bill Carney,* CBS, 1981.
Side by Side: The True Story of the Osmond Family, NBC, 1982.
Desperate Intruder, syndicated, 1983.
Emergency Room, syndicated, 1983.
This Wife for Hire, ABC, 1985.
Island Sons, ABC, 1987.

OTHER TELEVISION WORK; EXECUTIVE PRODUCER

(With Dick Clark and Paul Klein) *Valentine Magic on Love Island* (pilot), NBC, 1980.
(With Norman Gimbel and Philip Capice) *Private Sessions* (pilot), NBC, 1985.
The Alan King Show (special), CBS, 1986.

Also worked as executive producer for *Wedding Day,* 1981.

WRITINGS:

Freeway (novel), Macmillan, 1978.

Writer for the *Dick Cavett Show* and the *Helen Gurley Brown Show.*

ADAPTATIONS: The novel *Freeway* was adapted for film and released by New World, 1988.*

*   *   *

BATES, Kathy 1948-

PERSONAL: Full name, Kathleen Doyle Bates; born June 28, 1948, in Memphis, TN; daughter of Langdon Doyle (a mechanical engineer) and Bertye Kathleen (Talbot) Bates. *Education:* Southern Methodist University, B.F.A., 1969.

ADDRESSES: Agent—Susan Smith & Associates, 121 North San Vincente Blvd., Beverly Hills, CA 90211.

CAREER: Actress. Actors Theatre of Louisville, Louisville, KY, member of company, 1978-79, 1980-81, and 1984-85; member of Circle Repertory Company, Playwrights Horizons, City Center Young People's Company, and Lion Theatre Company, all New York City.

MEMBER: Actors Fund of America (life member), American Society of Composers, Authors, and Publishers, Women in Film, Academy of Motion Picture Arts and Sciences.

AWARDS, HONORS: Antoinette Perry Award nomination, outstanding performance by an actress in a play, and Outer Critics Circle Award, both 1983, Los Angeles Drama Critics Award and Dramalogue Award, both 1986, all for *'night, Mother;* Obie Award, *Village Voice,* Dramalogue Award, and Drama Desk nomination, all 1988, for *Frankie and Johnny in the Clair de Lune;* Academy Award, best performance by an actress in a leading role, 1990, and Golden Globe Award, best actress in a dramatic film, Hollywood Foreign Press Association, 1990, for *Misery;* Distinguished Artists Award, Club 100 of the Music Center, and Golden Globe nomination, best actress in a film comedy, both 1991, for *Fried Green Tomatoes.*

CREDITS:

FILM APPEARANCES

Selma Darin, *Straight Time,* Warner Brothers, 1978.
Stella May, *Come Back to the 5 & Dime, Jimmy Dean, Jimmy Dean,* Viacom, 1982.
Furniture man's wife, *Two of a Kind,* Twentieth Century-Fox, 1983.
Woman on Mateo Street, *The Morning After,* Twentieth Century-Fox, 1986.
Ruth Stanton, *Summer Heat,* Atlantic Releasing, 1987.
Mrs. Canby, *Arthur 2 on the Rocks,* Warner Brothers, 1988.
Jill, *High Stakes* (also known as *Melanie Rose*), Vidmark, 1989.
Mary Beth Alder, *Signs of Life* (also known as *One for Sorrow, Two for Joy*), Avenue, 1989.
Lisa Coleman, *Men Don't Leave,* Warner Brothers, 1990.
Mrs. Green, *Dick Tracy,* Touchstone/Buena Vista, 1990.
Rosemary Powers, *White Palace,* Universal, 1990.
Annie Wilkes, *Misery,* Columbia, 1990.
Evelyn Couch, *Fried Green Tomatoes,* Universal, 1991.
Hazel Quarrier, *At Play in the Fields of the Lord,* Universal, 1991.
Elsa Barlow, *The Road to Mecca,* L & O, 1991.
Bibby, *Used People,* Largo, 1992.
Prostitute, *Shadows and Fog,* Orion, 1992.
Mrs. Blier, *Prelude to a Kiss,* Twentieth Century-Fox, 1992.

Also appeared as BoBo, *Taking Off,* 1971, and as Helen Blake, *My Best Friend Is a Vampire,* 1988.

STAGE APPEARANCES

Duck and others, *Virginia Folk Tales,* Wayside Children's Theatre, Middletown, VA, 1973.
Casserole, Playwrights Horizons, New York City, 1975.
A Quality of Mercy, Playwrights Horizons, 1975.
Joanne, *Vanities,* Chelsea Westside Theater, New York City, 1976, then Westwood Theatre, Los Angeles, CA, and Drury Lane Theatre, Chicago, IL, both 1977.
Semmelweiss, Studio Arena Theatre, Buffalo, NY, 1977, then Hartman Theatre, Stamford, CT, 1981.
Colette, *Music-Hall Sidelights,* Lion Theatre, New York City, 1978.
Lenny MaGrath, *Crimes of the Heart,* Actors Theatre of Louisville, Louisville, KY, 1978.
Herrick Simmons, *The Art of Dining,* Public/Newman Theatre, New York City, 1979, then Eisenhower Theatre, Kennedy Center, Washington DC, 1979-1980.
Chocolate Cake, Actors Theatre of Louisville, c. 1980.
Final Placement, Actors Theatre of Louisville, c. 1980.
Isabel, *Goodbye Fidel,* New Ambassador Theatre, New York City, 1980.
Extremities, Actors Theatre of Louisville, 1981, then International Theatre Festival, Baltimore, MD, 1981.
Stella May, *Come Back to the 5 & Dime, Jimmy Dean, Jimmy Dean,* Martin Beck Theatre, New York City, 1982.
Jessie Cates, *'night, Mother,* American Repertory Theatre, Cambridge, MA, then Golden Theatre, New York City, 1983, then Mark Taper Forum, Los Angeles, CA, 1983.
Ella, *Curse of the Starving Class,* INTAR Theatre, 1985, then Promenade Theatre, New York City, 1985.
Aunt Dan, *Aunt Dan and Lemon,* Taper Too Theatre, Los Angeles, CA, c. 1986.
Frankie, *Frankie and Johnny in the Clair de Lune,* Manhattan Theatre Club, New York City, 1987, then Mark Taper Forum, 1988.
Elsa Barlow, *The Road to Mecca,* Promenade Theatre, 1988, then Eisenhower Theatre, Kennedy Center, 1989.

Also appeared in *5th of July,* and *The Shadow Box,* New York City; appeared with Folger Theatre Group, Washington, DC; spent two summers with O'Neill Playwrights Conference, Waterford, CT; spent three summers with Sundance Playwrights Lab.

TELEVISION APPEARANCES; EPISODIC

(Television debut) *The Love Boat,* ABC, 1977.

OTHER TELEVISION APPEARANCES

Katrine Kovacs, *Johnny Bull* (movie), ABC, 1986.
Jessie, *Roe vs. Wade* (movie), NBC, 1989.
Bonnie Cooper, *No Place Like Home* (movie; also known as *Homeless*), CBS, 1989.

Also appeared as Bobbi Burk, *Murder Ordained* (miniseries), 1987, and as Belle Bodeker, *All My Children* (series), ABC.

WRITINGS:

Author of the song "And Even the Horses Had Wings," 1971.

* * *

BEAUMONT, Ralph 1926-

PERSONAL: Born March 5, 1926, in Pocatello, ID; son of Nels Peter (a painter) and Florence Marie (Feldsted) Bergendorf. *Education:* Attended San Francisco City College, 1946-48; studied dance, acting, and speech at the American Theatre Wing, 1948-50.

ADDRESSES: Office—c/o The Ahmanson Theatre, 135 North Grand Ave., Los Angeles, CA 90012.

CAREER: Dancer and choreographer. Starlight Operetta, Dallas, TX, assistant choreographer for musical productions, 1950. Center Theatre Group, Ahmanson Theatre, Los Angeles, CA, production administrator, 1973—. *Military service:* U.S. Army, 1944-46; attained rank of sergeant.

MEMBER: American Federation of Radio and Television Artists, American Guild of Variety Artists, Society of Stage Directors and Choreographers, Actors' Equity Association, Screen Actors Guild, Beta Phi Beta.

CREDITS:

STAGE APPEARANCES

(Stage debut) *Inside America,* Hanna Theatre, Cleveland, OH, 1949.
Dancer, *Guys and Dolls,* Curran Theatre, San Francisco, CA, 1951.
(Broadway debut) Dancer, *Can-Can,* Shubert Theatre, New York City, 1953.
Dancer, *Shangri-La* (also see below), Winter Garden Theatre, New York City, 1956.

STAGE WORK; AS CHOREOGRAPHER EXCEPT WHERE INDICATED

Assistant choreographer, *Shangri-La,* Winter Garden Theatre, 1956.
Wonderful Town, New York City Center, 1958.
Saratoga, Winter Garden Theatre, 1959.
The Most Happy Fella, Coliseum Theatre, London, 1960.
Rinaldo in Campo, Teatro Sistina, Rome, 1961.
Enrico, Teatro Sistina, 1961.
Gentleman Prefer Blondes, Prince's Theatre, London, 1962.
Babilonia, Teatro Sistina, 1962.
Babes in the Wood, Orpheum Theatre, New York City, 1964.
The Yearling, Alvin Theatre, New York City, 1965.
(And director) *The Most Happy Fella,* New York City Center, 1966.
Guys and Dolls, New York City Center, 1966.
A Funny Thing Happened on the Way to the Forum, Playhouse, Pennsylvania State University, State College, 1966.
Wonderful Town, New York City Center, 1967.
A Funny Thing Happened on the Way to the Forum, Lunt-Fontanne Theatre, New York City, 1972.

FILM APPEARANCES; DANCER

April in Paris (also see below), Warner Brothers, 1952.
She's Back on Broadway (also see below), Warner Brothers, 1952.
The Band Wagon (also see below), Metro-Goldwyn-Mayer (MGM), 1952.
Gentlemen Prefer Blonds (also see below), Twentieth Century-Fox, 1952.

FILM WORK; ASSISTANT CHOREOGRAPHER

April in Paris, Warner Brothers, 1952.
She's Back on Broadway, Warner Brothers, 1952.
The Band Wagon, MGM, 1952.
Gentlemen Prefer Blonds, Twentieth Century-Fox, 1952.

TELEVISON APPEARANCES; DANCER; EPISODIC

Holiday Hotel (also see below), ABC, 1950.
The Ed Sullivan Show (also see below), CBS, 1952.
The Martha Raye Show (also see below), NBC, 1954.
The Sid Caesar Show (also see below), NBC, 1955.
The Milton Berle Show (also see below), NBC, 1956.

TELEVISION WORK; CHOREOGRAPHER

Holiday Hotel, ABC, 1950.
The Ed Sullivan Show, CBS, 1952.
The Martha Raye Show, NBC, 1954.
The Sid Caesar Show, NBC, 1955.
The Milton Berle Show, NBC, 1956.
Senore Della Venturo (also known as *Mr. Nine O'Clock*), RAI, Rome, Italy, 1962.
The Jack Parr Show, NBC, 1963.

TELEVISON WORK; MOVIES

Choreographer, *Wonderful Town,* CBS, 1958.*

* * *

BEDELIA, Bonnie 1952-

PERSONAL: Born March 25, 1952, in New York, NY; daughter of Philip (a journalist) and Marian (a writer and editor; maiden name, Wagner) Culkin; children: Yuri, Jonah. *Education:* Attended Professional Children's School, New York; attended Hunter College; studied ballet with George Balanchine at New York City Ballet; studied for the theatre at Herbert Berghof Studios with Uta Hagen and at the Actors Studio with Lee Strasberg.

ADDRESSES: Office—Jamner, Pariser, and Meschures, 760 North La Cienega Blvd., Los Angeles, CA 90069. *Agent*—Michael Black, International Creative Management, 8899 Beverly Blvd., Los Angeles, CA 90048.

CAREER: Actress and dancer. Inner City Repertory Company, Los Angeles, CA, original member; Los Angeles Classics Theatreworks, co-founder.

MEMBER: Actors Equity Association, American Federation of Television and Radio Artists, Screen Actors Guild.

AWARDS, HONORS: Scholarship, New York City Ballet, 1959-64; *Theatre World* Award, 1967, for *My Sweet Charlie;* Golden Globe nomination, 1983, for *Heart Like a Wheel.*

CREDITS:

STAGE APPEARANCES

(Stage debut) Jackie, *Dr. Praetorius,* North Jersey Playhouse, 1957.
Dancer, *Medea,* New York City Ballet, New York City, 1958-60.
(Broadway debut) Kathy Lanen, *Isle of Children,* Cort Theatre, New York City, 1962.
Wanda, *Enter Laughing,* Henry Miller's Theatre, New York City, 1964.
Pauline, *The Playroom,* Brooks Atkinson Theatre, New York City, 1965.
Sarah Mills, *Happily Never After,* Eugene O'Neill Theatre, New York City, 1966.
Marlene Chambers, *My Sweet Charlie,* Longacre Theatre, New York City, 1966.
Laura, *The Glass Menagerie,* Inner City Repertory Theatre, Los Angeles, CA, 1967.
Nina, *The Seagull,* Inner City Repertory Theatre, Los Angeles, 1968.
Helena, *A Midsummer Night's Dream,* Inner City Repertory Theatre, Los Angeles, 1968.

Also appeared as Clara in *The Nutcracker.*

MAJOR TOURS

Performed in a national tour with New York City Opera, 1960-61; also performed in summer stock tours.

FILM APPEARANCES

Annie Burke, *The Gypsy Moths,* Metro-Goldwyn-Mayer (MGM), 1969.
Ruby, *They Shoot Horses, Don't They?,* Cinerama, 1969.
Susan Henderson, *Lovers and Other Strangers,* Cinerama, 1970.
Title role, *The Strange Vengeance of Rosalie* (also known as *Rosalie* and *The Strange Vengeance*), Cinecrest Films, 1971, Twentieth Century-Fox, 1972.
Ellie, *Between Friends,* Clearwater, 1973.
Suzanne, *The Big Fix,* Universal, 1978.
Shirley Muldowney, *Heart Like a Wheel,* Twentieth Century-Fox, 1983.
Grace, *Death of an Angel,* Twentieth Century-Fox, 1985.
Charlene, *The Boy Who Could Fly,* Twentieth Century-Fox, 1986.
Ruth Squires, *Violets Are Blue,* Columbia, 1986.
Alice Kildee, *The Stranger,* Columbia, 1987.
Holly Gennaro McClane, *Die Hard,* Twentieth Century-Fox, 1988.
Pam Marshetta, *The Prince of Pennsylvania,* New Line Cinema, 1988.
Kitty Oppenheimer, *Fat Man and Little Boy,* Paramount, 1989.
Holly Gennaro McClane, *Die Hard 2: Die Harder,* Twentieth Century-Fox, 1990.
Barbara Sabich, *Presumed Innocent,* Warner Brothers, 1990.

TELEVISION APPEARANCES; SERIES

Sandy Porter, *Love of Life,* CBS, 1961-66.
Anna Larsen, *The New Land,* ABC, 1974.

TELEVISION APPEARANCES; MOVIES

Temple Brooks, *Then Came Bronson,* NBC, 1969.
Jenna Hampshire, *Sandcastles,* CBS, 1972.
Edith Dayton-Thomas, *Hawkins on Murder,* CBS, 1973.
Janet Thatcher, *A Message to My Daughter,* ABC, 1973.
A Time for Love, NBC, 1973.
Laura Taylor, *Heatwave!,* ABC, 1974.
Joan Saltzman, *A Question of Love,* NBC, 1978.
Susan Norton, *Salem's Lot* (two-part broadcast), CBS, 1979.
Dr. Rand, *Walking Through the Fire,* CBS, 1979.
Aleta, *Fighting Back* (also known as *The Story of Rocky Blier*), ABC, 1980.
Marcia Miller, *Million Dollar Infield,* CBS, 1982.
Cass, *Memorial Day,* CBS, 1983.
Janet Weston, *The Lady from Yesterday,* CBS, 1985.
Carol Deford, *Alex: The Life of a Child,* ABC, 1986.
When the Time Comes, ABC, 1987.
Hannah McGrath, *Somebody Has to Shoot the Picture,* HBO, 1990.
Regina Twigg, *Switched at Birth,* NBC, 1991.

TELEVISION APPEARANCES; EPISODIC

"The Death Farm," *Judd for the Defense,* ABC, 1968.
"My Father and My Mother," *CBS Playhouse,* CBS, 1968.
"The Deceivers," *High Chaparral,* NBC, 1968.
"The Unwanted," *Bonanza,* NBC, 1969.

"Forever," *Bonanza,* NBC, 1972.
"Love Came Laughing," *Love Story,* NBC, 1973.

Also appeared in episodes of *The Defenders,* CBS, *East-Side, West-Side,* CBS, and *Naked City,* ABC.

TELEVISION APPEARANCES; SPECIALS

Appeared in presentations of *The Hallmark Hall of Fame, U.S. Steel Hour, Playhouse 90,* and *Armstrong Circle Theatre.*

RECORDINGS:

SONGS

"The Best Things in Life Are Free," from *They Shoot Horses, Don't They?,* original soundtrack recording, ABC Records.

OTHER

Has recorded *Babbit, Are You Now or Have You Ever Been, An Evening with Raymond Carver,* and *Once in a Lifetime,* for Los Angeles Classics Theatreworks.

* * *

BELLAMY, Ralph 1904-1991

OBITUARY NOTICE—See index for *CTFT* sketch: Full name, Ralph Rexford Bellamy; born June 17, 1904, in Chicago, IL; died of a lung ailment, November 29, 1991, in Los Angeles, CA. Actor and author. A veteran of more than one hundred films, Bellamy won his greatest acclaim for portraying Franklin D. Roosevelt in the Broadway play *Sunrise at Campobello,* which earned him an Antoinette Perry Award for best actor in 1958. He began his acting career with repertory theater troupes in the Midwest. After some short-lived roles on Broadway he went into films in the 1930s; he appeared in approximately sixty during the decade, giving an Academy Award-nominated performance with Cary Grant in *The Awful Truth.* In 1942 Bellamy left Hollywood for television and stage work. His theater successes in the 1940s included *Tomorrow the World* and *Detective Story.* On television he appeared in numerous leading series, notably *Man against Crime,* for which he won a best actor award from the Academy of Radio and Television Arts and Sciences in 1950. He also received four Emmy Award nominations for his work in programs such as the movie *Missiles of October* and the miniseries *The Winds of War,* in which he once again played Roosevelt. Among Bellamy's later film roles were appearances in *Rosemary's Baby, Trading Places,* and *Pretty Woman.* He received an honorary Academy Award for his body of work in film in 1987 and the first annual Hal Roach Entertainment Award. Bellamy was a founding director of the Screen Actors Guild, and as president of Actors' Equity he helped unionize the Off-Broadway theater and establish actors' pension funds. He chronicled his career in his 1979 memoir, *When the Smoke Hit the Fan.*

OBITUARIES AND OTHER SOURCES:

BOOKS

Who's Who in America, 46th edition supplement, Marquis, 1991.

PERIODICALS

Chicago Tribune, November 30, 1991, section 2, p. 21; December 1, 1991, section 2, p. 10.
Los Angeles Times, November 30, 1991, p. B1.
New York Times, November 30, 1991, p. 9.
Times (London), December 2, 1991, p. 16.
Variety, December 2, 1991, p. 101.
Washington Post, November 30, 1991, p. B6.

* * *

BELLISARIO, Donald P. 1935-

PERSONAL: Born August 8, 1935, in Charleroi, PA; son of Albert and Dana (Lapcevic) Bellisario; children: seven. *Religion:* Catholic. *Politics:* Independent.

ADDRESSES: Office—Bellisarius Productions, Universal Studios, Universal City, CA 91608. *Agent*—Norman Kurland, Broder-Kurland-Webb-Uffner Agency, 8439 Sunset Blvd., Suite 402, Los Angeles, CA 90069.

CAREER: Television writer, director, and producer.

MEMBER: Writers Guild of America, Directors Guild of America.

AWARDS, HONORS: Edgar Allen Poe Award, Mystery Writers of America, best television series episode, 1981, for "China Doll," *Magnum, P.I.;* Emmy Award nominations, outstanding drama series, 1981 and 1982, for *Magnum, P.I.;* Emmy Award nominations, outstanding drama series, 1989 and 1990, and Writers Guild of America Award nomination, best television episode, 1991, for *Quantum Leap.*

CREDITS:

TELEVISION WORK; SERIES

Director and producer, *Black Sheep Squadron* (also known as *Baa Baa Black Sheep;* also see below), NBC, 1977-78.
Executive producer, *Quincy, M.E.* (also see below), NBC, 1978.
Director and supervising producer, *Battlestar Galactica* (also see below), ABC, 1978-79.

Creator with Glen A. Larson, director, and executive producer, *Magnum, P.I.* (also see below), CBS, 1980-88.
Executive producer with Stephen J. Cannell, *Stone* (also see below), ABC, 1980.
Creator and executive producer, *Tales of the Gold Monkey* (also see below), ABC, 1982-83.
Creator, director, and executive producer, *Airwolf* (also see below), CBS, 1984.
Creator, director, and executive producer, *Quantum Leap* (also see below), NBC, 1989-90.
Creator, director, and executive producer, *Tequila and Bonetti* (also known as *Tequila and Boner;* also see below), CBS, 1992.

TELEVISION WORK; PILOTS

Worked on pilot episodes for the series *Tequila and Bonetti,* CBS, 1992; *Magnum, P.I.; Airwolf; Tales of the Gold Monkey;* and *Quantum Leap.*

TELEVISION WORK; MOVIES

Creator, director, and executive producer, *Three on a Match* (also see below), NBC, 1987.

FILM WORK

Director and executive producer, *Last Rites* (also see below), Metro-Goldwyn-Mayer/United Artists (MGM/UA), 1988.

WRITINGS:

TELEVISION SERIES

Kojak, CBS, beginning in 1973.
Black Sheep Squadron (also known as *Baa Baa Black Sheep*), NBC, 1977-78.
(Coauthor) *Battlestar Galactica,* ABC, 1978-79.
Quincy, M.E., NBC, 1979.
Stone, ABC, 1980.
Magnum, P.I. (includes episode "China Doll"), CBS, between 1981 and 1984.
Tales of the Gold Monkey, ABC, 1982-83.
Airwolf, CBS, 1984.
Quantum Leap, NBC, 1989-92.
Tequila and Bonetti, CBS, 1992.

TELEVISION PILOTS

Magnum, P.I., CBS, 1980.
Tales of the Gold Monkey, ABC, 1982.
Airwolf, CBS, 1983.
Quantum Leap, NBC, 1989.
Tequila and Bonetti, CBS, 1992.

TELEVISION MOVIES

Three on a Match, NBC, 1987.

SCREENPLAYS

Last Rites, MGM/UA, 1988.

ADAPTATIONS: The television pilot *Tales of the Gold Monkey* was adapted by Judy Alexander for a book entitled *Tales of the Gold Monkey Storybook,* published by Putnam, 1983.

* * *

BERG, Jeff 1947-

PERSONAL: Born May 26, 1947, in Los Angeles, CA; son of Dick Berg (a television producer); married, wife's name Denise (a clinical psychologist). *Education:* University of California, Berkeley, B.A., 1969.

ADDRESSES: Office—International Creative Management (ICM), 8899 Beverly Blvd., Los Angeles, CA 90048.

CAREER: Executive. Creative Management Associates, Los Angeles, CA, vice-president and head of literary division, 1969-75; International Creative Management, vice-president of motion picture department, 1975-80, president, 1980-85, chairman and chief executive officer, 1985—. Director of Joseph International Industries.

OTHER SOURCES:

PERIODICALS

American Film, July-August, 1981.

* * *

BERGEN, Candice 1946-

PERSONAL: Born May 9, 1946, in Beverly Hills, CA; daughter of Edgar (a ventriloquist, comedian, and actor) and Frances (Westerman) Bergen; married Louis Malle (a film director), September 27, 1980; children: Chloe. *Education:* Attended University of Pennsylvania.

ADDRESSES: Agent—William Morris Agency, 151 El Camino, Beverly Hills, CA 90212.

CAREER: Actress, photographer, and writer. Formerly a model; spokesperson for Sprint long distance telephone service.

AWARDS, HONORS: Academy Award nomination, best supporting actress, 1979, for *Starting Over;* Emmy Awards, outstanding lead actress in a comedy series, 1988 and 1989, Golden Apple Award, star of the year, 1989, Viewers for Quality Television Award, best actress in a comedy series, 1989, Golden Globe Award, best actress in a comedy series, 1989 and 1992, Emmy Award nomination, outstanding lead actress in a comedy series, 1990, People's Choice Award, best female television performer, 1992, American Comedy Award, funniest actress in a television series, all for *Murphy Brown.*

CREDITS:

TELEVISION APPEARANCES; SERIES

Title role, *Murphy Brown,* CBS, 1988—.

TELEVISION APPEARANCES; EPISODIC

Guest, *You Bet Your Life,* NBC, 1957.
"The Rebel," *Coronet Blue,* CBS, 1967.
Commentator, *Today Show,* NBC, 1975.
Guest, *The Muppet Show,* syndicated, 1976.
Host, *Saturday Night Live,* NBC, 1986.
Barbara, "Moving Day," *Trying Times,* PBS, 1987.
Guest, *Tonight Show,* NBC, 1988.
Guest, *Late Night with David Letterman,* NBC, 1988.
Guest, *CBS This Morning,* CBS, 1988.
Guest, *Entertainment Tonight,* syndicated, 1988 and 1989.
Guest, *Good Morning America,* ABC, 1988 and 1989.
Guest, *The Pat Sajak Show,* CBS, 1989.
Guest, *The Phil Donahue Show,* syndicated, 1989.
Host, *Paris '89,* TBS, 1989.
"TV's 50th Anniversary Special," *Today Show,* NBC, 1989.

TELEVISION APPEARANCES; SPECIALS

The Woody Allen Special, NBC, 1969.
The Way They Were, syndicated, 1981.
Bugs Bunny/Looney Tunes All-Star 50th Anniversary, CBS, 1986.
Memories Now and Then, CBS, 1988.
The Barbara Walters Special, ABC, 1989.
The 41st Annual Primetime Emmy Awards Presentation, FOX, 1989.
The 61st Annual Academy Awards Presentation, ABC, 1989.
CBS Premiere Review Spectacular, CBS, 1989.
The 42nd Annual Primetime Emmy Awards Presentation, FOX, 1990.
Presenter, *The 62nd Annual Primetime Emmy Awards Presentation,* ABC, 1990.
CBS Comedy Bloopers, CBS, 1990.
CBS Comedy Bloopers II, CBS, 1990.
Comic Relief IV, HBO, 1990.
Time Warner Presents the Earth Day Special, ABC, 1990.
The 43rd Annual Primetime Emmy Awards Presentation, FOX, 1991.
Big Bird's Birthday or Let Me Eat Cake, PBS, 1991.
Funny Women of Television: A Museum of Television and Radio Tribute, NBC, 1991.
A User's Guide to Planet Earth: The American Environment Test, ABC, 1991.

Also appeared as herself in *It's up to Us: The Giraffe Project,* 1988.

OTHER TELEVISION APPEARANCES

Elaine Conti, *Hollywood Wives* (mini-series), ABC, 1985.
Morgan Le Fey, *Arthur the King* (movie), CBS, 1985.
Ewa Berwid, *Murder: By Reason of Insanity* (movie), CBS, 1985.
Sydney Biddle Barrows, *Mayflower Madam* (movie), CBS, 1987.

RADIO APPEARANCES

Made debut on *The Chase and Sanborn Show Starring Edgar Bergen and Charlie McCarthy,* 1952.

FILM APPEARANCES

(Film debut) Lakey Eastlake, *The Group,* United Artists (UA), 1966.
Shirley Eckert, *The Sand Pebbles,* Twentieth Century-Fox, 1966.
Electra, *The Day the Fish Came Out,* International Classics, 1967.
Candice, *Live for Life* (also known as *Vivre pour Vivre* and *Vivere pour Vivere*), UA-Lopert, 1967.
Lily/Julie, *The Magus,* Twentieth Century-Fox, 1968.
Sue Ann Daley, *The Adventurers,* Paramount, 1970.
Jan, *Getting Straight,* Columbia, 1970.
Cresta Marybelle Lee, *Soldier Blue,* Avco Embassy, 1970.
Susan, *Carnal Knowledge,* Avco Embassy, 1971.
Title role, *T. R. Baskin* (also known as *Date with a Lonely Girl*), Paramount, 1971.
Maren, *11 Harrowhouse* (also known as *Anything for Love*), Twentieth Century-Fox, 1974.
Miss Jones, *Bite the Bullet,* Columbia, 1975.
Eden Pedecaris, *The Wind and the Lion,* Metro-Goldwyn-Mayer (MGM)/UA, 1975.
Melissa Ruger, *The Hunting Party,* UA, 1977.
Ellie Tucker, *The Domino Principle* (also known as *The Domino Killings*), Avco Embassy, 1977.
Lizzy, *The End of the World (in Our Usual Bed in a Night Full of Rain),* Warner Brothers, 1978.
Marcie Bonwit, *Oliver's Story,* Paramount, 1978.
Jessica Potter, *Starting Over,* Paramount, 1979.
Merry Noel Blake, *Rich and Famous,* MGM/UA, 1981.
Margaret Bourke-White, *Gandhi,* Columbia, 1982.
Kyle McLaren, *Stick,* Universal, 1985.

STAGE APPEARANCES

(Stage debut) *Sabrina Fair,* Westbury Music Fair, Westbury, NY, 1967.
(Broadway debut) Darlene, *Hurlyburly,* Ethel Barrymore Theatre, 1985.

WRITINGS:

Knock Wood (autobiography), Linden Press, 1984.

Also author of a play titled *The Freezer,* 1968; contributor of articles and photographs to periodicals, including *Life, Esquire, Interview, Cosmopolitan, Vogue,* and *National Geographic.*

OTHER SOURCES:

BOOKS

Newsmakers 90, Issue 1, Gale, 1990, pp. 22-25.

PERIODICALS

Chicago Tribune, April 5, 1984, pp. 1, 17.
New York Times, April 13, 1984.
People, April 9, 1984, p. 97.*

* * *

BERGMAN, Alan

PERSONAL: Born September 11, in Brooklyn, NY; son of Samuel and Ruth (Margulies) Bergman; married Marilyn Keith (a lyricist) February 9, 1958; children: Julie Rachel. *Education:* Attended Ethical Culture School; received B.A. from University of North Carolina (studied music and theatre arts); received M.A. from University of California at Los Angeles. *Avocational interests:* Tennis, antique and art collecting.

ADDRESSES: Agent—c/o The Lantz Office, 888 Seventh Ave., No. 2501, New York, NY 10016; Gorfaine-Schwartz, 3301 Barham Blvd., No. 201, Los Angeles, CA 90068.

CAREER: Lyricist. Worked as a television director in Philadelphia, PA. *Military service:* U.S. Army, 1943-45.

MEMBER: Academy of Motion Picture Arts and Sciences (member of executive committee of music branch; member of board of governors), National Academy of Songwriters (member of board of directors), American Society of Composers, Authors, and Publishers.

AWARDS, HONORS: All with wife, Marilyn Bergman: Grammy Award nomination (wife under name Marilyn Keith; with Lew Spence), National Academy of Recording Arts and Sciences, best song of the year, 1960, for "Nice 'N' Easy"; Academy Award, best song, 1968, and Golden Globe Award, best original song, 1969 (both with Michel Legrand), both for "The Windmills of Your Mind"; Academy Award nomination (with Legrand), best song, 1969, for "What Are You Doing the Rest of Your Life?"; Academy Award nomination (with Legrand), best song, 1970, for "Pieces of Dreams"; Academy Award nomination (with Henry Mancini), best song, 1971, for "All His Children"; Grammy Award nomination (with Legrand), best song of the year, 1972, for "The Summer Knows"; Academy Award nomination (with Maurice Jarre), best song, 1972, for "Marmalade, Molasses and Honey"; Grammy Award, best song of the year, 1973, Academy Award, best song, 1973, Golden Globe Award, best original song, 1974 (all with Marvin Hamlisch), all for "The Way We Were," and Grammy Award (with Hamlisch), best original score in a motion picture or television special, 1974, for *The Way We Were* (film); Emmy Award nominations (with Billy Goldenberg), best dramatic underscore and best special musical material, both 1975, for *Queen of the Stardust Ballroom;* received grant from American Film Institute, 1976; Emmy Award (with Leonard Rosenman), best dramatic underscore, 1976, for *Sybil;* Grammy Award nomination (with Rupert Holmes, Barbra Streisand, Paul Williams, and others), best original score in a motion picture or television special, 1977, for *A Star Is Born* (film); Academy Award nomination (with Hamlisch), best song, 1978, for "The Last Time I Felt Like This"; Grammy Award nomination (with Neil Diamond), best song of the year, 1978, for "You Don't Bring Me Flowers"; Grammy Award nomination (with Billy Goldenberg and Larry Morton), best cast show album, 1979, for *Ballroom;* Academy Award nomination (with David Shire), best song, 1979, for "I'll Never Say 'Goodbye.' "

Inducted into Songwriters Hall of Fame, 1980; Academy Award nomination (with Legrand), best song, 1982, for "How Do You Keep the Music Playing?"; Academy Award nomination (with John Williams), best song, 1982, for "If We Were in Love"; Academy Award nomination (with Dave Grusin), best song, 1982, for "It Might Be You," and Grammy Award nomination (with Grusin), best original score in a motion picture or television special, 1983, for *Tootsie* (film); Academy Award nomination (with Legrand), best original song, 1983, for "Papa, Can You Hear Me?," Academy Award nomination (with Legrand), best original song, 1983, for "The Way He Makes Me Feel," and Academy Award, best original song score or adaptation score, 1983, and Grammy Award nomination, best original score in a motion picture or television special, 1984 (both with Legrand), both for *Yentl* (film); Singers Salute to the Songwriter Award, Clooney Foundation, 1986; Aggie Award, Songwriter's Guild, 1987; Academy Award nomination, best original song, 1989, Golden Globe nomination, 1990, and Grammy Award nomination, 1990 (all with Marvin Hamlisch), all for "The Girl Who Used to Be Me"; recipient of three People's Choice Awards.

CREDITS:

TELEVISION WORK; SERIES

Producer and director, *Kid Gloves,* CBS, 1951.
Director, *The M and M Candy Carnival,* CBS, 1952-53.

TELEVISION WORK; SPECIALS; WITH WIFE, MARILYN BERGMAN

Executive producer, *The Music Makers: An ASCAP Celebration of American Music at Wolf Trap,* PBS, 1987.

Also executive producer of *Barbra Streisand: One Voice,* 1986.

TELEVISION APPEARANCES

Night of 100 Stars III (special), NBC, 1990.

WRITINGS:

FILM LYRICS; WITH MARILYN BERGMAN

(Wife under name Marilyn Keith) Title song (composed by Lew Spence), *The Marriage-Go-Round,* Twentieth Century-Fox, 1960.
Title song (composed by George Duning), *Any Wednesday* (also known as *Bachelor Girl Apartment*), Warner Brothers, 1966.
"Make Me Rainbows" (composed by John Williams), *Fitzwilly* (also known as *Fitzwilly Strikes Back*), United Artists (UA), 1967.
Score (composed by Quincy Jones), *In the Heat of the Night,* UA, 1967.
"The Windmills of Your Mind" and "His Eyes, Her Eyes" (both composed by Michel Legrand), *The Thomas Crown Affair* (also known as *Thomas Crown and Company* and *The Crown Caper*), UA, 1968.
"You Must Believe in Spring" (composed by Legrand), *Young Girls of Rochefort,* Warner Brothers-Seven Arts, 1968.
"Maybe Tomorrow" (composed by Jones), *John and Mary,* Twentieth Century-Fox, 1969.
"Tomorrow Is My Friend" and "There's Enough to Go Around" (both composed by Henry Mancini), *Gaily, Gaily* (also known as *Chicago, Chicago*), UA, 1969.
"A Smile, A Mem'ry and an Extra Shirt" (composed by Dave Grusin), *A Man Called Gannon,* Universal, 1969.
"Sugar in the Rain" (composed by Sid Ramin), *Stiletto,* Avco Embassy, 1969.
"What Are You Doing the Rest of Your Life?" (composed by Legrand), *The Happy Ending,* UA, 1969.
"I Was Born in Love with You" (composed by Legrand), *Wuthering Heights,* American International, 1970.
"Sweet Gingerbread Man" and "Nobody Knows" (both composed by Legrand), *The Magic Garden of Stanley Sweetheart,* Metro-Goldwyn-Mayer (MGM), 1970.
Title song (composed by Marvin Hamlisch), *Move,* Twentieth Century-Fox, 1970.
Title song and "Little Boy Lost" (both composed by Legrand), *Pieces of Dreams,* UA, 1970.
"The Costume Ball" (composed by Elmer Bernstein), *Doctors' Wives,* Columbia, 1971.
"All His Children" (composed by Mancini), *Sometimes a Great Notion,* Universal, 1971.
"Rain Falls Anywhere It Wants To" (composed by Laurence Rosenthal), *The African Elephant,* National General, 1971.
"The Summer Knows" (composed by Legrand), *Summer of '42,* Warner Brothers, 1971.
"Face in the Crowd" (composed by Legrand), *Le Mans,* National General, 1971.
"Marmalade, Molasses and Honey" (composed by Maurice Jarre), *The Life and Times of Judge Roy Bean,* National General, 1972.
"Love's the Only Game in Town" (composed by J. Williams), *Pete and Tillie,* Universal, 1972.
Molly and Lawless John, Producers Distributors Corp., 1972.
Title song (composed by Hamlisch), *The Way We Were,* Columbia, 1973.
"Breezy's Song" (composed by Legrand), *Breezy,* Universal, 1973.
"In Every Corner of the World" (composed by Legrand), *Forty Carats,* Columbia, 1973.
Title song (composed by Mandel), *Summer Wishes, Winter Dreams,* Columbia, 1973.
"Easy Baby" (composed by Mancini), *99 and 44/100% Dead,* Twentieth Century-Fox, 1974.
"There'll Be Time" (composed by Legrand), *Ode to Billy Joe,* Warner Brothers, 1975.
"Evening Sun, Morning Moon" (composed by Grusin), *The Yakuza* (also known as *Brotherhood of the Yakuza*), Warner Brothers-Toei, 1975.
"I Believe in Love" (composed by Kenny Loggins), *A Star Is Born,* Warner Brothers-First Artists, 1976.
"I'm Harry, I'm Walter" (composed by David Shire), *Harry and Walter Go to New York,* Columbia, 1976.
"Hello and Goodbye" (composed by Bernstein), *From Noon to Three,* UA, 1976.
Title song (composed by Grusin), *Bobby Deerfield,* Columbia, 1977.
"The Last Time I Felt Like This" (composed by Hamlisch), *Same Time Next Year,* Universal, 1978.
Title song, *The One and Only,* Paramount, 1978.
"There's Something Funny Goin' On" (composed by Grusin), *. . . And Justice for All,* Columbia, 1979.
"I'll Never Say 'Goodbye' " (composed by David Shire), *The Promise,* Universal, 1979.
"Where Do You Catch the Bus for Tomorrow?," *A Change of Seasons,* Twentieth Century-Fox, 1980.

"Ask Me No Questions" (composed by Mancini), *Back Roads,* Warner Brothers, 1981.

"How Do You Keep the Music Playing?" and "Think about Love" (both composed by Legrand), *Best Friends,* Warner Brothers, 1982.

"Comin' Home to You" (composed by Grusin), *Author! Author!,* Twentieth Century-Fox, 1982.

Title song and "It Might Be You" (both composed by Grusin), *Tootsie,* Columbia, 1982.

"If We Were in Love" (composed by J. Williams), *Yes, Giorgio,* MGM/UA, 1982.

Title song (composed by Legrand), *Never Say Never Again,* Warner Brothers, 1983.

"Papa, Can You Hear Me?," "The Way He Makes Me Feel," "Will Someone Ever Look at Me That Way?," and others (all composed by Legrand), *Yentl,* MGM/UA, 1983.

"Little Boys" (composed by Mancini), *The Man Who Loved Women,* Columbia, 1983.

"Something New in My Life" (composed by Legrand), *Micki and Maude,* Columbia, 1984.

"The Music of Goodbye" (theme song), *Out of Africa,* Universal, 1985.

"I Know the Feeling" (composed by Hamlisch), *January Man,* MGM, 1989.

"The Girl Who Used to Be Me" (composed by Hamlisch), *Shirley Valentine,* Paramount, 1989.

Title song (composed by Mancini), *Welcome Home,* Columbia, 1989.

"Most of All You" (composed by James Newton Howard), *Major League,* Paramount, 1989.

"Dreamland," *For the Boys,* Twentieth Century-Fox, 1991.

"Places That Belong to You," *The Prince of Tides,* Columbia, 1991.

"It's All There," *Switch,* Warner Brothers, 1991.

Also lyricist of other songs in films.

TELEVISION SERIES MUSIC

Theme song (lyrics by Marilyn Bergman), *All That Glitters,* syndicated, 1977.

TELEVISION SERIES LYRICS; WITH MARILYN BERGMAN

"Worlds" (theme song; composed by David Rose), *Bracken's World,* NBC, 1969-70.

"The Kind of Girl She Is" (theme song; composed by Dave Grusin) *The Sandy Duncan Show,* CBS, 1972.

Theme song (composed by Grusin), *Maude,* CBS, 1972-78.

Theme song (composed by Grusin), *Good Times,* CBS, 1974-79.

"Nancy's Blues" (theme song; composed by Marvin Hamlisch) *The Nancy Walker Show,* ABC, 1976.

"All Good Things Come in Pairs" (theme song; composed by Billy Goldenberg) *The Dumplings,* NBC, 1976.

"There's a New Girl in Town" (theme song; composed by David Shire), *Alice,* CBS, 1976-82.

Theme song, *Julie Farr, M.D.,* ABC, 1978 and 1979.

Theme song, *In the Heat of the Night,* NBC, 1988—.

"Just over the Brooklyn Bridge" (theme song), *Brooklyn Bridge,* CBS, 1991—.

Theme song, *The Powers That Be,* NBC, 1992.

TELEVISION MOVIE LYRICS; WITH MARILYN BERGMAN

"The Hands of Time" (composed by Michel Legrand), *Brian's Song,* ABC, 1971.

"Who Gave You Permission?," "Pennies and Dreams," "Suddenly There's You," and others (all composed by Billy Goldenberg), *Queen of the Stardust Ballroom* (dramatic musical; also see below), CBS, 1975.

Score (composed by Leonard Rosenman), *Sybil,* NBC, 1976.

"Too Many Springs" (composed by Don Sebesky), *Hollow Image,* ABC, 1979.

TELEVISION PILOT LYRICS; WITH MARILYN BERGMAN

"Dear Mom and Dad" (theme song; composed by Henry Mancini) *Co-Ed Fever,* CBS, 1979.

Theme song, *P.O.P.,* NBC, 1984.

TELEVISION SPECIAL LYRICS; WITH MARILYN BERGMAN

"America, the Dream Goes On," *I Love Liberty,* ABC, 1982.

STAGE LYRICS; WITH MARILYN BERGMAN

Score (composed by Sammy Fain) *Something More,* Eugene O'Neill Theatre, New York City, 1964.

Score (composed by Billy Goldenberg) *Ballroom* (adapted from television movie *Queen of the Stardust Ballroom*), Majestic Theatre, New York City, 1978.

Score (composed by Leonard Rosenman), *The Lady and the Clarinet,* Center Theatre Group, Mark Taper Forum, Los Angeles, 1980.

SONG LYRICS; WITH MARILYN BERGMAN

Lyricist of albums and numerous songs, including "You Don't Bring Me Flowers" (composed by Neil Diamond), for Barbra Streisand and Diamond, c. late 1970s; *The Ballad of the Blues* (album), for Jo Stafford; *Never Be Afraid* (album) and "I Love To Dance Like They Used to Dance," both for Bing Crosby; "On Rainy Afternoons," "A Child Is Born," "After the Rain," "One Day," "Ask Yourself Why," "If I Close My Eyes," "Two People," and "Why Let It Go?," all for Streisand; "On My Way to You," for Maureen McGovern and Streisand; "Nice 'N' Easy" (wife under name Marilyn Keith), "L.A. Is My Lady," "Sleep Warm," "Love Looks So Well on You," and "Sentimental Baby," all for Frank Sinatra; "Someone in the Dark," for Michael Jackson; "The Island," for Patti Austin and Sarah Vaughn; "Yellow Bird" for Norman Luboff; "The Trouble with Hello Is Goodbye," for Carmen Macrae; "Cinnamon and Clove" and "Like a Lover," both for Sergio Mendes and Macrae; "Look Around," for Mendes; "What Matters Most," for Kenny Rankin; "The World Goes On," for Quincy Jones; "Live It Up," for Johnny Mathis; "Raggedy Anne and Raggedy Andy," for Liza Minelli; "Where Do You Start?" and "I Can Hardly Wait," both for Michael Feinstein; and songs for children.

* * *

BERGMAN, Marilyn (Marilyn Keith)

PERSONAL: Full name, Marilyn Keith Bergman; born November 10, in Brooklyn, NY; daughter of Albert A. and Edith (Arkin) Katz; married Alan Bergman (a lyricist), February 9, 1958; children: Julie Rachel. *Education:* Attended High School of Music and Art, New York, NY; received B.A. from New York University (studied psychology and English). *Avocational interests:* Tennis, antique and art collecting.

ADDRESSES: Agent—c/o The Lantz Office, 888 Seventh Ave., No. 2501, New York, NY 10016; Gorfaine-Schwartz, 3301 Barham Blvd., No. 201, Los Angeles, CA 90068.

CAREER: Lyricist.

MEMBER: Academy of Motion Picture Arts and Sciences (member of executive committee of music branch), National Academy of Songwriters (member of board of directors), American Society of Composers, Authors, and Publishers (member of board of directors).

AWARDS, HONORS: All with husband, Alan Bergman: Grammy Award nomination (under name Marilyn Keith; with Lew Spence), National Academy of Recording Arts and Sciences, best song of the year, 1960, for "Nice 'N' Easy"; Academy Award, best song, 1968, and Golden Globe Award, best original song, 1969 (both with Michel Legrand), both for "The Windmills of Your Mind"; Academy Award nomination (with Legrand), best song, 1969, for "What Are You Doing the Rest of Your Life?"; Academy Award nomination (with Legrand), best song, 1970, for "Pieces of Dreams"; Academy Award nomination (with Henry Mancini), best song, 1971, for "All His Children"; Grammy Award nomination (with Legrand), best song of the year, 1972, for "The Summer Knows"; Academy Award nomination (with Maurice Jarre), best song, 1972, for "Marmalade, Molasses and Honey"; Grammy Award, best song of the year, 1973, Academy Award, best song, 1973, Golden Globe Award, best original song, 1974 (all with Marvin Hamlisch), all for "The Way We Were," and Grammy Award (with Hamlisch), best original score in a motion picture, 1974, for *The Way We Were* (film); Emmy Award nominations (with Billy Goldenberg), best dramatic underscore and best special musical material, both 1975, for *Queen of the Stardust Ballroom;* received grant from American Film Institute, 1976; Emmy Award (with Leonard Rosenman), best dramatic underscore, 1976, for *Sybil;* Grammy Award nomination (with Rupert Holmes, Barbra Streisand, Paul Williams, and others), best original score in a motion picture, 1977, for *A Star Is Born* (film); Academy Award nomination (with Hamlisch), best song, 1978, for "The Last Time I Felt Like This"; Grammy Award nomination (with Neil Diamond), best song of the year, 1978, for "You Don't Bring Me Flowers"; Grammy Award nomination (with Billy Goldenberg and Larry Morton), best cast show album, 1979, for *Ballroom;* Academy Award nomination (with David Shire), best song, 1979, for "I'll Never Say 'Goodbye.' "

Inducted into Songwriters Hall of Fame, 1980; Academy Award nomination (with Legrand), best song, 1982, for "How Do You Keep the Music Playing?"; Academy Award nomination (with John Williams), best song, 1982, for "If We Were in Love"; Academy Award nomination (with Dave Grusin), best song, 1982, for "It Might Be You," and Grammy Award nomination (with Grusin), best original score in a motion picture or television special, 1983, for *Tootsie* (film); Academy Award nomination (with Legrand), best original song, 1983, for "Papa, Can You Hear Me?," Academy Award nomination (with Legrand), best original song, 1983, for "The Way He Makes Me Feel," and Academy Award, best original song score, 1983, and Grammy Award nomination, best original score in a motion picture, 1984 (both with Legrand), both for *Yentl* (film); Singers Salute to the Songwriter Award, Clooney Foundation, 1986; Aggie Award, Songwriter's Guild, 1987; Academy Award nomination, best original song, 1989, Golden Globe nomination, 1990, and Grammy Award nomination, 1990 (all with Marvin Hamlisch), all for "The Girl Who Used to Be Me"; recipient of three People's Choice Awards.

CREDITS:

TELEVISION WORK; SPECIALS; WITH HUSBAND, ALAN BERGMAN

Executive producer, *The Music Makers: An ASCAP Celebration of American Music at Wolf Trap,* PBS, 1987.

Also executive producer of *Barbra Streisand: One Voice,* 1986.

TELEVISION APPEARANCES

Night of 100 Stars III (special), NBC, 1990.

WRITINGS:

FILM LYRICS; WITH ALAN BERGMAN

(Under name Marilyn Keith) Title song (composed by Lew Spence), *The Marriage-Go-Round,* Twentieth Century-Fox, 1960.

Title song (composed by George Duning), *Any Wednesday* (also known as *Bachelor Girl Apartment*), Warner Brothers, 1966.

"Make Me Rainbows" (composed by John Williams), *Fitzwilly* (also known as *Fitzwilly Strikes Back*), United Artists (UA), 1967.

Score (composed by Quincy Jones), *In the Heat of the Night,* UA, 1967.

"The Windmills of Your Mind" and "His Eyes, Her Eyes" (both composed by Michel Legrand), *The Thomas Crown Affair* (also known as *Thomas Crown and Company* and *The Crown Caper*), UA, 1968.

"You Must Believe in Spring" (composed by Legrand), *Young Girls of Rochefort,* Warner Brothers-Seven Arts, 1968.

"Maybe Tomorrow" (composed by Jones), *John and Mary,* Twentieth Century-Fox, 1969.

"Tomorrow Is My Friend" and "There's Enough to Go Around" (both composed by Henry Mancini), *Gaily, Gaily* (also known as *Chicago, Chicago*), UA, 1969.

"A Smile, A Mem'ry and an Extra Shirt" (composed by Dave Grusin), *A Man Called Gannon,* Universal, 1969.

"Sugar in the Rain" (composed by Sid Ramin), *Stiletto,* Avco Embassy, 1969.

"What Are You Doing the Rest of Your Life?" (composed by Legrand), *The Happy Ending,* UA, 1969.

"I Was Born in Love with You" (composed by Legrand), *Wuthering Heights,* American International, 1970.

"Sweet Gingerbread Man" and "Nobody Knows" (both composed by Legrand), *The Magic Garden of Stanley Sweetheart,* Metro-Goldwyn-Mayer (MGM), 1970.

Title song (composed by Marvin Hamlisch), *Move,* Twentieth Century-Fox, 1970.

Title song and "Little Boy Lost" (both composed by Legrand), *Pieces of Dreams,* UA, 1970.

"The Costume Ball" (composed by Elmer Bernstein), *Doctors' Wives,* Columbia, 1971.

"All His Children" (composed by Mancini), *Sometimes a Great Notion,* Universal, 1971.

"Rain Falls Anywhere It Wants To" (composed by Laurence Rosenthal), *The African Elephant,* National General, 1971.

"The Summer Knows" (composed by Legrand), *Summer of '42,* Warner Brothers, 1971.

"Face in the Crowd" (composed by Legrand), *Le Mans,* National General, 1971.

"Marmalade, Molasses and Honey" (composed by Maurice Jarre), *The Life and Times of Judge Roy Bean,* National General, 1972.

"Love's the Only Game in Town" (composed by J. Williams), *Pete and Tillie,* Universal, 1972.

Molly and Lawless John, Producers Distributors Corp., 1972.

Title song (composed by Hamlisch), *The Way We Were,* Columbia, 1973.

"Breezy's Song" (composed by Legrand), *Breezy,* Universal, 1973.

"In Every Corner of the World" (composed by Legrand), *Forty Carats,* Columbia, 1973.

Title song (composed by Johnny Mandel), *Summer Wishes, Winter Dreams,* Columbia, 1973.

"Easy Baby" (composed by Mancini), *99 and 44/100% Dead,* Twentieth Century-Fox, 1974.

"There'll Be Time" (composed by Legrand), *Ode to Billy Joe,* Warner Brothers, 1975.

"Evening Sun, Morning Moon" (composed by Grusin), *The Yakuza* (also known as *Brotherhood of the Yakuza*), Warner Brothers-Toei, 1975.

"I Believe in Love" (composed by Kenny Loggins), *A Star Is Born,* Warner Brothers-First Artists, 1976.

"I'm Harry, I'm Walter" (composed by David Shire), *Harry and Walter Go to New York,* Columbia, 1976.

"Hello and Goodbye" (composed by Bernstein), *From Noon to Three,* UA, 1976.

Title song (composed by Grusin), *Bobby Deerfield,* Columbia, 1977.

"The Last Time I Felt Like This" (composed by Hamlisch), *Same Time Next Year,* Universal, 1978.

Title song, *The One and Only,* Paramount, 1978.

"There's Something Funny Goin' On" (composed by Grusin), *. . . And Justice for All,* Columbia, 1979.

"I'll Never Say 'Goodbye' " (composed by David Shire), *The Promise,* Universal, 1979.

"Where Do You Catch the Bus for Tomorrow?," *A Change of Seasons,* Twentieth Century-Fox, 1980.

"Ask Me No Questions" (composed by Mancini), *Back Roads,* Warner Brothers, 1981.

"How Do You Keep the Music Playing?" and "Think about Love" (both composed by Legrand), *Best Friends,* Warner Brothers, 1982.

"Comin' Home to You" (composed by Grusin), *Author! Author!,* Twentieth Century-Fox, 1982.

Title song and "It Might Be You" (both composed by Grusin), *Tootsie,* Columbia, 1982.

"If We Were in Love" (composed by J. Williams), *Yes, Giorgio,* MGM/UA, 1982.

Title song (composed by Legrand), *Never Say Never Again,* Warner Brothers, 1983.

"Papa, Can You Hear Me?," "The Way He Makes Me Feel," "Will Someone Ever Look at Me That Way?," and others (all composed by Legrand), *Yentl,* MGM/UA, 1983.

"Little Boys" (composed by Mancini), *The Man Who Loved Women,* Columbia, 1983.

"Something New in My Life" (composed by Legrand), *Micki and Maude,* Columbia, 1984.

"The Music of Goodbye" (theme song), *Out of Africa,* Universal, 1985.

"I Know the Feeling" (composed by Hamlisch), *January Man,* MGM, 1989.

"The Girl Who Used to Be Me" (composed by Hamlisch), *Shirley Valentine,* Paramount, 1989.

Title song (composed by Mancini), *Welcome Home,* Columbia, 1989.

"Most of All You" (composed by James Newton Howard), *Major League,* Paramount, 1989.

"Dreamland," *For the Boys,* Twentieth Century-Fox, 1991.

"Places That Belong to You," *The Prince of Tides,* Columbia, 1991.

"It's All There," *Switch,* Warner Brothers, 1991.

Also lyricist of other songs in films.

TELEVISION SERIES LYRICS; WITH ALAN BERGMAN, EXCEPT AS NOTED

"Worlds" (theme song; composed by David Rose), *Bracken's World,* NBC, 1969-70.

"The Kind of Girl She Is" (theme song; composed by Dave Grusin) *The Sandy Duncan Show,* CBS, 1972.

Theme song (composed by Grusin), *Maude,* CBS, 1972-78.

Theme song (composed by Grusin), *Good Times,* CBS, 1974-79.

"Nancy's Blues" (theme song; composed by Marvin Hamlisch), *The Nancy Walker Show,* ABC, 1976.

"All Good Things Come in Pairs" (theme song; composed by Billy Goldenberg), *The Dumplings,* NBC, 1976.

"There's a New Girl in Town" (theme song; composed by David Shire), *Alice,* CBS, 1976-82.

Theme song (composed by Alan Bergman), *All That Glitters,* syndicated, 1977.

Theme song, *Julie Farr, M.D.,* ABC, 1978 and 1979.

Theme song, *In the Heat of the Night,* NBC, 1988—.

"Just over the Brooklyn Bridge" (theme song), *Brooklyn Bridge,* CBS, 1991—.

Theme song, *The Powers That Be,* NBC, 1992.

TELEVISION MOVIE LYRICS; WITH ALAN BERGMAN

"The Hands of Time" (composed by Michel Legrand), *Brian's Song,* ABC, 1971.

"Who Gave You Permission?," "Pennies and Dreams," "Suddenly There's You," and others (all composed by Billy Goldenberg), *Queen of the Stardust Ballroom* (dramatic musical; also see below), CBS, 1975.

Score (composed by Leonard Rosenman), *Sybil,* NBC, 1976.

"Too Many Springs" (composed by Don Sebesky), *Hollow Image,* ABC, 1979.

TELEVISION PILOT LYRICS; WITH ALAN BERGMAN

"Dear Mom and Dad" (theme song; composed by Henry Mancini) *Co-Ed Fever,* CBS, 1979.

Theme song, *P.O.P.,* NBC, 1984.

TELEVISION SPECIAL LYRICS; WITH ALAN BERGMAN

"America, the Dream Goes On," *I Love Liberty,* ABC, 1982.

STAGE LYRICS; WITH ALAN BERGMAN

Score (composed by Sammy Fain) *Something More,* Eugene O'Neill Theatre, New York City, 1964.

Score (composed by Billy Goldenberg) *Ballroom* (adapted from television movie *Queen of the Stardust Ballroom*), Majestic Theatre, New York City, 1978.

Score (composed by Leonard Rosenman), *The Lady and the Clarinet,* Center Theatre Group, Mark Taper Forum, Los Angeles, 1980.

SONG LYRICS; WITH ALAN BERGMAN

Lyricist of albums and numerous songs, including "You Don't Bring Me Flowers" (composed by Neil Diamond), for Barbra Streisand and Diamond, c. late 1970s; *The Ballad of the Blues* (album), for Jo Stafford; *Never Be Afraid* (album) and "I Love to Dance Like They Used to Dance," both for Bing Crosby; "On Rainy Afternoons," "A Child Is Born," "After the Rain," "One Day," "Ask Yourself Why," "If I Close My Eyes," "Two People," and "Why Let It Go?," all for Streisand; "On My Way to You," for Maureen McGovern and Streisand; "Nice 'N' Easy" (under name Marilyn Keith), "L.A. Is My Lady," "Sleep Warm," "Love Looks So Well on You," and "Sentimental Baby," all for Frank Sinatra; "Someone in the Dark," for Michael Jackson; "The Island," for Patti Austin and Sarah Vaughn; "Yellow Bird" for Norman Luboff; "The Trouble with Hello Is Goodbye," for Carmen Macrae; "Cinnamon and Clove" and "Like a Lover," both for Sergio Mendes and Macrae; "Look Around," for Mendes; "What Matters Most," for Kenny Rankin; "The World Goes On," for Quincy Jones; "Live It Up," for Johnny Mathis; "Raggedy Anne and Raggedy Andy," for Liza Minelli; "Where Do You Start?" and "I Can Hardly Wait," both for Michael Feinstein; and songs for children.

* * *

BERKOFF, Steven 1937-

PERSONAL: Born August 3, 1937, in Stepney, London, England; son of Alfred (a tailor) and Pauline (Hyman)

Berkoff; married Shelley Lee (a dancer and choreographer), August 21, 1976 (marriage ended). *Education:* Studied acting at Webber-Douglas Academy, London, England, 1958-59, and Ecole Jacques Le Coq, Paris, France, 1965.

ADDRESSES: Agent—(stage) Joanna Marston, 4 Hereford Sq., London S.W.7, England; (literary) International Creative Management, 388/396 Oxford St., London W.1, England.

CAREER: Actor, director, and writer. Worked with various repertory companies; founding member, actor, director, writer, and adapter of plays for London Theatre Group, London, England.

CREDITS:

STAGE APPEARANCES

Louis, *A View from the Bridge,* Empire Theatre, Finsbury Park, England, 1959.
Bellboy, *Oh Dad, Poor Dad,* Lyric Theatre, Hammersmith, England, 1961.

Also appeared as Gregor, *Metamorphosis,* 1969, Mark Taper Forum, Los Angeles, CA, c. 1982, later Ethel Barrymore Theatre, New York City, 1989; as Titorelli, *The Trial,* 1971; in title role, *Agamemnon,* 1973; and as Usher, *The Fall of the House of Usher,* 1974. Appeared in *Knock at the Manor Gate,* 1972; *Miss Julie versus Expressionism,* 1973; *Miss Julie* and *The Zoo Story* (double bill); and *Arturo Ui.* Toured Israel, Europe, and the United States with London Theatre Group.

STAGE WORK

Director, *Hamlet,* Edinburgh Festival, Edinburgh, Scotland, 1979.
Director, *Kvetch,* Westside Arts Theatre, New York City, 1987.
Director, *Coriolanus,* Delacorte Theater, New York City, 1988.

Also director of *Greek,* Croydon Warehouse, Croydon, England, then Actors Playhouse Theatre, New York City, 1983; presented a one-man show at Donmar Warehouse, 1985-86.

FILM APPEARANCES

John, *Prehistoric Women,* Twentieth Century-Fox, 1967.
Constable, *A Clockwork Orange,* Warner Brothers, 1971.
Pankratov, *Nicholas and Alexandra,* Columbia, 1971.
Lord Ludd, *Barry Lyndon,* Warner Brothers, 1975.
Stephen, *The Passenger* (also known as *Profession: Reporter*), Metro-Goldwyn-Mayer (MGM)/United Artists (UA), 1975.
Sagan, *Outland,* Warner Brothers, 1981.
Harrison, *McVicar,* Crown International, 1982.
General Orlov, *Octopussy,* MGM/UA, 1983.
Victor Maitland, *Beverly Hills Cop,* Paramount, 1984.
Podovsky, *Rambo: First Blood, Part II,* Tri-Star, 1985.
Sergeant Jones, *Revolution,* Warner Brothers, 1985.
Hugo Motherskille, *Underworld* (also known as *Transmutations*), Limehouse Pictures, 1985.
The fanatic, *Absolute Beginners,* Orion, 1986.
Mr. Sharon, *Under the Cherry Moon,* Warner Brothers, 1986.
Streets of Yesterday, Perfect Features, 1989.
George Cornell, *The Krays,* Rank, 1990.

Also appeared in *Buster 1988* and *The Passenger.*

TELEVISION APPEARANCES; MOVIES

Atoman, *Coming Out of the Ice,* CBS, 1982.
Karl Von Eiderfeld, *Sins,* CBS, 1986.
Jack McFarland, *Prisoner of Rio,* Samba, 1988.
Adolf Hitler, *War and Remembrance,* TNT, 1988.
Girolamo Savonarola, *Season of Giants,* TNT, 1991.
Intruders, CBS, 1992.

WRITINGS:

East and Other Plays (includes *East,* produced at Edinburgh Festival, Edinburgh, Scotland, 1975), J. Calder, 1977.
Gross Intrusion (stories), J. Calder, 1977.
(Adapter) *The Trial* [and] *Metamorphosis* (plays), Amber Lane, 1981.

Also author of *Kvetch* (play), c. 1986; *Steven Berkoff's America,* 1988; *I Am Hamlet,* 1989; and *A Prisoner in Rio,* Hutchinson. Author or adapter of such plays as *Greek, Agamemnon, Decadence,* and *The Fall of the House of Usher.**

* * *

BERNHARD, Sandra 1955-

PERSONAL: Born June 6, 1955, in Flint, MI; daughter of Jerome (a proctologist) and Jeanette (a painter) Bernhard. *Education:* Attended high school in Scottsdale, AZ.

ADDRESSES: Office—10100 Santa Monica Blvd., No. 1600, Los Angeles, CA 90067; and c/o Enigma Records,

136 West 18th St., New York, NY 10011. *Agent*—Terry Danuser, Management Company Entertainment Group, 11355 West Olympic Blvd., Suite 500, Los Angeles, CA 90064; and William Morris Agency, 151 El Camino Dr., Beverly Hills, CA 90212.

CAREER: Actress, comedienne, and singer. Worked on a kibbutz in Israel; manicurist-pedicurist at a beauty salon in Beverly Hills, CA; stand-up comedienne at nightclubs in and around Beverly Hills, 1974-78.

MEMBER: Screen Actors Guild.

AWARDS, HONORS: Award, National Society of Film Critics, c. 1983, for *The King of Comedy;* Charlie Local and National Comedy Award, funniest show off-Broadway, Association of Comedy Artists, 1988, for *Without You I'm Nothing.*

CREDITS:

FILM APPEARANCES

Angie, *Cheech and Chong's Nice Dreams,* Columbia, 1981.
Masha, *The King of Comedy,* Twentieth Century-Fox, 1983.
Grouch waitress, *Sesame Street Presents: Follow That Bird,* Warner Brothers, 1985.
Nurse Stein, *Track 29,* Island, 1988.
Without You I'm Nothing, Management Company Entertainment Group, 1990.
Minerva Mayflower, *Hudson Hawk,* Tri-Star, 1991.

Appeared as actress/comedienne, *Heavy Petting,* 1988; also appeared in *Perfect,* Columbia, 1985, *The Whoopee Boys,* Paramount, 1986, and *Casual Sex?,* Universal, 1988.

STAGE APPEARANCES

Sandra Bernhard: Without You I'm Nothing (solo show; also see below), Orpheum Theatre, New York City, 1988.

TELEVISION APPEARANCES; SPECIALS

Just for Laughs, Showtime, 1987.
The Prince's Trust Gala, TBS, 1989.
Decade, MTV, 1989.
Save the Planet: A CBS/Hard Rock Cafe Special, CBS, 1990.
Host, *Living in America,* syndicated, 1990.

TELEVISION APPEARANCES; EPISODIC

"Top Billing," *Tales From the Crypt,* HBO, 1991.

Regular guest on *The Richard Pryor Show* and *Late Night With David Letterman.*

RECORDINGS:

ALBUMS

I'm Your Woman, Mercury, 1985.

Also recorded *Without You I'm Nothing,* 1989.

WRITINGS:

Without You I'm Nothing (solo stage show), 1988, adaptation (with John Boskovich) released as a feature film, Management Company Entertainment Group, 1990.
Confessions of a Pretty Lady, Harper, 1988.

Co-author of eight songs for the record album *I'm Your Woman,* Mercury, 1985. Contributor to magazines, including *Interview, Spin,* and *Vanity Fair.*

OTHER SOURCES:

BOOKS

Newsmakers 89, Gale, 1989, p. 32-33.

PERIODICALS

Daily News (New York), March 27, 1988; May 29, 1988.
Interview, August, 1989, p. 130; March, 1990, p. 136.
New York, February 21, 1983, p. 36.
People, September 10, 1990, p. 67.
Rolling Stone, November 3, 1988, p. 76.*

* * *

BIGELOW, Kathryn

PERSONAL: Daughter of a paint factory manager and a librarian. *Education:* Studied painting at San Francisco Art Institute; attended Whitney Museum Independent Study Program, 1972; graduate study at Columbia University School of Film, c. 1978.

ADDRESSES: Agent—Paula Wagner, Creative Artists Agency, 9830 Wilshire Blvd., Beverly Hills, CA 90212.

CAREER: Director. Began career as assistant to Vito Acconci.

MEMBER: Screen Directors Guild.

CREDITS:

FILM WORK; DIRECTOR, EXCEPT WHERE INDICATED

(With Monty Montgomery) *The Loveless* (also see below), Mainline, 1982.
Near Dark (also see below), DEG, 1987.
Blue Steel, Metro-Goldwyn-Mayer/United Artists, 1990.
Point Break (also known as *Riders on the Storm* and *Johnny Utah*), Twentieth Century-Fox, 1991.

Script supervisor for *Union City,* 1980.

FILM APPEARANCES

Newspaper editor, *Born in Flames,* First Run Features, 1983.

WRITINGS:

SCREENPLAYS

(With Monty Montgomery) *The Loveless,* Mainline, 1982.
(With Eric Red) *Near Dark,* DEG, 1987.

OTHER SOURCES:

PERIODICALS

Interview, August, 1989, p. 84; March, 1990, p. 20.
Premiere, April, 1990, p. 45.
Rolling Stone, September 21, 1989, p. 47.*

* * *

BIRCH, Patricia 1934(?)-

PERSONAL: Born c. 1934 in Scarsdale, NY; married William Becker (president of Janus Films); children: Jonathan, Peter, one daughter. *Education:* Professional dance training with Merce Cunningham and with Martha Graham; attended School of American Ballet.

ADDRESSES: Agent—William Morris Agency, 1350 Ave. of Americas, New York, NY 10019.

CAREER: Choreographer, director, and actress. Began theatre career as a dancer in Martha Graham Dance Company; later served as instructor and rehearsal director for same organization; first appeared on stage as actress and dancer in musical comedies.

AWARDS, HONORS: Antionette Perry Award nomination and Drama Desk Award, best choreographer, both 1972, both for *Grease;* Drama Desk Award, choreography, 1974, for *Candide;* Antionette Perry Award nomination and Drama Desk Award, best choreographer, 1974, for *Over Here!;* Antionette Perry Award nomination, best choreographer, 1976, for *Pacific Overtures;* Antionette Perry Award nomination, best choreographer, 1977, for *Music Is;* Emmy Award nomination, outstanding achievement in Choreography and Emmy Award, outstanding directing in a variety or music program (with Humphrey Burton), 1988, both for *Celebrating Gershwin.*

CREDITS:

STAGE WORK; CHOREOGRAPHER, EXCEPT WHERE NOTED

(Assistant to director) *You're a Good Man, Charlie Brown,* Little Fox Theatre, San Francisco, California, 1968.
Up Eden, Jan Hus Playhouse, 1968.
You're a Good Man, Charlie Brown (also see below), Coconut Grove Playhouse, Miami, FL, 1968.
(Director of special sequences) *Fireworks,* Village South Theatre, 1969.
The Me Nobody Knows, Orpheum Theatre and Helen Hayes Theatre, both New York City, both 1970.
F. Jasmine Adams, Circle in the Square, New York City, 1971.
Grease (also see below), Broadhurst Theatre and Royale Theatre, both New York City, both 1972, and Eden Theatre, New York City, 1972-79.
The Real Inspector Hound [and] *After Magritte* (double bill), Theatre Four, New York City, 1972-73.
A Little Night Music (also see below), Sam S. Shubert Theatre, New York City, 1973.
Candide (also see below), Broadway Theatre, New York City, 1974.
Diamond Studs (also known as *The Life of Jesse James*), Westside Theatre, New York City, 1975, and Ford's Theatre Society, Washington, DC, 1975.
(And director) *Truckload,* Lyceum Theatre, New York City, 1975.
Music Is, St. James Theatre, New York City, 1976.
Pacific Overtures, Winter Garden Theatre, New York City, 1976.
(Choreographer and director, both with Robert Kalfin) *Happy End,* Martin Beck Theatre, New York City, and Brooklyn Academy of Music, Brooklyn, NY, both 1977.
Hot Grog, The Phoenix Theatre, Marymount Manhattan Theatre, Manhattan, NY, 1977.
Gilda Radner Live from New York (also see below), Winter Garden Theatre, 1979.
They're Playing Our Song, Center Theatre Group, Ahmanson Theatre, Los Angeles, CA, 1978, Imperial Theatre, New York City, 1979.
(Production supervisor) *V.I.P. Night on Broadway,* Sam S. Shubert Theatre, 1979.
Zoot Suit, Winter Garden Theatre, 1979.
(And director) *Really Rosie,* Chelsea Theatre Center/Upstairs, New York City, 1980, and American Place Theatre, New York City, 1980-81.
(And director) *El Bravo!,* Entermedia Theatre, 1981.
(And director) *American Passion,* Joyce Theater, 1983.
(And director) *Raggedy Ann,* Nederlander Theatre, New York City, 1986.
Roza, Center Theatre Group, Mark Taper Forum, Los Angeles, 1986-87, and Royale Theatre, 1987.
(And director) *A Walk on the Wild Side,* Musical Theatre Works, City Stage Company (CSC) Theatre, New York City, 1988.
Elvis: A Rockin' Remembrance, Beacon Theatre, New York City, 1989.
Love's Labour's Lost, The Acting Company, Marymount Manhattan Theatre, 1989.
Welcome to the Club, Music Box, New York City, 1989.

Birch staged the tango sequence in the Broadway production of *The Prime of Miss Jean Brodie,* 1968; worked on playwright Arthur Miller's *The Creation of the World and Other Business,* New York, 1972; also staged the opera *Falstaff* at the Kennedy Center, Washington, DC.

STAGE APPEARANCES; DANCER

Brigadoon, New York City Light Opera Company, City Center Theatre, 1957.
Carousel, New York City Light Opera Company, 1957.
Oklahoma!, New York City Light Opera Company, 1958.
Goldilocks, Lunt-Fontanne, New York City, 1958.

STAGE APPEARANCES; ACTRESS

(Dramatic debut) Anybodys, *West Side Story,* Winter Garden Theatre, 1960.
Constance, *Fortuna,* Maidman Playhouse, 1962.

FILM WORK; CHOREOGRAPHER, EXCEPT WHERE NOTED

The Wild Party, American International Pictures, 1975.
A Little Night Music, New World Pictures, 1977.
Roseland, Cinema Shares International, 1977.
Grease, Paramount, 1978.
Sgt. Pepper's Lonely Hearts Club Band, Universal, 1978.
Zoot Suit, Universal, 1981.
Grease Two (also see below), Paramount, 1982.
Big, Twentieth Century-Fox, 1988.
Elvira, Mistress of the Dark, New World Pictures, 1988.
Stella, Samuel Goldwyn/Buena Vista, 1991.

Choreographed filmed production of *Gilda Radner Live From New York,* released as motion picture.

FILM WORK; DIRECTOR

Grease two, Paramount, 1982.

Also directed 1980 film *Angel.*

TELEVISION WORK; CHOREOGRAPHER

(Resident choreographer) *The Electric Company,* PBS, 1971-74.
The Goldie Hawn Special, CBS, 1978.
Saturday Night Live, NBC, 1979.
The Robert Klein Show, NBC, 1981.
The New Show, NBC, 1984.
Candide (also known as *Live from Lincoln Center*), PBS, 1986.
(With Humphrey Burton) *Celebrating Gershwin* (also known as *The Jazz Age* and *'S Wonderful*), PBS, 1987.

TELEVISION WORK; DIRECTOR

Three By Three (also known as *Dance in America*), PBS, 1985.

OTHER SOURCES:

PERIODICALS

New York Times, October 29, 1972.*

*   *   *

BIROC, Joe
See BIROC, Joseph

*   *   *

BIROC, Joseph 1903(?)-
(Joseph F. Biroc; Joe Biroc)

PERSONAL: Full name Joseph F. Biroc; born February 12, 1903 (one source says 1900), in New York, NY.

CAREER: Cinematographer. Began working at Paragon Studios film lab, Ft. Lee, NJ, at age 18; became assistant cameraman in the 1920s; worked as camera operator in the 1920s and 1930s; during World War II, led one of the first teams to film the liberation of Paris. *Military service:* United States Signal Corps.

MEMBER: American Society of Cinematographers.

AWARDS, HONORS: Academy Award nomination, black and white cinematography, 1964, for *Hush . . . Hush, Sweet Charlotte;* Emmy Award, outstanding achievement in cinematography for entertainment programming for a special or feature length program, 1972, for *Brian's Song;* Academy Award, cinematography, 1974, for *The Towering Inferno;* Emmy Award nomination, outstanding cinematography in entertainment programming for a single episode of a regular or limited series, 1977, for part one of *The Moneychangers;* Emmy Award nomination, outstanding cinematography in entertainment programming for a special or feature length program, 1978, for *A Family Upside Down;* Emmy Award nomination, outstanding cinematography in entertainment programming for a single episode of a regular or limited series, 1978, for part one of *Washington: Behind Closed Doors;* Emmy Award nomination, outstanding cinematography for a single episode of a regular series, 1979, for part two of *Little Women;* Emmy Award nomination, outstanding cinematography for a special, 1980, for *Kenny Rogers as the Gambler;* Emmy Award, outstanding cinematography for a single episode of a regular series, 1983, for "The Masterbuilder's Woman," *Casablanca;* Emmy Award nomination, outstanding cinematography for a special, 1985, for *A Death in California;* American Society of Cinematographers Lifetime Achievement Award, 1989.

CREDITS:

FILM WORK; CINEMATOGRAPHER; UNDER NAME JOSEPH BIROC, EXCEPT AS INDICATED

(With Joseph Walker) *It's a Wonderful Life,* RKO Radio Pictures, 1946.
(Under name Joseph F. Biroc) *Magic Town,* RKO Radio Pictures, 1947.
(With John Seitz, Ernest Laszlo, Gordon Avil, and Edward Cronjager) *On Our Merry Way* (also known as *A Miracle Can Happen*), United Artists (UA), 1948.
My Dear Secretary, UA, 1948.
(Under name Joseph F. Biroc) *Roughshod,* RKO Radio Pictures, 1949.
Mrs. Mike, UA, 1949.
Johnny Allegro (released in England as *Hounded*), Columbia, 1949.
The Killer That Stalked New York, Columbia, 1950.
(Under name Joseph F. Biroc) *Cry Danger,* RKO Radio Pictures, 1951.
(Under name Joseph F. Biroc) *Without Warning* (also known as *The Story Without a Name*), UA, 1952.
The Bushwackers (released in England as *The Rebel*), Real Art, 1952.
Red Planet Mars, UA, 1952.
Loan Shark, Lippert, 1952.
Bwana Devil, UA, 1953.
(Under name Joseph F. Biroc) *Vice Squad* (released in England as *The Girl in Room 17*), UA, 1953.
The Twonky, UA, 1953.
Donovan's Brain, UA, 1953.
(Under name Joseph F. Biroc) *The Glass Wall,* Columbia, 1953.
The Tall Texan, Lippert, 1953.
Appointment in Honduras, RKO Radio Pictures, 1953.
Charade, Monarch, 1953.
(Under name Joseph F. Biroc) *World for Ransom,* Allied Artists, 1954.
Down Three Dark Streets, UA, 1954.
(With John Alton) *The Steel Cage,* UA, 1954.
Bengazi, RKO Radio Pictures, 1955.
(Under name Joseph F. Biroc) *Ghost Town,* UA, 1956.
(Under name Joseph F. Biroc) *Quincannon, Frontier Scout,* UA, 1956.
(Under name Joe Biroc) *Nightmare* UA, 1956.
Attack!, UA, 1956.
The Black Whip, Twentieth Century-Fox, 1956.
Tension at Table Rock, RKO Radio Pictures, 1956.
The Ride Back, UA, 1957.
The Garment Jungle, Columbia, 1957.
China Gate, Twentieth Century-Fox, 1957.
Run of the Arrow, Universal, 1957.
The Unknown Terror, Twentieth Century-Fox, 1957.
Forty Guns (also known as *Woman with a Whip*), Twentieth Century-Fox, 1957.
The Amazing Colossal Man, American International Pictures, 1957.
(With Lamar Boren) *Underwater Warrior,* Metro-Goldwyn-Mayer (MGM), 1958.
(Under name Joseph F. Biroc) *Home before Dark,* Warner Brothers, 1958.
(Under name Joseph F. Biroc) *Born Reckless,* Warner Brothers, 1959.
The FBI Story, Warner Brothers, 1959.
Verboten!, Columbia, 1959.
The Bat, Allied Artists, 1959.
Ice Palace, Warner Brothers, 1960.
Thirteen Ghosts, Columbia, 1960.
Gold of the Seven Saints, Warner Brothers, 1961.
Operation Eichmann, Allied Artists, 1961.
The Devil at Four O'Clock, Columbia, 1961.
Sail a Crooked Ship, Columbia, 1961.
Convicts Four (also known as *Reprieve*), Allied Artists, 1962.
Hitler (also known as *Women of Nazi Germany*), Allied Artists, 1962.
Confessions of an Opium Eater (also known as *Souls for Sale* and *Secrets of a Soul;* released in England as *Evils of Chinatown*), Allied Artists, 1962.
Bye Bye Birdie, Columbia, 1963.
(Under name Joseph F. Biroc) *Toys in the Attic,* UA, 1963.
Under the Yum-Yum Tree, Columbia, 1963.
Viva Las Vegas (released in England as *Love in Las Vegas*), MGM, 1963.
(Under name Joseph F. Biroc) *Gunfight at Comanche Creek,* Allied Artists, 1964.
(Under name Joe Biroc) *Bullet for a Badman* (also known as *Renegade Posse*), Universal, 1964.
Ride the Wild Surf, Columbia, 1964.
Kitten with a Whip, Universal, 1964.
Hush . . . Hush, Sweet Charlotte, Twentieth Century-Fox, 1964.
The Young Lovers, MGM, 1964.
I Saw What You Did, Universal, 1965.
The Flight of the Phoenix, Twentieth Century-Fox, 1965.
The Russians Are Coming, The Russians Are Coming, UA, 1966.
The Swinger, Paramount, 1966.
To Trap a Spy, MGM, 1966.
Who's Minding the Mint?, Columbia, 1967.
Enter Laughing, Columbia, 1967.
Warning Shot, Paramount, 1967.
Tony Rome, Twentieth Century-Fox, 1967.
Fitzwilly (released in England as *Fitzwilly Strikes Back*), UA, 1967.
(Under name Joe Biroc) *The Detective,* Twentieth Century-Fox, 1968.
The Legend of Lylah Clare, MGM, 1968.

(With Ricou Browning) *Lady in Cement,* Twentieth Century-Fox, 1968.
Whatever Happened to Aunt Alice, Cinerama, 1969.
Too Late the Hero (also known as *Suicide Run*), Cinerama, 1970.
Mrs. Pollifax—Spy, UA, 1971.
The Organization, UA, 1971.
The Grissom Gang, Cinerama, 1971.
Escape from the Planet of the Apes, Twentieth Century-Fox, 1971.
Ulzana's Raid, Universal, 1972.
Emperor of the North Pole (also known as *Emperor of the North*), Twentieth Century-Fox, 1973.
Cahill, United States Marshal, Warner Brothers, 1973.
Shanks, Paramount, 1974.
The Longest Yard, Paramount, 1974.
Blazing Saddles, Warner Brothers, 1974.
(With Fred Koenekamp) *The Towering Inferno,* Twentieth Century-Fox/Warner Brothers, 1974.
Hustle, Paramount, 1975.
The Duchess and the Dirtwater Fox, Twentieth Century-Fox, 1976.
The Choirboys, Universal, 1977.
Beyond the Poseidon Adventure, Warner Brothers, 1979.
Airplane!, Paramount, 1980.
All the Marbles (released in England as *The California Dolls*) UA, 1981.
(With Philip Lathrop) *Hammett,* Warner Brothers, 1982.
Airplane II: The Sequel, Paramount, 1982.

Also cinematographer for *All That I Have,* 1951; *Promises, Promises* (also known as *Promise Her Anything*), 1963; *The Killing of Sister George,* 1968; *Lone Wolf; T-Men in Action; Man Behind the Badge; Dear Phoebe;* and *Garden of Cucumbers.*

TELEVISION WORK; CINEMATOGRAPHER

Alcoa Theatre (series), 1957.
Brian's Song (movie), ABC, 1971.
Playmates (movie), ABC, 1972.
Gidget Gets Married (movie), ABC, 1972.
The Crooked Hearts (movie), ABC, 1972.
Ghost Story (series), NBC, 1972.
Honky Tonk (pilot), NBC, 1974.
Wonder Woman (pilot), ABC, 1974.
Thursday's Game (movie), ABC, 1974.
Arthur Hailey's "The Moneychangers" (pilot), NBC, 1976.
SST—Death Flight (movie; also known as *SST: Disaster in the Sky*), ABC, 1977.
Washington: Behind Closed Doors (pilot), ABC, 1977.
The Clone Master (pilot), NBC, 1978.
Little Women (movie), NBC, 1978.
A Family Upside Down (movie), NBC, 1978.
Scruples (movie), CBS, 1980.
Kenny Rogers as the Gambler (movie), CBS, 1980.
Desperate Lives (pilot), CBS, 1982.
Casablanca (series), NBC, 1983.
The Jerk, Too (movie; also known as *Another Jerk*), NBC, 1984.
Father of Hell Town (movie; also known as *Hell Town U.S.A.*), NBC, 1985.
A Death in California (movie), ABC, 1985.
A Winner Never Quits (movie), ABC, 1986.
Outrage! (movie), CBS, 1986.

Also cinematographer for episodes of *Superman,* syndicated; and for *The Honeymoon Is Over; Four Star Theatre; Readers Digest; Solo; Ghost Breakers; Take Her She's Mine; Heaven Help Us; House Detective; Richard Diamond, Private Detective; Flag;* and *Time out for Dad.*

OTHER SOURCES:

BOOKS

The International Dictionary of Films and Filmmakers, Volume 4, St. James Press, 1987.*

* * *

BIROC, Joseph F.
See BIROC, Joseph

* * *

BLEASDALE, Alan 1946-

PERSONAL: Born March 23, 1946, in Liverpool, England; son of George (a foreman) and Margaret (a shop assistant; maiden name, Grant) Bleasdale; married Julia Moses, December 28, 1970; children: Timothy, Jamie, Tamana. *Education:* Padgate Teachers Training College, teachers certificate, 1967. *Avocational interests:* Rowing.

ADDRESSES: Agent—Harvey Unna and Stephen Durbridge Ltd., 24-32 Pottery Ln., London W11 4LZ, England.

CAREER: Writer. St. Columbus Secondary Modern School, Huyton, England, teacher, 1967-71; King George V School, Gilbert and Ellice Islands (now Kiribati), teacher, 1971-74; Halewood Grange Comprehensive School, Lancashire, England, teacher, 1974-75; full-time writer, beginning in 1975. Liverpool Playhouse, resident playwright, 1975-76; Contact Theatre, resident playwright, 1976-78; Liverpool Playhouse, joint artistic director, 1981-84, associate director, 1984-86; GBH Films, director, 1988—; JAB Films, director, 1990—.

AWARDS, HONORS: Broadcasting Press Guild Television Award, best series, 1982, for *Boys from the Black-*

stuff; Writer of the Year, Royal Television Society, 1982; British Academy of Film and Television Arts Award, television writing, 1982; *Evening Standard* Drama Award, best musical, 1985, for *Are You Lonesome Tonight?;* ITV Achievement of the Decade Award, best British television drama of the decade, 1989, for *Boys from the Blackstuff;* honorary degree, Liverpool Polytechnic, 1991.

WRITINGS:

PLAYS

Fat Harold and the Last Twenty-Six, first produced at Liverpool Playhouse, Liverpool, 1975.
The Party's Over, produced at Playhouse Theatre, Liverpool, 1975.
(With others) *Scully* (adaptation of Bleasdale's novel of the same title; also see below), produced at Everyman Theatre, Liverpool, 1975.
Down the Dock Road, produced at Playhouse Theatre, 1976.
(With Kenneth Alan Taylor) *Franny Scully's Christmas Stories,* produced at Playhouse Theatre, 1976.
It's a Madhouse, produced at Contact Theatre, Manchester, 1976 (also see below).
Should Auld Acquaintance, produced at Contact Theatre, 1976.
No More Sitting on the Old School Bench, produced at Contact Theatre, 1977, published by Woodhouse, 1979, published with David Calcutt's *Detention* by Heinemann, 1987.
Crackers, produced at The Playhouse, Leeds, 1978.
Pimples, produced at Contact Theatre, 1978.
Love Is a Many Splendoured Thing (for children), produced in Redditch, Worcestershire, 1986, published in *Act I,* edited by David Self and Ray Speakman, Hutchinson, 1979.
Having a Ball, first produced at the Coliseum, Oldham, Lancashire, 1981 (also see below).
Young People Today (sketch), produced in *The Big One* in London, 1983.
Are You Lonesome Tonight? (musical), first produced at Liverpool Playhouse, 1985, published by Faber, 1985.
Having a Ball [and] *It's a Madhouse,* Faber, 1986.

TELEVISION SERIES

Boys from the Blackstuff (five-part series), BBC, 1982, published by Hutchinson, edited by David Self, 1985.
Scully (adapted from Bleasdale's novel of the same title; also see below), 1984, television script published by Hutchinson, edited by Self, 1984.
The Monocled Mutineer (four-part series; adapted from the book by William Allison and John Farley), BBC, 1986, television script published by Hutchinson, 1986.

Also author of *G.B.H.,* a seven-part series broadcast in 1991.

TELEVISION PLAYS

Early to Bed, BBC, 1975.
Dangerous Ambition, BBC, 1976.
Scully's New Year's Eve, BBC, 1978.
The Black Stuff, BBC, 1980.
The Muscle Market, BBC, 1981.

SCREENPLAYS

No Surrender, Norstar, 1986, published as *No Surrender: A Deadpan Farce* by Faber, 1986.

NOVELS

Scully, Hutchinson, 1975.
Who's Been Sleeping in My Bed?, Hutchinson, 1977, revised edition published as *Scully and Mooey,* Corgi, 1984.

* * *

BLINN, William 1937-

PERSONAL: Full name, William Frederick Blinn; born July 21, 1937. *Education:* Graduate of American Academy of Dramatic Arts.

ADDRESSES: Office—16041 Jeanne Lane, Encino, CA 91436. *Agent*—Len Rosenberg, William Morris Agency, 151 South El Camino Dr., Beverly Hills, CA 90212.

CAREER: Producer and writer. Blinn-Thorpe Productions, partner, 1977-84; Echo Cove Productions.

AWARDS, HONORS: Emmy Award, outstanding writing in a dramatic adaptation, George S. Peabody Award, and Writers Guild of America Award, all 1971, for *Brian's Song;* Emmy Award (with Ernest Kinoy), outstanding writing in a drama series, and Television Critics' Award, both 1977, for *Roots: Part II;* Humanitas Award, 1977, for *Roots: Part IV;* Image Award, National Association for the Advancement of Colored People, for *The Rookies;* Image Award, 1980, for "All God's Children," *ABC Movie of the Week;* Emmy Award nomination (with Mel Swope), outstanding drama series, 1982, and Emmy Award nomination (with Ken Ehrlich), outstanding drama series, 1983, both for *Fame.*

CREDITS:

TELEVISION WORK; SERIES

Producer, *The Rookies* (also see below), ABC, 1972-73.
Creator and executive producer, *The New Land,* ABC, 1974.
Executive producer (with Jerry Thorpe), *The Lazarus Syndrome* (also see below), ABC, 1979.

Executive producer (with Mace Neufeld and Jerry Thorpe), *The American Dream* (also known as *The Novacks;* also see below), ABC, 1981.
Executive producer, *Fame* (also see below), NBC, 1982-83, syndicated, 1983-84.
Executive producer (with Jerry Thorpe), *Our House* (also see below), NBC, 1987-88.
Creator and executive producer, *The Boys of Twilight* (also see below), CBS, 1992.

TELEVISION WORK; MINI-SERIES

Producer (with Jerry Thorpe), *The MacKenzies of Paradise Cove* (also see below), ABC, 1979.

TELEVISION WORK; MOVIES

Executive producer (with Jerry Thorpe), *A Question of Love* (also known as *A Purely Legal Matter;* also see below), NBC, 1978.
Producer (with Jerry Thorpe), *All God's Children* (featured on *ABC Movie of the Week;* also see below), ABC, 1980.
Executive producer (with Jerry Thorpe), *Happy Endings* (also known as *House of Cards;* also see below), NBC, 1983.
Executive producer, *Davy Crockett* (featured on *The Magical World of Disney*), NBC, 1988.
Executive producer, *Polly* (featured on *The Magical World of Disney;* also see below), NBC, 1989.
Executive producer, *Wild Jack* (also known as *Jack of the Wild, McCall!,* and *McCall of the Wild;* featured on *The Magical World of Disney;* also see below), NBC, 1989.
Executive producer, *Appearances* (also see below), NBC, 1990.
Executive producer, *Polly Comin' Home!* (also known as *Polly—One More Time!;* also see below), NBC, 1990.

Also worked as co-producer of *Eight Is Enough: A Family Reunion* (also see below).

TELEVISION WORK; PILOTS

Creator, *Starsky and Hutch* (also see below), ABC, 1975.
Producer (with Jerry Thorpe), *Stickin' Together* (also see below), ABC, 1978.
Creator and executive producer, *Aaron's Way* (also see below), NBC, 1988.

TELEVISION WORK; SPECIALS

Executive producer, *Bridges to Cross,* CBS, 1986.

WRITINGS:

TELEVISION SERIES

(With Michael Gleason) *My Favorite Martian,* CBS, 1963-66.
(With David Shaw, Ernest Kinoy, Richard McDonagh, and others) *Shane,* ABC, 1966.
(With George Eckstein, Anthony Wilson, Don Brinkley, and others) *The Invaders,* ABC, 1967-68.
(With Sandor Stern, Skip Webster, Mark Slade, and others) *The Rookies,* ABC, 1972-76.
(With Hindi Brooks, Arnold Laven, Peter Lefcourt, and others) *Eight Is Enough,* ABC, 1977-81.
(With Ronald M. Cohan, Barbara Corday, Ted Hecht, and others) *The American Dream* (also known as *The Novacks*), ABC, 1981.
(With Christopher Gore, Lee H. Grant, and others) *Fame,* NBC, 1982-83, syndicated, 1983-84.
Our House, NBC, 1987-88.
The Boys of Twilight, CBS, 1992.

TELEVISION MINI-SERIES

(With Ernest Kinoy, James Lee, and M. Charles Cohen) *Roots,* ABC, 1977.
A Man Called Intrepid, NBC, 1979.
The MacKenzies of Paradise Cove, ABC, 1979.

TELEVISION MOVIES

Brian's Song (featured on *ABC Movie of the Week*), ABC, 1971.
A Question of Love (also known as *A Purely Legal Matter*), NBC, 1978.
All God's Children (featured on *ABC Movie of the Week*), ABC, 1980.
An Eclipse of Reason (featured on *ABC Movie of the Week*), ABC, 1980.
Happy Endings (also known as *House of Cards;* also see below), NBC, 1983.
Polly (featured on *The Magical World of Disney*), NBC, 1989.
Wild Jack (also known as *Jack of the Wild, McCall!,* and *McCall of the Wild;* featured on *The Magical World of Disney*), NBC, 1989.
The Outside Woman (featured on *CBS Movie of the Week*), ABC, 1989.
Appearances, NBC, 1990.
Polly Comin' Home! (also known as *Polly—One More Time!*), NBC, 1990.

Also author of *Eight Is Enough: A Family Reunion.*

TELEVISION PILOTS

The Rookies, ABC, 1972.
Starsky and Hutch, ABC, 1975.
Hunter, CBS, 1976.
Stickin' Together, ABC, 1978.
The Lazarus Syndrome, ABC, 1979.
For Heaven's Sake, ABC, 1979.
The Naturals, NBC, 1983.
City, ABC, 1986.

Aaron's Way, NBC, 1988.
Half 'n' Half, ABC, 1988.

SCREENPLAYS

Purple Rain, Warner Brothers, 1984.

BOOKS

Brian's Song, Bantam, 1983.

* * *

BLOODWORTH, Linda
See BLOODWORTH-THOMASON, Linda

* * *

BLOODWORTH-THOMASON, Linda 1947(?)- (Linda Bloodworth)

PERSONAL: Born c. 1947, in Poplar Bluff, MO; married Harry Thomason (a television and film producer and director), 1983.

ADDRESSES: Office—Mozark Productions, Columbia Television, Columbia Plaza E., Burbank, CA 91505.

CAREER: Television writer, creator, and producer. Co-owner (with husband Harry Thomason) of Mozark Productions.

AWARDS, HONORS: Emmy Award nomination, outstanding writing in a comedy series, 1987, for *Designing Women;* Emmy Award nominations, outstanding comedy series, 1988, 1989, and 1990, all for *Designing Women;* Writers Guild of America award nomination, best writing for episodic comedy, 1992, for "A Day in the Life of Wood Newton," *Evening Shade.*

CREDITS:

TELEVISION COEXECUTIVE PRODUCER, WITH HARRY THOMASON

(And creator) *Lime Street* (series), ABC, 1985.
(And creator) *Designing Women* (series), CBS, 1986—.
(And creator) *Evening Shade* (series), CBS, 1990—.
The Designing Women Special: Their Finest Hour (special; also see below), CBS, 1990.

TELEVISION PRODUCER; UNDER NAME LINDA BLOODWORTH

Dribble (pilot; also see below), NBC, 1980.
Filthy Rich (series; also see below), CBS, 1982.
London and Davis in New York (pilot; also see below), CBS, 1984.

TELEVISION APPEARANCES

*Memories of M*A*S*H* (special), CBS, 1991.

WRITINGS:

TELEVISION SERIES

(Under name Linda Bloodworth) *Rhoda,* CBS, 1974-78.
(Under name Linda Bloodworth) *Designing Women,* CBS, 1990—.

Also contributed to the series *M*A*S*H* under the name Linda Bloodworth.

TELEVISION EPISODES

Evening Shade (includes premiere episode and "A Day in the Life of Wood Newton"), CBS, 1990—.

OTHER TELEVISION WRITINGS

(Under name Linda Bloodworth) *Over and Out* (pilot), NBC, 1976.
Lime Street (premiere), ABC, 1985.
The Designing Women Special: Their Finest Hour, CBS, 1990.

OTHER SOURCES:

PERIODICALS

New York Times, March 3, 1991, pp. 29-30.
People, January 28, 1991, pp. 49, 52-53.*

* * *

BOAM, Jeffrey 1949-

PERSONAL: Full name Jeffrey David Boam; born November 30, 1949, in Rochester, NY; married Paula Mary Ann Haggar; children: Tessa Bianca, Mia Catherine-Maria. *Education:* Sacramento State College, B.A., 1970; University of California, Los Angeles, M.F.A., 1972.

ADDRESSES: Agent—Creative Artists Agency, 9830 Wilshire Blvd., Beverly Hills, CA 90212.

CAREER: Producer, director, and screenwriter.

MEMBER: Writers Guild, Authors League of America, Academy of Motion Picture Arts and Sciences.

CREDITS:

FILM WORK

Assistant director, *Straight Time* (also see below), Warner Brothers, 1978.
Associate producer, *The Dead Zone* (also see below), Paramount, 1983.

FILM APPEARANCES

Lydia's interview, *Innerspace* (also see below), Warner Brothers, 1987.

WRITINGS:

SCREENPLAYS

(With Alvin Sargent and Edward Bunker) *Straight Time* (based on Bunker's novel *No Beast So Fierce*), Warner Brothers, 1978.

The Dead Zone (based on the novel by Stephen King) Paramount, 1983.

(With Janice Fischer and James Jeremias) *The Lost Boys* (based on a story by Fischer and Jeremias) Warner Brothers, 1987.

(With Chip Proser) *Innerspace* (based on a story by Proser), Warner Brothers, 1987.

Funny Farm (based on the book by Jay Cronley), Warner Brothers, 1988.

Lethal Weapon 2 (based on a story by Shane Black and Warren Murphy), Warner Brothers, 1989.

Indiana Jones and the Last Crusade, Paramount, 1989.

(With Robert Mark Kamen) *Lethal Weapon 3,* Warner Brothers, 1992.*

* * *

BOGDANOV, Michael 1938-

PERSONAL: Born Michael Bogdin, December 15, 1938, in London, England; son of Francis Benzion and Rhoda (Rees) Bogdin; married Patricia Ann Warwick, December 17, 1966; children: Malachi, Jethro, Ffion. *Education:* Studied at the University of Paris (Sorbonne), 1958, and University of Munich, 1962; Trinity College, M.A.(modern languages), 1963. *Avocational interests:* Cricket, wine, music, sheep, reading.

ADDRESSES: Office—English Shakespeare Company, 38 Bedford Square, London WC1B 3EG, England. *Agent*—(Literary) Michael Imison, 28 Almeida St., London, NI 1TD, England.

CAREER: Artistic director. Telefis Eireann, Dublin, Ireland, director and producer, 1966-68; Oxford Playhouse, Oxford, England, director, 1969; Royal Court Theatre, London, England, director, 1969; Royal Shakespeare Company, Stratford-on-Avon, England, assistant director, 1970-71; Tyneside Theatre Company, Newcastle-upon-Tyne, England, assistant director, 1971-1973; Leicester Theatre Trust, Leicester, England, associate director, and Phoenix Theatre, Leicester, director, both 1973-78; Young Vic Theatre, London, artistic director, 1978-1980; National Theatre, London, associate director, 1980-1988; English Shakespeare Company, London, co-founder and joint artistic director, 1986—; Abbey Theatre, Dublin, associate director, 1986—; Deutsche Schauspielhaus, Hamburg, Germany, intendant, 1989-1993.

AWARDS, HONORS: Laurence Olivier Award, Society of West End Theatres (London), director of the year, 1979, for *The Taming of the Shrew;* Tokyo Critics Award, best director, 1984, for *Romeo and Juliet;* Dublin Critics Award, best director, 1984, for *Hamlet;* Outstanding Achievement Award, *Drama Magazine,* 1986; Manchester (England) Critics Award, 1987; Laurence Olivier Award, Society of West End Theatres (London), director of the year, 1989, for *The Wars of the Roses.*

CREDITS:

STAGE WORK; ARTISTIC DIRECTOR, EXCEPT AS INDICATED

The Bootleg Gentleman (musical; also see below), Oxford Playhouse, Oxford, England, 1968.

A Comedy of the Changing Years, Royal Court Theatre, London, 1969.

Assistant director, *Rabelais,* Royal Shakespeare Company, Stratford-on-Avon, England, 1970.

Assistant director, *A Midsummer Night's Dream,* Royal Shakespeare Company, London, 1970, then New York City, then Ahmanson Theatre, Los Angeles, CA, both 1971, later world cities, 1972.

Assistant director, *Two Gentlemen of Verona,* Teatro Escobar, Sau Paulo, Brazil, 1971.

The Magic Drum, Phoenix Theatre, Leicester, England, then National Theatre, London, both 1973.

He That Plays the King: Richard III, Hamlet, The Tempest, Phoenix Theatre, 1974.

The Recruiting Officer, Haymarket Theatre, London, 1975.

Sir Gawain and the Green Knight (also see below), National Theatre, 1977.

The Hunchback of Notre Dame, National Theatre, 1977.

Bartholomew Fair, Young Vic Theatre, London, 1978.

The Canterbury Tales (also see below), Young Vic Theatre, 1978.

The Action Man Trilogy: Richard III, Hamlet, The Tempest, Young Vic Theatre, 1978, then Stuttgart and Dusseldorf, Germany, 1979.

The Taming of the Shrew, Royal Shakespeare Company, 1978-79.

Faust!, Young Vic Theatre, 1979.

The Seagull, Toho Theatre Company, Tokyo, Japan, 1980.

The Shadow of a Gunman, Royal Shakespeare Company, The Other Place Theatre, London, 1980, then Warehouse Theatre, London, 1981.

The Romans in Britain, National Theatre, 1980.

Hiawatha (Christmas production; also see below), National Theatre, 1980-83.

The Knight of the Burning Pestle, Royal Shakespeare Company, Alwych Theatre, London, 1981.

One-Woman Plays (includes "Waking Up," "The Same Old Story," "A Woman Alone," and "Medea"), National Theatre, 1981.
The Hypochondriac (also see below), National Theatre, 1981.
The Mayor of Zalamea, or, The Best Garrotting Ever Done, National Theatre, 1981-82, then Washington, DC, 1984.
Uncle Vanya, National Theatre, 1982.
The Caucasian Chalk Circle, National Theatre, 1982.
The Spanish Tragedy, National Theatre, 1982-83, then Lyttleton Theatre, London, 1984.
Hamlet, Abbey Theatre, Dublin, Ireland, 1983.
Romeo and Juliet, Imperial Theatre, Tokyo, Japan, 1983.
Lorrenzaccio, National Theatre, 1983.
Macbeth (workshop presentation), National Theatre Company, Cottesloe Theatre, London, then British school tour, 1983.
You Can't Take It With You, National Theatre, 1983-84.
Strider: The Story of a Horse, National Theatre, 1984.
The Ancient Mariner (also see below), National Theatre, 1984-85.
Donnerstag Aus Licht (opera), Covent Garden, London, 1985.
Measure for Measure, Stratford Festival Theatre, Ontario, Canada, 1985.
Mutiny! (musical), Picadilly Theatre, London, 1985-86.
Julius Caesar (also see below), Deutsche Schauspielhaus, Hamburg, Germany, 1986.
Romeo and Juliet, Royal Shakespeare Company, Stratford-on-Avon, 1986, then Barbican Theatre, London, 1987.
The Henrys: Henry IV, Parts 1 and 2, and Henry V (inaugural production), English Shakespeare Company, Theatre Royal, Plymouth, England, 1986, then British cities, then international cities, 1986-87.
The Wars of the Roses: Richard II, Henry IV Parts 1 and 2, Henry V, Henry VI: House of Lancaster, Henry VI: House of York, Richard III, English Shakespeare Company, Theatre Royal, Bath, England, then British cities, then international cities, then Old Vic, London, 1987-89.
The Canterbury Tales (also see below), Prince of Wales' Theatre, London, 1987.
Reineke Fuchs (also see below), Deutsche Schauspielhaus, 1987.
Montag aus Licht, Stockhausen Opera, La Scala, Milan, Italy, 1988.
Hamlet, Deutsche Schauspielhaus, 1989.
Mary Stuart, Deutsche Schauspielhaus, 1990.
The Tempest, Deutsche Schauspielhaus, 1990.
The Ginger Man, Deutsche Schauspielhaus, 1991.

Also director of the English Shakespeare Company touring productions of *Coriolanus* and *The Winter's Tale* which travelled to Japan, Australia, and India, as well as throughout Great Britain.

TELEVISION WORK; ARTISTIC DIRECTOR

And producer, *Broad and Narrow* (series), Telefis Eireann/ATV, 1966-68.
Hiawatha (also see below), Channel 4, 1981.
And host, *Shakespeare Lives,* Channel 4, 1983.

WRITINGS:

(With Terence Brady) *Broad and Narrow* (television series), ATV, 1965.
The Bootleg Gentleman (musical adaptation of *Le Bourgeois Gentilhomme* by Moliere), first produced at Oxford Playhouse, Oxford, England, 1968.
Sir Gawain and the Green Knight (adaptation of anonymous medieval tale), first produced at National Theatre, London, 1977.
(With Phil Woods) *Canterbury Tales* (adaptation of selections from *The Canterbury Tales* by Geoffrey Chaucer), first produced at Young Vic Theatre, London, 1978.
The Hypochondriac (musical adaptation of Alan Drury's translation of *Le Malade Imaginaire* by Moliere), first produced at National Theatre, 1981.
Hiawatha: Longfellow's classic poem adapted by Michael Bogdanov (stage-play), Heinemann, 1981.
The Play of the Ancient Mariner: Dramatised by Michael Bogdanov from the poem by Samuel Taylor Coleridge, Heinemann, 1984.
(With Michael Pennington) *The English Shakespeare Company: The Story of 'The Wars of the Roses,' 1986-89,* Hern, 1991.

Also author of plays, stage adaptations, and children's plays.

ADAPTATIONS: Bogdanov's production of *Julius Caesar* was filmed by ZDF-TV, Hamburg, Germany, 1986.

OTHER SOURCES:

BOOKS

Contemporary Authors, Volume 129, Gale, 1990, p. 51.

* * *

BONET, Lisa 1967-

PERSONAL: Born November 16, 1967, in San Francisco, CA; daughter of Arlene Bonet (a teacher); married Lenny Kravitz (a musician), 1987 (separated, 1991); children: Zoe. *Education:* Studied at Celluloid Actor's Studio.

ADDRESSES: Office—151 South El Camino Dr., Beverly Hills, CA 90212.

CAREER: Actress.

AWARDS, HONORS: Youth in Film Award, best young actress in a television series, and Emmy Award nomination, best supporting actress in a comedy series, 1986, both for *The Cosby Show.*

CREDITS:

TELEVISION APPEARANCES; SERIES

Denise Huxtable, *The Cosby Show,* NBC, 1984-87, then as Denise Huxtable Kendall, 1989-92.
Denise Huxtable, *A Different World,* NBC, 1987-88.

Also appeared in *The Two of Us.*

TELEVISION APPEARANCES; EPISODIC

"The Satanic Piano," *Tales from the Dark Side,* syndicated, 1985.
"Home for the Weekend," *The Cosby Show,* NBC, 1988.
"Together Again and Again," *The Cosby Show,* NBC, 1988.
"The Physical," *The Cosby Show,* NBC, 1988.
"Rudy's All-Nighter," *The Cosby Show,* NBC, 1988.
"Move It" (also known as "Baby Games"), *The Cosby Show,* NBC, 1988.
The Arsenio Hall Show, syndicated, 1989.
"Denise: The Saga Continues," *The Cosby Show,* NBC, 1989.

Also appeared in *St. Elsewhere,* NBC.

TELEVISION APPEARANCES; SPECIALS

Carrie, "Don't Touch," *The ABC Afterschool Special,* ABC, 1985.
Andy Williams and the NBC Kids Search for Santa, NBC, 1985.
Battle of the Network Stars XVIII, ABC, 1985.
The 37th Annual Prime Time Emmy Awards, ABC, 1985.
Disney World Celebrity Circus, NBC, 1987.
Our Common Future, Arts and Entertainment, 1989.
Time Warner Presents the Earth Day Special, ABC, 1990.

Also appeared in *Night of 100 Stars II, Fast Copy,* and *Motown Returns to the Apollo,* all 1985; and *Funny, You Don't Look 200,* 1987.

FILM APPEARANCES

Epiphany Proudfoot, *Angel Heart,* Tri-Star, 1987.

OTHER SOURCES:

PERIODICALS

Ebony, December, 1987, p. 150.
Essence, February, 1990, p. 54.
Interview, April, 1987, p. 42.
People, March 16, 1987.
Seventeen, July, 1985, p. 73; April, 1987, p. 79.*

* * *

BOORSTIN, Jon

PERSONAL: Married Leni Isaacs (a public affairs manager); children: Ariel, Eric. *Education:* Harvard University, B.A., 1967; attended Trinity College, Cambridge, and California Institute for the Arts.

ADDRESSES: Agent—David Wardlow, Camden Artists-ITG, 822 South Robertson, Suite 200, Los Angeles, CA 90035.

CAREER: Writer, producer, and documentary filmmaker. U.S. Information Agency, lecturer; National Film and Television Institute of India, teacher of screenwriting and film production.

MEMBER: International P.E.N., Academy of Motion Picture Arts and Sciences, Writers Guild of America, Phi Beta Kappa.

AWARDS, HONORS: Academy Award nomination, best documentary short subject, 1974, for *The Exploratorium;* Grand Prix, Festival International du Film Fantastique, 1986, for *Dream Lover;* Prix du Public, International Imax-Omnivax Film Festival, 1989, for *To the Limit;* other awards for documentary films include Chris Awards, CINE Golden Eagle awards, IFPA Film and Video Communicators Blue Ribbon; Knox fellow in England; Fulbright fellow in India.

CREDITS:

FILM WORK

Associate producer, *All the President's Men,* Warner Brothers, 1976.
Producer (with Alan J. Pakula), *Dream Lover* (also see below), Metro-Goldwyn-Mayer/United Artists, 1986.
To The Limit, Imax Films, 1989.
Eureka!, Imax Films, 1992.

Also worked as producer of *The Exploratorium* (documentary short subject; also see below), 1974, *Kid City,* and *People Who Make Things.*

TELEVISION WORK; SERIES

Co-producer, *Dark Shadows* (also see below), NBC, 1991.

WRITINGS:

SCREENPLAYS

Dream Lover, Metro-Goldwyn-Mayer/United Artists, 1986.

Also author of *The Exploratorium* (documentary short subject), 1974, and *Sleepless,* ABC; author of additional screenplays, including *Love and Again, Brother's Keeper, Please Please Me, Rescue Me,* and *Do No Harm.*

TELEVISION WRITINGS

Dark Shadows (series), NBC, 1991.

Also author of the pilot *Mercy Street,* NBC, and the miniseries *The Great Satan,* HBO.

OTHER

The Hollywood Eye: What Makes Movies Work, HarperCollins, 1991.

Author of the column "Letters to My Mother-in-Law," *Los Angeles Times;* contributor of articles to *New York Times* and *Bombay Sunday Observer.*

* * *

BOURNE, Mel 1923-

PERSONAL: Born in 1923, in Newark, NJ; son of Max and Frieda Bourne; married; children: Timothy, Tristan, Travis. *Education:* Purdue University, B.S., chemical engineering, 1945; Yale School of Drama, 1945-48. Assistant to designer Robert Edmond Jones.

ADDRESSES: Office—165 Duane St., New York, NY 10013.

CAREER: Production designer. Designer of television commercials during 1960s; worked with filmmaker Woody Allen, late 1970s-1984.

AWARDS, HONORS: Academy Award nomination (with Daniel Robert), best art direction, 1978, for *Interiors;* Academy Award nomination, best art direction, 1984, for *The Natural;* Academy Award nomination, best art direction, 1991, for *The Fisher King.*

CREDITS:

FILM WORK; PRODUCTION DESIGNER

Interiors, United Artists (UA), 1978.
Nunzio, Universal, 1978.
Manhattan, UA, 1979.
Windows, UA, 1980.
Stardust Memories, UA, 1980.
Thief, UA, 1981.
A Midsummer Night's Sex Comedy, Orion/Warner Brothers, 1982.
Still of the Night, Metro-Goldwyn-Mayer/UA, 1982.
Zelig, Orion/Warner Brothers, 1983.
Broadway Danny Rose, Orion, 1984.
The Natural, Tri-Star, 1984.
F/X, Orion, 1986.
Manhunter, DEG, 1986.
Fatal Attraction, Paramount, 1987.
Cocktail, Buena Vista, 1988.
The Accused (also known as *Reckless Endangerment*), Paramount, 1988.
Rude Awakening, Orion, 1989.
Reversal of Fortune, Warner Brothers, 1990.
The Fisher King (also see below), Tri-Star, 1991.
Man Trouble, Twentieth Century-Fox, 1991.

Also worked as production designer for American unit of *Luna,* 1979.

FILM WORK; ART DIRECTOR

That Night, Universal, 1957.
(With George Jenkins) *The Miracle Worker,* United Artists (UA), 1962.
Annie Hall, UA, 1977.
The Greek Tycoon, Universal, 1978.

FILM APPEARANCES

Carmichael, *The Fisher King,* Tri-Star, 1991.

TELEVISION WORK; SERIES

Production designer for the series *Kojak,* 1972, and for television series of the 1950s, including *The Aldrich Family, Howdy Doody, Believe It or Not, Mr. Own, The Robert Quinlan Show, The Lux Video Theatre, We the People, Hallmark Hall of Fame, The Goldbergs, Armstrong Circle Theatre, Goodyear-Philco Playhouse,* and *Star Star Stage.*

OTHER TELEVISION WORK

Art director, *The Silence* (movie), NBC, 1975.
Art director, *The Quinns* (movie), ABC, 1977.
Art director, *The Mike Wallace Profiles* (special), CBS, 1981.
Production designer, *Miami Vice* (pilot), NBC, 1985.
Production designer, *Equal Justice* (pilot), ABC, 1990.

STAGE WORK; PRODUCTION DESIGNER

Designer of Broadway productions in the 1950s, including *The Male Animal, Seagulls over Sorrento, The Millionairess,* and *End as a Man,* and the Los Angeles Light Opera production of *Carousel.*

OTHER SOURCES:

PERIODICALS

Theatre Crafts, January, 1984; April, 1991.

* * *

BOVASSO, Julie 1930-1991

OBITUARY NOTICE—See index for *CTFT* sketch: Full name, Julia Anne Bovasso; born August 1, 1930, in

Brooklyn, NY; died of cancer, September 14, 1991, in New York, NY. Performer, director, producer, educator, and playwright. Bovasso began her career as a stage actress in the 1940s, appearing in New York City productions of *The Importance of Being Earnest* and *Faustina.* In 1953 Bovasso founded the Tempo Playhouse, which earned her the Obie Award for best experimental theatre in 1956. In this forum she directed, produced, and performed in *The Typewriter* and *The Lesson,* and received an Obie Award for her performance in twentieth-century French author Jean Genet's *The Maids.* Bovasso continued to perform throughout the 1960s, but shifted her focus to education, serving as drama instructor at the New School for Social Research, Brooklyn College of the City University of New York, and Sarah Lawrence College. During the late 1960s and early 1970s Bovasso was involved with La Mama Experimental Theatre Club, directing and performing in her own experimental plays, such as *Schubert's Last Serenade* and *Angelo's Wedding,* and winning a Triple Obie Award as playwright, director, and actress for *Gloria and Esperanza* in 1969. Bovasso explored other media in the 1970s and 1980s, appearing on episodes of the television series *Miami Vice* and *Cagney and Lacey* as well as in the feature films *Saturday Night Fever, The Verdict,* and *Moonstruck.*

OBITUARIES AND OTHER SOURCES:

BOOKS

The Writers Directory, 1990-1992, ninth edition, St. James Press, 1990, p. 108.

PERIODICALS

Variety, September 23, 1991, p. 90.

* * *

BOX, John 1920-

PERSONAL: Born January 27, 1920, in London, England. *Education:* Studied at Bartlett School of Architecture, London.

CAREER: Art director and production designer. Worked as draftsman for London Films, 1947, then as assistant art director to Alex Vetchinsky and Carmen Dillon. *Military service:* British Army, 1939-45.

AWARDS, HONORS: Academy Award, art direction—set decoration, 1962, for *Lawrence of Arabia;* Academy Award, art direction—set decoration, 1965, for *Doctor Zhivago;* British Academy Award, 1967, for *A Man for All Seasons;* Academy Award, art direction—set decoration, 1968, for *Oliver!;* Academy Award, art direction—set decoration, 1971, for *Nicholas and Alexandra;* Academy Award nomination, art direction—set decoration, 1972, for *Travels with My Aunt;* British Academy Award, 1974, for *The Great Gatsby;* British Academy Award, 1975, for *Rollerball;* Academy Award nomination, art direction, 1984, for *A Passage to India;* Special Award, film crafts, British Academy of Film and Television Arts, 1991.

CREDITS:

FILM WORK; ART DIRECTOR

The Gamma People, Columbia, 1957.
Zarak, Columbia, 1957.
Fire Down Below, Columbia, 1958.
High Flight, Columbia, 1958.
Tank Force (also known as *No Time to Die*), Columbia, 1958.
The Inn of the Sixth Happiness, Twentieth Century-Fox, 1958.
Our Man in Havana, Columbia, 1959.
The World of Suzie Wong, Paramount, 1960.

Also worked as art director for *The Million Pound Note* (also known as *Man with a Million*), 1953; *The Black Knight,* 1954; *A Prize of Gold,* 1956; *Cockleshell Heroes,* 1956; *How to Murder a Rich Uncle,* 1958; and *Two-Way Street,* 1960.

FILM WORK; PRODUCTION DESIGNER

Lawrence of Arabia, Columbia, 1962.
Of Human Bondage, Metro-Goldwyn-Mayer (MGM), 1964.
Doctor Zhivago, MGM, 1965.
The Wild Affair, Bryanston/Goldstone, 1966.
A Man for All Seasons, Columbia, 1966.
Oliver!, Columbia, 1968.
Nicholas and Alexandra, Columbia, 1971.
Travels with My Aunt, MGM, 1972.
The Great Gatsby, Paramount, 1974.
Rollerball, United Artists, 1975.
Sorcerer, Universal/Paramount, 1977.
The Keep, Paramount, 1983.
A Passage to India, Columbia, 1984.

FILM WORK; PRODUCER

The Looking Glass War, Columbia, 1970.

TELEVISION WORK; PRODUCTION DESIGNER

Murder by the Book (special), Arts and Entertainment, 1990.*

* * *

BOYLE, Lara Flynn 1971(?)-

PERSONAL: Born c. 1971, in Davenport, IA. *Education:* Studied acting at Chicago Academy for the Arts.

ADDRESSES: Agent—Judy Schoen and Associates, 606 North Larchmont Blvd., Suite 309, Los Angeles, CA 90004.

CAREER: Actress.

AWARDS, HONORS: ACE Award nomination, National Cable Television Association, best actress in a dramatic series, 1991, for "Splinters of Privacy," *The Hidden Room.*

CREDITS:

TELEVISION APPEARANCES; SERIES

Donna Hayward, *Twin Peaks* (also known as *Northwest Passage*), ABC, 1990.

TELEVISION APPEARANCES; MOVIES

Laura Taggart, *Terror on Highway 91,* CBS, 1989.
Jennifer Levin, *The Preppie Murder,* ABC, 1989.

TELEVISION APPEARANCES; EPISODIC

Nicole, "Splinters of Privacy," *The Hidden Room,* Lifetime, 1991.

OTHER TELEVISION APPEARANCES

Jackie Bradford, *Amerika* (mini-series; also known as *Topeka, Kansas . . . U.S.S.R.*), ABC, 1987.
Jennifer Cullen, *Gang of Four* (pilot), ABC, 1989.

FILM APPEARANCES

Donna Gardner, *Poltergeist III,* Metro-Goldwyn-Mayer/United Artists, 1988.
Jessica Kailo, *How I Got into College,* Twentieth Century-Fox, 1989.
Sarah, *The Rookie,* Warner Brothers, 1990.
Mara Motes, *Mobsters* (also known as *Gangsters*), Universal, 1991.
Rosarita, *The Dark Backward,* Greycat Films, 1991.
Heather, *Where the Day Takes You,* New Line Cinema, 1992.
Stacy, *Wayne's World,* Paramount, 1992.

Also appeared as Ginny Danburry, *Dead Poets Society,* 1989; and Camille, *May Wine,* 1990.

OTHER SOURCES:

PERIODICALS

Rolling Stone, October 4, 1990, p. 68.*

* * *

BRACCO, Lorraine 1955(?)-

PERSONAL: Born c. 1955; married Harvey Keitel (an actor), (separated); children: Stella. *Education:* Studied acting at the Actors Studio, and with Stella Adler, Ernie Martin, and John Strasberg.

ADDRESSES: Agent—Creative Artists Agency, Inc., 9830 Wilshire Blvd., Beverly Hills, CA 90212.

CAREER: Actress. Began career as a model in Europe.

AWARDS, HONORS: Academy Award nomination, best performance by an actress in a supporting role, 1990, for *Goodfellas.*

CREDITS:

FILM APPEARANCES

Carla, *The Pick-Up Artist,* Twentieth Century-Fox, 1987.
Ellie Keegan, *Someone to Watch over Me,* Columbia, 1987.
Riley, *The Dream Team,* Universal, 1989.
Karen Hill, *Goodfellas,* Warner Brothers, 1990.
Bobbie Henderson, *Talent for the Game,* Paramount, 1991.
Sheila Faxton, *Switch,* Warner Brothers, 1991.
Dr. Rae Crane, *Medicine Man,* Buena Vista, 1992.
Mary, *Radio Flyer,* Columbia, 1992.

Also appeared as Bubble, *Duos sur canape,* 1979; Miss Lombardo, *Sing,* 1989; and Sheila, *In una notte di chiaro di luna,* 1989. Appeared in *Goose and Tom Tom, Un complicato intrigo di Donne,* and *Vicole e Delitti,* 1985.

OTHER SOURCES:

PERIODICALS

Hollywood Reporter, March 23, 1992, p. S-10.
Interview, February, 1989, p. 84; February, 1990, p. 80.
Premiere, April, 1989, p. 60.*

* * *

BRADBURY, Malcolm 1932-

PERSONAL: Full name, Malcolm Stanley Bradbury; born September 7, 1932, in Sheffield, England; son of Arthur and Doris Ethel (Marshall) Bradbury; married Elizabeth Salt, October, 1959; children: Matthew, Dominic. *Education:* University of Leicester, B.A. (with first-class honors), 1953; Queen Mary College, London, M.A., 1955; further graduate study at Indiana University—Bloomington, 1955-56; Victoria University of Manchester, Ph.D., 1964.

ADDRESSES: Office—School of English and American Studies, University of East Anglia, Norwich, Norfolk NR4 7TJ, England. *Agent*—John Cushman Associates, Inc., 25 West 43rd St., New York, NY 10036.

CAREER: Writer and critic. Indiana University—Bloomington, teaching fellow, 1955-56; Yale University,

New Haven, CT, junior fellow, 1958-59; University of Hull, Hull, England, staff tutor in literature, 1959-61; University of Birmingham, Birmingham, England, lecturer, 1961-65; University of East Anglia, Norwich, England, lecturer, 1965-67, senior lecturer, 1967-69, reader in English, 1969-70, professor of American studies, 1970—. Harvard University, fellow, 1965-66; University of California, Davis, visiting professor, 1966; Oxford University, visiting fellow of All Souls College, 1969; University of Zurich, visiting professor, 1972; Washington University, St. Louis, MO, Fanny Hurst Professor of Writing, 1982; University of Queensland, Davis Professor, 1983; Griffith University, visiting professor 1983. British Council, chair of English studies seminar, 1976-84; Booker McConnell Prize for Fiction, chair of judges, 1981; Radio Broadland (independent radio station), director.

MEMBER: International P.E.N., Society of Authors, British Association of American Studies, Royal Society of Literature (fellow).

AWARDS, HONORS: Junior fellow in the United States, British Association of American Studies, 1958-59; fellow, American Council of Learned Societies, 1965-66; Heinemann Prize, Royal Society of Literature, 1975, for *The History Man;* named among twenty best British writers by Book Marketing Council, 1982; D.Litt., University of Leicester, 1986; shortlisted for Booker McConnell Prize for Fiction, 1987, for *Rates of Exchange;* D.Litt., University of Birmingham, 1989; honorary fellow of Queen Mary College, London; Commander, Order of the British Empire.

WRITINGS:

PLAYS

(With David Lodge and James Duckett) *Between These Four Walls* (stage revue), first produced in Birmingham, England, 1963.

(With Lodge, Duckett, and David Turner) *Slap in the Middle* (stage revue), first produced in Birmingham, England, 1965.

Congress (radio play), BBC, 1980.

Co-author of the radio play *This Sporting Life,* 1974-75.

TELEVISION PLAYS

(With Chris Bigsby) *The After Dinner Game* (also see below), BBC, 1975.

(With Bigsby) *Stones,* BBC, 1976.

Love on a Gunboat, BBC, 1977.

The Enigma (based on a story by John Fowles), BBC, 1980.

Standing In for Henry, BBC, 1980.

OTHER TELEVISION WRITINGS

Rates of Exchange (series; based on his novel of the same name; also see below), BBC, 1985.

Blott on the Landscape (series; adapted from a novel by Tom Sharpe), BBC, 1985.

Porterhouse Blue (adapted from work by Sharpe), Channel 4, 1987.

The Green Man (movie; based on novel by Kingsley Amis), A&E, 1991.

Also author of *Imaginary Friends* (adapted from work by Alison Lurie), 1987, and writer for the serials *Anything More Would Be Greedy,* 1989, and *The Gravy Train,* 1990.

BOOKS

Eating People Is Wrong (novel), Secker & Warburg, 1959, Knopf, 1960.

Phogey! or, How to Have Class in a Classless Society (also see below), Parrish, 1960.

All Dressed Up and Nowhere to Go: The Poor Man's Guide to the Affluent Society (also see below), Parrish, 1962.

Evelyn Waugh, Oliver & Boyd, 1964.

Stepping Westward (novel), Secker & Warburg, 1965, Houghton, 1966.

(With Allan Rodway) *Two Poets* (verse), Byron Press, 1966.

What Is a Novel?, Edward Arnold, 1969.

The Social Context of Modern English Literature, Schocken, 1971.

Possibilities: Essays on the State of the Novel, Oxford University Press, 1973.

The History Man (novel), Secker & Warburg, 1975, Houghton, 1976.

Who Do You Think You Are? Stories and Parodies, Secker & Warburg, 1976.

The Outland Dart: American Writers and European Modernism, Oxford University Press, 1978.

The After Dinner Game: Three Plays for Television, Arrow Books, 1982.

Saul Bellow, Methuen, 1982.

All Dressed Up and Nowhere to Go (contains revised versions of *Phogey!* and *All Dressed Up and Nowhere to Go*), Pavilion, 1982.

Rates of Exchange (novel), Knopf, 1983.

The Modern American Novel, Oxford University Press, 1983.

Why Come to Slaka?, Secker & Warburg, 1986.

Cuts: A Very Short Novel (novella), Harper, 1987.

My Strange Quest for Mensonge, Penguin, 1988.

No, Not Bloomsbury (collected essays), Columbia University Press, 1988.

Unsent Letters: Irreverent Notes from a Literary Life, Penguin, 1988.

The Modern World: Ten Great Writers, Penguin, 1989.

(With Richard Ruland) *From Puritanism to Postmodernism: A History of American Literature,* Routledge & Kegan Paul, 1991.

Also author of *The Novel Today,* 1990.

EDITOR

Forster: A Collection of Critical Essays, Prentice-Hall, 1966.
Mark Twain, *"Pudd'nhead Wilson" and "Those Extraordinary Twins",* Penguin, 1969.
E. M. Forster, *"A Passage to India": A Casebook,* Macmillan, 1970.
(With David Palmer) *Contemporary Criticism,* Edward Arnold, 1970, St. Martin's, 1971.
(With Eric Mottram and Jean France) *The Penguin Companion to American Literature,* McGraw, 1971 (published in England as *The Penguin Companion to Literature,* Volume III: *U.S.A.,* Allen Lane, 1971), published as *The Avenal Companion to English and American Literature,* Avenal Books, 1981.
(With Palmer) *Metaphysical Poetry,* Indiana University Press, 1971.
(With Palmer) *The American Novel and the 1920s,* Edward Arnold, 1971.
(With Palmer) *Shakespearian Comedy,* Edward Arnold, 1972.
(With James McFarlane) *Modernism, 1890-1930,* Penguin, 1976.
The Novel Today: Contemporary Writers on Modern Fiction, Rowman & Littlefield, 1977.
(With Palmer) *Decadence and the 1890s,* Edward Arnold, 1979.
(With Palmer) *The Contemporary English Novel,* Edward Arnold, 1979.
(With Palmer) *Contemporary Theatre,* Holmes & Maier, 1979.
(With Howard Temperley) *An Introduction to American Studies,* Longman, 1980.
Stephen Crane, *The Red Badge of Courage* (critical edition), Dent, 1983.
(With Palmer) *Shakespearean Tragedy,* Holmes & Meier, 1984.
The Penguin Book of Modern British Short Stories, Penguin, 1988.

OTHER

Work represented in anthologies, including *Prose Models,* edited by G. Levin, Harcourt, 1964; *Modern American Poetry,* edited by J. R. Brown and B. Harris, Edward Arnold, 1965; and *The Calendar of Modern Letters: March, 1925-July, 1927,* Barnes & Noble, 1966. Series editor, "Arnold Stratford-upon-Avon Studies," Edward Arnold, 1970-81, and "Contemporary Writers," Methuen. Contributor of articles, stories, and reviews to periodicals.

ADAPTATIONS: The History Man has been adapted as a four-part television series by Christopher Hampton, released by BBC, 1979.

OTHER SOURCES:

BOOKS

Contemporary Authors New Revision Series, Volume 33, Gale, 1991.
Contemporary Literary Criticism, Volume 32, Gale, 1985.
Dictionary of Literary Biography, Volume 14: *British Novelists since 1960,* 2 parts, Gale, 1983.*

* * *

BRADBURY, Ray 1920-
(Douglas Spaulding)

PERSONAL: Full name, Ray Douglas Bradbury; born August 22, 1920, in Waukegan, IL; son of Leonard Spaulding and Esther (Moberg) Bradbury; married Marguerite Susan McClure, September 27, 1947; children: Susan, Ramona, Bettina, Alexandra. *Education:* Attended public schools in Waukegan, IL, and Los Angeles, CA. *Politics:* Independent. *Religion:* Unitarian Universalist. *Avocational interests:* Swimming, walking.

ADDRESSES: Contact—USA Network, 1230 Avenue of the Americas, New York, NY 10020.

CAREER: Writer and producer. Once worked as a newsboy in Los Angeles, CA, 1940-43. The Pandemonium Theatre Company, founder, producer, and director, 1963.

MEMBER: Writers Guild of America, Science Fiction Fantasy Writers Association, Screen Writers Guild, Pacific Art Foundation (vice president).

AWARDS, HONORS: O'Henry Short Story Prize, 1947 and 1948; Benjamin Franklin Award for best short story of 1953-54 in an American magazine, for "Sun and Shadow" in *Reporter;* award for contribution to American literature, National Institute of Arts and Letters, 1954; Commonwealth Club of California Gold Medal, 1954, for *Fahrenheit 451;* Boys' Clubs of America Junior Book Award, 1956, for *Switch on the Night;* Golden Eagle Award, 1957, for screenwriting; Academy Award nomination, best short film, 1963, for *Icarus Montgolfier Wright;* Mrs. Ann Radcliffe Awards, Count Dracula Society, 1965 and 1971; Valentine Davies Award, Writers Guild of America, West, 1974; World Fantasy Award, 1977, for life achievement; D.Litt, Whittier College, 1979; Balrog Award, 1979, for Best Poet; Aviation and Space Writers Award, 1979, for television documentary; award from PEN, 1985, for body of work; Gandalf Award (Grand Master), Science Fiction Achievement, 1989; the play version of *The Martian Chronicles* won five Los Angeles Drama Critics Circle Awards; ACE Award nomination, best dramatic series, 1991, for *The Ray Bradbury Theater.*

CREDITS:

TELEVISION WORK; SERIES

Creator, editor, executive producer (with Peter Sussman and Larry Wilcox), and host, *The Ray Bradbury Theater* (includes adaptations of Bradbury's stories, such as "The Playground," "The Crowd," "Banshee," "The Screaming Woman," "The Town Where No One Got Off," "The Lake," "The Pedestrian," "The Chicago Abyss," and "The Veldt"; also see below), HBO, 1985-87, then USA, 1987—.

TELEVISION APPEARANCES

Appeared on the special *Neptune All Night,* 1989; and on the *Today* show. Has been interviewed on numerous Larry King shows, as well as on many talk shows.

FILM APPEARANCES

Literary party guest, *Rich and Famous,* Metro-Goldwyn-Mayer/United Artists, 1981.

Also appeared in *The Fantasy Film World of George Pal,* 1986.

STAGE WORK

Producer, with S. L. Stebel and Charles Rome Smith, of the play *Next in Line* (also see below), Pandemonium Theatre Company, New Ivar Theatre, 1992.

WRITINGS:

STAGE PLAYS

The Meadow, first produced at Huntington Hartford Theatre, Hollywood, CA, 1960.

Way in the Middle of the Air, first produced at Desilu Gower Studios, Hollywood, 1962.

The Anthem Sprinters, and Other Antics (four one-acts), first produced at Beverly Hills Playhouse, Beverly Hills, CA, 1967, published by Dial Press, 1963.

The World of Ray Bradbury (three one-acts: *The Pedestrian* [also see below], *The Veldt* [also see below], and *To the Chicago Abyss* [also see below]), first produced at Coronet Theatre, Los Angeles, 1964, then Orpheum Theatre, New York City, 1965.

The Wonderful Ice Cream Suit (also see below), first produced at Coronet Theater, Los Angeles, 1965, later Bouwerie Lane Theatre, New York City, 1981, published by Dramatic Publishing, 1986.

The Day It Rained Forever (one-act), published by Samuel French, 1966.

The Pedestrian (one-act), published by Samuel French, 1966.

Dandelion Wine (based on his novel of the same title; music composed by Billy Goldenberg; also see below), first produced at Forum Theatre, New York City, 1967, later Goodman Theatre, Chicago, IL, 1976, then Arena Stage, Washington, DC, 1982-83, published by Dramatic Publishing, 1988.

Christus Apollo (music by Jerry Goldsmith), first produced at Royce Hall, University of California, Los Angeles, 1969.

Leviathan 99 (also see below), first produced at Stage 9 Theatre, 1972.

The Wonderful Ice Cream Suit and Other Plays (contains *The Wonderful Ice Cream Suit, The Veldt,* and *To the Chicago Abyss*), published by Bantam, 1972, published in England as *The Wonderful Ice Cream Suit and Other Plays for Today, Tomorrow, and Beyond Tomorrow,* Hart-Davis, 1973.

Madrigals for the Space Age (for chorus and narrator; music composed by Lalo Schifrin) first produced at Dorothy Chandler Pavilion, Los Angeles, 1973, published by Music Publishers, 1972.

Pillar of Fire (also see below), first produced at Little Theatre, California State College, Fullerton, CA, 1973.

Pillar of Fire and Other Plays for Today, Tomorrow, and Beyond Tomorrow (contains *Pillar of Fire, Kaleidoscope* [also see below], and *The Foghorn* [based on his story of same title; also see below]), published by Bantam, 1975.

That Ghost, That Bride of Time: Excerpts from a Play-in-Progress, published by Roy A. Squires Press, 1976.

The Martian Chronicles (based on his novel of same title; also see below), first produced at the Colony Theater, Los Angeles, 1977, published by Dramatic Publishing, 1986.

Fahrenheit 451 (musical; based on his story of same title; also see below), first produced at the Colony Theater, 1979, published by Dramatic Publishing, 1986.

The Veldt (based on his story of the same title), first produced in London, 1980, published by Dramatic Publishing, 1989.

A Device Out of Time, published by Dramatic Publishing, 1986.

The Flying Machine, published by Dramatic Publishing, 1986.

Kaleidoscope, published by Dramatic Publishing, 1986.

Falling Upward, first produced at the Melrose Theatre, Los Angeles, 1988, published by Dramatic Publishing, 1989.

To the Chicago Abyss, published by Dramatic Publishing, 1989.

Also author of *Any Friend of Nicholas Nickleby Is a Friend of Mine* (also see below), 1968; plays also produced at Royal Shakespeare Festival Theatre, London.

SCREENPLAYS

The Beast from 20,000 Fathoms (based on his story *The Foghorn*), Warner Bros., 1953.

(With John Huston) *Moby Dick,* Warner Bros., 1956.

(With George C. Johnson) *Icarus Montgolfier Wright,* Format Films, 1962.

(Author of narration and creative consultant) *An American Journey,* U.S. Government for United States Pavilion at New York World's Fair, 1964.

(As Douglas Spaulding; with Ed Weinberger) *Picasso Summer,* Warner Bros./Seven Arts, 1972.

Something Wicked This Way Comes (based on his novel of same title; also see below), Buena Vista, 1983.

TELEVISION PLAYS

"The Burning Man," *The Twilight Zone,* CBS, 1985.

The Ray Bradbury Theater (series), HBO, 1985-87, then USA, 1987—.

"The Elevator," *The Twilight Zone,* CBS, 1986.

Also author of specials *Any Friend of Nicholas Nickleby Is a Friend of Mine,* 1982, "The Invisible Boy," *Robbers, Rooftops and Witches,* 1982, and *Walking on Air,* 1987. Author during the 1950s of the episode "The Jail," *Alcoa Premiere.* Also author of scripts for episodes of *Alfred Hitchcock Presents, Jane Wyman's Fireside Theatre, Suspense, Steve Canyon, Trouble Shooters, Twilight Zone, Alcoa Premiere,* and *The Curiosity Shop.*

RADIO PLAYS

Leviathan 99, BBC, 1966.

"Bradbury 13," *NPR Playhouse,* National Public Radio, 1984.

Forever and the Earth (limited edition), published by Croissant & Co., 1984.

Also contributed to *CBS Radio Playhouse,* c. 1940s.

OTHER

Dark Carnival (short story collection), Arkham, 1947, revised edition, Hamish Hamilton, 1948.

The Martian Chronicles, Doubleday, 1950, revised edition published as *The Silver Locusts,* Hart-Davis, 1951.

The Illustrated Man, (short story collection), Doubleday, 1951, revised edition, Hart-Davis, 1952.

(Editor and contributor) *Timeless Stories for Today and Tomorrow,* Bantam, 1952.

Fahrenheit 451 (collection; contains "Fahrenheit 451," "The Playground," and "And the Rock Cried Out"), Ballantine, 1953.

The Golden Apples of the Sun (short story collection; also see below), Doubleday, 1953, revised edition, Hart-Davis, 1953.

Fahrenheit 451 (previously published as part of collection), Hart-Davis, 1954.

The October Country (short story collection), Ballantine, 1955.

Switch on the Night (juvenile), Pantheon, 1955.

(Editor) *The Circus of Dr. Lao and Other Improbable Stories,* Bantam, 1956.

Dandelion Wine (novel), Doubleday, 1957.

A Medicine for Melancholy (short story collection; also see below), Doubleday, 1959, revised edition published in England as *The Day It Rained Forever,* Hart-Davis, 1959.

The Small Assassin (short story collection), Ace Books, 1962.

Something Wicked This Way Comes (novel), Simon & Schuster, 1962.

R Is for Rocket (juvenile; short story collection), Doubleday, 1962.

The Machineries of Joy (short story collection), Simon & Schuster, 1964.

The Vintage Bradbury (short story collection), Vintage Books, 1965.

S Is for Space (juvenile; short story collection), Doubleday, 1966.

Twice Twenty-Two (contains *The Golden Apples of the Sun* and *A Medicine for Melancholy*), Doubleday, 1966.

(With Lewy Olfson) *Teacher's Guide: Science Fiction* (essay), Bantam, 1968.

(With Robert Bloch) *Bloch and Bradbury: Ten Masterpieces of Science Fiction,* Tower, 1969, published in England as *Fever Dreams and Other Fantasies,* Sphere, 1970, published as *Whispers from Beyond,* Peacock Press, 1972.

I Sing the Body Electric! (short story collection), Knopf, 1969.

Old Ahab's Friend, and Friend to Noah, Speaks His Piece: A Celebration (poem), Roy A. Squires Press, 1971.

The Halloween Tree (juvenile; novel), Knopf, 1972.

When Elephants Last in the Dooryard Bloomed: Celebrations for Almost Any Day in the Year (poems; also see below), Knopf, 1973.

(With Bruce Murray, Arthur C. Clarke, Walter Sullivan, and Carl Sagan) *Mars and the Mind of Man* (verse and essays), Harper, 1973.

Zen and the Art of Writing (essays), Capra Press, 1973.

That Son of Richard III: A Birth Announcement (poem), Roy A. Squires Press, 1974.

Ray Bradbury (short story collection), Harrap, 1975.

Long after Midnight (short story collection), Knopf, 1976.

The Best of Bradbury, Bantam, 1976.

Where Robot Mice and Robot Men Run Round in Robot Towns (poems; also see below), Knopf, 1977.

Twin Hieroglyphs That Swim the River Dust (poems), Lord John, 1978.

The Bike Repairman (poem), Lord John, 1978.

The Mummies of Guanajuato (short story), Abrams, 1978.

The Author Considers His Resources (poem), Lord John, 1979.

(And author of introduction) *To Sing Strange Songs* (short story collection), Wheaton, 1979.

The Aqueduct (short story), Roy A. Squires Press, 1979.

The Attic Where the Meadow Greens (poems), Lord John, 1979.

Beyond 1984: Remembrance of Things Future (articles and poems), Targ, 1979.

The Stories of Ray Bradbury, Knopf, 1980.

(And author of introduction) *The Last Circus* (two short stories), Lord John, 1980.

About Norman Corwin (essay), California State University, Northridge, 1980.

The Haunted Computer and the Android Pope (poems; also see below), Knopf, 1981.

The Ghosts of Forever (five poems, a story, and an essay), Rizzoli, c. 1981.

The Complete Poems of Ray Bradbury (contains *Where Robot Mice and Robot Men Run Round in Robot Towns, The Haunted Computer and the Android Pope,* and *When Elephants Last in the Dooryard Bloomed*), Ballantine, 1982.

Dinosaur Tales (verse and short story collection), Bantam, 1983.

The Love Affair (a short story and two poems), Lord John, 1983.

(And author of introduction) *A Memory for Murder* (short story collection), Dell, 1984.

(Author of text) *Los Angeles,* Skyline Press, 1984.

(Author of text) *Orange County,* Skyline Press, 1985.

(Author of text) *The Art of "Playboy,"* Alfred Van der Mack, 1985.

Death Is a Lonely Business (novel), Knopf, 1985.

Death Has Lost Its Charm for Me (verse), Lord John, 1987.

The April Witch (juvenile; short story collection), Creative Education, Inc., 1987.

The Other Foot (juvenile; short story collection), Creative Education, Inc., 1987.

The Foghorn (juvenile; short story collection), Creative Education, Inc., 1987.

The Veldt (juvenile; short story collection), Creative Education, Inc., 1987.

Fever Dream (juvenile; short story collection), St. Martin's, 1987.

The Toynbee Convector (short story collection), Knopf, 1988.

A Graveyard for Lunatics (novel), Knopf, 1990.

The Smile (juvenile; short story collection), Creative Education, Inc., 1991.

Author of forwards and prologues for other publications and authors. Bradbury's work is represented in seven hundred anthologies (many of which are school texts), including *Best American Short Stories,* 1946, 1948, 1952, and 1958, and *The Ghoul Keepers,* Pyramid Books, 1961. Contributor of short stories and articles, sometimes under pseudonyms, to *Reporter, Playboy, Saturday Review, Weird Tales, Magazine of Fantasy and Science Fiction, Omni, Life,* and other publications.

ADAPTATIONS: Fahrenheit 451 was adapted into a screenplay, released by Universal, 1966, and it was adapted as an opera, by Georgia Holof and David Mettere, first produced at the Indiana Civic Theater, Fort Wayne, IN, 1988; *The Illustrated Man* was adapted into a screenplay, released by Warner Bros., 1969; the story "The Screaming Woman" was filmed for television in 1972; the story "Murderer" was filmed for television by WGBH-TV, Boston, MA, 1976; *The Martian Chronicles* was filmed as a television mini-series, c. 1980; "The Electric Grandmother" has been adapted into a teleplay, by Jeffrey Kindley, *Peacock Theatre,* NBC, 1983; the story "Next in Line" was adapted as a play by S. L. Stebel and Charles Rome Smith, Pandemonium Theatre Company, New Ivar Theatre, 1992; other Bradbury works have been adapted into other mediums, including sound recordings. *The Autumn People,* Ballantine, 1965, and *Tomorrow Midnight,* Ballantine, 1966, are comic adaptations of some of Bradbury's stories.

OTHER SOURCES:

BOOKS

Contemporary Literary Criticism, Gale, Volume 1, 1973, Volume 3, 1975, Volume 10, 1979, Volume 15, 1980, Volume 42, 1987.

Dictionary of Literary Biography, Gale, Volume 2: *American Novelists since World War II,* 1978, Volume 8, *Twentieth Century American Science Fiction Writers,* 1981.

Greenberg, Martin H., and Joseph D. Olander, editors, *Ray Bradbury,* Taplinger, 1980.

Johnson, Wayne L., *Ray Bradbury,* Ungar, 1980.

Nolan, William F., *The Ray Bradbury Companion,* Gale, 1974.

PERIODICALS

Starlog, April, 1990, p. 29.

BRANDO, Marlon 1924-

PERSONAL: Born April 3, 1924, in Omaha, NE; son of Marlon (a chemical feed and pesticide manufacturer) and Dorothy Pennebaker (an actress; maiden name, Myers) Brando; married Anna Kashfi, October, 1957 (divorced, 1959); married Motiva Castenada, 1960 (divorced); married Tarita; children: (first marriage) Christian Devi; (second marriage) Miko, Rebecca; (third marriage) Simon (Tehotu), Cheyenne. *Education:* Attended Shattuck Military Academy, 1939-41; attended New School for Social Research, Dramatic Workshop, 1943; studied acting with Elia Kazan and Stella Adler.

ADDRESSES: Agent—c/o Screen Actors Guild, 7950 West Sunset Blvd., Hollywood, CA 90046.

CAREER: Actor.

AWARDS, HONORS: Theatre World Promising Personalities Award, 1945; Academy Award nomination, best actor, 1951, for *A Streetcar Named Desire;* British Academy Award, best foreign actor, Cannes International Film Festival, best actor, and Academy Award nomination, best actor, all 1952, all for *Viva Zapata!;* British Academy Award, best foreign actor, and Academy Award nomination, best actor, both 1953, both for *Julius Caesar;* Academy Award, best actor, 1954, British Academy Award, best foreign actor, 1954, and Golden Globe Award, best actor, 1955, all for *On The Waterfront;* Golden Globe Award, World Film Favorite, 1956, 1973, and 1974; Academy Award nomination, best actor, 1957, for *Sayonara;* Academy Award, best actor, 1972, and Golden Globe Award, best actor, 1973, both for *The Godfather;* Academy Award nomination, best actor, 1973, for *Last Tango in Paris;* Emmy Award, outstanding supporting actor in a mini-series, 1979, for *Roots: The Next Generations;* Tokyo International Film Festival, best actor, and Academy Award nomination, best supporting actor, both 1989, both for *A Dry White Season.*

CREDITS:

FILM APPEARANCES

(Debut) Ken, *The Men,* United Artists (UA), 1950.
Stanley Kowalski, *A Streetcar Named Desire,* Warner Brothers/Twentieth Century-Fox, 1951.
Emiliano Zapata, *Viva Zapata!,* Twentieth Century-Fox, 1952.
Marc Antony, *Julius Caesar,* Metro-Goldwyn-Mayer (MGM), 1953.
Johnny, *The Wild One,* Columbia, 1953.
Napoleon Bonaparte, *Desiree,* Twentieth Century-Fox, 1954.
Terry Malloy, *On The Waterfront,* Columbia, 1954.
Sky Masterson, *Guys and Dolls,* MGM, 1955.
Sakini, *The Teahouse of the August Moon,* MGM, 1956.
Maj. Lloyd Gruver, *Sayonara,* Warner Brothers, 1957.
Christian Diestl, *The Young Lions,* Twentieth Century-Fox, 1958.
Val Xavier, *The Fugitive Kind,* UA, 1960.
Rio, *One-Eyed Jacks* (also see below), Paramount, 1961.
Fletcher Christian, *Mutiny on the Bounty,* MGM, 1962.
Harrison Carter MacWhite, *The Ugly American,* Universal, 1963.
Freddy, *Bedtime Story,* Universal, 1964.
Robert Crain, *Morituri,* Twentieth Century-Fox, 1965.
Matt Fletcher, *The Appaloosa,* Universal, 1966.
Sheriff Calder, *The Chase,* Columbia, 1966.
Ogden Mears, *A Countess From Hong Kong,* Universal, 1967.
Maj. Weldon Pendelton, *Reflections in a Golden Eye,* Warner Brothers, 1967.
Grindl, *Candy,* Cinerama, 1968.
Bud the Chauffeur, *The Night of the Following Day,* UA, 1969.
Sir William Walker, *Burn!,* UA, 1970.
Peter Quint, *The Night Comers,* Avco Embassy, 1971.
Don Vito Corleone, *The Godfather,* Paramount, 1972.
Paul, *Last Tango in Paris,* UA, 1973.
Lee Clayton, *The Missouri Breaks,* UA, 1976.
Jor-El, *Superman,* Warner Brothers, 1978.
Colonel Walter E. Kurtz, *Apocalypse Now,* UA, 1979.
Adam Steiffel, *The Formula,* MGM, 1980.
Ian McKenzie, *A Dry White Season,* MGM, 1989.
Carmine Sabatini, *The Freshman,* Tri-Star, 1990.

Also provided narration for the film *Raoni: The Fight for the Amazon,* 1979.

FILM WORK

Director, *One-Eyed Jacks,* Paramount, 1961.

TELEVISION APPEARANCES; MINI-SERIES

George Lincoln Rockwell, *Roots: The Next Generations* (also see below), episode VII, CBS, 1979.

TELEVISION APPEARANCES; EPISODIC

"I'm No Hero", *Actor's Studio,* CBS, 1949.
"Miracle on 44th Street: A Portrait of the Actors Studio," *American Masters,* PBS, 1991.

TELEVISION APPEARANCES; SPECIALS

Person to Person, CBS, 1955.

TELEVISION WORK; MINI-SERIES

Director (episode VII), *Roots: The Next Generations,* CBS, 1979.

STAGE APPEARANCES

Bobino, Adelphi Theatre, New York City, 1944.

Nels, *I Remember Mama,* Music Box Theatre, New York City, 1944.
Stanley Kowalski, *A Streetcar Named Desire,* Ethel Barrymore Theatre, New York City, 1947.

Also appeared in *Truckline Cafe,* New York City, 1946; *Candida,* New York City, 1946; and *A Flag is Born,* New York City, 1947.

OTHER SOURCES:

BOOKS

Jordon, Rene, *Marlon Brando,* Pyramid, 1973.
Morella, Joe, and Edward Z. Epstein, *Marlon Brando; The Unauthorized Biography,* Crown, 1973.
Offen, Ron, *Brando,* Regnery, 1973.
Thomas, Bob, *Marlon: Portrait of the Rebel as an Artist,* Random House, 1974.

PERIODICALS

Esquire, November, 1989, p. 156.
Film Comment, July/August, 1991, p. 30.
Life, Autumn, 1990, p. 64.
Los Angeles Magazine, March, 1989, p. 208; September, 1990, p. 183.
Newsweek, May 28, 1990, p. 25.*

* * *

BRAZZI, Rossano 1916-
(Edward Ross)

PERSONAL: Born September 18, 1916, in Bologna, Italy; son of Adelmo (a leather goods manufacturer) and Maria (Ghedini) Brazzi; married Countess Lydia Bertolini, January 25, 1940. *Education:* Studied law at University of San Marco.

ADDRESSES: Office—Via G. B. Martini 13, Rome, Italy.

CAREER: Actor and director. Lawyer's apprentice in Rome, Italy, 1937. Appeared on Italian radio; reader of poetry on Italian television.

AWARDS, HONORS: Silver Ribbon Award, best performer in a motion picture, 1942, for *Noi vivi* (which had not yet been released); Italy's Golden Microphone Award, for poetry readings on television; Golden Star Award, for most popular radio performer of the year.

CREDITS:

FILM APPEARANCES

Una signora dell'ovest, Scalera, 1942.
Renzo Gamba, *The Great Dawn* (also known as *La grande aurura*), Scalera, 1946.
Antonio, *Furia,* Franchini-AGIC, 1947.
Francesco I, *The King's Jester* (also known as *Il re si diverte*), Scalera, 1947.
Prince Mdwani, *The White Devil* (also known as *Il diavolo bianco*), Manenti, 1947.
Vladimir Dubrowski, *Return of the Black Eagle,* Lux, 1949.
Professor Bhaer, *Little Women,* Metro-Goldwyn-Mayer (MGM), 1949.
Stefano, *Bullet for Stefano* (also known as *Il passatore*), Lux, 1950.
Donato, *Volcano* (also known as *Vulcano*), MGM, 1953.
Georgio, *Three Coins in the Fountain,* Twentieth Century-Fox, 1954.
Vincenzo Torlato-Favrini, *The Barefoot Contessa,* United Artists (UA), 1954.
Nino, *Angela,* Twentieth Century-Fox, 1955.
Renato Di Rossi, *Summertime* (also known as *Summer Madness*), UA, 1955.
Bertrand, *Loser Takes All,* British Lion, 1957.
Paul Bonnard, *Legend of the Lost,* UA, 1957.
Tonio Fischer, *Interlude,* Universal, 1957.
Carlo Landi, *The Story of Esther Costello* (also known as *Golden Virgin*), Columbia, 1957.
Emile De Becque, *South Pacific,* Twentieth Century-Fox, 1958.
Luc, *A Certain Smile,* Twentieth Century-Fox, 1958.
Charles-Edouard de Valhubert, *Count Your Blessings,* MGM, 1958.
Lucien Bonaparte, *Austerlitz* (also known as *The Battle of Austerlitz*), Lux, 1960.
Signor Naccarelli, *Light in the Piazza,* MGM, 1961.
Roberto Orlandi, *Rome Adventure* (also known as *Lovers Must Learn*), Warner Brothers, 1962.
Archimedes, *The Siege of Syracuse* (also known as *Archimede*), Paramount, 1962.
Leo, "The Tortoise and the Hare," *Three Fables of Love,* Janus, 1963.
Count Paolo Barbarelli, *Dark Purpose* (also known as *L'intrigo*), Universal, 1964.
Lorenzo, *The Battle of the Villa Fiorita* (also known as *Affair at the Villa Fiorita*), Warner Brothers, 1965.
Mario, *Engagement Italiano* (also known as *La ragazza in prestito*), Centro Cinematografico, 1966.
Phineas T. Prune, *The Christmas That Almost Wasn't* (also see below), Childhood Production, 1966.
Carlos Matabosch, *The Bobo,* Warner Brothers, 1967.
Giorgio, *Woman Times Seven,* Twentieth Century-Fox, 1967.
Carlo Rocchi, *Guilt Is Not Mine* (also known as *L'ingiusta condanna* and *Quelli che non muoiono*), Zeus-Electron/Hoffberg, 1968.
Dr. Hamilton, *One Step to Hell* (also known as *Caccio ai violenti, Rey de Africa,* and *King of Africa*), World, 1969.

Giovanni Borghese, *Krakatoa, East of Java* (also known as *Volcano*), Security/Cinerama, 1969.

Beckerman, *The Italian Job,* Paramount, 1969.

Baron de Coyne, *The Adventurers,* Paramount, 1970.

Brigoli, *Psychout for Murder* (also see below; also known as *Salvare la faccia*), Times Film, 1971.

Baron Tedesco, *The Great Waltz,* MGM, 1972.

Count Frankenstein, *House of Freaks* (also known as *Frankenstein's Castle of Freaks* and *El castello dell'orrore*), Aquarius, 1973.

Drummer of Vengeance, Times Film, 1974.

Ambassador Lara, *Political Asylum* (also known as *Detras de esa puerta*), Panamericana, 1975.

Father DeCarlo, *The Final Conflict,* Twentieth Century-Fox, 1981.

Carmine, *Fear City,* Zupnick-Curtis Enterprises, 1984.

Don LaManna, *Final Justice,* Mediterranean-Arista, 1985.

Dr. Sernich, *Formula for Murder,* Fulvia International, 1986.

Marini, *Russicum i giorni del diavolo,* Columbia, 1988.

Leo Kovalensky, *We the Living* (also known as *Noi vivi*), Scalera-Duncan Scott/Angelika, 1988.

Also appeared in *Processo e morte di Socrato,* 1939; *Il ponto di vetro, Ritorno, La forza bruta, E caduta una donna, Provesso e morte di Socrate,* and *La Tosca* (also known as *The Story of Tosca*), all 1940; *Kean* and *Il bravo di Venezia,* both 1941; *Damals, I due Foscari, La gorgona,* and *Treno crociato,* all 1942; *Baruffe chiozzotte* and *Silenzio, si gira,* both 1943; *La resa di Titi* (also known as *The Merry Chase*), *Malia,* and *I dieci commandamenti* (also known as *The Ten Commandments*), all 1945; *Aquila Nera,* 1946; *Il corriere del re, Eleanora Duse,* and *La monaca di Monza,* all 1947; *I contrabbandieri del mare,* 1949; *Romanza d'amore, Gli inesorabilia,* and *La corona negra,* all 1950; *La leggenda de Genofeffa, La cendetta di Aquila Nera,* and *Incantesimo tragico,* all 1951; *La prigionera della torre dell fuoco, La donna che inventa l'amore, Il boia di Lilla, Eran trecento,* and *Il figlio di Lagardere,* all 1952; *Il fuco nelle vene* (also known as *Flesh and Desire*) and *C'era una volta Angelo Musco,* both 1953; *La Castiglione* and *Carne de horca* (also known as *Il terrore dell 'Andalusia*), both 1954; *Un amore,* 1965; *La ragazzo del bersagliere* and *Per amore . . .per magia* (also known as *For Love . . .for Magic*), both 1966; *La schiava del paradiso,* 1967; *Sette uomini e un cervello* (also see below), 1968; *Intimita proibite di una giovane sposa* and *Il sesso di diavolo,* both 1970; *Cappucetto rosso, Cenerentola . . .et voi ci credete* (also see below), *De aire y fuego,* and *Il castello di paura,* all 1972; *Mr. Kingstreet's War,* 1973; *Storia del pugliato degli antichi ad oggi,* 1974; *Il cavaliere Costante Nicosia indemontiato ovvero Dracula in Brianza, Il tempo degli assassino, Gli angeli dalle mani bendate,* and *La farina del diavolo,* all 1975; *I telefoni bianchi* (also known as *White Telephones*), 1976; *Maestro d'amore* (also known as *Master of Love*), 1977; Arthur, *Io e Caterina,* 1980; priest, *The Voice,* 1982; *The Third Solution,* 1989; and *Michelangelo and Me.*

FILM WORK; DIRECTOR

The Christmas That Almost Wasn't, Childhood Production, 1966.

Psychout for Murder (also known as *Salvare la faccia*), Times Film, 1971.

Also director of *Sette uomini e un cervello* (under pseudonym Edward Ross), 1968; and *Cappucetto rosso, Cenerentola . . .et voi ci credete,* 1972.

TELEVISION APPEARANCES; MINI-SERIES

The Rana of Bhitbor, *The Far Pavilions,* HBO, 1984.

TELEVISION APPEARANCES; MOVIES

Captain Devilla, *Honeymoon with a Stranger,* ABC, 1969.

Fillipo Fillici, *A Time for Miracles,* ABC, 1980.

Diego Ortiz De Vilhegas, *Christopher Columbus,* CBS, 1985.

TELEVISION APPEARANCES; SERIES

Riakos, *The Survivors,* ABC, 1969-70.

TELEVISION APPEARANCES; EPISODIC

"Big Nick," *Douglas Fairbanks, Jr., Presents the Rheingold Theater,* NBC, 1955.

"Slip of the Tongue," *June Allyson Show,* CBS, 1960.

"Our Man in Rome," *June Allyson Show,* CBS, 1961.

"Keep My Share of the World," *Run for Your Life,* NBC, 1966.

"Don't Wait for Tomorrow," *Bob Hope Chrysler Theater,* NBC, 1967.

"The Skin Game," *Name of the Game,* NBC, 1970.

"The Naples Beat," *Madigan,* NBC, 1973.

"You Don't See Many Pirates These Days," *Hawaii Five-O,* CBS, 1977.

"The Young and the Fair," *Police Woman,* NBC, 1978.

"Angels on Skis," *Charlie's Angels,* ABC, 1979.

Fantasy Island, ABC, 1981.

"The Gigolo," *The Love Boat,* ABC, 1982.

"Straight through the Hart," *Hart to Hart,* ABC, 1983.

Also appeared in *The Dinah Shore Chevy Show* and *The Rosemary Clooney Show.*

STAGE APPEARANCES

Appeared as the husband, *Strange Interlude,* 1948.*

BRIDGES, Beau 1941-

PERSONAL: Born Lloyd Vernet Bridges III, December 9, 1941, in Los Angeles, CA; son of Lloyd Vernet (an actor) and Dorothy (Simpson) Bridges; married, wife's name, Julie; children: Casey (daughter). *Education:* Attended University of California, Los Angeles, and University of Hawaii at Manoa.

ADDRESSES: Agent—Creative Artists Agency, 1888 Century Park E., Suite 1400, Los Angeles, CA 90067.

CAREER: Actor.

AWARDS, HONORS: Golden Globe Award, and ACE Award, best actor in a mini-series or motion picture made for television, both 1991, both for *Without Warning: The James Brady Story;* ACE Award nomination, best actor in a dramatic series, 1991, for "Abra Cadaver," *Tales from the Crypt.*

CREDITS:

FILM APPEARANCES

Frankie Tucker, *Force of Evil,* Metro-Goldwyn-Mayer (MGM), 1948.
Bertram, *No Minor Vices,* MGM, 1948.
Beau, *The Red Pony,* Republic, 1949.
Tommy, *Zamba* (also known as *Zamba the Gorilla*), Eagle Lion, 1949.
Mark, *The Explosive Generation,* United Artists (UA), 1961.
Fred, *Village of the Giants,* Embassy, 1965.
PFC Felix Teflinger, *The Incident,* Twentieth Century-Fox, 1967.
Tim Austin, *For Love of Ivy,* Cinerama, 1968.
Ben Harvey, *Gaily, Gaily* (also known as *Chicago, Chicago*), UA, 1969.
Elgar Enders, *The Landlord,* UA, 1970.
Franklin Cane, *The Christian Licorice Store,* National General, 1971.
Adam, *Adam's Woman* (also known as *Return of the Boomerang*), Warner Brothers, 1972.
Paul Reis, *Child's Play,* Paramount, 1972.
Billy Breedlove, *Hammersmith Is Out,* Cinerama, 1972.
Charlie, *Your Three Minutes Are Up,* Cinerama, 1973.
Johnny, *Lovin' Molly* (also known as *The Wild and the Sweet*), Columbia, 1974.
Dick Buek, *The Other Side of the Mountain* (also known as *A Window to the Sky*), Universal, 1975.
Jesse Arlington, *One Summer Love* (also known as *Dragonfly*), American International, 1976.
Major Folly, *Swashbuckler* (also known as *The Scarlet Buccaneer*), Universal, 1976.
Mike Ramsay, *Two-Minute Warning,* Universal, 1976.
King Louis and Philippe, *Behind the Iron Mask* (also known as *The Fifth Musketeer*), Columbia, 1977.
Hutch, *Greased Lightning,* Warner Brothers, 1977.
Sonny, *Norma Rae,* Twentieth Century-Fox, 1979.
Toby, *The Runner Stumbles,* Twentieth Century-Fox, 1979.
Duane Hansen, *Honky Tonk Freeway,* Universal/Anchor, 1981.
Jack Hansen, *Love Child,* Warner Brothers, 1982.
Gunter Wetzel, *Night Crossing,* Buena Vista, 1982.
Bruce McBride, *Silver Dream Racer,* Almi, 1982.
Connie Kalitta, *Heart Like a Wheel,* Twentieth Century-Fox, 1983.
Win Berry, *The Hotel New Hampshire,* Orion, 1984.
Sheriff Sam Wayburn, *The Killing Time,* New World, 1987.
Joe Jennings, *The Wild Pair* (also known as *Devil's Odds;* also see below), Trans World Entertainment, 1987.
Judge John Eden, *Seven Hours to Judgment* (also see below), Trans World, 1988.
Frank Baker, *The Fabulous Baker Boys,* Twentieth Century-Fox, 1989.
Captain Keene, *The Iron Triangle,* Scotti Brothers, 1989.
John Alder, *Signs of Life* (also known as *One for Sorrow, Two for Joy*), Avenue, 1989.
Sam Woods, *The Wizard,* Universal, 1989.
Orville, *Daddy's Dyin' . . . Who's Got the Will?,* MGM/UA, 1990.

Also appeared in *Mutual Respect,* 1974, and *Married to It.*

FILM WORK: DIRECTOR

The Wild Pair (also known as *Devil's Odds*), Trans World Entertainment, 1987.
Seven Hours to Judgment, Trans World, 1988.

TELEVISION APPEARANCES; MOVIES

Frederick Ingham, *The Man without a Country,* ABC, 1973.
Chris Schroeder, *The Stranger Who Looks Like Me,* ABC, 1974.
Dr. Steve Drucker, *Medical Story,* NBC, 1975.
Harry Feversham, *The Four Feathers,* NBC, 1978.
Ben Morton, *The President's Mistress,* CBS, 1978.
David Rodman, *The Child Stealer,* ABC, 1979.
Ray Johnson, *Dangerous Company,* CBS, 1982.
Bud Herren, *The Kid from Nowhere* (also see below), NBC, 1982.
Leonard Vole, *Witness for the Prosecution,* CBS, 1982.
Frank Powell, *The Red-Light Sting,* CBS, 1984.
Unicorn, *Alice in Wonderland,* CBS, 1985.
Thad Taylor, *A Fighting Choice,* ABC, 1986.
Brad Gordon, *Outrage!,* CBS, 1986.
Hank Tilby, *The Thanksgiving Promise* (also see below), ABC, 1986.

Police Chief Richard Czech, *Everybody's Baby: The Rescue of Jessica McClure* (also known as *The Jessica McClure Story*), ABC, 1989.
Arnold Zimmerman, *Guess Who's Coming for Christmas?* (also known as *UFO Cafe* and *George Walters Will Be Away for the Holidays*), NBC, 1990.
Jack Perkins, *Wildflower,* Lifetime, 1991.
Title role, *Without Warning: The James Brady Story* (also known as *Thumbs Up*), HBO, 1991.

TELEVISION APPEARANCES; SERIES

Seaman Howard Spicer, *Ensign O'Toole,* NBC, 1962-63.
Pat Knowland, *Mr. Novak,* NBC, 1963-65.
Richard Chapin, *United States,* NBC, then A&E, 1980.

TELEVISION APPEARANCES; MINI-SERIES

Randy Claggart, *James A. Michener's "Space",* CBS, 1985.

TELEVISION APPEARANCES; PILOTS

Brandon Drood, *Frank Marshall,* CBS, 1966.
Charlie Gordon, *Three of a Kind,* ABC, 1989.

TELEVISION APPEARANCES; SPECIALS

Guest, *Robert Young and the Family,* CBS, 1973.
Young Benjamin Franklin, *The Whirlwind,* CBS, 1974.
Guest, *The Dorothy Hamill Winter Carnival Special,* ABC, 1977.
Mom, I Want to Come Home Now, syndicated, 1981.
The 61st Annual Academy Awards Presentation, ABC, 1989.
America's All-Star Tribute to Elizabeth Taylor (also known as *The Second Annual America's Hope Award*), ABC, 1989.
Presenter, *The 11th Annual ACE Awards* (also known as *The Golden ACE Awards*), syndicated, 1990.
Presenter, *The 62nd Annual Academy Awards Presentation,* ABC, 1990.
The 4th Annual American Comedy Awards, ABC, 1990.
Night of One Hundred Stars III, NBC, 1990.
Presenter, *The 48th Annual Golden Globe Awards,* TBS, 1991.
The Meaning of Life, CBS, 1991.

TELEVISION APPEARANCES; EPISODIC

"Brotherly Love," *My Three Sons,* ABC, 1960.
Sea Hunt, CBS, 1960.
"Image of a Drawn Sword," *Zane Grey Theater,* CBS, 1961.
Sea Hunt, CBS, 1961.
"A Lesson in Any Language," *My Three Sons,* ABC, 1961.
"The Rich Boy," *The Real McCoys,* ABC, 1962.
"A Pair of Boots," *The Lloyd Bridges Show,* CBS, 1962.
"The Skippy Maddox Story," *The Lloyd Bridges Show,* CBS, 1963.
"The Echo of a Silent Cheer," *Ben Casey,* ABC, 1963.
"Incident at Paradise," *Rawhide,* CBS, 1963.
"Pay the Two Dollars," *Mr. Novak,* NBC, 1963.
"Sparrow on the Wire," *Mr. Novak,* NBC, 1964.
My Three Sons, ABC, 1964.
"Cannibal Plants, They Eat You Alive," *The Eleventh Hour,* NBC, 1964.
"The Child Between," *Dr. Kildare,* NBC, 1964.
"The Short Day of Private Putnam," *Combat,* ABC, 1964.
"Mike Wears the Pants," *My Three Sons,* ABC, 1964.
"Honor—And All That," *Mr. Novak,* NBC, 1965.
"Then Came the Mighty Hunter," *12 O'Clock High,* ABC, 1965.
"An Elephant Is Like a Rope," *The FBI,* ABC, 1965.
"Stroke of Genius," *The Fugitive,* ABC, 1966.
"The Mourners for Johnny Sharp," *The Loner,* CBS, 1966.
"Nice Day for a Hanging," *Branded,* NBC, 1966.
"My Father's Guitar, *Gunsmoke,* CBS, 1966.
"Justice," *Bonanza,* NBC, 1967.
"The Other Side of the Coin," *The Fugitive,* ABC, 1967.
"The Legend of Jud Star," *Cimarron Strip,* CBS, 1967.
"Ordeal by Terror," *Felony Squad,* ABC, 1967.
"The Poker Game," *Insight,* syndicated, 1969.
"The Last of My Brothers," *Insight,* syndicated, 1969.
"Incident on Danker Street," *Insight,* syndicated, 1970.
Joe Grant, "My Dad Lives in a Downtown Hotel," *ABC Afterschool Special,* ABC, 1973.
"A Picture in Sobel's Window," *Insight,* syndicated, 1976.
Stubby Pringle, "Stubby Pringle's Christmas," *Hallmark Hall of Fame,* NBC, 1978.
"Vanessa in the Garden," *Amazing Stories,* NBC, 1985.
Mr. Tauscher, "Can a Guy Say No?, *ABC Afterschool Special,* ABC, 1986.
Jack Grant, "Just Another Secret," *Frederick Forsyth Presents,* USA, 1989.
Breen, "The Man in the Brooks Brothers Suit," in "Women and Men: Stories of Seduction," *HBO Showcase,* HBO, 1990.
"To Be Free: The National Literacy Honors from the White House," *Bell Atlantic Showcase,* ABC, 1990.
"Abra Cadaver," *Tales from the Crypt,* HBO, 1991.

TELEVISION WORK; DIRECTOR

The Kid from Nowhere (movie), NBC, 1982.
The Thanksgiving Promise (movie), ABC, 1986.

Also worked as director of *Don't Touch* (special), 1985.

STAGE APPEARANCES

(Broadway debut) Tom, *Where's Daddy?,* Billy Rose Theatre, New York City, 1966.

The Trial of the Catonsville Nine, Center Theatre Group, New Theatre for Now, New York City, 1970-71.
Arlo Forrest Buffy, *Who's Who in Hell,* Lunt-Fontanne Theatre, New York City, 1974.
Love Letters, Canon Theatre, Los Angeles, CA, 1990.*

* * *

BRIDGES, Jeff 1949(?)-

PERSONAL: Born December 4, 1949 (some sources say 1951), in Los Angeles, CA; son of Lloyd Vernet (an actor) and Dorothy (Simpson) Bridges; married Susan Gaston (a photographer); children: three. *Education:* Studied acting with Uta Hagen at Hagen-Berghof Studio. *Avocational interests:* Composing songs, painting, writing.

ADDRESSES: Agent—Creative Artists Agency Inc., 1888 Century Park E., Suite 1400, Los Angeles, CA 90067.

CAREER: Actor. Cofounder of End Hunger Network. *Military service:* Served in U.S. Coast Guard Reserves.

AWARDS, HONORS: Academy Award nomination, best supporting actor, 1971, for *The Last Picture Show;* Academy Award nomination, best supporting actor, 1974, for *Thunderbolt and Lightfoot;* named Discovery of the Year, Hollywood Women's Press Club, 1975; Academy Award nomination, best actor, 1984, for *Starman;* Presidential End Hunger Award—Celebrity, Agency for International Development, 1988; NATO/ShoWest Male Star of the Year, National Association of Theatre Owners, 1990; Golden Globe Award nomination, best actor in a musical or comedy, 1991, for *The Fisher King.*

CREDITS:

FILM APPEARANCES

(Film debut) Douglas, *Halls of Anger,* United Artists (UA), 1970.
Duane Jackson, *The Last Picture Show,* Columbia, 1971.
Jake Rumsey, *Bad Company,* Paramount, 1972.
Ernie, *Fat City,* Columbia, 1972.
Don Parritt, *The Iceman Cometh,* American Film Theatre, 1973.
Elroy Jackson, Jr., *The Last American Hero* (also known as *Hard Driver*), Twentieth Century-Fox, 1973.
Zack Feather, *Lolly-Madonna XXX* (also known as *The Lolly-Madonna War*), Metro-Goldwyn-Mayer (MGM), 1973.
Lightfoot, *Thunderbolt and Lightfoot,* UA, 1974.
Lewis Tater, *Hearts of the West* (also known as *Hollywood Cowboy*), MGM/UA, 1975.
Jack McKee, *Rancho Deluxe,* UA, 1975.
Jack Prescott, *King Kong,* Paramount, 1976.
Craig Blake, *Stay Hungry,* UA, 1976.
Jerry Green, *Somebody Killed Her Husband,* Columbia, 1978.
Nick Kegan, *Winter Kills,* Avco Embassy, 1979.
Harry, *The American Success Company,* Columbia, 1980.
John H. Bridges, *Heaven's Gate,* 1980.
Richard Bone, *Cutter and Bone* (also released as *Cutter's Way*), UA, 1981.
Rupert Baines, *Kiss Me Goodbye,* Twentieth Century-Fox, 1982.
Voice of Prince Lir, *The Last Unicorn* (animated), ITC, 1982.
Kevin Flynn/Clu, *Tron,* Buena Vista, 1982.
Terry Brogan, *Against All Odds,* Columbia, 1984.
Title role, *Starman,* Columbia, 1984.
Matthew Scudder, *Eight Million Ways to Die,* Tri-Star, 1985.
Jack Forrester, *The Jagged Edge,* Columbia, 1985.
Turner Kendall, *The Morning After,* Twentieth Century-Fox, 1986.
Vernon Hightower, *Nadine,* Tri-Star, 1987.
Preston Tucker, *Tucker: The Man and His Dream,* Paramount, 1988.
Jack Baker, *The Fabulous Baker Boys,* Twentieth Century-Fox, 1989.
Larry Livingston, *See You in the Morning,* Warner Bros., 1989.
Duane Jackson, *Texasville,* Columbia, 1990.
Bartender, *Cold Feet,* Avenue, 1990.
Jack Lucas, *The Fisher King,* Tri-Star, 1991.

Also appeared in *The Yin and Yang of Dr. Go,* 1972.

TELEVISION APPEARANCES; EPISODIC

(Television debut) *Sea Hunt,* syndicated, c. 1957.
"Gentlemen in Blue," *The Lloyd Bridges Show,* CBS, 1962.
"To Walk with the Stars," *The Lloyd Bridges Show,* CBS, 1963.
"The Ordeal of Bud Windom," *The Loner,* ABC, 1965.
"Boomerang," *The FBI,* ABC, 1969.
"Nightbirds," *The Most Deadly Game,* ABC, 1970.
"Rapunzel," *Faerie Tale Theatre,* Showtime, 1983.

TELEVISION APPEARANCES; MOVIES

Young John, *Silent Night, Lonely Night,* NBC, 1969.
Mike Olson, *In Search of America,* ABC, 1971.
Neighbor, *The Thanksgiving Promise* (also known as *The Thanksgiving Story*), ABC, 1986.

TELEVISION APPEARANCES; SPECIALS

The 59th Annual Academy Awards Presentation, ABC, 1987.
Superstars and Their Moms, TBS, 1989.
The 61st Annual Academy Awards Presentation, ABC, 1989.

The 62nd Annual Academy Awards Presentation, ABC, 1990.

The 63rd Annual Academy Awards Presentation, ABC, 1991.

A User's Guide to Planet Earth: The American Environment Test, ABC, 1991.

Also appeared in *The American Film Institute Salute to John Huston,* 1983.

OTHER TELEVISION APPEARANCES

Naked Hollywood (documentary), Arts and Entertainment, 1991.

STAGE APPEARANCES

Toured with father, Lloyd Bridges, in *Anniversary Waltz,* New England cities.

OTHER SOURCES:

BOOKS

Celebrity Register, 5th edition, Gale, 1990, p. 52.

PERIODICALS

American Film, October, 1990, p. 26.
New York Times, November 2, 1975.
People, October 27, 1986, p. 112.*

* * *

BRILEY, John 1925-

PERSONAL: Full name, John Richard Briley; born June 25, 1925, in Kalamazoo, MI; son of William Treve (in sales) and Mary Stella (in sales; maiden name, Daly) Briley; married Dorothy Louise Reichart, August 23, 1950; children: Dennis Patrick, Paul Christian, Mary Sydney, Shaun William. *Education:* Attended Western Michigan College of Education (now Western Michigan University), 1943; University of Michigan, B.A., 1951, M.A., 1952; University of Birmingham, Ph.D., 1960. *Avocational interests:* Swimming, tennis, skiing.

ADDRESSES: Office—24 Highland Rd., Amersham, Buckinghamshire, England; and 5150 Wilshire Blvd., Suite 505, Los Angeles, CA 90069. *Agent*—Michael Levy, 6169 Sunset Blvd., Los Angeles, CA 90069; and Douglas Rae Management Ltd., 28 Charing Cross Rd., London WC2H 0DB, England; and International Creative Management, 40 West 57th St., New York, NY 10019.

CAREER: Writer. General Motors Corp., Detroit, MI, in public relations department, 1947-50; U.S. Air Force, South Ruislip, England, director of orientation activities, 1955-60; Metro-Goldwyn-Mayer (MGM), Elstree, England, staff writer, 1960-64; free-lance writer, 1964—. University of Michigan, visiting lecturer, 1969. Chesham Theatre Club, president. *Military service:* U.S. Air Force, 1943-46; became captain.

MEMBER: Writers Guild of Great Britain (member of executive council, 1975-85), Writers Guild of America West, Authors Guild, Dramatists Guild, Phi Beta Kappa, Phi Kappa Phi, Amersham Swimming Club.

AWARDS, HONORS: Academy Award, best original screenplay, and Golden Globe Award, best screenplay, both 1982, for *Gandhi;* Christopher Awards, 1983, 1985, and 1988.

CREDITS:

FILM WORK

Producer (with Richard Attenborough and Norman Spencer), *Cry Freedom* (also see below), Universal, 1987.

FILM APPEARANCES

Sergeant, *Situation Hopeless—But Not Serious,* Paramount, 1965.

WRITINGS:

SCREENPLAYS

(With Jack Trevor Story) *Invasion Quartet* (based on a novel by Norman Collins), Metro-Goldwyn-Mayer (MGM), 1961.

(With Story) *Postman's Knock* (based on a story by Story), MGM, 1962.

Children of the Damned, MGM, 1964.

Pope Joan (also known as *The Devil's Imposter*), Columbia, 1972.

That Lucky Touch, Allied Artists, 1975.

(With Jack Gold) *The Medusa Touch* (based on a novel by Peter Van Greenaway), Warner Brothers, 1978.

Eagle's Wing (based on a story by Michael Syson), Rank, 1979.

Gandhi, Columbia, 1982.

Enigma (based on a novel by Michael Barak), Embassy, 1983.

Marie, MGM/United Artists, 1986.

(With Stanley Mann) *Tai-Pan* (based on a novel by James Clavell), De Laurentiis Entertainment Group, 1986.

Cry Freedom (based on books by Donald Woods), Universal, 1987.

Sandino, Tri-Star, 1990.

Other screenplays include *A Fragile Life; West with the Night; Why Did I Ever Leave Horses?; Captain Barnes, Lieutenant Farnum; Offering; To Die a Stranger; The Veil; The Great Baby Blue; How Sleep the Brave; Mister God, This Is Anna; The Big Apple; The Deadly Inheritance; The Crucible; White Fang;* and *The Fourth Season.*

PLAYS

Seven Bob a Buck, produced at Hampstead Theatre Club, then Comedy Theatre, both London, 1964.

So Who Needs Men!, produced at Northampton Repertory Theatre, Northampton, England, then New London Theatre, both 1976.

Also author of the play *See America First.*

TELEVISION SERIES

Hits and Misses, BBC, 1962.

The Airbase, BBC, 1965.

NOVELS

The Traitors, Putnam, 1968, published in England as *How Sleep the Brave,* Transworld, 1971.

The Last Dance, Secker & Warburg, 1978.

OTHER

Contributor to periodicals, including *Shakespeare Survey* and *Shakespeare Quarterly.*

OTHER SOURCES:

BOOKS

Contemporary Authors, Volume 101, Gale, 1981.*

* * *

BRODKIN, Herbert 1912-1990(?)

PERSONAL: Born November 9, 1912, in New York, NY; died c. 1990 in New York, NY. *Education:* University of Michigan, B.A.; Yale University, M.F.A., directing and design.

CAREER: Producer. Worked as designer for summer stock and repertory theatre productions and as scenery designer in Hollywood, CA; designed plays and operas for City Center and Theater Guild; scenery designer, production manager, and director at Bucks County Playhouse and Westport Country Playhouse; Columbia Broadcasting System, began as scenic designer; Titus Productions, founder, producer, and chief operating officer, beginning 1960. *Military service:* U.S. Army, Signal Corps, directed forty films on military subjects; Special Services, supervised production of three hundred plays for United Service Organizations and Army; became major.

AWARDS, HONORS: Emmy Award nominations, outstanding producer—live series, 1955, for *The Alcoa Hour,* outstanding dramatic program, 1967-68, for "Dear Friends," and 1968, for "The People Next Door," both *CBS Playhouse,* and outstanding special—drama or comedy (with Buzz Berger), 1974, for "Missiles of October," *ABC Theatre;* Emmy Award, outstanding limited series, 1978, for *Holocaust;* Emmy Award nomination, outstanding drama special, 1981, and Hugh M. Hefner First Amendment Award—Motion Pictures and Television (with Robert Berger, Ernest Kinoy, and Herbert Wise), Playboy Foundation, 1982, for "producing a powerful dramatization of the recent free-speech struggles," both for *Skokie.*

CREDITS:

TELEVISION PRODUCER; SERIES

(With William Brown, Gordon Duff, Norman Felton, Felix Jackson, Fletcher Markle, Worthington Miner, Paul Nickell, Franklin Schaffner, and Charles H. Schultz) *Studio One* (also broadcast as *Studio One Summer Theatre*), CBS, 1948-57, broadcast as *Studio One in Hollywood,* 1958.

(With Carlo De'Angelo, Walter Tibbals, and Leonard White) *Charlie Wild, Private Detective,* CBS, 1950-51, ABC, 1951-52, DuMont Network, 1952.

ABC Album, ABC, 1953.

The Motorola Television Hour, CBS, 1953-54.

The Elgin Hour, NBC, 1954-55.

(With Philip Barry, Samuel Chotzinoff, Vincent M. Fennelly, Gene Roddenberry, and Alex Segal) *The Alcoa Hour* (also known as *Alcoa-Goodyear Theatre*), 1955-57.

(With Herbert Hirschman) *Espionage,* NBC, 1963-64.

(With Denne Petitclerc) *Shane,* ABC, 1966.

TELEVISION PRODUCER; PILOTS

Colonel Humphrey J. Flack, ABC, 1953.

Jamie, ABC, 1953.

Jet Fighter, ABC, 1953.

Justice, ABC, 1953.

Mr. Glencannon Takes All, ABC, 1953.

Sketchbook, ABC, 1953.

"The Defender" (pilot for *The Defenders;* also see below), *Studio One,* CBS, 1957.

Light's Out, NBC, 1972.

Also produced pilot *One-Eyed Jacks Are Wild* for ABC in 1966 (never broadcast).

TELEVISION PRODUCER; MOVIES

"Dear Friends," *CBS Playhouse,* CBS, c. 1967.

"The People Next Door," *CBS Playhouse,* CBS, 1968.

(With Buzz Berger) "Missiles of October," *ABC Theatre,* ABC, 1974.

Also producer of *Pueblo,* 1973.

TELEVISION EXECUTIVE PRODUCER; SERIES

(And creator) *Brenner,* CBS, 1959, 1961, 1962, and 1964.

The Defenders, CBS, 1961-65.

The Nurses, CBS, 1962-64, broadcast as *The Doctors and the Nurses,* 1964-65.
For the People, CBS, 1965.
Coronet Blue, CBS, 1967.

TELEVISION EXECUTIVE PRODUCER; PILOTS

The Happeners, syndicated, 1967.
Rx for the Defense, ABC, 1973.
Land of Hope, CBS, 1976.
The Four of Us, ABC, 1977.
The Firm, NBC, 1983.

TELEVISION EXECUTIVE PRODUCER; MINI-SERIES

Holocaust, NBC, 1978.

TELEVISION EXECUTIVE PRODUCER; MOVIES

Crawlspace, CBS, 1972.
F. Scott Fitzgerald and "The Last of the Belles," ABC, 1974.
F. Scott Fitzgerald in Hollywood, ABC, 1976.
The Deadliest Season, CBS, 1977.
The Last Tenant, ABC, 1978.
Siege, CBS, 1978.
Hollow Image, ABC, 1979.
Doctor Franken, NBC, 1980.
Death Penalty, NBC, 1980.
F. D. R.—The Last Year, NBC, 1980.
The Henderson Monster, CBS, 1980.
King Crab, ABC, 1980.
Skokie, CBS, 1981.
Benny's Place, ABC, 1982.
My Body, My Child, ABC, 1982.
Ghost Dancing, ABC, 1983.
Sakharov, HBO, 1984.
(With Robert "Buzz" Berger) *Doubletake,* CBS, 1985.
Johnny Bull, ABC, 1986.
Murrow, HBO, 1986.
Welcome Home, Bobby, CBS, 1986.
Mandela, HBO, 1987.
Night of Courage, ABC, 1987.
Internal Affairs, CBS, 1988.
"Stones for Ibarra," *Hallmark Hall of Fame,* CBS, 1988.
Murder Times Seven, CBS, 1990.
Murder in Black and White, CBS, 1990.

FILM PRODUCER

(With Michael Powell) *Sebastian,* Paramount, 1968.
The People Next Door, Avco Embassy, 1970.

STAGE PRODUCER

Something about a Soldier, Ambassador Theatre, New York City, 1962.

OBITUARIES AND OTHER SOURCES:

PERIODICALS

Channels: The Business of Communications, November, 1989, p. 66.
Time, November 12, 1990, p. 86.*

* * *

BROOK, Peter 1925-

PERSONAL: Full name, Peter Stephen Paul Brook; born March 21, 1925, in London, England; son of Simon (a chemist) and Ida (a chemist; maiden name, Jansen) Brook; married Natasha Parry (an actress), November 3, 1951; children: one son, one daughter. *Education:* Magdalen College, Oxford, B.A., 1944 (one source cites 1945), M.A. *Avocational interests:* The theatre and cinema, air travel, playing the piano, and painting.

ADDRESSES: *Office*—CICT, 56 rue de l'Universite, 75007 Paris.

CAREER: Director, designer, and producer for stage, film, and television. Has worked on more than fifty productions, including plays, films, and operas in England, the United States, and France. Spent a year away from school working at a film studio, learning script writing, cutting, and direction, c. 1941; formed the Oxford University Film Society, early 1940s; worked as a writer and director for Crown Film Unit, preparing shorts and advertising films, c. 1945; director of productions for Royal Opera House, Covent Garden, London, England, 1948-49; codirector of the Royal Shakespeare Theatre, 1962—; founded with Micheline Rozan, experimental International Center for Theater Research, 1970-80. Director of Centre International de Creations Theatrales, Paris.

MEMBER: Association of Cinematographers and Allied Technicians, Society of Stage Directors and Choreographers.

AWARDS, HONORS: Antoinette Perry Award nomination for best director, 1959, for *The Visit;* Antoinette Perry Award nomination for best director of a musical, 1961, for *Irma La Douce;* best director award, London Critics' Poll, 1964, best director award, *Variety* New York Drama Critics' Poll, Antoinette Perry Award for best director, and Outer Circle Award, all 1965, all for *Marat/Sade;* Commander of the Order of the British Empire and Chevalier de l'Ordre des Arts et des Lettres, both 1965; Drama Desk Award for best director, Antoinette Perry Award for best director, and best director award, New York Drama Critics' Poll, all 1970, all for *A Midsummer Night's Dream;* Shakespeare Award, Freiherr von Stein Foundation, 1973; Grand Prix Dominique and Brigadier Prize, both

1975, both for *Timon of Athens;* Common Wealth Award of Distinguished Service, Bank of Delaware, 1980; SWET award for outstanding contribution by English theatre artist to U.S. theatre season, 1983; Antoinette Perry Special Award and Prix Italia, both 1984, both for *La Tragedie de Carmen;* honorary member of American Academy of Arts and Sciences, 1986; Officier de l'Ordre des Arts et des Lettres, Legion of Honour (France), 1987; Obie Award for best direction, 1988, for *The Mahabharata;* honorary doctorate, Birmingham; first prize, Artists Theatre Union, Moscow, U.S.S.R. (now Commonwealth of Independent States), for vital contribution in the domain of universal theatre, 1988; Europa Prize for theatre, Taormina Arte, Italy, 1989; Nonino Prize, Percoto, 1991; Inamori Foundation Award, Kyoto, Japan, 1991; The Wexner Prize, USA, 1992; D.Litt., Birmingham University and Strathclyde University; Grand Officer of the Order of Sant'Iago da Espada, Portugal.

CREDITS:

STAGE WORK; DIRECTOR

Dr. Faustus, Torch Theatre, London, England, 1943.
Man and Superman, Birmingham Repertory Theatre, London, 1945.
King John, Birmingham Repertory Theatre, 1945.
The Lady from the Sea, Birmingham Repertory Theatre, 1945.
The Barretts of Wimpole Street, "Q," Theatre, London, 1945.
The Infernal Machine, Chanticleer Theatre, London, 1945.
The Brothers Karamazov, Lyric Theatre, London, 1946.
Love's Labour's Lost, Shakespeare Memorial Theatre, Stratford-on-Avon, 1946.
Romeo and Juliet, Shakespeare Memorial Theatre, 1947.
Men without Shadows, Lyric Theatre, 1947.
The Respectable Prostitute, Lyric Theatre, 1947.
Boris Godunov, Royal Opera House, Covent Garden, London, 1948.
La Boheme, Covent Garden, 1948.
Dark of the Moon, Ambassadors' Theatre, London, 1949.
The Marriage of Figaro, Covent Garden, 1949.
The Olympians, Covent Garden, 1949.
Salome, Covent Garden, 1949.
Ring 'Round the Moon, Globe Theatre, London, 1950.
The Little Hut, Lyric Theatre, 1950.
Measure for Measure, Shakespeare Memorial Theatre, 1950, then Paris, France, 1970.
Salome, Royal Opera House, 1950.
Penny for a Song, Haymarket Theatre, London, 1951.
The Winter's Tale, Phoenix Theatre, London, 1951.
Figure of Fun, Aldwych Theatre, London, 1951.
La Mort d'un commis voyageur, Theatre National, Brussels, Belgium, 1951.
Colombe, New Theatre, London, 1951.
(U.S. stage debut) *Faust,* Metropolitan Opera House, New York City, 1953.
Venice Preserv'd, Lyric Theatre, 1953, then New York City, 1953.
The Dark is Light Enough, Aldwych Theatre, 1954.
Both Ends Meet, Apollo Theatre, London, 1954.
House of Flowers, Alvin Theatre, New York City, 1954.
The Lark, Lyric Theatre, 1955.
(And designer) *Titus Andronicus* (also see below), Shakespeare Memorial Theatre, 1955.
Hamlet, Phoenix Theatre, 1955, then Mayakovsky Theatre, Moscow, U.S.S.R (now Commonwealth of Independent States), 1955.
The Power and the Glory (also see below), Phoenix Theatre, 1956.
(And set designer) *The Family Reunion,* Phoenix Theatre, 1956.
(And designer) *A View from the Bridge,* Comedy Theatre, London, 1956, then Theatre Antoine, Paris, 1958.
(And designer) *La Chatte sur un toit brulant* (title means "Cat on a Hot Tin Roof"), Theatre Antoine, 1956.
(And designer) *The Tempest* (also see "Writings" below), Shakespeare Memorial Theatre, 1957.
Eugene Onegin, Metropolitan Opera House, 1957.
The Visit, Lunt-Fontanne, New York City, 1958, then Royalty Theatre, London, 1960.
Irma La Douce, Lyric Theatre, 1959, then Plymouth Theatre, New York City, 1960.
The Fighting Cock, ANTA Theatre, New York City, 1959.
(And designer) *La Balcon* (title means "The Balcony"), Gymnase Theatre, Paris, 1960.
(And designer) *King Lear* (also see below), Royal Shakespeare Theatre, Stratford-on-Avon, 1962, then Aldwych Theatre, 1962, later New York State Theatre, New York City, 1964.
(With Clifford Williams) *The Tempest,* Royal Shakespeare Theatre, 1963.
(And designer) *Serjeant Musgrave's Dance,* Theatre de l'Athenee, Paris, 1963.
Marat/Sade (also known as *The Persecution and Assassination of Marat as Performed by the Inmates of the Asylum of Charenton under the Direction of the Marquis de Sade;* also see below), Royal Shakespeare Company, Aldwych Theatre, 1964, then Martin Beck Theatre, New York City, 1965.
The Physicists, Martin Beck Theatre, 1964.
The Investigation, Aldwych Theatre, 1965.
U.S. (also see below), Aldwych Theatre, 1966.
(And designer) *Oedipus,* Old Vic Theatre, London, 1968.
The Tempest, Round House Theatre, London, 1968.
A Midsummer Night's Dream, Royal Shakespeare Company, 1971, then Billy Rose Theatre, New York City,

1971, later Ahmanson Theatre, Los Angeles, CA, 1973.

(And producer, with Ted Hughes) *Orghast,* International Centre of Theatre Research (ICTR), staged at the site of the ancient Persepolis, near Shiraz, Iran, 1971.

(And producer, with Hughes) *The Conference of the Birds* (also see below), ICTR, Theatre Bouffes du Nord, Paris, France, 1972, then Australia and New York, 1980.

Kaspar, ICTR, Mobilier National Theatre, Paris, 1972.

Timon of Athens, ICTR, Theatre Bouffes du Nord, 1974.

Les Iks, ICTR, Theatre Bouffes du Nord, 1975, then London, 1976.

Ubu au Bouffes, La Mama Theatre, New York City, 1977, then Paris, 1977, later Young Vic Theatre, New York City, 1978.

Measure for Measure, Theatre Bouffes du Nord, 1978.

Anthony and Cleopatra, Royal Shakespeare Company, 1978, then Aldwych Theatre, 1979.

Conference of the Birds (part of double bill), Avignon Festival, Paris, then Majestic Theatre, New York City, later Australia, 1979-80.

The Cherry Orchard, Paris, 1981, then Majestic Theatre, New York City, 1988.

La Tragedie de Carmen (also see below), Paris, 1981, then Vivian Beaumont Theater, New York City, 1984, later Tramway Theatre, Glasgow, Scotland, 1989.

Tchin, Tchin, Theatre Montparnasse, Paris, 1984.

The Mahabharata (in French; also see below), Theatre Bouffes du Nord, 1985, then (in English) Majestic Theatre, New York City, 1987-88, later Glasgow, 1988.

Also directed *The Vicious Cycle* in London, 1946, and *Time and Again,* 1957.

MAJOR TOURS; DIRECTOR

Pygmalion, Entertainments National Service Association, tour for British armed forces, 1945.

Titus Andronicus (also see below), London and European cities, 1957.

Irma La Douce, U.S. cities, 1962.

(And producer) *The Conference of the Birds,* five West African countries, 1972-73, and included in presentation at Brooklyn Academy of Music, New York City, 1973.

Directed tour of *The Perils of Scobie Prilt,* 1963; directed and produced tour of *The Mahabharata* in European cities. With International Centre of Theatre Research, produced numerous world tours throughout the 1970s.

FILM WORK; DIRECTOR

Sentimental Journey, Oxford University Film Society, 1944.

The Beggar's Opera, Warner Brothers, 1953.

Moderato Cantabile (also see below), Royal International, 1960.

(And editor) *Lord of the Flies* (also see below), Continental Distributing, 1963.

Marat/Sade (also known as *The Persecution and Assassination of Jean-Paul Marat as Performed by the Inmates of the Asylum of Charenton under the Direction of the Marquis de Sade*), United Artists, 1967.

(And producer) *Tell Me Lies,* Continental Distributing, 1968.

King Lear (also see below), Altura, 1971.

Meetings with Remarkable Men (also see below), Libra, 1979.

La Tragedie de Carmen (also see below), MK2/Alby Films/Antenne-2, 1983.

The Mahabharata (also see below), Reiner Moritz, 1989.

TELEVISION WORK; DIRECTOR

Box for One (also see below), BBC, 1949.

King Lear (also see below), Ford Foundation Program, 1953.

Heaven and Earth, ABC, 1957.

The Mahabharata (three part mini-series; also see below), PBS, 1990.

TELEVISION APPEARANCES

The Magic of Peter Brook, Camera Three, CBS, 1971.

WRITINGS:

STAGE SCRIPTS

U.S., Aldwych Theatre, 1966.

(With Jean-Claude Carriere and Marius Constant) *La Tragedie de Carmen* (adapted from the novel by Prosper Merimee), Paris, 1981, then Vivian Beaumont Theater, 1984, later Tramway Theatre, 1989.

(With Carriere) *The Mahabharata* (adapted from the original Sanskrit poem; also see below), Bouffes du Nord, 1985.

STAGE SCORES

Titus Andronicus, Shakespeare Memorial Theatre, 1955.

The Power and the Glory, Phoenix Theatre, 1956.

The Tempest, Shakespeare Memorial Theatre, 1957.

FILM SCRIPTS

(With Marguerite Duras and Gerard Jarlot) *Moderato Cantabile* (adapted from the novel by Duras), Royal International, 1960.

Lord of the Flies (adapted from the novel by William Golding), 1962.

King Lear (adapted from the play by William Shakespeare), Altura, 1971.

(With Jeanne de Salzmann) *Meetings with Remarkable Men* (adapted from the book by G. I. Gurdjieff), Libra, 1979.
La Tragedie de Carmen, MK2/Alby Films/Antenne-2, 1983.
(With Volker Schlondorff, Carriere, and Marie-Helene Estienne) *Swann in Love* (adapted from the novel *Un Amour de Swann* by Marcel Proust), Orion Classics, 1984.
(With Carriere and Estienne) *The Mahabharata* (also see below), Reiner Moritz, 1989.

TELEVISION SCRIPTS

Box for One, BBC, 1949.
King Lear, Ford Foundation Program, 1953.
(With Carriere and Estienne) *The Mahabharata,* PBS, 1990.

Also author of television play, *The Birthday Present,* for television, broadcast in 1955.

BOOKS

The Empty Space (nonfiction), Atheneum, 1968.
The Shifting Point (autobiography), Bessie Books, 1988.
Le Diable c'est L'Ennui, Acte Sud, 1991.

Also author of *Forty Years of Theatrical Exploration, 1946-1987,* 1988.

OTHER SOURCES:

BOOKS

Celebrity Register, 5th edition, Gale, 1990, p. 55.
Contemporary Authors, Volume 105, Gale, 1982, pp. 87-89.

PERIODICALS

New York Times, January 22, 1989; September 28, 1989.
New York Times, January 15, 1971.
Times (London), April 2, 1989, p. C9.
Voice, February 2, 1988, pp. 97, 100.

* * *

BROOKS, James L. 1940-

PERSONAL: Born May 9, 1940, in Brooklyn, NY (one source says North Bergen, NJ); son of Edward M. and Dorothy Helen (Sheinheit) Brooks; married Marianne Catherine Morrissey, July 7, 1964 (divorced); married Holly Beth Holmberg (a television writer), July 23, 1978; children: (first marriage) Amy Lorraine; (second marriage) Chloe, Cooper. *Education:* Attended New York University, 1958-60.

ADDRESSES: Agent—International Creative Management, 8899 Beverly Blvd., Los Angeles, CA 90048. *Office*—Gracie Films/Twentieth Century-Fox, Bungalow Nine, 10201 West Pico Blvd., Los Angeles, CA 90035.

CAREER: Director, screenwriter, and producer of motion pictures and television programs. Started in television as copy boy for CBS News; news writer and reporter for CBS, 1964-66; writer and producer of documentaries for Wolper Productions, 1966-67; executive story editor for ABC-TV, Los Angeles, CA. Guest lecturer at Stanford Graduate School of Communications.

MEMBER: Directors Guild of America, Writers Guild of America, Television Academy of Arts and Sciences, Screen Actors Guild, and Academy of Motion Picture Arts and Sciences.

AWARDS, HONORS: Emmy awards, outstanding writing in a comedy series, 1971, 1974, 1975, 1976, and 1977, and outstanding comedy series, 1975, 1976, and 1977, Emmy Award nominations, outstanding comedy series, 1971, 1972, 1973, and 1974, and outstanding writing in a comedy series, 1973, Writers Guild of America award nomination, best comic episode, 1972, Peabody Award, Writers Guild of America award nomination, best teleplay, TV Critics Achievement in Comedy award, TV Critics Achievement in Series award, and Humanitas prize, Human Family Educational and Cultural Institute, all 1977, all for *The Mary Tyler Moore Show;* Golden Globe Award, 1974, Emmy Award nominations, outstanding writing in a comedy series and outstanding comedy series, both 1975, and Humanitas prizes, 1977 and 1982, all for *Rhoda;* Emmy Award, outstanding writing in drama, 1978, 1979, 1980, 1981, and 1982, Emmy Award nomination, outstanding drama series, 1978, and Peabody awards, 1977 and 1978, all for *Lou Grant;* Emmy awards, outstanding comedy series, 1979, 1980, and 1981, Emmy Award nominations, outstanding comedy series, 1982 and 1983, TV Film Critics Circle awards, achievement in comedy and achievement in a series, 1977, Golden Globe awards, best comedy series, 1978, 1979, and 1980, and Humanitas prize, 1979, all for *Taxi;* Writers Guild of America award nomination, outstanding script, 1978, for *Cindy;* Writers Guild of America award nomination, best screen comedy adaptation, 1979, for *Starting Over;* Golden Globe awards, best screenplay and best picture, Academy awards, best film, best direction, and best screenplay, and Directors Guild of America award, best director, all 1983, for *Terms of Endearment;* Academy Award nominations, best screenplay and best picture, New York Film Critics awards, best picture, best direction, and best screenplay, and Directors Guild of America award nomination, best director, all 1987, for *Broadcast News;* Emmy Award nominations, outstanding variety or comedy program, 1987, 1988, and 1990, outstanding writing in a variety or music show, 1987, 1988, and 1989, and outstanding variety, music, or comedy special, 1990, and Emmy awards, outstanding variety, music, or comedy program, 1989, and outstanding writing in a variety or music program (with others), 1990, all for *The Tracey Ullman Show;* NATO award, producer of the year, 1989; People's Choice Award, favorite comedy motion picture, 1988, for *Big;* Emmy Award nomination, outstanding animated program (for Christmas special), 1990, and Emmy awards, outstanding animated program (for series), 1990 and 1991, all for *The Simpsons.*

CREDITS:

FILM DIRECTOR

Terms of Endearment (also see below), Paramount, 1983.
Broadcast News (also see below), Twentieth Century-Fox, 1987.

FILM PRODUCER, EXCEPT WHERE NOTED

(With Alan J. Pakula) *Starting Over* (also see below), Paramount, 1979.
(With Penney Finkelman and Martin Jurow) *Terms of Endearment* (also see below), Paramount, 1983.
Between Friends, Orion, 1986.
(With Penney Finkelman Cox) *Broadcast News* (also see below), Twentieth Century-Fox, 1987.
(With Robert Greenhut) *Big,* Twentieth Century-Fox, 1988.
(Executive producer) *Say Anything,* Twentieth Century-Fox, 1989.
War of the Roses, Twentieth Century-Fox, 1989.

FILM APPEARANCES

Evaluator, *Real Life,* Paramount, 1979.
David, *Modern Romance,* Columbia, 1981.

TELEVISION EXECUTIVE PRODUCER; SERIES, EXCEPT WHERE NOTED

(And creator with Allan Burns) *The Mary Tyler Moore Show* (also see below), CBS, 1970-77.
(And creator with Burns) *Paul Sands in Friends and Lovers,* CBS, 1974-75.
(With Charlotte Brown and Burns) *Rhoda* (also see below), CBS, 1974-78.
(With Burns and Gene Reynolds) *Lou Grant* (also see below), CBS, 1977-82.
(With Stan Daniels, Ed Weinberger, and David Davis) *Taxi,* ABC, 1978-82, NBC, 1982-83.
(With Daniels and Weinberger, and creator with Daniels, Weinberger, and Charlie Hauck) *The Associates* (also see below), ABC, 1979-80, The Entertainment Channel, 1982.
(And creative consultant) *The Tracey Ullman Show* (created by Brooks, Burns, Jerry Belson, Heidi Perlman, and Ken Estin; also see below), Fox, 1986-90.
(With Matt Groening and Sam Simon) *The Simpsons,* Fox, 1990—.
(And creative consultant) *Sibs* (also known as *Grown-Ups*), ABC, 1991.
Mary Tyler Moore: The Twentieth Anniversary Show (special), CBS, 1991.

TELEVISION PRODUCER, EXCEPT WHERE NOTED

Creator, *Room 222* (series), ABC, 1969.
(With Burns), *Friends and Lovers* (pilot; also see below), CBS, 1974.
Thursday's Game (film; also see below), ABC, 1974.
(With Daniels, Davis, and Weinberger), *Cindy* (film; also see below), ABC, 1978.

TELEVISION APPEARANCES

The Forty-first Annual Emmy Awards, Fox, 1989.
Naked Hollywood, Arts and Entertainment, 1991.

WRITINGS:

SCREENPLAYS FOR FILMS

Starting Over, Paramount, 1979.
Terms of Endearment, Paramount, 1983.
Broadcast News, Twentieth Century-Fox, 1987.

SCREENPLAYS FOR TELEVISION FILMS

Thursday's Game, ABC, 1974.
(With Daniels and Davis) *Cindy,* ABC, 1978.
(With others) *The Munsters' Revenge,* NBC, 1981.

SCREENPLAYS FOR TELEVISION; SERIES, EXCEPT WHERE NOTED

(With Ernie Frankel and Robert Hamner) *My Friend Tony,* NBC, 1969.
(With others) *The Mary Tyler Moore Show,* CBS, 1970-77.
(With Michael Zagor) *Going Places* (pilot), NBC, 1973.
(With Burns) *Friends and Lovers,* CBS, 1974.
(With others) *Rhoda,* CBS, 1974-78.
(With Lorenzo Music, Carl Gottlieb, Jerry Davis, and Burns) *The New Lorenzo Music Show* (pilot), ABC, 1976.
(With Burns) *Lou Grant,* CBS, 1977-82.
(With Burns) *The Associates,* ABC, 1979-80, The Entertainment Channel, 1982.
(With Burns) *Duck Factory,* NBC, 1984.
(With Burns) *The Tracey Ullman Show,* Fox, 1986-90.
(With Burns) *The Days and Nights of Molly Dodd,* NBC, 1987-88, Lifetime, 1989.
(With Burns) *Eisenhower and Lutz,* CBS, 1988.

OTHER SOURCES:

PERIODICALS

New York Times, April 8, 1984; January 7, 1988, p. C19.
Premiere, February, 1988, pp. 84 and 86.*

BROOKS, Richard 1912-1992

PERSONAL: Born May 18, 1912, in Philadelphia, PA; died of congestive heart failure, March 11, 1992, in Beverly Hills, CA; married Harriett Levin, 1945 (marriage ended); married Jean Simmons (an actress), 1961 (divorced, 1976); children: Kate, Tracy. *Education:* Attended Temple University; trained as a journalist.

CAREER: Producer, director, and screenwriter. Metro-Goldwyn-Mayer, Hollywood, CA, director, beginning in 1946; independent film producer, beginning in 1965. Reporter for *Atlantic City Press Union,* beginning in 1932; reporter for *New York World Telegram;* radio writer, narrator, and commentator for National Broadcasting Company (NBC); director for Mill Pond Theatre, New York City, beginning in 1940. *Military service:* U.S. Marine Corps.

MEMBER: Writers Guild of America, Academy of Motion Picture Arts and Sciences, Directors Guild of America.

AWARDS, HONORS: Academy Award nomination, best screenplay, 1955, for *The Blackboard Jungle;* Academy Award nominations, best screenplay based on material from another medium and best director, both 1958, both for *Cat on a Hot Tin Roof;* Academy Award, best screenplay based on material from another medium, and Writers Guild of America Best-Written American Drama Award, both 1960, both for *Elmer Gantry;* Academy Award nominations, best screenplay based on material from another medium and best director, both 1966, both for *The Professionals;* Academy Award nominations for best screenplay based on material from another medium and best director, and Writers Guild of America Laurel Award, all 1967, all for *In Cold Blood;* Lifetime Achievement Award, joint award from Writers Guild of America West and Directors Guild of America, 1990.

CREDITS:

FILM WORK; DIRECTOR

Crisis (also see below), Metro-Goldwyn-Mayer (MGM), 1950.
The Light Touch (also see below), MGM, 1951.
Deadline U.S.A. (also see below), Twentieth Century-Fox, 1952.
Take the High Ground, MGM, 1953.
Battle Circus (also see below), MGM, 1953.
The Last Time I Saw Paris (also see below), MGM, 1954.
The Flame and the Flesh, MGM, 1954.
The Blackboard Jungle (also see below), MGM, 1955.
The Last Hunt (also see below), MGM, 1956.
The Catered Affair (released in England as *Wedding Breakfast*), MGM, 1956.
Something of Value (also see below), MGM, 1957.
The Brothers Karamazov (also see below), MGM, 1958.
Cat on a Hot Tin Roof (also see below), MGM, 1958.
Elmer Gantry (also see below), United Artists (UA), 1960.
Sweet Bird of Youth (also see below), MGM, 1962.
(And producer) *Lord Jim* (also see below), Columbia, 1965.
(And producer) *The Professionals* (also see below), Columbia, 1966.
(And producer) *In Cold Blood* (also see below), Columbia, 1967.
(And producer) *The Happy Ending* (also see below), UA, 1969.
$ ([*Dollars*]; released in England as *The Heist*; also see below), Columbia, 1971.
(And producer) *Bite the Bullet* (also see below), Columbia, 1975.
Looking for Mr. Goodbar (also see below), Paramount, 1977.
(And producer) *Wrong Is Right* (also see below), Columbia, 1982.
Fever Pitch (also see below), MGM/UA, 1985.

WRITINGS:

SCREENPLAYS, EXCEPT WHERE INDICATED

White Savage (based on the story by Peter Milne), Universal, 1943.
(With Gene Lewis) *Cobra Woman* (based on the story by W. Scott Darling), Universal, 1944.
My Best Gal (story), Republic, 1944.
Swell Guy (based on Gilbert Emery's play *The Hero*), Universal-International, 1947.
Brute Force (based on the story by Robert Patterson), Universal-International, 1947.
To the Victor, Warner Brothers, 1948.
(With John Huston) *Key Largo,* Warner Brothers, 1948.
Any Number Can Play (based on the novel by Edward Heth), Metro-Goldwyn-Mayer (MGM), 1949.
(With Sydney Boehm) *Mystery Street* (based on the story by Leonard Spigelgass), MGM, 1950.
(With Daniel Fuchs) *Storm Warning,* Warner Brothers, 1950.
Crisis (based on George Tabori's *The Doubters*), MGM, 1950.
The Light Touch (based on the story by J. Harris and T. Reed), MGM, 1951.
Deadline U.S.A., Twentieth Century-Fox, 1952.
Battle Circus (based on the story by Allen Rinkin and Laura Kerr), MGM, 1953.
(With Julius J. Epstein and Philip G. Epstein) *The Last Time I Saw Paris* (based on *Babylon Revisited* by F. Scott Fitzgerald), MGM, 1954.
The Blackboard Jungle (based on the novel by Evan Hunter), MGM, 1955.

The Last Hunt (based on the novel by Milton Lott), MGM, 1956.
Something of Value (based on the novel by Robert C. Ruark), MGM, 1957.
The Brothers Karamazov (based on the novel by Fyodor Dostoyevsky) MGM, 1958.
(With James Poe) *Cat on a Hot Tin Roof,* (based on the play by Tennessee Williams), MGM, 1958.
Elmer Gantry (based on the novel by Sinclair Lewis), UA, 1960.
Sweet Bird of Youth (based on the play by Tennessee Williams), MGM, 1962.
Lord Jim (based on the novel by Joseph Conrad), Columbia, 1965.
The Professionals (based on *A Mule for the Marquesa* by Frank O'Rourke), Columbia, 1966.
In Cold Blood (based on the novel by Truman Capote), Columbia, 1967.
The Happy Ending, UA, 1969.
$ ([*Dollars*]; released in England as *The Heist*), Columbia, 1971.
Bite the Bullet, Columbia, 1975.
Looking for Mr. Goodbar (based on the novel by Judith Rossner), Paramount, 1977.
Wrong Is Right (based on the novel by Charles McCarry), Columbia, 1982.
Fever Pitch, MGM/UA, 1985.

ADDITIONAL DIALOGUE FOR FILMS

Men of Texas, Universal, 1942.
Sin Town, Universal, 1942.
Don Winslow of the Coast Guard, Universal, 1943.

NOVELS

The Brick Foxhole, Harper, 1945.
The Boiling Point, Harper, 1948.
The Producer, Simon & Schuster, 1951.

ADAPTATIONS: The Brick Foxhole was adapted as the film *Crossfire* by RKO Radio Pictures, 1947.

OBITUARIES AND OTHER SOURCES:

BOOKS

The International Dictionary of Films and Filmmakers, Volume 2, St. James Press, 1984.

PERIODICALS

Hollywood Reporter, March 12, 1992, pp. 1, 8.*

* * *

BROWNE, Coral 1913-1991

OBITUARY NOTICE—See index for *CTFT* sketch: Born July 23, 1913, in Melbourne, Australia; died of breast cancer, May 29, 1991, in Los Angeles, CA. Performer. Browne began her career as a vaudeville and comedy actress in the early 1930s in Melbourne, Australia, before moving to London in 1934, where she became known for her comic portrayals in such productions as *Lover's Leap* and *The Man Who Came to Dinner.* In the 1950s the actress shifted her focus to drama, appearing as Lady Macbeth in *Macbeth* and as Helen in *Troilus and Cressida.* It was on a Soviet tour of *Hamlet* that Browne encountered British spy Guy Burgess. The meeting inspired *An Englishman Abroad,* a televised film for which Browne received the 1983 best actress award from the British Academy of Film and Television Arts. In addition to her later stage performances in *Charley's Aunt* and *The Importance of Being Earnest,* Browne appeared in several motion pictures during the 1970s and 1980s, including *The Ruling Class* and *American Dreamer.* Browne met horror-film actor Vincent Price during the filming of the 1971 film *Theater of Blood,* and they were married three years later.

OBITUARIES AND OTHER SOURCES:

BOOKS

Who's Who, 1991, St. Martin's, 1991, p. 241.

PERIODICALS

Variety, June 3, 1991, p. 69; March 16, 1992, p. 75.

* * *

BRYCELAND, Yvonne 1925-1992

OBITUARY NOTICE—See index for *CTFT* sketch: Born November 18, 1925, in Cape Town, South Africa; died of cancer, January 13, 1992, in London, England. Performer. Bryceland is best known for her work in the productions of contemporary South African playwright and actor Athol Fugard. She began her career as a stage actress in Cape Town in the late 1940s with credits in *Stage Door, Ring round the Moon,* and *The Chalk Garden.* Bryceland first worked with Fugard in 1969, when she starred in his *People are Living There,* and she later appeared in *Boesman and Lena,* Fugard's play about a black homeless couple, and in *Statements after an Arrest under the Immorality Act.* In 1972 Bryceland cofounded the Cape Town Space Theatre—one of the first racially integrated theatres in South Africa—with her husband, Brian Astbury. There Bryceland appeared in *The Glass Menagerie* and in the title role in *Medea.* Bryceland moved to London in 1978, the same year that South African theatres integrated, because she continued to feel frustrated with the country's racist policies. Bryceland's portrayal of an unconventional artist in Fugard's *The Road to Mecca*—which marked her New York theatre debut—earned her several best actress prizes, both in New York and in London. Bryceland reprised her roles in *People are Living There* and *Hello and Goodbye* for television, and in *Boesman and Lena* and *The Road to Mecca* for film.

OBITUARIES AND OTHER SOURCES:

PERIODICALS

New York Times, April 10, 1988, pp. 1, 51.
Variety, January 20, 1992, p. 154.

* * *

BUMSTEAD, Henry 1915-

PERSONAL: Born March 17, 1915, in Ontario, CA; son of Lloyd and Emma Bumstead; married, first wife's name, Betty, 1937 (marriage ended), married, second wife's name, Lena, 1983; children: four children by first marriage. *Education:* University of Southern California, B.A., 1937.

ADDRESSES: Agent—Smith/Gosnell Agency, Inc., 1515 Palisades Dr., Suite N, Pacific Palisades, CA 90272.

CAREER: Art director and production designer.

MEMBER: International Alliance of Theatrical Stage Employees and Moving Picture Machine Operators of the United States and Canada.

AWARDS, HONORS: Academy Award nomination (with Hal Pereira), best art direction—set decoration, 1958, for *Vertigo;* Academy Award (with Alexander Golitzen), best art direction—set decoration, 1962, for *To Kill a Mockingbird;* Academy Award, best art direction—set decoration, 1973, for *The Sting.*

CREDITS:

FILM WORK; ART DIRECTOR

(With Hans Dreier) *Saigon,* Paramount, 1948.
(With Dreier) *The Sainted Sisters,* Paramount, 1948.
(With Dreier) *My Own True Love,* Paramount, 1948.
(With Dreier) *Song of Surrender,* Paramount, 1949.
(With Dreier) *Top o' the Morning,* Paramount, 1949.
(With Dreier) *My Friend Irma,* Paramount, 1949.
(With Dreier) *Streets of Laredo,* Paramount, 1949.
(With Dreier) *The Furies,* Paramount, 1950.
(With Dreier) *No Man of Her Own* (also known as *The Lie*), Paramount, 1950.
(With Dreier) *My Friend Irma Goes West,* Paramount, 1950.
(With Hal Pereira) *The Goldbergs* (also known as *Molly*), Paramount, 1950.
(With Pereira) *The Redhead and the Cowboy,* Paramount, 1950.
(With Pereira) *Rhubarb,* Paramount, 1951.
(With Pereira) *Submarine Command,* Paramount, 1951.
(With Pereira) *Jumping Jacks,* Paramount, 1952.
(With Pereira) *The Stars Are Singing,* Paramount, 1953.
(With Pereira) *Little Boy Lost,* Paramount, 1953.
(With Pereira) *The Bridges at Toko-Ri,* Paramount, 1954.
(With Pereira) *Run for Cover,* Paramount, 1955.
(With Pereira) *Lucy Gallant* (also known as *Oil Town*), Paramount, 1955.
(With Pereira) *The Man Who Knew Too Much,* Paramount, 1956.
(With Pereira) *That Certain Feeling,* Paramount, 1956.
(With Pereira) *The Leather Saint,* Paramount, 1956.
(With Pereira) *The Vagabond King,* Paramount, 1956.
(With Pereira) *Hollywood or Bust,* Paramount, 1956.
(With Pereira) *I Married a Monster from Outer Space,* Paramount, 1958.
(With Pereira) *Vertigo,* Paramount, 1958.
(With Pereira) *The Hangman,* Paramount, 1959.
(With Pereira) *The Bellboy,* Paramount, 1960.
(With Pereira) *Cinderfella,* Paramount, 1961.
Come September, Universal, 1961.
(With Alexander Golitzen) *The Spiral Road,* Universal, 1962.
(With Golitzen) *To Kill a Mockingbird,* Universal, 1962.
(With Golitzen) *A Gathering of Eagles,* Universal, 1964.
(With Golitzen) *Father Goose,* Universal, 1964.
(With Golitzen) *The War Lord,* Universal, 1965.
(With Golitzen) *Gunpoint,* Universal, 1966.
(With Golitzen) *Tobruk,* Universal, 1966.
(With Golitzen) *The Secret War of Harry Frigg,* Universal, 1968.
(With Golitzen) *What's So Bad about Feeling Good?* Universal, 1968.
(With Golitzen) *Tell Them Willie Boy Is Here,* Universal, 1969.
(With Golitzen) *A Man Called Gannon,* Universal, 1969.
(With Golitzen) *One More Train to Rob,* Universal, 1971.
(With Golitzen) *Raid on Rommel,* Universal, 1971.
(With Golitzen) *Joe Kidd,* Universal, 1972.
High Plains Drifter, Universal, 1973.
The Sting, Universal, 1973.
(With Golitzen) *Showdown,* Universal, 1973.
The Front Page, Universal, 1974.
The Great Waldo Pepper, Universal, 1975.

Also worked as art director for *Aaron Slick from Punkin Crick,* 1952; *Come Back, Little Sheba,* 1952; *Knock on Wood,* 1954; *As Young as We Are,* 1958; *The Great Imposter,* 1961; *The Brass Bottle,* 1964; *Bullet for a Badman,* 1964; *Beau geste,* 1966; *Blindfold,* 1966; and *Banning,* 1967.

FILM WORK; PRODUCTION DESIGNER

Topaz, Universal, 1969.
Slaughterhouse-Five (also see below), Universal, 1972.

Family Plot, Universal, 1976.
Slap Shot, Universal, 1977.
Rollercoaster, Universal, 1977.
Same Time Next Year, Universal, 1978.
House Calls, Universal, 1978.
The Concorde—Airport '79 (also known as *Airport 80: The Concorde*), Universal, 1979.
A Little Romance, Orion, 1979.
Smokey and the Bandit, Part II (also known as *Smokey and the Bandit Ride Again*), Universal, 1980.
The World according to Garp, Warner Brothers, 1982.
Harry and Son, Orion, 1984.
The Little Drummer Girl, Warner Brothers, 1984.
Warning Sign, Twentieth Century-Fox, 1985.
Psycho III, Universal, 1986.
Funny Farm, Warner Brothers, 1988.
A Time of Destiny, Columbia, 1988.
Her Alibi, Warner Brothers, 1989.
Ghost Dad, Universal, 1990.
Almost an Angel, Paramount, 1990.
Cape Fear, Universal, 1991.

FILM APPEARANCES

Elliot Rosewater, *Slaughterhouse-Five,* Universal, 1972.
Colonel in Italy, *A Time of Destiny,* Columbia, 1988.

TELEVISION WORK; ART DIRECTOR; MOVIES

The Movie Murderer, NBC, 1970.
McCloud: Who Killed Miss U.S.A.? (also known as *Portrait of a Dead Girl,* NBC, 1970.
The Adventures of Nick Carter, NBC, 1972.
Don't Push, I'll Charge When I'm Ready, NBC, 1977.
Amateur Night at the Dixie Bar and Grill, NBC, 1979.

Also worked as art director for *The Birdmen,* 1971; *The Victim,* 1972; and *Honky Tonk,* 1974.

TELEVISION WORK; ART DIRECTOR; PILOTS

Laugh!s (also known as *Laughs, Funny Farm,* and *Catch a Rising Star*), Showtime, 1990.

OTHER SOURCES:

PERIODICALS

American Cinematographer, May, 1974.
Premiere, December, 1991.

* * *

BURNS, Francis
See GELBART, Larry

BURROUGHS, William S. 1914-
(William Lee)

PERSONAL: Full name, William Seward Burroughs; born February 5, 1914, in St. Louis, MO; son of Perry Mortimer (in business) and Laura (Lee) Burroughs; married Ilse Herzfeld Klapper, 1937 (divorced, 1946); married Joan Vollmer Adams, January 17, 1946 (accidentally shot and killed by Burroughs, 1951); children: (second marriage) William S. Burroughs, Jr. (deceased). *Education:* Harvard University, A.B., 1936; graduate work at Harvard University; studied medicine in Vienna.

ADDRESSES: Office—c/o James Grauerholz, William Burroughs Communications, P.O. Box 147, Lawrence, KS 66044. *Agent*—Andrew Wylie, Wylie, Aitken & Stone Inc., 250 West 57th St., Suite 2106, New York, NY 10107; Gillon Aitken and Sally Riley, Aitken & Stone Ltd., 29 Fernshaw Rd., London SW10 0TG, England. *Publicist*—Ira P. Silverberg, Ira Silverberg Communications, 401 West Broadway, #2, New York, NY 10012.

CAREER: Writer and actor. Worked as a private detective, exterminator, factory worker, bartender, newspaper reporter, and advertising copywriter, 1936-44. Lecturer, City College of New York, and Naropa Institute for Contemplative Education, Boulder, CO; appeared at international conventions on psychoanalysis in Milan, 1980, and New York City, 1981. *Military service:* Entered the U.S. Army 1942, and discharged six months later for psychological reasons.

MEMBER: American Academy and Institute of Arts and Letters, Commander de l'Ordre des Arts et des Lettres.

AWARDS, HONORS: A series of lectures, panels, films, exhibitions, theater performances, readings, and concerts were held in Burroughs's honor at the Nova Convention, New York, 1978, the Final Academy, London, 1982, and the River City Reunion, Lawrence, KS, 1987.

CREDITS:

STAGE APPEARANCES

Has given over 160 public readings from his works in Europe and the United States, 1965-89.

FILM APPEARANCES

Opium Jones, *Chappaqua,* Regional, 1967.
Mafia Don, *It Don't Pay to Be an Honest Man* (also known as *It Don't Pay to Be an Honest Citizen*), Object, 1985.
Home of the Brave, Cinecom, 1986.
Tom the priest, *Drugstore Cowboy,* Avenue, 1989.
Man in barn, *Twister,* Vestron, 1989.
A Thanksgiving Prayer (also see below), Island, 1990.

Also appeared in *Bill and Tony* (also see below), 1962; *Towers Open Fire* (also see below), 1963; *The Cut-Ups* (also see below), 1965; *Underground and Emigrants,* 1976; Energy Czar, *Energy and How to Get It,* 1981; *Poetry in Motion,* 1982; *Fried Shoes, Cooked Diamonds,* 1982; *Kerouac,* 1983; *Burroughs,* 1983; *What Happened to Kerouac?,* 1985; *The Beat Generation—An American Dream,* 1987; Butler, *Bloodhounds of Broadway,* 1989; *Heavy Petting,* 1989; *Rub Out the Word,* 1989; *Ghosts at No. 9.*

FILM WORK

Burroughs collaborated with Brion Gysin and Antony Balch on three short films, *Bill and Tony,* 1962, *Towers Open Fire,* 1963, and *The Cut-Ups,* 1965.

TELEVISION APPEARANCES

Saturday Night Live (episode), NBC, 1981.
A Thanksgiving Prayer, USA, 1990.

RECORDINGS:

Author of "Call Me Burroughs," 1965; "William S. Burroughs/John Giorno," 1975; "You're the Guy I Want to Share My Money With," 1981; "Nothing Here Now but The Recordings," 1981; "Abandoned Artifacts b/w on the Nova Lark," 1981; "Revolutions per Minute (The Art Record)," 1982; "Myths, I.," 1983; "Mister Heartbreak," 1984; "Break Through in Grey Room," 1986; "Seven Souls," 1990; "Dead City Radio," 1990.

WRITINGS:

STAGE

Naked Lunch (based on Burroughs's book of the same title; also see below), New York Shakespeare Festival, Public Theatre, New York City, 1974.
The Last Words of Dutch Schultz (also see below), first produced at Prop Theater, Chicago, 1988.
The Junky's Christmas, first produced at Prop Theater, 1990.
(Author of libretto) *The Black Rider,* music by Robert Wilson with songs by Tom Waits, first produced at Thalia Theater, Hamburg, Germany, 1990.

SCREENPLAYS

(With Tom Huckabee and Paul Cullum) *Taking Tiger Mountain,* The Players Chess Club, 1983.

OTHER

(As William Lee) *Junkie: Confessions of an Unredeemed Drug Addict* (bound with *Narcotic Agent,* by Maurice Helbrant), Ace, 1953, published under name William S. Burroughs, Ace, 1964, published as *Junky,* Penguin, 1977.
The Naked Lunch, Olympia (Paris), 1959, reprinted as *Naked Lunch,* Grove, 1962.
(With Gregory Corso and Brion Gysin) *Minutes to Go,* Two Cities (Paris), 1960, Beach Books, 1968.
(With Gysin) *The Exterminator,* Auerhahn, 1960.
(Contributor) *A Casebook on the Beat,* Crowell, 1961.
The Soft Machine (also see below), Olympia, 1962, Grove, 1966.
The Ticket That Exploded, Olympia, 1962, Grove, 1967.
Dead Fingers Talk, Olympia, 1963.
(With Allen Ginsberg) *The Yage Letters,* City Lights, 1963.
Nova Express (also see below), Grove, 1964.
Time, "C" Press, 1965.
Darazt, Lovebooks, 1965.
The White Subway (also see below), Aloes Books, 1965.
Valentine's Day Reading, American Theatre of Poets, 1965.
Health Bulletin APO-33: A Metabolic Regulator, F— You Press, 1965, published as *APO-33: A Report on the Synthesis of the Apomorphine Formula,* Beach, 1966.
(With Claude Pelieu and Carl Weissner) *So Who Owns Death TV?,* Beach Book Texts and Documents, 1967.
They Do Not Always Remember, Delacorte, 1968.
(Author of preface) Jeff Nuttall, *Pig,* Fulcrum Press, 1969.
Ali's Smile, Unicorn Books, 1969.
The Dead Star, Nova Broadcast Press, 1969.
(With Daniel Odier) *Entretiens avec William Burroughs,* Editions Pierre Belfond, 1969, revised and enlarged edition published as *The Job: Interviews with William S. Burroughs,* Grove, 1970, 2nd revised and enlarged edition, 1974.
The Last Words of Dutch Schultz, Cape Goliard Press, 1970, expanded edition published as *The Last Words of Dutch Schultz: A Fiction in the Form of a Film Script,* Viking, 1975.
(With Gysin) *The Third Mind,* Grove, 1970.
(With Weissner) *The Braille Film,* Nova Broadcast Press, 1970.
Electronic Revolution and Other Writings, Blackmoor Head Press, 1971.
The Wild Boys: A Book of the Dead (also see below), Grove, 1971.
(With Pelieu) *Jack Kerouac* (in French), L'Herne (Paris), 1971.
(With Gysin and Ian Somerville) *Brion Gysin Let the Mice In,* Something Else Press, 1973.
Mayfair Academy Series More or Less, Urgency Press Rip-Off, 1973.
Exterminator!, Viking/Richard Seaver, 1974.
The Book of Breeething, OU Press (Ingatestone, England), 1974, Blue Wind, 1975, 2nd edition, 1980.
Port of Saints, Covent Garden Press, 1975, Blue Wind Press, 1979.
(With Charles Gatewood) *Sidetripping,* Strawberry Hill, 1975.

(With Eric Mottram) *Snack: Two Tape Transcripts,* Aloes Books, 1975.

Cobblestone Gardens (also see below), Cherry Valley Editions, 1976.

The Retreat Diaries (also see below), City Moon, 1976.

Naked Scientology, Expanded Media Productions (Bonn, West Germany), 1978.

Doctor Benway: A Variant Passage from "The Naked Lunch," Bradford Morrow, 1979.

Roosevelt after Inauguration and Other Atrocities, City Lights, 1979.

Ah Pook Is Here, Calder, 1979.

Blade Runner: A Movie, Blue Wind Press, 1979.

The Soft Machine, Nova Express, [and] *The Wild Boys,* Grove, 1980.

Early Routines, Cadmus Editions, 1981.

Cities of the Red Night, Holt, 1981.

Letters to Allen Ginsberg, 1953-1957, Full Court Press, 1981.

A William Burroughs Reader, Pan Books, 1982.

(Contributor) Roger Ely, editor, *The Final Academy: Statements of a Kind,* Final Academy, 1982.

The Place of Dead Roads, Holt, 1984.

The Burroughs File (includes *The White Subway, Cobblestone Gardens,* and *The Retreat Diaries*), City Lights, 1984.

Queer, Viking, 1985.

The Adding Machine: Collected Essays, Calder, 1985, Seaver, 1986.

The Western Lands, Viking, 1987.

Interzone, Viking, 1989.

Also author of *Takis,* an exhibition catalog, 1963; author (with Pelieu and Weissner) of *Fernseh-Tuberkulose,* 1969; and (with Jack Kerouac) "And the Hippos Were Boiled in Their Tanks," an unpublished novel, 1944. Also composer of song, "Old Lady Sloan," recorded by Mortal Micronotz, 1982. Contributor to periodicals, including *Evergreen Review* and *Harper's.*

ADAPTATIONS: Paul Stephen Lim adapted *Queer* in his stage production, *Lee and the Boys in the Backroom,* first produced at Lawrence Community Theatre, Lawrence, KS, 1987; *The Last Words of Dutch Schultz* has been optioned for film production.

OTHER SOURCES:

BOOKS

Maynard, Joe, and Barry Miles, editors, *William S. Burroughs: A Bibliography, 1953-1973,* University of Virginia Press, 1978.

BURROWS, James 1940-

PERSONAL: Born December 30, 1940, in Los Angeles, CA; son of Abe (a writer, composer, and director) and Ruth Burrows. *Education:* Received B.A. from Oberlin College; received M.F.A. from Yale University.

ADDRESSES: Contact—c/o Bob Broder, Broder, Kurland, Webb, Uffner, 8439 Sunset Blvd., Suite 402, Los Angeles, CA 90069.

CAREER: Director.

AWARDS, HONORS: Emmy Awards, outstanding directing in a comedy series, 1980 and 1981, and Emmy Award nomination, outstanding directing in a comedy series, 1982, all for *Taxi;* Emmy Awards, outstanding directing in a comedy series, 1983 and 1991, Emmy Award nominations, outstanding directing in a comedy series, 1984, 1985, 1986, 1987, 1988, 1989, and 1990, Emmy Awards, outstanding comedy series, 1983, 1984, 1989, and 1991, Emmy Award nominations, outstanding comedy series, 1985, 1986, 1987, 1988, and 1990, and Outstanding Directorial Achievement Award for Television, Directors Guild of America, 1990, all for *Cheers;* Emmy Award nomination, outstanding informational special, 1990, for *Cheers: Special 200th Episode Celebration.*

CREDITS:

TELEVISION WORK; SERIES; DIRECTOR, EXCEPT AS NOTED

(With Jay Sandrich, Doug Rogers, and others) *The Mary Tyler Moore Show,* CBS, 1970-77.

(With Michael Zinberg, Richard Kinon, and others) *The Bob Newhart Show,* CBS, 1972-78.

(With Robert Morse, Jay Sandrich, Alan Rafkin, and others) *Paul Sand in Friends and Lovers,* CBS, 1974-75.

(With Alan Rafkin, Tony Mordente, and others) *Rhoda,* CBS, 1974-78.

(With Richard Kinon and Alan Arkin) *Fay,* NBC, 1975-76.

(With Mel Shapiro, Doug Rogers, Joan Darling, Noam Pitlik, and others) *Phyllis,* CBS, 1975-77.

(With Michael Zinberg, Asaad Kelada, Tony Mordente, Harvey Medlinsky, and others) *The Tony Randall Show,* ABC, 1976-77, then CBS, 1977-78.

(With Alan Rafkin, Alan Myerson, Jay Sandrich, and others) *Laverne and Shirley,* ABC, 1976-83.

(With Tony Mordente, Alan Myerson, and others) *Busting Loose,* CBS, 1977.

(With Michael Zinberg, Lee H. Bernhardi, Will MacKenzie, Tony Mordente, and Harvey Medlinsky) *We've Got Each Other,* CBS, 1977-78.

(With Doug Rogers, Burt Brinckerhoff, Harvey Medlinsky, Bill Persky, and Noam Pitlik) *The Betty White Show,* CBS, 1977-78.

(With Lee H. Bernhardi, Charles W. Liotta, Noam Pitlik, Mel Shapiro, and Doug Rogers) *On Our Own,* CBS, 1977-78.

(With Peter Bonerz, Alan Myerson, Jeremiah Morris, and Richard S. Harwood) *Szysznyk,* CBS, 1977-78.

(With Gene Reynolds, Alexander Singer, and others) *Lou Grant,* CBS, 1977-82.

(With Hal Cooper) *Free Country,* ABC, 1978.

(With Alan Myerson, Bill Persky, and Marc Daniels) *Husbands, Wives and Lovers,* CBS, 1978.

(With Howard Storm, Jerry Paris, Joel Zwick, and Marty Cohan) *The Ted Knight Show,* CBS, 1978.

(With Will MacKenzie, Noam Pitlik, Danny DeVito, and others) *Taxi,* ABC, 1978-82, then NBC, 1982-83.

(With Tony Mordente) *The Associates,* ABC, 1979-80, then TEC, 1982.

(With Jeff Bleckner, Jay Sandrich, and Will MacKenzie) *The Stockard Channing Show,* CBS, 1980.

(With Jeff Chambers, Steve Gordon, and Mark Gordon) *Good Time Harry,* NBC, 1980.

(With Will MacKenzie, Doug Rogers, Jeff Chambers, Ed Weinberger, and Howard Storm) *Best of the West,* ABC, 1981-82.

(And creator with Glen Charles and Les Charles; producer with Glen Charles, Les Charles, Ken Levine, and David Isaacs; and executive producer with Glen Charles and Les Charles) *Cheers,* NBC, 1982—.

(With Asaad Kelada, Jay Sandrich, Reinhold Weege, and Jeff Melman) *Night Court,* NBC, beginning in 1984.

(And executive producer) *All Is Forgiven,* NBC, 1986.

(And executive producer) *The Tortellis,* NBC, 1987.

The Marshall Chronicles, ABC, 1990.

The Fanelli Boys (also known as *The Boys Are Back*), NBC, 1990.

Executive producer (with Glen Charles and Les Charles) and consultant, *Flesh 'n' Blood* (also see below), NBC, 1991.

TELEVISION WORK; PILOTS; DIRECTOR

Bumpers, NBC, 1977.

Calling Dr. Storm, M.D., NBC, 1977.

Roosevelt and Truman, CBS, 1977.

The Plant Family, CBS, 1978.

Your Place or Mine?, CBS, 1978.

Butterflies, NBC, 1979.

Every Stray Dog and Kid, NBC, 1981.

Goodbye Doesn't Mean Forever, NBC, 1982.

At Your Service, NBC, 1984.

P.O.P., NBC, 1984.

"In the Lion's Den," *CBS Summer Playhouse,* CBS, 1987.

Channel 99, NBC, 1988.

Down Home, NBC, 1990.

Wings, NBC, 1990.

Roc, Fox, 1991.

Flesh 'n' Blood, NBC, 1991.

Pacific Station, NBC, 1991.

TELEVISION WORK; SPECIALS

Director, *Big Shots in America,* NBC, 1985.

Segment director, *Time Warner Presents the Earth Day Special,* ABC, 1990.

Segment director, "Cheers," *Disneyland's 35th Anniversary Celebration,* NBC, 1990.

Director and executive producer, *Cheers: Special 200th Episode Celebration,* NBC, 1990.

TELEVISION WORK; EPISODIC; DIRECTOR

The Hogan Family (also known as *Valerie* and *Valerie's Family*), NBC, 1986-90, then CBS, 1990.

Dear John, NBC, beginning in 1988.

TELEVISION WORK; MOVIES; DIRECTOR

More Than Friends, ABC, 1978.

TELEVISION APPEARANCES

The 43rd Annual Primetime Emmy Awards Presentation, Fox, 1991.

STAGE WORK; DIRECTOR

The Castro Complex, Stairway Theatre, 1970.

Last of the Red Hot Lovers, Arlington Park Theatre, Arlington Heights, IL, 1972-73.

Goodbye, Charlie, Arlington Park Theatre, 1972-73.

Charley's Aunt, Arlington Park Theatre, 1972-73.

FILM WORK; DIRECTOR

Partners, Paramount, 1982.*

* * *

BURTT, Ben 1948-

PERSONAL: Full name, Benjamin Burtt, Jr.; born in 1948, in Syracuse, NY; *Education:* Allegheny College, B.S. in physics; studied film at University of Southern California.

CAREER: Sound technician. Sound designer for Lucasfilm; sound designer for radio series *Star Wars.*

AWARDS, HONORS: Academy Award, special achievement, 1977, for *Star Wars;* Academy Award, special achievement, 1981, for *Raiders of the Lost Ark;* Academy Award, sound effects editing, 1982, for *E.T.—The Extra-Terrestrial;* Academy Award nominations, sound effects editing and sound, both 1984, for *Return of the Jedi;* Academy Award nomination, best achievement in sound effects, 1988, for *Willow;* Academy Award, best achievement in sound effects editing, and Academy Award nomination, best achievement in sound, both 1989, for *Indiana Jones and the Last Crusade.*

CREDITS:

FILM WORK; SOUND TECHNICIAN

The Milpitas Monster, Samuel Golden Ayer Productions, 1976.
Star Wars (also known as *Star Wars, Episode 4: A New Hope*), Twentieth Century-Fox, 1977.
The Invasion of the Body Snatchers, United Artists (UA), 1978.
More American Graffiti, Universal, 1979.
The Empire Strikes Back, Twentieth Century-Fox, 1980.
Raiders of the Lost Ark, Paramount, 1981.
E.T.—The Extra-Terrestrial, Universal, 1982.
The Dark Crystal, Universal, 1982.
Return of the Jedi (also known as *Star Wars: Episode 6*), Twentieth Century-Fox, 1983.
Indiana Jones and the Temple of Doom, Paramount, 1984.
The Dream Is Alive (documentary), Imax Corp., 1985.
Nutcracker: The Motion Picture, Atlantic Releasing, 1986.
Howard the Duck, Universal, 1986.
Willow, Metro-Goldwyn-Mayer/UA, 1988.
Always, Universal, 1989.
Blue Planet (documentary), Imax Corp., 1990.
The True Story of "Glory" Continues, Columbia, 1991.

Also worked as editor and sound technician for *Niagara: Miracles, Myths, and Magic* (also see below), 1992.

FILM WORK; DIRECTOR

Blue Planet (documentary), Imax Corp., 1990.
The True Story of "Glory" Continues, Columbia, 1991.

OTHER FILM WORK

Also worked on *Indiana Jones and the Last Crusade,* Paramount, 1989.

TELEVISION WORK; SOUND TECHNICIAN

Worked on the British television movie *Killdozer,* 1974.

TELEVISION APPEARANCES; SERIES

SST: Screen, Stage, Television, ABC, 1989.

WRITINGS:

The Great Heep (television special), ABC, 1986.

Also screenwriter, with Kieth Merrill, of *Niagara: Miracles, Myths, and Magic,* 1992.

OTHER SOURCES:

PERIODICALS

Film Comment, November-December, 1983.*

BUSCH, Charles 1954-

PERSONAL: Born August 23, 1954, in New York, NY. *Education:* Graduated from New York's High School of Music and Art; received degree in drama from Northwestern University.

ADDRESSES: *Office*—Theatre-in-Limbo, 123 West 3rd St., Suite C, New York, NY 10012. *Agent*—Gregory Lane, William Morris Agency, 1350 Avenue of the Americas, New York, NY 10019.

CAREER: Actor and playwright. Worked variously as a quick-sketch portrait artist and an office receptionist. Cofounder, actor, and writer for Theatre-in-Limbo, which was originally formed to do *Vampire Lesbians of Sodom* as a lark.

AWARDS, HONORS: Charlie Local and National Comedy Award, Association of Comedy Artists, 1985, for special contribution to the art of comedy.

CREDITS:

STAGE APPEARANCES

Hollywood Confidential (one-man show; also see below), One Sheridan Square Theatre, New York City, 1978.
(Off-Broadway debut) Fauna Alexander, "Sleeping Beauty or Coma," *Vampire Lesbians of Sodom,* and A Virgin Sacrifice and Madeleine Astarte, "Vampire Lesbians of Sodom," *Sleeping Beauty or Coma* (double-bill; also see below), Theatre-in-Limbo, Limbo Lounge, New York City, 1984, then Provincetown Playhouse, New York City, 1985-86.
Irish O'Flanagan, *Times Square Angel* (also see below), Theatre-in-Limbo, Provincetown Playhouse, 1985-86.
Chicklet, *Psycho Beach Party* (also see below), Theatre-in-Limbo, Players Theatre, New York City, 1987-88.
Gertrude Garnet, *The Lady in Question* (two-act; also see below), Theatre-in-Limbo, WPA Theatre, New York City, 1988, then Orpheum Theatre, New York City, 1989.

Also appeared in one-man show, *Charles Busch Alone with a Cast of Thousands* (also see below), which toured the U.S. for six years; appeared in other Theatre-in-Limbo productions (also see below) at the Limbo Lounge: as Maria Garbanza and Marquesa del Drago in *Pardon My Inquisition, or Kiss the Blood off My Castanets,* and Empress Theodora in *Theodora, She-Bitch of Byzantium.*

STAGE WORK; ASSOCIATE DIRECTOR

Ankles Aweigh (musical; also see below), Goodspeed Opera House, East Haddam, CT, 1988-89.

FILM APPEARANCES

Voice of Gemnen, *Light Years* (animated), Miramax, 1988.

WRITINGS:

PLAYS

Hollywood Confidential (one-man show), produced at One Sheridan Square Theatre, New York City, 1978.

Vampire Lesbians of Sodom [and] *Sleeping Beauty or Coma,* produced at the Limbo Lounge, New York City, 1984, then Provincetown Playhouse, New York City, 1985-90, later Coronet Theatre, Los Angeles, CA, 1990.

Times Square Angel, produced at Provincetown Playhouse, 1985-86.

Psycho Beach Party, produced at Players Theatre, New York City, 1987-88.

The Lady in Question (two-act), first produced at WPA Theatre, New York City, 1988, then Orpheum Theatre, New York City, 1989.

(Adaptor) Guy Bolton and Eddie Davis, *Ankles Aweigh* (musical), produced at Goodspeed Opera House, East Haddam, CT, 1988-89.

Also author of one-man show, *Charles Busch Alone with a Cast of Thousands,* which toured the U.S. for six years; author of other Theatre-in-Limbo productions, including *Pardon My Inquisition, or Kiss the Blood off My Castanets* and *Theodora, She-Bitch of Byzantium.*

OTHER

Contributor to magazines, including *Interview* and *New York Times Book Review.*

OTHER SOURCES:

PERIODICALS

New York Times, July 23, 1989.*

C

CALDWELL, Zoe 1933-

PERSONAL: Born September 14, 1933, in Hawthorn, Victoria, Australia; daughter of A. E. (a plumber) and Zoe (a singer and dancer) Caldwell; married Robert Whitehead, May 9, 1968; children: William Edgar (Sam), Charlie. *Education:* Attended Methodist Ladies College, Melbourne, Australia.

ADDRESSES: c/o Robert Whitehead Productions, 1564 Broadway, New York, NY 10036.

CAREER: Actress and director.

AWARDS, HONORS: Antoinette Perry Award, best supporting dramatic actress, 1966, for "The Gnadiges Fraulein," *Slapstick Tragedy;* Drama League Distinguished Performance Award, 1968; Antoinette Perry Award, best dramatic actress, 1968, for *The Prime of Miss Jean Brodie;* Drama Desk Award, outstanding performance, 1970, for *Colette;* Order of the British Empire, 1970; Andrew Allen Award, best acting performance in radio, 1981; Drama Desk Award, best actress, and Antoinette Perry Award, best dramatic actress, both 1982, for *Medea.*

CREDITS:

STAGE APPEARANCES

Title role, *Major Barbara,* Union Theatre Repertory Company, Melbourne, Australia, 1953.

Bubba, *The Seventeenth Doll,* Elizabethan Theatre Trust, Sydney, Australia, 1954.

Ophelia, *Hamlet,* Elizabethan Theatre Trust, 1954.

Twelfth Night, Royal Shakespeare Company (RSC), Stratford-upon-Avon, England, 1958.

Hamlet, RSC, 1958.

Daughter of Antiochus, *Pericles,* RSC, 1958.

Margaret, *Much Ado about Nothing,* RSC, 1958.

Bianca, *Othello,* RSC, 1959.

Cordelia, *King Lear,* RSC, 1959.

Helen, *All's Well That Ends Well,* RSC, 1959.

(London debut) Whore, "Cob and Leach," in *Trials by Logue* (double-bill), Royal Court Theatre, London, England, 1960.

Ismene, *Antigone,* Royal Court Theatre, 1960.

Isabella, *The Changeling,* Royal Court Theatre, 1961.

Jacqueline, *Jacques,* Royal Court Theatre, 1961.

Rosaline, *Love's Labour's Lost,* Stratford Shakespeare Festival of Canada, Stratford, Ontario, 1961.

Sonja Downfahl, *The Canvas Barricade,* Stratford Shakespeare Festival of Canada, 1961.

Pegeen Mike, *The Playboy of the Western World,* Manitoba Theatre Center, Winnipeg, Manitoba, Canada, 1961.

Title role, *Saint Joan,* Adelaide Festival of the Arts, Adelaide, Australia, 1962.

Ham Funeral, Elizabethan Theatre Trust, 1962.

Nola Boyle, *The Season at Sarsaparilla,* Union Theatre Repertory Company, 1962.

Frosine, *The Miser,* Minnesota Theatre Company, Minneapolis, 1963.

Natalia, *The Three Sisters,* Minnesota Theatre Company, 1963.

Woman, *Death of a Salesman,* Minnesota Theatre Company, 1963.

Elizabeth Von Ritter, *A Far Country,* Crest Theatre, Toronto, Ontario, 1964.

Title role, *Mother Courage,* Manitoba Theatre Center, 1964.

Countess Aurelia, *The Madwoman of Chaillot,* Goodman Memorial Theatre, Chicago, IL, 1964.

Millamant, *The Way of the World,* Minnesota Theatre Company, 1965.

Grusha Vashnadze, *The Caucasian Chalk Circle,* Minnesota Theatre Company, 1965.

Frosine, *The Miser,* Minnesota Theatre Company, 1965.

(Broadway debut) Sister Jean, *The Devils,* Helen Hayes Theatre, New York City, 1966.
Polly, "The Gnadiges Fraulein," in *Slapstick Tragedy* (double-bill), Longacre Theatre, New York City, 1966.
Orinthia, *The Apple Cart,* Shaw Festival, Niagara-on-the-Lake, Ontario, 1966.
Lena Szczepanowska, *Misalliance,* Shaw Festival, 1966.
Lady Anne, *Richard III,* Stratford Shakespeare Festival of Canada, 1967.
Mrs. Page, *The Merry Wives of Windsor,* Stratford Shakespeare Festival of Canada, 1967.
Cleopatra, *Antony and Cleopatra,* Stratford Shakespeare Festival of Canada, 1967.
Title role, *The Prime of Miss Jean Brodie,* Helen Hayes Theatre, New York City, 1968.
Title role, *Colette,* Ellen Stewart Theatre, New York City, 1970.
Lady Hamilton, *A Bequest to the Nation,* Haymarket Theatre, London, 1970.
Eve, *The Creation of the World and Other Business,* Shubert Theatre, New York City, 1972.
Love and Master Will, Opera House, John F. Kennedy Center for the Performing Arts, Washington, DC, 1973.
Alice, *Dance of Death,* Vivian Beaumont Theatre, Lincoln Center, New York, 1974.
Mary Cavan Tyrone, *Long Day's Journey into Night,* Eisenhower Theatre, John F. Kennedy Center for the Performing Arts, 1975, then Brooklyn Academy Opera House, New York City, 1976.
The Neighborhood Playhouse at 50: A Celebration, Shubert Theatre, 1978.
Title role, *Medea,* Cort Theatre, New York City, 1982, then Clarence Brown Company, Knoxville, TN, 1982.
Title role, *Lillian* (one-woman show), Ethel Barrymore Theatre, New York City, 1986.

STAGE WORK

Director, *An Almost Perfect Person,* Belasco Theatre, New York City, 1977.
Director, *These Men,* Harold Clurman Theatre, New York City, 1980.
Assistant director, *Macbeth,* Mark Hellinger Theatre, New York City, 1988.
Director, *Park Your Car in Harvard Yard,* American National Theatre Academy, Music Box Theatre, New York City, 1991.

Also stage director, Stratford Shakespeare Festival of Canada, 1979.

FILM APPEARANCES

Countess, *The Purple Rose of Cairo,* Orion, 1985.

TELEVISION APPEARANCES

The 43rd Annual Tony Awards (special), CBS, 1989.
Mrs. Kennedy, *Lantern Hill* (movie), Disney Channel, 1990.
Avonlea (special), Disney Channel, 1990.

Also appeared in movie *Sarah Bernhardt,* 1977.*

* * *

CALLAHAN, Gene 1923(?)-1990

PERSONAL: Born c. 1923; died of a heart attack, December 26, 1990.

CAREER: Set decorator and production designer. Designer for opera productions at Louisiana State University in the 1940s.

AWARDS, HONORS: Academy Award (with Harry Horner), best art direction—set decoration (black and white), 1961, for *The Hustler;* Academy Award, best art direction—set decoration (black and white), 1963, for *America, America;* Academy Award nomination, best art direction—set decoration, 1963, for *The Cardinal;* Emmy Award nomination (with Jack Wright, Jr.), individual achievements in entertainment—art directors and set decorators, 1964, for *Carol for Another Christmas;* Academy Award nomination (with Jack Collis and Jerry Wunderlich), best art direction—set decoration, 1976, for *The Last Tycoon;* Academy Award nomination, for *Annie.*

CREDITS:

FILM WORK; SET DECORATOR

The Hustler, Twentieth Century-Fox, 1961.
Mad Dog Coll, Columbia, 1961.
Splendor in the Grass, Warner Brothers, 1961.
The Connection, Allen-Clarke, 1962.
David and Lisa, Continental, 1962.
Lilith, Columbia, 1964.

FILM WORK; PRODUCTION DESIGNER

Harvey Middleman, Fireman, Columbia, 1965.
The Group, United Artists (UA), 1966.
Hurry Sundown, Paramount, 1967.
Funny Girl, Columbia, 1968.
(With Peter Dohanos) *Truman Capote's Trilogy,* Allied Artists, 1969.
The Magic Garden of Stanley Sweetheart, Metro-Goldwyn-Mayer (MGM), 1970.
Dealing; or, The Berkeley-to-Boston Forty-Brick Lost-Bag Blues, Warner Brothers, 1971.
Doc, UA, 1971.
The Effect of Gamma Rays on Man-in-the-Moon Marigolds, Twentieth Century-Fox, 1972.

The Candidate, Warner Brothers, 1972.
The Friends of Eddie Coyle, Paramount, 1973.
The Happy Hooker, Cannon, 1975.
The Stepford Wives, Columbia, 1975.
The Last Tycoon, Paramount, 1976.
The Next Man, Allied Artists, 1976.
(With Willy Holt and Carmen Dillon) *Julia,* Twentieth Century-Fox, 1977.
Bloodbrothers, Warner Brothers, 1978.
Eyes of Laura Mars, Columbia, 1978.
King of the Gypsies, Paramount, 1978.
Chapter Two, Columbia, 1979.
Seems Like Old Times, Columbia, 1980.
Whose Life Is It Anyway?, MGM/UA, 1981.
Grease 2, Paramount, 1982.
The Survivors, Columbia, 1983.
Places in the Heart, Tri-Star, 1984.
The Jagged Edge, Columbia, 1985.
Children of a Lesser God, Paramount, 1986.
Black Widow (also see below), Twentieth Century-Fox, 1987.
Arthur 2 on the Rocks, Warner Brothers, 1988.
Little Nikita, Columbia, 1988.
(With Edward Pisoni) *Steel Magnolias,* Tri-Star, 1989.
The Man in the Moon, MGM-Pathe, 1991.

Also worked as production designer for *The Last Married Couple in America,* 1979; and *Big Trouble,* 1985.

OTHER FILM WORK

Art director, *For Pete's Sake* (also known as *July Pork Bellies*), Columbia, 1977.

Also worked as art director for *America, America,* 1963; and as art direction consultant for *Stop,* 1970. Other film work credits include *The Cardinal,* 1963; *Butterfield 8; Long Day's Journey into Night;* and *Annie.*

FILM APPEARANCES

Mr. Foster, *Black Widow,* Twentieth Century-Fox, 1987.

TELEVISION WORK

Art director, *Carol for Another Christmas* (also known as *Xerox Special*), ABC, 1964.
Art director, *Panic in Echo Park* (movie), NBC, 1977.

OBITUARIES AND OTHER SOURCES:

PERIODICALS

Theatre Crafts, March, 1991, p. 18.*

CAMERON, James 1954-

PERSONAL: Born August 16, 1954, in Kapuskasing, Ontario, Canada; immigrated to United States, 1971; son of an electrical engineer (father); married second wife, Gale Anne Hurd, 1985 (divorced); married Katheryn Bigelow (a motion picture director). *Education:* Attended California State University at Fullerton, majored in physics.

ADDRESSES: *Agent*—International Creative Management, 8899 Beverly Blvd., Los Angeles, CA 90048. *Office*—c/o Alexandra Drobac, Lightstorm Entertainment, 3100 Damon Way, Burbank, CA 91505.

CAREER: Director and screenwriter. Worked as a truck driver. Served various functions for Roger Corman's New World Pictures, including production assistant, second unit director, production designer and miniature set builder; head of Lightstorm Entertainment, under five-year contract with Twentieth-Century Fox, beginning in 1992.

MEMBER: Directors Guild of America.

CREDITS:

FILM WORK; DIRECTOR, EXCEPT WHERE INDICATED

(With Ovidio Assonitis) *Piranha II: The Spawning* (also known as *The Spawning* and *Piranha II: Flying Killers*), Columbia, 1981.
The Terminator (also see below), Orion, 1984.
Aliens (also see below), Twentieth Century-Fox, 1986.
The Abyss (also see below), Twentieth Century-Fox, 1989.
(And producer) *Terminator 2: Judgement Day* (also known as *T2;* also see below), Tri-Star, 1991.

Worked as art director for *Battle beyond the Stars* and production designer for *Galaxy of Terror.* Also worked with director John Carpenter, creating special effects for *Escape from New York.*

FILM WORK; EXECUTIVE PRODUCER

Point Break, Twentieth Century-Fox, 1991.

WRITINGS:

SCREENPLAYS

(With Gale Anne Hurd and William Wisher, Jr.) *The Terminator,* Orion, 1984.
(With Sylvester Stallone) *Rambo: First Blood, Part II,* Tri-Star, 1985.
Aliens (based on story by Cameron, David Giler and Walter Hill; based on characters created by Dan O'Bannon and Ronald Shusett) Twentieth Century-Fox, 1986.
The Abyss, Twentieth Century-Fox, 1989.
(With Wisher) *Terminator 2: Judgement Day* (also known as *T2*), Tri-Star, 1991.

OTHER SOURCES:

BOOKS

Film Directors: A Complete Guide, Lone Eagle Press, 1987, pp. 3-5, 8-9.

PERIODICALS

Hollywood Reporter, April 22, 1992, pp. 1, 6.
Los Angeles Times, July 2, 1991, pp. F1, F4-5.
People, August 11, 1986, pp. 93-95.
Starlog, January, 1990, pp. 29-32, 62.*

* * *

CAMERON, Kirk 1970(?)-

PERSONAL: Born October 20, 1970 (one source says 1971), in Canoga Park, CA; son of Robert (a junior high school physical education teacher) and Barbara (son's business manager) Cameron; married Chelsea Noble (an actress), 1991. *Avocational interests:* Working out at the gym, playing guitar.

ADDRESSES: Agent—United Talent Agency, 9560 Wilshire Blvd., 5th Floor, Beverly Hills, CA 90212.

CAREER: Actor. Began his career in television commercials at age nine. Spokesperson for "Just Say No" anti-drug campaign.

AWARDS, HONORS: Best Actor Award, Family Television and Film Awards Organization, 1988; People's Choice Awards, favorite young television performer, Proctor & Gamble Productions, 1988 and 1989; Golden Globe Award nomination for *Growing Pains.*

CREDITS:

TELEVISION APPEARANCES; SERIES

Eric Armstrong, *Two Marriages,* ABC, 1983-1984.
Mike Seaver, *Growing Pains,* ABC, 1985-92.

TELEVISION APPEARANCES; MOVIES

Gary, *Star Flight: The Plane That Couldn't Land,* ABC, 1983.
Mickey, *Children in the Crossfire,* NBC, 1984.
Will Loomis, *A Little Piece of Heaven,* NBC, 1991.

Also appeared in *Goliath Awaits,* 1981, and *Honor Bright,* 1991.

TELEVISION APPEARANCES; SPECIALS

The Wildest West Show of the Stars, CBS, 1986.
Bob Hope's High-Flying Birthday Extravaganza, NBC, 1987.
The 39th Annual Emmy Awards, Fox, 1987.
Happy Birthday, Bob: Fifty Stars Salute Your Fifty Years with NBC, NBC, 1988.
Superstars and Their Moms, ABC, 1988.
Super Bloopers and New Practical Jokes, NBC, 1988 and 1990.
The Hollywood Christmas Parade, syndicated, 1988 and 1989.
Host, *The Ice Capades with Kirk Cameron,* ABC, 1988.
Comic Relief III, HBO, 1989.
Bob Hope's Love Affair with Lucy, NBC, 1989.
The 41st Annual Emmy Awards, Fox, 1989.
The 15th Annual People's Choice Awards, CBS, 1989.
Host, *Dick Clark's New Year's Rockin' Eve,* ABC, 1990.
Ole! It's Bob Hope's Acapulco Spring Fling of Comedy and Music, NBC, 1990.
The Walt Disney Company Presents the American Teacher Awards (also known as *The Magical World of Disney*), Disney Channel, 1990.
Happy Birthday, Bugs: Fifty Looney Years, CBS, 1990.
The Greatest Practical Jokes of All Time, NBC, 1990.
America's All-Star Tribute to Oprah Winfrey, ABC, 1990.
The 4th Annual American Comedy Awards, ABC, 1990.
The 16th Annual People's Choice Awards, CBS, 1990.
Presenter, *The 42nd Annual Primetime Emmy Awards Presentation,* Fox, 1990.
The 17th Annual People's Choice Awards, CBS, 1991.
Special events chairperson, *Children's Miracle Network Telethon,* syndicated, 1991.
Presenter, *The 48th Annual Golden Globe Awards,* TBS, 1991.

TELEVISION APPEARANCES; EPISODIC

"Just One of the Guys," *Full House,* ABC, 1988.

TELEVISION APPEARANCES; PILOTS

Bobby, *Mickey Spillane's Mike Hammer: More Than Murder,* CBS, 1984.

TELEVISION WORK

Second assistant director of *Out of Sight, Out of Mind,* 1990; and *Sight Unseen,* 1991.

FILM APPEARANCES

Teddy, *The Best of Times,* Universal, 1986.
Chris Hammond, *Like Father, Like Son,* Tri-Star, 1987.
Tucker Muldowney, *Listen to Me,* Columbia, 1989.

OTHER SOURCES:

PERIODICALS

People, December 15, 1986, p. 177; August 5, 1991, pp. 88-89.

CAMP, Colleen 1953-

PERSONAL: Born in 1953 in San Francisco, CA.

CAREER: Actress. Worked as a bird trainer at Busch Gardens.

CREDITS:

FILM APPEARANCES

(Film debut) *Battle for the Planet of the Apes,* Twentieth Century-Fox, 1973.
The Last Porno Flick (also known as *The Mad, Mad Moviemakers*), Bryanston, 1974.
Connie Thompson (Miss Imperial County), *Smile,* United Artists (UA), 1975.
Donna, *Death Game,* Levitt-Pickman, 1977.
Billie Jean, *Love and the Midnight Auto Supply,* Producers Capitol, 1978.
Playmate, *Apocalypse Now,* UA, 1979.
Ann Morris, *The Game of Death* (also known as *Goodbye Bruce Lee: His Last Game of Death*), Columbia, 1979.
Cindy, *Cloud Dancer,* Blossom, 1980.
Christy Miller, *They All Laughed,* Twentieth Century-Fox/UA, 1981.
Robin, *The Seduction,* Avco Embassy, 1982.
Dusty Trails, *Smokey and the Bandit, Part 3,* Universal, 1983.
Sarah Richman, *Valley Girl,* Atlantic, 1983.
Rose, *The City Girl,* Moon, 1984.
Liz Sampson, *Joy of Sex,* Paramount, 1984.
Tracy King, *Rosebud Beach Hotel,* Almi, 1984.
Elaine Fox, *D.A.R.Y.L.,* Paramount, 1985.
Yvette, *Clue,* Paramount, 1985.
Nancy Catlett, *Doin' Time,* Ladd/Warner Brothers, 1985.
Kirkland, *Police Academy 2: Their First Assignment,* Warner Brothers, 1985.
Mrs. Kirkland-Tackleberry, *Police Academy 4: Citizens on Patrol,* Warner Brothers, 1987.
Rhonda Shand, *Walk Like a Man,* Metro-Goldwyn-Mayer (MGM)/UA, 1987.
Arlanda, *Track 29,* Island, 1988.
Molly Gilbert, *Illegally Yours,* MGM/UA, 1988.
Jenny, *Wicked Stepmother,* MGM/UA, 1989.
Margaret Snow, *My Blue Heaven,* Warner Brothers, 1990.

Also appeared as Mary Ann, *The Swinging Cheerleaders,* 1974, Randy, *Who Fell Asleep?* 1979, and Liberty Jean, *Loose Ends,* 1983. Also appeared in *Cats in the Cage,* 1968, *Ebony, Ivory, and Jade,* 1977, *The Seducers,* 1980, *Screwball Academy,* 1986, *Funny Lady,* and *Gumball Rally.*

FILM WORK

Associate producer, *The City Girl,* Moon, 1984.

TELEVISION APPEARANCES: SERIES

Vickie St. John, *Rich Man, Poor Man, Book II,* ABC, 1976-77.
Kristin Shepard, *Dallas,* CBS, 1979.

TELEVISION APPEARANCES: MOVIES

Starlet, *Amelia Earhart,* NBC, 1976.
Rosette, *Lady of the House,* NBC, 1978.
Backfield in Motion, ABC, 1991.

Also appeared as Ellie Snyder, *Addicted to His Love,* 1988, and in *Sisterhood.*

TELEVISION APPEARANCES: EPISODIC

Cartoonist's wife, "Korman's Kalamity," *Tales from the Crypt,* HBO, 1990.

Also appeared on *The Dean Martin Show* (television debut), NBC, and on episodes of *Happy Days,* ABC, *The Dukes of Hazzard,* CBS, *WKRP in Cincinnati,* CBS, *Magnum, P.I.,* CBS, and *Murder, She Wrote,* CBS.

TELEVISION APPEARANCES: SPECIALS

Appeared on *George Burns Comedy Week,* and *Going Home Again.**

* * *

CAMPION, Jane 1955(?)-

PERSONAL: Born c. 1955, in Wellington, New Zealand; daughter of Richard (a director) and Edith (an actress). *Education:* Attended art school; attended Australian Film and Television School.

ADDRESSES: Contact—New Zealand Film Commission, P.O. Box 11546, Wellington, New Zealand 4/859-754.

CAREER: Director and screenwriter. Worked in short film medium and television in mid-1980s.

AWARDS, HONORS: Palme d'Or (short film category), Cannes International Film Festival, 1986, for *Peel;* best Australian feature award and best director award, Australian Film Critics' Circle, both 1989, both for *Sweetie.*

CREDITS:

FILM WORK; DIRECTOR

(And editor) *Peel: An Exercise in Discipline* (also see below), Unexpected Film Company, 1982.
A Girl's Own Story (also see below), Unexpected Film Company, 1983.
(And producer, cinematographer, and camera operator) *Passionless Moments* (also see below), Unexpected Film Company, 1984.
Sweetie (also see below), Avenue Pictures, 1989.

Angel at My Table (originally broadcast as a mini-series on Australian television; adaptation of New Zealand author Janet Frame's autobiography), Circle Releasing, 1990.

Also director of *After Hours,* 1984.

TELEVISION WORK; DIRECTOR

Two Friends, Australian Broadcasting Company, 1986.

WRITINGS:

SCREENPLAYS

Peel: An Exercise in Discipline, Unexpected Film Company, 1982.
A Girl's Own Story, Unexpected Film Company, 1983.
Passionless Moments, Unexpected Film Company, 1984.
(With Gerard Lee) *Sweetie* (based on Campion's idea), Union Generale Cinematographique, 1989.

FILM MUSIC

"Feel the Cold," *A Girl's Own Story,* Unexpected Film Company, 1983.

OTHER SOURCES:

PERIODICALS

Washington Post, March 4, 1990.*

* * *

CARDIFF, Jack 1914-

PERSONAL: Born September 18, 1914, in Yarmouth, England; son of John Joseph and Florence Cardiff; married Julia Lily Mickleboro, 1940; children: three sons. *Education:* Attended school in Hertfordshire, England.

ADDRESSES: Agent—Eric L'Epine Smith, 10 Wyndham Pl., London W.1, England; Grace Lyons Management, 8350 Melrose Ave., Suite 202, Los Angeles, CA 90069.

CAREER: Cinematographer and director. Child actor, beginning in 1918; became camera operator, 1928, and director, 1958. British Ministry of Information, photographer with Film Unit, 1942.

MEMBER: Association francaise de cameramen (honorary member), BSC.

AWARDS, HONORS: Academy Award, best cinematography (color), 1947, and Golden Globe Award, cinematography, Hollywood Foreign Press Association, 1948, both for *Black Narcissus;* Film Achievement Award, *Look* magazine; French Coup ce soir, 1951; Dr. Art, University of Rome, 1953; Academy Award nomination, best cinematography (color), 1956, and BSC Award, both for *War and Peace;* Academy Award nomination, best directing, 1960, Golden Globe Award, outstanding director, 1961, and New York Critics Award, best film direction, all for *Sons and Lovers;* Academy Award nomination, best cinematography (color), 1961, for *Fanny.*

CREDITS:

FILM WORK: CINEMATOGRAPHER

(With Hal Rosson) *As You Like It,* Twentieth Century-Fox, 1936.
(With Harry Stradling and Bernard Browne) *Knight without Armor,* United Artists (UA), 1937.
(With Ray Rennahan and Henry Imus) *Wings of the Morning,* Twentieth Century-Fox, 1937.
(With Georges Perinal and Osmond Borradaile) *The Four Feathers,* UA, 1939.
(With Claude Friese-Greene) *The Great Mr. Handel,* Midfilm, 1942.
(With Perinal) *Colonel Blimp* (also known as *The Life and Death of Colonel Blimp*), General Films Distributors, 1945.
(With Frederick A. Young, Robert Krasker, and Jack Hildyard) *Caesar and Cleopatra,* Eagle Lion, 1946.
Stairway to Heaven (also known as *A Matter of Life and Death*), Universal, 1946.
Black Narcissus, General Films Distributors, 1947.
The Red Shoes, Eagle Lion/Rank, 1948.
Scott of the Antarctic, Eagle Lion/Pyramid, 1949.
(With Paul Beeson, Ian Craig, David McNeilly, and Jack Haste) *Under Capricorn,* Warner Brothers, 1949.
The Black Rose, Twentieth Century-Fox, 1950.
The African Queen, US, 1951.
Pandora and the Flying Dutchman, Metro-Goldwyn-Mayer (MGM), 1951.
It Started in Paradise, General Films Distributors, 1952.
The Magic Box, British Lion, 1952.
The Master of Ballantrae, Warner Brothers, 1953.
The Barefoot Contessa, UA, 1954.
Crossed Swords (also known as *Il maestro di Don Giovanni*), UA, 1954.
The Brave One, RKO Radio Pictures, 1956.
(With Aldo Tonti) *War and Peace,* Paramount, 1956.
Legend of the Lost, UA, 1957.
The Prince and the Showgirl, Warner Brothers, 1957.
The Vikings, UA, 1958.
(With William C. Mellor) *The Diary of Anne Frank,* Twentieth Century-Fox, 1959.
Fanny, Warner Brothers, 1961.
The Big Money, Lopert, 1962.
Scalawag, Paramount, 1973.
Ride a Wild Pony, Buena Vista, 1976.
Behind the Iron Mask (also known as *The Fifth Musketeer*), Columbia, 1977.
Death on the Nile, Paramount, 1978.

Crossed Swords (also known as *The Prince and the Pauper*), Warner Brothers, 1978.
Avalanche Express, Twentieth Century-Fox, 1979.
A Man, a Woman, and a Bank (also known as *A Very Big Withdrawal*), Avco Embassy, 1979.
The Awakening, Warner Brothers, 1980.
The Dogs of War, UA, 1980.
Ghost Story, Universal, 1981.
The Wicked Lady, MGM/UA, 1983.
Conan the Destroyer, Universal, 1984.
Scandalous, Orion, 1984.
Cat's Eye, MGM/UA, 1985.
Rambo: First Blood, Part II, Tri-Star, 1985.
Million Dollar Mystery, DEG, 1987.
Call from Space, Showscan Film Corp., 1989.
The Magic Balloon, Showscan Film Corp., 1990.

Also worked as cinematographer for *Western Approaches,* c. 1942; *Beyond This Place,* 1959; *The Freakmaster,* 1973; *Penny Gold,* 1974; *Tai-Pan,* 1986; and *Blue Velvet.*

FILM WORK; DIRECTOR

Intent to Kill, Twentieth Century-Fox, 1958.
Scent of Mystery (also known as *Holiday in Spain*), Michael Todd, Jr., 1960.
Sons and Lovers, Twentieth Century-Fox, 1960.
The Lion, Twentieth Century-Fox, 1962.
My Geisha, Paramount, 1962.
The Long Ships, Columbia, 1964.
Young Cassidy, MGM, 1965.
The Liquidator, MGM, 1966.
Dark of the Sun (also known as *The Mercenaries*), MGM, 1968.
(And producer) *The Girl on a Motorcycle* (also known as *Naked Under Leather*), Claridge, 1968.
The Mutations, Columbia, 1974.

TELEVISION WORK

Photographer, *The Far Pavilions,* HBO, 1984.
Photographer, *The Last Days of Pompeii,* ABC, 1984.

WRITINGS:

Author of an autobiography, published in 1975. Contributor to periodicals, including *American Cinematographer.**

* * *

CARRADINE, Keith 1949-

PERSONAL: Full name, Keith Ian Carradine; born August 8, 1949, in San Mateo, CA; son of John Richmond Reed (an actor) and Sonia Sorel (an actress and artist; maiden name, Henius) Carradine; married Sandra Will, February 6, 1982; children: Martha Campbell Plimpton, Cade Richmond, Sorel. *Education:* Studied drama at Colorado State University, 1967. *Politics:* Democrat. *Religion:* Episcopalian.

ADDRESSES: *Agent*—Ed Limato, William Morris Agency, 1350 Ave. of Americas, New York, NY 10019.

CAREER: Actor, singer, songwriter.

MEMBER: Academy of Motion Picture Arts and Sciences, Greenpeace Foundation, Cousteau Society, Sierra Club.

AWARDS, HONORS: Academy Award, best song, and Golden Globe Award, best song, 1975, both for "I'm Easy" from the motion picture *Nashville;* Emmy Award nomination, outstanding supporting actor in a limited series or special, 1983, for *Chiefs;* Outer Critics Circle award, outstanding debut, 1983, for *Foxfire;* Antionette Perry Award nomination, best performance by a leading actor in a musical, 1991, for *The Will Rogers Follies.*

CREDITS:

STAGE APPEARANCES

(Broadway debut) Woof (understudy), *Hair,* Biltmore Theater, New York City, 1969-70.
Dude, *Tobacco Road,* Alhambra Dinner Theatre, Jacksonville, FL, 1970.
Orpheus, *Wake Up, It's Time to Go to Bed,* New York Shakespeare Festival, LuEsther Theater, New York City, 1979.
Benjamin Hubbard, *Another Part of the Forest,* Seattle Repertory Theatre, Seattle, WA, 1981-82.
Dillard Nations, *Foxfire,* Ethel Barrymore Theatre, New York City, 1982-83, later at Ahmanson Theatre, Los Angeles, CA, 1985-86.
Charlie, *Detective Story,* Center Theatre Group, Ahmanson Theatre, 1983-84.
Will Rogers, *The Will Rogers Follies,* Palace Theatre, New York City, 1991—.

Appeared as Claude in Los Angeles production of *Hair,* 1969.

FILM APPEARANCES

(Film debut) Cowboy, *A Gunfight,* Paramount, 1971.
Cowboy, *McCabe and Mrs. Miller,* Warner Brothers, 1971.
Cigaret, *Emperor of the North Pole* (also known as *Emperor of the North*), Twentieth Century-Fox, 1973.
Whizzer, *Hex,* Twentieth Century-Fox, 1973.
Bowie, *Thieves Like Us,* United Artists, 1974.
Arthur, *Idaho Transfer,* Cinemation, 1975.
Tom Frank, *Nashville* (also see below), Paramount, 1975.
David Foster, *Lumiere,* New World, 1976.

Carroll Barber, *Welcome to L.A.* (also see below), United Artists, 1976.
D'Hubert, *The Duellists,* Paramount, 1977.
E. J. Bellocq, *Pretty Baby,* Paramount, 1978.
Hall, *An Almost Perfect Affair,* Paramount, 1979.
Wayne Van Til, *Old Boyfriends,* Avco-Embassy, 1979.
Jim Younger, *The Long Riders,* United Artists, 1980.
Spencer, *Southern Comfort,* Twentieth Century-Fox, 1981.
Mickey, *Choose Me,* Island Alive, 1984.
Clarence Butts, *Maria's Lovers,* Cannon, 1985.
Coop, *Trouble in Mind,* Alive, 1985.
L'Inchiesta (title means "The Inquest"; also known as *The Investigation* and *The Inquiry*), Sacis, 1986.
Nick Hart, *The Moderns,* Alive, 1988.
Reed, *Backfire,* Vidmark, 1989.
Clarence, *Daddy's Dyin'. . . Who's Got the Will?,* Metro-Goldwyn-Mayer (MGM)/United Artists, 1990.
Monte Latham, *Cold Feet,* Avenue, 1990.
Marvin Macy, *The Ballad of the Sad Cafe,* Angelika Films, 1991.
John Cross, *Crisscross,* MGM, 1992.

Appeared in *Run, Run, Joe!,* 1974, *Antione et Sebastien, You and Me, Street of No Return,* and *Dr. Grassler.* Made cameo appearance in *Sgt. Pepper's Lonely Hearts Club Band,* Universal, 1978.

TELEVISION APPEARANCES; MOVIES

Middle Caine, *Kung Fu,* ABC, 1972.
Danny Brown, *Man on a String,* CBS, 1972.
Lt. Lewis, *The Godchild,* ABC, 1974.
John Boslett, *Scorned and Swindled,* CBS, 1984.
Allen Devlin/Ed Vinson, *Blackout,* HBO, 1985.
Pete Gray, *A Winner Never Quits,* ABC, 1986.
J.J., *Half a Lifetime,* HBO, 1986.
Jim Lee, *Eye on the Sparrow,* NBC, 1987.
Richard Everton, *Stones for Ibarra,* CBS, 1988.
Elmo Zumwalt III, *My Father, My Son,* CBS, 1988.
Captain Tom Watkins, *The Forgotten* (also see below), USA Network, 1989.
Pierre Guitry, *Judgement* (also known as *Sacraments* and *Vermillion Parish*), HBO, 1990.
Liam Devlin, *Confessional,* Harmony Gold (syndicated), 1990.
Peter "Mac" MacAllister, *Payoff,* Showtime, 1991.

TELEVISION APPEARANCES; MINISERIES

Lt. Murph McCoy, *A Rumor of War,* CBS, 1980.
Foxy Funderburke, *Chiefs,* CBS, 1983.
John Rule, *Murder Ordained* (also known as *Broken Commandments* and *Kansas Gothic*), CBS, 1987.
Agent Michael Rourke, *The Revenge of Al Capone,* NBC, 1989.

TELEVISION APPEARANCES; SPECIALS

Forty-fifth Annual Tony Awards, CBS, 1991.

TELEVISION APPEARANCES; EPISODIC

Made television debut in episode of *Bonanza,* 1971, also appeared in episode of *The Fall Guy,* ABC, 1984, and *An American Portrait,* CBS, 1986.

RECORDINGS:

ALBUMS

I'm Easy (also see below), Asylum, 1977.
Lost and Found, Asylum, 1978.

Contributed music to the film *Welcome to L.A.* (also see below).

WRITINGS:

FILM MUSIC

"I'm Easy," *Nashville,* Paramount, 1975.
Welcome to L.A., United Artists, 1976.
Lyricist, "Maria's Song," *Maria's Lovers,* Cannon, 1985.

OTHER SOURCES:

PERIODICALS

New York Times, April 7, 1977.*

* * *

CARVEY, Dana 1955-

PERSONAL: Born April 2, 1955, in Missoula, MT; married Paula Zwaggerman. *Education:* Studied communication arts at San Francisco State University.

ADDRESSES: Office—NBC-TV, 30 Rockefeller Plaza, New York, NY 10112. *Agent*—International Creative Management, 8899 Beverly Blvd., Los Angeles, CA 90048.

CAREER: Actor. Stand-up comedian in San Francisco and Los Angeles, CA.

AWARDS, HONORS: Emmy Award nominations, outstanding individual performance in a variety or music program, 1989, 1990, and 1991, and American Comedy Awards, funniest supporting male in television, George Schlatter Productions, 1989, 1990, and 1991, all for *Saturday Night Live;* winner of San Francisco Stand-Up Comedy Competition.

CREDITS:

TELEVISION APPEARANCES; SERIES

Adam Shields, *One of the Boys,* NBC, 1982.
Clinton "Jafo" Wonderlove, *Blue Thunder,* ABC, 1984.

Saturday Night Live, NBC, 1986—.

TELEVISION APPEARANCES; PILOTS

Michael Elliott, *Alone at Last,* NBC, 1980.
Simon, *Whacked Out,* NBC, 1981.

TELEVISION APPEARANCES; SPECIALS

Comic Relief II, HBO, 1987.
Elliot Clinton, *Slickers,* NBC, 1987.
The 2nd Annual American Comedy Awards, ABC, 1988.
Host, *Superman's 50th Anniversary: A Celebration of the Man of Steel,* CBS, 1988.
Saturday Night Live 15th Anniversary, NBC, 1989.
The 41st Annual Emmy Awards, Fox, 1989.
The Tonight Show Starring Johnny Carson: 28th Anniversary Special, NBC, 1990.
Comic Relief IV, HBO, 1990.
The 4th Annual American Comedy Awards, ABC, 1990.
Saturday Night Live Goes Commercial, NBC, 1991.
MTV's 1991 Video Music Awards, MTV, 1991.
The 19th Annual American Film Institute Life Achievement Award: A Salute to Kirk Douglas, CBS, 1991.
Toonces, The Cat Who Could Drive a Car, NBC, 1992.

Also appeared on *Salute to the Improvisation.*

FILM APPEARANCES

Assistant, *Halloween II,* Universal, 1981.
Baby Face, *Racing with the Moon,* Paramount, 1984.
Mime waiter, *This Is Spinal Tap,* Embassy, 1984.
Richie Evans, *Tough Guys,* Buena Vista, 1986.
Brad Williams, *Moving,* Warner Brothers, 1988.
Eddie Farrell, *Opportunity Knocks,* Universal, 1990.
Garth Algar, *Wayne's World,* Paramount, 1992.

Also appeared in *Hot Shots,* 1986, and on *Superbowl of Comedy.*

OTHER SOURCES:

PERIODICALS

Gentlemen's Quarterly, August, 1989, p. 230.
People Weekly, May 4, 1987, p. 101.
Rolling Stone, October 22, 1987, p. 29.
San Francisco, May, 1981, p. 61.*

* * *

CATES, Gilbert 1934-

PERSONAL: Born Gilbert Katz, June 6, 1934, in New York, NY; son of Nathan (a dress manufacturer) and Nina (Peltzman) Katz; married Betty Jane Dubin, February 9, 1957 (divorced); married Judith Reichman, January 25, 1987; children: (first marriage) Melissa Beth, Jonathan Michael, David Sawyer, Gilbert Lewis. *Education:* Attended DeWitt Clinton High School, Bronx, NY; studied at Neighborhood Playhouse School of the Theatre, New York City, 1953; Syracuse University, B.A., 1955, M.A., 1965; studied with Robert Lewis, New York City, 1959. *Avocational interests:* Fencing, photography.

ADDRESSES: Agent—William Morris Agency, 151 South El Camino Dr., Beverly Hills, CA 90212.

CAREER: Producer and director. Syracuse University, Syracuse, NY, instructor in speech and drama, 1955; Childville, Inc., New York City, member of board of directors, 1966-73.

MEMBER: Directors Guild of America (vice-president of eastern region, 1965, and western region, 1980—; president, 1984-87), Academy of Motion Picture Arts and Sciences (member of board of governors; chair of board of directors), American Academy of Television Arts and Sciences, Actors Equity Association (member of eastern regional board of directors, 1962-63), League of New York Theaters, Tau Delta Phi, Friars Club (Los Angeles; member of board of governors, 1980—).

AWARDS, HONORS: Best short film award, International Film Importers and Distributors, 1962; San Francisco Film Festival citation, 1963, for *The Painting;* Image Award, National Association for the Advancement of Colored People, and TV Scout Award, excellence in television, both 1972, for *To All My Friends on Shore;* Chancellor's Medal, Syracuse University, 1974; Emmy Award nomination, outstanding directing in a limited series or special, 1985, for "Consenting Adult," *An ABC Theatre Presentation;* Robert B. Aldrich Award, Directors Guild of America, 1989; Emmy Award nomination, outstanding variety, music, or comedy special, 1989, for *The 62nd Annual Academy Awards;* Emmy Award nomination, outstanding directing in a mini-series or special, 1989, for *Do You Know the Muffin Man?;* Emmy Award, outstanding variety, music, or comedy program, 1990, for *The 63rd Annual Academy Awards;* Emmy Award nomination, outstanding directing in a mini-series or special, 1991, for *Absolute Strangers;* Citation Award, Edinburgh Film Festival.

CREDITS:

TELEVISION WORK; MOVIES

Director and producer, *To All My Friends on Shore,* CBS, 1972.
Director, *The Affair* (also known as *Love Song*), ABC, 1973.
Director, *Johnny, We Hardly Knew Ye,* NBC, 1977.
Director and supervising producer, *Country Gold,* CBS, 1982.
Producer, *The Kid from Nowhere,* NBC, 1982.

Director, *Hobson's Choice,* CBS, 1983.

Director and producer, *Burning Rage* (also known as *Coalfire*), CBS, 1984.

Director and producer, *Child's Play* (also known as *Who Hears the Child's Cry*), CBS, 1986.

Director and producer, *Fatal Judgment* (also known as *Fatal Dosage*), CBS, 1988.

Director, *My First Love* (also known as *Second Chance* and *One More Time*), ABC, 1989.

Director, *Do You Know the Muffin Man?,* CBS, 1989.

Director and producer, *Call Me Anna* (also known as *My Name Is Anna*), ABC, 1990.

Director and producer, *Absolute Strangers* (also known as *Matter of Privacy*), CBS, 1991.

Executive producer (with Donna Mills) *In My Daughter's Name,* CBS, 1992.

TELEVISION WORK; SPECIALS

Producer and director, *After the Fall,* NBC, 1974.

Producer and director (with brother Joseph Cates), *Circus Lions, Tigers, and Melissas Too,* NBC, 1977.

Executive producer (with Joseph Cates), *Country Night of Stars,* NBC, 1978.

Executive producer (with Joseph Cates), *Country Night of Stars II,* NBC, 1978.

Executive producer, *Stubby Pringle's Christmas,* NBC, 1978.

Executive producer (with Joseph Cates), *Country Stars of the 70s,* NBC, 1979.

Executive producer (with Joseph Cates), *Skinflint,* NBC, 1979.

Executive producer (with Joseph Cates), *Elvis Remembered: Nashville to Hollywood,* NBC, 1980.

Executive producer (with Joseph Cates), *Fifty Years of Country Music,* NBC, 1981.

Producer and director, *Country Gold,* CBS, 1982.

Director, *Johnny Cash Christmas, 1983,* CBS, 1983.

Director (with Joseph Cates), *Johnny Cash: Christmas on the Road,* CBS, 1984.

Director, *The 10th Anniversary Johnny Cash Christmas Special,* CBS, 1985.

Producer, *The 62nd Annual Academy Awards,* ABC, 1989.

Producer, *The 63rd Annual Academy Awards,* ABC, 1990.

Also worked as producer and director of specials featuring Ice Follies, the World's Fair, and Aquacade, all ABC, 1965.

TELEVISION WORK; EPISODIC

Executive producer (with Joseph Cates), "Have I Got a Christmas for You," *Hallmark Hall of Fame,* NBC, 1977.

Executive producer (with Joseph Cates), "Fame," *Hallmark Hall of Fame,* NBC, 1978.

Producer and director, *Faerie Tale Theatre,* Showtime, 1982.

Director, "Consenting Adult," *An ABC Theatre Presentation,* ABC, 1985.

TELEVISION WORK; SERIES

Producer (with Roger Peterson and Chester Feldman), *I've Got a Secret* (game show), CBS, 1952-67.

Producer and director, *Mother's Day* (game show), ABC, c. 1958-59.

Haggis Baggis (game show), NBC, 1958-59.

Producer and director, *Camouflage* (game show), ABC, 1961-62.

Creator, producer, and director, *Hootenanny,* ABC, 1962.

Executive producer and director, *International Showtime,* NBC, 1962-64.

OTHER TELEVISION WORK

Producer and director, *Electric Showcase,* ABC, 1965.

Producer, *Off Campus* (pilot), CBS, 1977.

Producer and director, *One More Time,* ABC, 1988.

FILM DIRECTOR AND PRODUCER, EXCEPT WHERE INDICATED

The Painting (short subject), Union Films, 1962.

Rings around the World, Columbia, 1967.

I Never Sang for My Father (also see below), Columbia, 1970.

Director, *Summer Wishes, Winter Dreams,* Columbia, 1973.

One Summer Love (also known as *Dragonfly*), American International, 1976.

Director, *The Promise* (also known as *Face of a Stranger*), Universal, 1979.

Director, *The Last Married Couple in America,* Universal, 1980.

Oh God! Book II, Warner Brothers, 1980.

Director, *Backfire,* Vidmark, 1989.

FILM APPEARANCES

Appeared in *50 Years of Action!,* 1986.

STAGE WORK

Stage manager, *Shinbone Alley,* Broadway Theatre, New York City, 1957.

Associate producer (with Joseph Cates), *Spoon River Anthology* (later *Spoon River*), Booth Theatre, New York City, 1963, then Royal Court Theatre, London, 1964.

Producer (with Jack Farren), *You Know I Can't Hear You When the Water's Running* (also see below), Ambassador Theatre, New York City, 1967-68, then Broadhurst Theatre, New York City, 1968.

Producer, *I Never Sang for My Father,* Longacre Theatre, New York City, 1968.

Producer, *The Chinese and Dr. Fish,* Ethel Barrymore Theatre, New York City, 1970.
Producer (with Roy N. Nevans and Albert J. Schiff), *Solitaire/Double Solitaire,* John Golden Theatre, New York City, 1971.
Director, *The Price,* Long Wharf Theatre, New Haven, CT, 1971.
Director, *Voices,* Ethel Barrymore Theatre, 1972.
Producer (with Matthew Alexander) and director, *Tricks of the Trade,* Brooks Atkinson Theatre, New York City, 1980.

Also worked as producer of *You Know I Can't Hear You When the Water's Running* (tour), U.S. cities, 1967, and London, 1968.

OTHER SOURCES:

PERIODICALS

Hollywood Reporter, November 30, 1988, pp. 16 and 20.*

* * *

CATES, Phoebe 1964(?)-

PERSONAL: Born c. 1964 (some sources say 1963), in New York City; daughter of Joseph Cates (a television producer); married Kevin Kline (an actor), 1989; children: Owen Joseph. *Education:* Attended Professional Children's School; studied with Actors Circle theatre group.

ADDRESSES: *Agent*—InterTalent Agency, Inc., 131 South Rodeo Dr., Suite 300, Beverly Hills, CA 90212.

CAREER: Actress. Worked as a model prior to 1984.

MEMBER: Screen Actors Guild.

CREDITS:

TELEVISION APPEARANCES; MINI-SERIES

Lilli, *Lace,* ABC, 1984.
Lilli, *Lace 2,* ABC, 1985.

TELEVISION APPEARANCES; EPISODIC

Entertainment Tonight, syndicated, 1989.

OTHER TELEVISION APPEARANCES

Annie Burroughs, *Baby Sister* (movie), ABC, 1983.
Presenter, *The 63rd Annual Academy Awards Presentation* (special), ABC, 1991.

Also appeared as Marguerite, *Vaclav Havel's largo desolato* (special), 1990; appeared briefly in the series *Mr. and Mrs. Dracula.*

FILM APPEARANCES

Linda Barrett, *Fast Times at Ridgmont High,* Universal, 1982.
Sarah, *Paradise,* Embassy, 1982.
Christine Ramsay, *Private School,* Universal, 1983.
Kate, *Gremlins,* Warner Brothers, 1984.
Patty Winston, *Date with an Angel,* DEG, 1987.
Amanda, *Bright Lights, Big City,* Metro-Goldwyn-Mayer/United Artists, 1988.
Carson McBride, *Shag,* Tri-Star, 1988.
Aiken Reed, *Heart of Dixie,* Tri-Star, 1990.
Kate Beringer, *Gremlins 2: The New Batch,* Warner Brothers, 1990.
Elizabeth Cronin, *Drop Dead Fred,* New Line Cinema, 1991.

STAGE APPEARANCES

Ariadna Koromyslova, *The Nest of the Wood Grouse,* New York Shakespeare Festival (NYSF), Public Theatre, New York City, 1984.
Jill, *Rich Relations,* Second Stage Theatre, New York City, 1985.
Rosaria, *Women and Football,* Manhattan Punch Line, New York City, 1988.
Juliet, *Romeo and Juliet,* Goodman Theatre, Chicago, IL, c. 1988.
Hero, *Much Ado about Nothing,* NYSF, New York City, 1988.
Evelyn Foreman, *The Tenth Man,* Vivian Beaumont Theatre, New York City, 1989.

OTHER SOURCES:

PERIODICALS

New York Post, June 28, 1984.
People, June 14, 1982, p. 36.*

* * *

CATON-JONES, Michael 1958-

PERSONAL: Born in 1958 in Broxburn, Scotland.

ADDRESSES: *Agent*—Creative Artists Agency, 1888 Century Park East, 14th Floor, Los Angeles, CA 90067.

CAREER: Director.

CREDITS:

FILM DIRECTOR

Scandal, Miramax Films, 1989.
Memphis Belle, Warner Brothers, 1990.
Doc Hollywood, Warner Brothers, 1991.

FILM APPEARANCES

Maitre d', *Doc Hollywood,* Warner Brothers, 1991.*

* * *

CAULFIELD, Maxwell 1959-

PERSONAL: Born November 23, 1959, in Derby, England (some sources list Glasgow, Scotland); immigrated to United States, 1978; son of Peter Nelby and Oriole Caulfield; married Juliet Mills (an actress), December 2, 1980. *Education:* Left school at fifteen.

ADDRESSES: Agent—Irv Schecter Agency, 9300 Wilshire Blvd., Beverly Hills, CA 90212.

CAREER: Actor. Began career in show business as a nude dancer at the Windmill Theatre in London, England.

MEMBER: Screen Actors Guild, Actors Equity Association (U.S. and British chapters).

AWARDS, HONORS: Theatre World Award, 1979, for *Class Enemy.*

CREDITS:

STAGE APPEARANCES

Demetrius, *Hot Rock Hotel,* Truck and Warehouse Theater, New York City, 1978.
Understudy, *Once a Catholic,* Helen Hayes Theatre, New York City, 1979.
Iron (Herron), *Class Enemy,* Players Theatre, New York City, 1979.
Ralph, *Hitting Town,* Zephyr Theatre, Los Angeles, CA, 1980.
Horace, *The Inheritors,* Mirror Repertory Co., Real Theatre/Theatre at St. Peter's Church, New York City, c. 1980s.
Captain Stanhope, *Journey's End,* Cast Theatre, Los Angeles, c. 1980s.
Winston Smith, *1984,* Cast Theatre, Los Angeles, c. 1980s.
Ben Gordon, *Paradise Lost,* Mirror Repertory Co., Real Theatre/Theatre at St. Peter's Church, c. 1980s.
Frazer, *Crimes and Dreams,* Theatre Four, New York City, 1980.
Sloane, *Entertaining Mr. Sloane,* Westside Mainstage and Cherry Lane Theatre, New York City, 1981, Mark Taper Forum, Los Angeles, 1987.
Peter, *Salonika,* New York Public Theatre, New York City, 1985.
Dennis, *Loot,* Mark Taper Forum, 1987.
Richard Loeb, *Never the Sinner,* Citadel Theatre, Canada, 1991.

MAJOR TOURS

John Merrick, *The Elephant Man,* Florida, c. 1980s.
Milo Tindle, *Sleuth,* national tour, 1988.

FILM APPEARANCES

Michael Carrington, *Grease 2,* Paramount, 1982.
Bill, *Electric Dreams,* Metro-Goldwyn-Mayer (MGM)/United Artists, 1984.
Roy Alston, *The Boys Next Door,* New World-Republic, 1985.
Lt. Ray Ellis, *The Supernaturals,* Republic, 1987.
Eric Garrison, *Mindgames,* MGM, 1989.
George Abbot, *Project Alien,* ITC, 1990.
Shane, *Sundown,* Vestron, 1991.

TELEVISION APPEARANCES; SERIES

Miles Colby, *Dynasty II: The Colbys* (also known as *The Colbys*), ABC, 1985-87.

Also appeared in *Dynasty* mini-series, 1991.

TELEVISION APPEARANCES; MOVIES

Jeff, *The Parade,* CBS, 1984.
Alain Marais, *Judith Krantz's Till We Meet Again* (also known as *Till We Meet Again*), CBS, 1989.
Phil Serulla, *Blue Bayou* (also known as *Orleans*), NBC, 1990.

SIDELIGHTS: Favorite roles: Captain Stanhope in *Journey's End* and John Merrick in *The Elephant Man.*

OTHER SOURCES:

PERIODICALS

New York Times, September 4, 1981.
People, April 29, 1985, p. 128.*

* * *

CHANG, Gary 1953-

PERSONAL: Full name, Gary Kington Chang; born February 22, 1953, in Minneapolis, MN; son of Melvin and Diana (Lee) Chang; married Margaret Ann Craig, February 14, 1982. *Education:* Carnegie-Mellon University, B.F.A., music composition, 1975; California Institute of Arts, M.F.A., music composition, 1977. *Avocational interests:* Cooking and tennis.

ADDRESSES: Office—23352 Alamos Lane, Newhall, CA 91321. *Agent*—Milander-Schleussner-Kaufman Agency, Inc., 4146 Lankershim Blvd., North Hollywood, CA 91602.

CAREER: Consultant, studio musician, and film music composer. Fairlight Instruments, West Los Angeles, CA, product specialist, 1980-82; Gary Chang Co., Newhall, CA, freelance composer and studio musician, 1982-85; Rolandcorp USA, Los Angeles CA, product consultant, 1985-89; Gary Chang Music Co., Inc., Newhall, film music composer, 1985—.

MEMBER: American Federation of Musicians, Society of Composers and Lyricists.

AWARDS, HONORS: National Endowment for the Arts grant, 1977.

CREDITS:

FILM WORK; SONG PRODUCER

"Dream Montage," *The Breakfast Club,* Universal, 1985.
"Bring Me a Dream," *Death Warrant,* Metro-Goldwyn-Mayer/United Artists, 1990.
"Standing in the Shadows" and "Dangerous," *The Perfect Weapon,* Paramount, 1991.

WRITINGS:

FILM MUSIC

(With Keith Forsey) *The Breakfast Club,* Universal, 1985.
3:15, The Moment of Truth, Dakota Entertainment, 1986.
52 Pick-Up, Cannon, 1986.
Firewalker, Cannon, 1986.
Sticky Fingers, Spectrafilm, 1988.
(With Michael Kamen) *Dead-Bang,* Warner Brothers, 1989.
A Shock to the System, Corsair, 1990.
Death Warrant, Metro-Goldwyn-Mayer/United Artists, 1990.
Miami Blues, Orion, 1990.
The Perfect Weapon, Paramount, 1991.

TELEVISION MUSIC; SERIES

The Marshall Chronicles, ABC, 1990.
WIOU, CBS, 1990.
Eerie, Indiana, NBC, 1991.

TELEVISION MUSIC; MOVIES

A Killer Among Us, CBS, 1990.
Rising Son, Turner Network Television, 1990.
Eighty-three Hours 'til Dawn, CBS, 1990.
Donor, CBS, 1990.
Murder in New Hampshire: The Pamela Smart Story, CBS, 1991.
The Nightman, NBC, 1992.
Standoff at Marion, NBC, 1992.

TELEVISION MUSIC; EPISODIC

"Hunger Chic," *Trying Times,* PBS, 1989.
"The Boss," *Trying Times,* PBS, 1989.
"Death and Taxes," *Trying Times,* PBS, 1989.
"Harold Clurman: A Life of Theatre," *American Masters,* PBS, 1989.

* * *

CHARNIN, Martin 1934-

PERSONAL: Full name, Martin Jay Charnin; born November 24, 1934, in New York, NY; son of William (an opera singer) and Birdie (Blakeman) Charnin; married Lynn Ross (a dancer), March 2, 1958 (divorced, 1961); married Genii Prior (a dancer), January 8, 1962 (divorced); married Jade Hobson, December, 1984; children: (first marriage) Randy; (second marriage) Sasha. *Education:* Cooper Union, B.A., 1955.

ADDRESSES: Office—c/o Richard Ticktin, 1345 Avenue of the Americas, New York, NY 10105.

CAREER: Director, lyricist, author, and producer. Began career as an actor in musical productions.

MEMBER: American Society of Composers, Authors, and Publishers, American Guild of Authors and Composers, Directors Guild of America, Writers Guild of America, Dramatists Guild, Society of Stage Directors and Choreographers (executive board member), National Academy of Recording Arts and Sciences, New York Theatre Actors Society.

AWARDS, HONORS: Emmy Award, outstanding variety or musical program, 1970, for *Annie, the Woman in the Life of a Man;* Emmy Awards, outstanding single program—variety or musical, and outstanding director—comedy, variety, or music special (with Walter C. Miller), and Emmy Award nomination, outstanding writing—comedy, variety, or music special, all 1972, for "Jack Lemmon in 'S Wonderful, 'S Marvelous, 'S Gershwin," *Bell System Family Theatre;* gold record, Recording Industry Association of America, 1972, for "The Best Thing You've Ever Done"; Emmy Award nomination (with Dave Wilson), outstanding director—comedy, variety, or music special, 1973, for *Jack Lemmon—Get Happy;* Drama Desk awards, best lyrics and best director of a musical, 1977, Antoinette Perry Award, best score of a Broadway musical, Antoinette Perry Award nomination, best director of a Broadway musical, and New York Drama Critics' Circle Award, best new musical, all 1977, for *Annie* (stage musical); Grammy Award, best cast show album (with Charles Strouse), 1977, for *Annie* (album); Antoinette Perry Award nominations, best book of a musical and best direction of a musical, both 1981, for *The First;* gold and platinum records for stage and film albums of *Annie;* Standard Award, most performed song of the decade, American Society of Composers, Authors, and Publishers, for "Tomorrow."

CREDITS:

STAGE DIRECTOR

Ballad for a Firing Squad, Theatre de Lys, New York City, 1968.
Nash at Nine (adaptation of the works of Ogden Nash; conceived by Charnin), Helen Hayes Theatre, New York City, 1973.
Music! Music!, City Center Theatre, New York City, 1974.
The National Lampoon Show, New Palladium, New York City, 1975.
Annie (all theatres in New York City; also see below), Alvin Theatre, 1977-81, American National Theatre Academy, 1981, Eugene O'Neill Theatre, 1981, Uris Theatre, 1981.
The First (also see below), Martin Beck Theatre, New York City, 1981.
A Little Family Business, Ahmanson Theatre Group, Ahmanson Theatre, Los Angeles, then Martin Beck Theatre, both 1982.
Upstairs (conceived by Charnin), O'Neal's Forty-third Street Theatre, New York City, 1982.
A Backer's Audition (conceived by Charnin, Douglas Bernstein, and Denis Markell), Manhattan Theatre Club/Upstage, New York City, 1983-84.
Jokers, Goodspeed Opera House, East Haddam, CT, 1986-87.
No Frills Revue (conceived by Charnin), City Stage Company Theatre, New York City, 1988.
Cafe Crown, Brooks Atkinson Theatre, New York City, 1989.
Laughing Matters, Arts Common at St. Peter's Church, 1989.
Sid Caesar and Company: Does Anybody Know What I'm Talking About?, John Golden Theatre, New York City, 1989.
Annie Two: Miss Hannigan's Revenge (also see below), John F. Kennedy Center for the Performing Arts, Washington, DC, 1989-90.
Annie Warbucks (also see below), Goodspeed Opera House, 1990, then Marriot Hotel Theatre, Lincolnshire, England, 1992, later Drury Lane Theatre, Chicago, IL, 1992.
Winchell (also see below), Depot Theatre, Westport, NY, 1991, then Brooks Atkinson Theatre Workshop, 1991.

Also directed *The Bar Mitzvah Boy,* London, 1978.

OTHER STAGE WORK

Producer, *Kaleidoscope Revue* (also see below), Provincetown Playhouse, Boston, MA, 1957.
Production supervisor, *On the Swing Shift,* Manhattan Theatre Club/Downstage, New York City, 1982.
Production supervisor, *Mike,* Walnut Street Theatre, Philadelphia, PA, 1987-88.

MAJOR TOURS

Lyricist, *Zenda,* California cities, 1963.
Lyricist and director, *Annie,* U.S. cities and London, beginning in 1978.
Lyricist, with others, *Lena Horne: The Lady and Her Music,* U.S. cities, beginning in 1982.

Also lyricist for touring production of *Little Revue,* 1960.

STAGE APPEARANCES

(Stage debut) Big Deal, *West Side Story,* Winter Garden Theatre, New York City, 1957.
Noel Schwartz, *The Girls against the Boys,* Alvin Theatre, New York City, 1959.
Big Deal, *West Side Story,* Winter Garden Theatre, 1960.

TELEVISION WORK; SPECIALS

Producer, *Annie, the Woman in the Life of a Man* (also see below), CBS, 1970.
Director (with Walter C. Miller) and producer, *George M!* (also see below), NBC, 1970.
Producer, *Dames at Sea,* NBC, 1972.
Director (with Miller) and producer, "Jack Lemmon in 'S Wonderful, 'S Marvelous, 'S Gershwin" (also see below), *Bell System Family Theatre,* NBC, 1972.
Producer and creator, *Cole Porter in Paris,* NBC, 1973.
Director (with Dave Wilson) and producer, *Jack Lemmon—Get Happy* (also known as *Get Happy: The Music of Harold Arlen*), NBC, 1973.
Director and producer, *Annie and the Hoods* (also see below), ABC, 1974.
Producer, *George M!* (also see below), CBS, 1976.

Produced pilot program for Children's Television Workshop, 1973; produced *The Annie Christmas Show* and *C'mon Saturday,* both 1977.

TELEVISION APPEARANCES

Judge, *Opryland: Night of Stars and Future Stars* (pilot), NBC, 1981.
Broadway Plays Washington, PBS, 1982.
Music by Richard Rodgers, PBS, 1990.

RECORDINGS:

(Lyricist) *Annie* (stage cast show album; music by Charles Strouse), Columbia, 1977.

Also lyricist for song "The Best Thing You've Ever Done," 1972, and film cast album *Annie.*

WRITINGS:

LYRICS FOR STAGE PRODUCTIONS

Kaleidoscope Revue, produced at Provincetown Playhouse, Boston, MA, 1957.
Fallout Revue (also see below), produced at Renata Theatre, New York City, 1959.
Pieces of Eight, Upstairs at the Downstairs Theatre, New York City, 1959.
Hot Spot, produced at Majestic Theatre, New York City, 1963.
Mata Hari, produced at National Theatre, Washington, DC, 1967.
Two by Two, produced at Imperial Theatre, New York City, 1970-71.
Annie (includes song "Tomorrow"), produced at Alvin Theatre, 1977-81.
I Remember Mama, produced at Majestic Theatre, 1979.
(With others) *The Madwoman of Central Park West,* produced at Twenty-two Steps Theatre, New York City, 1979.
(With others) *Lena Horne: The Lady and Her Music,* produced at Nederlander Theatre, New York City, 1980-81.
The First (also see below), produced at Martin Beck Theatre, New York City, 1981.
Annie Two: Miss Hannigan's Revenge, produced at John F. Kennedy Center for the Performing Arts, Washington, DC, 1989-90.
Annie Warbucks, produced at Goodspeed Opera House, East Haddam, CT, 1990.
Winchell (also see below), produced at Depot Theatre, Westport, NY, 1991, produced at Brooks Atkinson Theatre Workshop, New York City, 1991.

SCRIPTS FOR STAGE PRODUCTIONS

(Coauthor) *Kaleidoscope Revue,* produced at Provincetown Playhouse, 1957.
Fallout Revue, produced at Renata Theatre, 1959.
Wet Paint, produced at Renata Theatre, 1965.
(With Joel Siegel) *The First,* produced at Martin Beck Theatre, 1981.
(With Keith Levinson) *Winchell,* produced at Depot Theatre, 1991, produced at Brooks Atkinson Theatre, 1991.

Author and director of nightclub acts for various stars, including Shirley Jones, Abbe Lane, Dionne Warwick, Nancy Wilson, Leslie Uggams, Jose Ferrer, Larry Kert, and Andrea McArdle.

LYRICS FOR TELEVISION PROGRAMS

Feathertop, ABC, 1961.
Jackie Gleason Show, CBS, 1961.
(With others) *Annie, the Woman in the Life of a Man,* CBS, 1970.

SCRIPTS FOR TELEVISION SPECIALS

George M!, NBC, 1970.
"Jack Lemmon in 'S Wonderful, 'S Marvelous, 'S Gershwin," *Bell System Family Theatre,* NBC, 1972.
(With others) *Annie and the Hoods,* ABC, 1974.

BOOKS

The Giraffe Who Sounded Like Ol' Blue Eyes (juvenile), illustrations by Kate Draper, Dutton, 1976.
Annie: A Theatre Memoir, Dutton, 1977.

OTHER

Lyricist for songs, including "The Best Thing You've Ever Done," 1972, and "Maman."

ADAPTATIONS: The musical *Annie* was adapted for film by screenwriter Carol Sobieski, directed by John Huston, for Columbia, 1982.

OTHER SOURCES:

BOOKS

Contemporary Authors, Volume 103, Gale, 1982, pp. 77-78.

PERIODICALS

New York Daily News, January 6, 1988, p. 31.

* * *

CHILDRESS, Alice 1920-

PERSONAL: Surname is pronounced "*chill*-dress"; born October 12, 1920, in Charleston, SC; married second husband, Nathan Woodard (a musician), July 17, 1957; children: (first marriage) Jean (Mrs. Richard Lee). *Education:* Attended public schools in New York City; studied acting with Venzella Jones and Nadja Romanov.

ADDRESSES: Agent—Flora Roberts, Inc., 157 West 57th St., Penthouse A, New York, NY 10019.

CAREER: Playwright, novelist, actress, and director. American Negro Theatre, New York City, actress and director, c. 1941-52. Radcliffe Institute for Independent Study (now Mary Ingraham Bunting Institute), visiting scholar, 1966-68; lecturer at schools and universities. Frances Delafield Hospital, member of governing board.

MEMBER: International P.E.N., Dramatists Guild (member of council), American Federation of Television and Radio Artists, Writers Guild of America East (member of council), Harlem Writers Guild.

AWARDS, HONORS: Obie Award, best original Off-Broadway play, *Village Voice,* 1956, for *Trouble in Mind;* John Golden Fund for Playwrights grant, 1957; Rockefeller grant, 1967; Outstanding Book of the Year citation, *New York Times Book Review,* 1973, Woodward School Book Award, Jane Addams Children's Book Honor Award, young adult novel, Jane Addams Peace Association, and National Book Award nomination, all 1974, Lewis Carroll Shelf Award, University of Wisconsin, 1975, and Best Young Adult Book citation, American Library Association, 1975, all for *A Hero Ain't Nothin' but a Sandwich* (novel); named honorary citizen of Atlanta, GA, 1975, for opening of play *Wedding Band: A Love/Hate Story in Black and White;* Sojourner Truth Award, National Association of Negro Business and Professional Women's Clubs, 1975; best screenplay award, Virgin Islands Film Festival, and first Paul Robeson Award for Outstanding Contributions to the Performing Arts, Black Filmmakers Hall of Fame, both 1977, for *A Hero Ain't Nothin' but a Sandwich* (screenplay); "Alice Childress Week" officially observed in Charleston and Columbia, SC, 1977, to celebrate opening of play *Sea Island Song; Rainbow Jordan* was named one of *School Library Journal*'s Best Books of 1981, one of the Outstanding Books of the Year by the *New York Times,* 1982, a notable children's trade book in the social studies by National Council for the Social Studies and Children's Book Council, 1982, and received an honorable mention, Coretta Scott King Award, 1982; Radcliffe Medal, 1984; Audelco Pioneer Award, 1986.

CREDITS:

STAGE APPEARANCES

(Stage debut) *On Striver's Row,* Library Theatre, New York City, 1940.

Sistuh Bessie, *Natural Man,* Library Theatre, 1941.

Three's a Family, Library Theatre, 1943.

Blanche, *Anna Lucasta,* Library Theatre, then Mansfield Theatre, both 1944.

Sadie, *Rain,* American Negro Theatre Playhouse, New York City, 1947.

Almost Faithful, American Negro Theatre Playhouse, 1948.

Title role, *Florence* (also see below), American Negro Theatre, New York City, 1949.

The Candy Story, New Playwrights Theatre, New York City, 1951.

The mother, *The Emperor's Clothes,* Greenwich Mews Theatre, New York City, 1953.

Mrs. Thurston, *The Cool World,* Eugene O'Neill Theatre, New York City, 1960.

STAGE DIRECTOR

Florence (also see below), American Negro Theatre, New York City, 1949.

Trouble in Mind (also see below), Greenwich Mews Theatre, New York City, 1955.

(With Joseph Papp) *Wedding Band: A Love/Hate Story in Black and White* (also see below), University of Michigan, Ann Arbor, 1966, then New York Shakespeare Festival, Public Theatre, New York City, 1972-73.

FILM APPEARANCES

Uptight, Paramount, 1968.

WRITINGS:

PLAYS

Florence (one-act), first produced at American Negro Theatre, New York City, 1949.

Just a Little Simple (based on stories by Langston Hughes), first produced at Club Baron Theatre, New York City, 1950.

Gold through the Trees, first produced at Club Baron Theatre, 1952.

Trouble in Mind, first produced at Greenwich Mews Theatre, New York City, 1955, revised version published in *Black Theatre: A Twentieth-Century Collection of the Work of Its Best Playwrights,* edited by Lindsay Patterson, Dodd, 1971.

Wedding Band: A Love/Hate Story in Black and White, first produced at University of Michigan, Ann Arbor, 1966, then New York Shakespeare Festival, Public Theatre, New York City, 1972, published by Samuel French, 1973.

String (one-act; based on a story by Guy de Maupassant; also see below), first produced by Negro Ensemble Company, St. Mark's Playhouse, New York City, 1969.

Young Martin Luther King (originally titled *The Freedom Drum;* music by husband Nathan Woodard), produced as a touring production at Performing Arts Repertory Theatre, 1969-71.

Mojo: A Black Love Story (one-act; also see below), produced at New Heritage Theatre, New York City, 1970.

When the Rattlesnake Sounds: A Play about Harriet Tubman (juvenile), illustrated by Charles Lilly, published by Coward, 1975.

Let's Hear It for the Queen: A Play (juvenile), published by Coward, 1976.

Sea Island Song, produced in Charleston, SC, 1977, produced as *Gullah,* University of Massachusetts at Amherst, 1984.

Mojo [and] *String,* published by Dramatists Play Service, 1971, produced in a double-bill at Inner City Cultural Center, Los Angeles, 1978-79.

(And author, with Woodard, of music and lyrics) *Moms: A Praise Play for a Black Comedienne* (based on the life of Jackie "Moms" Mabley), first produced by Green Plays, Art Awareness, 1986, then Hudson Theatre Guild, New York City, 1987.

Other plays include *The World on a Hill,* published in *Plays to Remember,* Macmillan, 1968; *Martin Luther King at Montgomery, Alabama* (music by Woodard), 1969; *A Man Bearing a Pitcher,* 1969; *The African Garden* (music by Woodard), 1971; and *Vashti's Magic Mirror.*

SCREENPLAYS

A Hero Ain't Nothin' but a Sandwich (based on Childress's novel of the same title; also see below), New World Pictures, 1978.

RADIO PLAYS

Wine in the Wilderness: A Comedy-Drama, broadcast by WGBH-TV, 1969, published by Dramatists Play Service, 1969, produced as a stage play, National Black Theatre, New York City, 1978.

BOOKS

Like One of the Family: Conversations from a Domestic's Life, Independence Publishers, 1956, reprinted with an introduction by Trudier Harris, Beacon Press, 1986.

(Editor) *Black Scenes* (collection of scenes from plays written by Afro-Americans about the black experience), Doubleday, 1971.

A Hero Ain't Nothin' but a Sandwich (novel), Coward, 1973.

A Short Walk (novel), Coward, 1979.

Rainbow Jordan (novel), Coward, 1981.

Many Closets, Coward, 1987.

Also author of *Those Other People,* 1989.

OTHER

Work represented in anthologies, including *Best Short Plays of the World Theatre, 1968-1973,* edited by Stanley Richards, Crown, 1973; *Anthology of the Afro-American in the Theatre: A Critical Approach,* edited by Lindsay Patterson, Publishers Agency, 1978; and *Black American Literature and Humanism,* edited by R. Baxter Miller, University Press of Kentucky, 1981. Author of column "Here's Mildred," *Baltimore Afro-American,* 1956-58. Contributor of plays, articles, and reviews to periodicals, including *Masses and Mainstream, Black World, Freedomways, Essence,* and *Negro Digest.*

ADAPTATIONS: Wedding Band: A Love/Hate Story in Black and White has been adapted for television, broadcast by ABC, 1973; *String* has been adapted for television, broadcast as an episode of *Vision,* PBS, 1979.

OTHER SOURCES:

BOOKS

Abramson, Doris E., *Negro Playwrights in the American Theatre, 1925-1959,* Columbia University Press, 1969.

Betsko, Kathleen, and Rachel Koenig, *Interviews with Contemporary Women Playwrights,* Beech Tree Books, 1987.

Children's Literature Review, Volume 14, Gale, 1988.

Contemporary Authors New Revision Series, Volume 27, Gale, 1989.

Contemporary Literary Criticism, Gale, Volume 12, 1980, Volume 15, 1980.

Dictionary of Literary Biography, Gale, Volume 7: *Twentieth-Century American Dramatists,* 1981, Volume 38: *Afro-American Writers after 1955: Dramatists and Prose Writers,* 1985.

Donelson, Kenneth L., and Alleen Pace Nilson, *Literature for Today's Young Adults,* Scott, Foresman, 1980.

Evans, Mari, editor, *Black Women Writers (1950-1980): A Critical Evaluation,* Doubleday-Anchor, 1984.

Hatch, James V., *Black Theater, U.S.A.: Forty-five Plays by Black Americans,* Free Press, 1974.

Mitchell, Loften, editor, *Voices of the Black Theatre,* James White, 1975.

Street, Douglas, editor, *Children's Novels and the Movies,* Ungar, 1983.*

* * *

CHURCHILL, Caryl 1938-

PERSONAL: Born September 3, 1938, in London, England; daughter of Robert Churchill (a political cartoonist) and his wife (a fashion model); married David Harter (a barrister), 1961; children: three sons. *Education:* Lady Margaret Hall, Oxford, B.A., 1960.

ADDRESSES: Agent—Margaret Ramsay Ltd., 14A Goodwin's Court, London WC2N 4LL, England.

CAREER: Playwright. Royal Court Theatre, London, England, resident writer, 1974, tutor to Young Writers' Group.

AWARDS, HONORS: Richard Hillary Memorial Prize, 1961; Obie Award, play writing, *Village Voice,* 1981, for *Cloud Nine;* Obie Award, play writing, 1982, and runner-up for Susan Smith Blackburn Prize, 1983, both for *Top Girls;* Susan Smith Blackburn Prize, 1984, for *Fen;* Obie Award, best new play, 1987, for *Serious Money.*

WRITINGS:

PLAYS

Downstairs, first produced at Oriel College, Oxford University, Oxford, England, 1958, then London, 1959.

Having a Wonderful Time, first produced by Oxford Players, Oxford University, 1960.

Easy Death, first produced at Oxford University, 1962.

Schreber's Nervous Illness, first produced at King's Head Lunchtime Theatre, London, 1972.

Owners (also see below), first produced at Royal Court Theatre Upstairs, London, 1972, produced at Thirteenth Street Theatre, New York City, 1973, published by Eyre Methuen, 1973.

Perfect Happiness, first produced at Soho Polytechnic Lunchtime Theatre, London, 1974.

Moving Clocks Go Slow, first produced at Royal Court Theatre Upstairs, London, 1975.

Objections to Sex and Violence, first produced at Royal Court Theatre, London, 1975.

Light Shining in Buckinghamshire (also see below), first produced at Traverse Theatre, Edinburgh, Scotland, 1976, published by Pluto Press, 1978.

Vinegar Tom (also see below), first produced at Hull Arts Centre, Hull, England, 1976, published by Theatre Quarterly Publications, 1978.

(With David Bradford, Bryony Lavery, and Michelene Wandor) *Floorshow,* first produced at North London Poly Theatre, London, 1977.

Traps (also see below), first produced at Royal Court Theatre Upstairs, 1977, published by Pluto Press, 1978, produced at Remains Theatre, New York City, 1983.

Cloud Nine (also see below), first produced at Royal Court Theatre, 1979, published by Pluto Press, 1979, produced at Lucille Lortel's Theatre de Lys (now Lucille Lortel Theatre), New York City, 1981-83.

Three More Sleepless Nights, first produced at Soho Polytechnic Theatre, 1980.

Top Girls, first produced at Royal Court Theatre, then Public Theatre, New York City, 1982-83, published by Samuel French, 1982, revised edition published by Methuen, 1984.

Fen (also see below), published by Methuen, 1983, first produced at Almeida Theatre, London, produced at Public/Newman Theatre, New York City, 1984, published as *Fen: A Drama,* Samuel French, 1984.

Softcops (also see below), produced by Royal Shakespeare Company, London, 1984, published by Methuen, 1984.

Churchill: Plays One (includes *Owners, Light Shining in Buckinghamshire, Vinegar Tom, Traps,* and *Cloud Nine*), published by Methuen, 1985.

(With David Lan) *A Mouthful of Birds,* first produced at Royal Court Theatre, 1986.

Serious Money, first produced at Royal Court Theatre, 1987, then Public Theatre/LuEsther Hall, New York City, 1987.

TELEVISION SCRIPTS

Author of *The Judge's Wife,* 1972; *Turkish Delight,* 1974; *The After Dinner Joke,* 1978; *Crimes,* 1981; and *The Legion Hall Bombing.*

RADIO SCRIPTS

Author of *The Ants,* 1962, published in *Penguin New English Dramatists 12,* Penguin, 1968; *Lovesick,* 1967; *Identical Twins,* 1968; *Abortive,* 1971; *Not, Not, Not, Not, Not Enough Oxygen,* 1972; *Henry's Past,* 1972; and *Perfect Happiness,* 1973.

OTHER SOURCES:

BOOKS

Contemporary Authors New Revision Series, Volume 22, Gale, 1988.

Contemporary Literary Criticism, Volume 31, Gale, 1985.

Dictionary of Literary Biography, Volume 13: *British Dramatists since World War II,* Gale, 1982.

PERIODICALS

New York Times, January 9, 1983; November 22, 1987.*

* * *

CLARK, James
See CLARK, Jim

* * *

CLARK, Jim 1931-
(James Clark)

PERSONAL: Born May 24, 1931, in Boston, Lincolnshire, England; son of Vernon (a company director) and Florence (a housewife; maiden name, Deal) Clark; married Laurence Mery (a film editor), in July, 1963; children: David, Kate, Sybil.

ADDRESSES: Agent—Tim Corrie, c/o Peters, Fraser, & Dunlop, The Chamber, Chelsea Harbour, London S.W.10, England.

CAREER: Film editor and director.

MEMBER: Directors Guild of America, Academy of Motion Picture Arts and Sciences, Association of Cinematograph, Television, and Allied Technicians (Canada).

AWARDS, HONORS: Academy Award, film editing, 1984, for *The Killing Fields;* Academy Award nomination, film editing, 1986, for *The Mission.*

CREDITS:

FILM EDITOR; AS JAMES CLARK

One Wish Too Many (also known as *The Magic Marble*), Sterling Educational Films-Children's Film Foundation, 1956.
Surprise Package, Columbia, 1960.
The Grass Is Greener, Universal, 1960.
The Innocents, Twentieth Century-Fox, 1961.
Term of Trial, Warner Bros., 1962.
Charade, Universal, 1963.
The Pumpkin Eater, Royal-Columbia, 1964.
Darling, Embassy, 1965.

FILM EDITOR

X Y & Zee (also known as *Zee and Co.*), Columbia, 1972.
The Day of the Locust, Paramount, 1975.
The Adventures of Sherlock Holmes' Smarter Brother, Twentieth Century-Fox, 1975.
Marathon Man, Paramount, 1976.
(With Arthur Schmidt) *The Last Remake of Beau Geste,* Universal, 1977.
Agatha, Warner Bros., 1979.
Yanks, Universal, 1979.
Honky Tonk Freeway, Universal-AFD, 1981.
Privates on Parade, HandMade Films, 1982, Orion Classics, 1984.
The Killing Fields, Warner Bros., 1984.
The Frog Prince, Goldcrest-Warner Bros., 1985, released in United States as *French Lesson,* Warner Bros., 1986.
The Mission, Warner Bros., 1986.
(With Bryan Oates) *Il giovane Toscanini* (also known as *Toscanini* and *Young Toscanini*), Italian International Films, 1988.
Memphis Belle, Warner Bros., 1990.
Meeting Venus, Warner Bros., 1991.

FILM DIRECTOR

(Under name James Clark) *The Christmas Tree* (also see below), CFF, 1966.
Think Dirty (also known as *Every Home Should Have One*), British Lion, 1970.
Rentadick, Virgin, 1972.
Madhouse, American International, 1974.

OTHER FILM WORK

Creative consultant, *Midnight Cowboy,* United Artists, 1969.

WRITINGS:

SCREENPLAYS; AS JAMES CLARK

(With Michael Barnes) *The Christmas Tree* (based on a story by Ed Harper), CFF, 1966.

COLEMAN, Dabney 1932-

PERSONAL: Full name, Dabney W. Coleman; born January 3, 1932, in Austin, TX; son of Melvin Randolph and Mary (Johns) Coleman; married Ann Courtney Harrell, December 21, 1957 (divorced, June 1959); married Carol Jean Hale (an actress), December 11, 1961 (divorced); children: Kelly Johns, Randolph, Mary. *Education:* Attended Virginia Military Institute, 1949-51; received degree from University of Texas, c. 1954; attended University of Texas Law School until 1957; studied theatre at the Neighborhood Playhouse School, 1958-60. *Religion:* Episcopalian.

ADDRESSES: Agent—International Creative Management, 8899 Beverly Blvd., Los Angeles, CA 90048. *Contact*—c/o Fox Television, 5746 Sunset Blvd., Hollywood, CA 90028.

CAREER: Actor in New York City, 1960-62, and Los Angeles, CA, 1962—. *Military service:* U.S. Army, 1953-55.

MEMBER: Screen Actors Guild, Phi Delta Theta.

AWARDS, HONORS: Emmy Award nominations, outstanding lead actor in a comedy series, 1983 and 1984, both for *Buffalo Bill;* Emmy Award, outstanding supporting actor in a special, 1987, for *Sworn to Silence;* Golden Globe Award, best actor in a comedy, and Emmy Award nomination, outstanding lead actor in a comedy series, both 1988, both for *The "Slap" Maxwell Story;* Emmy Award nomination, outstanding supporting actor in a special, 1988, for *Baby M;* Emmy Award nomination, outstanding guest actor in a drama series, 1991, for *Columbo.*

CREDITS:

FILM APPEARANCES

Charlie, *The Slender Thread,* Paramount, 1965.
Salesman, *This Property Is Condemned,* Paramount, 1966.
Jed, *The Scalp Hunters,* United Artists (UA), 1968.
Harrison Wilby, *The Trouble with Girls (and How to Get into It)* (also known as *The Chautauqua*), Metro-Goldwyn-Mayer (MGM), 1969.
Mayo, *Downhill Racer,* Paramount, 1969.
Frank Donnelly, *I Love My Wife,* Universal, 1970.
Executive officer, *Cinderella Liberty,* Twentieth Century-Fox, 1973.
Charles Huntley, *The Dove,* Paramount, 1974.
Assistant fire chief, *The Towering Inferno,* Twentieth Century-Fox/Warner Brothers, 1974.
Jack Parker, *Bite the Bullet,* Columbia, 1975.
Dave McCoy, *The Other Side of the Mountain* (released in England as *A Window to the Sky*), Universal, 1975.
Captain Murray Arnold, *Midway* (released in England as *The Battle of Midway*), Universal, 1976.

Maxwell, *Rolling Thunder,* American International Pictures, 1977.

Ralph Thompson, *Viva Knievel!* (also known as *Seconds to Live*), Warner Brothers, 1977.

Emmett, *North Dallas Forty,* Paramount, 1979.

Jack Heintzel, *How to Beat the High Cost of Living,* American International Pictures, 1980.

Judge Keith Hayes, *Melvin and Howard,* Universal, 1980.

Tom Dickerson, *Nothing Personal,* American International/Filmways, 1980.

Franklin Hart, Jr., *Nine to Five,* Twentieth Century-Fox, 1980.

Mark, *Modern Problems,* Twentieth Century-Fox, 1981.

Bill Ray, *On Golden Pond,* Universal, 1981.

Ron, *Tootsie,* Columbia, 1982.

Dr. Joseph Prang, *Young Doctors in Love,* Twentieth Century-Fox, 1982.

McKittrick, *Wargames,* MGM/UA, 1983.

Jack Flack/Hal Osborne, *Cloak and Dagger,* Universal, 1984.

Producer, *The Muppets Take Manhattan,* Tri-Star, 1984.

Cooper, *The Man with One Red Shoe,* Twentieth Century-Fox, 1985.

Jerry Caesar, *Dragnet,* Universal, 1987.

Walter Sawyer, *Hot to Trot,* Warner Brothers, 1988.

Stewart McBain, *Where the Heart is,* Buena Vista, 1990.

Burt Simpson, *Short Time,* Twentieth Century-Fox, 1990.

Aunt Bea, *Meet the Applegates* (also known as *The Applegates*), Triton Pictures, 1991.

Also appeared in the films *Bogard,* 1975, and *The Black Street Fighter,* 1976.

TELEVISION APPEARANCES; SERIES

Dr. Leon Bessemer, *That Girl,* ABC, 1966-67.

Dr. Tracy Graham, *Bright Promise* (also see below), NBC, 1969-72.

Lt. Lloyd Daggett, *Cannon,* CBS, 1971-76.

Reverend Merle Jeeter, *Mary Hartman, Mary Hartman,* syndicated, 1976-77.

Reverend Merle Jeeter, *Forever Fernwood,* syndicated, 1977.

"Fast" Eddie Barnes, *Apple Pie,* ABC, 1978.

Bill Bittinger, *Buffalo Bill,* NBC, 1983-84.

"Slap" Maxwell, *The "Slap" Maxwell Story,* ABC, 1987-88.

Otis Drexell, *Drexell's Class* (also known as *Oh No, Not Drexell!* and *Shut Up, Kids;* also see below), Fox, 1991—.

Also appeared on the syndicated series *Fernwood 2-Night,* a spin-off from the shows *Mary Hartman, Mary Hartman* and *Forever Fernwood.*

TELEVISION APPEARANCES; EPISODIC

The Comedy Zone, CBS, 1984.

Hugh Creighton, "Columbo and the Murder of a Rock Star," *Columbo,* ABC, 1991.

Also appeared as a guest on *The Mary Tyler Moore Show* on CBS.

TELEVISION APPEARANCES; PILOTS

Captain Walter Jones, *Egan,* ABC, 1973.

Captain Logan, *Kiss Me, Kill Me,* ABC, 1976.

TELEVISION APPEARANCES; MOVIES, EXCEPT WHERE NOTED

The Brotherhood of the Bell, CBS, 1970.

Bob Mitchell, *Dying Room Only,* ABC, 1973.

Senator Burt Haines, *The President's Plane Is Missing,* ABC, 1973.

Ted Seligson, *Savage* (also known as *Watch Dog*), NBC, 1973.

Mr. Wood, *Bad Ronald,* ABC, 1974.

Paul Mathison, *Attack on Terror: The FBI versus the Ku Klux Klan,* CBS, 1975.

Al Stephensen, *Returning Home,* ABC, 1975.

McCallum, *Maneaters Are Loose!,* CBS, 1978.

Josh Harrington, *More Than Friends,* ABC, 1978.

Jack Wilson, *When She Was Bad . . .* (also known as *A New Life*), ABC, 1979.

Randall Bordeaux, *Callie and Son,* CBS, 1981.

William S. Paley, *Murrow,* HBO, 1986.

Tyler Cane, *Fresno* (miniseries), CBS, 1986.

The Return of Mickey Spillane's Mike Hammer, CBS, 1986.

Ed Siegel, *Guilty of Innocence: The Lenell Geter Story* (also known as *Justice Delayed: The Lenell Geter Story*), CBS, 1987.

Jessie Kiplinger, *Plaza Suite,* ABC, 1987.

Hal Gilbert, *Maybe Baby* (also known as *Sooner or Later*), NBC, 1988.

William Cox, *Never Forget* (also known as *The Promise*), TNT, 1991.

TELEVISION APPEARANCES; SPECIALS

The Night of One Hundred Stars Two (also see below), ABC, 1985.

Comic Relief Two, HBO, 1987.

Happy Birthday, Hollywood, ABC, 1987.

Marty Costigan, *Sworn to Silence* (also known as *Privileged Information*), ABC, 1987.

Gary N. Skoloff, *Baby M* (also known as *The Baby M Story*), ABC, 1988.

Host, "The Aspen Comedy Festival," *Showtime Presents,* Showtime, 1989.

TELEVISION WORK; EXECUTIVE CONSULTANT

Drexell's Class, Fox, 1991—.

STAGE APPEARANCES

(With Tania Velia) American couple, *A Call on Kuprin,* Broadhurst Theater, New York City, 1961.
The Night of One Hundred Stars Two, Radio City Music Hall, New York City, 1985.

WRITINGS:

TELEVISION

Bright Promise, NBC, 1972.

OTHER SOURCES:

BOOKS

Celebrity Register, 5th edition, Gale, 1990, pp. 91-92.
Newsmakers, Issue 3, Gale, 1988, pp. 75-78.

PERIODICALS

Los Angeles Magazine, February, 1988, p. 16.
Newsweek, July 18, 1983, p. 71.
People, July 11, 1983, p. 71.
Rolling Stone, November 19, 1987, p. 39.
TV Guide, March 2, 1984, p. 36; January 2, 1988, p. 26.*

* * *

COLUMBUS, Chris 1959-

PERSONAL: Full name, Christopher Columbus; born in 1959 in Spangler, PA; son of Alex (a coal miner and aluminum plant worker) and Irene (a factory worker) Columbus; married Monica Devereux (a dancer). *Education:* Graduated from New York University film school, 1980.

ADDRESSES: Agent—Jack Rapke, Creative Artists Agency, 9830 Wilshire Blvd., Beverly Hills, CA 90212.

CAREER: Director and screenwriter.

CREDITS:

FILM DIRECTOR

Adventures in Babysitting, Buena Vista, 1987.
Heartbreak Hotel (also see below), Buena Vista, 1988.
Home Alone, Twentieth Century-Fox, 1990.
Only the Lonely (also see below), Twentieth Century-Fox, 1991.

TELEVISION WORK

Developer, *Galaxy High School* (animated series), CBS, 1986.

WRITINGS:

SCREENPLAYS

Reckless, Metro-Goldwyn-Mayer/United Artists, 1984.
Gremlins, Warner Brothers, 1984.
Young Sherlock Holmes, Paramount, 1985.
The Goonies, Warner Brothers, 1985.
Heartbreak Hotel, Buena Vista, 1988.
Only the Lonely, Twentieth Century-Fox, 1991.

TELEVISION SERIES

Galaxy High School (animated), CBS, 1986.

OTHER SOURCES:

PERIODICALS

Daily News (New York), June 30, 1985.
Daily News Magazine (New York), June 28, 1987, p. 12.
Rolling Stone, March 27, 1986, p. 107.*

* * *

COMDEN, Betty 1919-

PERSONAL: Born Elizabeth Cohen, May 3, 1919, in Brooklyn, NY; daughter of Leo (a lawyer) and Rebecca (a school teacher; maiden name, Sadvoransky) Cohen; married Steven Kyle (a designer and businessman), January 4, 1942; children: Susanna, Alan. *Education:* New York University, B.S., drama, 1938.

ADDRESSES: Office—c/o The Dramatists Guild, 234 West 44th St., New York, NY 10036.

CAREER: Lyricist, writer, and actress. Appeared in cabaret group, "The Revuers," at a number of clubs, including the Village Vanguard, the Rainbow Room, and the Blue Angel, and on a variety of television shows, 1939-44.

MEMBER: Writers Guild of America (East and West), American Federation of Television and Radio Artists, Screenwriters Guild, American Guild of Variety Artists, American Society of Composers, Authors, and Publishers, Dramatists Guild (member of council, 1948—), Actors' Equity Association.

AWARDS, HONORS: All with Adolph Green: Theatre World Award, 1944, and Screenwriters Guild Award, 1949, both for *Our Town;* Screenwriters Guild Award, 1952, Antoinette Perry Award nomination, best book, 1986, voted one of the best American films of all times by the American Film Institute, and named one of the ten best films of all time (internationally) by *Sight & Sound,* all for *Singin' in the Rain;* Antoinette Perry Award, outstanding musical, New York Drama Critics' Circle Award, best new musical, and Donaldson Award, all

1953, all for *Wonderful Town;* Academy Award nomination, best story and screenplay, 1953, for *The Band Wagon;* Academy Award nomination, best story and screenplay, and Screenwriters Guild of America Award, both 1955, both for *It's Always Fair Weather;* Antoinette Perry Award nomination, outstanding musical, 1957, Screenwriters Guild Award, and Grammy Award nomination, best sound track album—original cast, motion picture or TV, both 1960, all for *Bells Are Ringing;* Obie Award, *Village Voice,* and Grammy Award nomination, best comedy-musical, both 1959, both for *A Party with Betty Comden and Adolph Green;* Grammy Award nomination, song of the year, 1961, for "Make Someone Happy" from the musical *Do Re Mi;* Antoinette Perry Award nomination, best musical, and Grammy Award nomination, best original cast show album, both 1961, both for *Do Re Mi;* Grammy Award nomination, best score from an original cast show album, 1967, Antoinette Perry Awards, best score, best lyrics, and best musical play, all 1968, all for *Hallelujah, Baby!;* Antoinette Perry Award, best musical, 1970, for *Applause;* Antoinette Perry Awards, best book and best score, and Grammy Award nomination, best cast show album, 1978, all for *On the Twentieth Century;* Antoinette Perry Award nominations, best book and best score, both 1983, both for *A Doll's Life;* Antoinette Perry Award, best original score, and New York Drama Critics' Circle Award, best new musical, both 1991, and Grammy Award, best musical show album, 1992, all for *The Will Rogers Follies;* Kennedy Center Honor, 1991.

Woman of Achievement Award, New York University Alumni Association, 1978; New York City's Mayor Award of Art and Culture, 1978; named to Songwriters Hall of Fame, 1980; named Lion of the Performing Arts, New York Public Library, 1987; named to Theatre Hall of Fame.

CREDITS:

STAGE APPEARANCES

(Broadway debut) Claire, *On the Town* (also see below), Adelphi Theatre, New York City, 1944.

A Party (revue based on collection of Comden and Green's previously written songs and sketches; also see below), Cherry Lane Theatre, New York City, 1958, then expanded version at Golden Theatre, New York City, as *A Party with Betty Comden and Adolph Green,* 1958, later new version at Morosco Theatre, New York City, 1977, then on tour.

Lyrics and Lyricists, Kaufman Auditorium, New York City, 1971.

George Abbott . . . A Celebration, Shubert Theatre, New York City, 1976.

Tasha Blumberg, *Isn't It Romantic* (two-act), Playwrights Horizons Theatre, New York City, 1983-84, then Lucille Lortel Theatre, New York City, 1984-85.

Happy Birthday, Mr. Abbott!; or, Night of 100 Years, Palace Theatre, New York City, 1987.

The Players Club Centennial Salute, Shubert Theatre, 1989.

Also appeared in *An Evening with Betty Comden and Adolph Green,* 1971.

FILM APPEARANCES

The Revuers, *Greenwich Village,* Twentieth Century-Fox, 1944.

Garbo, *Garbo Talks,* United Artists, 1984.

Mrs. Wheeler, *Slaves of New York,* Tri-Star, 1989.

TELEVISION APPEARANCES; SPECIALS

The Fabulous 50s, CBS, 1960.

The American Film Institute Salute to Gene Kelly (also known as *The AFI Salute to Gene Kelly*), CBS, 1985.

Evening at Pops, PBS, 1987 and 1988.

Tony Bennett (also known as *On Stage at Wolf Trap*), PBS, 1988.

The Kennedy Center Honors: A Celebration of the Performing Arts, CBS, 1988 and 1991.

The 45th Annual Tony Awards, CBS, 1991.

TELEVISION APPEARANCES; EPISODIC

"Follies in Concert," *Great Performances,* PBS, 1986.

"Bernstein at 70," *Great Performances,* PBS, 1989.

"Music by Richard Rodgers," *Great Performances,* PBS, 1990.

"Broadway Sings: The Music of Jule Styne," *Great Performances,* PBS, 1991.

WRITINGS:

STAGE LYRICS, EXCEPT WHERE INDICATED; WITH ADOLPH GREEN

(And sketches) *Two on the Aisle,* produced at Mark Hellinger Theatre, New York City, 1951.

Wonderful Town (two-act musical), produced at Winter Garden Theatre, New York City, 1953.

Additional lyrics, *Peter Pan* (three-act musical), produced at Winter Garden Theatre, 1954.

Say, Darling, produced at American National Theatre and Academy, New York City, 1958.

Do Re Mi (two-act musical; includes song "Make Someone Happy"), produced at St. James Theatre, New York City, 1960.

(And others) *Leonard Bernstein's Theatre Songs,* produced at Theatre De Lys, New York City, 1965.

Hallelujah, Baby! (two-act musical), produced at Martin Beck Theatre, New York City, 1967.

Lorelei (two-act musical; based on *Gentlemen Prefer Blondes*), produced at Civic Center Music Hall, Oklahoma City, OK, 1973, then at Palace Theatre, 1974.

(With others) *By Bernstein,* produced at Chelsea Theater Center Westside, New York City, 1975.

(And music; with others) *The Madwoman of Central Park West* (one-woman show), produced at 22 Steps Theatre, New York City, 1979.

(And others) *Diamonds* (two-act musical), produced at Circle in the Square Downtown, New York City, 1984-85.

The Will Rogers Follies, produced at Palace Theatre, 1991.

STAGE BOOK AND LYRICS; WITH GREEN

On the Town (two-act musical based on the ballet *Fancy Free* by Jerome Robbins; also see below), produced at Adelphi Theatre, 1944.

Billion Dollar Baby, produced at Alvin Theatre, New York City, 1945.

Bonanza Bound, produced at Shubert Theatre, Philadelphia, PA, 1947.

Bells Are Ringing (two-act musical; also see below), produced at Shubert Theatre, 1956, published by Random House, 1957.

Subways Are for Sleeping (two-act musical), produced at St. James Theatre, 1961-62.

Fade Out—Fade In, produced at Mark Hellinger Theatre, 1964, published by Random House, 1965.

On the Twentieth Century (two-act musical), produced at St. James Theatre, 1978, published by Drama Book Publishers, 1981.

A Doll's Life (two-act musical), produced at Mark Hellinger Theatre, 1982.

STAGE BOOK; WITH GREEN

Applause (two-act musical; based on film *All about Eve;* also see below), produced at Palace Theatre, 1970-72, published by Random House, 1971.

STAGE MUSIC; WITH GREEN

(And others) *Straws in the Wind* (two-act musical), produced at American Place Theatre, 1975.

PLAYS; WITH GREEN

A Party (revue based on collection of Comden and Green's previously written songs and sketches), first produced at Cherry Lane Theatre, 1958, expanded version produced at Golden Theatre as *A Party with Betty Comden and Adolph Green,* 1958, new version produced at Morosco Theatre, 1977, then on tour.

Singin' in the Rain (two-act musical; adaptation of movie of same title; also see below), produced at Gershwin Theatre, New York City, 1985-86.

(And others) *Jerome Robbins' Broadway,* produced at Imperial Theatre, New York City, 1989-90.

SCREENPLAYS, EXCEPT WHERE INDICATED; WITH GREEN

Good News (based on the musical comedy by Lawrence Schwab, Frank Mandel, Buddy De Sylva, Lew Brown, and Ray Henderson), Metro-Goldwyn-Mayer (MGM), 1947.

The Barkleys of Broadway, MGM, 1949.

(And lyrics) *On the Town* (based on the musical play by Comden, Green, and Leonard Bernstein), MGM, 1949.

Lyrics, *Take Me Out to the Ballgame,* MGM, 1949.

(And lyrics) *Singin' in the Rain,* MGM, 1952, published by Viking, 1972.

(And lyrics) *The Band Wagon,* MGM, 1953.

(And lyrics) *It's Always Fair Weather,* MGM, 1955.

Auntie Mame (based on the novel *Mame* by Patrick Dennis and the play by Jerome Lawrence and Robert E. Lee), Warner Brothers, 1958.

(And lyrics) *Bells Are Ringing* (based on the musical play), MGM, 1960.

(And lyrics) *What a Way To Go* (based on a story by Gwen Davis), Twentieth Century-Fox, 1964.

TELEVISION SPECIALS; WITH GREEN

Let's Celebrate, ABC, 1972.

Applause (adapted from musical of same title), CBS, 1973.

Also author of various other musical comedy specials for ABC.

TELEVISION SERIES; WITH GREEN

(And Nat Hiken) *Buick Circus Hour,* NBC, 1952-53.

OTHER

Comden and Green on Broadway, Drama Book Publishers, 1981.

Also author, with Green, of music, book, and lyrics for cabaret group, "The Revuers," 1939-44. Contributor to periodicals, including *Esquire, Cahiers du Cinema* and *Vogue.*

RECORDINGS:

A Party with Betty Comden and Adolph Green, Capitol.

OTHER SOURCES:

BOOKS

Contemporary Authors New Revision Series, Volume 2, Gale, 1981.*

CONNERY, Sean 1930-

PERSONAL: Born Thomas Connery, August 25, 1930, in Edinburgh, Scotland; son of Joseph and Euphania C. Connery; married Diane Cilento, 1962 (divorced); married Micheline Roquebrune, 1979; children: (first marriage) Jason; (second marriage) one stepdaughter.

ADDRESSES: Agent—Creative Artists Agency, 1888 Century Park E., Suite 1400, Los Angeles, CA 90067.

CAREER: Actor, director, and producer. Tantallon Films Ltd., director, 1972—. *Military service:* Served with Royal Navy.

MEMBER: Royal Scottish Academy of Music and Drama (fellow).

AWARDS, HONORS: Shared Golden Globe Award, male world film favorite, Hollywood Foreign Press Association, 1972; D.Litt., Heriot-Watt University, 1981; Hasty Pudding Man of the Year Award, 1984; named Star of the Year, National Association of Theatre Owners (NATO), 1987; commander, Order of Arts and Literature of France; British Academy of Film and Television Arts Award, best actor in a leading role, 1987, for *The Name of the Rose;* Academy Award, best supporting actor, 1987, and Golden Globe Award, best actor in a supporting role, 1988, both for *The Untouchables;* Golden Globe Award nomination, best supporting actor, for *Indiana Jones and the Last Crusade;* named NATO/ShoWest Worldwide Star of the Year, 1990; American Cinematheque Award, 1992.

CREDITS:

FILM APPEARANCES

Let's Make Up, United Artists (UA), 1955.
Spike, *No Road Back,* RKO Radio Pictures, 1957.
Mike, *Action of the Tiger,* Metro-Goldwyn-Mayer (MGM), 1957.
Mark Trevor, *Another Time, Another Place,* Paramount, 1958.
Johnny, *Hell Drivers,* Rank, 1958.
A Night to Remember, Rank, 1958.
Welder, *Time Lock,* Romulus-Beaconsfield, 1959.
O'Bannion, *Tarzan's Greatest Adventure,* Paramount, 1959.
Michael McBride, *Darby O'Gill and the Little People,* Buena Vista, 1959.
Private Flanagan, *The Longest Day,* Twentieth Century-Fox, 1962.
Paddy Damion, *The Frightened City,* Allied Artists, 1962.
James Bond, *Doctor No,* UA, 1963.
James Bond, *From Russia with Love,* UA, 1964.
James Bond, *Goldfinger,* UA, 1964.
Anthony Richmond, *Woman of Straw,* UA, 1964.
Mark Rutland, *Marnie,* Universal, 1964.
James Bond, *Thunderball,* UA, 1965.
Joe Roberts, *The Hill,* MGM, 1965.
Pedlar Pascoe, *Operation Snafu* (also known as *On the Fiddle* and *War Head*), American International, 1965.
Samson Shillitoe, *A Fine Madness,* Warner Brothers, 1966.
James Bond, *You Only Live Twice,* UA, 1967.
Shalako, *Shalako,* Cinerama, 1968.
Jack Kehoe, *The Molly Maguires,* Paramount, 1970.
Roald Amundson, *The Red Tent,* Paramount, 1971.
Anderson, *The Anderson Tapes,* Columbia, 1971.
James Bond, *Diamonds Are Forever,* UA, 1971.
Detective Sergeant Johnson, *The Offence* (also known as *Something Like the Truth*), UA, 1973.
Zed, *Zardoz,* Twentieth Century-Fox, 1974.
Colonel Arbuthnot, *Murder on the Orient Express,* Paramount, 1974.
Mulay el Raisuli, *The Wind and the Lion,* MGM, 1975.
Daniel Dravot, *The Man Who Would Be King,* Allied Artists/Columbia, 1975.
Nils Tahlvik, *The Terrorists,* Twentieth Century-Fox, 1975.
Robin Hood, *Robin and Marian,* Columbia, 1976.
Kahlif Abdul-Muhsen, *The Next Man,* Allied Artists, 1976.
Major General Urquhart, *A Bridge Too Far,* UA, 1977.
Edward Pierce, *The Great Train Robbery,* UA, 1979.
Dr. Paul Bradley, *Meteor,* American International, 1979.
Robert Dapes, *Cuba,* UA, 1979.
O'Neil, *Outland,* Warner Brothers, 1981.
King Agamemnon, *Time Bandits,* Embassy, 1981.
Patrick Hale, *Wrong Is Right,* Columbia, 1982.
Green Knight, *Sword of the Valiant,* Cannon, 1982.
Douglas, *Five Days One Summer,* Warner Brothers, 1982.
James Bond, *Never Say Never Again,* Warner Brothers, 1983.
Ramirez, *Highlander,* Twentieth Century-Fox, 1986.
William of Baskerville, *The Name of the Rose,* Twentieth Century-Fox, 1986.
James Malone, *The Untouchables,* Paramount, 1987.
Lieutenant Colonel Alan Caldwell, *The Presidio,* Paramount, 1988.
Himself, *Memories of Me,* MGM/UA, 1988.
Dr. Henry Jones, *Indiana Jones and the Last Crusade,* Paramount, 1989.
Jessie McMullen, *Family Business,* Tri-Star, 1989.
Captain Marko Ramius, *The Hunt for Red October,* Paramount, 1990.
Barley Blair, *Russia House,* MGM/UA, 1990.
Juan Villa-Lobos Ramirez, *Highlander 2020: The Quickening,* Interstar, 1991.

King Richard, *Robin Hood: Prince of Thieves,* Warner Brothers, 1991.
Dr. Robert Campbell, *Medicine Man,* Buena Vista, 1992.

Also appeared in *Ransom,* 1974; *Happy Anniversary 007: Twenty-Five Years of James Bond,* 1987; and *100% Bonded,* 1987.

FILM WORK

Producer and director of *The Bowler and the Bonnet* (documentary).

TELEVISION APPEARANCES; SPECIALS

The Barbara Walters Special, ABC, 1987.
The 60th Annual Academy Awards Presentation, ABC, 1988.
Host, *The Prince's Trust Gala,* TBS, 1989.
The 61st Annual Academy Awards Presentation, ABC, 1989.
Premiere: Inside the Summer Blockbuster, Fox, 1989.
Sinatra 75: The Best Is Yet to Come, CBS, 1990.

Also appeared in *Rich and Famous: 1988 World's Best,* 1988.

TELEVISION APPEARANCES; MOVIES

Anna Karenina, syndicated, 1964.

Also appeared in *Requiem for a Heavyweight,* 1957; *Anna Christie; Boy with the Meataxe; Women in Love; The Crucible; Riders to the Sea; Adventure Story;* and a Canadian production of *Macbeth.*

TELEVISION APPEARANCES; EPISODIC

"Jack in Rome," *Jack Benny Program,* CBS, 1957.
"The Hollow Crown," *Age of Kings,* syndicated, 1961.
"The Road to Shrewsbury," *Age of Kings,* syndicated, 1961.
"Mademoiselle Colombe," *Festival of the Arts,* syndicated, 1962.
"The Deposing of a King," *Age of Kings,* syndicated, 1963.
"Male of the Species," *On Stage,* NBC, 1969.

Also appeared as guest host of *Sammy and Company.*

OTHER SOURCES:

PERIODICALS

Hollywood Reporter, April, 1988, p. 42.
New York Times, June 7, 1987.
Sunday Times, April 22, 1990, p. E1.*

CONTI, Tom 1941-

PERSONAL: Full name, Thomas Antonio Conti; born November 22, 1941, in Paisley, Scotland; son of Alfonso (a hairdresser) and Mary (a hairdresser; maiden name, McGoldrick) Conti; married Kara Drummond Wilson (an actress), July 2, 1967; children: Nina. *Education:* Attended Royal Scottish Academy of Music and Drama, Glasgow, Scotland. *Avocational interests:* Playing flamenco guitar.

ADDRESSES: Agent—c/o John Gaines, Agency for the Performing Arts, 9000 Sunset Blvd., Los Angeles, CA 90069.

CAREER: Actor and director. Acted at Citizens' Theatre, Glasgow, Scotland.

MEMBER: Garrick Club (London).

AWARDS, HONORS: Laurence Olivier Award, actor of the year—new play, Society of West End Theatre, and Variety Club of Great Britain award, both 1978, and Antoinette Perry Award, best actor, 1979, all for *Whose Life Is It Anyway?;* Academy Award nomination, best actor, 1983, for *Reuben, Reuben;* West End Theatre Managers Award; Royal Television Society Award.

CREDITS:

STAGE APPEARANCES

(Stage debut) *The Roving Boy,* Citizen's Theatre, Glasgow, Scotland, 1959.
Harry Vine, *The Black and White Minstrels,* Edinburgh Festival, Edinburgh, Scotland, 1972.
Ben, *Let's Murder Vivaldi,* King's Head Theatre, Islington, England, 1972.
(London debut) Carlos, *Savages,* Royal Court Theatre, then Comedy Theatre, both 1973.
Harry Vine, *The Black and White Minstrels,* Hampstead Theatre, London, 1974.
Enrico Zamati, *Other People,* Hampstead Theatre, 1974.
Title role, *Don Juan,* Hampstead Theatre, 1976.
Dick Dudgeon, *The Devil's Disciple,* Royal Shakespeare Company, Aldwych Theatre, London, 1976.
Ken Harrison, *Whose Life Is It Anyway?,* Mermaid Theatre, then Savoy Theatre, both London, 1978.
(New York debut) Ken Harrison, *Whose Life Is It Anyway?,* Trafalgar Theatre, 1979.
An Italian Straw Hat, Shaftesbury Theatre, London, 1986.
Dave, *Treats,* Hampstead Theatre, 1989.
Title role, *Jeffrey Bernard Is Unwell,* Apollo Theatre, London, 1990.
The Ride Down Mt. Morgan, Wyndham's Theatre, London, 1991-92.

Also appeared in *They're Playing Our Song,* 1980; *Romantic Comedy,* 1982; and *Two into One.*

STAGE DIRECTOR

Last Licks, Longacre Theatre, New York City, 1979.
Before the Party, Oxford Playhouse, then Queen's Theatre, London, 1980.
The Housekeeper, Apollo Theatre, London, 1982.

FILM APPEARANCES

(Film debut) Andrea Sarti as a man, *Galileo,* American Film Theatre, 1975.
Seymour, *Flame,* VPS/Goodtimes, 1975.
Mark, *Full Circle,* Fester, 1977, released as *The Haunting of Julia,* Discovery, 1981.
Jacquin, *The Duellists,* Paramount, 1977.
Colonel John Lawrence, *Merry Christmas Mr. Lawrence,* Universal, 1982.
Gowan McGland, *Reuben, Reuben,* Twentieth Century-Fox, 1983.
Alan McMann, *American Dreamer,* Warner Bros., 1983.
Pope Leo XIV, *Saving Grace,* Columbia, 1986.
Vic Mathews, *The Gospel According to Vic* (also known as *Heavenly Pursuits*), Skouras, 1986.
Dr. Stuart Framingham, *Beyond Therapy,* New World, 1987.
Dr. Roger Briggs, *Miracles,* Orion, 1987.
Costas Caldes, *Shirley Valentine,* Paramount, 1989.

Also appeared as Tom/Geoffrey, *Eclipse,* 1976; Andrija Gavrilovic, *That Summer of White Roses,* 1989; Daniel, *Blade on the Feather,* 1989; appeared in *Two Brothers Running.*

TELEVISION APPEARANCES; MOVIES

Dolek Berson, *The Wall,* CBS, 1982.
Serge Klarsfeld, *Nazi Hunter: The Beate Klarsfeld Story,* ABC, 1986.
David Rose, *Lily,* CBS, 1986.
Duncan McKaskel, *The Quick and the Dead,* HBO, 1987.
Joe Bradley, *Roman Holiday,* NBC, 1987.
Pat Piscitelli, *Fatal Judgment,* CBS, 1988.
Dr. Phillips, *Voices Within: The Lives of Truddi Chase* (also known as *When Rabbit Howls*), ABC, 1990.

OTHER TELEVISION APPEARANCES

Bruno Varella, "If It's a Man, Hang Up" (special), *Thriller,* ABC, 1975.
Norman, *The Norman Conquests,* BBC, 1978.
Gus, *The Dumb Waiter* (special), ABC, 1987.

Also appeared in *Mother of Men,* 1959; appeared as Charles Bovary, *Madame Bovary,* 1976; Adam Morris, *The Glittering Prizes,* BBC; and appeared in *Treats; The Beaux Stratagem;* and *Princess and the Pea.*

OTHER SOURCES:

PERIODICALS

New York Times, April 22, 1979.

* * *

CONVY, Bert 1934-1991

OBITUARY NOTICE—See index for *CTFT* sketch: Born July 23, 1934, in St. Louis, MO; died of cancer, July 15, 1991, in Los Angeles, CA. Performer. Convy is best remembered as the host of the television game shows *Tattletales, Super Password,* and *Win, Lose or Draw,* and as a film, television, and stage actor. Convy played baseball for a Philadelphia Phillies farm team for two seasons in the early 1950s before embarking upon a full-time acting career. His theatrical credits include stage musicals, such as the original cast performances of *Cabaret* and *Fiddler on the Roof,* and other plays, including *A Tree Grows in Brooklyn* and *The Front Page.* He appeared on numerous television shows—*Perry Mason, The Partridge Family, Love of Life,* and *The Snoop Sisters*—and also hosted his own variety program, *The Late Summer, Early Fall Bert Convy Show* in the 1970s. Convy's film credits include *Semi-Tough* and *John Goldfarb, Please Come Home,* as well as the made-for-television *Dallas Cowboy Cheerleaders* and *Man in the Santa Claus Suit.* He received an Emmy for best game show host in 1977 for *Tattletales.* He also appeared as a singer and comedian in nightclubs, was co-executive producer for *Win, Lose or Draw,* and directed the 1986 film *Weekend Warriors.*

OBITUARIES AND OTHER SOURCES:

BOOKS

Who's Who in America, 46th edition, Marquis, 1990, p. 655.

PERIODICALS

Variety, July 22, 1991, p. 69.

* * *

COOGAN, Keith 1970(?)-

PERSONAL: Born c. 1970; son of Leslie Mitchell (a stand-up comic and son's business manager); grandson of Jackie Coogie (an actor); partner of Dominique Cole (an actress).

ADDRESSES: Agent—Harry Gold Agency, 3500 West Olive Ave., Suite 1400, Burbank, CA 91505.

CAREER: Actor. Appeared in television commercials beginning at age five.

MEMBER: Screen Actors Guild.

CREDITS:

FILM APPEARANCES

Brad Anderson, *Adventures in Babysitting,* Buena Vista, 1987.
Patrick Morenski, *Hiding Out,* DEG, 1987.
Ted Johnson, *Cheetah,* Buena Vista, 1989.
Mitch Kozinski, *Cousins,* Paramount, 1989.
Andy, *Under the Boardwalk,* New World, 1989.
Kenny Crandell, *Don't Tell Mom the Babysitter's Dead* (also known as *The Real World*), Warner Brothers, 1991.
Snuffy Bradberry, *Toy Soldiers,* Tri-Star, 1991.

Also appeared as Jonathan in *The Great O'Grady,* and as Crutch Kane in *Book of Love,* 1990.

TELEVISION APPEARANCES; EPISODIC

Erik Nelson, "A Town's Revenge," *ABC Afterschool Special,* 1989.
Matt Thompson, "Over the Limit," *ABC Afterschool Special,* 1990.

Also appeared as a child in *CHiPs, The Love Boat,* and *Fantasy Island.*

OTHER TELEVISION APPEARANCES

The 61st Annual Academy Awards (special), ABC, 1989.
D. G. Reynolds, *Spooner* (movie), Disney Channel, 1989.

OTHER SOURCES:

PERIODICALS

People, July 8, 1991.*

* * *

COPPOLA, Carmine 1910-1991

OBITUARY NOTICE—See index for *CTFT* sketch: Born June 11, 1910, in New York, NY; died after a stroke, April 26, 1991, in Northridge, CA. Musician and composer. Coppola was best known as the creator of musical scores for movies, including *The Godfather* and *Apocalypse Now.* A 1933 graduate of the Juilliard School of Music, he later played flute and composed and arranged music for the Radio City Music Hall orchestra. Coppola then held first flute positions with the Detroit Symphony and the NBC Symphony. After receiving his master's degree from the Manhattan School of Music in 1950, he worked variously as a musician, composer, and arranger for numerous New York City stage productions, including *Kismet* and *Stop the World—I Want to Get Off.* The father of film director Francis Ford Coppola and actress Talia Shire, he began working as music composer on many of his son's films. As co-composer with Nino Rota, the elder Coppola received the Academy award in 1975 for Best Musical Score for *The Godfather, Part II.* His additional film score credits include *The Black Stallion* and *Gardens of Stone,* and he contributed music to *Tucker: The Man and His Dream* and *New York Stories.* Coppola was also composer and conductor for live orchestra performances accompanying the restored 1927 film *Napoleon,* and served as the music director for the Los Angeles Civic Opera. Coppola made brief appearances in some of his son's films, including *One from the Heart* and *New York Stories.*

OBITUARIES AND OTHER SOURCES:

BOOKS

Who's Who in America, 46th edition, Marquis, 1990.

PERIODICALS

The Hollywood Reporter, April 29, 1991, p. 1.

* * *

CORBIN, Barry 1940-

PERSONAL: Born October 16, 1940, in Le Mesa, TX; son of Kilmer Blaine and Alma LaMerle (Scott) Corbin; married Marie Elyse Soape, March 15, 1965 (divorced, April, 1972); married Susan James Berger, May 29, 1976; children: James Barry, Christopher Clayton, Shannon Ross. *Education:* Attended Texas Tech University, 1959-64, and University of Colorado, 1964. *Politics:* Democrat. *Avocational interests:* Owning and riding cutting horses.

ADDRESSES: Agent—Judy Schoen and Assoc., 606 North Larchmont, Hollywood, CA 90048. *Publicist*—Wilkinson/Lipsman, 8170 Beverly Blvd, Suite 205, Los Angeles, CA 90048.

CAREER: Actor and writer. American Shakespeare Festival, Stratford, CT, member of company, 1968-69; Actors Theatre of Louisville, Louisville, KY, member of company, 1975-79. North Carolina State University, member of faculty, 1966-67. *Military service:* U.S. Marine Corps Reserve, active duty, 1962-64.

MEMBER: Screen Actors Guild (member of board of directors, 1985 and 1987-90), Actors Equity Association, American Federation of Television and Radio Artists, Dramatists Guild, Academy of Motion Picture Arts and Sciences, American Quarter Horse Association, National Cutting Horse Association.

AWARDS, HONORS: Theatre USA Award, 1974, for *Suckerrod Smith and the Cisco Kid.*

CREDITS:

TELEVISION APPEARANCES; SERIES

Merit Sawyer, *Boone,* NBC, 1983-84.
Maurice Minnifeld, *Northern Exposure,* CBS, 1990—.

TELEVISION APPEARANCES; MINI-SERIES

Pete, *The Thorn Birds,* ABC, 1983.

TELEVISION APPEARANCES; MOVIES

Sixth resident, *Rage,* NBC, 1980.
Dr. Agajanian, *Bitter Harvest,* NBC, 1981.
Gus Lobell, *A Few Days in Weasel Creek,* CBS, 1981.
Nick Hanson, *The Killing of Randy Webster,* CBS, 1981.
I. D. Masters, *Murder in Texas,* NBC, 1981.
Lieutenant Fletcher, *This House Possessed,* ABC, 1981.
Naylor, *Fantasies,* ABC, 1982.
Bob Austin, *Prime Suspect,* CBS, 1982.
Franz Grebner, *Fatal Vision,* NBC, 1984.
Bert Hamilton, *Flight 90: Disaster on the Potomac,* NBC, 1984.
Judge J. Samuel Perry, *The Jesse Owens Story,* syndicated, 1984.
Colonel, *The Ratings Game,* The Movie Channel, 1984.
Jim Heusdens, *Death in California,* ABC, 1985.
Floyd Carpenter, *The Defiant Ones,* ABC, 1986.
Captain Johnson, *Firefighter,* CBS, 1986.
The director, *C.A.T. Squad,* NBC, 1986.
Max Ball, *Warm Hearts, Cold Feet* (also known as *Babytalk*), CBS, 1987.
Judge Wirtz, *LBJ: The Early Years,* NBC, 1987.
Sheriff Wallace, *Secret Witness* (also known as *No Secrets*), CBS, 1988.
Roy "Big Mac" McCleary, *Man Against the Mob* (also known as *Trouble in the City of Angels*), NBC, 1988.
Malcolm Bryce, *The People across the Lake,* NBC, 1988.
Gil Rosine, *Stranger on My Land,* ABC, 1988.
Red King, White Knight, HBO, 1989.
I Know My First Name Is Steven, NBC, 1989.
Roscoe Brown, *Lonesome Dove,* CBS, 1989.
Principal Haskin, *Spooner,* Disney, 1989.
Police Officer Bob Wallis, *The Chase,* NBC, 1991.
Charlie McCloud, *Conagher,* TNT, 1991.

TELEVISION APPEARANCES; EPISODIC

Jenkins, "John Henry," *Shelley Duvall's Tall Tales and Legends,* Showtime, 1987.
Elmore, "Young Henry Houdini," *The Disney Sunday Movie,* ABC, 1987.
Bob Berg, "Last Flight Out," *AT&T Presents,* NBC, 1990.

OTHER TELEVISION APPEARANCES

Vernon Witchard, *Norma Rae* (pilot), NBC, 1981.
Sheriff Ames, *Travis McGee* (pilot), ABC, 1982.
Thomas Brady, *Spies* (special), CBS, 1987.
Governor Howard James, *Camp California* (pilot; also known as *Club Fed*), ABC, 1989.

Also appeared as Jimmy Scott Farnsworth, *Maggie* (special), 1986, and in *Texas 150: A Celebration Special,* 1986.

FILM APPEARANCES

Fat Zack, *Any Which Way You Can,* Warner Brothers, 1980.
Warden Walter Beatty, *Stir Crazy,* Columbia, 1980.
Uncle Bob, *Urban Cowboy,* Paramount, 1980.
Phil, *Dead and Buried,* Avco Embassy, 1981.
Wimbush, *The Night the Lights Went Out in Georgia,* Avco Embassy, 1981.
Derwood Arnspringer, *Honkytonk Man,* Warner Brothers, 1982.
Sheriff, *Six Pack,* Twentieth Century-Fox, 1982.
C. J., *The Best Little Whorehouse in Texas,* Universal, 1982.
Abernathy, *The Ballad of Gregorio Cortez,* Embassy, 1983.
Roy, *The Man Who Loved Women,* Columbia, 1983.
General Beringer, *Wargames,* Metro-Goldwyn-Mayer (MGM)/United Artists (UA), 1983.
Frank Burton, *Hard Traveling,* Shire, 1985.
Lew Harlan, *My Science Project,* Buena Vista, 1985.
Andrew Woolridge, *Nothing in Common,* Tri-Star, 1986.
Leon, *What Comes Around,* AWO Associates, 1986.
Off the Mark (also known as *Crazy Legs*), Fries Entertainment, 1987.
Sergeant Irwin Lee, *Under Cover,* Cannon, 1987.
Harv, *Critters II: The Main Course,* New Line, 1988.
Jim Sinclair, *Permanent Records,* Paramount, 1988.
George Lawrence, *It Takes Two,* MGM/UA, 1988.
P. J. Downing, *Who's Harry Crumb?,* Tri-Star, 1989.
Captain, *Short Time,* Twentieth Century-Fox, 1990.
Mr. Collins, *Ghost Dad,* Universal, 1990.
Sheriff, *The Hot Spot,* Orion, 1990.
Officer Don, *Career Opportunities,* Universal, 1991.

STAGE APPEARANCES

Forester, *As You Like It,* American Shakespeare Festival Theatre, Stratford, CT, 1968.
Mercade, *Love's Labour's Lost,* American Shakespeare Festival Theatre, Stratford, CT, 1968.
(Broadway debut) Gower, *Henry V,* ANTA Theatre, New York City, 1969.
Othello, American Shakespeare Festival, New York City, 1969.
Sir William Cecil/Lord Burghley/Sir Robert Cecil, *Masquerade,* Theatre Four, New York City, 1971.
Detective, *Crystal and Fox,* McAlpin Rooftop Theatre, 1973.

Bennie, *Getting Out,* Marymount Manhattan Theatre, New York City, 1978.

Also appeared in *Holy Ghosts.*

WRITINGS:

PLAYS

Author of *Suckerrod Smith and the Cisco Kid,* 1974, and *Throckmorton, Texas 76083,* 1983.

SCREENPLAYS

Author of *The Wildcatters,* 1986.

* * *

COURAGE, Alexander 1938-

PERSONAL: Born in 1938.

CAREER: Music director, composer, orchestrator, and arranger. Orchestrator for John Williams, Jerry Goldsmith, Adolph Deutsch, Hugo Friedhofer, Alex North, David Raksin, and Andre Previn. Instructor at University of Southern California.

AWARDS, HONORS: Academy Award nomination (with Lionel Newman), best scoring of music—adaptation or treatment, 1965, for *The Pleasure Seekers;* Academy Award nomination (with Newman), best scoring of music—adaptation or treatment, 1967, for *Doctor Doolittle;* Emmy Award nomination, best music composition in a series or single program of a series, 1973, for *Medical Center;* Emmy Award (with Ian Fraser, Chris Boardman, and Angela Morley), best music direction, 1987, for *Julie Andrews: The Sound of Christmas.*

CREDITS:

FILM WORK; MUSIC DIRECTOR

Sierra Stranger (also see below), Columbia, 1957.
Undersea Girl (also see below), Allied Artists, 1957.
(With Lionel Newman) *The Pleasure Seekers,* Twentieth Century-Fox, 1964.
(With Newman) *Doctor Doolittle* (also see below), Twentieth Century-Fox, 1967.
Superman IV: The Quest for Peace (also see below), Warner Brothers, 1987.

FILM WORK; ORCHESTRATOR

The Island of Doctor Moreau, American International, 1977.
Heart Like a Wheel, Twentieth Century-Fox, 1983.
Legend, Universal, 1985.
Lionheart, Orion, 1987.
L'Ours, AMLF, 1988.
Gremlins 2: The New Batch (also see below), Warner Brothers, 1990.

OTHER FILM WORK

Music coordinator, *Yes, Giorgio,* United Artists, 1982.

Also worked as music arranger for numerous films, including *Showboat, Seven Brides for Seven Brothers, Oklahoma, Kismet, Gigi,* and *Bells Are Ringing,* all for Metro-Goldwyn-Mayer (MGM), and *My Fair Lady, Porgy and Bess,* and *Fiddler on the Roof.*

TELEVISION WORK

Music arranger (with Chris Boardman, Ian Fraser, and Angela Morley), *Julie Andrews: The Sound of Christmas* (special), ABC, 1987.

WRITINGS:

FILM SCORES, EXCEPT WHERE INDICATED

Hot Rod Rumble, Allied Artists, 1957.
Shake, Rattle, and Rock!, American International, 1957.
Sierra Stranger, Columbia, 1957.
(With Hugo Friedhofer) *The Sun Also Rises,* Twentieth Century-Fox, 1957.
Undersea Girl, Allied Artists, 1957.
Handle with Care, MGM, 1958.
The Left-Handed Gun, Warner Brothers, 1958.
Tokyo After Dark, Paramount, 1959.
(With Ron Goodwin) *Follow the Boys,* MGM, 1963.
Doctor Doolittle, Twentieth Century-Fox, 1967.
"Fanfare" (theme song from *Star Trek* television series; also see below), *Star Trek II: The Wrath of Khan,* Paramount, 1982.
"Fanfare," *Star Trek III: The Search for Spock,* Paramount, 1984.
"Fanfare," *Star Trek IV: The Voyage Home,* Paramount, 1986.
(With John Williams) *Superman IV: The Quest for Peace,* Warner Brothers, 1987.
"Schatzilein" and "Colossus," *Triumph of the Spirit,* Triumph, 1989.
"Fanfare," *Star Trek V: The Final Frontier,* Paramount, 1990.
Source music, *Gremlins 2: The New Batch,* Warner Brothers, 1990.

TELEVISION MUSIC; SERIES

"Fanfare" and original theme, *Star Trek,* NBC, 1966-69.
Judd, for the Defense, ABC, 1967-69.
(With Jerry Goldsmith and Arthur Morton) *The Waltons,* CBS, 1972-81.
"Fanfare," *Star Trek: The Next Generation,* syndicated, 1987—.

TELEVISION MUSIC; EPISODIC

Wagon Train, NBC, 1957-62, then ABC, 1962-65.
The Untouchables, ABC, 1959-63.
Voyage to the Bottom of the Sea, ABC, 1964-68.
Daniel Boone, NBC, 1964-70.
Lost in Space, CBS, 1965-68.
Medical Center, CBS, 1969-76.

TELEVISION MUSIC; MOVIES

A Wedding on Walton's Mountain, NBC, 1982.
Mother's Day on Walton's Mountain, NBC, 1982.
A Day for Thanks on Walton's Mountain, NBC, 1982.

TELEVISION MUSIC; PILOTS

"The Cage," *Star Trek,* NBC, 1966.

* * *

COX, Alex 1954-

PERSONAL: Born December 15, 1954, in Liverpool, England; immigrated to United States, 1977. *Education:* Attended Oxford University; studied film production at Bristol University; attended University of California, Los Angeles Film School, 1977-80.

ADDRESSES: Agent—Stephanie Mann & Associates, 8323 Blackburn, No. 5, Los Angeles, CA 90048. *Contact*—P.O. Box 1002, Venice, CA 90291.

CAREER: Director and screenwriter.

MEMBER: Directors Guild of America.

CREDITS:

FILM WORK; DIRECTOR

Repo Man (also see below), Universal, 1984.
Sid and Nancy (also see below), Samuel Goldwyn, 1986.
Straight to Hell (also see below), Island, 1987.
(And editor, with Carlos Puente Ortega) *Walker,* Universal/Northern Distribution, 1987.

FILM APPEARANCES

Repo Man (also see below), Universal, 1984.

WRITINGS:

SCREENPLAYS

Repo Man, Universal, 1984.
(With Abbe Wool) *Sid and Nancy,* Samuel Goldwyn, 1986.
(With Dick Rude) *Straight to Hell,* Island, 1987.

OTHER SOURCES:

PERIODICALS

American Film, November, 1986, pp. 34-35.
Rolling Stone, September 10, 1987, pp. 29, 32, 90.
Scene, October, 1986, p. 32.
Village Voice, October 21, 1986, pp. 58, 60.*

* * *

CROFT, Paddy

PERSONAL: Born in Worthing, Sussex, England. *Education:* Attended Avondale College.

ADDRESSES: Agent—Select Artists' Representatives, 337 West 43rd St., Suite 1B, New York, NY 10036.

CAREER: Actress. Member of acting companies at Playhouse in the Park, Cincinnati, OH, 1965, Charles Playhouse, Boston, MA, 1968-69, and Hartford Stage Company, Hartford, CT, 1972-73; worked with repertory companies in Coventry, Canterbury, Preston, and Amersham, England.

AWARDS, HONORS: Vernon Rice Award (with others), Drama Desk, 1971, for *Long Day's Journey into Night.*

CREDITS:

STAGE APPEARANCES

(New York debut) Meg Dillon, *The Hostage,* One Sheridan Square Theatre, 1961.
Mrs. Whitefield and Miss Ramsden, *Man and Superman,* Phoenix Theatre, New York City, 1964.
Alice Fisher, *Billy Liar,* Gate Theatre, New York City, 1965.
Mrs. Jackson, *Live Like Pigs,* Actors' Playhouse, New York City, 1965.
Understudy for role of Mrs. Mercy, *The Killing of Sister George,* Belasco Theatre, New York City, 1966.
Josie Finn, *Hogan's Goat,* East 74th Theatre, 1966-67.
Miss McKay, *The Prime of Miss Jean Brodie,* Helen Hayes Theatre, New York City, 1968.
Understudy for title role, *Candida,* Longacre Theatre, New York City, 1970.
Cathleen, *Long Day's Journey into Night,* Promenade Theatre, New York City, 1971.
Mrs. Henderson, *The Shadow of a Gunman,* Sheridan Square Playhouse, New York City, 1972.
Mrs. Pearce, *Pygmalion,* Queens Playhouse, New York City, 1972.
Woman, *The Plough and the Stars,* Vivian Beaumont Theatre, New York City, 1973.
Juno and the Paycock, Hartford Stage Company, Hartford, CT, 1973.
Mary, *Crown Matrimonial,* Helen Hayes Theatre, 1973.

You Never Can Tell, McCarter Theatre, Princeton, NJ, 1974.
Miss Erikson, *Present Laughter,* John F. Kennedy Center for the Performing Arts, Washington, DC, 1975.
The Real Inspector Hound, Center Stage, Baltimore, MD, 1976.
Black Comedy, Center Stage, 1976.
The Rivals, Center Stage, 1977.
The Runner Stumbles, Center Stage, 1977.
Blithe Spirit, Center Stage, 1978.
Catchpenny Twist, Hartford Stage Company, 1978.
The Hostage, Whole Theatre Company, Montclair, NJ, 1979.
Rummy Mitchens, *Major Barbara,* Circle in the Square, New York City, 1980.
The Admirable Crichton, Long Wharf Theatre, New Haven, CT, 1980.
Going Over, Yale Repertory Theatre, New Haven, 1981.
Clara, *Hay Fever,* Center Theatre Group, Ahmanson Theatre, Los Angeles, 1982.
The Hostage, Long Wharf Theatre, 1983.
The Importance of Being Earnest, Repertory Theatre of St. Louis, St. Louis, MO, 1983.
"The Public Eye" and "Black Comedy," *Light Comedies* (double bill), Hartman Theatre, Stamford, CT, 1984.
Understudy for the role of Grace, *Joe Egg,* Longacre Theatre, 1985.
Understudy for the role of Mrs. McGee, *Corpse!,* Helen Hayes Theatre, 1986.
Flights of Devils, Long Island Stage, Rockville Centre, NY, 1987.
Receptionist, *Two into One,* Paper Mill Playhouse, Millburn, NJ, 1987.
Bessie, *The Plough and the Stars,* Irish Repertory Theatre, 18th Street Playhouse, New York City, 1988.
Lizzy Sweeney, *Philadelphia, Here I Come!,* Irish Repertory Theatre, South Street Theatre, New York City, 1990.
Nurse Eaton, *Starting Monday,* Workshop of the Players Art, WPA Theatre, New York City, 1990.
Adventures in the Skin Trade, Long Wharf Theatre, 1991.

Also appeared in *Charley's Aunt,* Williamstown Theatre and Repertory Theatre of St. Louis; *Mary Stuart,* Guthrie Theatre, Minneapolis, MN; and *Kill.*

MAJOR TOURS

Shatov, *A Matter of Gravity,* U.S. cities, 1976-77.

Also toured as Monica, *Present Laughter.*

FILM APPEARANCES

Celebrant, *Finnegans Wake* (also known as *Passages from "Finnegans Wake"* and *Passages from James Joyce's "Finnegans Wake"*), Grove Press, 1965.
Just Tell Me What You Want, Warner Bros., 1980.
Housekeeper, *The Beneker Gang,* Lorimar, 1986.
Bridget, *Masquerade,* Metro-Goldwyn-Mayer/United Artists, 1988.

TELEVISION APPEARANCES; MOVIES

Powers' sister, *Johnny, We Hardly Knew Ye,* NBC, 1977.

* * *

CROWDER, Jack
See RASULALA, Thalmus

* * *

CRYSTAL, Billy 1947(?)-

PERSONAL: Full name, William Crystal; born March 14, 1947 (some sources say 1948), in Long Beach (some sources say Long Island or Manhattan), NY; son of Jack (a record store owner, record company executive, and producer of jazz concerts) and Helen Crystal; married Janice Goldfinger, 1970; children: Jennifer, Lindsay. *Education:* Attended Marshall University; graduated from Nassau Community College; New York University, B.F.A., television and film direction, 1970. *Avocational interests:* Softball, tennis, cooking Japanese food, collecting New York Yankees memorabilia and miniature furniture.

ADDRESSES: Office—Rollins, Joffe, Morra, & Brezner, 5555 Melrose Ave., Los Angeles, CA 90038. *Agent*—International Creative Management, 8899 Beverly Blvd., Los Angeles, CA 90048.

CAREER: Actor, comedian, and writer. Briefly worked as a substitute teacher at Long Beach Junior High School; worked with Alumni Theatre Group at Nassau Community College; member of improvisational comedy troupe variously called We the People, Comedy Jam, and Three's Company, 1971-75; stand-up comedian, 1975—, performing at clubs including Catch a Rising Star, Playboy clubs, and the Comedy Store.

MEMBER: Screen Actors Guild.

AWARDS, HONORS: Emmy Award nomination, best actor in a variety program, 1985, for *Saturday Night Live;* Grammy Award nomination, best comedy recording, 1985, for *Mahvelous!;* two ACE awards and other ACE Award nominations, National Cable Television Association, 1986, for *On Location: Billy Crystal—Don't Get Me Started;* Emmy Award nomination, outstanding individual performance in a variety or music program, 1987, for *The Twenty-ninth Annual Grammy Awards;* Emmy Award nomination, outstanding individual performance in a variety or music program, 1988, for *An All-Star Toast to the Improv;* Emmy Award, outstanding performance in special events, 1989, for *The Thirty-first Annual Grammy Awards;* Golden Apple Award, star of the year, Women's Press Club, 1989; Emmy Award (cowinner), outstanding writing, and Emmy Award nominations, outstanding individual performance in a variety or music program and outstanding variety, music, or comedy special, all 1989, for *Midnight Train to Moscow;* American Comedy Award, funniest actor in a motion picture, 1989, for *When Harry Met Sally . . . ;* Emmy awards for outstanding writing and outstanding individual performance in a variety or music program, both 1991, for *The Sixty-third Annual Academy Awards;* Golden Globe Award nomination, best actor in a musical or comedy, and American Comedy Award, both 1991, for *City Slickers;* American Comedy Award, 1992, for work on Academy Awards presentation show.

CREDITS:

FILM APPEARANCES

Lionel, *Rabbit Test,* Avco Embassy, 1978.
Animalympics (animated film), Barber Rose International Films, 1979.
Morty the Mime, *This Is Spinal Tap,* Embassy Pictures, 1984.
Danny Costanzo, *Running Scared,* Metro-Goldwyn-Mayer/United Artists (MGM/UA), 1986.
Miracle Max, *The Princess Bride,* Twentieth Century-Fox, 1987.
Larry Donner, *Throw Momma from the Train,* Orion, 1987.
Dr. Abbie Polin, *Memories of Me* (also see below), MGM/UA, 1988.
Harry Burns, *When Harry Met Sally. . . ,* Nelson Entertainment, 1989.
Mitch Robbins, *City Slickers* (also see below), Columbia, 1991.

Also appeared in *Goodnight Moon,* 1987.

FILM WORK

Producer (with Alan King and Michael Hertzberg), *Memories of Me* (also see below), MGM/UA, 1988.
Executive producer, *City Slickers* (also see below), Columbia, 1991.

TELEVISION APPEARANCES; SERIES

Jodie Dallas, *Soap,* ABC, 1977-81.
The Billy Crystal Comedy Hour (also see below), NBC, 1982.
Saturday Night Live (also see below), NBC, 1984-85.

TELEVISION APPEARANCES; EPISODIC

Guest, *Saturday Night Live with Howard Cosell,* ABC, 1976.
Guest, *Saturday Night Live,* NBC, 1976.
"New Year's Wedding," *All in the Family,* CBS, 1976.
The Kissing Bandit, "The Kissing Bandit," *The Love Boat,* ABC, 1978.
Third Pig, "The Three Little Pigs," *Faerie Tale Theatre,* Showtime, 1984.
Robert Klein Time, USA, 1988.

Appeared on numerous talk shows, including *The Tonight Show, That Was the Year That Was, Dinah,* and *The Mike Douglas Show.*

TELEVISION APPEARANCES; SPECIALS

ABC team member, *Battle of the Network Stars,* ABC, 1976.
ABC team member, *Battle of the Network Stars,* ABC, 1977.
ABC team member, *Battle of the Network Stars.* ABC, 1978.
Guest, *The Thirty-six Most Beautiful Girls in Texas,* ABC, 1978.
ABC team member, *Battle of the Network Stars,* ABC, 1979.
Host (with Howard Cosell), *Battle of the Network Stars,* ABC, 1979.
Player, *The Celebrity Football Classic,* NBC, 1979.
Regular performer, *The TV Show* (also see below), ABC, 1979.
Guest, *Doug Henning's World of Magic V,* NBC, 1982.
Billy Crystal: A Comic's Line (also see below), HBO, 1984.
Host, *A Comedy Salute to Baseball* (also see below), NBC, 1985.
Guest, *The Night of One Hundred Stars Two,* ABC, 1985.
Guest performer, *Richard Lewis I'm in Pain Concert,* Showtime, 1985.
Host (with Robin Williams and Whoopi Goldberg), *Comic Relief,* HBO, 1986.
Host, Fernando, Sandy, and Buddy, *On Location: Billy Crystal—Don't Get Me Started* (also see below), HBO, 1986.
Guest, *Kraft Salutes the George Burns Ninetieth Birthday Special,* CBS, 1986.
The Twenty-eighth Annual Grammy Awards, CBS, 1986.
Host (with Williams and Goldberg), *Comic Relief Two,* HBO, 1987.
The Lost Minutes of Billy Crystal, HBO, 1987.
Host, *The Twenty-ninth Annual Grammy Awards,* CBS, 1987.
An All-Star Celebration: The 1988 Vote, ABC, 1988.
An All-Star Toast to the Improv, HBO, 1988.
Life's Most Embarrassing Moments, syndicated, 1988.

The Sixtieth Annual Academy Awards, ABC, 1988.
Host, *The Thirtieth Annual Grammy Awards,* CBS, 1988.
All-Star Tribute to Kareem Abdul-Jabbar, NBC, 1989.
The Barbara Walters Special, ABC, 1989.
Host (with Williams and Goldberg), *Comic Relief Three,* HBO, 1989.
Grand Slam, syndicated, 1989.
Midnight Train to Moscow (also see below), HBO, 1989.
Saturday Night Live Fifteenth Anniversary, NBC, 1989.
The Sixty-first Annual Academy Awards, ABC, 1989.
Host, *The Thirty-first Annual Grammy Awards,* CBS, 1989.
Host (with Williams and Goldberg), *Comic Relief Four,* HBO, 1990.
The Fourth Annual American Comedy Awards, ABC, 1990.
Overtime . . . with Pat O'Brien, CBS, 1990.
Guest, *Robert Wuhl's World Tour,* HBO, 1990.
Host, *The Sixty-second Annual Academy Awards,* ABC, 1990.
The World of Jewish Humor, PBS, 1990.
Wolf Trap Salutes Victor Borge: An Eightieth Birthday Celebration, PBS, 1990.
A Comedy Salute to Michael Jordan, NBC, 1991.
Entertainers '91: The Top Twenty of the Year, ABC, 1991.
Host, *The Sixty-third Annual Academy Awards* (also see below), ABC, 1991.
Voices That Care, Fox Broadcasting Company, 1991.
Muhammad Ali's Fiftieth Birthday Celebration, ABC, 1992.
Host, *The Sixty-fourth Annual Academy Awards Presentation,* ABC, 1992.
Host (with Williams and Goldberg), *Comic Relief V,* HBO, 1992.

Also appeared in *Comic Relief: Backstage Pass,* 1986.

TELEVISION APPEARANCES; MOVIES

David, *SST—Death Flight,* ABC, 1977.
Angel Myles Gordon, *Human Feelings,* NBC, 1978.
Danny Doyle, *Breaking Up Is Hard to Do,* ABC, 1979.
Lieutenant Jake Beser, *Enola Gay: The Men, the Mission, the Atomic Bomb,* NBC, 1980.

TELEVISION WORK

Director, *On Location: Billy Crystal—Don't Get Me Started* (also see below), HBO, 1986.
Executive producer, *Midnight Train to Moscow* (also see below), HBO, 1989.
Executive producer, *Sessions* (also see below), HBO, 1991.

STAGE APPEARANCES

Appeared as Master of Ceremonies in summer stock production of *Cabaret,* Ohio, 1981.

STAGE WORK

House manager for production of *You're a Good Man, Charlie Brown,* New York City, 1971.

RECORDINGS:

Mahvelous! (comedy album), A & M Records, 1985.

Also recorded song "You Look Mahvelous." Crystal has appeared in numerous video releases, including *Your Favorite Laughs from "An Evening at the Improv,"* 1984, and *Big City Comedy,* 1985.

WRITINGS:

FOR TELEVISION

(With others) *The TV Show,* ABC, 1979.
(With others) *The Billy Crystal Comedy Hour,* NBC, 1982.
(With Rocco Urbisci) *Billy Crystal: A Comic's Line,* HBO, 1984.
(With others) *Saturday Night Live,* NBC, 1984-85.
A Comedy Salute to Baseball, NBC, 1985.
On Location: Billy Crystal—Don't Get Me Started, HBO, 1986.
(With others) *Midnight Train to Moscow,* HBO, 1989.
(And creator) *Sessions,* HBO, 1991.
(Special material) *The Sixty-third Annual Academy Awards,* ABC, 1991.

FOR FILM

(With Eric Roth) *Memories of Me* (screenplay), MGM/UA, 1988.
City Slickers (story idea), Columbia, 1991.

Author of screenplay for *Goodnight Moon,* 1987.

OTHER

(With Dick Schaap) *Absolutely Mahvelous* (autobiography), Putnam, 1986.

Contributor to periodicals, including *New York Times* and *Playboy.*

OTHER SOURCES:

BOOKS

Celebrity Register, 5th edition, Gale, 1990, p. 104.
Contemporary Newsmakers 1985 Cumulation, Gale, 1986, pp. 71-74.
Crystal, Billy, and Dick Schaap, *Absolutely Mahvelous,* Putnam, 1986.

PERIODICALS

American Film, July/August, 1989, pp. 30-33 and 48.
Cosmopolitan, June, 1986, p. 80.
Gentlemen's Quarterly, August, 1989, p. 199.

Life, July, 1989, p. 68; April, 1990, p. 90.
McCall's, July, 1991, p. 58.
People, September 30, 1985, p. 40.
Playboy, September, 1985, p. 140; March, 1988, p. 47.
Rolling Stone, October 24, 1985, p. 49.
TV Guide, November 15, 1980, p. 30; March 24, 1990, p. 5.*

* * *

CULHANE, Shamus 1908-

PERSONAL: Born November 12, 1908, in Ware, MA; son of James Henry (a telegrapher) and Alma (a homemaker; maiden name, Lapierre) Culhane; married Maxine Marx, June, 1947 (divorced, 1959); married Juana Hegarty (a psychotherapist), June 30, 1959; children: Brian, Kevin. *Education:* Studied at Walt Disney Art School, 1935-39, and Chouinard Art School, 1942-47. *Politics:* Liberal Democrat. *Avocational interests:* Reading history.

ADDRESSES: Office—325 West End Ave., New York, NY 10023. *Agent*—Perry Knowlton, Curtis Brown Ltd., 10 Astor Place, New York, NY 10003.

CAREER: Animator and author. Began career as an errand boy for Bray Studios, New York City, 1924-29; Krazy Kat Studios, New York City, inker, 1929-30; Max Fleischer Studios, New York City, animator, director, 1930-32; Ub Iwerks Studio, Los Angeles, CA, animator, director, 1932-34; Van Bueren Studio, New York City, director, 1935; Walt Disney Productions, Los Angeles, animator, 1935-39; Max Fleischer Studios, Miami, FL, director, 1939-41; Warner Brothers, Los Angeles, animator, 1943; Walter Lantz Studio, Los Angeles, director, 1943-46; Shamus Culhane Productions, Los Angeles and New York City, producer, director, and animator, 1947-58, producer, director, 1967-80; free-lance animation work, New York City, 1958-62; Hal Seeger Productions, New York City, director, animator, 1962-64; Paramount/Famous Studios, New York City, producer, director, 1966-67; MG Films, New York City, Milan, Italy, and London, England, executive producer, director, 1972-76; Westfall Productions, New York City, producer, director, 1975-77; writer, 1980—.

MEMBER: International Animated Film Association—East (president, 1967-70; member of board of directors, 1970-86), Directors Guild of America.

AWARDS, HONORS: Directors Awards, 1948-58, for television commercials; Christopher Award, 1958, for *Hemo the Magnificent;* Clio Awards for Milestones in Television, 1959, for commercials for Muriel Cigars, Ajax, and Esso; Golden Award, Motion Picture Cartoonists, 1984; Fifty Years Award, International Animated Film Association, 1985; Annie Award, International Animated Film Association—Hollywood, 1986, for distinguished contributions to the art of animation.

CREDITS:

FILM WORK; ANIMATOR

Snow White and the Seven Dwarfs, Walt Disney Studios, 1938.
Pinnochio, Walt Disney Studios, 1939.
Gulliver's Travels, Fleischer Studios, 1940.
Mr. Bug Goes to Town, Fleischer Studios, 1941.
(Animator of title sequence) *Around the World in Eighty Days,* United Artists, 1956.
Hemo the Magnificent, Shamus Culhane Productions, 1958.

FILM WORK; DIRECTOR, ANIMATED SHORTS

Pass the Biscuits Mirandy, Walter Lantz Studio, 1943.
Boogie Woogie Man, Walter Lantz Studio, 1943.
Meatless Tuesday (Andy Panda), Walter Lantz Studio, 1943.
The Greatest Man in Siam, Walter Lantz Studio, 1944.
Barber of Seville (Woody Woodpecker), Walter Lantz Studio, 1944.
Jungle Jive, Walter Lantz Studio, 1944.
Fish Fry (Andy Panda), Walter Lantz Studio, 1944.
Abou Ben Boogie, Walter Lantz Studio, 1944.
The Beach Nut (Woody Woodpecker), Walter Lantz Studio, 1944.
Ski for Two (also known as *Woody Plays Santa;* Woody Woodpecker), Walter Lantz Studio, 1944.
The Painter and the Pointer (Andy Panda), Walter Lantz Studio, 1944.
The Pied Piper of Basin Street, Walter Lantz Studio, 1945.
Chew-Chew Baby (Woody Woodpecker), Walter Lantz Studio, 1945.
Woody Dines Out (Woody Woodpecker), Walter Lantz Studio, 1945.
Dippy Diplomat (Woody Woodpecker), Walter Lantz Studio, 1945.
Loose Nut (Woody Woodpecker), Walter Lantz Studio, 1945.
Mousie Come Home (Andy Panda), Walter Lantz Studio, 1946.
The Reckless Driver (Woody Woodpecker), Walter Lantz Studio, 1946.
Fair Weather Friends (Woody Woodpecker), Walter Lantz Studio, 1946.
A Balmy Knight, Paramount/Famous Studios, 1966.
Potions and Notions (Honey Halfwitch), Paramount/Famous Studios, 1966.
My Daddy, the Astronaut (also see below) Paramount/Famous Studios, 1967.
The Space Squid, Paramount/Famous Studios, 1967.

Think or Sink, Paramount/Famous Studios, 1967.
The Trip, Paramount/Famous Studios, 1967.
Alter Egotist (Honey Halfwitch), Paramount/Famous Studios, 1967.
The Squaw Path, Paramount/Famous Studios, 1967.
The Plumber, Paramount/Famous Studios, 1967.
Halt, Who Grows There?, Paramount/Famous Studios, 1967.
Robin Hoodwinked, Paramount/Famous Studios, 1967.
From Orbit to Obit, Paramount/Famous Studios, 1967.
High but Not Dry (Honey Halfwitch), Paramount/Famous Studios, 1967.
Brother Bat (Honey Halfwitch), Paramount/Famous Studios, 1967.
Forget-Me-Nuts, Paramount/Famous Studios, 1967.
The Stuck-up Wolf, Paramount/Famous Studios, 1967.
The Stubborn Cowboy, Paramount/Famous Studios, 1967.
(Finished by Ralph Bakshi) *The Opera Caper,* Paramount/Famous Studios, 1967.

TELEVISION WORK; SPECIALS

Producer, with Frank Capra, of three Bell Telephone science specials, 1954-57; director of *The Night the Animals Talked,* 1969; director and producer of *Noah's Animals* (also see below), 1974.

WRITINGS:

SCREENPLAYS FOR ANIMATED FILMS

(Coauthor) *My Daddy, the Astronaut,* Paramount/Famous Studios, 1967.

Author of numerous screenplays for *Noah's Animals, Professor Kitzel, Spirit of '76,* and *Spirit of Independence.* Also coauthor of screenplays *The Maine Stein Song, The Herring Murder Case,* and *Last of the Red-Hot Dragons.*

BOOKS

Talking Animals and Other People (autobiography), St. Martin's, 1986.
Animation from Script to Screen, St. Martin's, 1988.

Contributor of articles to *Cartoonist Profiles* and *Animafilms.*

OTHER SOURCES:

BOOKS

Maltin, Leonard, *Of Mice and Magic,* McGraw, 1980.
Solomon, Charles, *The History of Animation: Enchanted Drawings,* Knopf, 1989.

CULKIN, Macaulay 1980(?)-

PERSONAL: Born August 26, 1980 (some sources say 1981), in New York, NY; son of Christopher (an actor under the name Kit Culkin) and Patricia Culkin. *Education:* Student at St. Joseph's School of Yorkville, New York City; studies dance at George Balanchine's School of American Ballet.

ADDRESSES: Agent—Paul Feldshar, International Creative Management, 8899 Beverly Blvd., Los Angeles, CA 90048.

CAREER: Actor. Appeared in television commercials, including those for Apple Computers, Gilette, Kraft Foods, and Dr. Pepper.

AWARDS, HONORS: American Comedy Award, funniest lead actor in a motion picture, George Schlatter Productions, 1991, for *Home Alone.*

CREDITS:

FILM APPEARANCES

(Film debut) Cy Blue Black, *Rocket Gibraltar,* Columbia, 1988.
Miles Russell, *Uncle Buck,* Universal, 1989.
Billy, *See You in the Morning,* Warner Brothers, 1989.
Gabe, *Jacob's Ladder,* Tri-Star, 1990.
Kevin McAllister, *Home Alone,* Twentieth Century-Fox, 1990.
Thomas J. Sennett, *My Girl,* Columbia, 1991.
Billy, *Only the Lonely,* Twentieth Century-Fox, 1991.

TELEVISION APPEARANCES; SPECIALS

Entertainers '91: The Top Twenty of the Year, ABC, 1991.
Dangerous (also known as *Black or White*), FOX, 1991.
Bob Hope's Cross-Country Christmas, NBC, 1991.
The 5th Annual American Comedy Awards, ABC, 1991.
The 43rd Annual Primetime Emmy Awards Presentation, FOX, 1991.
The 17th Annual People's Choice Awards, CBS, 1991.
Voice of Nicholas McClary, *WishKid Starring Macaulay Culkin,* NBC, 1991.
Presenter, *The 63rd Annual Academy Awards Presentation,* ABC, 1991.
Presenter, *The 48th Annual Golden Globe Awards,* TBS, 1991.

TELEVISION APPEARANCES; EPISODIC

Appeared on *The Equalizer.*

STAGE APPEARANCES

(Stage debut) *Bach Babies* (one source says *Beach Babies*), Symphony Space, New York City, c. 1985.
Sammy, "After School Special," *Evening B,* Ensemble Studio Theatre, New York City, 1987.

Buster, "Buster B. and Olivia," *Marathon '88,* Ensemble Studio Theatre, 1988.

Also appeared in *H.M.S. Pinafore,* Light Opera Theatre of Manhattan, New York City; *The Nutcracker,* New York City Ballet, Lincoln Center; and *Mrs. Softee,* Ensemble Studio Theatre.

OTHER SOURCES:

PERIODICALS

Interview, July, 1991, p. 94.
People Weekly, December 17, 1990, p. 127; spring, 1991, p. 104.
Premiere, November, 1991, p. 90.*

* * *

CUNNINGHAM, John 1932-

PERSONAL: Born June 22, 1932, in Auburn, NY. *Education:* Graduated from Yale University and Dartmouth University.

ADDRESSES: *Contact*—Gage Agency, 9255 Sunset Blvd., Suite 515, Los Angeles, CA 90069.

CAREER: Actor.

CREDITS:

STAGE APPEARANCES

Tullus Aufidius, *The Tragedy of Coriolanus,* American Shakespeare Festival, Stratford, CT, 1965.
Mercutio, *The Tragedy of Romeo and Juliet,* American Shakespeare Festival, 1965.
Petruchio, *The Taming of the Shrew,* American Shakespeare Festival, 1965.
Edmund, *The Tragedy of King Lear,* American Shakespeare Festival, 1965.
Prince Henry/Henry V, *Falstaff (Henry IV, Part II),* American Shakespeare Festival Theatre, Stratford, 1966.
Sir Richard Brito, *Murder in the Cathedral,* American Shakespeare Festival Theatre, 1966.
Orsino, *Twelfth Night,* American Shakespeare Festival Theatre, 1966.
Clifford Bradshaw, *Cabaret,* Broadhurst Theatre, New York City, c. 1966-67, then Imperial Theatre, New York City, c. 1967-68.
Malcolm, *Macbeth,* American Shakespeare Festival Theatre, 1967.
Bassanio, *The Merchant of Venice,* American Shakespeare Festival Theatre, 1967.
Demetrius, *A Midsummer Night's Dream,* American Shakespeare Festival Theatre, 1967.
Count Orsino, *Love and Let Love,* Sheridan Square Playhouse, New York City, 1968.
Nikos, *Zorba,* Imperial Theatre, 1968-69.
John Adams, *1776,* 46th Street Theatre, New York City, c. 1969-71.
Peter, *Company,* Alvin Theatre, New York City, c. 1970-71.
The Good Doctor, Eugene O'Neill Theatre, New York City, c. 1973-74.
Male Lecturer, *The Bone Room,* Portfolio Studio, 1975.
Two for the Seesaw, Playwrights Horizons Theatre, New York City, 1976.
Dancing in the Dark, Manhattan Theatre Club, New York City, 1979.
Tom, *Father's Day,* American Place Theatre, New York City, 1979.
Russell, *Snapshot,* Hudson Guild Theatre, New York City, 1980.
Geoffrey, *Rose,* Cort Theatre, New York City, 1981.
Punchinello, *Head over Heels,* Harold Clurman Theatre, 1981-82.
Quartermaine's Terms, Long Wharf Theatre, New Haven, CT, c. 1982-83.
Henry Windscape, *Quartermaine's Terms,* Playhouse 91, New York City, 1983.
Arthur, *Wednesday,* Hudson Guild Theatre, New York City, 1983.
Richard, *On Approval,* Roundabout Theatre, New York City, 1984.
Ted Fine, *Miami,* Playwrights Horizons Theatre, 1986.
Tony, *The Perfect Party,* Playwrights Horizons Theatre, 1986, then Astor Place Theatre, New York City, 1986.
Narrator/Wolf/Steward, *Into the Woods,* Old Globe Theatre, San Diego, CA, c. 1986-87.
Lawrence Wood, *Birds of Paradise,* Promenade Theatre, New York City, 1987.
Anthony Anderson, *The Devil's Disciple,* Circle in the Square, New York City, c. 1988-89.
Andrew Makepeace Lad III, *Love Letters,* Long Wharf Theatre, c. 1988-89, Promenade Theatre, 1989.
Stage Two: A Dance Lesson, Long Wharf Theatre, c. 1989-90.
Flan, *Six Degrees of Separation,* Mitzi E. Newhouse Theatre, New York City, 1990, then Vivian Beaumont Theatre, New York City, 1990.

Standby for *California Suite,* Eugene O'Neill Theatre, 1976-77; also appeared in *Hot Spot,* 1963, *Love Me a Little,* and *Pimpernel.*

MAJOR TOURS

Zoltan Karpathy, *My Fair Lady,* U.S. Cities, 1957-c. 1962.
Narrator, *The Fantasticks,* North American Cities, c. 1968.

FILM APPEARANCES

Hawthorne, *The Big Fix,* Universal, 1978.
Dave Holter, *Matilda,* American International, 1978.
Lenny, *Lost and Found,* Columbia, 1979.
Sloane, *Key Exchange,* TCL, 1985.
Bruce Holt, *Hello Again,* Buena Vista, 1987.
Mr. Anderson, *Dead Poets Society,* Buena Vista, 1989.

Also appeared as John Grau in *The Money Juggler,* 1988.

TELEVISION APPEARANCES; SERIES

Dr. Dan Shearer, *Another World,* NBC, 1970-71.
Dr. Wade Collins, *Search for Tomorrow,* CBS, 1971-77.
Garth Slater, *Loving,* ABC, 1983.

TELEVISION APPEARANCES; MOVIES

Paul Rodgers, *Private Sessions,* NBC, 1985.

TELEVISION APPEARANCES; SPECIALS

Dr. MacIntyre, *Happy Endings,* ABC, 1975.

TELEVISION APPEARANCES; PILOTS

Roger Vincent, *Nick and the Dobermans,* NBC, 1980.
Mr. Watkins, *Gabe and Walker,* ABC, 1981.

OTHER TELEVISION APPEARANCES

George Markell, *Adam's Apple,* CBS, 1986.

Also appeared as Fitzjames O'Brien in *Song of Myself,* 1976.*

* * *

CURTEIS, Ian 1935-

PERSONAL: Full name, Ian Bayley Curteis; born May 1, 1935, in London, England; married Dorothy Joan Armstrong, 1964 (divorced, 1984); married Joanna Trollope, 1985; children: (first marriage) Tobit, Mikol; stepchildren: Louise, Antonia. *Education:* Attended London University.

ADDRESSES: Agent—David Higham Associates, Ltd., 5-8 Lower John St., Golden Square, London W1R 4HA, England.

CAREER: Screenwriter, director, and actor. Actor and director at theatres in England, 1956-63; British Broadcasting Corporation (BBC), London, television script reader, 1956-63, drama director, 1963-67; Associated Television, drama director, 1963-67; full-time screenwriter, 1967—.

MEMBER: Royal Society of Literature, Writer's Guild of Great Britain (chairman of committee on censorship, 1981-85), Beefsteak Club, Garrick Club.

AWARDS, HONORS: British Academy of Film and Television Arts award nominations, play of the year, 1977, for *Philby, Burgess and Maclean,* and 1979, for *Churchill and the Generals* and *Suez 1956;* Grand Prize, best program of 1980, New York International Film and TV Festival, for *Churchill and the Generals;* International Emmy Award nomination, International Council of the National Academy of Television Arts and Sciences, 1981, for *Miss Morison's Ghosts.*

CREDITS:

FILM DIRECTOR

The Projected Man, Universal, 1967.

TELEVISION WORK

Creator of numerous drama series (also see below), including *The Regiment; Doomwatch; Owen M.D.; Z-Cars; Barlow at Large; Sutherland's Law; Crown Court; Spytrap; Justice; The One in Line; Hadleigh; The Cedar Tree; The Duchess of Duke Street; Rough Justice;* and *The Prince Regent.*

WRITINGS:

TELEPLAYS; MOVIES

The Folly, Independent Television (ITV), 1968.
The Haunting, ITV, 1969.
Beethoven, BBC-TV, 1970.
Sir Alexander Fleming, BBC-TV, 1970.
A Distinct Chill, BBC-TV, 1971.
Second Time Round, ITV, 1971.
Long Voyage out of War (trilogy), BBC-TV, 1971, published by J. Calder, 1971.
Mr. Rolls and Mr. Royce, BBC-TV, 1972.
The Portland Millions, ITV, 1976.
Philby, Burgess and Maclean, ITV, 1977.
"Childhood," *Great Performances,* PBS, 1977.
The Rudolph Hess Business, ITV, 1978.
The Atom Spies, ITV, 1979.
Churchill and the Generals, BBC-TV, 1979, published by BBC, 1979.
Suez 1956, BBC-TV, 1979, published by BBC, 1979.
Miss Morison's Ghosts, ITV, 1981.
The Mitford Girls, ITV, 1981.
The Falklands Play, published by Century Hutchinson, 1987.
The Nightmare Years, TNT, 1989.

Also author of television adaptation of Graham Greene's novel *The Man Within,* 1983; author of teleplays *The Trials of Lady Sackville,* BBC-TV, *The Contract* (trilogy), *Eureka, The Nightmare Years,* and *Cecil Rhodes, 1990.*

TELEPLAYS; SERIES

People Like Us, LWE, 1978.

Writer for numerous drama series, including *The Regiment, Doomwatch, Owen M.D., Z-Cars, Barlow at Large, Sutherland's Law, Crown Court, Spytrap, Justice, The One in Line, Hadleigh, The Cedar Tree, The Duchess of Duke Street, Rough Justice,* and *The Prince Regent.*

TELEPLAYS; EPISODIC

"Lost Empires" (adaptation of J. B. Priestly's work of same title), *Masterpiece Theatre,* PBS, 1987.

OTHER

A Personal Affair (play), produced at Yvonne Arnaud Theatre, Guildford, England, 1982, produced at Globe Theatre, London, 1982.

Screenwriter for *Man's Fate* (adaptation of Andre Malraux's *La Condition humaine*), 1982, and *Tom Paine,* 1983.

OTHER SOURCES:

BOOKS

Contemporary Authors, Volume 103, Gale, 1981.

* * *

CURTIS, Dan 1928-

PERSONAL: Full name, Daniel Mayer Curtis; born August 12, 1928, in Bridgeport, CT; son of Edward Philip and Mildred Bernice Cherkass; married Norma May Klein, June 22, 1952; children: Linda, Cathy, Tracy. *Education:* Attended University of Bridgeport, 1947; Syracuse University, B.A., 1950.

ADDRESSES: Office—Dan Curtis Productions Inc., 10000 West Washington Blvd., Suite 3014, Culver City, CA 90232. *Agent*—International Creative Management, 8899 Beverly Blvd., Los Angeles, CA 90048. *Manager*—Michael Rutman, Breslauer, Jacobson & Rutman, 10345 Olympic Blvd., Los Angeles, CA 90064.

CAREER: Producer, director, and writer. National Broadcasting Company, head of sales in film division, 1952-61; MCA, New York City, network television program sales representative, 1961-62; Dan Curtis Productions, Los Angeles, CA, founder and owner, 1962—. *CBS Golf Classic,* owner, 1963-73. *Military service:* U.S. Naval Reserve, active duty, 1945-47.

MEMBER: Directors Guild of America, Sigma Alpha Mu, Riviera Country Club.

AWARDS, HONORS: Emmy Award nomination, outstanding dramatic program, 1968, for *The Strange Case of Dr. Jekyll and Mr. Hyde;* Emmy Award nominations, outstanding limited series and outstanding directing in a limited series or special, both 1983, for *The Winds of War;* Emmy Award, outstanding mini-series, Emmy Award nomination, outstanding directing in a mini-series or special, Distinguished Service Award for the Performing Arts, Simon Wiesenthal Center, and Outstanding Directorial Achievement Award for Television, dramatic specials, Directors Guild of America, all 1988, for *War and Remembrance.*

CREDITS:

TELEVISION WORK; MINI-SERIES

Producer and director, *The Winds of War,* ABC, 1983.
Executive producer and director, *War and Remembrance* (also see below), ABC, 1988.

TELEVISION WORK; SERIES

Director (with Lela Swift and others), creator, and executive producer, *Dark Shadows,* ABC, 1966-71.
Director (with Charles S. Dubin, Barry Crane, and others) and executive producer, *Supertrain,* NBC, 1979.
Director (with others) and executive producer, *Dark Shadows,* NBC, 1991.

TELEVISION WORK; PILOTS

Producer and director, *In the Dead of Night* (also see below), ABC, 1969.
Producer, *The Night Stalker,* ABC, 1972.
Producer and director, *The Night Strangler,* ABC, 1973.
Producer and director, *The Norliss Tapes,* NBC, 1973.
Producer and director, *Melvin Purvis: G-Man,* ABC, 1974.
Executive producer and director, *The Long Days of Summer,* ABC, 1980.
Executive producer, *The Big Easy,* NBC, 1982.

TELEVISION WORK; MOVIES

Producer, *The Strange Case of Dr. Jekyll and Mr. Hyde,* ABC, 1968.
Producer, *Frankenstein,* ABC, 1973.
Producer, *The Picture of Dorian Gray,* ABC, 1973.
Producer and director, *Scream of the Wolf,* ABC, 1974.
Producer and director, *The Great Ice Rip-Off,* ABC, 1974.
Producer and director, *Dracula,* CBS, 1974.
Producer and director, *Turn of the Screw,* ABC, 1974.
Producer and director, *The Kansas City Massacre,* ABC, 1975.
Producer and director, *Trilogy of Terror* (includes "Julie," "Millicent and Therese," and "Amelia"), ABC, 1975.
Executive producer and director, *Curse of the Black Widow,* ABC, 1977.
Producer and director, *When Every Day Was the Fourth of July* (also see below), NBC, 1978.
Executive producer and director, *The Last Ride of the Dalton Gang,* NBC, 1979.

Executive producer and director, *Mrs. R's Daughter,* NBC, 1979.
Executive producer, *Johnny Ryan* (also known as *Ryan's Way, G-Men,* and *Against the Mob*), NBC, 1990.
Creator, executive producer, and director, *Dark Shadows,* NBC, 1991.

OTHER TELEVISION WORK

Producer, *CBS Golf Classic,* CBS, 1963-73.

TELEVISION APPEARANCES; SPECIALS

War and Remembrance: A Living History, ABC, 1988.
The 41st Annual Emmy Awards, Fox, 1989.

FILM WORK; PRODUCER AND DIRECTOR

House of Dark Shadows, Metro-Goldwyn-Mayer (MGM), 1970.
Night of Dark Shadows (also known as *Curse of Dark Shadows*), MGM, 1971.
Burnt Offerings (also see below), United Artists, 1976.

WRITINGS:

TELEVISION PLAYS

In the Dead of Night (pilot), ABC, 1969.
(Author of original story with Lee Hutson) *When Every Day Was the Fourth of July* (movie), NBC, 1978.
War and Remembrance (mini-series), ABC, 1988.

SCREENPLAYS

Burnt Offerings, United Artists, 1976.

OTHER SOURCES:

PERIODICALS

Hollywood Reporter, November 22, 1988, pp. 10 and 40.

* * *

CURTIS, Ken 1916-1991

PERSONAL: Born Curtis Gates, July 2, 1916, in Lamar, CO; died April 28, 1991, in Fresno, CA; married wife, Torrie; children: two. *Education:* Attended Colorado College.

CAREER: Actor and director. Worked previously as a big band singer with such groups as the Tommy Dorsey Orchestra, the Shep Fields Band, and the Sons of the Pioneers. *Military Service:* U.S. Army, served in infantry and anti-aircraft unit during World War II.

CREDITS:

TELEVISION APPEARANCES; SERIES

Jim Buckley, *Ripcord,* syndicated, 1961.
Deputy Festus Hagen, *Gunsmoke* (also known as *Marshal Dillon*), CBS, 1964-75.
Hoyt Coryell, *The Yellow Rose,* NBC, 1983-84.

TELEVISION APPEARANCES; MOVIES

Howard Jakes, *Black Beauty,* NBC, 1978.
Kentuck, *California Gold Rush,* NBC, 1981.
Kelly Sutton, *Once upon a Texas Train,* CBS, 1988.
Seaborn Tay, *Conagher* (also known as *Louis L'Amour's Conagher*), TNT, 1991.

Also appeared in the serial *Don Daredevil Rides Again,* 1951.

TELEVISION APPEARANCES; SPECIALS

When the West Was Fun: A Western Reunion, ABC, 1979.

Also appeared in *The Whirlwind,* 1974.

TELEVISION APPEARANCES; EPISODIC

Appeared as a guest on television series, including *Gunsmoke* (before becoming a regular cast member), *Perry Mason, Rawhide,* and *Have Gun, Will Travel.*

FILM APPEARANCES

Cowboy Blues, Columbia, 1946.
Buck Clayton, *Out of the Depths,* Columbia, 1946.
Curt Benson, *Stallion Canyon,* Astor, 1949.
Regimental singer, *Rio Grande,* Republic, 1950.
Dermot Fahy, *The Quiet Man,* Republic, 1952.
Specialty Bit, *The Long Gray Line,* Columbia, 1955.
Dolan, *Mister Roberts,* Warner Brothers, 1955.
Charlie McCorry, *The Searchers,* Warner Brothers, 1956.
Al, *Spring Reunion,* United Artists (UA), 1957.
John Dale Price, *The Wings of Eagles,* Metro-Goldwyn-Mayer, 1957.
Monsignor Killian, *The Last Hurrah,* Columbia, 1958.
Fred Mueller, *The Missouri Traveler,* Buena Vista, 1958.
Burch, *Escort West,* UA, 1959.
Wilkie, *The Horse Soldiers,* UA, 1959.
Jerry Lacer, *The Killer Shrews* (also see below), McLendon Radio Pictures, 1959.
Lee Hearn, *The Young Land,* Columbia, 1959.
Capt. Almeron Dickinson, *The Alamo,* UA, 1960.
Wessner, *Freckles,* Twentieth Century-Fox, 1960.
Dr. Lusk, *My Dog, Buddy* (also see below), Columbia, 1960.
Greely Clegg, *Two Rode Together,* Columbia, 1961.
Ben, Union Corporal, *How the West Was Won,* Cinerama, 1962.
Homer, *Cheyenne Autumn,* Warner Brothers, 1964.
Voice of Nutsy, *Robin Hood* (animated), Disney-Buena Vista, 1973.
Jed, *Pony Express Rider,* Doty-Dayton, 1976.

Also appeared in *Rhythm Round-up,* 1945, *Song of the Prairie,* 1945, *Lone Star Moonlight,* 1946, *Singing on the Trail,* 1946, *That Texas Jamboree,* 1946, *Throw a Saddle on a Star,* 1946, *Over the Santa Fe Trail,* 1947, *Call of the Forest,* 1949, *Riders of the Pony Express,* 1949, *Legend of the Wild,* 1981, *Lost,* 1983, and *Texas Guns,* 1990.

FILM PRODUCER

The Giant Gila Monster, McLendon Radio Pictures, 1959.
The Killer Shrews, McLendon Radio Pictures, 1959.
My Dog, Buddy, Columbia, 1960.

OBITUARIES AND OTHER SOURCES:

PERIODICALS

Hollywood Reporter, April 30, 1991.*

D

DALY, Bob 1936-

PERSONAL: Full name, Robert Anthony Daly; born December 8, 1936, in Brooklyn, NY; son of James and Eleanor Daly; married Nancy MacNeil, 1961; children: Linda Marie, Robert Anthony, Brian James. *Education:* Attended Brooklyn College of the City University of New York. *Religion:* Roman Catholic.

ADDRESSES: Office—Warner Brothers, Inc., 4000 Warner Blvd., Burbank, CA 91522.

CAREER: Motion picture company executive. CBS-TV, began as director of business affairs, became successively vice-president for business affairs and executive vice-president of network, 1955-80; Warner Brothers, Inc., Burbank, CA, chairman and chief executive officer, 1981—. CBS Entertainment Co., president, 1977—. National Conference of Christians and Jews, member of board of directors.

MEMBER: Academy of Motion Picture Arts and Sciences, American Film Institute (member of board of directors and board of trustees), National Academy of Television Arts and Sciences, Hollywood Radio and Television Society, Motion Picture Pioneers, Bel Air Country Club.*

* * *

DANIELE, Graciela 1939-

PERSONAL: Born December 8, 1939, in Buenos Aires, Argentina; immigrated to United States, 1963; daughter of Raul and Rosa (Almoina) Daniele. *Education:* Graduated from Theater Colon, Bellas Artes; studied jazz dance with Matt Mattox in New York City. *Avocational interests:* Gardening.

ADDRESSES: Agent—Howard Rosenstone, Rosenstone/Wender, 3 East 48th St., fourth floor, New York, NY, 10017.

CAREER: Choreographer and director.

MEMBER: Society of Stage Directors and Choreographers (member of executive board, 1985—).

AWARDS, HONORS: Los Angeles Critics' Award, 1981, and Drama Desk Award nomination, 1981, both for *The Pirates of Penzance;* Antoinette Perry Award nominations, best choreography, 1981, for *The Pirates of Penzance,* 1984, for *The Rink,* 1986, for *The Mystery of Edwin Drood,* 1990, for *Dangerous Games,* and 1991, for *Once on This Island;* San Diego Theatre Critics Award, best road show, 1989, for *Dangerous Games;* Antoinette Perry Award nomination, best direction of a musical, 1991, for *Once on This Island.*

CREDITS:

STAGE WORK; CHOREOGRAPHER, EXCEPT WHERE INDICATED

Yerma, Greenwich Mews Theatre, New York City, 1971.

Assistant to choreographer, *So Long, 174th Street,* Harkness Theatre, New York City, 1976.

Joseph and the Amazing Technicolor Dreamcoat, Brooklyn Academy of Music, Brooklyn Academy of Music Opera House, Brooklyn, NY, 1976-77.

Musical staging, *A History of the American Film,* ANTA Theatre, New York City, 1978.

A Lady Needs a Change, Manhattan Theatre Club, New York City, 1978.

Twelfth Night; or, What You Will, American Shakespeare Theatre, Stratford, CT, 1978.

The Most Happy Fella, Majestic Theatre, New York City, 1979.

Girls, Girls, Girls, New York Shakespeare Festival (NYSF), Public/Other Stage, New York City, 1980.
Alice in Concert, NYSF, Public/Anspacher Theatre, New York City, 1980-81.
The Pirates of Penzance, NYSF, Delacorte Theatre, New York City, 1980; Uris Theatre, New York City, 1981.
A Midsummer Night's Dream, NYSF, Delacorte Theatre, 1982.
Zorba, U.S. cities, 1983.
The Rink, Martin Beck Theatre, New York City, 1984.
America's Sweetheart, Hartford Stage Company, Hartford, CT, 1984-85.
The Mystery of Edwin Drood, NYSF, Delacorte Theatre, New York City, 1985.
The Knife, NYSF, Public/Newman Theatre, New York City, 1987.
(And director) *Tango Apasionado,* Westbeth Theatre Center, New York City, 1987.
(And director) *Dangerous Games,* Nederlander Theatre, New York City, 1989.
(And director) *In a Pig's Valise,* Second Stage, New York City, 1989.
Production supervisor, *Rendezvous with Romance,* Joyce Theatre, New York City, 1989.
(And director) *Once on This Island,* Playwrights Horizons, New York City, 1990.
Director, *Falsetto Land,* Hartford Stage, 1991.
Director, *Marcet of the Falsettos,* Hartford Stage, 1991.
Snowball, Old Globe Theatre, Hartford, CT, 1991.

Also choreographed *Naughty Marietta* for the New York City Opera and *Die Fledermaus* for the Opera Company, Boston, MA. Worked on three ballets for Ballet Hispanico of New York, 1989-91.

STAGE APPEARANCES

Faith, *Here's Where I Belong,* Billy Rose Theatre, New York City, 1968.
Clancy's employee, *Promises, Promises,* Shubert Theatre, New York City, 1968-69.
Claire, *Coco,* Mark Hellinger Theatre, New York City, 1969-70.
Dancer, *Oklahoma!,* New York State Theatre, New York City, 1969.
Mariposa, *El Maleficio de la Mariposa,* Puerto Rican Traveling Theatre, city parks, New York City, 1970.
Young Vanessa, *Follies,* Winter Garden, New York City, 1971.
Hunyak, *Chicago,* Forty-Sixth Street Theatre, New York City, 1975.

Made Broadway debut in *What Makes Sammy Run?,* 1964.

FILM WORK; CHOREOGRAPHER

The Pirates of Penzance, Universal, 1983.
Haunted Honeymoon, Orion, 1986.
Driving Me Crazy, First Run Features, 1988.
(Additional choreography) *Naked Tango,* New Line Cinema, 1990.

TELEVISION WORK; CHOREOGRAPHER

"The Most Happy Fella," *Great Performances* (special), PBS, 1980.
Mirrors (movie), NBC, 1985.

TELEVISION APPEARANCES

"On the Move: The Central Ballet of China," *Great Performances* (special), PBS, 1988.

* * *

DAVIAU, Allen 1942-

PERSONAL: Born June 14, 1942, in New Orleans, LA; son of George and Alice Daviau. *Education:* Graduated from Loyola High School, Los Angeles, CA, 1960.

ADDRESSES: Agent—Spyros Skouras, Sanford, Skouras & Gross Agency, 1015 Gayley Ave., Suite 300, Los Angeles, CA 90024.

CAREER: Cinematographer.

MEMBER: American Society of Cinematographers.

AWARDS, HONORS: Academy Award nomination, best cinematography, 1982, for *E.T.: The Extraterrestrial;* Academy Award nomination, best cinematography, 1985, for *The Color Purple;* Academy Award nomination, best achievement in cinematography, 1987, American Society of Cinematographers Award, 1987, British Academy of Film and Television Artists Award, 1988, all for *Empire of the Sun;* Academy Award nomination, best achievement in cinematography, and American Society of Cinematographers Award nomination, outstanding achievement in a theatrical feature, both 1990, for *Avalon;* Academy Award nomination, best achievement in cinematography, and American Society of Cinematographers Award nomination, outstanding achievement in a theatrical feature, both 1991, for *Bugsy.*

CREDITS:

FILM WORK; CINEMATOGRAPHER, EXCEPT WHERE INDICATED

Additional photography, *Close Encounters of the Third Kind,* Columbia, 1977.
The Boy Who Drank Too Much, MTM Enterprises, 1980.
Harry Tracy—Desperado, Quartet, 1982.
E.T.: The Extraterrestrial, Universal, 1982.

(With Steven Larner and John Hora) "Terror at 20,000 Feet" and "Kick the Can," *Twilight Zone: The Movie,* Warner Brothers, 1983.
Indiana Jones and the Temple of Doom, Paramount, 1984.
The Falcon and the Snowman, Orion, 1985.
The Color Purple, Warner Brothers, 1985.
Harry and the Hendersons, Universal, 1987.
Empire of the Sun, Warner Brothers, 1987.
Avalon, Tri-Star, 1990.
Defending Your Life, Warner Brothers, 1991.
Bugsy, Tri-Star, 1991.

TELEVISION WORK; MOVIES

Cinematographer, *Rage,* NBC, 1980.
Cinematographer, *Legs,* ABC, 1983.

Also worked on *Streets of L.A.,* CBS, 1979.

TELEVISION WORK; EPISODIC

Director of photography, *Amazing Stories,* NBC, 1985.

Also director of photography for the pilot episode of *Ghost Train.*

* * *

DAVID, Lolita
See DAVIDOVICH, Lolita

* * *

DAVIDOVICH, Lolita 1961(?)-
(Lolita David)

PERSONAL: Born c. 1961, in Ontario, Canada.

ADDRESSES: Contact—International Creative Management, 8899 Beverly Blvd., Los Angeles, CA 90048.

CAREER: Actress.

AWARDS, HONORS: ACE Award nomination, National Cable Television Association, best actress in a movie or mini-series, 1991, for "Parole Board," *Prison Stories: Women on the Inside.*

CREDITS:

FILM APPEARANCES

Blaze Starr, *Blaze,* Buena Vista, 1989.
Joan, *The Object of Beauty,* Avenue Entertainment, 1991.
Anastasia Sanshin, *The Inner Circle,* Columbia, 1991.

Also appeared under name Lolita David in *Adventures in Babysitting* and *The Big Town.*

TELEVISION APPEARANCES; MOVIES

First motel girl, *Class,* USA, 1983.
Uncut Gem, TBS, 1990.
Ellen, *Keep the Change,* TNT, 1992.

Also appeared in *Two Fathers' Justice,* 1985.

TELEVISION APPEARANCES; EPISODIC

Loretta, "Parole Board," *Prison Stories: Women on the Inside* (also known as *Women in Prison* and *Doing Time: Women in Prison*), HBO, 1991.*

* * *

DAVIDSON, Martin 1939-

PERSONAL: Born November 7, 1939, in New York, NY; son of Murray and Lillian Davidson; married, 1968; wife's name, Sandra. *Education:* Attended Syracuse University and American Academy of Dramatic Arts.

ADDRESSES: Agent—Frank Wuliger, Harris and Goldberg Talent and Literary Agency, 2121 Avenue of the Stars, Suite 950, Los Angeles, CA 90211. *Contact*—c/o Directors Guild of America, 7920 Sunset Blvd., Hollywood, CA 90046.

CAREER: Director, screenwriter, and television writer. Appeared in and directed Off-Broadway plays.

MEMBER: Directors Guild of America, Writers Guild of America.

CREDITS:

FILM DIRECTOR

(With Stephen Verona) *The Lords of Flatbush* (also see below), Columbia, 1974.
Almost Summer (also see below), Universal, 1978.
Hero at Large, Metro-Goldwyn-Mayer/United Artists, 1980.
Eddie and the Cruisers (also see below), Embassy, 1983.
(And executive producer) *Heart of Dixie,* Orion, 1989.
Hard Promises, Columbia, 1992.

TELEVISION WORK; SERIES; DIRECTOR

And executive producer, *Flatbush/Avenue J* (also see below), ABC, 1976.
Call to Glory, ABC, 1984.
Our Family Honor, ABC, 1985.
Law and Order, NBC, 1990.
My Life and Times, ABC, 1991.

TELEVISION WORK; MOVIES

Director, *Long Gone,* HBO, 1987.

TELEVISION WORK; PILOTS

Director, *Hardesty House,* ABC, 1986.

WRITINGS:

The Bob Newhart Show (television series), CBS, 1972.
(With Stephen Verona) *The Lords of Flatbush* (screenplay), Columbia, 1974.
Flatbush/Avenue J (television series), ABC, 1976.
(With others) *Almost Summer* (screenplay), Universal, 1978.
(With Joe Brooks) *If I Ever See You Again* (screenplay), Columbia, 1978.
(With Arlene Davidson) *Eddie and the Cruisers* (screenplay; adapted from the novel by P. F. Kluge), Embassy, 1983.

* * *

DAVIS, Brad 1949-1991

OBITUARY NOTICE—See index for *CTFT* sketch: Full name, Robert Davis; born November 6, 1949, in Tallahassee, FL; died of complications resulting from Acquired Immune Deficiency Syndrome (AIDS), September 8 (one source says August 8), 1991, in Studio City, CA. Performer. Davis is best remembered for his leading role in the 1978 film *Midnight Express,* based on a true story of an American jailed in Turkey for drug smuggling. He began acting in stage productions in Atlanta, later moving to New York City, where he studied at the American Academy of Dramatic Arts and made his Broadway debut in *Crystal and Fox* in 1973. After winning the 1978 Golden Globe award for best new actor for his *Midnight Express* role, Davis went on to appear in films such as *Chariots of Fire, Querelle, Cold Steel, Rosalie Goes Shopping,* and *The Player.* His television credits include *Sybil, Roots, Robert Kennedy and His Times, Unspeakable Acts, The Plot to Kill Hitler, The Rope, A Habitation of Dragons,* and *Child of Darkness, Child of Light.* He also performed in several stage productions during his career, most notably one of the first plays to deal with the subject of AIDS, the critically-acclaimed 1985 drama *The Normal Heart,* in addition to roles in *Entertaining Mr. Sloane* and *Metamorphosis.*

OBITUARIES AND OTHER SOURCES:

BOOKS

International Motion Picture Almanac, Quigley, 1991, p. 80.

PERIODICALS

Hollywood Reporter, September 10, 1991, p. 3.
New York Times, September 10, 1991. p. B5.
Variety, September 16, 1991, p. 102.

DAVIS, Donald 1928-

PERSONAL: Full name, Donald George Davis; born February 26, 1928, in Newmarket, Ontario, Canada; son of E. J. Davis, Jr. (a manufacturer), and Dorothy (Chilcott) Davis. *Education:* Attended St. Andrew's College, 1946; University of Toronto, B.A., 1950. *Avocational interests:* Rusticating.

ADDRESSES: Agent—Caldwell & Co., 219 Dufferin St., Suite 305, Toronto, Ontario, Canada M6K 1Y9.

CAREER: Actor, director, and producer. Straw Hat Players, founder with brother, Murray Davis, 1948; Crest Theatre, Toronto, Ontario, Canada, founder with Murray Davis, 1954.

MEMBER: Actors' Equity Association (Canadian Advisory Committee, 1956-59; councillor, 1965-69), Association of Canadian Television and Radio Artists, American Federation of Television and Radio Artists, Screen Actors Guild.

AWARDS, HONORS: Obie Award, *Village Voice,* 1960, for *Krapp's Last Tape.*

CREDITS:

STAGE APPEARANCES

(Debut) Sir Toby Belch, *Twelfth Night,* Hart House Theatre, Toronto, Ontario, Canada, 1937.
Henry Bevan, *The Barretts of Wimpole Street,* Woodstock Playhouse, Woodstock, NY, 1947.
Title role, *Noah,* Canadian Repertory Theatre, Ottawa, Ontario, 1951.
Claudius, *Hamlet,* Canadian Repertory Theatre, 1951.
Angelo, *Measure for Measure,* Stratford Shakespearean Festival Company, Stratford, Ontario, c. 1955.
Tiresias, *Oedipus Rex,* Stratford Shakespearean Festival Company, c. 1955.
Marc Antony, *Julius Caesar,* Stratford Shakespearean Festival Company, c. 1955.
Westmoreland, *Henry V,* Stratford Shakespearean Festival Company, c. 1955.
Pistol, *The Merry Wives of Windsor,* Stratford Shakespearean Festival Company, c. 1955.
Tiresias, *Oedipus Rex,* Edinburgh Festival, Edinburgh, Scotland, 1956.
Westmoreland, *Henry V,* Edinburgh Festival, 1956.
(Broadway debut) Agydas, *Tamburlaine the Great,* Winter Garden Theatre, 1956.
(London debut) Angus McBane, *The Glass Cage,* Piccadilly Theatre, London, England, 1957.
Narrator, *Oedipus Rex* (opera), City Centre Theatre, New York City, 1959.

Title role, *Krapp's Last Tape,* Provincetown Playhouse, New York City, 1960, then Arena Theatre, Washington, DC, 1961.

Orsino, *Twelfth Night,* American Shakespeare Festival (ASF), Stratford, CT, 1960.

Domitius Enobarbus, *Antony and Cleopatra,* ASF, 1960.

Roar Like a Dove, Royal Poinciana Playhouse, Palm Beach, FL, 1961.

Duncan, *Macbeth,* ASF, 1961.

Jacques, *As You Like It,* ASF, 1961.

Achilles, *Troilus and Cressida,* ASF, 1961.

Gustav, *Creditors,* Mermaid Theatre, New York City, then Theatre Group, University of California, Los Angeles, both 1962.

Title role, *Becket,* Goodman Memorial Theatre, Chicago, IL, 1962.

George, *Who's Afraid of Virginia Woolf?,* Billy Rose Theatre, New York City, 1962.

Sam 40, *Photo Finish,* Brooks Atkinson Theatre, New York City, 1963.

Title role, *Macbeth,* Institute for Advanced Studies in the Theatre Arts, New York City, 1964.

Henry Macy, *The Ballad of the Sad Cafe,* Goodman Memorial Theatre, 1965.

An Evening's Frost, Mendelssohn Theatre, Ann Arbor, MI, then Theatre de Lys, New York City, both 1965.

George, *Who's Afraid of Virginia Woolf?,* Manitoba Theatre Center, Winnipeg, Manitoba, Canada, 1965.

Thomas Jefferson, *Brother to Dragons,* American Place Theatre, New York City, 1965.

David Bliss, *Hay Fever,* Bucks County Playhouse, New Hope, PA, 1965.

Lord Essex, *Elizabeth the Queen,* City Centre Theatre, 1966.

The Oresteia and *The Birds* (double-bill), Ypsilanti Greek Theatre, Ypsilanti, MI, 1966.

Archie Rice, *The Entertainer,* Springfield Theatre Co., Springfield, MA, 1968.

James Tyrone, *Long Day's Journey into Night,* Springfield Theatre Co., 1968.

Father, *The Death of Bessie Smith,* Studio Arena Theatre, Buffalo, NY, 1968.

Daddy, *The American Dream,* Studio Arena Theatre, 1968.

Peter, *The Zoo Story,* Studio Arena Theatre, then Billy Rose Theatre, both 1968.

Title role, *Krapp's Last Tape,* Studio Arena Theatre, then Billy Rose Theatre, both 1968.

Henry II, *The Lion in Winter,* Studio Arena Theatre, 1968.

Orgon, *Tartuffe,* Stratford Shakespearean Festival, Avon Theatre, Stratford, Ontario, 1969.

Shylock, *The Merchant of Venice,* Stratford Shakespearean Festival, Festival Theatre, Stratford, Ontario, 1970.

Judge Black, *Hedda Gabler,* Stratford Shakespearean Festival, Festival Theatre, 1970.

The Sorrows of Frederick, Mainstage Theatre, Vancouver, British Columbia, Canada, 1971.

Brigadier General Ezra Mannon, *Mourning Becomes Electra,* Circle in the Square, New York City, 1972.

Title role, *Lear,* Yale Repertory Theatre, New Haven, CT, 1973.

Azrielka, *The Dybbuk,* Manitoba Theatre Center, 1974.

Play and Other Plays, Manhattan Theatre Club, New York City, 1977-78.

Nikolayevich, *Old World,* Philadelphia Drama Guild, Philadelphia, PA, 1980-81.

Bam, *What Where,* Harold Clurman Theatre, New York City, 1983.

The director, *Ohio Impromptu,* Harold Clurman Theatre, 1983.

Also appeared as Papa, *Papa Is All,* Crocker-Harris, *The Browning Version,* Mr. Winslow, *The Winslow Boy,* and Sir Henry Harcourt-Reilly, *The Cocktail Party,* all with Straw Hat Players, 1948-55; appeared as Baptista, *The Taming of the Shrew,* Bassanio, *The Merchant of Venice,* and Joseph Surface, *The School for Scandal,* and in *The River Line,* all in Great Britain, 1950-53; appeared as Thomas a Becket, *Murder in the Cathedral,* Malvolio, *Twelfth Night,* Creon, *Antigone,* Vershinin, *The Three Sisters,* Jack the Skinner, *Jig for the Gypsy,* Mr. Stuart, *Hunting Stuart,* and Angus McBane, *The Glass Cage,* and in *Haste to the Wedding,* all at Crest Theatre, 1954-59; also appeared as Father Farley, *Mass Appeal,* Norman Thayer, *On Golden Pond,* and Stalin, *Master Class,* all at Belfry Theatre; appeared as Pozzo, *Waiting for Godot,* and Dodge, *Buried Child,* both at Toronto Free Theatre; appeared as Dilwyn Knox, *Breaking the Code,* National Arts Center; Daddy Warbucks, *Annie,* Citadel Theatre; Zrak, *Prague,* Centaur Theatre; Gardner Church, *Painting Churches,* Grand Theatre; and the man, *That Time,* Manhattan Theatre Club and Arena Stage, Washington, DC.

STAGE WORK

Coproducer, *The Glass Cage,* Piccadilly Theatre, 1957.

Director, *Deathwatch,* Richard Barr's Festival of the Absurd, Cherry Lane Theatre, New York City, 1961-62.

Director, *Toy for the Clowns,* Richard Barr's Theatre '62 Playwright Series, Cherry Lane Theatre, 1962.

Director, *The Imaginary Invalid,* Studio Arena Theatre, 1967.

Director, *The Royal Family,* Shaw Festival, Niagara-on-the-Lake, Ontario, 1972.

Also produced and directed *Laura* and *French without Tears* and produced various other productions, all with Straw Hat Players, 1948-55; directed *Bright Sun at Midnight* and *The Crest Revue,* both with Crest Theatre.

MAJOR TOURS

Coproducer, *The Drunkard,* Canadian cities, c. 1950.
Coproducer, *There Goes Yesterday,* Canadian cities, c. 1950.
The Wind and the Rain, Ontario cities, 1950.
Angus McBane, *The Glass Cage,* British cities, 1957.

TELEVISION APPEARANCES; EPISODIC

The Defenders, CBS, 1962, 1963, and 1965.
The Nurses, CBS, 1962.
The Doctors and the Nurses, CBS, 1964.
Mission Impossible, CBS, 1966.

Also appeared in *Street Legal; Hitchcock; Adderly; Judge; For the Record; The Newcomers; The F.B.I.;* and *Get Smart.*

OTHER TELEVISION APPEARANCES

FBI agent, *I Made News,* BBC, 1951.
Title role, *The Trial and Death of Socrates,* CBS, 1961.
Abraham Lincoln, *A Season of War,* CBS, 1963.
Look up and Live, CBS, 1966.

Also appeared in *And Then We Die; Sarah; The Great Detective; Beaverbrook; The Man Inside;* and *Tiger at the Gate.*

RADIO APPEARANCES

Appeared in Canadian programs including *The Stage Series; CBC Wednesday Night; Buckingham Theatre; Ford Theatre;* and *CBC Schools Program.*

FILM APPEARANCES

Tiresias, *Oedipus Rex* (also known as *King Oedipus*), Motion Pictures, 1957.
Anthony Bird, *Joy in the Morning,* Metro-Goldwyn-Mayer, 1965.
Alexander, *Agency,* Farley, 1981.
Bishop Strachan, *Samuel Lount,* Moonshine Productions, 1986.

Also appeared in *The Phoenix* and *Then Came You.*

* * *

DAVIS, Geena 1957-

PERSONAL: Born January 21, 1957, in Wareham, MA; married Richard Emmolo (divorced); married Jeff Goldblum (an actor), November 1, 1987 (divorced). *Education:* Attended New England College; Boston University, B.F.A. (acting), 1979; studied flute, piano, and organ.

ADDRESSES: Publicist—Susan Geller and Associates, 335 North Maple Dr., Suite 254, Beverly Hills, CA 90210.

CAREER: Actress. Actress with Mount Washington Repertory Theatre Company, North Conway, NH; model for Zoli Agency, New York City; appeared in television commercials.

AWARDS, HONORS: Academy Award, best supporting actress, 1988, for *The Accidental Tourist;* Academy Award nomination, best actress, British Academy of Film and Television Arts Award nomination, best actress in a leading role, and Golden Globe Award nomination, best actress, all 1991, for *Thelma and Louise.*

CREDITS:

FILM APPEARANCES

April, *Tootsie,* Columbia, 1982.
Larry, *Fletch,* Universal, 1985.
Odette, *Transylvania 6-5000,* New World, 1985.
Veronica Quaife, *The Fly,* Twentieth Century-Fox, 1986.
Barbara Maitland, *Beetlejuice,* Warner Brothers, 1988.
Muriel Pritchett, *The Accidental Tourist,* Warner Brothers, 1988.
Valerie Dale, *Earth Girls Are Easy,* Vestron, 1989.
Phyllis, *Quick Change,* Warner Brothers, 1990.
Thelma, *Thelma and Louise,* Metro-Goldwyn-Mayer, 1991.
Dottie Hinson, *A League of Their Own,* Columbia, 1992.

TELEVISION APPEARANCES; SERIES

Wendy Killian, *Buffalo Bill* (also see below), NBC, 1983-84.
Sara McKenna, *Sara,* NBC, 1985.
Daphne, *Hit List,* PBS, 1989.

TELEVISION APPEARANCES; MOVIES

Tamara Reshevsky, *Secret Weapons,* NBC, 1985.

TELEVISION APPEARANCES; EPISODIC

"Kitt the Cat," *Knight Rider,* NBC, 1983.
Housekeeper, "Help Wanted," *Family Ties,* NBC, 1984.
"Karen 2, Alex 0," *Family Ties,* NBC, 1984.
"Don Juan's Last Affair," *Fantasy Island,* ABC, 1984.
Melba Bozinski, "Raiders of the Lost Sub," *Riptide,* NBC, 1984.
"Dream, Dream, Dream," *George Burns Comedy Week,* CBS, 1985.
"Steele in the Chips," *Remington Steele,* NBC, 1985.
Late Night with David Letterman, NBC, 1988.
The Today Show, NBC, 1988.

CBS in the Morning, CBS, 1989.
Hostess, *Saturday Evening Live,* NBC, 1989.
Hollywood Insider, USA, 1989.

TELEVISION APPEARANCES; SPECIALS

Day to Day Affairs, HBO, 1985.
The 61st Annual Academy Awards Presentation, ABC, 1989.
Time Warner Presents the Earth Day Special, ABC, 1990.
The 62nd Annual Academy Awards Presentation, ABC, 1990.
Big Bird's Birthday; or, Let Me Eat Cake, PBS, 1991.
Presenter, *The 63rd Annual Academy Awards Presentation,* ABC, 1991.

STAGE APPEARANCES

Appeared in *One Flew Over the Cuckoo's Nest, Harvey,* and *Play It Again, Sam,* all Mount Washington Repertory Theatre, North Conway, NH.

WRITINGS:

TELEPLAYS

(With others) *Buffalo Bill* (series), NBC, 1983-84.

OTHER SOURCES:

PERIODICALS

American Premiere, May-June, 1991, p. 17.
Esquire, August, 1989, p. 86.
Gentlemen's Quarterly, June, 1989, p. 222.*

* * *

DAVISON, Jon 1949-

PERSONAL: Born July 21, 1949, in Haddonfield, NJ. *Education:* New York University film school.

ADDRESSES: *Office*—Sony Studios, TriStar Bldg., Room 226, 10202 West Washington Blvd., Culver City, CA 90232.

CAREER: Producer. New World Pictures, national director of publicity and advertising, 1972-77, named in charge of production, 1977; independent producer, 1980—. Once taught film history at New York University, where he also ran the New York University Cinema for two years.

CREDITS:

FILM PRODUCER

Hollywood Boulevard, New World, 1976.
Grand Theft Auto, New World, 1977.
Piranha, New World, 1978.
Airplane!, Paramount, 1980.
White Dog (also known as *Trained to Kill*), Paramount, 1982.
Top Secret!, Paramount, 1984.
Robocop 2, Orion, 1990.

OTHER FILM WORK

Associate producer, *Big Bad Mama,* New World, 1974.
Second unit director, *Rock 'n' Roll High School,* New World, 1979.
Second unit director, *The Howling,* Avco Embassy, 1980.
Associate producer, *Twilight Zone—The Movie,* Warner Brothers, 1983.
Executive producer, *Robocop,* Orion, 1987.

* * *

DEARDEN, James 1949-

PERSONAL: Born September 14, 1949, in London, England; son of Basil Dearden (a film director). *Education:* Attended Oxford University.

ADDRESSES: *Agent*—International Creative Management, 8899 Beverly Blvd., Los Angeles, CA 90048.

CAREER: Screenwriter and director.

AWARDS, HONORS: Silver Bear from Berlin Film Festival, for *The Contraption;* Special Jury Prize from Avoriaz Film Festival, 1985, and Special Jury Prize for young director from Oxford Film Festival, both for *The Cold Room;* Academy Award nomination, best screenplay based on material from another medium, 1987, for *Fatal Attraction.*

CREDITS:

FILM DIRECTOR

Pascali's Island (also see below), Avenue, 1988.
A Kiss Before Dying (also see below), Universal, 1991.

Also director of short films, including *The Contraption* and *Diversion* (also see below).

TELEVISION DIRECTOR; MOVIES

The Cold Room (also see below), HBO, 1984.

WRITINGS:

SCREENPLAYS

Fatal Attraction (from his original screenplay *Diversion;* also see below), Paramount, 1987.
Pascali's Island (based on a novel by Barry Unsworth), Avenue, 1988.
A Kiss Before Dying (based on a novel by Ira Levin), Universal, 1991.

Also creator of short films, including *The Contraption* and *Diversion.*

TELEVISION MOVIES

The Cold Room (based on a novel by Jeffrey Caine), HBO, 1984.

OTHER SOURCES:

PERIODICALS

Film Comment, July-August, 1988, p. 17.
Vogue, September, 1988, p. 558.*

* * *

DEHNER, John 1915-1992

OBITUARY NOTICE—See index for *CTFT* sketch: Full name, John Forkum Dehner; born November 23, 1915, in Staten Island, NY; died of emphysema and diabetes, February 4, 1992, in Santa Barbara, CA. Performer, animator, and broadcaster. Dehner, whose prolific career in the entertainment industry spanned six decades, is best known for playing villainous film characters. He began acting on the New York stage in the 1930s, debuting in *Bridal Crown* and later directing *Alien Summer.* Relocating to California when he became an animator for Walt Disney Studios, he worked on such films as *Fantasia* and *The Reluctant Dragon,* as well as numerous cartoon shorts. After serving in the army during World War II, Dehner began working in radio—first as an announcer, and later appearing on serials such as *Gunsmoke, Lone Ranger, Suspense, Sam Spade,* and *Have Gun, Will Travel.* His first film part was in 1944's *Thirty Seconds Over Tokyo,* and he went on to play roles in more than one hundred films, such as *State Fair, Lorna Doone, Scaramouche, The Sign of Zorro, Support Your Local Gunfighter, Slaughterhouse-Five, Fun with Dick and Jane, The Right Stuff,* and *The Jagged Edge.* He also made numerous television appearances, in both series such as *Twilight Zone, Andy Griffith Show, The Doris Day Show,* and *Young Maverick,* as well as in movies and mini-series including *Bare Essence, Winds of War,* and *War and Remembrance.*

OBITUARIES AND OTHER SOURCES:

PERIODICALS

Variety, February 10, 1992, p. 95.

* * *

DELANY, Dana 1956-

PERSONAL: Some sources spell surname Delaney; born March 13, 1956, in New York, NY. *Education:* Phillips Andover Academy, graduated, 1974; graduated from Wesleyan University, Middletown, CT.

ADDRESSES: Agent—International Creative Management, 8899 Beverly Blvd., Los Angeles, CA 90048.

CAREER: Actress.

AWARDS, HONORS: Emmy Award, outstanding lead actress in a drama series, 1988, Emmy Award nomination, outstanding lead actress in a drama series, Women at Work Commissioners' Award, National Commission on Working Women, and Quality Award, best actress in a drama series, Viewers for Quality Television, all 1989, and Emmy Award nomination, outstanding lead actress in a drama series, 1990, all for *China Beach.*

CREDITS:

TELEVISION APPEARANCES; SERIES

Amy Russell, *Love of Life,* CBS, 1979-80.
Hayley Wilson, *As the World Turns,* CBS, 1981.
Georgia Holden, *Sweet Surrender,* NBC, 1987.
Colleen McMurphy, *China Beach,* ABC, 1988-90.

TELEVISION APPEARANCES; MOVIES

Laura Shaper, *Threesome,* CBS, 1984.
Moya Trevor, *Liberty,* NBC, 1986.
Nora, *A Winner Never Quits,* ABC, 1986.
Jane Goodrich, *A Promise to Keep* (also known as *Angels without Wings*), NBC, 1990.

TELEVISION APPEARANCES; SPECIALS

May Thayer, *The City,* ABC, 1986.
The 41st Annual Emmy Awards, Fox, 1989.
Time Warner Presents the Earth Day Special, ABC, 1990.
The 47th Annual Golden Globe Awards, TBS, 1990.
Presenter, *The 42nd Annual Primetime Emmy Awards,* Fox, 1990.
An American Saturday Night, ABC, 1991.
Host, *The 48th Annual Golden Globe Awards,* TBS, 1991.

TELEVISION APPEARANCES; EPISODIC

"Knowing Her," *Moonlighting,* ABC, 1985.
"L.A.," *Magnum, P.I.,* CBS, 1986.
"Out of Sync," *Magnum, P.I.,* CBS, 1987.
"South by Southwest," *thirtysomething,* ABC, 1988.

TELEVISION APPEARANCES; PILOTS

Jeannie, *The Streets* (also known as *Street Heat*), NBC, 1984.

FILM APPEARANCES

Linda, *The Fan,* Paramount, 1981.
Susan McCall, *Almost You,* Twentieth Century-Fox/TLC, 1984.

Sister Ana, *Where the River Runs Black,* Metro-Goldwyn-Mayer/United Artists (MGM/UA), 1986.
Jenny, *Moon over Parador,* Universal, 1988.
Celina, *Patty Hearst,* Atlantic-Zenith, 1988.
Anne Briscoe, *Masquerade,* MGM/UA, 1988.
Marianne, *Light Sleeper,* New Line Cinema, 1992.
Becky Metcalf, *Housesitter,* Universal, 1992.

STAGE APPEARANCES

The Resistible Rise of Arturo Ui, Hartman Theatre Company, Stamford, CT, 1979-80.
(Broadway debut) Dorothy, *A Life,* Morosco Theatre, New York City, 1980-81.
Manya, *Blood Moon,* Production Company Theatre, then Actors and Directors Theatre, both New York City, 1983.
Rocket to the Moon, Hartman Theatre, 1984.
Beloved Friend, Hartman Theatre, 1984-85.

* * *

DEMY, Jacques 1931-1990

OBITUARY NOTICE—See index for *CTFT* sketch: Born June 5, 1931, in Pont Chateau, France; died of leukemia, October 27, 1990, in Paris, France. Director and screenwriter. As a young man, Demy studied art and filmmaking in France, attending the Ecole Nationale de Photographie et Cinematographie and working with animator Paul Grimault and documentarist Georges Rouquier. In the early 1960s he began making feature-length movies, which became noted for their fairy-tale motif and elements of both romance and melodrama. Among the best known of his films are *Lola, La Baie des anges (Bay of the Angels), Les Demoiselles de Rochefort (The Young Girls of Rochefort), The Model Shop, Peau d'ane (Donkey Skin, The Magic Donkey),* and *Les Parapluies de Cherbourg (The Umbrellas of Cherbourg),* for which he won the Palm d'Or at the 1964 Cannes Film Festival.

OBITUARIES AND OTHER SOURCES:

BOOKS

The Annual Obituary, 1990, St. James Press, 1991, pp. 599-601.

* * *

De NIRO, Robert 1943-

PERSONAL: Born August 17, 1943, in New York City; son of Robert (an artist) and Virginia (a painter; maiden name, Admiral) De Niro; married Diahnne Abbott (an actress); children: Drena, Raphael. *Education:* Studied with Stella Adler and Lee Strasberg at the Actors Studio.

ADDRESSES: Agent—Creative Artists, 9830 Wilshire Blvd., Beverly Hills, CA 90212.

CAREER: Actor. Founder of Tribeca Film Center, New York City.

MEMBER: Screen Actors Guild, Actors Equity Association.

AWARDS, HONORS: New York Film Critics Award, best supporting actor, 1973, for *Bang the Drum Slowly;* New York Film Critics Award, best supporting actor, 1973, for *Mean Streets;* Academy Award, best supporting actor, 1974, for *The Godfather, Part II;* Academy Award nomination, best actor, 1976, for *Taxi Driver;* Academy Award nomination, best actor, 1978, for *The Deer Hunter;* Hasty Pudding Man of the Year Award, Harvard University, 1979; Academy Award, best actor, 1980, and Golden Globe Award, best actor in a film or drama, Hollywood Foreign Press Association, 1981, for *Raging Bull;* Academy Award nomination, best performance by an actor in a leading role, 1990, for *Awakenings;* Academy Award nomination, best actor, and Golden Globe Award nomination, best actor in a drama, both 1991, for *Cape Fear.*

CREDITS:

FILM APPEARANCES

Greetings, Sigma III, 1968.
Sam, *Sam's Song* (also known as *The Swap*), Cannon, 1969.
Cecil, *The Wedding Party,* Ajay, 1969.
Lloyd Barker, *Bloody Mama,* American International, 1970.
John Rubin, *Hi, Mom* (also known as *Confessions of a Peeping John*), Sigma III, 1970.
Gypsy cab driver, *Jennifer on My Mind,* United Artists (UA), 1971.
Danny, *Born to Win,* UA, 1971.
Mario, *The Gang That Couldn't Shoot Straight,* Metro-Goldwyn-Mayer (MGM), 1971.
Bruce Pearson, *Bang the Drum Slowly,* Paramount, 1973.
Johnny Boy, *Mean Streets,* Warner Brothers, 1973.
Vito Corleone, *The Godfather, Part II,* Paramount, 1974.
Travis Bickle, *Taxi Driver,* Columbia, 1976.
Monroe Stahr, *The Last Tycoon,* Paramount, 1977.
Jimmy Doyle, *New York, New York,* UA, 1977.
1900, Paramount, 1977.
Michael Vronsky, *The Deer Hunter,* Warner Brothers, 1978.
Jake LaMotta, *Raging Bull,* UA, 1980.
Des Spellacy, *True Confessions,* UA, 1981.
Rupert Pupkin, *The King of Comedy,* Twentieth Century-Fox, 1983.

David "Noodles" Aaronson, *Once upon a Time in America,* Warner Brothers, 1984.
Frank Raftis, *Falling in Love,* Paramount, 1984.
Archibald "Harry" Tuttle, *Brazil,* Universal, 1985.
Captain Rodrigo Mendoza, *The Mission,* Warner Brothers, 1986.
Louis Cypher, *Angel Heart,* Tri-Star, 1987.
Al Capone, *The Untouchables,* Paramount, 1987.
Jack Walsh, *Midnight Run,* Universal, 1988.
Joseph "Megs" Megessey, *Jacknife,* Cineplex Odeon, 1989.
Ned, *We're No Angels* (also see below), Paramount, 1989.
Stanley Cox, *Stanley and Iris,* MGM/UA, 1990.
James Conway, *Goodfellas,* Warner Brothers, 1990.
Leonard Lowe, *Awakenings,* Columbia, 1990.
Himself, *Hollywood Mavericks,* Roxie Releasing, 1990.
Max Cady, *Cape Fear,* Universal, 1991.
Donald Rimgale, *Backdraft,* Universal, 1991.
David Merrill, *Guilty by Suspicion,* Warner Brothers, 1991.

Also appeared in *Addict,* 1971; *America at the Movies,* 1976; as Alfredo Berlinghieri, *Novecento,* 1976; *Acting: Lee Strasberg and the Actors Studio,* 1981; *Hello Actors Studio,* 1987; and as narrator, *Dear America: Letters Home from Vietnam.*

FILM WORK

Executive producer, *We're No Angels,* Paramount, 1989.

STAGE APPEARANCES

(Off-Broadway debut) Boy, *One Night Stands of a Noisy Passenger,* Actors Playhouse, New York City, 1970.
Douglas One and Fatboy, *Kool Aid,* Forum Theatre, Repertory Theatre of Lincoln Center, New York City, 1971.
Night of 100 Stars, Radio City Music Hall, New York City, 1982.
Cuba, *Cuba and His Teddy Bear,* New York Shakespeare Festival, Public Theatre, New York City, 1986.

Also appeared in *Strange Show,* 1982.

TELEVISION APPEARANCES; EPISODIC

"Martin Scorsese Directs," *American Masters,* PBS, 1990.

TELEVISION APPEARANCES; SPECIALS

The Night of 100 Stars II, ABC, 1985.
The New Hollywood, NBC, 1990.
The Godfather Family: A Look Inside, HBO, 1990.
Presenter, *The 62nd Annual Academy Awards Presentation,* ABC, 1990.

OTHER SOURCES:

PERIODICALS

New York Times, March, 1977.
Sunday Times (London), April 22, 1990, p. G1.*

* * *

DENNIS, Sandy 1937-1992

PERSONAL: Full name, Sandra Dale Dennis; born April 27, 1937, in Hastings, NE; died of ovarian cancer, March 2, 1992, in Westport, CT; cremated; daughter of Jack (a postal clerk) and Yvonne (a secretary) Dennis; married Gerry Mulligan (a jazz musician), June, 1965 (separated, 1976). *Education:* Attended Lincoln High School, Lincoln, NE; attended Nebraska Wesleyan University and University of Nebraska; studied acting at Herbert Berghof Studios, New York City.

ADDRESSES: Agent—Lantz Office, 9255 Sunset Blvd., Suite 505, Los Angeles, CA 90069.

CAREER: Actress. Professional acting debut in summer stock, New London Players, London, NH; also worked with Lincoln Community Theatre, Lincoln, NE.

MEMBER: Actors Studio.

AWARDS, HONORS: Antoinette Perry Award, best supporting actress, New York Critics Poll Award, *Variety,* and *Theatre World* Award, all 1962, for *A Thousand Clowns;* Antoinette Perry Award, best dramatic actress, and New York Critics Poll Award, *Variety,* both 1964, for *Any Wednesday;* Academy Award, best supporting actress, 1966, for *Who's Afraid of Virginia Woolf?;* Silver Star Award, best actress, Moscow Film Festival, 1967, for *Up the Down Staircase;* Straw Hat Award, best actress, 1971, for *And Miss Reardon Drinks a Little.*

CREDITS:

FILM APPEARANCES

(Film debut) Kay, *Splendor in the Grass,* Warner Brothers, 1961.
Honey, *Who's Afraid of Virginia Woolf?,* Warner Brothers, 1966.
Jill, *The Fox,* Warner Brothers, 1967.
Sylvia Barrett, *Up the Down Staircase,* Warner Brothers, 1967.
Sara Deever, *Sweet November,* Warner Brothers/Seven Arts, 1968.
The Millstone, Palomar Pictures International, c. 1968.
Rosamund Stacey, *Thank You All Very Much* (also known as *A Touch of Love*), Columbia, 1969.
Frances Austen, *That Cold Day in the Park,* Commonwealth United Entertainment, 1969.

Gwen Kellerman, *The Out of Towners,* Paramount, 1970.
Jane Gwilt, *Mr. Sycamore,* Film Venture, 1975.
Martha Nicholas, *God Told Me To* (also known as *Demon*), New World, 1976.
Winifred, *Nasty Habits,* Brut, 1976.
Irina, *The Three Sisters* (also see below), NTA, 1977.
Anne Callan, *The Four Seasons,* Universal, 1981.
Mona, *Come Back to the Five and Dime, Jimmy Dean, Jimmy Dean* (also see below), Viacom, 1982.
Claire, *Another Woman,* Orion, 1988.
Aunt Lucy, *976-EVIL,* New Line, 1988.
Millie Drew, *Parents,* Vestron, 1989.
Mother, *The Indian Runner,* Metro-Goldwyn-Mayer/Pathe, 1991.

Also appeared in *The Animals Film,* 1981.

TELEVISION APPEARANCES; MOVIES

Dr. Enid Bingham, *The Man Who Wanted to Live Forever* (also known as *Heartfarm* and *The Only Way Out Is Dead*), ABC, 1970.
Marjorie Worden, *Something Evil,* CBS, 1972.
Sophie Rosenman, *Perfect Gentlemen,* CBS, 1978.
Elsa Spahn, *The Execution,* NBC, 1985.

TELEVISION APPEARANCES; EPISODIC

The Guiding Light, CBS, 1956.
"Idylls of a Running Back," *Naked City,* ABC, 1962.
"Carrier," *Naked City,* ABC, 1963.
"The Other Side of the Mountain," *The Fugitive,* ABC, 1963.
"Somewhat Lower Than Angels," *Arrest and Trial,* ABC, 1964.
"Don't Mention My Name in Sheboygan," *Mr. Broadway,* CBS, 1964.
"Day of Terror, Night of Fear," *Police Story,* NBC, 1978.
"Out of the Blue," *The Love Boat,* ABC, 1985.
"Arthur," *Alfred Hitchcock Presents,* NBC, 1985.
Kay, "Out of the Past," *The Equalizer,* CBS, 1986.

TELEVISION APPEARANCES; SPECIALS

Celia Pope, *A Hatful of Rain,* ABC, 1968.
Irina, *The Three Sisters,* syndicated, 1968.
Patricia Benson, *The Trouble with Mother,* syndicated, 1979.
Martha James, *Wilson's Reward,* syndicated, 1980.

STAGE APPEARANCES

Hilde, *The Lady from the Sea,* Tempo Theatre, New York City, 1956.
(Broadway debut) Understudy for roles of Flirt Conroy and Reenie Flood, *The Dark at the Top of the Stairs* (also see below), Music Box Theatre, New York City, 1957.
Elma Duckworth, *Bus Stop,* Royal Poinciana Playhouse, Palm Beach, FL, 1957.
Mordeen, *Burning Bright,* Theatre East, New York City, 1959.
Millicent Bishop, *Face of a Hero,* Eugene O'Neill Theatre, New York City, 1960.
Nancy, *Motel,* Wilbur Theatre, Boston, MA, 1960.
Sister Gabrielle, *Port Royal,* Grace Protestant Episcopal Church, New York City, 1960.
Ann Howard, *The Complaisant Lover,* Ethel Barrymore Theatre, New York City, 1961-62.
Sandra Markowitz, *A Thousand Clowns,* Eugene O'Neill Theatre, 1962.
Ellen Gordon, *Any Wednesday,* Music Box Theatre, 1964.
Irina, *The Three Sisters,* World Theatre, Aldwych, England, 1965.
Title role, *Daphne in Cottage D,* Longacre Theatre, New York City, 1967.
Cherry, *Bus Stop,* Ivanhoe Theatre, Chicago, IL, 1970-71.
Teresa Phillips, *How the Other Half Loves,* Royale Theatre, New York City, 1971.
Hannah Heywood, *Let Me Hear You Smile,* Biltmore Theatre, New York City, 1973.
Blanche DuBois, *A Streetcar Named Desire,* Ivanhoe Theatre, 1973-74.
Eva, *Absurd Person Singular,* Music Box Theatre, 1974-75.
Doris, *Same Time, Next Year,* Brooks Atkinson Theatre, New York City, 1975-78.
Fallen Angels, Paper Mill Playhouse, Millburn, NJ, 1977-78.
Sally, *The Supporting Cast,* Biltmore Theatre, 1981.
Mona, *Come Back to the Five and Dime, Jimmy Dean, Jimmy Dean,* Martin Beck Theatre, New York City, 1982.
Sophia Bowsky, *Buried inside Extra,* Public Theatre/Martinson Hall, New York City, 1983.

MAJOR TOURS

Reenie Flood, *The Dark at the Top of the Stairs,* U.S. cities, 1959.
Catherine Reardon, *And Miss Reardon Drinks a Little,* U.S. cities, 1971.
Anna Reardon, *And Miss Reardon Drinks a Little,* U.S. cities, 1972.
Billie Dawn, *Born Yesterday,* U.S. cities, 1974.
Maggie, *Cat on a Hot Tin Roof,* U.S. cities, 1975.

OBITUARIES AND OTHER SOURCES:

PERIODICALS

Detroit Free Press, March 5, 1992, p. 2B.
Variety, March 9, 1992, p. 67.*

DePATIE, David H. 1930-

PERSONAL: Full name, David Hudson DePatie; born December 24, 1930, in Los Angeles, CA; son of Edmond LaVoie and Dorothy (Hudson) DePatie; married Marcia Lee MacPherson, June, 1972; children: David Hudson, Steven Linn, Michael Linn. *Education:* Studied at University of the South, 1947-48; University of California at Berkeley, A.B., 1951. *Politics:* Republican. *Religion:* Episcopalian.

ADDRESSES: *Office*—DePatie-Freleng Enterprises, Inc., 3425 Stiles Ave., Camarillo, CA 93010; The DePatie Vineyards, 21491 Greenwood Rd., Philo, CA 95466.

CAREER: Producer and executive producer. Warner Brothers Pictures, Inc., 1951-63, became vice-president, general manager of commercial and cartoon films division, 1963; DePatie-Freleng Enterprises, Inc., Van Nuys, CA, president, 1963—; The DePatie Vineyards, founder and proprietor, 1983—.

MEMBER: Academy of Motion Picture Arts and Sciences, Society of Motion Picture Editors, Phi Gamma Delta.

AWARDS, HONORS: All with Friz Freleng: Academy Award nomination, best short film (cartoon), 1964, for *The Pink Phink;* Academy Award nomination, best short film (cartoon), 1966, for *The Pink Blueprint;* Emmy Award nomination (with Ted Geisel), best children's special, 1975, for *Dr. Seuss' The Hoober-Bloob Highway;* Emmy Award nomination, best children's entertainment series, 1975, for *The Pink Panther;* Emmy Award (with Bob Chenault), best children's informational special, 1977, for "My Mom's Having a Baby," *ABC Afterschool Specials;* Emmy Award nomination (with Geisel), best animated program, 1980, for *Dr. Seuss' Pontoffel Pock, Where Are You?;* Emmy Award nomination, best animated program, 1980, for *Pink Panther in Olym-Pinks;* Emmy Award (with Geisel), best animated program, 1982, for *The Grinch Grinches the Cat in the Hat.*

Double Gold awards, California State Fair, 1983 and 1985, for best zinfandel wine; champion zinfandel wine, *Wine & Spirits* magazine, 1984 and 1986.

CREDITS:

TELEVISION WORK; SERIES; ANIMATED CARTOONS

Producer (with Friz Freleng) *The Super Six,* NBC, 1966-69.
Producer (with Freleng) *Super President,* NBC, 1967-68.
Producer (with Freleng) *Here Comes the Grump,* NBC, 1969-71.
Producer (with Freleng) *The Pink Panther,* NBC, 1969-79.
Producer (with Freleng) *Doctor Dolittle,* NBC, 1970-72.
Producer (with Freleng) *The Houndcats,* NBC, 1972-73.
Producer (with Freleng) *The Barkleys,* NBC, 1972-73.
Producer (with Freleng) *Bailey's Comets,* NBC, 1973-74.
Producer (with Freleng), *Return to the Planet of the Apes,* NBC, 1975-76.
Producer (with Freleng) *The Oddball Couple,* ABC, 1975-77.
Producer (with Freleng) *Baggy Pants and the Nitwits,* NBC, 1977-78.
Producer (with Freleng) *What's New Mr. Magoo?,* CBS, 1977-78.
Executive producer (with Freleng) *Spider-Woman,* ABC, 1979-80.
Executive producer (with Lee Gunther) *Spider-Man and His Amazing Friends,* NBC, 1981-82.
Executive producer (with Fred Silverman), *Pandamonium,* CBS, 1982-83.
Executive producer (with Silverman), *Meatballs and Spaghetti,* CBS, 1982-83.
Executive producer (with Gunther) *Dungeons and Dragons,* CBS, 1983.
Producer (with Kay Wright), *Pink Panther and Sons,* NBC, 1984.
Executive producer, *The Charmkins,* syndicated, 1985.

Also worked as producer (with Freleng) of *The Fantastic Four,* 1978-79.

TELEVISION WORK; SPECIALS

Executive producer, *Dr. Seuss' Horton Hears a Who* (animated; also known as *Horton Hears a Who*), CBS, 1970.
Executive producer, *Dr. Seuss' "The Cat in the Hat"* (animated; also known as *The Cat in the Hat*), CBS, 1971.
Executive producer, *Dr. Seuss' "The Lorax"* (animated; also known as *The Lorax*), CBS, 1972.
Executive producer, *Dr. Seuss on the Loose* (animated), CBS, 1973.
Executive producer, *Dr. Seuss' The Hoober-Bloob Highway* (animated), CBS, 1975.
Producer, *The Bugs Bunny Easter Special* (animated), CBS, 1977.
Executive producer, *Halloween Is Grinch Night* (animated), ABC, 1977.
Producer, *Michel's Mixed-Up Musical Bird,* ABC, 1978.
Sequence producer and sequence director, *Bugs Bunny's Looney Christmas Tales* (animated), CBS, 1979.
Producer, *The Bear Who Slept Through Christmas* (animated), CBS, 1979.
Executive producer (with Friz Freleng), *Dr. Seuss' Pontoffel Pock, Where Are You?,* ABC, c. 1980.
Producer (with Freleng), *Pink Panther in Olym-Pinks,* ABC, c. 1980.
Producer, *Daffy Duck's Easter Show* (animated), NBC, 1980.

Producer (with Freleng) *Dennis the Menace: Mayday for Mother* (animated), NBC, 1981.
Producer, *Bugs Bunny's Howl-oween Special* (animated), CBS, 1981.
Executive producer, *The Grinch Grinches the Cat in the Hat* (animated), ABC, 1982.

TELEVISION WORK; EPISODIC

Producer, "The Incredible, Indelible, Magical, Physical Mystery Trip" (animated), *ABC Afterschool Specials,* ABC, 1973.
Producer, "The Magical Mystery Trip Through Little Red's Head" (animated), *ABC Afterschool Specials,* ABC, 1974.
Executive producer (with Friz Freleng), "My Mom's Having a Baby," *ABC Afterschool Specials,* ABC, 1977.
Executive producer, "The Tiny Tree" (animated), *Bell System Family Theatre,* CBS, 1977.
Executive producer, "Where Do Teenagers Come From?," *ABC Afterschool Specials,* ABC, 1980.

TELEVISION WORK; PILOTS

Executive producer (with Joe Bacal and Tom Griffin), *G. I. Joe: A Real American Hero* (animated), syndicated, 1983.

FILM WORK

Producer (with Friz Freleng) *The Pink Phink* (cartoon short), United Artists (UA), c. 1964.
Producer (with Freleng) *The Pink Blueprint* (cartoon short), UA, c. 1966.

WRITINGS:

FILM

Creator of characters, with Friz Freleng, upon which *The Trail of the Pink Panther,* United Artists (UA), 1982, and *Curse of the Pink Panther,* Metro-Goldwyn-Mayer/UA, 1983, are based.*

* * *

DEPP, Johnny 1963-

PERSONAL: Full name, John Christopher Depp; born June 9, 1963, in Owensboro, KY; son of John (an engineer) and Betty Sue (a homemaker) Depp; divorced.

ADDRESSES: Agent—Tracey Jacobs, International Creative Management, 8899 Beverly Blvd., Los Angeles, CA 90048.

CAREER: Actor. Guitarist in the rock bands The Flames, The Kids, and Rock City Angels.

AWARDS, HONORS: Male Star of Tomorrow Award, NATO/ShoWest, 1990.

CREDITS:

FILM APPEARANCES

Glen Lantz, *A Nightmare on Elm Street,* New Line Cinema, 1984.
Jack Marshall, *Private Resort,* Tri-Star, 1985.
Lerner, *Platoon,* Orion, 1986.
Wade "Cry-Baby" Walker, *Cry-Baby,* Universal, 1990.
Title role, *Edward Scissorhands,* Twentieth Century-Fox, 1990.
Cameo appearance, *Freddy's Dead: The Final Nightmare,* New Line Cinema, 1991.

TELEVISION APPEARANCES; SERIES

Officer Tom Hanson, *21 Jump Street,* FOX, 1987-89.

TELEVISION APPEARANCES; EPISODIC

Appeared in an episode of *Hotel,* ABC.

OTHER TELEVISION APPEARANCES

Donnie Fleischer, *Slow Burn* (movie), Showtime, 1986.
The 41st Annual Emmy Awards (special), FOX, 1989.
Idols (special), FOX, 1991.

OTHER SOURCES:

PERIODICALS

Interview, April, 1990, p. 84.*

* * *

DERN, Laura 1967(?)-

PERSONAL: Full name, Laura Elizabeth Dern; born February 10, 1967 (some sources say 1966), in Santa Monica, CA; daughter of Bruce (an actor) and Diana (an actress; maiden name, Ladd) Dern. *Education:* Attended University of California, Los Angeles; studied acting at Lee Strasberg Theatre Institute and Royal Academy of Dramatic Art.

ADDRESSES: Agent—Judy Hofflund, Intertalent, 9200 Sunset Blvd., Penthouse 25, Los Angeles, CA 90069. *Publicist*—Annett Wolf, Inc., 1033 Gayley Ave., Suite 208, Los Angeles, CA 90024.

CAREER: Actress.

AWARDS, HONORS: New Generation Award, Los Angeles Film Critics, 1985, for *Smooth Talk* and *Mask;* Academy Award nomination, best actress, 1991, for *Rambling Rose.*

CREDITS:

FILM APPEARANCES

Debbie, *Foxes,* United Artists (UA), 1980.
Jessica McNeil, *Ladies and Gentlemen: The Fabulous Stains,* Paramount, 1982.
Diane, *Teachers,* Metro-Goldwyn-Mayer/United Artists, 1984.
Diana, *Mask,* Universal, 1985.
Connie, *Smooth Talk,* Spectrafilm, 1985.
Sandy Williams, *Blue Velvet,* DiLaurentiis, 1986.
Kathleen Robinson, *Fat Man and Little Boy,* Paramount, 1988.
Lula Pace Fortune, *Wild at Heart,* Samuel Goldwyn, 1990.
Rose, *Rambling Rose,* New Line Cinema, 1991.

Also appeared as Claire Clairmont, *Haunted Summer,* 1977; also appeared in *White Lightning,* 1973, and *Alice Doesn't Live Here Anymore,* 1975.

TELEVISION APPEARANCES; MOVIES

Audrey Constantine, *Happy Endings,* NBC, 1983.
Mrs. Harduvel, *Afterburn,* HBO, 1992.

Also appeared as Crissy, *The Three Wishes of Billy Grier,* 1984.

TELEVISION APPEARANCES; EPISODIC

Rebecca Laymon, "The Strange Case of Dr. Jekyll and Mr. Hyde," *Nightmare Classics,* Showtime, 1989.

Also appeared in *Secret Storm.*

STAGE APPEARANCES

Charlene Loody, *The Palace of Amateurs,* Minetta Lane Theatre, New York City, 1988.

Also appeared in productions of *Hamlet* and *A Midsummer Night's Dream.*

OTHER SOURCES:

PERIODICALS

American Film, October, 1989, p. 46.
Interview, March, 1986, p. 146; September, 1990, p. 118.
New York Times, May 4, 1986.
People, April 29, 1985, p. 107; October 8, 1990, p. 59.
Premiere, September, 1990, p. 86.*

* * *

DeSCENNA, Linda 1949-

PERSONAL: Born November 14, 1949, in Warren, OH; daughter of Jack Loveless (an accountant) and Dorothy (a homemaker; maiden name, Sabey) DeScenna; married Ric McElvin (a lead man), December 8, 1984. *Education:* Graduated from Kent State University, 1971, with degrees in cinematography and painting.

ADDRESSES: Contact—c/o I.A.T.S.E. Local 44, 11500 Burbank Blvd., North Hollywood, CA 98601.

CAREER: Set decorator. Worked as a studio secretary and cocktail waitress, Hollywood, CA; worked on the crews for various set decorators; worked as lead for John Anderson.

MEMBER: International Alliance of Theatrical Stage Employees and Moving Picture Operators of the U.S. and Canada (I.A.T.S.E.).

AWARDS, HONORS: Academy Award nominations, best set decoration, 1979, for *Star Trek: The Motion Picture,* 1982, for *Blade Runner,* 1985, for *The Color Purple,* and 1988, for *Rain Man.*

CREDITS:

FILM WORK; SET DECORATOR

Star Trek: The Motion Picture, Paramount, 1979.
Fatso, Twentieth Century-Fox, 1979.
It's My Turn, Columbia, 1980.
Blade Runner, Warner Brothers, 1982.
Second Thoughts, Universal, 1982.
Brainstorm, United Artists, 1983.
Spacehunter: Adventures in the Forbidden Zone, Columbia, 1983.
The Lonely Guy, Universal, 1984.
The Adventures of Buckaroo Banzai: Across the Eighth Dimension, Twentieth Century-Fox, 1984.
The Falcon and the Snowman, Orion, 1985.
The Goonies, Warner Brothers, 1985.
The Color Purple, Warner Brothers, 1985.
Back to School, Orion, 1986.
Harry and the Hendersons, Universal, 1987.
Summer School, Paramount, 1987.
Someone to Watch Over Me, Columbia, 1987.
Moving, Warner Brothers, 1988.
Scrooged, Paramount, 1988.
Rain Man, Metro-Goldwyn-Mayer/United Artists, 1988.
Back to the Future Part II, Universal, 1989.
Avalon, Tri-Star, 1990.
Defending Your Life, Warner Brothers, 1991.
The Rocketeer, Buena Vista, 1991.
Honeymoon in Vegas, Lobel Bergman Productions, 1992.
Toys, Fox-Baltimore Pictures, 1992.

TELEVISION WORK; SET DECORATOR

Worked on several television series, including *Logan's Run* and *Fantastic Journey.*

DEVINE, Loretta

PERSONAL: Born in Houston, TX; daughter of James (a laborer) and Eunice (a beautician; maiden name, O'Neal) Devine. *Education:* University of Houston, B.A., speech and drama education, 1971; Brandeis University, M.F.A., theater arts, 1976; studied acting with Ed Koven and improvisation with Gary Austin. *Politics:* Democrat. *Religion:* Baptist.

ADDRESSES: Agent—Writers and Artists, 11726 San Vicente, Suite 300, Los Angeles, CA 90049.

CAREER: Actress, singer, songwriter, and writer. Julia C. Hester House, youth program director and activity coordinator, 1971-72, founder of Hester House Players and Hester House Dancers, 1971; Black Arts Center, Houston, TX, director of theater department, 1972-74; Brandeis University, Waltham, MA, instructor in English, 1974-76. Texas Southern University, instructor, summer, 1974; Harvard University, instructor, summers, 1975-76. Ethnic Arts Center Players, founder, 1972-74.

MEMBER: National Association for the Advancement of Colored People, Alpha Kappa Alpha.

AWARDS, HONORS: Citizen Advocates for Justice Award, 1984; Best Actress Award nomination, National Association for the Advancement of Colored People, 1988, Certificate of Recognition, Hollywood Dramalogue, 1988, and Hollywood Dramalogue Critics Award, best ensemble performance, 1989, all for *The Colored Museum;* San Diego Critics Circle Award nomination, best actress, 1989-90, for *Lady Day at Emerson's Bar and Grill;* Best Supporting Actress Award, National Association for the Advancement of Colored People, 1990, for *Woman from the Town;* Dramalogue Award for acting, 1991, for *Rabbit's Foot.*

CREDITS:

STAGE APPEARANCES

Minister, *Godsong,* La Mama Etc., New York City, 1977.
(Broadway debut) Dionne, *Hair—Revival,* Biltmore Theatre, New York City, 1977.
Soloist, *Langston Hughes,* AMAS Repertory Theatre, 1977.
Title role, *Karma,* Richard Allen Center, New York City, 1977.
Gloria, *Verandah,* New Dramatists, 1977.
Soloists, *Seasons Reasons,* Henry Street Settlement Playhouse, New York City, 1977.
Yenta lady, *A Broadway Musical,* Lunt-Fontanne Theatre, New York City, 1978.
Loretta, *Miss Truth,* Apollo Theatre, New York City, 1978.
Bones, Circle in the Square, New York City, 1978.
Ms. Dabney, *Mahalia,* Henry Street Settlement Playhouse, 1978.
Virtue, *The Blacks,* Richard Allen Center, New York City, 1978.
Young Mary, *Comin' Uptown,* Winter Garden Theatre, New York City, 1979.
Jewel, *Lion and the Jewel,* Lincoln Center, New York City, 1980.
Precious, *Dementos,* City Center, New York City, 1980.
Lorell Robinson, *Dreamgirls,* Imperial Theatre, New York City, 1981.
The Casting of Kevin Christian, Shepherd Street Art Gallery, 1983.
Mermaid, *Gotta Getaway!* Radio City Music Hall, New York City, 1984.
Janeen Earl-Taylor, *Long Time Since Yesterday,* Henry Street Settlement Playhouse, New York City, 1985.
Lilly, *Big Deal,* Broadway Theater, New York City, 1986.
Lala, Wigs, and model, *The Colored Museum,* Public Theaters/Susan Stein Shiva Theater, New York City, 1986.
Delia, *Spunk,* Mark Taper Forum, Los Angeles, CA, 1990.
Billy Holiday, *Lady Day at Emerson's Bar and Grill,* Old Globe Theatre, San Diego, CA, 1990, then Little Theatre, Phoenix, AZ, 1991.
Holly Day, *Rabbit Foot,* Los Angeles Theatre Center, Los Angeles, CA, 1991.
Charlesetta, *East Texas Hot Links,* The Met, Los Angeles, CA, 1991.
Soloist, *Rodgers, Hart, Hammerstein Tribute,* Embassy Theatre, 1991.
Soloist, *Big Moments on Broadway,* Kennedy Center Opera House, Washington, DC, 1991.

Also appeared as Cissy, *Woman From the Town,* 1990; and in *Spunk.*

STAGE WORK; DIRECTOR

Who's Got His Own, Black Arts Center, Houston, TX, 1972.
El Majj Malik, Black Arts Center, 1972.
Black Cycle, Black Arts Center, 1973.
The Warning: A Theme for Linda, Black Arts Center, 1973.
Niggers Still Your First Name, Black Arts Center, 1974.
Black Girl, Black Arts Center, 1974.
Shoes, Black Arts Center, 1974.

FILM APPEARANCES

Verna McLaughlin, *Little Nikita,* Columbia, 1987.
Diane, *Sticky Fingers,* Spectrafilm, 1988.
Bertha, *Stanley and Iris,* Metro-Goldwyn-Mayer/United Artists, 1988.
Judy, *Oklahoma Hotel,* EAE, 1990.

Nadine, *Living Large,* Samuel Goldwyn, 1991.
Janine Brown, *Class Act,* Warner Brothers, 1991.

TELEVISION APPEARANCES; SERIES

Stevie Rollins, *A Different World,* NBC, 1987.
Aunt Loretta, *Sugar and Spice,* CBS, 1988.
Valerie, *Reasonable Doubts,* NBC, 1991.
Ellie, *Simple Folks,* CBS, 1992.

TELEVISION APPEARANCES; EPISODIC

Lydia, *Amen,* NBC, 1988.
Nurse Hawkings, *Murphy Brown,* CBS, 1990.
Juror, *Cop Rock,* Fox, 1990.
Nurse Tilda, *STAT,* Disney, 1991.

OTHER TELEVISION APPEARANCES

Cheryl Kelly, "Sirens," *CBS Summer Playhouse* (pilot), CBS, 1987.
Anne Maude Carter, *The Murder of Mary Phagan* (mini-series), NBC, 1988.
Lorraine, *Heart and Soul* (pilot), ABC, 1989.
Thelma, *Parent Trap III* (movie), NBC, 1989.
Aunt Charlotte, *In the House* (pilot), NBC, 1991.

WRITINGS:

Author of *Managing the Hunks,* an unsold television pilot.

* * *

DEXTER, John 1925(?)-1990

PERSONAL: Born August 2, 1925 (some sources say 1935), in Derby, England; died of heart failure, March 23, 1990, in London, England; son of Harry James (a plumber) and Rose Dexter. *Education:* Attended schools in England to age fourteen; became George Devine's directing protege at the Royal Court Theatre.

CAREER: Director, designer, and actor. English Stage Company, London, England, associate director, 1957; National Theatre, London, associate director, 1963-66 and 1971-75; Metropolitan Opera Company, New York City, production supervisor, 1974-81; named artistic director of Stratford Shakespeare Festival, Stratford, Ontario, 1980 (post rescinded after protests that he was not a Canadian). Appeared on radio and television. *Military service:* Served in British Army during World War II.

AWARDS, HONORS: London Drama Critics Award, 1962, for *Chips with Everything;* Antoinette Perry Award nominee, best director, 1967, for *Black Comedy; Best Plays* Award, best director, 1974-75, for *The Misanthrope; Best Plays* Award, best director, 1974-75, Drama Desk Award, 1974-75, and Antoinette Perry Award, best director, 1975, all for *Equus;* Antoinette Perry Award, best director, and Drama Desk Award, both 1988, both for *M. Butterfly.*

CREDITS:

STAGE WORK; DIRECTOR

Yes—and After, English Stage Company, Royal Court Theatre, London, England, 1957.
Each in His Own Wilderness, English Stage Company, Royal Court Theatre, 1957.
Chicken Soup with Barley, English Stage Company, Royal Court Theatre, 1958 and 1960.
Roots, English Stage Company, Royal Court Theatre, 1959.
Last Day in Dreamland and *A Gift of the Sea* (double bill), English Stage Company, Royal Court Theatre, 1959.
This Year, Next Year, English Stage Company, Royal Court Theatre, 1960.
I'm Talking about Jerusalem, English Stage Company, Royal Court Theatre, 1960.
Toys in the Attic, Royal Court Theatre, 1960.
The Kitchen, English Stage Company, Royal Court Theatre, 1961.
(Broadway debut) *Chips with Everything,* Plymouth Theatre, New York City, 1963.
The Royal Hunt of the Sun, ANTA Theatre, New York City, 1965.
Do I Hear a Waltz, Forty-sixth Street Theatre, New York City, 1965.
"Black Comedy" and "White Lies," in *Black Comedy* (double bill), Ethel Barrymore Theatre, New York City, 1967.
The Unknown Soldier and His Wife, Vivian Beaumont Theatre, New York City, 1967.
Hamlet, American Shakespeare Festival, Stratford, CT, 1969.
In Praise of Love, Morosco Theatre, New York City, 1973.
Equus, Plymouth Theatre, 1974, then Helen Hayes Theatre, 1976.
The Misanthrope, St. James Theatre, New York City, 1975.
Phaedra Britannica, National Theatre Company, London, 1975.
The Merchant, Plymouth Theatre, 1977.
Pygmalion, Center Theatre Group, Ahmanson Theatre, Los Angeles, 1978.
One Night Stand, Nederlander Theatre, New York City, 1980.
Gallileo and *As You Like It* (double bill), National Theatre Company, 1980.
Shoemaker's Holiday, National Theatre Company, 1981.
The Portage to San Cristobal of A. H., Mermaid Theatre, 1982.
The Glass Menagerie, Eugene O'Neill Theatre, New York City, 1983.

The Nightingale, Covent Garden Opera Company, London, 1983.
Portraits, Savoy Theatre, London, 1987.
M. Butterfly, National Theatre, Washington, D.C., then Eugene O'Neill Theatre, 1988, later Shaftesbury Theatre, London, 1989.
The 3 Penny Opera, National Theater, then Lunt-Fontanne Theatre, New York City, 1989.

Also directed *Gigi,* 1985, and *The Cocktail Party,* 1986.

STAGE WORK; ASSOCIATE DIRECTOR; NATIONAL THEATRE COMPANY, OLD VIC THEATRE, LONDON

Chicken Soup with Barley, 1961.
This Time Next Year, 1961.
I'm Talking about Jerusalem, 1961.
The Kitchen, 1961.
South, 1961.
The Keep, 1961 and 1962.
(Codirector) *Chips with Everything,* 1962.
My Place, 1962.
England, Our England, 1962.
The Blood of the Bambergs, 1962.
The Sponge Room and *Squat Betty* (double bill), 1962.
Jackie the Jumper, 1962.
Half a Sixpence, 1962.
Saint Joan, then Chichester and Edinburgh Festivals, 1962.
Hobson's Choice, 1964.
Othello, 1964.
(Codirector) *The Royal Hunt of the Sun,* then Chichester Festival, 1964.
(Codirector) *Armstrong's Last Goodnight,* then Chichester Festival, 1966.
Black Comedy, then Chichester Festival, 1966.
A Bond Honoured, 1966.
The Storm, 1966.
Wise Child, 1967.
A Woman Killed with Kindness, 1971.
(Codirector) *Tyger,* 1971.
The Goodnatured Man, 1971.
The Old Ones, 1972.
The Misanthrope, 1973.
Equus, 1973.
In Praise of Love, 1973.
The Party, 1973.
Pygmalion, then Albery Theatre, 1974.

MAJOR TOURS; DIRECTOR

Equus, U.S. cities, 1975.

OPERA; DIRECTOR

(Opera directing debut) *Benvenuto Cellini,* Covent Garden, London, 1966.
From the House of the Dead, Hamburg Opera, Hamburg, Germany, 1967.
Billy Budd, Hamburg Opera, 1967.
Il Ballo in Maschera, Hamburg Opera, 1967.
Boris Godurov, Hamburg Opera, 1967.
I Vespri Siciliani, Hamburg Opera, 1967.
Aida, Metropolitan Opera Company, 1974.
La Gioconda, Metropolitan Opera Company, 1974.
I Vespri Siciliani, Metropolitan Opera Company, 1974, then Paris Opera, Paris, France, 1975.
The Devils, Sadler's Wells Theatre, London, 1975.
La Forza del Destino, Metropolitan Opera Company, then Paris Opera, 1975.
La Gioconda, Paris Opera, 1975.
Aida, Paris Opera, 1976.
Le Prophete, Metropolitan Opera Company, 1977.
Dialogues of the Carmelites, Metropolitan Opera Company, 1977.
Lulu, Metropolitan Opera Company, 1977.
Rigoletto, Metropolitan Opera Company, 1977.
Billy Budd, Metropolitan Opera Company, 1978.
The Bartered Bride, Metropolitan Opera Company, 1978.
Don Pasquale, Metropolitan Opera Company, 1978.
Don Carlo, Metropolitan Opera Company, 1979.
Die Enfuhrung aus dem Serail, Metropolitan Opera Company, 1979.
The Rise and Fall of the City of Mahagonny, Metropolitan Opera Company, 1979.
Rossignol, Le Sacre du Printemps, and *Oedipus Rex* (triple bill), 1981.
Parade (triple bill), Metropolitan Opera Company, 1981.
Stravinsky (triple bill), Metropolitan Opera Company, 1981.
The Portage to San Cristobal, Metropolitan Opera Company, 1982.
The Devil and the Good Lord, Buxton Opera Festival, 1985.
La Buone Figlio, Buxton Opera Festival, 1985.
Il Filosofo di Campagna, Buxton Opera Festival, 1985.

Also director for American Shakespeare Festival, Stratford, CT, 1969. Director of *Nabucco,* produced in Zurich, Switzerland, 1986.

OPERA PRODUCER; METROPOLITAN OPERA COMPANY

Lulu, 1980.
Don Carlo, 1980.
Rigoletto, 1981.
La Forza del Destino, 1984.
Don Carlo, 1984.
Aida, 1985.
Dialogues of the Carmelites, 1987.

FILM APPEARANCES

Jacoby, *Laura,* Twentieth Century-Fox, 1944.

Tom Russell, *Buffalo Bill Rides Again,* Screen Guild, 1947.

FILM WORK; DIRECTOR

Othello, Eagle/Warner Brothers, 1966.
The Virgin Soldiers, Columbia, 1968.
The Sidelong Glances of a Pigeon Kicker (also known as *Pigeons*), Saturn Pictures/Metro-Goldwyn-Mayer-Plaza, 1970.
I Want What I Want, Marayan/Cinerama, 1972.

TELEVISION WORK; SPECIALS

Also director of *Mahagonny,* 1979, *Lulu,* 1980, and *Twelfth Night,* Grenada TV.

OBITUARIES AND OTHER SOURCES:

PERIODICALS

New York Times, March 27, 1990.
Variety, March 28, 1990.*

* * *

DIETRICH, Marlene 1901(?)-1992

PERSONAL: Born Maria Magdalena von Losch, in Berlin, Germany, December 27, 1901 (some sources say 1900 and 1904); immigrated to the U.S., 1930; naturalized U.S. citizen, 1939; died May 6, 1992, in Paris, France; daughter of Edward (a police officer) and Josephine (Felsing) von Losch; married Rudolf Sieber (an assistant director), May 13, 1924 (separated, 1939; died, 1976); children: Maria Riva. *Education:* Attended Augusta Victoria School, Berlin; studied violin at Musik Konservatorium, Weimar, Germany, 1919, and at Berlin Music Academy; prepared for the stage with Max Reinhardt. *Avocational interests:* Tennis.

ADDRESSES: Agent—Regency Artists Ltd., 9200 Sunset Blvd., Suite 823, Los Angeles, CA 90069.

CAREER: Actress, singer, entertainer. Appeared in films in Germany beginning in 1922; stage debut in Max Reinhardt's production of *Broadway,* Berlin, 1926; came to U.S. to make films, 1930, and remained in Hollywood for many years; entertained troops and made anti-Nazi broadcasts in Europe and throughout the world during World War II; recording and cabaret performer in the 1950s, appearing all over the world.

AWARDS, HONORS: Academy Award nomination, best actress, 1930, for *Morocco;* Medal of Freedom for her efforts in World War II, 1947; Antoinette Perry Special Award, 1968; Legion d'Honneur of France, Chevalier, 1951, Officier, 1972, Commandeur, 1990.

CREDITS:

FILM APPEARANCES

Lola Frohlich, *The Blue Angel* (originally *Der Blaue Engel,* 1930), Paramount, 1930.
Amy Jolly, *Morocco,* Paramount, 1930.
X-27, *Dishonored,* Paramount, 1931.
Helen Faraday, *Blonde Venus,* Paramount, 1932.
Shanghai Lily, *Shanghai Express,* Paramount, 1932.
Lily Czepanek, *Song of Songs,* Paramount, 1933.
Sophia Frederica, Catherine II, *The Scarlet Empress,* Paramount, 1934.
Concha Perez, *The Devil Is a Woman,* Paramount, 1935.
Madeleine de Beaupre, *Desire,* Paramount, 1936.
Domini Enfilden, *The Garden of Allah,* United Artists, 1936.
Maria Barker, *Angel,* Paramount, 1937.
Alexandra Vladinoff, *Knight without Armor,* United Artists, 1937.
Frenchy, *Destry Rides Again,* Universal, 1939.
Bijou Blanche, *Seven Sinners* (also known as *Cafe of the Seven Sinners*), Universal, 1940.
Claire Ledeux, *The Flame of New Orleans,* Universal, 1941.
Fay Duval, *Manpower,* Warner Brothers, 1941.
Elizabeth Madden, *The Lady Is Willing,* Columbia, 1942.
Josie Winters, *Pittsburgh,* Universal, 1942.
Cherry Malotte, *The Spoilers,* Universal, 1942.
Herself, *Follow the Boys,* Universal, 1944.
Jamilla, *Kismet* (also known as *Oriental Dream*), Metro-Goldwyn-Mayer, 1944.
Lydia, *Golden Earrings,* Paramount, 1947.
Erika von Schluetow, *A Foreign Affair,* Paramount, 1948.
Blanche Ferrand, *The Room Upstairs* (originally *Martin Roumagnac,* 1946), Lopert, 1948.
Nightclub patron, *Jigsaw* (also known as *Gun Moll*), United Artists, 1949.
Charlotte Inwood, *Stage Fright,* Warner Brothers, 1950.
Monica Teasdale, *No Highway in the Sky* (also known as *No Highway*), Twentieth Century-Fox, 1951.
Altar Keane, *Rancho Notorious,* RKO Radio Pictures, 1952.
Hostess, *Around the World in Eighty Days,* United Artists, 1956.
Marquise Maria de Crevecoeur, *The Monte Carlo Story,* United Artists, 1957.
Christine "Helm" Vole, *Witness for the Prosecution,* United Artists, 1957.
Tanya, *Touch of Evil,* Universal, 1958.
Mme. Bertholt, *Judgment at Nuremberg,* United Artists, 1961.
Party guest, *Paris When It Sizzles,* Paramount, 1964.
Baroness von Semering, *Just a Gigolo,* United Artists, 1979.

Also appeared in numerous films, many of them silent: Kathrin in *So sind die Maenner* (also known as *Napoleons kleiner Brueder, Der kleine Napoleon, Men Are Like This, Napoleon's Little Brother,* and *The Little Napoleon*), 1922; Lucie in *Tragoedie der Liebe* (also known as *The Tragedy of Love*), 1923; *Der Mensch am Wege* (also known as *Man by the Roadside*), 1923; *Der Sprung ins Leben* (also known as *They Leap into Life*), 1924; *Die freudlose Gasse* (also known as *The Joyless Street,* and *The Street of Sorrow*), 1925; Micheline in *Manon Lescaut,* 1926; *Eine DuBarry von Heute* (also known as *A Modern Dubarry*), 1926; Edmee Marchand in *Kopf hoch, Charly!* (also known as *Heads Up, Charley*), 1926; *Madame wuenscht keine Kinder* (also known as *Madame Wants No Children*), 1926; Yvette in *Sein groesster Bluff* (also known as *Er oder Dich* and *His Greatest Bluff*), 1927; Erni in *Cafe Electric* (also known as *Wenn ein Weib den Weg verliert* and *When a Woman Loses Her Way*), 1927; Sophie in *Der Juxbaron* (also known as *The Imaginary Baron*), 1927; Chicotte de Gastone in *Prinzessin Olala* (also known as *Princess Olala* and *Art of Love*), 1928; *Die glueckliche Mutter,* 1928; Laurence Gerard in *Ich kuesse Ihre Hand, Madame* (also known as *I Kiss Your Hand Madame*), 1929; Stascha in *Die Frau, nach der Man sich sehnt* (also known as *The Woman One Longs For* and *Three Loves*), 1929; Miss Ethel in *Das Schiff der Verlorenen Menschen* (also known as *Le Navire des hommes perdus, The Ship of Lost Men,* and *The Ship of Lost Souls*) 1929; Evelyn in *Liebesnaechte* (also known as *Gefahren der Brautzeit, Aus dem Tagebuch eines Verfuehrers, Eine Nacht der Libe, Liebesbriefe, Nights of Love,* and *Love Letters*), 1929; *Dangers of the Engagement Period,* 1929; *I Loved a Soldier,* 1936; *Screen Snapshots No. 103,* 1943; and *Marlene* (documentary), 1984. Narrator of *The Black Fox,* 1962.

STAGE APPEARANCES

(London debut) *Marlene Dietrich* (one-woman show), Queen's Theatre, London, 1964.

(Broadway debut) *Marlene Dietrich* (one-woman show), Lunt-Fontanne Theatre, New York City, 1967, later Mark Hellinger Theatre, New York City, 1968.

Appeared in productions for the Max Reinhardt company in Germany, 1926-1929. Has performed her one-woman show in theatres throughout the world, 1964-1975.

TELEVISION APPEARANCES; SPECIALS

Marlene Dietrich: I Wish You Love (adaptation of her one-woman stage show), CBS, 1973.

RADIO APPEARANCES

Appeared in radio series *Cafe Istanbul* and *Time for Love* in the 1950s.

WRITINGS:

Marlene Dietrich's ABC, Doubleday, 1962.

Nehmt nur mein Leben . . . : Reflexionen, Bertelsmann, 1979.

Ich bin, Gott sei Dank, Berlinerin (memoirs), Ullstein, 1987, translation by Salvator Attanasio published as *Marlene,* Grove Press, 1989.

OBITUARIES AND OTHER SOURCES:

BOOKS

Close-Ups: Intimate Profiles of Movie Stars by Their Co-Stars, Directors, Screenwriters, and Friends, edited by Danny Peary, Workman, 1978.

Griffith, Richard, *Marlene Dietrich: Image and Legend,* Doubleday, 1959.

Higham, Charles *Marlene: The Life of Marlene Dietrich,* Norton, 1977.

Kobal, John, *Marlene Dietrich,* Studio Vista, 1968.

Morley, Sheridan, *Marlene Dietrich,* Elm Tree Books, 1976.

Rosen, Marjorie, *Popcorn Venus: Women, Movies, and the American Dream,* Coward, McCann, & Geoghegan, 1973.

Silver, Charles, *Marlene Dietrich,* Pyramid Publications, 1974.

PERIODICALS

Hollywood Reporter, May 7, 1992, pp. 1, 7, 22.*

* * *

DIGNAM, Mark 1909-1989

PERSONAL: Born March 20, 1909, in London, England; died September 29, 1989, in London; son of Edmund Grattan and Agnes Mary (Sheen) Dignam; married Georgia MacKinnon (divorced); married Helen Christie (divorced); married Virginia Kirby. *Education:* Attended Mount St. Mary's College and Neuchatel; studied acting with the Sheffield Repertory Company. *Avocational interests:* Swimming.

CAREER: Actor. Member of several theatre companies in England, including the Croydon Repertory Company, Kingdom, 1936, the Old Vic Company, 1947-50, the Shakespeare Memorial Theatre Company, 1956-58, and the Royal Shakespeare Company and National Theatre Company, 1970s and 1980s. Journalist and frequent radio performer. *Military service:* British Army, served as a signaller with the Royal Artillery, 1941-44.

CREDITS:

STAGE APPEARANCES

(Stage debut) *The Lonely House,* County Theatre, St. Albans, England, 1930.

(London debut) Bleeding sergeant, *Macbeth,* Kingsway Theatre, London, 1932.

Adam Veryard, *A Cup of Happiness,* Royalty Theatre, London, 1932.

Gloucester, *Henry V,* Alhambra Theatre, London, 1934.

George Hemsby, *Libel!,* Playhouse Theatre, London, 1934.

Donado, *'Tis Pity She's a Whore,* Arts Theatre, London, 1934.

Henry Armiger, *Swords for Utopia,* Arts Theatre, 1935.

Strength, *Everyman,* Ambassadors' Theatre, London, 1935.

Bernardo, *Hamlet,* Old Vic Theatre, London, 1935.

Mantius, *Catiline,* Royalty Theatre, 1936.

Nicholas Dalziel, *Rain before Seven,* Arts Theatre, 1936.

Relling, *The Wild Duck,* Westminster Theatre, London, 1936-37.

Justin O'Connell, *Waste,* Westminster Theatre, 1936-37.

Professor Weissmann, *Crooked Cross,* Westminster Theatre, 1936-37.

Serebryakov, *Uncle Vanya,* Westminster Theatre, 1936-37.

Boss Mangan, *Heartbreak House,* Westminster Theatre, 1936-37.

Johnny the priest, *Anna Christie,* Westminster Theatre, 1936-37.

Ghost and first player, *Hamlet,* Westminster Theatre, 1936-37.

Schaaf, *A Month in the Country,* Westminster Theatre, 1936-37.

Colonel Pickering, *Pygmalion,* Old Vic Theatre, 1937.

Provost, *Measure for Measure,* Old Vic Theatre, 1937.

Buckingham, *Richard III,* Old Vic Theatre, 1937.

Ezra Mannon, *Mourning Becomes Electra,* Westminster Theatre, 1937-38.

Voltore, *Volpone,* Westminster Theatre, 1937-38.

Henry of York, *The Zeal of Thy House,* Westminster Theatre, 1937-38.

Bohun, QC, *You Never Can Tell,* Westminster Theatre, 1937-38.

Zhevakin, *Marriage,* Westminster Theatre, 1937-38.

(Broadway debut) Mr. E. H. Carson, *Oscar Wilde,* Fulton Theatre, New York City, 1938.

Charles Bendrex, *Music at Night,* Westminster Theatre, 1939-40.

Bill Walker, *Major Barbara,* Westminster Theatre, 1939-40.

Ephraim Cabot, *Desire under the Elms,* Westminster Theatre, 1939-40.

Bishop, *Getting Married,* Arts Theatre Festival, London, 1945.

James Mortimore, *The Thunderbolt,* Arts Theatre Festival, London, 1945.

Claudius, *Hamlet,* Arts Theatre, Cambridge, England, then Arts Theatre Festival, 1945.

Pra, *The Simpleton of the Unexpected Isles,* Arts Theatre, 1945.

Agrippa, *Antony and Cleopatra,* Piccadilly Theatre, London, 1946.

Dr. Wangel, *The Lady from the Sea,* Arts Theatre, 1946.

Mr. Robinson, *Exercise Bowler,* Arts Theatre, 1946.

John of Gaunt, *Richard II,* Edinburgh Festival, Edinburgh, Scotland, 1947.

Baptista, *The Taming of the Shrew,* Edinburgh Festival, 1947.

Harrison North, *Angel,* Strand Theatre, London, 1947.

Claudius, *Hamlet,* Old Vic Company, New Theatre, then Elsinore Castle, Denmark, both 1950.

Sea captain, *Twelfth Night,* Old Vic Theatre, 1950.

Zeal-of-the-Land Busy, *Bartholomew Fair,* Old Vic Theatre, 1950.

Exeter, *Henry V,* Old Vic Theatre, 1950.

Sir Howard Hallam, *Captain Brassbound's Conversion,* Old Vic Theatre, 1950.

Sir Hugh Evans, *The Merry Wives of Windsor,* Old Vic Theatre, 1950.

Seti the Second, *The Firstborn,* Winter Garden Theatre, London, 1952.

Dean Harry Kennedy, *Two Loves I Have . . . ,* Arts Theatre, 1952.

Colonel Ritter von und zu Ruppertshausen, *High Balcony,* Embassy Theatre, London, 1952.

William Corder, *Maria Marten,* Arts Theatre, 1952.

Izzy, *Five Philadelphia Physicians,* Embassy Theatre, 1953.

Major H. Maunsell, *Carrington, VC,* Westminster Theatre, 1953.

Presiding angel and principal, *The World of Sholom Aleichem,* Embassy Theatre, 1955.

Consalvo, *Summertime,* Apollo Theatre, London, 1955.

Mr. Kroll, *Rosmersholm,* Royal Court Theatre, London, 1959, then Comedy Theatre, London, 1960.

Auda Abu Tayi, *Ross,* Haymarket Theatre, London, 1960-62.

Humphrey Craik, *The Poison Tree,* Ashcroft Theatre, Croydon, England, 1963.

Shamrayev, *The Seagull,* Queen's Theatre, London, 1964.

Graham, *Saint Joan of the Stockyards,* Queen's Theatre, 1964.

Edgar, *A Scent of Flowers,* Duke of York's Theatre, London, 1964.

Alexander, *A Present for the Past,* Lyceum Theatre, Edinburgh, Scotland, 1966.

Mr. Hardcastle, *She Stoops to Conquer,* Oxford Playhouse, Oxford, England, 1966.
General, *The Balcony,* Oxford Playhouse, 1967.
Vicar, *Halfway up the Tree,* Queen's Theatre, 1967.
Polonius, *Hamlet,* Roundhouse Theatre, London, then Lunt-Fontanne Theatre, New York City, both 1969.
Courcy, Croissy, and Canavo, *The Hallelujah Boy,* Duchess Theatre, London, 1970.
Father, *A Voyage 'round My Father,* Greenwich Theatre, London, 1970.
Cecil, *Vivat! Vivat Regina!,* Piccadilly Theatre, 1971.
Menenius, *Coriolanus,* Royal Shakespeare Company (RSC), Stratford-on-Avon, 1972, then Aldwych Theatre, London, 1973.
Caesar, *Julius Caesar,* RSC, Stratford-on-Avon, 1972, then Aldwych Theatre, 1973.
Marcus Andronicus, *Titus Andronicus,* RSC, Stratford-on-Avon, 1972, then Aldwych Theatre, 1973.
Maurice Shanklin, *Duck Song,* Aldwych Theatre, 1974.
Philip IV and Valladares, *The Bewitched,* Aldwych Theatre, 1974.
Barry, *The Freeway,* National Theatre Company, Old Vic Theatre, 1974.
General Mercier, *Grand Manoeuvres,* National Theatre Company, Old Vic Theatre, 1974.
Nat, *Hindle Wakes,* Greenwich Theatre, 1978.
Vladimir, *Cousin Vladimir,* RSC, Aldwych Theatre, 1978.
Old Werk, *The Wild Duck,* National Theatre Company, Olivier Theatre, London, 1979.
Duke of Venice, *Othello,* National Theatre Company, Olivier Theatre, 1980.
Father Barre, *The Devils,* RSC, The Pit, London, 1984.
Thomas Bruckner, *Mephisto,* RSC, Barbican Theatre, London, 1986.
Nestor, *Troilus and Cressida,* RSC, Barbican Theatre, 1986.
Escalus, *Measure for Measure,* RSC, Stratford-on-Avon, 1987.

As a member of the Old Vic Company during the years 1947-50 appeared as Baptista, *The Taming of the Shrew;* John of Gaunt, *Richard II;* Peter Cauchon, *St. Joan;* Sicinius, *Coriolanus;* Malvolio, *Twelfth Night;* Petulant, *The Way of the World;* Lopahin, *The Cherry Orchard;* Holofernes, *Love's Labour's Lost;* Ignaty, *A Month in the Country;* Seigneur Anselm, *The Miser,* all New Theatre, London. Also appeared with the Stratford Company on their 1958 tour of Moscow and Leningrad, Russia.

STAGE APPEARANCES, SHAKESPEARE MEMORIAL THEATRE COMPANY, STRATFORD-ON-AVON, ENGLAND

Ghost, *Hamlet,* 1956.
Morocco, *The Merchant of Venice,* 1956.
Duke of Venice, *Othello,* 1956.
Provost, *Measure for Measure,* 1956.
Holofernes, *Love's Labour's Lost,* 1956.
Badger, *Toad of Toad Hall,* then Memorial Theatre, London, 1956.
Duke Frederick, *As You Like It,* 1957.
Pandulph, *King John,* 1957.
Casca, *Julius Caesar,* 1957.
Pisanio, *Cymbeline,* 1957.
Antonio, *The Tempest,* then Drury Lane Theatre, London, 1957.
Capulet, *Romeo and Juliet,* 1958.
Malvolio, *Twelfth Night,* 1958.
Claudius, *Hamlet,* 1958.
Simonides, *Pericles,* 1958.

MAJOR TOURS

Adam Veryard, *A Cup of Happiness,* U.K. cities, 1933.
Banquo, *Macbeth,* Old Vic Company, U.K. cities, 1940-41.
McCarthy, *The Time of Your Life,* Old Vic Company, U.K. cities, 1940-41.
His Excellency, U.K. cities, 1951.
Mr. James Formal, *The Gentleman Dancing Master,* U.K. cities, 1963.

Also toured with the Ben Greet Company, U.K. cities, 1931, and the Shakespeare Memorial Theatre Company, U.S.S.R. cities, 1958.

FILM APPEARANCES

First knight, *Murder in the Cathedral,* Classic, 1952.
Bolingbroke, "The Actor," *Train of Events,* Film Arts, 1952.
Mr. Burke, *Beau Brummell,* Metro-Goldwyn-Mayer, 1954.
Prosecutor, *Court Martial* (also known as *Carrington V.C.*), British Lion, 1954.
Inspector, *The Passing Stranger,* Independent Film Distributors/British Lion, 1954.
Doctor in the House, General Films Distributors, 1954.
Lease of Life, General Films Distributors, 1954.
Three Cornered Fate, Paramount, 1954.
Sykes, *Escapade,* Eros, 1955.
Governor, *The Prisoner,* Columbia, 1955.
Caleb, *Conscience Bay,* Cross 5 Channel, 1960.
Ark Royal captain, *Sink the Bismarck!,* Twentieth Century-Fox, 1960.
Prosecuting counsel, *The Pure Hell of St. Trinian's,* Continental Distributing, 1961.
In Search of the Castaways, Buena Vista, 1962.
King Arthur, *Siege of the Saxons,* Columbia, 1963.
Merlin, *Sword of Lancelot* (also known as *Lancelot and Guinevere*), Universal, 1963.
Lieutenant, *Tom Jones,* Lopert, 1963.
Master, *A Jolly Bad Fellow* (also known as *They All Died Laughing*), Continental Distributing, 1964.

Sydney Selwyn, *Escape by Night,* (also known as *Clash by Night*), Allied Artists, 1965.
Attorney general, *Game for Three Losers,* Avco Embassy, 1965.
Vincentio, *The Taming of the Shrew,* Columbia, 1967.
Airey, *The Charge of the Light Brigade,* United Artists, 1968.
Isadora (also known as *The Loves of Isadora*), Universal, 1968.
Polonius, *Hamlet,* Columbia, 1969.
Wedding reception guest, *There's a Girl in My Soup,* Columbia, 1970.
Macduff's son, *Macbeth,* Columbia, 1971.
News vendor and gardener, *Memoirs of a Survivor,* EMI, 1981.
Ambrose, *The Chain,* Rank, 1985.
Reverend Lambert, *On the Black Hill,* British Film Institute, 1987.

Also appeared in *Dead Cert,* 1974.

TELEVISION APPEARANCES

Samuel, *The Story of David* (movie), ABC, 1976.

Also appeared in *The Sea, Hess, Disraeli, The XYY Man, Suez,* and *A Voyage 'round My Father.*

OBITUARIES AND OTHER SOURCES:

PERIODICALS

Variety, October 11-17, 1989.*

* * *

DILLMAN, Bradford 1930-

PERSONAL: Born April 14, 1930, in San Francisco, CA; son of Dean (a stockbroker) and Josephine (Moore) Dillman; married Frieda Harding, June 16, 1956 (divorced April 4, 1962); married Suzy Parker (an actress and model), April 20, 1963; children: (first marriage) Jeffrey, Pamela; (second marriage) Diana, Christopher, Georgina Belle LaSalle (stepdaughter). *Education:* Yale University, B.A., English literature, 1951; studied with Lee Strasberg at Actors Studio, New York City, beginning in 1955, and with John Lehne, beginning in 1962.

ADDRESSES: Agent—Agency for the Performing Arts, 9000 Sunset Blvd., Suite 1200, Los Angeles, CA 90069.

CAREER: Actor. *Military service:* U.S. Marine Corps, 1952-53; became first lieutenant.

MEMBER: Actors Equity Association, American Federation of Television and Radio Artists, Screen Actors Guild, Players Club.

AWARDS, HONORS: Blum Award, outstanding new person in the theater, 1957; *Theatre World* Award, 1957, for *Long Day's Journey into Night;* Golden Globe Award, new male star of the year, Hollywood Foreign Press Association, 1959; Best Actor Award, Cannes International Film Festival, 1959, for *Compulsion;* Emmy Award nomination, outstanding single performance by an actor in a leading role, 1962, for "The Voice of Charlie Pont"; Emmy Award, outstanding actor in a daytime drama special, 1975, for "The Last Bride of Salem," *ABC Afternoon Playbreak.*

CREDITS:

FILM APPEARANCES

Bertrand, *A Certain Smile,* Twentieth Century-Fox, 1958.
Alan Newcombe, *In Love and War,* Twentieth Century-Fox, 1958.
Artie Straus, *Compulsion,* Twentieth Century-Fox, 1959.
Larnier and Claude, *Crack in the Mirror,* Twentieth Century-Fox, 1960.
Paul Raine, *Circle of Deception,* Twentieth Century-Fox, 1961.
Francis Bernardone, *Francis of Assisi,* Twentieth Century-Fox, 1961.
Gowan Stevens, *Sanctuary,* Twentieth Century-Fox, 1961.
Sidney Tale, *A Rage to Live,* United Artists (UA), 1965.
Lieutenant Stiles, *The Plainsman,* Universal, 1966.
The Helicopter Spies, Metro-Goldwyn-Mayer, 1968.
Jonathan Fields, *Jigsaw,* Universal, 1968.
Captain David Young, *Sergeant Ryker,* Universal, 1968.
Major Barnes, *The Bridge at Remagen,* UA, 1969.
Captain Myerson, *Suppose They Gave a War and Nobody Came?* (also known as *War Games*), Cinerama, 1970.
Lloyd Thomas, *Brother John,* Columbia, 1971.
Dr. Lewis Dixon, *Escape from the Planet of the Apes,* Twentieth Century-Fox, 1971.
Bill Delancey, *The Mephisto Waltz,* Twentieth Century-Fox, 1971.
Senator Zachary Wheeler, *The Resurrection of Zachary Wheeler,* Vidtronics, 1971.
Willie Oban, *The Iceman Cometh,* American Film Theatre, 1973.
J. J., *The Way We Were,* Columbia, 1973.
Peter Macomber, *Chosen Survivors,* Columbia, 1974.
Manfred Steyner, *Gold,* Allied Artists, 1974.
Big Eddie, *99 and 44/100 % Dead* (also known as *Call Harry Crown*), Twentieth Century-Fox, 1974.
James Parmiter, *Bug,* Paramount, 1975.
Captain McKay, *The Enforcer,* Warner Brothers, 1976.
John Wilkes Booth, *The Lincoln Conspiracy,* Sunn Classic, 1977.
Mastermind, Goldstone, 1977.
Odums, *The Amsterdam Kill,* Columbia, 1978.

Paul Grogan, *Piranha,* World, 1978.
Major Baker, *The Swarm,* Warner Brothers, 1978.
Brickman, *Love and Bullets,* Associated Film Distribution, 1979.
Dr. Gary Shaw, *Guyana, Cult of the Damned* (also known as *Guyana, Crime of the Century*), Universal, 1980.
Captain Briggs, *Sudden Impact,* Warner Brothers, 1983.
Clark, *Treasure of the Amazon,* Videocine-S.A., 1985.
Frank Simmons, *Man Outside,* Virgin Vision, 1987.
Hot Pursuit, Paramount, 1987.
Dobler, *Lords of the Deep,* Concorde, 1989.

Also appeared in *One Away,* 1980; in *Running Scared,* 1980; as Walt Simmons, *Heroes Stand Alone,* 1989; and in *Black Ribbon for Deborah.*

TELEVISION APPEARANCES; SERIES

Captain David Young, *Court-Martial,* ABC, 1966.
Paul Hollister, *King's Crossing,* ABC, 1982.
Darryl Clayton, *Falcon Crest,* CBS, 1982-83.

TELEVISION APPEARANCES; MOVIES

Paul Varney, *Fear No Evil,* NBC, 1969.
Lyle Fawcett, *Black Water Gold,* ABC, 1970.
Jim Meeker, *Five Desperate Women,* ABC, 1971.
Frank Klaner, *Revenge* (also known as *There Once Was a Woman*), ABC, 1971.
Andrew Rodanthe, *Moon of the Wolf,* ABC, 1972.
Steven Dennis, *Deliver Us from Evil,* ABC, 1973.
Major Mike Dunning, *The Disappearance of Flight 412,* NBC, 1974.
Sam Champion, *Murder or Mercy,* ABC, 1974.
Martin Reed, *Adventures of the Queen,* CBS, 1975.
Michael Dominick, *Force Five,* CBS, 1975.
Richard, *Widow,* NBC, 1976.
Dr. Eric Lake, *The Hostage Heart,* CBS, 1977.
Jack Mathews, *Before and After,* ABC, 1979.
Jason Eddington, *The Memory of Eva Ryker,* CBS, 1980.
Singer, *The Legend of Walks Far Woman,* NBC, 1982.
Eric Noble, *Covenant,* NBC, 1985.

TELEVISION APPEARANCES; PILOTS

Duke Paige, *Longstreet,* ABC, 1971.
Randy Jamison, *The Delphi Bureau,* ABC, 1972.
Jeffrey Winslow, *The Eyes of Charles Sand,* ABC, 1972.
Avery Stanton, *Kingston: The Power Play,* NBC, 1976.
Howard Bronstein, *Street Killing,* ABC, 1976.
Donald Prince, *Jennifer: A Woman's Story,* NBC, 1979.
Harry Flemington, *Tourist,* syndicated, 1980.

TELEVISION APPEARANCES; EPISODIC

Kraft Television Theater, NBC, 1953.
Eric Valkay, "There Shall Be No Night," *Hallmark Hall of Fame,* NBC, 1957.
The Eleventh Hour, NBC, 1962.
Charlie Pont, "The Voice of Charlie Pont," *Premiere, Presented by Fred Astaire,* ABC, c. 1962.
Naked City, ABC, 1963.
Espionage, NBC, 1963.
The Virginian, NBC, 1963.
Wagon Train, NBC, 1963.
Captain David Young, "The Case against Paul Ryker," *Kraft Suspense Theater,* NBC, 1963.
"To Catch a Butterfly," *Alfred Hitchcock Theater,* CBS, 1963.
"Chain Reaction," *Alcoa Premiere,* ABC, 1963.
Vito Fortunato, *The Greatest Show on Earth,* ABC, 1963-64.
The Nurses, CBS, 1964.
Ben Casey, ABC, 1964.
Dr. Kildare, NBC, 1964 and 1966.
Profiles in Courage, NBC, 1965.
12 O'Clock High, ABC, 1966.
Bob Hope Chrysler Theater, NBC, 1966 and 1967.
The FBI, ABC, 1966-68 and 1970-71.
The Man from U.N.C.L.E., NBC, 1967.
Judd for the Defense, ABC, 1968.
Mission: Impossible, CBS, 1968 and 1972.
Fear No Evil, NBC, 1969.
Marcus Welby, M.D., ABC, 1969.
Bonanza, NBC, 1971.
Night Gallery, NBC, 1971.
Columbo, NBC, 1972.
"The Last Bride of Salem," *ABC Afternoon Playbreak,* ABC, 1975.
Gary Stevens, "Death in Deep Water," *Thriller,* ABC, 1975.
Sam Kay, "Look Back in Darkness" (also known as "The Next Voice You See"), *Thriller,* ABC, 1975.
Victor Modrian, *Hot Pursuit,* NBC, 1984.
Peter Merkin, "Easy Come, Easy Go" (also known as "Christine Cromwell"), *ABC Saturday Movie,* ABC, 1989.

Also appeared on *Wide World of Mystery.*

STAGE APPEARANCES

Richard, *The Scarecrow,* Theatre de Lys, New York City, 1953.
Freddie, *Pygmalion,* Sharon Playhouse, Sharon, CT, 1953.
Marchbanks, *Candida,* Sharon Playhouse, 1953.
Hadrian, *You Touched Me,* Sharon Playhouse, 1953.
Understudy, *End as a Man,* Theatre de Lys, 1953.
Pierre, *The Madwoman of Chaillot,* Sharon Playhouse, 1954.
Happy, *Death of a Salesman,* Sharon Playhouse, 1954.
Young teacher, *The Browning Version,* Sharon Playhouse, 1954.
Danny, *Night Must Fall,* Sharon Playhouse, 1954.

Kip Ames, *Third Person,* President Theatre, New York City, 1955.
Extra, *Inherit the Wind,* National Theatre, New York City, 1955.
Morgan, *The Corn Is Green,* Sharon Playhouse, 1955.
Octavius, *The Barretts of Wimpole Street,* Sharon Playhouse, 1955.
Frederic and Hugo, *Ring 'round the Moon,* Sharon Playhouse, 1955.
The radical, *Counsellor-at-Law,* Sharon Playhouse, 1955.
Black Chiffon, University of Michigan, Ann Arbor, 1955.
Jimmy, *The Rainmaker,* Sharon Playhouse, 1956.
Edmund Tyrone, *Long Day's Journey into Night,* Helen Hayes Theatre, New York City, 1956-58.
Gil Stanford, *The Fun Couple,* Lyceum Theatre, New York City, 1962.*

* * *

DILLON, Melinda 1939-

PERSONAL: Full name, Melinda Ruth Dillon; born October 13, 1939, in Hope, AR; daughter of W. S. (a U.S. Army colonel) and E. Norine (Barnett) Dillon; married Richard Libertini (an actor), September 30, 1963; children: one son. *Education:* Attended Goodman Theatre School, 1958-61; studied acting with Lee Strasberg, 1962-64. *Avocational interests:* Singing, playing the banjo, studying acting, reading, watching old films, rearranging apartment.

CAREER: Actress. Understudy for *Second City,* Chicago, IL, 1958-61, then joined company as an ingenue-vocalist, 1961.

MEMBER: Screen Actors Guild, Actors' Equity Association.

AWARDS, HONORS: Antoinette Perry Award nomination, dramatic actress supporting or featured, *Variety* New York Drama Critics Poll Award, and *Theatre World* Award, all 1963, all for *Who's Afraid of Virginia Woolf?;* Academy Award nomination, supporting actress, 1977, for *Close Encounters of the Third Kind;* Academy Award nomination, supporting actress, 1981, for *Absence of Malice.*

CREDITS:

STAGE APPEARANCES

Understudy for the role of Rosalie, *Oh Dad, Poor Dad, Mama's Hung You in the Closet and I'm Feelin' So Sad,* Phoenix Theatre, New York City, 1962.
(Broadway debut) Honey, *Who's Afraid of Virginia Woolf?,* Billy Rose Theatre, New York City, 1962-63.
Conerico Was Here to Stay, Playwrights Unit, Village South Theatre, New York City, 1964.
Dorothy, "The Shock of Recognition," Jill, "The Footsteps of Doves," and Clarice, "I'll Be Home for Christmas," in *You Know I Can't Hear You When the Water's Running* (triple-bill), Ambassador Theatre, New York City, 1967-68, then Broadhurst Theatre, New York City, 1968.
Lilly Seltzer, *A Way of Life,* ANTA Theatre, New York City, 1969.
Marat/Sade, Arena Stage Theatre, Washington, DC, 1969.
Orson Bean, *A Round with Ring,* ANTA Matinee Series, Theatre de Lys, New York City, 1969.
Various roles, *Paul Sills' Story Theater,* Ambassador Theatre, 1970-71.
Ovid's Metamorphoses, Ambassador Theatre, 1971.

Also appeared as Grusche in *The Caucasian Chalk Circle,* as Caroline in *What Shall We Tell Caroline?,* as Sonja in *Uncle Vanya,* as Blanaid in *The Moon in the Yellow River,* as Irma in *The Madwoman of Chaillot,* as Felice in *The Burning of the Lepers,* and as Kitty in *The Time of Your Life,* all at the Arena Stage Theatre, 1961-62; appeared in other productions at the Arena Stage Theatre, 1968-69.

FILM APPEARANCES

Leslie Hopkins, *The April Fools,* National General, 1969.
Mary Guthrie, *Bound for Glory,* United Artists (UA), 1976.
Suzanne Hanrahan, *Slap Shot,* Universal, 1977.
Jillian Guiler, *Close Encounters of the Third Kind,* Columbia, 1977.
Anna Zerinkas, *F.I.S.T.,* UA, 1978.
Teresa, *Absence of Malice,* Columbia, 1981.
Mother, *A Christmas Story,* Metro-Goldwyn-Mayer/UA, 1983.
Honey Carder, *Songwriter,* Tri-Star, 1984.
Nancy Henderson, *Harry and the Hendersons,* Universal, 1987.
Eileen McDermott, *Staying Together,* Hemdale, 1989.
Nina, *Spontaneous Combustion,* Taurus, 1990.
Savannah Wingo, *The Prince of Tides,* Columbia, 1991.

Also appeared in *Strangers Came to Die,* 1964, and as Mrs. Rogers in *Captain America,* 1990.

TELEVISION APPEARANCES; MOVIES

Dr. Kris Lassiter, *The Critical List,* NBC, 1978.
Ann Hurley, *Transplant,* CBS, 1979.
Agnes, *The Shadow Box,* ABC, 1980.
Sherry Phillips, *Fallen Angel,* CBS, 1981.
Ruda Dwyer, *Right of Way,* HBO, 1983.
Joyce Mollencamp, *Shattered Spirits,* ABC, 1986.
Sharon, *Shattered Innocence* (also known as *Shattered Image, Images of Eileen,* and *Mourning Song*), CBS, 1988.

Paula Brown, *Nightbreaker* (also known as *Advance to Ground Zero*), TNT, 1989.

Also appeared in *Point of Departure, Mississippi,* and *Sara.*

TELEVISION APPEARANCES; MINI-SERIES

Rachel Mott, *James A. Michener's "Space,"* CBS, 1985.

TELEVISION APPEARANCES; PILOTS

Madam Arkadina, *Freeman,* ABC, 1976.
Dora Herren, *Enigma,* CBS, 1977.
Jeannie, *Marriage Is Alive and Well,* NBC, 1980.
Anne Gronouski, *Hellinger's Law,* CBS, 1981.

TELEVISION APPEARANCES; SERIES

Story Theater, syndicated, 1971.

TELEVISION APPEARANCES; SPECIALS

Dulcy Wintergreen, *The Juggler of Notre Dame,* syndicated, 1982.

Also appeared on the *Merv Griffin Special, Paul Sills' Story Theatre,* and *The Paul Sand Show.*

TELEVISION APPEARANCES; EPISODIC

The Defenders, CBS, 1963.
Penny, "A Little Peace and Quiet," *The Twilight Zone,* CBS, 1985.

Also appeared on *The Jeffersons, Good Morning America, The Today Show, Dick Cavett Show,* and the *Dinah Shore Show.*

OTHER TELEVISION APPEARANCES

Stacy, *The Poet and the Politician,* CBS, 1963.*

* * *

DIPHUSA, Patty
See ALMODOVAR, Pedro

* * *

DJOLA, Badja

PERSONAL: Full name, Badja Medu Djola.

ADDRESSES: Agent—Artist Agency, 10000 Santa Monica Blvd., Suite 305, Los Angeles, CA 90067.

CAREER: Actor, 1973—. Worked as drummer and dancer with Koumpo West African Dance Company.

CREDITS:

FILM APPEARANCES

Heavyweight in gym, *The Main Event,* Warner Brothers, 1979.
"Half-Dead" Johnson, *Penitentiary,* Jerry Gross, 1979.
Cleon, *Night Shift,* Warner Brothers, 1982.
Nate, *The Lightship,* Warner Brothers, 1985.
Gaston, *The Serpent and the Rainbow,* Universal, 1988.
Agent Monk, *Mississippi Burning,* Orion, 1988.
John Fitzgerald, *An Innocent Man,* Buena Vista, 1989.
Slim, *A Rage in Harlem,* Glinwood Films, 1991.

TELEVISION APPEARANCES; EPISODIC

African prince, "Grand Theft Hotel" (also known as "B. L. Stryker"), *The ABC Saturday Mystery,* ABC, 1990.

OTHER SOURCES:

PERIODICALS

Premiere, May, 1991, p. 48.*

* * *

DONALDSON, Roger 1945-

PERSONAL: Born November 15, 1945, in Ballarat, Australia; immigrated to New Zealand at age 19.

ADDRESSES: Agent—Creative Artists Agency, 1888 Century Park East, 14th Floor, Los Angeles, CA 90067.

CAREER: Producer and director. Founded a business in still photography.

CREDITS:

FILM DIRECTOR

(And producer) *Sleeping Dogs,* Satori, 1977.
(And producer) *Smash Palace,* Atlantic, 1981.
The Bounty, Orion, 1984.
Marie, Metro-Goldwyn-Mayer/United Artists, 1985.
No Way Out, Orion, 1987.
Cocktail, Buena Vista, 1988.
(And producer with Charles Roven) *Cadillac Man,* Orion, 1990.
White Sands, Warner Brothers, 1992.

Also director of *Nutcase,* 1983.

TELEVISION WORK

Directed *Winners and Losers* (short dramas) for New Zealand Television.*

* * *

DOZIER, William 1908-1991

PERSONAL: Born February 13, 1908, in Omaha, NB; died of a stroke, April 23, 1991, in Santa Monica, CA; son of Robert C. and Emma (McElroy) Dozier; married Katherine Foley, September 14, 1929 (marriage ended); married Joan Fontaine, May 2, 1946 (divorced, 1950); married Ann Rutherford, 1953; children: (first marriage) Robert J., (second marriage) Deborah Leslie Potter. *Education:* Creighton University, A.B., 1929; attended law school for two years.

ADDRESSES: Office—826 Greenway Dr., Beverly Hills, CA 90210; 19228 Pacific Coast Highway, Malibu, CA 90265.

CAREER: Motion picture and television producer, actor, and executive. Berg-Allenberg Writers and Artists Agency, representative, 1935; Paramount Studios, Hollywood, CA, head of story and writing department, 1941-44; RKO Radio Pictures, Hollywood, production executive, 1944-51, vice president in charge of production, 1955-56; Universal International Pictures, Hollywood, vice president and associate head of production, 1946-49; Columbia Pictures, producer, 1949-51; Columbia Broadcasting System (CBS), New York City and Hollywood, various positions including executive producer of dramatic programs, vice president in charge of programs, and president of the television division, beginning in 1951; Screen Gems, Hollywood, vice president in charge of production, 1959-64; founder and president of independent television production company, Greenway Productions, 1964-72; Mount St. Mary's College, West Los Angeles, CA, professor of creative TV and drama, 1972-78.

CREDITS:

TELEVISION WORK; SERIES

Producer, *Rod Brown of the Rocket Rangers,* CBS, 1953-54.
(With others) Producer, *Danger,* CBS, 1954-55.
Executive producer, *The Loner,* CBS, 1965-66.
Executive producer, *The Tammy Grimes Show,* ABC, 1966.
Executive producer, *Batman* (also see below), ABC, 1966-68.
Executive producer, *The Green Hornet,* ABC, 1966-67.

Also involved in *Playhouse 90* and *Studio One,* both CBS.

TELEVISION WORK; EPISODIC

Executive producer, *Pentagon U.S.A.* (first episode telecast under title *Pentagon Confidential*), CBS, 1953.
Producer, *Ben Hecht's Tales of the City* (also known as *Tales of the City*), NBC, 1963.

TELEVISION APPEARANCES; SERIES

Narrator, *Batman,* ABC, 1966-68.

TELEVISION APPEARANCES; MOVIES

Dr. Richard Sheppard, Sr., *Guilty or Innocent: The Sam Sheppard Murder Case,* NBC, 1975.
Senator Ferguson, *The Amazing Howard Hughes,* CBS, 1977.
William Bast, *Evening in Byzantium,* syndicated, 1978.
Chairman, *Crisis in Mid-Air,* CBS, 1979.
Mr. Caldwell, *Guyana Tragedy: The Story of Jim Jones,* CBS, 1980.
Julius Thompkins, *Not Just Another Affair,* CBS, 1982.

FILM PRODUCER

The Hour Before the Dawn, Paramount, 1944.
Harriet Craig, Columbia, 1950.
Two of a Kind, Columbia, 1951.
Batman, Twentieth Century-Fox, 1966.
The Big Bounce, Warner Brothers, 1969.

FILM APPEARANCES

Michelle's lawyer, *American Gigolo,* Paramount, 1980.

Also appeared in *Kino, the Padre on Horseback.*

OBITUARIES AND OTHER SOURCES:

PERIODICALS

The Hollywood Reporter, April 24, 1991, pp. 3-4.*

* * *

DUKE, Bill

PERSONAL: Education: Graduate of American Film Institute, Los Angeles, CA.

ADDRESSES: Agent—Jeremy Zimmer, United Talent, 9560 Wilshire Blvd., 5th Floor, Beverly Hills, CA 90048.

CAREER: Director, actor, and playwright. Weusi Kuumba Troupe, Brooklyn, NY, past director.

MEMBER: Screen Directors Guild.

AWARDS, HONORS: Audelco Recognition Award, 1977, for *Unfinished Women.*

CREDITS:

FILM DIRECTOR

A Rage in Harlem, Miramax, 1991.
Deep Cover, New Line Cinema, 1992.

Also director of *Maximum Security,* 1987.

FILM APPEARANCES

Duane, *Car Wash,* Universal, 1976.
Leon Jaimes, *American Gigolo,* Paramount, 1980.
Cooke, *Commando,* Twentieth Century-Fox, 1985.

Malcolm, *No Man's Land,* Orion, 1987.
Mac, *Predator,* Twentieth Century-Fox, 1987.
Captain Armbruster, *Action Jackson,* Lorimar, 1988.
Borel, *Sans espoir de retour* (also known as *Street of No Return*), Bac Films, 1988.
Albert Diggs, *Bird on a Wire,* Universal, 1990.

TELEVISION DIRECTOR; EPISODIC

Knots Landing, CBS, 1979-83.
Falcon Crest (also known as *The Vintage Years*), CBS, 1981.
Flamingo Road, NBC, 1981-82.
Emerald Point, N.A.S. (also known as *Navy*), CBS, 1983-84.
Hunter, NBC, 1984-85.
"The Killing Floor," *American Playhouse,* PBS, 1985.
"Raisin in the Sun," *American Playhouse,* PBS, 1989.

Also director for *McGruder and Loud,* ABC. Director of more than seventy other episodes of television series, including *Miami Vice,* NBC, *Cagney and Lacey,* CBS, *Hill Street Blues,* NBC, and *Dallas,* CBS.

TELEVISION DIRECTOR; SPECIALS

Me and Mom, ABC, 1985.
Hell Town, NBC, 1985.
Heartbeat (also known as *Private Practice* and *Women's Medical*), ABC, 1988.
The Meeting, PBS, 1989.

TELEVISION DIRECTOR; MOVIES

Johnnie Mae Gibson: FBI (also known as *The Johnnie Gibson Story* and *Agent Gibson: Undercover FBI*), CBS, 1986.

TELEVISION DIRECTOR; SERIES

Brewster Place, ABC, 1990.

TELEVISION APPEARANCES

"Happy" Jordan, *Love Is Not Enough* (movie), NBC, 1978.
Sergeant Matlovich vs. the U.S. Air Force (movie), NBC, 1978.
Luther Freeman, *Palmerstown, U.S.A.* (series), CBS, 1980-81.
Seith Foster, *Dallas: The Early Years* (movie), CBS, 1986.

Appeared as Sanda in specials *Santiago's Ark,* 1972, and *Santiago's America,* 1975.

STAGE DIRECTOR

The Secret Place, Playwrights Horizons, New York City, 1972.
Unfinished Women, New York Shakespeare Festival, Mobile Theatre, 1977.
No Place to Be Somebody, Matrix Theatre, 1987.

Also directed more than thirty other Off-Broadway plays.

STAGE APPEARANCES

Akano, *Slave Ship,* Brooklyn Academy of Music, Brooklyn, NY, 1969-70.
Industrialist, "Day of Absence," *Brotherhood and Day of Absence* (double bill), Negro Ensemble Company, St. Mark's Playhouse, New York City, 1970.
Garrett Morris, *Ain't Supposed to Die a Natural Death,* Ethel Barrymore Theatre, New York City, 1971, then Ambassador Theatre, New York City, 1971-72.

WRITINGS:

PLAYS

An Adaptation: Dream (one-act), produced by Negro Ensemble Company, New York City, 1971.
Sonata, produced by Theatre Genesis, St. Mark's Playhouse, New York City, 1975.

TELEVISION EPISODES

Good Times, CBS, 1974-79.

OTHER

Author of the book *Bill Duke's 24-Hours L.A.* Contributor of articles and poems to magazines and newspapers, including *Black Creation.*

OTHER SOURCES:

PERIODICALS

Premiere, April, 1991, pp. 40-42.*

* * *

DUNNE, Irene 1901(?)-1990

PERSONAL: Full name, Irene Marie Dunne; born December 20, 1901 (other sources say 1898, 1904, or 1907), in Louisville, KY; died September 4, 1990, in Hollywood, CA; daughter of Joseph John and Adelaide Antoinette (Henry) Dunne; married Francis D. Griffin, July 16, 1928 (died, 1965); children: Mary Frances. *Education:* Loretta Academy; received diploma from the Chicago College of Music.

CAREER: Actress and singer. Began career in musical comedy and theatre with the Ziegfeld Follies. Technicolor Inc., member of board of directors, 1965—. Active in the Republican party. Appointed as an alternate delegate to the United Nations 12th General Assembly, 1957.

AWARDS, HONORS: Academy Award nominations, best actress, 1931, for *Cimarron,* 1936, for *Theodora Goes*

Wild, 1937, for *The Awful Truth,* 1939, for *Love Affair,* and 1948, for *I Remember Mama;* Laetare Medal for most outstanding Catholic lay person, University of Notre Dame, 1949; Kennedy Center Honors, John F. Kennedy Center for the Performing Arts, 1985.

CREDITS:

STAGE APPEARANCES

(Broadway debut) Tessie, *The Clinging Vine,* Knickerbocker Theatre, New York City, 1922.
Grace Bartlett, *The City Chap,* Liberty Theatre, New York City, 1925.
Diana, *Yours Truly,* Shubert Theatre, New York City, 1927.
Polly, *She's My Baby,* Globe Theatre, New York City, 1928.
Arlette, *Luckee Girl,* Casino Theatre, New York City, 1928.

Made stage debut in *Irene,* Chicago, 1920; also appeared in *Lollipop,* as Magnolia in *Show Boat,* and in a touring production of *Sweetheart Time.*

FILM APPEARANCES

Delphine, *Leathernecking* (also known as *Present Arms*), RKO Radio Pictures, 1930.
Helene Andrews, *Bachelor Apartment,* RKO Radio Pictures, 1931.
Sabra Cravat, *Cimarron,* RKO Radio Pictures, 1931.
Mary, *Consolation Marriage* (also known as *Married in Haste*), RKO Radio Pictures, 1931.
Diana Page, *The Great Lover,* Metro-Goldwyn-Mayer (MGM), 1931.
Back Street, Universal, 1932.
Jessica, *Symphony of Six Million* (also known as *Melody of Life*), RKO Radio Pictures, 1932.
Laura Stanhope, *Thirteen Women,* RKO Radio Pictures, 1932.
Title role, *Ann Vickers,* RKO Radio Pictures, 1933.
Sarah Cazenove, *If I Were Free* (also known as *Behold We Live*), RKO Radio Pictures, 1933.
Sally, *The Secret of Madame Blanche,* MGM, 1933.
Anna Stanley, *No Other Woman,* RKO Radio Pictures, 1933.
Christina Phelps, *The Silver Cord,* RKO Radio Pictures, 1933.
Countess Ellen Olenska, *Age of Innocence,* RKO Radio Pictures, 1934.
Hilda Bouverie, *Stingaree,* RKO Radio Pictures, 1934.
Toni Dunlap, *This Man Is Mine,* RKO Radio Pictures, 1934.
Stephanie, *Roberta,* RKO Radio Pictures, 1934.
Helen Hudson, *Magnificent Obsession,* Universal, 1935.
Adeline Schmidt, *Sweet Adeline,* Warner Bros., 1935.
Magnolia Hawks, *Show Boat,* Universal, 1936.
Theodora Lynn, *Theodora Goes Wild,* Columbia, 1936.
Lucy Warriner, *The Awful Truth,* Columbia, 1937.
Sally Watterson, *High Wide and Handsome,* Paramount, 1937.
Margaret "Maggie" Garret, *Joy of Living,* RKO Radio Pictures, 1938.
Terry McKay, *Love Affair,* RKO Radio Pictures, 1939.
Eleanor Wayne, *Invitation to Happiness,* Paramount, 1939.
Helen, *When Tomorrow Comes,* Universal, 1939.
Ellen Arden, *My Favorite Wife,* RKO Radio Pictures, 1940.
Julie Gardiner Adams, *Penny Serenade,* Columbia, 1941.
Nancy Andrews, *Unfinished Business,* Universal, 1941.
Jane Palmer, *Lady in a Jam,* Universal, 1942.
Dorinda Durston, *A Guy Named Joe,* MGM, 1943.
Susan Dunn Ashwood, *The White Cliffs of Dover,* MGM, 1944.
Anne Crandall, *Together Again,* Columbia, 1944.
Paula Wharton, *Over 21,* Columbia, 1945.
Anna, *Anna and the King of Siam,* Twentieth Century-Fox, 1946.
Vinnie Day, *Life with Father,* Warner Bros., 1947.
Mama, *I Remember Mama,* RKO Radio Pictures, 1948.
Kay, *Never a Dull Moment,* RKO Radio Pictures, 1950.
Queen Victoria, *The Mudlark,* Twentieth Century-Fox, 1950.
Polly Baxter, *It Grows on Trees,* Universal, 1952.

Also appeared in *The Stolen Jools* (also known as *The Slippery Pearls*), 1931.

TELEVISION APPEARANCES

Hostess, *Playhouse of Stars* (anthology), CBS, 1952.
Hostess, *Schlitz Playhouse of Stars* (series), CBS, 1952.

Appeared in *Kennedy Center Honors: A Celebration of the Performing Arts,* CBS, 1985, *It's Showtime, Ford Television Theatre, The June Allyson Show, The Loretta Young Show,* and *The General Electric Theatre.*

RADIO APPEARANCES

Recreated numerous film roles for the Lux Radio Theatre, 1940-51.

OBITUARIES AND OTHER SOURCES:

PERIODICALS

Film Comment, January-February, 1980.
New York Times, September 6, 1990, p. D21.*

DUNNOCK, Mildred 1900(?)-1991

OBITUARY NOTICE—See index for *CTFT* sketch: Born January 25, 1900 (one source says 1906), in Baltimore, MD; died July 5, 1991, in Martha's Vineyard, MA. Performer and director. Dunnock enjoyed a long and prolific career on both the stage and screen. Originally a school teacher, she began acting professionally in the early 1930s and made her Broadway debut as Miss Pinty in *Life Begins* in 1932. She continued to teach during the day and perform in the evenings for many years. Some of her notable stage appearances were in *The Corn Is Green, Lute Song, Another Part of the Forest,* the original production of *Death of a Salesman, Cat on a Hot Tin Roof,* and *Tartuffe.* After reprising her role as Miss Ronberry in the 1945 film version of *The Corn Is Green,* she went on to appear in numerous films, including *Viva Zapata, The Trouble with Harry, Butterfield 8, Sweet Bird of Youth, Seven Women,* and *The Pick-Up Artist.* Dunnock was twice nominated for Academy Awards for performances in *Death of a Salesman* and *Baby Doll.* Her acting career expanded further in the early 1950s to include television series such as *Gulf Playhouse, Broadway Television Theatre, Kraft Theatre,* and *Alfred Hitchcock Presents,* and, later, the television adaptation of *Death of a Salesman.* Later in her career, Dunnock directed two stage productions, *Graduation,* in 1965, and *Luminosity Without Radiance: A Self-Portrait,* in 1973. She also continued to make television appearances, most recently in *The Best Place to Be* and *The Patricia Neal Story.*

OBITUARIES AND OTHER SOURCES:

BOOKS

International Motion Picture Almanac, Quigley, 1991, p. 95.

PERIODICALS

Variety, July 15, 1991, p. 54.

E

EISNER, Michael D. 1942-

PERSONAL: Full name, Michael Dammann Eisner; born March 7, 1942, in Mount Kisco, NY; son of Lester, Jr., and Margaret (Dammann) Eisner; married Jane Breckenridge; children: Michael, Eric, Anders. *Education:* Denison University, B.A., 1964.

ADDRESSES: Office—Walt Disney Company, 500 South Buena Vista St., Burbank, CA 91521.

CAREER: Executive producer. CBS, worked in programming department; ABC-TV, manager of talent and specials, 1966, director of program development, director of program planning and executive assistant to the vice president in charge of programming, vice president of daytime television programming, and vice president of children's programs, 1966-75, ABC Entertainment, senior vice president of prime time production and development, 1976; Paramount Pictures, president and chief operating officer with creative responsibilities for all divisions, 1976-84; Walt Disney Company, chairman and chief executive officer, 1984—. Board of directors, Denison University, California Institute of Arts, American Film Institute, the Performing Arts Council of the Los Angeles Music Center, and Sega Enterprises, Inc. (amusement game manufacturer).

CREDITS:

TELEVISION APPEARANCES

Host, *Disney Sunday Movie,* ABC, 1986-88.
Host, *The Magical World of Disney,* NBC, 1988-90.

OTHER SOURCES:

PERIODICALS

Parade Magazine, November 15, 1987.*

ELFMAN, Danny 1953-

PERSONAL: Born May 29, 1953, in Los Angeles, CA; son of Milton (a teacher) and Blossom (a teacher and writer; maiden name, Bernstein) Elfman.

ADDRESSES: Contact—c/o The Kraft Agency, 6525 West Sunset Blvd., Los Angeles, CA 90028.

CAREER: Composer and musician. Singer and guitarist with the band Oingo Boingo, beginning in 1981.

AWARDS, HONORS: Grammy Award, best instrumental composition, 1989, for "The Batman Theme," from the movie *Batman;* Emmy Award nomination, outstanding achievement in main title theme music, 1990, for *The Simpsons.*

CREDITS:

FILM APPEARANCES

Singer, *Hot Tomorrows,* American Film Institute, 1978.
Oingo Boingo band member, *Back to School* (also see below), Orion, 1986.

RECORDINGS:

ALBUMS; WITH OINGO BOINGO

Oingo Boingo (EP), IRA, 1980.
Only A Lad, A&M, 1981.
Nothing to Fear, A&M, 1982.
Best O'Boingo, MCA, 1991.

Also recorded *Good for Your Soul,* A&M; *Dead Man's Party,* MCA; *Dark at the End of the Tunnel* (compilation), MCA; *Boingo Live,* MCA; *BOI-NGO,* MCA; and *Skeletons in the Closet* (compilation), A&M.

SOLO ALBUMS

Has recorded *So-lo,* MCA; and *Music for a Darkened Theatre* (compilation of Elfman's film and television music).

WRITINGS:

FILM MUSIC

Forbidden Zone, Borack, 1980.
Pee-wee's Big Adventure, Warner Brothers, 1985.
Back to School, Orion, 1986.
Wisdom (also see below), Twentieth Century-Fox, 1986.
Summer School, Paramount, 1987.
Beetlejuice, Warner Brothers, 1988.
Big Top Pee-wee, Paramount, 1988.
Hot to Trot, Warner Brothers, 1988.
Midnight Run, Universal, 1988.
Scrooged, Paramount, 1988.
Batman, Warner Brothers, 1989.
Darkman, Universal, 1990.
Dick Tracy, Touchstone-Buena Vista, 1990.
Edward Scissorhands, Twentieth Century-Fox, 1990.
Nightbreed (also see below), Twentieth Century-Fox, 1990.

SONGS USED IN FILMS

"Little Girls," *Tempest,* Columbia, 1982.
"Goodbye, Goodbye," *Fast Times at Ridgemont High,* Universal, 1982.
"Who Do You Want to Be Today," "Something Isn't Right," and "Bachelor Party Theme," *Bachelor Party,* Twentieth Century-Fox, 1983.
"Weird Science," *Weird Science,* Universal, 1985.
"Not My Slave," *Something Wild,* Orion, 1986.
"Tears Run Down" and "Rock Me Baby," *Wisdom,* Twentieth Century-Fox, 1986.
"Same Man I Was Before," *My Best Friend Is a Vampire* (also known as *I Was a Teenage Vampire*), Kings Road Entertainment, 1988.
"Flesh 'n Blood," *Ghostbusters II,* Columbia, 1989.
"Winning Side," *She's Out of Control,* Columbia, 1989.
"Skin," *Nightbreed,* Twentieth Century-Fox, 1990.
Main title theme and song, *Pure Luck,* Universal, 1991.

TELEVISION THEMES; SERIES

"Fast Times," *Fast Times,* CBS, 1986.
Sledge Hammer!, ABC, 1986.
Beetlejuice, ABC, Fox, 1989.
The Flash, CBS, 1990.
The Simpsons, Fox, 1990.

TELEVISION MUSIC; EPISODIC

Pee-wee's Playhouse, CBS, 1986.
Theme music, *Tales from the Crypt,* HBO, 1990-91.

TELEVISION MUSIC; SPECIALS

A Special Evening of Pee-wee's Playhouse, CBS, 1987.
Theme song, *Simpsons Roasting on an Open Fire* (also known as *The Simpsons Christmas Special*), Fox, 1989.

OTHER SOURCES:

PERIODICALS

American Film, February, 1991, p. 42.

* * *

ELLIOTT, Sumner Locke 1917-1991

OBITUARY NOTICE—See index for *CTFT* sketch: Born October 17, 1917, in Sydney, New South Wales, Australia; immigrated to the United States, 1948, naturalized citizen, 1955; died of colon cancer, June 24, 1991, in Manhattan, NY. Writer and actor. Elliott, whose early career was spent in theatre and television, was widely known for his best-selling novels, which often drew on his own past and featured well-drawn characters and vigorous prose. He began as an actor in his native Australia and eventually left the limelight to write television scripts and more than thirty plays. His first novel was the autobiographical *Careful, He Might Hear You,* a well-received work about a custody battle over an orphaned boy. Among his later novels are *Water under the Bridge,* for which he also wrote a television adaptation, *Waiting for Childhood,* and *Fairyland.* Elliott plays produced on Broadway included *Buy Me Blue Ribbons* and *John Murray Anderson's Almanac.*

OBITUARIES AND OTHER SOURCES:

BOOKS

The Writers Directory: 1990-1992, St. James Press, 1990.

PERIODICALS

New York Times, June 26, 1991, p. D22.
Variety, July 1, 1991, p. 49.

* * *

ERMAN, John 1935-
(Bill Sampson)

PERSONAL: Born August 3, 1935, in Chicago, IL; son of Milton G. (in sales) and Lucille Arlie (Straus) Erman. *Education:* University of California, Los Angeles, B.A., applied arts, 1957. *Politics:* Democrat. *Religion:* Jewish.

ADDRESSES: *Agent*—Jamner Pariser Meschures, 760 North La Cienega Blvd., Los Angeles, CA 90049.

CAREER: Director. Free-lance actor, 1959-63; Twentieth Century-Fox, casting director, 1959-63, head of television casting, 1960-61; Faculty Acting School, Los Angeles, CA, founder.

MEMBER: Directors Guild of America.

AWARDS, HONORS: Emmy Award nomination (with David Greene, Marvin J. Chomsky, and Gilbert Moses), outstanding directing in a drama series, 1977, for *Roots;* Humanitas Prize, 1977, for *Green Eyes;* Directors Guild of America Award and Christopher Award, both 1979, for *Roots: The Next Generations;* Emmy Award nomination, outstanding directing in a limited series or special, 1980, for *Moviola: The Scarlett O'Hara War;* Emmy Award, outstanding directing of a limited series or special, 1983, for *Who Will Love My Children?;* Directors Guild of America Award, outstanding directorial achievement for television, 1985, for *An Early Frost;* Emmy Award nomination, outstanding drama or mini-series, 1987, for *The Two Mrs. Grenvilles;* Emmy Award nominations, outstanding drama or comedy special and outstanding directing in a mini-series or special, 1988, for "The Attic: The Hiding of Anne Frank," *General Foods Golden Showcase;* Emmy Award nomination, outstanding drama or comedy special, 1988, for *David.*

CREDITS:

TELEVISION DIRECTOR; MINI-SERIES

(With David Greene, Marvin J. Chomsky, and Gilbert Moses) *Roots,* ABC, 1977.
(With Charles S. Dubin, Georg Stanford Brown, and Lloyd Richards) *Roots: The Next Generations,* ABC, 1979.

TELEVISION DIRECTOR; MOVIES

Alexander: The Other Side of Dawn, NBC, 1977.
(And producer) *Green Eyes,* ABC, 1977.
Just Me and You, NBC, 1978.
My Old Man, CBS, 1979.
Moviola: This Year's Blonde (also known as *The Secret Love of Marilyn Monroe*), NBC, 1980.
Moviola: The Scarlett O'Hara War, NBC, 1980.
Moviola: The Silent Lovers, NBC, 1980.
The Letter, ABC, 1982.
Eleanor: First Lady of the World, CBS, 1982.
Another Woman's Child (also known as *The Far Shore*), CBS, 1983.
Who Will Love My Children?, ABC, 1983.
A Streetcar Named Desire, ABC, 1984.
The Atlanta Child Murders, CBS, 1985.
An Early Frost, NBC, 1985.
Right to Kill?, ABC, 1985.
(And producer) *The Two Mrs. Grenvilles,* ABC, 1987.
(And producer) *When the Time Comes,* ABC, 1987.
(And producer) *David,* ABC, 1988.
(And supervising producer) *The Last Best Year* (also known as *The Last Best Year of My Life*), ABC, 1990.
(And supervising producer) *Carolina Skeletons,* NBC, 1991.
(And producer) *The Last to Go,* ABC, 1991.
(And supervising producer) *Our Sons,* ABC, 1991.

Also director of *Child of Glass,* 1978.

TELEVISION DIRECTOR; EPISODIC

The Outer Limits, ABC, 1963-65.
My Favorite Martian, CBS, 1963-66.
Please Don't Eat the Daisies, NBC, 1965-67.
That Girl, ABC, 1966-71.
"The Empath," *Star Trek,* NBC, 1968.
The Ghost and Mrs. Muir, NBC, 1968-69, ABC, 1969-70.
Bracken's World, NBC, 1969-71.
Karen, ABC, 1975.
Good Heavens, ABC, 1976.
Family, ABC, 1976-80.
(And supervising producer) "The Attic: The Hiding of Anne Frank," *General Foods Golden Showcase,* CBS, 1988.

Director of an episode of *Stoney Burke,* 1962.

TELEVISION DIRECTOR; OTHER

Letters From Three Lovers (pilot), ABC, 1973.
(With Philip Leacock) *The New Land* (series), ABC, 1974.

FILM DIRECTOR

Making It, Twentieth Century-Fox, 1971.
(Under pseudonym Bill Sampson) *Ace Eli and Rodger of the Skies,* Twentieth Century-Fox, 1973.
Stella, Buena Vista, 1990.*

* * *

ESTEVEZ, Emilio 1962-

PERSONAL: Born May 12, 1962, in New York, NY; son of Martin (an actor; original surname, Estevez) and Janet Sheen; children: Taylor, Paloma. *Education:* Graduated from Santa Monica High School, CA.

ADDRESSES: *Agent*—Andrea Jaffe, Inc., 9229 Sunset Blvd., Suite 401, Los Angeles, CA 90069.

CAREER: Actor, screenwriter, and director.

CREDITS:

FILM APPEARANCES

(Film debut) Extra, *Apocalypse Now,* United Artists, 1979.
Johnny Collins, *Tex,* Buena Vista, 1982.
Two-Bit Matthews, *The Outsiders,* Warner Brothers, 1983.

J. J. Conney ("The Bishop of Battle"), *Nightmares,* Universal, 1983.
Otto Maddox, *Repo Man,* Universal, 1984.
Andrew Clark, *The Breakfast Club,* Universal, 1985.
Kirbo, *St. Elmo's Fire,* Columbia, 1985.
Mark Jennings, *That Was Then . . . This Is Now,* Paramount, 1985.
Bill Robinson, *Maximum Overdrive,* Dino De Laurentiis, 1986.
John Wisdom, *Wisdom,* Twentieth Century-Fox, 1986.
Bill Reimers, *Stakeout,* Buena Vista, 1987.
William H. Bonney ("Billy the Kid"), *Young Guns,* Twentieth Century-Fox, 1988.
Tow-Truck Man, *Never on Tuesday,* Paramount Home Video, 1989.
William H. Bonney ("Billy the Kid"), *Young Guns II,* Twentieth Century-Fox, 1990.
James St. James, *Men at Work,* Triumph, 1990.
Alex Furlong, *Freejack,* Warner Brothers, 1992.

FILM WORK

Director, *Wisdom,* Twentieth Century-Fox, 1986.
Director, *Men at Work,* Triumph, 1990.

Also executive producer of *National Lampoon's Family Dies.*

TELEVISION APPEARANCES; MOVIES

Danny Caldwell, *In the Custody of Strangers,* ABC, 1982.
Dr. Alexander Brown—as a younger man, *Nightbreaker* (also known as *Advance to Ground Zero*), TNT, 1989.

Also appeared in "Seventeen Going on Nowhere," *ABC Afterschool Special,* ABC; *To Climb a Mountain,* and *Making the Grade.*

STAGE APPEARANCES

Appeared in theatrical productions, including *Echoes of an Era* (also see below), Santa Monica High School, CA; and *Mister Roberts,* Burt Reynolds Dinner Theatre, FL.

WRITINGS:

SCREENPLAYS

That Was Then . . . This Is Now (based on the novel of the same title by S. E. Hinton), Paramount, 1985.
Wisdom, Twentieth Century-Fox, 1986.
Men at Work, Triumph, 1990.

OTHER

Author of the play *Echoes of an Era,* produced at Santa Monica High School, CA.

OTHER SOURCES:

BOOKS

Contemporary Newsmakers 1985 Cumulation, Gale, 1986.

PERIODICALS

American Film, March, 1985, p. 42.
Nuestro, October, 1985, p. 12.
People, February 28, 1983, p. 63.
Seventeen, July, 1985, p. 49.
Teen, July, 1985, p. 41.*

* * *

EVANS, Bruce A. 1946-

PERSONAL: Born September 19, 1946, in Long Beach, CA; son of George A. and Jane (Wallace) Evans. *Education:* Attended University of Southern California and University of California, Los Angeles.

ADDRESSES: Office—Universal Studios, Universal City, CA. *Agent*—Creative Artists Agency, 1888 Century Park E., 14th Floor, Los Angeles, CA 90067.

CAREER: Screenwriter, director, and producer. Evans-Gideon Productions, partner. Worked as an art auctioneer in Los Angeles, CA.

AWARDS, HONORS: Academy Award nomination (with Raynold Gideon), best screenplay based on material from another medium, 1986, for *Stand by Me;* Writers Guild of America nomination; Golden Globe Award nomination; Independent Spirit Award.

CREDITS:

FILM WORK

Associate producer, *Starman* (also see below), Columbia, 1984.
Producer (with Andrew Scheinman and Raynold Gideon), *Stand by Me* (also see below), Columbia, 1986.
Producer (with Gideon and David Blocker), *Made in Heaven* (also see below), Lorimar, 1987.
Director, *Kuffs* (also known as *Hero Wanted;* also see below), Universal, 1992.

WRITINGS:

SCREENPLAYS

(With Raynold Gideon and Stuart Margolan) *A Man, a Woman, and a Bank* (based on a story by Gideon and Evans), [Canada], 1979, Blue Box, 1984.
(With Gideon) *Starman,* Columbia, 1984.
(With Gideon) *Stand by Me* (based on Stephen King's novella *The Body*), Columbia, 1986.
(With Gideon) *Made in Heaven,* Lorimar, 1987.

Kuffs (also known as *Hero Wanted*), Universal, 1992.

OTHER SOURCES:

BOOKS

Contemporary Authors, Volume 134, Gale, 1992.

* * *

EVANS, Damon 1950-

PERSONAL: Born Dickie Evans, November 24, 1950, in Baltimore, MD. *Education:* Studied at Children's Theater Association, Peabody Conservatory, Interlochen Arts Academy, and Boston Conservatory of Music; attended Manhattan School of Music, 1974.

ADDRESSES: Contact—c/o Old Vic Theatre, Waterloo Rd., London SE1, England.

CAREER: Actor.

MEMBER: Actors Equity Association.

CREDITS:

TELEVISION APPEARANCES

Lionel Jefferson, *The Jeffersons* (series), CBS, 1975-78.
Alex Haley as a young man, *Roots: The Next Generation* (movie), ABC, 1979.
"Celebrating Gershwin" (also known as "The Jazz Age" and "'S Wonderful"), *Great Performances* (special), PBS, 1987.

Also appeared in *The Silence,* 1975, *Black News,* 1976, and *The Tony Awards Show,* 1977.

TELEVISION APPEARANCES; EPISODIC

"The Tenth Level," *New CBS Playhouse 90,* CBS, 1975.

Appeared on *Love of Life,* 1973, *The Merv Griffin Show,* 1976, and *Captain Kangaroo,* 1976.

FILM APPEARANCES

Subway Cop, *Turk 182!* Twentieth Century-Fox, 1985.

Also appeared as a tenor aria performer, *Parting Glances,* 1986.

STAGE APPEARANCES

Godspell, Cherry Lane Theatre, New York City, 1971.
Matthew Kumalo, *Lost in the Stars,* Imperial Theatre, New York City, 1972.
Hels Mikelli, *Via Galactica,* Uris Theatre, New York City, 1972.
Arnold Wilkerson, *Don't Bother Me, I Can't Cope,* Playhouse Theatre, later Edison Theatre, both New York City, 1972.
Joe, *Carmen Jones,* Old Vic Theatre, London, 1991.
Made Off-Broadway debut in *A Day in the Life of Just About Everyone,* 1971. Also appeared in *Love Me, Love My Children,* 1971, *The Me Nobody Knows,* 1971, and *Two If by Sea.**

* * *

EYEN, Jerome
See EYEN, Tom

See EYEN, Tom

* * *

EYEN, Tom 1941-1991
(Jerome Eyen, Roger Short, Jr.)

OBITUARY NOTICE—See index for *CTFT* sketch: Born August 14, 1941, in Cambridge, OH; died of cardiac arrest, May 26, 1991, in Palm Beach, FL. Writer and director. Eyen is best known for his 1981 Tony Award-winning Broadway musical *Dreamgirls,* based loosely on the lives of the members of the female vocal trio The Supremes. Eyen, the author of more than thirty plays, was an innovator in the 1960s Off-Off Broadway experimental theatre movement and once had four plays showing simultaneously. After receiving a grant from the Rockefeller Foundation in the mid 1960s, he formed his own company, the Theatre of the Eye. With a formula that often included strong language, daring sexual content, comedy, nudity, profanity, and social criticism, Eyen wrote such cult hits as *The Dirtiest Show in Town, The White Whore and the Bit Player, Why Hanna's Skirt Won't Stay Down, Sarah B. Divine,* and *Women behind Bars.* He also directed many of his own plays, sometimes under the names Jerome Eyen and Roger Short, Jr. In 1976 he became a writer for the television program *Mary Hartman, Mary Hartman.*

OBITUARIES AND OTHER SOURCES:

PERIODICALS

Chicago Tribune, May 28, 1991.
Los Angeles Times, May 28, 1991.
New York Times, May 28, 1991.
Variety, June 3, 1991, p. 69.
Washington Post, May 29, 1991.

F

FAHEY, Jeff

ADDRESSES: Agent—William Morris Agency, 151 South El Camino Drive, Beverly Hills, CA 90212.

CAREER: Actor. Studied with the Joffrey Ballet for three years.

AWARDS, HONORS: Gemini Award nominee, best performance by a lead actor in a single dramatic program, 1986, for *The Execution of Raymond Graham.*

CREDITS:

STAGE APPEARANCES

John, *Pastorale,* The Second Stage Theatre, New York City, 1982.

Also appeared as Curly in *Oklahoma!,* U.S. cities, c. 1981. Appeared in stage productions of *Brigadoon* and *West Side Story.*

FILM APPEARANCES

Tyree, *Silverado,* Columbia, 1985.
Duane Duke, *Psycho III,* Universal, 1986.
Donnie, *Backfire,* Vidmark, 1987.
Ray McGuinn, *Split Decisions,* New Century-Vista, 1988.
Jake Bonner, *Alexander's Treasures* (also known as *Out of Time*), Motion Picture International, 1989.
Ricky Rodriguez, *The Last of the Finest,* Orion, 1989.
Creed, *Outback,* Samuel Goldwyn Company, 1989.
Jake Bonner, *The Serpent of Death,* Paramount Home Video/Prism, 1989.
Ray Trueblood, *True Blood,* Fries, 1989.
Stan Harris, *Impulse,* Warner Brothers, 1990.
Pete Verrill, *White Hunter, Black Heart,* Warner Brothers, 1990.
Bill Crushank, *Body Parts,* Paramount, 1991.
Barry, *Iron Maze,* Castle Hill, 1991.
Jobe Smith, *The Lawnmower Man,* New Line Cinema, 1992.

TELEVISION APPEARANCES

Gary Corelli, *One Life to Live* (series), ABC, 1982-1985.
Raymond Graham, *The Execution of Raymond Graham* (movie), ABC, 1985.
Michael Manus, *Curiosity Kills* (movie; also known as *Curiosity Kills the Cat*), USA, 1990.
Parker Kane, *Parker Kane* (movie), NBC, 1990.
Hamilton Jordan, *Iran: Days of Crisis* (movie; also known as *444 Days*), TNT, 1991.

OTHER SOURCES:

PERIODICALS

Cosmopolitan, June, 1990, p. 88.*

* * *

FALTERMEYER, Harold 1952-

PERSONAL: Born October 5, 1952, in D-Munich, Germany; son of Hugo (a construction businessman) and Anneliese (a homemaker; maiden name, Schmidt) Faltermeyer; married March 21, 1977; wife's name, Karin (a homemaker); children: Elena Melody, Bianca, Florian. *Education:* Attended the Music College of Munich.

ADDRESSES: Office—Unique Production Inc., J. Swartz, 9595 Wilshire Blvd., Suite 1020, Beverly Hills, CA 90212. *Agent*—Creative Artists Agency, 9830 Wilshire Blvd., Beverly Hills, CA 90212.

CAREER: Composer, music director, and arranger. Producer of Donna Summer, Jennifer Rush, and the Pet Shop Boys.

MEMBER: Academy of Motion Pictures and Sciences, American Society of Composers, Authors, and Publishers, National Academy of Recording Arts and Sciences.

AWARDS, HONORS: Grammy Award (with others), best original score—motion picture or a television special, 1984, for *Beverly Hills Cop;* Grammy Award nominations, best pop instrumental, and best instrumental composition, both 1984, both for "Axel F," from the movie *Beverly Hills Cop;* Grammy Award (with Steve Stevens), best pop instrumental, 1986, for "Top Gun Anthem," from the movie *Top Gun;* Grammy Award nomination, best instrumental composition, 1986, for "Top Gun Anthem," from the movie *Top Gun;* Academy Award nomination (with Keith Forsey and Bob Seger), best song, 1987, for "Shakedown," from the movie *Beverly Hills Cop II.*

CREDITS:

FILM WORK

Arranger, *Midnight Express,* Columbia, 1978.
Music director and arranger, *Foxes,* United Artists, 1980.
Song producer, "Top Gun Anthem," "Mighty Wings," and "Destination Unknown," *Top Gun* (also see below), Paramount, 1986.
Song producer, "Shakedown," *Beverly Hills Cop II* (also see below), Paramount, 1987.

WRITINGS:

FILM MUSIC

Score and song (with Franie Golde), "Bit by Bit (Theme from *Fletch*)," *Fletch,* Universal, 1984.
Score and songs, "Axel F" and "The Heat Is On," *Beverly Hills Cop,* Paramount, 1984.
Score, *Thief of Hearts,* Paramount, 1984.
Score and songs, "Top Gun Anthem" (with Steve Stevens) and "Mighty Wings," *Top Gun,* Paramount, 1986.
Score and song (with Keith Forsey), "Shakedown," *Beverly Hills Cop II,* Paramount, 1987.
Score and song, "Sin City," *Fatal Beauty,* Metro-Goldwyn-Mayer/United Artists, 1987.
Score and song, "Fire and Ice," *Fire and Ice,* Concorde, 1987.
Score and song, "Running Away with You," *The Running Man,* Tri-Star, 1987.
Score, *Blue Blood* (also known as *Scandalous*), Atlas International, 1988.
(With Forsey) "Hunger of Love," *She's Out of Control,* Columbia, 1989.
Score, *Fletch Lives,* Universal, 1989.
Score, *Tango and Cash,* Warner Brothers, 1989.
Score, *Fire, Ice and Dynamite,* Odyssey/Cinecom International Films, 1990.
Score, *Kuffs,* Universal, 1992.

Also composer of score for *Didi der Doppelganger,* 1984.

* * *

FELDMAN, Edward S. 1929-

PERSONAL: Born, September 5, 1929, in New York, NY. *Education:* Attended Michigan State University.

ADDRESSES: Office—c/o Feldman/Meeker Company, Paramount Pictures Corp., 5555 Melrose Ave., Los Angeles, CA 90038.

CAREER: Producer. Twentieth Century-Fox, Los Angeles, CA, trade press contact, magazine and newspaper contact, 1950; Dover Air Force Base, Dover, DE, director of information services, 1954-56; Paramount Pictures Corp., Los Angeles, publicity coordinator, *The World of Suzie Wong,* 1959; Embassy films, Los Angeles, director of publicity, 1959; Seven Arts Production, Los Angeles, vice president in charge of advertising and publicity, 1962; Warner-7 Arts Production, Los Angeles, vice president and executive assistant to head producer, 1967; Filmways, Los Angeles, president of publicity department, 1970; Edward S. Feldman Company (later F/M Entertainment), Los Angeles, founder (with Charles Meeker), 1978, president, 1978—.

AWARDS, HONORS: Emmy nomination, outstanding special, 1977, for *The ABC Sunday Night Movie;* Emmy nomination, outstanding limited series, 1978, for *King;* Academy Award nomination, best picture, 1985, for *Witness.*

CREDITS:

FILM WORK; PRODUCER, EXCEPT AS NOTED

Executive producer, *What's the Matter with Helen?,* Untied Artists, 1971.
Executive producer, *Save the Tiger,* Paramount, 1973.
The Other Side of the Mountain, Universal, 1975.
Two-Minute Warning, Universal, 1976.
The Other Side of the Mountain—Part 2, Universal, 1978.
(With John Herman Shaner) *The Last Married Couple in America,* Universal, 1980.
The Sender, Paramount, 1982.
Executive producer, *Six Pack,* Twentieth Century-Fox, 1982.
(With Mike Marvin) *Hot Dog . . . The Movie,* Metro-Goldwyn-Mayer/United Artists, 1984.
(With David Bombyk) *Explorers,* Paramount, 1985.
Witness, Paramount, 1985.
(With Robert D. Wachs) *The Golden Child,* Paramount, 1986.
(With Charles R. Meeker) *Hamburger,* F/M Entertainment, 1986.
Executive producer, *The Hitcher,* Tri-Star, 1986.

Executive producer, *Near Dark,* DeLaurentiis, 1987.
(With Meeker) *Wired,* F/M-Lion Screen/Taurus, 1990.
Executive producer, *The Doctor,* Buena Vista, 1991.

Also the executive producer of *Fuzz,* 1972, and *Green Card,* 1990.

TELEVISION WORK; EXECUTIVE PRODUCER; MOVIES

Moon of the Wolf, ABC, 1972.
Pioneer Woman, ABC, 1973.
Murdoch's Gang, CBS, 1973.
The Stranger Who Looks Like Me, ABC, 1974.
My Father's House, ABC, 1975.
21 Hours at Munich, ABC, 1976.
Smash-Up on Interstate 5, ABC, 1976.
Valentine, ABC, 1979.
Three Hundred Miles for Stephanie, NBC, 1981.
Not in Front of the Children, CBS, 1982.
Charles & Diana: A Royal Love Story, ABC, 1982.
Obsessed With a Married Woman, ABC, 1985.
Midas Valley, ABC, 1985.

TELEVISION WORK; EXECUTIVE PRODUCER; PILOTS

Flamingo Road, NBC, 1980.

TELEVISION WORK; EXECUTIVE PRODUCER; MINISERIES

King, NBC, 1978.*

* * *

FENN, Sherilyn

ADDRESSES: Agent—The Agency, 10351 Santa Monica Blvd., Suite 211, Los Angeles, CA 90069.

CAREER: Actress.

AWARDS, HONORS: Emmy Award nomination, best supporting actress in a drama series, 1990, for *Twin Peaks.*

CREDITS:

TELEVISION APPEARANCES; SERIES

Audrey Horne, *Twin Peaks,* ABC, 1990.

TELEVISION APPEARANCES; MOVIES

Monica, *Silence of the Heart,* CBS, 1984.
Billie Frechette, *Dillinger* (also known as *The Last Days of John Dillinger*), ABC, 1991.

TELEVISION APPEARANCES; SPECIALS

Betty, "A Table at Ciro's," (also known as "Tales From the Hollywood Hills") *Great Performances,* PBS, 1987.
Lorraine, *Divided We Stand,* ABC, 1988.
Beth, "A Family Again," *ABC Family Theater,* ABC, 1988.
MTV's 1990 Video Music Awards, MTV, 1990.
Presenter, *42nd Annual Primetime Emmy Awards,* Fox, 1990.

FILM APPEARANCES

Penny Hallin, *The Wild Life,* Universal, 1984.
Sandy, *Just One of the Guys,* Columbia, 1985.
Katie, *Out of Control,* New World, 1985.
Velvet, *Thrashin',* Fries Entertainment, 1986.
Keri Johnson, *The Wraith,* New Century-Vista, 1986.
Suzi, *Zombie High,* Cinema Group, 1987.
April Delongpre, *Two Moon Junction,* Lorimar, 1988.
Helen, *Crime Zone,* Concorde, 1988.
Girl in accident, *Wild at Heart,* Samuel Goldwyn, 1990.
Lucy Costello, *Backstreet Dreams,* Vidmark, 1990.
Candy Cane, *Ruby,* Triumph Releasing, 1992.
Bridey De Soto, *Desire and Hell at Sunset Motel,* Two Moon Releasing, 1992.
Jain, *Diary of a Hitman,* Vision International, 1992.
Curley's wife, *Of Mice and Men,* Metro-Goldwyn-Mayer, 1992.

Also appeared as Jennifer in *True Blood,* Fries Entertainment, and as Catherine in *Meridian: Kiss of the Beast.*

OTHER SOURCES:

PERIODICALS

Rolling Stone, October 14, 1990.*

* * *

FIELD, Sally 1946-

PERSONAL: Full name, Sally Margaret Field; born November 5, 1946, in Pasadena, CA; daughter of Maggie Field O'Mahoney (one source says Mahoney; an actress); stepdaughter of Jock Mahoney (an actor); married Steve Craig, September, 1968 (divorced, 1975); married Alan Greisman (a film producer), December, 1984; children: (first marriage) Peter, Eli; (second marriage) Samuel. *Education:* Attended Actor's Studio, 1968 and 1973-75; studied acting with David Craig.

ADDRESSES: Agent—Creative Artists Agency, 1888 Century Park E., Suite 1400, Los Angeles, CA 90067.

CAREER: Actress. Fogwood Films Ltd., producer, beginning in 1984.

MEMBER: Screen Actors Guild, American Federation of Television and Radio Artists.

AWARDS, HONORS: Emmy Award, outstanding lead actress in a drama or comedy special, 1976, for *Sybil;* Best Actress Award, Cannes International Film Festival, Academy Award, best actress, New York Film Critics

Award, and National Society of Film Critics Award, all 1979, and Golden Globe Award, best actress in a dramatic film, Hollywood Foreign Press Association, 1980, all for *Norma Rae;* NATO Star of the Year Award, National Association of Theatre Owners, 1981; People's Choice Award (with Jane Fonda), best motion picture actress, Proctor & Gamble Productions, 1982; Golden Apple Award (with John Forsythe), star of the year, Hollywood Women's Press Club, 1984; Academy Award, best actress, 1984, and Golden Globe Award, best actress in a dramatic film, 1985, both for *Places in the Heart;* Hasty Pudding Woman of the Year Award, Hasty Pudding Theatricals, 1986.

CREDITS:

FILM APPEARANCES

(Film debut) Mercy McBee, *The Way West,* United Artists (UA), 1967.
Mary Tate Farnsworth, *Stay Hungry,* UA, 1976.
Carol Bell, *Heroes,* Universal, 1977.
Carrie, *Smokey and the Bandit,* Universal, 1977.
Gwen, *Hooper,* Warner Brothers, 1978.
Mary Ellen, *The End,* UA, 1978.
Title role, *Norma Rae,* Twentieth Century-Fox, 1979.
Celeste Whitman, *Beyond the Poseidon Adventure,* Warner Brothers, 1979.
Carrie, *Smokey and the Bandit II* (also known as *Smokey and the Bandit Ride Again*), Universal, 1980.
Amy Post, *Back Roads,* Warner Brothers, 1981.
Megan Carter, *Absence of Malice,* Columbia, 1981.
Kay Villano, *Kiss Me Goodbye,* Twentieth Century-Fox, 1982.
Edna Spalding, *Places in the Heart,* Tri-Star, 1984.
Emma Moriarty, *Murphy's Romance* (also see below), Columbia, 1985.
Daisy Morgan, *Surrender,* Warner Brothers, 1987.
Lilah Krytsick, *Punchline,* Columbia, 1988.
M'Lynn Eatenton, *Steel Magnolias,* Tri-Star, 1989.
Betty Mahmoody, *Not without My Daughter,* Metro-Goldwyn-Mayer/Pathe, 1991.
Celeste Talbert, *Soapdish,* Paramount, 1991.

FILM WORK

Executive producer, *Murphy's Romance,* Columbia, 1985.
Producer, *Dying Young* (also known as *Choice of Love*), Twentieth Century-Fox, 1991.

TELEVISION APPEARANCES; SERIES

Frances "Gidget" Lawrence, *Gidget,* ABC, 1965-66.
Sister Bertrille, *The Flying Nun,* ABC, 1967-70.
Sally Burton, *The Girl with Something Extra,* NBC, 1973-74.

TELEVISION APPEARANCES; MOVIES

Denise Miller, *Maybe I'll Come Home in the Spring,* ABC, 1971.
Jane Duden, *Marriage: Year One,* NBC, 1971.
Vicki, *Mongo's Back in Town,* CBS, 1971.
Christine Morgan, *Home for the Holidays,* ABC, 1972.
Roselle Bridgeman, *Hitched* (also known as *Westward the Wagon*), NBC, 1973.
Jennifer Melford, *Bridger,* ABC, 1976.
Sybil Dorsett, *Sybil,* NBC, 1976.

TELEVISION APPEARANCES; SPECIALS

Narrator, *California Girl* (documentary), ABC, 1968.
Beth Barber, *Lily for President,* CBS, 1982.
Punchline Party, HBO, 1988.
The New Hollywood, NBC, 1990.
Hostess/narrator, *Barbara Stanwyck: Fire and Desire,* TNT, 1991.
Voices That Care, Fox, 1991.
First Person with Maria Shriver, NBC, 1991.

Also appeared in *American Film Institute Salute to Lillian Gish,* 1984; *American Film Institute Salute to Billy Wilder,* 1986; as presenter, *The 58th Annual Academy Awards Presentation,* 1986; and *James Stewart: A Wonderful Life,* 1987.

TELEVISION APPEARANCES; EPISODIC

Bonnie Banner, "Woody, Can You Spare a Sister?," *Hey, Landlord,* NBC, 1967.
Bonnie Banner, "Sharin' Sharon," *Hey, Landlord,* NBC, 1967.
Bonnie Banner, "Big Brother Is Watching You," *Hey, Landlord,* NBC, 1967.
Bonnie Banner, "A Little Off the Top," *Hey, Landlord,* NBC, 1967.
"Jenny, Who Bombs Buildings," *Bracken's World,* NBC, 1970.
"I Can Hardly Tell You Apart," *Marcus Welby, M.D.,* ABC, 1971.
Clementine Hale, "Dreadful Sorry Clementine," *Alias Smith and Jones,* ABC, 1971.
Clementine Hale, "The Clementine Incident," *Alias Smith and Jones,* ABC, 1972.
"Whisper," *Night Gallery,* NBC, 1973.
Molly Follett, "All the Way Home," *NBC Live Theater,* NBC, 1981.

OTHER SOURCES:

PERIODICALS

American Film, October, 1982, p. 58.
New York Times, September 16, 1984.
People, October 15, 1984, p. 112; October 15, 1988, p. 90.*

FIELD, Ted 1952(?)-

PERSONAL: Born c. 1952; son of Marshall Field IV and Kay Fanning (editor of the *Christian Science Monitor*); married Judith Erickson, c. 1975 (divorced c. 1988); children: Judith Danielle. *Education:* Attended University of Chicago and Pomona College.

ADDRESSES: Office—Interscope Group, 10900 Wilshire Blvd., Suite 1400, Los Angeles, CA 90024.

CAREER: Producer. Race car driver, early 1970s-c. 1983; Field Enterprises, Chicago, IL, owner with half-brother Marshall Field V, c. 1977-84; Interscope Communications (production company), Los Angeles, CA, founder with Peter Samuelson, c. 1979—.

AWARDS, HONORS: Emmy Award nomination, 1987, for *Murder Ordained;* Emmy Award (with others), outstanding children's program, 1989, for "A Mother's Courage: The Mary Thomas Story," *The Magical World of Disney.*

CREDITS:

FILM WORK; PRODUCER

(With Peter Samuelson) *Revenge of the Nerds,* Twentieth Century-Fox, 1984.
(With Rene Dupont) *Turk 182!,* Twentieth Century-Fox, 1985.
(With Robert W. Cort) *Critical Condition,* Paramount, 1987.
(With Cort, Peter V. Herald, Scott Kroopf, and Martin Mickelson) *Outrageous Fortune,* Buena Vista, 1987.
(With Cort and Edward Teets) *Three Men and a Baby,* Buena Vista, 1987.
(With Cort and Peter Bart) *Revenge of the Nerds II: Nerds in Paradise,* Twentieth Century-Fox, 1987.
(With Cort) *The Seventh Sign,* Tri-Star, 1988.
(With Cort) *Cocktail,* Buena Vista, 1988.
(With Cort and Neil A. Machlis) *An Innocent Man,* Buena Vista, 1989.
Collision Course (also known as *East/West Cop*), Recorded Releasing, 1990.
(With Cort) *Three Men and a Little Lady,* Buena Vista, 1990.
Class Action, Twentieth Century-Fox, 1991.
(With Cort and Karen Murphy) *The Cutting Edge,* Metro-Goldwyn-Mayer, 1992.

FILM WORK; EXECUTIVE PRODUCER

Bill and Ted's Excellent Adventure, Orion, 1989.
Renegades, Universal, 1989.
The First Power (also known as *Transit* and *Pentagram*), Orion, 1990.
Bird on a Wire, Universal, 1990.
(Co-executive producer) *Arachnophobia* (also known as *Along Came a Spider*), Buena Vista, 1990.
Bill and Ted's Bogus Journey (also known as *Bill and Ted Go to Hell*), Orion, 1991.
Paradise, Buena Vista, 1991.
(With Cort and Rick Jaffa) *Hand That Rocks the Cradle,* Hollywood Pictures, 1992.

Also executive producer of *Eve of Destruction,* 1991.

TELEVISION WORK; EXECUTIVE PRODUCER; MOVIES

(With Dick Berg) *American Geisha,* CBS, 1986.
(Co-executive producer) *The Father Clements Story,* NBC, 1987.
Murder Ordained (also known as *Broken Commandments* and *Kansas Gothic*), CBS, 1987.
Crossing the Mob (also known as *Philly Boy*), NBC, 1988.
My Boyfriend's Back, NBC, 1989.
Aftermath: A Test of Love, CBS, 1991.
The Secret Life of Archie's Wife, CBS, 1991.
Shoot First: A Cop's Vengeance, NBC, 1991.

TELEVISION WORK; EPISODIC

Executive producer (with Robert W. Cort) "A Mother's Courage: The Mary Thomas Story" (also known as "Long Shot"), *The Magical World of Disney,* NBC, 1989.

OTHER TELEVISION WORK

Producer, *Marlo and the Magic Movie Machine* (series), CBS, 1977-81.
Producer, *The Real Adventures of Sherlock Jones and Proctor Watson,* PBS, 1987.
Co-executive producer, *Everybody's Baby: The Rescue of Jessica McClure* (special; also known as *The Jessica McClure Story*), ABC, 1989.

OTHER SOURCES:

PERIODICALS

Forbes, June 27, 1988, p. 14.
People Weekly, December 12, 1983, p. 50.

* * *

FLICK, Stephen Hunter 1949-

PERSONAL: Born June 21, 1949, in Evanston, IL; son of C. E. and Margret Ann Flick. *Education:* Attended University of Southern California, Film School, 1973-75; received B.F.A. from San Jose State University.

ADDRESSES: Office—Weddington Productions, 11036 Weddington St., North Hollywood, CA 91601.

CAREER: Sound effects creator/editor and sound editor. Director of commercials, including spots for Dos Equis beer; sound editor for trailers and picture editor for Roger Corman's New World Pictures.

MEMBER: Motion Picture and Video Tape Editor's Guild.

AWARDS, HONORS: Academy Award nomination for best sound effects editing, 1982, for *Poltergeist;* Academy Award for best sound effects editing, 1987, for *Robocop;* Academy Award nomination for best sound effects editing, 1988, for *Die Hard;* Academy Award nomination for best sound editing, 1990, for *Total Recall.*

CREDITS:

FILM WORK; SOUND EDITING

Star Trek: The Motion Picture, Paramount, 1979.
Pennies from Heaven, Metro-Goldwyn-Mayer/United Artists, 1981.
Raiders of the Lost Ark, Paramount, 1981.
Under Fire, Orion, 1983.
(Supervisor) *Streets of Fire,* Universal, 1984.
(Supervisor) *Body Double,* Columbia, 1984.
(Supervisor) *Weird Science,* Universal, 1985.
(Supervisor) *Brewster's Millions,* Universal, 1985.
(Supervisor) *Robocop 2* (also see below), Orion, 1990.

FILM WORK; SOUND EFFECTS

(Editor) *The Final Countdown,* United Artists, 1980.
Dr Heckyl and Mr. Hype, Cannon, 1980.
Poltergeist, Metro-Goldwyn-Mayer, 1981.
(Editor supervisor) *Forty-eight Hours,* Paramount, 1982.
(Supervisor) *Robocop,* Orion, 1987.
(Supervisor) *Die Hard,* Twentieth Century-Fox, 1988.
(Supervisor) *Total Recall,* Tri-Star, 1990.
(Supervisor) *Robocop 2,* Orion, 1990.
(Supervisor) *Predator 2,* Twentieth Century-Fox, 1990.
Point Break, Largo Entertainment, 1991.
Basic Instinct, Carolco, 1992.

OTHER SOURCES:

PERIODICALS

The Hollywood Reporter Craft Series: Sound Editors and Mixers, February 4, 1991, pp. S-10, S-12.

* * *

FONDA, Bridget 1965(?)-

PERSONAL: Born c. 1965; daughter of Peter (an actor, director, producer, and writer) and Susan Fonda. *Education:* Attended Lee Strasberg Theatre Institute; studied with Harold Gruskin and David Mamet.

ADDRESSES: Agent—United Talent Agency, 9560 Wilshire Blvd., 5th Floor, Beverly Hills, CA 90212.

CAREER: Actress.

CREDITS:

FILM APPEARANCES

One of the lovers, *Aria,* Warner Brothers, 1987.
Voice of historian/head, *Light Years* (animated), Miramax, 1988.
Peggy Kellogg, *You Can't Hurry Love,* Lightning, 1988.
Melaina Buller, *Shag: The Movie,* Tri-Star, 1988.
Mandy Rice-Davies, *Scandal,* Miramax, 1989.
Amy Hempel, *Strapless,* Atlantic Releasing, 1989.
Mary Godwin Shelley, *Frankenstein Unbound,* Twentieth Century-Fox, 1990.
Grace Hamilton, *The Godfather, Part III,* Paramount, 1990.
Claudi, *Leather Jackets,* Triumph Releasing, 1991.
Nancy Lee, *Doc Hollywood,* Warner Brothers, 1991.
Out of the Rain (also known as *Remains*), Vision International, 1991.
Allie, *Single White Female,* Columbia, 1992.
Singles, Warner Brothers, 1992.

TELEVISION APPEARANCES; EPISODIC

21 Jump Street, Fox, 1989.
Louise Bradshaw, "Jacob Have I Loved," *WonderWorks,* PBS, 1989.
Dorite, "Professional Man," *The Edge,* HBO, 1989.

STAGE APPEARANCES

Sissy, *Class 1 Acts,* Nat Horne Theatre, New York City, 1988.

Also appeared in *Confession,* Warren Robertson Workshop, and *Pastels,* Lee Strasberg Theatre Institute.

OTHER SOURCES:

PERIODICALS

Interview, June, 1989, p. 86.
Rolling Stone, April 20, 1989, p. 40.
US, May 29, 1989.*

* * *

FONTEYN, Margot 1919-1991

PERSONAL: Full name, Margot Fonteyn de Arias; born Margaret Hookham, May 18, 1919, in Reigate, Surrey, England; died of cancer, February 21, 1991, in Panama City, Panama; daughter of Felix John (an engineer) and Hilda (Fontes) Hookham; married Roberto E. Arias (an attorney, politician, and diplomat), February 6, 1955 (died, 1989). *Education:* Educated privately and in schools in England, China, and the United States; studied dance with Serafine Astafieva and others; attended Vic-Wells and Sadler's Wells Ballet School (now Royal Ballet) beginning in 1933.

ADDRESSES: *Office*—c/o Royal Ballet, Royal Opera House, Covent Garden, London WC2, England. *Agent*—David Higham Associates Ltd., 5-8 Lower John St., Golden Sq., London W1R 4HA, England.

CAREER: Ballerina and author. Vic-Wells and Sadler's Wells Ballet (became Royal Ballet Company in 1956), London, England, mid-1930s to mid-1970s, began as ballerina, became prima ballerina, later guest artist; toured and performed on stage and television with Royal Ballet Company; partner, with Rudolf Nureyev, 1962-79; writer. Appeared with Royal Ballet Company at Metropolitan Opera House, New York City, 1949 and 1950; performed at Granada Musical Festival, 1953 and 1954. Guest artist at numerous theatres and with numerous companies, including Yugoslav National Ballet, Belgrade, Yugoslavia, 1954, Ballets de Paris, Stuttgart Ballet, National Ballet (Washington, DC), Scottish Ballet, New London Ballet, Marie Rambert's Ballet, Australian Ballet, and Royal Opera House, Copenhagen, Denmark. Dance coach of American Ballet Theatre; artistic adviser to various companies, including National Ballet Company of Panama. Chancellor of Durham University, 1982-91. Model and mentor for world-famous ballerinas, dancewear designer; lecturer.

MEMBER: British Royal Academy of Dancing (president, 1954-91).

AWARDS, HONORS: Commander of the Order of the British Empire, 1951; Dame Commander of the Order of the British Empire, 1956; Order of the Finnish Lion, 1960; Order of Estacio de Sa (Brazil), 1973; Benjamin Franklin Medal from Royal Society of the Arts, 1974; Chevalier of the Order of Merit of Duarte, Sanchez, and Mella (Dominican Republic), 1975; International Artist Award from Philippine Government, 1976; International Shakespeare Prize from F.V.S. Foundation of Hamburg, 1977; honoree of Royal Opera House gala, Covent Garden, London, c. 1990. Litt.D. from University of Leeds, 1953, and University of Manchester, 1966; Mus.D. from Oxford University, 1959, and University of London; LL.D. from Cambridge University, 1962, and University of Edinburgh, 1963; Hon. Dr. from Durham University, 1982; and D.H. from Philippine Women's University.

CREDITS:

STAGE APPEARANCES

Snowflake, *The Nutcracker Suite,* Sadler's Wells Theatre, London, 1934.

Soloist, *The Haunted Ballroom,* Sadler's Wells Theatre, 1934.

Princess Aurora, *The Sleeping Beauty,* Metropolitan Opera House, New York City, 1949.

Guest artist, *The Sleeping Beauty,* La Scala Theatre, Milan, Italy, 1950.

Title role, *The Sleeping Beauty,* Opera Theatre, Paris, 1954.

Juliet, *Romeo and Juliet,* Royal Ballet Company, Covent Garden, London, 1965.

Guest artist, "Romeo and Juliet," *The Royal Ballet,* Metropolitan Opera House, 1967.

Lady Capulet, *Romeo and Juliet,* Milan, then Metropolitan Opera House, both 1981.

Also appeared in principal roles of numerous productions, including *Rio Grande,* 1934; *Le Baiser de la fee,* 1935; *Giselle* and *Apparitions,* both 1936; *Les Patineurs* and *A Wedding Bouquet,* both 1937; *Horoscope* and *The Sleeping Beauty,* both 1938; *Swan Lake,* 1939; *The Wise Virgins,* and *The Sleeping Beauty,* both 1940; *Hamlet* and *Comus,* both 1942; *The Quest,* 1943; *Les Sirenes* and, as Spirit of the Air, *The Fairy Queen,* both 1946; *The Three-Cornered Hat* and *Mam'zelle Angot,* both 1947; *Scenes de ballet, Les Demoiselles de la nuit,* and, as Death, *Don Juan,* all 1948; *Cinderella, Giselle, Les Sylphides, Le Lac des Cygnes, The Sleeping Beauty, Dante Sonata,* and *Symphonic Variations,* all 1949; *Ballet Imperial,* 1950; *Daphnis and Chloe* and *Tiresias,* both 1951; *Sylvia,* 1952; *Homage to the Queen,* 1953; *The Firebird* and, as soloist, *The Entry of Madame Butterfly,* Madrid, Spain, both 1954; *Ondine,* 1958; *Marguerite and Armand,* 1963; *The Corsair, La Bayadere,* and *Raymonda,* all 1966; *Paradise Lost,* 1967; *Pelleas et Melisande* and *Poeme de l'extase,* both 1970; *Coppelia;* and also performed, with Frederick Ashton, in Metropolitan Opera House centennial gala, 1984.

MAJOR TOURS

Toured English cities during 1940s and U.S. cities during early 1950s.

FILM APPEARANCES

Herself, *The Little Ballerina,* Universal, 1951.

Juliet, *Romeo and Juliet,* Embassy, 1966.

The Swan Lake, United Productions of America-Seven Arts, 1967.

Ballet dancer, *I Am a Dancer,* Anglo-EMI, 1972.

Also appeared in *The Royal Ballet,* 1960.

TELEVISION APPEARANCES; SERIES

Host and narrator, *The Magic of Dance,* BBC, 1979, PBS, 1982.

TELEVISION APPEARANCES; SPECIALS

Princess Aurora, "Sleeping Beauty," *Producers' Showcase,* NBC, 1955.
Title role, "Cinderella," *Producers' Showcase,* NBC, 1957.
The Kennedy Center Honors: A Celebration of the Performing Arts, CBS, 1986.
The Margot Fonteyn Story, PBS, 1990.

WRITINGS:

(Contributor to commentary) Keith Money, *The Art of Margot Fonteyn* (photographic study), M. Joseph, 1965.
Margot Fonteyn: Autobiography, W. H. Allen, 1975, Knopf, 1976.
A Dancer's World: An Introduction, W. H. Allen, 1978, published as *A Dancer's World: An Introduction for Parents and Students,* Knopf, 1979.
The Magic of Dance, Knopf, 1979.
Pavlova: Portrait of a Dancer, Viking, 1984, published in England as *Pavlova: Impressions,* Weidenfeld & Nicolson, 1984.

OBITUARIES AND OTHER SOURCES:

PERIODICALS

Chicago Tribune, February 22, 1991; February 24, 1991.
Detroit Free Press, February 23, 1991.
Hollywood Reporter, February 22, 1991.
Los Angeles Times, February 22, 1991.
New York Times, March 6, 1980; February 22, 1991.
Times (London), February 22, 1991.
Washington Post, February 22, 1991.*

* * *

FORD, Tennessee Ernie 1919-1991

PERSONAL: Full name, Ernest Jennings Ford; born February 13, 1919, in Bristol, TN; died of liver failure, October 17, 1991, in Reston, VA; son of Clarence T. (a postal worker and fiddle player) and Maude (Long) Ford; married Betty Jean Heminger, September 18, 1942 (died, February, 1989); married Beverly Wood-Smith, June, 1989; children: (first marriage) Jeffrey Bucknew (Buck), Brion Leonard; (second marriage) Stevie (stepdaughter). *Education:* Attended Virginia Intermount College, 1937-39, and Cincinnati Conservatory of Music, 1939.

CAREER: Actor and singer. Worked as a radio announcer for WOPI-Radio, Bristol, TN, 1937-39, WATL-Radio, Atlanta, GA, 1939-41, a station in Knoxville, TN, and several stations in California; Capitol Records, recording artist, 1949-76; Betford Corp., San Francisco, CA, president, 1956-90. *Military service:* U.S. Army Air Forces, navigator and instructor, 1942-45; became lieutenant.

AWARDS, HONORS: Emmy Award nomination, best new personality, 1954; *Motion Picture Daily* Award, best television program, 1956-57, for *The Tennessee Ernie Ford Show;* Grammy Award, best gospel performance, 1964, for *Great Gospel Songs;* Presidential Medal of Freedom, 1984; inducted into Country Music Hall of Fame, 1990; Minnie Pearl Award, lifetime achievement, *TNN Music City News* and Group W Satellite Communications, 1990.

CREDITS:

TELEVISION APPEARANCES; SERIES

Host, *Kay Kyser's Kollege of Musical Knowledge* (quiz show), NBC, 1954.
Host, *The Tennessee Ernie Ford Show,* NBC, 1955-57 and 1958-60, ABC, 1962-65.

Appeared on *Old American Barn Dance,* 1953.

TELEVISION APPEARANCES; SPECIALS

Tennessee Ernie Ford Meets King Arthur, NBC, 1960.
Sir Joseph Porter, *H.M.S. Pinafore,* NBC, 1960.
Friends and Nabors, CBS, 1966.
Andy Griffith's Uptown-Downtown Show, CBS, 1967.
Host, *The Tennessee Ernie Ford Special,* CBS, 1967.
The Wonderful World of Burlesque III, NBC, 1967.
One More Time, ABC, 1968.
Looking Back, CBS, 1969.
Host, *The Peapicker in Piccadilly,* NBC, 1969.
Cohost, *City vs. Country,* ABC, 1971.
Host, *The Fabulous Fordies,* NBC, 1972.
Host, *Tennessee Ernie Ford's White Christmas,* NBC, 1972.
Host, *Country Music Hit Parade,* NBC, 1973.
Host, *The Stars and Stripes Show,* NBC, 1973.
Opryland U.S.A., NBC, 1973.
Host, *Tennessee Ernie's Nashville-Moscow Express,* NBC, 1975.
Cohost, *The Stars and Stripes Show,* NBC, 1976.
Cohost, *Country Night of the Stars,* NBC, 1978.
Host, *Tennessee Ernie Ford's America,* PBS, 1985.
Tennessee Ernie Ford: Fifty Golden Years, TNN, 1990.
Dinah Shore: A Special Conversation with Tennessee Ernie Ford, TNN, 1991.

Also appeared on *Country Comes Home,* 1984.

TELEVISION APPEARANCES; EPISODIC

Appeared on *I Love Lucy,* 1954, and on episodes of *The Red Skelton Show, The Perry Como Show, The George Gobel Show, Lux Music Hall, The Danny Thomas Show, The Lucy Show,* and *Here's Lucy.*

RADIO APPEARANCES

Soloist, *Hometown Jamboree,* 1948.

STAGE APPEARANCES

Festival at Ford's, Circle in the Square/Ford's Theatre, Washington, DC, 1971.

Performed at the Palladium Theatre, London, 1953. Nightclub performer, beginning in 1950.

RECORDINGS:

ALBUMS

Spirituals, Capitol, 1958.
Nearer the Cross, Capitol, 1958.
Gather 'Round, Capitol, 1959.
Sixteen Tons, Capitol, 1960.
Sing a Hymn, Capitol, 1960.
Civil War Songs of the North, Capitol, 1961.
Civil War Songs of the South, Capitol, 1961.
Hymns at Home, Capitol, 1961.
I Love to Tell the Story, Capitol, 1962.
Favorite Hymns, Capitol, 1962.
Sing a Hymn with Me, Capitol, 1962.
Sing a Spiritual with Me, Capitol, 1962.
This Lusty Land, Capitol, 1963.
Hymns, Capitol, 1963.
Tennessee Ernie Ford, Capitol, 1963.
We Gather Together, Capitol, 1963.
Long, Long Ago, Capitol, 1963.
Great Gospel Songs, Capitol, 1964.
Tennessee Ernie Ford's Country Hits, Capitol, 1964.
The World's Best Loved Hymns, Capitol, 1965.
Favorite Hymns, Ranwood, 1987.

Other recordings include *Christmas Special,* Capitol; *Amazing Grace,* Pickwick; *Jesus Loves Me,* Pickwick; *Make a Joyful Noise,* Capitol; *The Need for Prayer,* Pickwick; *Rock of Ages,* Pickwick; *America the Beautiful,* Capitol; *Faith of Our Fathers,* Capitol; *For the 83rd Time,* Capitol; *Tennessee Ernie Ford Sings His Great Love,* Capitol; *25th Anniversary,* Capitol; *The Story of Christmas,* Capitol; *The Star Carol,* Capitol; *The Very Best of Tennessee Ernie Ford,* Capitol; (with Glen Campbell) *Ernie Sings and Glen Picks,* Capitol; *Precious Memories,* Capitol; *He Touched Me,* Capitol; *Tennessee Ernie Ford Sings 22 Favorite Hymns,* Ranwood; *Swing Wide Your Golden Gate,* Word; *Tell Me the Old Story,* Word; and *There's a Song in My Heart,* Word.

WRITINGS:

Author of the autobiography *This Is My Song, This Is My Story,* 1963. Songwriter.

OBITUARIES AND OTHER SOURCES:

PERIODICALS

Detroit News and Free Press, October 18, 1991, p. 3B.
Variety, October 21, 1991, p. 86.*

*   *   *

FORNES, Maria Irene 1930-

PERSONAL: Born May 14, 1930, in Havana, Cuba; immigrated to the United States, 1945, naturalized citizen, 1951; daughter of Carlos Luis (a public servant) and Carmen Hismenia (Collado) Fornes. *Education:* Attended public schools in Havana, Cuba. *Politics:* Democrat. *Religion:* Roman Catholic.

ADDRESSES: Office—1 Sheridan Sq., New York, NY 10014. *Agent*—Berttia Case, 345 West 58th St., New York, NY 10019.

CAREER: Playwright and director. Theatre for the New City, New York City, teacher of playwriting, 1972-73; New York Theatre Strategy, New York City, president, 1973-80; Padua Hills Festival, Claremont, CA, teacher of playwriting, 1978—; International Arts Relations (INTAR) Hispanic American Theatre, New York City, teacher of playwriting, 1981—, director of Playwrights Laboratory. Also worked as a textile designer.

MEMBER: Dramatists Guild, American Society of Composers, Authors, and Publishers, League of Professional Theatre Women, Authors League of America.

AWARDS, HONORS: Grants from John Hay Whitney Foundation, 1961-62, Centro Mexicano de Escrivatores, 1962-63, University of Minnesota, 1965, Cintas Foundation, 1967-68, Yale University, 1968-69, Creative Artists Public Service (CAPS), 1972, and National Endowment for the Arts, 1974, 1984, and 1985; Obie Award, best scripts, *Village Voice,* 1965, for *Promenade* and *The Successful Life of Three;* Guggenheim fellow, 1972-73; Obie Award, best script, 1978, for *Fefu and Her Friends;* Obie Award, best direction, 1979, for *Eyes on the Harem;* Obie Award, sustained achievement, 1982; Obie Award, best scripts and direction, 1984, for *The Danube, Sarita,* and *Mud;* Obie Award, best play or production, 1985, for *The Conduct of Life;* Academy-Institute Award for Literature, American Academy and Institute of Arts and Letters, 1985; HBO Translation Award, 1985, for *Cold Air;* Obie Award, best new play, 1988, for *Abingdon Square.*

CREDITS:

STAGE WORK; DIRECTOR

The Successful Life of Three (also see below), Open Theatre, New York City, 1965, then Judson Church, New York City, 1967.

Promenade (also see below), Judson Church, 1965.

Tango Palace (also known as *There! You Died;* also see below), Firehouse Theatre, Minneapolis, MN, 1965.

A Vietnamese Wedding (also see below), Washington Square Church, New York City, 1967, then Promenade Theatre, New York City, 1969-70.

The Annunciation (also see below), Judson Church, 1967.

The Curse of the Langston House (also see below), Cincinnati Playhouse, Cincinnati, OH, 1972.

Aurora (also see below), New York Theatre Strategy, New York City, 1973.

Dr. Kheal (also see below), Theatre Genesis, New York City, 1973.

Molly's Dream (also see below), New York Theatre Strategy, 1973.

Fefu and Her Friends (also see below), American Place Theatre, New York City, 1978.

Going to New England, INTAR Hispanic American Theatre/Stage 2, New York City, 1980.

Life Is a Dream (also see below), INTAR Hispanic American Theatre, 1981.

A Visit (also see below), Theatre for the New City, New York City, 1981-82.

Exiles, INTAR Hispanic American Theatre/Stage Two, 1982-83.

Mud (also see below), Theatre for the New City, 1983.

Sarita (also see below), INTAR Hispanic American Theatre, 1984.

The Danube (also see below), American Place Theatre, 1984.

The Conduct of Life (also see below), Theatre for the New City, 1985.

Cold Air (also see below), INTAR Hispanic American Theatre, 1985.

Lovers and Keepers (also see below), INTAR Hispanic American Theatre, 1986.

Abingdon Square (also see below), American Place Theatre, 1987.

Uncle Vanya (also see below), CSC Repertory, Classic Stage Company, New York City, 1987-88.

"Hunger" (also see below), *Three Pieces for a Warehouse* (triple bill), 500 Greenwich Street Theatre, New York City, 1988.

Also directed *A Vietnamese Wedding* (tour; also see below), U.S. cities, 1967-68; and *Eyes on the Harem* (also see below), 1979.

OTHER STAGE WORK

Costume designer, *Two Camps by Koutoukas,* Actors Playhouse, New York City, 1968.

WRITINGS:

PLAYS

Tango Palace (also known as *There! You Died*), produced at Actors Workshop, San Francisco, CA, 1964, then Theatre Genesis, New York City, 1973, later toured as part of a U.S. Information Agency production in Calcutta, India, 1973.

The Successful Life of Three, produced at Firehouse Theatre, Minneapolis, MN, then Open Theatre, New York City, 1965, later toured U.S. cities, 1971-72.

(Author of book and lyrics) *Promenade,* produced at Judson Church, New York City, 1965 and 1969, then Promenade Theatre, New York City, 1969-70, later Theatre Off Park, New York City, 1983, then toured U.S. cities, 1972 and 1975.

The Office, produced at Henry Miller's Theatre, New York City, 1966.

A Vietnamese Wedding, produced at Washington Square Church, New York City, 1967, then toured U.S. cities, 1967-68.

The Annunciation, produced at Judson Church, 1967.

Dr. Kheal, produced at Village Gate Theatre, New York City, 1968, then Festival of Short Plays, American Place Theatre, New York City, 1974.

The Red Burning Light, produced at Open Theatre, Zurich, Switzerland, 1968, then La Mama ETC, New York City, 1969.

Molly's Dream, produced at Tanglewood Workshop, Boston University, Boston, MA, 1968, then New York Theatre Strategy, New York City, 1973.

The Curse of the Langston House, produced at Cincinnati Playhouse, Cincinnati, OH, 1972.

Aurora, produced at New York Theatre Strategy, 1973.

Fefu and Her Friends, produced at American Place Theatre, 1978.

(Adapter) *Life Is a Dream* (based on the play by Pedro Calderon de La Barca), produced at INTAR Hispanic American Theatre, New York City, 1981.

A Visit, produced at Theatre for the New City, New York City, 1981-82.

Mud, produced at Theatre for the New City, 1983, then Westbeth Theatre Center, New York City, 1986.

Sarita, produced at INTAR Hispanic American Theatre, 1984.

The Danube, produced at American Place Theatre, 1984.

The Conduct of Life, produced at Theatre for the New City, 1985.

(Adapter) *Cold Air* (based on the play by Pinera), produced at INTAR Hispanic American Theatre, 1985.

(Adapter) "Drowning" (based on the play by Anton Chekhov), *Orchards* (seven dramatizations), produced at Lucille Lortel Theatre, New York City, 1985.

Lovers and Keepers, produced at INTAR Hispanic American Theatre, 1986.

Abingdon Square, produced at American Place Theatre, 1987.

(Author of revision) *Uncle Vanya* (based on the work by Chekhov), CSC Repertory, Classic Stage Company, New York City, 1987-88.

And What of the Night?, Milwaukee Repertory Theatre, Milwaukee, WI, 1988.

"Hunger," *Three Pieces for a Warehouse* (triple bill), 500 Greenwich Street Theatre, New York City, 1988.

Also author of other plays, including *The Widow,* 1963; *Cap-a-Pie,* 1975; *Lolita in the Garden,* 1977; *In Service,* 1978; *Eyes on the Harem,* 1979; *Evelyn Brown (A Diary),* 1980; (adapter) *Blood Wedding* (based on the play by Garcia Lorca), 1981; *No Time,* 1985; *The Trial of Joan of Arc on a Matter of Faith,* 1986; *The Mothers* (also known as *Charley*), 1986; and *Art,* 1986. Contributor of music and lyrics to *Carmines Sings Whitman Sings Carmines,* Playwrights Horizons, New York City, 1985.*

* * *

FORREST, George 1915-

PERSONAL: Full name, George Forrest Chichester, Jr.; born July 31, 1915, in Brooklyn, NY; son of George Forrest (a banker and investment counselor) and Isabel (Paine) Chichester. *Education:* Studied with Marion Andre in Lake Worth, FL, and with Fannie Greene in New York City. *Avocational interests:* Theatre, concerts, opera, and travel.

CAREER: Lyricist and composer. Worked as a dance orchestra leader and pianist, night-club entertainer, and accompanist.

MEMBER: American Society of Composers, Authors, and Publishers, American Guild of Authors and Composers, Dramatists Guild.

AWARDS, HONORS: Academy Award nomination (with Robert Wright), best song, 1937, for "Donkey Serenade" from *The Firefly;* Antoinette Perry Award (with Wright), outstanding musical, 1954, for *Kismet;* Antoinette Perry Award nomination (with Wright and Maury Yeston), best original score written for the theatre, 1990, for *Grand Hotel.*

CREDITS:

STAGE WORK; WITH ROBERT WRIGHT

Director, *The Gypsy Lady* (also see below), Century Theatre, New York City, 1946, produced under title *Romany Love,* His Majesty's Theatre, London, 1947.

WRITINGS:

FILM MUSIC; LYRICS, EXCEPT WHERE INDICATED; WITH ROBERT WRIGHT

Music, *New Shoes,* Metro-Goldwyn-Mayer (MGM), 1936.

The Longest Night, MGM, 1936.

After the Thin Man, MGM, 1936.

Libeled Lady, MGM, 1936.

Sinner Take All, MGM, 1936.

The Firefly, MGM, 1937.

The Good Old Soak, MGM, 1937.

London by Night, MGM, 1937.

Madame "X", MGM, 1937.

Mama Steps Out, MGM, 1937.

Mannequin, MGM, 1937.

Man of the People, MGM, 1937.

Maytime, MGM, 1937.

Navy Blue and Gold, MGM, 1937.

Parnell, MGM, 1937.

Saratoga, MGM, 1937.

Bad Man of Brimstone, MGM, 1938.

You're Only Young Once, MGM, 1938.

Boys' Town, MGM, 1938.

The First Hundred Years, MGM, 1938.

Lord Jeff, MGM, 1938.

Marie Antoinette, MGM, 1938.

Paradise for Three, MGM, 1938.

Sweethearts, MGM, 1938.

Three Comrades, MGM, 1938.

The Toy Wife, MGM, 1938.

Vacation from Love, MGM, 1938.

Happily Buried, MGM, 1938.

The Magician's Daughter, MGM, 1938.

Nuts and Bolts, MGM, 1938.

Our Gang Follies, MGM, 1938.

Snow Gets in Your Eyes, MGM, 1938.

Broadway Serenade, MGM, 1939.

The Girl Downstairs, MGM, 1939.

The Hardys Ride High, MGM, 1939.

Honolulu, MGM, 1939.

Let Freedom Ring, MGM, 1939.

Balalaika, MGM, 1939.

These Glamour Girls, MGM, 1939.

The Women, MGM, 1939.

Florian, MGM, 1940.

New Moon, MGM, 1940.

Strange Cargo, MGM, 1940.

Music in My Heart, Columbia, 1940.
Dance, Girl, Dance, RKO Radio Pictures, 1940.
South of Pago-Pago, United Artists (UA), 1940.
Kit Carson, UA, 1940.
Blondie Goes Latin, Columbia, 1941.
Cubana, Hal Roach, 1941.
Fiesta, Hal Roach, 1941.
I Married an Angel, MGM, 1942.
Kismet (adaptation of the musical of the same title; also see below), MGM, 1955.
Music, *Song of Norway* (adaptation of the musical of the same title; also see below), Cinerama, 1970.
Songs, *Taking Off,* Universal, 1971.
(And music) *The Great Waltz* (adaptation of the musical of the same title; also see below), MGM, 1972.

STAGE MUSIC; WITH ROBERT WRIGHT

Lyrics and music, *Thank You, Columbus,* Hollywood Playhouse, CA, 1940.
Lyrics for additional music, *Naughty Marietta,* Curran Theatre, San Francisco, CA, 1941, Philharmonic Auditorium, Los Angeles, 1941.
Lyrics for additional music, *Rio Rita,* Curran Theatre, 1941, Philharmonic Auditorium, 1941.
Music, *Fun for the Money,* Hollywood Playhouse, 1941.
Lyrics and music (based on themes of the music of Edvard Grieg), *Song of Norway,* Imperial Theatre, New York City, 1944.
Lyrics and music, *Spring in Brazil,* U.S. cities, 1945.
Lyrics (with score derived from the Victor Herbert operettas *The Fortune Teller* and *Serenade*), *The Gypsy Lady,* Century Theatre, New York City, 1946, produced under title *Romany Love,* His Majesty's Theatre, London, 1947.
Lyrics and musical adaptation (based on the music by Hector Villa-Lobos), *Magdalena,* Ziegfeld Theatre, New York City, 1948.
Lyrics, *The Great Waltz,* Curran Theatre, 1949, Philharmonic Auditorium, 1949, produced with additional lyrics at the same theatres, 1953, revival produced with additional musical adaptation, Music Center, Los Angeles, 1965.
Lyrics and music (based on themes of the music of Alexander Borodin) *Kismet,* first produced at Ziegfeld Theatre, 1953.
Book, lyrics, and music, *The Carefree Heart* (also see below), U.S. cities, 1957.
Lyrics and music, *At the Grand,* Philharmonic Auditorium, 1958, Curran Theatre, 1958.
Music, *The Love Doctor* (revised version of *The Carefree Heart*), Piccadilly Theatre, London, 1959.
Lyrics and music, *Kean,* Broadway Theatre, New York City, 1961.
Lyrics and music (based on themes of the music of Sergei Rachmaninoff), *Anya,* Ziegfeld Theatre, 1965.
Lyrics and music, *Cyrano de Bergerac,* U.S. cities, 1973.
Lyrics and music (based on themes of the music of Alexander Borodin and African folk music), *Timbuktu!* (based on the musical *Kismet*), Mark Hellinger Theatre, New York City, 1978.
Songs, *Grand Hotel,* Martin Beck Theatre, New York City, 1989.

Also composed music for Camp Tamiment summer revues, Tamiment Playhouse, Stroudsburg, PA, 1942; contributed material to *Ziegfeld Follies,* Winter Garden, New York City, 1943.

RADIO MUSIC; LYRICS AND MUSIC; WITH ROBERT WRIGHT

Vicks Radio Hour, NBC, 1936.
Maxwell House Good News, NBC, 1937.
Tune-Up Time, NBC, 1940.
Treasury Story Parade, all networks, 1942-43.

TELEVISION MUSIC; WITH ROBERT WRIGHT

Revues, *Startime Hour,* The DuMont Network, 1950.

OTHER MUSIC

Contributor with Wright of material to nightclub acts, including "Folies Bergere Revue," New York City, 1942; "Vaughn Monroe's Commodore Hotel Revue," New York City, 1942-43; four Copacabana revues, New York City, 1942-43; and three Colonial Inn revues, Hollywood, FL, 1945-48. Creator with Wright of nightclub acts for Jane Froman, 1942-56; Celeste Holm, 1943; and Anne Jeffreys and Robert Sterling, 1952-53. Author of song "Stranger in Paradise."*

* * *

FOWLER, Clement 1924-

PERSONAL: Born December 27, 1924, in Detroit, MI; son of Morris (in business) and Lillian Fowler; married Edith Samuel (a book designer), April 7, 1951. *Education:* Attended Wayne State University, 1941-43, 1946-48, received B.A.; studied for the theatre with Sanford Meisner and Harold Clurman.

ADDRESSES: Manager—Beverly Chase Management, 162 West 54th Street, New York, NY 10019.

CAREER: Actor. PAF Playhouse, Huntington Station, NY, member of theatrical company, 1970-73. *Military service:* U.S. Army Air Corps, 1943-45; became staff sergeant.

CREDITS:

STAGE APPEARANCES

(Stage debut) Jack, *The Importance of Being Earnest,* Actors Company of Detroit, Detroit, MI, 1947.

Exton, *Richard II,* City Center Theatre, New York City, 1951.

Bibinski, *Silk Stockings,* Rye Music Theatre, 1957.

Van Buren, *Damn Yankees,* Rye Music Theatre, 1957.

Sosia, *A God Slept Here,* Provincetown Playhouse, New York City, 1958.

Starkeeper, *Carousel,* Rye Music Theatre, 1958.

Rosencrantz, *Hamlet,* Lunt-Fontanne Theatre, New York City, 1964.

Who's Afraid of Virginia Woolf?, Hartford Stage Company, Hartford, CT, 1966-67.

Spoon River Anthology, PAF Playhouse, Huntington Station, NY, 1970-71.

The Odd Couple, PAF Playhouse, 1971-72.

Understudy for the role of Al, *The Sunshine Boys,* Broadhurst Theatre, New York City, 1972.

Henry IV, Part One, Folger Theatre Group, Washington, DC, 1974-75.

Henry V, Folger Theatre Group, 1975-76.

All's Well that Ends Well, Folger Theatre Group, 1975-76.

Much Ado About Nothing, Folger Theatre Group, 1976-77

Jacob, *Awake and Sing!,* Counterpoint Theatre, New York City, 1977.

Events from the Life of Ted Snyder, PAF Playhouse, 1977-78.

A Small Winter Crisis, The New Dramatists, Inc., New York City, 1977-78

Berenger the First, *Exit the King,* Counterpoint Theatre, New York City, 1978.

Louis Epstein and Printer and Dumond, *Joley,* Northstage Theatre, Glen Cove, NY, 1979.

Herr Shaaf, German tutor, *A Month in the Country,* Roundabout Stage One, New York City, 1979.

An Attempt at Flying, Yale Repertory Theatre, New Haven, CT, 1980-81.

A Man for All Seasons, Center Stage, Baltimore, MD, 1980-81.

House Music, American Jewish Theatre, New York City, 1981.

Northumberland, *Henry IV, Part One,* New York Shakespeare Festival (NYSF), Delacorte Theatre, New York City, 1981.

She Stoops to Conquer, Studio Arena Theatre, Buffalo, NY, 1982-83.

Grandfather, *The Transfiguration of Benno Blimpie,* Playwrights Horizons Theatre, New York City, 1983.

Paradise Lost, Mirror Repertory Company, Real Theatre/Theatre at St. Peter's Church, New York City, 1983-84.

Rain, Mirror Repertory Company, Real Theatre/Theatre at St. Peter's Church, 1983-84.

The Inheritors, Mirror Repertory Company, Real Theatre/Theatre at St. Peter's Church, 1983-84.

Bishop of Ely, Erpingham, and Governor of Harfleur, *Henry V,* NYSF, Delacorte Theatre, 1984.

The Madwoman of Chaillot, Mirror Repertory Company, Theatre at St. Peter's Church, 1985.

Vivat! Vivat Regina!, Mirror Repertory Company, Theatre at St. Peter's Church, 1985.

Clarence, Mirror Repertory Company, Theatre at St. Peter's Church, 1985.

Children of the Sun, Mirror Repertory Company, Theatre at St. Peter's Church, 1985-86.

The Time of Your Life, Mirror Repertory Company, Theatre at St. Peter's Church, 1985-86.

The Circle, Mirror Repertory Company, Theatre at St. Peter's Church, 1986.

Sergei and Don, *Highest Standard of Living,* Playwrights Horizons Theatre, 1986.

Sarcophagus, Yale Repertory Theatre, New Haven, CT, 1987.

Dinner at Eight, Long Wharf Theatre, New Haven, 1988.

Fathers and Sons, Long Wharf Theatre, 1988.

Cymbeline, NYSF, Public/Newman Theatre, New York City, then London, England, 1989.

The Crucible, Long Wharf Theatre, 1989.

A Flea in Her Ear, Long Wharf Theatre, 1989.

Hamlet, Public Theatre, 1990.

The Sea Gull, Alliance Theatre, Atlanta, GA, 1991.

Also appeared in *Legend of Lovers* (Broadway debut), 1951. Appeared as Pfc. Bernstein, *Fragile Fox,* New York City, 1954; *He Who Gets Slapped,* Hartford Stage Company, Hartford, CT; *The Diary of Anne Frank,* American Stage Company, Teaneck, NJ; *King Lear* and *Six Characters in Search of an Author,* American Conservatory Theatre, Pittsburgh, PA; *The Fantasticks,* PAF Playhouse; *Juno and the Paycock, The Good Doctor,* Rutgers University, New Brunswick, NJ; *The Cold Wind and the Warm, Kipling,* and *The Eagle Has Two Heads,* New York City. Appeared in productions for the New Jersey Shakespeare Festival, Madison, NY, 1983-84 and 1987; Mirror Repertory Company, The Real Theatre at St. Peter's Church, 1983-84 and 1985-86.

FILM APPEARANCES

Rosencrantz, *Hamlet,* Warner Brothers, 1964.

Doctor, *The Chosen,* Metro-Goldwyn-Mayer (MGM), 1981.

Eddie's father, *Diner,* MGM/United Artists, 1982.

Banker Williams, *Playing for Keeps,* Universal, 1986.

Also appeared in *The Borgia Stick,* Universal, and *The Pursuit of Happiness.*

TELEVISION APPEARANCES

Appeared in *I Cover Times Square* (television debut), 1950; *Nurse,* NBC; *The Winter's Tale,* PBS; *King Lear,* PBS.

TELEVISION APPEARANCES; EPISODIC

Appeared in *As the World Turns,* NBC; *The Doctors,* ABC; *The Guiding Light,* CBS; *Loving,* ABC; and *Ryan's Hope,* ABC. Also appeared in *Studio One, Robert Montgomery Presents, Danger, Omnibus, The Web, Hallmark Hall of Fame, Suspense, Decoy,* and *The Big Story.*

* * *

FOXX, Redd 1922-1991

PERSONAL: Original name, John Elroy Sanford; born December 9, 1922, in St. Louis, MO; died of a heart attack, October 11, 1991, in Los Angeles, CA; son of Fred (an electrician) and Mary Alma (a minister; maiden name, Hughes) Sanford; married Evelyn Killibrew (divorced, 1951); married Betty Jean Harris (a singer), 1956 (divorced, 1976); married Yunchi Chung, 1978 (divorced, 1982); married Ka Ha Cho, July, 1991; children: (first marriage) Debraca (stepdaughter). *Education:* Attended public schools in Chicago, IL.

CAREER: Actor and comedian. Recording artist with Dooto Records, beginning in 1955, and Loma Records; owner of a nightclub in Hollywood, CA, a cosmetics factory, and a beauty salon.

AWARDS, HONORS: Golden Globe Award, best actor in a musical or comedy series, Hollywood Foreign Press Association, 1973, and Emmy Award nominations, outstanding continued performance by an actor in a leading role in a comedy series, 1971, 1972, and best lead actor in a comedy series, 1973, all for *Sanford and Son.*

CREDITS:

TELEVISION APPEARANCES; SERIES

Fred Sanford, *Sanford and Son,* NBC, 1972-77.
Host, *The Redd Foxx Comedy Hour,* ABC, 1977-78.
Fred Sanford, *Sanford,* NBC, 1980-81.
Al Hughes, *The Redd Foxx Show,* ABC, 1986.
Alexander Royal, *The Royal Family,* CBS, 1991.

TELEVISION APPEARANCES; SPECIALS

. . . And Beautiful, syndicated, 1969.
The Bob Hope Show, NBC, 1973.
Keep U.S. Beautiful, NBC, 1973.
The Rowan and Martin Special, NBC, 1973.
Show Business Salute to Milton Berle, NBC, 1973.
Cotton Club '75, NBC, 1974.
Jack Benny's Second Farewell Show, NBC, 1974.
Bob Hope Special: Bob Hope's Christmas Party, NBC, 1975.
Lola, ABC, 1976.
Celebrity Challenge of the Sexes 1, CBS, 1977.
Bob Hope Special: Happy Birthday, Bob!, NBC, 1978.
Celebrity Challenge of the Sexes 4, CBS, 1979.
The 37th Annual Prime Time Emmy Awards, ABC, 1985.
Motown Merry Christmas, NBC, 1987.
A Laugh, a Tear, syndicated, 1990.
Motown Merry Christmas, syndicated, 1990.

TELEVISION APPEARANCES; EPISODIC

"A Time for Laughter," *ABC Stage '67,* ABC, 1967.
"Paul Shaffer: Viva Shaf Vegas," *Cinemax Comedy Experiment,* Cinemax, 1987.

Appeared on *Today,* 1964, and on episodes of *The Lucy Show, The Addams Family, Mr. Ed, Green Acres, The Name of the Game, The Johnny Carson Show, The Merv Griffin Show, Steve Allen, Mike Douglas,* and *The Flip Wilson Show.*

OTHER TELEVISION APPEARANCES

The Krofft Komedy Hour (pilot), ABC, 1978.
Woodrow "Buddy" Johnson, *My Buddy* (pilot; also see below), NBC, 1979.
Ivory Clay, *Ghost of a Chance,* CBS, 1987.

TELEVISION WORK; PILOTS

Executive producer, *My Buddy,* NBC, 1979.

FILM APPEARANCES

Uncle Bud, *Cotton Comes to Harlem,* United Artists, 1970.
Ben Chambers, *Norman . . .Is That You?,* Metro-Goldwyn-Mayer/United Artists, 1976.
Bennie Wilson, *Harlem Nights,* Paramount, 1989.

STAGE APPEARANCES

Musician with the Bon Bons, Chicago, IL, 1939-41; teamed with Slappy White, 1947-51; appeared at Carnegie Hall, New York City, 1975; performed in nightclubs in most major U.S. cities.

RECORDINGS:

ALBUMS

Involved in more than fifty recordings, including *Laff of the Party,* 1956, *On the Loose, Live—Las Vegas!, Bare Facts, Both Sides, Foxx-a-Delic, In a Nutshell, Matinee Idol,* and *Pass the Apple, Eve.*

WRITINGS:

(Editor with Norma Miller) *The Redd Foxx Encyclopedia of Black Humor,* Ritchie, 1977.

OBITUARIES AND OTHER SOURCES:

BOOKS

Contemporary Authors, Volume 89-92, Gale, 1980, pg. 174.

PERIODICALS

New York Times, February 6, 1972; June 19, 1976; July 30, 1982.

Variety, October 21, 1991, p. 86.*

* * *

FRANCISCUS, James 1934-1991

OBITUARY NOTICE—See index for *CTFT* sketch: Full name, James Grover Franciscus; born January 31, 1934, in Clayton, MO; died of emphysema, July 8, 1991, in Los Angeles, CA. Actor and producer. Franciscus first garnered critical recognition for playing the title role in the mid-1960s series *Mr. Novak,* about a secondary English instructor. Prior to *Mr. Novak,* Franciscus played Detective Jim Halloran in the ABC television series *Naked City* for fifteen years, beginning in 1948. Other television roles included the title characters in *Longstreet, Doc Elliot,* and the mid-1970s series *Hunter,* as well as appearances in *Wagon Train, Alfred Hitchcock Presents, The June Allyson Show, Ben Casey,* and *The Twilight Zone.* He also appeared in television movies, including *Jacqueline Bouvier Kennedy,* in which he portrayed John F. Kennedy. A cofounder of Omnibus Productions, Franciscus produced the films *Heidi, David Copperfield, Jane Eyre,* starring George C. Scott, *Kidnapped,* and *The Red Pony,* starring Henry Fonda. His film appearances included *Youngblood Hawke* in 1964, *Hell Boats* in 1968, *Cat O' Nine Tails* in 1971, *Puzzle* in 1977, *City on Fire* in 1979, and *The Courageous* in 1982. Toward the mid-1980s he became dissatisfied with the roles offered him and turned his energies to screenwriting. During the 1970s he founded the James Franciscus Celebrity Tennis Tournament as a fund-raiser to fight multiple sclerosis.

OBITUARIES AND OTHER SOURCES:

BOOKS

Who's Who in America, Volume 88, Marquis, 1988, p. 1026.

PERIODICALS

Variety, July 15, 1991, p. 54.

FRANKLIN, Richard 1948-

PERSONAL: Born July 15, 1948, in Melbourne, Australia; son of Rea Richard (an engineering company director) and Margaret Anne (a housewife; maiden name, Jacobson) Franklin; married Denise Elizabeth Baldwin (a teacher), December 15, 1972; children: Rebecca, David, Toby. *Education:* Attended Monash University (Melbourne, Australia), studied English, 1966, and University of Southern California, studied cinema, 1967-69. *Avocational interests:* Musical theater.

ADDRESSES: *Agent*—Larry Becsey, Chasen Agency, 910 North Canon, Beverly Hills, CA 90210.

CAREER: Director and producer.

MEMBER: Directors Guild of America.

AWARDS, HONORS: Grand Prix-Avoriaz, Best Foreign Film, Academy of Science Fiction (United States), for *Patrick;* Jury Prize-Avoriaz, Academy of Science Fiction, for *Link.*

CREDITS:

FILM DIRECTOR, EXCEPT WHERE INDICATED

Belinda, Aquarius, 1972.

Loveland, Illustrated, 1973.

(And producer) *The True Story of Eskimo Nell* (also see below), Filmways, 1975.

Fantasm, Filmways Australasian, 1976.

(And producer with Anthony I. Ginnane) *Patrick,* Filmways, 1979.

Producer (with Randal Kleiser), *The Blue Lagoon,* Columbia, 1980.

(And producer with Barbi Taylor) *Road Games,* Avco Embassy, 1981.

Psycho II, Universal, 1983.

Cloak and Dagger, Universal, 1984.

(And producer) *Link,* Cannon, 1986.

F/X 2: The Deadly Art of Illusion, Orion, 1991.

TELEVISION DIRECTOR; PILOTS

Beauty and the Beast, CBS, 1987.

A Fine Romance, ABC, 1988.

OTHER TELEVISION WORK

Director of *Homicide,* 1970.

WRITINGS:

SCREENPLAYS

The True Story of Eskimo Nell, Filmways, 1975.

OTHER

(With Wayne Levy) *Fred Ott Sneezes for Edison,* Methuen (Australia), 1976.

SIDELIGHTS: Richard Franklin began 8-mm filmmaking at age 10.

* * *

FRENCH, Antonia
See KUREISHI, Hanif

* * *

FRIEL, Brian 1929-

PERSONAL: Born Bernard Patrick Friel, January 9, 1929, in Omagh, County Tyrone, Northern Ireland; son of Patrick (a teacher) and Christina (MacLoone) Friel; married Anne Morrison, December 27, 1955 (one source says 1954); children: Paddy (daughter), Mary, Judy, Sally, David. *Education:* Attended St. Columb's College, Derry, 1941-46; St. Patrick's College, Maynooth, B.A., 1948; graduate study at St. Joseph's Teachers Training College (now St. Joseph's College of Education), Belfast, 1949-50.

ADDRESSES: Office—Drumaweir House, Greencastle, County Donegal, Ireland. *Agent*—Jack Tantleff, 375 Greenwich St., No. 700, New York, NY 10013; Curtis Brown, 162-168 Regent St., London W1R 5TB, England.

CAREER: Playwright. Worked as a primary and post-primary schoolteacher in Northern Ireland, 1950-60; Tyrone Guthrie Theatre, Minneapolis, MN, guest, 1963; Field Day (theater company), Derry, co-founder, 1980. Member of Irish Senate.

MEMBER: National Association of Irish Artists, Irish Academy of Letters, Aosdana.

AWARDS, HONORS: Arts Council grant, 1963; Macaulay fellow, Irish Arts Council, 1965; Antoinette Perry Award nomination, best play, 1966, for *Philadelphia, Here I Come!,* for which the author was also named most promising new Broadway playwright by *Variety* poll of New York drama critics; Antoinette Perry Award nomination, best dramatic play, 1969, for *Lovers;* D.Litt., Rosary College, Chicago, IL, 1974; Christopher Ewart-Biggs Memorial Prize, British Theatre Association Award, and *Plays and Players* Award, best new play, all 1981, for *Translations;* D.Litt., National University of Ireland, 1983, and New University of Ulster, 1986; London *Evening Standard* Drama Award, best play, 1988, and New York Drama Critics' Circle Award, best foreign play, 1989, both for *Aristocrats;* Lucille Lortel Award, outstanding play, 1991, for *Aristocrats; Evening Standard* Drama Award, best play, 1991, Laurence Olivier Award, best play, 1991, and Antoinette Perry Award, best play, 1992, all for *Dancing at Lughnasa.*

WRITINGS:

PLAYS

A Sort of Freedom, produced by BBC-Radio, 1958.

To This Hard House, produced by BBC-Radio, 1958.

The Francophile, produced at Group Theatre, Belfast, Northern Ireland, c. 1959, then produced as *The Doubtful Paradise,* Belfast, 1960.

The Enemy Within (three-act), produced at Abbey Theatre, Dublin, Ireland, 1962, published by Proscenium, 1975.

The Blind Mice, produced at Eblana Theatre, Dublin, 1963.

Philadelphia, Here I Come! (also see below), first produced at Dublin Theatre Festival, Gaiety Theatre, Dublin, 1964, then Helen Hayes Theatre, New York City, 1966, later toured U.S. cities, 1966-67, published by Faber, 1965, Farrar, Straus, 1966.

The Loves of Cass McGuire, first produced at Helen Hayes Theatre, 1966, published by Farrar, Straus, 1967.

Lovers (two one-acts, "Winners" and "Losers"), first produced at Gate Theatre, Dublin, 1967, then Vivian Beaumont Theatre, later Music Box Theatre, both New York City, 1968, published by Farrar, Straus, 1968.

Crystal and Fox (also see below), first produced at Gaiety Theatre, 1968, then Mark Taper Forum, Los Angeles, CA, c. 1970, later McAlpin Rooftop Theatre, New York City, c. 1973.

The Mundy Scheme (also see below), first produced at Olympia Theatre, Dublin, 1969, then Royale Theatre, New York City, 1969.

Crystal and Fox [and] *The Mundy Scheme,* published by Farrar, Straus, 1970.

The Gentle Island (two-act), first produced at Olympia Theatre, 1971, then Lyric Theatre, Belfast, 1972, published by Davis-Poynter, 1973.

The Freedom of the City (two-act), first produced at Abbey Theatre, 1972, then Goodman Theatre Center, Chicago, IL, 1973-74, later Alvin Theatre, New York City, 1974, published by Samuel French, 1974.

Volunteers, first produced at Abbey Theatre, 1975, published by Faber, 1979.

Living Quarters, first produced at Abbey Theatre, 1977, published by Faber, 1978.

The Faith Healer, produced at Longacre Theatre, New York City, 1979, then Royal Court Theatre, London, 1992, published by Faber, 1980.

Aristocrats (three-act), produced in Dublin, 1979, published by Gallery Press, 1980.

Translations, produced in Derry, 1980, then Manhattan Theatre Club, New York City, 1981, published by Faber, 1981.

(Translator) *Anton Chekhov's "Three Sisters,"* produced in Derry, 1981, published by Gallery Books, 1981.

The Communication Cord, produced in Derry, 1982, then ACT/A Contemporary Theatre, Seattle, WA, 1984-85, published by Faber, 1983.

Selected Plays of Brian Friel, published by Faber, 1984, Catholic University Press, 1986.

(Adapter) *Fathers and Sons* (based on a novel by Ivan Turgenev), first produced at National Theatre, London, 1987, then Long Wharf Theatre, New Haven, CT, 1988.

Dancing at Lughnasa, produced at Plymouth Theatre, London, c. 1990, then Plymouth Theatre, New York, 1991.

Also author of *American Welcome,* produced in New York City, 1980, published in *The Best Short Plays of 1981,* Chilton, 1981. Other plays include *Making History,* produced in London, 1988. Author of plays for British and Irish radio and television.

OTHER WRITINGS

A Saucer of Larks (stories), Doubleday, 1962.

The Gold in the Sea (stories), Doubleday, 1966.

Selected Stories, Gallery Books, 1979.

The Diviner: Brian Friel's Best Short Stories, Devin, 1983.

(Editor) Charles McGlinchey, *The Last of the Name,* Blackstaff Press, 1986.

Author of screen adaptation of his play *Philadelphia, Here I Come!,* c. 1970. Also contributor of stories to periodicals, including *New Yorker.*

ADAPTATIONS:

The Loves of Cass McGuire was adapted for television and produced in Dublin.

OTHER SOURCES:

BOOKS

Contemporary Authors New Revisions Series, Volume 33, Gale, 1991, pp. 153-154.

Contemporary Literary Criticism, Gale, Volume 5, 1976, Volume 42, 1987.

Dantanus, Ulf, *Brian Friel: The Growth of an Irish Dramatist,* Faber, 1987.

Dictionary of Literary Biography, Volume 13: *British Dramatists since World War II,* Gale, 1982.

Maxwell, D. E. S., *Brian Friel,* Bucknell University Press, 1973.

PERIODICALS

New York Times, April 30, 1989, p. 7.

* * *

FURST, Anton 1944(?)-1991

OBITUARY NOTICE—See index for *CTFT* sketch: Full name, Anthony Francis Furst; born c. 1944; committed suicide, November 24, 1991, in Los Angeles, CA. Special effects designer. Furst founded the London-based special effects firm, Holoco, which designed and staged holograph shows including "The Light Fantastic," for a tour of the rock group The Who. Furst was one of the leaders in the introduction of laser special effects to motion pictures and his firm, Holoco, went on to design effects for such films as *Star Wars, Alien, Superman, Outland,* and *Moonraker.* Broadening his expertise to include production design, Furst served as art director for the films *Full Metal Jacket, The Company of Wolves, Awakenings,* and *Batman,* the latter for which he received an Academy Award in 1990 with associate set-decorator, Peter Young. Furst also employed his creative talents outside the film industry with the design of the New York restaurant Planet Hollywood.

OBITUARIES AND OTHER SOURCES:

PERIODICALS

Variety, December 2, 1991, p. 101.

G

GABLE, June 1945-

PERSONAL: Born June 5, 1945, in Brooklyn, NY; daughter of Joseph and Shirl Galup. *Education:* Carnegie-Mellon University, B.F.A., drama, 1968.

ADDRESSES: Office—P.O. Box 5617, Beverly Hills, CA 90210. *Agent*—Agency for the Performing Arts, 888 Seventh Ave., New York, NY 10019.

CAREER: Actress, dancer, director, singer, and writer. Certified yoga teacher.

MEMBER: Actors Equity Association, Screen Actors Guild, American Federation of Television and Radio Artists, Himalayan Institute.

AWARDS, HONORS: Antoinette Perry Award nomination, best supporting actress in a musical play, 1974, for *Candide;* Obie Award, *Village Voice,* 1976, for *Comedy of Errors.*

CREDITS:

STAGE APPEARANCES

Beatnik witch, *MacBird!,* Village Gate Theatre, New York City, 1967, then Circle in the Square, New York City, 1969.

Alice Whitfield, *Jacques Brel Is Alive and Well and Living in Paris* (also see below), Village Gate Theatre, 1968-70.

Member of chorus of women, *Mod Donna,* New York Shakespeare Festival (NYSF), Public Theatre, New York City, 1969-70.

Gloria, *In Three Zones,* Charles Playhouse, Boston, MA, 1970.

Penny, *A Day in the Life of Just About Everyone,* Bijou Theatre, New York City, 1971.

Shorty, *Wanted,* Cherry Lane Theatre, New York City, 1972.

Lucy Lockit, *The Beggar's Opera,* Chelsea Theatre Center, then McAlpin Rooftop Theatre, New York City, 1972.

Alicia, *Lady Audley's Secret* (also see below), Eastside Playhouse, New York City, 1972.

Standby, *Nash at Nine* (revue), Helen Hayes Theatre, New York City, 1973.

Lois Lane, *Kiss Me Kate,* Playhouse in the Park, Cincinnati, OH, 1973.

Old woman, *Candide,* Chelsea Theatre, Brooklyn, NY, 1973, then Broadway Theatre, New York City, 1974.

Googie Gomez, *The Ritz,* Longacre Theatre, New York City, 1975.

Adriana, *The Comedy of Errors,* NYSF, Delacorte Theatre, New York City, 1975.

Mahagonny, Yale Repertory Theatre, New Haven, CT, 1978-79.

Tamara, *Chinchilla,* Marymount Manhattan Theatre, New York City, 1979.

Elaine, *Star Treatment,* Lion Theatre, New York City, 1980.

Teri Sterling, *Coming Attractions,* Playwrights Horizons Theatre, New York City, 1980-81.

Bette, *A History of the American Film,* Mark Taper Forum, Los Angeles, 1981-82.

Snooks Keene, *Moose Murders,* Eugene O'Neill Theatre, New York City, 1983.

Yvette Guilbert, Countess Adele Tapie de Celeyran, Something Fancy, and Nini Leg-in-the-Air, *Times and Appetites of Toulouse-Lautrec,* American Place Theatre, New York City, 1985.

Maria, *Twelfth Night; or, What You Will,* Hartford Stage Company, Hartford, CT, 1985-86.

Wilma, *The Perfect Party,* Playwrights Horizons Theatre, 1986.

Karla Mendez, *The Art of War,* New Theatre of Brooklyn, Brooklyn, NY, 1987.

No Way to Treat a Lady, Hudson Guild Theatre, New York City, 1987.
Magda La Selva, *Magda and Callas,* Philadelphia Festival Theatre, Philadelphia, PA, 1987-88.
Carnival, Cleveland Playhouse, Cleveland, OH, 1988-89.

Also appeared in *Shoe Palace Murray.*

MAJOR TOURS

Alice Whitfield, *Jacques Brel Is Alive and Well and Living in Paris,* London, England, 1969.
Alicia, *Lady Audley's Secret,* U.S. cities, 1971-72.
Sonia Walsk, *They're Playing Our Song,* U.S. cities, 1981-82.
Retta, *Pump Boys and Dinettes,* U.S. cities, 1983-84.

TELEVISION APPEARANCES; SERIES

Detective Battista, *Barney Miller,* ABC, 1976-77.
Laugh-In, NBC, 1977-78.
Sha Na Na, syndicated, 1978-81.

TELEVISION APPEARANCES; PILOTS

Shirley Tinker, *Newman's Drugstore,* NBC, 1976.
Gail, *The Bay City Amusement Company,* NBC, 1977.

TELEVISION APPEARANCES; EPISODIC

Appeared as Lucy, *Beggar's Opera,* 1976; and on episodes of *The Tonight Show* and *Merv Griffin,* 1980, *It's All in Your Head,* and *Camera Three,* CBS.

FILM APPEARANCES

Realtor, *She-Devil,* Orion, 1989.
Luba, *Brenda Starr,* Triumph, 1992.*

* * *

GARFIELD, Allen 1939-

PERSONAL: Born Allen Goorwitz, November 22, 1939, in Newark, NJ; has made occasional appearances under real name since 1978; son of Philip and Alice (Lavroff) Goorwitz. *Education:* Attended Upsala College; graduated from Anthony Mannino Studio, New York City, 1965; studied with Lee Strasberg, Harold Clurman, and Elia Kazan.

ADDRESSES: Office—c/o Burton Moss Agency, 113 North San Vincente Blvd., Beverly Hills, CA 90211.

CAREER: Actor. Began career as a journalist, moving from copyboy to sports reporter for the *Newark Star Ledger,* and then staff writer for Australia's *Sunday Morning Herald;* film debut in *Greetings,* 1967; broadway debut in *Inquest,* Music Box Theatre, 1970. The Actors Shelter, founder and teacher.

MEMBER: Actors Studio.

AWARDS, HONORS: Numerous West Coast theater awards for roles in *Nuts, A View from the Bridge, The Transfiguration of Benno Blimpie,* and . . . *Are You Now, or Have You Ever Been. . . .*

CREDITS:

FILM APPEARANCES

Martin Axborough, *March of the Spring Hare* (also known as *Roommates*), Pantages, 1969.
Elias, Jr., *Putney Swope,* Cinema V Distributing, 1969.
Dress shop proprietor, *The Owl and the Pussycat,* Columbia, 1970.
Joe Banner, *Hi, Mom!* (also known as *Confessions of a Peeping John*), SIGMA III, 1970.
Benjy, *The Organization,* United Artists, 1971.
Herby Moss, *You've Got to Walk It Like You Talk It or You'll Lose That Beat,* J.E.R., 1971.
Man on cross, *Bananas,* United Artists, 1971.
Stutter, *Believe In Me,* Metro-Goldwyn-Mayer, 1971.
Norman, *Taking Off,* Universal, 1971.
Vic, *Get to Know Your Rabbit,* Warner Brothers, 1972.
Taxi driver, *Top of the Heap,* Fanfare, 1972.
Howard Klein, *The Candidate,* Warner Brothers, 1972.
Vincent J. Palmer, *Slither,* Metro-Goldwyn-Mayer, 1973.
Rizzo, *Busting,* United Artists, 1974.
Bernie Moran, *The Conversation,* Paramount, 1974.
Kruger, *The Front Page,* Universal, 1974.
Barnett, *Nashville,* Paramount, 1975.
The Commitment, Borden, 1976.
Louis B. Mayer, *Gable and Lombard,* Universal, 1976.
Harry Fishbine, *Mother, Jugs and Speed,* Twentieth Century-Fox, 1976.
Manny Bloom, *Skateboard,* Universal, 1978.
(Under name Allen Goorwitz) Vinnie Costa, *The Brink's Job,* Universal, 1978.
(Under name Allen Goorwitz) Sam, *The Stunt Man,* Twentieth Century-Fox, 1980.
(Under name Allen Goorwitz) Cal Van Damp, *One-Trick Pony,* Warner Brothers, 1980.
(Under name Allen Goorwitz) Howard McDermotte, *Continental Divide,* Universal, 1981.
(Under name Allen Goorwitz) Restaurant owner, *One from the Heart,* Columbia, 1982.
Juicy Brucey, *Deadhead Miles,* Paramount, 1982.
(Under name Allen Goorwitz) Kurr, *The Black Stallion Returns,* United Artists, 1983.
(Under name Allen Goorwitz) Gordon, *The State of Things,* Artificial Eye, 1983.
(Under name Allen Goorwitz) Max Wolfe, *Get Crazy,* Embassy, 1983.
Abbadabba Berman, *The Cotton Club,* Orion, 1984.
Rosenberg, *Teachers,* United Artists, 1984.
Phil Hanner, *Irreconcilable Differences,* Warner Brothers, 1984.

Mr. Mosol, *Desert Bloom,* Columbia, 1986.
Harold Lutz, *Beverly Hills Cop II,* Paramount, 1987.
Ben Sydney, *Chief Zabu,* IFM, 1988.
Greenberg, *Let It Ride,* Paramount, 1989.
Zachary Willard, *Night Visitor* (also known as *Never Cry Devil*), Metro-Goldwyn-Mayer/United Artists, 1990.
Reporter, *Dick Tracy,* Touchstone/Buena Vista, 1990.
Bernie, *Until the End of the World,* Warner Brothers, 1991.
Harrison Farnsworth IV, *Club Fed,* Prism Entertainment, 1991.

Has also appeared in *Greetings,* 1967, *Cry Uncle,* 1973, *The Good, the Bad, and the Beautiful,* 1975, and *Paco,* 1976.

TELEVISION APPEARANCES; MOVIES

Brewster, *Footsteps,* CBS, 1972.
Mario Portello, *The Marcus-Nelson Murders,* CBS, 1973.
Leo Ritchie, *The Virginia Hill Story,* NBC, 1974.
Lieutenant Ralph Fogerty, *The Million Dollar Rip-Off,* NBC, 1976.
Herbie Stoltz, *Nowhere to Run,* NBC, 1978.
Damon Runyon, *Ring of Passion,* NBC, 1978.
(Under name Allen Goorwitz) Dr. Arthur Abrams, *Leave 'em Laughing,* CBS, 1981.
District Attorney Randall Hale, *Killer in the Mirror,* NBC, 1986.
Adam Gore, *Sins* (mini-series) CBS, 1986.

Also appeared as the principal in *Growing Pains: Number One,* 1976, *Sketches of a Strangler,* 1978, and as Uncle Howie in *You Ruined My Life,* 1987.

TELEVISION APPEARANCES; EPISODIC

"Welcome to Our City," *Mod Squad,* ABC, 1971.
"The Whimper of Whipped Dogs," *Young Lawyers,* ABC, 1971.
"A Little Plot in Tranquil Valley," *McCloud,* NBC, 1972.
"A Date with Death," *Banyon,* NBC, 1972.
"Let's Get Away from It Almost," *Bob Newhart Show,* CBS, 1973.
Love, American Style, ABC, 1973.
"The Unwritten Law," *Adam's Rib,* ABC, 1973.
"The Double-Edged Sword," *Ironside,* NBC, 1973.
"Incident at Vichy," *Conflicts,* PBS, 1973.
Judgment: The Trial of Ethel and Julius Rosenberg (special), ABC, 1974.
Rhoda, CBS, 1975.
"The Fires of Ignorance," *Gunsmoke,* CBS, 1975.
"But Who Will Bless Thy Daughter, Norah?," *Kate McShane,* CBS, 1975.
"In Again, Out Again," *McCoy,* NBC, 1976.
"Crime and Punishment," *Taxi,* NBC, 1982.
"The Deal," *Tales from the Darkside,* syndicated, 1988.

TELEVISION APPEARANCES; PILOTS

Sonny Waller, *Sonny Boy,* CBS, 1974.
Professor, *Serpico: The Deadly Game,* NBC, 1976.
"Lottery," *Lottery,* ABC, 1983.
Mitchell Franklin, *Never Again,* ABC, 1984.

TELEVISION APPEARANCES; SERIES

Ben Rutledge, *Taxi,* ABC, 1978-82, NBC, 1982-83.
Arnie, *The Boys,* Showtime, 1989.

STAGE APPEARANCES

Witness (double-bill with *Sweet Eros*), Gramercy Arts Theatre, 1968.
(Broadway debut) Clerk, *Inquest,* Music Box Theatre, New York City, 1970.

Also appeared in *Dream of a Blacklisted Actor, Nuts, A View from the Bridge, The Transfiguration of Benno Blimpie,* and *. . . Are You Now, or Have You Ever Been. . . .**

* * *

GARR, Teri 1949(?)-

PERSONAL: Full name, Teri Ann Garr; born December 11, 1949 (some sources say 1952), in Los Angeles, CA (some sources say Lakewood, OH); daughter of Eddie (a vaudeville performer) and Phyllis (a dancer and model; maiden name, Lind) Garr. *Education:* Studied speech and drama at California State University, Northridge.

ADDRESSES: Office—Bill Treusch Associates, 853 Seventh Ave., No. 9A, New York, NY 10019. *Agent*—Rick Nicita, Creative Artists Agency, 1888 Century Park E., Suite 1400, Los Angeles, CA 90067. *Publicist*—Pat Kingsley, PMK Public Relations, Inc., 955 South Camillo Dr., No. 200, Los Angeles, CA 90048.

CAREER: Actress.

MEMBER: Screen Actors Guild, American Federation of Television and Radio Artists.

AWARDS, HONORS: Academy Award nomination, best supporting actress, 1982, for *Tootsie.*

CREDITS:

FILM APPEARANCES

For Pete's Sake!, Worldwide, 1966.
Testy True, *Head,* Columbia, 1968.
Terri, *Maryjane,* American International, 1968.
Changes, Cinerama, 1969.
Tourist's wife, *The Moonshine War,* Metro-Goldwyn-Mayer (MGM), 1970.
Amy, *The Conversation,* Paramount, 1974.
Inga, *Young Frankenstein,* Twentieth Century-Fox, 1974.

Fluffy Peters, *Won Ton Ton, the Dog Who Saved Hollywood,* Paramount, 1976.
Ronnie Neary, *Close Encounters of the Third Kind,* Columbia, 1977.
Bobbie Landers, *Oh, God!,* Warner Brothers, 1977.
Alec's mother, *The Black Stallion,* United Artists (UA), 1979.
Ericka, *Honky Tonk Freeway,* Universal/Anchor, 1981.
Arlene, *The Escape Artist,* Orion/Warner Brothers, 1982.
Frannie, *One from the Heart,* Columbia, 1982.
Sandy, *Tootsie,* Columbia, 1982.
Alec's mother, *The Black Stallion Returns,* MGM/UA, 1983.
Caroline, *Mr. Mom* (also known as *Mr. Mum*), Twentieth Century-Fox, 1983.
Veronica, *The Sting II,* Universal, 1983.
Wendy, *Firstborn,* Paramount, 1984.
Julie, *After Hours,* Warner Brothers, 1985.
Jean Briggs, *Miracles,* Orion, 1987.
Louise, *Full Moon in Blue Water,* Trans World, 1988.
Sunny Cannald, *Out Cold,* Hemdale, 1988.
Pam Trotter, *Let It Ride,* Paramount, 1989.
Carolyn Simpson, *Short Time,* Twentieth Century-Fox, 1990.

Played Margaret Lightman, *Witches' Brew,* 1978; appeared in *Stiffs,* 1988; played Kay Harris, *Waiting for the Light,* 1990; also appeared in *Lies* and *Viva Las Vegas.*

TELEVISION APPEARANCES; SERIES

Dancer, *Shindig,* ABC, 1965-66.
The Ken Berry "Wow" Show, ABC, 1972.
Mabel, *Banyon,* NBC, 1972-73.
The Burns and Schreiber Comedy Hour, ABC, 1973.
Amber, *The Girl with Something Extra,* NBC, 1973-74.
The Sonny and Cher Comedy Hour, CBS, 1973-74.
The Sonny Comedy Review, ABC, 1974.

Appeared on *Cher,* 1975-76.

TELEVISION APPEARANCES; MOVIES

Rita Wusinski, *Law and Order,* NBC, 1976.
Kelli Fisher, *Doctor Franken* (also known as *The Franken Project*), NBC, 1980.
Amy McCleary, *Prime Suspect* (also known as *Cry of Innocence*), CBS, 1982.
Mary Hawley, *John Steinbeck's "The Winter of Our Discontent,"* CBS, 1983.
Hannah Winter, *To Catch a King,* HBO, 1984.
Sally Bierston, *Intimate Strangers,* CBS, 1986.
Jill, *Mother Goose Rock 'n' Rhyme,* Disney, 1990.
Randi Thompson, *Stranger in the Family* (also known as *My Son's Memories*), ABC, 1991.
Susan Woolley, *Deliver Them from Evil: The Taking of Alta View,* CBS, 1992.

Appeared in *The History of White People in America, Part I,* 1985.

TELEVISION APPEARANCES; SPECIALS

"Death at Dinner," *The Booth,* PBS, 1985.
Deja Vu, syndicated, 1985.
The Night of 100 Stars II (also see below), ABC, 1985.
The 58th Annual Academy Awards Presentation, ABC, 1986.
David Letterman's 2nd Annual Holiday Film Festival, NBC, 1986.
David Letterman's Old-Fashioned Christmas, NBC, 1987.
Hostess, *Jackie Gleason: The Great One* (also known as *How Sweet It Is: A Wake for Jackie Gleason*), CBS, 1988.
Memories Then and Now, CBS, 1988.
Denise, *Good and Evil,* ABC, 1991.
Hostess, *Celebration of Country,* ABC, 1991.
Hostess, *Love Laughs,* Lifetime, 1991.
An American Saturday Night, ABC, 1991.
The Best of Disney: Fifty Years of Magic, ABC, 1991.
Math: Who Needs It?, PBS, 1991.
The Movie Awards, CBS, 1991.
TGIF Comedy Preview, ABC, 1991.
David Steinberg's Biased and Insensitive Review of the Year, Arts and Entertainment, 1992.

TELEVISION APPEARANCES; EPISODIC

Roberta Lincoln, "Assignment: Earth," *Star Trek,* NBC, 1968.
Helen Schaefer, "Pack of Lies," *Hallmark Hall of Fame,* CBS, 1987.
Robin Stone, "Drive, She Said," *Trying Times,* PBS, 1987.
"Martin Mull Live! From North Ridgeville," *HBO Comedy Hour,* HBO, 1987.
"Paul Reiser: Out on a Whim," *On Location,* HBO, 1987.
Helen Eagles, "Teri Garr in Flapjack Floozie," *Cinemax Comedy Experiment,* Cinemax, 1988.
"The Trap" (also known as "Loved to Death" and "Carrion Death"), *Tales from the Crypt,* HBO, 1991.
"A Quiet Little Neighborhood, a Perfect Little Murder" (also known as "Honey, Let's Kill the Neighbors"), *The Don and Judy Show,* NBC, 1991.

Also appeared in "The Tale of the Frog Prince," *Faerie Tale Theatre,* Showtime, and in episodes of *McCloud* and *Star Trek.*

TELEVISION APPEARANCES; MINI-SERIES

Talon Kensington, *Fresno,* CBS, 1986.

STAGE APPEARANCES

Helen, *One Crack Out,* Marymount Manhattan Theatre, New York City, 1978.

Billie Moore, *Broadway,* Wilbur Theatre, Boston, MA, 1978.

"The Good Parts," *Second Annual New Plays Festival,* Actors Studio, New York City, 1979.

Ladyhouse Blues, Queens Theatre, New York City, 1979.

Night of 100 Stars II, Radio City Music Hall, New York City, 1985.

"Play," and Mommy, "The American Dream," *50/60 Vision: Plays and Playwrights That Changed the Theatre! Thirteen Plays in Repertory,* Center Theatre Group, Mark Taper Forum, Los Angeles, 1989-90.

Toured as a dancer in *West Side Story,* U.S. cities; also danced with the San Francisco Ballet and the Los Angeles Ballet.

RECORDINGS:

VIDEOS

Appeared on *Mr. Mike's Mondo Video,* 1979.

OTHER SOURCES:

BOOKS

Newsmakers, 1988 cumulation, Gale, 1989.

PERIODICALS

Cosmopolitan, July, 1983, p. 72.
Glamour, September, 1983, p. 346.
Interview, May, 1990, p. 32.
People, February 21, 1983, p. 43; October 28, 1991, p. 89.
Playboy, May, 1988, p. 114.
Redbook, August, 1990, p. 66.*

* * *

GELBART, Larry 1928-
(Francis Burns)

PERSONAL: Full name, Larry Simon Gelbart; born February 25, 1928, in Chicago, IL; son of Harry (a barber) and Frieda (Sturner) Gelbart; married Patricia Marshall (a singer and actress), November 25, 1956; children: Cathy, Gary, Paul, Adam, Becky. *Education:* Attended John Marshall High School, Chicago, IL, and Fairfax High School, Los Angeles, CA.

ADDRESSES: Office—807 North Alpine Dr., Beverly Hills, CA 90210. *Agent*—Louis Blau, Loeb & Loeb, 10100 Santa Monica Blvd., Suite 2200, Los Angeles, CA 90067.

CAREER: Writer and producer. *Military service:* U.S. Army, 1946-47.

MEMBER: International P.E.N., Writers Guild of America, Dramatists Guild, American Society of Composers, Authors, and Publishers, Directors Guild of America, Authors League, Motion Picture Academy of Arts and Sciences (member of board of governors), Writers Guild of Great Britain.

AWARDS, HONORS: Emmy Award nominations, best comedy writing, 1955, 1956, and 1957, all for *Caesar's Hour;* Emmy Award nomination, best writing of a single musical or variety program, 1958, for *Sid Caesar's Chevy Show;* Sylvania Award, 1958, for specials starring Art Carney; Emmy Award nomination, outstanding writing achievement in a comedy or variety show, 1963, for *The Danny Kaye Show;* Antoinette Perry Award (with Burt Shevelove), best musical play, 1963, for *A Funny Thing Happened on the Way to the Forum;* Emmy Award nomination, outstanding writing achievement in comedy, 1972, Writers Guild of America Awards, 1972, both for *M*A*S*H;* Emmy Award nomination, best writing in comedy-variety, variety, or music, 1973, for *Barbra Streisand . . .and Other Musical Instruments;* Emmy Award, outstanding comedy series, 1973, Writers Guild of America Awards, 1974, Emmy Award nominations, outstanding comedy series, 1974 and 1975, outstanding writing achievement in comedy, 1975, George Foster Peabody Award, 1975, and Humanitas Award, all for *M*A*S*H;* Academy Award nomination, best screenplay based on material from another medium, 1977, Edgar Allan Poe Award, Mystery Writers of America, and Writers Guild Award, all for *Oh, God!;* Writers Guild Award and Christopher Award, both for *Movie, Movie;* Academy Award nomination, best screenplay written directly for the screen, 1982, Los Angeles Film Critics Award, New York Film Critics Award, and National Society of Film Critics Award, all for *Tootsie;* Emmy Award nomination, outstanding directing in a comedy series, 1983, for *AfterM*A*S*H;* Doctor of Letters, Union College, 1986; Drama Desk Award, best book of a musical, 1989, and Antoinette Perry Award, best book of a musical, 1990, both for *City of Angels.* Best New Musical citation, New York Drama Critics Circle, Outer Critics Circle Award, outstanding Broadway musical, Edgar Allan Poe Award, best mystery play, all 1990, all for *City of Angels.* Outer Critics Circle Award for contribution to comedy, 1990, for *City of Angels* and *Mastergate.* Lee Strasberg Award for Lifetime Achievement in the Arts and Sciences, 1990.

CREDITS:

TELEVISION WORK; SERIES

Producer (with Gene Reynolds), *M*A*S*H* (also see below), CBS, 1972-76.

Producer (with Gene Reynolds), *Roll Out!* (also see below), CBS, 1973-74.

Executive producer (with Gene Reynolds), *Karen* (also see below), ABC, 1975.

Creator and executive producer, *United States* (also see below), NBC, then A&E, 1980.
Developer, *AfterM*A*S*H* (also see below), CBS, 1983-84.

Developed *M*A*S*H* for television.

TELEVISION WORK; PILOTS

Producer (with Gene Reynolds), *If I Love You, Am I Trapped Forever?* (also see below), CBS, 1974.

TELEVISION APPEARANCES; SPECIALS

Producer (with Gregory Peck, Robert Wise, and Gene Allen), *The 57th Annual Academy Awards,* ABC, 1985.
Presenter, *The 58th Annual Academy Awards Presentation,* ABC, 1986.
*Memories of M*A*S*H,* CBS, 1991.

FILM WORK

Associate producer, *The Wrong Box,* Columbia, 1966.
Executive producer, *Blame It on Rio* (also see below), Twentieth Century-Fox, 1984.

WRITINGS:

TELEVISION SERIES

The All-Star Revue, NBC, 1950-53.
(With Neil Simon, Woody Allen, Mel Brooks, and Mel Tolkin) *Caesar's Hour,* NBC, 1955-57.
The Red Buttons Show, CBS, 1952-54, then NBC, 1954-55.
(With Hal Collins) *Honestly, Celeste!,* CBS, 1954.
The Patrice Munsel Show, ABC, 1954-62.
Caesar's Hour, NBC, c. 1955-57.
The Pat Boone Chevy Showroom, ABC, 1957-60.
The Danny Kaye Show, CBS, 1963.
The Marty Feldman Comedy Machine, ABC, 1972.
*M*A*S*H,* CBS, 1972-76.
Roll Out!, CBS, 1973-74.
Karen, ABC, 1975.
United States, NBC, then A&E, 1980.
*AfterM*A*S*H,* CBS, 1983-84.

TELEVISION PILOTS

Eddie (also known as *Bel Air Patrol*), CBS, 1971.
My Wives Jane, CBS, 1971.
If I Love You, Am I Trapped Forever?, CBS, 1974.
Riding High, NBC, 1977.

TELEVISION SPECIALS

(With Woody Allen) *The Sid Caesar Show,* NBC, 1958.
Sid Caesar's Chevy Show, NBC, c. 1958.
(With Sheldon Keller) *The Art Carney Show,* NBC, 1959.
The Rosalind Russell Show, NBC, 1959.
(With Sheldon Keller) *The Best of Anything,* NBC, 1960.
Four for Tonight (also known as *Star Parade*), NBC, 1960.
(With Woody Allen) *Hooray for Love,* CBS, 1960.
(With Gary Belkin) *The Chevrolet Golden Anniversary Show,* CBS, 1961.
Opening Tonight, CBS, 1962.
Judy Garland and Her Guests, Phil Silvers and Robert Goulet, CBS, 1963.
Barbra Streisand . . .and Other Musical Instruments, CBS, 1973.

SCREENPLAYS

(With Blake Edwards) *The Notorious Landlady* (based on a story by Margery Sharp), Columbia, 1962.
(With Carl Reiner) *The Thrill of It All* (based on a story by Reiner and Gelbart), Universal, 1963.
(With Burt Shevelove) *The Wrong Box* (based on a novel by Robert Louis Stevenson and Lloyd Osbourne), Columbia, 1966.
(With Norman Panama and Peter Barnes) *Not with My Wife, You Don't* (based on a story by Panama and Melvin Frank), Warner Brothers, 1966.
(With Luigi Magni) *The Chastity Belt* (also known as *On My Way to the Crusades, I Met a Girl Who . . .;* based on a story by Ugo Liberatore), Warner Brothers/Seven Arts, 1968.
(With Francesco Maselli, Luisa Montagnana, and Virgil C. Leone) *A Fine Pair* (based on a story by Montagnana), National General, 1969.
Oh, God! (based on a novel by Avery Corman), Warner Brothers, 1977.
(With Sheldon Keller) *Movie, Movie,* Warner Brothers, 1978.
(Under pseudonym Francis Burns) *Rough Cut,* Paramount, 1980.
Neighbors (based on a novel by Thomas Berger), Columbia, 1981.
(With Murray Schisgal) *Tootsie* (based on a story by Gelbart and Don McGuire), Columbia, 1982.
(With Charlie Peters) *Blame It on Rio* (based on screenplay by Claude Berri), Twentieth Century-Fox, 1984.

STAGE PLAYS

(With Bill Manhoff and Laurence Marks) *My L.A.,* Forum Theatre, Los Angeles, CA, 1948.
The Conquering Hero, produced at American National Theatre Academy, New York City, 1960.
(With Burt Shevelove) *A Funny Thing Happened on the Way to the Forum,* produced at Alvin Theatre, New York City, 1962, then Lunt-Fontanne Theatre, New York City, 1972, later toured U.S. cities, 1974 and 1980-87.
Sly Fox, produced at Broadhurst Theatre, New York City, 1976-77, then toured U.S. cities, 1978-81.

One, Two, Three, Four, Five, workshop production at Manhattan Theatre Club, New York City, 1987 and 1988.
Mastergate, produced at American Repertory Theatre, Cambridge, MA, then Criterion Center Theatre, New York City, 1989.
City of Angels, produced at Virginia Theatre, New York City, 1989.
(Co-author) *Jerome Robbins' Broadway,* produced at Imperial Theatre, New York City, 1989.

Other plays include *My L.A.,* 1950; *Jump,* produced in London, 1972; and *Power Failure.*

RADIO SERIES

Maxwell House Coffee Time with Danny Thomas, CBS, 1946.
Duffy's Tavern, NBC, 1946.
Command Performance, Armed Forces Radio Service, 1946-47.
The Jack Paar Show, CBS, 1949.
The Joan Davis Show, CBS, 1949.
The Bob Hope Show, NBC, 1949-52.

Also writer for *The Eddie Cantor Show,* 1946, and for *Jack Carson,* 1947-48.

OTHER SOURCES:

BOOKS

Contemporary Authors, Volume 73, Gale, 1978, pp. 234-235.
Laube, Abe, *Broadway's Greatest Musicals,* Funk, 1970.

PERIODICALS

New York Times, January 5, 1977; December 10, 1989, p. H5.
New York Times Magazine, October 8, 1989, pp. 53-56, 89-91.
Theatre Week, December 18, 1989, p. 14.

* * *

GIERASCH, Stefan 1926-

PERSONAL: Born February 5, 1926, in New York, NY.

CAREER: Actor. Member of company, Milwaukee Repertory Theatre, Milwaukee, WI, 1965-66, Trinity Square Repertory Company, Providence, RI, 1966-67, A.P.A., Phoenix, AZ, 1967-68, Studio Arena Theatre, Buffalo, NY, 1967-68, Long Wharf Theatre, New Haven, CT, 1971-72, and Los Angeles Theatre Center, Los Angeles, CA, 1987-91.

MEMBER: Actors Equity Association, Screen Actors Guild, Actors Studio.

CREDITS:

TELEVISION APPEARANCES; MINI-SERIES

Gannon, *Captains and the Kings,* NBC, 1976.
Niendorf, *Beggarman, Thief,* NBC, 1979.
Real estate agent, *The Winds of War,* ABC, 1983.
Trenor Park, *Dream West,* CBS, 1986.
Judge Watts, *Cruel Doubt,* NBC, 1992.

TELEVISION APPEARANCES; MOVIES

Carmedly, *This Is the West That Was,* NBC, 1974.
Mordecai Gur, *Victory at Entebbe,* ABC, 1976.
Al Davis, *Return to Earth,* ABC, 1976.
Axel Kalb, *Stunts Unlimited,* ABC, 1980.
Michael Curtiz, *My Wicked, Wicked Ways . . . The Legend of Errol Flynn,* CBS, 1985.
Otto Wilshke, *Incident at Dark River* (also known as *Dark River—A Father's Revenge* and *The Smell of Money*), TNT, 1989.

TELEVISION APPEARANCES; EPISODIC

Sideshow owner, "Lower Berth," *Tales from the Crypt,* HBO, 1990.

OTHER TELEVISION APPEARANCES

Dr. Nate Tishman, *Kate McShane* (pilot), CBS, 1975.
Dr. Sidney Gelson, *The Million Dollar Face* (pilot), NBC, 1981.
Shannon's Deal (pilot), NBC, 1989.
Professor Woodard and Joshua Collins, *Dark Shadows* (series), NBC, 1991.

Also appeared as Michael Skrobotov, *Enemies,* 1974; Robert F. Powell, *Hazard's People,* 1976; J. Powell Karbo, *A.E.S. Hudson Street* (series), 1978; Sam Purdy, *Big Bend Country,* 1981; and chef, *Gabe and Walker,* 1981.

FILM APPEARANCES

Billy, *The Young Don't Cry,* Columbia, 1957.
Stage Struck, Buena Vista, 1957.
Preacher, *The Hustler,* Twentieth Century-Fox, 1961.
Willy Herzallerliebst, *The Traveling Executioner,* Metro-Goldwyn-Mayer (MGM), 1970.
Del Que, *Jeremiah Johnson,* Warner Brothers, 1972.
Landlord, *The New Centurions* (also known as *Precinct 45: Los Angeles Police*), Columbia, 1972.
Fritz, *What's Up, Doc?,* Warner Brothers, 1972.
Mayor Jason Hobart, *High Plains Drifter,* Universal, 1973.
Sanitation foreman, *Claudine,* Twentieth Century-Fox, 1974.
Sergeant Danaher, *Cornbread, Earl and Me,* American International, 1975.

Robert Simon, *The Great Texas Dynamite Chase* (also known as *Dynamite Women*), New World Pictures, 1976.
Principal Morton, *Carrie,* United Artists (UA), 1976.
Johnson/Professor Schreiner, *Silver Streak,* Twentieth Century-Fox, 1976.
Lieutenant Jennings, *Blue Sunshine,* Cinema Shares, 1978.
Charlie Goodman, *The Champ,* MGM/UA, 1979.
Dimitros, Jerry Gross Organization, 1981.
Charlie, *Perfect,* Columbia, 1985.
Edgar De Witt, *Spellbinder,* MGM/UA, 1988.
Dr. Vogel, *Megaville,* Amazing Movies, 1990.

Also appeared as Mr. Bowtie in *Looking for Mr. Goodbar.*

STAGE APPEARANCES

Dexter and understudy, *Kiss and Tell,* Biltmore Theatre, New York City, 1943.
Get Away, Old Man, Cort Theatre, New York City, 1943.
Third legionnaire, *Snafu,* Hudson Theatre, New York City, 1944.
Newsboy, *Billion Dollar Baby,* Alvin Theatre, New York City, 1945.
Soldier, *Montserrat,* Fulton Theatre, New York City, 1949.
Marty, *Night Music,* American National Theatre Academy, 1951.
Valentin, *Maya,* Theatre de Lys, New York City, 1953.
Micah, *The Scarecrow,* Theatre de Lys, 1953.
Sanathanaka, *The Little Clay Cart,* Theatre de Lys, 1953.
The drunk, *Mardi Gras,* Locust Theatre, Philadelphia, PA, 1954.
Smith, *The Threepenny Opera,* Theatre de Lys, 1955.
Matvai, *A Month in the Country,* Phoenix Theatre, New York City, 1956.
Postmaster, *Purple Dust,* Cherry Lane Theatre, New York City, 1956.
Max Steiner, *Compulsion,* Ambassador Theatre, New York City, 1957.
The guard, *Deathwatch,* Theatre East, New York City, 1958.
Tommy Owens, *The Shadow of a Gunman,* Bijou Theatre, New York City, 1958.
Herr Zeller, *The Sound of Music,* Lunt-Fontanne Theatre, New York City, 1959.
Patch Keegan, *Little Moon of Alban,* Longacre Theatre, New York City, 1960.
Jimmy Beales, *Roots,* Mayfair Theatre, New York City, 1961.
Gus, *The Collection* (double bill with *The Dumbwaiter*), Cherry Lane Theatre, 1962.
Leon Hallett, *Isle of Children,* Cort Theatre, 1962.
Kenneth O'Keefe, *The Ginger Man,* Orpheum Theatre, New York City, 1963.
Jacobson, *The Deputy,* Brooks Atkinson Theatre, New York City, 1964.
The Tempest, Milwaukee Repertory Theatre, Milwaukee, WI, 1965.
Under Milk Wood, Milwaukee Repertory Theatre, 1965.
Pantagleize, Milwaukee Repertory Theatre, 1965.
Saint Joan, Milwaukee Repertory Theatre, 1965.
The Time of Your Life, Milwaukee Repertory Theatre, 1965.
Mother Courage, Milwaukee Repertory Theatre, 1966.
The Glass Menagerie, Milwaukee Repertory Theatre, 1966.
Henry IV, Part I, Milwaukee Repertory Theatre, 1966.
Saint Joan, Trinity Square Playhouse, Providence, RI, 1966.
Pierre, *War and Peace,* Lyceum Theatre, New York City, 1967.
Ah! Wilderness, Trinity Square Playhouse, 1967, then Circle in the Square/Ford's Theatre, Washington, DC, 1969-70.
Enrico IV, Studio Arena Theatre, Buffalo, NY, 1968.
Duke of York, *Richard II,* American Shakespeare Festival Theatre, Stratford, CT, 1968.
Holofernes, *Love's Labour's Lost,* American Shakespeare Festival Theatre, 1968.
Jaques, *As You Like It,* American Shakespeare Festival Theatre, 1968.
Zelo Shimansky, *Seven Days of Mourning,* Circle in the Square, New York City, 1969-70.
Perowne, *AC/DC,* Chelsea Theatre Center, Brooklyn, NY, 1971.
Arsenic and Old Lace, Circle in the Square/Ford's Theatre, 1971.
Hamlet, Long Wharf Theatre, New Haven, CT, 1972.
Clegg, *Owners,* Mercer-Shaw Theatre, New York City, 1973.
Moke, *Nellie Toole & Co.,* Theatre Four, New York City, 1973.
Harry Hope, *The Iceman Cometh,* Circle in the Square/Joseph E. Levine Theatre, New York City, 1973-74.
Candy, *Of Mice and Men,* Brooks Atkinson Theatre, 1974-75.
Orgon, *Tartuffe,* Circle in the Square, 1977.
Semmelweiss, Eisenhower Theatre, Kennedy Center for the Performing Arts, Washington, DC, 1978.
"The Man with the Flower in His Mouth," *A Special Evening* (double bill), Ensemble Studio Theatre, New York City, 1979.
Park Your Car in the Harvard Yard, Los Angeles Actors' Theatre, Los Angeles, CA, 1981-82.
Jack, *Brighton Beach Memoirs,* Alvin Theatre, 1983-84.
Big Daddy, *Cat on a Hot Tin Roof,* Long Wharf Theatre, 1984-85.

Akbar, *Nanawatai,* Los Angeles Theatre Center, Los Angeles, CA, 1985-86.

Mr. Crampton, *You Never Can Tell,* Circle in the Square, 1986-87.

Earl of Gloucester, *King Lear,* Los Angeles Theatre Center, 1987-88.

Sand and Stone, Sundays at the Itchey Foot, 1988-89.

The Marriage of Bette and Boo, Los Angeles Theatre Center, 1989-90.

* * *

GIMBEL, Roger 1925-

PERSONAL: Born March 11, 1925. *Education:* Attended Yale University.

ADDRESSES: Office—Roger Gimbel Productions, Inc., 8439 Sunset Blvd., Suite 201, Los Angeles, CA 90069.

CAREER: Producer and studio executive. RCA Victor Television, copy and creative chief; NBC-TV, associate producer of *The Tonight Show,* head of program development for daytime programming, and producer of specials for *NBC Tonight, The Jack Paar Show,* and *The Ernie Kovacs Show;* CBS-TV, producer of the *Glen Campbell Goodtime Hour,* beginning in 1969, and vice-president in charge of production for Tomorrow Entertainment, beginning in 1971; Roger Gimbel's Tomorrow Enterprises, Inc., founder, 1975; EMI-TV, U.S. president, 1976; Peregrine Producers Group, Inc., president and chief executive officer, 1984; Roger Gimbel Productions, founder, 1987, president, 1991—; Carolco/Gimbel Productions, president and executive producer, 1988-90.

AWARDS, HONORS: Emmy Award (with George Schaefer), outstanding single program, drama or comedy, 1972, for *A War of Children;* Television Movie Producer of the Year, American Film Institute, 1992.

CREDITS:

TELEVISION WORK; MOVIES; EXECUTIVE PRODUCER

Gargoyles, CBS, 1972.

Truman Capote's "The Glass House," CBS, 1972.

A War of Children, CBS, 1972.

Birds of Prey, CBS, 1973.

I Heard the Owl Call My Name, CBS, 1973.

Tell Me Where It Hurts, CBS, 1974.

The Amazing Howard Hughes, CBS, 1977.

The Girl Called Hatter Fox, CBS, 1977.

(With Edward L. Rissien) *Minstrel Man,* CBS, 1977.

(With Tony Converse) *Betrayal,* NBC, 1978.

(With Converse) *Deadman's Curve,* CBS, 1978.

Deathmoon, CBS, 1978.

Forever, CBS, 1978.

Just Me and You, NBC, 1978.

(With Converse) *One in a Million: The Ron LeFlore Story,* CBS, 1978.

Special Olympics (also known as *A Special Kind of Love*), CBS, 1978.

(With Converse) *Steel Cowboy* (also known as *Fast Lane Fever*), NBC, 1978.

(With Converse) *Can You Hear the Laughter?: The Story of Freddie Prinze,* CBS, 1979.

(With Converse) *The Cracker Factory,* ABC, 1979.

(With Converse and Marian Rees) *Orphan Train,* CBS, 1979.

(With William S. Gilmore) *S.O.S. Titanic,* ABC, 1979.

(With Converse) *Survival of Dana,* CBS, 1979.

(With Converse) *My Kidnapper, My Love,* NBC, 1980.

(With Herbert Hirschman) *Sophia Loren: Her Own Story,* NBC, 1980.

(With Converse) *Broken Promise,* CBS, 1981.

(With Converse) *The Killing of Randy Webster* (also known as *The Throwdown*), CBS, 1981.

(With Converse) *Deadly Encounter* (also known as *American Eagle*), CBS, 1982.

(With Converse) *The Legend of Walks Far Woman,* NBC, 1982.

(With Converse) *A Piano for Mrs. Cimino,* CBS, 1982.

(With Converse) *A Question of Honor,* CBS, 1982.

(With Converse) *Packin' It In,* CBS, 1983.

(With Converse) *Sessions,* ABC, 1983.

Aurora (also known as *Aurora by Night* and *My Three Loves*), NBC, 1984.

(With Freyda Rothstein) *Blackout,* HBO, 1985.

Apology, HBO, 1986.

(With Rothstein) *Rockabye,* CBS, 1986.

Shattered Dreams (also known as *The Charlotte Fedders Story*), CBS, 1990.

Montana, TNT, 1990.

Chernobyl: The Final Warning (also known as *The Chernobyl Story* and *The Dr. Robert Gale Story*), TNT, 1991.

OTHER TELEVISION WORK

Producer, *With Love, Sophia* (special), ABC, 1967.

Producer, *Hollywood Stars of Tomorrow* (special), ABC, 1968.

Producer, *Monte Carlo, C'est la rose* (special), ABC, 1968.

Executive producer (with Tony Converse), *Gossip* (pilot; also see below), NBC, 1979.

Executive producer (with Converse), *The Manions of America* (mini-series), ABC, 1981.

Executive producer (with Harry Colomby), *Report to Murphy* (series), CBS, 1982.

Other television credits include *The Autobiography of Miss Jane Pittman; Born Innocent; Brand New Life; In This House of Brede; I Love You, Goodbye; Larry; Miles to Go; Queen of the Stardust Ballroom;* and *Things in Their Season.*

FILM WORK; EXECUTIVE PRODUCER

Lady Ice, National General, 1973.
The Gravy Train, Columbia, 1974.

WRITINGS:

TELEVISION SCRIPTS

Gossip (pilot), NBC, 1979.

* * *

GIVENS, Robin 1964(?)-

PERSONAL: Born November 27, 1964 (one source says 1965), in New York, NY; daughter of Ruth Roper; married Mike Tyson (a boxer), February 7, 1988 (divorced, 1988). *Education:* Attended Sarah Lawrence College and Harvard University.

ADDRESSES: Agent—Triad Artists, 10100 Santa Monica Blvd., Suite 1600, Los Angeles, CA 90067.

CAREER: Actress. Founder and director, Never Blue Productions, 1990—.

CREDITS:

TELEVISION APPEARANCES; SERIES

Darlene Merriman, *Head of the Class,* ABC, 1986-91.

TELEVISION APPEARANCES; EPISODIC

"Theo and the Older Woman," *The Cosby Show,* NBC, 1985.
"The Big Bribe," *Diff'rent Strokes,* ABC, 1986.
"Crime below the Waist," *Sonny Spoon,* NBC, 1988.
20/20, ABC, c. 1988.
"Picking Up the Pieces," *People Magazine on TV,* CBS, 1989.

OTHER TELEVISION APPEARANCES

April Baxter, *Beverly Hills Madam* (movie), NBC, 1986.
Dinah St. Clair, *The Penthouse* (movie), ABC, 1989.
Kiswana Browne, *The Women of Brewster Place* (movie), NBC, 1989.

Also appeared on *The 15th Annual People's Choice Awards* (special), 1989.

FILM APPEARANCES

Imabelle, *A Rage in Harlem,* Miramax, 1991.

OTHER SOURCES:

PERIODICALS

Interview, July, 1987, p. 68; March, 1991, p. 38.
People Weekly, May 11, 1987, p. 127; February 22, 1988, p. 32; October 17, 1988, p. 60; October 24, 1988, pp. 56-58.
Time, October 17, 1988, p. 65.*

* * *

GOLD, Jack 1930-
(John Gould)

PERSONAL: Born June 28, 1930, in London, England; married Denyse Macpherson, 1957; children: two sons, one daughter. *Education:* London University, B.Sc., economics, and LL.B. *Avocational interests:* Music, reading.

ADDRESSES: Agent—InterTalent Agency, 9200 Sunset Blvd., Penthouse 25, Los Angeles, CA 90069.

CAREER: Director. British Broadcasting Corporation (BBC) Radio, London, England, assistant studio manager, 1954-55; BBC film department, editor, 1955-60.

AWARDS, HONORS: British Academy of Film and Television Arts (BAFTA) Award, television—documentary programme, 1964, for *Death in the Morning;* BAFTA Award, 1968, for *World of Coppard;* Grand Prix Award, Monte Carlo, 1971, for *Mad Jack;* BAFTA Award, 1972, for *Stocker's Copper; Evening News* Best Comedy Award, 1973, for *The National Health;* Peabody Award, 1974, for *Catholics;* Desmond Davies Award, BAFTA, 1975, for services to television; Italia Prize, International Emmy Award, and Critics Award, all 1976, all for *The Naked Civil Servant; Evening News* Best Film Award, 1976, for *Aces High;* Martin Luther King Memorial Prize (joint winner), 1980, Monte Carlo Catholic Award, and Monte Carlo Critics Award, both 1981, all for *The Sailor's Return;* Christopher Award, 1981, for *Little Lord Fauntleroy;* International Emmy Award, 1981, for *A Lot of Happiness;* Association of Cable Enterprises Award, 1984, for *Sakharov;* Association of Cable Enterprises Award, 1986, for *Murrow;* Golden Globe Award and Emmy Award nomination, outstanding directing in a miniseries or a special, both 1987, both for *Escape from Sobibor.*

CREDITS:

TELEVISION DIRECTOR; MOVIES

Catholics, CBS, 1973.
The Naked Civil Servant, Thames TV, 1978.
Little Lord Fauntleroy, CBS, 1980.
Sakharov, HBO, 1984.
Murrow, HBO, 1986.
Escape from Sobibor, CBS, 1987.

The Rose and the Jackal, TNT, 1990.

Also directed a number of other television films, including *Tonight, Death in the Morning, Modern Millionairess, Famine, Dispute, 90 Days, Dowager in Hot Pants, World of Coppard, Mad Jack, Stocker's Copper, Arturo Ui, The Lump, Thank You Comrades, Marya, A Walk in the Forest, Merchant of Venice, Bavarian Night, A Lot of Happiness,* 1981, *Macbeth,* 1982, *L'Elegance,* 1982, *Good and Bad at Games,* 1983, and *Masterclass,* 1989.

TELEVISION DIRECTOR; EPISODIC

"Me and the Girls" (also known as "Star Quality: Noel Coward Stories," and "Noel Coward Stories") *Masterpiece Theatre,* PBS, 1987.
"Stones for Ibarra," *Hallmark Hall of Fame* (also see below), CBS, 1988.
"Graham Greene's 'The Tenth Man,' " *Hallmark Hall of Fame,* CBS, 1988.
"She Stood Alone" (also known as "A Mighty Fortress"), *Disney Night at the Movies,* NBC, 1991.

TELEVISION DIRECTOR; SPECIALS

Praying Mantis (also see below), 1985.

FILM DIRECTOR

The Bofors Gun, Universal, 1968.
The Reckoning, Columbia, 1969.
The National Health, or Nurse Norton's Affair, Columbia, 1973.
Who? (also known as *Man without a Face, Prisoner of the Skull,* and *The Man in the Steel Mask;* also see below), Lorimar, 1975.
Man Friday, Avco Embassy, 1975.
Aces High, EMI, 1977.
The Medusa Touch (also see below), Warner Brothers, 1978.
The Sailor's Return, Osprey, 1978.
Charlie Muffin, Euston Films Ltd., 1980.
Praying Mantis, Channel Four, 1982.
Red Monarch, Goldcrest Films and Television Ltd., 1983.
The Chain, J. Arthur Rank, 1985.
Ball-Trap on the Cote Sauvage, BBC Enterprises, 1989.

Also director of *Stones for Ibarra,* 1988.

FILM PRODUCER

(With Anne V. Coates) *The Medusa Touch* (also see below), Warner Brothers, 1978.

STAGE DIRECTOR

The Devil's Disciple, Aldwych Theatre, London, 1976.
This Story of Yours, Hampstead Theatre Club, London, 1987.
"I Can't Remember Anything," and "Clara," *Danger: Memory!* (double-bill), Hampstead Theatre Club, 1988.

WRITINGS:

SCREENPLAYS

(Under name John Gould) *Who?* (based on the novel by Algis Budrys), Lorimar, 1975.
(With John Briley) *The Medusa Touch* (based on the novel by Peter Van Greenaway), Warner Brothers, 1978.*

* * *

GOLDBERG, Gary David 1944-

PERSONAL: Born June 25, 1944, in Brooklyn, NY; son of George (a postal worker) and Anne (Prossman) Goldberg; married Diana Meehan; children: Shana, Cailin Elizabeth. *Education:* Attended Brandeis University, 1962-64; San Diego State University, B.A., 1975.

ADDRESSES: Office—UBU Productions, 5555 Melrose Ave., Suite 206, Los Angeles, CA 90038. *Agent*—Jim Preminger, The Jim Preminger Agency, 1650 Westwood Blvd., No. 140, Los Angeles, CA 90069.

CAREER: Writer, creator, producer, and director of works for television and film; founder and president of UBU Productions.

MEMBER: Actors' Equity Association, American Federation of Television and Radio Artists (AFTRA), Writers Guild of America, West.

AWARDS, HONORS: Writers Guild Award, outstanding episodic comedy television script, 1978; Emmy Award, outstanding drama series, 1978, for *Lou Grant;* Peabody Award, 1979; Writers Guild nomination, 1982; Humanitas Award, 1984; Emmy nominations, outstanding comedy series, 1983, 1984, 1985, and 1986, for *Family Ties;* Emmy Award, outstanding writing in a comedy series, 1986, with Alan Uger, for *Family Ties* episode "My Name is Alex."

CREDITS:

TELEVISION WORK; SERIES

Coproducer and story editor, *Tony Randall Show* (also see below), ABC, 1976-77.
Coproducer, *Tony Randall Show,* ABC, 1976-77, then CBS, 1977-78.
Coproducer, *Lou Grant* (also see below), CBS, 1978-79.
Creator and coproducer, *The Last Resort* (also see below), CBS, 1979-80.
Creator, director, and executive producer, *Making the Grade,* CBS, 1982.

Creator and executive producer, *Family Ties* (also see below), NBC, 1982-89.
Creator (with Ruth Bennett) and executive producer, *Sara* (also see below), ABC, 1985.
Creator and executive producer, *The Bronx Zoo,* NBC, 1987.
Creator and executive producer, *Day by Day,* NBC, 1988.
Executive producer (with Susan Seeger), *American Dreamer* (also see below), NBC, 1990.
Executive producer, *Brooklyn Bridge* (also see below), CBS, 1991—.

Also creator and executive producer of *Duet,* for FOX, and *Taking It Home.*

OTHER TELEVISION WORK

Producer, *The Last Resort* (pilot), CBS, 1979.
Executive producer, *Famous Lives* (pilot), NBC, 1983.
Executive producer, *Family Ties Vacation* (movie; also see below), NBC, 1985.

TELEVISION APPEARANCES

Himself, *Inside "Family Ties": Behind the Scenes of a Hit* (special), NBC, 1988.
Guest, *It's Only Television* (series), Nickelodeon, 1991.

Also appeared on *Today at Night, Volume II.*

FILM WORK

Producer (with Joseph Stern) and director, *Dad* (also see below), Universal, 1989.

WRITINGS:

TELEVISION SERIES

Bob Newhart Show, CBS, 1976.
Alice, CBS, 1976.
Tony Randall Show, ABC, 1976-77, then CBS, 1977-78.
The Last Resort, CBS, 1979.
Lou Grant, CBS, 1979.
Family Ties, NBC, 1982-87.
Sara, ABC, 1985.

TELEVISION EPISODES

*M*A*S*H,* CBS, 1979.
American Dreamer, NBC, 1990.
Brooklyn Bridge, CBS, 1991.

OTHER TELEVISION WRITINGS

Family Ties Vacation (movie), NBC, 1985.
Brooklyn Bridge (pilot), CBS, 1991.

FILM

Dad, Universal, 1989.
(With Ronald Shusett and Dan O'Bannon) *Total Recall,* Tri-Star, 1990.
(With Chuck Pfarrer) *Navy Seals,* Orion, 1990

Also screenwriter for *Coming of Age in New York City, Son of Grease, Silky,* and *Reel to Reel.*

OTHER SOURCES:

BOOKS

Newsmakers 89, Issue 4, Gale, 1989, pp. 152-153.

PERIODICALS

Newsweek, May 9, 1988, p. 77.*

* * *

GOLDTHWAIT, Bob 1962-
(Bobcat Goldthwait)

PERSONAL: Born in May, 1962, in Syracuse, NY; son of Tom (a sheet metal worker) and Kathleen (a department store employee) Goldthwait; married Ann Luly (a film production associate); children: Tyler (stepson), Tasha.

ADDRESSES: Publicist—Michael Levine Public Relations, 14 East 60th St., Suite 908, New York, NY 10022.

CAREER: Comedian and actor. Performed with comedy troupe "The Generic Comics," beginning in 1980.

AWARDS, HONORS: Charlie Comedy Award, best male comedian—West Coast, Association of Comedy Artists, 1988.

CREDITS:

MAJOR TOURS

Meat Bob '88, U.S. cities, 1988.

FILM APPEARANCES

Zed, *Police Academy 2: Their First Assignment,* Warner Bros., 1985.
(As Bobcat Goldthwait) Egg Stork, *One Crazy Summer,* Warner Bros., 1986.
(As Bobcat Goldthwait) Cadet Zed, *Police Academy 3: Back in Training,* Warner Bros., 1986.
Carl Hefler, *Burglar,* Warner Bros., 1987.
(As Bobcat Goldthwait) Zed, *Police Academy 4: Citizens on Patrol,* Warner Bros., 1987.
Fred P. Chaney, *Hot To Trot,* Warner Bros., 1988.
(As Bobcat Goldthwait) Eliot Loudermilk, *Scrooged,* Paramount, 1988.
(As Bobcat Goldthwait) Title role, *Shakes the Clown* (also see below), IRS Releasing, 1992.

FILM DIRECTOR

(As Bobcat Goldthwait) *Shakes the Clown,* IRS Releasing, 1992.

TELEVISION APPEARANCES; SPECIALS

Bob Goldthwait: Don't Watch This Show, Cinemax, 1986.
The American Comedy Awards, ABC, 1987.
Comic Relief 2, HBO, 1987.
Bob Goldthwait: Share the Warmth, HBO, 1987.
Twenty-ninth Annual Grammy Awards, CBS, 1987.
Bob Goldthwait: Is He Like That All the Time? (also see below), HBO, 1988.
The Ninth Annual Awards for Cable Excellence: The ACE Awards, HBO, 1988.
The Second Annual American Comedy Awards, ABC, 1988.
Comic Relief 3, HBO, 1989.
The First International Rock Awards, ABC, 1989.
Montreal International Comedy Festival 1989, HBO, 1989.
Bob Saget: In the Dream State, HBO, 1990.
Comic Relief 4, HBO, 1990.
The Fourth Annual American Comedy Awards, ABC, 1990.
Host, *Save the Planet: A CBS/Hard Rock Cafe Special* (also see below), CBS, 1990.
(As Bobcat Goldthwait) *A Party for Richard Pryor,* CBS, 1991.

TELEVISION APPEARANCES; MOVIES

(As Bobcat Goldthwait) Kevin Costner, *Medusa: Dare to Be Truthful,* Showtime, 1991.

TELEVISION APPEARANCES; SERIES

(As Bobcat Goldthwait) Voice, *Capitol Critters* (animated), ABC, 1992.

TELEVISION APPEARANCES; EPISODIC

Bobby Green, *Apartment 2-C Starring George Carlin,* HBO, 1985.
Young Man, "The Ventriloquist's Dummy," *Tales from the Crypt,* HBO, 1990.

Also appeared on *Good Morning America, Late Night with David Letterman,* and *The Tonight Show.*

TELEVISION DIRECTOR; SPECIALS

Bob Goldthwait: Is He Like That All the Time? (also see below), HBO, 1988.

RECORDINGS:

VIDEOS

Also appeared in *Star Shorts,* during 1980s.

ALBUMS

Recorded *Meat Bob,* Chrysalis.

WRITINGS:

SCREENPLAYS

(As Bobcat Goldthwait) *Shakes the Clown,* IRS Releasing, 1992.

TELEVISION SPECIALS

Bob Goldthwait: Is He Like That All the Time?, HBO, 1988.
(With Adam Barr, Garry Bormet, Peter Ocko, and Martin Olson) *Save the Planet: A CBS/Hard Rock Cafe Special,* CBS, 1990.

OTHER SOURCES:

PERIODICALS

Interview, December, 1986, p. 40.
New York Daily News, November 30, 1986; March 19, 1987.
People, June 9, 1986, p. 55.
Sun-Times (Chicago), March 27, 1986, p. 84.*

* * *

GOLDTHWAIT, Bobcat
See GOLDTHWAIT, Bob

* * *

GORDON, Charles

PERSONAL: Born in Belzoni, MS.

ADDRESSES: Office—Lawrence Gordon Productions, Twentieth Century-Fox, 10201 West Pico Blvd., Bldg. 86, Los Angeles, CA 90035.

CAREER: Film and television producer. Began career as talent agent with William Morris Agency, Los Angeles, CA; later, developer of television programs; currently motion picture and television producer, frequently with brother, Lawrence Gordon. Gordon Company, president and chief executive officer; Daybreak Productions, president and chief executive officer; affiliated with Lawrence Gordon Productions, Los Angeles, CA.

AWARDS, HONORS: Academy Award nomination, best picture, 1989, for *Field of Dreams.*

CREDITS:

FILM PRODUCER

Night of the Creeps, Tri-Star, 1986.
(With Ronald E. Frazier) *The Wrong Guys,* New World, 1988.
(With Lawrence Gordon) *Field of Dreams,* Universal, 1989.

(With Lawrence Gordon) *K-9,* Universal, 1989.
(With Lawrence Gordon) *Lock Up,* Tri-Star, 1989.
(With Lawrence Gordon and Joel Silver) *Die Hard 2* (also known as *Die Harder*), Twentieth Century-Fox, 1990.
(With Lawrence Gordon) *The Rocketeer,* Buena Vista, 1991.
The Super, Twentieth Century-Fox, 1991.

FILM EXECUTIVE PRODUCER

Die Hard, Twentieth Century-Fox, 1988.
(With Lawrence Gordon) *Leviathan,* Metro-Goldwyn-Mayer/United Artists, 1989.

TELEVISION WORK; PILOTS

Producer, *The Renegades* (also see below), ABC, 1982.
Executive producer (with Lawrence Gordon), *Lone Star,* NBC, 1983.
Executive producer (with Lawrence Gordon and Stuart Sheslow), *The Streets,* NBC, 1984.
Executive consultant (with Lawrence Gordon), *The Brotherhood,* ABC, 1991.

TELEVISION WORK; SERIES

Executive producer (with Lawrence Gordon), *The Renegades,* ABC, 1983.
Producer (with others), *Just Our Luck,* ABC, 1983-84.
Creator and executive producer (with Lawrence Gordon), *Our Family Honor,* ABC, 1985.*

* * *

GORDON, Lawrence 1936-

PERSONAL: Born March 25, 1936, in Belzoni, MS. *Education:* Studied business administration at Tulane University.

ADDRESSES: Office—Lawrence Gordon Productions, Twentieth Century-Fox, 10201 West Pico Blvd., Bldg. 86, Los Angeles, CA 90035.

CAREER: Film and television producer. Four Star Television, assistant to producer Aaron Spelling, 1964; later, writer and associate producer for some of Spelling's shows; ABC-TV, head of West Coast talent development, 1965; Bob Banner Associates, television and motion picture executive, beginning c. 1966; American International Pictures, vice-president in charge of product development, beginning in 1968; Screen Gems (television division of Columbia Pictures), vice-president, 1971; American International Pictures, vice-president in charge of worldwide production; Twentieth Century-Fox, president, 1984-86; currently independent producer with Twentieth Century-Fox. Lawrence Gordon Productions, founder; Largo Entertainment, chair and chief executive officer.

AWARDS, HONORS: Academy Award nomination, best picture, 1989, for *Field of Dreams.*

CREDITS:

FILM PRODUCER

Hard Times (also known as *The Streetfighter*), Columbia, 1975.
The Driver, Twentieth Century-Fox, 1978.
The End, United Artists, 1978.
The Warriors, Paramount, 1979.
Xanadu, Universal, 1980.
(With Hank Moonjean) *Paternity,* Paramount, 1981.
Jekyll and Hyde . . . Together Again, Paramount, 1982.
(With Joel Silver) *Forty-eight Hours,* Paramount, 1982.
(With Silver) *Streets of Fire,* Universal-RKO Radio Pictures, 1984.
(With Silver) *Brewster's Millions,* Universal, 1985.
(With Silver) *Jumpin' Jack Flash,* Twentieth Century-Fox, 1986.
(With Silver and John Davis) *Predator,* Twentieth Century-Fox, 1987.
The Couch Trip, Orion, 1988.
(With Silver) *Die Hard,* Twentieth Century-Fox, 1988.
(With Charles Gordon) *Field of Dreams,* Universal, 1989.
(With Charles Gordon) *K-9,* Universal, 1989.
(With Charles Gordon) *Lock Up,* Tri-Star, 1989.
Family Business, Tri-Star, 1989.
(With Robert D. Wachs) *Another Forty-eight Hours,* Paramount, 1990.
(With Silver and Charles Gordon) *Die Hard 2* (also known as *Die Harder*), Twentieth Century-Fox, 1990.
(With Silver and John Davis) *Predator 2,* Twentieth Century-Fox, 1990.
(With Charles Gordon) *The Rocketeer,* Buena Vista, 1991.

Also producer of *Lucas,* 1986.

FILM EXECUTIVE PRODUCER

The Wrong Guys, New World Pictures, 1988.
(With Charles Gordon) *Leviathan,* Metro-Goldwyn-Mayer/United Artists, 1989.

Also executive producer of *Dillinger,* 1973, *It's Not the Size That Counts,* 1974, *Rolling Thunder,* 1977, and *Hooper,* 1978.

TELEVISION EXECUTIVE PRODUCER, EXCEPT WHERE INDICATED; PILOTS

Home Cookin', ABC, 1975.
Dog and Cat (also see below), ABC, 1977.
Lacy and the Mississippi Queen, NBC, 1978.
The Nightengales, NBC, 1979.
Stunts Unlimited, ABC, 1980.

The Renegades (based on the story by Gordon; also see below), ABC, 1982.
(With Charles Gordon) *Lone Star,* NBC, 1983.
(With Charles Gordon and Stuart Sheslow) *The Streets,* NBC, 1984.
Executive consultant (with Charles Gordon), *The Brotherhood,* ABC, 1991.

TELEVISION EXECUTIVE PRODUCER, EXCEPT WHERE INDICATED; SERIES

Dog and Cat, ABC, 1977.
(With Aaron Spelling and Douglas S. Cramer) *Matt Houston,* ABC, 1982.
(With Charles Gordon) *The Renegades* (based on the story by Gordon; also see below), ABC, 1983.
Creator and executive producer (with Charles Gordon), *Our Family Honor,* ABC, 1985.

TELEVISION EXECUTIVE PRODUCER; MOVIES

The Missing Are Deadly, ABC, 1975.

STAGE WORK; PRODUCER

(With Howard Feuer, Jeremy Ritzer, and Sidney Shlenker) *Entertaining Mr. Sloane,* Cherry Lane Theatre, New York City, 1981-82.
(With Richard M. Kagan and Sidney Shlenker), *Smile,* Lunt-Fontaine Theatre, New York City, 1986-87.

WRITINGS:

Author of stories "Five Desperate Women" (also see below) and "The Renegades."

ADAPTATIONS: "Five Desperate Women" was adapted by Marc Norman and Walter Black for a television movie of the same title, produced by Aaron Spelling, 1971.*

* * *

GOULD, John
See GOLD, Jack

* * *

GRAHAM, William A. 1930(?)-

ADDRESSES: Agent—Creative Artists Agency, 1888 Century Park E., 14th Floor, Los Angeles, CA 90067.

CAREER: Director.

AWARDS, HONORS: Emmy Award nomination, outstanding directing in a limited series or special, 1980, for *Guyana Tragedy: The Story of Jim Jones.*

CREDITS:

TELEVISION DIRECTOR; MOVIES

The Doomsday Flight, NBC, 1966.
Then Came Bronson, CBS, 1969.
Trial Run, NBC, 1969.
The Intruders (also known as *Death Dance at Madelia*), NBC, 1970.
Congratulations, It's a Boy! (also known as *So's Your Old Man!*), ABC, 1971.
Marriage: Year One, NBC, 1971.
Thief, ABC, 1971.
Magic Carpet, ABC, 1972.
Birds of Prey, CBS, 1973.
Mr. Inside/Mr. Outside, NBC, 1973.
Shirts/Skins, ABC, 1973.
Larry, CBS, 1974.
Trapped Beneath the Sea, ABC, 1974.
Beyond the Bermuda Triangle (also known as *Beyond This Place There Be Dragons*), NBC, 1975.
Perilous Voyage (also known as *The Revolution of Antonio DeLeon*), NBC, 1976.
Shark Kill, NBC, 1976.
21 Hours at Munich, ABC, 1976.
The Amazing Howard Hughes, CBS, 1977.
Contract on Cherry Street, NBC, 1977.
Minstrel Man, CBS, 1977.
And I Alone Survived, NBC, 1978.
Cindy, ABC, 1978.
One in a Million: The Ron LeFlore Story, CBS, 1978.
Orphan Train, CBS, 1979.
Transplant, CBS, 1979.
Guyana Tragedy: The Story of Jim Jones, CBS, 1980.
Rage, NBC, 1980.
Deadly Encounter (also known as *American Eagle*), CBS, 1982.
M.A.D.D.: Mothers Against Drunk Drivers, NBC, 1983.
Women of San Quentin, NBC, 1983.
Calendar Girl Murders, ABC, 1984.
Secrets of a Married Man (also known as *Trick Eyes* and *Portrait of a John*), NBC, 1984.
Mussolini: The Untold Story, NBC, 1985.
George Washington II: The Forging of a Nation, CBS, 1986.
The Last Days of Frank and Jesse James, NBC, 1986.
Proud Men (also known as *The Tall Men*), ABC, 1987.
Police Story: The Freeway Killings (also known as *Police Story II*), NBC, 1987.
Street of Dreams, CBS, 1988.
Gore Vidal's Billy the Kid, TNT, 1989.
Truck One, NBC, 1989.
Montana, TNT, 1990.
Bed of Lies (also known as *Deadly Blessing*), ABC, 1992.

Director of *The Outsider,* 1967, and *The Legend of Custer,* 1968.

TELEVISION DIRECTOR; PILOTS

Jigsaw (also known as *Man on the Move*), ABC, 1972.
The Police Story, NBC, 1973.
Get Christie Love!, ABC, 1974.
The Last Ninja, ABC, 1983.

TELEVISION DIRECTOR; SERIES

Supercarrier, ABC, 1988.
True Blue, NBC, 1989-90.

Director of *Otherworld,* 1985.

FILM DIRECTOR

Waterhole No. 3, Paramount, 1967.
Change of Habit, Universal, 1969.
Submarine X-1, United Artists (UA), 1969.
Honky, Jack H. Harris, 1971.
Count Your Bullets (also known as *Cry for Me, Billy; Face to the Wind;* and *Naked Revenge*), Brut, 1972.
Together Brothers, Twentieth Century-Fox, 1974.
Where the Lilies Bloom, UA, 1974.
Sounder, Part 2, Gamma III, 1976.
Harry Tracy—Desperado, Quartet, 1982.
Return to the Blue Lagoon, Columbia, 1991.

Director of *The Last Generation,* 1971, and *Face to the Wind,* 1972.*

* * *

GRANT, David
See GRANT, David Marshall

* * *

GRANT, David Marshall 1955-
(David Grant)

PERSONAL: Born June 21, 1955, in New Haven, CT (one source says Westport, CT); son of two physicians. *Education:* Attended Connecticut College; studied at Juilliard School of Drama, Weber Douglas Academy of Dramatic Arts, and National Theater Institute; Yale School of Drama, certificate of fine arts, 1978.

ADDRESSES: Agent—International Creative Management, 8899 Beverly Blvd., Los Angeles, CA 90048.

CAREER: Actor.

CREDITS:

STAGE APPEARANCES

Sganarelle, Yale Repertory Theatre, New Haven, CT, 1977-78.
(Off-Broadway debut) Valere, "The Flying Doctor," Alcidas, "The Forced Marriage," and "A Dumb Show," in *Sganarelle: An Evening of Moliere Farces* (triple-bill), New York Shakespeare Festival, Public/Newman Theatre, New York City, 1978.
Table Settings, Playwrights Horizons Theatre, New York City, 1979.
(Broadway debut) Rudy, *Bent,* New Apollo Theatre, New York City, 1979-80.
Jacek, *The Survivor,* Morosco Theatre, New York City, 1981.
The Further Adventures of Sally and *The Wind-Up Toys,* Center Stage Theatre, Baltimore, MD, 1980-81.
Lakeboat, Long Wharf Theatre, New Haven, 1981-82.
Ferdinand, *The Tempest,* New York Shakespeare Festival, Delacorte Theatre, New York City, 1981.
Roche, *Rat in the Skull,* Mark Taper Forum, Los Angeles, CA, 1985-86.
Jeff, *Making Movies,* Promenade Theatre, New York City, 1990.

Also appeared in *The Marriage of Bette and Boo,* Los Angeles Theatre Center, Los Angeles, and *True West.* Appeared in productions with Yale Repertory Company, including *The Ghost Sonata, Julius Caesar,* and *Tom Jones.*

STAGE WORK

Director of *Streamers,* Fig Tree Theatre, Hollywood, CA, and *Bent,* Coast Playhouse, Los Angeles.

FILM APPEARANCES

(Film debut) Alex, *French Postcards,* Paramount, 1979.
The Awakening, Orion, 1980.
Randy Hastings, *Happy Birthday, Gemini,* United Artists, 1980.
Robert, *The End of August,* Quartet, 1982.
(As David Grant) David Sommers, *American Flyers,* Warner Brothers, 1985.
Sonny Binkley, *The Big Town,* Columbia, 1987.
Ross Carver, *Bat 21,* Tri-Star, 1988.
Rob Diehl, *Air America,* Tri-Star, 1990.
David, *Strictly Business,* Warner Brothers, 1991.

TELEVISION APPEARANCES; MOVIES

Sid Lewis, *Legs,* ABC, 1983.
Josh, *Sessions,* NBC, 1983.
(As David Grant) Willard 'Digger' Barnes, *Dallas: The Early Years,* CBS, 1986.
Colonel Osterman, *Breaking Point,* TNT, 1989.

Also appeared as Tom, *Kent State,* 1981. Appeared in *Jessie,* ABC.

OTHER TELEVISION APPEARANCES

To the Moon, Alice (special), Showtime, 1990.

Provided the voice of Mike Doonesbury, *A Doonesbury Special* (animated), c. 1977; also appeared as Bob, *The Shady Hill Kidnapping,* 1982, and as Russell, *thirtysomething,* ABC.

OTHER SOURCES:

PERIODICALS

New York Times, January 4, 1980.*

* * *

GRAZER, Brian 1951-

PERSONAL: Born July 12, 1951, in Los Angeles, CA; children: Sage, Riley. *Education:* Attended University of Southern California; studied law during the early 1980s. *Avocational interests:* Surfing.

ADDRESSES: Office—Imagine Films Entertainment Inc., 1925 Century Park E., Suite 2300, Los Angeles, CA 90067.

CAREER: Producer. Warner Brothers, intern in legal department, early 1980s; Brut/Faberge, script reader; worked as a talent agent; affiliated with Edgar J. Scherick-Daniel Blatt Co.; Imagine Films Entertainment Inc. (independent movie and television production company), co-chief executive with filmmaker Ron Howard, c. 1986—.

AWARDS, HONORS: Academy Award nomination (with Lowell Ganz, Babaloo Mandel, and Bruce Jay Friedman), outstanding original screenplay, 1984, for *Splash;* named Producer of the Year, National Association of Theatre Owners and ShoWest, 1992.

CREDITS:

FILM WORK; PRODUCER, EXCEPT AS NOTED

Night Shift, Warner Brothers, 1982.
Splash (also see below), Buena Vista, 1984.
Real Genius, Tri-Star, 1985.
(With George Folsey, Jr.) *Spies Like Us,* Warner Brothers, 1985.
(With James Keach) *Armed and Dangerous* (also see below), Columbia, 1986.
(With David Valdes) *Like Father, Like Son,* Tri-Star, 1987.
Vibes, Columbia, 1988.
The 'Burbs, Universal, 1989.
Parenthood, Universal, 1989.
Executive producer (with Jim Abrahams), *Cry-Baby,* Universal, 1990.
Kindergarten Cop, Universal, 1990.
Executive producer, *Closet Land,* Universal, 1991.
Executive producer, *Backdraft,* Universal, 1991.
My Girl, Columbia, 1991.
Executive producer, *The Doors,* Tri-Star, 1991.
Housesitter, Universal, 1992.
(With Ron Howard) *Far and Away,* Universal, 1992.
Boomerang, Paramount, 1992.

FILM APPEARANCES

Made a brief appearance in *Splash,* Buena Vista, 1984.

TELEVISION WORK; MOVIES

Producer (with S. Bryan Hickox), *Thou Shalt Not Commit Adultery,* NBC, 1978.
Producer (with Bruce Cohn Curtis), *Zuma Beach,* NBC, 1978.
Executive producer, *Ask Max* (also known as *Disney Sunday Movie*), ABC, 1986.
Executive producer, *Splash, Too* (also known as *Disney Sunday Movie*), ABC, 1988.

TELEVISION WORK; SERIES

Executive producer, *Shadow Chasers* (also see below), ABC, 1985.
Executive producer, *Take Five,* CBS, 1987.
Executive producer, *Ohara,* ABC, 1987.
Executive producer, *Parenthood* (based on the 1989 film of the same name), NBC, 1990.

OTHER TELEVISION WORK

Producer, *Poison* (special), Showtime, 1988.
Executive producer, *Mutts* (special; also known as *Conversations with My Dog*), ABC, 1988.
Executive producer, *Smart Guys* (pilot), NBC, 1988.

TELEVISION APPEARANCES; SPECIALS

The New Hollywood, NBC, 1990.
Naked Hollywood (also known as *A&E Premieres*), A&E, 1991.

WRITINGS:

STORIES ADAPTED INTO FILMS

(With Bruce Jay Friedman) *Splash,* screenplay by Lowell Ganz, Babaloo Mandel, and Friedman, Buena Vista, 1984.
(With Harold Ramis and James Keach) *Armed and Dangerous,* screenplay by Harold Ramis and Peter Torokvei, Columbia, 1986.

STORIES ADAPTED FOR TELEVISION

Shadow Chasers (original story for series), ABC, 1985.

OTHER SOURCES:

PERIODICALS

Hollywood Reporter, February 20, 1992, pp. S1-S35.
New York Times, August 25, 1989.*

* * *

GREEN, Adolph 1915-

PERSONAL: Born December 2, 1915, in New York, NY; son of Daniel and Helen (Weiss) Green; married Phyllis Newman (an actress), January 31, 1960; children: Adam, Amanda.

ADDRESSES: Agent—John Springer Associates, 667 Madison Ave., New York, NY 10021.

CAREER: Lyricist, writer, and actor. Worked formerly as a Wall Street runner. Appeared in cabaret group, "The Revuers," at a number of clubs, including the Village Vanguard, the Rainbow Room, and the Blue Angel, and on a variety of television shows, 1939-44.

AWARDS, HONORS: All with Betty Comden: Theatre World Award, 1944, and Screenwriters Guild Award, 1949, both for *Our Town;* Screenwriters Guild Award, 1952, Antoinette Perry Award nomination, best book, 1986, voted one of the best American films of all times by the American Film Institute, and named one of the ten best films of all time (internationally) by *Sight & Sound,* all for *Singin' in the Rain;* Antoinette Perry Award, outstanding musical, New York Drama Critics' Circle Award, best new musical, and Donaldson Award, all 1953, all for *Wonderful Town;* Academy Award nomination, best story and screenplay, 1953, for *The Band Wagon;* Academy Award nomination, best story and screenplay, and Screenwriters Guild of America Award, both 1955, both for *It's Always Fair Weather;* Antoinette Perry Award nomination, outstanding musical, 1957, Screenwriters Guild Award, and Grammy Award nomination, best sound track album—original cast, motion picture or TV, both 1960, all for *Bells Are Ringing;* Obie Award, *Village Voice,* and Grammy Award nomination, best comedy-musical, both 1959, both for *A Party with Betty Comden and Adolph Green;* Grammy Award nomination, song of the year, 1961, for "Make Someone Happy," from the musical *Do Re Mi;* Antoinette Perry Award nomination, best musical, and Grammy Award nomination, best original cast show album, both 1961, both for *Do Re Mi;* Grammy Award nomination, best score from an original cast show album, 1967, Antoinette Perry Awards, best score, best lyrics, and best musical play, all 1968, all for *Hallelujah, Baby!;* Antoinette Perry Award, best musical, 1970, for *Applause;* Antoinette Perry Awards, best book and best score, and Grammy Award nomination, best cast show album, 1978, all for *On the Twentieth Century;* Antoinette Perry Award nominations, best book, and best score, both 1983, both for *A Doll's Life;* Antoinette Perry Award, best original score, and New York Drama Critics' Circle Award, best new musical, both 1991, and Grammy Award, best musical show album, all for *The Will Rogers Follies;* Kennedy Center Honor, 1991.

Named to Songwriters Hall of Fame, 1980; named Lion of the Performing Arts, New York Public Library, 1987.

CREDITS:

STAGE APPEARANCES

(Broadway debut) Ozzie, *On the Town* (also see below), Adelphi Theatre, New York City, 1944.

A Party (revue based on collection of Green and Comden's previously written songs and sketches; also see below), Cherry Lane Theatre, New York City, 1958, then expanded version at Golden Theatre, New York City, as *A Party with Betty Comden and Adolph Green,* 1958, later new version at Morosco Theatre, New York City, 1977, then on tour.

The Cradle Will Rock, Philharmonic Hall, New York City, 1964.

Lyrics and Lyricists, Kaufman Auditorium, New York City, 1971.

George Abbott . . . A Celebration, Shubert Theatre, New York City, 1976.

Voice over characters, *Phyllis Newman in Vamps and Rideouts,* Berkshire Theatre Festival, Stockbridge, MA, 1982.

Shimmel Shitzman and Jerry Hollingsworth, *The New Yorkers,* Morse Center Trinity Theatre, New York City, 1984.

Happy Birthday, Mr. Abbott!; or, Night of 100 Years, Palace Theatre, New York City, 1987.

The Players Club Centennial Salute, Shubert Theatre, 1989.

Also appeared in *An Evening with Betty Comden and Adolph Green,* 1971.

FILM APPEARANCES

The Revuers, *Greenwich Village,* Twentieth Century-Fox, 1944.

Commune leader, *Simon,* Warner Brothers, 1980.

Leo Silver, *My Favorite Year,* Metro-Goldwyn-Mayer (MGM)/United Artists, 1982.

Himself, *Garbo Talks,* United Artists, 1984.

Jerry Silber, *Lily in Love* (also known as *Playing for Keeps*), New Line Cinema, 1985.

Funny, Original Cinema, 1988.

Joey Wellman, *Je veux rentrer a la maison* (also known as *I Want to Go Home*), MK2 Diffusion, 1989.

TELEVISION APPEARANCES; SPECIALS

The American Film Institute Salute to Gene Kelly (also known as *The AFI Salute to Gene Kelly*), CBS, 1985.
Evening at Pops, PBS, 1987 and 1988.
The Kennedy Center Honors: A Celebration of the Performing Arts, CBS, 1988 and 1991.
The 45th Annual Tony Awards, CBS, 1991.

TELEVISION APPEARANCES; EPISODIC

Song performer, "Follies in Concert," *Great Performances,* PBS, 1986.
Song performer, "Broadway Sings: The Music of Jule Styne," *Great Performances,* PBS, 1987.
"Music by Richard Rodgers," *Great Performances*, PBS, 1990.

WRITINGS:

STAGE LYRICS, EXCEPT WHERE INDICATED; WITH BETTY COMDEN

(And sketches) *Two on the Aisle,* produced at Mark Hellinger Theatre, New York City, 1951.
Wonderful Town (two-act musical), produced at Winter Garden Theatre, New York City, 1953.
Additional lyrics, *Peter Pan* (three-act musical), produced at Winter Garden Theatre, 1954.
Say, Darling, produced at American National Theatre and Academy, New York City, 1958.
Do Re Mi (two-act musical; includes song "Make Someone Happy"), produced at St. James Theatre, New York City, 1960.
(And others) *Leonard Bernstein's Theatre Songs,* produced at Theatre de Lys, New York City, 1965.
Hallelujah, Baby! (two-act musical), produced at Martin Beck Theatre, New York City, 1967.
Lorelei (two-act musical; based on *Gentlemen Prefer Blondes*), produced at Civic Center Music Hall, Oklahoma City, OK, 1973, then at Palace Theatre, 1974.
(With others) *By Bernstein,* produced at Chelsea Theater Center Westside, New York City, 1975.
(And music; with others) *The Madwoman of Central Park West* (one-woman show), produced at 22 Steps Theatre, New York City, 1979.
(And others) *Diamonds* (two-act musical), produced at Circle in the Square Downtown, New York City, 1984-85.
The Will Rogers Follies, produced at Palace Theatre, 1991.

STAGE BOOK AND LYRICS; WITH COMDEN

On the Town (two-act musical based on the ballet *Fancy Free* by Jerome Robbins; also see below), produced at Adelphi Theatre, 1944.
Billion Dollar Baby, produced at Alvin Theatre, New York City, 1945.
Bonanza Bound, produced at Shubert Theatre, Philadelphia, PA, 1947.
Bells Are Ringing (two-act musical; also see below), produced at Shubert Theatre, 1956, published by Random House, 1957.
Subways Are for Sleeping (two-act musical), produced at St. James Theatre, 1961-62.
Fade Out—Fade In, produced at Mark Hellinger Theatre, 1964, published by Random House, 1965.
On the Twentieth Century (two-act musical), produced at St. James Theatre, 1978, published by Drama Book Publishers, 1981.
A Doll's Life (two-act musical), produced at Mark Hellinger Theatre, 1982.

STAGE BOOK; WITH COMDEN

Applause (two-act musical; based on film *All about Eve;* also see below), produced at Palace Theatre, 1970-72, published by Random House, 1971.

STAGE MUSIC; WITH COMDEN

(And others) *Straws in the Wind* (two-act musical), produced at American Place Theatre, 1975.

PLAYS; WITH COMDEN

A Party (revue based on collection of Green and Comden's previously written songs and sketches), first produced at Cherry Lane Theatre, 1958, expanded version produced at Golden Theatre as *A Party with Betty Comden and Adolph Green,* 1958, new version produced at Morosco Theatre, 1977, then on tour.
Singin' in the Rain (two-act musical; adaptation of movie of same title; also see below), produced at Gershwin Theatre, New York City, 1985-86.
(And others) *Jerome Robbins' Broadway,* produced at Imperial Theatre, New York City, 1989-90.

SCREENPLAYS, EXCEPT WHERE INDICATED; WITH COMDEN

Good News (based on the musical comedy by Lawrence Schwab, Frank Mandel, Buddy De Sylva, Lew Brown, and Ray Henderson), MGM, 1947.
The Barkleys of Broadway, MGM, 1949.
(And lyrics) *On the Town* (based on the musical play by Green, Comden, and Leonard Bernstein), MGM, 1949.
Lyrics, *Take Me Out to the Ballgame,* MGM, 1949.
(And lyrics) *Singin' in the Rain,* MGM, 1952, published by Viking, 1972.
(And lyrics) *The Band Wagon,* MGM, 1953.
(And lyrics) *It's Always Fair Weather,* MGM, 1955.

Auntie Mame (based on the novel *Mame* by Patrick Dennis and the play by Jerome Lawrence and Robert E. Lee), Warner Brothers, 1958.
(And lyrics) *Bells Are Ringing* (based on the musical play), MGM, 1960.
(And lyrics) *What a Way To Go* (based on a story by Gwen Davis), Twentieth Century-Fox, 1964.

FILM MUSIC; SONGS

"Mamushka," *The Addams Family,* Paramount, 1991.

TELEVISION SERIES; WITH COMDEN

(And Nat Hiken) *Buick Circus Hour,* NBC, 1952-53.

TELEVISION SPECIALS; WITH COMDEN

Let's Celebrate, ABC, 1972.
Applause (adapted from musical of same title), CBS, 1973.

Also author of various other musical comedy specials for ABC.

OTHER

Also author, with Comden, of music, book, and lyrics for cabaret group, "The Revuers," 1939-44.

RECORDINGS:

A Party with Betty Comden and Adolph Green, Capitol.

OTHER SOURCES:

BOOKS

Celebrity Register 1990, Gale, 1990.
Contemporary Authors, Volume 110, Gale, 1984.*

* * *

GREEN, Patricia

PERSONAL: Full name Patricia M. Green.

ADDRESSES: Agent—Cindy Turtle, The Turtle Agency, 12456 Ventura Blvd., Suite 1, Studio City, CA 91604.

CAREER: Writer, editor, and producer.

MEMBER: Writers Guild of America.

AWARDS, HONORS: Emmy Award, outstanding writing in a drama series, 1985, for *Cagney & Lacey* episode "Who Said It's Fair, Part II"; Emmy Award, outstanding drama series, 1986, for *Cagney & Lacey;* Emmy Award nomination, outstanding drama series, 1989, for *China Beach;* Humanitas Prize, sixty minute category, 1989, for *China Beach* episode "Promised Land"; Emmy Award, outstanding drama series, and Emmy Award nomination, outstanding writing in a drama series, both 1991, both for *L.A. Law.*

CREDITS:

TELEVISION WORK

Story editor, *North and South* (also see below), ABC, 1985.
Co-producer, *Cagney & Lacey* (also see below), CBS, 1985-86.
Supervising producer, *China Beach,* ABC, 1988-89.
Supervising producer, *L.A. Law* (also see below), NBC, 1990-91.
Co-executive producer, *L.A. Law,* NBC, 1991-92.

WRITINGS:

TELEVISION SERIES

Shirley, NBC, 1979-80.
Eight Is Enough, ABC, 1979-81.
The Mississippi, CBS, 1983-84.
Cagney & Lacey, CBS, 1984-85.
Scarecrow and Mrs. King, CBS, 1986.
L.A. Law, NBC, 1990-91.

TELEVISION EPISODES

Better Late Than Never, NBC, 1979.
American Dream, ABC, 1981.
King's Crossing, ABC, 1982.
Knots Landing, CBS, 1982.
Two Marriages, ABC, 1984.

OTHER TELEVISION WRITINGS

I'll Love You When You're More Like Me (special), ABC, 1979.
North and South (mini-series), ABC, 1985.
Perry Mason: The Case of the Murdered Madam (movie), NBC, 1987.
Hope Division (pilot), ABC, 1987.*

* * *

GREENAWAY, Peter 1942-

PERSONAL: Born April 5, 1942, in Newport, Wales; children: two daughters. *Education:* Studied painting and art history at Walthamstow College of Art.

ADDRESSES: Contact—c/o Miramax Films, 18 East 48th St., Suite 1601, New York, NY 10017.

CAREER: Director and screenwriter. British Film Institute, caretaker, beginning 1965; British Government Central Office of Information, director and editor of documentaries. Exhibited paintings at Lord's Gallery, 1964.

AWARDS, HONORS: Co-winner of special award, British Film Institute, 1980, for *The Falls;* best short film, Melbourne Film Festival, 1981, for *Act of God;* best artistic contribution, Cannes Film Festival, 1988, for *Drowning by Numbers;* two prizes at the Festival International du Nouveau Cinema et de la Video, 1990, for *A TV Dante.*

CREDITS:

FILM DIRECTOR

(And editor) *A Walk through H,* British Film Institute, 1978 (also see below).
(And editor and producer) *Vertical Features Remake,* British Film Institute, 1978 (also see below).
(And editor) *The Falls,* British Film Institute, 1980, released in the United States, 1983 (also see below).
The Draughtsman's Contract, British Film Institute, 1982, released in the United States by United Artists Classics, 1983 (also see below).
A Zed and Two Noughts, British Film Institute, 1985, released in the United States by Skouras, 1985 (also see below).
The Belly of an Architect, Hemdale, 1987 (also see below).
Drowning by Numbers, Film Four-Elsevier Vendex, 1988 (also see below).
The Cook, the Thief, His Wife, and Her Lover, Miramax, 1989 (also see below).
Prospero's Books (based on *The Tempest* by William Shakespeare), Miramax, 1991 (also see below).

Director of the films *Train,* 1966; *Tree,* 1966; *Five Postcards from Capital Cities,* 1967; *Revolution,* 1967; *Intervals,* 1969; *Erosion,* 1971; *H Is for House,* 1973; *Water,* 1975; *Water Wrackets,* 1975; *Windows,* 1975; *Goole by Numbers,* 1976; *Dear Phone,* 1977; *1-100* (one source says *1-1C0*), 1978; *Making a Splash,* 1984; *A TV Dante—Canto Five,* 1984; *Inside Rooms: The Bathroom,* 1985; *A TV Dante,* 1989; *Death in the Seine,* 1989 (also see below). Also director of *Twenty-six Bathrooms.*

FILM DIRECTOR; DOCUMENTARIES

Act of God, British Film Institute, 1981.
Zandra Rhodes, Central Office of Information (England), 1981.
Modern American Composers 1: Cage and Monk, Trans Atlantic Films/Channel Four, 1984.
Modern American Composers 2: Glass and Ashley, Trans Atlantic Films/Channel Four, 1984.

WRITINGS:

A Walk through H (screenplay), British Film Institute, 1978.
Vertical Features Remake (screenplay), British Film Institute, 1978.
The Falls (screenplay), British Film Institute, 1980, released in the United States, 1983.
The Draughtsman's Contract (screenplay), British Film Institute, 1982, released in the United States by United Artists Classics, 1983.
A Zed and Two Noughts (screenplay), British Film Institute, 1985, Skouras, 1985, published by Faber, 1986.
The Belly of an Architect (screenplay), Hemdale, 1987.
Drowning by Numbers (screenplay), Film Four-Elsevier Vendex, 1988, published by Faber, 1988.
The Cook, the Thief, His Wife, and Her Lover (screenplay), Miramax, 1989.
Prospero's Books (screenplay; based on *The Tempest* by William Shakespeare), Miramax, 1991.

Also author of the screenplay, *Death in the Seine,* 1989, and a novel, *Fifty-five Men on Horseback,* 1990.

OTHER SOURCES:

BOOKS

Contemporary Authors, Volume 127, Gale, 1989, p. 174.

PERIODICALS

Film Comment, May-June, 1990, p. 54.
Interview, March, 1990, p. 120.
New York Times, April 1, 1990, p. H27; April 26, 1991, p. C7.*

*　　*　　*

GREENE, Ellen 1952(?)-

PERSONAL: Born February 22, c. 1952, in Brooklyn, NY; daughter of a dentist and a guidance counselor; companion of Marty Robinson (a puppeteer), since 1982. *Education:* Attended Rider College.

ADDRESSES: *Agent*—Joan Hyler, William Morris Agency, 151 El Camino Dr., Beverly Hills, CA 90212.

CAREER: Actress and singer. Performed in a musical road show and in a cabaret act in various clubs in New York City, including The Brothers and the Sisters Club and Reno Sweeney's.

AWARDS, HONORS: Antoinette Perry Award nomination, best actress in a featured role in a Broadway musical, 1977, for *Threepenny Opera.*

CREDITS:

STAGE APPEARANCES

(Broadway debut) Title role/Barbara's voice, *Rachel Lily Rosenbloom and Don't You Ever Forget It!,* Broadhurst Theatre, New York City, 1973.
Chrissy, *In the Boom Boom Room,* New York Shakespeare Festival (NYSF), NYSF Public/Anspacher Theatre, New York City, 1974.

Jenny Towler, *Threepenny Opera,* NYSF, Vivian Beaumont Theatre, New York City, 1976, and Delacorte Theatre, New York City, 1977.
Funny Face, Studio Arena Theatre, Buffalo, NY, 1978-79.
Wake Up, It's Time to Go to Bed!, NYSF, Public/LuEsther Theatre, New York City, 1979.
Disrobing the Bride, Music-Theatre Group/Lenox Arts Center, The Cubiculo, New York City, 1981.
Suzanne/Little Rose, *The Little Prince and the Aviator,* Alvin Theatre, New York City, 1981-82.
Audrey, *Little Shop of Horrors* (also see below), Workshop of the Players Art (WPA) Theatre, New York City, 1982, then Orpheum Theatre, New York City, 1982.
Ellis, *Starting Monday,* WPA Theatre, 1990.

Also appeared in *The Sorrows of Stephen,* NYSF, New York City; *Stage Directions,* NYSF, New York City; *The Seven Deadly Sins,* produced with *The Berlin Requiem* as *Two By Brecht and Weill,* American Repertory Theatre, Cambridge, MA; *The Nature and Purpose of the Universe,* New York City; and *Teeth 'n' Smiles,* New York City. Appeared as Audrey in productions of *Little Shop of Horrors* (also see below) at Westwood Playhouse, Los Angeles, and in London.

MAJOR TOURS

Sonia Walsk, *They're Playing Our Song,* U.S. cities, 1979.

Toured as a singer and dancer in *George M!,* U.S. cities, 1970-71.

FILM APPEARANCES

(Film debut) Sarah, *Next Stop, Greenwich Village,* Twentieth Century-Fox, 1976.
Karen Mulligan, *I'm Dancing as Fast as I Can,* Paramount, 1982.
Audrey, *Little Shop of Horrors,* Warner Brothers, 1986.
Annette Uttanzi, *Me and Him,* Columbia, 1988.
Ellen, *Talk Radio,* Universal, 1988.
Jan Emerson, *Pump Up the Volume,* New Line Cinema, 1990.
Voice of Goldie, *Rock-a-Doodle* (animated), Samuel Goldwyn, 1991.

Also appeared in *Little Feet,* 1990, and as Judy in *Fathers and Sons,* 1992.

TELEVISION APPEARANCES; MOVIES

Paula, *Seventh Avenue,* NBC, 1977.
Kitty Packard, *Dinner at Eight,* TNT, 1989.
Sister Ruth, *Glory! Glory!,* HBO, 1989.
Sally Maggio, *Road Show,* CBS, 1989.

TELEVISION APPEARANCES; EPISODIC

Darlene, *Miami Vice,* NBC, 1981.

OTHER TELEVISION APPEARANCES

Jess, *The Rock Rainbow* (pilot; one source says *Rock Follies*), ABC, 1978.
Superman's Fiftieth Anniversary: A Celebration of the Man of Steel (special), CBS, 1988.

OTHER SOURCES:

PERIODICALS

People, January 12, 1987, p. 43.*

* * *

GRESHAM, Gloria 1946(?)-

PERSONAL: Born c. 1946.

ADDRESSES: Agent—Gersh Agency, 250 North Canon Dr., Beverly Hills, CA 90210.

CAREER: Costume designer. Worked on Broadway and Off-Broadway and worked as a design assistant on films.

MEMBER: Costume Designers Guild.

AWARDS, HONORS: Academy Award nomination, best achievement in costume design, 1990, for *Avalon.*

CREDITS:

FILM WORK; COSTUME DESIGNER

Just Tell Me What You Want, Warner Brothers, 1980.
Urban Cowboy, Paramount, 1980.
Zorro, the Gay Blade, Twentieth Century-Fox, 1981.
Author! Author!, Twentieth Century-Fox, 1982.
Diner, Metro-Goldwyn-Mayer/United Artists, 1982.
The Escape Artist, Orion/Warner Brothers, 1982.
Without a Trace, Twentieth Century-Fox, 1983.
Body Double, Columbia, 1984.
(With Francine Jamison and Jim Tyson) *Fletch,* Universal, 1984.
(With Kendall Errair and Barton K. James) *Footloose,* Paramount, 1984.
(With Bernie Pollack) *The Natural,* Tri-Star, 1984.
Eight Million Ways to Die, Tri-Star, 1986.
Tin Men, Buena Vista, 1987.
Outrageous Fortune, Buena Vista, 1987.
Midnight Run, Universal, 1988.
Twins, Universal, 1988.
Ghostbusters II, Columbia, 1989.
The War of the Roses, Twentieth Century-Fox, 1989.
When Harry Met Sally, Columbia, 1989.
Avalon, Tri-Star, 1990.
Kindergarten Cop, Universal, 1990.
Misery, Columbia, 1990.
V. I. Warshawski (also known as *Fully Loaded*), Buena Vista, 1991.

Beethoven, Universal, 1992.

STAGE WORK; COSTUME DESIGNER

A Black Quartet, Tambellini's Gate Theatre, then Frances Adler Theatre, 1969.
The Way It Is!!!, New Lincoln Theatre, 1969.
Show Me Where the Good Times Are, Edison Theatre, New York City, 1970.
Forty Carats, tour of U.S. cities, 1974.
Weekend with Feathers, Shubert Theatre, New Haven, CT, then on tour of U.S. cities, 1976.

TELEVISION WORK

Assistant costume designer for television movies.

SIDELIGHTS: Favorite Films: Avalon and *Diner.*

OTHER SOURCES:

PERIODICALS

People Weekly, spring, 1990, p. 122.*

* * *

GRIECO, Richard 1965(?)-

PERSONAL: Born c. 1965, in Watertown, NY. *Education:* Attended Central Connecticut State University.

ADDRESSES: Agent—Creative Artists Agency, 9830 Wilshire Blvd., Beverly Hills, CA 90212. *Publicist*—Diane Passarelli, Manager of Public Relations, Stephen J. Cannell Productions, Inc., 7083 Hollywood Blvd., Hollywood, CA 90028.

CAREER: Actor. Worked as a model in New York City before beginning acting career.

CREDITS:

TELEVISION APPEARANCES; SERIES

Rick Gardener, *One Life to Live,* ABC, 1986-87.
Officer Dennis Booker, *21 Jump Street,* Fox, 1987-89.
Officer Dennis Booker, *Booker,* Fox, 1989-90.

TELEVISION APPEARANCES; EPISODIC

Appeared in *Rags to Riches; Who's the Boss? The Bronx Zoo;* and *Facts of Life.*

TELEVISION APPEARANCES; SPECIALS

Golden Globe Awards, TBS, 1990.
17th Annual People's Choice Awards, CBS, 1991.

FILM APPEARANCES

Michael Corben, *If Looks Could Kill* (also known as *Teen Agent*), Warner Brothers, 1991.
Benny "Bugsy" Siegel, *Mobsters* (also known as *Gangsters*), Universal, 1991.

OTHER SOURCES:

PERIODICALS

People Weekly, June 12, 1989, p. 61.*

* * *

GRIFFITH, Andy 1926-

PERSONAL: Full name, Andrew Samuel Griffith; born June 1, 1926, in Mount Airy, NC; son of Carl Lee and Geneva (Nunn) Griffith; married Barbara Edwards, 1949 (divorced); married Cindi Knight, April 2, 1983; children: (first marriage) Andy Sam, Dixie Nunn. *Education:* University of North Carolina at Chapel Hill, B.A. in music, 1949. *Avocational interests:* Swimming and skeet and trap shooting.

ADDRESSES: Office—P.O. Box 1968, Manteo, NC 27954-1968. *Agent*—William Morris Agency, 151 El Camino, Beverly Hills, CA 90212.

CAREER: Actor. Taught at Goldsboro High School, Goldsboro, NC; stand-up comic at the Blue Angel nightclub in New York City, 1954, and at other clubs across the country.

AWARDS, HONORS: Theatre World Award, 1955-56, and Antoinette Perry Award nomination, outstanding supporting or featured dramatic actor, 1956, both for *No Time for Sergeants;* named best male lead in a musical by *Variety,* 1959, for *Destry Rides Again;* Antoinette Perry Award nomination, best actor in a musical, 1960, for *Destry Rides Again;* Tarheel Award, 1961; Outstanding Television Personality Award, Advertising Club of Baltimore, 1968; Emmy Award nomination, outstanding supporting actor in a limited series or special, 1981, for *Murder in Texas;* People's Choice Award, male performer in a new program, 1987, for *Matlock.*

CREDITS:

TELEVISION APPEARANCES; SERIES

The Steve Allen Show, NBC, 1959-60.
Andy Taylor, *The Andy Griffith Show* (also see below), CBS, 1960-68.
Andy Thompson, *Headmaster,* CBS, 1970-71.
Andy Sawyer, *The New Andy Griffith Show,* CBS, 1972.
Sheriff Sam Adams, *Adams of Eagle Lake* (also see below), 1975.
Harry Broderick, *Salvage 1* (also see below), ABC, 1978.
Carroll Yeager, *The Yeagers,* ABC, 1980.
Lamont Devereaux, *Best of the West,* ABC, 1981-82.

Title role, *Matlock* (also see below), NBC, 1986-1992, ABC, 1992—.

TELEVISION APPEARANCES; MOVIES

Will Stockdale, "No Time for Sergeants," *The U.S. Steel Hour,* ABC, 1955.
Artie Sawyer, *The Strangers in 7A,* CBS, 1972.
Priest, *Go Ask Alice,* ABC, 1973.
Sam Farragut, *Pray for the Wildcats,* ABC, 1974.
Horton Maddock, *Savages,* ABC, 1974.
"Six Characters in Search of an Author," *Hollywood Television Theatre,* PBS, 1976.
Gus Brenner, *Street Killing,* ABC, 1976.
Ash Robinson, *Murder in Texas,* NBC, 1981.
Guy Harris, *The Demon Murder Case,* NBC, 1983.
John Wallace, *Murder in Coweta County,* CBS, 1983.
Victor Worheide, *Fatal Vision,* NBC, 1984.
Judge Julius Sullivan, *Crime of Innocence,* NBC, 1985.
Andy Taylor, *Return to Mayberry* (also see below; based on *The Andy Griffith Show*), NBC, 1986.
Noah Talbot, *Under the Influence,* CBS, 1986.

TELEVISION APPEARANCES; MINI-SERIES

Esker Scott Anderson, *Washington: Behind Closed Doors,* ABC, 1977.
Lewis Venor, *Centennial,* NBC, 1978-79.
General Barney Slater, *From Here to Eternity,* NBC, 1979.
Commander Robert Munroe, *Roots: The Next Generation,* ABC, 1979.

TELEVISION APPEARANCES; SPECIALS

The Andy Williams Special, NBC, 1962.
The Bob Hope Show, NBC, 1963.
The Andy Williams Show, NBC, 1964.
Cohost, *The Andy Griffith-Don Knotts-Jim Nabors Show,* CBS, 1965.
Friends and Nabors, CBS, 1966.
Host, *Andy Griffith's Uptown-Downtown Show,* CBS, 1967.
The Don Knotts Special, CBS, 1967.
The Tennessee Ernie Ford Special, CBS, 1967.
Host, *Looking Back* (also see below), CBS, 1969.
Don Knotts' Nice Clean, Decent, Wholesome Hour, CBS, 1970.
Mr. Already Married, *Dinah in Search of the Ideal Man,* NBC, 1973.
Mitzi and a Hundred Guys, CBS, 1975.
Celebration: The American Spirit, ABC, 1976.
Voice of Story Teller, *Frosty's Winter Wonderland,* ABC, 1979.
The Nashville Palace, ABC, 1980.
The Fourteenth Annual People's Choice Awards, CBS, 1988.
Tennessee Ernie Ford: Fifty Golden Years, The Nashville Network, 1990.
The All-Star Salute to Our Troops, CBS, 1991.

Also appeared in *City vs. Country,* 1971.

TELEVISION APPEARANCES; PILOTS

Guest, *The Jud Strunk Show,* ABC, 1972.
Guest, *The NBC Follies,* NBC, 1973.
Sheriff Sam McNeill, *Winter Kill* (for series *Adams of Eagle Lake*), ABC, 1974.
Abel Marsh, *The Girl in the Empty Grave* (also known as *Abel*), NBC, 1977.
Abel Marsh, *Deadly Game* (sequel to *The Girl in the Empty Grave*), ABC, 1977.
Harry Broderick, *Salvage* (for series *Salvage 1*), ABC, 1979.
Vernon Bliss, *For Lovers Only,* ABC, 1982.
Benjamin J. Matlock, *Diary of a Perfect Murder* (for series *Matlock*), NBC, 1986.

TELEVISION APPEARANCES; EPISODIC

Monologist, *Ed Sullivan Show,* CBS, 1954.

Also appeared on *Hotel,* ABC.

TELEVISION WORK; EXECUTIVE PRODUCER

(With Richard O. Linke) *Mayberry, R.F.D.* (series), CBS, 1968-71.
Return to Mayberry (movie), NBC, 1986.

FILM APPEARANCES

(Debut) Lonesome Rhodes, *A Face in the Crowd,* Warner Brothers, 1957.
Will Stockdale, *No Time for Sergeants,* Warner Bros., 1958.
Al Woods, *Onionhead,* Warner Bros., 1958.
Pat Collins, *The Second Time Around,* Twentieth Century-Fox, 1961.
Sam, *Angel in My Pocket,* Universal, 1969.
Howard Pike, *Hearts of the West* (also known as *Hollywood Cowboy*), United Artists, 1975.
Colonel Ticonderoga, *Rustler's Rhapsody,* Paramount, 1985.

Also appeared in *The Treasure Chest Murder,* 1975.

STAGE APPEARANCES

Ko-Ko, *The Mikado,* University of North Carolina Players, c. 1947.
Sir Walter Raleigh, *The Lost Colony* (annual outdoor drama pageant), Roanoake Island, NC, c. 1947-53.
(Broadway debut) Will Stockdale, *No Time for Sergeants,* Alvin Theatre, New York City, 1955.
Tom Destry, *Destry Rides Again,* Imperial Theatre, New York City, 1959-60.

RECORDINGS:

What It Was, Was Football, Capitol, 1953.

Also released a comedic version of *Romeo and Juliet.*

WRITINGS:

TELEVISION SCREENPLAYS

Looking Back, CBS, 1969.

OTHER SOURCES:

PERIODICALS

People, April 14, 1986, p. 90.*

* * *

GROENING, Matt 1954-

PERSONAL: Surname is pronounced "*gray*-ning" (rhymes with "raining"); born February 15, 1954, in Portland OR; son of Homer (a filmmaker) and Margaret (a teacher) Groening; married Deborah Caplan (his manager and business partner), October 29, 1986; children: Homer, Abraham. *Education:* Evergreen State College, B.A., 1977. *Avocational interests:* Watching badly translated foreign films, nurturing ducks.

ADDRESSES: Contact—Susan A. Grode (attorney-representative), 2029 Century Park E., No. 3590, Los Angeles, CA 90067.

CAREER: Writer, cartoonist, producer, and business executive. Worked variously as a cemetery landscaper, dishwasher, clerk, and ghost writer/chauffeur to an elderly filmmaker, Los Angeles, CA, 1977-79; *Los Angeles Reader,* Los Angeles, positions included circulation manager, editor, writer, cartoonist, and author of "Sound Mix" music column, 1979-84; formed Life in Hell Cartoon Co. and Acme Features Syndicate, with wife, Deborah Caplan, in the 1980s.

AWARDS, HONORS: Won short story contest, *Jack and Jill,* 1962; Emmy Award nominations, outstanding writing in a variety or music program, 1987, 1988, 1989, all for *The Tracy Ullman Show;* Emmy Awards, outstanding animated program, 1989, 1990, for *The Simpsons;* Emmy Award nomination, outstanding animated program, 1990, for *The Simpsons Roasting on an Open Fire.*

CREDITS:

TELEVISION WORK; CREATOR, DEVELOPER, AND ANIMATOR

(And director and producer) *The Tracy Ullman Show* (televised debut of *The Simpsons;* also see below), Fox, 1987-89.

(Executive producer, with James L. Brooks and Sam Simon) *Simpsons Roasting on an Open Fire* (Christmas special; also see below), Fox, 1989.

(And director of voice recording sessions, and executive producer, with Brooks and Simon) *The Simpsons* (also see below), Fox, 1990—.

RECORDINGS:

ALBUMS

(Executive producer) *The Simpsons Sing the Blues* (also see below), Geffen, 1991.

WRITINGS:

"LIFE IN HELL" CARTOON STRIP BOOKS

Love is Hell, privately printed, 1984, revised, Pantheon, 1985.

Work is Hell, Pantheon, 1986.

School is Hell, Pantheon, 1987.

Childhood is Hell, Pantheon, 1988.

Akbar and Jeff's Guide to Life, Pantheon, 1989.

Greetings from Hell, Pantheon, 1989.

The Big Book of Hell, Pantheon, 1990.

With Love from Hell: A Postcard Book, HarperCollins, 1991.

How to Go to Hell, HarperCollins, 1991.

Life in Hell appeared as a privately printed comic strip beginning in the late 1970s, and first appeared in *Wet,* 1978, then as a regular feature in *The Los Angeles Reader,* 1980-86, and in *L.A. Weekly,* 1984—. The strip is syndicated to two hundred periodicals worldwide through Acme Features Syndicate, beginning in the 1980s. Groening also created "The Life in Hell Fun Calendars" published by Pantheon, 1985-89, and HarperCollins, 1990—.

"THE SIMPSONS" BOOKS

The Simpsons Xmas Book (adapted from a screenplay by Mimi Pond), HarperCollins, 1990.

The Simpsons Rainy Day Fun Book, HarperCollins, 1990.

Greetings from the Simpsons, HarperCollins, 1990.

(With sister, Maggie Groening) *Maggie Simpson's Alphabet Book,* HarperCollins, 1991.

(With Maggie Groening) *Maggie Simpson's Book of Animals,* HarperCollins, 1991.

(With Maggie Groening) *Maggie Simpson's Book of Colors and Shapes,* HarperCollins, 1991.

(With Maggie Groening) *Maggie Simpson's Counting Book,* HarperCollins, 1991.

Simpsons Student Diary, Trielle Publishers (Australia), 1991.

Simpsons Uncensored Family Album, HarperCollins, 1991.

Simpsons Fun in the Sun Book, HarperCollins, 1992.

Groening is also the creator of Simpsons calendars, published by HarperCollins, 1990—, and *Simpsons Illustrated* magazine, published by Welsh.

OTHER BOOKS

(With Steve Vance) *Postcards That Ate My Brain,* Pantheon, 1990.

Also creator, with Vance, of "Postcards That Ate My Brain" calendars. Contributor to periodicals, including *Jack and Jill* and *Film Comment.*

SONGS

(With D. J. Jazzy Jeff), "Deep, Deep Trouble," from *The Simpsons Sing the Blues,* Geffen, 1991.

TELEVISION SCRIPTS

The Tracy Ullman Show (fifty animated *Simpsons* segments), Fox, 1987-89.
(With others) *The Simpsons,* Fox, 1990—.
(Animated character dialogue) *The Ice Capades Fiftieth Anniversary Special,* ABC, 1990.

OTHER SOURCES:

BOOKS

Authors and Artists for Young Adults, Volume 8, Gale, 1992, pp. 73-83.

PERIODICALS

Advocate, February 26, 1991, p. 30.
Detroit Free Press, July 16, 1990, p. A13.
Los Angeles Magazine, February, 1985, p. 22.
Los Angeles Times, April 29, 1990, pp. D1-7.
Mother Jones, December, 1989, p. 28.
Playboy, July, 1990, p. 130.
Saturday Review, April, 1985, p. 50.
Washington Post, December 18, 1988, pp. F16-18.

* * *

GROVER, Stanley 1926-

PERSONAL: Born Stanley Grover Nienstedt, March 28, 1926, in Woodstock, IL; son of Harry B. (an insurance broker) and Maude (Grover) Nienstedt; married Linda Glavey (a government secretary), April 7, 1956 (divorced, February 28, 1974); children: two sons, one daughter. *Education:* University of Missouri, A.B., 1949; studied with John Daggett Howell, 1949-66; attended Roosevelt University, 1949-50. *Avocational interests:* Swimming, water skiing, maps and geography, travel.

ADDRESSES: Office—c/o Atkins Associates, 303 South Crescent Heights Blvd., Los Angeles, CA 90048.

CAREER: Actor. Page boy for National Broadcasting Company (NBC), Chicago, IL. Performed in nightclubs in Chicago, Washington, DC, New York City, Puerto Rico, and Montreal, Quebec. *Military service:* U.S. Naval Reserve, active duty, 1944-46; served in Pacific theater.

MEMBER: Actors Equity Association, Screen Actors Guild, American Federation of Television and Radio Artists, American Guild of Variety Artists, Players Club (New York City), Phi Mu Alpha Sinfonia.

CREDITS:

TELEVISION APPEARANCES; SERIES

That Was the Week That Was, NBC, 1964.
Dr. Kevin Reed, *The Edge of Night,* CBS, 1971-72.
Mark Mercer, *Somerset,* NBC, 1972.
Bert Baker, *Married: The First Year,* CBS, 1979.
Judge Richard Lobel, *L.A. Law,* NBC, 1989-92.

Played Lieutenant Bernie Green, *Love Is a Many-Splendored Thing,* CBS.

TELEVISION APPEARANCES; MOVIES

Fireman, *Nicky's World,* CBS, 1974.
The French Atlantic Affair, ABC, 1979.
Mr. Sandusky, *Marriage Is Alive and Well,* NBC, 1980.
Enola Gay, NBC, 1980.
Alexander Haig, *The Betty Ford Story,* ABC, 1987.
Hiram Carey, *Nutcracker: Money, Madness, and Murder,* NBC, 1987.
Shannon's Deal, NBC, 1989.
John Montaine, *False Arrest* (also known as *Reasonable Doubt*), ABC, 1991.

Also appeared as Mr. McKenzie in *Together,* 1991.

TELEVISION APPEARANCES; SPECIALS

The Good Years, CBS, 1961.
Drink, Drank, Drunk, PBS, c. 1975.
Desperate, ABC, 1987.
Werewolf, Fox, 1987.

TELEVISION APPEARANCES; EPISODIC

Contestant, *Arthur Godfrey's Talent Scouts,* CBS, 1950.
The Mike Wallace Show, ABC, 1952.
Chance of a Lifetime, ABC, 1955-56.
Music for a Summer Night, ABC, 1959.
The Andros Targets, CBS, 1977.
Capital News, ABC, 1990.
"Mrs. Cage," *American Playhouse,* PBS, 1992.

Also appeared on *The Libby Show,* 1955 and 1956, and as the father on *Sisters.* Appeared on episodes of other shows, including *Murder, She Wrote; Stingray; Hardcastle and McCormick; Dallas; Fame; Lou Grant; Eight Is Enough; Barnaby Jones; Starsky and Hutch; The Waltons; Hart to*

Hart; Capitol; CHiPs; Falcon Crest; Knots Landing; Love of Life; General Hospital; and *Hill Street Blues.*

FILM APPEARANCES

Jack Snowden, *Network,* Metro-Goldwyn-Mayer/United Artists (UA), 1976.
Powell's second lawyer, *The Onion Field,* Avco Embassy, 1979.
March, *North Dallas Forty,* Paramount, 1979.
Baldwin Bureau, *Being There,* UA, 1979.
Reporter, *Ghostbusters,* Columbia, 1984.
Phil's dad, *Fandango,* Warner Brothers, 1985.
NSA inspector, *The Falcon and the Snowman,* Orion, 1985.
Consul Saunders, *Old Gringo,* Columbia, 1989.

Also appeared in *The Law at Randado.*

STAGE APPEARANCES

(New York debut) Member of chorus, *Seventeen,* Broadhurst Theatre, New York City, 1951.
Fred and understudy, *Wish You Were Here* (also see below), Imperial Theatre, 1952.
Woody Mahoney, *Finian's Rainbow,* Starlight Theatre, Kansas City, MO, 1955, then New York City Center, New York City, 1967.
Caliph, *Kismet,* Valley Forge Music Fair, Devon, PA, 1956, then Meadowbrook Dinner Theatre, Cedar Grove, NJ, 1960.
Peter, *Plain and Fancy,* Lambertville Music Circus, Lambertville, NJ, 1956, then Meadowbrook Dinner Theatre, 1959.
Understudy for title role, *Candide,* Martin Beck Theatre, New York City, 1956.
The singer, *Time Remembered,* Morosco Theatre, New York City, 1957.
Marius, *Fanny,* South Shore Music Circus, Cohasset, MA, 1958.
Willoughby, *Thirteen Daughters,* 54th Street Theatre, New York City, 1961.
Lieutenant Cable, *South Pacific* (also see below), New York City Center, 1961.
Chick, *Wish You Were Here,* Imperial Theatre, New York City, 1952, later Cape Cod Melody Tent, Hyannis, MA, 1961.
Carver, *Let It Ride!,* Eugene O'Neill Theatre, New York City, 1961.
Charley Wayne, *Mr. President,* St. James Theatre, New York City, 1962.
Red Shadow, *Desert Song,* Cape Cod Melody Tent, 1963.
Tony, *West Side Story,* Casa Manana, Fort Worth, TX, 1963.
Lun Tha, *The King and I,* New York City Center, 1968.
Dr. Taylor, *Allegro,* Goodspeed Opera House, East Haddam, CT, 1968.
Michael, *I Do! I Do!,* Woodstock Playhouse, Woodstock, NY, 1969.
Bob Primm, *Lyle,* McAlpin Rooftop Theatre, New York City, 1970.
Larry, *Company,* Alvin Theatre, New York City, 1970-71.
Captain Paul Fontaine, *Desert Song,* Kennedy Center for the Performing Arts, Washington, DC, then Uris Theatre, New York City, 1973.
Gregory Schaeffer, *Don't Call Back,* Helen Hayes Theatre, New York City, 1975.
Tintypes, South Coast Repertory Theatre, Costa Mesa, CA, 1981-82.
Legion commander, *The Petrified Forest,* Los Angeles Theatre Center, Los Angeles, CA, 1985-86.
Celebrating Josh, Shubert Theatre, New York City, 1989.

Also appeared as Tommy, *Brigadoon* (also see below), Chautauqua, NY, 1959; as Curly, *Oklahoma!,* San Juan, PR, 1959; in *Tribute to Oscar Hammerstein,* 46th Street Theatre, New York City; and in *Baby.*

MAJOR TOURS

Chick, *Wish You Were Here,* U.S. cities, 1956 and 1959.
Spofford, *Gentlemen Prefer Blondes,* northeastern U.S. cities, 1966.
Sid, *Pajama Game,* northeastern U.S. cities, 1966.
Oscar, *Sweet Charity,* Ohio cities, 1967.
Eddie, *Do I Hear a Waltz?,* Ohio cities, 1967.

Also toured as Lieutenant Cable, *South Pacific,* 1952-54; Jack, *Where's Charley?,* 1960; and Tommy, *Brigadoon,* 1962.

RADIO APPEARANCES

Commentator from the ship S.S. *Liberte,* 1952.

RECORDINGS:

ALBUMS

RCA Reader's Digest: Treasury of Great Operettas, RCA, 1962.

Also recorded *All-Time Broadway Hit Parade,* 1965.

* * *

GRUSIN, Dave 1934-

PERSONAL: Born June 26, 1934, in Littleton (some sources say Denver), CO; son of Henri (a violinist) and Rosabelle (a pianist; maiden name, De Poyster) Grusin. *Education:* University of Colorado, B. Music, piano, 1956; graduate study at Manhattan School of Music, 1959-60.

ADDRESSES: Office—GRP Records, Inc., 555 West 57th St., New York, NY 10019. *Agent*—Gorfaine-

Schwartz Agency, 3301 Barham Blvd., Suite 201, Los Angeles, CA 90068.

CAREER: Pianist, keyboardist, composer, conductor, arranger, and record producer. Worked and performed with Quincy Jones, beginning in early 1960s; worked and performed with numerous artists, including Mel Torme, Peggy Lee, Ruth Price, Sergio Mendes, Tom Scott, Gerry Mulligan, Lee Ritenour, Sarah Vaughan, Carmen McRae, Jon Lucien, Roberta Flack, and Aretha Franklin; record producer, with Larry Rosen, beginning in 1976; owner, with Rosen, of GRP Records, Inc., 1983—. *Military service:* U.S. Navy, involved with air operations, 1956-58.

MEMBER: Phi Mu Alpha.

AWARDS, HONORS: Grammy Award nomination, best arrangement accompanying vocalists, 1968, for "Fool on the Hill"; Grammy Award (with Paul Simon), best album or original instrumental score for a motion picture or television special, 1968, for *The Graduate;* Grammy Award nomination, best arrangement accompanying vocalists, 1973, for "Lady Love"; Grammy Award nomination, best arrangement accompanying vocalists, 1973, for "Rashida"; Grammy Award nomination (with Quincy Jones and Louis Johnson), best instrumental composition, 1976, for "Midnight Soul Patrol"; Academy Award nomination, best original score, 1978, for *Heaven Can Wait;* Academy Award nomination, best original score, 1979, for *The Champ.*

Grammy Award nomination, best instrumental arrangement, 1980, for "Marcosinho," from *The Hawk* (album); Grammy Award nomination, best instrumental arrangement, 1981, for "Mountain Dance," from *Mountain Dance* (album); Academy Award nomination, best original score, 1981, and Grammy Award nomination, best original score in a motion picture or a television special, 1982, both for *On Golden Pond;* Academy Award nomination (with Alan and Marilyn Bergman), best song, 1982, for "It Might Be You," from *Tootsie* (film), Grammy Award nomination, best instrumental composition, 1983, and Grammy Award nomination (with the Bergmans), best original score in a motion picture or television special, 1983, all for *Tootsie;* Grammy Award nomination, best instrumental composition, 1983, for "An Actor's Life"; Grammy Award, best instrumental arrangement, 1983, for "Summer Sketches '82," from *Dave Grusin and the N.Y./L.A. Dream Band* (album); Grammy Award (with Lee Ritenour), best instrumental arrangement, 1985, for "Early A.M. Attitude," and Grammy Award nomination (with Ritenour), best arrangement accompanying vocals, 1985, for "Harlequin," both from *Harlequin* (album), and Grammy Award nomination (with Ritenour), best pop instrumental, 1985, for *Harlequin.* Grammy Award nomination (with Ritenour), best instrumental composition, 1986, for "Earth Run," from *Earth Run* (album); Grammy Award nomination, best pop instrumental, for "It Might Be You," and Grammy Award nomination, best instrumental arrangement, for "The Heart Is a Lonely Hunter," both 1987, from *Cinemagic* (album), and Grammy Award nomination (with Don Murray, Keith Grant, and Josiah Gluck), best recording engineering, non-classical, 1987, for *Cinemagic;* Academy Award, best original score, 1988, for *The Milagro Beanfield War,* and Grammy Award, best arrangement on an instrumental, 1989, for "Suite from *The Milagro Beanfield War,*" from *Migration* (album); Academy Award nomination, best original score, 1989, for *The Fabulous Baker Boys* (film), Grammy Award, best instrumental arrangement accompanying vocals, 1989, for "My Funny Valentine," from *The Fabulous Baker Boys Motion Picture Soundtrack* (album), and Grammy Award, best album of original instrumental background score written for a motion picture or television, 1989, for *The Fabulous Baker Boys Motion Picture Soundtrack;* Golden Globe Award nomination, best original score, and Academy Award nomination, best original score, both 1990, for *Havana;* Golden Globe Award nomination, best original score, 1991, for *For the Boys;* Grammy Award, best arrangement on an instrumental, 1992, for "Medley: Bess You Is My Woman/I Love You Porgy," from *The Gershwin Connection* (album).

Honorary doctorates from Berklee, 1988, and University of Colorado, 1989.

CREDITS:

FILM WORK; ARRANGER

"My Funny Valentine," by Richard Rodgers and Oscar Hammerstein, *The Fabulous Baker Boys* (also see below), Twentieth Century-Fox, 1989.

TELEVISION WORK

Arranger and orchestra leader, *The Andy Williams Show* (series), NBC, 1960-64.

Also worked as music director for *Disney World—A Gala Opening—Disneyland East,* 1971.

TELEVISION APPEARANCES

Evening at Pops (special), PBS, 1988.

SONG ARRANGER

Arranger of numerous songs, including "Fool on the Hill," for Sergio Mendes & Brasil '66, A & M, c. 1968; "Lady Love" and "Rashida," both for Jon Lucien, RCA, c. 1973; "Mountain Dance," from *Mountain Dance* (also see below), 1979; "Marcosinho," from *The Hawk,* c. 1980; "Summer Sketches '82," from *Dave Grusin and the N.Y./*

L.A. Dream Band (also see below), c. 1983; "Early A.M. Attitude" and "Harlequin" (both with Lee Ritenour), from *Harlequin* (also see below), 1985; "The Heart Is a Lonely Hunter," from *Cinemagic* (also see below), 1987; "Suite from *The Milagro Beanfield War,*" from *Migration* (also see below), 1989; and "Medley: Bess You Is My Woman/I Love You Porgy," from *The Gershwin Connection,* c. 1992.

RECORDINGS:

ALBUMS

Subways Are for Sleeping, Epic, 1960.
Piano, Strings, and Moonlight, Epic, 1961.
Kaleidoscope, Columbia, 1963.
One of a Kind, GRP/Arista, 1976.
Discovered Again, Sheffield Treas., c. 1977.
Mountain Dance, GRP/Arista, 1979.
Out of the Shadows, GRP, 1981.
Dave Grusin and the N.Y./L.A. Dream Band, GRP, c. 1983.
Night Lines, GRP, 1984.
(With Lee Ritenour) *Harlequin,* GRP, 1985.
(With Ritenour) *Earth Run* (also see below), GRP, c. 1986.
Cinemagic, GRP, 1987.
(With GRP All-Stars) *GRP Super Live in Concert,* GRP, 1988.
(With brother Don Grusin) *Sticks and Stones,* GRP, 1988.
Dave Grusin Collection, GRP, 1989.
(With Ritenour) *Festival,* GRP, 1989.
Migration, GRP, 1989.
The Fabulous Baker Boys Motion Picture Soundtrack, GRP, c. 1989.

Also performed on other recordings, including *Rio* and *On the Line* (both with Ritenour), Elektra/Musician; *Body Heat* and *I Heard That!* (both with Quincy Jones), A & M; *Earl Klugh* and *Living Inside Your Love* (both with Earl Klugh), Blue Note; *Marching in the Street* (with Harvey Mason), Arista; *Barefoot Ballet* (with John Klemmer), ABC; *My Favorite Things* (with Sergio Mendes), Atlantic; *A Secret Place* (with Grover Washington, Jr.), Kudu; *Face to Face* (with Kevin Eubanks); *Little Big Horn* (with Gerry Mulligan); *Blackwood* (with Eddie Daniels); *Brown's Bag* (with Ray Brown); and *Crawl Space* (with Art Farmer).

WRITINGS:

FILM SCORES, EXCEPT AS INDICATED

Divorce American Style, Columbia, 1967.
(With Paul Simon) *The Graduate,* Embassy, 1967.
Waterhole No. 3 (includes "The Code of the West," with Robert Wells), Paramount, 1967.
Candy, Cinerama, 1968.
The Heart Is a Lonely Hunter, Seven Arts, 1968.
Where Were You When the Lights Went Out?, Metro-Goldwyn-Mayer (MGM), 1968.
Generation (also known as *A Time for Giving*), Avco Embassy, 1969.
The Mad Room, Columbia, 1969.
A Man Called Gannon (includes "A Smile, a Mem'ry and an Extra Shirt," lyrics by Alan and Marilyn Bergman), Universal, 1969.
Tell Them Willie Boy Is Here, Universal, 1969.
Winning, Universal, 1969.
Adam at 6 A.M., National General Pictures, 1970.
Halls of Anger (includes "Reachin' Out to You," with Norman Gimbel), United Artists (UA), 1970.
The Gang That Couldn't Shoot Straight, MGM, 1971.
The Pursuit of Happiness, Columbia, 1971.
Shoot Out, Universal, 1971.
Fuzz, UA, 1972.
The Great Northfield, Minnesota Raid, Universal, 1972.
The Friends of Eddie Coyle, Paramount, 1973.
The Midnight Man, Universal, 1974.
The Nickel Ride, Twentieth Century-Fox, 1974.
W. W. and the Dixie Dancekings, Twentieth Century-Fox, 1975.
Three Days of the Condor, Paramount, 1975.
The Yakuza (also known as *Brotherhood of the Yakuza;* includes "Evening Sun, Morning Moon," lyrics by the Bergmans), Warner Brothers-Toei, 1975.
The Front, Columbia, 1976.
Murder By Death, Columbia, 1976.
Bobby Deerfield (includes title song, lyrics by the Bergmans), Columbia, 1977.
Fire Sale, Twentieth Century-Fox, 1977.
The Goodbye Girl, Warner Brothers, 1977.
Mr. Billion, Twentieth Century-Fox, 1977.
Heaven Can Wait, Paramount, 1978.
. . . And Justice for All (includes "There's Something Funny Goin' On," lyrics by the Bergmans), Columbia, 1979.
The Champ, MGM, 1979.
The Electric Horseman, Universal, 1979.
My Bodyguard, Twentieth Century-Fox, 1980.
"Cheryl's Theme," *All Night Long,* Universal, 1981.
Absence of Malice, Columbia, 1981.
On Golden Pond, ITC/IPC/Universal/AFD, 1981.
(With Stephen Sondheim) *Reds,* Paramount, 1981.
Author! Author! (includes "Comin' Home to You," lyrics by the Bergmans), Twentieth Century-Fox, 1982.
Tootsie (includes title song and "It Might Be You," lyrics for both by the Bergmans), Columbia, 1982.
Falling in Love, Paramount, 1984.
The Little Drummer Girl (includes "Always in Love" and "Eyes of Fire," with Sylvester Levay), Warner Brothers, 1984.

The Pope of Greenwich Village, MGM/UA, 1984.
Racing with the Moon, Paramount, 1984.
Scandalous (includes "It's Scandalous," with Don Black), Orion, 1984.
The Goonies, Warner Brothers, 1985.
Lucas, Twentieth Century-Fox, 1986.
The Milagro Beanfield War, Universal, 1988.
Clara's Heart, Warner Brothers, 1988.
Tequila Sunrise, Warner Brothers, 1988.
A Dry White Season, MGM/UA, 1989.
The Fabulous Baker Boys, Twentieth Century-Fox, 1989.
"Tri-Star Logo Theme," *Look Who's Talking Too,* Tri-Star, 1990.
Havana, Universal, 1990.
Bonfire of the Vanities, Warner Brothers, 1990.
For the Boys, Twentieth Century-Fox, 1991.

TELEVISION MUSIC; SERIES

Theme song and additional music, *Dan August,* ABC, 1970.
"The Kind of Girl She Is" (theme song; lyrics by Alan and Marilyn Bergman), *The Sandy Duncan Show,* CBS, 1972.
Assignment: Vienna, ABC, 1972.
Theme song (lyrics by the Bergmans), *Maude,* CBS, 1972.
Roll Out!, CBS, 1973.
The Girl with Something Extra, NBC, 1973.
Theme song (lyrics by the Bergmans), *Good Times,* CBS, 1974.
"Keep Your Eye on the Sparrow" (theme song), and additional music, *Baretta,* ABC, 1975.
Theme song and additional music, *St. Elsewhere,* NBC, 1982.
"The Smithsonian and the Presidency," *This Is America, Charlie Brown,* CBS, 1988.
Theme music, *Capital News* (also known as *Powerhouse*), ABC, 1990.

Also composer of themes and music for other series, including *The Bold Ones* and *The Name of the Game,* both NBC.

TELEVISION MUSIC; MOVIES

The Intruders, NBC, 1970.
Sarge: The Badge or the Cross, NBC, 1971.
A Howling in the Woods, NBC, 1971.
The Forgotten Man, ABC, 1971.
The Deadly Dream, ABC, 1971.
The Family Rico, CBS, 1972.
The Death Squad, ABC, 1974.
Eric, NBC, 1975.
The Trial of Chaplain Jensen, ABC, 1975.

Also composer of music for *Prescription: Murder* and *Scorpio Letters.*

TELEVISION MUSIC; SPECIALS

Oath: The Sad and Lonely Sundays, ABC, 1976.
Oath: 33 Hours in the Life of God, ABC, 1976.
Colorado C. I., CBS, 1978.
You Don't Look 40, Charlie Brown!, CBS, 1990.

OTHER TELEVISION MUSIC

Amanda Fallon (pilot), NBC, 1973.
Three of a Kind (pilot), ABC, 1989.

Also composer of music for *P. O. P.,* 1984, and *On the Edge,* 1987.

OTHER MUSICAL COMPOSITIONS

"An Actor's Life" (song), Golden Horizon Music Corporation, c. 1983.
(With Lee Ritenour) *Harlequin* (album), GRP, 1985.
(With Ritenour) "Earth Run" (song), *Earth Run,* GRP, c. 1986.
"It Might Be You" (song), *Cinemagic,* GRP, 1987.

Also composer of other songs, including "Midnight Soul Patrol" (with Quincy Jones and Louis Johnson), c. 1976.

OTHER SOURCES:

BOOKS

Contemporary Musicians, Volume 7, Gale, 1992.
Contemporary Newsmakers 1987 Cumulation, Gale, 1988, p. 150.

PERIODICALS

Audio, January, 1985; March, 1985.
down beat, March, 1985, pp. 59, 61; July 1989, p. 24.
Stereo Review, June, 1983; September, 1985.

* * *

GUILLEM, Sylvie 1965-

PERSONAL: Surname is pronounced "Gee-*em*"; born February 23, 1965, in Le Blanc-Mesnil, France; daughter of a factory foreman and a gymnast. *Education:* Attended Paris Opera Ballet School, 1976-81.

ADDRESSES: Office—Royal Ballet, Royal Opera House, London WC2E 9DD, England.

CAREER: Ballerina. Originally trained to be a gymnast; began the study of ballet at the Paris Opera Ballet School, 1976; joined the Paris Ballet Company as *quadrille,* 1981, promoted to *coryphee,* 1982, to *sujet,* 1983, then *premiere danseuse* and later *etoile* (lead dancer), 1984; joined the Royal Ballet, London, as principle guest artist, 1989.

AWARDS, HONORS: Prize for excellence and gold medal, Varna International Dance Competition, Bulgaria,

1983; Prix Carpeau, 1984; Commander des Arts et Lettres, 1988; Hans Christian Andersen Ballet Prize, Royal Danish Theatre, 1988, for *Swan Lake.*

CREDITS:

STAGE APPEARANCES

Raymonda, Paris Opera Ballet, Paris, 1983.
Odette/Odile, *Swan Lake,* Paris Opera Ballet, 1984, then with Royal Ballet, Covent Garden, London, 1989.
Le Corsaire, Lincoln Center, New York City, 1986.
Cinderella, Paris Opera Ballet, Metropolitan Opera House, New York City, 1987, then with Royal Ballet, Covent Garden, 1989.
Giselle, Royal Ballet, Covent Garden, 1987.
Sebastien I, *Le Martyre de Saint-Sebastien,* Metropolitan Opera House, 1988.
Grand Pas Classique, Royal Ballet, Covent Garden, 1989.
La Bayadere, Royal Ballet, Covent Garden, 1989.
The Sleeping Beauty, Royal Ballet, Covent Garden, 1989.
Apollo, Royal Ballet, Covent Garden, 1989.

Also appeared in *Washington Square, Arepo, Romeo and Juliet, Don Quixote, Notre Dame de Paris, Cendrillon, In the Middle,* and *Magnificat.*

MAJOR TOURS

Toured the United States with the Paris Opera Ballet, 1986 and 1988, and with the Royal Ballet, 1991. Principal guest artist with the American Ballet Theatre, 1991.

TELEVISION APPEARANCES; SPECIALS

The Hans Christian Andersen Awards 1988, PBS, 1990.

TELEVISION APPEARANCES; EPISODIC

"The Night of Music: A Global Celebration," *Great Performances,* PBS, 1986.
"Nureyev's Cinderella," *Great Performances,* PBS, 1988.

FILM APPEARANCES

Yvette Chauvire: Une etoile pour l'exemple (also known as *Yvette Chauvire: A Star for Example*), Films du Prieure, 1988.

OTHER SOURCES:

BOOKS

Newsmakers 88, Gale, 1988.

PERIODICALS

Interview, July, 1989.
People Weekly, July 28, 1986.
Time, June 23, 1986.*

GUZMAN, Pato 1933(?)-1991

PERSONAL: Born c. 1933; died after a brief illness, January 2, 1991, in Santiago, Chile; married; wife's name, Rita.

ADDRESSES: Agent—Gersh Agency, 250 North Canon Dr., Beverly Hills, CA 90210.

CAREER: Producer, production designer, and art director. Sketch artist, assistant art director, and later art director, for Desilu Studios, beginning in the mid-1950s.

MEMBER: International Alliance of Theatrical Stage Employees and Moving Picture Machine Operators of the United States and Canada.

CREDITS:

FILM PRODUCTION DESIGNER

The President's Analyst, Paramount, 1967.
I Love You, Alice B. Toklas! (also known as *Kiss My Butterfly*), 1968, Warner Brothers.
Art director, *The Lawyer,* Paramount, 1969.
Bob and Carol and Ted and Alice, Columbia, 1969.
Alex in Wonderland, Metro-Goldwyn-Mayer (MGM), 1970.
The Marriage of a Young Stockbroker, Twentieth Century-Fox, 1971.
Visual consultant, *Count Your Bullets* (also known as *Cry for Me, Billy, Face to the Wind,* and *Naked Revenge*), Brut, 1972.
Play It as It Lays, Universal, 1972.
Blume in Love, Samuel Bronston, 1973.
An Unmarried Woman, Twentieth Century-Fox, 1978.
The In-Laws, Warner Brothers, 1979.
Hide in Plain Sight, MGM/United Artists, 1980.
Willie and Phil, Twentieth Century-Fox, 1980.
(And producer with Paul Mazursky) *Tempest,* Columbia, 1982.
(And producer with Mazursky) *Moscow on the Hudson,* Columbia, 1984.
(And producer with Mazursky) *Down and out in Beverly Hills,* Buena Vista, 1986.
(And producer with Mazursky and Geoffrey Taylor) *Moon over Parador,* Universal, 1988.
(And producer with Mazursky and Irby Smith) *Enemies, a Love Story,* Twentieth Century-Fox, 1989.
(And producer with Mazursky) *Scenes from a Mall,* Buena Vista, 1991.

TELEVISION WORK; EPISODIC

Art director for episodes of *I Love Lucy* and *The Untouchables;* also art director for pilot episode of *Star Trek.*

OBITUARIES AND OTHER SOURCES:

PERIODICALS

Theatre Crafts, March, 1991, p. 20.
Variety, January 14, 1991, p. 126.*

H

HADARY, Jonathan 1948-

PERSONAL: Born October 11, 1948, in Chicago, IL. *Education:* Attended Tufts University.

ADDRESSES: *Agent*—Peter Strange, 1500 Broadway, Suite 2001, New York, NY 10036.

CAREER: Actor. Studio Arena Theatre, Buffalo, NY, member of company, 1968-69; member of Alley Theatre, Houston, TX.

MEMBER: Screen Actors Guild.

AWARDS, HONORS: Obie Award nomination, performance, *Village Voice,* 1985, for *As Is;* Antoinette Perry Award nomination, best performance by a featured actor in a musical, 1990, for *Gypsy.*

CREDITS:

STAGE APPEARANCES

Songs from Pins and Needles, Manhattan Theatre Club, New York City, 1976.
Gemini, Playwrights Horizons, New York City, 1976.
Herschel Weinberger, *Gemini,* Little Theatre (now Helen Hayes Theatre), New York City, 1977.
Marshall Lowenstein, *Gemini,* Circle Repertory Theatre, New York City, 1977.
Pushing Thirty (one-man show), Circle Repertory Theatre, 1978.
Norman Mushari, *God Bless You, Mr. Rosewater,* WPA Theatre, New York City, 1979.
Scrambled Feet, Village Gate Upstairs, New York City, 1979.
Sammy Dazzle, *Coming Attractions,* Mainstage Theatre, New York City, 1980.
Tomfoolery, Village Gate Upstairs, 1981.
Torch Song Trilogy, Helen Hayes Theatre, 1982.
Saul, *As Is* (also see below), Lyceum Theatre, New York City, 1985.
Charley, *Charley Bacon and His Family,* Ark Theatre, New York City, 1985.
Dack, *One Two Three Four Five,* City Center Stage II, New York City, 1987.
Vince Corey, *Wenceslas Square,* Public Theatres/Martinson Hall, New York City, 1988.
Herbie, *Gypsy,* St. James Theatre, New York City, 1989.
Guiteau, Garfield's assassin, *Assassins,* Playwrights Horizons, 1991.

Toured U.S. cities as Schroeder, *You're a Good Man, Charlie Brown,* 1968-70. Made off-Broadway debut in *White Nights,* 1974; also appeared in *El Grande de Coca-Cola.*

TELEVISION APPEARANCES

Saul, *As Is* (movie), Showtime, 1986.
Song performer, *The 45th Annual Tony Awards* (special), CBS, 1991.

OTHER SOURCES:

PERIODICALS

New York Daily News, January 3, 1990, pp. 29, 33.*

* * *

HAINES, Randa 1945-

PERSONAL: Born February 20, 1945, in Los Angeles, CA. *Education:* Studied acting with Lee Strasberg; attended School of Visual Arts; attended American Film Institute, beginning in 1975.

ADDRESSES: *Contact*—Directors Guild of America, 7950 Sunset Blvd., Hollywood, CA 90046.

CAREER: Director. Also worked as a script supervisor.

MEMBER: Directors Guild of America.

AWARDS, HONORS: Emmy Award nomination, director of a limited series or special, 1984, for *Something about Amelia.*

CREDITS:

TELEVISION DIRECTOR

Something about Amelia (movie), ABC, 1984.
Under the Sky (special), PBS, 1979.

TELEVISION DIRECTOR; SERIES

Knots Landing, CBS, 1979.
Tucker's Witch, CBS, 1982.
For Love and Honor, NBC, 1983.
The Family Tree, NBC, 1983.

TELEVISION DIRECTOR; EPISODIC

"The Jilting of Granny Weatherall," *Learning in Focus* (also known as *American Short Story*), PBS, 1980.
Hill Street Blues, NBC, 1981.
"Just Pals," *After School Special,* CBS, 1982.
"Bang! You're Dead!," *Alfred Hitchcock Presents,* NBC, 1985.
"Judy You're Not Yourself Today," *Tales from the Crypt,* HBO, 1990.

FILM DIRECTOR

Children of a Lesser God, Paramount, 1986.
The Doctor, Buena Vista, 1991.

Also directed the film short *August/September,* during 1970s.

FILM APPEARANCES

As herself, *Calling the Shots* (documentary), World Artists, 1988.

STAGE APPEARANCES

Appeared in Off-Off-Broadway productions.

WRITINGS:

TELEVISION SCRIPTS

Worked as writer for *Family* (series), ABC, c. 1970s.

OTHER SOURCES:

PERIODICALS

Films in Review, December, 1986, pp. 601-605.
People Weekly, spring, 1991, p. 75.*

HALE, Billy 1934-

PERSONAL: Also known professionally as William Hale; born July 11, 1934, in Rome, Italy; son of William and Alma (Harbour) Hale; married January, 1980; wife's name, Trudy; children: Tempe, Charlie. *Education:* Attended University of Southern California. *Religion:* Unitarian. *Politics:* Democrat. *Avocational interests:* Hiking, music.

ADDRESSES: Office—P.O. Box 1322, Topanga, CA 90290. *Agent*—Alan Greenspan, International Creative Management, 8899 Beverly Blvd., Los Angeles, CA 90048.

CAREER: Director.

AWARDS, HONORS: Emmy Award and Golden Globe nomination, 1981, for *Murder in Texas;* Emmy Award, best miniseries, Peabody Award, and Christopher Award, all 1988, for *The Murder of Mary Phagan;* awards at the Chicago, Australia, and Edinburgh film festivals for various short films, including *The Towers* and *Grand Central Market.*

CREDITS:

TELEVISION DIRECTOR; MINISERIES

(And producer) *Murder in Texas,* NBC, 1981.
Lace, ABC, 1984.
Lace II, ABC, 1985.
Harem, ABC, 1986.
The Murder of Mary Phagan (also known as *The Ballad of Mary Phagan;* also see below), NBC, 1988.

TELEVISION DIRECTOR; SERIES

Run for Your Life, NBC, 1964.
The Bob Hope Chrysler Theater, NBC, 1965.
The Felony Squad, ABC, 1966.
Judd, for the Defense, ABC, 1966.
The FBI, ABC, 1967.
The Invaders, ABC, 1967-68.
Lancer, CBS, 1969.
Barnaby Jones, CBS, 1970.
Night Gallery, NBC, 1972.
The Streets of San Francisco, ABC, 1973.
Kojak, CBS, 1974.
Caribe, ABC, 1975.
The Paper Chase, CBS, 1978.

TELEVISION DIRECTOR; MOVIES

How I Spent My Summer Vacation, Universal TV, 1967.
The Great Niagara, ABC, 1974.
Nightmare, CBS, 1974.
The Killer Who Wouldn't Die, ABC, 1976.
Stalk the Wild Child, NBC, 1976.
Red Alert, CBS, 1977.

S.O.S. Titanic, ABC, 1979.
One Shoe Makes It Murder, CBS, 1982.
The Demon Murder Case (also known as *The Rhode Island Murders*), NBC, 1983.
Liberace, ABC, 1988.
People Like Us, NBC, 1990.

TELEVISION DIRECTOR; PILOTS

Kojak, CBS, 1974.
Crossfire, NBC, 1975.

FILM DIRECTOR

Lonnie, Futuramic, 1963.
Deadly Roulette, Universal, 1966.
Gunfight in Abilene, Universal, 1967.
Journey to Shiloh, Universal, 1968.

Also director of short films, including *The Towers* and *Grand Central Market.*

WRITINGS:

(Coauthor) *The Murder of Mary Phagan* (miniseries; also known as *The Ballad of Mary Phagan*), NBC, 1988.

* * *

HALL, Ed 1931-1991

OBITUARY NOTICE—See index for *CTFT* sketch: Full name, Edward C. Hall; born January 11, 1931, in Roxbury, MA; died of cancer, July 30, 1991, in Providence, RI. Actor. Hall appeared in more than eighty plays with the Trinity Repertory Company from 1965 to the time of his death, and was the company's first African-American member. A nominee for both the New York Drama Desk Award and the Helen Hayes Award in 1988 for his performance in *Joe Turner's Come and Gone,* Hall performed major roles in such plays as *A Christmas Carol* and *Driving Miss Daisy.* Seen regularly in several television series, including *Medical Center* and *Baby, I'm Back,* Hall also starred in episodes of *The F.B.I., Barnaby Jones, Another World,* and *Streets of San Francisco.* Among his last appearances was in 1991's television movie *Separate But Equal.*

OBITUARIES AND OTHER SOURCES:

BOOKS

Who's Who Among Black Americans, 1992/1993, Gale, 1992, p. 582.

PERIODICALS

Variety, August 12, 1991, p. 56.

HALL, Kevin Peter 1955(?)-1991

PERSONAL: Born May 9, c. 1955, in Pittsburgh, PA; died of pneumonia-related complications in 1991 in California; married Alaina Reed (an actress); children: two. *Education:* Received degree in theatre arts from George Washington University.

CAREER: Actor. Founder and owner, with Jay Fenichel, First Team Entertainment production company, c. 1988.

CREDITS:

FILM APPEARANCES

Eddie, *One Dark Night,* ComWorld, 1983.
Bouncer, *The Wild Life,* Universal, 1984.
Monster, *Monster in the Closet,* Troma, 1987.
Title role, *Predator,* Twentieth Century-Fox, 1987.
Harry, *Harry and the Hendersons,* Universal, 1987.
Big John, *Big Top Pee Wee,* Paramount, 1988.
Twins, Universal, 1988.
Title role, *Predator II,* Twentieth Century-Fox, 1990.

TELEVISION APPEARANCES; SERIES

Dr. Elvin "El" Lincoln, *Misfits of Science,* NBC, 1985-86.
Harry, *Harry and the Hendersons,* syndicated, 1991.

Also appeared in the series *227.*

TELEVISION APPEARANCES; MOVIES

Gorvil, *Rona Jaffe's "Mazes and Monsters",* CBS, 1982.
Shannon's Deal, NBC, 1989.

TELEVISION APPEARANCES; SPECIALS

Rodney Dangerfield "Opening Night at Rodney's Palace" (also known as *On Location*), HBO, 1989.

TELEVISION APPEARANCES; EPISODIC

E/R, CBS, 1984.
Night Court, NBC, 1984.
Dukes of Hazzard, CBS, 1985.

STAGE APPEARANCES

Appeared in *In Five,* Tiffany Theatre, 1988; and as Queequeg, *Moby Dick Rehearsed,* Mark Taper Forum, Los Angeles, CA. Toured with Jay Fenichel in children's show *Little Bob and Big Billy's Fractured Fairytales* and in a two-man comedy revue.

OBITUARIES AND OTHER SOURCES:

PERIODICALS

Ebony, November, 1988, p. 116.
Hollywood Reporter, April 12, 1991, p. 4.
People, July 13, 1987, p. 89.*

HAMILTON, Joe 1929-1991

OBITUARY NOTICE—See index for *CTFT* sketch: Full name, Joseph Henry Michael Hamilton, Jr.; born January 6, 1929, in Los Angeles, CA; died of cancer, June 9, 1991, in Los Angeles. Producer and musician. Hamilton began his career as a vocalist with the Skylarks, appearing on television's *Dinah Shore Show* in the 1950s. In 1958, he shifted careers and began producing television programs, including the comedy-variety series *The Garry Moore Show.* He also served as executive producer of such popular series as *The Tim Conway Show, Mama's Family,* and the long-running *Carol Burnett Show,* which featured his then-wife, Burnett. During his long career in the television industry, Hamilton garnered five Emmy Awards, three of which were for work on *The Carol Burnett Show,* as well as ten Emmy nominations for variety programs he produced for Burnett.

OBITUARIES AND OTHER SOURCES:

PERIODICALS

Variety, June 17, 1991, p. 84.

* * *

HAMMER, Jan 1948-

PERSONAL: Name pronounced "Yon Hommer"; born April 17, 1948, in Prague, Czechoslovakia; came to the United States, 1968; father was a physician and a jazz musician; mother was a jazz singer; married; wife's name Ivona; children: one daughter, one son. *Education:* Academy of Muse Arts (Prague), 1966-68; Berklee College of Music (Boston, MA), 1968.

ADDRESSES: Home and studio—Holmes, NY. *Agent*—Elliott Sears Management, 120 West 44th St., Suite 303, New York, NY 10036.

CAREER: Musician (keyboardist), composer, music arranger. Composed musical scores for television programs and motion pictures in Prague, Czechoslovakia, 1966-67; performed as pianist in jazz clubs in Czechoslovakia, Poland, and West Germany, 1967-68; worked as a musician in the Boston, MA, area, 1968-70; musical arranger and piano accompanist for jazz vocalist Sarah Vaughan, 1970-71; keyboardist in musical group Mahavishnu Orchestra with John McLaughlin, 1971-73; involved in numerous musical performance groups and recording projects as keyboardist, 1973—. Has performed with Jeremy Steig, Elvin Jones, Billy Cobham, Jeff Beck, John Abercrombie, Jack de Johnette, Fernando Saunders, Al Dimeola, Carlos Santana, John McLaughlin, Mick Jagger, Neal Schon, James Young, and Tony Williams.

AWARDS, HONORS: Winner of International Music Competition, Vienna, Austria, 1966; *Keyboard Magazine* best lead synthesist, 1978, 1979, 1980, 1981, 1982, 1983, and 1984; *Keyboard Magazine* best studio synthesist, 1985 and 1986; Emmy Award nominations for outstanding achievement in music composition for a series, 1985 and 1986, for *Miami Vice;* Grammy Awards for best instrumental composition and best pop instrumental, both 1985, for *Miami Vice Theme;* Diamond Award (Belgium), 1987, for best instrumental artist in Europe.

RECORDINGS:

ALBUMS

(With Mahavishnu Orchestra) *The Inner Mounting Flame,* Columbia, 1972.
(With Mahavishnu Orchestra) *Birds of Fire,* Columbia, 1973.
(With Mahavishnu Orchestra) *Between Nothingness and Eternity,* Columbia, 1973.
(With Carlos Santana and John McLaughlin) *Love, Devotion, Surrender,* Columbia, 1973.
(With Billy Cobham) *Spectrum,* Atlantic, 1973.
(With Stanley Clarke), *Stanley Clarke,* Nemperor, 1974.
(With Jerry Goodman), *Like Children,* Nemperor, 1974.
(With John Abercrombie), *Timeless,* ECM, 1974.
The First Seven Days, Nemperor, 1975.
(With Tommy Bolin) *Teaser,* Nemperor, 1975.
(With Elvin Jones) *On the Mountain,* P.M., 1975.
Make Love, MPS, 1976.
(With Jan Hammer Group) *Oh, Yeah?,* Nemperor, 1976.
(With Jeff Beck) *Wired,* Epic, 1976.
Jeff Beck with the Jan Hammer Group, Nemperor, 1976.
(With Jan Hammer Group) *Melodies,* Nemperor, 1977.
(With Al Di Meola) *Elegant Gypsy,* Columbia, 1977.
(With Jan Hammer Group) *Black Sheep,* Asylum, 1978.
(With Glen Moore) *Introducing Glen Moore,* Elektra, 1978.
(With Hammer) *Hammer,* Asylum, 1979.
(With Tony Williams) *The Joy of Flying,* Columbia, 1979.
(With A. Di Meola) *Splendido Hotel,* Columbia, 1980.
(With J. Beck) *There and Back,* Epic, 1980.
(With Neal Schon) *Untold Passion,* Columbia, 1981.
(With A. Di Meola) *Electric Rendezvous,* Columbia, 1982.
(With Mahavishnu Orchestra) *Best of Mahavishnu Orchestra,* Columbia, 1982.
(With N. Schon) *Here to Stay,* Columbia, 1983.
(With A. Di Meola) *Tour de Force—Live,* Columbia, 1983.
(With J. Abercrombie) *Night,* ECM, 1984.
(With A. Di Meola) *Scenario,* Columbia, 1984.
Music from the Television Series "Miami Vice" (omnibus compilation), MCA, 1985.
(With J. Beck) *Flash,* Epic, 1985.
(With Mick Jagger) *She's the Boss,* Columbia, 1985.

(With James Young) *City Slicker,* Passport, 1985.
The Early Years (retrospective compilation), Nemperor, 1986.
Escape from Television, MCA, 1987.
Snapshots, MCA, 1989.
(With Clarence Clemons) *An Evening with Mr. C,* Columbia, 1989.

Album recordings also include *Time Is Free; Some Shapes to Come* with Steve Grossman; and *Energy* with Jeremy Steig.

WRITINGS:

FILM SCORES

A Night in Heaven, Twentieth-Century Fox, 1983.
Gimme an "F", Twentieth-Century Fox, 1984.
Secret Admirer, Orion, 1985.
I Come in Peace, Triumph, 1991.
The Taking of Beverly Hills, Columbia, 1991.
Midnight Heat, New Line, 1992.

TELEVISION MUSIC: MOVIES

Two Fathers' Justice (also known as *Two Fathers*), NBC, 1985.
Charley Hannah, ABC, 1986.
Clinton and Nadine (also known as *Night Hunt* and *Blood Money: The Story of Clinton and Nadine*), HBO, 1988.
K-9000, Fox Broadcasting Company, 1991.
Knight Rider 2000, NBC, 1991.
Curiosity Kills (also known as *Curiosity Killed the Cat*), USA, 1991.

TELEVISION MUSIC; SPECIALS

Les Paul: He Changed the Music (also known as *Cinemax Sessions*), Cinemax, 1988.
Capital News, ABC, 1990.
Czeslaw Milosz: The Poet Remembers, PBS, 1990.

TELEVISION MUSIC; SERIES

(Theme) *Miami Vice,* MCA, 1985.
"Evan," *Miami Vice,* NBC, 1985.
"Bushido," *Miami Vice,* NBC, 1986.
Chancer (British), Central Television, 1991.

Also scored two episodes for *Tales from the Crypt,* and the pilot for *News at 12,* 1991.

OTHER SOURCES:

BOOKS

Contemporary Newsmakers, Volume 87, issue 3, Gale, 1988.
Coryell, Julie, and Laura Friedman, *Jazz-Rock Fusion: The People, the Music,* Delta, 1978.

PERIODICALS

Chicago Tribune, December 15, 1985.
Contemporary Keyboard, October, 1978; May, 1982; September, 1985.
Crawdaddy, November, 1973.
Crescendo International, May, 1981.
Detroit News, April 20, 1987.
down beat, April 26, 1973; March 11, 1976; October 21, 1976, January 26, 1978; November, 1980; March, 1983; June, 1985; September, 1986.
Guitar Player, December, 1981; December, 1982.
Los Angeles Times, December 7, 1983; October 27, 1985.
Musical Journal, July/August, 1979.
Musician, August, 1986.
New York Times, May 19, 1985; October 16, 1985.
People, February 21, 1983.
Rolling Stone, April 14, 1983; March 28, 1985.
Stereo Review, March, 1984; March, 1986; September, 1986.
USA Today, February 26, 1986.
Variety, October 21, 1981.

* * *

HARLIN, Renny 1959(?)-

PERSONAL: Born Renny Lauri Mauritz Harjola (some sources spell surname Harjula), c. 1959, in Helsinki (one source says Riihimaeki), Finland; son of a physician and a nurse. *Education:* Studied visual communications at University of Helsinki.

CAREER: Director. Larmark Productions, Finland, founder, with Marcus Selin; Larmark Productions, Los Angeles, CA, partner.

AWARDS, HONORS: Award for best short subject, Finnish Film Board, 1982, for *Hold On.*

CREDITS:

FILM DIRECTOR, EXCEPT AS INDICATED

Born American (also known as *Arctic Heat;* also see below), Concorde, 1986.
Prison, Empire, 1988.
A Nightmare on Elm Street 4: The Dream Master, New Line, 1988.
Die Hard 2 (also known as *Die Harder*), Twentieth Century-Fox, 1990.
The Adventures of Ford Fairlane, Twentieth Century-Fox, 1990.
Producer, *Rambling Rose,* Seven Arts, 1991.

Also worked on *Hold On* (short documentary), 1982.

TELEVISION DIRECTOR

Directed *Freddy's Nightmares,* 1988.

TELEVISION APPEARANCES

Naked Hollywood (also known as *A&E Premieres*), Arts and Entertainment, 1991.

WRITINGS:

SCREENPLAYS

(With Marcus Selin) *Born American* (also known as *Arctic Heat*), Concorde, 1986.

OTHER SOURCES:

PERIODICALS

Interview, June, 1990, p. 61.
People Weekly, September 10, 1991, pp. 102-104.*

*   *   *

HARRELSON, Woody 1962(?)-

PERSONAL: Born July 23, c. 1962, in Midland, TX; son of Charles V. Harrelson. *Education:* Received B.A. in theater arts and English from Hanover College. *Avocational interests:* Sports (basketball, baseball, football, surfing, skiing), writing, juggling, chess, playing guitar and piano.

ADDRESSES: Office—NBC-TV, 30 Rockefeller Plaza, New York, NY 10112. *Agent*—Creative Artists Agency, Inc., 9830 Wilshire Blvd., Beverly Hills, CA 90212. *Publicist*—Maggie Begley, Mahoney/Wasserman & Associates, 420 Lexington Ave., New York, NY 10017.

CAREER: Actor. Partner of Sun International (merchandising company specializing in beach accessories).

AWARDS, HONORS: Emmy Award nominations, 1986, 1987, 1989, and 1991, and Emmy Award, 1988, all outstanding supporting actor in a comedy series, all for *Cheers;* American Comedy Award, best newcomer.

CREDITS:

TELEVISION APPEARANCES; SERIES

Woody Boyd, *Cheers,* NBC, 1985—.

TELEVISION APPEARANCES; MOVIES

Slater, *Bay Coven* (also known as *Strangers in Town* and *Eye of the Demon*), NBC, 1987.
Charlie Daimler, *Killer Instinct* (also known as *Over the Edge*), NBC, 1988.
Lou the Lamb, *Mother Goose Rock 'n' Rhyme,* Disney, 1990.

TELEVISION APPEARANCES; EPISODIC

"Paul Reiser: Out on a Whim," *On Location,* HBO, 1987.
"Mickey's 60th Birthday Special," *The Magical World of Disney,* NBC, 1988.
"Disneyland's 35th Anniversary Celebration," *The Magical World of Disney,* NBC, 1990.

TELEVISION APPEARANCES; SPECIALS

Super Bloopers and New Practical Jokes, NBC, 1990.
Man on telephone, *AFI Presents "TV or Not TV?,"* NBC, 1990.
Host, *Showtime Comedy Club All-Stars IV,* Showtime, 1990.

FILM APPEARANCES

Krushinski, *Wildcats,* Warner Brothers, 1986.
Casualties of War, Columbia, 1989.
Dustin, *Cool Blue* (also known as *Creative Detour*), Columbia, 1990.
Homeless Vietnam veteran, *Ted and Venus* (also known as *Love and Venus* and *Love and Venice*), Double Helix, 1991.
Hank, *Doc Hollywood,* Warner Brothers, 1991.
Billy Hoyle, *White Men Can't Jump,* Twentieth Century-Fox, 1992.

STAGE APPEARANCES

Understudy for Roy Selridge and Joseph Wykowski, *Biloxi Blues,* Neil Simon Theatre, New York City, 1985.
Jack, *The Boys Next Door,* Lamb's Theatre, New York City, 1987.
Two on Two and *The Zoo Story* (double-bill), Court Theatre, Los Angeles, 1989.

Appeared in more than twenty-five plays at Hanover College, Indiana.

WRITINGS:

Author of plays.*

*   *   *

HARRIS, HYDE
See Timothy Harris

*   *   *

HARRIS, Mel

PERSONAL: Full name, Mary Ellen Harris; born July 12, in Bethlehem, PA; married David Hume Kennerly; children: Byron. *Education:* Attended Columbia University;

studied acting with Lee Strasberg, Betty Cashman, and Milton Katselas.

ADDRESSES: Office—ABC-TV, 1330 Avenue of the Americas, New York, NY 10019. *Agent*—Gersh Agency, Inc., 250 North Canon Dr., Beverly Hills, CA 90210. *Manager*—Litke/Gale Madden Associates, 10390 Santa Monica Blvd., No. 300, Los Angeles, CA 90025.

CAREER: Actress.

CREDITS:

TELEVISION APPEARANCES; SERIES

Hope Murdoch, *thirtysomething,* ABC, 1987-91.

TELEVISION APPEARANCES; EPISODIC

"Cementing Relationships," *M*A*S*H,* CBS, 1980.
"A Very Happy Ending," *Alfred Hitchcock Presents,* NBC, 1986.
"Working without a Net," *Heart of the City,* ABC, 1986.
The Wizard, CBS, 1986.
"First Love," *Rags to Riches,* NBC, 1987.
"Books," *American Treasury,* CBS, 1989.
"The S. S. Savannah," *American Treasury,* CBS, 1989.
"Automobiles," *American Treasury,* CBS, 1989.

OTHER TELEVISION APPEARANCES

Fay Salerno, *Harry's Hong Kong* (movie), ABC, 1987.
The 15th Annual People's Choice Awards (special), CBS, 1989.
Madge Oberholtzer, *Cross of Fire* (movie), NBC, 1989.
Hostess, *Hush Little Baby: The Challenge of Child Care* (special), Lifetime, 1989.
Eleanor Gilbert Rusher, *My Brother's Wife* (movie; also known as *Just Good Friends* and *Middle Ages*), ABC, 1989.
The Burden of Proof (movie), ABC, 1992.

Also appeared on the special *The Second Annual Valvoline National Driving Test* 1990.

FILM APPEARANCES

Terry, *Wanted: Dead or Alive,* New World, 1987.
Nora Haley, *Cameron's Closet,* SVS, 1988.
Tracy, *K-9,* Universal, 1989.

STAGE APPEARANCES

Carol Shartel, *Empty Hearts,* Circle Repertory Company, New York City, 1992.

OTHER SOURCES:

PERIODICALS

People, October 26, 1987, pg. 55.*

HARRIS, Tim
See Timothy Harris

* * *

HARRIS, Timothy 1946-
(Tim Harris, Hyde Harris)

PERSONAL: Full name Timothy Hyde Harris; born July 21, 1946, in Los Angeles, CA; son of Donald and Mary Helen (an artist; maiden name, McDermott) Harris; married Mary Bess Walker (a film director), March 21, 1980. *Education:* Peterhouse College, Cambridge, B.A. (with honors), 1969, M.A., 1974. *Politics:* Independent. *Religion:* "Pagan." *Avocational interests:* Travel (Europe and Africa), competitive saber fencing, spearfishing, skin diving, tennis (junior champion of Portugal, 1963).

ADDRESSES: Agent—Agency for the Performing Arts, Inc., 9000 Sunset Blvd., Suite 1200, Los Angeles, CA 90069.

CAREER: Screenwriter. Sailor, carpenter, and house painter, 1964—.

MEMBER: Writers Guild of America (West).

CREDITS:

TELEVISION WORK

Coexecutive producer, *Street of Dreams* (also see below), CBS, 1988.

TELEVISION APPEARANCES

Naked Hollywood (documentary series), Arts and Entertainment, 1991.

WRITINGS:

FILMS; WITH HERSCHEL WEINGROD

Cheaper to Keep Her, American Cinema, 1980.
Trading Places, Paramount, 1983.
Brewster's Millions (based on the novel by George Barr McCutcheon), Universal, 1985.
(With Jerico Weingrod, and Jonathan Reynolds) *My Stepmother Is an Alien,* Columbia, 1988.
(With William Davies, and William Osborne) *Twins,* Universal, 1988.
(With Murray Salem) *Kindergarten Cop* (based on a story by Salem), Universal, 1990.
Pure Luck (based on Francis Veber's *Le Chevre*) Universal, 1991.

Also wrote the following screenplays with Herschel Weingrod: (Under name Tim Harris) *Paint It Black,* Vestron; *Dummies; Siberian Express; The French Kiss; The Pied Piper; The Fugitive Pigeon; Bigfinger; Mickey;* and *Beauty School.*

TELEVISION MOVIES

Street of Dreams (adapted from Harris's novel *Good Night and Goodbye*), CBS, 1988.

NOVELS

Kronski/McSmash, M. Joseph, 1969, Doubleday, 1970.
Kyd for Hire, Dell, 1978, published in England under name Hyde Harris, Gollancz, 1978.
Goodnight and Goodbye, Delacorte, 1979.

OTHER SOURCES:

BOOKS

Contemporary Authors, Volume 101, Gale, 1981.*

* * *

HARRY, Jackee (Jackee, Jacqueline Harry)

PERSONAL: Given name is pronounced "Jack-*kay*"; full name, Jacqueline Yvonne Harry; born in Winston-Salem, NC; daughter of Flossie (a hospital secretary) Harry; married c. 1980 (divorced, 1984). *Education:* Attended Music and Art High School, New York City, where she studied opera with Bernice Wyatt; received B.A. from Brooklyn Center, Long Island University. *Religion:* Baptist.

CAREER: Actress. Worked as a teacher at Brooklyn Technical High School before beginning entertainment career.

MEMBER: Screen Actors Guild.

AWARDS, HONORS: Emmy Award, outstanding supporting actress in a comedy series, 1987, for *227.*

CREDITS:

TELEVISION APPEARANCES; SERIES

Lily Mason, *Another World,* NBC, 1983-85.
Sandra Clark, *227,* NBC, 1985-89.
(Under name Jackee) Ruth, *The Royal Family,* CBS, 1992.

TELEVISION APPEARANCES; MOVIES

Crash Course, NBC, 1988.
The Women of Brewster Place, ABC, 1989.

TELEVISION APPEARANCES; PILOTS

Friday Night Surprise, NBC, 1988.
The Cheech Show, NBC, 1988.
Jackee, NBC, 1989.

TELEVISION APPEARANCES; SPECIALS

Gina Lipman, *Alvin Goes Back to School,* NBC, 1986.
Ida Early, *The Incredible Ida Early,* NBC, 1987.
Countess, *ALF Loves a Mystery,* NBC, 1987.
The Patsy Awards, syndicated, 1987.
American Video Awards, syndicated, 1987.
The 19th Annual NAACP Image Awards, NBC, 1987.

TELEVISION APPEARANCES; EPISODIC

Host, *The Late Show,* Fox, 1986.
"Telling Whoppers," *One to Grow On,* NBC, 1988.
"A Slight Case of Murder," *Amen,* NBC, 1988.
"Self Confidence," *One to Grow On,* NBC, 1988.

FILM APPEARANCES

Dancer, *The Cotton Club,* Orion, 1984.
Moscow on the Hudson, Columbia, 1984.
(Under name Jackee) Julia Benson, *Ladybugs,* Paramount, 1992.

STAGE APPEARANCES

(Under name Jacqueline Harry) Nurse, "Going through Changes," *Two Plays by Richard Wesley,* Billie Holiday Theatre, New York City, 1973.
Melinda Bernard, *A Broadway Musical,* Lunt-Fontanne Theatre, New York City, 1978.
Alice, *I'm Getting My Act Together and Taking It on the Road,* Public/Anspacher Theatre, New York City, 1978-80.
Second Thoughts, Mitzi E. Newhouse Theater, New York City, 1979.
Cassie, *Child of the Sun,* Harry Dejur Henry Street Playhouse, New York City, 1981.
Colored People's Time, Cherry Lane Theatre, New York City, 1982.
Diamonds, Circle in the Square Downtown, New York City, 1984.

Also appeared on Broadway in *The Wiz* and *One Mo' Time,* in a touring production of *Eubie!,* and in a cabaret act at Sweetwater's, New York City.

OTHER SOURCES:

PERIODICALS

People, November 10, 1986, p. 108.*

* * *

HARRY, Jacqueline
See HARRY, Jackee

* * *

HATFIELD, Hurd 1920(?)-

PERSONAL: Full name, William Rukard Hurd Hatfield; born December 7, 1920 (some sources say 1918), in New

York, NY; son of William Henry and Adele Steele (McGuire) Hatfield. *Education:* Attended Bard College; studied acting at Chekhov Theatre Studio, Devonshire, England.

ADDRESSES: Office—Ballinterry House, Rathcormac, County Cork, Ireland.

CAREER: Actor.

MEMBER: Actors Equity Association, Screen Actors Guild, American Federation of Radio and Television Artists, Faculty Club of Columbia University, Players Club.

AWARDS, HONORS: Emmy Award nomination, best supporting actor, 1963, for "The Invincible Mr. Disraeli," *Hallmark Hall of Fame.*

CREDITS:

FILM APPEARANCES

Lao San, *Dragon Seed,* Metro-Goldwyn-Mayer (MGM), 1944.
Dorian Gray, *The Picture of Dorian Gray,* MGM, 1945.
Georges, *Diary of a Chambermaid,* United Artists (UA), 1946.
Oliver Keane, *The Unsuspected,* Warner Brothers, 1947.
Dr. John Wyatt, *The Beginning or the End,* MGM, 1947.
Creepy, *The Checkered Coat,* Twentieth Century-Fox, 1948.
Father Pasquerel, *Joan of Arc,* RKO Radio Pictures, 1948.
Clifford Ward, *Chinatown at Midnight,* Columbia, 1949.
Stretch Norton, *Destination Murder,* RKO Radio Pictures, 1950.
Prince, *Tarzan and the Slave Girl* (also known as *Tarzan and the Jungle Queen*), RKO Radio Pictures, 1950.
Moultrie, *The Left-Handed Gun,* Warner Brothers, 1958.
Pontius Pilate, *King of Kings,* MGM, 1961.
Count Arias, *El Cid,* Allied Artists, 1961.
Castle, *Mickey One,* Columbia, 1965.
Father, *The Double-Barrelled Detective Story,* Saloon Productions, 1965.
Paul Bern, *Harlow,* Magna, 1965.
Terence Huntley, *The Boston Strangler,* Twentieth Century-Fox, 1968.
Anthony Fokker, *Von Richtofen and Brown* (also known as *The Red Baron*), UA, 1970.
Ahimelech, *King David,* Paramount, 1985.
Old Grandaddy, *Crimes of the Heart,* DD Entertainment, 1986.
Troppa, *Her Alibi,* Warner Brothers, 1988.

TELEVISION APPEARANCES; EPISODIC

"The Rivals," *Masterpiece Theater,* NBC, 1950.
"The Importance of Being Earnest," *Masterpiece Theater,* NBC, 1950.
"Mademoiselle Fifi," *Story Theater,* syndicated, 1950.
"Tiger in the Closet," *The Web,* CBS, 1952.
"The Nativity Play," *Studio One,* CBS, 1952.
"Greed," *Summer Studio,* CBS, 1953.
"Seventh Heaven," *Broadway Television Theater,* syndicated, 1953.
"The Hasty Heart," *Broadway Television Theater,* syndicated, 1953.
"The Pistol Shot," *Suspense,* CBS, 1954.
"The Hunchback of Notre Dame," *Robert Montgomery Presents,* NBC, 1954.
"The King's Bounty," *Kraft Theater,* NBC, 1955.
"I Was Accused," *Armstrong Circle Theater,* NBC, 1955.
"The Hanging Judge," *Climax,* CBS, 1956.
"The Perfect Murder," *Alfred Hitchcock Presents,* CBS, 1956.
"The Eric Vincent Story," *The Millionaire,* CBS, 1956.
"The Fog," *Climax,* CBS, 1956.
"None Are So Blind," *Alfred Hitchcock Presents,* CBS, 1956.
"The Trial of Poznan," *Armstrong Circle Theater,* NBC, 1957.
"The Prince and the Pauper," *DuPont Show of the Month,* CBS, 1957.
"Beyond This Place," *DuPont Show of the Month,* CBS, 1957.
"The Last Man," *Playhouse 90,* CBS, 1958.
"Cabin B-13," *Climax,* CBS, 1958.
"The Count of Monte Cristo," *DuPont Show of the Month,* CBS, 1958.
"Various Temptations," *Lux Playhouse,* CBS, 1959.
"Too Bad about Sheila Troy," *Oldsmobile Music Theater,* NBC, 1959.
"The Curse of Aden," *The Further Adventures of Ellery Queen,* NBC, 1959.
"I, Don Quixote," *DuPont Show of the Week,* CBS, 1959.
"Don Juan in Hell," *Play of the Week,* syndicated, 1960.
"The Invincible Mr. Disraeli," *Hallmark Hall of Fame,* NBC, 1963.
"One Day in the Life of Ivan Denisovich," *Bob Hope Chrysler Theater,* NBC, 1963.
Frederick, "A Cry of Angels," *Hallmark Hall of Fame,* NBC, 1963.
"The Cry Beneath the Sea," *Voyage to the Bottom of the Sea,* ABC, 1964.
Sagredo Niccolini, "Lamp at Midnight," *Hallmark Hall of Fame,* NBC, 1966.
"Ten Blocks on the Camino Real," *N.E.T. Playhouse,* National Educational Television, 1966.
"The Movers," *New York Television Theater,* National Educational Television, 1966.
"Night of the Man-Eating House," *Wild Wild West,* CBS, 1966.
"Night of the Undead," *Wild Wild West,* CBS, 1968.
"Montserrat," *Hollywood Television Theater,* PBS, 1971.

"The Hunters," *The FBI,* ABC, 1972.
"Between Time and Timbuktu," *Playhouse New York,* PBS, 1972.
"The Bullet," *Search,* NBC, 1972.
"The House and the Brain," *Wide World of Mystery,* ABC, 1973.
"A Hair Trigger Away," *Kojak,* CBS, 1976.
"Death Takes a Curtain Call," *Murder, She Wrote,* CBS, 1984.
"Knave of Diamonds, Ace of Hearts," *Blacke's Magic,* NBC, 1986.
"One Good Bid Deserves a Murder," *Murder, She Wrote,* CBS, 1986.
"Gershwin's Trunk," *Amazing Stories,* NBC, 1987.

OTHER TELEVISION APPEARANCES

Host, *Hollywood Screen Test* (series), ABC, 1948-53.
Herman Gray, *Thief* (movie), ABC, 1971.
Charles Langdon, *The Norliss Tapes* (movie), NBC, 1973.
Benjamin Franklin: The Rebel (special), CBS, 1975.
Cedric Plummer, *The Word* (mini-series), CBS, 1978.
Foxhall Edwards, *You Can't Go Home Again* (movie), CBS, 1979.
British agent, *The Manions of America* (mini-series), ABC, 1981.
Aaron DeMessina, *Lime Street* (pilot), ABC, 1985.

Also appeared as John Church, *The Rebel,* 1975.

STAGE APPEARANCES

(Debut) The Baron, *The Lower Depths,* Chekhov Theatre Studio, Devonshire, England, 1939.
(Broadway debut) Kirilov, *The Possessed,* Lyceum Theatre, New York City, 1939.
The religious man, *The Strings, My Lord, Are False,* Theatre Royale, 1942.
Richard Halton, *On Approval,* Shubert Theatre, New Haven, CT, 1948.
John Forster, *The Ivy Green,* Lyceum Theatre, 1949.
Dominic, *Venus Observed,* Century Theatre, New York City, 1952.
Sir Nathaniel, *Love's Labour's Lost,* New York City Center, 1953.
Lord Byron and Don Quixote, *Camino Real,* National Theatre, 1953.
Domingo Salamanca, *Bullfight,* Theatre de Lys, New York City, 1954.
Prince Paul, *Anastasia,* Lyceum Theatre, 1954.
Title role, *Julius Caesar,* American Shakespeare Festival and Academy, Stratford, CT, 1955.
Gonzolo, *The Tempest,* American Shakespeare Festival and Academy, Stratford, CT, 1955.
Father Grigoris, *The Lowers,* Martin Beck Theatre, New York City, 1956.
Narrator, *L'Histoire du Soldat* (opera), New York City Center, 1956.
The cardinal, *The Duchess of Malfi,* Phoenix Theatre, San Francisco, CA, 1957.
Grandiet, *The Devils,* Arena Stage, Washington, DC, 1963.
Marat/Sade, Center Stage, Baltimore, MD, 1970.
Dr. Austin Sloper, *Washington Square,* Washington Theatre Club, Washington, DC, 1972.
Jones, *Victory,* Yale Repertory Theatre, New Haven, CT, 1974.
A Doll's House, Seattle Repertory Theatre, Seattle, WA, 1975.

Also appeared as the senator's son, *The Respectful Prostitute,* Coronet Theatre, Hollywood, CA; as the son, *The Skin of Our Teeth,* produced in California; and as the witch boy, *Dark of the Moon,* produced in California. Toured eastern and southern U.S. cities as Sir Andrew Aguecheek, *Twelfth Night,* as Caleb Plummer, *Cricket on the Hearth,* and as Gloucester, *King Lear.*

RECORDINGS:

Recordings include *The Mind of Poe,* 1987; *The Picture of Dorian Gray; The Tempest;* and *Romeo and Juliet.**

* * *

HAWTHORNE, Nigel 1929-

PERSONAL: Full name, Nigel Barnard Hawthorne; born April 5, 1929, in Coventry, England; son of Charles Barnard and Agnes Rosemary (Rice) Hawthorne. *Education:* Attended Christian Brothers College and University of Cape Town. *Avocational interests:* Drawing, gardening, and swimming.

ADDRESSES: Agent—Ken McReddie, 91 Regent St., London W1, England.

CAREER: Actor.

AWARDS, HONORS: Clarence Derwent Award and SWET Award, both for best supporting actor, 1977, for *Privates on Parade;* Broadcasting Press Guild Award, best actor, c. 1981; British Academy of Film and Television Arts awards, television light entertainment performance, 1981 and 1982, both for *Yes Minister;* British Academy of Film and Television Arts awards, television light entertainment performance, 1986 and 1987, both for *Yes Minister;* University of Sheffield, honorary M.A., 1987; Outer Critics Circle Award, outstanding actor in a play on or off Broadway, and Antoinette Perry Award, best performance by a leading actor in a play, both 1991, both for *Shadowlands;* Laurence Olivier Award, 1992, for *The Madness of George III.*

CREDITS:

STAGE APPEARANCES

(Debut) Archie Fellowes, *The Shop at Sly Corner,* Hofmeyr Theatre, Cape Town, South Africa, 1950.
(London debut) Donald, *You Can't Take It with You,* Embassy Theatre, 1951.
Fancy Dan, *Talking to You,* Duke of York's Theatre, London, 1962.
Nymphs and Satires, Apollo Theatre, London, 1965.
Angry Neighbor, *In at the Death,* Phoenix Theatre, London, 1967.
Sir Oswald Stoll, *The Marie Lloyd Story,* Theatre Royal, Stratford, England, 1967.
Roy Jenkins, *Mrs. Wilson's Diary,* Criterion Theatre, London, 1967.
Prince Albert, *Early Morning,* Royal Court Theatre, London, 1968.
Total Eclipse, Royal Court Theatre, 1968.
Count Wermuth, *The Tutor,* Royal Court Theatre, 1968.
Lord Touchwood, *The Double Dealer,* Royal Court Theatre, 1969.
Prince Albert, *Early Morning,* Royal Court Theatre, 1969.
Commander Pemberton, *Insideout,* Royal Court Theatre, 1969.
Commodore, *Narrow Road to the Deep North,* Royal Court Theatre, 1969.
Falstaff, *Henry IV,* Sheffield Playhouse, London, 1970.
Title role, *Macbeth,* Sheffield Playhouse, 1970.
Niall, *Curtains,* Traverse Theatre, 1970, then Edinburgh Festival, Scotland, 1970, later at Open Space Theatre, London, 1971.
The Player, *Rosencrantz and Guildenstern Are Dead,* Cambridge Theatre, London, 1971.
Christopher, *West of Suez,* Royal Court Theatre, then Cambridge Theatre, 1971.
Face, *The Alchemist,* Young Vic Theatre, London, 1972.
Brutus, *Julius Caesar,* Young Vic Theatre, 1972.
Chairman, *A Sense of Detachment,* Royal Court Theatre, 1972.
Baptista, *The Taming of the Shrew,* Young Vic Theatre, 1972.
Judge, *The Trial of St. George,* Soho Poly Theatre, London, 1972.
Philip, *The Philanthropist,* May Fair Theatre, London, 1973.
The Ride across Lake Constance, Hampstead Theatre, London, then May Fair Theatre, 1973.
(Broadway debut) Touchstone, *As You Like It,* Mark Hellinger Theatre, New York City, 1974.
Colonel, *Bird Child,* Theatre Upstairs, London, 1974.
Cutler Walpole, *The Doctor's Dilemma,* Mermaid Theatre, London, 1975.
Stephen, *Otherwise Engaged,* Queen's Theatre, London, 1975.
Touchstone, *As You Like It,* Riverside Studios, London, 1976.
Owen, *Clouds,* Hampstead Theatre, 1976.
Brian, *Blind Date,* King's Head Theatre, London, 1977.
Abbe de Pradts, *The Fire That Consumes,* Mermaid Theatre, London, 1977.
Major Giles Flack, *Privates on Parade,* Royal Shakespeare Company (RSC), Aldwych Theatre, London, 1977.
Julius Sagamore, *The Millionairess,* Haymarket Theatre, London, 1978.
Title role, *Uncle Vanya,* Hampstead Theatre, 1979.
Morgenhall, "The Dock Brief," *John Mortimer's Casebook,* Young Vic Theatre, London, 1982.
Orgon, *Tartuffe; or, The Imposter,* Barbican Theatre, London, then Pit Theatre, London, 1983.
Solveig's father, *Peer Gynt,* RSC, Pit Theatre, London, 1983.
Douglas, *Across from the Garden of Allah,* Comedy Theatre, London, 1986.
Colonel Tadeusz, *Jacobowsky and the Colonel,* National Theatre Company (NTC), National Theatre, London, 1986.
Mr. Posket, *The Magistrate,* NTC, National Theatre, 1986.
Blair, *Hapgood,* Aldwych Theatre, 1988.
C. S. Lewis, *Shadowlands,* Queen's Theatre, 1989, then Brooks Atkinson Theatre, New York City, 1990-91.
King George III, *The Madness of George III,* Lyttelton Theatre, 1991—.
C. S. Lewis, *Shadowlands,* Brooks Atkinson Theatre, New York City, 1992.

MAJOR TOURS

Touchstone, *As You Like It,* North American cities, 1974.
Dr. Sloper, *The Heiress,* British cities, 1983.

FILM APPEARANCES

Boer Sentry, *Young Winston,* Columbia, 1972.
*S*P*Y*S,* Twentieth Century-Fox, 1974.
Pastor De Ruiter, *The Hiding Place,* World Wide, 1975.
Dilke, *Sweeney 2,* EMI, 1978.
Voice of Campion, *Watership Down* (animated), Avco Embassy, 1978.
Official, *History of the World, Part 1,* Twentieth Century-Fox, 1981.
Victorian Father, *Memoirs of a Survivor,* EMI, 1981.
Pyote Baranovich, *Firefox,* Warner Brothers, 1982.
Kinnoch, *Gandhi,* Columbia, 1982.
Voice of Dr. Robert Boycott, *The Plague Dogs* (animated), United International, 1984.
Voice of Fflewddur, *The Black Cauldron* (animated), Buena Vista, 1985.

Dreamchild, Universal, 1985.
Mr. Thorn, *The Chain,* J. Arthur Rank, 1985.
Publisher, *Turtle Diary,* Samuel Goldwyn, 1985.
Voice, *Rarg* (animated short), Expanded Entertainment, 1988.
Ted Walker, *En Handfull tid* (also known as *A Handful of Time*), Norsk Film, 1989.
Achmet, *King of the Wind,* Shapiro/Glickenhaus Entertainment, 1990.

Also appeared in *S,* 1974; *The House,* 1984; and *Tartuffe,* 1990.

TELEVISION APPEARANCES; MOVIES

Stryver, *A Tale of Two Cities,* CBS, 1980.
Esmerelda Trial Magistrate, *The Hunchback of Notre Dame,* CBS, 1982.
King Abdullah, *A Woman Called Golda,* Operation Prime Time, 1982.
Cardinal Stefan Wyszynski, *Pope John Paul II,* CBS, 1984.
Colonel, *Jenny's War,* Operation Prime Time, 1985.
Fleabites, BBC, 1992.

TELEVISION APPEARANCES; SERIES

Holocaust (mini-series), NBC, 1978.
Edward and Mrs. Simpson, Thames TV, 1978.
Humphrey Appleby, *Yes Minister,* The Entertainment Channel, 1982-83.
Georgie Pillson, *Mapp & Lucia,* PBS, 1986.
The Trials of Oz, BBC, 1992.

Also appeared in *Yes Minister,* 1980-83 and 1985-86; and *Yes, Prime Minister,* 1986-87.

TELEVISION APPEARANCES; EPISODIC

Archdeacon Grantly, "The Barchester Chronicles," *Masterpiece Theatre,* PBS, 1984.
Harpagon, "The Miser," *Great Performances,* PBS, 1988.
Philip, "Relatively Speaking," *Great Performances,* PBS, 1989.
The 45th Annual Tony Awards (special), CBS, 1991.

Also appeared as Stephano in *The Tempest,* 1980; appeared in *Marie Curie,* 1977, *Destiny,* 1978, *The Knowledge,* 1979, *The Critic,* 1982, *Tartuffe,* 1985, and *The Shawl,* 1989.

OTHER SOURCES:

PERIODICALS

Interview, December, 1990, p. 80.

HECKERLING, Amy 1954-

PERSONAL: Born May 6, 1954, in New York,. NY; daughter of an accountant; married second husband, Neal Israel (a film director and writer), July, 1984; children: (second marriage) Mollie Sara. *Education:* Received degree in film and television from New York University, 1975.

ADDRESSES: *Agent*—David Gersh, The Gersh Agency, 250 North Canon Drive, Beverly Hills, CA 90210.

CAREER: Producer, director and writer. American Film Institute, fellow in directing program.

CREDITS:

FILM DIRECTOR

Fast Times at Ridgemont High, Universal, 1982.
Johnny Dangerously, Twentieth-Century Fox, 1984.
National Lampoon's European Vacation, Warner Brothers, 1985.
Look Who's Talking, Tri-Star, 1989.
Look Who's Talking Too, Tri-Star, 1990.

Also director of several short films, including *Modern Times, High Finance,* and *Getting It Over With,* 1974.

FILM APPEARANCES

Ship's waitress, *Into the Night,* Universal, 1985.

TELEVISION WORK; EPISODIC

Director, *Fast Times* (also see below), CBS, 1986.

OTHER TELEVISION WORK

Supervising producer, *Fast Times* (series; also see below), CBS, 1986.
Supervising producer, *Tough Cookies* (series), CBS, 1986.
Producer, *Life on the Flipside* (pilot; also known as *Flipside, Homeward Bound,* and *Pop Rock*), NBC, 1988.

WRITINGS:

SCREENPLAYS

Look Who's Talking, Tri-Star, 1989.
(With Neal Israel) *Look Who's Talking Too,* Tri-Star, 1990.

TELEVISION SERIES

Fast Times, CBS, 1986.

OTHER

(With Pamela Pettler) *The No-Sex Handbook,* illustrated by Jack Ziegler, Warner Books, 1990.

ADAPTATIONS: The television series *Baby Talk,* ABC, 1991, was based on *Look Who's Talking* and *Look Who's Talking Too.*

OTHER SOURCES:

BOOKS

Contemporary Newsmakers: 1987 Cumulation, Gale, 1988, pp. 166-167.
Film Directors: A Complete Guide, Lone Eagle, 1987, pp. 22-24.

PERIODICALS

People, May 13, 1985, pp. 103-106.*

* * *

HEDAYA, Dan

PERSONAL: Born in Brooklyn, NY. *Education:* Tufts University.

ADDRESSES: Agent—International Creative Management, 8899 Beverly Blvd., Los Angeles, CA 90048.

CAREER: Actor.

CREDITS:

FILM APPEARANCES

Yaacov, *The Passover Plot,* Atlas, 1976.
Alex Heller, *The Seduction of Joe Tynan,* Universal, 1979.
Sergeant Otis Barnes, *Night of the Juggler,* Columbia, 1980.
Howard Terkel, *True Confessions,* United Artists (UA), 1981.
Peck, *Endangered Species,* Metro-Goldwyn-Mayer (MGM)/UA, 1982.
Dr. Klein, *I'm Dancing as Fast as I Can,* Paramount, 1982.
Lieutenant Allegrezza, *The Hunger,* MGM/UA, 1983.
John Gomez, *The Adventures of Buckaroo Banzai: Across the 8th Dimension,* Twentieth Century-Fox, 1984.
Julian Marty, *Blood Simple,* Circle, 1984.
Peter Daniels, *Reckless,* MGM/UA, 1984.
Detective Molinari, *Tightrope,* Warner Brothers, 1984.
Arius, *Commando,* Twentieth Century-Fox, 1985.
Captain Logan, *Running Scared,* MGM/UA, 1986.
Anthony Castelo, *Wise Guys,* MGM/UA, 1986.
Waturi, *Joe versus the Volcano,* Warner Brothers, 1990.
Loan officer, *Pacific Heights,* Twentieth Century-Fox, 1990.
Robert Quince, *Tune In Tomorrow,* Cinecom, 1990.
Tully Alford, *The Addams Family,* Paramount, 1991.

TELEVISION APPEARANCES; MOVIES

Hot dog vendor, *The Prince of Central Park,* CBS, 1977.
Detective Ralph Corso, *Death Penalty,* NBC, 1980.
Skyros, *The Dollmaker,* ABC, 1984.
John Fosh, *Courage* (also known as *Mother Courage*), CBS, 1986.
Simon Fleischer, *Slow Burn,* Showtime, 1986.
Harry, *A Smoky Mountain Christmas,* ABC, 1986.
Captain Bates, *That Secret Sunday* (also known as *Betrayal of Trust*), CBS, 1986.
John Fraser, *Double Your Pleasure* (also known as *Double Trouble, Reluctant Agent,* and *Reluctant Spy*), NBC, 1989.
Vincent, *The Whereabouts of Jenny,* ABC, 1991.

TELEVISION APPEARANCES; SERIES

Carmine Howard, *Good Time Harry,* NBC, 1980.
Detective Ralph Macafee, *Hill Street Blues,* NBC, 1981.
Nick Tortelli, *Cheers,* NBC, 1982-87.
Nick Tortelli, *The Tortellis,* NBC, 1987.
Ernie, *One of the Boys,* NBC, 1989.

TELEVISION APPEARANCES; PILOTS

Cal, *The Earthlings,* ABC, 1984.
Arthur Willis, *The Flamingo Kid,* ABC, 1989.
Dr. Robert Smiley, *The Rock,* CBS, 1990.

OTHER TELEVISION APPEARANCES

The Regis Philbin Show (special), Lifetime, 1987.
Mickey, *Mama's Boy,* NBC, 1987.
Uncle Lucky, *Just Like Family,* Disney, 1989.
Louis Bonatto, "Veronica's Aunt," *Veronica Clare,* Lifetime, 1991.

Appeared on an episode of *L.A. Law,* NBC.

STAGE APPEARANCES

Dr. Schon/Harlequin, *Lulu (Earth Spirit),* Sheridan Square Playhouse, New York City, 1970.
Angel Ruz Covarrubias, *The Last Days of British Honduras,* Public Theatre/Other Stage, New York City, 1974.
Tokio, *Golden Boy,* Manhattan Theatre Club, New York City, 1975.
Peter Ziff and second guard, *Museum,* Public Theatre/LuEsther Hall, New York City, 1977.
Smitty, *Conjuring an Event,* American Place Theatre, New York City, 1978.
Survivors, Second Annual New Plays Festival, Actors Studio, New York City, 1979.
Pistol, *Henry V,* New York Shakespeare Festival, Delacorte Theatre/Central Park, New York City, 1984.

Appeared in *The Basic Training of Pavlo Hummel,* 1977, and in *Scenes From Everyday Life.**

HELGENBERGER, Marg

PERSONAL: Education: Attended Northwestern University.

ADDRESSES: Agent—S.T.E. Representation, 888 Seventh Ave., 18th Floor, New York, NY 10106.

CAREER: Actress.

AWARDS, HONORS: Quality Award, best supporting actress in a drama, Viewers for Quality Television, 1989, Emmy Award, outstanding supporting actress in a drama series, 1990, and Emmy Award nomination, outstanding supporting actress in a drama series, 1991, all for *China Beach.*

CREDITS:

TELEVISION APPEARANCES; SERIES

Siobhan Ryan Novak, *Ryan's Hope,* ABC, 1984-86.
Natalie Thayer, *Shell Game,* CBS, 1987.
K. C., *China Beach,* ABC, 1988-91.

TELEVISION APPEARANCES; EPISODIC

"An Eye for an Eye," *Spenser: For Hire,* ABC, 1987.
"It Was Fascination," *Karen's Song,* Fox, 1987.
"Weaning," *thirtysomething,* ABC, 1987.
"The Gambler," *Matlock,* NBC, 1987.
"Top Secret," *Buck James,* ABC, 1988.
Mrs. Cooper, "Peacemaker" (also known as "Triple Play II"), *American Playhouse,* PBS, 1991.
"Deadline," *Tales from the Crypt,* HBO, 1991.

OTHER TELEVISION APPEARANCES

Hostess, *Dick Clark's New Year's Rockin' Eve* (special), ABC, 1988.
Cohost, *Home,* ABC, 1989.
Virginia Whitelaw, *Blind Vengeance* (movie), USA, 1990.
Death Dreams (movie), Lifetime, 1991.
Narrator, *Not on the Frontline* (documentary), PBS, 1991.
A friend in need, *The Hidden Room,* Lifetime, 1991.
Deadline (pilot; also known as *Bay City Story* and *Manhattan Exclusive*), ABC, 1991.

FILM APPEARANCES

Rachel, *Always,* United Artists (UA)/Universal, 1989.
Alex, *After Midnight,* Metro-Goldwyn-Mayer (MGM)/UA, 1989.
Jenetta, *Crooked Hearts,* MGM/Pathe, 1991.*

HENRITZE, Bette (Bette Howe)

PERSONAL: Surname is pronounced "hen-rit-*see*"; born May 23, in Betsy Layne, KY. *Education:* Attended University of Tennessee; studied at American Academy of Dramatic Arts.

ADDRESSES: Agent—Triad Artists, Inc., 888 Seventh Ave., Suite 1602, New York, NY 10106.

CAREER: Actress. Arena Stage, Washington, DC, guest artist, 1988-89.

AWARDS, HONORS: Obie Award, *Village Voice,* 1967, for *Measure for Measure,* the Wilder plays, *The Displaced Person,* and *The Rimers of Eldritch.*

CREDITS:

STAGE APPEARANCES

(New York debut; under name Bette Howe) Mary Delaney, *Jenny Kissed Me,* Hudson Theatre, New York City, 1948.
Cloyne, *Purple Dust,* Cherry Lane Theatre, New York City, 1956.
Various roles, *Pictures in the Hallway,* Playhouse Theatre, New York City, 1956.
Peasant woman, *The Power and the Glory,* Phoenix Theatre, New York City, 1958.
Nirodyke, *Lysistrata,* Phoenix Theatre, 1959.
Peer Gynt, Phoenix Theatre, 1960.
Pimple, *She Stoops to Conquer,* Phoenix Theatre, 1960.
Bessie Burgess, *The Plough and the Stars,* Phoenix Theatre, 1960.
Mrs. Peyton, *The Octoroon,* Phoenix Theatre, 1961.
Margaret, *Much Ado about Nothing,* New York Shakespeare Festival (NYSF), Wollman Memorial Skating Rink, New York City, 1961.
Duchess of York, *King Richard II,* NYSF, Wollman Memorial Skating Rink, 1961.
Mrs. Gensup, *Giants, Sons of Giants,* Alvin Theatre, New York City, 1962.
Nerissa, *The Merchant of Venice,* NYSF, New York City, 1962.
Goneril, *King Lear,* NYSF, 1962.
Mary Todd, *Abe Lincoln in Illinois,* Anderson Theatre, New York City, 1963.
Cross-Lane Nora, *The Lion in Love,* One Sheridan Square Theatre, New York City, 1963.
Charmian, *Antony and Cleopatra,* NYSF, Delacorte Theatre, New York City, 1963.
Paulina, *The Winter's Tale* (also see below), NYSF, Delacorte Theatre, 1963.
Mrs. Hasty Malone, *The Ballad of the Sad Cafe,* Martin Beck Theatre, New York City, 1963.

Various roles, *The White House,* Henry Miller's Theatre, New York City, 1964.

Emilia, *Othello,* NYSF, Delacorte Theatre, then Martinique Theatre, New York City, 1964.

Louise, Maja, landlady, and young lady, *Baal,* Martinique Theatre, 1965.

Mariana, *All's Well That Ends Well,* NYSF, Delacorte Theatre, 1966.

Mariana, *Measure for Measure,* NYSF, Delacorte Theatre, 1966.

Ermengarde, "The Long Christmas Dinner," and Mademoiselle Pointevin, "Queens of France," *Thornton Wilder's Triple Bill,* Cherry Lane Theatre, 1966.

Mrs. Shortley, *The Displaced Person,* St. Clement's Church, New York City, 1966.

Mary Windrod, *The Rimers of Eldritch,* Cherry Lane Theatre, 1967.

Bea Schmidt, *Dr. Cook's Garden,* Belasco Theatre, New York City, 1967.

Mrs. Bacon, *Here's Where I Belong,* Billy Rose Theatre, New York City, 1968.

Edna, "The Acquisition," *Trainer, Dean, Liepolt and Co.* (triple-bill), American Place Theatre, New York City, 1968-69.

Jessie Mason, *Crimes of Passion,* Astor Place Theatre, New York City, 1969.

Understudy, *Hello and Goodbye,* Sheridan Square Playhouse, New York City, 1969.

Margaret Jourdain, *Henry VI, Part I,* NYSF, Delacorte Theatre, 1970.

Duchess of York, *Henry VI, Part II,* NYSF, Delacorte Theatre, 1970.

Duchess of York, *Richard III,* NYSF, Delacorte Theatre, 1970.

Anna Ames, *The Happiness Cage,* Estelle Newman Theatre, New York City, 1970.

Fay, Clarice, Wendy, and the woman, *Older People,* Public/Anspacher Theatre, New York City, 1972.

Ursula, *Much Ado about Nothing,* Delacorte Theatre, 1972, then Winter Garden Theatre, New York City, 1972-73.

Trixie, *Lotta; or, The Best Thing Evolution's Come Up With,* Public/Anspacher Theatre, 1973.

Mother, *Over Here!,* Sam S. Shubert Theatre, New York City, 1974.

Margaret, *Richard III,* Mitzi E. Newhouse Theatre, New York City, 1974.

Mrs. Soames, *Our Town,* American Shakespeare Theatre, Stratford, CT, 1975.

Pauline, *The Winter's Tale,* American Shakespeare Theatre, 1975.

Elizabeth, *Angel Street,* Lyceum Theatre, New York City, 1975-76.

Nora, *Home,* Long Wharf Theatre, New Haven, CT, 1976.

Mrs. Mihaly Almasi, *Catsplay,* Manhattan Theatre Club, then Promenade Theatre, both New York City, 1978.

Susan Ramsden, *Man and Superman,* Circle in the Square, New York City, 1978-79.

Anna, *A Month in the Country* (also see below), Roundabout Theatre, New York City, 1979-80.

Understudy for Margie, *One Night Stand,* Nederlander Theatre, New York City, 1980.

Essie, *Ah! Wilderness,* Indiana Repertory Theatre, Indianapolis, 1981.

Mother Superior, *Agnes of God,* GeVa Theatre, Rochester, NY, 1981.

Second witch, *Macbeth,* Circle in the Square, 1982.

Miss Ericson and Monica Reed, *Present Laughter,* Circle in the Square, 1982-83.

Emily Stilson, *Wings,* Center Stage Theatre, Baltimore, MD, 1983.

Rabbi's wife, *The Golem,* NYSF, Delacorte Theatre, 1984.

Mary Margaret Donovan, *The Octette Bridge Club,* Music Box Theatre, New York City, 1985.

Mom, *Daughters,* Westside Arts Theatre, New York City, 1986.

Nurse Guinness, *Heartbreak House,* Yale Repertory Theatre, New Haven, CT, 1986.

Grace Tanner, *Amazing Grace,* Alliance Theatre, Atlanta, GA, 1987.

Ouiser, *Steel Magnolias,* WPA Theatre, New York City, 1987, then Lucille Lortel Theatre, New York City, 1987-89.

Mrs. Hedges, *Born Yesterday,* Philadelphia Drama Guild, Philadelphia, PA, 1987-88.

Eva Temple, *Orpheus Descending,* Neil Simon Theatre, New York City, 1989.

Miss Framer, *Lettice and Lovage,* Ethel Barrymore Theatre, New York City, 1990.

Demetria Riffle, *On Borrowed Time,* Circle in the Square, 1991.

Appeared at Manasquan Theatre, NJ, 1951.

MAJOR TOURS

Paulina, *The Winter's Tale,* New Jersey and Connecticut cities, 1976.

Mrs. Putnam, *The Crucible,* New Jersey and Connecticut cities, 1976.

Anna, *A Month in the Country,* New Jersey and Pennsylvania cities, 1976.

Jenny, *The Torch-Bearers,* New Jersey and Pennsylvania cities, 1976.

Also toured Virginia cities with the Barter Theatre Company, 1950; and toured as Helga Ten Dorp in *Deathtrap,* summers, 1979-80.

FILM APPEARANCES

Mrs. Kimball, *The Hospital,* United Artists, 1971.
Anna Kraus, *The Happiness Cage* (also known as *The Mind Snatchers*), Cinerama, 1972.
Sarah Parker, *Rage,* Warner Brothers, 1972.
All That Jazz, Twentieth Century-Fox, 1979.
Sally Devlin, *The World according to Garp,* Warner Brothers, 1982.
Mrs. Murphy, *Brighton Beach Memoirs,* Universal, 1986.
Emma, *Other People's Money,* Warner Brothers, 1991.

TELEVISION APPEARANCES; EPISODIC

Appeared in episodes of *Omnibus, Love of Life,* and *Another World,* all NBC; *The Defenders, The Doctors and the Nurses, CBS Repertory Theatre,* and *As the World Turns,* all CBS; *N.Y.P.D., All My Children, The Edge of Night, One Life to Live,* and *Ryan's Hope,* all ABC; "The Plough and the Stars," *Play of the Week;* and *Hidden Faces.**

* * *

HERSHEY, Barbara 1948- (Barbara Seagull)

PERSONAL: Born Barbara Herzstein, February 5, 1948, in Hollywood, CA; daughter of Arnold H. (a horse racing columnist) Herzstein; lived with David Carradine (an actor), 1969-75; children: Tom (name legally changed from Free). *Education:* Attended public high school in Hollywood, CA. *Avocational interests:* Gardening, drawing, cooking, playing flute and piano.

ADDRESSES: Agent—Creative Artists Agency, 1888 Century Park E., Suite 1400, Los Angeles, CA 90067. *Publicist*—John West, P/M/K Public Relations, Inc., 955 South Camillo Dr., No. 200, Los Angeles, CA 90048.

CAREER: Actress.

AWARDS, HONORS: Golden Palm Award, best actress in a full-length film, Cannes International Film Festival, 1987, for *Shy People;* Golden Palm Award, best actress in a full-length film, 1988, for *A World Apart;* Emmy Award, outstanding lead actress in a mini-series or special, 1990, and Golden Globe Award, best actress in a mini-series or motion picture made for television, Hollywood Foreign Press Association, 1991, both for *A Killing in a Small Town;* Emmy Award nomination, outstanding lead actress in a mini-series or special, 1991, for *Paris Trout.*

CREDITS:

FILM APPEARANCES

(Film debut; under name Barbara Seagull) Stacey Iverson, *With Six You Get Eggroll* (also known as *A Man in Mommy's Bed*), National General Pictures, 1968.
Leloopa, *Heaven with a Gun,* Metro-Goldwyn-Mayer, 1969.
Sandy, *Last Summer,* Allied Artists, 1969.
Tish Gray, *The Baby Maker,* National General, 1970.
Nella Mundine, *The Liberation of L. B. Jones,* Columbia, 1970.
Susan, *Dealing; or, The Berkeley-to-Boston Forty-Brick Lost-Bag Blues,* Warner Brothers, 1971.
Jane Kauffman, *The Pursuit of Happiness,* Columbia, 1971.
Title role, *Boxcar Bertha,* American International, 1972.
(Under name Barbara Seagull) Zanni, *The Crazy World of Julius Vrooder* (also known as *Vrooder's Hooch*), Twentieth Century-Fox, 1974.
(Under name Barbara Seagull) Sally, *Diamonds,* Avco Embassy, 1975.
Marion, *Dirty Knight's Work* (also known as *Trial by Combat* and *Choice of Arms*), Warner Brothers, 1976.
Susan Burgade, *The Last Hard Men,* Twentieth Century-Fox, 1976.
Nina Franklin, *The Stunt Man,* Twentieth Century-Fox, 1980.
Girl, *Americana,* Sherwood, 1981.
J.M. Halstead, *Take This Job and Shove It,* Avco Embassy, 1981.
Carla Moran, *The Entity,* Twentieth Century-Fox, 1982.
Glennis Yeager, *The Right Stuff,* Warner Brothers, 1983.
Harriet Bird, *The Natural,* Tri-Star, 1984.
Lee, *Hannah and Her Sisters,* Orion, 1986.
Myra Fleener, *Hoosiers,* Orion, 1986.
Ruth Sullivan, *Shy People,* Cannon, 1987.
Nora Tilley, *Tin Men,* Buena Vista, 1987.
Mary Magdalene, *The Last Temptation of Christ,* Universal, 1988.
Hillary Whitney Essex, *Beaches,* Touchstone, 1988.
Diana Roth, *A World Apart,* Atlantic, 1988.
Aunt Julia, *Tune In Tomorrow,* Cinecom, 1990.
T.K. Katwuller, *Defenseless,* Seven Arts, 1991.

Appeared under the name Barbara Seagull as Angela, *Angela: Love Comes Quietly,* 1974, and in *You and Me,* 1975.

TELEVISION APPEARANCES; MOVIES

Mary Cutler, *Flood,* NBC, 1976.
Ellen Lange, *In the Glitter Palace,* NBC, 1977.
Nikki Klausing, *Just a Little Inconvenience,* NBC, 1977.
Cody, *Sunshine Christmas,* NBC, 1977.
Madelaine, *A Man Called Intrepid,* NBC, 1979.
Julie, *Angel on My Shoulder,* ABC, 1980.
Lili Damita, *My Wicked Ways . . . The Legend of Errol Flynn,* CBS, 1985.
Julia Maitland, *Passion Flower,* CBS, 1986.
Candy Morrison, *A Killing in a Small Town* (also known as *Evidence of Love*), CBS, 1990.

Hanna Trout, *Paris Trout* (also known as *Rage*), Showtime, 1991.
Jimmie Sue Finger, *Stay the Night*, ABC, 1992.

TELEVISION APPEARANCES; SERIES

Kathleen Monroe, *The Monroes*, ABC, 1966-67.
Karen Holmes, *From Here to Eternity*, NBC, 1980.

TELEVISION APPEARANCES; EPISODIC

Betty, "Chivalry Is Not Dead," *Gidget*, ABC, 1965.
"The Rise and Fall of Steven Morley," *The Farmer's Daughter*, ABC, 1966.
Betty, "Love and the Single Gidget," *Gidget*, ABC, 1966.
Betty, "Ask Helpful Hannah," *Gidget*, ABC, 1966.
Martha's daughter, "Holloway's Daughters," *Bob Hope Chrysler Theater*, NBC, 1966.
"The King's Shilling," *Daniel Boone*, NBC, 1967.
"Sara Jane, You Never Whispered Again," *Run for Your Life*, NBC, 1968.
"Thc Miraclc," *The Invaders*, ABC, 1968.
"The Peace Maker," *High Chapparal*, NBC, 1968.
"Secrets," *CBS Playhouse*, CBS, 1968.
"Besieged: Death on Cold Mountain," *Kung Fu*, ABC, 1974.
"Besieged: Cannon at the Gate," *Kung Fu*, ABC, 1974.
"Three Blonde Mice," *Switch*, CBS, 1978.
"Weekend," *American Playhouse*, PBS, 1982.
"The Nightingale," *Faerie Tale Theater*, Showtime, 1983.
"Wake Me When I'm Dead" (also known as "Murder Me Twice"), *Alfred Hitchcock Presents*, NBC, 1985.
The Today Show, NBC, 1988.
Entertainment Tonight, syndicated, 1988.
"Martin Scorsese Directs" (documentary), *American Masters*, PBS, 1990.

Also appeared in *Love Story*, 1973.

OTHER TELEVISION APPEARANCES:

Working (special), Showtime, 1981.
Guest, *Twilight Theater II* (pilot), NBC, 1982.
Champlin on Film, Bravo, 1989.
The 61st Annual Academy Awards Presentation (special), ABC, 1989.
Larry King TNT Extra (also known as *The Larry King Special . . . Inside Hollywood*), TNT, 1991.

Also appeared as Lenore, *Weekend* (special), 1982.

STAGE APPEARANCES

Appeared in *Einstein and the Polar Bear*, on Broadway, 1981.

OTHER SOURCES:

PERIODICALS

New York Times, March 29, 1987.*

HILL, Arthur 1922-

PERSONAL: Full name, Arthur Edward Spence Hill; born August 1, 1922, in Melfort, Saskatchewan, Canada; son of Olin Drake (a lawyer) and Edith Georgina (Spence) Hill; married Peggy Hassard, September, 1942; children: Douglas, Jennifer. *Education:* University of British Columbia, B.A., and graduate study in law.

ADDRESSES: Agent—Creative Artists Agency, 1888 Century Park E., Suite 1400, Los Angeles, CA 90067.

CAREER: Actor. *Military service:* Royal Canadian Air Force, mechanic, 1942-45.

MEMBER: Screen Actors Guild, Actors Equity Association, American Federation of Radio and Television Artists, British Actors Equity Association.

AWARDS, HONORS: Antoinette Perry Award, and Drama Desk Critics Award, both best actor in a drama, both 1963, both for *Who's Afraid of Virginia Woolf?*

CREDITS:

STAGE APPEARANCES

(Stage debut) Finch, *Home of the Brave*, Wimbledon Theatre, London, 1948, then produced as *The Way Back*, Westminster Theatre, London, 1949.
Tommy Turner, *The Male Animal*, Arts Theatre, London, 1949.
Hector Malone, *Man and Superman*, New Theatre, then Prince's Theatre, London, 1951.
Paul Unger, *Winter Journey* (also known as *The Country Girl*), St. James's Theatre, London, 1952.
(Broadway debut) Cornelius Hackl, *The Matchmaker*, Edinburgh Festival, Edinburgh, Scotland, then Haymarket Theatre, London, 1954, later Royale Theatre, New York City, 1955.
Ben Gant, *Look Homeward, Angel*, Ethel Barrymore Theatre, New York City, 1957.
Bruce Bellingham, *The Gang's All Here*, Ambassador Theatre, New York City, 1959.
Jay Follet, *All the Way Home* (also known as *A Death in the Family*), Belasco Theatre, New York City, 1960.
George, *Who's Afraid of Virginia Woolf?*, Billy Rose Theatre, New York City, 1962.
Bill Deems, *Something More!*, Eugene O'Neill Theatre, New York City, 1964.
Harold Potter, *The Porcelain Year*, Locust Theatre, Philadelphia, PA, 1965.
Simon Harford, *More Stately Mansions*, Ahmanson Theatre, Los Angeles, CA, then Morosco Theatre, New York City, 1967.
Captain Robert Falcon Scott, *Terra Nova*, Yale Repertory Theatre, New Haven, CT, 1977.

Toured U.S. cities as Cornelius Hackl in *The Matchmaker.* Member of Long Island Festival Repertory, 1968.

FILM APPEARANCES

Robin King, *The Body Said No!,* New World Angel, 1950.
The Undefeated, Associated British Pathe, 1951.
Shaw, *Scarlet Thread,* Butchers, 1951.
Miss Pilgrim's Progress, Grand National, 1952.
Cranmer Guest, *Paul Temple Returns,* Butchers, 1952.
Ted Harrison, *Salute the Toff,* Butchers, 1952.
Al, *A Day to Remember,* General Films Distributors, 1953.
Slim Cassidy, *Family Affair* (also known as *Life with the Lyons*), Exclusive, 1954.
Jackie Jackson, *The Deep Blue Sea,* Twentieth Century-Fox, 1955.
Raising a Riot, Continental Distributing, 1957.
Tomaselli, *The Young Doctors,* United Artists (UA), 1961.
Sam Bonner, *In the Cool of the Day,* Metro-Goldwyn-Mayer (MGM), 1963.
Grainger, *The Ugly American,* Universal, 1963.
Albert Graves, *Harper* (also known as *The Moving Target*), Warner Brothers, 1966.
Neil Stanton, *Moment to Moment,* Universal, 1966.
Barney, *Petulia,* Warner Brothers, 1968.
Shelby, *The Chairman,* Twentieth Century-Fox, 1969.
Robert, *Don't Let the Angels Fall,* National Film Board of Canada, 1969.
Reverend Jack Eccles, *Rabbit, Run,* Warner Brothers, 1970.
Dr. Stone, *The Andromeda Strain,* Universal, 1971.
John Popper, *The Pursuit of Happiness,* Columbia, 1971.
Cap Collis, *The Killer Elite,* UA, 1975.
Duffy, *Futureworld,* American International, 1976.
Tough colonel, *A Bridge Too Far,* UA, 1977.
Wyoming governor, *Butch and Sundance: The Early Days,* Twentieth Century-Fox, 1979.
Mike, *The Champ,* MGM/UA, 1979.
Richard King, *A Little Romance,* Orion, 1979.
Bert Prosser, *Dirty Tricks,* Avco Embassy, 1981.
Brewer, *The Amateur,* Twentieth Century-Fox, 1982.
Henry, *Making Love,* Twentieth Century-Fox, 1982.
Narrator, *Something Wicked This Way Comes,* Buena Vista, 1983.
Caleb Grainger, *One Magic Christmas,* Buena Vista, 1985.

Also narrated *The Glacier Fox,* 1978; appeared in *Riel,* 1982, and *Henry Fonda: The Man and His Movies,* 1984.

TELEVISION APPEARANCES; PILOTS

Owen Marshall, *Owen Marshall: A Pattern of Morality,* ABC, 1971.

TELEVISION APPEARANCES; SERIES

Owen Marshall, *Owen Marshall, Counselor at Law,* ABC, 1971-74.
Carl Palmer, *Hagen,* CBS, 1980.
Charles Hardwicke, *Glitter,* ABC, 1984.

TELEVISION APPEARANCES; MOVIES

Paul Maitland, *The Other Man,* NBC, 1970.
Arnold Greer, *Vanished,* NBC, 1971.
Richard Damian, *Ordeal,* ABC, 1973.
General Thomas Ewing, *The Ordeal of Dr. Mudd,* CBS, 1980.
Dr. Curtis McDonald, *The Return of Frank Cannon,* CBS, 1980.
Dale "Diz" Corbett, *Revenge of the Stepford Wives,* NBC, 1980.
Michael Eaton, *Angel Dusted,* NBC, 1981.
Glenn Gorham, *Tomorrow's Child,* ABC, 1982.
Dr. Steve Holliston, *Intimate Agony,* ABC, 1983.
General Keating, *Prototype,* CBS, 1983.
Dr. Phil Julian, *The Guardian,* HBO, 1984.
Vice-president, *Murder in Space,* Showtime, 1985.
Andrew Kingsley, *Christmas Eve,* NBC, 1986.
Thomas Shea, *Perry Mason: The Case of the Notorious Nun,* NBC, 1986.

TELEVISION APPEARANCES; EPISODIC

"Dream Stuff," *Douglas Fairbanks, Jr., Presents,* NBC, 1954.
Paul Verrall, "Born Yesterday," *Hallmark Hall of Fame,* NBC, 1956.
"The Morning Face," *Studio One,* CBS, 1957.
"The Enemies," *U.S. Steel Hour,* CBS, 1958.
"Human Interest Story," *Alfred Hitchcock Presents,* CBS, 1959.
Walter Hartright, "The Woman in White," *The Dow Hour of Great Mysteries,* NBC, 1960.
"The Closing Door," *Play of the Week,* syndicated, 1960.
Narrator, "Ethan Frome," *DuPont Show of the Month,* CBS, 1960.
"The Girl Who Knew Too Much," *U.S. Steel Hour,* CBS, 1960.
"Game of Hearts," *U.S. Steel Hour,* CBS, 1960.
"The Stone Boy," *Robert Herridge Theater,* CBS, 1960.
"The Man Who Found the Money," *Alfred Hitchcock Presents,* NBC, 1960.
"The Invincible Teddy," *Our American Heritage,* NBC, 1961.
"Mother and Daughter," *Special for Women,* NBC, 1961.
"Who's the Finest One of All?," *Great Ghost Tales,* NBC, 1961.
"The Boy Between," *The Defenders,* CBS, 1961.
"Keep Me Company," *Alfred Hitchcock Presents,* NBC, 1961.

"The Sweet Kiss of Madness," *Ben Casey,* ABC, 1961.
"Come Again to Carthage," *Westinghouse Presents,* CBS, 1961.
"The Battle of Hearts," *Armstrong Circle Theater,* CBS, 1961.
"Canada Run," *The Untouchables,* ABC, 1962.
"The Big Laugh," *U.S. Steel Hour,* CBS, 1962.
"I've Got It Made," *Frontiers of Faith,* syndicated, 1962.
"The Last Six Months," *The Defenders,* CBS, 1962.
"Kiss the Maiden All Forlorn," *Route 66,* CBS, 1962.
"Night Shift," *The Nurses,* CBS, 1962.
"Remember the Dark Sins of Youth?," *Slattery's People,* CBS, 1964.
"The Go-Between," *The Defenders,* CBS, 1964.
"Vote for Murder," *The Reporter,* CBS, 1964.
"Flight to Harbin," *The FBI,* ABC, 1966.
"The Monster from the Inferno," *Voyage to the Bottom of the Sea,* ABC, 1966.
"The Plague Merchant," *The FBI,* ABC, 1966.
"The Carriers," *Mission: Impossible,* CBS, 1966.
"The Fatal Mistake," *Bob Hope Chrysler Theater,* NBC, 1966.
"The Leeches," *The Invaders,* ABC, 1967.
"The Assassin," *Run for Your Life,* NBC, 1967.
"'Atta Girl Kelly," *The World of Disney,* NBC, 1967.
"Death of a Very Small Killer," *The Fugitive,* ABC, 1967.
"By Force and Violence," *The FBI,* ABC, 1967.
"Secrets," *CBS Playhouse,* CBS, 1968.
"My Client, the Fool," *Judd, for the Defense,* ABC, 1968.
"Warburton's Edge," *Lancer,* CBS, 1969.
"Attorney," *The FBI,* ABC, 1969.
"All the Beautiful Young Girls," *Bracken's World,* NBC, 1969.
"Echo of a Nightmare," *The Name of the Game,* NBC, 1970.
"Giants Never Kneel," *Bold Ones: The Doctors,* NBC, 1970.
"Aquarius Descending," *The Name of the Game,* NBC, 1970.
"Men Who Care," *Marcus Welby, M.D.,* ABC, 1971.
John Gunther, "Death Be Not Proud," *Tuesday Night Movie of the Week,* ABC, 1975.
Abraham Lincoln, "The Rivalry," *Hallmark Hall of Fame,* NBC, 1975.
"Journey into Spring," *Little House on the Prairie,* NBC, 1976.
Porter McPhail, "Tell Me My Name," *G.E. Theater,* CBS, 1977.
Shrike, "Miss Lonelyhearts," *American Playhouse,* PBS, 1983.
"The Murder of Sherlock Holmes," *Murder, She Wrote,* CBS, 1984.
Mr. Frank, "Love Leads the Way," *The Disney Sunday Movie,* ABC, 1986.
Governor, "Agenda for Murder," *Columbo* (also known as *The ABC Saturday Night Mystery*), ABC, 1990.

Also appeared in "People Don't Do Such Things," *Tales of the Unexpected,* 1979.

TELEVISION APPEARANCES; SPECIALS

The Sacco-Vanzetti Story, NBC, 1960.
Focus, NBC, 1962.
Dan Hillard, *The Desperate Hours,* ABC, 1967.
Judge James Edwin Horton, *Judge Horton and the Scottsboro Boys,* NBC, 1976.
Churchill and the Generals, NBC, 1981.
The Love Boat Fall Preview Party, ABC, 1984.*

* * *

HIPP, Paul

PERSONAL: Born in Philadelphia, PA; son of Jack and Nancy Hipp.

ADDRESSES: Agent—Stone Manners, 9113 Sunset Blvd., Los Angeles, CA 90069.

CAREER: Actor, singer and songwriter.

MEMBER: Screen Actors Guild, Actors Equity Association, American Federation of Television and Radio Artists.

AWARDS, HONORS: Antoinette Perry Award nomination, best performance by a leading actor in a musical, 1991, Laurence Olivier Award nomination, best performance by an actor in a musical, 1991, Theater World Award, Outer Critics Circle Award, Drama Desk nomination, and Dora Award nomination, all for *Buddy: The Buddy Holly Story.*

CREDITS:

STAGE APPEARANCES

Title role, *Buddy: The Buddy Holly Story,* Shubert Theatre, New York City, 1990.

FILM APPEARANCES

Nino, *China Girl,* Great American/Vestron, 1987.
Michael, *Sticky Fingers,* Spectrafilm, 1988.
Doogie, *Fathers and Sons,* RCA/Columbia, 1991.
Dr. Shorts, *Lethal Weapon III,* Warner Brothers, 1992.

TELEVISION APPEARANCES

Elvis Presley, *Liberace: Behind the Music* (movie), CBS, 1988.
Singer, *Macy's Thanksgiving Day Parade* (special), NBC, 1990.

Also appeared as Jarret in an episode of *The Equalizer,* CBS, and on episodes of *Entertainment Tonight, Good Morning America, Today,* and numerous other television programs in the United States and England.

RECORDINGS:

Hipp recorded the main theme for the film *China Girl,* and is recording an album of original material with his band, Paul Hipp and the Heroes.

WRITINGS:

Co-author, with Carole King, of the songs "I Can't Stop Thinking About You" and "Time Heals All Wounds," for her 1990 album, *City Streets.*

OTHER SOURCES:

PERIODICALS

Interview, September, 1990, p. 64.*

* * *

HOCKNEY, David 1937-

PERSONAL: Born July 9, 1937, in Bradford, Yorkshire, England; son of Kenneth and Laura Hockney. *Education:* Attended Bradford College of Art, 1953-57; graduated from Royal College of Art, 1962.

ADDRESSES: Office—7506 Santa Monica Blvd., Los Angeles, CA 90046.

CAREER: Artist, photographer, set and costume designer, and author. Has worked as a painter, photographic and graphic artist since 1962, with works exhibited throughout the world, including a large retrospective presented at the Los Angeles County Museum of Art, Los Angeles, the Tate Gallery, London, and the Metropolitan Museum of Modern Art, New York City. Art instructor at University of Iowa, 1964, University of Colorado at Boulder, 1965, University of California, Los Angeles, 1966, and University of California, Berkeley, 1967.

AWARDS, HONORS: Hockney has received numerous awards for his paintings, including: Guinness Award, 1961; first prize at the Eighth International Exhibition of Drawings, Lugano, Italy, 1964; Infinity Award, International Center of Photography, 1985, for "the painter, sculptor, or graphic artist who has made important use of photography in his art;" Progress Medal, Royal Photographic Society of Great Britain, 1988; and Praemium Imperiale, Japan Art Association, 1991; honorary degree from University of Aberdeen, Scotland, 1988.

CREDITS:

STAGE WORK; SET AND COSTUME DESIGNER

Ubu Roi, Royal Court Theatre, London, 1966.
Rake's Progress, Glyndebourne Opera, England, 1975.
The Magic Flute, Glyndebourne Opera, 1978.
"Parade," "Les Mamelles de Tiresias," and "L'Enfant et les Sortileges," in *Parade* (triple-bill), Metropolitan Opera, New York City, 1981.
"Le Sacre du Printemps," "Le Rossignol," and "Oedipus Rex" (triple-bill), Metropolitan Opera, 1981.
Varii Capricci, Royal Ballet, New York City, 1983.
Tristan und Isolde, Los Angeles Music Center Opera, 1987.
(with Ian Falconer) *Turandot,* Chicago Lyric Opera, 1992, then San Francisco Opera.
(with Ian Falconer) *Die Frau Ohne Schatten,* Royal Opera House, Covent Garden, England, 1992, then Los Angeles Music Center Opera.

FILM WORK

Hockney's paintings of California swimming pools appeared in *California Suite,* Columbia, 1978, and his photographic montage of Theresa Russell titled "Nude 17th June 1984" was created for *Insignificance,* Island Alive, 1985.

FILM APPEARANCES

Painter, *A Bigger Splash,* Buzzy Enterprises, 1984.
Himself, *Superstar: The Life and Times of Andy Warhol* (documentary), Aries, 1990.

Also appeared as himself in the documentary *Godzilla Meets Mona Lisa.*

TELEVISION WORK

Artwork, *What Ever Happened to Baby Jane?* (movie), ABC, 1991.
Costume and set designer, *The Magic Flute* (special), PBS, 1991.

TELEVISION APPEARANCES

Himself, *Pablo Picasso: The Legacy of a Genius* (documentary), PBS, 1982.
Himself, *Omnibus* (documentary series), ABC, 1988.
Himself, *The Painter's World: Changing Constants of Art from the Renaissance to the Present* (documentary), PBS, 1989.

WRITINGS:

SCREENPLAYS

A Day on the Grand Canal with the Emperor of China, or Surface Is Illusion But So Is Depth (documentary), New Yorker Films, 1988.

OTHER

David Hockney by David Hockney, edited by Nikos Stangos, Thames & Hudson, 1976, Abrams, 1977.
Paper Pools, Abrams, 1980.
The Artist's Eye, National Gallery, 1981.
(With Stephen Spender) *China Diary,* Abrams, 1982.
Cameraworks, Knopf, 1984.
(With Paul Joyce) *Hockney on Photography,* Harmony Books, 1988.
David Hockney: A Retrospective, Abrams, 1988.

Hockney has published collections of his work in various mediums, and has illustrated books for others, including *Six Fairy Tales of the Brothers Grimm.*

SIDELIGHTS: Internationally-known artist, photographer, and set designer David Hockney told *Chicago Tribune* music critic John von Rhein that he makes no distinction between his painting, his high-tech experiments with fax machines, laser printers and videocameras, and his theatre designs: "I don't divide up my work, really; it's all one. If I agree to do an opera, everything goes into it. I give it 100 percent of my time until I've finished it; it's not a sideline."

OTHER SOURCES:

BOOKS

Freidman, Martin L., *Hockney Paints the Stage,* Abbeville Press, 1983.
Livingstone, Marco, *David Hockney,* Thames & Hudson, 1981.
Newsmakers: 1988 Cumulation, Gale, 1989, pp. 182-185.

PERIODICALS

Art in America, November, 1985, p. 144; June 1990, p. 185.
ARTNews, January 1980, p. 52; October, 1986, p. 91.
Film Comment, July-August, 1989, p. 53.
Interview, December, 1986, p. 160; January, 1988, p. 51.
Life, February, 1988, p. 53.
Newsweek, February 15, 1988, p. 64.
New York, February 28, 1981, p. 36.
New Yorker, July 7, 1979, p. 35; July 9, 1984, p. 60.
Opera News, May, 1980, p. 12.
Rolling Stone, December 13, 1990, p. 178.
Smithsonian, February, 1988, p. 62.
Time, June 20, 1988, p. 76.
USA Today, July, 1988, p. 76.

* * *

HOGARTH, Emmett
See POLONSKY, Abraham

HOLDER, Geoffrey 1930(?)-

PERSONAL: Full name, Geoffrey Lamont Holder; born August 1, 1930 (one source cites 1931), in Port-of-Spain, Trinidad, West Indies; son of Arthur (a sales representative) and Louise (De Frense) Holder; married Carmen de Lavallade (an actress, dancer, and college professor), June 26, 1955; children: Leo Anthony Lamont (one source lists Ed). *Education:* Attended Queens Royal College, Port-of-Spain, 1948.

ADDRESSES: Office—c/o Donald Buchwald Associates, 10 East Forty-fourth St., New York, NY 10017. *Contact*—215 West Ninety-second St., New York, NY 10025.

CAREER: Dancer, choreographer, director, actor, costume designer, singer, composer, painter, cook, and writer. Worked for the Government of Trinidad, port services; started stage career as costume designer for brother Boscoe Holder's dance company; first stage appearance as dancer with brother's dance company, 1942; became head of his own dance touring company, 1950; Holder and his company performed in Puerto Rico and throughout the islands of the West Indies, 1953; made first stage appearance in U.S. with company at several venues, including the White Barn Theatre in Westport, CT, and the Jacob's Pillow Dance Festival in Lee, MA, 1953; appeared with dance company in biannual concerts at Kaufmann Auditorium, New York City, 1956-60; starred in calypso revue at Loew's Metropolitan Theatre, Brooklyn, NY, 1957; appeared in Festival of Two Worlds, Spoleto, Italy, 1958; designed costumes and appeared with the John Butler Dance Theatre, New York City, 1958; danced in the Vancouver B.C. Festival, 1960; appeared as solo dancer at International Festival in Lagos, Nigeria, 1962; danced with his company at the Harkness Dance Festival in New York City, 1963, and choreographed and designed the costumes for the same festival in 1966; WNBC-TV, drama critic, beginning in 1973. Various exhibits of paintings, including shows at the Barbados Museum in Puerto Rico, the Gropper Gallery in Cambridge, MA, Grinnel Galleries in Detroit, MI, and the Barone Gallery in New York City, 1955-59.

MEMBER: Screen Actors Guild, Actors Equity Association, American Guild of Variety Artists, American Federation of Television and Radio Artists, American Guild of Musical Artists.

AWARDS, HONORS: Guggenheim Fellowship in painting, 1957; United Caribbean Youth Award, 1957; Drama Desk Award, best costume design, Antoinette Perry Awards for best costume design and best director of a musical, all 1975, all for *The Wiz;* Antoinette Perry Award nomination, outstanding costume designer of a Broadway play, 1978, for *Timbuktu!;* Monarch Award, National Council of Culture and Arts, 1982; Ellis Island Medal of

Honor, National Ethnic Coalition of Organizations, 1986; Liberty Award, 1986.

CREDITS:

STAGE APPEARANCES; DANCER

(Broadway debut) *House of Flowers,* Alvin Theatre, New York City, 1954.

Solo dancer, *Aida,* Metropolitan Opera Association, New York City, 1956.

Solo dancer, *La Perichole,* Metropolitan Opera Association, 1956.

Specialty dancer, *Show Boat,* Jones Beach Marine Theatre, New York City, 1957.

Josephine Baker's Revue, Brooks Atkinson Theatre, New York City, 1964.

Holder appeared with his company in three revues: *Ballet Congo, Bal Creole,* and *Bal Negre.*

STAGE APPEARANCES; ACTOR

Lucky, *Waiting for Godot,* Ethel Barrymore Theatre, New York City, 1957.

Twelfth Night, Cambridge Drama Festival, MA, 1960.

Good Dragon, *The Masque of St. George and the Dragon,* Actors Studio, New York City, 1973.

Yeshu, *From the Memoirs of Pontius Pilate,* Actors Studio, 1976.

Night of One Hundred Stars Two, Radio City Music Hall, New York City, 1985.

The Players Club Centennial Salute, Sam S. Shubert Theatre, New York City, 1989.

Night of One Hundred Stars Three, Radio City Music Hall, 1990.

STAGE WORK; DIRECTOR

The Wiz (also see below), Majestic Theatre, New York City, 1975-78, Broadway Theatre, New York City, 1978-84, Lunt-Fontanne Theatre, New York City, 1984.

Timbuktu! (also see below), Mark Hellinger Theatre, New York City, 1978.

STAGE WORK; CHOREOGRAPHER

Brouhaha, Folksbiene Playhouse, 1960.

Mhil Daiim, Actors Studio, 1964.

Three Songs for One (also see below), Ted Shawn Theatre, 1964.

I Got a Song, Studio Arena Theatre, Buffalo, NY, 1974.

Timbuktu! (also see below), Mark Hellinger Theatre, 1978.

(And staging, with others) *Fifty Golden Years of Showstoppers,* Radio City Music Hall, 1982.

STAGE WORK; COSTUME DESIGNER

The Twelve Gates, Ted Shawn Theatre, 1964.

Three Songs for One, Ted Shawn Theatre, 1964.

The Wiz, Majestic Theatre, 1975-78, Broadway Theatre, 1978-84, Lunt-Fontanne Theatre, 1984.

Timbuktu!, Mark Hellinger Theatre, 1978.

MAJOR TOURS

(Director and costume designer) *The Wiz,* opened at Ahmanson Theatre in Los Angeles, CA, 1977, toured major U.S. cities.

FILM APPEARANCES

Dancer, *All Night Long,* J. Arthur Rank, 1961.

Willie Shakespeare, *Doctor Dolittle,* Twentieth Century-Fox, 1967.

Bazooki man, *Krakatoa, East of Java* (also known as *Volcano*), Cinerama, 1969.

Sorcerer, *Everything You Always Wanted to Know about Sex, but Were Afraid to Ask,* United Artists, 1972.

Baron Samedi, *Live and Let Die,* United Artists, 1973.

Cudjo, *Swashbuckler* (released in England as *The Scarlet Buccaneer*), Universal, 1976.

Punjab, *Annie,* Columbia, 1982.

Narrator, *Dance Black America,* Horizon Releasing, 1985.

Nelson, *Boomerang,* Paramount, 1992.

Also appeared in *Edgar Allan Poe's The Gold Bug,* 1990.

FILM WORK

Holder made a documentary film, based on a story he had written, in the 1950s with members of his dance company.

TELEVISION APPEARANCES; MOVIES

Mr. Johnson, *Ghost of a Chance,* CBS, 1987.

TELEVISION APPEARANCES; SPECIALS

(With dance company) *Alladin,* CBS, 1957.

Lion, *Androcles and the Lion,* NBC, 1967.

Slave on ship, *The Man without a Country,* ABC, 1973.

Ghost of Christmas Future, *John Grin's Christmas,* ABC, 1986.

Sixteenth Annual Black Filmmakers Hall of Fame, syndicated, 1989.

Sixty-second Annual Academy Awards, ABC, 1990.

Narrated *The Bottle Imp* in a televised U.S. Steel Theatre Guild production, 1957.

OTHER TELEVISION APPEARANCES

Holder appeared in a series of popular television ads in the late seventies and early eighties for products such as Seven-Up soft drinks.

TELEVISION WORK; CHOREOGRAPHER

"Dance Theatre of Harlem" (also known as "Dance in America"), *Great Performances,* PBS, 1977.

(Opening theme choreography) *The Cosby Show,* NBC, 1984.

Choreographed productions for station WELI, Boston, MA. Choreographer and solo dancer for CBS in 1962.

RECORDINGS:

ALBUMS

Recorded *Geoffrey Holder and His Trinidad Hummingbirds* on the Riverside label; also recorded an album of song stories for Mercury records.

WRITINGS:

Author (with Tom Harshman) of *Black Gods, Green Islands* (a collection of five novellas), 1957; author and illustrator of *Geoffrey Holder's Caribbean Cookbook,* 1974. Contributor of articles to *New York Times Magazine, Show, Saturday Review,* and *Playbill.*

OTHER SOURCES:

PERIODICALS

New York Times, May 25, 1975.*

* * *

HOLLY, Ellen 1931-

PERSONAL: Full name, Ellen Virginia Holly; born January 16, 1931, in New York, NY; daughter of William (a chemical engineer) and Grayce (a librarian; maiden name, Arnold) Holly. *Education:* Hunter College (now Hunter College of the City University of New York), B.A., 1952; studied acting at Perry-Mansfield School of the Theater, and with Charlotte Perry, Barney Brown, Uta Hagen, Mira Rostova, and Eli Rill. *Avocational interests:* Writing.

ADDRESSES: Agent—Starkman Agency, 1501 Broadway, Suite 301A, New York, NY 10036.

CAREER: Actress.

MEMBER: Actors Equity Association, Screen Actors Guild, American Federation of Television and Radio Artists, Delta Sigma Theta.

CREDITS:

STAGE APPEARANCES

(Off-Broadway debut) Tatiana, "The Anniversary" and Naida Gisben and Sharon Guilders, "A Switch in Time," *Two for Fun* (double-bill), Greenwich Mews Theatre, New York City, 1955.

Slave girl, *Salome,* Davenport Theatre, New York City, 1955.

Bianca, *A Florentine Tragedy,* Davenport Theatre, 1955.

(Broadway debut) Stephanie, *Too Late the Phalarope,* Belasco Theatre, New York City, 1956.

Rich woman's daughter, *Tevya and His Daughters,* Carnegie Hall Playhouse, New York City, 1957.

Desdemona, *Othello,* Belvedere Lake Theatre, 1958.

Elizabeth Falk, *Face of a Hero,* Eugene O'Neill Theatre, New York City, 1960.

Rosa, *Moon on a Rainbow Shawl,* East Eleventh Street Theatre, New York City, 1962.

Cille Morris, *Tiger, Tiger, Burning Bright,* Booth Theatre, New York City, 1962.

Iras, *Antony and Cleopatra,* New York Shakespeare Festival (NYSF), Delacorte Theatre, New York City, 1963.

Duchess of Hapsburg, *Funny House of a Negro,* East End Theatre, New York City, 1964.

Tatiana, *A Midsummer Night's Dream,* NYSF, Delacorte Mobile Theatre, 1964.

Katherine, *King Henry V,* NYSF, Delacorte Mobile Theatre, 1965.

Katherine, *The Taming of the Shrew,* NYSF, Delacorte Mobile Theatre, 1965.

"Clara Passmore Who Is the Virgin Mary Who Is the Bastard Who Is the Owl," *The Owl Answers,* White Barn Theatre, Westport, CT, then Theatre de Lys, New York City, 1965.

Lady Macbeth, *Macbeth,* NYSF, Delacorte Mobile Theatre, 1966.

An Evening of Negro Poetry and Folk Music, Delacorte Theatre, 1966, produced as *A Hand Is on the Gate,* Longacre Theatre, New York City, 1966.

Marguerite Gautier, *Camino Real,* Playhouse in the Park, Cincinnati, OH, 1968.

Gypsy palmist and courtesan, *The Comedy of Errors* (also see below), Ford's Theatre, Washington, DC, 1968.

Crime on Goat Island, Playhouse in the Park, Cincinnati, 1968.

Varya, *The Cherry Orchard,* NYSF, Public/Anspacher Theatre, New York City, 1973.

Regan, *King Lear,* NYSF, Delacorte Theatre, 1973.

Also appeared in several roles, including Sally Dupre and narrator for Aunt Bess, in *John Brown's Body;* appeared in *Orchids in the Moonlight,* American Repertory Theatre, Cambridge, MA; member of company, Playhouse in the Park, Cincinnati, OH, 1968.

MAJOR TOURS

Gypsy palmist and courtesan, *The Comedy of Errors,* National Repertory Theatre, U.S. cities, 1967.

Hippolita, *'Tis Pity She's a Whore,* U.S. cities, 1974-75.

FILM APPEARANCES

Carol, *Take a Giant Step,* United Artists (UA), 1959.
Secretary, *Cops and Robbers,* UA, 1973.
Odrie McPherson, *School Daze,* Columbia, 1988.

TELEVISION APPEARANCES; SERIES

Carla Gray, *One Life to Live,* ABC, 1968-81 and 1983-85.
Judge Frances Collier, *The Guiding Light,* CBS, 1989—.

Also appeared as Sally Travers, *Love of Life,* CBS.

TELEVISION APPEARANCES; MOVIES

Amy, *Sergeant Matlovich vs. the U.S. Air Force,* NBC, 1978.

TELEVISION APPEARANCES; EPISODIC

Tituba, *Odyssey,* CBS, 1957.
Regan, "King Lear," *Theater in America* (also known as *Great Performances*), PBS, 1974.
Mrs. Robbins, "High School Narc," *ABC Afterschool Special,* ABC, 1985.

Also appeared in episodes of *The Big Story,* NBC; *Confidential File,* syndicated; *The Nurses,* CBS; *The Defenders,* CBS; *Sam Benedict,* ABC; *Look Up and Live,* CBS; and *Dr. Kildare,* NBC.

* * *

HOLT, Andrew
See ANHALT, Edward

* * *

HORNER, James

ADDRESSES: Agent—Gorfaine-Schwartz Agency, 3301 Barham Blvd., Suite 201, Los Angeles, CA 90068.

CAREER: Music director, composer, arranger, and producer.

AWARDS, HONORS: Academy Award nomination, best original score, and Grammy Award nomination, best instrumental composition, both 1986, both for *Aliens;* Academy Award nomination (with Barry Mann and Cynthia Weil), best song, 1986, and Grammy Awards (with Mann and Weil), song of the year, and best song written for motion picture or television, both 1987, all for "Somewhere Out There," from movie *An American Tail;* Grammy Award nomination, best album of original instrumental background score for motion picture or television, 1987, for *An American Tail;* Academy Award nomination, best original score, 1989, for *Field of Dreams;* Grammy Award, best album or original instrumental score for a motion picture or for television, 1990, for *Glory.*

CREDITS:

FILM WORK

Music adaptor, *The Lady in Red* (also known as *Guns, Sin and Bathtub Gin;* also see below), New World, 1979.
Music conductor, *The Dresser* (also see below), Columbia, 1983.
Music designer, *Krull* (also see below), Columbia, 1983.
Music director, *Star Trek III: The Search for Spock* (also see below), Paramount, 1984.
Music producer, *Commando* (also see below), Twentieth Century-Fox, 1985.
Music conductor and arranger, *Aliens* (also see below), Twentieth Century-Fox, 1986.

WRITINGS:

FILM SCORES

The Lady in Red, New World, 1979.
Battle beyond the Stars, New World, 1980.
Humanoids from the Deep (also known as *Monster*), New World, 1980.
Deadly Blessing, United Artists (UA), 1981.
The Hand, Warner Brothers, 1981.
The Pursuit of D. B. Cooper, Universal, 1981.
Wolfen, Warner Brothers, 1981.
Star Trek II: The Wrath of Khan, Paramount, 1982.
48 Hours, Paramount, 1982.
Brainstorm, UA, 1983.
The Dresser, Columbia, 1983.
Gorky Park, J. Arthur Rank, 1983.
Krull, Columbia, 1983.
Something Wicked This Way Comes, Buena Vista, 1983.
Space Raiders (also known as *Star Child*), New World, 1983.
Testament, Paramount, 1983.
Uncommon Valor, Paramount, 1983.
Star Trek III: The Search for Spock, Paramount, 1984.
The Stone Boy, Twentieth Century-Fox, 1984.
(With Chris Young) *Barbarian Queen,* Concorde-Cinema Group, 1985.
Cocoon, Twentieth Century-Fox, 1985.
Commando, Twentieth Century-Fox, 1985.
Heaven Help Us (also known as *Catholic Boys*), Tri-Star, 1985.
The Journey of Natty Gann, Buena Vista, 1985.
Volunteers, Tri-Star, 1985.
Wizards of the Lost Kingdom, New Horizons-Concorde-Cinema Group, 1985.
Aliens, Twentieth Century-Fox, 1986.
An American Tail (also see below), Universal, 1986.
The Name of the Rose, Twentieth Century-Fox, 1986.
Off Beat, Touchstone Films-Silver Screen Partners II, 1986.

Where the River Runs Black, Metro-Goldwyn-Mayer (MGM)/UA, 1986.
Batteries Not Included, Universal, 1987.
P. K. & the Kid, Lorimar Home Video, 1987.
Project X, Twentieth Century-Fox, 1987.
Cocoon: The Return, Twentieth Century-Fox, 1988.
Red Heat, Tri-Star, 1988.
Vibes, Columbia, 1988.
Willow, MGM/UA, 1988.
The Land before Time (also see below), Universal, 1988.
Dad, Universal, 1989.
Field of Dreams, Universal, 1989.
Glory, Tri-Star, 1989.
Honey, I Shrunk the Kids, Buena Vista, 1989.
In Country, Warner Brothers, 1989.
I Love You to Death, Tri-Star, 1990.
Another 48 Hours, Paramount, 1990.
(With Ernest Troost) *Andy Colby's Incredibly Awesome Adventure* (also known as *Andy and the Airwave Rangers*), Concorde, 1990.
Class Action, Twentieth Century-Fox, 1991.
My Heroes Have Always Been Cowboys, Samuel Goldwyn, 1991.
Once Around, Universal, 1991.
The Rocketeer, Buena Vista, 1991.
An American Tale: Fievel Goes West (also see below), Universal, 1991.
Patriot Games, Paramount, 1992.

Also composer of score for *In Her Own Time,* 1985.

ANIMATED FILM SHORTS

Score, *Tummy Trouble,* Buena Vista, 1989.

FILM MUSIC; SONGS

(With Barry Mann and Cynthia Weil) "Somewhere Out There," *An American Tail,* Universal, 1986.
(With Will Jennings) "If We Hold on Together," *The Land before Time,* Universal, 1988.
"Way Out West," "Dreams to Dream," "Dreams to Dream (finale version)," and "The Girl I Left Behind," *An American Tale: Fievel Goes West,* Universal, 1991.

TELEVISION MUSIC; EPISODIC

"Cutting Cards" (also known as "Dead Right" and "The Switch"), *Tales from the Crypt,* HBO, 1990.

TELEVISION MUSIC; MOVIES

Angel Dusted, NBC, 1981.
A Few Days in Weasel Creek, CBS, 1981.
A Piano for Mrs. Cimino, CBS, 1982.
Between Friends, HBO, 1983.
Surviving, ABC, 1985.
Extreme Close-Up (also known as *Home Video*), NBC, 1990.

Also composer of score for *Rascals and Robbers—The Secret Adventures of Tom Sawyer and Huck Finn,* 1982.*

* * *

HORSFORD, Anna Maria 1947-

PERSONAL: Born March 6, 1947, in New York, NY; daughter of Victor A. (an investment real estate broker) and Lilian Agatha (Richardson) Horsford. *Education:* High School of Performing Arts, drama major, 1964; attended Inter-American University of Puerto Rico, 1966-67.

ADDRESSES: c/o Monty Silver, 200 West 57th St., New York, NY 10019.

CAREER: Actress and producer. WNET-13, National Educational Television, New York City, worked variously as temporary office worker, then production secretary, became producer, 1970-81; College of New Rochelle, New Rochelle, NY, teacher, 1978-79, and 1981.

MEMBER: Black Women in American Theatre (president, 1983-84), Variety Club of America, Hale House for Addictive Babies.

AWARDS, HONORS: Outstanding Leadership Award, National Association for the Advancement of Colored People (Gary, IN chapter), 1973.

CREDITS:

STAGE APPEARANCES

(Stage debut) Maiden Lady, *Coriolanus,* New York Shakespearean Theatre, New York City, 1965.
Young Woman, "Great Goodness of Life (A Coon Show)", in *A Black Quartet* (quadruple-bill), Tambellini's Gate Theatre, New York City, 1969.
Secretary, *The Well of the House,* Public Theatre, New York City, 1972.
Perfection, *Perfection in Black,* Negro Ensemble Company, New York City, 1973.
Les Femmes Noires, Public Theatre, 1974.
Rita, *Sweet Talk,* Public Theatre, 1975.
Red, Blue, Purple, *For Colored Girls Who Have Considered Suicide/When the Rainbow is Enuf,* Booth Theatre, New York City, 1978.
Amazon, *Peep,* South Street Theatre, New York City, 1981.
Women, *N.O.T.,* Lion Theatre, New York City, 1981.

Also appeared with the Actors Theatre of Louisville, Louisville, KY, 1984-85.

FILM APPEARANCES

Rosie Washington, *Times Square,* AFD, 1980.
Emily Stolz, *The Fan,* Paramount, 1981.
Mara, *Love Child,* Warner Brothers, 1982.
Amy Zon, *An Almost Perfect Affair,* Paramount, 1983.
Maggie, *Class,* Orion, 1983.
Slam Dunk, *Crackers,* Universal, 1984.
Naomi, *St. Elmo's Fire,* Columbia, 1985.
Della, *Heartburn,* Paramount, 1986.
Harriet, *Street Smart,* Golan-Globus/Cannon, 1987.
Eugenia, *Presumed Innocent,* Warner Brothers, 1990.

TELEVISION APPEARANCES; MOVIES

Monica, *Hollow Image,* ABC, 1979.
Marge Keating, *Bill,* CBS, 1981.
Charmaine, *Benny's Place,* ABC, 1982.
Kathy Thomas, *Muggable Mary: Street Cop,* CBS, 1982.
Sgt. Johnson, *The Firm,* NBC, 1983.
Hilly the letter carrier, *Murder Ink,* CBS, 1983.
Leigh Williams, *A Doctor's Story,* NBC, 1984.
Collins, *Stone Pillow,* CBS, 1985.
Virginia Cates, *A Case of Deadly Force,* CBS, 1986.
Mrs. Raines, *C.A.T. Squad,* NBC, 1986.
Nurse Betty, *Nobody's Child,* CBS, 1986.
Edith Sperling, *If It's Tuesday, It (Still) Must Be Belgium,* NBC, 1987.
Hillary, *Who Gets the Friends?,* CBS, 1988.
Mrs. Pierson, *Taken Away,* CBS, 1989.
District Attorney Barbara Evans, *A Killer Among Us,* NBC, 1990.
Veronica Perry, *Murder Without Motive: The Edmund Perry Story,* NBC, 1992.

TELEVISION APPEARANCES; SERIES

Thelma Frye, *Amen,* NBC, 1986-89.

Also appeared as Clara Jones on *The Guiding Light,* CBS, and on *The Doctors,* NBC.

TELEVISON APPEARANCES; EPISODIC

Jessica, "Starstruck," *After School Specials,* 1981.
Hannah, "Chalotte Forten's Mission: Experiment in Freedom," *American Playhouse,* PBS, 1985.
Guest, *At Rona's,* NBC, 1989.

TELEVISION APPEARANCES; SPECIALS

National Aids Awareness Test: What Do You Know About Acquired Immune Deficiency Syndrome, syndicated, 1987.
Hollywood Christmas Parade, syndicated, 1989.*

HOSKINS, Bob 1942-

PERSONAL: Full name, Robert William Hoskins; born October 26, 1942, in Bury St. Edmonds, Suffolk, England; son of Robert (a bookkeeper) and Elsie (a cook; maiden name Hopkins) Hoskins; married Jane Livesey (divorced); married Linda Banwell (a former schoolteacher); children: (first marriage) Alex, Sarah; (second marriage) Rosa, Jack. *Education:* Attended Stroud Green School, Finsbury Park; studied commercial art; studied accounting for three years. *Avocational interests:* Photography, listening to music, writing, gardening, playgoing.

ADDRESSES: Agent—Hutton Management Ltd., 200 Fulham Rd., London SW10 9PN, England.

CAREER: Actor. Previously worked as a laborer, porter, window cleaner, merchant seaman, circus fire-eater, agricultural worker on a *kibbutz* in Israel, and truck driver.

AWARDS, HONORS: British Academy of Film and Television Arts Award nominations, best actor, 1978, for *Pennies from Heaven,* and 1982, for *The Long Good Friday; Evening Standard* Best Actor Award, 1982, for *The Long Good Friday;* Academy Award nomination, British Academy of Film and Television Arts Award, Cannes International Film Festival award, New York Drama Critics Circle Award, and Golden Globe Award, Hollywood Press Association, all for best actor, all 1986, all for *Mona Lisa.*

CREDITS:

FILM APPEARANCES

Foster, *The National Health; or, Nurse Norton's Affair,* Columbia, 1973.
Policeman, *Royal Flash,* Twentieth Century-Fox, 1975.
Big Mac, *Inserts,* United Artists (UA), 1976.
Sergeant Major Williams, *Zulu Dawn,* Warner Brothers, 1980.
Harold, *The Long Good Friday,* Embassy, 1982.
Rock and Roll Manager, *Pink Floyd—The Wall,* Metro-Goldwyn-Mayer (MGM)/UA, 1982.
Colonel Perez, *Beyond the Limit* (released in England as *The Honorary Consul*), Paramount, 1983.
Owney Madden, *The Cotton Club,* Orion, 1984.
Becker, *Lassiter,* Warner Brothers, 1984.
Morrie Mendelsohn, *The Dunero Boys,* Jethro Films, 1985.
George, *The Woman Who Married Clark Gable,* Set 2 Films, 1985.
Spoor, *Brazil,* Universal, 1985.
George, *Mona Lisa,* Island/Handmade, 1986.
Stanley Gould, *Sweet Liberty,* Universal, 1986.
James Madden, *The Lonely Passion of Judith Hearne,* Island, 1987.
Father Da Costa, *A Prayer for the Dying,* Samuel Goldwyn, 1987.

Eddie Valiant, *Who Framed Roger Rabbit?,* Buena Vista, 1988.
Darky, *The Raggedy Rawney* (also see below), Island, 1988.
Jack Moony, *Heart Condition,* New Line, 1990.
Lou Landsky, *Mermaids,* Orion, 1990.
Smee, *Hook,* Tristar, 1991.
Gus Klein, *Shattered* (also known as *Troubles*), MGM/Pathe, 1991.
Beria, *The Inner Circle,* Columbia, 1991.
Louis Aubinard, *The Favor, the Watch and the Very Big Fish,* Trimark, 1992.
Johhny Scanlan, *Passed Away,* Buena Vista, 1992.

Also made the following film appearances: Secret Policeman's voice, *The Secret Policeman's Third Ball;* and *That All Men Should Be Brothers.*

FILM DIRECTOR

The Raggedy Rawney, Island, 1988.

STAGE APPEARANCES

(Stage debut) Peter, *Romeo and Juliet,* Victoria Theatre, Stoke on Trent, England, 1969.
Pinchwife, *The Country Wife,* Century Theatre, London, 1970.
The Baby Elephant, Theatre Upstairs, London, 1971.
Uriah Shelley, *Man Is Man,* Royal Court Theatre, London, 1971.
Lenny, *The Homecoming,* Hull Arts Center Theatre, 1971.
Title role, *Richard III,* Hull Arts Center Theatre, 1971.
Bernie the Volt, *Veterans,* Royal Court Theatre, 1971.
Butcher Brunt, *Cato Street,* Young Vic Theatre, London, 1971.
Azdak, *The Caucasian Chalk Circle,* Northcott Theatre, Exeter, England, 1971.
Soldiers, *Lear,* Royal Court Theatre, 1971.
Title role, *King Lear,* Dartington Hall Theatre, 1972.
Sextus Pompeius, *Antony and Cleopatra,* Bankside Globe Theatre, London, 1973.
Geography of a Horse Dreamer, Royal Court Theatre, 1974.
Doolittle, *Pygmalion,* Albert Theatre, London, 1974.
Touchstone, *As You Like It,* Oxford Playhouse, 1974.
Bill Cracker, *Happy End,* Oxford Playhouse, then Lyric Theatre, London, 1974-75.
Rocky, *The Iceman Cometh,* Royal Shakespeare Company, Aldwych Theatre, London, 1976.
Borkov, *Ivanov,* Royal Shakespeare Company, Aldwych Theatre, 1976.
Sergeant, *The Devil's Disciple,* Royal Shakespeare Company, Aldwych Theatre, 1976.
Jake, *England, England,* Jeannetta Cochrane Theatre, London, 1977.
The World Turned Upside Down, Cottesloe Theatre, London, 1978.
Joe Veriatio, *Has Washington Legs?,* Cottesloe Theatre, 1978.
Bosola, *The Duchess of Malfi,* Manchester Royal Exchange, The Roundhouse Theatre, London, 1981.
Lee, *True West,* National Theatre, London, 1981.
Nathan Detroit, *Guys and Dolls,* National Theatre, 1982.

Also made the following stage appearances: Hiring, *The Anniversary,* Century Theatre; Menelaus, *The Trojan Woman,* Hull Arts Center Theatre; Doolittle, *Pygmalion,* Albery Theatre, London; Common Man, *A Man for All Seasons,* Manchester 69 Company; Borkov, *Ivanov,* Royal Shakespeare Company, London; Marker, *A View from the Bridge.*

TELEVISION APPEARANCES; MOVIES

Woodbine, *Her Majesty's Pleasure,* BBC, 1972.
Sexton, *If There Weren't Any Blacks . . . ,* LWT, 1973.
Dobbs, *Thick as Thieves,* LWT, 1973.
Schmoedipus, BBC, 1974.
Title role, *Sheppey,* BBC, 1980.
Iago, *Othello,* BBC, 1981.
Eddie Reed, *You Don't Have to Walk to Fly,* LWT, 1982.
Benito Mussolini, *Mussolini: The Decline and Fall of Il Duce* (also known as *Mussolini and I*), HBO, 1985.

TELEVISION APPEARANCES; SERIES

Arthur Parker, *Pennies from Heaven,* BBC, 1977-78.
Arnie Cole, *Flickers,* ATV, 1980.

TELEVISION APPEARANCES; EPISODIC

"Cry Terror" (also known as "Kill Two Birds"), *Thriller,* ABC, 1975.

OTHER TELEVISION APPEARANCES

Roger Rabbit and the Secrets of Toontown (special; also known as *In Search of Toontown*), CBS, 1988.
Michael Caine: Breaking the Mold (special; also known as *Crazy about the Movie*), Cinemax, 1991.

Also made the following television appearances: (Television debut) *Villains on the High Road,* 1972; *Softly, Softly,* 1973; *The Gentle Rebellion,* 1974; *On the Move,* 1975; Joe Grimaldi, "It Must Be Something in the Water," *Omnibus,* BBC; Knocker, *The Villains,* LWT; *And All Who Sail in Her,* BBC; *On the Road,* BBC; *Crown Court,* Granada; *New Scotland Yard,* LWT; *Shoulder to Shoulder,* BBC; "On Brecht," *Omnibus,* BBC; *Three Piece Suit,* BBC; *In the Looking Glass,* BBC; Napoleon, *Penninsular,* BBC; Chorus, *Mycenae and Men,* BBC; *The Beggars Opera,* BBC; Mussolini, *Mussolini and I,* RAI, Italy; and *Rock Follies.*

WRITINGS:

SCREENPLAYS

(With Nicole De Wilde) *The Raggedy Rawney,* Island, 1988.

SIDELIGHTS: Favorite roles: Bernie the Volt, *Veterans;* title role, *Richard III;* title role, *King Lear.*

OTHER SOURCES:

BOOKS

Newsmakers 89, Gale, 1990, pp. 206-209.

PERIODICALS

New York Times, April 16, 1982; June 20, 1982; June 8, 1986.
New York Times Magazine, December 6, 1987, pp. 52, 54, 60, 56-68.

* * *

HOTY, Dee 1952-

PERSONAL: Born August 16, 1952, in Lakewood, OH. *Education:* Attended Otterbein College.

CAREER: Actress. Cleveland Playhouse, Cleveland, OH, member of company, 1974-76 and 1977-78, guest artist, 1976-77.

AWARDS, HONORS: Antoinette Perry Award nomination, best performance by a leading actress in a musical, 1991, for *The Will Rogers Follies.*

CREDITS:

STAGE APPEARANCES

Cora Wainwright, *The Five O'Clock Girl,* Helen Hayes Theatre, New York City, 1981.
Chairy Barnum, *Barnum,* Saenger Performing Arts Center, New Orleans, LA, 1981.
Forbidden Broadway, Comedy Store, Los Angeles, CA, 1983.
Maybe I'm Doing It Wrong, Chuck Martinez and La Jolla Playhouse, La Jolla, CA, 1984.
Alaura Kingsley, *City of Angels* (also see below), Virginia Theatre, New York City, 1989-90.
Wife of Will Rogers, *The Will Rogers Follies,* Palace Theatre, New York City, 1991.

Also appeared in *The Golden Apple* (Off-Broadway debut), 1979; as Claire, *Personals,* Minetta Lane Theatre, 1985; Lady Jacqueline Carstone, *Me and My Girl,* Marquis Theatre, 1986; on Broadway in *Shakespeare's Cabaret;* and Off-Broadway in *Tah-Dah!*

FILM APPEARANCES

Second beauty, *Harry and Walter Go to New York,* Columbia, 1976.

TELEVISION APPEARANCES; MOVIES

Martha Lowrie, *An Uncommon Love,* CBS, 1983.

RECORDINGS:

ALBUMS

Performed on original cast recording of *City of Angels,* c. 1990.*

* * *

HOWE, Bette
See HENRITZE, Bette

* * *

HUDSON, Hugh

PERSONAL: Born in England. *Education:* Attended Eton College.

ADDRESSES: Agent—Creative Artists Agency, 1888 Century Park E., 14th floor, Los Angeles, CA 90067.

CAREER: Film producer and director. Head of casting department for a London, England, advertising agency; worked for small film company in Paris, France; organized Cammell-Hudson-Brownjohn Film Company (production house), London; director of television commercials with Ridley Scott; Hudson Films, founder, 1975.

AWARDS, HONORS: Academy Award nomination, best director, 1981, for *Chariots of Fire.*

CREDITS:

FILM DIRECTOR

Fangio (also see below), Hudson Films, 1977.
Midnight Express, Columbia, 1978.
Chariots of Fire, Warner Brothers, 1981.
(And producer, with Stanley S. Carter) *Greystoke: The Legend of Tarzan, Lord of the Apes,* Warner Brothers, 1984.
Revolution, Warner Brothers, 1985.
Lost Angels, Orion, 1989.

Also director of *Twelve Squadron Bucaneers,* 1978.

WRITINGS:

SCREENPLAYS

Fangio, Hudson Films, 1977.*

HUNTLEY, Raymond 1904-1990

PERSONAL: Born April 23, 1904, in Birmingham, England; died June 15, 1990, in London, England; son of Alfred and Fannie (Walsh) Huntley; married June Bell (marriage dissolved). *Education:* King Edward's School, Birmingham, England.

CAREER: Actor.

CREDITS:

STAGE APPEARANCES

(Stage debut) *A Woman Killed with Kindness,* Birmingham Repertory Theatre, Birmingham, England, 1922.
(London debut) Acis, *As Far as Thought Can Reach, Part V: Back to Methuselah,* Court Theatre, London, 1924.
Reverend Septimus Tudor, *The Farmer's Wife,* Court Theatre, 1924.
Count Dracula, *Dracula,* Little Theatre, London, 1927.
(New York debut) Angelo Querini, *The Venetian Glass Nephew,* Vanderbilt Theatre, New York City, 1931.
Reverend Septimus Tudor, *The Farmer's Wife,* Queen's Theatre, London, 1932.
Pettingwaite, *Clear All Wires,* Garrick Theatre, London, 1933.
Cookson, *What Happened Then?,* Fortune Theatre, London, 1933.
Major Kilpatrick, Stringer, and Chatham, *Clive of India,* Wyndham's Theatre, London, 1934.
Alexei Turbin, *The White Guard,* Ambassadors' Theatre, London, 1934.
Ex-officer and Fletcher, *Cornelius,* Duchess Theatre, London, 1935.
Hastings, *Richard III,* Old Vic Theatre, London, 1936.
Sir George Cockburn, *St. Helena,* Daly's Theatre, London, 1936.
Slivers, *Bees on the Boat Deck,* Lyric Theatre, London, 1936.
Chapman, *Follow Your Saint,* Queen's Theatre, 1936.
Dr. Reuchlin, *Young Madame Conti,* Savoy Theatre, London, 1936, then Music Box Theatre, New York City, 1937.
Reverend John Fulton, *The First Legion,* Daly's Theatre, 1937.
Alan, *Time and the Conways,* Duchess Theatre, 1937.
Kashdak, *Susannah and the Elders,* Duke of York's Theatre, London, 1937.
Professor Hans Skaedia, *Glorious Morning,* Duchess Theatre, 1938.
Councillor Albert Parker, *When We Are Married,* St. Martin's Theatre, London, 1938.
Captain Guy Felton, *Rhondda Roundabout,* Globe Theatre, London, 1939.
Frank Crawley, *Rebecca,* Queen's Theatre, 1940, then Strand Theatre, London, 1942.
Malcolm Stritton, *They Came to a City,* Globe Theatre, 1943.
Victor Prynne, *Private Lives,* Apollo Theatre, London, 1944.
Mr. Arcularis, *Fear No More,* Lyric/Hammersmith Theatre, London, 1946.
Colonel Sanderson, DSO, *The Day of Glory,* Embassy Theatre, London, 1946.
Clive, *The Anonymous Lover,* Duke of York's Theatre, 1947.
Henry Martin, *The Late Edwina Black,* Ambassador's Theatre, 1949.
Robert Christie, *Black Chiffon,* 48th Street Theatre, New York City, 1950.
Frank Kemp, *And This Was Odd,* Criterion Theatre, London, 1951.
Theodore Brumfit, *Lords of Creation,* Vaudeville Theatre, London, 1952.
Sir Mohammed D'Urt, *No Sign of the Dove,* Savoy Theatre, 1953.
James Rice, *The Bombshell,* Westminster Theatre, London, 1954.
Manning, *The Shadow of Doubt,* Saville Theatre, London, 1955.
Ernest Fanshaw, *Double Image,* Savoy Theatre, 1956.
Sir Norman Tullis, *Any Other Business?,* Westminster Theatre, 1958.
Det. Superintendent Coates, *The Woman on the Stair,* Westminster Theatre, 1959.
Dr. Rodd, *Caught Napping,* Piccadilly Theatre, London, 1959.
Sir Nicholas Ennor, *The Landing Place,* Repertory Players, Phoenix Theatre, 1961.
John Freyling, *Difference of Opinion,* Garrick Theatre, 1963.
Edgar, *A Family and a Fortune,* Arnaud Theatre, Guildford, England, 1966.
Earl of Caversham, *An Ideal Husband,* Garrick Theatre, 1966.
Collins, *Getting Married,* Strand Theatre, 1967.
Paymaster General, *Soldiers,* New Theatre, London, 1968.
Mr. Fowler, *Separate Tables,* Apollo Theatre, 1977.

Company member, Alexandra Stock Company, Birmingham, England, 1931, and Reando Company, Edinburgh and Glasgow, Scotland, 1932.

MAJOR TOURS

Curdles Ash, *The Farmer's Wife,* English cities, 1925-26.
Philip Voaze, *Interference,* English cities, 1927-28.
Dracula, U.S. cities, 1928-1930.
Count Dunbarry, *The Dunbarry,* English cities, 1932-33.
Frank Crawley, *Rebecca,* English cities, 1941.
Count Barras, *Ah! Josephine,* English cities, 1945.

Edgar, *A Family and a Fortune,* English cities, 1966.

Also toured in repertory with actor Hamilton Deane, 1926-27.

FILM APPEARANCES

What Happened Then?, Wardour, 1934.
Dolan, *Can You Hear Me Mother?,* New Ideal, 1935.
Ludvig, *Rembrandt,* United Artists (UA), 1936.
Gibout, *Dinner at the Ritz,* Twentieth Century-Fox, 1937.
White officer, *Knight without Armor,* UA, 1937.
Kampenfeldt, *Night Train* (also known as *Gestapo* and *Night Train to Munich*), Twentieth Century-Fox, 1940.
Mr. Humphries, *The Ghost of St. Michaels,* Associated British Films, 1941.
John Price, *The Ghost Train,* General Film Distributors, 1941.
Dr. Kerbishley, *Mail Train* (also known as *Inspector Hornleigh Goes to It*), Twentieth Century-Fox, 1941.
Prison Governor, *Once a Crook,* Twentieth Century-Fox, 1941.
Rabenau, *A Voice in the Night* (also known as *Freedom Radio*), Columbia, 1941.
Marx, *Pimpernel Smith* (also known as *Mister V*), UA, 1942.
Albert Parker, *When We Are Married,* Anglo-American/British National, 1943.
Malcom Stritton, *They Came to a City,* Ealing, 1944.
Davenport, *The Way Ahead,* (also known as *The Immortal Battalion*), Twentieth Century-Fox, 1945.
Miller, *The Adventuress* (also known as *I See a Dark Stranger*) General Film Distributors, 1946.
Professor Laxton Jones, *School for Secrets* (also known as *Secret Flight*), General Film Distributors, 1946.
Moy-Thompson, *Mr. Perrin and Mr. Traill,* Eagle-Lion, 1948.
Henry Courtney, *So Evil My Love,* Paramount, 1948.
Mr. Wix, *Passport to Pimlico,* Eagle-Lion, 1949.
Williams, *It's Hard to Be Good,* General Film Distributors, 1950.
Mr. Chester, *Trio,* Paramount, 1950.
Mr. Throstle, *I'll Never Forget You* (also known as *The House on the Square*), Twentieth Century-Fox, 1951.
Chief Inspector Sullivan, *The Long Dark Hall,* Eagle-Lion, 1951.
Clive, *Man Bait* (also known as *The Last Page*), Lippert, 1952.
Tom Forester, *Glad Tidings,* Eros, 1953.
Mr. Patterson, *Meet Mr. Lucifer,* General Film Distributors, 1953.
Wright, *Mr. Denning Drives North,* Carroll Pictures, 1953.
Reverend Maurice, *Aunt Clara,* British Lion, 1954.
Nathaniel Beenstock, *Robson's Choice,* British Lion, 1954.
Samuel Pettigrew, *Scotch on the Rocks* (also known as *Laxdale Hall*), International, 1954.
Edward Marshall, *Broken Journey,* Twentieth Century-Fox, 1954.
J. F. Hassett, *The Constant Husband,* British Lion, 1955.
Laboratory official, *The Dam Buster,* Warner Brothers, 1955.
Captain Beamish, *Doctor at Sea,* J. Arthur Rank, 1955.
The general, *The Prisoner,* Columbia, 1955.
Maurice Miller, *The Teckman Mystery,* Associated Artists, 1955.
Attorney General, *The Last Man to Hang,* Columbia, 1956.
Prisoner Governor, *Rotten to the Core,* Cinema V, 1956.
Rawlins, *Wee Geordie,* Times, 1956.
Tatlock, *Brothers in Law,* British and Colonial, 1957.
Sir Gregory Upshoot, *The Green Man,* Distributors Corporation of America, 1957.
Dr. Reese, *Town on Trial,* Columbia, 1957.
Magistrate, *I'm All Right, Jack,* British Lion, 1959.
Harold, *Innocent Meeting,* UA, 1959.
Joseph Whemple, *The Mummy,* Universal, 1959.
Colonel Bellamy, *Orders Are Orders,* British Lion, 1959.
Mr. Hoylake, *Room at the Top,* Romulus, 1959.
Garrick Jones, *Bottoms Up,* Associated British Films, 1960.
Special branch chief, *Follow That Horse,* Warner Brothers, 1960.
Inspector Pape, *Make Mine Mink,* Continental, 1960.
Foreign Office Minister, *Man in a Cocked Hat* (also known as *Carlton-Brown of the F.O.*), Show, 1960.
Forbes, *Next to No Time,* Show, 1960.
Army officer, *Our Man in Havana,* Columbia, 1960.
Bossom, *Sands of the Desert,* Warner Brothers/Pathe, 1960.
Rev. Edwin Peake, *A French Mistress,* British Lion, 1960.
Judge, *The Pure Hell of St. Trinian's,* Continental Distributing, 1961.
Sir George Gatling, *The Risk* (also known as *Suspect*), Kingsley International, 1961.
Sir Ronald Ackroyd, *On the Beat,* J. Arthur Rank, 1962.
Vernon, *Only Two Can Play,* Kingsley/Columbia, 1962.
President of court martial, *Waltz of the Toreadors* (also known as *The Amorous General*), Continental Distributing, 1962.
Wagstaffe, *Crooks Anonymous,* Janus, 1963.
Mr. Wedgewood, *Father Came Too,* J. Arthur Rank, 1964.
Harry Halburton, *Gutter Girls* (also known as *The Yellow Teddy Bears* and *Thrill Seekers*), Topaz Film Corp., 1964.
Vicar, *Nurse on Wheels,* Janus, 1964.
Colonel Wentworth, *The Black Torment,* Compton-Tekl, 1965.

The minister, *The Great St. Trinian's Train Robbery,* Braywild/British Lion, 1966.
John Naylor, *Hostile Witness,* UA, 1968.
Bayswater, *Hot Millions,* Metro-Goldwyn-Mayer, 1968.
Smither, *The Adding Machine,* Regal Films, 1969.
Young Winston, Columbia, 1972.
Symptoms, Bryantson, 1976.

TELEVISION APPEARANCES

Superintendent Dode, *Destiny of a Spy* (movie), NBC, 1969.
Sir Geoffrey Dillon, *Upstairs, Downstairs* (series), BBC, 1970-75.

Also appeared in the series *Uncle Charles* and in *That's Your Funeral.*

OBITUARIES AND OTHER SOURCES:

PERIODICALS

Hollywood Reporter, June 20, 1990.
New York Times, June 20, 1990.*

* * *

HYMAN, Dick 1927-

PERSONAL: Full name, Richard Roven Hyman; born March 8, 1927, in New York, NY. *Education:* Studied with Teddy Wilson.

CAREER: Jazz artist, pianist, organist, composer and arranger. Played with Red Norvo, 1949-50; toured Europe with Benny Goodman, 1950; recorded for MGM, 1954-58; musical director for Arthur Godfrey, 1958-61; studio work as composer and arranger. *Military service:* U.S. Navy, 1945-46.

AWARDS, HONORS: Emmy Award, musical composition, 1980, for "Sunshine's On the Way," *NBC Special Treat;* Emmy Award, outstanding achievement in music direction, 1983, for "Eubie Blake: A Century of Music," *Kennedy Center Tonight.*

CREDITS:

FILM APPEARANCES

The Great Rocky Mountain Jazz Party (documentary), Great Rocky Mountain Jazz Party, 1977.

FILM WORK

Arranger, *Scott Joplin,* Universal, 1977.
Arranger, *Stardust Memories,* United Artists (UA), 1980.
Music supervisor, *Radio Days,* Orion, 1987.
Arranger and pianist, *Billy Bathgate,* Buena Vista, 1991.

STAGE WORK

Orchestrator with Luther Henderson and Sy Oliver, *Doctor Jazz,* Winter Garden Theater, New York City, 1975.
Orchestrator, *Sugar Babies,* Curran Theatre, San Francisco, then Mark Hellinger Theatre, both, 1979, later U.S. cities.
Orchestrator and musical arranger, *Black Broadway,* Town Hall Theatre, New York City, 1980.
Music director and principal arranger, *Eubie Blake: A Century of Music* (also see below), John F. Kennedy Center for the Performing Arts, New York City, 1983.

TELEVISION APPEARANCES; SPECIALS

Pianist (with Benny Carter Quartet), *In Performance at the White House* (also known as *The House I Live In;* also see below), PBS, 1989.
In Performance at the White House (also known as *The House I Live In;* also see below), PBS, 1990.

TELEVISION WORK

Music director, orchestrator, and principal arranger, "Eubie Blake: A Century of Music," *Kennedy Center Tonight* (also see below), PBS, 1983.
Musical supervisor, *Benny Goodman—Let's Dance—A Musical Tribute,* PBS, 1986.
Music director, "Ask Me Again" (also known as "An Old-Fashioned Story"), *American Playhouse,* PBS, 1989.
Music director, *In Performance at the White House* (also known as *The House I Live In*), PBS, 1989.
Music director, *In Performance at the White House* (also known as *The House I Live In*), PBS, 1990.

Played the organ for television game show, *Beat the Clock.* Also served as music director for David Frost's television specials.

RECORDINGS:

Recorded *The Electric Eclectics of Dick Hyman* and *Pieces for Moog* on the Command label; *Traditional Jazz Piano* and *Solo Piano Fantomfingers* on Project 3; *Genius at Play* and *Shakespeare, Sullivan, and Hyman,* with Maxine Sullivan, on Monmouth-Evergreen; *Theme and Variations on "A Child is Born"* on Chiaroscuro; *Let It Happen* on RCA by the Jazz Piano Quartet with Hank Jones, Marian McPartland, and Roland Hanna; *Jelly Roll Morton Orchestral Transcriptions* on Columbia; *Satchmo Remembered* on Atlantic; and *Waltz Dressed as Blue* on Grapevine. Also recorded with Ruby Braff on Chairoscuro. Hyman's settings of William Shakespeare were recorded by Earl Wrightson as *Shakespeare's Greatest Hits,* 1964.

Wrote arrangements for Enoch Light's band and, in 1965, composed *Duets in Odd Meters and Far-Out Rhythms.*

WRITINGS:

FILM MUSIC

French Quarter, Crown International, 1978.
Stardust Memories, UA, 1980.
The Chosen, Contemporary Films, 1981.
Zelig, Warner Brothers, 1983.
Broadway Danny Rose, Orion, 1984.
Mask, Universal, 1985.
The Purple Rose of Cairo, Orion, 1985.
Moonstruck, United Artists, 1987.
(And lyrics, with others) *Radio Days,* Orion, 1987.
Leader of the Band (also known as *Leader of the Pack*), New Century/Vista, 1987.
Thelonius Monk: Straight, No Chaser (documentary), Warner Brothers, 1988.
The Lemon Sisters, Miramax, 1989.

TELEVISION MUSIC; MOVIES

The Deadliest Season, CBS, 1977.
The Last Tenant, ABC, 1978.
The Henderson Monster, CBS, 1980.
King Crab, ABC, 1980.
Johnny Bull, ABC, 1986.

TELEVISION MUSIC; SERIES

This Will Be the Year That Will Be, ABC, 1973.
That Was the Year That Was, ABC, 1973.

TELEVISION MUSIC; SPECIALS

"Sunshine's on the Way," *NBC Special Treat,* NBC, 1980.
"Robbers, Rooftops and Witches," *CBS Library,* CBS, 1982.
"Eubie Blake: A Century of Music," *Kennedy Center Tonight,* PBS, 1983.
"Natica Jackson," *Great Performances: Tales from the Hollywood Hills,* PBS, 1987.
"A Table at Ciro's," *Great Performances: Tales from the Hollywood Hills,* PBS, 1987.
"Pat Hobby Teamed with Genius," *Great Performances: Tales from the Hollywood Hills,* PBS, 1987.
"The Old Reliable," *Great Performances: Tales from the Hollywood Hills,* PBS, 1988.
"Golden Land," *Great Performances: Tales from the Hollywood Hills,* PBS, 1988.
"The Closed Set," *Great Performances: Tales from the Hollywood Hills,* PBS, 1988.
"As Me Again" (also known as "An Old-Fashioned Story"), *American Playhouse,* PBS, 1989.
In Performance at the White House (also known as *The House I Live In*), PBS, 1989.
"Broadway Dreamers: The Legacy of the Group Theatre," *American Masters,* PBS, 1989.
In Performance at the White House (also known as *The House I Live In*), PBS, 1990.*

J

JACKEE
See HARRY, Jackee

* * *

JACKSON, Ernestine

PERSONAL: Born September 18, in Corpus Christi, TX. *Education:* Attended Del Mar College, Juilliard School of Music, and Hunter College of the City University of New York.

ADDRESSES: Agent—Ambrosio Mortimer, 301 North Cannon Dr., Suite 305, Beverly Hills, CA 90210.

CAREER: Actress and singer. Coconut Grove Playhouse, Coconut Grove, FL, member of company, 1987-88.

MEMBER: Actors Equity Association.

AWARDS, HONORS: Antoinette Perry Award nomination, best supporting actress in a musical play, and *Theatre World* Award, both 1974, for *Raisin;* Antoinette Perry Award nomination, best actress in a Broadway musical, 1977, for *Guys and Dolls.*

CREDITS:

STAGE APPEARANCES

Townsperson, *Hello, Dolly!* (also see below), St. James Theatre, New York City, 1964-70.
(Debut) Member of chorus, *Show Boat,* New York State Theatre, New York City, 1966.
Singer, *Finian's Rainbow,* New York City Center Theatre, New York City, 1967.
Member of chorus, *Applause,* Palace Theatre, New York City, 1970.
Jesus Christ Superstar, Mark Hellinger Theatre, New York City, 1971.
Ruth Younger, *Raisin,* Arena Stage, Washington, DC, 1972-73, then 46th Street Theatre, New York City, 1973-75, later Lunt-Fontanne Theatre, New York City, 1975.
Ernestina, *Tricks,* Alvin Theatre, New York City, 1973.
Sister Sarah Brown, *Guys and Dolls,* Broadway Theatre, New York City, 1976-77.
Hot Dishes!, Harry DeJur Playhouse, New York City, 1978.
Member of chorus, *The Bacchae,* Circle in the Square, New York City, 1980.
Lil, *Louis,* Harry DeJur Playhouse, 1981.
Singer, *Some Enchanted Evening* (concert), St. Regis-Sheraton Hotel, New York City, 1983, then American Stage Company, Teaneck, NJ, 1986-87, later on tour.
Rap Master Ronnie, Village Gate Theatre Upstairs, New York City, 1984.
Jill Donovan, *Jack and Jill,* Riverwest Theatre, New York City, 1985.
Rosie, *Black Girl,* Second Stage Theatre, New York City, 1986.
Mary, *Brownstone,* Roundabout Theatre, New York City, 1986.
Mollie, *Sophie,* Jewish Repertory Theatre, New York City, 1987.
Standby for Molly, Martha, Bertha, and Mattie, *Joe Turner's Come and Gone,* Ethel Barrymore Theatre, New York City, 1988.

Appeared in *Money Notes.* Toured U.S. cities as Irene Molloy, *Hello, Dolly!,* 1970-71.

FILM APPEARANCES

Cleo, *Aaron Loves Angela,* Columbia, 1975.
Media jackal, *Bonfire of the Vanities,* Warner Brothers, 1990.*

JACKSON, Samuel L. 1949(?)-

PERSONAL: Born c. 1949; married LaTanya Richardson (an actress); children: Zoe. *Education:* Attended Morehouse College.

ADDRESSES: Agent—Ambrosio/Mortimer & Associates, Inc., 165 West 46th St., Suite 1109, New York, NY 10036.

CAREER: Actor. Worked in street theater, repertory theater, and developmental theater; appeared in television commercials.

AWARDS, HONORS: Special Jury Prize, best supporting actor in a full-length film, Cannes International Film Festival, 1991, for *Jungle Fever.*

CREDITS:

FILM APPEARANCES

Ragtime, Paramount, 1981.
Holdup man, *Coming to America,* Paramount, 1988.
Leeds, *School Daze,* Columbia, 1988.
Black guy, *Sea of Love,* Universal, 1989.
Ulysses, *A Shock to the System,* Corsair, 1990.
Def by Temptation, Troma, 1990.
Mickey, *Betsy's Wedding,* Buena Vista, 1990.
Madlock, *Mo' Better Blues,* Universal, 1990.
Dream blind man, *The Exorcist III,* Twentieth Century-Fox, 1990.
Stacks Edwards, *Goodfellas,* Warner Brothers, 1990.
Gator Purify, *Jungle Fever,* Universal, 1991.
Monroe, *Strictly Business* (also known as *Go Natalie, Go Beverly*), Warner Brothers, 1991.
Meeker, *White Sands,* Warner Brothers, 1992.
Robby, *Patriot Games,* Paramount, 1992.

Also appeared as Eddie's uncle, *Eddie Murphy Raw,* 1987.

STAGE APPEARANCES

Lucky, *Mobile Theater: The Mighty Gents,* New York Shakespeare Festival, Delacorte Theatre/Central Park, New York City, 1979.
Sergeant/Kiowa man/soldier/Klansman, *Mother Courage and Her Children,* Public/Newman Theatre, New York City, 1980.
Cephus, *Home,* Negro Ensemble Company, Theatre Four, New York City, 1981.
Private Louis Henson, *A Soldier's Play,* Negro Ensemble Company, Theatre Four, 1981.
Ohio Tip-Off, Center Stage Theatre, Baltimore, MD, 1983.
Actor 7, *District Line,* Negro Ensemble Company, Theatre Four, 1984.
Native Speech, Center Stage Theatre, 1984.
Lyons, *Fences,* Seattle Repertory Theatre, Seattle, WA, 1985.
The Piano Lesson, Yale Repertory Theatre, New Haven, CT, 1987.
Prince, *We: Part I-Sally/Part II-Prince,* Negro Ensemble Company, Theatre Four, 1988.
Two Trains Running, Yale Repertory Theatre, 1989.

TELEVISION APPEARANCES; MOVIES

George Harris, *Uncle Tom's Cabin,* Showtime, 1987.
Reverend Bob McClain, *Common Ground,* CBS, 1990.
Hatcher, *Dead and Alive: The Race for Gus Farace,* ABC, 1991.

TELEVISION APPEARANCES; EPISODIC

"The Trial of the Moke," *Great Performances,* PBS, 1978.

OTHER SOURCES:

PERIODICALS

New York Times, June 9, 1991, p. H16.*

* * *

JACOBS, David 1939-

PERSONAL: Born August 12, 1939, in Baltimore, MD; son of Melvin and Ruth (Levenson) Jacobs; married Diana Pietrocarli, February 12, 1977; children: Aaron Michael, Molly Sarah. *Education:* Maryland Institute, College of Art, B.F.A., 1961. *Avocational interests:* Photography.

ADDRESSES: Office—10202 West Washington Blvd., Culver City, CA 90230.

CAREER: Television producer, director, and writer; creator of television series. *The Book of Knowledge, Inc.,* art articles editor, 1961-65; American Heritage Publishing, New York City, editor and writer, 1965-68; previously a painter.

MEMBER: American Film Institute (member of board of directors, 1987), Academy of Television Arts and Sciences, Writers Guild of America.

AWARDS, HONORS: Humanitas Prize (with Carol Evan McKeand), sixty minute category, 1978, for *Family* episode "Annie Laurie."

CREDITS:

TELEVISION EXECUTIVE PRODUCER

(With Lee Rich and Michael Filerman; and creator) *Knots Landing* (series; also see below), CBS, 1979-83.
(With Rich) *A Perfect Match* (movie), CBS, 1980.
(With Rich and Filerman; and creator) *Secrets of Midland Heights* (series; also see below), CBS, 1980-81.

(With Filerman) *Behind the Screen* (series; also see below), CBS, 1981-82.
(With Gary Adelson) *Lace* (mini-series), ABC, 1984.
(And creator) *Berrenger's* (series; also see below), NBC, 1985.
(With Malcolm Stuart) *Dallas: The Early Years* (movie; also see below), CBS, 1986.
(And creator) *Paradise* (series; also known as *Guns of Paradise;* also see below), CBS, 1988-91.
Homefront (series; also known as *1945*), ABC, 1991—.

TELEVISION DIRECTOR

Knots Landing (series), CBS, 1981-83.
Guns of Paradise (premiere; also known as *Paradise*), CBS, 1988.

OTHER TELEVISION WORK

Story editor, *Family* (series), ABC, 1977-78.
Creator and executive story consultant, *Dallas,* CBS, 1978.
Producer and creator, *Married: The First Year,* CBS, 1979.

WRITINGS:

TELEVISION SERIES

The Blue Knight, CBS, 1976.
Knots Landing, CBS, 1979-83.
Secrets of Midland Heights, CBS, 1980-81.
Behind the Screen, CBS, 1981-82.

OTHER TELEVISION WRITING

Dallas: The Early Years (movie), CBS, 1986.
Guns of Paradise (also known as *Paradise;* premiere), CBS, 1988.

NONFICTION, WITH THE EDITORS OF HORIZON MAGAZINE

Master Builders of the Middle Ages, American Heritage Publishing, 1969.
Constantinople: City on the Golden Horn, American Heritage Publishing, 1969.
Beethoven, American Heritage Publishing, 1970.
Constantinople and the Byzantine Empire, Cassell, 1971.

OTHER NONFICTION

(With Anthony E. Neville) *Bridges, Canals & Tunnels,* American Heritage Publishing, 1968.
Master Painters of the Renaissance, Viking, 1968.
An American Conscience: Woodrow Wilson's Search for World Peace, Harper, 1973.
Architecture, Newsweek Books, 1974.
Chaplin, the Movies, & Charlie, Harper, 1975.
Disney's America on Parade: A History of the U.S.A. in a Dazzling, Fun-Filled Pageant, Abrams, 1975.
(With Sara Ann Friedman) *Police!: A Precinct at Work,* Harcourt, 1975.*

* * *

JAFFE, Herb 1921(?)-1991

OBITUARY NOTICE—See index for *CTFT* sketch: Born c. 1921, in New York, NY; died of cancer, December 7, 1991, in Beverly Hills, CA. Producer, studio executive, and literary agent. Jaffe will be remembered for his work in the field of major motion pictures. After beginning his career as a freelance press and talent agent for MCA, Jaffe embarked on a six year tenure with the studio's newly formed television division. In 1957 he formed Herb Jaffe Associates, a literary agency that represented such writers as Paddy Chayefsky, Philip Roth, and Joseph Heller, but later sold the agency and returned to the film industry. In the mid-sixties Jaffe moved to a vice presidential position with United Artists, and eventually became the studio's head of worldwide production. Under Jaffe's leadership the studio released such films as *Midnight Cowboy* and *Last Tango in Paris.* He left UA in the 1970s to work as an independent producer on numerous motion pictures, including *The Wind and the Lion, The Lords of Discipline,* and both *Fright Night* films. In addition to his work as a producer, Jaffe also served on the board of governors for the Academy of Motion Picture Arts and Sciences from 1985 to 1988.

OBITUARIES AND OTHER SOURCES:

BOOKS

International Motion Picture Almanac, Quigley, 1991, p. 160.

PERIODICALS

Variety, December 16, 1991, p. 74.

* * *

JAFFE, Stanley R. 1940-

PERSONAL: Full name, Stanely Richard Jaffe; born July 31, 1940, in New Rochelle, NY; son of Leo and Dora (Bressler) Jaffe; married Melinda Long; children: Bobby, Betsy, Katie, Alexander. *Education:* University of Pennsylvania, B.S., 1962.

ADDRESSES: Office—c/o Paramount Communications, Inc., 15 Columbus Circle, New York, NY 10023-7780.

CAREER: Film producer and director. Seven Arts Associates, Hollywood, CA, creator, writer, director and producer, 1962-63, director of East Coast programming for

Seven Arts TV, 1963-64, executive assistant to president, 1964, director of programming, 1965-67; Paramount Pictures, Hollywood, executive vice president and chief corporate officer, 1969-70, president of Paramount TV, 1970-71; Jaffilms, Inc., Hollywood, president, 1971; independent producer, beginning in 1971; Columbia Pictures, Hollywood, executive vice president of worldwide production, 1975-76; Jaffe/Lansing Productions, cofounder, 1982; Paramount Communications, New York City, president and chief operating officer, 1991—. Served on board of trustees for Rippowam Cisqua School, the board of advisors for the graduate school of the Wharton School of Finance and Commerce, and the presidents' council of Memorial Sloan Kettering; chair of the board of the Robert Steel Pediatric Cancer Research Foundation.

MEMBER: Academy of Motion Picture Arts and Sciences, City Athletic Club, Quaker Ridge Golf Club.

AWARDS, HONORS: Academy Award, best picture, and Di Donatello award, both 1979, both for *Kramer vs. Kramer;* Academy Award nomination, best picture, 1987, for *Fatal Attraction.*

CREDITS:

FILM WORK; PRODUCER

Goodbye, Columbus, Paramount, 1969.
(With David Greene) *I Start Counting,* United Artists, 1970.
Bad Company, Paramount, 1972.
The Bad News Bears, Paramount, 1976.
Kramer vs. Kramer, Columbia, 1979.
(With Howard B. Jaffe) *Taps,* Twentieth Century-Fox, 1981.
(And director) *Without a Trace,* Twentieth Century-Fox, 1983.
(With Sherry Lansing) *Fatal Attraction,* Paramount, 1987.
(With Lansing) *The Accused,* Paramount, 1988.
(With Lansing) *Black Rain,* Paramount, 1989.

FILM WORK; EXECUTIVE PRODUCER

Firstborn, Paramount, 1984.
Racing with the Moon, Paramount, 1984.

Also executive producer of *Man on a Swing,* 1973.

TELEVISION WORK

Executive producer, *Johny Cypher* (series), syndicated, 1965.
Executive producer, *When the Time Comes,* ABC, 1987.

Also creator and associate producer for *The Professionals,* 1963.

JEAKINS, Dorothy 1914-

PERSONAL: Born January 11, 1914, in San Diego, CA; daughter of George Tyndall (a bank clerk) and Sophie-Marie (a couture dressmaker; maiden name, von Kempf) Jeakins; married; children: Stephen Dane, Peter Dane. *Education:* Attended Otis Art Institute, 1931-34. *Avocational interests:* cooking, bird-watching, gardening, reading books.

ADDRESSES: Contact—2926 Torito Rd., Santa Barbara, CA 93108.

CAREER: Costume designer for stage and film. Art Students League, Los Angeles, CA, 1935; worked on WPA Federal Art Project, 1935-36; assistant to Ernst Dryden, 1938; photo research, *Voyage to America* (documentary for U.S. Pavilion), New York World's Fair, 1964; curator of costume and textiles, Los Angeles County Museum of Art, 1968.

MEMBER: Costume Designers Guild.

AWARDS, HONORS: Academy Award (with Karinska), best costume design (color), 1948, for *Joan of Arc;* Academy Award (with others), best costume design (color), 1950, for *Samson and Delilah;* Academy Award nomination (with Edith Head and Miles White), best costume design (color), 1952, for *The Greatest Show on Earth;* Academy Award nomination, best costume design (black-and-white), 1952, for *My Cousin Rachel;* Academy Award nomination (with others), best costume design (color), 1956, for *The Ten Commandments;* Antoinette Perry Award nomination, 1957, best costume design, for *Major Barbara* and *Too Late the Phalarope;* Antoinette Perry Award nomination, best costume design, 1959, for *The World of Suzie Wong;* Academy Award nomination, best costume design (black-and-white), 1961, for *The Children's Hour;* Academy Award nomination, best costume design (color), 1962, for *The Music Man;* Academy Award, best costume design (black and white), 1964, for *The Night of the Iguana;* Academy Award nomination, best costume design (color), 1965, for *The Sound of Music;* Academy Award nomination, best costume design (color), 1966, for *Hawaii;* Academy Award nomination (with Moss Mabry), best costume design, 1973, for *The Way We Were;* Academy Award nomination, best costume design, 1987, for *The Dead;* Crystal Award, Women in Film, 1987; honorary doctorate awarded by the Otis Art Institute of the Parson School of Design, 1987; Vesta Award, 1989. Guggenheim Foundation fellow, 1962.

CREDITS:

FILM WORK; COSTUME DESIGNER

(Assistant to designer) *Dr. Rhythm,* Paramount, 1938.
(With Karinska) *Joan of Arc,* RKO Radio Pictures, 1948.

(With Edith Head, Gus Peters, Gwen Wakeling, and Elois Jenssen) *Samson and Delilah,* Paramount, 1949.
Cyrano de Bergerac, United Artists (UA), 1950.
Belles on Their Toes, Twentieth Century-Fox, 1952.
The Big Sky, RKO Radio Pictures, 1952.
(With Head and Miles White) *The Greatest Show on Earth,* Paramount, 1952.
Les Miserables, Twentieth Century-Fox, 1952.
My Cousin Rachel, Twentieth Century-Fox, 1952.
(Costumes for Grace Kelly) *High Noon,* UA, 1952.
The Outcasts of Poker Flats, Twentieth Century-Fox, 1952.
Stars and Stripes Forever, Twentieth Century-Fox, 1952.
(With Charles LeMaire) *Treasure of the Golden Condor,* Twentieth Century-Fox, 1952.
Beneath the Twelve-Mile Reef, Twentieth Century-Fox, 1953.
Niagara, Twentieth Century-Fox, 1953.
Titanic, Twentieth Century-Fox, 1953.
White Witch Doctor, Twentieth Century-Fox, 1953.
Three Coins in the Fountain, Twentieth Century-Fox, 1954.
Prince Valiant, Twentieth Century-Fox, 1954.
(With Bert Henrikson) *Friendly Persuasion,* Allied Artists, 1956.
(With others) *The Ten Commandments,* Paramount, 1956.
The Young Stranger, RKO Radio Pictures/Universal, 1957.
South Pacific, Twentieth Century-Fox, 1958.
Desire under the Elms, Paramount, 1959.
Green Mansions, Metro-Goldwyn-Mayer (MGM), 1959.
Elmer Gantry, UA, 1960.
Let's Make Love, Twentieth Century-Fox, 1960.
The Unforgiven, UA, 1960.
The Children's Hour, UA, 1961.
All Fall Down, MGM, 1962.
The Music Man, Warner Brothers, 1962.
The Best Man, UA, 1964.
Ensign Pulver, Warner Brothers, 1964.
The Night of the Iguana, MGM, 1964.
The Fool Killer (also known as *Violent Journey*), Allied Artists, 1965.
The Sound of Music, Twentieth Century-Fox, 1965.
Any Wednesday, Warner Brothers, 1966.
Hawaii, UA, 1966.
The Flim-Flam Man, Twentieth Century-Fox, 1967.
Reflections in a Golden Eye, Warner Brothers, 1967.
Finian's Rainbow, Seven Arts, 1968.
The Fixer, MGM, 1968.
(With Seth Banks and Grace Harris) *The Stalking Moon,* National General, 1968.
True Grit, Paramount, 1969.
Little Big Man, National General, 1970.
The Molly Maguires, Paramount, 1970.
Fat City, Columbia, 1972.
Fuzz, UA, 1972.
When the Legends Die, Twentieth Century-Fox, 1972.
The Iceman Cometh, American Film Theater, 1973.
(With Moss Mabry) *The Way We Were,* Columbia, 1973.
The Savage is Loose, Campbell/Devon, 1974.
Young Frankenstein, Twentieth Century-Fox, 1974.
The Hindenburg, Universal, 1975.
The Yazuka (also known as *Brotherhood of the Yazuka*), Warner Brothers/Toei (Japan), 1975.
(With Sheldon Levine and Shirlee Strahm) *Audrey Rose,* UA, 1977.
The Betsy, Allied Artists, 1978.
Love and Bullets, Associated Film Distribution, 1979.
North Dallas Forty, Paramount, 1979.
(And casting director) *On Golden Pond,* Universal/AFD/ITC/IPC, 1981.
The Postman Always Rings Twice, Paramount, 1981.
The Dead, Vestron-Zenith, 1987.

STAGE WORK; COSTUME DESIGNER

Affairs of State, Royale Theatre, New York City, 1950.
King Lear, National Theatre, New York City, 1950.
Too Late the Phalarope, Belasco Theatre, New York City, 1956.
Major Barbara, Martin Beck Theatre, New York City, 1956.
The Taming of the Shrew, American Shakespeare Festival Theatre (ASFT), Stratford, CT, 1956.
The Taming of the Shrew, Phoenix Theatre, New York City, 1957.
Winesburg, Ohio, National Theatre, 1958.
The World of Suzie Wong, Broadhurst Theatre, New York City, 1958.
Cue for Passion, Henry Miller's Theatre, New York City, 1958.
A Winter's Tale, ASFT, 1958.
Romeo and Juliet, ASFT, 1959.
All's Well That Ends Well, ASFT, 1959.
A Taste of Honey, Lyceum Theatre, New York City, 1960.
My Mother, My Father and Me, Plymouth Theatre, New York City, 1963.

Also designed costumes for productions of University of California—Los Angeles Theatre Group, including *Murder in the Cathedral, Three Sisters, Comedies of Despair,* and *The Prodigal,* all 1960; *Six Characters in Search of an Author,* and *The Iceman Cometh,* both 1961; *Burlesque,* 1963; *The Seagull,* and *King Lear,* both 1964; and *Yeats and Company,* 1965. Designed costumes and sets for productions of Center Theater Group, Mark Taper Forum, Los Angeles, including costumes for *Naked,* 1965, *Who's Happy Now?,* 1967, *Crystal & Fox,* 1970, *Othello,* 1971, *Juno and the Paycock,* 1974, *The Duchess of Malfi,* 1975.

Also designed costumes for touring productions of *A Taste of Honey,* National Tour Company, National Theatre, Washington, DC, then Blackstone Theatre, Chicago, IL, 1961; *Othello,* National Tour Company, Dorothy Chandler Pavilion Theatre, Los Angeles, then Curran Theatre, 1973; and *Oliver!,* National Tour Company, Dorothy Chandler Pavilion, then Curran Theatre, c. 1973. Designed costumes for touring productions of Los Angeles Civic Light Opera, Los Angeles, including *Carousel,* 1953; *Peter Pan,* 1954; *Kiss Me, Kate,* 1955; *Rosalinda,* 1956; *South Pacific,* and *Annie Get Your Gun,* both 1957; *Oklahoma!,* 1959; *Show Boat,* 1960; *The Sound of Music,* 1961; *Oliver!,* 1962; *Carousel,* 1963.

SIDELIGHTS: Jeakins was the first recipient of an Academy Award for costume design for her work on *Joan of Arc* in 1948.

OTHER SOURCES:

BOOKS

International Dictionary of Films and Filmmakers, Volume 4: *Writers and Production Artists,* St. James Press, 1987, p. 230-231.

PERIODICALS

New York Times, March 13, 1988, pp. 23-24.

* * *

JENKINS, George 1908-

PERSONAL: Full name, George Clarke Jenkins; born November 19, 1908 Baltimore, MD; son of Benjamin Wheeler (a merchant) and Jane (Clarke) Jenkins; married Phyllis Adams, May 6, 1955; children: (previous marriage) Jane Jenkins Dumaise; Alexandra Kirkland Marsh (stepdaughter; deceased). *Education:* Studied architecture at University of Pennsylvania, 1929-31.

ADDRESSES: Office—740 Kingman Ave., Santa Monica, CA 90402; and 220 East 66th St., New York, NY 10021.

CAREER: Stage and lighting designer, motion picture production designer. Interior and industrial designer, 1934-35; assistant to Jo Mielziner, 1937-41; Simmons Aerocessories Co., plant engineer, 1941-43; CBS-TV, art director in charge of color, 1953-54; University of California, Los Angeles, professor of motion picture design, 1985-88. American National Theatre and Academy, member of Board of Standards and Planning for Living Theatre, 1953-65; theatre consultant to Hopkins Center, Dartmouth College, Marine Stadium, Miami, FL, Annenbire Theatre Complex, University of Pennsylvania.

MEMBER: Society of Motion Picture Art Directors, United Scenic Artists, Directors Guild of America, Delta Phi.

AWARDS, HONORS: Donaldson Award, set design, Billboard Publications, 1945, for *I Remember Mama;* Antoinette Perry Award nomination, scenic design, 1957, for *The Happiest Millionaire* and *Too Late the Phalarope;* Antoinette Perry Award nomination, scenic design in a drama, 1960, for *The Miracle Worker;* Antoinette Perry Award nomination, scenic design in a musical, 1961, for *Thirteen Daughters;* Academy Award, art direction, 1976, for *All the President's Men;* Academy Award nomination, art direction, 1979, for *The China Syndrome.*

CREDITS:

FILM WORK; ART DIRECTOR, EXCEPT WHERE INDICATED

The Best Years of Our Lives, RKO Radio Pictures, 1946.
The Secret Life of Walter Mitty, RKO Radio Pictures, 1947.
The Bishop's Wife, RKO Radio Pictures, 1948.
Enchantment, RKO Radio Pictures, 1948.
A Song Is Born, RKO Radio Pictures, 1948.
Roseanna McCoy, RKO Radio Pictures, 1949.
The San Francisco Story, Warner Brothers, 1952.
Monsoon, United Artists (UA), 1953.
At War with the Army, Paramount, 1956.
The Miracle Worker, UA, 1962.
Mickey One, Columbia, 1965.
Up the Down Staircase, Warner Brothers, 1967.
Wait Until Dark, Warner Brothers, 1967.
No Way to Treat a Lady, Paramount, 1968.
The Subject Was Roses, Metro-Goldwyn-Mayer (MGM), 1968.
Me, Natalie, National General, 1969.
The Angel Levine, UA, 1970.
Klute, Warner Brothers, 1971.
The Pursuit of Happiness, Columbia, 1971.
1776, Columbia, 1972.
The Paper Chase, Twentieth Century-Fox, 1973.
The Parallax View, Paramount, 1974.
Funny Lady, Columbia, 1975.
Night Moves, Warner Brothers, 1975.
All the President's Men, Warner Brothers, 1976.
Comes a Horseman, UA, 1978.
The China Syndrome, Columbia, 1979.
Starting Over, Paramount, 1979.
The Postman Always Rings Twice, Paramount, 1981.
Rollover, Warner Brothers, 1981.
Sophie's Choice, Universal, 1982.
Dream Lover, MGM/UA, 1986.
Orphans, Lorimar, 1987.
See You in the Morning, Warner Brothers, 1989.
Presumed Innocent, Warner Brothers, 1990.

STAGE WORK; SET DESIGNER

Mexican Hayride, Winter Garden Theatre, New York City, 1944.
Lost in the Stars, Music Box Theatre, New York City, 1949.
Three Wishes for Jamie, Mark Hellinger Theatre, New York City, 1952.
The Immoralist, Royale Theatre, New York City, 1954.
The Merry Widow, City Center, New York City, 1957.
Jennie, Majestic Theatre, New York City, 1963.
The Only Game in Town, Broadhurst Theatre, New York City, 1968.
Sly Fox, Broadhurst Theatre, 1976.

Also worked as set designer for *The Trial,* London, 1951; *Ice Capades,* 1959-61; and *The Student Prince,* San Francisco, CA, 1966. Set designer for *Cosi Fan Tutte,* 1956, *Ariadne auf Naxos,* 1957, and *La Boheme,* 1958, all for San Francisco Opera Association.

STAGE WORK; LIGHTING DESIGNER

I Remember Mama, Music Box Theatre, 1944.
Bell, Book, and Candle, Ethel Barrymore Theatre, New York City, 1950.
Song of Norway, Jones Beach Marine Theatre, Jones Beach, NY 1958.
Critic's Choice, Ethel Barrymore Theatre, 1960.
Hit the Deck, Jones Beach Marine Theatre, 1960.
Paradise Island, Jones Beach Marine Theatre, 1961.
Around the World in Eighty Days, Jones Beach Marine Theatre, 1963.

STAGE WORK; SET AND LIGHTING DESIGNER

Early to Bed, Broadhurst Theatre, City, 1943.
Allah Be Praised, Adelphi Theatre, New York City, 1944.
Dark of the Moon, 46th Street Theatre, New York City, 1945.
Common Ground, Fulton Theatre, 1945.
Strange Fruit, Royale Theatre, 1945.
Are You with It?, Century Theatre, New York City, 1945.
Gently Does It, Playhouse Theatre, New York City, 1953.
The Bad Seed, 46th Street Theatre, 1954.
Ankles Aweigh, Mark Hellinger Theatre, 1955.
The Desk Set, Broadhurst Theatre, 1955.
Too Late the Phalarope, Belasco Theatre, New York City, 1956.
The Happiest Millionaire, Lyceum Theatre, New York City, 1956.
Rumble, Alvin Theatre, New York City, 1957.
Annie Get Your Gun, City Center, 1958.
Two for the See-Saw, Booth Theatre, New York City, 1958.
Tall Story, Belasco Theatre, 1959.
Jolly's Progress, Longacre Theatre, New York City, 1959.
The Miracle Worker (also see below), Playhouse Theatre, 1959.
One More River, Ambassador Theatre, New York City, 1960.
Thirteen Daughters, 54th St. Theatre, New York City, 1961.
A Thousand Clowns, Eugene O'Neill Theatre, New York City, 1962, then Comedy Theatre, London, 1964.
Everybody out, the Castle Is Sinking, Colonial Theatre, Boston, MA, 1964.
Catch Me If You Can, Morosco Theatre, New York City, 1965.
Mardi Gras, Jones Beach Marine Theatre, 1965.
Generation (also see below), Morosco Theatre, 1965.
(And production supervisor, with Ben Edwards), *The Royal Hunt of the Sun,* ANTA Theatre, New York City, 1965.
Wait Until Dark (also see below), Ethel Barrymore Theatre, then Strand Theatre, London, 1966.
Night Watch, Morosco Theatre, 1972.

MAJOR TOURS; SET AND LIGHTING DESIGNER

The Miracle Worker, U.S. cities, 1961-62.
Generation, U.S. cities, 1967.
Wait Until Dark, U.S. cities, 1967.

TELEVISION WORK; SET DESIGNER, EXCEPT AS INDICATED

New Revue, CBS, 1953-54.
The Royal Family, CBS, 1954.
Annie Get Your Gun, NBC, 1957.
An Afternoon with Mary Martin, NBC, 1959.
An Evening with Mary Martin, NBC, 1959.
Carmen (opera), NBC, 1959.
The Dollmaker (movie), ABC, 1984.

Also director of pilot film of Four Star Playhouse, CBS, 1952; art director and director, *Out of the Dark,* 1953.

* * *

JEROME, Timothy 1943-

PERSONAL: Born December 29, 1943, in Los Angeles, CA. *Education:* Graduate of Ithaca College.

ADDRESSES: *Agent*—The Gersh Agency, Inc., 130 West 42nd St., No. 1804, New York, NY 10036.

AWARDS, HONORS: Antoinette Perry Award nomination, featured actor in a musical, 1987, for *Me and My Girl.*

CAREER: Actor.

CREDITS:

STAGE APPEARANCES

(Broadway debut) Dr. Carrasco, *Man of La Mancha* (also see below), ANTA Washington Square Theatre, New York City, 1965, then Martin Beck Theatre, New York City, 1968, later Mark Hellinger Theatre, New York City, 1971.

Nathan Rothschild, *The Rothschilds,* Lunt-Fontanne Theatre, New York City, 1970.

Macheath, *The Beggar's Opera,* Brooklyn Academy of Music, Brooklyn, NY, 1972.

Understudy for the roles of Lucifer and God, *The Creation of the World and Other Business,* Shubert Theatre, New York City, 1972.

Reader, *The Winter Calligraphy of Ustad Selim,* AMDA Theatre, 1974.

Pretzels, Theatre Four, New York City, 1974.

Feldman, *The Magic Show,* Cort Theatre, New York City, 1974.

St. Joan, Long Wharf Theatre, New Haven, CT, 1976.

The Mooney Shapiro Songbook, Morosco Theatre, New York City, 1981.

Bustopher Jones/Asparagus/Growltiger, *Cats,* Winter Garden Theatre, New York City, 1982-86.

Willy, *Colette Collage,* York Theatre Company, Church of the Heavenly Rest, 1983.

Dr. Glass/Senator Blake, *Room Service,* Roundabout Theatre, New York City, 1986.

Herbert Parchester, *Me and My Girl,* Marquis Theatre, New York City, 1986-89.

General Director Preysing, *Grand Hotel,* Martin Beck Theatre, 1989.

Romance in Hard Times, New York Shakespeare Festival, Anspacher Theatre, 1989.

Also appeared Off-Broadway in *Civilization and Its Discontents* and *The Little Prince.* Member of McCarter Repertory Company, Princeton University, 1967-68; and Arena Stage, Washington, DC, 1978-79 and 1979-80.

MAJOR TOURS

Dr. Carrasco, *Man of La Mancha,* U.S. cities, 1969.

The teacher, *The Baker's Wife,* U.S. cities, 1976.

FILM APPEARANCES

Rabbi, *Compromising Positions,* Paramount, 1985.

Jud/bartender, *Betrayed* (also known as *Summer Lightning Sundown*), Metro-Goldwyn-Mayer, 1988.*

JOHNSON, Lamont 1922-

PERSONAL: Full name, Ernest Lamont Johnson, Jr.; born September 30, 1922, in Stockton, CA; son of Ernest Lamont (a realtor) and Ruth Alice (Fairchild) Johnson; married Toni Merrill (an actress), July 27, 1945; children: Jeremy Caroline, Christopher. *Education:* Graduated from Pasadena Junior College; attended University of California, Los Angeles, 1942-43; studied acting with Sanford Meisner at the Neighborhood Playhouse School of the Theatre, 1948, and with Lee Strasberg, 1949-50. *Avocational interests:* Collecting recordings.

ADDRESSES: Agent—The Brandt Company, 12700 Ventura Blvd., Suite 340, Studio City, CA 91604.

CAREER: Director, actor, and producer. University of California, Los Angeles Theatre Group (now Centre Theatre Group), founding member and member of executive committee, beginning in 1959. Previously employed as a radio actor and announcer.

MEMBER: Actors' Equity Association, Screen Actors Guild, Directors Guild of America, Writers Guild of America.

AWARDS, HONORS: Screen Directors Guild, most distinguished directorial achievement in television award, 1964, for premiere of *Profiles in Courage;* Emmy Award nomination, outstanding directorial achievement in drama, 1969, and Directors Guild of America Award, most distinguished directorial achievement in television award, 1970, both for *My Sweet Charlie;* Director's Guild of America awards, most distinguished directorial achievement in television, 1972 and 1973, and Emmy Award nomination, outstanding directorial achievement in drama, 1973, both for *That Certain Summer;* Emmy Award nomination, best direction in drama, 1974, for *The Execution of Private Slovik;* Emmy Award nomination, outstanding directing in a special program, 1975, for *Fear on Trial;* Emmy Award nomination, outstanding directing in a limited series or special, 1984, for *Ernie Kovacs: Between the Laughter;* Emmy Award, outstanding direction in a limited series, 1985, for *Wallenberg: A Hero's Story;* Emmy Award nomination, outstanding directing in a special, 1986, for *Unnatural Causes;* Emmy Award, outstanding directing in a mini-series or a special, 1987, for *Gore Vidal's Lincoln;* Emmy Award nomination, outstanding directing in a mini-series, 1990, for *The Kennedys of Massachusetts.*

CREDITS:

TELEVISION APPEARANCES

(Debut) Marullus and Cinna, *Julius Caesar,* CBS, 1949.

Title role, *Aesop,* NBC, 1952.

Mike, *Prize Winner* (series), NBC, 1953-54.

TELEVISION DIRECTOR; MOVIES

Losers Weepers, NBC, 1967.
Deadlock, NBC, 1969.
My Sweet Charlie, NBC, 1970.
That Certain Summer, ABC, 1972.
The Execution of Private Slovik, NBC, 1974.
Fear on Trial, CBS, 1975.
Off the Minnesota Strip, ABC, 1980.
Crisis at Central High, CBS, 1981.
Escape from Iran: The Canadian Caper, CBS, 1981.
Dangerous Company, CBS, 1982.
Life of the Party: The Story of Beatrice, CBS, 1982.
Gore Vidal's Lincoln (also known as *Lincoln*), NBC, 1988.
(And coproducer) *Voices Within: The Lives of Truddi Chase* (also known as *When Rabbit Howls*), ABC, 1990.

TELEVISION DIRECTOR; SERIES

Matinee Theatre, NBC, 1956-58.
Have Gun—Will Travel, CBS, 1957-63.
The Rifleman, ABC, 1958-63.
Peter Gunn, NBC, 1958-60, then ABC, 1960-61.
Johnny Ringo, CBS, 1959-60.
Naked City, ABC, 1960-63.
The Defenders, CBS, 1961-65.
The Twilight Zone, CBS, 1962.
Coronet Blue, CBS, 1967.

TELEVISION DIRECTOR; EPISODIC

Profiles in Courage, NBC, 1964.
"Paul's Case," *American Short Story,* PBS, 1979.

Also directed episodes of *Dr. Kildare* and *The Richard Boone Show,* both NBC, and *Studio One,* CBS.

TELEVISION DIRECTOR; PILOTS

Midnight Mystery, NBC, 1957.
The Virginian, NBC, 1958.
Angel, CBS, 1960.
The Search, CBS, 1968.
Deadlock, NBC, 1969.

OTHER TELEVISION WORK

Director, *Faerie Tale Theater* (premiere), Showtime, 1982.
Director, *Ernie Kovaks: Between the Laughter* (special), ABC, 1984.
Director and producer, *Wallenberg: A Hero's Story* (mini-series), NBC, 1985.
Director, *Unnatural Causes* (special), NBC, 1986.
Producer, *Suomi's Children* (series), PBS, 1987.
Director, *The Kennedys of Massachusetts* (also known as *The Fitzgeralds and the Kennedys;* mini-series), ABC, 1990.
Director, *Crash Landing,* ABC, 1992.

RADIO WORK

Performed in *The F.B.I. in Peace and War, Columbia Workshop, Let's Pretend, Lux Radio Theatre, Theatre Guild on the Air,* and *Suspense.*

STAGE APPEARANCES

Tadeusz, *Manya,* Pasadena Playhouse, Los Angeles, 1939.
Yes Is for a Very Young Man (also see below), Pasadena Playhouse, 1946, then Cherry Lane Theatre, New York City, 1949.
Ainger, *Young Woodley,* Westport Country Playhouse, Westport, CT, 1946.
(Broadway debut) Lord, *Macbeth,* National Theatre, 1948.
Weldon "Pete" Carter, *The Pony Cart,* Theatre de Lys, New York City, 1954.
A Christmas Carol, Players State Theatre, Coconut Grove, FL, 1980-81.

Also appeared as Peter Santard in a European tour of *Kind Lady* with United Service Organizations (USO), 1945.

STAGE WORK; DIRECTOR

Yes Is for a Very Young Man, Cherry Lane Theatre, 1949.
The Potting Shed, La Jolla Playhouse, La Jolla, CA, 1957.
The Man in the Moon, Hollywood Opera Theatre, Hollywood, CA, 1957.
The Skin of our Teeth, La Jolla Playhouse, 1958.
Under Milk Wood, Schoenberg Hall, Theatre Group, University of California at Los Angeles (UCLA), 1959.
4 Comedies of Despair, Schoenberg Hall, Theatre Group, UCLA, 1960.
The Egg, Schoenberg Hall, Theatre Group, UCLA, 1961, then Cort Theatre, New York City, 1962.
The Perfect Setup, Cort Theatre, 1962.
Peribanez, Schoenberg Hall, Theatre Group, UCLA, 1963.
'Tis Pity She's a Whore, Schoenberg Hall, Theatre Group, UCLA, 1963.
Iphigenia in Tauris, Los Angeles Concert Opera, Philharmonic Auditorium, Los Angeles, 1964.
Semiramide, Los Angeles Concert Opera, Philharmonic Auditorium, 1964.
The Adventures of the Black Girl in Her Search for God, Centre Theatre Group, Mark Taper Forum, 1969.
Nanawatai, Los Angeles Theatre Centre, Los Angeles, 1985-86.
The Eighties, George Street Playhouse, New Brunswick, NJ, 1988, then Westwood Playhouse, 1989.
Orfeo, Santa Fe Opera, Santa Fe, NM, 1990, then Los Angeles Music Center Opera, Los Angeles, 1990.

OTHER STAGE WORK

Producer, *Yes Is for a Very Young Man,* Pasadena Playhouse, 1946, then Cherry Lane Theatre, 1949.

FILM APPEARANCES

Willy, *Sally and Saint Anne,* Universal, 1952.
Captain Tink O'Grady, *Retreat Hell!,* Warner Brothers, 1952.
Captain Adams, *The Glory Brigade,* Twentieth Century-Fox, 1953.
Lannigan, *The Human Jungle,* Allied Artists, 1954.
Carl Holt, *Please Murder Me,* 78m Distributors Corp. of America, 1956.
Peter Malaks, *The Brothers Rico,* Columbia, 1957.
Barry Brunz, *One on One* (also see below), Warner Brothers, 1977.

FILM WORK; DIRECTOR

Thin Ice, Twentieth Century-Fox, 1961.
A Covenant with Death, Warner Brothers, 1966.
(And producer) *Kona Coast,* Warner Brothers, 1968.
The McKenzie Break, United Artists (UA), 1970.
A Gunfight, Paramount, 1971.
The Groundstar Conspiracy, Universal, 1972.
You'll Like My Mother, Universal, 1972.
The Last American Hero (also known as *Hard Driver*), Twentieth Century-Fox, 1973.
Visit to a Chief's Son, UA, 1974.
Lipstick, Paramount, 1976.
One on One, Warner Brothers, 1977.
Somebody Killed Her Husband, Columbia, 1978.
Cattle Annie and Little Britches, Universal, 1981.
Spacehunter: Adventures in the Forbidden Zone (also known as *Road Gangs, Adventures in the Creep Zone*), Columbia, 1983.

* * *

JOHNSON, Mary Lea 1926-

PERSONAL: Born August 20, 1926, in New Jersey; daughter of John Seward (an industrialist) and Ruth R. (Dill) Johnson; married second husband, Martin Richards (a producer), August 11, 1978; children: (first marriage) Quentin, Eric, Seward, Roderick, Hillary, Alice. *Education:* Attended The Masters School, Dobbs Ferry, NY, and American Academy of Dramatic Arts, NY; studied costume design at La Sorbonne, Paris, France.

ADDRESSES: Office—The Producer Circle Co., 1350 Avenue of the Americas, New York, NY 10019.

CAREER: Film and theatrical producer. The Producer Circle Co., New York City, founder with husband and producer, 1976—. Past member of board of directors for Second Stage Theatre, New York City and Phoenix, NY; Merriwold Art Gallery, Far Hills, NJ, owner, 1971-76; has served on the board of directors for Easton Hospital, Easton, MD, and Somerset Hospital, Somerset, NJ.

MEMBER: League of New York Theatres and Producers.

AWARDS, HONORS: Antoinette Perry Award nomination, best Broadway musical, 1978, for *On the Twentieth Century;* Antoinette Perry Award, best Broadway musical, 1979, for *Sweeney Todd;* Antoinette Perry Award nomination, best play, 1982, for *Crimes of the Heart;* Antoinette Perry Award nomination, outstanding musical, 1985, for *Grind;* Antoinette Perry Award nomination, best musical, 1990, for *Grand Hotel;* also winner of numerous other Antoinette Perry awards as well as New York Drama Critics awards; Citizen of the Year honoree, Mental Health Association of New Jersey.

CREDITS:

STAGE WORK; PRODUCER

The Norman Conquests, Morosco Theatre, New York City, 1976.
(With others) *On the Twentieth Century,* St. James Theatre, New York City, 1978.
(With others) *Sweeney Todd: The Demon Barber of Fleet Street,* Uris Theatre, New York City, 1979.
(With others) *Goodbye Fidel,* New Ambassador Theatre, New York City, 1980.
(With others) *Crimes of the Heart,* John Golden Theatre, New York City, 1981.
(With others) *March of the Falsettos,* Westside Arts/Cheryl Crawford Theatre, 1981.
(With others) *A Doll's Life,* Mark Hellinger Theatre, New York City, 1982.
(With others) *Foxfire,* Ethel Barrymore Theatre, New York City, 1982.
(With others) *Grind,* Mark Hellinger Theatre, 1985.
(With others) *Mayor,* Top of the Gate Theatre, New York City, 1985.
(With others) *Roza,* Royale Theatre, New York City, 1987.
(With others) *Grand Hotel,* Martin Beck Theatre, New York City, 1989.

FILM WORK

Involved in the production of *The Boys from Brazil,* Twentieth Century-Fox, 1978, *The Shining,* Warner Brothers, 1980, and *Fort Apache, The Bronx,* Twentieth Century-Fox, 1981.*

JOHNSTONE, Iain 1943-

PERSONAL: Full name, Iain Gilmour Johnstone; born April 8, 1943, in Reading, England; son of John (a civil servant) and Ethel (Gilmour) Johnstone; married Maureen Hammond (a researcher), September, 1980 (one source says 1957); children: two daughters, one named Sophie. *Education:* University of Bristol, LL.B. (with honors), 1964. *Politics:* Social Democrat. *Religion:* Presbyterian.

ADDRESSES: *Office*—76 Campden Hill Rd., London W.8, England; *Sunday Times*, 1 Pennington St., London E1 9XW, England. *Agent*—Anthony Sheil Associates Ltd., 2-3 Morwell St., London WC1B 3AR, England.

CAREER: Critic and writer. Independent Television News, London, England, newscaster, 1966-67; *Times*, London, reporter, 1967; BBC-TV, London, producer and news broadcaster, 1968-82; Paramount-TV, London, correspondent for *Entertainment Tonight*, 1982—; film critic for *Sunday Times*, London. Managing director of Kentel Ltd.

MEMBER: Queens Club.

AWARDS, HONORS: British Academy of Film and Television Arts Award nomination, 1982, for documentary film *Snowdon on Camera*.

WRITINGS:

The Arnhem Report, W. H. Allen, 1977.
Snowdon on Camera (television script), BBC, 1981.
The Man with No Name, Plexus, 1981, Morrow, 1982.
The Making of "Superman" and "Superman II" (television script), ABC, 1982.
(And director) *"Santa Claus": The Making of the Movie* (television script), ABC, 1987.*

* * *

JONES, Cherry 1956-

PERSONAL: Born November 21, 1956, in Paris, TN. *Education:* Attended Carnegie-Mellon University.

CAREER: Actress. American Repertory Theatre, Cambridge, MA, member of company, 1980—; Arena Stage, Washington, DC, guest artist, 1983-84.

AWARDS, HONORS: Antoinette Perry Award nomination, best performance by a leading actress in a play, 1991, for *Our Country's Good*.

CREDITS:

STAGE APPEARANCES

Rosalind, *As You Like It*, American Repertory Theatre, Cambridge, MA, 1980.
Dorcas, *The Winter's Tale*, Helen Owen Carey Playhouse, Brooklyn, NY, 1980.
Millicent, *He and She*, BAM Playhouse, 1980.
A Midsummer Night's Dream, American Repertory Theatre, 1981.
Irina, *Three Sisters*, American Repertory Theatre, 1983.
The Boys from Syracuse, American Repertory Theatre, 1983.
Liz, *The Philanthropist*, Manhattan Theatre Club, New York City, 1983.
Kitty Chase, *The Ballad of Soapy Smith*, New York Shakespeare Festival, Public/Newman Theatre, New York City, 1984.
Love's Labour's Lost, American Repertory Theatre, 1984.
Sally Bowles, *I Am a Camera*, American Jewish Theatre, 1984.
Cecily Cardew, *The Importance of Being Earnest*, Samuel Beckett Theatre, 1985.
Lynne, *Stepping Out*, John Golden Theatre, New York City, 1987.
Sara Littlefield, *Claptrap*, Manhattan Theatre Club, 1987.
Dorine, *Tartuffe*, Portland Stage Company, Portland, ME, 1987.
Fran, *Big Time: Scenes from a Service Economy*, American Theatre Exchange, Joyce Theatre, New York City, 1988.
Lady Macbeth, *Macbeth*, Mark Hellinger Theatre, New York City, 1988.
Light Shining in Buckinghamshire, Perry Street Theatre, New York City, 1991.
Liz, *Our Country's Good*, Nederlander Theatre, New York City, 1991.
Anna, the sister, *The Baltimore Waltz*, Circle Repertory Theatre, 1992.

Also appeared in other American Repertory Theatre productions, including as Viola, *Twelfth Night;* in title role, *Major Barbara; Sganarelle; The Journey of the Fifth Horse; Ghosts; The School for Scandal; Baby with the Bath Water;* and *The Caucasian Chalk Circle*.

TELEVISION APPEARANCES

Secretary, *O'Malley* (pilot), NBC, 1983.
Tina Crawford, *Alex: The Life of a Child* (movie), ABC, 1986.
Janice Eaton, *Adam's Apple* (pilot), CBS, 1986.

FILM APPEARANCES

Ginger McDonald, *The Big Town* (also known as *The Arm*), Columbia, 1987.
Cindy Montgomery, *Light of Day* (also known as *Born in the U.S.A.*), Tri-Star, 1987.

OTHER SOURCES:

PERIODICALS

New York Times, May 26, 1991, p. H5.*

* * *

JOY, Robert 1951-

PERSONAL: Born August 17, 1951, in Montreal, Canada; son of Clifton Joseph and Flora Louise (Pike) Joy; married Mary Shontkroff; children: Ruby. *Education:* Graduated from Newfoundland Memorial University and attended Oxford University; attended Sundance Film Institute, 1985.

ADDRESSES: Agent—Jeff Hunter, Triad Artists, Inc., 888 7th Ave., Suite 1602, New York, NY 10106.

CAREER: Actor and composer. Worked for three years as an actor, writer, and composer with the Newfoundland Company CODCO. Member of Ensemble Studio Theatre; active with the Manhattan Class Company.

AWARDS, HONORS: Rhodes Scholar; Genie Award nomination, best performance by an actor in a supporting role, 1981, for *Atlantic City;* Genie Award nomination, best original song, 1987, for *The Adventure of Faustus Bidgood;* Gemini Award nomination, best performance by a supporting actor, 1987, for *American Playhouse*'s "The Prodigious Hickey"; Los Angeles Drama-Logue Award for *Romeo and Juliet.*

CREDITS:

STAGE APPEARANCES

(Off-Broadway debut) Peter Van Daan, *The Diary of Anne Frank,* Theatre Four, New York City, 1978-79.

Privates on Parade, Long Wharf Theatre, New Haven, CT, 1979.

Fables for Friends, Playwrights Horizons Theatre, New York City, 1980.

Jude Emerson, *Lydie Breeze,* American Place Theatre, New York City, 1982.

Welcome to the Moon, Ensemble Studio Theatre, New York City, 1982.

Robert Buie, *The Death of Von Richthofen as Witnessed from Earth,* New York Shakespeare Festival (NYSF), Public/Newman Theatre, New York City, 1982.

Ted, *What I Did Last Summer,* Circle Repertory Company, Circle Repertory Theatre, New York City, 1983.

Title role, *Lenny and the Heartbreakers* (musical), NYSF, Public/Newman Theatre, 1983-84.

Huck, *Big River: The Adventures of Huckleberry Finn,* American Repertory Theatre, Cambridge, MA, 1983-84.

Mike, *Found a Peanut,* NYSF, Public/Anspacher Theatre, New York City, 1984.

Man #2, *Field Day,* Young Playwrights Festival, Playwrights Horizons Theatre, 1985.

(Broadway debut) Simon Bliss, *Hay Fever,* Music Box Theatre, New York City, 1985-86.

Rick Steadman, *The Nerd,* Helen Hayes Theatre, New York City, 1987.

Julian Hyde, *Hyde in Hollywood* (also see below) American Place Theatre, 1989.

Tranio, *The Taming of the Shrew,* NYSF, Delacorte Theatre, New York City, 1990.

Buffalo Bill, *Indians,* McCarter Theatre, Princeton, NJ, 1991.

Clive Beaumont and Mark Beaumont, *Shimada,* Broadhurst Theatre, New York City, 1992.

Also appeared as Mercutio in *Romeo and Juliet,* La Jolla Playhouse, La Jolla, CA; *Stem of the Briar,* Kenyon Festival Theatre, Gambier, OH; *Harold and Maude,* Citadel Theatre, Edmonton, Alberta, Canada; and *Life and Limb,* Playwrights Horizons Theatre.

FILM APPEARANCES

Dave, *Atlantic City* (also known as *Atlantic City, U.S.A.*), Paramount, 1981.

Harry K. Thaw, *Ragtime,* Paramount, 1981.

Patrick, *Ticket to Heaven,* United Artists, 1981.

David Art, *Threshold,* Twentieth Century-Fox, 1983.

Elliot West, *Amityville 3-D,* Orion, 1983.

Jim, *Desperately Seeking Susan,* Orion, 1985.

Colin Fraser, *Joshua Then and Now,* Twentieth Century-Fox, 1985.

Dr. Harvey Rimmer, *Terminal Choice,* Almi, 1985.

Eddy Peddle, *The Adventure of Faustus Bidgood* (also see below), Atlantic Region, 1986.

Dickie, *Big Shots,* Twentieth Century-Fox, 1987.

Fred, *Radio Days,* Orion, 1987.

Michael Collins, *The Suicide Club,* Suicide Productions, 1987, Angelika, 1988.

Sherman the Robot, *Millennium,* Twentieth Century-Fox, 1989.

Also appeared as Paul in *She's Back,* 1989; as Clawson in *The Dark Half,* 1990; as Neal Lessee in *Cool World;* and as Hans Spiro's assistant in *Shadows and Fog,* 1991.

FILM WORK; MUSIC DIRECTOR

The Adventure of Faustus Bidgood (also see below), Atlantic Region, 1986.

TELEVISION APPEARANCES; EPISODIC

Lorenzo Blackstone, "The Prodigious Hickey," *American Playhouse,* PBS, 1987.

Mr. Tapping, "The Return of Hickey," *American Playhouse,* PBS, 1988.

Mr. Tapping, "The Beginning of the Firm," *American Playhouse,* PBS, 1989.

Julian Hyde, "Hyde in Hollywood," *American Playhouse,* PBS, 1991.

Also appeared in "Longtime Companion," *American Playhouse,* PBS; appeared as a guest on television series, including *The Equalizer, Moonlighting, Miami Vice,* and *One Life to Live.*

TELEVISION APPEARANCES: MOVIES

Mark Lijek, *Escape from Iran: The Canadian Caper,* CBS, 1981.

Hans, *Sword of Gideon,* HBO, 1986.

Judgment (also known as *Sacrament* and *Vermillion Parish*), HBO, 1990.

WRITINGS:

FILM SCORES

(With Paul Steffler and Pamela Morgan) *The Adventure of Faustus Bidgood,* Atlantic Region, 1986.

K

KARKALITS, Patti
See KARR, Patti

* * *

KARR, Patti 1932-
(Patti Karkalits)

PERSONAL: Born Patsy Lou Karkalits, July 10, 1932, in St. Paul, MN; daughter of C. F. (a fruit and vegetable broker) and Estelle (Klebold) Karkalits. *Education:* Attended Texas Christian University, 1949-50; studied dancing with Margaret Craske, Anthony Tudor, Frank Wagner, Don Farnworth, and Matt Mattox; studied voice with John Bartis, Henry Rosenblatt, and Rosalie Snyder, 1964; studied acting with Joseph Leon, Ezra Stone, Danny Levin, and Jane White.

ADDRESSES: Office—336 West End Ave., New York, NY 10023. *Agent*—Michael Hardeling Agency, 114 East 28th St., New York, NY 10016.

CAREER: Actress, singer, and dancer. Dancer in Summertime Light Opera Company, Houston, TX, 1950; appeared as Beatrice in the dance team Gomez and Beatrice, hotels and clubs in Florida, 1952; dancer at the Sheraton Mount Royal Hotel, Montreal, Quebec, 1954.

MEMBER: Actors Equity Association, American Guild of Variety Artists.

CREDITS:

STAGE APPEARANCES

(Under name Patti Karkalits; Broadway debut) Dancer, *Maggie,* National Theatre, New York City, 1953.

(Under name Patti Karkalits) Dancer, *Carnival in Flanders,* New Century Theatre, New York City, 1953.

Dancer, *Bells Are Ringing,* Shubert Theatre, New York City, 1956.

Dancer, *New Girl in Town,* 46th Street Theatre, New York City, 1957.

Dancer, *The Body Beautiful,* Broadway Theatre, New York City, 1958.

Dancer and understudy, *Redhead* (also see below), 46th Street Theatre, 1959.

Dancer and understudy, *Once upon a Mattress,* Phoenix Theatre, New York City, 1959.

Dancer and understudy for Rose Grant, *Bye Bye Birdie* (also see below), Martin Beck Theatre, New York City, 1960.

Animal girl and member of dance team, *Do Re Mi,* St. James Theatre, New York City, 1961.

New Faces of 1962, Alvin Theatre, New York City, 1962.

Lucy McPherson and press representative, *Come On Strong,* Morosco Theatre, New York City, 1962.

Rosalie, *Carnival,* Starlight Theatre, Kansas City, MO, 1963.

Ellie, *Show Boat,* Starlight Theatre, 1963.

To Broadway with Love, Texas Pavilion, New York World's Fair, 1964.

Gladys, *Pajama Game,* Music Circus Theatre, Sacramento, CA, 1965.

Skits-Oh-Frantics! (revue), Bert Wheeler Theatre, New York City, 1967.

Gwen, *Month of Sundays,* Theatre de Lys, New York City, 1968.

Desiree Wildwood, *Up Eden,* Jan Hus Playhouse, New York City, 1968.

Juanita, *Look to the Lilies,* Lunt-Fontanne Theatre, New York City, 1970.

Understudy for all female roles, *A Funny Thing Happened on the Way to the Forum,* Lunt-Fontanne Theatre, 1972.

Mrs. Hepplewhite's mother and Kimberly Langley, *Different Times,* American National Theatre Academy, New York City, 1972.

Theta, *Lysistrata,* Brooks Atkinson Theatre, New York City, 1972.

Fastrada, *Pippin,* Imperial Theatre, New York City, 1972-77, then Minskoff Theatre, New York City, 1977.

Gittel Mosco, *Seesaw,* Uris Theatre, New York City, 1973.

Helen McFudd, *Irene,* Minskoff Theatre, 1973-74.

Maggie Simpson, *A Broadway Musical,* Lunt-Fontanne Theatre, 1978.

Antwerp, *Got Tu Go Disco,* Minskoff Theatre, 1979.

Lillian, *Musical Chairs,* Rialto Theatre, New York City, 1980.

Janet, *Snapshot,* Hudson Guild Theatre, New York City, 1980.

Flora, *The Housewives' Cantata,* Theatre Four, New York City, 1980.

Chiquita, *Something for the Boys,* AMDA Studio One, New York City, 1981.

"What People Do When They're All Alone," in *Scenes Dedicated to My Brother* (double-bill), South Street Theatre, New York City, 1982.

Doris, *Baseball Wives,* American Renaissance Theatre, New York City, 1982.

Understudy for Anna, *The Rink,* Martin Beck Theatre, 1984.

I Can Get It for You Wholesale, American Jewish Theatre, New York City, 1991.

Also appeared in *The Threepenny Opera* and *Hello Out There,* both Green Mansions, New York, summers, 1954-56; appeared in *Pipe Dream* and in a Japanese production of *West Side Story,* Tokyo, Japan.

MAJOR TOURS

Dancer, *Brigadoon,* U.S. cities, 1950-51.

Essie Whimple, *Redhead,* eastern U.S. cities, 1960.

Rose Grant, *Bye Bye Birdie,* U.S. cities, 1962, 1963, and 1965.

Millie Michaels, *California Suite,* eastern U.S. cities, 1977-78.

Also toured as Dorothy Shaw in *Gentlemen Prefer Blondes.*

FILM APPEARANCES

Dorothy Mills, *Tax Season,* Prism, 1990.*

KATZENBERG, Jeffrey 1950-

PERSONAL: Born in 1950; married; wife's name, Marilyn (a kindergarten teacher). *Education:* Attended Fieldston School, New York City.

ADDRESSES: Office—Walt Disney Co., 500 South Buena Vista St., Burbank, CA 91521.

CAREER: Motion picture company executive. Paramount Pictures, New York City, assistant to the chairman, 1975-77, executive director of marketing, 1977, moved to the West Coast as vice-president for television programming, 1977-78, vice-president for feature production, 1978-80, senior vice-president for production, Motion Picture Division, 1980-82, president of production for motion pictures and television, 1982-84; Walt Disney Co., Burbank, CA, chairman of Walt Disney Studios, 1984—.

OTHER SOURCES:

PERIODICALS

New York Times, February 7, 1988, p. 29.*

* * *

KATZMAN, Leonard

PERSONAL: Full name, Leonard S. Katzman.

ADDRESSES: Agent—The Agency, 10351 Santa Monica Blvd., No. 211, Los Angeles, CA, 90025. *Contact*—Writers Guild of America, 8955 Beverly Blvd., West Hollywood, CA, 90048.

CAREER: Producer and writer.

AWARDS, HONORS: Emmy Award nominations, outstanding drama series, for *Dallas,* 1980 and 1981.

CREDITS:

TELEVISION PRODUCER; SERIES

(With Norman MacDonnell and Joseph Drackow) *Gunsmoke,* CBS, 1955-75.

(With others) *The Wild, Wild West* (also see below), CBS, 1965-70.

(With others) *Hawaii Five-O,* CBS, between 1968 and 1980.

(And director with others) *Dirty Sally* (also see below), CBS, 1974.

Petrocelli, NBC, 1974-76.

The Fantastic Journey (also see below), NBC, 1977.

Logan's Run (based on the feature film [also see below]), CBS, 1977-78.

(Later executive producer; and director with others) *Dallas* (also see below), CBS, 1978-91.

OTHER TELEVISION WORK

Executive producer, *Our Family Honor* (series), ABC, 1985-86.
Executive producer and creator (with David Paulsen), *Dangerous Curves* (movie; also see below), CBS, 1992.

FILM DIRECTOR

Space Monster, American International Pictures, 1965.

WRITINGS:

TELEVISION SERIES

(With others) *The Wild, Wild West,* between 1965 and 1970.
(With others) *Dirty Sally,* CBS, 1974.
(With others) *The Fantastic Journey,* NBC, 1977.
(With others) *Logan's Run,* between 1977 and 1978.
(With others) *Dallas,* CBS, 1979-1989.
Private Benjamin (based on the feature film), CBS, 1983.
The Dukes of Hazzard, CBS, 1984.

TELEVISION MOVIES

(With David Paulsen) *Dangerous Curves,* CBS, 1992.

SCREENPLAYS

Space Monster, American International Pictures, 1965.*

* * *

KAZAN, Nicholas

PERSONAL: Son of Elia (director) and Molly Day (a playwright; maiden name, Thacher) Kazan.

ADDRESSES: Agent—Sanford, Skouras, Gross & Associates, 1015 Gayley Ave., Suite 300, Los Angeles, CA 90024.

CAREER: Screenwriter and producer. Mark Taper Forum, Los Angeles, CA, writer for Improvisational Theatre Project's Impact Company, 1977-78 season.

MEMBER: Screen Writers Guild.

AWARDS, HONORS: Academy Award nomination, best screenplay based on material from another medium, 1990, and Writers Guild nomination, best adapted screenplay, for *Reversal of Fortune.*

CREDITS:

FILM WORK

Co-producer, *Reversal of Fortune* (also see below), Warner Brothers, 1990.

TELEVISION WORK; SPECIAL

Director, "The Professional Man," *The Edge* (anthology), HBO, 1989.

WRITINGS:

SCREENPLAYS

(With Eric Bergren and Christopher DeVore) *Frances,* Universal, 1982.
At Close Range (based on story by Elliott Lewitt and Kazan), Orion, 1986.
Patty Hearst (based on *Every Secret Thing* by Patricia Campbell Hearst with Alvin Moscow), Atlantic/Zenith, 1988.
Reversal of Fortune (based on the book by Alan Dershowitz), Warner Brothers, 1990.
Mobsters, Universal, 1991.

Also author of *Showboat 1988,* 1977.

TELEVISION

"Indian Poker" and "Professional Man," *The Edge* (anthology), HBO, 1989.

PLAYS

April 2, 1979: The Day the Blanchardville, N.C. Political Action and Poker Club Got the Bomb, produced at WPA Theatre, New York City, 1978.
Safe House, produced at Mark Taper Forum, Los Angeles Music Center, Los Angeles, CA, then at Manhattan Theatre Club, New York City, 1978.
Blood Moon, produced at The Production Company, New York City, 1983, published by Samuel French, 1984.
Just Horrible, segment of *Class 1 Acts,* Nat Horne Theatre, New York City, 1988.

Wrote for The Impact Company of the Improvisational Theatre Project.*

* * *

KEITH, Marilyn
See BERGMAN, Marilyn

* * *

KENNEDY, Arthur 1914-1990
(J. Arthur Kennedy, John Kennedy)

PERSONAL: Full name, John Arthur Kennedy; born February 17, 1914, in Worcester, MA; died of a brain tumor, January 5, 1990, in Branford, CT; son of J. T. (a doctor) and Helen (Thompson) Kennedy; married Mary Cheffey (an actress; died, 1975); children: Laurie, Terence. *Education:* Carnegie Institute of Technology, B.A., drama, 1936. *Avocational interests:* Swimming, tennis, travel.

CAREER: Actor. *Military service:* U.S. Army Air Force, 1943-45; served in 1st Motion Picture Unit; made training films.

MEMBER: Actors' Equity Association, Screen Actors Guild, American Federation of Television and Radio Artists, Phi Kappa Psi.

AWARDS, HONORS: Antoinette Perry Award, best supporting or featured dramatic actor, 1949, for *Death of a Salesman;* Academy Award nomination, best supporting actor, 1949, for *Champion;* New York Film Critics Award, and Academy Award nomination, best actor, both 1951, both for *Bright Victory;* Golden Globe Award, and Academy Award nomination, best supporting actor, both 1955, both for *Trial;* Academy Award nominations, best supporting actor, 1957, for *Peyton Place,* and 1958, for *Some Came Running;* Carnegie Institute of Technology Award of Merit, 1959; Film Daily Award, Filmdom's Famous Five, and Limelight Award, all 1960, all for *Elmer Gantry.*

CREDITS:

STAGE APPEARANCES

(As John Kennedy; Broadway debut) Bushy, *Richard II* (also see below), St. James Theatre, New York City, 1937.

(As John Kennedy) Sir Richard Vernon, *Henry IV, Part I,* St. James Theatre, 1939.

(As J. Arthur Kennedy) Jerry Dorgan, *Life and Death of an American,* Maxine Elliott Theatre, New York City, 1939.

Smithers, *International Incident,* Ethel Barrymore Theatre, New York City, 1940.

Chris Keller, *All My Sons,* Coronet Theatre, New York City, 1947.

Biff, *Death of a Salesman,* Morosco Theatre, New York City, 1949-50.

Dave Rickes, *See the Jaguar,* Cort Theatre, New York City, 1952.

John Proctor, *The Crucible,* Martin Beck Theatre, New York City 1953.

Lieutenant Colonel William F. Edwards, *Time Limit!,* Booth Theatre, New York City, 1956.

Patrick Flannigan, *The Loud Red Patrick,* Ambassador Theatre, New York City, 1956.

Title role, *Becket* (also see below), Hudson Theatre, New York City, 1961.

Walter Franz, *The Price,* Morosco Theatre, 1968.

Man, *Veronica's Room,* Music Box Theatre, New York City, 1973.

MAJOR TOURS

Thomas Becket, *Becket,* national tour, opening Colonial Theatre, Boston, MA, then U.S. cities, 1961.

Also toured Midwest with Globe Theatre, 1936; toured as Bushy, *Richard II,* 1937.

FILM APPEARANCES

(Film debut) Eddie Kenny, *City for Conquest,* Warner Bros., 1940.

Jim Younger, *Bad Men of Missouri,* Warner Bros., 1941.

Red Hattery, *High Sierra,* Warner Bros., 1941.

George Foster, *Highway West,* Warner Bros., 1941.

Johnny Rocket, *Knockout,* First National/Warner Bros., 1941.

Joe Geary, *Strange Alibi,* Warner Bros., 1941.

Flying Officer, Jed Forrest, *Desperate Journey,* Warner Bros., 1942.

Ned Sharp, *They Died with Their Boots On,* Warner Bros., 1942.

Lieutenant Tommy McMartin, *Air Force,* Warner Bros., 1943.

Branwell Bronte, *Devotion,* Warner Bros., 1946.

John Waldron, *Boomerang,* Twentieth Century-Fox, 1947.

Sundance Kid, *Cheyenne,* (also known as *The Wyoming Kid*), Warner Bros., 1947.

Connie Kelly, *Champion,* United Artists (UA), 1949.

Tommy Ditinan, *Chicago Deadline,* Paramount, 1949.

Alan Palmer, *Too Late for Tears,* UA, 1949.

Chalk, *The Walking Hills,* Columbia, 1949.

Mr. Woodry, *The Window,* RKO Radio Pictures, 1949.

Tom Wingfield, *The Glass Menagerie,* Warner Bros., 1950.

Larry Nevins, *Bright Victory* (also known as *Lights Out*), Universal, 1951.

Land Waldron, *Red Mountain,* Paramount, 1951.

Cole Garret, *Bend of the River* (also known as *Where the River Bends*), Universal, 1952.

Dr. Ben Barringer, *The Girl in White* (also known as *So Bright the Flame*), Metro-Goldwyn-Mayer (MGM), 1952.

Wes Merritt, *The Lusty Men,* RKO Radio Pictures, 1952.

Vern Haskeoo, *Rancho Notorious,* RKO Radio Pictures, 1952.

Joe Quinn, *Crash Out,* Filmakers, 1955.

Jesse Bard, *The Desperate Hours,* Paramount, 1955.

Alan Curtis, *Impulse,* Eros, 1955.

Vic Hansbro, *The Man From Laramie,* Columbia, 1955.

Santiago, *The Naked Dawn,* Universal, 1955.

Barney Castle, *Trial,* MGM, 1955.

Rick Harpe, *The Rawhide Years,* Universal, 1956.

Lucas Cross, *Peyton Place,* Twentieth Century-Fox, 1957.

First Mate Ramsay, *Twilight for the Gods,* Universal, 1958.
Frank Hirsh, *Some Came Running,* MGM, 1958.
Willie O'Reilly, *Home is the Hero,* British Lion/Showcorporation, 1959.
Bart Hunter, *A Summer Place,* Warner Bros., 1959.
Jim Lefferts, *Elmer Gantry,* UA, 1960.
Clyde Inglish, *Claudelle Inglish* (also known as *Young and Eager*), Warner Bros., 1961.
Dr. Quimper, *Murder She Said* (also known as *Meet Miss Marple*), MGM, 1961.
Dr. Adams, *Adventures of a Young Man* (also known as *Hemingway's Adventures of a Young Man*), Twentieth Century-Fox, 1962.
Pontius Pilate, *Barabbas,* Columbia, 1962.
Jackson Bently, *Lawrence of Arabia,* Columbia, 1962.
Doc Holliday, *Cheyenne Autumn,* Warner Bros., 1964.
Ferro Maria Ferri, *Italiano brava gente* (also known as *Italiani brava gente, Oni shli na vostok,* and *Attack and Retreat*), Embassy, 1965.
Patrick Brown, *Joy in the Morning,* MGM, 1965.
Captain Love, *Murieta* (also known as *Vendetta* and *Joaquino Murrieta*), Warner Bros., 1965.
Dr. Duval, *Fantastic Voyage* (also known as *Microscopia* and *Strange Journey*), Twentieth Century-Fox, 1966.
Bill Bowdre, *Nevada Smith,* Paramount, 1966.
Monday's Child (also known as *Il chica del Lunes*), Andre Du Rona, 1967.
Stay Away, Joe, MGM, 1968.
General Lesly, *Anzio* (also known as *The Battle for Anzio*), Columbia, 1968.
Forbes, *Days of the Evil Gun,* MGM, 1968.
Roy Colby, *A Minute to Pray, A Second to Die* (also known as *Un minuto per pregari, uni stante pe morire* and *Dead or Alive*), Cinerama, 1968.
Albert Dixon, *Hail, Hero,* National General, 1969.
Doc, *Shark* (also known as *Un arma de dos filos* and *Maneaters*), Fuller, 1970.
Walter Pell, *Glory Boy,* (also known as *My Old Man's Place*), Cinerama, 1971.
Inspector McCormack, *Don't Open the Window* (also known as *Non si seve profanare ol sonne die morte, Breakfast at Manchester Morgue,* and *The Living Dead at Manchester Morgue*), Hallmark, 1974.
Franchino, *The Sentinel,* Universal, 1977.
Bishop, *The Tempter* (also known as *L'Anti Cristo*), Avco/Embassy, 1978.
Owen Coughlin, *Signs of Life,* Avenue Pictures, 1989.

Also appeared in *Santa Fe Trail,* 1940; *Bacciamo le mani* (also known as *Ferrente, Kiss My Hand* and *Mafia War*), 1973; *Ricco,* 1973; *La polizia ha le mani legate* (also known as *The Police Can't Move* and *Killer Cop*), 1974; *Roma a mano armato* (also known as *Rome Armed to the Teeth* and *Brutal Justice*), 1976; *La spiaggia del desiderio* (also known as *Emmanuelle on Taboo Island*), 1976; *Novi ospiti per un delitto* (also known as *Nine Guests for Crime*), 1976; *Ab Morgen sind wir reich und ehrlich* (also known as *Rich and Respectable*), 1977; *Gli ultimi angeli* (also known as *L'avventurosa fuga* and *Last Angels*), 1977; *Ciclon* (also known as *Cyclone*), 1977; *Sono stato un'agente CIA* (also known as *Covert Action*), 1978; *Bermuda: La fossa maledetta* (also known as *La cueva de los tiburones, The Sharks Cave,* and *Cave of Sharks*), 1978; *Porco mondo,* 1978; and *Grandpa,* 1990. Appeared as narrator, *The Brave Rifles,* 1966.

TELEVISION APPEARANCES; EPISODIC

"People Need People," *Alcoa Premiere,* ABC, 1961.
Dupont Show of the Week, NBC, 1963.
Espionage, NBC, 1964.

Also appeared in *Kraft Suspense Theatre,* NBC; *The Ethel Barrymore Theatre; General Electric Theatre;* and *Playhouse 90.*

OTHER TELEVISION APPEARANCES

Narrator, *F. D. R.* (special), ABC, 1965.
Angus MacGregor, *The Movie Murderer* (movie), NBC, 1970.
Marvin Hirsh, *A Death of Innocence* (movie), CBS, 1971.
Albert Graves, *Crawlspace* (movie), CBS, 1972.
Gunther Damon, *The President's Plane Is Missing* (movie), ABC, 1973.
Sheriff Sam Jericho, *Nakia* (series), ABC, 1974.

Also appeared in *The Third Commandment.*

OBITUARIES AND OTHER SOURCES:

PERIODICALS

New York Times, April 30, 1989, p. H24; January 7, 1990.
Variety, January 10, 1990.*

* * *

KENNEDY, J. Arthur
See KENNEDY, Arthur

* * *

KENNEDY, John
See KENNEDY, Arthur

* * *

KERSHNER, IRVIN 1923-

PERSONAL: Born April 29, 1923, in Philadelphia, PA. *Education:* Attended Temple University Tyler School of

Fine Arts, 1946, and University of Southern California Art Center School.

CAREER: Director and screenwriter. United States Information Services, documentary filmmaker in the Middle East, 1950-52.

MEMBER: Directors Guild of America.

AWARDS, HONORS: Emmy Award nomination, outstanding directing in a special program—drama, 1977, for *Raid on Entebbe.*

CREDITS:

FILM DIRECTOR

Stakeout on Dope Street, Warner Brothers, 1958.
The Young Captives, Paramount, 1959.
The Hoodlum Priest, United Artists, 1961.
A Face in the Rain, Embassy, 1963.
The Luck of Ginger Coffey, Continental Distributing, 1964.
A Fine Madness, Warner Brothers, 1966.
The Flim-Flam Man (released in England as *One Born Every Minute*), Twentieth Century-Fox, 1967.
Loving, Columbia, 1970.
Up the Sandbox, National General, 1972.
*S*P*Y*S,* Twentieth Century-Fox, 1974.
The Return of a Man Called Horse, United Artists, 1976.
Eyes of Laura Mars, Columbia, 1978.
The Empire Strikes Back, Twentieth Century-Fox, 1980.
Never Say Never Again, Warner Brothers, 1983.
Robocop 2, Orion, 1990.

OTHER FILM WORK

Executive producer for *Wildfire,* 1988.

FILM APPEARANCES

Zebedee, *The Last Temptation of Christ,* Universal, 1988.

TELEVISION DIRECTOR; MOVIES

Raid on Entebbe, NBC, 1977.
Traveling Man, HBO, 1989.

TELEVISION DIRECTOR; EPISODIC

The Rebel, ABC, between 1959 and 1961.
Naked City, ABC, between 1960 and 1963.
Ben Casey, ABC, between 1961 and 1966.

OTHER TELEVISION WORK

Director and cinematographer for documentary segment of syndicated program *Confidential File* (also known as *Paul Coates's Confidential File*) in the mid-1950s.

WRITINGS:

Author of an uncredited screenplay titled *A Man Called Horse,* produced by National General Pictures in 1970.

OTHER SOURCES:

PERIODICALS

American Film, January/February, 1981, pp. 45-51.*

* * *

KERT, Larry 1930(?)-1991

OBITUARY NOTICE—See index for *CTFT* sketch: Full name, Frederick Lawrence Kert; born December 5, 1930 (one source lists 1934), in Los Angeles, CA; died of complications from AIDS, June 5, 1991, in New York. Actor, singer, and dancer. Kert will best be remembered for originating the role of Tony in the Broadway production of *West Side Story.* He began his career with Bill Norvas and the Upstarts, a song and dance troupe that was featured in various stage shows. Kert sang and acted in supporting parts until 1957, when he won the lead role of Tony in *West Side Story.* Kert acted the role for three years of its original Broadway run, and on tour in later years. He appeared in numerous productions throughout the fifties and sixties, including *Breakfast at Tiffany's, Cabaret,* and *La Strada.* In 1970, Kert replaced Dean Jones in the role of Robert in the musical *Company.* His work in *Company* earned him a Tony nomination, giving Kert the distinction of being the only replacement actor to win such an honor. In 1987 Kert appeared in two Gershwin musicals, *Let Them Eat Cake* and *Of Thee I Sing.* Prior to his death, Kert appeared at the Rainbow and Stars nightclub, where he performed songs from *West Side Story* with his original costar Carol Lawrence. In addition to his stage work, Kert also appeared in films and on numerous television programs.

OBITUARIES AND OTHER SOURCES:

BOOKS

Notable Names in the American Theatre, James White, 1976, p. 885.

PERIODICALS

Variety, June 10, 1991, p. 86.

* * *

KIDD, Michael 1919-

PERSONAL: Born Milton Greenwald, August 12, 1919, in Brooklyn, NY; son of Abraham (a barber and union official) and Lillian Greenwald; married Mary Heater (a dancer), July 30, 1940 (marriage dissolved); married Shelah Hackett; children: (first marriage) Kristine, Susan; (second marriage) one son, one daughter. *Education:* Attended City College of New York, studied chemical engineering, 1936-37; attended School of American Ballet, 1937-39; studied with Blanche Evan, Ludmilla Scholler, Muriel Stewart, and Anatole Vilzak. *Avocational interests:* Photography.

ADDRESSES: Contact—c/o Samuel Liff, William Morris Agency, 1350 Avenue of the Americas, New York, NY 10019.

CAREER: Choreographer and dancer. Worked early in career as a copy boy and a dance photographer. American Ballet and Lincoln Kirstein's Ballet Caravan, dancer, 1937-c. 1940; Eugene Loring's Dance Players, assistant director and soloist, 1941-c. 1942; Ballet Theatre, soloist, 1942-47.

MEMBER: American Guild of Musical Artists, Society of Stage Directors and Choreographers, Screen Actors Guild, Screen Directors Guild.

AWARDS, HONORS: Antoinette Perry Award for outstanding dance direction, 1947, for *Finian's Rainbow;* Antoinette Perry awards for choreographer, 1951, for *Guys and Dolls,* 1954, for *Can-Can,* 1957, for *Li'l Abner,* and 1960 for *Destry Rides Again;* Antoinette Perry Award nomination for director of a musical play, 1960, for *Destry Rides Again;* Antoinette Perry Award nominations for choreographer, 1962, for *Subways Are for Sleeping,* 1966, for *Skyscraper,* and 1971, for *The Rothschilds;* Antoinette Perry Award nomination for director of a musical play, 1971, for *The Rothschilds;* Emmy Award nomination for choreography (with Peter Anastos), 1982, for *Baryshnikov in Hollywood.*

CREDITS:

STAGE CHOREOGRAPHER, EXCEPT WHERE INDICATED

(And scenarist) *On Stage!* (also see below), Ballet Theatre, Boston Opera House, Boston, MA, 1945.
Finian's Rainbow, 46th Street Theatre, New York City, 1947, then Palace Theatre, London, 1947.
Hold It!, National Theatre, New York City, 1948.
Love Life, 46th Street Theatre, 1948.
Arms and the Girl, 46th Street Theatre, 1950.
Guys and Dolls, 46th Street Theatre, 1950, then Coliseum Theatre, London, 1953.
Can-Can, Shubert Theatre, New York City, 1953.
(And producer and director; all with Norman Panama and Melvin Frank) *Li'l Abner,* St. James Theatre, New York City, 1956.
(And director) *Destry Rides Again,* Imperial Theatre, New York City, 1959.
(And director; and producer with N. Richard Nash) *Wildcat,* Alvin Theatre, New York City, 1960.
(And director) *Subways Are for Sleeping,* St. James Theatre, 1961-62.
Here's Love, Shubert Theatre, 1963.
(And associate director) *Wonderworld,* New York World's Fair, New York City, 1964.
(And coproducer and director) *Ben Franklin in Paris,* Lunt-Fontanne Theatre, New York City, 1964.
Skyscraper, Lunt-Fontanne Theatre, 1965-66.
Holly Golightly (also known as *Breakfast at Tiffany's*), Forrest Theatre, Philadelphia, PA, 1966, then Majestic Theatre, New York City, 1966.
(And director) *The Rothschilds,* Lunt-Fontanne Theatre, 1970-71, then Curran Theatre, San Francisco, CA, 1972.
Director, *Cyrano,* Palace Theatre, New York City, 1973.
Director, *Good News,* St. James Theatre, 1974-75.
Director, *Pal Joey '78,* Center Theatre Group, Ahmanson Theatre, Los Angeles, CA, c. 1977-78.
(And director) *The Music Man,* City Center Theatre, New York City, 1980.

MAJOR TOURS

Choreographer and director, *The Music Man,* U.S. cities, 1979-80.

STAGE APPEARANCES

(Stage debut) Understudy for the role of Adversary's Follower, *The Eternal Road,* Manhattan Opera House, New York City, 1937.
Billy the Kid, Lincoln Kirstein's Ballet Caravan, Chicago Opera House, Chicago, IL, 1938.
Railroads on Parade, New York World's Fair, New York City, c. 1939.
American Jubilee, New York World's Fair, New York City, c. 1940.
City Portrait, Eugene Loring's Dance Players, c. 1941-42.
Harlequin for President, Dance Players, c. 1941-42.
The Man from Midian, Dance Players, c. 1941-42.
Jinx, Dance Players, Erie Theatre, Schenectady, NY, 1942.
Pillar of Fire, Ballet Theatre, Metropolitan Opera House, New York City, 1942.
Another Reflection, *Dim Lustre,* Metropolitan Opera House, 1943.
Fancy Free, Metropolitan Opera House, 1944.
Interplay (ballet; part of *Concert Varieties*), Ziegfeld Theatre, New York City, 1945.
Handyman, *On Stage!,* Ballet Theatre, Boston Opera House, Boston, MA, 1945.
Undertow, Metropolitan Opera House, 1945.

Also soloist with Ballet Theatre in productions, including *Helen of Troy, Petrouchka,* and *Three Virgins and a Devil;*

also appeared in ballets, including *Bluebeard, Coppelia, Giselle, Romeo and Juliet,* and *Tricorne.* Appeared in *Aurora's Wedding.*

FILM CHOREOGRAPHER, EXCEPT WHERE INDICATED

Where's Charley?, Warner Bros., 1952.
The Band Wagon, Metro-Goldwyn-Mayer (MGM), 1953.
Knock on Wood, Paramount, 1954.
Seven Brides for Seven Brothers, MGM, 1954.
Guys and Dolls, MGM, 1955.
(And director) *Merry Andrew,* MGM, 1958.
Li'l Abner, Paramount, 1959.
Star (also known as *Those Were Happy Times*), Twentieth Century-Fox, 1968.
Hello, Dolly!, Twentieth Century-Fox, 1969.
Movie Movie, (also see below), Warner Bros., 1978.

FILM APPEARANCES

Angie Valentine, *It's Always Fair Weather,* MGM, 1955.
Tommy French, *Smile,* United Artists, 1975.
Pop Popchik, *Movie Movie,* Warner Bros., 1978.
Dr. Westerford, *Skin Deep,* Twentieth Century-Fox, 1989.

Also appeared in the films *Actor* and *Change.*

TELEVISION CHOREOGRAPHER

Baryshnikov in Hollywood, CBS, 1982.
Sixtieth Annual Academy Awards Presentation, ABC, 1988.

OTHER TELEVISION WORK

Director, *Laverne and Shirley,* ABC, 1976.
Stage director, *Julie Andrews in Concert,* PBS, 1990.

TELEVISION APPEARANCES; SPECIALS, EXCEPT WHERE INDICATED

The Bob Hope Show, NBC, 1950.
For the Love of It (movie), ABC, 1980.
Fortieth Annual Tony Awards, CBS, 1986.
Everybody Dance Now, PBS, 1991.*

* * *

KIDMAN, Nicole 1968(?)-

PERSONAL: Born c. 1968, in Hawaii; daughter of a biochemist and a nurse; married Tom Cruise (an actor), 1991. *Education:* Studied at St. Martin's Youth Theatre, Melbourne, Australia, Australian Theatre for Young People, Sydney, and Philip Street Theatre.

ADDRESSES: Agent—Creative Artists Agency, 9830 Wilshire Blvd., Beverly Hills, CA 90212. *Publicist*—Nancy Seltzer and Associates, 6220 Del Valle Dr., Los Angeles, CA 90048.

CAREER: Actress.

MEMBER: Screen Actors Guild.

AWARDS, HONORS: Awards, best actress in a mini-series, Australian Film Institute, for *Bangkok Hilton* and *Vietnam;* named Female Star of Tomorrow by NATO/ShoWest, 1991; Golden Globe Award nomination, best supporting actress, 1992, for *Billy Bathgate.*

CREDITS:

FILM APPEARANCES

Judy, *BMX Bandits,* Nilsen Premiere, 1983.
Helen, *Bush Christmas,* Hoyts Release, 1983.
Julia Matthews, *Wills and Burke—The Untold Story,* Greater Union, 1985.
Jade, *Windrider,* Hoyts Release, 1986.
Mary McAllister, *The Bit Part,* Comedia, 1987.
Helen Davey, *Emerald City,* Greater Union, 1989.
Rae Ingram, *Dead Calm,* Warner Brothers, 1989.
Dr. Claire Lewicki, *Days of Thunder,* Paramount, 1990.
Nicole Radcliffe, *Flirting,* Warner Brothers, 1991.
Drew Preston, *Billy Bathgate,* Buena Vista, 1991.
Shannon, *Far and Away,* Universal, 1992.

Appeared as Petra, *Chase Through the Night,* 1985. Also appeared in *Prince and the Great Race,* 1983; *Night Master,* 1987; *Watch the Shadows Dance,* 1988; and *Breaking Loose,* 1988.

TELEVISION APPEARANCES; MINI-SERIES

Katrina Stanton, *Bangkok Hilton,* TBS, 1990.

Also appeared in *Vietnam.*

TELEVISION APPEARANCES; EPISODIC

Carol Trig, "Room to Move," *WonderWorks,* PBS, 1987.

OTHER SOURCES:

PERIODICALS

People, spring, 1991, p. 66.
Rolling Stone, July 12, 1990, p.56.*

* * *

KIESER, Ellwood E. 1929-

PERSONAL: Full name, Ellwood Eugene Kieser; born March 27, 1929; son of Ellwood Eugene and Helen Marie (Kleinsmith) Kieser. *Education:* La Salle College, B.A., 1950; St. Paul's College, M.A., 1953; Graduate Theological Union, Ph.D., 1973.

ADDRESSES: Office—Paulist Productions Inc., 17575 Pacific Coast Highway, Pacific Palisades, CA 90272.

CAREER: Producer and writer. Ordained Roman Catholic priest, 1956. Paulist Productions, Pacific Palisades, CA, president and executive producer, 1960—; University of California—Los Angeles, department of philosophy, instructor.

*MEMBER:*American Academy of Television Artists, Writers Guild of America, West.

AWARDS, HONORS: Emmy Award nomination, outstanding achievement in religious programming, 1972 and 1973, and Emmy Award, outstanding achievement in religious programming, 1981, 1982, 1983, and 1984, all for *Insight;* Emmy Award, outstanding achievement in religious programming, 1983, for *The Juggler of Notre Dame.*

CREDITS:

FILM PRODUCER

Romero, Four Seasons, 1990.

TELEVISION EXECUTIVE PRODUCER; SPECIALS

It Can't Happen to Me, syndicated, 1979.
Princess, syndicated, 1980.
When, Jenny? When, syndicated, 1980.
The Trouble with Grandpa, syndicated, 1981.
(With Lan O'Kun) *The Juggler of Notre Dame,* syndicated, 1982.
Leadfoot, syndicated, 1982.
Josie, syndicated, 1983.
Packy, syndicated, 1987.

TELEVISION EXECUTIVE PRODUCER; SERIES

(And creator) *Insight* (also see below), syndicated, 1960.

TELEVISION EXECUTIVE PRODUCER; MOVIES

Executive producer of *The Fourth Wiseman,* 1984, and *We Are the Children,* 1986.

TELEVISION APPEARANCES; SERIES

Host, *Insight,* syndicated, 1960.

* * *

KING, Larry 1933-

PERSONAL: Full name, Lawrence Harvey Zeiger; born November 19, 1933, in Brooklyn, NY; son of Eddie (a bar-and-grill owner and defense plant worker) and Jennie (a bar-and-grill owner and garment worker) Zeiger; married Alene Akins, 1961 (divorced, 1963); married Mickey Sutphin, 1964 (divorced, 1966); remarried Akins, 1967 (divorced, 1971); married Sharon Lepore (a math teacher), 1976 (divorced, 1982); married Julia Alexander, October 7, 1989; children: (with Akins) Chaia (daughter); (with Alexander) Andy.

ADDRESSES: Office—Mutual Broadcasting System Inc., 1755 South Jefferson Davis Hwy., Arlington, VA 22202.

CAREER: Talk show host and writer. Worked various jobs, including delivery boy and mail clerk, in Brooklyn, NY, during 1950s; WAHR-Radio (now WMBM-Radio), Miami, FL, disc jockey, 1957-c. 1958; WKAT-Radio, Miami, disc jockey, beginning in 1958; Pumpernik's Restaurant, Miami, host of on-location program, broadcast on WKAT, c. 1958-c. 1962, and on WIOD-Radio, Miami, 1962-c. 1963; WIOD, host of on-location program, beginning c. 1963; WLBW-TV, Miami, host of late-night talk show, c. 1963-64; WTVJ-TV, Miami, host of weekend show, beginning 1964; broadcaster and free-lance writer, 1972-75; WIOD, talk show host, 1975-78; Mutual Broadcasting System, Arlington, VA, host of radio talk show first run out of Miami, 1978, then out of Arlington, 1978—; Cable News Network (CNN), host of television talk show, 1985—. Worked in public relations for horse-racing track in Shreveport, LA, 1974-75; football commentator for Miami Dolphins and Shreveport Steamers.

AWARDS, HONORS: Peabody Award, University of Georgia School of Journalism, 1982 (one source says 1987), for *The Larry King Show;* Radio Award, National Association of Broadcasters, 1985; Jack Anderson Investigative Reporting Award, 1985; Larry King was named best radio talk show host by *Washington Journalism Review,* 1986; Awards for Cablecasting Excellence (ACE) Awards, 1987, 1988, and 1989, for *Larry King Live;* Larry King was named broadcaster of the year by International Radio and Television Society, 1989; ACE nomination, 1991, for *Larry King Live;* named to Emerson Hall of Fame.

CREDITS:

RADIO APPEARANCES

Host, *The Larry King Show,* Mutual Broadcasting System, 1978—.

Also conducts interviews for *Talk to America,* Voice of America.

TELEVISION APPEARANCES

Host, *Larry King Live* (talk show), CNN, 1985—.
Larry King Extra (special), TNT, 1991.

Also host of *Let's Talk Washington,* WJLA-TV; also provided voice for an episode of *The Simpsons* (animated), Fox.

FILM APPEARANCES

Ghostbusters, Columbia, 1984.
Lost in America, Warner Bros., 1985.
T.V. Talk Show Host, *Eddie and the Cruisers II: Eddie Lives!,* Scotti, 1989.
Himself, *The Exorcist III,* Twentieth Century-Fox, 1990.

WRITINGS:

(With Emily Yoffe) *Larry King by Larry King* (autobiography), Simon & Schuster, 1982.
(With Peter Occhiogrosso) *Tell It to the King* (also see below), Putnam, 1988.
(With B. D. Colen) *"Mr. King, You're Having a Heart Attack": How a Heart Attack and Bypass Surgery Changed My Life,* Delacorte, 1989.
(With Occhiogrosso) *Tell Me More* (companion book to *Tell It to the King*), Putnam, 1990.

Also author of columns for *Miami Beach Sun-Reporter,* beginning c. 1965, *Miami Herald, Miami News, Sporting News,* and *USA Today.* Writer for entertainment sections of the *Miami Herald.**

* * *

KING, Larry L. 1929-

PERSONAL: Full name, Lawrence Leo King; born January 1, 1929, in Putnam, TX; son of Clyde Clayton (a farmer) and Cora Lee (a homemaker; maiden name, Clark) King; married Jeanne Casey, November 25, 1950 (divorced, 1964); married Rosemarie Kline, February 20, 1965 (died, June 8, 1972); married Barbara S. Blaine (an attorney), May 6, 1978; children: (first marriage) Alexandria, Kerri, Bradley; (third marriage) Lindsay, Blaine. *Education:* Attended Texas Technological College (now Texas Tech University), 1949-50, and Harvard University, 1969-70. *Politics:* Democrat. *Religion:* None.

ADDRESSES: Office and agent—Barbara S. Blaine, 700 Thirteenth St., N.W., Suite 1000, Washington, DC 20005.

CAREER: Writer and actor. Oil field worker in Texas, 1944-46; newspaper reporter in Hobbs, NM, 1949, Midland, TX, 1951-52, and Odessa, TX, 1953-54; radio station KCRS, Midland, news director, 1951-52; U.S. Congress, Washington, DC, administrative assistant, 1955-64; *Capitol Hill* (magazine), Washington, DC, editor, 1965; Princeton University, Princeton, NJ, Ferris Professor of Journalism and Political Science, 1974-75. Member of Kennedy-Johnson campaign team, traveling in Southwest, 1960; fellow in communications at Duke University, 1975-76; Texhouse Corporation, president, beginning in 1979; Southwest Texas State University, Distinguished Lyndon B. Johnson Lecturer, 1991. *Military service:* U.S. Army, Signal Corps, writer, 1946-49; became staff sergeant.

MEMBER: PEN International, National Writer's Union, Authors League of America, Dramatists Guild, Screenwriters Guild East, Washington Independent Writers, Texas Institute of Letters.

AWARDS, HONORS: American Librarians' awards, for magazine articles "My Hero LBJ" and "Everybody's Louie"; Texas Writers Roundup Award for nonfiction book, 1968, for *. . . And Other Dirty Stories;* Mark Twain Citation for topical humor in contemporary writing, Samuel Clemens Society of Missouri, 1969; Nieman fellow, 1969-70; Theta Sigma Phi Award of Excellence, Professional Organization of Women in Journalism and Communications, and National Book Award nomination, both 1971, for *Confessions of a White Racist;* Stanley Walker Journalism Award, Texas Institute of Letters, 1972, for magazine article "The Lost Frontier"; (with Peter Masterson) Antoinette Perry Award nomination, best book of a Broadway musical, 1979, for *The Best Little Whorehouse in Texas;* (with Philip Buton, Jr.) Emmy Award, writing, 1981, for documentary *The Best Little Statehouse in Texas;* named Literary Lion by Friends of Dallas Public Library, 1986, for "distinguished career in literature"; elected to Texas Walk of Stars in Austin, TX, by Sixth Street Preservation Society, 1987; Children's Choice Award, 1988, for *Because of Lozo Brown;* Helen Hayes Award, best new play, Mary Goldwater Award, best new play, Theater Lobby, both 1988, New York Outer Circle Critics award nomination, best production of a new play, 1989, all for *The Night Hank Williams Died.*

CREDITS:

STAGE APPEARANCES

(Stage debut) The Captain, *Mr. Roberts,* Permian Playhouse, Odessa, TX, 1953.
Steve, *A Streetcar Named Desire,* Theatre Midland, Midland, TX, 1953.
Detective Story, Permian Playhouse, 1954.
T.V. announcer and Sheriff Ed Earl Dodd, *The Best Little Whorehouse in Texas* (also see below), 46th Street Theatre, New York City, 1978-82.
Gus Gilbert, *The Night Hank Williams Died* (also see below), New Playwrights Theatre, Washington, DC, 1988, then Orpheum Theatre, New York City, 1989.

TELEVISION APPEARANCES

Narrator, "The Best Little Statehouse in Texas," *CBS Reports* (special; also see below), CBS, 1981.
Special correspondent, *MacNeil-Lehrer Newshour,* PBS, 1984.
Special correspondent, *Adam Smith's Money World,* PBS, 1986.

WRITINGS:

STAGE PLAYS

(With Peter Masterson; music and lyrics by Carol Hall) *The Best Little Whorehouse in Texas* (book for musical; also see below), first produced at Actor's Studio, New York City, 1977, produced at Entermedia Theatre, New York City, 1978, and 46th Street Theatre, New York City, 1978-82, published by Samuel French, c. 1978.

(With Ben Z. Grant) *The Kingfish,* first produced at New Playwrights Theatre, Washington, DC, 1979, produced at John Houseman Theatre, New York City, 1991, published by Southern Methodist University Press, 1992.

The Night Hank Williams Died (with music and lyrics; also see below), first produced at Memphis State University, Memphis, TN, 1985, new version produced at New Playwrights Theatre, 1988, WPA Theatre, New York City, 1989, and Orpheum Theatre, New York City, 1989, published by Southern Methodist University Press, 1989.

Christmas: 1933 (one-act; based on his book *That Terrible Night Santa Got Lost in the Woods;* also see below), produced at Circuit Playhouse, Memphis, TN, 1986, published by Samuel French, 1987.

The Golden Shadows Old West Museum, first produced at Arkansas Repertory Theatre, Little Rock, AR, 1989, produced at American Playwrights Theatre, Washington, DC, 1989.

The Best Little Whorehouse in Texas is also anthologized in *Best Plays of 1977-78.*

SCREENPLAYS

(With Colin Higgins and Peter Masterson) *The Best Little Whorehouse in Texas* (based on musical by King and Masterson; music and lyrics by Carol Hall), Universal, 1982.

TELEVISION DOCUMENTARIES

How a Bill Becomes a Law, PBS, 1970.

(With Philip Buton, Jr.) "The Best Little Statehouse in Texas," *CBS Reports* (special), CBS, 1981.

FICTION

The One-Eyed Man (novel), New American Library, 1966.

That Terrible Night Santa Got Lost in the Woods, drawings by Pat Oliphant, Encino Press, 1981.

Because of Lozo Brown (children's book), illustrated by Amy Schwartz, Viking 1988.

NONFICTION

. . .And Other Dirty Stories (collected articles), World, 1968.

Confessions of a White Racist, Viking, 1971.

The Old Man and Lesser Mortals (collected articles), Viking, 1974.

(With Bobby Baker) *Wheeling and Dealing: Confessions of a Capitol Hill Operator,* Norton, 1978.

Of Outlaws, Con Men, Whores, Politicians, and Other Artists (collected articles), Viking, 1980.

The Whorehouse Papers, Viking, 1982.

None but a Blockhead: On Being a Writer, Viking, 1986.

Warning: Writer at Work, Texas Christian University Press, 1986.

OTHER

Contributor to numerous periodicals, including *Esquire, Life, Playboy, Rolling Stone,* and *Sports Illustrated;* contributing editor to periodicals, including *Texas Observer,* 1964-75, *Harper's,* 1965-71, *New Times,* 1974-77, *Texas Monthly,* 1974-80, and *Parade,* 1982—.

OTHER SOURCES:

BOOKS

Bennett, Patrick, *Talking with Texas Writers,* Texas A & M University Press, 1980.

Carlson, Satch, *Runnin' on Empty,* Sundog Books, 1988.

Carr, John, *Kite-Flying and Other Irrational Acts: Conversations with Twelve Southern Writers,* Louisiana State University Press, 1972.

Strickland, Ron, *Texans: Oral Histories from the Lone Star State,* Paragon House, 1991.

PERIODICALS

Dallas Morning News, December 22, 1991.

New York Times, April 10, 1988, p. H5.

Southwest Review, winter, 1983.

* * *

KINSKI, Klaus 1926(?)-1991

OBITUARY NOTICE—See index for *CTFT* sketch: Born Nikolaus Gunther Nakszynski (one source transliterates name as Nicolaus Naksznski), October 18, 1926 (one source cites 1928), in Sopot, Danzig (now Poland); died November 23, in Lagunitas, CA. Actor. Kinski will be remembered for his performances in both foreign and domestic films, which total more than one hundred and eighty. His career began on the German stage, where he worked after serving in the German army in World War II. He eventually drifted into film roles, including parts in Italian "Spaghetti Westerns" such as *For a Few Dollars*

More. In the early seventies Kinski accepted the starring role in *Aguirre, the Wrath of God,* a film by German director Werner Herzog. Kinski would later act in Herzog's *Nosferatu, the Vampire, Woyzeck,* and *Fitzcarraldo.* Praised for his ability to accurately convey such human conditions as insanity, pathos, and megalomania, Kinski became a favorite of critics. In 1982 he moved to America and began making films. Among the many American films he has made are *Creature, Love and Money,* and *The Little Drummer Girl,* for which he received high critical praise. In addition to his film work, Kinski also appeared on several television programs, including HBO's anthology series *The Hitchhiker.* He also directed and starred in *Paganini.*

OBITUARIES AND OTHER SOURCES:

BOOKS

Contemporary Newsmakers 1987 Cumulation, Gale, 1988, p. 209-12.

The International Who's Who, 53rd edition, Europa, 1989, p. 837.

PERIODICALS

Variety, December 2, 1991, p. 101.

* * *

KLAUSEN, Ray 1939-

PERSONAL: Full name, Raymond Jens Klausen; born May 29, 1939, in Jamaica, NY; son of Jens (a cabinetmaker) and Ane Kathrine (Jensen) Klausen. *Education:* Hofstra University, B.A., 1961; New York University, M.A., art, 1963; Yale University, M.F.A., theatre design, 1967.

CAREER: Production designer. Theatrical set designer, beginning in 1967; free-lance television production designer, 1970—; set designer for national tours of Kenny Rogers and Lionel Richie, 1984, and Travis Tritt, 1992. Sculptor, exhibiting at galleries, including Multiple Gallery, New York City, 1971; McKenzie Gallery, Los Angeles, CA, 1970-73; Gallery Moos, Toronto, Ontario, 1973; Upstairs Gallery, Long Beach, CA, 1974; Dirks Perri Gallery, Studio City, CA, 1976-77; JLB Gallery, Newport Beach, CA, 1990; Gallery Sanyo, Tokyo, Japan, 1991; Zantman Gallery, Carmel, CA, 1991; Wade Gallery, Los Angeles, 1991; and Ruth Bachofner Gallery, Los Angeles, 1992. *Military service:* U.S. Army, 1962-63.

AWARDS, HONORS: Emmy Award, outstanding art direction for a comedy-variety or music series, 1975, for *Cher;* Emmy Award nomination, outstanding individual achievement—special events, 1980, for *The Fifty-second Annual Academy Awards Presentation;* Emmy Award nomination, outstanding art direction for a variety or music program, 1981, for *Lynda Carter's Celebration;* Emmy Award, outstanding art direction for a variety or music program, 1982, for *The Fifty-fourth Annual Academy Awards Presentation;* Emmy Award, outstanding art direction for a variety or music program, 1983, for *The Fifty-fifth Annual Academy Awards Presentation;* Emmy Award nomination, outstanding art direction for a variety or music program, 1984, for *The Sixth Annual Kennedy Center Honors: A Celebration of the Performing Arts;* Emmy Award nomination, outstanding art direction for a variety or music program, 1985, for *The 1985 American Music Awards;* Emmy Award nomination, outstanding art direction for a variety or music program, 1986, for *The Eighth Annual Kennedy Center Honors: A Celebration of the Performing Arts;* Emmy Award nomination, outstanding art direction for a variety or music program, 1987, for *Happy Birthday, Hollywood!;* Emmy Award nomination, outstanding art direction for a variety or music program, 1990, for *The 1990 American Music Awards;* Emmy Award nomination, outstanding art direction for a variety or music program, 1991, for *The Sixty-second Annual Academy Awards Presentation.* Bates travel fellow (Europe), 1967.

CREDITS:

TELEVISION WORK; PRODUCTION DESIGNER; SERIES, EXCEPT WHERE INDICATED

Cher, CBS, 1975.
The Monte Carlo Show, syndicated, 1980.
Show Business, ABC, 1981.
The Love Connection, syndicated, 1983—.
Let's Make a Deal, syndicated, 1984.
You Are the Jury (pilot), NBC, 1984.
Rock n' Roll Summer Action, NBC, 1985.
Perfect Match, syndicated, 1986.
You Are the Jury, NBC, 1986.
The Smothers Brothers Comedy Hour, CBS, 1988.
America's Funniest People, ABC, 1990—.

TELEVISION WORK; ARTISTIC DIRECTOR; SPECIALS

Sandy in Disneyland, CBS, 1974.
The John Davidson Christmas Show, NBC, 1975.
The Dorothy Hamill Special, ABC, 1976.
Ted Knight Musical Comedy Variety Special Special, CBS, 1976.
Paul Anka . . . Music My Way, ABC, 1977.
The John Davidson Christmas Show, ABC, 1977.
Eddie and Herbert, CBS, 1977.
The Beatrice Arthur Special, CBS, 1980.
Lynda Carter's Special, CBS, 1980.
Lynda Carter: Encore, CBS, 1980.
John Denver and the Muppets: A Christmas Together, ABC, 1980.

The Fifty-second Annual Academy Awards Presentation, ABC, 1980.
Omnibus, ABC, 1980.
Lynda Carter's Celebration, CBS, 1981.
Jubilee (also see below), Metro-Goldwyn-Mayer, 1981.
The American Film Institute Salute to Frank Capra, CBS, 1982.
Lynda Carter: Street Lights, CBS, 1982.
The Fantastic Miss Piggy Show, ABC, 1982.
The Fifty-fourth Annual Academy Awards Presentation, ABC, 1982.
Magic with the Stars, NBC, 1982.
Texaco Star Theater: Opening Night, NBC, 1982.
The Fifty-fifth Annual Academy Awards Presentation, ABC, 1983.
Hollywood's Private Home Movies, ABC, 1983.
The American Film Institute Salute to Lillian Gish, CBS, 1984.
Hollywood Stars' Screen Tests, NBC, 1984.
The Sixth Annual Kennedy Center Honors: A Celebration of the Performing Arts, CBS, 1984.
The 1985 American Music Awards, ABC, 1985.
The Seventh Annual Kennedy Center Honors: A Celebration of the Performing Arts, CBS, 1985.
NBC's Sixtieth Anniversary Celebration, NBC, 1985.
The Thirty-ninth Annual Tony Awards, CBS, 1985.
The 1986 American Music Awards, ABC, 1986.
Nell Carter—Never Too Old to Dream, NBC, 1986.
The Eighth Annual Kennedy Center Honors: A Celebration of the Performing Arts, CBS, 1986.
The Fortieth Annual Tony Awards, CBS, 1986.
Miss Hollywood, 1986, ABC, 1986.
The Thirty-eighth Annual Emmy Awards, NBC, 1986.
The 1987 American Music Awards, ABC, 1987.
Happy Birthday, Hollywood!, ABC, 1987.
The Ninth Annual Kennedy Center Honors: A Celebration of the Performing Arts, CBS, 1987.
Motown Merry Christmas, NBC, 1987.
Superstars and Their Moms—1987, ABC, 1987.
The American Film Institute Salute to Jack Lemmon, CBS, 1988.
Friday Night Surprise! (also known as *Surprise!*), NBC, 1988.
The Tenth Annual Kennedy Center Honors: A Celebration of the Performing Arts, CBS, 1988.
The Smothers Brothers Comedy Special, CBS, 1988.
The Smothers Brothers Thanksgiving Special, CBS, 1988.
Superstars and Their Moms—1988, ABC, 1988.
The 1989 American Music Awards, ABC, 1989.
Fifty Years of Television: A Golden Celebration, CBS, 1989.
Friday Night Surprise!, NBC, 1989.
The Sixty-first Annual Academy Awards Presentation, ABC, 1989.
The 1990 American Music Awards, ABC, 1990.
Night of One Hundred Stars III, NBC, 1990.
The 1991 American Music Awards, ABC, 1991.
The Eleventh Annual Kennedy Center Honors: A Celebration of the Performing Arts, CBS, 1991.
The Ace Awards, NCTA, 1991.
The Eighteenth Annual Daytime Emmy Awards, CBS, 1991.
The Sixty-third Annual Academy Awards Presentation, ABC, 1991.
The 1992 American Music Awards, ABC, 1992.
The Ace Awards, NCTA, 1992.

STAGE WORK; ARTISTIC DIRECTOR

Hello, Hollywood, Hello!, Bally's Grand Theatre, Las Vegas, NV, 1978-88.
Jubilee, Bally's Grand Theatre, 1981—.

Set designer, The Repertory Theatre, St. Louis, MO, 1967-68 and 1968-69 seasons; designer, Center Theatre Group, Mark Taper Forum Theatre, Los Angeles, CA, 1968-69 season; designer, New Theatre for Now, New York City, 1969-70 season.

OTHER SOURCES:

PERIODICALS

Entertainment Weekly, March 22, 1991, p. 22.
New York Times, March 24, 1991, p. H-11.

* * *

KLINE, Kevin 1947-

PERSONAL: Full name, Kevin Delaney Kline; born October 24, 1947, in St. Louis, MO; son of Robert Joseph (a toy and record store owner and singer) and Peggy (Kirk) Kline; married Phoebe Cates (an actress), 1989. *Education:* Indiana University, B.A., speech and theatre, 1970; Juilliard Drama Center, studied with Harold Guskin, diploma, 1972. *Avocational interests:* Musical composition, travel, sports.

ADDRESSES: Agent—Creative Artists Agency, 1888 Century Park E., Suite 1400, Los Angeles, CA 90067.

CAREER: Actor. Acting Company, New York City, founding member, 1972-76, artistic associate, 1987-88.

MEMBER: Actors' Equity Association, Screen Actors Guild.

AWARDS, HONORS: Antoinette Perry Award, best supporting or featured actor in a musical, 1978, for *On the Twentieth Century;* Drama Desk Award, Obie Award, *Village Voice,* and Antoinette Perry Award, all for best actor in a musical, 1980, for *The Pirates of Penzance* (play); Obie Award for sustained excellence, 1986; Academy Award, best supporting actor, 1988, for *A Fish Called Wanda;* William Shakespeare Award for Classical Theatre, Shakespeare Theatre at the Folger, 1989; Golden Globe Award nomination, best actor in a musical or comedy, 1991, for *Soapdish.*

CREDITS:

STAGE APPEARANCES

Henry VI, Part I, New York Shakespeare Festival (NYSF), Delacorte Theatre, New York City, 1970.
Soldier, *Henry VI, Part II,* NYSF, Delacorte Theatre, 1970.
Tressel, *Richard III,* NYSF, Delacorte Theatre, 1970.
Charles Surface, *The School for Scandal,* City Center Acting Company, Good Shepherd-Faith Church, New York City, 1972.
Guardiano, *Women Beware Women,* City Center Acting Company, Good Shepherd-Faith Church, 1972.
Vaskal Pepel, *The Lower Depths,* City Center Acting Company, Good Shepherd-Faith Church, 1972.
IRA officer, *The Hostage,* City Center Acting Company, Good Shepherd-Faith Church, 1972.
Colonel Vershinin, *The Three Sisters,* City Center Acting Company, Billy Rose Theatre, New York City, 1973.
MacHeath, *The Beggar's Opera,* City Center Acting Company, Billy Rose Theatre, 1973.
Friar Peter, *Measure for Measure,* City Center Acting Company, Billy Rose Theatre, 1973.
Leandre, *Scapin,* City Center Acting Company, Billy Rose Theatre, 1973.
Jamie Lockhart, *The Robber Bridegroom,* Acting Company, Harkness Theatre, New York City, 1975.
Lancaster, *Edward II,* Acting Company, Harkness Theatre, 1975.
Understudy for the roles of Tom and Wesley, *The Time of Your Life,* Acting Company, Harkness Theatre, 1975.
Understudy for the roles of the Baron and Colonel, *The Three Sisters,* Acting Company, Harkness Theatre, 1975.
Daniel, *Beware the Jubjub Bird,* Theatre Four, New York City, 1976.
Son, *Playing with Fire,* Counterpoint Theatre Company, Counterpoint Theatre, New York City, 1977.
Clym Yeobright, *Dance on a Country Grave,* Hudson Guild Theatre, New York City, 1977.
Carr, *Nest of Vipers,* New Dramatists Theatre, New York City, 1977.
The Promise, Bucks County Playhouse, Pennsylvania, 1977.
Understudy for the role of MacHeath, *The Threepenny Opera,* NYSF, Vivian Beaumont Theatre, New York City, 1978.
Bruce Granit, *On the Twentieth Century,* St. James Theatre, New York City, 1978.
Paul, *Loose Ends,* Circle in the Square, New York City, 1979.
V.I.P. Night on Broadway, Shubert Theatre, New York City, 1979.
Pirate king, *The Pirates of Penzance,* NYSF, Delacorte Theatre, 1980, then Uris (now Gershwin) Theatre, later Minskoff Theatre, New York City, 1981.
Johnny, *Holiday,* Center Theatre Group, Ahmanson Theatre, Los Angeles, 1980-81.
Title role, *Richard III,* NYSF, Delacorte Theatre, 1983.
Hart Farrell, *Isn't It Romantic,* Playwrights Horizons Theatre, New York City, 1983, then Lucille Lortel Theatre, New York City, 1984.
Title role, *Henry V,* NYSF, Delacorte Theatre, 1984.
Captain Bluntschli, *Arms and the Man,* Circle in the Square, 1985.
Title role, *Hamlet,* NYSF, Public/Newman Theatre, New York City, 1986.
Benedick, *Much Ado about Nothing,* NYSF, Delacorte Theatre, 1988.
Title role, *Hamlet* (also see below), NYSF, Public/Anspacher Theatre, New York City, 1990.

Also appeared in productions for the Arena Stage company, 1978-79. Appeared in touring productions as Tony Lumpkin, *She Stoops to Conquer,* and Tom, *The Knack,* both for the Acting Company, 1974.

STAGE WORK; DIRECTOR

Hamlet, NYSF, Public/Anspacher Theatre, 1990.

FILM APPEARANCES

(Film debut) Nathan Landau, *Sophie's Choice,* Universal, 1982.
Pirate king, *Pirates of Penzance,* Universal, 1983.
Harold, *The Big Chill,* Columbia, 1983.
Paden, *Silverado,* Columbia, 1985.
Henry Squires, *Violets Are Blue,* Columbia, 1986.
Donald Woods, *Cry Freedom,* Universal, 1987.
Otto, *A Fish Called Wanda,* Metro-Goldwyn-Mayer/United Artists (MGM/UA), 1988.
Nick Starkey, *The January Man,* MGM/UA, 1989.
Joey Boca, *I Love You to Death,* Tri-Star, 1990.
Jeffrey Anderson, *Soapdish,* Paramount, 1991.
Mack, *Grand Canyon,* Twentieth Century-Fox, 1991.

TELEVISION APPEARANCES; SERIES

Wood Reed, *Search for Tomorrow,* CBS, 1976-77.

TELEVISION APPEARANCES; SPECIALS

McCarthy, "The Time of Your Life," *Great Performances,* PBS, 1976.
Title role, "Hamlet," *Great Performances,* PBS, 1990.

The 62nd Annual Academy Awards Presentation, ABC, 1990.
The 44th Annual Tony Awards, CBS, 1990.
The 63rd Annual Academy Awards Presentation, ABC, 1991.

OTHER SOURCES:

BOOKS

Celebrity Register, 5th edition, Gale, 1990, p. 238.

PERIODICALS

Newsday, July 13, 1988, Part II, pp. 4-5.
New York Times, June 23, 1978; January 4, 1981; December 12, 1982.*

* * *

KOPELSON, Arnold 1935-

PERSONAL: Born February 14, 1935, in New York, NY. *Education:* New York University, B.S.; New York Law School, J.D., 1959.

ADDRESSES: Office—Inter-Ocean Film Sales, Ltd., 6100 Wilshire, Suite 1500, Los Angeles, CA 90048.

CAREER: Producer, financier, and distributor of films. Film Packages International, chairman; Inter-Ocean Film Sales, Ltd., co-chairman.

AWARDS, HONORS: Academy Award, best picture, 1986, for *Platoon.*

CREDITS:

FILM WORK; PRODUCER

Foolin' Around, Columbia, 1980.
Jungle Warriors, Aquarius Films, 1984.
Platoon, Orion, 1986.
Hot Pursuit, Paramount, 1987.
(With Shimon Arama) *Triumph of the Spirit,* Triumph, 1989.
Out for Justice, Warner Brothers, 1991.

Also producer of *Rote Hitze,* 1985.

FILM WORK; EXECUTIVE PRODUCER

Lost and Found, Columbia, 1979.
The Legacy, Universal, 1979.
Night of the Juggler, Columbia, 1980.
Final Assignment, Inter-Ocean, 1980.
Dirty Tricks, AVCO Embassy, 1981.
Gimme an "F", Twentieth Century-Fox, 1984.
Warlock, Trimark, 1989.
Fire Birds, (also known as *Wings of the Apache*), Touchstone, 1990.

Also executive producer of *Model Behavior,* 1984.

TELEVISION APPEARANCES; EPISODIC

Judge, *The 1987 Miss Universe Pageant,* CBS, 1987.*

* * *

KOTCHEFF, Ted 1931-
(William T. Kotcheff)

PERSONAL: Full name, William Theodore Kotcheff; born April 7, 1931, in Toronto, Ontario, Canada.

CAREER: Director, producer, and screenwriter. Affiliated with Canadian Broadcasting Corp. (CBC), 1952-57, and American Broadcasting Companies, Inc. (ABC-TV) in London, England, 1957.

MEMBER: Directors Guild of America.

AWARDS, HONORS: British Guild of Television Producers and Directors Merit Award for drama, 1959; British Society of Film and Television Arts Award, best single play, 1971, for *Edna, the Inebriate Woman;* Golden Bear Award, best picture, Berlin Film Festival, 1974, for *The Apprenticeship of Duddy Kravitz;* Genie Award nomination, best achievement in direction, Canadian Department of Communications Film Festival Bureau, 1986, for *Joshua Then and Now.*

CREDITS:

FILM WORK; DIRECTOR, EXCEPT WHERE NOTED

(Under name William T. Kotcheff) *Tiara Tahiti,* Zenith, 1962.
Life at the Top, Columbia, 1965.
Two Gentlemen Sharing, American International, 1969.
Outback, United Artists, 1971.
Billy Two Hats (also known as *The Lady and the Outlaw*), United Artists, 1973.
The Apprenticeship of Duddy Kravitz, Paramount, 1974.
Fun with Dick and Jane, Columbia, 1977.
Production consultant, *Why Shoot the Teacher,* Ambassador-Quartet, 1977.
Who Is Killing the Great Chefs of Europe? (released in England as *Too Many Chefs;* also known as *Someone Is Killing the Great Chefs of Europe*), Warner Brothers, 1978.
North Dallas Forty (also see below), Paramount, 1979.
First Blood, Orion, 1982.
(And producer) *Split Image,* Orion, 1982.
(And executive producer) *Uncommon Valor,* Paramount, 1983.
Joshua Then and Now, Twentieth Century-Fox, 1985.
Switching Channels, Tri-Star, 1988.
Weekend at Bernie's (also known as *Hot and Cold;* also see below), Twentieth Century-Fox, 1989.

Winter People, Columbia, 1989.
Folks, Twentieth Century-Fox, 1992.

FILM APPEARANCES

Jack Parker, *Weekend at Bernie's* (also known as *Hot and Cold*), Twentieth Century-Fox, 1989.

TELEVISION DIRECTOR; SPECIALS

The Desperate Hours, ABC, 1967.
"The Human Voice," *ABC Stage '67,* ABC, 1967.
Of Mice and Men, ABC, 1968.

TELEVISION DIRECTOR; PILOTS

Director, *Rx for the Defense,* ABC, 1973.

STAGE WORK

Director of London productions of *Progress the Park, Play with a Tiger, Luv, Maggie May, The Au Pair Man,* and *Have You Any Dirty Washing, Mother Dear?* Also worked on a production of *Edna the Inebriate Woman,* ca. 1971.

WRITINGS:

(With Frank Yablans and Peter Gent) *North Dallas Forty* (screenplay; based on the novel by Gent), Paramount, 1979.

* * *

KOTCHEFF, William T.
See KOTCHEFF, Ted

* * *

KULP, Nancy 1921-1991

OBITUARY NOTICE—See index for *CTFT* sketch: Full name, Nancy Jane Kulp; born August 28, 1921, in Harrisburg, PA; died of cancer, February 4, 1991, in Palm Desert, CA. Actress. Kulp was best known to television audiences as the intellectual, man-starved bank secretary Jane Hathaway on *The Beverly Hillbillies,* a role that earned Kulp an Emmy nomination in 1967. Kulp recreated the role for the 1981 television movie *Return of the Beverly Hillbillies.* She began her acting career with several non-speaking film parts before appearing in a talking role in the film *The Model and the Marriage Broker* in 1952. After the *Hillbillies* Kulp appeared in the series *The Brian Keith Show* from 1973 to 1974. For the remainder of the seventies, throughout the eighties, and into the nineties Kulp made guest appearances on various television shows, including *Sanford and Son, Simon and Simon,* and *Quantum Leap.* Among her numerous film credits are *The Three Faces of Eve* and *The Parent Trap.* Kulp also made several stage appearances in the early eighties, including productions of *Accent on Youth* and *Mornings at Seven.* Aside from her acting career, Kulp also made a bid for Congress in Port Royal, Pennsylvania in 1984.

OBITUARIES AND OTHER SOURCES:

BOOKS

Who's Who of American Women, 17th edition, Marquis, 1991, p. 562.

PERIODICALS

New York Times, February 5, 1991.

* * *

KUREISHI, Hanif 1954(?)-
(Antonia French)

PERSONAL: Surname is pronounced "koor-*ee*-shee"; born December 5, 1954 (one source says 1956), in London, England; father clerked and worked as a political journalist. *Education:* King's College, London, B.A., philosophy.

ADDRESSES: Agent—Sheila Lemon, Lemon & Durbridge Ltd., 24 Pottery Lane, London W11 4LZ, England.

CAREER: Writer. Worked in various capacities in theater, including scene shifter, stage manager, and box-office clerk; Royal Court Theatre, London, England, writer in residence, 1981 and 1985-86.

AWARDS, HONORS: Thames Television Playwright Award, 1980, for *The Mother Country;* George Devine Award, 1981; *Evening Standard* Award, screenplay, 1985; New York Film Critics Circle award, National Society of Film Critics award, best screenplay, 1986, and Academy Award nomination, best screenplay written directly for the screen, 1986, all for *My Beautiful Laundrette;* Whitbread Book of the Year award, first novel, Booksellers Association of Great Britain and Ireland (United Kingdom), 1990, for *The Buddha of Suburbia.*

WRITINGS:

STAGE PLAYS

Soaking Up the Heat, produced at Theatre Upstairs, London, 1976.
The Mother Country, produced at Riverside Studios, London, 1980.
The King and Me (also see below), produced at Soho Poly Theatre, London, 1980.
Borderline, produced at Royal Court, London, 1981, published by Methuen as part of the Royal Court writers series, 1981.
Cinders (adapted from a play by Janusz Glowacki), produced in London, 1981.

Outskirts (also see below), produced by Royal Shakespeare Company at Royal Shakespeare Company Warehouse, London, 1981.

Tomorrow—Today! (also see below), produced in London, 1981.

(Translator with David Leveaux) Alexander Ostrovsky, *Artists and Admirers,* produced in London, 1982, produced by City Stage Company (CSC) at CSC Repertory Theatre, New York City, 1986.

Birds of Passage, produced in London, 1983, published by Amber Lane Press, 1983.

Outskirts [and] *The King and Me* [and] *Tomorrow—Today!,* Riverrun Press, 1983.

Mother Courage (adapted from a play by Bertolt Brecht), produced by Royal Shakespeare Company, London, 1984.

SCREENPLAYS FOR FILM AND TELEVISION

My Beautiful Laundrette (also see below), broadcast in England by Channel Four, 1985, distributed in United States by Orion Classics, 1986, film script published with autobiographical essay "The Rainbow Sign" by Faber & Faber, 1986.

Sammy and Rosie Get Laid, Cinecom, 1987, published by Penguin, 1988.

RADIO PLAYS

Author of *You Can't Go Home,* 1980, and *The Trial* (from a novel by Franz Kafka), 1982.

OTHER

The Buddha of Suburbia (novel), Viking, 1990.

Also wrote the novella *With Your Tongue Down My Throat,* which appeared in *Granta;* contributor of short story to *Harper's;* wrote additional material under various pseudonyms, including Antonia French.

OTHER SOURCES:

PERIODICALS

Economist, July 21, 1990, p. 92.

Film Comment, October, 1986, p. 50.

Hollywood Reporter, March 21, 1988.

Interview, July, 1987, p. 94; April, 1990, p. 138.

Los Angeles Times, May 25, 1990, p. E1.

New York Times, November 8, 1987, p. 25; May 24, 1990, p. C17.

Observer (London), April 19, 1981, p. 34.*

L

LAIRD, Jack 1923-1991

OBITUARY NOTICE—See index for *CTFT* sketch: Born May 8, 1923, in Bombay, India; died of cancer, December 3, 1991, in Los Angeles, CA. Writer, producer, and performer. During his lifetime, Laird involved himself in all areas of the performing arts. He appeared in his first movie, *The Circus Clown,* in 1934, and later went on to act on stage, in films, and on television. His film appearances include *Mr. Belvedere Goes to College* and *Journey into Light,* and his television appearances include episodes of *Fireside Theatre, Ben Casey* and *Ironside.* Laird was also a prolific and versatile writer, scripting episodes of *My Three Sons, Dragnet, The Wild Wild West* and *Kojak.* Laird produced many of the episodes he wrote, as well as numerous others. At the time of his death, Laird was working on a television series based on stories by thriller writer Robert Ludlum.

OBITUARIES AND OTHER SOURCES:

BOOKS

Who's Who in America, 44th edition, Marquis, 1986, p. 1607.

PERIODICALS

Variety, January 20, 1992, p. 155.

* * *

LANDON, Michael 1936-1991

OBITUARY NOTICE—See index for *CTFT* sketch: Born Eugene Maurice Orowitz, October 31, 1936, in Forest Hills, NY; died of liver and pancreatic cancer, July 1, 1991, in Malibu, CA. Actor, producer, writer, and director. Landon is best known for his acting in three popular television series, *Bonanza, Little House on the Prairie,* and *Highway to Heaven.* He began acting in television anthology series in the mid-1950s before making his feature film debut in *I Was a Teenage Werewolf* in 1957. From 1959 to 1973 Landon starred as Little Joe Cartwright in the NBC western *Bonanza,* which, at one point in its run, earned the distinction of being the most watched television show in the world. Landon began writing and directing episodes of *Bonanza* in the early sixties. Following *Bonanza,* Landon created, produced, and starred in *Little House on the Prairie,* a series based on Laura Ingalls Wilder's books that he also predominantly wrote and directed. When *Little House* ended in 1983, he served similar functions on a new series, *Highway to Heaven,* which he starred in from 1984 to 1988. When *Highway to Heaven* concluded its run it marked the end of a thirty-five year relationship between Landon and NBC, a feat many believe to be the longest-running association between a network and a star in television history. In addition to his work in series television, Landon was also prolific in the creation of movies for television. He was the producer/writer/director, as well as supporting actor, on such productions as *The Loneliest Runner* and *Where Pigeons Go to Die,* and the producer and director of the films *The Killing Stone* and *It's Good to Be Alive.* He also wrote, directed, and appeared in the theatrical release *Sam's Son.* Throughout his career, Landon strove to create entertainment that was both thought-provoking and uplifting—he was said to have been drawn to optimistic themes due to an unhappy childhood. At the time he learned of his illness, Landon's new series *US,* in which he was to play a travelling reporter, had been accepted by CBS for the network's 1991 fall lineup. At Landon's request, the two hour pilot for the series was aired after his death.

OBITUARIES AND OTHER SOURCES:

BOOKS

Who's Who in America, 46th edition, Marquis, 1990, p. 1900.

PERIODICALS

Detroit News and Free Press, April 9, 1991.
Variety, July 8, 1991, pp. 61-62.

* * *

LANDSBURG, Alan 1933-

PERSONAL: Full name, Alan William Landsburg; born May 10, 1933, in White Plains, NY; son of Harry and Fannie (Koslowe) Landsburg; married Sally Breit (divorced, 1975); married Linda Otto (a film producer), March 7, 1976; children (first marriage): Valerie, Michael. *Education:* New York University, B.A., 1953.

ADDRESSES: Office—22432 Pacific Coast Highway, Malibu, CA 90265.

CAREER: Producer, director, and writer. Affiliated with National Broadcasting Company (NBC), 1951-59; affiliated with Columbia Broadcasting System (CBS), 1959-60; Wolper Productions/Metromedia Producers, executive producer, 1961-70; Alan Landsburg Productions, chair of board of directors, 1970-85. University of California, Los Angeles, instructor, 1968-70. *Military service:* U.S. Army, 1953-55.

MEMBER: Writers Guild of America, Directors Guild of America, Academy of Television Arts and Sciences, Academy of Motion Picture Arts and Sciences.

AWARDS, HONORS: George Foster Peabody Broadcasting Award, Henry W. Grady School of Journalism and Mass Communications, University of Georgia, 1964, for *Biography;* George Foster Peabody Broadcasting Award, 1966, for *National Geographic Specials;* Emmy Award, outstanding dramatic program, 1969, for "A Storm in Summer," *Hallmark Hall of Fame;* Academy Award nomination, feature documentary, 1971, for *Alaska Wilderness Lake;* Emmy Award nomination, outstanding drama special, 1975, for *Fear on Trial;* Emmy Award nomination, outstanding informational series, 1977, for *Between the Wars;* Emmy Award nomination, outstanding drama special, 1983, for *Bill;* Emmy Award nomination (with Joan Barnett), outstanding drama special, 1983, for *Adam.*

CREDITS:

TELEVISION EXECUTIVE PRODUCER; MOVIES

(With Laurence D. Savadore) *Fear on Trial,* CBS, 1975.
(With Merrill Grant and Don Kirshner) *The Savage Bees,* NBC, 1976.
Tarantulas: The Deadly Cargo, CBS, 1977.
It Happened at Lake Wood Manor, ABC, 1977.
Terror out of the Sky, CBS, 1978.
Ruby and Oswald, CBS, 1978.
The Chisholms, CBS, 1979.
(With Grant and Kirshner) *The Triangle Factory Fire Scandal,* NBC, 1979.
(With Sonny Fox) *And Baby Makes Six,* NBC, 1979.
Mysterious Island of Beautiful Women, CBS, 1979.
Baby Comes Home, CBS, 1980.
Marathon, CBS, 1980.
(With Tom Kuhn) *A Long Way Home,* ABC, 1981.
Bill, CBS, 1981.
Mysterious Two, NBC, 1982.
Bill: On His Own, CBS, 1983.
(With Joan Barnett) *Adam,* NBC, 1983.
(With Barnett) *Adam: His Song Continues,* NBC, 1986.
(With Barnett) *The George McKenna Story,* CBS, 1986.
(With Barnett) *Parent Trap II,* The Disney Channel, 1986.
Strange Voices, NBC, 1987.
Long Gone, HBO, 1987.
Too Young the Hero, CBS, 1988.
A Stoning in Fulham County (also known as *The Stoning, The Amish Story,* and *Incident at Tile Mill Road*), NBC, 1988.
Quiet Victory: The Charlie Wedemeyer Story, CBS, 1988.
A Place at the Table (also known as *The Best Kept Secret, No Child Shall Go Hungry,* and *A Million Children*), NBC, 1988.
The Ryan White Story, ABC, 1989.
Unspeakable Acts (also see below), ABC, 1990.
In Defense of a Married Man, ABC, 1990.
A Triumph of the Heart: The Ricky Bell Story, CBS, 1991.
A Nightmare in Columbia County, CBS, 1991.

Also executive producer of *Bluegrass.*

TELEVISION EXECUTIVE PRODUCER; SERIES

It Was a Very Good Year, ABC, 1971.
(With Don Kirshner) *The Kids from C.A.P.E.R.,* NBC, 1976-77.
In Search Of . . . , syndicated, 1976-82.
Between the Wars, syndicated, 1978.
The Chisholms, CBS, 1980.
No Holds Barred, CBS, 1980.
(With Merrill Grant) *That's Incredible,* ABC, 1980-84.
(With Grant and Woody Fraser) *The Krypton Factor* (gameshow), ABC, 1981.
(With Fraser) *People Do the Craziest Things,* ABC, 1984.
True Confessions (also see below), syndicated, 1986.
High Risk (also see below), CBS, 1988.

Also executive producer of *National Geographic Specials,* 1965-70, *The American Idea,* and *March of Time.*

TELEVISION EXECUTIVE PRODUCER; SPECIALS

(With Laurence D. Savadore) *Alan King in Las Vegas, Part I,* ABC, 1973.
(With Savadore) *Alan King in Las Vegas, Part II,* ABC, 1973.
(With Merrill Grant and David Auerbach) *The World's Funniest Commercial Goofs,* ABC, 1983, 1984.
(With Woody Fraser) *Life's Most Embarrassing Moments,* ABC, 1983.
Life's Most Embarrassing Moments II, ABC, 1983.
(With Fraser) *Life's Most Embarrassing Moments III,* ABC, 1984.
(With Kay Hoffman and Fraser) *Life's Most Embarrassing Moments IV,* ABC, 1984.
Getting the Last Laugh, ABC, 1985.
To Protect the Children, TBS, 1986.
Wanted: A Room With Love, syndicated, 1986.
Destined to Live: 100 Roads to Recovery, NBC, 1988.
Maggie's Secret, CBS, 1990.

Also executive producer of *Alaska Wilderness Lake,* 1971.

TELEVISION EXECUTIVE PRODUCER; EPISODIC

Executive producer of *ABC Afterschool Special* and *The Undersea World of Jacques Cousteau,* both ABC.

TELEVISION EXECUTIVE PRODUCER; PILOTS

(With Merrill Grant) *The Future: What's Next,* CBS, 1981.
The Mysterious Two, NBC, 1982.
(With Woody Fraser) *Success: It Can Be Yours,* ABC, 1982.
(With Mort Lachman and Fraser) *It Only Hurts When You Laugh,* NBC, 1983.
(With Fraser) *Personal and Confidential,* NBC, 1983.
(With Fraser) *People Do the Craziest Things,* ABC, 1984.
(With Fraser and Grant) *People to People,* ABC, 1984.
(And creator and director) *Under Fire: The Real Story,* ABC, 1989.

TELEVISION DIRECTOR

(With Jack Haley, Jr.; and associate producer) *Biography* (series), syndicated, 1962.
(And producer) *Men in Crisis* (series), syndicated, 1964.
(And producer) *Black Water Gold* (movie), ABC, 1970.
Real Life Stories (pilot), CBS, 1981.
High Risk (premiere), CBS, 1988.

TELEVISION DIRECTOR; EPISODIC

True Confessions, syndicated, 1986.
High Risk, CBS, 1988.

OTHER TELEVISION WORK

Producer, *Mirror, Mirror, off the Wall* (special), NBC, 1969.
Producer, "A Storm in Summer," *Hallmark Hall of Fame,* PBS, 1969.
Supervising producer with Woody Fraser and Merrill Grant, *Those Amazing Animals* (series), ABC, 1980-81.

FILM WORK

Coexecutive producer, *Jaws 3-D,* Universal, 1983.
Coexecutive producer, *Porky's II: The Next Day,* Twentieth Century-Fox, 1983.

Also producer of *The Outer Space Connection,* 1974.

WRITINGS:

TELEVISION WRITING

True Confessions, syndicated, 1986.
Unspeakable Acts (movie), ABC, 1990.
With Reason to Suspect (movie), ABC, 1992.

OTHER

(With Sally Landsburg) *In Search of Ancient Mysteries,* foreword by Rod Serling, Bantam, 1974.
(With S. Landsburg) *The Outer Space Connection,* photographs by Andrew Reichline, Bantam, 1975.
In Search of Magic and Witchcraft, foreword by Leonard Nimoy, Bantam, 1977.
In Search of Strange Phenomena, foreword by Nimoy, Bantam, 1977.
In Search of Myths and Monsters, foreword by Nimoy, Bantam, 1977.
In Search of . . . : Lost Civilizations, Extraterrestrials, Magic and Witchcraft, Strange Phenomena, Myths and Monsters, Doubleday, 1978.
(With Edward Garrick) *The Insects Are Coming,* Warner Books, 1978.
Secrets of the Bermuda Triangle, Warner Books, 1978.
In Search Of. . . , Doubleday, 1978.

Also author of *In Search of Extraterrestrials,* 1977.

Landsburg's works have been translated into Spanish and French.

* * *

LANE, Nathan 1956-

PERSONAL: Born February 3, 1956, in Jersey City, NJ.

ADDRESSES: Agent—Schiffman, Ekman, Morrison & Marx, 156 Fifth Ave., Suite 523, New York, NY 10010.

CAREER: Actor. Performed at dinner theaters and in summer stock.

AWARDS, HONORS: Drama Desk Award, best actor in a play, 1989, for *The Lisbon Traviata;* Drama Desk Award nomination, best actor in a musical, and Antoinette Perry Award nomination, best performance by a leading actor in a musical, both 1992, both for *Guys and Dolls.*

CREDITS:

STAGE APPEARANCES

(Off-Broadway debut) *A Midsummer Night's Dream,* Equity Library Theatre, New York City, 1978.
(Broadway debut) Roland Maule, *Present Laughter,* Circle in the Square, New York City, 1982-83.
Prince Fergus, *Merlin,* Mark Hellinger Theatre, New York City, 1983.
Harry, *Love,* Audrey Wood Theatre, New York City, 1984.
Patrick, "Raving," *One-Act Play Marathon '84,* Ensemble Studio Theatre, New York City, 1984.
Tony Lumpkin, *She Stoops to Conquer,* Roundabout Theatre, New York City, 1984.
The Common Pursuit, Long Wharf Theatre, New Haven, CT, 1984-85.
Leonard, Haji Rahaji, and Jed Rubin, *A Backers' Audition,* Manhattan Theatre Club, New York City, 1985.
Toad, *Wind in the Willows,* Nederlander Theatre, New York City, 1985.
Pompey, *Measure for Measure,* New York Shakespeare Festival, Delacorte Theatre, New York City, 1985.
Nick Finchling, *The Common Pursuit,* Promenade Theatre, New York City, 1986-87.
Harvey Wheatcraft, *Claptrap,* City Center Theatre, New York City, 1987.
Stanley, *Broadway Bound,* Shubert Theatre, New Haven, CT, 1987, then Center Theatre Group, Ahmanson Theatre, Los Angeles, CA.
"Hidden in This Picture" (one-act), *Uncounted Blessings,* St. Clement's Church, New York City, 1988.
Jonathan Balton, *The Film Society,* Second Stage Theatre, New York City, 1988.
Mendy, *The Lisbon Traviata,* City Center Theatre, 1989, then Promenade Theatre, 1989-90.
A Pig's Valise, Second Stage Theatre, 1989.
Henry McNeil, *Some Americans Abroad,* Vivian Beaumont Theatre, New York City, 1990.
Hugh Gumbs, *Bad Habits,* Manhattan Theatre Club, 1990.
Sam Truman, *Lips Together, Teeth Apart,* Manhattan Theatre Club, 1991.
Mr. Brink, *On Borrowed Time,* Circle in the Square, 1991.
Nathan Detroit, *Guys and Dolls,* Martin Beck Theatre, New York City, 1992.

TELEVISION APPEARANCES

Stage manager, *Jacqueline Suzann's "Valley of the Dolls"* (mini-series), CBS, 1981.
Jonathan Burns, *One of the Boys* (series; also known as *O'Malley*), NBC, 1982.
Macy's Thanksgiving Day Parade (special), NBC, 1985.

FILM APPEARANCES

Harold Allen, *Ironweed,* Tri-Star, 1987.
Charlie Sorrel, *The Lemon Sisters,* Miramax, 1990.
Baw-Waponi advance man, *Joe Versus the Volcano,* Warner Brothers, 1990.
Wally Thurman, *He Said, She Said,* Paramount, 1991.
Tim, *Frankie and Johnny,* Paramount, 1991.*

* * *

LANSING, Robert 1928-

PERSONAL: Born Robert Howell Brown, June 5, 1928, in San Diego, CA; son of Robert George (a real estate broker) and Alice Lucille (Howell) Brown; married Emily McLaughlin (an actress), June 6, 1956 (divorced); married Garifalia Hardy, 1969 (divorced); married Anne Cecile Erde Pivar, 1981; children: (first marriage) Robert; (second marriage) Alice. *Education:* Attended University High School, West Los Angeles, CA, and Beverly Hills High School. *Politics:* Democrat. *Avocational interests:* Swimming, painting.

ADDRESSES: Office—1165 Park Ave., New York, NY 10028. *Agent*—Don Buchwald and Associates, 10 East 44th St., New York, NY 10017.

CAREER: Actor. *Military service:* U.S. Army, 1946-47.

MEMBER: Actors Equity Association, American Federation of Television and Radio Artists, Screen Actors Guild (member of board of directors; national vice-president), Directors Guild of America, Academy of Magical Arts (life member), Players Club.

CREDITS:

FILM APPEARANCES

Scott Nelson, *4D Man* (also known as *The Master of Terror* and *The Evil Force*), Universal, 1959.
Steve Carella, *The Pusher,* United Artists (UA), 1960.
Sergeant Banning, *A Gathering of Eagles,* Universal, 1963.
Charles, *Under the Yum-Yum Tree,* Columbia, 1963.
Talion, *An Eye for an Eye,* Embassy, 1966.
Hank Donner, *Namu, the Killer Whale,* UA, 1966.
Tony Gunther, *It Takes All Kinds,* Commonwealth, 1969.
Dave Fenner, *The Grissom Gang,* Cinerama, 1971.

Major Reason, *Black Jack* (also known as *Wild in the Sky*), American International, 1973.
Howard, *Bittersweet Love,* Avco Embassy, 1976.
Dr. Phillip Reynolds, *Scalpel* (also known as *False Face*), United International, 1976.
Dan Stokely, *Empire of the Ants,* American International, 1977.
Acapulco Gold, Riddle, 1978.
Island Claws (also known as *The Night of the Claw*), Island Claws, 1981.
Mayor Elias Johnson, *The Nest,* Concorde, 1988.
C. A. Thomas, *After School* (also known as *Private Tutor*), Moviestore, 1988.
Driver, *Jungle Fever,* Universal, 1991.

Also appeared in *Blind Vengeance,* 1990.

TELEVISION APPEARANCES; MOVIES

John Phillips, *The Astronaut,* ABC, 1972.
Harold, *Widow,* NBC, 1976.
General McAllister, *Bionic Showdown: The Six Million Dollar Man and the Bionic Woman,* NBC, 1989.

TELEVISION APPEARANCES; SERIES

Peter Brooks, *Young Dr. Malone,* NBC, 1958-63.
Detective Steve Carella, *87th Precinct,* NBC, 1961-62.
Brigadier General Frank Savage, *Twelve O'Clock High,* ABC, 1964-67.
Peter Murphy and Mark Wainwright, *The Man Who Never Was,* ABC, 1966-67.
Lieutenant Jack Curtis, *Automan,* ABC, 1983-84.
Control, *The Equalizer,* CBS, 1985.

TELEVISION APPEARANCES; PILOTS

Warren Claman, *Killer by Night* (also known as *The City by Night*), CBS, 1972.
Alex Norton, *The Crime Club,* CBS, 1975.
Charles Cole, *Deadly Triangle,* NBC, 1977.
Owen Hooper, *S*H*E,* CBS, 1980.

TELEVISION APPEARANCES; EPISODIC

"Shadow of Suspicion," *Kraft Theatre,* NBC, 1956.
"The Square Egghead," *U.S. Steel Hour,* CBS, 1959.
"The Case of Julia Walton," *U.S. Steel Hour,* CBS, 1959.
"Big Doc's Girl," *U.S. Steel Hour,* CBS, 1959.
"The Great Gold Mountain," *U.S. Steel Hour,* CBS, 1960.
Edward Stevens, "The Burning Court," *The Dow Hour of Great Mysteries,* NBC, 1960.
"Wanted: Someone Innocent," *U.S. Steel Hour,* CBS, 1962.
Sam Benedict, NBC, 1962, 1963.
"Fair Young Ghost," *U.S. Steel Hour,* CBS, 1963.
The Virginian, NBC, 1963, 1965, 1967.
Wagon Train, ABC, 1964.
Twilight Zone, CBS, 1964.
Ironside, NBC, 1968.
Gary Seven, "Assignment: Earth," *Star Trek,* NBC, 1968.
Name of the Game, NBC, 1969.
Gunsmoke, CBS, 1969.
Medical Center, CBS, 1969.
Bonanza, NBC, 1970.
Mannix, CBS, 1970, 1971.
The Evil Touch, syndicated, 1973.
Horace Bixby, "Life on the Mississippi," *Great Performances,* PBS, 1980.
Sam Penny, "The Shadow of Sam Penny," *Simon & Simon,* CBS, 1983.
Hotel, ABC, 1986.

Appeared in episodes of *General Electric Theater,* CBS, in "The Vampire Hunter," an episode of *Monsters,* and on *Alfred Hitchcock Presents* and *Camera Three.*

STAGE APPEARANCES

(New York debut) Dunbar, *Stalag 17* (also see below), 48th Street Theatre, New York City, 1948.
A cadet of Gascoyne, *Cyrano de Bergerac,* New York City Center Theatre, 1953.
Jack Chesney, *Charley's Aunt,* New York City Center Theatre, 1953.
Marquis of Dorset, *Richard III,* New York City Center Theatre, 1953.
Herstal de la Crux, *The Lovers,* Martin Beck Theatre, New York City, 1956.
Lloyd Hilton, *Cue for Passion,* Henry Miller's Theatre, New York City, 1958.
Dr. Cukrowicz, "Suddenly Last Summer," *Garden District* (double bill), York Theatre, New York City, 1958.
William A. Brown, *Great God Brown,* Coronet Theatre, New York City, 1959.
All about Love, Drury Lane Theatre, New York City, 1959.
Paul Carr, *Cut of the Axe,* Ambassador Theatre, New York City, 1960.
Under the Yum-Yum Tree, Playhouse on the Mall, Paramus, NJ, 1963.
Antony, *Antony and Cleopatra,* MacArthur Park Theatre, Los Angeles, CA, 1967.
Daniel Brightower, *Brightower,* John Golden Theatre, New York City, 1970.
Jeff Cooper, *Finishing Touches* (also see below), Plymouth Theatre, New York City, 1973.
The captain, *The Father,* Roundabout Theatre, New York City, 1973.
"The Line" and "Phaedra," *The O'Neill Sea Plays,* Long Wharf Theatre, New Haven, CT, 1977.
S.S. Glencairn, Long Wharf Theatre, 1977-78.
The Dance of Death, Seattle Repertory Company, Seattle, WA, 1980-81.

Damien (one-man show), PAF Playhouse, Long Island, NY, 1981.
Benjamin, *The Little Foxes* (also see below), Ahmanson Theatre, Los Angeles, CA, 1981.
The Bathers, Long Wharf Theatre, 1983-84.
Alexander, *The Cost of Living,* Judith Anderson Theatre, New York City, 1985.
John Brown's Body, Williamstown Theatre Festival, Williamstown, NY, 1989.
Ajay, *Mi Vida Loca,* Manhattan Theatre Club/City Center Stage II, New York City, 1990.

MAJOR TOURS

Dunbar, *Stalag 17,* national tour, 1952-53.
Jeff Cooper, *Finishing Touches,* national tour, 1973-74.
Benjamin, *The Little Foxes,* London, 1981.

OTHER SOURCES:

PERIODICALS

Starlog, December, 1989.*

* * *

LaPAGLIA, Anthony 1959(?)-

PERSONAL: Full name, Anthony M. LaPaglia; born c. 1959.

ADDRESSES: *Agent*—J. Michael Bloom, 9200 Sunset Blvd., Suite 710, Los Angeles, CA 90069.

CAREER: Actor.

MEMBER: Screen Actors Guild.

CREDITS:

FILM APPEARANCES

Henry, *Slaves of New York,* Tri-Star, 1989.
Stevie Dee, *Betsy's Wedding,* Buena Vista, 1990.
Mark, *He Said, She Said,* Paramount, 1991.

Also appeared as Vito in *Mortal Sins,* 1989; as Frank Pesce, Jr., in *29th Street,* 1991; and as Stevie Diroma in *One Good Cop,* 1991.

TELEVISION APPEARANCES; MOVIES

(As Anthony M. LaPaglia) Officer Petrelli, *Gladiator School* (also known as *Police Story*), ABC, 1988.
Title role, *Frank Nitti: The Enforcer* (also known as *The Frank Nitti Story*), ABC, 1988.
Raskin, *Sleep Well, Professor Oliver* (also known as *Gideon Oliver*), ABC, 1988.
David Ringel, *Criminal Justice,* HBO, 1990.
The killer, *Keeper of the City,* Showtime, 1991.

TELEVISION APPEARANCES; SERIES

Nicholas Gennaro, *The Brotherhood,* ABC, 1991.

TELEVISION APPEARANCES; EPISODIC

Cable television installer, "Spoiled," *Tales From the Crypt,* HBO, 1991.

STAGE APPEARANCES

(As Anthony M. LaPaglia) Les, *Bouncers,* Minetta Lane Theatre, New York City, 1987.

OTHER SOURCES:

PERIODICALS

Premiere, May, 1991, p. 45.*

* * *

LASSALLY, Walter 1926-

PERSONAL: Born December 18, 1926, in Berlin, Germany; immigrated to England, 1939.

ADDRESSES: *Contact*—International Photographers, 7715 Sunset Blvd., Suite 300, Hollywood, CA 90046.

CAREER: Cinematographer. Worked as clapper boy for Riverside Studios; began professional career as cinematographer working on short films.

MEMBER: International Photographers.

AWARDS, HONORS: Academy Award for best cinematography, 1964, for *Zorba the Greek.*

CREDITS:

FILM WORK; CINEMATOGRAPHER OF FULL-LENGTH FILMS

The Passing Stranger, Independent Film Distributors/British Lion, 1954.
Together, Connoisseur, 1956.
Electra, Lopert Pictures, 1962.
The Loneliness of the Long Distance Runner (also known as *Rebel with a Cause*), Continental Distributing, 1962.
A Taste of Honey, Continental Distributing, 1962.
Tom Jones, Lopert Pictures, 1963.
Psyche Fifty-nine, Columbia/Royal, 1964.
Zorba the Greek, Twentieth Century-Fox, 1964.
Madalena, Greek Motion Pictures, 1965.
The Day the Fish Came Out, International Classics, 1967.
Joanna, Twentieth Century-Fox, 1968.
Oedipus the King, Universal, 1968.
The Adding Machine, Regal Films, 1969.
Three into Two Won't Go, Universal, 1969.

Something for Everyone (also known as *The Rook;* released in England as *Black Flowers for the Bride*), National General Pictures, 1970.

Le Mans (uncredited; filmed racetrack sequences), National General Pictures, 1971.

Lola (released in England as *Twinky*), American International Pictures, 1971.

Savages, Angelika Films, 1972.

To Kill a Clown, Twentieth Century-Fox, 1972.

Happy Mother's Day . . . Love George (also known as *Run, Stranger, Run*), Cinema 5, 1973.

Malachi's Cove (also known as *The Seaweed Children*), Impact Quadrant, 1973.

The Wild Party, American International Pictures, 1975.

Autobiography of a Princess, Merchant-Ivory Productions, 1975.

Pleasantville, Visions, 1976.

Ansichten eines Clowns (also known as *The Clown*), Constantin, 1976.

The Great Bank Hoax (also known as *The Great Georgia Bank Hoax* and *Shenanigans*), Jacoby, 1977.

Die Frau gegenuber (also known as *Woman across the Way*), DNS-Film, 1978.

The Pilot, Summit, 1979.

Something Short of Paradise, American International Pictures, 1979.

The Blood of Hussain, Cinegate, 1980.

Der Preis furs uberleben (also known as *The Price for Survival* and *Le Prix de la survie*), Popular Film, 1980.

Memoirs of a Survivor, EMI Productions, 1981.

Engel aus Eisen (also known as *Angels of Iron*), Independent Film Productions, 1981.

Too Far to Go (also see below), Zoetrope, 1982.

Private School, Universal, 1983.

Heat and Dust, Curzon/Universal, 1983.

The Bostonians, Almi Pictures, 1984.

The Perfect Murder, Enterprise, 1988.

The Deceivers, Cinecom, 1988.

Fragments of Isabella, National Film Theatre, 1989.

Kamilla og tyven II (also known as *Kamilla and the Thief Part 2: Kamilla's Friend*), Penelope Films, 1989.

That's Adequate, South Gate Entertainment/Manley Productions, 1989.

Border Shootout (also known as *The Law at Randado* and *The Law at Randada*), Turner Home Entertainment, 1990.

Switch (also known as *Dans la peau d'une blonde*), Warner Brothers, 1991.

The Ballad of the Sad Cafe, Angelika Films, 1991.

One Good Cop, Buena Vista, 1991.

Father of the Bride, Buena Vista, 1991.

Terror in Beverly Hills, Double Helix Films, 1991.

OTHER FILM WORK; CINEMATOGRAPHER

To koritsi me ta mavra (also known as *A Girl in Black*), 1955.

Another Sky, 1955.

To telefteo psema (also known as *A Matter of Dignity*), 1957.

We Are the Lambeth Boys, 1958.

Jago hua savera (also known as *Day Shall Dawn*), 1958.

Beat Girl (also known as *Wild for Kicks*), 1960.

Eroica (also known as *Our Last Spring*), 1960.

Aliki sto naftiko (also known as *Aliki in the Navy*), 1960.

I Liza kai i alli (also known as *Liza and Her Double*), 1961.

Anikti epistoli (also known as *Open Letter*), 1968.

Olimpiada en Mexico (also known as *The Olympics in Mexico*), 1968.

Turnkey, 1970.

Gun Before Butter, 1972.

Bilocation (also known as *Within Hail*), 1973.

Apres le vent des sables (also known as *La Trame*), 1974.

Henry Cotton: This Game of Golf, 1974.

Requiem for a Village, 1975.

Fluchtversuch, 1976.

Morgensterne, 1977.

Tuxedo Warrior, 1983.

The Case of Marcel Duchamp, 1983.

Indian Summer, 1987.

FILM WORK; CINEMATOGRAPHER FOR SHORT FILMS

(And coproducer and codirector) *Smith, Our Friend,* 1946.

Dancing with Crime, 1947.

This Was a Woman, 1947.

What's in a Number, 1948.

Things Happen at Night, 1948.

Night and the City, 1950.

Every Five Minutes, 1950.

From Plan into Action, 1951.

Forward a Century, 1951.

Festival, 1952.

At Whose Door?, 1952.

We Who Are Young, 1952.

The Pleasure Garden, 1952.

Three Installations, 1952.

Wakefield Express, 1952.

Power Signal Lineman, 1953.

High Speed; Sunday by the Sea, 1953.

One Great Vision, 1953.

Thursday's Children, 1953.

Bow Bells, 1954.

Friends of the Family, 1954.

Green and Pleasant Land, 1955.

Henry, 1955.

Continuous Observation, 1955.

The Children Upstairs, 1955.
A Hundred Thousand Children, 1955.
Foot and Mouth, 1955.
The Brighton Story, 1956.
The Gentle Corsican, 1956.
Momma Don't Allow, 1956.
Return from the Sun, 1956.
Simon, 1956.
The Simpson and Godlee Story, 1956.
Children's Corner, 1956.
Every Day Except Christmas, 1957.
A River Speaks, 1957.
Ten Bridges, 1957.
George Bernard Shaw, 1957.
Blue Peter, 1958.
A.B.C. (also known as *Aruba, Bonaire, Curazao*), 1958.
Alone with the Monsters, 1958.
A Song for Prince Charlie, 1958.
Refuge England, 1959.
Enquiry into General Practice, 1959.
Midsummer Music, 1960.
Let My People Go, 1961.
Why Bri?, 1961.
London University, 1961.
The Peaches, 1964.
Lila, 1964.
Mao le veut, 1965.
Labyrinth, 1967.
Henry Moore at the Tate Gallery, 1970.
Can Horses Sing?, 1971.
Carved in Ivory, 1974.
W.S.P., 1974.
Ernst Fuchs, 1976.

Served as assistant editor on *House of Blackmail,* 1953.

FILM APPEARANCES

Appeared as himself in *How the Myth Was Made: A Study of Robert Flaherty's Man of Aran,* 1978.

TELEVISION WORK; CINEMATOGRAPHER

Stone Pillow, CBS, 1985.
Mrs. Delafield Wants to Marry, CBS, 1986.
Adventure of Huckleberry Finn (featured on *American Playhouse*), PBS, 1986.
My Africa (featured on *CBS Summer Playhouse*), CBS, 1988.

Cinematographer for other television movies and specials, including *Adventures of a Brown Man in Search of Civilisation; In the Beginning; Hullabaloo over Georgie and Bonnie's Pictures;* "The Highest" (episode of *Visions of Eight*), 1973; *Too Far to Go; Life on the Mississippi; Ganguin the Savage; The Private History of the Campaign that Failed; Pudd'nhead Wilson; Children in the Crossfire;* and *The Mysterious Stranger.*

WRITINGS:

Contributor of articles to periodicals and professional journals, including *Sight and Sound, Film,* and *American Cinematographer.*

OTHER SOURCES:

PERIODICALS

Films and Filming (London), December, 1954.
Focus on Film (London), Number 13, 1973.*

* * *

LAURIE, Piper 1932-

PERSONAL: Born Rosetta Jacobs, January 22, 1932, in Detroit, MI; married Joseph Morgenstern, 1962; children: Anne. *Education:* Attended Los Angeles High School, Los Angeles, CA; studied at Neighborhood Playhouse.

ADDRESSES: *Agent*—Triad Artists, Inc., 10100 Santa Monica Blvd., 16th Floor, Los Angeles, CA 90067.

CAREER: Actress.

MEMBER: Screen Actors Guild, American Federation of Television and Radio Artists, Academy of Motion Picture Arts and Sciences.

AWARDS, HONORS: Emmy Award nominations, best single performance by an actress, 1957, for an episode of *Studio One,* and 1958, for "The Days of Wine and Roses," *Playhouse 90;* Academy Award nomination, best actress, 1961, for *The Hustler;* named Hasty Pudding Woman of the Year, Hasty Pudding Theatricals, 1962; Academy Award nomination, best supporting actress, 1976, for *Carrie;* Emmy Award nomination, outstanding supporting actress in a limited series or special, 1981, for *The Bunker;* Emmy Award nomination, outstanding supporting actress in a limited series or special, and Golden Globe Award, Hollywood Foreign Press Association, both 1983, for *The Thorn Birds;* Emmy Award nomination, outstanding supporting actress in a drama series, 1983, for *St. Elsewhere;* Academy Award nomination, best supporting actress, 1986, for *Children of a Lesser God;* Emmy Award, outstanding supporting actress in a mini-series or special, 1986, for "Promise," *Hallmark Hall of Fame;* Emmy Award nominations, outstanding lead actress in a drama series, and outstanding supporting actress in a drama series, both 1990, both for *Twin Peaks.*

CREDITS:

FILM APPEARANCES

Cathy Norton, *Louisa,* Universal, 1950.

Chris Abbott, *The Milkman,* Universal, 1950.
Frances Travers, *Francis Goes to the Races,* Universal, 1951.
Tina, *The Prince Who Was a Thief,* Universal, 1951.
Millicent, *Has Anybody Seen My Gal?,* Universal, 1952.
Lee Kingshead, *No Room for the Groom,* Universal, 1952.
Kiki, *Son of Ali Baba,* Universal, 1952.
Princess Khairuzan, *The Golden Blade,* Universal, 1953.
Angelique Duroux, *The Mississippi Gambler,* Universal, 1953.
Louise Graham, *Dangerous Mission,* RKO Radio Pictures, 1954.
Rannah Hayes, *Dawn at Socorro,* Universal, 1954.
Liz Fielding, *Johnny Dark,* Universal, 1954.
Sarah Hatfield, *Ain't Misbehavin',* Universal, 1955.
Laura Evans, *Smoke Signal,* Universal, 1955.
Delia Leslie, *Until They Sail,* Metro-Goldwyn-Mayer, 1957.
Mina Van Runkel, *Kelly and Me,* Universal, 1957.
Sarah Packard, *The Hustler,* Twentieth Century-Fox, 1961.
Margaret White, *Carrie,* United Artists, 1976.
Ruby Claire, *Ruby,* Dimension, 1977.
Mary Horton, *Tim,* Satori, 1981.
Aunt Em, *Return to Oz,* Buena Vista, 1985.
Mrs. Norman, *Children of a Lesser God,* Paramount, 1986.
Mrs. Emily Boynton, *Appointment With Death,* Cannon, 1988.
Margot, *Distortions,* Cori, 1988.
Frances Warsaw, *Tiger Warsaw,* Sony, 1988.
Gene Ettinger, *Dream a Little Dream,* Vestron, 1989.
Bea Sullivan, *Other People's Money,* Warner Brothers, 1991.

Appeared in *The Boss' Son,* 1988, and *Mother, Mother,* 1989.

TELEVISION APPEARANCES; SERIES

Jo Skagska, *Skag,* NBC, 1980, syndicated, 1982.
St. Elsewhere, NBC, 1983.
Catherine Martell, *Twin Peaks* (also known as *Northern Passage*), ABC, 1990.

TELEVISION APPEARANCES; MINI-SERIES

Anne Mueller, *The Thorn Birds,* ABC, 1983.

TELEVISION APPEARANCES; MOVIES

Julie Quinlan, *In the Matter of Karen Ann Quinlan,* NBC, 1977.
Ethel Gumm, *Rainbow,* NBC, 1978.
Magda Goebbels, *The Bunker,* CBS, 1981.
Matilda West, *Mae West,* ABC, 1982.
Christine Groda, *Love, Mary,* CBS, 1985.
Darlene Marsh, *Toughlove,* ABC, 1985.
Margo, *Toward the Light* (also known as *Go to the Light*), CBS, 1988.
Martha Robinson, *Rising Son,* TNT, 1990.

TELEVISION APPEARANCES; EPISODIC

Billie Moore, "Broadway," *The Best of Broadway,* CBS, 1955.
Viola, "Twelfth Night," *Hallmark Hall of Fame,* NBC, 1957.
"The Days of Wine and Roses," *Playhouse 90,* CBS, 1958.
Miriamme, "Winterset," *Hallmark Hall of Fame,* NBC, 1959.
Anne Gilbert, "Promise," *Hallmark Hall of Fame,* CBS, 1986.

Also appeared in "The Life of Margaret Sanger," *Nova,* PBS; "The Road That Led Afar," *General Electric Theater,* CBS; "Murder at the Oasis," *Murder, She Wrote,* CBS; appeared on episodes of *Studio One,* CBS, 1957; *Robert Montgomery Presents,* CBS; *General Electric Theater,* CBS; *The Desilu Playhouse,* CBS; and *Play of the Week.*

OTHER TELEVISION APPEARANCES

The Bob Hope Show (special), NBC, 1962.
The 49th Annual Golden Globe Awards (special), Fox, 1992.

Also appeared on *Tender Is the Night,* Showtime; *The Deaf Heart; The Ninth Day;* and *The Woman Rebel.*

STAGE APPEARANCES

Flo Varney, *Rosemary,* and Candy Simpson, *The Alligators* (double bill), York Playhouse, New York City, 1960.
The daughter, *The Glass Menagerie,* Brooks Atkinson Theatre, New York City, 1965.
The Innocents, Ivanhoe Theatre, Chicago, IL, 1970-71.
Marion Froude, *Biography,* Manhattan Theatre Club, New York City, 1980.

OTHER SOURCES:

PERIODICALS

People, April 30. 1990, p. 27.*

* * *

LEACOCK, Philip 1917-1990

PERSONAL: Born October 8, 1917, in London, England; died July 14, 1990, in London; married; (second marriage) Carolyn Slater; children: Jonathan, Rebecca; (previous marriage) Timothy, Louisa. *Avocational interests:* Environmental issues.

CAREER: Producer and director.

MEMBER: Sierra Club, Temescal Canyon Association, Citizen's Commission on State Parks.

CREDITS:

FILM DIRECTOR, EXCEPT WHERE INDICATED

Life in Her Hands, United Artists (UA), 1951.
The Brave Don't Cry, Associated British Films, 1952.
Appointment in London, British Lion, 1953.
The Little Kidnappers (also known as *The Kidnappers*), UA, 1954.
Escapade, Eros, 1955.
High Tide at Noon, J. Arthur Rank, 1957.
The Spanish Gardener, J. Arthur Rank, 1957.
Innocent Sinners, J. Arthur Rank, 1958.
The Rabbit Trap, UA, 1959.
Take a Giant Step, UA, 1959.
Hand in Hand, Columbia, 1960.
Let No Man Write My Epitaph, Columbia, 1960.
Thirteen West Street, Columbia, 1962.
The War Lover, Columbia, 1962.
Reach for Glory, Columbia, 1963.
Tamahine, Metro-Goldwyn-Mayer, 1964.
Producer, *Firecreek,* Warner Brothers, 1968.
Adam's Woman (also known as *Return of the Boomerang*), Warner Brothers, 1972.

Also director of documentaries during the 1940s, including *Island People* (with Paul Rotha): *The Story of Wool; Out of True;* and *Festival in London.*

TELEVISION DIRECTOR; MOVIES

The Birdmen, ABC, 1971.
When Michael Calls, ABC, 1972.
Dying Room Only, ABC, 1973.
The Great Man's Whiskers, NBC, 1973.
Killer on Board, NBC, 1977.
The Curse of King Tut's Tomb, NBC, 1980.
Angel City, CBS, 1980.
The Two Lives of Carol Letner, CBS, 1981.
"Three Sovereigns for Sarah," *American Playhouse,* PBS, 1985.

TELEVISION DIRECTOR; PILOTS

The Daughters of Joshua Cabe, ABC, 1972.
(And producer), *Baffled!,* NBC, 1973.
Key West, NBC, 1973.
Wild and Wooley, ABC, 1978.
Heaven on Earth, NBC, 1981.
The Wild Women of Chastity Gulch, ABC, 1982.
(With others) *Finder of Lost Loves,* ABC, 1984.
Bridges to Cross, CBS, 1986.

TELEVISION WORK; SERIES

Executive producer (with Michael Garrison), *The Wild Wild West,* CBS, 1965-70.
Executive producer, *Cimarron Strip,* CBS, 1967-68, 1971.
Executive producer (with others), *Gunsmoke* (also see below), CBS, 1955-75.
Executive producer (with others), *Hawaii Five-O* (also see below), CBS, 1968-80.
Director (with John Erman) and producer, *The New Land,* ABC, 1974.
Director, *Born to the Wind* (also known as *Indians*), BBC, then NBC, 1982.

TELEVISION DIRECTOR; EPISODIC

Dirty Sally, CBS, 1974.
Kate Loves a Mystery, NBC, 1979.
Sweepstakes, NBC, 1979.
Little Women, NBC, 1979.

Also director of episodes of *Alfred Hitchcock Presents; Gunsmoke,* CBS; *Route 66,* CBS; *Hawaii Five-O,* CBS; *The Defenders,* CBS; *The Virginian,* NBC; *The FBI,* ABC; *The Mod Squad,* ABC; *The Men from Shiloh,* NBC; *The Waltons,* CBS; *Apple's Way,* CBS; *Family,* ABC; *Eight Is Enough,* ABC, 1977-81; *The Paper Chase,* CBS; *Fantasy Island,* ABC; *Buck Rogers in the 25th Century,* NBC; *Nurse,* CBS; *Dynasty,* ABC; and *Hotel,* ABC.

OBITUARIES AND OTHER SOURCES:

PERIODICALS

New York Times, July 21, 1990.
Variety, July 25, 1990.*

* * *

LEAN, David 1908-1991

OBITUARY NOTICE—See index for *CTFT* sketch: Born March 25, 1908, in Croydon, England; died April 16, 1991, in London, England. Film editor and director. Although the director of only sixteen movies, Lean is remembered as an important filmmaker distinguished by the scope and style of his work. Beginning his film career as an editor, he was invited by playwright Noel Coward in the early 1940s to codirect his *In Which We Serve,* considered by critics to be a classic war movie. Lean went on to successfully film adaptations of Coward's plays as well as adaptations of nineteenth-century author Charles Dickens's *Oliver Twist* and *Great Expectations.* He is best known for directing the epic films *Bridge on the River Kwai, Doctor Zhivago,* and *Lawrence of Arabia,* all made between 1957 and 1965. His last work was the 1984 *Passage to India,* and he had begun preparations for a film based on Joseph Conrad's novel *Nostromo.* Lean received Academy awards for *Bridge on the River Kwai* and *Lawrence of Arabia,* was knighted in 1984, and received the American Film Institute Life Achievement Award in 1990.

OBITUARIES AND OTHER SOURCES:

BOOKS

Anderegg, Michael A., *David Lean,* Twayne, 1984.
Who's Who in America, 46th edition, Marquis, 1990, p. 1936.

PERIODICALS

American Film, March 1990, pp. 20.
Hollywood Reporter, February 17, 1989, p. 12; March 12, 1990, pp. 1, 8; April 17, 1991, pp. 1, 7, 19, 21.
New York Times, October 17, 1989, p. C17.
Sunday Times (London), April 21, 1991.

* * *

LEE, Leslie 1935-

PERSONAL: Full name, Leslie E. Lee; born in 1935 in Bryn Mawr, PA. *Education:* University of Pennsylvania, B.A., biology and English; Villanova University, M.A., theatre.

CAREER: Playwright and author. Worked as a medical technician at Valley Forge Army Hospital, PA, and as a bacteriologist at the Pennsylvania State Department of Health; affiliated with La Mama E.T.C., New York City, 1969-70; College of Old Westbury, NY, instructor in playwriting, 1975-76; University of Pennsylvania, Philadelphia, playwright-in-residence, beginning in 1980; Frederick Douglass Creative Arts Center, NY, instructor in playwriting. New York State Council on the Arts, theatre panelist, 1982-84; Negro Ensemble Company, coordinator for playwriting workshop, 1985.

MEMBER: Writers Guild of America, Dramatists Guild.

AWARDS, HONORS: Rockefeller Foundation playwriting grant, 1966-68; Shubert Foundation playwriting grants, 1971 and 1972; Obie Award, best play, 1975, Antoinette Perry Award nomination, best play, 1976, Special Mention by Black Filmmakers, 1977, John Gassner Medallion for Playwriting, Outer Circle Critics, and Mississippi ETV Award, all for *The First Breeze of Summer;* Eugene O'Neill Playwriting Conference playwriting fellowship, 1980; National Endowment for the Humanities playwriting grant, 1982; Audience Development Committee (AUDELCO) Award nomination, best play, 1983, for *Colored People's Time;* first prize, National Black Film Consortium, 1984, for *The Killing Floor;* Isabelle Strickland Award for excellence in the fields of arts and human culture.

CREDITS:

STAGE WORK

Director, *Darkness, Fierce Winds,* American Folk Theatre, Theatre at Holy Name House, New York City, 1980.

WRITINGS:

PLAYS

Elegy to a Down Queen (two-act), produced at Cafe La Mama (now La Mama E.T.C.), New York City, 1969, musical version produced at La Mama E.T.C., 1972.

Cops and Robbers (one-act), produced at Cafe La Mama, 1970-71.

As I Lay Dying, a Victim of Spring, produced by New Dramatists, New York City, 1972.

The Night of the No-Moon, produced by New Dramatists, New York City, 1973.

The War Party, produced by New Dramatists, New York City, 1974.

Between Now and Then (two-act), produced by New Dramatists, New York City, 1975, published by Samuel French, 1984.

The First Breeze of Summer (two-act; also see below), produced by Negro Ensemble Company (NEC), St. Marks Playhouse, then Palace Theatre, both New York City, 1975, published by Samuel French, 1975.

The Book of Lambert, produced at Theatre at St. Clements, New York City, 1977.

Nothin' Comes Easy, produced at Village Gate Theatre, New York City, 1978.

(With June Carroll and Arthur Siegel) *Life, Love, and Other Minor Matters* (musical revue), produced at Village Gate Theatre, 1980.

Colored People's Time (two-act), produced by NEC, Cherry Lane Theatre, New York City, 1982, published by Samuel French, 1983.

Willie (two-act), produced by O'Neill Center's National Playwright's Conference, Waterford, CT, 1983.

(With Charles Strouse and Lee Adams) *Golden Boy* (revision of the 1964 musical), produced at Billie Holiday Theatre, Brooklyn, NY, 1984.

The Wig Lady, produced at Harold Clurman Theatre, New York City, 1984.

Phillis (musical; book by Lee, music and lyrics by Micki Grant), produced at Apollo Theatre, Harlem, NY, 1986.

Hannah Davis, produced at Crossroads Theatre, New Brunswick, NJ, 1987.

Martin Luther King, Jr. (musical biography for children), produced by Theatreworks/USA, Brooklyn Center for the Performing Arts, Brooklyn, 1987.
Black Eagles, produced at Crossroads Theatre, c. 1989.
Ground People (two-act; with music), produced at American Place Theatre, New York City, 1990.

Also author of *Killing Time* (with music), produced at Village Gate Theatre.

TELEVISION PLAYS; EPISODIC

"Almos' a Man" (adapted from the story by Richard Wright), *The American Short Story,* PBS, 1977.
"The Killing Floor," *American Playhouse,* PBS, 1984.

Author of the script "Langston Hughes," PBS, c. 1986.

TELEVISION SERIES

Summer Father, shown on *Vegetable Soup* series, PBS, 1978.
Another World, NBC, 1982-83.

TELEVISION SPECIALS

Voices and Visions (documentary), PBS, 1988.

SCREENPLAYS

(With Gus Edwards) *Go Tell It on the Mountain* (adaptation of the novel by James Baldwin), Learning in Focus, 1984.

OTHER

The Day after Tomorrow (novella), Scholastic Book Services, 1974.

Also author of the novella *Never the Time and Place,* 1985.

ADAPTATIONS: The First Breeze of Summer was filmed for the PBS series *Great Performances,* 1976.*

* * *

LEE, William
See BURROUGHS, William S.

* * *

Le GALLIENNE, Eva 1899-1991

OBITUARY NOTICE—See index for *CTFT* sketch: Born January 11, 1899, in London, England; died of heart failure, June 3, 1991, in Weston, CT. Actress, producer, director, and writer. One of the premiere celebrities of the American theater, Le Gallienne made her Broadway debut in 1915 and gained widespread recognition six years later for her performance as Julie in *Liliom.* "Considered by many the country's prime devotee of classical drama," wrote Burt A. Folkart in the *Los Angeles Times,* "she believed that plays, like books, should be plentiful and convenient." In 1926, Le Gallienne founded the Civic Repertory Theatre, conceived as a national theater to rival England's Old Vic; she directed thirty-two plays before the company folded in 1933. Later, with two other actresses, she created the short-lived American Repertory Company. She received an Academy Award nomination for her role in the film *Resurrection* and won an Emmy Award for a television production of *The Royal Family,* a play loosely based on the Barrymores. Her last stage appearance was as the White Queen in the 1982 Broadway revival of the stage musical *Alice in Wonderland.* In 1986, President Ronald Reagan awarded her the National Medal of Arts. Her writings include two volumes of memoirs, a children's book, a translation of *Seven Tales by Hans Christian Andersen,* and a biography of Eleanor Duse, *The Mystic in the Theatre.*

OBITUARIES AND OTHER SOURCES:

BOOKS

Who's Who, 143rd edition, St. Martin's, 1991.

PERIODICALS

Chicago Tribune, June 5, 1991, section 1, p. 10.
Los Angeles Times, June 5, 1991, p. A18.
New York Times, June 5, 1991, p. B6.
Times (London), June 10, 1991, p. 16.
Variety, June 10, 1991, p. 86.
Washington Post, June 6, 1991, p. B6.

* * *

LEIGH-HUNT, Barbara 1935-

PERSONAL: Born December 14, 1935, in Bath, England; daughter of Chandos Austin and Elizabeth (Jones) Leigh-Hunt; married Richard Pasco (an actor), November 18, 1967; stepchildren: William. *Education:* Studied at Bristol Old Vic Theatre School, 1952-54.

ADDRESSES: Contact—Michael Whitehall Ltd., 125 Gloucester Rd., London SW7 4TE, England.

CAREER: Actress. Governor and associate artist with Royal Shakespeare Company.

MEMBER: Theatrical Ladies Guild, Royal Theatrical Fund (member of board).

AWARDS, HONORS: Bristol *Evening Post* Award to most promising student, 1953; Clarence Derwent Award for best supporting actress, 1980, for portrayal of Gertrude in *Hamlet.*

CREDITS:

STAGE APPEARANCES

The Merry Gentleman, Bristol Old Vic, 1953.

A Midsummer Night's Dream (also see below), Old Vic company, Edinburgh Festival, 1954, then Metropolitan Opera House, New York City, 1954.

Portia, *The Merchant of Venice,* Old Vic company, c. 1959-60.

Helena, *A Midsummer Night's Dream,* Old Vic company, c. 1959-60.

Maria, *Twelfth Night,* Old Vic company, c. 1959-60.

Viola, *Twelfth Night,* Nottingham Playhouse, London, 1962.

Beatrice, *Much Ado about Nothing,* Bristol Old Vic Repertory Company, 1963.

Rosemary, *A Severed Head,* Bristol Old Vic Repertory Company, Theatre Royal, then Criterion Theatre, London, 1963.

Kate Hardcastle, *She Stoops to Conquer,* Bath Festival, 1965.

Hedda, *Hedda Gabler,* Bristol Old Vic, 1966.

Isabella, *Measure for Measure* (also see below), Bristol Old Vic Repertory Company, Theatre Royal, then City Center Theatre, New York City, 1967.

Ophelia, *Hamlet* (also see below), Bristol Old Vic Repertory Company, Theatre Royal, then City Center Theatre, 1967.

Anita Hill, *Mrs. Mouse, Are You Within?,* Bristol Old Vic Repertory Company, Duke of York's Theatre, London, 1968.

Maggie, *The Formation Dancers,* Hampstead Theatre Club, London, 1971.

Don Juan in Love, Edinburgh Festival, 1973.

Amanda, *Private Lives,* Bristol Theatre, 1973.

Madge Larrabee, *Sherlock Holmes,* Royal Shakespeare Company (RSC), Aldwych Theatre, London, 1974, then at Broadhurst Theatre, New York City, 1974-75.

Krupskaya (Lenin's Wife), *Travesties,* RSC, Aldwych Theatre, 1974.

The Grand Tour, Brighton Festival, 1975.

Mistress Ford, *The Merry Wives of Windsor,* Stratford Theatre, London, 1975, then Aldwych Theatre, 1976.

Queen Elizabeth, *Richard III,* The Other Place Theatre, 1975.

Helen, *Troilus and Cressida,* Stratford Theatre, 1976.

Paulina, *The Winter's Tale,* Stratford Theatre, 1976.

Teacher, *Every Good Boy Deserves Favour,* Royal Festival Hall, 1977.

Orbison, *That Good between Us,* Warehouse Theatre, London, 1977.

Arkadina, *The Seagull,* Bristol Theatre, 1978.

Gertrude, *Hamlet,* Stratford Theatre, c. 1980.

Queen Margaret, *Richard III,* Stratford Theatre, c. 1980.

The Hollow Crown, RSC, Fortune Theatre, London, 1981.

Pleasure and Repentance, Fortune Theatre, 1981.

Raissa Pavlovna Goormizhaskaya, *The Forest,* RSC, Warehouse Theatre, 1981.

Hamlet, RSC, Aldwych Theatre, 1981.

Queen Margaret, *Richard III,* RSC, Aldwych Theatre, 1981-82.

The actress, *La Ronde,* RSC, Aldwych Theatre, 1982.

The Forest, RSC, Aldwych Theatre, 1982.

Helen Kroger, *Pack of Lies,* Lyric Theatre, London, 1983.

Big Mama, *Cat on a Hot Tin Roof,* Lyttleton Theatre, London, 1988.

The Vinegar Fly, Soho Polytechnic Theatre, London, 1988.

Mrs. Voysey, *The Voysey Inheritance,* Cottesloe Theatre, London, 1989.

Heather Espy, *Racing Demon,* National Theatre Company, Cottesloe Theatre, 1990.

Lady Hunstanton, *A Woman of No Importance,* Barbican Theatre, 1991.

Also appeared as Bet Bouncer, *She Stoops to Conquer,* 1960; Belvidera, *Venice Preserv'd,* 1970; Goneril, *King Lear,* 1977; and Ann, *Canaries Sometimes Sing,* 1979. Appeared with Bristol Old Vic Repertory Company as Lady Macbeth, *Macbeth;* and The Woman, *Don Juan in Love.* Also appeared in *Bartholemew Fair,* Olivier Theatre. Performed at Lowestoft and Colwyn Bay, 1955-56; toured Europe and performed in minor roles with Old Vic company, 1957-58; performed at Guilford Repertory Theatre, 1959; performed with Bristol Old Vic Repertory Company, 1963-69, and Royal Shakespeare Company, 1975-77; performed extensive anthology work at major festivals; appeared with Medici Quartet as narrator.

MAJOR TOURS

Rosaline, *Love's Labour's Lost,* Bristol Old Vic Repertory Company, Israeli and European cities, 1964.

Title role, *Saint Joan,* Bristol Old Vic Repertory Company, United Kingdom cities, 1965.

Victoria, *Portrait of a Queen,* United Kingdom cities, 1966.

Lady Hunstanton, *A Woman of No Importance,* United Kingdom cities, 1992.

Appeared in major North American tours with Old Vic company in *A Midsummer Night's Dream* and with Bristol Old Vic company as Isabella in *Measure for Measure* and Ophelia in *Hamlet.* Appeared as the Mayoress, *Getting Married,* United Kingdom cities.

FILM APPEARANCES

Helena, *A Midsummer Night's Dream,* Showcorporation, 1961.

Brenda Blaney, *Frenzy,* Universal, 1972.

Catherine Parr, *Henry VIII and His Six Wives,* Metro-Goldwyn-Mayer-EMI, 1972.
Catherine Matcham, *The Nelson Affair* (also known as *Bequest to the Nation*), Universal, 1973.
Margaret, *Oh, Heavenly Dog!,* Twentieth Century-Fox, 1980.
Queen Mother, *Wagner,* Alan Landsburg, 1983.
Voice of Farmer's Wife, *The Plague Dogs* (animated), United International, c. 1984.

Also appeared as Celia Mumford, *Paper Mask,* 1990.

TELEVISION APPEARANCES

Isabel Arundell Burton, *Search for the Nile* (documentary), NBC, 1972.
Jean Lawrence, *Tumbledown* (movie), Arts & Entertainment, 1990.
Blanche Copley-Barnes, *The Infernal Serpent* (also known as *Inspector Morse, Series IV* and *Mystery!*), PBS, 1991.

Also appeared in *The Brontes, Cold Feet, Every Good Boy Deserves Favour, Macbeth, Mary's Wife, Mrs. Mouse, Are You Within?, One Chance in Four,* and *A Perfect Hero.*

RADIO APPEARANCES

Has performed extensively on radio.

RECORDINGS:

Has performed on numerous albums and audiocassettes.

* * *

LEISURE, David 1950(?)-

PERSONAL: Born c. 1950, in San Diego, CA; married wife, Kelly; children: Maya. *Education:* Studied drama at Grossmont College and San Diego State University.

ADDRESSES: Agent—Harris & Goldberg, 1999 Avenue of the Stars, Suite 2850, Los Angeles, CA 90067; J. Carter Gibson Agency, 9000 Sunset Blvd., Suite 801, Los Angeles, CA 90069.

CAREER: Actor. Appeared in numerous award-winning television commercials.

MEMBER: Screen Actors Guild.

CREDITS:

TELEVISION APPEARANCES; SERIES

Charley, *Empty Nest,* NBC, 1988—.

TELEVISION APPEARANCES; MOVIES

Andrew Selsky, *If It's Tuesday, It Still Must Be Belgium,* NBC, 1987.
Jimmy, *The Goddess of Love,* NBC, 1988.
Derek, *Perfect People,* ABC, 1988.
Newscaster/host, *Mother Goose Rock 'n' Rhyme,* Disney, 1990.

TELEVISION APPEARANCES; SPECIALS

Policeman, *Wait until Dark,* HBO, 1982.
NBC Presents the American Film Institute Comedy Special, NBC, 1987.
The 14th Annual Circus of the Stars, CBS, 1989.
The 4th Annual American Comedy Awards, ABC, 1990.
Host, *Live! The World's Greatest Stunts,* Fox, 1990.
Host, *The World's Funniest, Cleverest, Most Imaginative Commercials,* CBS, 1990.
Tube Test Two, ABC, 1991.

TELEVISION APPEARANCES; EPISODIC

Host, "All-American Sports Nuts" (also known as "The All-American Sports Comedy Hour"), *The Magical World of Disney,* NBC, 1988.
Mark's replacement, "Championship Game," *First in Ten: In Your Face!,* HBO, 1990.
Super Bloopers and New Practical Jokes, NBC, 1990.

Also appeared as co-host in the syndicated *Hour Magazine;* in NBC's *Alf* and *227;* ABC's *Sledge Hammer!;* and *Super Password.*

OTHER TELEVISION APPEARANCES

Appeared in more than sixty television commercials, including the role of Joe Isuzu, the spokesperson for Isuzu cars and trucks, and as Joe Friday, for Bell Atlantic Yellow Pages.

FILM APPEARANCES

First Krishna, *Airplane!,* Paramount, 1980.
Religious zealot, *Airplane II: The Sequel,* Paramount, 1982.
Peter Newcomb, *You Can't Hurry Love,* Lightning, 1988.

STAGE APPEARANCES

Appeared on stage in Off-Broadway and California productions, including Emery in *Boys in the Band,* San Diego, 1972, and *Richard III,* Old Globe Theatre, San Diego.

OTHER SOURCES:

PERIODICALS

Daily News (New York), January 28, 1988.
New York Newsday, October 31, 1988.
People, November 10, 1986.*

LEONARD, Elmore 1925-

PERSONAL: Full name, Elmore John Leonard, Jr.; born October 11 (one source says October 29), 1925, in New Orleans, LA; son of Elmore John (in sales) and Flora Amelia (Rive) Leonard; married Beverly Cline, July (one source says August) 30, 1949 (divorced May 24, 1977); married Joan Shephard, September 15, 1979; children: (first marriage) Jane Jones, Peter, Christopher, William, Katherine. *Education:* University of Detroit, Ph.B., 1950. *Religion:* Roman Catholic.

ADDRESSES: Agent—H. N. Swanson, 8523 Sunset Blvd., Los Angeles, CA 90069.

CAREER: Writer. Campbell-Ewald Advertising Agency, Detroit, MI, copywriter, 1950-61; free-lance copywriter and author of educational and industrial films, 1961-63; affiliated with Elmore Leonard Advertising Company, 1963-66. *Military service:* U.S. Naval Reserve, 1943-46.

MEMBER: Writers Guild of America, Mystery Writers of America, Western Writers of America, Authors League of America, Authors Guild.

AWARDS, HONORS: Hombre was named one of the twenty-five best western novels of all time by the Western Writers of America, 1977; Edgar Allan Poe Award, Mystery Writers of America, 1983, for *LaBrava;* Literary Lions award, New York Public Library, 1989.

CREDITS:

TELEVISION WORK; MOVIES

Creator, *Desperado: Badlands Justice,* NBC, 1989.

WRITINGS:

SCREENPLAYS

The Moonshine War (based on the novel by Leonard; also see below), Metro-Goldwyn-Mayer, 1970.
Joe Kidd, Universal, 1972.
Mr. Majestyk (based on the novel by Leonard; also see below), United Artists, 1974.
(With Joseph C. Stinson) *Stick* (based on the novel by Leonard; also see below), Universal, 1985.
(With John Steppling) *Fifty-two Pick-Up* (based on the novel by Leonard; also see below), Cannon, 1986.
(With Fred Walton) *The Rosary Murders* (based on the novel by William X. Kienzle), New Line Cinema, 1987.

Author, with Joe Borrelli and Alan Sharp, of *Cat Chaser* (based on the novel by Leonard; also see below), 1989; also author of film scripts for Encyclopaedia Brittanica Films, including "Settlement of the Mississippi Valley," "Boy of Spain," "Frontier Boy," and "Julius Caesar"; author of a recruiting film for the Franciscans.

TELEVISION MOVIES

High Noon, Part Two: The Return of Will Kane, CBS, 1980.
Desperado, NBC, 1987.

WESTERN NOVELS

The Bounty Hunters, Houghton, 1953.
The Law at Randado (also see below), Houghton, 1955.
Escape from Five Shadows, Houghton, 1956.
Last Stand at Saber River, Dell, 1957, published in England as *Lawless River,* R. Hale, 1959, and as *Stand on the Saber,* Corgi, 1960.
Hombre (also see below), Ballantine, 1961.
Valdez Is Coming (also see below), Gold Medal, 1970.
Forty Lashes Less One, Bantam, 1972.
Gunsights, Bantam, 1979.

CRIME NOVELS

The Big Bounce (also see below), Gold Medal, 1969, revised edition, Armchair Detective, 1989.
The Moonshine War (also see below), Doubleday, 1969.
Mr. Majestyk (also see below), Dell, 1974.
Fifty-two Pick-Up (also see below), Delacorte, 1974.
Swag (also see below), Delacorte, 1976, published as *Ryan's Rules,* Dell, 1976.
Unknown Man, No. 89, Delacorte, 1977.
The Hunted (also see below), Dell, 1977.
The Switch, Bantam, 1978.
City Primeval: High Noon in Detroit (also see below), Arbor House, 1980.
Gold Coast (also see below), Bantam, 1980, revised edition, 1985.
Split Images, Arbor House, 1981.
Cat Chaser, Arbor House, 1982.
Stick, Arbor House, 1983.
LaBrava, Arbor House, 1983.
Glitz (also see below), Arbor House, 1985.
Bandits, Arbor House, 1987.
Touch, Arbor House, 1987.
Freaky Deaky, Morrow, 1988.
Killshot, Morrow, 1989.
Get Shorty, Delacorte, 1990.

OMNIBUS VOLUMES

Elmore Leonard's Dutch Treat (contains *The Hunted, Swag,* and *Mr. Majestyk*), introduction by George F. Will, Arbor House, 1985.
Elmore Leonard's Double Dutch Treat (contains *City Primeval: High Noon in Detroit, The Moonshine War,* and *Gold Coast*), introduction by Bob Greene, Arbor House, 1986.

OTHER

Notebooks, Lord John, 1990.

Also author of *Eight Black Horses,* Mysterious Press. Contributor to *The Courage to Change: Personal Conversations about Alcoholism,* edited by Dennis Wholey, Houghton, 1984. Contributor of short stories and novelettes, including "3:10 to Yuma" and "The Tall T" (also see below), to periodicals, including *Dime Western, Argosy, Saturday Evening Post,* and *Zane Grey's Western Magazine.*

ADAPTATIONS: "3:10 to Yuma" was adapted for film by Halsted Welles and released by Columbia, 1957; "The Tall T" was adapted for film by Burt Kennedy and released by Columbia, 1957; *Hombre* was adapted for film by Irving Ravetch and Harriet Frank and released by Twentieth Century-Fox, 1967; *The Big Bounce* was adapted for film by Robert Dozier and released by Warner Brothers, 1969; *Valdez Is Coming* was adapted for film by Roland Kibbee and David Rayfiel and released by United Artists, 1971; *Fifty-Two Pick-Up* was adapted for film by Max Jack and released as *The Ambassador* by Cannon, 1984; *Glitz* was filmed for television by NBC, 1988; *The Law at Randado* was adapted for film and released as *Border Shootout* by Turner Home Entertainment, 1990.

OTHER SOURCES:

BOOKS

Bestsellers 89, Issue 1, Gale, 1989, p. 42.

Contemporary Authors New Revision Series, Volume 28, Gale, 1990, p. 282.

Contemporary Literary Criticism, Gale, Volume 28, 1984, p. 233; Volume 34, 1985, p. 212.

PERIODICALS

New York Times, December 30, 1984.*

* * *

LEWIS, Joseph H. 1900(?)-

PERSONAL: Born April 6, 1900 (one source says 1907), in New York, NY.

CAREER: Editor and director. Began as camera boy for Metro-Goldwyn-Mayer; worked as an assistant editor for Republic Pictures, in charge of film editing; became director in charge of second units for Universal Studios. *Military service:* Served in U.S. Signal Corps, during World War II.

MEMBER: Directors Guild of America.

CREDITS:

FILM WORK; EDITOR

(With Ray Curtis) *Harmony Lane,* Republic, 1935.
The Headline Woman, Mascot, 1935.
Ladies Crave Excitement, Mascot, 1935.
Streamline Express, Republic, 1935.
One Frightened Night, Mascot, 1935.
The Devil on Horseback, Grand National, 1936.
(With Lester Orlebeck) *King of the Pecos,* Republic, 1936.
(With Murray Seldeen) *Laughing Irish Eyes,* Republic, 1936.

FILM WORK; DIRECTOR, EXCEPT WHERE INDICATED

Courage of the West, Universal, 1937.
Singing Outlaw, Universal, 1937.
Border Wolves, Universal, 1938.
The Last Stand, Universal, 1938.
The Spy Ring (also known as *International Spy*), Universal, 1938.
Blazing Six Shooters (released in England as *Stolen Wealth*), Columbia, 1940.
Boys of the City (also known as *The Ghost Creeps*), Monogram, 1940.
The Man from Tumbleweeds, Columbia, 1940.
The Return of Wild Bill, Columbia, 1940.
Texas Stagecoach (released in England as *Two Roads*), Columbia, 1940.
That Gang of Mine, Monogram, 1940.
Two-Fisted Rangers, Columbia, 1940.
Arizona Cyclone, Universal, 1941.
The Invisible Ghost, Monogram, 1941.
Pride of the Bowery, Monogram, 1941.
Criminals Within, Producers Releasing Corporation, 1941.
The Boss of Hangtown Mesa, Universal, 1942.
Bombs over Burma, Producers Releasing Corporation, 1942.
The Mad Doctor of Market Street, Universal, 1942.
Secrets of a Co-Ed (released in England as *Silent Witness*), Producers Releasing Corporation, 1942.
The Silver Bullet, Universal, 1942.
Minstrel Man, Producers Releasing Corporation, 1944.
The Falcon in San Francisco, RKO Radio Pictures, 1945.
My Name is Julia Ross, Columbia, 1945.
(Director of choreography sequences) *The Jolson Story,* Columbia, 1946.
So Dark the Night, Columbia, 1946.
The Swordsman, Columbia, 1947.
The Return of October, Columbia, 1948.
The Undercover Man, Columbia, 1949.
Gun Crazy (also known as *Deadly Is the Female*), United Artists (UA), 1949.
A Lady without Passport, Metro-Goldwyn-Mayer (MGM), 1950.
Retreat, Hell, Warner Brothers, 1952.
Desperate Search, MGM, 1952.
Cry of the Hunted, MGM, 1953.
The Big Combo, Allied Artists, 1955.

A Lawless Street, Columbia, 1955.
Seventh Calvalry, Columbia, 1956.
The Halliday Brand, UA, 1957.
Terror in a Texas Town, UA, 1958.

Made directorial debut on *Navy Spy,* 1937, sharing the credit with Crane Wilbur. Also directed *The Last Stand,* 1938.

TELEVISION WORK; EPISODIC DIRECTOR

Alcoa/Goodyear Theater, NBC, 1958-60.
The Rifleman, ABC, 1958-63.
The Detectives, ABC, 1959-61 (thirty minute episodes), and 1961-62 (sixty minute episodes).
The Defenders, CBS, 1961-65.
The Investigators, CBS, 1961.
The Dick Powell Show, NBC, 1961-63.
Branded, NBC, 1965-66.
The Big Valley, ABC, 1965-69.

Contributed to *The Barbara Stanwyck Show.**

* * *

LEWIS, Richard 1949(?)-

PERSONAL: Born June 29, c. 1949, in Brooklyn, NY (one source says New Jersey); son of Bill (a caterer) and Blanche (an actress) Lewis. *Education:* Ohio State University, degree in marketing, 1970.

ADDRESSES: Contact—9200 Sunset Blvd., No. 428, Los Angeles, CA 90069.

CAREER: Comedian, actor, writer. Copywriter in a New Jersey advertising agency, c. 1970-71; stand-up comedian at nightclubs in New York City, Las Vegas, NV, Atlantic City, NJ, and elsewhere, 1971—.

AWARDS, HONORS: Cited on *GQ*'s Twentieth Century's Most Influential Humorists list.

CREDITS:

TELEVISION APPEARANCES; SPECIALS

Richard Lewis: I'm in Pain (comedy), Showtime, 1985.
Comic Relief, HBO, *I,* c. 1987, *III,* 1989, *IV,* 1990.
Joey, *King of the Building* (comedy pilot), CBS, 1987.
Richard Lewis: I'm Exhausted (comedy), HBO, 1988.
An All-Star Toast to the Improv, HBO, 1988.
Montreal International Comedy Festival, HBO, 1989.
Two Years . . . Later (interview), NBC, 1990.
The World of Jewish Humor (documentary), PBS, 1990.
Richard Lewis: I'm Doomed (comedy), HBO, 1990.
Host, *The Fourteenth Annual Young Comedians Show,* HBO, 1991.
Host, *An American Saturday Night,* ABC, 1991.
George Burns' Ninety-fifth Birthday Party, CBS, 1991.
Here He Is. . . the One, the Only. . . Groucho (documentary), HBO, 1991.
Host, *Living against the Odds* (also see below), PBS, 1991.

Has appeared on *Life's Most Embarrassing Moments,* 1988, *Salute to The Improv,* HBO, and *No Life to Live,* HBO; has also appeared on numerous awards programs, including *The Annual People's Choice Awards, The Primetime Emmy Awards Presentation,* and *The Annual ACE Awards.*

TELEVISION APPEARANCES; SERIES

Richard, *Harry,* ABC, 1987.
Marty Gold, *Anything but Love,* ABC, beginning in 1989.

Has made more than forty guest appearances on *The David Letterman Show,* NBC, 1982—.

FILM APPEARANCES

Richard, *The Wrong Guys,* New World, 1988.
Pimples, *That's Adequate* (satire), South Gate Entertainment, 1989.

Also appeared in *Diary of a Young Comic* (also see below), 1979, and *Once Upon a Crime,* 1992.

WRITINGS:

(Coauthor) *Living against the Odds* (television script), PBS, 1991.

Coauthor of screenplay *Diary of a Young Comic,* 1979; writer for *The Steve Landesberg Television Show,* NBC, 1983.

OTHER SOURCES:

PERIODICALS

GQ, July, 1990, p. 148.
People, June 20, 1988, p. 103.*

* * *

LIGHT, Judith 1949(?)-

PERSONAL: Full name, Judith Ellen Light; born February 9, c. 1949, in Trenton, NJ; daughter of Sidney (an accountant) and Pearl Sue (a model; maiden name, Hollander) Light; married Robert Desiderio, 1985. *Education:* Carnegie-Mellon University, B.F.A., drama, 1970.

ADDRESSES: Agent—International Creative Management, 8899 Beverly Blvd., Los Angeles, CA 90048.

CAREER: Actress. United Service Organizations (USO), member of European tour, 1968; California Shakespeare Festival, member of company, 1969; Milwaukee Repertory Theatre, Milwaukee, WI, member of company, 1970-72, guest artist, 1972-73; Seattle Repertory Theatre, Seattle, WA, member of company, 1972-73; Milwaukee Repertory Theatre, member of company, 1973-74.

MEMBER: Screen Actors Guild, Actors' Equity, AFTRA.

AWARDS, HONORS: Emmy Awards, best actress in a daytime drama, 1980 and 1981, Soapy Awards, best actress, 1980 and 1981, and Hall of Fame Award, *Daytime TV,* 1981, all for *One Life to Live.*

CREDITS:

TELEVISION APPEARANCES; SERIES

Karen Wolek, *One Life to Live,* ABC, 1977-82.
Angela Bower, *Who's the Boss?,* ABC, 1984—.

TELEVISION APPEARANCES; MOVIES

Marsha Sarno, *Intimate Agony,* ABC, 1983.
Cathy Proctor, *Dangerous Affection* (also known as *Stamp of a Killer*), NBC, 1987.
Vicki Vine, *My Boyfriend's Back,* NBC, 1989.
Jeanne White, *The Ryan White Story,* ABC, 1989.
Laura Simmons, *In Defense of a Married Man,* ABC, 1990.
Marie Hilley, *Wife, Mother, Murderer,* ABC, 1991.

TELEVISION APPEARANCES; EPISODIC

"Monkey on a String," *Kojak,* CBS, 1977.
"Dog Day Hospital," *St. Elsewhere,* NBC, 1983.
Stacey, "Not an Affair to Remember," *Family Ties,* NBC, 1983.
Mississippi, CBS, 1984.
"Dreams of Steele," *Remington Steele,* NBC, 1984.
Famous People/Private Lives, syndicated, 1989.

TELEVISION APPEARANCES; SPECIALS

The Love Boat Fall Preview Party, ABC, 1984.
The 37th Annual Prime Time Emmy Awards, ABC, 1985.

TELEVISION APPEARANCES; PILOTS

Elizabeth Harding, *You Are the Jury,* NBC, 1984.

STAGE APPEARANCES

Helene, *A Doll's House,* Vivian Beaumont Theatre, New York City, 1974.
Stella, *A Streetcar Named Desire,* Theatre Plus, Toronto, Ontario, 1975.
Stag at Bay, Hartman Theatre, Stamford, CT, 1975.
Understudy, *Jesse and the Bandit Queen,* New York Shakespeare Festival (NYSF), Public Theatre, New York City, 1975-76.
Julie Herzl, *Herzl,* Palace Theatre, New York City, 1976.
Francisca, *Measure for Measure,* NYSF, Delacorte Theater, New York City, 1976.

Also starred in Milwaukee Repertory production of *Our Town,* Seattle Repertory production of *Camino Real,* Eugene O'Neill Playwrights Foundation production of *Uncommon Women and Others,* a U.S.O. production of *Guys and Dolls,* and, in 1976, a New York City production of *The Seagull.*

OTHER SOURCES:

PERIODICALS

People, November 16, 1981, p. 70.

* * *

LINNEY, Romulus 1930-

PERSONAL: Born September 21, 1930, in Philadelphia, PA; son of Romulus Zachariah and Maitland Thompson (Clabaugh) Linney; married Ann Leggett Sims, April 14, 1963 (divorced, 1966); married Margaret Jane Andrews (an actress), September 14, 1967; children: (first marriage) Laura; (second marriage) Susan. *Education:* Oberlin College, A.B., 1953; Yale School of Drama, M.F.A., 1958; attended New School of New York City, 1960. *Avocational interests:* The arts and sports, especially water sports.

ADDRESSES: Agent—Gilbert Parker, William Morris Agency, 1350 Avenue of the Americas, New York, NY 10019.

CAREER: Writer and director. Six summers of professional equity stock as actor and director; Actors' Studio, New York City, stage manager, 1960; University of North Carolina at Chapel Hill, visiting associate professor of dramatic arts, 1961; North Carolina State College, Raleigh, director of fine arts, beginning in 1962; Manhattan School of Music, Manhattan, NY, faculty member, 1964-72. Visiting professor at institutions, including Columbia University, 1972-74; Connecticut College, 1979; University of Pennsylvania, 1979-86; and Princeton University, 1982-85. *Military service:* U.S. Army, 1954-56.

MEMBER: Authors League of America, Authors Guild, PEN, Directors Guild, Actor's Equity Association.

AWARDS, HONORS: Grant from National Endowment for the Arts, 1974; Guggenheim fellow, 1980; Obie Award, for playwriting, *Village Voice,* 1980, for *Tennessee;* Mishma Prize, fiction, 1981; Academy-Institute Award, for literature, American Academy and Institute of Arts and Letters, 1984; Rockefeller fellow, 1986.

CREDITS:

STAGE WORK; DIRECTOR

Holy Ghosts (also see below), Alley Theatre, Houston, TX, 1982-83.
Sand Mountain Matchmaking (also see below), Henry St. Settlement Theatre, 1989.

Director for *F.M.* (also see below), produced in Philadelphia, PA, 1982.

WRITINGS:

STAGE PLAYS

The Sorrows of Frederick (also see below), published by Harcourt, 1966, produced at Mark Taper Forum Theatre, Los Angeles, 1967; one-act version, produced at Actors Theatre of Louisville, Louisville, KY, as part of anthology *'84 Shorts,* 1984-1985.
Democracy and Esther (also see below), produced at H B Studio, 1969; produced as *Democracy* by Virginia Museum Theatre Repertory Company, Richmond, 1973-74, published as *Democracy* by Dramatists Play Service, 1976.
The Love Suicide at Schofield Barracks (also see below), produced at ANTA Theatre, New York City, 1972; one-act version, produced at Actors Theatre of Louisville, 1984-85, published in *The Best Short Plays 1986,* edited by Ramon Delgado, Applause, 1986.
Democracy and Esther [and] *The Love Suicide at Schofield Barracks,* published by Harcourt, 1973.
Two by Linney (contains the plays *The Seasons* and *Man's Estate*), produced by Equity Library Theatre, New York City, 1974.
Holy Ghosts (also see below), produced at Cubiculo Theatre, New York City, 1976, also produced at American Revels Company Theatre, Richmond, VA, 1979-80.
Childe Byron, produced by Virginia Museum Theatre Repertory Company, 1976-77, published by Dramatists Play Service, 1978; revised version produced at Circle Repertory Theatre, New York City, 1981.
Holy Ghosts [and] *The Sorrows of Frederick,* published by Harcourt, 1977.
Old Man Joseph and His Family, produced at Colonnades Theatre Lab, 1977-78, then at Chelsea Theatre Center, New York City, 1978, later at Chelsea Westside Theatre, New York City, 1978, published by Dramatists Play Service, 1978.
Tennessee (one-act; also see below), published by Dramatists Play Service, 1980.
El Hermano, published by Dramatists Play Service, 1981.
The Captivity of Pixie Shedman, produced at Marymount Manhattan Theatre, New York City, 1981, published by Dramatists Play Service, 1981.
April Snow, produced at South Coast Repertory Theatre, Costa Mesa, CA, 1982-83.
F.M. (also see below), produced in Philadelphia, PA, 1982, produced at Shandol Theatre, 1988.
The Death of King Philip, produced at Actors Theatre of Louisville as part of anthology *'83 Shorts,* 1983-84, published by Dramatists Play Service, 1984.
Laughing Stock (contains the plays *Goodbye, Howard, F.M.,* and *Tennessee*), produced at Lion Theatre, 1984, published by Dramatists Play Service, 1984.
Wrath (part of *The Show of the Seven Deadly Sins,* included in *Faustus in Hell* [adapted and directed by Nagle Jackson]), produced at McCarter Theatre, 1984-85.
A Woman without a Name, staged reading given at Denver Center Theatre Company, Denver, CO, as part of anthology *Primafacie I,* 1984-85, produced at Denver Center Theatre Company, 1985-86, published by Dramatists Play Service, 1986.
Sand Mountain (includes the one-act plays *Sand Mountain Matchmaking* [also see below] and *Why the Lord Come to Sand Mountain* [also see below]), produced at The Whole Theatre, Montclair, NJ, 1985-86, published by Dramatists Play Service, 1985.
Why the Lord Come to Sand Mountain, produced by Delaware Theatre Company, Wilmington, as part of *Christmas Mysteries,* 1986-87.
Pops, produced at The Whole Theatre, 1986-87, published by Dramatists Play Service, 1987.
April Snow, produced at City Center Theatre, New York City, 1988.
Juliet, produced at Ensemble Studio Theatre, New York City, 1988.
Heathen Valley (adapted from his novel of the same title; also see below), produced at Theater for the New City, New York City, 1988-89.
Precious Memories, produced at Milwaukee Repertory Theatre, Milwaukee, WI, 1988-89.
2 Plays, produced at Actors Theatre of Louisville, 1989-90.
Sand Mountain Matchmaking, produced at Henry St. Settlement Theatre, 1989.
Three Poets, produced at Theater for the New City, 1989.

Also author of *Just Folks,* 1978, *Yzucey,* 1988, and *Gardens of Eden.*

TELEVISION PLAYS

The Thirty-fourth Star, CBS, 1976.
Feelin' Good (series), PBS, 1976-77.

NOVELS

Heathen Valley, Atheneum, 1962.
Slowly, by Thy Hand Unfurled, Harcourt, 1965.
Jesus Tales, North Point Press, 1980.

EDITOR, WITH NORMAN A. BAILEY AND DOMENICK CASCIO

Ten Plays for Radio, Burgess, 1954.
Radio Classics, Burgess, 1956.

OTHER

Contributor to literary periodicals.

OTHER SOURCES:

PERIODICALS

New York Times, December 3, 1989, p. H5.*

* * *

LINSON, Art

PERSONAL: Born in Chicago, IL. *Education:* University of California, Los Angeles, LL.D., 1967.

ADDRESSES: Office—c/o Directors Guild of America, 110 West 57th St., New York, NY 10019.

CAREER: Producer and director. Rock music manager with Lou Adler; owner of Spin Dizzy (record company) prior to film career.

MEMBER: Directors Guild of America.

CREDITS:

FILM WORK; PRODUCER, EXCEPT WHERE INDICATED

(With Michael Gruskoff) *Rafferty and the Gold Dust Twins* (also known as *Rafferty and the Highway Hustlers*), Warner Brothers, 1975.
(With Gary Stromberg) *Car Wash,* Universal, 1976.
American Hot Wax, Paramount, 1978.
(With Don Phillips) *Melvin and Howard,* Universal, 1980.
(And director) *Where the Buffalo Roam,* Universal, 1980.
(With Irving Azoff) *Fast Times at Ridgemont High,* Universal, 1982.
(With Cameron Crowe and Don Phillips; and director) *The Wild Life,* Universal, 1984.
The Untouchables, Paramount, 1987.
(With Richard Donner and Ray Hartwick) *Scrooged,* Paramount, 1988.
(With Fred Caruso) *Casualties of War,* Columbia, 1989.
We're No Angels, Paramount, 1989.
Executive producer (with Barrie M. Osborne and Floyd Mutrux), *Dick Tracy,* Buena Vista, 1990.

Also worked on *Singles.*

TELEVISION APPEARANCES; SPECIALS

The New Hollywood, NBC, 1990.*

LLOYD, Michael 1948-

PERSONAL: Full name, Michael Jeffrey Lloyd; born November 3, 1948, in New York, NY; son of John Sutton and Suzanne Lloyd; married Patricia Ann Varble (a writer and artist), September 6, 1980; children: Michael, Christopher, Jeni, Deborah. *Education:* Attended the University of Southern California.

ADDRESSES: Office—12121 Wilshire Blvd., Suite 1041, Santa Monica, CA 90025.

CAREER: Composer, lyricist, producer, and actor. Vice-president of artists and repertoire for MGM Records, Inc., 1969-73; independent record producer, 1973—; president of Heaven Productions, 1975—, Michael Lloyd Productions, 1979—, and Taines-Lloyd Productions, 1984—. Has worked with numerous artists, including Barry Manilow, Belinda Carlisle, Eric Carmen, Stryper, The Monkees, Shaun Cassidy, and The Osmonds. Visiting professor at University of California, Los Angeles; guest lecturer at colleges, including Pepperdine College, and at conferences, including Music Publishers Forum and Billboard Gospel Music Forum.

MEMBER: American Society of Composers, Authors, and Publishers (ASCAP), American Federation of Musicians, National Association of Recording Arts and Sciences, American Federation of Television and Radio Artists, Screen Actors Guild.

AWARDS, HONORS: 43 Gold Album awards, 18 Platinum Album awards, 28 Gold and Platinum awards, 36 Chart Album awards, 78 Chart Single awards, 12 ASCAP awards, and 10 Broadcast Music Inc. awards.

CREDITS:

FILM WORK

Music director, *The Van,* Crown, 1977.
Song producer, *The North Avenue Irregulars* (also see below), Buena Vista, 1979.
Song producer, *Somewhere in Time,* Universal, 1980.
Song producer, *The Earthling* (also see below), Filmways, 1981.
Song producer, *Out of the Blue,* Discovery, 1982.
Producer (with Hal Taines), *Lovelines* (also see below), Tri-Star, 1984.
Music supervisor and song producer, *Dirty Dancing* (also see below), Vestron, 1987.
Co-producer, *The Garbage Pail Kids Movie* (also see below), Atlantic Entertainment Group, 1987.
Song producer, *Spaceballs,* Metro-Goldwyn-Mayer (MGM), 1987.
Song producer, *Date with an Angel,* De Laurentiis, 1987.
Song producer, *Teen Wolf Too,* Atlantic Releasing, 1987.
Song producer, *Mac and Me,* Orion, 1988.

Song producer, *Gleaming the Cube,* Twentieth Century-Fox, 1988.
Music supervisor, *The Iron Triangle* (also see below), Scotti Brothers, 1989.
Song producer, *Major League,* Paramount, 1989.
Song producer, *All Dogs Go to Heaven* (also see below), United Artists (UA), 1989.

Also worked as song producer for *Nights of the City,* New World.

FILM APPEARANCES

Strawberry Shortcake, *The North Avenue Irregulars,* Buena Vista, 1979.
Lloyd Sidewalk, *Lovelines,* Tri-Star, 1984.

TELEVISION WORK; SERIES

Song producer, *Joanie Loves Chachi* (also see below), ABC, 1982-83.
Song producer and music supervisor, *Dancin' to the Hits,* syndicated, 1986.
Music director, *The Spectacular World of Guinness Records* (also see below), syndicated, 1987.
Song producer, *Dirty Dancing* (also see below), CBS, 1988-89.

Also worked as music producer for *The Kidsongs TV Show* (also see below), 1987; and song producer for *The Hardy Boys, Happy Days,* and *Kids Inc.*

TELEVISION WORK; MOVIES

Music supervisor, *Kent State,* NBC, 1981.
Music supervisor, *Living Proof: The Hank Williams, Jr., Story,* NBC, 1983.
Song producer, *A Summer to Remember. . . ,* CBS, 1985.
Producer and music supervisor, *Swimsuit* (also see below), NBC, 1989.

TELEVISION WORK; SPECIALS

Worked on *ABC Funshine Saturday, Shaun Cassidy Special,* and *Leif Garrett Special.*

STAGE WORK

Music producer and recorder, *The Triumph of the Spider Monkey,* Los Angeles Theatre Center, Los Angeles, CA, 1985-86.

RECORDINGS:

Executive producer of *The Christmas Album—A Gift of Love,* 1990, and *The Christmas Album—A Gift of Hope,* 1991, both for Children's Hospital, Nationwide; also worked on children's audio and videocassettes, including *Kidsongs* video series, released by Warner Brothers/Viewmaster, *The Baby Album,* released by New Beginnings, and *Land of OZ,* released by Kushner/Locke.

WRITINGS:

FILM MUSIC

Composer, *The Pom Pom Girls,* Crown, 1976.
Composer, *The Earthling,* Filmways, 1981.
Score composer and song composer, *Beach Girls,* Crown, 1982.
Song composer, *If You Could See What I Hear,* Jensen Farley, 1982.
Song composer, *Heart Like a Wheel,* Twentieth Century-Fox, 1982.
Score composer and song composer, *Tough Enough,* Twentieth Century-Fox, 1983.
Composer (with John D'Andrea), *Savage Streets,* Motion Picture Marketing, 1984.
Score composer and song composer, *Tomboy,* Crown, 1985.
Composer of Latin dance music (with others), *Dirty Dancing,* Vestron, 1987.
Score composer and song composer, *The Garbage Pail Kids Movie,* Atlantic Entertainment Group, 1987.
Score composer and song composer, *Body-Slam,* De Laurentiis, 1987.
Composer and lyricist, *All Dogs Go to Heaven,* UA, 1989.
Composer, *The Iron Triangle,* Scotti Brothers, 1989.

Also composed music for *Amblin'.*

TELEVISION MUSIC; SERIES

Theme song composer, *Monty Nash,* syndicated, 1971.
Composer (with others), *Sigmund and the Sea Monsters,* NBC, 1973-75.
Composer (with others), *Land of the Lost,* NBC, 1974.
Composer (with Reg Powell), *Far Out Space Nuts,* CBS, 1975.
Composer, *Shipshape* (also see below), CBS, 1978.
Composer, *Me and Maxx,* NBC, 1980.
Song composer, *Joanie Loves Chachi,* ABC, 1982-83.
Composer, *The Spectacular World of Guinness Records,* syndicated, 1987.
Composer, *Dirty Dancing,* CBS, 1988-89.
Composer, *The Challengers,* syndicated, 1990.

Also composed music for the series *The Staff of Life,* 1985; *The Kidsongs TV Show,* 1987; *That's Incredible!,* ABC; *The David Viscott Show; Heroes—Made in the U.S.A.;* and *Dick Clark's Golden Greats.*

TELEVISION MUSIC; MOVIES

Composer (with John D'Andrea), *Love's Dark Ride,* NBC, 1978.
Composer (with D'Andrea), *Stranger in Our House,* NBC, 1978.
Composer (with D'Andrea), *Grambling's White Tiger,* NBC, 1981.

Composer (with D'Andrea), *Swimsuit,* NBC, 1989.

Also composed music for *Summer of Fear,* 1978.

OTHER TELEVISION MUSIC

Shipshape (pilot), CBS, 1978.

Also composed music (with others) for an episode of *Three's a Crowd,* ABC, 1984; and for the special *Ultimate Stuntman: A Tribute to Dar Robinson,* 1987.

STORIES ADAPTED INTO SCREENPLAYS

(With Chip Hand and William Hillman) *Lovelines,* by Hand and Hillman, Tri-Star, 1984.

* * *

LUCAS, Craig 1951-

PERSONAL: Born April 30, 1951, in Atlanta, GA; adopted son of Charles S. and Eleanore Lucas. *Education:* Boston University, B.F.A. (cum laude), 1973.

ADDRESSES: Agent—William Morris Agency, 1350 Avenue of the Americas, New York, NY 10019.

CAREER: Playwright and screenwriter.

MEMBER: Dramatists Guild (council member), Circle Repertory (New York City).

AWARDS, HONORS: George and Elisabeth Marton Award for Playwriting from Foundation of the Dramatists Guild, 1984-85, and Los Angeles Drama Critics Award for outstanding writing, 1985-86, both for *Blue Window;* Guggenheim fellow, 1987; Rockefeller fellow, 1989; Drama Desk Award nomination for best play, 1989, for *Reckless;* Audience Award for best dramatic film, Sundance U.S. Film Festival, 1990, for *Longtime Companion;* Antoinette Perry Award nomination for best play, Drama Desk Award nomination for best play, Outer Critics Circle Award for best new play, and Obie Award for best new play from *Village Voice,* all 1990, for *Prelude to a Kiss.*

WRITINGS:

STAGE PLAYS

(Conceiver and developer of concept with Norman Rene) *Marry Me a Little* (musical revue; songs written by Stephen Sondheim), produced at Production Company Theatre, 1980, then at Actors' Playhouse, New York City, 1981.

Missing Persons, produced at Production Company Theatre (now defunct), 1981.

Reckless (two-act), produced at South Coast Repertory Theatre, Costa Mesa, CA, c. 1984-c. 1985, produced at Circle Repertory Theatre (revision of 1983 Off-Off-Broadway production), New York City, 1988-89.

Blue Window (also see below), produced by The Production Company at Theatre Guinevere, 1984, published by Samuel French, c. 1985.

Three Postcards (book for one-act musical; music and lyrics by Craig Carnelia), produced at Playwrights Horizons Theatre, New York City, 1987, published in *Best Plays of 1986-1987,* Dodd, 1988.

Prelude to a Kiss (three-act), first produced at South Coast Repertory Theatre, 1988, new version (two-act), produced at Berkeley Repertory Theatre, Berkeley, CA, 1989, further revision, produced at Circle Repertory Theatre, New York City, 1990, then at Helen Hayes Theatre, New York City, 1990.

The Scare, Home for Contemporary Theatre and Art, 1988.

Throwing Your Voice, Naked Angels, 1991.

Oedipus at Westbury, A.R.T., 1992.

Also author of librettos for operas *Breedlove* and *Orpheus in Love* (music for both composed by Gerald Burby).

SCREENPLAYS

Longtime Companion, Samuel Goldwyn, 1990.

Prelude to a Kiss, Twentieth Century-Fox, 1992.

TELEVISION PLAYS

Blue Window (presented as part of "American Playhouse" series), PBS, 1987.

OTHER SOURCES:

PERIODICALS

Los Angeles Times, June 5, 1990, p. F1.

New York Times, March 11, 1990; March 18, 1990.

Washington Post, May 25, 1990, p. D1.

* * *

LUNDEN, Joan 1950-

PERSONAL: Born Joan Blunden, September 9, 1950, in Fair Oaks, CA; daughter of Erle Murray (a physician) and Gladyce Lorraine (Somervill) Blunden; married Michael Krauss (a television producer), September 10, 1978 (separated); children: Jamie Beryl, Lindsay Leigh, Sarah Emily. *Education:* Attended Universidad de Las Americas, 1968-72; American River Junior College, A.A., 1972.

ADDRESSES: Office—c/o ABC-TV, Good Morning America, 1965 Broadway, New York, NY 10023.

CAREER: Television news anchor, talk show host, and author. Opened and managed charm and modeling school, Sacramento, CA, 1972-73; KCRA-TV and radio,

Sacramento, coanchor and producer, 1973-75; WABC-TV, New York City, *Eyewitness News,* reporter, 1975-80, coanchor of weekend newscasts, 1976-80, *Good Morning America,* cohost, 1980—. Spokesperson for Beechnut baby food, Revlon Care for Kids products, and American Lung Association pregnancy and smoking campaign.

AWARDS, HONORS: Outstanding Mother of the Year, National Mother's Day Committee, 1982-83; Spirit of Achievement Award, Albert Einstein College of Yeshiva University; Young Women's Christian Association (YWCA) Outstanding Women's Awards Speaker; National Women's Political Caucus Award; New Jersey Division on Civil Rights Award; Baylor University Outstanding Woman of the Year Award.

CREDITS:

TELEVISION APPEARANCES; TALK SHOWS

Contributor, *Good Morning America,* ABC, 1975, cohost, 1980—.
Host, *Mother's Day,* Lifetime, 1984.
Everyday with Joan Lunden, syndicated, 1989.

Also appeared in *Mothers' Minutes,* a series of informational spots broadcast on weekday afternoons.

TELEVISION APPEARANCES; SPECIALS

Secret World of the Very Young, CBS, 1984.
Host, *Walt Disney World Happy Easter Parade,* ABC, 1985, 1987-91.
Host, *Walt Disney World Very Merry Christmas Parade,* ABC, 1986-91.
Whatta Year . . . 1986, ABC, 1986.
Our Kids and the Best of Everything, ABC, 1987.
Host, *100th Tournament of Roses Parade,* ABC, 1989.
Host, *101st Tournament of Roses Parade,* ABC, 1990.
American Red Cross Emergency Test, ABC, 1990.
Host, *102nd Tournament of Roses Parade,* ABC, 1991.

TELEVISION APPEARANCES; EPISODIC

Herself, *Murphy Brown,* CBS, 1992.

FILM APPEARANCES

Cameo, *What About Bob,* Buena Vista, 1991.

Also had bit part as saloon hostess in *Macho Callahan,* 1970.

RECORDINGS:

VIDEOS

Narrator, *Your Newborn Baby, Everything You Need to Know,* 1990.

WRITINGS:

Coauthor, with Ardy Friedburg, of autobiography *Good Morning, I'm Joan Lunden,* 1986; also coauthor, with Michael Krauss, of *Joan Lunden's Mothers' Minutes,* 1986, and *Your Newborn Baby;* author of syndicated column *Parent's Notes.* *

M

MACCHIO, Ralph 1962-

PERSONAL: Born November 4, 1962, on Long Island (one source says in Huntington), NY; married a nurse, c. 1987.

ADDRESSES: Office—451 Deerpark Ave., Dix Hills, NY 17746. *Agent*—Writers and Artists Agency, 11726 San Vicente Blvd., Suite 300, Los Angeles, CA 90049.

CAREER: Actor. Began career appearing in television commercials.

CREDITS:

FILM APPEARANCES

Chooch, *Up the Academy* (also known as *The Brave Young Men of Weinberg*), Warner Brothers, 1980.
Johnny Cade, *The Outsiders,* Warner Brothers, 1983.
Daniel LaRusso, *The Karate Kid,* Columbia, 1984.
Eddie, *Teachers,* Metro-Goldwyn-Mayer/United Artists, 1984.
Eugene Martone, *Crossroads,* Columbia, 1986.
Daniel LaRusso, *The Karate Kid Part II,* Columbia, 1986.
Jack Lambert, *Distant Thunder,* Paramount, 1988.
Daniel LaRusso, *The Karate Kid Part III,* Columbia, 1989.
Frank Della Rocca, Jr., *Too Much Sun,* New Line Cinema, 1991.
William, *My Cousin Vinny,* Twentieth Century-Fox, 1992.

TELEVISION APPEARANCES

Jeremy Andretti, *Eight Is Enough* (series), ABC, 1980-81.
Denny Brody, *Dangerous Company* (movie), CBS, 1982.
Title role, *The Three Wishes of Billy Grier* (movie), ABC, 1984.

Also appeared as Tony Barnett, *Journey to Survival,* 1982.

STAGE APPEARANCES

(Off-Broadway and Broadway debut) Teddy, *Cuba and His Teddy Bear,* Longacre Theatre, then New York Shakespeare Festival, Public Theatre, both New York City, 1986.
Only Kidding, Westside Arts Theatre, New York City, 1989.

OTHER SOURCES:

PERIODICALS

People Weekly, August 27, 1984, p. 74.*

* * *

MacLEOD, Gavin 1931-

PERSONAL: Born February 28, 1931, in Mount Kisco, NY; married second wife, Patti Steele (a singer and dancer), c. 1974 (divorced, 1982); remarried Steele, 1985; children: Keith, David, Julie, Meghan; stepchildren: Tommy, Stephanie, Andrew. *Education:* Received B.F.A. from Ithaca College.

ADDRESSES: Agent—Shapira and Associates, Inc., 15301 Ventura Blvd., Suite 345, Sherman Oaks, CA 91403.

CAREER: Actor. *Military service:* Served in U.S. Air Force.

CREDITS:

TELEVISION APPEARANCES; SERIES

Happy Hanes, *McHale's Navy,* ABC, 1962-64.
Murray Slaughter, *The Mary Tyler Moore Show,* CBS, 1970-77.
Captain Merrill Stubing, *The Love Boat* (also see below), ABC, 1977-86.

TELEVISION APPEARANCES; MOVIES

Warden, *The Intruders* (also known as *Death Dance at Madelia*), NBC, 1970.
Jordan Robbins, *Only with Married Men,* ABC, 1974.
Curt Arvey, *Scruples,* CBS, 1980.
Captain Merrill Stubing, *The Love Boat: A Valentine Voyage* (also known as *The Love Boat: A Summer Cruise* and *Valentine's Day Love Boat Reunion*), CBS, 1990.

TELEVISION APPEARANCES; PILOTS

Honeymoon Suite, ABC, 1973.
Captain Merrill Stubing, *The New Love Boat* (also known as *The Love Boat II*), ABC, 1977.
Yankee Sullivan, *Ransom for Alice!,* NBC, 1977.
Lieutenant Nojack, *Murder Can Hurt You!,* ABC, 1980.
Host, *Whatever Became of. . . ?,* ABC, 1982.

TELEVISION APPEARANCES; SPECIALS

Mitzi and a Hundred Guys, CBS, 1975.
Mitzi . . . What's Hot, What's Not, CBS, 1978.
Alan King's Third Annual Final Warning!!, ABC, 1979.
Celebrity Challenge of the Sexes 3, CBS, 1979.
The Dean Martin Celebrity Roast, NBC, 1984.
Host, *The ABC All-Star Spectacular,* ABC, 1985.
Captain Merrill Stubing, "The Shipshape Cruise," *The Love Boat Special,* ABC, 1986.
Captain Merrill Stubing, "The Christmas Cruise," *The Love Boat Special,* ABC, 1986.
Captain Merrill Stubing, "Who Killed Maxwell Thorn?," *The Love Boat Special,* ABC, 1987.
Himself and Murray Slaughter, *Mary Tyler Moore: The 20th Anniversary Show,* CBS, 1991.

Also appeared as host, *The New and Spectacular Guinness Book of World Records,* 1980; and in *The 37th Annual Prime Time Emmy Awards,* 1985.

TELEVISION APPEARANCES; EPISODIC

"Baby Face Killer," *The Whirlybirds,* syndicated, 1957.
"Act of Folly," *Walter Winchell File,* ABC, 1957.
"The Arraignment," *U.S. Marshal,* syndicated, 1958.
"The Walkout," *Walter Winchell File,* ABC, 1958.
"The Kill," *Peter Gunn,* NBC, 1958.
"The Robbery," *Steve Canyon,* NBC, 1959.
Mr. Lucky, CBS, 1959.
"The Tri-State Gang," *The Untouchables,* ABC, 1959.
"The Informer," *U.S. Marshal,* syndicated, 1960.
"Hair of the Dog," *Mr. Lucky,* CBS, 1960.
"Take Five for Murder," *Peter Gunn,* ABC, 1960.
"Tinge of Red," *Dan Raven,* NBC, 1960.
"The Big Train," *The Untouchables,* ABC, 1961.
"The Case of the Grumbling Grandfather," *Perry Mason,* CBS, 1961.
"Crime and Commitment," *Cain's Hundred,* NBC, 1961.
"Rules of Guidance," *Cain's Hundred,* NBC, 1961.
"Winter Harvest," *Dr. Kildare,* NBC, 1961.
"Doyle against the House," *The Dick Powell Show,* NBC, 1961.
"Style of Living," *The Investigators,* CBS, 1961.
"The Heist," *Straightaway,* CBS, 1961.
"Loophole," *The Untouchables,* ABC, 1961.
"Empress Carlotta's Necklace," *The Dick Van Dyke Show,* CBS, 1961.
"Man in the Middle," *The Untouchables,* ABC, 1962.
"Romance, Roses, and Rye Bread," *The Dick Van Dyke Show,* CBS, 1964.
"Sleeping Cutie," *The Munsters,* CBS, 1964.
"The Meeting," *Rawhide,* CBS, 1964.
"Dance, Marine, Dance," *Gomer Pyle, USMC,* CBS, 1965.
"The Hong Kong Shilling Affair," *The Man from U.N.C.L.E.,* NBC, 1965.
"The Case of the Grinning Gorilla," *Perry Mason,* CBS, 1965.
"TV or Not TV," *The Andy Griffith Show,* CBS, 1965.
"The Taylors in Hollywood," *The Andy Griffith Show,* CBS, 1965.
"The Case of the Runaway Racer," *Perry Mason,* CBS, 1965.
"Who's Got a Secret?," *My Favorite Martian,* CBS, 1965.
"Man from Uncle Martin," *My Favorite Martian,* CBS, 1966.
Dr. Charles Norwood, "Baby Crazy," *Summer Fun,* ABC, 1966.
Hogan's Heroes, CBS, 1966.
"Then Suddenly, Panic!," *Ben Casey,* ABC, 1966.
"The Fatal Chase Raid," *The Rat Patrol,* ABC, 1966.
"The Shock of Recognition," *Run for Your Life,* NBC, 1966.
"The Masquers," *Combat,* ABC, 1967.
"Brother Love," *The Big Valley,* ABC, 1967.
"The Eighty-Seven-Dollar Bride," *The Road West,* NBC, 1967.
"Six Hours to Sky High," *Iron Horse,* ABC, 1967.
"Black Market," *Garrison's Gorillas,* ABC, 1967.
"Return of the Hero," *Ironside,* NBC, 1968.
"Presumed Dead," *The Big Valley,* ABC, 1968.
"And They Painted Daisies on His Coffin," *Hawaii Five-O,* CBS, 1968.
"A Star Is Reborn," *The Flying Nun,* ABC, 1969.
"The Box," *Hawaii Five-O,* CBS, 1969.
"Alias Nellie Handley," *The Big Valley,* ABC, 1969.
Hogan's Heroes, CBS, 1969.
"Visitation," *Judd, for the Defense,* ABC, 1969.
"Rock Bye-Bye," *It Takes a Thief,* ABC, 1969.
"The Black Angel," *Lancer,* CBS, 1969.
"An Evening with Alistir Mundy," *It Takes a Thief,* ABC, 1970.

"Jenny Wilde Is Drowning," *Name of the Game,* NBC, 1970.
"Love and the Image Makers," *Love, American Style,* ABC, 1974.
"Rhoda's Wedding," *Rhoda,* CBS, 1974.
"The Fine Art of Crime," *The New Adventures of Wonder Woman,* CBS, 1978.
"Love Boat Angels," *Charlie's Angels,* ABC, 1979.
Guest host, *The Big Show,* NBC, 1980.
"Fallen Idols," *Hotel,* ABC, 1985.
Vice-principal Durfner, "Student Exchange," *The Disney Sunday Movie,* ABC, 1987.
Michael Holmes, "The Last Act Is a Solo," *General Motors Playwrights Theater,* Arts and Entertainment, 1991.

Also appeared on episodes of *The DuPont Show of the Week, Death Valley Days,* and *The Mike Douglas Show.*

OTHER TELEVISION APPEARANCES

Also appeared as Myron Selznick, *The Scarlett O'Hara Wars;* and as Mr. Goldberger, *The Day the Bubble Burst.*

FILM APPEARANCES

Lieutenant, *I Want to Live!,* United Artists (UA), 1958.
Padua, *Compulsion,* Twentieth Century-Fox, 1959.
Ernest Huckle, *Operation Petticoat,* Universal, 1959.
Thayer, *High Time,* Twentieth Century-Fox, 1960.
Private Crotty, *War Hunt,* UA, 1962.
Seaman Joseph "Happy" Hanes, *McHale's Navy,* Universal, 1964.
Seaman Joseph "Happy" Hanes, *McHale's Navy Joins the Air Force,* Universal, 1965.
Hulagu Khan, *The Sword of Ali Baba,* Universal, 1965.
Crosley, *The Sand Pebbles,* Twentieth Century-Fox, 1966.
Emil, *Deathwatch,* Beverly Pictures, 1966.
C. S. Divot, *The Party,* UA, 1968.
First director, *The Comic,* Columbia, 1969.
Lou, *A Man Called Gannon,* Universal, 1969.
Sergeant Kruger, *The 1,000 Plane Raid,* UA, 1969.
Moriarty, *Kelly's Heroes,* Metro-Goldwyn-Mayer, 1970.

Also appeared in *The Late Show; The Jerk; Serial;* and *My Favorite Year.*

STAGE APPEARANCES

Harry Locke, *The Captains and the Kings,* Playhouse Theatre, New York City, 1962.
Night of 100 Stars, Radio City Music Hall, New York City, 1982.

Also appeared in *Night of 100 Stars II,* 1985; *A Hatful of Rain* (Broadway debut); *Chapter Two,* Chicago, IL; *Carousel; Middle of the Night; The Egg; An Evening of the Absurd; Lullabye; The Webb and the Rock; Awake and Sing; The Balcony; The Roost; And Miss Reardon Drinks a Little; Once More with Feeling; A Funny Thing Happened on the Way to the Forum; Gypsy; The Seven-Year Itch; Annie Get Your Gun; The Connection; Mass Appeal; High Button Shoes; Love Letters;* and *Never Too Late.*

* * *

MacMURRAY, Fred 1908-1991

OBITUARY NOTICE—See index for *CTFT* sketch: Full name, Frederick Martin MacMurray; born August 30, 1908, in Kankakee, IL; died of pneumonia, November 5, 1991, in Santa Monica, CA. Actor. MacMurray is best known for his portrayal of the warmhearted father on *My Three Sons*—one of television's longest-running series—but that role came late in his busy acting career. The versatile actor, who was comfortable with both comedy and drama, appeared in over fifty films beginning with the 1934 *Friends of Mr. Sweeney.* He won widespread critical recognition with the 1944 classic *Double Indemnity,* and also appeared in *The Caine Mutiny, Miracle of the Bells,* and *The Apartment.* MacMurray displayed his comedic skills in such Walt Disney films as *The Absent-Minded Professor, Son of Flubber* and *The Shaggy Dog.*

OBITUARIES AND OTHER SOURCES:

BOOKS

The International Dictionary of Films and Filmmakers, Volume 3: *Actors and Actresses,* St. James Press, 1986, pp. 397-98.
Who's Who in America, 46th edition, Marquis, 1990, p. 2078.

PERIODICALS

Detroit Free Press, November 6, 1991, p. 4B.
Variety, November 11, 1991, p. 68.

* * *

MAHARIS, George 1938-

PERSONAL: Born September 1, 1938, in Astoria, NY. *Education:* Studied with Sanford Meisner and Lee Strasberg.

ADDRESSES: Office—13150 Mulholland Dr., Beverly Hills, CA 90210.

CAREER: Actor.

AWARDS, HONORS: Theatre World Award, 1959-60, for *The Zoo Story;* Emmy Award nomination, outstanding continued performance by a lead actor in a series, 1961, for *Route 66.*

CREDITS:

FILM APPEARANCES

Yaov, *Exodus,* United Artists (UA), 1960.
Peter Santelli, *Quick, Before It Melts,* Metro-Goldwyn-Mayer, 1964.
Lee Barrett, *The Satan Bug,* UA, 1965.
Alan Macklin, *Sylvia,* Paramount, 1965.
Ben Lewis, *A Covenant with Death,* Warner Brothers, 1966.
Taurus, *The Happening,* Columbia, 1967.
Jacob Galt, *The Desperados,* Columbia, 1969.
Paul Cardenas, *Land Raiders* (also known as *Day of the Landgrabbers*), Columbia, 1969.
Sergeant Chips Slater, *The Last Day of the War,* Sagittarius, 1969.
Machelli, *The Sword and the Sorcerer,* Group One, 1982.

TELEVISION APPEARANCES; SERIES

Buzz Murdock, *Route 66,* CBS, 1960-63.
Jonathan Croft, *The Most Deadly Game* (also known as *Zig Zag*), ABC, 1970-71.

TELEVISION APPEARANCES; MOVIES

Joe Walden, *Escape to Mindanao,* NBC, 1968.
Gus Monk, *The Monk* (pilot), ABC, 1969.
Ben Chappel, *The Victim,* ABC, 1972.
Robert Davenport, *Murder on Flight 502,* ABC, 1975.
Guy Woodhouse, *Look What's Happened to Rosemary's Baby* (also known as *Rosemary's Baby II*), ABC, 1976.
Les Phillips, *SST-Death Flight* (also known as *Flight of the Maiden, Death Flight,* and *SST: Disaster in the Sky*), ABC, 1977.
Evan Walsh, *Crash,* ABC, 1978.
Lyle Benson, *Return to Fantasy Island* (pilot; also known as *Fantasy Island II*), ABC, 1978.

Also appeared in *A Small Rebellion.*

TELEVISION APPEARANCES; EPISODIC

Husband, "The Brave and the Free," *Of Men and Women,* ABC, 1972.
Mark, "Murder Is a One-Act Play" (also known as "Death of Sister Mary"), *Thriller,* ABC, 1974.

Also appeared as Budd Gardner on *Search for Tomorrow,* and on *Naked City.*

TELEVISION APPEARANCES; MINI-SERIES

Joey Quales, *Rich Man, Poor Man—Book I,* ABC, 1976.

STAGE APPEARANCES

The Best Little Whorehouse in Texas, Claridge Hotel, Atlantic City, NJ, 1984.

Also appeared off-Broadway in *I, Too, Have Lived in Arcadia, Deathwatch, The Saintliness of Margery Kempe,* and *The Zoo Story.**

* * *

MANCINI, Henry 1924-

PERSONAL: Born April 16 (some sources say 24), 1924, in Cleveland, OH; son of Quinto (a steelworker and musician) and Anna (Pece) Mancini; married Virginia O'Connor (a vocalist), September 13, 1947; children: Christopher, Monica, Felice. *Education:* Attended Carnegie Institute of Technology School of Music and Juilliard School of Music, both 1942; studied privately with Mario Castelnuovo-Tedesco, Ernst Krenek, and Alfred Sendry; apprenticed under David Tamke of Universal Studios. *Avocational interests:* Collecting sculpture.

ADDRESSES: Agent—Rogers & Cowan, Inc., 9665 Wilshire Blvd., Beverly Hills, CA 90212. *Contact*—c/o RCA, 1133 Avenue of the Americas, New York, NY 10036.

CAREER: Composer, arranger, conductor, performer, author. Pianist and arranger for Tex Beneke Orchestra, 1945-47; composer of musical scores for radio shows, 1947-52; staff composer and arranger for Universal Pictures, 1952-58; free-lance composer, 1958—; affiliated with RCA records, 1959—. Affiliated with Share, Inc. (organization for mentally retarded children). *Military service:* U.S. Army Air Forces, 1943-45, served in infantry; performed with Air Forces band upon recommendation by Glenn Miller.

MEMBER: American Society of Composers, Authors, and Publishers, Composers and Lyricists Guild of America (executive board member).

AWARDS, HONORS: Academy Award nomination for best film score, 1954, for *The Glenn Miller Story;* Grammy awards for album of the year and best arrangement of the year and Grammy nominations for best performance by orchestra and best original cast album, all 1958, all for *The Music from Peter Gunn;* Emmy nomination for best musical score, 1958, for *Peter Gunn;* Grammy nominations for album of the year, best performance by orchestra, best performance by jazz group, best composition more than five minutes, and best arrangement, all 1959, all for *More Music from Peter Gunn;* citation as instrumental album of the year, *Billboard* magazine, Grammy awards for best arrangement and best performance by orchestra, and Grammy nomination for best soundtrack album, all 1959, all for *Music from Mr. Lucky.*

Grammy Award for best performance by large jazz group and Grammy nomination for best performance by band for dancing, both 1960, both for *The Blues and the Beat;* Grammy awards for record of the year, song of the year, best performance by orchestra, best recording of score from motion picture, and best arrangement, and Academy awards for best film score and best song, all 1961, all for "Moon River" and score from *Breakfast at Tiffany's;* Academy Award nomination, 1961, for theme song from *Bachelor in Paradise;* Grammy nomination for best performance by orchestra for dancing, 1961, for *Mr. Lucky Goes Latin;* Grammy Award for best instrumental arrangement and Grammy nominations for best instrumental theme, best original jazz composition, and best performance by orchestra or instrumentalist with orchestra, all 1962, all for "Baby Elephant Walk" and score from *Hatari!;* Grammy awards for record of the year, song of the year, and best background arrangement, and Academy Award, all 1963, all for theme song and score from *Days of Wine and Roses;* Grammy nomination for best performance by orchestra or instrumentalist with orchestra, 1963, for *Our Man in Hollywood;* Academy Award nomination for best song and Grammy nomination for best performance by chorus, both 1963, for theme song and music from *Charade;* Grammy awards for best instrumental arrangement, best instrumental composition, and best instrumental performance, Grammy nominations for album of the year and best original score, and Academy Award nomination for best score, all 1964, all for theme and score from *The Pink Panther;* Grammy nominations for song of the year and best performance by chorus and Academy Award nomination for best song, all 1964, all for theme from *Dear Heart;* Academy Award nomination for best song and Grammy nomination for best instrumental performance, both 1965, for theme song and score from *The Great Race;* Grammy nomination for best performance by chorus, 1965, for *Dear Heart and Other Songs about Love;* Grammy nominations for best instrumental theme, best original score, and best instrumental arrangement, all 1966, all for *Arabesque;* Grammy nomination for best performance by chorus, 1966, for *Henry Mancini Presents the Academy Award Songs;* Grammy Award for best instrumental arrangement and Grammy nominations for record of the year and best contemporary instrumental performance, all 1969, all for "Love Theme from Romeo and Juliet"; Grammy nomination for best original score, 1969, for *Me, Natalie.*

Grammy awards for best instrumental arrangement and best contemporary instrumental performance, both 1970, for "Theme from Z" and *Theme from Z and Other Film Music;* Grammy nomination for best instrumental composition, 1970, for "Love Theme" from *Sunflower;* Grammy nomination for best original score and Academy Award nominations for best original song score and best song, all 1970, respectively for score, theme song, and "Whistling Away the Dark" from *Darling Lili;* Grammy nomination for best pop instrumental, 1971, for "Theme from Love Story"; Academy Award nomination for best song, 1971, for "All His Children" from *Sometimes a Great Notion;* Grammy nomination for best instrumental arrangement, 1972, for theme from *The Mancini Generation;* Grammy nomination for instrumental composition and best pop instrumental performance by an arranger, conductor, and/or choral leader, 1972, for *Brass on Ivory;* Grammy nomination for best original score, 1975, for *The Return of the Pink Panther;* Grammy nomination for best instrumental arrangement, 1976, for "The Disaster Movie Suite"; Academy Award nomination for best song, 1976, for "Come to Me" from *The Pink Panther Strikes Again;* Grammy nomination for best instrumental composition, 1976, for theme from *The White Dawn;* Grammy nomination for best pop instrumental, 1978, for "The Pink Panther Theme"; Grammy nomination for best original score, 1978, for *Revenge of the Pink Panther;* Grammy nomination for best pop instrumental and Academy Award nominations for best song and best original score, all 1979, respectively for "Ravel's 'Bolero,' " "It's Easy to Say," and score from *"10".*

Academy Award for best original score, 1982, and Grammy nomination for best score, both 1982, both for *Victor/Victoria;* Grammy nomination for best instrumental composition and Emmy nomination for best dramatic underscore for limited series, both 1983, for theme song and score from *The Thorn Birds;* Grammy nomination for best instrumental arrangement, 1983, for "Cameo for Flute . . . for James" from *In the Pink;* Academy Award nomination for best song, 1986, for "Life in a Looking Glass" from *That's Life;* Grammy nominations for best instrumental composition and best album of original background score, both 1987, respectively for "The Blues in Three" and *The Glass Menagerie;* Grammy nomination for best arrangement accompanying vocals, 1987, for "It Might As Well Be Spring" from *The Hollywood Musicals.*

Named honorary alumnus of University of California, Los Angeles (U.C.L.A.), 1974; D.Mus. from Duquesne University, 1977; honorary mayor of Northridge, CA; endowed annual music scholarships at U.C.L.A. and Juilliard School of Music.

CREDITS:

FILM WORK; ARRANGER

The Glenn Miller Story (music by Joseph Gershenson), Universal, 1954.

(With Sol Yaged, Alan Harding, and Harold Brown) *The Benny Goodman Story,* (music by Gershenson), Universal, 1956.

TELEVISION WORK

Music conductor, *Mancini and Friends* (also see below), PBS, 1987.

Music director of *Monsanto Presents Mancini* (also see below), 1971, *The Mancini Generation* (also see below), 1972, and *Ann Margret—When You're Smiling,* 1973; music arranger of *The Mancini Generation* (also see below), 1972; title song conductor of *The Sex Symbol,* 1974.

TELEVISION APPEARANCES; SERIES

Host of weekly syndicated variety program *The Mancini Generation* (also see below), 1972.

TELEVISION APPEARANCES; SPECIALS

Host, *On Parade,* NBC, 1964.
Play It Again, Uncle Sam, PBS, 1975.
Perry Como's Music from Hollywood, ABC, 1977.
100 Years of America's Popular Music, NBC, April, 1981.
100 Years of Golden Hits, NBC, July, 1981.
Whatta Year . . . 1986, ABC, 1986.
A Capitol Fourth, PBS, 1986, 1989, and 1990.
Mancini and Friends, PBS, 1987.
The Television Academy Hall of Fame, Fox, 1990.
Seriously . . . Phil Collins, CBS, 1990.
National Memorial Day Concert (also see below), PBS, 1990.

Also hosted *Monsanto Presents Mancini,* a series of three specials, 1971, and appeared on numerous awards programs.

STAGE APPEARANCES

Festival at Ford's, Circle in the Square at Ford's Theatre, Washington, DC, c. 1970 and c. 1971.

SONG ARRANGER

"Love Theme from Romeo and Juliet" (also see below), RCA, 1969.
(With John Williams, Herb Spencer, and Al Woodbury, and conductor) "The Disaster Movie Suite" (also see below), RCA, 1976.

RECORDINGS:

ALBUMS

The Music from Peter Gunn (also see below), RCA, 1958.
More Music from Peter Gunn (also see below), RCA, 1959.
Music from Mr. Lucky (also see below), RCA, 1959.
The Blues and the Beat, RCA, 1960.
Breakfast at Tiffany's (also see below), RCA, 1961.
Mr. Lucky Goes Latin, RCA, 1961.
Hatari! (also see below), RCA, 1962.
Days of Wine and Roses (also see below), RCA, 1963.
Our Man in Hollywood, RCA, 1963.
Charade (also see below), RCA, 1963.
The Pink Panther (also see below), RCA, 1964.
Dear Heart (also see below), RCA, 1964.
Sarah Vaughan Sings the Henry Mancini Songbook, Mercury, 1965.
The Great Race (also see below), RCA, 1965.
Dear Heart and Other Songs about Love, RCA, 1965.
Arabesque (also see below), RCA, 1966.
Henry Mancini Presents the Academy Award Songs, RCA, 1966.
Me, Natalie (also see below), Columbia, 1969.
Theme from Z and Other Film Music, RCA, 1970.
Sunflower (also see below), RCA, 1970.
(With Doc Severinsen) *Brass on Ivory,* RCA, 1971.
The Return of the Pink Panther (also see below), RCA, 1975.
The White Dawn (also see below), RCA, 1976.
Revenge of the Pink Panther (also see below), lyrics by Leslie Bricusse, United Artists (UA), 1978.
The Thorn Birds (also see below), Warner Brothers, 1983.
In the Pink (also see below), RCA, c. 1983.
Victor/Victoria (also see below), Polygram, 1986.
The Hollywood Musicals (also see below), Columbia, 1986.

Music released on more than sixty albums, including *Combo, Experiment in Terror* (also see below), and *Uniquely Mancini.*

SELECTED AWARD-WINNING SINGLES

"Moon River," lyrics by Johnny Mercer, *Breakfast at Tiffany's* (also see below), RCA, 1961.
"Baby Elephant Walk," *Hatari!* (also see below), RCA, 1962.
"Love Theme from Romeo and Juliet," RCA, 1969.
"The Disaster Movie Suite," RCA, 1976.
"Cameo for Flute . . . for James," *In the Pink* (flute played by James Galway), RCA, c. 1983.
"It Might As Well Be Spring," *The Hollywood Musicals,* (vocals by Johnny Mathis), Columbia, 1986.

Other award-winning singles include theme song (lyrics by Mack Davis) from *Bachelor in Paradise* (also see below), 1961; theme song from *The Second Time Around,* 1961; theme song (lyrics by Mercer) from *Days of Wine and Roses* (also see below), 1962; theme song (lyrics by Mercer) from *Charade* (also see below), 1963; theme song (lyrics by Jay Livingston and Ray Evans) from *Dear Heart* (also see below), 1964; "The Sweetheart Tree" (lyrics by Mercer) from *The Great Race* (also see below), 1965; theme and "Whistling Away the Dark" from *Darling Lili* (also see below), 1970; "Love Theme" from *Sunflower* (also see below), 1970; "Theme from Love Story" (also see below), 1971; "All His Children" (lyrics by Alan and Marilyn Bergman) from *Sometimes a Great Notion* (also see below), 1971; "Come to Me" (lyrics by Don Black), from *The Pink Panther Strikes Again* (also see below), 1976; "It's Easy to Say" (lyrics by Robert Wells) and "Ravel's 'Bolero,'" both from *"10"* (also see below), 1979; "Life in a Looking Glass" (lyrics by Leslie Bricusse) from *That's Life!* (also see below), 1986.

WRITINGS:

FILM SCORES; COMPOSER

Tarantula, Universal, 1955.
Rock, Pretty Baby, Universal, 1956.
Man Afraid, Universal, 1957.
Touch of Evil, Universal, 1958.
Damn Citizen, Universal, 1958.
Flood Tide, Universal, 1958.
Summer Love, Universal, 1958.
Voice in the Mirror, Universal, 1958.
High Time, Twentieth Century-Fox, 1960.
The Great Imposter, Universal, 1960.
Bachelor in Paradise, Metro-Goldwyn-Mayer, 1961.
Breakfast at Tiffany's, Paramount, 1961.
Mr. Hobbs Takes a Vacation, Twentieth Century-Fox, 1962.
Hatari! (also known as *The African Story*), Paramount, 1962.
Experiment in Terror (also known as *Grip of Fear*), Columbia, 1962.
Days of Wine and Roses, Warner Brothers, 1962.
Charade, Universal, 1963.
Soldier in the Rain, Allied Artists, 1963.
The Pink Panther, UA, 1964.
Man's Favorite Sport(?), Universal, 1964.
A Shot in the Dark, UA, 1964.
Dear Heart, Warner Brothers, 1964.
The Great Race, Warner Brothers, 1965.
Arabesque, Universal, 1966.
Moment to Moment, Universal, 1966.
What Did You Do in the War, Daddy?, UA, 1966.
Gunn, Paramount, 1967.
Two for the Road, Twentieth Century-Fox, 1967.
Wait until Dark, Warner Brothers, 1967.
The Party, UA, 1968.
Gaily, Gaily, UA, 1969.
Me, Natalie, National General, 1969.
Darling Lili, Paramount, 1970.
The Hawaiians, UA, 1970.
The Molly Maguires, Paramount, 1970.
The Night Visitor, UMC, 1970.
Sunflower, Avco Embassy, 1970.
(And musical director) *Sometimes a Great Notion* (also known as *Never Give an Inch*), Universal, 1971.
Oklahoma Crude, Columbia, 1973.
The Thief Who Came to Dinner, Warner Brothers, 1973.
The White Dawn, Paramount, 1974.
The Girl from Petrovka, Universal, 1974.
99 44/100 Percent Dead, Twentieth Century-Fox, 1974.
The Great Waldo Pepper, Universal, 1975.
The Return of the Pink Panther, UA, 1975.
Once Is Not Enough, Paramount, 1975.
Alex and the Gypsy, Twentieth Century-Fox, 1976.
W.C. Fields and Me, Universal, 1976.
The Pink Panther Strikes Again, UA, 1976.
Silver Streak, Twentieth Century-Fox, 1976.
Angela, Montreal Travel Co., 1977.
Revenge of the Pink Panther, UA, 1978.
Who Is Killing the Great Chefs of Europe? (released in Great Britain as *Too Many Chefs*), Warner Brothers, 1978.
House Calls, Universal, 1978.
The Prisoner of Zenda, Universal, 1979.
Nightwing, Columbia, 1979.
"10," Warner Brothers, 1979.
Little Miss Marker, Universal, 1980.
A Change of Seasons, Twentieth Century-Fox, 1980.
Back Roads, Warner Brothers, 1981.
Condorman, Buena Vista, 1981.
S.O.B., Paramount, 1981.
Mommie Dearest, Paramount, 1981.
Victor/Victoria, UA, 1982.
The Trail of the Pink Panther, UA, 1982.
Better Late Than Never, Warner Brothers, 1983.
Curse of the Pink Panther, UA, 1983.
The Man Who Loved Women, Columbia, 1983.
Second Thoughts, Universal, 1983.
Harry and Son, Orion, 1984.
Lifeforce, Tri-Star, 1985.
Santa Claus: The Movie, Tri-Star, 1985.
A Fine Mess, Columbia, 1986.
The Great Mouse Detective, Buena Vista, 1986.
That's Life!, Columbia, 1986.
Blind Date, Tri-Star, 1987.
The Glass Menagerie, Cineplex Odeon, 1987.
Sunset, Tri-Star, 1988.
Without a Clue, Orion, 1988.
Physical Evidence, Columbia, 1989.
Ghost Dad, Universal, 1990.
Switch, Warner Brothers, 1991.

Also composed "Theme from Love Story," 1971, and music for *Visions of Eight,* 1973, *That's Dancing!,* 1985, and *Mother, Mother,* 1989; contributed to more than one hundred scores for Universal during 1950s.

TELEVISION MUSIC; COMPOSER

Peter Gunn (also see below), NBC, 1958.
"How Soon," theme song for *Richard Boone Show,* BBC, 1963.

The Thorn Birds (mini-series), ABC, 1983.
If It's Tuesday, It Still Must Be Belgium (movie), NBC, 1987.
Circus, ABC, 1987.
Justin Case (movie), ABC, 1988.
Welcome Home (movie), USA, 1989.
The 75th Anniversary of Beverly Hills, ABC, 1989.
Peter Gunn (movie), ABC, 1989.
Tic Tac Dough, ITC Domestic Television, 1990.
Fear (movie), Showtime, 1990.
National Memorial Day Concert, PBS, 1990.
The Democrats: A Presidential Debate, NBC, 1991.
Never Forget (movie; also known as *The Promise*), TNT, 1991.

Also composed music for *Mr. Lucky,* 1959; *Columbo,* 1971; *Curiosity Shop,* 1971; *Cade's County,* 1971; *The Mancini Generation,* 1972; *Blue Knight,* 1975; *The Invisible Man,* 1975; *The Moneychangers* (movie), 1976; *What's Happening,* 1976; *Kingston: Confidential,* 1977; *Sanford Arms,* 1977; *A Family Upside Down* (movie), 1978; *Co-Ed Fever,* 1979; *The Best Place to Be* (movie), 1979; *The Shadow Box* (movie), 1980; *Remington Steele,* 1982; *Ripley's Believe It or Not,* 1982; *Newhart,* 1982; *Hotel,* 1983; and NBC news.

STAGE MUSIC; COMPOSER

A Woman of Independent Means, Biltmore Theatre, New York City, 1983, Ford's Theatre, Washington, DC, 1987.

ORCHESTRAL WORKS

Beaver Valley '37, first performed by Pittsburgh Symphony, May, 1970.

OTHER

Sounds and Scores: A Practical Guide to Professional Orchestration, Northridge, 1962.

OTHER SOURCES:

BOOKS

Contemporary Musicians, Volume 1, Gale, 1989.*

* * *

MANTEGNA, Joe 1947-

PERSONAL: Full name, Joseph Anthony Mantegna; born November 13, 1947, in Chicago, IL; son of Joe Anthony (an insurance salesman) and Mary Ann (a shipping clerk; maiden name, Novelli) Mantegna; married Arlene Urhel, December 3, 1975; children: two daughters, including Mia. *Education:* Attended Morton Junior College; trained for the stage at Goodman School of Drama.

ADDRESSES: Agent—Peter Spring Associates, 1500 Broadway, Suite 2001, New York, NY 10036.

CAREER: Actor. Organic Theatre, Chicago, IL, member of company, 1973-78. Columbia College, Chicago, teacher, 1976-77.

AWARDS, HONORS: Joseph Jefferson Award, 1979, New York Dramatists Guild Award, 1979, and Emmy Award, 1980, all for *Bleacher Bums;* Antoinette Perry Award, featured actor in a play, Drama Desk Award, and Joseph Jefferson Award, all 1984, all for *Glengarry Glen Ross;* Venice Film Festival Award, best actor, 1988, for *Things Change.*

CREDITS:

FILM APPEARANCES

Chris, *Towing* (also known as *Fun Girls* and *Who Stole My Wheels?*), United International/Condor, 1978.
Orderly, *Second Thoughts,* Universal, 1983.
Bruce Fleckstein, *Compromising Positions,* Paramount, 1985.
Art Shirk, *The Money Pit,* Universal, 1986.
Pete Peterson, *Off Beat,* Touchstone Films/Silver Screen Partners II, 1986.
Harry Flugleman, *Three Amigos!,* Orion, 1986.
Chambers, *Critical Condition,* Paramount, 1987.
Mike, *House of Games,* Orion, 1987.
Assistant U.S. attorney Charlie Stella, *Suspect,* Tri-Star, 1987.
Carmine, *Weeds,* De Laurentiis Entertainment Group, 1987.
Jerry, *Things Change,* Columbia, 1988.
Joe, *Alice,* Orion, 1990.
Joey Zasa, *The Godfather Part III,* Paramount, 1990.
George Raft, *Bugsy,* Tri-Star, 1991.
Bobby Gold, *Homicide,* Triumph Releasing, 1991.
Al, *Queen's Logic,* Seven Arts, 1991.

Played the nephew, *Medusa Challenge,* 1977, and Svevo Bandini, *Wait until Spring, Bandini,* 1989.

STAGE APPEARANCES

A Life in the Theatre, Goodman Theatre, Chicago, IL, 1976-77.
Decker, *Bleacher Bums* (also see below), Organic Theatre, Chicago, IL, 1977.
Migrant worker and interstate trucker, *Working,* Goodman Theatre, 1977-78, then 46th Street Theatre, New York City, 1978.
The Disappearance of the Jews, Goodman Theatre, 1982-83.
Richard Roma, *Glengarry Glen Ross* (also see below), Goodman Theatre, 1983-84, then John Golden Theatre, New York City, 1984.

Bobby Gould, *Speed-the-Plow,* Royale Theatre, New York City, 1988.

Played Michael, *Mattress,* LaMama Theatre, Los Angeles, CA; at the Organic Theatre, played Gomez in *The Wonderful Ice Cream Shirt,* Corvino in *Volpone,* Jack Rolf in *Cops,* and appeared in *Sirens of Titan.*

MAJOR TOURS

Berger, *Hair,* Chicago, 1969-70.
Judas, *Godspell,* Chicago, 1972-73.
Understudy, *Lenny,* Chicago, 1974.
Richard Roma, *Glengarry Glen Ross,* U.S. cities, 1985-86.

Played Duke in *Huckleberry Finn* and Jack Rackam in *Bloody Bess,* on a tour of European cities.

STAGE WORK

Director, *Bleacher Bums* (also see below), Organic Theatre, 1977.

TELEVISION APPEARANCES; SPECIALS

Jovan "Joey" Shagula, *Big Shots in America,* NBC, 1985.
The Kennedy Center Honors: A Celebration of the Performing Arts, CBS, 1988.
The 42nd Annual Tony Awards, CBS, 1988.

Appeared in *Bleacher Bums* (also see below), PBS.

TELEVISION APPEARANCES; EPISODIC

Juan One, *Soap,* ABC, 1982.
Narrator, "Crack U.S.A.," *America Undercover,* HBO, 1989.
Narrator, "Death on the Job," *America Undercover,* HBO, 1991.

Also appeared in episodes of *Greatest American Hero,* CBS, *Making a Living,* ABC, *Bosom Buddies,* ABC, *Archie Bunker's Place,* CBS, *Simon and Simon,* CBS, and *Magnum, P.I.,* CBS.

OTHER TELEVISION APPEARANCES

Joe Esposito, *Elvis* (movie), ABC, 1979.
Ernie, *Now We're Cookin'* (pilot), CBS, 1983.
Yuri, *The Outlaws* (pilot), ABC, 1984.
The Comedy Zone (series), CBS, 1984.

Appeared in the pilot *Open All Night,* ABC.

WRITINGS:

PLAYS

(Coauthor) *Bleacher Bums* (Organic Theatre, Chicago, IL, then American Place Theatre, New York City, 1977), Samuel French, 1977.

Author of *Leonardo,* Lee Strasberg Institute, Los Angeles, CA.

OTHER SOURCES:

PERIODICALS

American Theatre, September, 1991, pp. 18-25, 69.
New York Times, May 18, 1984; November 15, 1987; May 16, 1988.
Premiere, October, 1991, pp. 68-72.*

*   *   *

MARGULIES, David 1937-

PERSONAL: Surname is pronounced "mar-gyoo-lies"; full name, David Joseph Margulies; born February 19, 1937, in New York City; son of Harry David (a lawyer) and Runya (a nurse and museum worker; maiden name, Zeltzer) Margulies; married Carol Grant, March 17, 1969 (marriage ended); married Lois Smith (an actress); children: (first marriage) Jonathan. *Education:* Attended School of Performing Arts and DeWitt Clinton High School, New York City; City College (now of the City University of New York), B.A., 1958; studied with Morris Carnovsky and Phoebe Brand at American Shakespeare Festival Academy; also studied with William Hickey.

ADDRESSES: Office—320 West 88th St., New York, NY 10024. *Agent*—Bret Adams Ltd., 449 West 44th St., New York, NY 10036.

CAREER: Actor and director. Loft Theatre, New York City, artistic director, 1967; Theatre of the Living Arts, Southwark Theatre School, Philadelphia, PA, acting teacher, 1967-68; Circle in the Square Theatre School, New York City, acting teacher, 1969-72; Lincoln Center Student Program, New York City, artist in the schools, 1969-75; Johnson State College, Johnson, VT, artist in residence, 1973; gave private acting lessons in New York City, 1973; Ensemble Studio Theatre, New York City, member of executive board, 1973—. *Military service:* U.S. Army, 1961-62.

MEMBER: Actors Equity Association, American Federation of Television and Radio Artists, Society of Stage Directors and Choreographers, Screen Actors Guild, Actors Studio.

CREDITS:

STAGE APPEARANCES

Postumus, *The Golden Six,* York Theatre, New York City, 1958.
Grimaldi, *'Tis Pity She's a Whore,* Orpheum Theatre, then Player's Theatre, New York City, 1958.
Romeo and Juliet, American Shakespeare Festival (ASF), Stratford, CT, 1959.
A Midsummer Night's Dream, ASF, 1959.
All's Well That Ends Well, ASF, 1959.

The gaoler, the old shepherd, the mariner, and the servant, *The Winter's Tale,* ASF, 1960.

Freddie, *The Disenchanted,* Tenthouse Theatre, Highland Park, IL, 1960.

Orlov, *Who Was That Lady I Saw You With?,* Tenthouse Theatre, 1960.

Understudy, *Under Milk Wood* (also see below), Circle in the Square, New York City, 1961.

David, *Six Characters in Search of an Author* (also see below), Martinique Theatre, New York City, 1963.

Benjamin, *Thistle in My Bed,* Grammercy Arts Theatre, New York City, 1963.

Clarin, *Life Is a Dream,* Astor Place Playhouse, New York City, 1964.

The pope and second scholar, *The Tragical Historie of Dr. Faustus,* Phoenix Theatre, New York City, 1964.

Title role, *Lorenzaccio,* Equity Library Theatre, New York City, 1965.

The director, *Six Characters in Search of an Author,* American Conservatory Theatre (ACT), Pittsburgh Playhouse, Pittsburgh, PA, 1965.

Truffaldino, *The Servant of Two Masters,* ACT, Pittsburgh Playhouse, 1965.

Apollo, *Apollo of Bellac,* ACT, Pittsburgh Playhouse, 1965.

Bernard, *Death of a Salesman,* ACT, Pittsburgh Playhouse, 1965.

Eisenring, *The Firebugs,* Studio Arena Theatre, Buffalo, NY, 1966.

Elbow, *Measure for Measure,* New York Shakespeare Festival (NYSF), Delacorte Theatre, New York City, 1966.

Cristoforu, *The Public Eye,* Academy Playhouse, Wilmette, IL, 1967.

Berenger, *The Rhinoceros,* Academy Playhouse, 1967.

Davies, *The Caretaker,* Theatre of the Living Arts, Philadelphia, PA, 1967.

Arthur, *Tango,* Pocket Theatre, New York City, 1969.

Rosario Chiarchiaro, *The Man with the Flower in His Mouth* (also see below), Sheridan Square Playhouse, New York City, 1969.

Reverend Dupas, *Little Murders,* Circle in the Square, 1969.

Feivel Leishik, *Seven Days of Mourning,* Circle in the Square, 1969-70.

Bertram, *The Last Analysis,* Circle in the Square, 1971.

Dr. Rance, *What the Butler Saw,* Academy Playhouse, Lake Forest, IL, 1971.

Fermin Asla Polo, alias Ismael de Lugo, *The Interrogation of Havana,* Brooklyn Academy of Music, Brooklyn, NY, 1971-72.

Norman, *The Opening,* Tappan Zee Playhouse, Nyack, NY, 1972.

Liphitz, *Happy Days Are Here Again,* Manhattan Theatre Club, New York City, 1972.

Member of company, *The Revue,* Moon Theatre, East Hampton, NY, 1972.

Aaron Silver, *An Evening with the Poet-Senator,* Playhouse Two, New York City, 1973.

Hugo Kalmar, *The Iceman Cometh,* Circle in the Square, 1973-74.

Harvey Appleman, *Kid Champion,* Public/Anspacher Theatre, New York City, 1975.

The director, *Rehearsal* (also see below), American Place Theatre, New York City, 1975.

The doctor, *Zalmen; or, The Madness of God,* Lyceum Theatre, New York City, 1976.

Sammy Samuels, *The Comedians,* Music Box Theatre, New York City, 1976-77.

Hold Me, Chelsea Westside Theatre, New York City, 1977.

Teddy, *Every Place Is Newark,* First Aspen Playwrights Conference, Aspen, CO, 1978.

"The Man with the Flower in His Mouth," *A Special Evening* (double bill), Ensemble Studio Theatre, New York City, 1979.

Imre Laszlo, *Break a Leg,* Palace Theatre, New York City, 1979.

First player and player king, *Hamlet,* Sanctuary Theatre, New York City, 1979.

Norbe and Gregory, *Walter and the Flatulist,* Sanctuary Theatre, 1980.

Moe and the farmer, *The American Clock,* Harold Clurman Theatre, New York City, 1980.

Serge Barrescu, *The West Side Waltz* (also see below), Ethel Barrymore Theatre, New York City, 1981-82.

David Ben-Gurion, *David and Paula,* American Jewish Theatre, New York City, 1982.

Title role, *King Lear,* Shakespeare in Delaware Park, Buffalo, NY, 1983.

Wes, *The Perfect Party,* Playwrights Horizon Theatre, New York City, 1986.

Foppy Schwartz, *Just Say No,* WPA Theatre, New York City, 1988.

Mendel Polan, *Cafe Crown,* Brooks Atkinson Theatre, New York City, 1989.

Appeared in the revue *The Second City* with Second City, Chicago, IL, 1962; also appeared in *The Old Tune* and *Cabal of Hypocrites.*

MAJOR TOURS

(Debut) Soldier in Cassio's army, *Othello,* NYSF, Playhouse in the Park, Philadelphia, PA, and Belvedere Lake Theatre, New York, 1958.

Philostrate, *A Midsummer Night's Dream,* ASF, Colonial Theatre, Boston, MA, then in Baltimore, MD, and Cleveland, OH, 1960.

Sol Stern, *The Tender Trap,* Paper Mill Playhouse, Millburn, NJ, and Mineola Playhouse, Mineola, NY, 1964.
The girl's father, *The Fantasticks,* U.S. cities, 1964.
Harry Metzger, *The Prince of Grand Street,* Forrest Theatre, Philadelphia, PA, and Shubert Theatre, Boston, MA, 1978.
Serge Barrescu, *The West Side Waltz,* San Francisco, Los Angeles, and San Diego, CA, Denver, CO, Philadelphia, PA, Seattle, WA, Washington, DC, Boston, MA, and Chicago, IL, 1980-82.
Jack, *Broadway Bound,* Shubert Theatre, New Haven, CT, and Ahmanson Theatre, Los Angeles, 1987.

STAGE WORK; DIRECTOR EXCEPT WHERE INDICATED

Stage manager, *Under Milk Wood,* Circle in the Square, 1961.
The Oresteia, Theatre of the Living Arts, 1968.
Next, Berkshire Theatre Festival, Stockbridge, MA, 1968.
The Christmas Dinner, Berkshire Theatre Festival, 1970.
The Complete Works of Studs Edsel, Folger Theatre Group, Folger Museum, Washington, DC, 1972.
Where Do We Go from Here?, Johnson State College, Johnson, VT, 1973, then Public/Newman Theatre, New York City, 1974.
Actors, Ensemble Studio Theatre, Johnson, VT, 1973.
The Merry Wives of Windsor, NYSF, Delacorte Theatre, 1974.
(With Jack Gelber) *Rehearsal,* American Place Theatre, 1975.
End of the War, Ensemble Studio Theatre, New York City, 1978.
"Bite the Hand," *One-Act Play Marathon '84,* Ensemble Studio Theatre, New York City, 1984.

FILM APPEARANCES

(Debut) Doorman, *A New Leaf,* Paramount, 1971.
Sunday Breakfast (short subject), shown at New York Film Festival, 1971.
Bill Phelps, *The Front,* Columbia, 1976.
Larry Goldie, *All That Jazz,* Twentieth Century-Fox, 1979.
Rabbi Joshua Drexel, *Last Embrace,* United Artists (UA), 1979.
Dr. Levy, *Dressed to Kill,* Filmways, 1980.
Dr. Jack Zymansky, *Times Square,* Anchor, 1980.
Detective Reilly, *Hide in Plain Sight,* UA, 1980.
Dr. Duberstein, *Daniel,* Paramount, 1983.
Mr. Farber, *Brighton Beach Memoirs,* Universal, 1986.
Harvey, *9-1/2 Weeks,* Metro-Goldwyn-Mayer/UA, 1986.
Magic Sticks, Tale Film, 1987.
Mr. Clarke, *Ishtar,* Columbia, 1987.
Lawyer, *Candy Mountain,* Les Films Vision, 1988.
Dr. Jonah Reiff, *Running on Empty,* Warner Brothers, 1988.
The mayor of New York, *Ghostbusters II,* Columbia, 1989.
Dr. Benjamin, *Funny about Love,* Paramount, 1989.

Played Walter Mitty, *Scarecrow in a Garden of Cucumbers,* 1972.

TELEVISION APPEARANCES; EPISODIC

Justin, "Divorced Kids' Blues," *ABC Afterschool Special,* ABC, 1987.
Bernard Yudwitz, "The Trial of Bernhard Goetz," *American Playhouse,* PBS, 1988.
Weyland Payne, "Ariana," *Kojak* (also known as *The ABC Saturday Night Movie*), ABC, 1989.
First visitor, "Vaclav Havel's 'Largo Desolato'," *Great Performances,* PBS, 1990.

Appeared in episodes of *Kojak,* 1977, *Ryan's Hope, One Life to Live,* and *All My Children.*

OTHER TELEVISION APPEARANCES

Pete, *A Mother for Janek,* PBS, 1965.
Chubby, *My Old Man* (movie), CBS, 1979.
Russell, *A Doctor's Story* (movie), NBC, 1984.
Rabbi Hier, *Never Forget* (movie; also known as *The Promise*), TNT, 1991.
Manning, *An Inconvenient Woman* (movie), ABC, 1991.
Leonard Sorkin, *STAT,* NBC, 1991.

Played David in *Six Characters in Search of an Author,* 1964, and the brother in law in *The Death of Ivan Ilyich,* 1978.*

* * *

MARKS, Richard 1943-

PERSONAL: Born November 10, 1943, in New York, NY; son of Ben and Irene (Epstein) Marks; married Barbara Joan Fallick, January 15, 1967; children: Leslie Sharon. *Education:* Attended New York University; received B.A. from City College of the City University of New York.

ADDRESSES: Contact—American Cinema Editors, 2401 Beverly Blvd., Suite 1, Los Angeles, CA 90057.

CAREER: Film editor. Free-lance film editor in New York City and Los Angeles, CA, 1964—.

MEMBER: American Cinema Editors, Motion Picture Academy of Arts and Science.

AWARDS, HONORS: Academy Award nominations, best achievement in film editing, 1979, for *Apocalypse*

Now, 1983, for *Terms of Endearment,* and 1987, for *Broadcast News.*

CREDITS:

FILM EDITOR

Parades (also known as *Break Loose*), Cinerama, 1972.
Bang the Drum Slowly, Paramount, 1973.
(With Dede Allen) *Serpico,* Paramount, 1973.
(With Peter Zinner and Barry Malkin) *The Godfather, Part II,* Paramount, 1974.
(With Mario Morra) *Three Tough Guys,* Paramount, 1974.
(With Edward Beyer) *Lies My Father Told Me,* Columbia, 1975.
The Last Tycoon, Paramount, 1976.
Apocalypse Now, United Artists, 1979.
The Hand, Warner Brothers, 1981.
Pennies from Heaven, Metro-Goldywn-Mayer, 1981.
Max Dugan Returns, Twentieth Century-Fox, 1983.
(With Sidney Wolinsky) *Terms of Endearment,* Paramount, 1983.
(With George Bowers) *The Adventures of Buckaroo Banzai: Across the Eighth Dimension,* Twentieth Century-Fox, 1984.
St. Elmo's Fire, Columbia, 1985.
Pretty in Pink, Paramount, 1986.
Broadcast News, Twentieth Century-Fox, 1987.
Say Anything, Twentieth Century-Fox, 1989.
(And second unit director) *Dick Tracy,* Touchstone-Buena Vista, 1990.
One Good Cop, Buena Vista, 1991.
Father of the Bride, Buena Vista, 1991.

TELEVISION EDITOR

Song of Myself, CBS, 1976.*

* * *

MARTIN, Barney

PERSONAL: Born in New York. *Avocational interests:* Golf, billiards.

ADDRESSES: *Agent*—Gores/Fields Agency, 10100 Santa Monica Blvd., No. 700, Los Angeles, CA 90067.

CAREER: Actor. Previously worked as a police officer.

CREDITS:

FILM APPEARANCES

Sidney, *Love with the Proper Stranger,* Paramount, 1963.
German officer in play, *The Producers,* Embassy, 1967.
Hank, *Charly,* Cinema Releasing Corp., 1968.
Motorcycle cop, *Movie Movie,* Warner Brothers, 1978.
Kiley, *Hot Stuff,* Columbia, 1979.
Ralph Marolla, *Arthur,* Warner Brothers, 1981.
A Fine Mess, Columbia, 1986.
Ralph Marolla, *Arthur 2 on the Rocks,* Warner Brothers, 1988.

Appeared as Rudy, *Pucker Up and Bark Like a Dog,* 1989. Also appeared in *Deadly Weapon,* 1989; and in *Tips.*

TELEVISION APPEARANCES; SERIES

Jackie Gleason and His American Scene Magazine, CBS, 1962-66.
Jack Terwilliger, *The Tony Randall Show,* ABC, 1976-77, then CBS, 1977-78.
Horace Batterson, *Number 96,* NBC, 1980-81.
Brothers Napa and Sonoma, *Zorro and Son,* CBS, 1983.
Ray, *Sydney,* CBS, 1990.

Also appeared on *Kraft Music Hall Presents the Dave King Show,* 1959.

TELEVISION APPEARANCES; MOVIES

Uncle Willie, *It Happened One Christmas,* ABC, 1977.
Eddie Mannix, *Moviola: This Year's Blonde* (also known as *The Secret Love of Marilyn Monroe*), NBC, 1980.
Eddie Mannix, *Moviola: The Silent Lovers,* NBC, 1980.
George Piper, *For Love or Money,* CBS, 1984.
Dr. Sloane, *Killer in the Mirror* (also known as *Stolen Dreams*), NBC, 1986.
Jack Hayes, *Us,* CBS, 1991.

TELEVISION APPEARANCES; EPISODIC

Herb Needler, "Splash, Too," *Disney Sunday Movie,* ABC, 1988.
Willard, "Sky High" (also known as "Wings"), *The Magical World of Disney,* NBC, 1990.

Also appeared in episodes of other shows, including *21 Jump Street,* Fox; *Highway to Heaven,* NBC; *Hill Street Blues,* NBC; *St. Elsewhere,* NBC; *Hart to Hart,* ABC; *Happy Days,* ABC; Lieutenant Hanratty, *Murder, She Wrote,* CBS; *Scarecrow and Mrs. King,* CBS; *Diff'rent Strokes,* NBC; *What a Country!,* syndicated; *Trapper John, M.D.,* CBS; *No Honestly;* and *Kids Incorporated.*

OTHER TELEVISION APPEARANCES

Zero Hour (special), ABC, 1967.
McGurk, *A Dog's Life* (pilot), NBC, 1979.
George Kosovich, *Sam* (pilot), ABC, 1985.
Isidore Morton, Sr., *Morton's by the Bay* (pilot), NBC, 1989.

STAGE APPEARANCES

Big Mike, *What a Killing,* Folksbiene Theatre, New York City, 1961.

Head immigration officer, assistant coach, and red stern, *All American,* Winter Garden Theatre, New York City, 1962.

Skits-Oh-Frantics!, Bert Wheeler Theatre, New York City, 1967.

Luther Billis, *South Pacific,* Jones Beach Theatre, New York City, 1968.

Saul, *Tonight in Living Color,* Actors Playhouse, New York City, 1969.

The Fantasticks, Arlington Park Theatre, Arlington Heights, IL, 1972-73.

Detective Peterson, *All over Town,* Booth Theatre, New York City, 1974-75.

Amos Hart, *Chicago,* Forty-Sixth Street Theatre, New York City, 1975-77.

Sid Ball, *The Roast,* Winter Garden Theatre, 1980.

Jess Smith, *Villager,* Lion Theatre, New York City, 1981.

Isn't It Romantic, Los Angeles Stage Company Theatre, Los Angeles, CA, 1984.

Clothespins and Dreams, Pasadena Civic Auditorium, Pasadena, CA, 1990.

Also appeared in *A Funny Thing Happened on the Way to the Forum,* Pasadena; *Helly Dolly!,* Pittsburgh, PA; *First Time Anywhere;* and *How Now Dow Jones.*

MAJOR TOURS

Jesse Vanderhof, *Promises, Promises,* U.S. cities, 1970-71.

Sergeant O'Mara, *Turtlenecks,* U.S. cities, 1973.*

* * *

MARTIN, Leila 1936-

PERSONAL: Born Leila Markowitz, August 22, 1936, in New York City; daughter of Seymour and Irma Markowitz; married Leonard Green (a manager and producer), December 24, 1955 (divorced, 1981); children: one son, one daughter. *Education:* Studied acting in New York City with Lee Strasberg and Sanford Meisner.

ADDRESSES: Agent—Select Artists, 337 West 43rd St., Suite 1B, New York, NY 10036.

CAREER: Actress.

MEMBER: Actors Equity Association, Screen Actors Guild, American Federation of Television and Radio Artists.

CREDITS:

STAGE APPEARANCES

Gussie, *Wish You Were Here,* Imperial Theatre, New York City, 1952.

Sarah Brown, *Guys and Dolls,* New York City Center Theatre, 1955.

The Mermaid in Lock 7, American Wind Symphony, Pittsburgh, PA, 1956.

Linda, *The Best House in Naples,* Lyceum Theatre, New York City, 1956.

Standby for Ellen Spelding, *Visit to a Small Planet,* Booth Theatre, New York City, 1957.

Standby for Louise, *Gypsy,* Broadway Theatre, New York City, 1959.

Gwendolyn Fairfax, *Ernest in Love,* Grammercy Arts Theatre, New York City, 1960.

Magnolia, *Show Boat,* Pinebrook Theatre, Pinebrook, NJ, 1960.

Polly, *The Boy Friend,* Pinebrook Theatre, 1960.

Teddy Stern, *Wish You Were Here,* Pinebrook Theatre, 1960.

Rutka Mazur, *The Wall,* Billy Rose Theatre, New York City, 1960.

Standby for Diana and Lysistrata, *The Happiest Girl in the World,* Martin Beck Theatre, New York City, 1961.

Dilla, *The Automobile Graveyard,* 41st Street Theatre, New York City, 1961.

Dunreath Henry, *King of Hearts,* Playhouse on the Mall, Paramus, NJ, 1963.

Lady Blakeney, *Pimpernell,* Grammercy Arts Theatre, 1964.

Bellabruna, *Blossom Time,* Paper Mill Playhouse, Millburn, NJ, 1966.

Standby for Stella, *Henry, Sweet Henry,* Palace Theatre, New York City, 1967.

Gutele Rothschild, *The Rothschilds,* Lunt-Fontanne Theatre, New York City, 1970-71.

Polly Peachum, *The Beggar's Opera,* Brooklyn Academy of Music, Brooklyn, NY, then McAlpin Rooftop Theatre, New York City, 1972.

Etiquette lady, *The King of the United States,* St. Clement's Church, New York City, 1974.

The wife, *Philemon,* Portfolio Studio Theatre, New York City, 1975.

Understudy, *Travesties,* Ethel Barrymore Theatre, New York City, 1975-76.

Countess, *A Little Night Music,* Studio Arena Theatre, Buffalo, NY, 1975-76.

Mademoiselle Emery and Mademoiselle Germaine, *The Umbrellas of Cherbourg,* Public/Cabaret Theatre, New York City, 1979.

Understudy for Dorothy and Maggie, *Forty-Second Street,* Winter Garden Theatre, New York City, 1980, then Majestic Theatre, New York City, 1981.

Jerry's Girls, Onstage Theatre, New York City, 1981.

Madame Giry, *Phantom of the Opera,* Majestic Theatre, 1988—.

Also appeared in *Peepshow,* 1944, and in *Two in the Aisle.* Played Maria, *West Side Story,* on tours of U.S. cities,

1959-60, and Canadian cities, 1962-63; played the sister and the crow, *Zorba,* on a tour of U.S. cities, 1984-86.

FILM APPEARANCES

Momar, *Santa Claus Conquers the Martians,* Embassy, 1964.
Nurse Jackson, *God Told Me To* (also known as *The Demon*), New World Pictures, 1976.

TELEVISION APPEARANCES; SERIES

Juliet Goodwin, *The Golden Windows,* NBC, 1954.

TELEVISION APPEARANCES; EPISODIC

Modern Romances, CBS, 1957.
The Max Liebman Spectaculars, NBC, 1957.
True Story, CBS, 1957.
Valiant Lady, CBS, 1957.
The Patti Page Show, ABC, 1959.
Naked City, ABC, 1963.
The Doctors, NBC, 1963.
The Nurses, NBC, 1964-65.
Loving, ABC, 1989.

* * *

MATALON, Vivian 1929-

PERSONAL: Born October 11, 1929, in Manchester, England; son of Moses and Rose (Tawil) Matalon. *Education:* Attended Munro College, Jamaica; graduated from Neighborhood Playhouse, New York City, 1950.

ADDRESSES: *Agent*—Clifford Stevens, STE Representation Ltd., 888 7th Ave., New York, NY 10019.

CAREER: Director and actor. Hampstead Theatre Club, London, England, artistic director, 1970-73; Brandeis University, Waltham, MA, visiting professor of drama, 1977-78. Artistic director, Academy Festival Theatre, Lake Forest, IL; professor, State University of New York at Stony Brook.

AWARDS, HONORS: Antoinette Perry Award, outstanding director of Broadway play, and Drama Desk Award, director of a play, both 1980, both for *Morning's at Seven;* Antoinette Perry Award nomination, director of a musical, 1984, for *The Tap Dance Kid.*

CREDITS:

STAGE DIRECTOR

The Admiration of Life, Arts Theatre, 1960.
Season of Goodwill, Queen's Theatre, London, 1964.
The Chinese Prime Minister, Globe Theatre, London, 1965.
The Glass Menagerie, Haymarket Theatre, London, 1965.
"A Song at Twilight," "Shadows of the Evening," and "Come into the Garden, Maud," *Suite in Three Keys* (triple-bill), Queen's Theatre, 1966.
After the Rain, Hampstead Theatre Club, London, 1966, later John Golden Theatre, New York City, 1967.
First Day of a New Season, Theatre Royal, Brighton, England, 1967.
Two Cities, Palace Theatre, London, 1969.
Papp, Hampstead Theatre Club, 1969.
Girlfriend, Apollo Theatre, London, 1970.
I Never Sang for My Father, Duke of York's Theatre, London, 1970.
"A Song at Twilight," and "Come into the Garden, Maud," *Noel Coward in Two Keys* (double-bill), Ethel Barrymore Theatre, New York City, 1974.
P.S. Your Cat Is Dead, John Golden Theatre, 1975.
Eve, Stratford Festival Theatre, Stratford, Ontario, Canada, 1976.
No Sex Please, We're British, Paper Mill Playhouse, Millburn, NJ, 1979.
The Master Builder, Seattle Repertory Theatre, Seattle, WA, 1979.
Heartbreak House, McCarter Theatre Company, Princeton, NJ, 1979.
Morning's at Seven, Lyceum Theatre, New York City, 1980.
Brigadoon, Majestic Theatre, New York City, 1980.
The American Clock, Biltmore Theatre, New York City, 1980.
Morning's at Seven, Ahmanson Theatre, Los Angeles, 1982.
The Corn Is Green, Lunt-Fontanne Theatre, New York City, 1983.
The Tap Dance Kid, Broadhurst Theatre, New York City, 1983, later Minskoff Theatre, New York City, 1984.
Morning's at Seven, Westminster Theatre, London, 1984.
Oliver Oliver, Long Wharf Theatre, New Haven, CT, then Manhattan Theatre Club, New York City, 1985.
Beautiful Bodies, The Whole Theatre, Montclair, NJ, 1987.
The Miracle Worker, Roundabout Theatre, New York City, 1987.

MAJOR TOURS; DIRECTOR

Noel Coward in Two Keys, U.S. Cities, 1975.

Also directed *The Signalman's Apprentice,* 1969, *The Gingerbread Lady,* 1974, *Bus Stop,* 1976, and *Season of Goodwill.*

STAGE PRODUCER

The Formation Dancers, Hampstead Theatre Club, 1970.
Disabled, Hampstead Theatre Club, 1970.
Awake and Sing, Hampstead Theatre Club, 1970.
High Time, Hampstead Theatre Club, 1972.

The Garden, Hampstead Theatre Club, 1972.
Small Craft Warnings, Hampstead Theatre Club, 1973.

STAGE APPEARANCES

Maya, Theatre De Lys, New York City, 1953.
Trip, *The School for Scandal,* Theatre De Lys, 1953.
Shampooer, *The Little Clay Cart,* Theatre De Lys, 1953.
Signalman Urban, *Caine Mutiny Court Martial,* Hippodrome, London, 1956.
Apples, *A Hatful of Rain,* Princes Theatre, London, 1957.
Don Paritt, *The Iceman Cometh,* Arts Theatre, London, 1958.

TELEVISION DIRECTOR

Emergency in Ward 10 (series), BBC, 1961-63.
"Private Contentment," *American Playhouse* (episodic), PBS, 1982.
"Merry Christmas, Baby," *General Motors Playwrights Theater* (episodic), Arts and Entertainment, 1992.

Directed *The Chopping Block, John Paddington, The Quails, A Case of Character, The Navigators,* and *Mr. Fowlds,* all for BBC.

TELEVISION APPEARANCES

Third Director, *For Ladies Only* (movie), NBC, 1981.
"Sanford Meisner: The Theatre's Best Kept Secret," *American Masters* (episodic), PBS, 1990.

FILM APPEARANCES

The Weapon, Republic, 1957.
U.S. Sailor, *Fire Down Below,* Columbia, 1957.
Floods of Fear, Universal, 1958.
Stefan, *Subway in the Sky,* United Artists, 1959.
Young man at Buvette, *Crack in the Mirror,* Twentieth Century-Fox, 1960.
Larry Webster, *Too Young To Love,* Rank, 1960.
Padre, *King and Country,* Allied Artists, 1964.*

* * *

MAYES, Wendell 1919-1992

PERSONAL: Full name, Wendell Curran Mayes; born July 21, 1919, in Hayti, MO; died of cancer, March 28, 1992, in Santa Monica, CA; son of Von (a lawyer) and Irene (a teacher; maiden name, Haynes) Mayes. *Education:* Attended Central College (now Central Methodist College), Fayette, MO, 1937-38, Johns Hopkins University, 1939-40, and Columbia University, 1941-42.

ADDRESSES: Office—1504 Bel-Air Rd., Los Angeles, CA 90077. *Agent*—George Diskant, 1033 Gayley Ave., Los Angeles, CA 90024.

CAREER: Screenwriter. Actor, 1946-53; television writer, 1953-60. *Military service:* U.S. Navy, 1942-45; served in Pacific theater.

MEMBER: Academy of Motion Picture Arts and Sciences, Writers Guild of America.

AWARDS, HONORS: Academy Award nomination, best screenplay based on material from another medium, award nomination, Writers Guild of America, and New York Film Critics writing award, all 1959, all for *Anatomy of a Murder;* award nomination, Writers Guild of America, 1978, for *Go Tell the Spartans.*

CREDITS:

FILM WORK

Producer, *Hotel* (also see below), Warner Brothers, 1967.

WRITINGS:

SCREENPLAYS

(With Billy Wilder and Charles Lederer) *The Spirit of St. Louis,* Warner Brothers, 1957.
The Enemy Below, Twentieth Century-Fox, 1957.
The Way to the Gold, Twentieth Century-Fox, 1957.
(With Robert Buckner) *From Hell to Texas* (also known as *Manhunt*), Twentieth Century-Fox, 1958.
The Hunters, Twentieth Century-Fox, 1958.
(With Halsted Welles) *The Hanging Tree,* Warner Brothers, 1959.
Anatomy of a Murder, Columbia, 1959.
(With John Lee Mahin, Martin Rackin, and Claude Binyon) *North to Alaska,* Twentieth Century-Fox, 1960.
Advise and Consent, Columbia, 1962.
(With Joseph Landon) *Von Ryan's Express,* Twentieth Century-Fox, 1965.
In Harm's Way, Paramount, 1965.
Hotel, Warner Brothers, 1967.
(With Alvin Sargent) *The Stalking Moon,* National General Pictures, 1968.
The Revengers, National General Pictures, 1972.
(With Stirling Silliphant) *The Poseidon Adventure,* Twentieth Century-Fox, 1972.
Death Wish, Paramount, 1974.
Bank Shot, United Artists, 1974.
Go Tell the Spartans, Avco Embassy, 1978.
(With John Melson) *Love and Bullets,* Associated Film Distribution, 1979.
(With Abraham Polonsky) *Monsignor,* Twentieth Century-Fox, 1982.

Also author of the screenplay for *Charlie.*

TELEVISION SCRIPTS

"The Most Blessed Woman," *Kraft Theater,* NBC, 1957.

Savage: In the Orient (pilot), CBS, 1983.
Criminal Behavior (movie; based on the novel *The Ferguson Affair,* by Ross MacDonald), ABC, 1992.

Also author of television scripts for *No Riders, Death Is a Spanish Dancer, Hang up My Guns, Cynara,* and *Profile in Courage;* writer for *Pond Theater* and *Studio One.*

OBITUARIES AND OTHER SOURCES:

PERIODICALS

Hollywood Reporter, April 6, 1992, p. 41.

* * *

MAYRON, Melanie 1952-

PERSONAL: Full name, Melanie Joy Mayron; born October 20, 1952, in Philadelphia, PA; daughter of David (a pharmaceutical chemist) and Norma (a real estate agent; maiden name, Goodman) Mayron. *Education:* Graduated from American Academy of Dramatic Arts, 1972; trained for the stage with Sandra Seacat, John Lehne, and Lee Strasberg.

ADDRESSES: Agent—Triad Artists, Inc., 10100 Santa Monica Blvd., 16th Floor, Los Angeles, CA 90067.

CAREER: Actress, writer, and producer. Partner, with Catlin Adams, of HighTop Films; member of Actors' Studio.

AWARDS, HONORS: British Academy Award nomination, best newcomer, and named best actress, Lucarno Film Festival, both 1979, both for *Girlfriends;* Emmy Award, outstanding supporting actress in a drama series, 1989, and Emmy Award nominations, outstanding supporting actress in a drama series, 1990 and 1991, all for *thirtysomething.*

CREDITS:

TELEVISION APPEARANCES; SERIES

Melissa Steadman, *thirtysomething,* ABC, 1987-91.

TELEVISION APPEARANCES; MOVIES

Dee Dee, *Hustling,* ABC, 1975.
Madelaine, *Katie: Portrait of a Centerfold,* NBC, 1978.
Marianne, *Playing for Time,* CBS, 1980.
Carol Link, *The Best Little Girl in the World,* ABC, 1981.
Sophie Rosenstein, *Will There Really Be a Morning?,* CBS, 1983.
Sonja Kahn, *Wallenberg: A Hero's Story,* NBC, 1985.

TELEVISION APPEARANCES; EPISODIC

Mrs. Eller, "Cindy Eller: A Modern Fairy Tale," *ABC Afterschool Specials,* ABC, 1985.
Sue, "Wanted: The Perfect Guy," *ABC Afterschool Specials,* ABC, 1986.

Also appeared on *Rhoda.*

OTHER TELEVISION APPEARANCES

Joyce Adams, *The New Love Boat* (pilot; also known as *The Love Boat III*), ABC, 1977.
Lily—Sold Out (special), CBS, 1981.
The 41st Annual Emmy Awards (special), Fox, 1989.
Time Warner Presents the Earth Day Special, ABC, 1990.
Hostess, *The Party's Over* (special documentary; also known as *Your Family Matters*), Lifetime, 1990.

FILM APPEARANCES

Ginger, *Harry and Tonto,* Twentieth Century-Fox, 1974.
Marsha, *Car Wash,* Universal, 1976.
Dixie, *Gable and Lombard,* Universal, 1976.
Annie Gerrard, *You Light Up My Life,* Columbia, 1977.
Susan Weinblatt, *Girlfriends,* Warner Brothers, 1978.
Lulu, *The Great Smokey Roadblock* (also known as *The Last of the Cowboys*), Dimension, 1978.
Susan, *Heartbeeps,* Universal, 1981.
Terry Simon, *Missing,* Universal, 1982.
Janet Keefer, *The Boss's Wife,* Tri-Star, 1986.
Lolly, *Sticky Fingers* (also see below), Spectrafilm, 1988.
Jenny Macklin, *Checking Out,* Warner Brothers, 1989.
Crystal Rybak, *My Blue Heaven,* Warner Brothers, 1990.

FILM WORK; PRODUCER

(With Catlin Adams) *Sticky Fingers* (also see below), Spectrafilm, 1988.
(With Adams) *Little Shiny Shoes* (also see below), Actors Make Movies, 1988.

STAGE APPEARANCES

Gilmer, *Godspell,* Marines Memorial Theatre, San Francisco, CA, 1974, then at La Mama Theatre, New York City, 1982.
Shulamith, *Gethsemane Springs,* Mark Taper Forum, Los Angeles, CA, 1976.
(Broadway debut) Nancy Scott, *The Goodbye People,* Belasco Theatre, New York City, 1979.
Bunny, Actors Studio, 1980.
Isabelle, *Crossing Delancey,* Jewish Repertory Theatre, 1985.

MAJOR TOURS

(Stage debut) Kate Draper, *Godspell,* U.S. cities, 1972-73.

WRITINGS:

(With Adams) *Sticky Fingers* (screenplay), Spectrafilm, 1988.

Also author of *Maggie & Mille;* with Adams, of the play *Little Shiny Shoes* and of the television screenplays *Tunes for a Small Harmonica* and *The Pretend Game;* and, with Lisa Harlow Stark, of the screenplay *The Laziest Man on Earth.*

* * *

McLAUGHLIN, Emily 1928-1991

OBITUARY NOTICE—See index for *CTFT* sketch: Born December 1, 1928, in White Plains, NY; died of cancer, April 26, 1991, in Los Angeles, CA. Actress. McLaughlin is best remembered for her role as nurse Jessie Brewer on the daytime television series *General Hospital.* After studying drama in New York City in the 1950s, she acted in Broadway and Off-Broadway productions and toured in *Richard III, Plaza Suite,* and *The Corn is Green.* She made her soap opera debut on *Young Doctor Malone* and was a performer on other television shows, including *Studio One, The Twilight Zone,* and *The Eleventh Hour.* McLaughlin was a member of the original cast of *General Hospital,* which was first broadcast in 1963, and continued her role until the time of her death in 1991.

OBITUARIES AND OTHER SOURCES:

PERIODICALS

Hollywood Reporter, April 29, 1991, p. 16.
Variety, May 6, 1991, p. 349.

* * *

MEDAVOY, Mike 1941-

PERSONAL: Born January 21, 1941, in Shanghai, China; immigrated to the United States, 1957; naturalized citizen, 1962; son of Michael and Dora Medavoy; married Patricia Duff; children: Melissa, Brian, Michael. *Education:* University of California, Los Angeles, B.A. (with honors), history, 1963.

ADDRESSES: Office—Tri-Star Pictures, 3400 Riverside Dr., Burbank, CA 91505.

CAREER: Motion picture executive. Universal Studios, member of casting department, 1963; Bill Robinson Associates, Los Angeles, CA, agent, 1963-64; GAC/CMA Co., vice-president of motion picture department, 1965-71; IFA Co., vice-president of motion picture department, 1971-74; United Artists Corp., senior vice-president for West Coast production, 1974-78; Orion Pictures Co., Burbank, CA, executive vice-president, 1978-90; Tri-Star Pictures, Burbank, chairman. Filmex, president, 1979—; Columbia Pictures, member of board of directors. Boston Museum of Fine Arts, member of visiting committee; Sundance Institute, member of board of governors; California Museum of Science and Industry, member of board of directors; University of California, Los Angeles, member of UCLA Foundation and UCLA Chancellors Associates; Tel Aviv University, member of advisory board.

MEMBER: Academy of Motion Picture Arts and Sciences (governor, 1977-81).

CREDITS:

TELEVISION APPEARANCES; EPISODIC

"Naked Hollywood," *A&E Premieres,* Arts and Entertainment, 1991.*

* * *

MERLIN, Joanna 1931-

PERSONAL: Name originally Joann Ratner; born July 15, 1931, in Chicago, IL; daughter of Harry (a grocer) and Toni (Merlin) Ratner; married Martin Lubner (an artist and teacher), December 17, 1950 (marriage ended, 1955); married David Dretzin (an attorney), March 1, 1964. *Education:* Attended University of California at Los Angeles, 1949-51, and American Shakespeare Festival Theatre and Academy, New York City, 1957-58; studied acting with Benjamin Zemach, 1947-50; Morris Carnovsky, 1948; Michael Chekhov, 1950-55; Fanny Bradshaw, 1957-58; Uta Hagen, 1961; and Tamara Daykarhanova, beginning in 1962.

ADDRESSES: Agent—Susan Smith and Associates, 192 Lexington Ave., Suite 1204, New York, NY 10016.

CAREER: Actress. Made first stage appearance in a Chicago, IL, production of *Too Many Marys,* 1942.

MEMBER: Actors Equity Association, American Federation of Television and Radio Artists, Screen Actors Guild.

CREDITS:

STAGE APPEARANCES

(Professional debut) Pilar, *Bullfight,* New Hampshire Playhouse, Hollywood, CA, 1956.
Athenian Girl and Myrrhina understudy, *Lysistrata,* Lenox Hill Playhouse, New York City, 1956.
Gina, *The Pidgeon,* Temple Theatre, New York City, 1957.
Hamlet, American Shakespeare Festival (ASF), Stratford, CT, 1958.
A Midsummer Night's Dream, ASF, Stratford, 1958.
Emilia, *The Winter's Tale,* ASF, Stratford, 1958.
Isolde, *Tunnel of Love,* Rockland County Playhouse, NY, 1959.

Mrs. Frank, *The Diary of Anne Frank,* Rockland County Playhouse, 1959.

Helena, *Look Back in Anger,* Rockland County Playhouse, 1959.

Esther, *The Flowering Peach,* Rockland County Playhouse, 1959.

Rosetta, *No Trifling with Love,* St. Marks Playhouse, New York City, 1959.

Barbara, *Major Barbara,* Murray Dodge Theatre, Princeton, NJ, 1960.

Catherine, *The Winslow Boy,* Tenthouse, Highland Park, IL, 1960.

Gina, *Right You Are,* McCarter Theatre, Princeton, 1960.

Anita di Speranza, *The Breaking Wall,* St. Marks Playhouse, 1960.

Silia Gala, *The Rules of the Game,* Gramercy Arts, 1960.

(Broadway debut) Gwendolyn, *Becket* (also see below), St. James Theatre, New York City, 1961, Hudson Theatre, New York City, 1961.

Martha Freud, *A Far Country* (also see below), Music Box, New York City, 1961.

Poppea Sabina, *The Emperor,* Maidman Theatre, New York City, 1963.

Stepdaughter, *Six Characters in Search of an Author,* Martinique Theatre, 1963.

Dawnthea, *Thistle in My Bed,* Gramercy Arts, 1963.

Rachel Apt, *The Wall,* Arena Stage, Washington, DC, 1964.

Tzeitl, *Fiddler on the Roof,* Imperial Theatre, New York City, 1964.

Gertrude Glass, *The Bird, the Bear and the Actress,* Eugene O'Neill Memorial Theatre, Waterford, CT, 1966.

Gloria, *Shelter,* John Golden Theatre, New York City, 1973.

Standby, *Uncle Vanya,* Circle in the Square, Joseph E. Levine Theatre, New York City, 1973.

Title role, *Clytemnestra,* The Cubiculo, New York City, 1976.

Pat, *Canadian Gothic/American Modern,* The Phoenix Theatre Company, Marymount Manhattan Theatre, New York City, 1976.

Anna Colonna, *The Grinding Machine,* American Place Theatre, New York City, 1978.

Leslie Nathan, *The Beach House,* Long Wharf Theatre, New Haven, CT, 1980.

Zlatke, *The Survivor,* Morosco Theatre, New York City, 1981.

Liz, *Solomon's Child,* Little Theatre, New York City, 1982.

Also appeared as Madame Ranevskaya in *The Cherry Orchard* and as Mrs. Patrick Campbell in *Dear Liar,* both at the John Drew Theatre in Long Island, New York.

MAJOR TOURS

Gwendolyn, *Becket,* U.S. Cities, 1960.

Martha Freud, *A Far Country,* 1961.

FILM APPEARANCES

Myra, *The Key* (documentary), Campus, 1957.

The Pusher, United Artists, 1960.

Josie, *Weddings and Babies,* Twentieth Century-Fox, 1960.

Anatomy of a Disease (documentary), Vision Association, 1962.

Nurse Pierce, *All That Jazz,* Twentieth Century-Fox, 1979.

Miss Berg, *Fame,* Metro-Goldwyn-Mayer/United Artist, 1980.

Superintendent Sturgis, *Love Child,* Warner Brothers, 1982.

Allan's Mother, *Soup for One,* Warner Brothers, 1982.

Mrs. Rosen, *Baby, It's You,* Paramount, 1983.

Schanberg's Sister, *The Killing Fields,* Warner Brothers, 1984.

Bag Lady, *Prince of Darkness,* Universal, 1987.

Margaret, *Mystic Pizza,* Samuel Goldwyn Productions, 1988.

Estelle Ward, *Class Action,* Twentieth Century-Fox, 1991.

TELEVISION APPEARANCES; FILMS

Mrs. Farelli, *The Last Tenant,* ABC, 1978.

Jacobo Timerman: Prisoner without a Name, Cell without a Number, NBC, 1983.

Dr. Bromberg, *Murder in Black and White* (also known as *Janek: Cause of Death*), CBS, 1990.

Frances Silvano, *In a Child's Name,* CBS, 1991.

TELEVISION APPEARANCES; DAYTIME SERIALS

Played Emily Cory on *Another World,* NBC.

TELEVISION APPEARANCES; EPISODIC

Great Jewish Stories, WOR, 1957.

"The Oresteia," *Omnibus,* NBC, 1960.

Seven Who Were Hanged, CBS, 1960.

Delgado's wife, *The Power and the Glory,* CBS, 1961.

Gloria, "King Stainislaus and the Knights of the Round Table," *Naked City,* ABC, 1962.

Lucia Lopez, "pilot episode," *East Side/West Side,* CBS, 1962.

Mrs. Martinez, "The Bagman," *The Defenders,* CBS, 1963.

Nan Riley, "pilot episode," *Nurse,* CBS, 1980.

Ellen Kennedy, *LA Law,* NBC, 1991.

Clara Bowman, *Law and Order,* NBC, 1992.

Gina Halbrook, *Baby Talk,* ABC, 1992.

TELEVISION WORK; SPECIALS

Inez Martin, "Starstruck," *ABC Afterschool Specials,* ABC, 1981.
Marian Rosenberg, "A Matter of Conscience" (also known as "Silent Witness"), *CBS Schoolbreak Specials,* CBS, 1989.
Emmy Stieglitz, "Marriage: Georgia O'Keefe and Alfred Stieglitz" (also known as "An American Place, O'Keefe and Stieglitz," and "The Eleventh Hour"), *American Playhouse,* PBS, 1991.

* * *

MICHAELS, Richard 1936-

PERSONAL: Born February 15, 1936, in Brooklyn, NY; children: Gregory, Meredith. *Education:* Attended Cornell University.

ADDRESSES: Agent—David Gersh, The Gersh Agency, 250 North Canon Dr., Beverly Hills, CA 90210.

CAREER: Director. Script supervisor, 1955-64; associate producer, 1965-70.

MEMBER: Directors Guild of America.

AWARDS, HONORS: Christopher Award, c. 1979, for *And Your Name Is Jonah;* Christopher Award, c. 1980, and Banff International Television Festival Special Jury Award, 1981, both for *Homeward Bound;* Scott Newman Drug Abuse Prevention Award, c. 1980, for *Scared Straight! Another Story.*

CREDITS:

TELEVISION DIRECTOR; MOVIES

Leave Yesterday Behind, ABC, 1978.
My Husband Is Missing (also known as *The Reach of Love*), NBC, 1978.
And Your Name Is Jonah, CBS, 1979.
Once upon a Family, CBS, 1980.
The Plutonium Incident, CBS, 1980.
Homeward Bound, CBS, 1980.
Scared Straight! Another Story, CBS, 1980.
Berlin Tunnel 21, CBS, 1981.
The Children Nobody Wanted, CBS, 1981.
One Cooks, the Other Doesn't, CBS, 1983.
Silence of the Heart, CBS, 1984.
Heart of a Champion: The Ray Mancini Story, CBS, 1985.
Rockabye, CBS, 1986.
Red River, CBS, 1988.
Indiscreet, CBS, 1988.
Love and Betrayal, CBS, 1989.
Leona Helmsley: The Queen of Mean, CBS, 1990.
A Triumph of the Heart: The Ricky Bell Story, CBS, 1991.
Her Wicked Ways, CBS, 1991.
Backfield in Motion, ABC, 1991.
Miss America: Behind the Crown, NBC, 1992.

TELEVISION DIRECTOR; SERIES

(And associate producer) *Bewitched,* ABC, 1968-72.
(With others) *Love, American Style,* ABC, 1969-74.
(With others) *The Brady Bunch,* ABC, 1969-74.
(With others) *Room 222,* ABC, 1969-74.
(With others) *Delvecchio,* CBS, 1976-77.
(With others) *Big Hawaii,* NBC, 1977.

TELEVISION DIRECTOR; EPISODIC

The Odd Couple, ABC, 1970-75.
Ellery Queen, NBC, 1975-76.

TELEVISION DIRECTOR; PILOTS

Kelly's Kids, ABC, 1974.
Charlie Cobb: Nice Night for a Hanging, NBC, 1977.
Having Babies II, ABC, 1977.
Jessie, ABC, 1984.
Kay O'Brien, CBS, 1986.
Leg Work, CBS, 1987.

TELEVISION DIRECTOR; MINISERIES

Once an Eagle, NBC, 1976-77.
Sadat, Operation Prime Time, 1983.
I'll Take Manhattan, CBS, 1987.

FILM DIRECTOR

How Come Nobody's on Our Side, American Films, 1975.
Death Is Not the End, Lipert Films International, 1976.
Blue Skies Again, Warner Brothers, 1983.

* * *

MILLER, Barry 1958-

PERSONAL: Born February 6 (one source says 8), 1958, in Los Angeles, CA (one source says New York, NY); married Marci Phillips, 1983.

ADDRESSES: Agent—Biff Liff, William Morris Agency, 1350 Avenue of the Americas, New York, NY 10019.

CAREER: Actor.

AWARDS, HONORS: Villager Award, best actor, 1981, for *Forty-Deuce;* Drama Desk Award, best featured actor in a play, 1984, Antoinette Perry Award, best featured actor in a dramatic role, Outer Critics Circle Award, and Theatre World Award, all 1985, all for *Biloxi Blues.*

CREDITS:

STAGE APPEARANCES

The City at 4 A.M., Actors Studio, New York City, 1979.

Bernie, *My Mother, My Father, and Me,* W.P.A. Theatre, New York City, 1980.
Ricky, *Forty-Deuce,* Perry Street Theatre, 1981.
Caliban, *The Tempest,* New York Shakespeare Festival, Delacorte Theatre, New York City, 1981.
Arnold Epstein, *Biloxi Blues,* Ahmanson Theatre, Los Angeles, CA, 1984, then Neil Simon Theatre, New York City, 1985-86.
Festival of One-Act Comedies, Judith Anderson Theatre, New York City, 1989.
Crazy He Calls Me, Walter Kerr Theatre, New York City, 1992.

FILM APPEARANCES

Young Lepke, *Lepke,* Warner Brothers, 1975.
Bobby C., *Saturday Night Fever,* Paramount, 1977.
Raymond Rothman, *Voices,* Metro-Goldwyn-Mayer (MGM)/United Artists (UA), 1979.
Raul Garcia/Ralph Garcy, *Fame,* MGM/UA, 1980.
Reuven Malter, *The Chosen,* Contemporary, 1982.
Parker, *The Journey of Natty Gann,* Buena Vista, 1985.
Richard Norvik, *Peggy Sue Got Married,* Tri-Star, 1986.
Dr. Nattore, *The Sicilian,* Twentieth Century-Fox, 1987.
Jeroboam, *The Last Temptation of Christ,* Universal, 1988.
Marty, *Love at Large,* Orion, 1990.

TELEVISION APPEARANCES; SERIES

Mark Vitale, *Joe and Sons,* CBS, 1975-76.
Bernard Fortwengler, *Szysznyk,* CBS, 1977-78.
Peter "Briggs" Brigman, *Equal Justice,* ABC, 1990-91.

TELEVISION APPEARANCES; EPISODIC

Henry Palamountain, "The Roommate," *American Playhouse,* PBS, 1986.

OTHER TELEVISION APPEARANCES

Staats, *Brock's Last Case* (pilot), NBC, 1973.
Kenneth McNamara, *Having Babies* (pilot; also known as *Giving Birth*), ABC, 1976.
Domenic, *The Death of Richie* (movie), NBC, 1977.
Jerry Rubin, *Conspiracy: The Trial of the Chicago Eight* (movie; also known as *The Truth and Nothing but the Truth: The Chicago Conspiracy Trial*), HBO, 1987.

Also appeared as Demos in *King of America,* 1982.*

* * *

MILLER, Dennis 1953-

PERSONAL: Born November 3, 1953, in Pittsburgh, PA. *Education:* Received degree in journalism from Point Park College.

CAREER: Comedian.

CREDITS:

TELEVISION APPEARANCES; SERIES

Saturday Night Live, NBC, 1985-91.
Host, *The Dennis Miller Show* (also see below), syndicated, 1992—.

Also appeared on *P.M. Magazine* in Pittsburgh, PA, and was host of *Punchline.*

TELEVISION APPEARANCES; SPECIALS

Comic Relief II, HBO, 1987.
Dennis Miller: Mr. Miller Goes to Washington, HBO, 1988.
Host, *Freedomfest: Nelson Mandela's 70th Birthday Celebration,* FOX, 1988.
Host, *A Rock 'n' Roll Christmas,* FOX, 1988.
Saturday Night Live 15th Anniversary, NBC, 1989.
Host, *The 13th Annual Young Comedians Show,* HBO, 1989.
Host, *The America's Choice Awards,* Turner Broadcasting System, 1990.
Comic Relief IV, HBO, 1990.
Dennis Miller: Black and White (also see below), HBO, 1990.
Time Warner Presents the Earth Day Special, ABC, 1990.
Two Years . . . Later, NBC, 1990.
Host, *Entertainers '91: The Top Twenty of the Year,* ABC, 1991.
Host, *The 43rd Annual Primetime Emmy Awards Presentation,* FOX, 1991.
Saturday Night Live Goes Commercial, NBC, 1991.

Also appeared on *The 10th Annual ACE Awards,* 1989.

TELEVISION APPEARANCES; EPISODIC

Appeared on *Late Night with David Letterman,* NBC.

TELEVISION EXECUTIVE PRODUCER

Dennis Miller: Black and White (special; also see below), HBO, 1990.
(With Brad Grey) *The Dennis Miller Show* (series; also see below), syndicated, 1992—.

WRITINGS:

TELEVISION

Dennis Miller: Black and White (special), HBO, 1990.
The Dennis Miller Show (series), syndicated, 1992—.

OTHER SOURCES:

PERIODICALS

Gentleman's Quarterly, August, 1989, p. 65.*

MILLER, Penelope
See MILLER, Penelope Ann

* * *

MILLER, Penelope Ann 1964-
(Penelope Miller)

PERSONAL: Born Penelope Andrea Miller, January 13, 1964, in Santa Monica, CA; daughter of Mark (an actor and filmmaker) and Beatrice (a journalist; maiden name, Ammidown) Miller. *Education:* Attended Menlo College; trained for the stage at Herbert Berghof Studios with Herbert Berghof.

ADDRESSES: *Agent*—Creative Artists Agency, 1888 Century Park E., 14th Floor, Los Angeles, CA 90067. *Manager*—Kincaid Management, 43 Navy St., 3rd Floor, Venice, CA 90291.

CAREER: Actress.

MEMBER: Actors Equity Association, American Federation of Television and Radio Artists.

AWARDS, HONORS: Antoinette Perry Award nomination, best performance by a featured actress in a play, 1989, for *Our Town.*

CREDITS:

FILM APPEARANCES

Brenda, *Adventures in Babysitting,* Buena Vista, 1987.
Daisy Hannigan, *Biloxi Blues,* Universal, 1988.
Winnie, *Big Top Pee-Wee,* Paramount, 1988.
Sally, *Miles from Home,* Cinecom, 1988.
Linda, *Dead-Bang,* Warner Brothers, 1989.
Lori Mitchell, *Downtown,* Twentieth Century-Fox, 1990.
Tina Sabatini, *The Freshman,* Tri-Star, 1990.
Joyce, *Kindergarten Cop,* Universal, 1990.
Paula, *Awakenings,* Columbia, 1990.
Kate Sullivan, *Other People's Money,* Warner Brothers, 1991.
Biddy, *A Very Good Year,* Castlerock, 1991.
Charlie, Carolco, 1991.
Betty Lou, *Gun in Betty Lou's Handbag,* Disney, 1992.
Margaret Harwood, *Year of the Comet,* Columbia, 1992.

TELEVISION APPEARANCES; SERIES

Nancy O'Hara, *The Guiding Light,* CBS, 1984.
Lee Melton, *As the World Turns,* CBS, 1984.
Gwen Stottlemeyer, *The Popcorn Kid,* CBS, 1987.

TELEVISION APPEARANCES; EPISODIC

Tina, "The Closed Set" (also known as "Tales from the Hollywood Hills"), *Great Performances,* PBS, 1988.
Emily Webb, "Our Town," *Great Performances,* PBS, 1989.

TELEVISION APPEARANCES; SPECIALS

Presenter, *The Movie Awards,* CBS, 1991.

STAGE APPEARANCES

(Under name Penelope Miller) Jody, *Quilters,* Arizona Theatre Company, 1983-84.
Meredith, *The People from Work,* Herbert Berghof Playhouse, New York City, 1984.
Daisy Hannigan, *Biloxi Blues,* Ahmanson Theatre, Los Angeles, CA, 1984, then (Broadway debut) Neil Simon Theatre, New York City, 1985-86.
Ruth, *Moonchildren,* Second Stage Theatre, New York City, 1987.
Emily Webb, *Our Town,* Lincoln Center Theatre, New York City, c. 1988, then Lyceum Theatre, New York City, 1988-89.

Member, under name Penelope Miller, of Denver Center Theatre Company, Denver, CO, 1984-85.

OTHER SOURCES:

PERIODICALS

Interview, December, 1988, p. 50.
Premiere, March, 1990, p. 49; September, 1991, p. 70.

* * *

MILLS, Alley

PERSONAL: Daughter of Ted Mills (a television executive). *Education:* Graduate (magna cum laude) of Yale University (drama) and Bennington College (art history).

ADDRESSES: *Agent*—Shapira and Associates, 15301 Ventura Blvd., Suite 345, Sherman Oaks, CA 91403.

CAREER: Actress.

CREDITS:

TELEVISION APPEARANCES; SERIES

Leslie Dunn, *The Associates,* NBC, 1979-80.
Sara Conover, *Making the Grade,* CBS, 1982.
Norma Arnold, *The Wonder Years,* ABC, 1988—.

TELEVISION APPEARANCES; MOVIES

Wanda, *Rape and Marriage: The Rideout Case,* CBS, 1980.
Allison Cross, *A Matter of Life and Death,* CBS, 1981.
Amy Vitelli, *The Other Woman,* CBS, 1983.
Dr. Rebecca Bishop, *Prototype,* CBS, 1983.
Amy Kennear, *The Atlanta Child Murders,* CBS, 1985.

TELEVISION APPEARANCES; PILOTS

Terry Robinson, *Poor Richard,* CBS, 1984.
Denise, *Second Edition,* CBS, 1984.
Charlotte Farnsworth, *Maggie,* CBS, 1986.
Pat, *Mr. President,* Fox, 1987.
Gloria, *I Love You Perfect,* ABC, 1989.

TELEVISION APPEARANCES; EPISODIC

"They've Taken Our Daughter," *Kaz,* CBS, 1979.
"Search," *Lou Grant,* CBS, 1981.
Tracy Renko, "Zen and the Art of Law Enforcement," *Hill Street Blues,* NBC, 1982.
Tracy Renko, "Personal Foul," *Hill Street Blues,* NBC, 1982.
Tracy Renko, "Hill Shooter," *Hill Street Blues,* NBC, 1982.
Tracy Renko, "Invasion of the Third World Mutant Body Snatchers," *Hill Street Blues,* NBC, 1982.
Tracy Renko, "A Hill of Beans," *Hill Street Blues,* NBC, 1983.
"Sprained Dreams," *Newhart,* CBS, 1983.
"The Man Who Cried Wife," *Moonlighting,* ABC, 1986.
"Where There's a Will, There's a Way," *I Married Dora,* ABC, 1987.
"West Coast Story," *I Married Dora,* ABC, 1987.
"To Heal a Nation," *General Electric Theater,* NBC, 1988.
Cohost, *Home,* ABC, 1989.
Linda Hatch, "Testing Dirty" (also known as "Drug Busters"), *ABC Afterschool Special,* ABC, 1990.

Also appeared on *The Patti Page Show.*

FILM APPEARANCES

Diary of a Mad Housewife, Universal, 1970.
Nancy Reese, *Going Berserk,* Universal, 1983.

STAGE APPEARANCES

The Little Foxes, Stage West, West Springfield, MA, 1977-78.
The Idol Makers, Mark Taper Forum, Los Angeles, CA, 1978-79.
Bella Phelan, *Says I, Says He,* Center Theatre Group, Mark Taper Forum, 1979-80.
Almost Perfect, Santa Monica Playhouse, Santa Monica, CA, 1986.

STAGE WORK

Associate director, *Hey, Rube,* Women's Interart Center, New York City, 1978.*

MILNER, Ron 1938-

PERSONAL: Full name, Ronald Milner; born May 29, 1938, in Detroit, MI. *Education:* Attended Highland Park Junior College, Detroit Institute of Technology, and Columbia University.

ADDRESSES: Agent— William Morris Agency, 151 South El Camino Dr., Beverly Hills, CA 90212. *Contact—* c/o Crossroads Theatre Co., 320 Memorial Parkway, New Brunswick, NJ 08901.

CAREER: Writer. Affiliated with Concept East Theatre, Detroit, MI, beginning in 1964; Lincoln University, Lincoln University, PA, writer in residence, 1966-67; Michigan State University, East Lansing, MI, instructor, 1971-72; Spirit of Shango Theatre Company, Detroit, founder and director; Wayne State University, Detroit, playwriting workshop leader.

AWARDS, HONORS: John Hay Whitney Foundation fellowship, 1962; Rockefeller grant.

CREDITS:

STAGE DIRECTOR

Brother Malcolm, National Black Touring Circuit, New Heritage Repertory Theatre, New York City, 1986.
Don't Get God Started (musical; also see below), Longacre Theatre, New York City, 1987.

WRITINGS:

PLAYS

Who's Got His Own (three-act; also see below), produced at American Place Theatre, New York City, 1966.
The Monster (one-act), produced at Louis Theatre Center, Chicago, IL, 1969, published in *Drama Review,* summer, 1968.
The Warning—A Theme for Linda (one-act), first produced with other plays in *A Black Quartet* at Chelsea Theatre Center, Brooklyn Academy of Music, Brooklyn, NY, 1969, published in *A Black Quartet: Four New Black Plays,* edited by Ben Caldwell and others, New American Library, 1970.
M(ego) and the Green Ball of Freedom (one-act), produced at Shango Theatre, Detroit, MI, 1971, published in *Black World,* April, 1971.
What the Wine Sellers Buy, produced at New Federal Theatre, New York City, 1973, published by Samuel French, 1974.
These Three, produced at Concept East Theatre, Detroit, 1974.
(And author of lyrics) *Season's Reasons* (musical), produced at Langston Hughes Theatre, Detroit, 1976.
Work, produced at Detroit Public Schools, Detroit, 1978.

(And author of lyrics) *Jazz-set* (musical), produced at Mark Taper Forum, Los Angeles, CA, 1980.
(And author of lyrics) *Crack Steppin'* (musical), produced at Music Hall, Detroit, 1981.
Roads of the Mountaintop, produced at Crossroads Theatre, New Brunswick, NJ, 1986.
Checkmates, produced at Westwood Playhouse, Los Angeles, 1987.
Don't Get God Started (musical), produced at Longacre Theatre, New York City, 1987.

Also author of *Life Agony* (one-act), produced at Unstable Theatre, Detroit, and *The Greatest Gift,* produced at Detroit Public Schools, Detroit.

OTHER

(Editor and author of introduction with Woodie King, Jr., and contributor) *Black Drama Anthology* (includes *Who's Got His Own*), New American Library, 1971.

Author of the screenplay *The James Brown Story.* Contributor to anthologies and other books, including *Best Short Stories by Negro Writers,* edited by Langston Hughes, Little, Brown, 1967; *Black Arts: An Anthology of Black Creations,* edited by Ahmed Alhamisi and Harun Kofi Wangara, Black Arts, 1969; *Five Black Writers,* edited by Donald B. Gibson, New York University Press, 1970; *The Black Aesthetic,* edited by Addison Gayle, Jr., Doubleday, 1971; *Nommo: An Anthology of Modern Black African and Black American Literature,* edited by William R. Robinson, Macmillan, 1972; *Black Short Story Anthology,* edited by Woodie King, Jr., Columbia University Press, 1972; and *Black Poets and Prophets,* edited by King and Earl Anthony, New American Library. Also contributor to periodicals, including *Negro Digest, Drama Review,* and *Black World.*

OTHER SOURCES:

BOOKS

Contemporary Authors, New Revision Series, Volume 24, Gale, 1988, pp. 322-24.
Contemporary Literary Criticism, Volume 56, Gale, 1989, pp. 220-29.
Dictionary of Literary Biography, Volume 38, Gale, 1985, pp. 201-07.*

* * *

MINGHELLA, Anthony 1954-

PERSONAL: Born January 6, 1954, in Ryde, Isle of Wight, England. *Education:* University of Hull, Yorkshire, B.A. (honours), 1975.

ADDRESSES: Agent—Judy Daish Associates, 83 Eastbourne Mews, London W2 6LQ, England; and William Morris Agency, 151 South El Camino Dr., Beverly Hills, CA 90212.

CAREER: Playwright and director. University of Hull, lecturer in drama, 1976-81.

AWARDS, HONORS: Plays and Players Award for most promising new playwright, 1984, for *A Little Like Drowning;* Plays and Players Award for best new play, 1986, for *Made in Bangkok;* British Academy of Film and Television Arts Award, best original screenplay, 1991, for *Truly, Madly, Deeply.*

CREDITS:

STAGE WORK; DIRECTOR

Mobius the Stripper (also see below) produced in Hull, England, 1975.
Child's Play (also see below), produced in Hull, 1978.
Whale Music (also see below), Haymarket Studio, Leicester, England, 1981, then New End Theatre, London, 1981.

FILM WORK; DIRECTOR

Truly, Madly, Deeply, Goldwyn, 1991.

WRITINGS:

PLAYS

Mobius the Stripper (adaptation of story by Gabriel Josipovici), produced in Hull, England, 1975.
Child's Play, produced in Hull, 1978.
Whale Music (also see below), produced at Haymarket Studio, Leicester, England, 1981, then New End Theatre, London, 1981.
A Little Like Drowning (also see below), produced at Hempstead Theatre, Hertfordshire, England, 1982, then London, 1984.
Two Planks and a Passion (also see below), produced in Exeter, England, 1983, then Greenwich Theatre, London, 1984.
Love Bites, produced in Derby, England, 1984.
(West End debut) *Made in Bangkok,* produced at Aldwych Theatre, London, 1986, then Mark Taper Forum, Los Angeles, 1988, published by Methuen, 1987.
Whale Music and Other Plays (contains *Whale Music, A Little Like Drowning,* and *Two Planks and a Passion*), published by Methuen, 1987.

Also author of *Interior: Room, Exterior: City* (three plays), 1989.

TELEVISION PLAYS

"Hans My Hedgehog" (also known as "The Grovelhog"), *The Storyteller,* NBC, 1987.
"Fearnot," *The Storyteller,* NBC, 1987.

"A Story Short," *The Storyteller,* NBC, 1988.
"The Luck Child," *The Storyteller,* NBC, 1988.
"Dead of Jericho," *Mystery* (part of the "Inspector Morse" series), PBS, 1988.
"The Heartless Giant," *The Jim Henson Hour* (also known as *Jim Henson Presents*), NBC, 1989.
"Deceived by Flight," *Mystery* (part of the "Inspector Morse" series), PBS, 1991.

Also author of television plays for the *Studio* series, 1983, and of *What If It's Raining,* 1986.

SCREENPLAYS

Truly, Madly, Deeply, Goldwyn, 1991.

Also adapted *Made in Bangkok* for film.

OTHER

On the Line (novelization of television series), Severn House, 1982.

Also author of radio plays.*

* * *

MIRREN, Helen 1946-

PERSONAL: Born in 1946 in England. *Education:* Attended convent school and teacher-training college.

ADDRESSES: Agent—Al Parker Ltd., 50 Mount Street, London W1, England.

CAREER: Actress. Performed at National Youth Theatre, 1963-64.

AWARDS, HONORS: Cannes International Film Festival Award, best actress, 1984, for *Cal;* British Academy of Film and Television Arts Award, best actress in a television program, 1992, for "Prime Suspect," an episode of *Mystery!*

CREDITS:

STAGE APPEARANCES

Cleopatra, *Anthony and Cleopatra,* Old Vic Theatre, London, 1965.
Kitty, *Charley's Aunt,* Manchester Theatre, Manchester, England, 1967.
Nerissa, *The Merchant of Venice,* Manchester Theatre, 1967.
Castiza, *The Revenger's Tragedy,* Royal Shakespeare Company, Stratford-on-Avon, England, 1967.
Diana, *All's Well That Ends Well,* Royal Shakespeare Company, Stratford-on-Avon, 1967.
Cressida, *Troilus and Cressida,* Aldwych Theatre, London, 1968.
Hero, *Much Ado about Nothing,* Aldwych Theatre, 1968-69.
Lady Anne, *Richard III,* Royal Shakespeare Company, Stratford-on-Avon, 1970.
Ophelia, *Hamlet,* Royal Shakespeare Company, Stratford-on-Avon, 1970.
Julia, *The Two Gentlemen of Verona,* Royal Shakespeare Company, Stratford-on-Avon, 1970.
Tatyana, *Enemies,* Royal Shakespeare Company, Aldwych Theatre, 1971.
Harriet, *The Man of Mode,* Royal Shakespeare Company, Aldwych Theatre, 1971.
Title role, *Miss Julie,* Royal Shakespeare Company, Aldwych Theatre, 1971.
Elayne, *The Balcony,* Royal Shakespeare Company, Aldwych Theatre, 1971.
Isabella, *Measure for Measure,* Riverside Studios Theatre, London, 1974.
Lady Macbeth, *Macbeth,* Royal Shakespeare Company, Stratford-on-Avon, 1974, then Aldwych Theatre, 1975.
Maggie, *Teeth 'n' Smiles,* Royal Court Theatre, London, 1975, then Wyndham's Theatre, London, 1976.
Nina, *The Seagull,* Lyric Theatre, London, 1975.
Ella, *The Bed before Yesterday,* Lyric Theatre, 1975.
Queen Margaret, *Henry VI, Parts I, II and III,* Royal Shakespeare Company, Stratford-on-Avon, 1977, then Aldwych Theatre, 1978.
Title role, *The Duchess of Malfi,* Royal Exchange Theatre, Manchester, England, 1980, then Mound House Theatre, London, 1981.
Grace, *Faith Healer,* Royal Court Theatre, 1981.
Cleopatra, *Antony and Cleopatra,* Pit Theatre, London, 1983.
Moll Cutpurse, *The Roaring Girl,* Barbican Theatre, London, 1983.
Marjorie, *Extremities,* Duchess Theatre, London, 1984.
Angela, "Some Kind of Love Story," and dying woman, "Elegy for a Lady," in *Two-Way Mirror* (double-bill), Young Vic Theatre, London, 1989.

Also appeared as Susie Monmican in *The Silver Lassie,* and as Win-the-Fight Littlewit in *Bartholomew Fair.*

FILM APPEARANCES

Herostradus, BBC, 1967.
Cora, *Age of Consent,* Columbia, 1969.
Gosh Smith-Boyde, *Savage Messiah,* Metro-Goldwyn-Mayer, 1972.
Patricia Burgess, *O Lucky Man!,* Warner Brothers, 1973.
Gertrude, *Hamlet,* Royal College of Art, 1976.
Caesonia, *Caligula,* Penthouse Films, 1979.
Victoria, *The Long Good Friday,* Embassy, 1979.
Alice Rage, *The Fiendish Plot of Dr. Fu Manchu,* Orion, 1980.

Morgana, *Excaliber,* Warner Brothers, 1981.
Priest of Love, Filmways, 1981.
Hermia, *A Midsummernight's Dream,* Eagle, 1982.
Marcella Morton, *Cal,* Warner Brothers, 1984.
Tanya Kirbuk, *2010,* United Artists, 1984.
Galina Ivanova, *White Nights,* Columbia, 1985.
Mother, *The Mosquito Coast,* Warner Brothers, 1986.
Ruth Chancellor, *The Gospel According to Vic* (also known as *Heavenly Pursuits*), Skouras, 1986.
Narrator, *Invocation Maya Deren* (documentary), Arts Council of Great Britain, 1987.
Narrator, *People of the Forest: The Chimps of Gombe* (documentary), National Geographic Society, 1988.
Lydia Neuman, *Pascali's Island,* Avenue, 1988.
Clemmie Jenkins, *When the Whales Came,* Twentieth Century-Fox, 1989.
Frances Penny Bethune, *Bethune: The Making of a Hero* (also known as *The Making of a Hero: The Story of Dr. Norman Bethune*), Filmstar, 1990.
Georgina Spica, the Wife, *The Cook, the Thief, His Wife and Her Lover,* Miramax, 1990.
Caroline, *The Comfort of Strangers,* Skouras, 1990.
Lilia Herriton, *Where Angels Fear to Tread,* Fine Line, 1991.

Also appeared as Beaty Simons in *Hussy,* 1979.

TELEVISION APPEARANCES; EPISODIC

"Cousin Bette," *Great Performances,* PBS, 1972.
Rosalind, "As You Like It," *The Shakespeare Plays,* PBS, 1979.
Princess Emilia, "The Little Mermaid," *Faerie Tale Theatre,* Showtime, 1987.
Alma Rattenbury, "Cause Celebre," *Mystery!,* PBS, 1988.
Detective Chief Inspector Jane Tennison, "Prime Suspect," *Mystery!,* PBS, 1992.

OTHER TELEVISION APPEARANCES

Stella MacKenzie, *Kiss Kiss, Kill Kill* (movie; also known as *A Coffin for the Bride*), ABC, 1974.
May Sloan, *S.O.S. Titanic* (movie), ABC, 1979.
Anna, *Red King, White Night* (movie), HBO, 1989.
The Siskel and Ebert Special, CBS, 1990.

Also appeared in a television production of *A Midsummernight's Dream,* 1978; appeared in *Miss Julie, The Applecart,* and *The Little Minister.*

OTHER SOURCES:

PERIODICALS

People, November 3, 1980, p. 99.
Variety, August 29, 1984, p. 6.*

MONTAND, Yves 1921-1991

OBITUARY NOTICE—See index for *CTFT* sketch: Born Ivo (some sources say Yvo) Livi, October 13, 1921, in Monsumano, Tuscany, Italy; died of a heart attack, November 9, 1991, in Senlis, France. Actor and singer. Beginning his entertainment career as a singer in France during World War II, Montand went on to gain fame as a stage and film actor. He made his film debut in the 1946 *Etoile sans lumiere* (also known as *Star without Light*). Working primarily in French and Italian movies, Montand first received international acclaim for his role in *Le Salaire de la peur* (also known as *The Wages of Fear*) in 1953. In the 1960s and 1970s he appeared in such well-received films as *Z, Tout va bien, Cesar et Rosalie,* and *Vincent, Francois, Paul, et les autres.* His last films included *Jean de Florette* and *Manon des sources* (also known as *Manon of the Spring*). Montand recorded many songs for movie soundtracks and in 1982 gave the first performance by a variety singer at the Metropolitan Opera in New York City. He also wrote a book of memoirs entitled *Du soleil plein la tete.*

OBITUARIES AND OTHER SOURCES:

BOOKS

Who's Who in the World, 11th edition, Marquis, 1991, p. 744.

PERIODICALS

Variety, November 18, 1991, pp. 44-45.

* * *

MONTGOMERY, Belinda J.

PERSONAL: Born in Winnipeg, Manitoba, Canada.

ADDRESSES: Contact—c/o *Doogie Howser, M.D.,* ABC Productions, 2020 Avenue of the Stars, 5th floor, Los Angeles, CA 90067.

CAREER: Actress. Child actress on Canadian television, radio, and the stage; also worked as a model.

CREDITS:

TELEVISION APPEARANCES; SERIES

Dr. Elizabeth Merrill, *The Man from Atlantis* (also see below), NBC, 1977-78.
Sarah Miller, *Aaron's Way,* NBC, 1988.
Katherine Howser, *Doogie Howser, M.D.,* ABC, 1989—.

Also appeared as Jennifer Brighton, *Dynasty,* ABC, beginning in 1981; Caroline Crockett, *Miami Vice,* NBC, beginning in 1981; and Pamela Crane, *Murder, She Wrote,* CBS, beginning in 1984.

TELEVISION APPEARANCES; MOVIES

Loey Wiley, *Ritual of Evil* (also known as *Next Time, My Love*), NBC, 1970.
Heller Chase, *The Bravos,* NBC, 1972.
Melinda, *Women in Chains,* ABC, 1972.
Diane Shaw, *The Devil's Daughter,* ABC, 1973.
Fiona, *The Hostage Heart,* CBS, 1977.
Peggy Ann West, *Murder in Music City* (also known as *The Country-Music Murders*), NBC, 1979.
Barbara Marciano, *Marciano,* ABC, 1979.
Melody Youngblood, *Bare Essence,* CBS, 1982.
Joan Donovan, *Uncommon Valor* (also known as *The Fire at County General*), CBS, 1983.
Libby Holland, *Dalton: Code of Vengeance II,* NBC, 1986.
Claire Graves, *Stark: Mirror Image,* CBS, 1986.
Myra Schmidbauer, *Adam: His Song Continues,* NBC, 1986.
Doc Stone, *Stone Fox,* NBC, 1987.
Terry Stillwell, *Casey's Gift: For Love of a Child* (also known as *In Memory of a Child* and *Maximum Liability*), NBC, 1990.

TELEVISION APPEARANCES; PILOTS

Luanne Gibson, *The D.A.: Conspiracy to Kill,* NBC, 1971.
Roselle Bridgeman, *Lock, Stock, and Barrel,* NBC, 1971.
Anne Dryden, *The Crime Club,* CBS, 1973.
Angie, "Dear Vincent," *Letters from Three Lovers,* ABC, 1973.
Dr. Elizabeth Merrill, *The Man from Atlantis,* NBC, 1977.
Kelly Kellogg, *Turnover Smith,* ABC, 1980.
Carrie Yeager, *Trouble in High Timber Country,* ABC, 1980.
Miami Vice, NBC, 1984.

TELEVISION APPEARANCES; EPISODIC

"A Touch of Hands," *The Virginian,* NBC, 1969.
"Twenty-Four Hours," *Medical Center,* CBS, 1969.
"Elegy for Edward Shelby," *Paris 7000,* ABC, 1970.
"Little Dog, Gone," *Ironside,* NBC, 1970.
"Nina," *Matt Lincoln,* ABC, 1970.
"Ride a Turquoise Pony," *Insight,* syndicated, 1971.
"The Day They Hanged Kid Curry," *Alias Smith and Jones,* ABC, 1971.
"Recurring Nightmare," *The FBI,* ABC, 1971.
Marcus Welby, M.D., ABC, 1971.
Owen Marshall, Counselor at Law, ABC, 1971.
"I Am Not Part of the Human World," *The Sixth Sense,* ABC, 1972.
"Desperate Runner," *The FBI,* ABC, 1972.
"Last Target," *Assignment: Vienna,* ABC, 1972.
"Stake Out," *Cannon,* CBS, 1972.
"A Deadly Velocity," *The Rookies,* ABC, 1972.
"A Collection of Eagles," *Streets of San Francisco,* ABC, 1973.
"The Guilty," *Medical Center,* CBS, 1973.
"Blind Terror," *Barnaby Jones,* CBS, 1973.
"The Word Is: Alternative," *The New Land,* ABC, 1974.
"Death in High Places," *Petrocelli,* NBC, 1974.
"Hoots," *Movin' On,* NBC, 1974.
"Sniper," *Police Story,* NBC, 1975.
"Jake's Okay," *Marcus Welby, M.D.,* ABC, 1975.
"Asylum," *Streets of San Francisco,* ABC, 1975.
"One Last Rebellion," *Medical Center,* CBS, 1975.
"A Lovely Way to Die," *City of Angels,* NBC, 1976.
Nashville 99, CBS, 1977.
"Night Scene," *Kingston: Confidential,* NBC, 1977.
"The Dutchman," *Most Wanted,* ABC, 1977.
"Accomplice to Murder," *Quincy,* NBC, 1978.
"Poison," *Lou Grant,* CBS, 1978.
Julie Farr, M.D., ABC, 1978.
"Dead Birds Don't Sing," *Sword of Justice,* NBC, 1978.
"Luke," *How the West Was Won,* ABC, 1979.
"Friday's Child," *Eischied,* NBC, 1979.
Fantasy Island, ABC, 1980.
"Girl under Glass," *Trapper John, M.D.,* CBS, 1980.
"El Dorado," *The Concrete Cowboys,* CBS, 1981.
Lobo, NBC, 1981.
"Lost and Found," *The Love Boat,* ABC, 1981.
"Ashes to Ashes and None Too Soon," *Simon and Simon,* CBS, 1982.
"The Baby," *Dynasty,* ABC, 1982.
"Mother and Son," *Dynasty,* ABC, 1982.
"Trained for Trouble," *Chips,* NBC, 1982.
"Bail Out," *Simon and Simon,* CBS, 1983.
"Walk a Straight Line," *T. J. Hooker,* ABC, 1983.
"Watch Out," *The Whiz Kids,* CBS, 1984.
"Payload," *Blue Thunder,* ABC, 1984.
"Miami: Sharing," *Lottery,* ABC, 1984.
Simon and Simon, CBS, 1984.
"Hit List," *Miami Vice,* NBC, 1984.
Magnum, P.I., CBS, 1984.
"Manna from Heaven," *Simon and Simon,* CBS, 1984.
"Calderone's Demise," *Miami Vice,* NBC, 1984.
"The Surrogate," *T. J. Hooker,* ABC, 1985.
"My Johnnie Lies over the Ocean," *Murder, She Wrote,* CBS, 1985.
"Wanted Dead or Alive," *Crazy Like a Fox,* CBS, 1985.
"Girls' Night Out," *Riptide,* NBC, 1985.
"Man at the Window," *Hitchhiker,* HBO, 1985.
"Murder Is a Novel Idea," *Street Hawk,* ABC, 1985.
Finders of Lost Loves, ABC, 1985.
"The Iron Man," *The Love Boat,* ABC, 1985.
Crazy Like a Fox, CBS, 1986.
"Competition: Who Needs It?," *Simon and Simon,* CBS, 1986.
"Child's Play," *Miami Vice,* NBC, 1987.

"To Have and to Hold," *Miami Vice,* NBC, 1989.
"Fifteen Forever," *In the Heat of the Night,* NBC, 1989.

Also appeared in *Days of Our Lives,* 1986.

TELEVISION APPEARANCES; SPECIALS

Cinderella, *Tales from Muppetland,* ABC, 1970.
Battle of the Network Stars III, ABC, 1977.
The 58th Annual Hollywood Christmas Parade, syndicated, 1989.

FILM APPEARANCES

Roberta, *The Todd Killings* (also known as *A Dangerous Friend* and *Skipper*), National General, 1971.
Audra-Jo, *The Other Side of the Mountain* (also known as *A Window to the Sky*), Universal, 1975.
Diana McBain, *Breaking Point,* Twentieth Century-Fox, 1976.
Annie Gallo, *Blackout,* Cinepix, 1978.
Audra-Jo, *The Other Side of the Mountain—Part 2,* Universal, 1978.
Sandy MacAuley, *Stone Cold Dead,* Dimension, 1980.
Dr. Joan Gilmore, *Silent Madness,* Almi, 1984.

Appeared in *Nightkillers,* 1983; and *Tell Me That You Love Me,* 1983.*

* * *

MONTY, Gloria 1921(?)-

PERSONAL: Born Gloria Montemuro, c. 1921, in Union City (one source says Weehawken), NJ; daughter of Joseph and Concetta M. (Mango) Montemuro; married Robert Thomas O'Byrne (a free-lance travel writer), January 8, 1952. *Education:* Received B.A. in drama and speech from New York University (one source says University of Iowa); received M.A. in drama from Columbia University.

ADDRESSES: Contact—c/o Directors Guild of America, 7950 Sunset Blvd., Los Angeles, CA 90046.

CAREER: Producer and director. New School for Social Research, New York City, director, 1952-53; Old Towne Theatre, Smithtown, NY, director, 1952-56; Abbey Theatre Workshop, New York City, director, 1952-56; Twentieth Century-Fox, executive producer in development for prime time television, 1987-90.

MEMBER: Directors Guild of America (member of executive committee), Women in Film, Stuntman's Association (honorary member), Thunderbird Country Club (Rancho Mirage, CA), Bel Air Country Club.

AWARDS, HONORS: Award from American Society of Lighting Directors, 1979; Emmy awards, best daytime drama series, 1981 and 1984, and Emmy Award nominations, best daytime drama series, 1982, 1983, 1985, and 1986, all for *General Hospital;* award for most successful show in the history of television, ABC, 1982; named Woman of the Year, Paulist Choristers of Southern California, 1986; Special Editors Award, *Soap Opera Digest.*

CREDITS:

TELEVISION WORK; SERIES

Director, *Secret Storm,* CBS, 1956-72.
Director (with Dick Franchot), *Bright Promise,* NBC, 1969-72.
Producer, then executive producer, *General Hospital* (also see below), ABC, 1978-87.
Executive producer, *The Hamptons,* ABC, 1983.

Also director of *This Child of Mine,* 1969.

TELEVISION WORK; MOVIES

Executive producer, *Confessions of a Married Man,* ABC, 1983.
Executive producer, *The Imposter* (also known as *The Snowman*), ABC, 1984.

TELEVISION WORK; EPISODIC

Director, *One Day at a Time,* CBS, 1975-84.
Director, *General Hospital* (also see below), ABC, beginning in 1978.

Also director of numerous episodes of *The ABC Wide World of Entertainment.*

TELEVISION WORK; SPECIALS

Producer of entertainment specials for ABC, beginning in 1972.

FILM WORK

Executive producer of *The Imposter,* 1988.

WRITINGS:

TELEVISION SERIES

(With others) *General Hospital,* ABC, beginning c. 1981.*

* * *

MOORE, Demi 1962-

PERSONAL: Given name, Demetria Gene; born November 11, 1962, in Roswell, NM; stepdaughter (some sources say daughter) of Danny (a journalist) and daughter of Virginia (King) Guynes; married Freddy (some sources say Rick) Moore (a musician), c. 1981 (divorced, 1983); married Bruce Willis (an actor), November 21, 1987; children:

Rumer Glenn, Scout La Rue (daughters). *Education:* Studied acting with Zina Provendie.

ADDRESSES: Agent—Creative Artists Agency, 9830 Wilshire Blvd., Beverly Hills, CA 90212.

CAREER: Actress and film producer. Has modeled for fashion magazines.

AWARDS, HONORS: Theatre World Award, 1987, for *The Early Girl.*

CREDITS:

FILM APPEARANCES

Patricia Welles, *Parasite,* Embassy, 1981.
Cameo, *Young Doctors in Love,* Twentieth Century-Fox, 1982.
Nicole Hollis, *Blame It on Rio,* Twentieth Century-Fox, 1984.
Laura Victor, *No Small Affair,* Columbia, 1984.
Jules, *St. Elmo's Fire,* Columbia, 1985.
Debbie Sullivan, *About Last Night,* Tri-Star, 1986.
Karen Simmons, *Wisdom,* Twentieth Century-Fox, 1986.
Cassandra, *One Crazy Summer,* Warner Brothers, 1986.
Abby Quinn, *The Seventh Sign,* Tri-Star, 1988.
Molly, *We're No Angels,* Paramount, 1989.
Molly Jensen, *Ghost,* Paramount, 1990.
Cynthia Kellogg, *Mortal Thoughts* (also see below), Columbia, 1991.
Diane Lightston, *Nothing but Trouble,* Warner Brothers, 1991.
Marina, *The Butcher's Wife,* Paramount, 1991.

Made film debut as Corri in *Choices,* 1981.

FILM WORK

Coproducer, *Mortal Thoughts,* Columbia, 1991.

TELEVISION APPEARANCES; SERIES

Jackie Templeton, *General Hospital,* ABC, 1982-83.

TELEVISION APPEARANCES; EPISODIC

"Max," *The Master,* NBC, 1984.
Host, *Saturday Night Live,* NBC, 1988.
"When Girls Collide," *Moonlighting,* ABC, 1989.
"Dead Right," *Tales from the Crypt,* HBO, 1990.
First Person with Maria Shriver, NBC, 1991.

Also appeared on episodes of *Kaz,* CBS, and *Vegas,* ABC.

TELEVISION APPEARANCES; SPECIALS

Nancy, *Bedrooms,* HBO, 1984.
Sandy Darden, *Judge Reinhold and Demi Moore in The New Homeowner's Guide to Happiness,* Cinemax, 1987.
61st Annual Academy Awards Presentation, ABC, 1989.
Entertainers '91: The Top 20 of the Year, ABC, 1991.

Also appeared in *Ron Reagan is the President's Son.*

STAGE APPEARANCES

Made Off-Broadway debut in *The Early Girl,* 1987.

OTHER SOURCES:

BOOKS

Newsmakers 91, Issue 4, Gale, 1991, pp. 282-284.

PERIODICALS

Daily News, March 31, 1988, pp. 51, 61.
Premiere, April, 1991, pp. 56-60, 620.*

* * *

MOORE, Edward James 1935-

PERSONAL: Born June 2, 1935, in Chicago, IL; son of Irwin J. (a truck driver) and Mary Elizabeth (Kase) Moore. *Education:* Attended Washburne Trade School; studied acting at Goodman Theatre and School of Drama, 1959-63, and Uta Hagen School of Acting, 1967-70.

ADDRESSES: Agent—c/o International Creative Management, 8899 Beverly Blvd., Los Angeles, CA 90048.

CAREER: Actor and playwright. Founder of the New York Playwright's Workshop of Greenwich Village, New York City. *Military service:* U.S. Navy, 1954-58.

MEMBER: American Federation of Radio and Television Artists, Actors' Equity Association, Screen Actors Guild, Dramatists Guild.

AWARDS, HONORS: Drama Desk Award, outstanding new playwright, 1974, for *The Sea Horse.*

CREDITS:

STAGE APPEARANCES

Palace guard, *Hippolytus,* Goodman Memorial Theatre, Chicago, IL, 1960.
Gendarme, *The Inspector,* Goodman Memorial Theatre, 1960.
Drum Major, *Woyzeck,* Goodman Memorial Theatre, 1961.
Mayor Berger, *Hannele,* Goodman Memorial Theatre, 1961.
Orsino, *Twelfth Night,* Goodman Memorial Theatre, 1961.
Mr. Akins, *Send Me No Flowers,* Red Barn Theatre, Saugatuck, MI, 1961.
Roger Henderson, *The Pleasure of His Company,* Red Barn Theatre, 1961.
Sunrise at Campobello, Red Barn Theatre, 1961.

Lt. Rooney, *Arsenic and Old Lace,* Red Barn Theatre, 1961.
Sandy Dean, *Brigadoon,* Red Barn Theatre, 1961.
Centuri, *Right You Are,* Goodman Memorial Theatre, 1962.
Hal Carter, *Picnic,* Goodman Memorial Theatre, 1962.
Tom, *Dinny and the Witches,* Goodman Memorial Theatre, 1962.
Cornelius Hackl, *The Matchmaker,* Goodman Memorial Theatre, 1962.
Bo Decker, *Bus Stop,* Goodman Memorial Theatre, 1962.
Dion Kapakos, *Critic's Choice,* Peninsula Players, Fish Creek, WI, 1962.
Mr. Tibbet, *Write Me a Murder,* Peninsula Players, 1962.
Freddie Vanderstuyt, *Romanoff and Juliet,* Peninsula Players, 1962.
Foley Thorndike, *Armored Dove,* Peninsula Players, 1962.
Anagnos, *The Miracle Worker,* Peninsula Players, 1962.
Anniello, *Hotel Paradiso,* Peninsula Players, 1962.
Ready-Money-Matt, *Threepenny Opera,* Peninsula Players, 1962.
Duke of Arudel, *Becket,* Goodman Memorial Theatre, 1962.
Ronny Heaslop, *A Passage to India,* Goodman Memorial Theatre, 1963.
Sergis Saranoff, *Arms and the Man,* Goodman Memorial Theatre, 1963.
Captain Absolute, *The Rivals,* Goodman Memorial Theatre, 1963.
Policeman, *The Madwoman of Chaillot,* Cleveland Playhouse, Cleveland, OH, 1964.
Matti, *Galileo,* Cleveland Playhouse, 1964.
Number 12, *Twelve Angry Men,* Cleveland Playhouse, 1965.
Roger, *Enter Laughing,* Cleveland Playhouse, 1965.
Murillo, *The Physicists,* Cleveland Playhouse, 1965.
Phil Matthews, *Nobody Loves an Albatross,* Candlelight Playhouse, Summit, IL, 1965.
Irvin Blanchard, *No Time for Sergeants,* Candlelight Playhouse, 1965.
Tom Stark, *All the King's Men,* Cleveland Playhouse, 1965.
Executioner, *The Balcony,* Hartford Stage Co., Hartford, CT, 1966.
Young man, *The American Dream,* Playhouse in the Park, Cincinnati, OH, 1966.
Roger, *The Pleasure of His Company,* Coconut Grove Playhouse, Miami Beach, FL, 1966.
(Broadway debut) His assistants, *After the Rain,* John Golden Theatre, New York City, 1967.
John Ken O'Dunc, *MacBird!,* Candlelight Playhouse, 1968.
Captain Fisby, *The Teahouse of the August Moon,* Candlelight Playhouse, 1968.
Arthur Brooks, *The Tenth Man,* Candlelight Playhouse, 1968.
Lt. Cutler, *The White House Murder Case,* Circle in the Square, New York City, 1970.
Andrew Mayo, *Beyond the Horizon,* McCarter Theatre, Princeton, NJ, 1974.
Harry Bales, *The Sea Horse* (also see below), Circle Repertory Theatre, New York City, 1974, then Westside Theatre, New York City, 1974.
Carl, *Serenading Louie,* Circle Repertory Theatre, 1976.
Antony, *Antony and Cleopatra,* Alliance Theatre Co., Atlanta, GA, 1981.
The Bicycle Man, Caldwell Playhouse, Boca Raton, FL, 1984.

TELEVISION APPEARANCES; MOVIES

Douglas Cornell, *F.D.R.—The Last Year,* NBC, 1980.
Wayne Peyton, *Dream House,* CBS, 1981.

TELEVISION APPEARANCES; EPISODIC

Andrew Mayo, "Beyond the Horizon," *Great Performances,* PBS, 1976.

Also appeared as Sam English, *The Edge of Night,* ABC; and Rick Latimer, *Love of Life,* CBS.

WRITINGS:

The Sea Horse, (two-act play; premiered at Westside Theatre, 1974) James T. White, 1974.

Also author of the play *The Bicycle Man.**

* * *

MORALES, Esai

PERSONAL: Born in Brooklyn, NY. *Education:* Attended New York High School of the Performing Arts.

CAREER: Actor. Established the production company Richport. Spokesperson for New York City Foster Care Program.

AWARDS, HONORS: Golden Eagle Award, most promising actor, NOSOTROS; named Entertainer of the Year, Latino Playwrights; New York Image Award.

CREDITS:

FILM APPEARANCES

Paco Moreno, *Bad Boys,* Universal, 1983.
Neekos Valdez, *Rainy Day Friends,* Signature-Powerdance, 1985.
Bob Morales, *La Bamba,* Columbia, 1987.
Raymi Rojas, *The Principal,* Tri-Star, 1987.
Handsome Jack Maddigan, *Bloodhounds of Broadway,* Columbia, 1989.

A Climate for Killing (also known as *A Row of Crows*), Propaganda Films, 1991.
Amazon, Bluebird Films, 1991.

Also appeared in *L.A. Bad,* 1985; as Zico Borenstein in *Naked Tango,* 1990; and in *Forty Deuce.*

TELEVISION APPEARANCES; MINI-SERIES

Rashid, *On Wings of Eagles,* NBC, 1986.

TELEVISION APPEARANCES; SPECIALS

Miguel Rados, "The Great Love Experiment," *ABC Afterschool Special,* ABC, 1984.

TELEVISION APPEARANCES; EPISODIC

Miguel, *The Equalizer,* CBS, 1985.
Felipe Cruz, *Miami Vice,* NBC, 1987.

STAGE APPEARANCES

Ariel, *The Tempest,* New York Shakespeare Festival, Delacorte Theatre, New York City, 1981.
Cupcakes, *Short Eyes,* Second Stage Theatre, New York City, 1984.
Hector, *Tamer of Horses,* Los Angeles Theatre Center, Los Angeles, CA, 1986.

Also appeared in title role, *El Hermano,* Ensemble Studio Theater, New York City.

OTHER SOURCES:

PERIODICALS

New York Times, July 4, 1986.*

*   *   *

MORIARTY, Cathy 1961(?)-

PERSONAL: Born c. 1961, in Bronx, NY; daughter of John (a warehouse worker) and Catherine Moriarty; married Carmine Dana (her business manager), 1981. *Education:* Attended Lincoln High School, Yonkers, NY.

CAREER: Actress. Worked variously as a waitress, sales clerk, fabric buyer, telephone solicitor, and receptionist.

AWARDS, HONORS: Academy Award nomination, best supporting actress, 1980, for *Raging Bull.*

CREDITS:

FILM APPEARANCES

Vickie LaMotta, *Raging Bull,* United Artists, 1980.
Ramona, *Neighbors,* Columbia, 1981.
Joan White, *White of the Eye,* Cannon, 1987.
Patti Smart, *Burndown,* Virgin, 1990.
Sylvester's mother, *Kindergarten Cop,* Universal, 1990.
Montana Moorehead, *Soapdish,* Paramount, 1991.
Lanna Lake, *The Mambo Kings,* Warner Brothers, 1992.

TELEVISION APPEARANCES; SPECIALS

The Hollywood Christmas Parade, syndicated, 1990.

OTHER SOURCES:

PERIODICALS

New York Times, November 15, 1980; December 13, 1981.
People Weekly, March 23, 1981, p. 99.*

*   *   *

MORODER, Giorgio 1941(?)-

PERSONAL: Born c. 1941, in Italy; immigrated to the United States.

ADDRESSES: *Agent*—Milander-Schleussner-Kaufman Agency, Inc., 4146 Lankershim Blvd., North Hollywood, CA 91602.

CAREER: Composer and producer.

AWARDS, HONORS: Academy Award, best original score, 1978, Grammy Award nomination (with others), best original score, 1978, and Golden Globe Award, best original score, 1979, all for *Midnight Express;* Grammy Award nominations (with Donna Summer and Pete Bellotte), album of the year and best disco recording, both 1979, both for *Bad Girls;* Academy Award (with Keith Forsey and Irene Cara), best original song, and Grammy Award nomination (with Cara), record of the year, both 1983, both for "Flashdance . . . What a Feeling," from *Flashdance;* Grammy Award, best instrumental composition, 1983, for "Love Theme from Flashdance"; Grammy Award nomination (with others), album of the year, 1983, Grammy Award (with others), best original score, 1983, and Golden Globe Award, best original score, 1984, all for the soundtrack from *Flashdance;* Academy Award (with Tom Whitlock), best song, 1986, for "Take My Breath Away," from *Top Gun.*

CREDITS:

FILM WORK

Music director, *Foxes* (also see below), United Artists (UA), 1980.
Music arranger, *Scarface* (also see below), Universal, 1983.
Associate producer, *Mamba* (also see below), Cinestar, 1988.

FILM APPEARANCES

Radio producer, *Electric Dreams* (also see below), Metro-Goldwyn-Mayer (MGM)-UA, 1984.

RECORDINGS:

Producer, with Pete Bellotte, of *Bad Girls,* recorded by Donna Summer, Casablanca, 1979, and six other albums by Summer; also producer of song "Love to Love You Baby," 1976, and of two songs on *Night Rains* by Janis Ian, 1979. Has recorded the solo albums *Battlestar Galactica, From Here to Eternity, Knights in White Satin,* and *E—MC2.*

WRITINGS:

FILM SCORES, EXCEPT WHERE INDICATED

Midnight Express, Columbia, 1978.
Songs, *Thank God It's Friday,* Columbia, 1978.
"Fly Too High," *Sunburn,* Paramount, 1979.
American Gigolo, Paramount, 1980.
(And songs) *Foxes,* UA, 1980.
(Title theme with David Bowie) *Cat People,* RKO Radio Pictures, 1982.
(And songs) *D.C. Cab,* Universal, 1983.
(And songs "Flashdance . . . What a Feeling," "Seduce Me Tonight," and "Love Theme from Flashdance") *Flashdance,* Paramount, 1983.
(And songs) *Scarface,* Universal, 1983.
Songs, *Superman III,* Warner Brothers, 1983.
(And songs) *Electric Dreams,* MGM-UA, 1984.
(With Klaus Doldinger; and song "The Neverending Story," with Keith Forsey) *The Neverending Story,* Warner Brothers, 1984.
"Thief of Hearts," *Thief of Hearts,* Paramount, 1984.
"Wings to Fly," *American Anthem,* Columbia, 1986.
"Quicksilver Lightning" (with Dean Pitchford), *Quicksilver,* Columbia, 1986.
Songs (including "Take My Breath Away," with Tom Whitlock), *Top Gun,* Paramount, 1986.
"All Revved Up" (with Whitlock), *Beverly Hills Cop II,* Paramount, 1987.
(And songs with Whitlock) *Over the Top,* Warner Brothers, 1987.
Another Way—D Kikan Joho (also known as *D Kikan Joho* and *Another Way*), Toho Company, Ltd., 1988.
(And songs) *Mamba,* Cinestar, 1988.
(And songs) *Let It Ride,* Paramount, 1989.
"Strike Like Lightning" and "Shadows," *Navy Seals,* Orion, 1990.

Composer of "Giving Up, Giving In," *The Bitch,* 1979; also composer of a new score for the film *Metropolis* (originally released by Deutsche Universum-Film AG [UFA], 1927), 1985.

OTHER SOURCES:

PERIODICALS

People, September 12, 1983, p. 62.*

* * *

MORRIS, Oswald 1915-

PERSONAL: Born November 22, 1915, in Ruislip, Middlesex, England.

CAREER: Cinematographer. Projectionist during school vacations; left school at age sixteen to work as an unpaid assistant and clapper boy for Wembley Studios; was lensman for cameraman Ronald Neame; became assistant cameraman and cameraman for BIP and Pinewood studios in 1938; developer of color film innovation with four-strip technicolor.

AWARDS, HONORS: British Academy Award for best cinematography, 1964, for *The Pumpkin Eater;* British Academy Award for best cinematography, 1965, for *The Hill;* British Academy Award for best cinematography, 1966, for *The Spy Who Came in from the Cold;* Academy Award nomination for best cinematography, 1968, for *Oliver!;* Academy Award for best cinematography, 1971, for *Fiddler on the Roof;* Academy Award nomination for best cinematography, 1978, for *The Wiz.*

CREDITS:

FILM WORK; CINEMATOGRAPHER

Captain Boycott, General Films Distributors, 1947.
Fools Rush In, General Film Distributors, 1949.
One Woman's Story, Universal, 1949.
Cairo Road, Associated British Films/Pathe, 1950.
The Adventurers (also known as *The Great Adventure* and *The Fortune in Diamonds*), Rank, 1951.
Circle of Danger, Eagle-Lion, 1951.
Moulin Rouge, United Artists (UA), 1952.
The Promoter, Universal, 1952.
Beat the Devil, UA, 1953.
So Little Time, MacDonald, 1953.
Beau Brummel, Metro-Goldwyn-Mayer (MGM), 1954.
The Golden Mask (released in England as *South of Algiers*), UA, 1954.
Lovers, Happy Lovers! (also known as *Lover Boy;* released in England as *Knave of Hearts*), Twentieth Century-Fox, 1955.
The Man Who Never Was, Twentieth Century-Fox, 1956.
Moby Dick, Warner Brothers, 1956.
(With Piero Portalupi) *A Farewell to Arms,* Twentieth Century-Fox, 1957.
Heaven Knows, Mr. Allison, Twentieth Century-Fox, 1957.

The Key, Warner Brothers, 1958.
Look Back in Anger, Warner Brothers, 1959.
The Entertainer, Bryanston/British Lion, 1960.
Our Man in Havana, Columbia, 1960.
The Guns of Navarone, Columbia, 1961.
Lolita, MGM, 1962.
Satan Never Sleeps (also known as *Flight from Terror;* released in England as *The Devil Never Sleeps*), Twentieth Century-Fox, 1962.
Term of Trial, Warner Brothers, 1962.
The Ceremony, UA, 1963.
Come Fly with Me, MGM, 1963.
Of Human Bondage, MGM, 1964.
The Pumpkin Eater, Royal/Columbia, 1964.
The Battle of the Villa Fiorita (also known as *Affair at the Villa Fiorita*), Warner Brothers, 1965.
The Hill, MGM, 1965.
Life at the Top, Columbia, 1965.
Mister Moses, UA, 1965.
The Spy Who Came in from the Cold, Paramount, 1965.
Stop the World—I Want to Get Off, Warner Brothers, 1966.
(With Luciano Trasatti) *The Taming of the Shrew,* Columbia, 1967.
Great Catherine, Warner Brothers, 1968.
Oliver!, Columbia, 1968.
The Winter's Tale, Warner Brothers, 1968.
Goodbye Mr. Chips, MGM, 1969.
Scrooge, National General, 1970.
Fiddler on the Roof, UA, 1971.
Fragment of Fear, Columbia, 1971.
Lady Caroline Lamb, UA, 1972.
Sleuth, Twentieth Century-Fox, 1972.
The Mackintosh Man, Warner Brothers, 1973.
The Man with the Golden Gun, UA, 1974.
The Odessa File, Columbia, 1974.
The Man Who Would Be King, Allied Artists, 1975.
Equus, UA, 1977.
The Seven-Per-Cent Solution, Universal, 1977.
The Wiz, Universal, 1978.
Just Tell Me What You Want, Warner Brothers, 1980.
The Great Muppet Caper, Universal, 1981.
The Dark Crystal, Universal/Associated Film, 1982.

FILM WORK; PHOTOGRAPHER

Green for Danger, General Films Distributors, 1946.
Golden Salamander, General Film Distributors, 1950.
Oliver Twist, Rank/UA, 1951.
Island of Desire (released in England as *Saturday Island*), RKO, 1952.
Indiscretion of an American Wife (also known as *Terminal Station Indiscretion*), Columbia, 1954.
The Roots of Heaven, Twentieth Century-Fox, 1958.
Reflections in a Golden Eye, Warner Brothers, 1967.

TELEVISION WORK; CINEMATOGRAPHER

Performed photography for the television movie *Dracula,* 1974.

OTHER SOURCES:

PERIODICALS

American Cinematographer, April, 1985.
Film Heritage, Number 3, 1977.
Filmmakers Newsletter, December, 1978.
Films and Filming (London), April, 1977.
Focus on Film (London), December, 1971.
Millimeter, November, 1978.
Screen International (London), November 22, 1975.*

* * *

MORRISON, Steve 1947-

PERSONAL: Full name, Stephen Roger Morrison; born March 3, 1947; son of Hyman Michael and Rebecca (Zolkwer) Morrison; married Gayle Valerie Broughall, 1979; children: three daughters. *Education:* University of Edinburgh, M.A. (with honors); studied at National Film School, Beaconsfield. *Avocational interests:* Tennis, reading, films and theatre, talking and dining, touring delicatessens.

ADDRESSES: Office—Granada Television, Manchester M60 9EA, England.

CAREER: Television executive. Affiliated with British Broadcasting Corp., Scotland, 1970-74; Granada Television, Manchester, England, producer and director with Northern Documentary Unit, 1974-77, editor of regional programs, 1977-81, head of arts and features, 1981-86, director of programs, 1987—.

MEMBER: National Film School (associate).

CREDITS:

FILM WORK

Executive producer, *28 Up* (documentary), First Run Features, 1985.
Producer, *The Magic Toyshop,* Roxie Releasing, 1986.
Producer, *The Fruit Machine* (also known as *Wonderland*), Vestron, 1988.
Executive producer, *My Left Foot,* Sovereign Pictures, 1989.
Executive producer and executive director, *The Field,* Avenue Entertainment, 1990.*

MORROW, Rob 1963(?)-

PERSONAL: Born c. 1963, in New Rochelle, NY; son of Murray (an industrial lighting manufacturer) and Diane (a dental hygienist) Morrow.

ADDRESSES: *Agent*—William Morris Agency, 151 South El Camino Dr., Beverly Hills, CA 90212.

CAREER: Actor. Has worked as a movie house assistant in Manhattan, NY, and as a waiter.

AWARDS, HONORS: Golden Globe nomination, best actor in a television drama series, 1992, for *Northern Exposure.*

CREDITS:

TELEVISION APPEARANCES; SERIES

Marco Bellini, *Tattinger's,* NBC, 1988.
Joel Fleischman, *Northern Exposure,* CBS, 1990—.

TELEVISION APPEARANCES; EPISODIC

The Forty-third Annual Primetime Emmy Awards Presentation, Fox, 1991.

STAGE APPEARANCES

Stuart Miller, *Escape from Riverdale,* Jewish Repertory Theatre, New York City, 1984.
Lincoln, *Slam!* (produced with other plays in *One-Act Play Marathon '84*), Ensemble Studio Theatre, New York City, 1984.
Understudy for the roles of Prick and Flem, *The Boys of Winter,* Biltmore Theatre, New York City, 1985.
Peter Sirutis, *The Shy and the Lonely* (produced with *Sailor off the Bremen* in double-bill entitled *I, Shaw*), Jewish Repertory Theatre, 1986.
Carlo, *The Return of Pinocchio,* 47th Street Theatre, New York City, 1986.
Reuven Malter, *The Chosen,* Second Avenue Theatre, New York City, 1987-88.
Max, *Soulful Scream of a Chosen Son,* Philadelphia Festival Theatre, Philadelphia, PA, c. 1988.
Marathon '88: Series B (four in a series of twelve one-act plays), Ensemble Studio Theatre, 1988.
The Substance of Fire, Long Wharf Theatre, New Haven, CT, c. 1990.

STAGE WORK

Assistant to director Michael Bennett for the production of *Dreamgirls,* Los Angeles, CA, 1983.

FILM APPEARANCES

Ben, *Private Resort,* Tri-Star, 1985.

OTHER SOURCES:

PERIODICALS

People, July 8, 1991, p. 73.*

* * *

MOSS, Arnold 1910-1989

PERSONAL: Born January 28, 1910, in Brooklyn, NY; died of lung cancer, December 15, 1989, in New York, NY; son of Jack (a pianist) and Essie (Joseph) Moss; married Stella Reynolds (a writer), June 3, 1933; children: Jeffrey, Andrea. *Education:* Received degree in Latin and Greek from College of the City of New York, 1928; Columbia University, A.M., 1934; New York University, Ph.D., theatre, 1973; received dramatic training with Eva Le Gallienne's Civic Repertory Theatre, 1928-30.

CAREER: Actor, producer, writer, and educator. Brooklyn College (now of the City University of New York), New York City, instructor in speech and theatre, 1933-40; Library of Congress, Washington, DC, producer, director, and performer for Whitall Poetry and Literature Series, 1955-73; instructor at American Shakespeare Theatre and Academy, Stratford, CT. Visiting professor and lecturer at numerous institutions, including University of Connecticut, 1973-74, Neighborhood Playhouse School of Theatre, 1974-76, Pace University, 1975, College of William and Mary, 1976, Purdue University, 1977, and University of Wyoming, 1985; artist in residence at Otterbein College. Touring lecturer for U.S. State Department as a "theatre specialist" in Latin America, 1961, and France and Africa, 1964.

MEMBER: Actors' Equity Association (former council member), Screen Actors Guild (former vice president), American Federation of Television and Radio Artists, Academy of Motion Picture Arts and Sciences, American Theatre Association, Players Club, Phi Beta Kappa.

AWARDS, HONORS: College of the City of New York, James K. Hackett Medal, 1968, Townsend Harris Medal, 1978; Founder's Day Certificate, New York University, 1973, for "the highest bracket of scholastic preferment" in the field of theatre study; certificate of appreciation, Layman's National Bible Company, 1977.

CREDITS:

STAGE APPEARANCES

(Stage debut) An Indian, *Peter Pan,* Eva La Gallienne's Civic Repertory Theatre, New York City, 1929.
(Broadway debut) Page Boy, *Wonder Boy,* Alvin Theatre, 1931.
Antonio, *The Fifth Column,* Alvin Theatre, 1940.

Fernando, *Hold on to Your Hats,* Shubert Theatre, New York City, 1940.

Howard Ingram, *Flight to the West,* Guild Theatre, New York City, 1940.

Ishmael, *Journey to Jerusalem,* National Theatre, New York City, 1940.

Count Czarniko, *The Land Is Bright,* Music Box Theatre, New York City, 1941.

Prospero, *The Tempest,* Alvin Theatre, 1945.

Walter Burns, *The Front Page,* Royale Theatre, New York City, 1946.

Malvolio, *Twelfth Night,* Empire Theatre, New York City, 1949.

Gloucester, *King Lear,* New York City, 1950.

Colonel Janek, *The Dark Is Light Enough,* ANTA Theatre, New York City, 1955.

Creon, *Medea,* Theatre Sarah Bernhardt, Paris, France, 1955.

King of France, *King John,* American Shakespeare Festival, Stratford, CT, 1956.

Duke of Vienna, *Measure for Measure,* American Shakespeare Festival, 1956.

Leaves of Grass (one-man show), Library of Congress, Washington, DC, 1956.

Duke of Vienna, *Measure for Measure,* Phoenix Theatre, New York City, 1957.

Prospero, *The Tempest,* Library of Congress, 1957.

Duke of Vienna, *Measure for Measure,* Library of Congress, 1958.

Society Man, *The Time of Your Life,* American Pavilion, Brussels World's Fair, Brussels, Belgium, 1958.

George Bernard Shaw, *Back to Methuselah,* Theatre Guild at Ambassador Theatre, New York City, 1958.

Don Armado, *Love's Labours Lost,* Library of Congress, 1959.

Narrator, and Mark, *Tristam,* Library of Congress, 1960.

Title role, *King Lear,* Library of Congress, 1960, University of Hawaii, 1965, University of Kentucky, 1966, Trenton State College, 1970, University of Connecticut, 1974, and College of William and Mary, 1976.

Malvolio, *Twelfth Night,* Library of Congress, 1961.

Title role, *Macbeth,* Library of Congress, 1962.

Various roles, *Come Woo Me!,* Library of Congress, 1963.

Don Armado, *Love's Labours Lost,* Otterbein College, 1964.

Prospero, *The Tempest,* University of Kansas, 1964.

Willy Loman, *Death of a Salesman,* Kent State University, 1969.

Dimitri Weissmann, *Follies,* Winter Garden Theatre, New York City, 1971.

Voice of God, *Paradise Lost,* Chicago Lyric Opera, Chicago, IL, 1979, then La Scala Opera, Milan, Italy, and the Vatican.

Shylock, *The Merchant of Venice,* Otterbein College, 1979.

Judge Wyler, *Whose Life Is It Anyway?,* Wilshire Theatre, Los Angeles, CA, 1980, then Morris Mechanic Theatre, Baltimore, MD, 1981.

Appeared with Eva Le Gallienne's Repertory Theatre, 1929-30. Also appeared as Master of Ceremonies with Milly Picon, Carnegie Hall, New York City, 1975; and as Frere Dominique, *Jeanne D'Arc au Bucher.* Narrator of concerts with Boston, Milwaukee, and Detroit symphony orchestras.

MAJOR TOURS

Seven Ages of Man (one-man show), U.S. cities, 1952.

Prospero, *The Tempest,* Shakespeare Festival Players, U.S. cities, 1959.

Duke of Vienna, *Measure for Measure,* Shakespeare Festival Players, U.S. cities, 1959.

Also toured in *A Goodly Heritage* (one-man show), U.S. cities; *Windows on America* (one-man show), U.S. cities; and *The Trembling Years* (one-man show), U.S. cities.

STAGE WORK

Co-producer, *Back to Methuselah,* Ambassador Theatre, 1958.

FILM APPEARANCES

(Film debut) Lieutenant Achmed, *Temptation,* Universal, 1946.

Colonel, *The Loves of Carmen,* Columbia, 1948.

Fouche, *The Black Book* (also known as *Reign of Terror*), Walter Wagner, 1949.

Zopilote, *Border Incident,* Metro-Goldwyn-Mayer (MGM), 1949.

Lurgan Sahib, *Kim,* MGM, 1950.

Colardi, *Mask of the Avenger,* Columbia, 1951.

Tasso, *My Favorite Spy,* Paramount, 1951.

Racelle, *Quebec,* Paramount, 1951.

Don Nacio, *Viva Zapata!,* Twentieth Century-Fox, 1952.

Micha, *Salome,* Columbia, 1953.

Rajah Karem Jee, *Bengal Brigade* (also known as *Bengal Rifles*), Universal, 1954.

The Doge of Venice, *Casanova's Big Night,* Paramount, 1954.

The General, *Jump into Hell,* Warner Brothers, 1955.

The Alien, *The 27th Day,* Columbia, 1957.

Reverend Spotts, *The Fool Killer* (also known as *Violent Journey*), Allied Artists, 1965.

Abdul, *Gambit,* Universal, 1966.

Mr. Shahari, *The Caper of the Golden Bulls* (also known as *Carnival of Thieves*), Embassy, 1967.

Also appeared as Paul Armand, *Hell's Island* (also known as *The Ruby Virgin; Love Is a Weapon;* and *South Seas Fury*), 1955.

TELEVISION APPEARANCES; EPISODIC

Kodos, the Executioner (alias Anton Karidian), "The Conscience of the King," *Star Trek* (episode), NBC, 1966.

OTHER TELEVISION APPEARANCES

Motorola Television Hour, CBC, 1954.
Niccolo, *Marco Polo* (special), NBC, 1956.
Joash, "Gideon," *The Hallmark Hall of Fame* (special), NBC, 1971.
Voice of Sergeant Muldoon, *Yes, Virginia, There Is a Santa Claus* (animated special), ABC, 1974.

Also appeared on *Studio One,* CBS; *Suspense,* CBS; *Theatre Guild on the Air,* CBS; *General Electric Theatre,* CBS; *You Are There,* CBS; *Alfred Hitchcock Presents,* CBS; *The Rifleman,* ABC; *Going My Way,* ABC; *Bonanza,* NBC; *Lights Out,* NBC; *Tales of Tomorrow,* ABC; *The Campbell Television Soundstage* (also known as *TV Soundstage*), NBC; and *The Clock.*

RADIO APPEARANCES; EPISODIC

Native, "Savage Encounter," *Columbia Presents Corwin,* CBS, 1944.

OTHER RADIO APPEARANCES

Also appeared in radio series as Philip Cameron, *Against the Storm,* NBC; Dr. Reed Bannister, *Big Sister,* CBS; Ted White, *The Guiding Light,* NBC; Frank Flippin, *The Man I Married,* NBC; and Giles Henning, *The Story of Mary Martin,* NBC. Appeared in episodes of *Grand Central Station,* NBC; *New York Philharmonic Symphony; Columbia Workshop; Great Novels; Spoon River Anthology; Archibald MacLeish Program; CBS Radio Mystery Theatre; Thomas Jefferson Series;* and *Great Plays Series.* Staff announcer, CBS, 1931.

RECORDINGS:

Recordings include role of Jason, *Medea; L'Histoire du Soldat,* 1961; narrator, *Come Woo Me!,* 1964; and *Many Voices: A Treasury of the Spoken Word.* Recorded more than seventy-five "Talking Books for the Blind," for the American Foundation for the Blind.

WRITINGS:

Author of more than sixty episodes of *CBS Radio Mystery Theatre;* author of *The Professional Actor as Performing Guest Artist in American Colleges and Universities.* Contributor to periodicals.

OBITUARIES AND OTHER SOURCES:

PERIODICALS

New York Times, December 17, 1989.*

* * *

MOUNT, Thom 1948-

PERSONAL: Full name, Thomas Henderson Mount; born May 26, 1948, in Durham, NC; son of Lillard H. and Bonnie Mount. *Education:* Attended Bard College, 1968-70; California Institute of Arts, M.F.A., filmmaking, 1973.

ADDRESSES: Office—The Mount Co., 3723 West Olive Ave., Burbank, CA 91505.

CAREER: Producer. Metro-Goldwyn-Mayer, assistant to the producer; Universal Studios, Studio City, CA, production executive, 1975-79, executive vice-president in charge of production, 1976-78, president and head of production, 1979-83; The Mount Co., Burbank, CA, independent film producer, 1983—.

CREDITS:

FILM PRODUCER

(With Tim Hampton) *Frantic,* Warner Brothers, 1987.
Can't Buy Me Love, Buena Vista, 1987.
(With Mark Burg) *Bull Durham,* Orion, 1988.
(With Hank Moonjean) *Stealing Home,* Warner Brothers, 1988.
Tequila Sunrise, Warner Brothers, 1988.

Also producer of *Roman Polanski's Pirates,* 1985, and *Frankenstein Unbound,* 1989.

TELEVISION PRODUCER

Producer of *Son of the Morning Star* and *Open Admissions.**

* * *

MULGREW, Kate 1955-

PERSONAL: Full name, Katherine Kiernan Mulgrew; born April 29, 1955, in Dubuque, IA; daughter of Thomas James (a contractor) and Joan Virginia (a painter; maiden name, Kiernan) Mulgrew; married Robert Harry Egan (a director), July 31, 1982; children: Ian Thomas, Alexander James. *Education:* Attended Northwestern University and University of Iowa; New York University, A.A., 1976; studied with Stella Adler; trained at Tyrone Guthrie Theater, Minneapolis, MN. *Religion:* Roman Catholic.

ADDRESSES: Publicist—Stan Rosenfield Public Relations, 9595 Wilshire Blvd., Suite 511, Beverly Hills, CA 90212.

CAREER: Actress. Cornish Institute, Seattle, WA, teacher of audition technique, 1982.

MEMBER: Actors Equity Association, Screen Actors Guild, American Federation of Television and Radio Artists, Committee for the Right to Life (member of board of directors).

AWARDS, HONORS: Golden Globe Award nomination, best dramatic actress in a series, 1979, for *Mrs. Columbo.*

CREDITS:

TELEVISION APPEARANCES; SERIES

Mary Ryan, *Ryan's Hope,* ABC, 1975-77 and 1985.
Kate Columbo, *Mrs. Columbo,* NBC, 1979.
Kate Callahan, *Kate Loves a Mystery,* NBC, 1979.
Dr. Joanne Springsteen, *Heart Beat,* ABC, 1987-88, then Dr. Joanne Halloran, 1988-89.

TELEVISION APPEARANCES; MINI-SERIES

Tony Nicholson, *The Word,* CBS, 1978.
Rachel Clement, *The Manions of America,* ABC, 1981.

TELEVISION APPEARANCES; MOVIES

Mother Elizabeth Bayley Seton, *A Time for Miracles,* ABC, 1980.
Kendall Murphy, *Roses Are for the Rich,* CBS, 1987.
Hattie Carraway, *Roots: The Gift,* ABC, 1988.
Sue Bradley, *The Fatal Friendship* (also known as *Friends and Enemies*), NBC, 1991.
Sarah Watson, *Danielle Steel's "Daddy",* NBC, 1991.

TELEVISION APPEARANCES; EPISODIC

"Alien Lover," *Mystery of the Week,* ABC, 1978.
"Act of Love," *Dallas,* CBS, 1978.
"McLaughlin's Flame," *Jessie,* ABC, 1984.
Trapper John, M.D., CBS, 1985.
"Time Heals," *St. Elsewhere,* NBC, 1986.
"Histories," *St. Elsewhere,* NBC, 1986.
"Ryan's Wedding," *Ryan's Hope,* ABC, 1986.
Janet Eldridge, "Strange Bedfellows," *Cheers,* NBC, 1986.
"Ryan's Doubts," *Ryan's Hope,* ABC, 1986.
"The Corpse Flew First Class," *Murder, She Wrote,* CBS, 1987.
"Reservations," *Hotel,* ABC, 1987.
"The Final Show," *Ryan's Hope,* ABC, 1989.
Murphy Brown, CBS, 1992.

OTHER TELEVISION APPEARANCES

Joan Russell, *Jennifer: A Woman's Story* (pilot), NBC, 1979.
Laura Adams, *My Town* (pilot), ABC, 1986.
Narrator, *Expecting Miracles* (special), PBS, 1989.
Hostess, *The Parent Survival Guide* (special), Lifetime, 1989.
Mayor Lisbeth Chardin, *Man of the People* (special), NBC, 1991.

Also appeared in the special *Carly Mills.*

FILM APPEARANCES

Sharon Martin, *A Stranger Is Watching,* Metro-Goldwyn-Mayer/United Artists, 1982.
Major Rayner Fleming, *Remo Williams: The Adventure Begins . . . ,* Orion, 1985.
Margaret, *Throw Momma from the Train,* Orion, 1987.

Also appeared as Isolt, *Lovespell.*

STAGE APPEARANCES

Blanche, *Widower's House,* Cyrano Repertory, New York City, 1974.
Emily, *Our Town,* American Shakespeare Theatre, Stratford, CT, 1975.
Desdemona, *Othello,* Hartman Theatre Company, Stamford, CT, 1977.
Regina, *Another Part of the Forest,* Seattle Repertory Theatre, Seattle, WA, 1981.
Title role, *Major Barbara,* Seattle Repertory Theatre, 1982.
Tracy, *The Philadelphia Story,* Alaska Repertory Theatre, Anchorage/Fairbanks, 1983.
Kitty Strong, *The Ballad of Soapy Smith,* Seattle Repertory Theatre, 1983.
Isabella, *Measure for Measure,* Center Theatre Group, Mark Taper Forum, Los Angeles, CA, 1984.
Charlotte, *The Real Thing,* Center Theatre Group, Mark Taper Forum, 1985.
Title role, *Hedda Gabler,* Center Theatre Group, Mark Taper Forum, 1985.
Tamora, *Titus Andronicus,* New York Shakespeare Festival, Delacorte Theatre, New York City, 1989.
Alice, *Aristocrats,* Center Theatre Group, Mark Taper Forum, 1989.

Also appeared as Maggie, *Cat on a Hot Tin Roof,* Syracuse Stage; and as Celemine, *The Misanthrope;* appeared in *Three Sisters,* New York City Center; *The Plow and the Stars,* Irish Rebel Theatre; and *Orpheus Descending,* Circle in the Square, New York City. Member of American Shakespeare Company, Stratford, CT, 1975.*

* * *

MULHARE, Edward 1923-

PERSONAL: Born April 8, 1923, in Cork, Ireland.

ADDRESSES: Agent—First Artists Agency, 10000 Riverside Dr., Suite 6, Toluca Lake, CA 91602.

CAREER: Actor.

AWARDS, HONORS: Emmy Award nomination, outstanding continued performance by an actor in a leading role in a comedy series, 1968, for *The Ghost and Mrs. Muir.*

CREDITS:

TELEVISION APPEARANCES; SERIES

Captain Daniel Gregg, *The Ghost and Mrs. Muir,* NBC, 1968-69, ABC, 1969-70.
Devon Miles, *Knight Rider,* NBC, 1982-86.

Appeared in *Robin Hood,* a British series.

TELEVISION APPEARANCES; MOVIES

Earnest, *Who's Earnest?,* CBS, 1957.
Alex MacLaughlin, *Gidget Grows Up,* ABC, 1969.
Devon Miles, *Knight Rider 2000,* NBC, 1991.

TELEVISION APPEARANCES; EPISODIC

"The Imposters," *The Adventures of Robin Hood,* CBS, 1956.
"The Ransom," *The Adventures of Robin Hood,* CBS, 1956.
"Peace and Quiet," *Aggie,* syndicated, 1957.
"Night of the Plague," *Kraft Theater,* NBC, 1957.
Larry Darant, "The First and the Last," *Kraft Theater,* NBC, 1957.
"The Sixth Finger," *Outer Limits,* ABC, 1963.
"He Who Can Does," *Mr. Novak,* NBC, 1963.
"Katy and the Prince," *The Farmer's Daughter,* ABC, 1964.
"The Ben Franklin Encounter," *Daniel Boone,* NBC, 1965.
"Empire of the Lost," *Daniel Boone,* NBC, 1965.
"The Duel," *Convoy,* NBC, 1965.
"Siren Voices," *12 O'Clock High,* ABC, 1966.
"The Savage Machine," *Run for Your Life,* NBC, 1966.
"The Mata Hari Affair," *Girl From UNCLE,* NBC, 1966.
"Duel at Monte Sainte Marie," *12 O'Clock High,* ABC, 1966.
"Hostage," *The FBI,* ABC, 1967.
"The Man Who Has Everything," *Cowboy in Africa,* ABC, 1967.
"The Secret Code," *Daniel Boone,* NBC, 1967.
"The Gauntlet," *Custer,* ABC, 1967.
"Operation Iceman," *Search,* NBC, 1972.
"Tower Beyond Tragedy," *Streets of San Francisco,* ABC, 1972.
"Death of a Hunter," *Cannon,* CBS, 1974.
"One Chance to Live," *Streets of San Francisco,* ABC, 1974.
"The Adventure of the Two-Faced Woman," *Ellery Queen,* NBC, 1976.
"Blue Bird Is Back," *Hunter,* CBS, 1977.
"The People Mover," *Most Wanted,* ABC, 1977.
"Experiment in Terra," *Battlestar Galactica,* ABC, 1979.
"The Man With the Jade Eyes," *Hart to Hart,* ABC, 1979.
"Whose Party Is This Anyway?," *Matt Houston,* ABC, 1983.
"One Good Bid Deserves a Murder," *Murder, She Wrote,* CBS, 1986.
"Stage Struck," *Murder, She Wrote,* CBS, 1986.
"Three for the Road," *MacGyver,* ABC, 1986.
"Past Tense/All the King's Men," *Hotel,* ABC, 1987.

Also appeared on *Studio One,* CBS, 1948-51.

TELEVISION APPEARANCES; SPECIALS

Lord Stormont, *Benjamin Franklin: The Ambassador,* CBS, 1974.
Host and narrator, *It's in the Closet. . .It's under the Bed,* syndicated, 1987.
Host, *Secrets and Mysteries,* syndicated, 1989.

FILM APPEARANCES

James Finnegan, *Hill 24 Doesn't Answer,* Continental Distributing, 1955.
Dr. Mark Fleming, *Signpost to Murder,* Metro-Goldwyn-Mayer (MGM), 1964.
Constanzo, *Von Ryan's Express,* Twentieth Century-Fox, 1965.
Malcolm Rodney, *Our Man Flint,* Twentieth Century-Fox, 1966.
Sir Jason Fox, *Caprice,* Twentieth Century-Fox, 1967.
Jean-Claude Ibert, *Eye of the Devil* (also known as *13*), MGM, 1967.
Byrne-White, *Megaforce,* Twentieth Century-Fox, 1982.

Narrator, *The Bengal Tiger,* 1972.

STAGE APPEARANCES

The First Mrs. Fraser, Opera House, Cork, Ireland, 1942.
Cassio, *Othello,* Opera House, Cork, 1942.
Max de Winter, *Rebecca,* Liverpool Repertory Company, London, 1950.
Lodovico, *Othello,* St. James's Theatre, London, 1951.
Henry Higgins, *My Fair Lady* (also see below), Mark Hellinger Theatre, New York City, 1957.
Paul Delville, *The Marriage-Go-Round,* Bucks County Playhouse, New Hope, PA, 1960.
Giacomo Nerone, *The Devil's Advocate,* Billy Rose Theatre, New York City, 1961.
Dirk Winsten, *Mary, Mary,* Helen Hayes Theatre, New York City, 1961-62.

A Man for All Seasons, Mummers Theatre, Oklahoma City, OK, 1970.
The devil, *Don Juan in Hell* (also see below), Palace Theatre, New York City, 1973.
Move Over, Mrs. Markham, Coconut Grove Playhouse, Coconut Grove, FL, 1989-90.

Appeared as Bill Walker in *Major Barbara,* Horace Giddens in *The Little Foxes,* and La Hire in *St. Joan,* all for Dublin Theatre Guild; appeared as Sidney Willis in *The Night of the Ball.* Toured as Henry Higgins, *My Fair Lady,* Russian cities, 1960, and U.S. cities, 1977-78; and as the devil, *Don Juan in Hell,* 1974-75.*

* * *

MULLIGAN, Robert 1925-

PERSONAL: Full name, Robert Patrick Mulligan; born August 23, 1925, in Bronx, NY; son of Robert Edward and Elizabeth (Gingell) Mulligan. *Education:* Graduate of Fordham University.

ADDRESSES: Agent—Robert Stein, United Talent, 9560 Wilshire Blvd., Suite 500, Beverly Hills, CA 90212.

CAREER: Director and producer.

AWARDS, HONORS: Emmy Award, outstanding directorial achievement in a drama, 1959, for *The Moon and Sixpence;* Academy Award nomination, outstanding directing, 1962, for *To Kill a Mockingbird.*

CREDITS:

FILM WORK; DIRECTOR, EXCEPT WHERE INDICATED

Fear Strikes Out, Paramount, 1957.
The Great Imposter, Universal, 1960.
The Rat Race, Paramount, 1960.
Come September, Universal, 1961.
The Spiral Road, Universal, 1962.
To Kill a Mockingbird, Universal, 1962.
Love with the Proper Stranger, Paramount, 1963.
Baby, the Rain Must Fall, Columbia, 1965.
(And producer with Alan J. Pakula) *Inside Daisy Clover,* Warner Brothers, 1965.
Up the Down Staircase, Warner Brothers, 1967.
The Stalking Moon, National General, 1969.
The Pursuit of Happiness, Columbia, 1971.
Summer of '42, Warner Brothers, 1971.
(And producer) *The Other,* Twentieth Century-Fox, 1972.
(And producer) *The Nickel Ride,* Twentieth Century-Fox, 1974.
Bloodbrothers, Warner Brothers, 1978.
Same Time, Next Year, Universal, 1978.
(And producer) *Kiss Me Goodbye,* Twentieth Century-Fox, 1982.
Clara's Heart, Warner Brothers, 1988.
The Man in the Moon, Metro-Goldwyn-Mayer/Pathe, 1991.

TELEVISION WORK; SPECIALS

Director, *Victor Borge's Comedy in Music I,* CBS, 1956.
Director, *Victor Borge's Comedy in Music II,* CBS, 1956.
Producer (with David Susskind) and director, *Member of the Wedding,* CBS, 1958.
Producer and director, *The Moon and Sixpence,* NBC (one source says CBS), 1959.

TELEVISION WORK; EPISODIC

Director, *The Alcoa Hour,* NBC, 1955-57.

OTHER TELEVISION WORK

Director, *The Defender* (pilot), CBS, 1957.

Also worked on *Billy Budd; Ah! Wilderness; A Tale of Two Cities; The Bridge of San Luis Rey; Playhouse 90; Hallmark Hall of Fame; Suspense;* and *The Jimmy Piersol Story.*

TELEVISION APPEARANCES; EPISODIC

"Natalie Wood," *Crazy about the Movies,* Cinemax, 1987.
"Gregory Peck: His Own Man," *Crazy about the Movies,* Cinemax, 1988.*

* * *

MYERS, Ruth

ADDRESSES: Agent—Sandra Marsh Management, 14930 Ventura Blvd., Suite 200, Sherman Oaks, CA 91403.

CAREER: Costume designer.

MEMBER: International Alliance of Theatrical Stage Employees and Moving Picture Machine Operators of the United States and Canada (Local 892), Association of Cinematograph, Television, and Allied Technicians (Canada).

AWARDS, HONORS: Academy Award nomination, costume design, 1992, for *The Addams Family.*

CREDITS:

FILM WORK; COSTUME DESIGNER

Smashing Time, Paramount, 1967.
Work Is a Four-Letter Word, Universal, 1968.
A Nice Girl Like Me, Avco Embassy, 1969.
Isadora, Universal, 1969.
Three Into Two Won't Go, Universal, 1969.
The Twelve Chairs, UMC, 1970.
The Virgin Soldiers, Columbia, 1970.

Romance of a Horse Thief, Allied Artists, 1971.
The Ruling Class, Avco Embassy, 1972.
A Touch of Class, Avco Embassy, 1973.
Little Malcolm and His Struggle Against the Eunuchs, Multicetera Investments, 1974.
That'll Be the Day, EMI, 1974.
The Adventures of Sherlock Holmes' Smarter Brother, Twentieth Century-Fox, 1975.
Stardust, Columbia, 1975.
Galileo, American Film Theatre, 1975.
The Romantic Englishwoman, New World, 1975.
(With Ed Wynigear, Phyllis Garr, Darryl Athons, and Carolina Ewart) *The World's Greatest Lover,* Twentieth Century-Fox, 1977.
Magic, Twentieth Century-Fox, 1978.
Silver Bears, Columbia, 1978.
. . . And Justice for All, Columbia, 1979.
The Main Event, Warner Brothers, 1979.
The Competition, Columbia, 1980.
In God We Trust, Universal, 1980.
It's My Turn, Columbia, 1980.
Altered States, Warner Brothers, 1980.
First Monday in October, Paramount, 1981.
(With others) *Sunday Lovers,* United Artists (UA), 1981.
Cannery Row, Metro-Goldwyn-Mayer (MGM)/UA, 1982.
Something Wicked This Way Comes, Buena Vista, 1983.
Crimes of Passion, New World, 1984.
Electric Dreams, MGM/UA, 1984.
(With Norman Burza and Michele Neely) *Teachers,* MGM/UA, 1984.
The Woman in Red, Orion, 1984.
Plenty, Twentieth Century-Fox, 1985.
Haunted Honeymoon, Orion, 1986.
The Accidental Tourist, Warner Brothers, 1988.
Vibes, Columbia, 1988.
Bert Rigby, You're a Fool, Warner Brothers, 1989.
Blaze, Buena Vista, 1989.
Blood Red, Hemdale, 1989.
The Russia House, MGM/UA, 1990.
The Marrying Man (also known as *Too Hot to Handle*), Buena Vista, 1991.
Another You (also known as *My Silent Partner*), Tri-Star, 1991.
The Addams Family, Paramount, 1991.

TELEVISION WORK; MOVIES

Costume designer, *Baja Oklahoma,* HBO, 1988.

OTHER SOURCES:

PERIODICALS

Theatre Crafts, October, 1991, pg. 36.*

N-O

NELSON, Craig T. 1946-

PERSONAL: Born April 4, 1946, in Spokane, WA; married; children: one. *Education:* Attended University of Arizona; studied at Oxford Theatre, Los Angeles, CA.

ADDRESSES: *Office*—Writers and Artists Agency, 11726 San Vicente Blvd., Suite 300, Los Angeles, CA 90049. *Agent*—International Creative Management, 8899 Beverly Blvd., Los Angeles, CA 90046.

CAREER: Actor and writer. Worked as a security guard and security analyst prior to acting career; appeared as "Mr. Peanut" in advertisements for a supermarket chain.

MEMBER: Screen Actors Guild.

AWARDS, HONORS: Oxford Theatre scholarship, Eddie Cantor Foundation, 1967; Emmy Award nominations, outstanding lead actor in a comedy series, 1990 and 1991, Golden Globe Award nomination, best actor in a musical or comedy, 1992, all for *Coach.*

CREDITS:

FILM APPEARANCES

Frank Bowers, *. . . And Justice for All,* Columbia, 1979.
Second geologist, *The Formula,* Metro-Goldwyn-Mayer (MGM), 1980.
Captain William Wooldridge, *Private Benjamin,* Warner Brothers, 1980.
Cop on stand, *Where the Buffalo Roam,* Universal, 1980.
Deputy Ward Wilson, *Stir Crazy,* Columbia, 1981.
Steve Freeling, *Poltergeist,* MGM/United Artists (UA), 1982.
Coach Nickerson, *All the Right Moves,* Twentieth Century-Fox, 1983.
Bernie Ackerman, *Man, Woman, and Child,* Paramount, 1983.
Bernard Osterman, *The Osterman Weekend,* Twentieth Century-Fox, 1983.
Winston, *Silkwood,* Twentieth Century-Fox, 1983.
Military attache, *The Killing Fields,* Warner Brothers, 1984.
Steve Freeling, *Poltergeist Two,* MGM/UA, 1986.
Godfrey/Percival, *Red Riding Hood,* Cannon, 1987.
Peter Dellaplane, *Action Jackson,* Lorimar, 1988.
Peter Karamis, *Me and Him,* Columbia, 1988.
Freddy Nefler, *Troop Beverly Hills,* Columbia, 1989.
Marlyn Huutula, *Rachel River,* Taurus, 1989.
Police Chief Hyde, *Turner and Hooch,* Buena Vista, 1989.

TELEVISION APPEARANCES; MOVIES, EXCEPT WHERE NOTED

How the West Was Won, ABC, 1978.
Major Landau, *The Promise of Love,* CBS, 1980.
Ray, *Rage,* NBC, 1980.
Daniels, *Inmates: A Love Story,* ABC, 1981.
Jack Ramsey, *Murder in Texas,* NBC, 1981.
Michael Caswell, *Paper Dolls,* ABC, 1983.
Frank Deford, *Alex: The Life of a Child,* ABC, 1986.
Senator Edward Kennedy, *The Ted Kennedy, Jr. Story,* NBC, 1986.
Major Harcourt, *Murderers among Us: The Simon Wiesenthal Story,* HBO, 1989.
Philip Toll, *Extreme Close-Up* (also known as *Home Video*), NBC, 1990.
Harley Steinmetz, *Drug Wars: The Camarena Story* (miniseries; also known as *Desperados: The Camarena Story*), NBC, 1990.
Walter Winchell, *The Josephine Baker Story,* HBO, 1991.

Also appeared in *Diary of a Teenage Hitchhiker,* 1979.

TELEVISION APPEARANCES; SERIES

Kenneth A. Dutton, *Chicago Story,* NBC, 1982.

Colonel Raynor Sarnac, *Call to Glory* (also known as *Air Force*), ABC, 1984-85.
Host, *Heroes: Made in the U.S.A.*, syndicated, 1986.
Hayden Fox, *Coach*, ABC, 1989—.

Appeared as a performer on the *Lohman and Barkley Show* (also see below).

TELEVISION APPEARANCES; EPISODIC

Wonder Woman, CBS, 1978.
Kenneth A. Dutton, pilot episode, *The Chicago Story*, NBC, 1981.

Also appeared on *The Mary Tyler Moore Show* on CBS, *Charlie's Angels* on ABC, and various talk shows.

TELEVISION APPEARANCES; SPECIALS

Golden Globe Awards, Turner Broadcasting System, 1990.
The Forty-third Annual Primetime Emmy Awards Presentation, Fox, 1991.

TELEVISION WORK

Producer of fifty-two episodes of *American Still*, a syndicated documentary series on American artists.

STAGE APPEARANCES

Harold "Okie" Peterson, *Friends*, Manhattan Theatre Club, Manhattan, NY, 1983-84.

Performed stand-up comedy routines with Barry Levinson at various clubs.

WRITINGS:

TELEVISION

(With Levinson and others) *The Tim Conway Comedy Hour*, CBS, 1970.
(With Levinson and others) *The John Byner Comedy Hour*, CBS, 1972.

Contributed, with Levinson, material to the *Lohman and Barkley Show* and to an Alan King special.

OTHER SOURCES:

PERIODICALS

Daily News, January 1, 1990, p. 66.*

* * *

NELSON, Tracy 1963-

PERSONAL: Born October 25, 1963, in Santa Monica, CA; daughter of Rick (an actor and singer) and Kristin (an actress; maiden name, Harmon) Nelson; married Billy Moses (an actor), 1987. *Education:* Attended Bard College; studied drama in northern England; also studied ballet.

ADDRESSES: Agent—STE Agency, 9301 Wilshire Blvd., Beverly Hills, CA 90212.

CAREER: Actress.

MEMBER: Screen Actors Guild.

CREDITS:

TELEVISION APPEARANCES; SERIES

Jennifer DiNuccio, *Square Pegs*, CBS, 1982-83.
Angela Timini, *Glitter*, ABC, 1984.
Sister Stephanie "Steve" Okowski, *Father Dowling Mysteries*, NBC, 1989, then ABC, 1990-91.

TELEVISION APPEARANCES; MOVIES

Annie Benton, *Pleasures*, ABC, 1982.
Patch Reed, *Kate's Secret*, NBC, 1986.
Jamie Davies, *Tonight's the Night*, ABC, 1987.
Randi Wainwright, *If It's Tuesday, It Still Must Be Belgium*, NBC, 1987.
Annie, *Highway Heartbreaker*, CBS, 1992.

TELEVISION APPEARANCES; PILOTS

Michelle, *Hearts of Steel*, ABC, 1986.
Susan Costigan, *Home*, ABC, 1987.
Sister Stephanie "Steve" Okowski, *Fatal Confession: A Father Dowling Mystery*, NBC, 1987.

TELEVISION APPEARANCES; SPECIALS

Battle of the Network Stars, ABC, 1983.
Circus of the Stars, CBS, 1984.
Lori, *The Drug Knot*, CBS, 1986.
The Barbour Report, ABC, 1986.
Performer, *The 61st Annual Academy Awards Presentation*, ABC, 1989.
Farm Aid IV, TNN, 1990.

Appeared in *Battle of the Network Stars XIV*, 1980.

TELEVISION APPEARANCES; EPISODIC

"Christmas With the Nelsons," *The Adventures of Ozzie and Harriet*, ABC, 1966.
"Blackout," *Hotel*, ABC, 1983.
"Ladies' Man," *Family Ties*, NBC, 1984.
"The Runaway," *The Love Boat*, ABC, 1985.
"Love and the Window Dresser," *New Love American Style*, ABC, 1986.
The Today Show, NBC, 1989.
Entertainment Tonight, syndicated, 1989.

FILM APPEARANCES

Germaine Beardsley, *Yours, Mine, and Ours*, United Artists, 1968.

Joanie, *Maria's Lovers,* Cannon, 1985.
Jenny Whiteman, *Down and Out in Beverly Hills,* Buena Vista, 1986.

Also appeared in *Banjoman,* 1975.

STAGE APPEARANCES

Fly Blackbird, Inner City Cultural Center, Los Angeles, CA, 1978.

RECORDINGS:

Recorded *Doin' It My Way* and *Come See about Me,* both 1980.

WRITINGS:

Author of *Homemade Songs,* 1988.

OTHER SOURCES:

PERIODICALS

Interview, September, 1984, p. 176.
People, December 13, 1982, p. 129; December 16, 1985, p. 121.
Redbook, October, 1989, p. 76.*

* * *

NEUWIRTH, Bebe

PERSONAL: Born December 31 in Newark, NJ; daughter of Lee Paul (a mathematician) and Sydney Anne (an artist) Neuwirth; married Paul Dorman (a theatre director), 1984. *Education:* Attended Juilliard School of Music, 1976-77. *Politics:* Democrat.

ADDRESSES: Contact—c/o NBC, 30 Rockefeller Plaza, New York, NY 10112.

CAREER: Dancer and actress. Moved to New York City to begin career at age seventeen.

AWARDS, HONORS: Antoinette Perry Award for best supporting actress in a musical, 1985, for *Sweet Charity;* Emmy awards for outstanding supporting actress in a comedy series, 1990 and 1991, for *Cheers.*

CREDITS:

TELEVISION APPEARANCES; SERIES

Lilith Sternin-Crane, *Cheers,* NBC, 1984—.

TELEVISION APPEARANCES; MOVIES

Gloria Allred, *Without Her Consent* (also known as *A Matter of Trust*), NBC, 1990.
Susan Maxwell, *Unspeakable Acts,* ABC, 1990.

TELEVISION APPEARANCES; SPECIALS

Disneyland's Thirty-fifth Anniversary Celebration, NBC, 1990.
Stand-Up Comics Take a Stand!, Family Channel, 1990.
The 43rd Annual Primetime Emmy Awards Presentation, Fox, 1991.

STAGE APPEARANCES

Boom, boom girl, *Little Me,* Eugene O'Neill Theatre, New York City, 1982.
Dancer, *Dancin',* Ambassador Theatre, New York City, 1982.
Upstairs at O'Neal's (satirical revue), O'Neal's 43rd Street Theatre, New York City, 1982-83.
Princess Dorothy, *The Road to Hollywood,* Guinevere Theatre, New York City, 1984.
Just So (musical adaptation of Rudyard Kipling's *Just So Stories*), Pennsylvania Stage Company, Allentown, PA, 1985.
Nickie, *Sweet Charity,* Minskoff Theatre, New York City, 1986-87.
Waitin' in the Wings: The Night the Understudies Take Centerstage (musical revue), Triplex Theatre, New York City, 1986.
Showing Off (musical revue), 45th Street Theatre, New York City, 1989.
Velma Kelly, *Chicago,* Long Beach Civic Light Opera, Long Beach, CA, 1992.

Also appeared in *West Side Story,* 1981, and was lead dancer in *Kicks* (also see below), 1984. Volunteer appearances in March of Dimes Telethon, Cystic Fibrosis Benefit Children's Ball, Ensemble Studio Theatre Benefit, and Circle Repertory Company Benefit, all 1986, all in New York City.

MAJOR TOURS

Lois, Cassie, Sheila, *A Chorus Line,* cities in U.S. and Canada, 1978-81.

STAGE WORK

Choreographer for *Kicks,* 1984.

FILM APPEARANCES

Mrs. Evans, *Say Anything,* Twentieth Century-Fox, 1989.
Lauren, *Green Card,* Buena Vista, 1990.
Felicia, *Penny Ante,* Motion Picture Corporation of America, 1990.
Countess di Frasso, *Bugsy,* TriStar, 1991.

OTHER SOURCES:

PERIODICALS

People, April 8, 1991, pp. 77-78.*

NEWMAN, Barry 1938-

PERSONAL: Full name, Barry Foster Newman; born November 7, 1938, in Boston, MA; son of Carl Henry and Sarah (Ostrovsky) Newman. *Education:* Brandeis University, B.A., anthropology, 1958.

ADDRESSES: Agent—Gersh Agency, Inc., 130 West 42nd St., Suite 1804, New York, NY 10036.

CAREER: Actor.

AWARDS, HONORS: Emmy Award nomination, best actor, and Golden Globe Award, best actor, Hollywood Foreign Press Association, both 1975, for *Petrocelli.*

CREDITS:

FILM APPEARANCES

Al Riccardo, *Pretty Boy Floyd,* Continental, 1960.
The Moving Finger, Moyer, 1963.
Tony Petrocelli, *The Lawyer,* Paramount, 1969.
Kowalski, *Vanishing Point,* Twentieth Century-Fox, 1971.
William Mathison, *The Salzburg Connection,* Twentieth Century-Fox, 1972.
John Talbot, *Fear Is the Key,* Paramount, 1973.
Dr. Frank Whitman, *City on Fire,* Avco Embassy, 1979.
Dr. Ben Corcoran, *Amy,* Buena Vista, 1981.
Barney Duncan, *Deadline,* Skouras, 1987.

TELEVISION APPEARANCES; MOVIES

Tony Petrocelli, *Night Games* (pilot), NBC, 1974.
Alan Fitch, *Sex and the Married Woman,* NBC, 1977.
Johnny Campana, *King Crab,* ABC, 1980.
Detective Flynn, *Fantasies,* ABC, 1982.
Peter Baylin, *Having It All,* ABC, 1982.
Bernie Segal, *Fatal Vision,* NBC, 1984.
Richard Chapman, *Second Sight: A Love Story* (also known as *Emma and I*), CBS, 1984.
Ben Taylor, *My Two Loves,* ABC, 1986.

TELEVISION APPEARANCES; SERIES

Tony Petrocelli, *Petrocelli,* NBC, 1974-76.

OTHER TELEVISION APPEARANCES

Garrett Braden, *Nightingales,* NBC, 1989.
Night of 100 Stars III (special; also see below), NBC, 1990.

Also appeared as John Barnes, *The Edge of Night.*

STAGE APPEARANCES

Detective Sergeant Trotter, *The Mousetrap,* Maidman Playhouse, New York City, 1960-61.
Young man, *Night Life,* Brooks Atkinson Theatre, New York City, 1962.
Sheik Orsini, *What Makes Sammy Run?,* 54th Street Theatre, New York City, 1964-65.
Night of 100 Stars III, Radio City Music Hall, New York City, 1990.*

* * *

NEWMAN, G. F. 1945-

PERSONAL: Full name Gordon F. Newman; born in 1945 in Kent, England; married Roberta Hall; children: two sons. *Avocational interests:* Animal rights, vegetarianism.

ADDRESSES: Agent—Elaine Steel.

CAREER: Writer and producer.

AWARDS, HONORS: Writer's Award, British Association of Film and Television Arts, 1991, for body of work.

WRITINGS:

SCREENPLAYS

Number One, Stageforum, 1985.

Also wrote screenplays for *Law & Order,* 1978; and *Sun in the Hunter's Eye.*

STAGE PLAYS

Operation Bad Apple, Royal Court Theatre, London, 1982.
An Honourable Trade, Royal Court Theatre, London, 1984.
The Testing Ground, Royal Court Theatre, London, 1989.

NOVELS

Sir, You Bastard, Simon & Schuster, 1970.
You Nice Bastard, New English Library, 1972.
The Player and the Guest, New English Library, 1972.
Billy: A Family Tragedy, New English Library, 1972.
The Split, New English Library, 1973.
Three Professional Ladies, New English Library, 1973.
The Price, New English Library, 1974, published as *You Flash Bastard,* Sphere Books, 1978.
The Guvnor, Hart-Davis, 1977.
The List, Secker & Warburg, 1980.
The Obsession, Granada, 1980.
Charlie and Joanna, Granada, 1981.
The Men with the Guns, Secker & Warburg, 1982.
Law and Order, Granada, 1983
The Nation's Health, Granada, 1984.
Set a Thief, Michael Joseph, 1986.
The Testing Ground, Michael Joseph, 1987.
Trading the Future, MacDonalds, 1991.

ADAPTATIONS: Sir, You Bastard was adapted as the film *The Take,* Columbia, 1974.

NORMAN, Marsha 1947-

PERSONAL: Born September 21, 1947, in Louisville, KY; daughter of Billie Lee (an insurance salesperson and realtor) and Bertha Mae (Conley) Williams; married Michael Norman (an English teacher; divorced, 1974); married Dann C. Byck, Jr. (a theatrical producer), November 23, 1978. *Education:* Agnes Scott College, B.A., philosophy, 1969; University of Louisville, M.A.T., teaching, 1971.

ADDRESSES: Office—c/o Jack Tantleff, 375 Greenwich St., Suite 700, New York, NY 10013. *Agent*—Martin Bauer, Bauer Benedek Agency, 9255 Sunset Blvd., No. 716, Los Angeles, CA 90069.

CAREER: Playwright and producer. Kentucky Department of Health, teacher, 1969-70; teacher of the gifted at public schools in Jefferson County, KY, 1970-72; Kentucky Arts Commission, filmmaker in the schools and director of special projects, 1972-76; *Louisville Times,* Louisville, KY, children's book reviewer and editor of the supplement *The Jellybean Journal,* 1974-79. Also worked with disturbed children at Kentucky Central State Hospital.

MEMBER: International PEN, Dramatists Guild, Writers Guild.

AWARDS, HONORS: Getting Out was named best play produced in regional theatre, American Theatre Critics Association, 1977-78; George Oppenheimer-*Newsday* Award, and John Glassner New Playwrights Medallion, Outer Critics Circle, both 1979, both for *Getting Out;* Pulitzer Prize, drama, Columbia University Graduate School of Journalism, Antoinette Perry Award nomination, best play, Susan Smith Blackburn Prize, and Elizabeth Hull-Kate Warriner Award, Dramatists Guild, all 1983, all for *'night, Mother;* Literary Lion Award, New York Public Library, 1986; Antoinette Perry Award, best book of a musical, Antoinette Perry Award nomination, best original score, and Drama Desk Award, best book of a musical, all 1991, all for *The Secret Garden.*

Received grants from National Endowment for the Arts, 1978-79, for Actors Theatre of Louisville; Rockefeller Foundation, 1979-80, for Mark Taper Forum; and American Academy and Institute for Arts and Letters.

CREDITS:

STAGE WORK

Director at Actors Theatre of Louisville, Louisville, KY, 1980-81.

TELEVISION APPEARANCES; SPECIALS

The 45th Annual Tony Awards, CBS, 1991.

WRITINGS:

STAGE PLAYS

Getting Out (two-act), produced at Actors Theatre of Louisville, Louisville, KY, 1977, later Phoenix Theatre, New York City, 1978, published by Avon, 1977.

Third and Oak: The Laundromat and *The Pool Hall* (two one-acts; also see below), produced at Actors Theatre of Louisville, 1978, published by Dramatists Play Service, 1978.

Circus Valentine (two-act), produced at Actors Theatre of Louisville, 1979.

The Holdup (two-act), produced at Actors Theatre of Louisville, 1980.

'night, Mother (also see below), produced at American Repertory Theatre, Cambridge, MA, later Golden Theatre, New York City, 1983.

Traveler in the Dark, produced at American Repertory Theatre, 1984.

Sarah and Abraham, produced at Actors Theatre of Louisville, 1987.

(Author of book and lyrics) *The Secret Garden* (children's musical), produced by Virginia Stage Company, Norfolk, 1989, later St. James Theatre, New York City, 1991.

Also author of the musical *Shakers.* Work represented in anthologies, including *The Best Plays of 1978-1979: The Burns Mantle Yearbook of the Theatre,* edited by Otis L. Guernsey, Jr., Dodd, 1980.

TELEVISION PLAYS; EPISODIC

"It's the Willingness," *Visions,* PBS, 1978.

"In Trouble at Fifteen," *Skag,* NBC, 1980.

"Third and Oak: The Pool Hall," *American Playwrights Theatre: The One Acts,* Arts and Entertainment, 1989.

OTHER TELEVISION PLAYS

The Laundromat, HBO, 1985.

Face of a Stranger (also known as *My Shadow;* also see below), CBS, 1991.

SCREENPLAYS

'night, Mother (based on Norman's play), Universal, 1986.

Also author of *The Children with Emerald Eyes,* Columbia; *Thy Neighbor's Wife,* United Artists; *The Bridge; Medicine Woman;* and *My Shadow.*

OTHER

Author of *The Fortune Teller* (novel), 1987; and *Four Plays by Marsha Norman,* 1988. Contributor to education journals and newspapers.

OTHER SOURCES:

BOOKS

Contemporary Authors, Volume 105, Gale, 1982.

PERIODICALS

Commonweal, October 12, 1979.
New Republic, July 7, 1979.
Newsweek, May 28, 1979.
New York, November 13, 1978; May 28, 1979.
New York Times, May 17, 1979; May 27, 1979; June 8, 1979; September 15, 1979; April 19, 1983.
Time, May 28, 1979.*

* * *

O'CONNOR, Kevin 1938-1991

OBITUARY NOTICE—See index for *CTFT* sketch: Born May 7, 1938, in Honolulu, HI; died of cancer, June 22, 1991, in New York, NY. Actor, director, producer, and teacher. Known for his stage acting career, O'Connor performed with the La Mama theatre company for many years, beginning in 1965. He appeared in three European tours with the company, acting in his last La Mama production, *The Dark and Mr. Stone,* in 1985. O'Connor's other stage credits included a number of Broadway and Off-Broadway shows, including *Samuel Beckett Plays, The Lady from Dubuque,* and *Devour the Snow.* He participated for several years at the Eugene O'Neill Playwrights Conference and appeared in a number of television and film productions. O'Connor also directed and produced stage works, most of which were performed at the Theatre at St. Clement's Church in the 1970s. An instructor of drama for fifteen years, he taught at New York University, St. Francis College, and Hunter College.

OBITUARIES AND OTHER SOURCES:

PERIODICALS

Variety, July 1, 1991, p. 49.

* * *

ONTKEAN, Michael 1946(?)-

PERSONAL: Born January 24, 1946 (some sources say 1950), in Vancouver, British Columbia, Canada; son of Leonard (an actor) and Muriel (an actress; maiden name, Cooper) Ontkean; *Education:* Attended University of New Hampshire.

ADDRESSES: Agent—Triad Artists, Inc., 888 Seventh Ave., No. 1602, New York, NY 10106.

CAREER: Actor. Acted at the age of four at father's repertory theatre; performed as a child actor at Stratford Shakespeare Festival, Stratford, Ontario, and for Canadian Broadcasting Corp. and Canada's National Film Board.

AWARDS, HONORS: Genie Award nomination, best performance by an actor in a supporting role, 1990, for *Bye Bye Blues.*

CREDITS:

TELEVISION APPEARANCES; SERIES

Officer Willie Gillis, *The Rookies* (also see below), ABC, 1972-74.
Sheriff Harry S. Truman, *Twin Peaks* (also known as *Northwest Passage*), ABC, 1990.

TELEVISION APPEARANCES; MOVIES

Officer Willie Gillis, *The Rookies* (pilot), ABC, 1972.
Jean Blomart, *The Blood of Others,* HBO, 1984.
John Ryan, *Kids Don't Tell,* CBS, 1985.
Chris Booth, *The Right of the People,* ABC, 1986.
Robert Simmons, *In Defense of a Married Man,* ABC, 1990.
Dr. Kenneth Z. Taylor, *In a Child's Name,* CBS, 1991.

Also appeared in *Man from the South* and *Summer.*

TELEVISION APPEARANCES; SPECIALS

Twin Peaks and Cop Rock: Behind the Scenes, ABC, 1990.
MTV's 1990 Video Music Awards, syndicated, 1990.
Presenter, *The 42nd Annual Primetime Emmy Awards Presentation,* Fox, 1990.
Presenter, *The 3rd Annual International Rock Awards,* ABC, 1991.

FILM APPEARANCES

Jeff, *The Peace Killers,* Transvue, 1971.
Frank Brandon, *Necromancy* (also known as *The Witching*), Cinerama, 1972.
Chuck, *Pickup on 101,* American International, 1972.
Hot Summer Week, Fanfare, 1973.
Ned Braden, *Slap Shot,* Universal, 1977.
Drew Rothman, *Voices,* Metro-Goldwyn-Mayer (MGM)/United Artists (UA), 1979.
Willie Kaufman, *Willie and Phil,* Twentieth Century-Fox, 1980.
Zack, *Making Love,* Twentieth Century-Fox, 1982.
Peter Nichols, *Just the Way You Are,* MGM/UA, 1984.
Mickey Leroi, *The Allnighter,* Universal, 1987.
Nick McGuire, *Maid to Order,* New Century/Vista, 1987.
Bill Hart, *Clara's Heart,* Warner Brothers, 1988.
Curt Flynn, *Street Justice,* Sandy Howard, 1989.
Teddy Cooper, *Bye Bye Blues,* Circle, 1990.
Robert Munch, *Postcards from the Edge,* Columbia, 1990.

Also appeared as Derek MacKenzie, *Cold Front,* 1989.

STAGE APPEARANCES

Has also made appearances at the Public Theatre, New York City, Williamstown Theatre Festival, Mark Taper Forum, Los Angeles, CA, and The Kitchen, Soho, London, England.*

* * *

OVITZ, Michael 1946-

PERSONAL: Born December 14, 1946, in Encino, CA; son of a liquor wholesaler; married Judy Reich, 1969; children: three. *Education:* University of California, Los Angeles, graduated, 1968; briefly attended law school.

ADDRESSES: Office—Creative Artists Agency, 9830 Wilshire Blvd., Beverly Hills, CA 90212.

CAREER: Talent agent and executive. William Morris Agency, Beverly Hills, CA, began as trainee, became talent agent, 1969-75; Creative Artists Agency, Beverly Hills, co-founder and talent agent, 1975—, currently president and chief stockholder.

MEMBER: Zeta Beta Tau.

OTHER SOURCES:

BOOKS

Newsmakers 90, Issue 1, Gale, 1990, p. 94.

PERIODICALS

New York Times, July 9, 1989.
Time, February 13, 1989, p. 58.*

P

PARKS, Bert 1914-1992

OBITUARY NOTICE—See index for *CTFT* sketch: Born December 30, 1914, in Atlanta, GA; died of a lung disease, February 2, 1992, in La Jolla, CA. Emcee and announcer. Parks hosted television's *Miss America Pageant* from the mid-1950s until 1979, making his signature song, "There She Is," part of the program's tradition for twenty-five years. He began his career in radio, first as a vocalist, then as a staff announcer for CBS, and first gained recognition as the emcee of *Stop the Music,* which he later hosted on television. His lengthy television career encompassed numerous quiz shows and prime-time telecasts, including *Break the Bank, Double or Nothing,* and *Two in Love,* as well as guest spots on such programs as *The Bionic Woman* and *Ellery Queen.* His cameo in the 1990 film *The Freshman* marked one of his last appearances.

OBITUARIES AND OTHER SOURCES:

BOOKS

International Motion Picture Almanac, Quigley Publishing Co., 1991, p, 246.

PERIODICALS

Variety, February 10, 1992, p. 95.

* * *

PATINKIN, Mandy 1952-

PERSONAL: Full name, Mandel Patinkin; born November 30, 1952, in Chicago, IL; son of Lester (a scrap metal dealer) and Doris (a homemaker; maiden name, Sinton) Patinkin; married Kathryn Grody (an actress), June 15, 1980; children: Isaac, Gideon. *Education:* Attended University of Kansas, 1970-72; studied drama at the Juilliard School of Music, 1972-74.

ADDRESSES: Agent—Triad, 888 Seventh Ave., 1602, New York, NY 10019. *Contact*—c/o CBS Records, 51 W. 52nd St., New York, NY 10019.

CAREER: Actor and singer. Active in regional theatre until joining the New York Shakespeare Festival, 1975-81; film appearances beginning in 1978; solo recording artist and concert performer, 1989—.

MEMBER: Actors' Equity Association, Screen Actors Guild, American Federation of Television and Radio Artists.

AWARDS, HONORS: Antoinette Perry Award, best actor in a featured role in a musical, 1980, for *Evita;* Antoinette Perry Award nomination, best actor in a musical, 1985, for *Sunday in the Park with George;* Drama League Musical Achievement Award, Drama League of New York, 1989.

CREDITS:

STAGE APPEARANCES

Durant Laxart, *Joan of Lorraine,* Good Shepherd/Faith Church Theatre, New York City, 1974.

Mr. Arthur Gower, *Trelawny of the 'Wells,'* New York Shakespeare Festival (NYSF), Vivian Beaumont Theater, New York City, 1975.

Fortinbras/Dumb Show King, *Hamlet,* NYSF, Vivian Beaumont Theater, 1975.

Major Robert Steele Strong, *Rebel Women,* NYSF, Public/Newman Theater, New York City, 1976.

Mark, *The Shadow Box,* Long Wharf Theatre, New Haven, CT, 1976, then Morosco Theatre, New York City, 1977.

Carlos, *Savages,* Hudson Guild Theatre, New York City, 1977.
Saverin, *Leave it to Beaver Is Dead,* NYSF, Public Theatre/Other Stage, 1979.
Che, *Evita,* Broadway Theatre, New York City, 1979.
Henry Percy, *Henry IV, Part I,* NYSF, Delacorte Theatre, New York City, 1981.
George, *Sunday in the Park with George* (also see below), Playwrights Horizons Theatre, New York City, 1983, then Booth Theatre, New York City, 1984.
"Follies" in Concert (also see below), Avery Fisher Hall, New York City, 1985.
Peter, *The Knife,* NYSF, Public/Newman Theatre, 1987.
Leontes, *The Winter's Tale,* NYSF, Public/Anspacher Theater, New York City, 1989.
Mandy Patinkin in Concert: Dress Casual (one-man show), NYSF, Public Theatre, 1989.

Also appeared as Hotspur in *Henry IV, Part I,* NYSF, Hudson Guild, New York City, as the title role in *Hamlet,* NYSF, and in *The Split.*

FILM APPEARANCES

Pool Man, *The Big Fix,* Universal, 1978.
Sayyid, *French Postcards,* Paramount, 1979.
Commuter, *Last Embrace,* United Artists (UA), 1979.
Cabbie, *Night of the Juggler,* Columbia, 1980.
Tateh, *Ragtime,* Paramount, 1981.
Paul Isaacson, *Daniel,* Paramount, 1983.
Avigdor, *Yentl,* Metro-Goldwyn-Mayer/UA, 1983.
Nick, *Maxie,* Orion, 1985.
Inigo Montoya, *The Princess Bride,* Twentieth Century-Fox, 1987.
Ray Salwen, *The House on Carroll Street,* Orion, 1988.
Sam Francisco, *Alien Nation,* Twentieth Century-Fox, 1988.
88 Keys, *Dick Tracy,* Touchstone/Buena Vista, 1990.
Alfred DeMusset, *Impromptu,* Hemdale, 1991.
John Palmeri, *True Colors,* Paramount, 1991.
Murray, *The Doctor,* Buena Vista, 1991.

TELEVISION APPEARANCES; EPISODIC

That Thing on ABC (comedy special; also see below), ABC, 1978.
That Second Thing on ABC (comedy special; sequel to *That Thing on ABC*), ABC, 1978.
"Sunday in the Park with George," *Broadway on Showtime,* Showtime, 1986.
" 'Follies' in Concert," *Great Performances,* PBS, 1986.

Also appeared in *Taxi* and *Midnight Special.*

TELEVISION APPEARANCES; MOVIES

Beaudine Croft, *Charleston,* NBC, 1979.

Also appeared in *Streets of Gold* and *Sparrow.*

RECORDINGS:

ALBUMS

Mandy Patinkin, CBS Records, 1989.

Also featured on albums, including *Evita* (original cast recording), *Sunday in the Park with George* (original cast recording), RCA, *"Follies" in Concert* (original cast recording), *South Pacific,* CBS Records, and *Mr. Arthur's Place.*

VIDEOS

Appeared in *South Pacific: The London Sessions,* 1986.

OTHER SOURCES:

BOOKS

Contemporary Musicians, Volume 3, Gale, 1990, pp. 175-76.

PERIODICALS

Cosmopolitan, January, 1988.
Esquire, April, 1989.
Hollywood Reporter, October 31, 1988, pp. 2, 13.
New Republic, May 8, 1989.
Newsweek, February 20, 1989; April 3, 1989.
New York Times, March 19, 1989.
People, February 17, 1986; May 8, 1989.
Starlog, November, 1988, pp. 30-32.*

* * *

PATRIC, Jason

PERSONAL: Son of Jason (an actor and writer) and Linda (Gleason) Miller.

ADDRESSES: Agent—David Schiff, InterTalent, 9200 Sunset Blvd., Penthouse 25, Los Angeles, CA 90069. *Manager*—Dolores Robinson Management, 355 North Maple Dr., Suite 250, Beverly Hills, CA 90210.

CAREER: Actor.

CREDITS:

FILM APPEARANCES

Jason, *Solarbabies,* Metro-Goldwyn-Mayer (MGM)/United Artists, 1986.
Michael, *The Lost Boys,* Warner Brothers, 1987.
Koverchenko, *The Beast,* Columbia, 1988.
Collie, *After Dark, My Sweet,* Avenue, 1990.
Lord Byron, *Frankenstein Unbound,* Twentieth Century-Fox, 1990.
Michael, *Denial* (also known as *Desire Loon*), Republic Pictures, 1991.
Jim Raynor, *Rush,* MGM/Pathe, 1991.

TELEVISION APPEARANCES; MOVIES

Gary Charters, *Toughlove,* ABC, 1985.

TELEVISION APPEARANCES; EPISODIC

Title role, "Teach 109," *American Playhouse,* PBS, 1988.

STAGE APPEARANCES

Appeared in *Beirut* at the Matrix Theatre, *Outta Gas on Lover's Leap* at the Coast Playhouse, and *The Tempest* and *Love's Labour's Lost* at the Champlain Shakespeare Festival.*

* * *

PENN, Sean 1960-

PERSONAL: Born August 17, 1960, in Santa Monica, CA; son of Leo Penn (an actor and director) and Eileen Ryan (an actress); married Madonna Louise Ciccone (a singer and actress), August, 1985 (divorced); children: (with actress Robin Wright) Frances Dylan Penn. *Education:* Graduated from Santa Monica High School, 1978; studied acting at Loft Studio and with Peggy Feury.

ADDRESSES: Office—1900 Avenue of the Stars, Suite 2200, Los Angeles, CA 90067. *Agent*—c/o Creative Artists Agency, 1888 Century Park East, Suite 1400, Los Angeles, CA 90067.

CAREER: Actor, director, and screenwriter. Worked as a production assistant for Los Angeles Group Repertory Theatre, Los Angeles, CA, 1978-80; also worked as an assistant to actor and director Pat Hingle.

CREDITS:

STAGE APPEARANCES

(Stage debut) *Earthworms,* Los Angeles Repertory Theatre, Los Angeles, c. 1980.
(Broadway debut) James, *Heartland,* Century Theatre, New York City, 1981.
George "Spanky" Farrell, slab boy, *Slab Boys,* Playhouse Theatre, New York City, 1983.

Also appeared in *The Girl on the Via Flaminia,* Gene Dynarski Theatre, Hollywood, CA; *Hurlyburly,* 1988.

STAGE WORK

Directed *Terrible Jim Fitch,* Group Repertory Theatre.

FILM APPEARANCES

(Film debut) Alex Dwyer, *Taps,* Twentieth Century-Fox, 1981.
Jeff Spicoli, *Fast Times at Ridgemont High,* Universal, 1982.
Mick O'Brien, *Bad Boys,* Universal, 1983.
Garvey, *Crackers,* Universal, 1984.
Henry "Hoppper" Nash, *Racing with the Moon,* Paramount, 1984.
Daulton Lee, *The Falcon and the Snowman,* Orion, 1985.
Brad Whitewood, Jr., *At Close Range,* Orion, 1986.
Glendon Wasey, *Shanghai Surprise,* Metro Goldwyn-Mayer (MGM), 1986.
Danny McGavin, *Colors,* Orion, 1988.
Gunther X, *Judgment in Berlin,* New Line Cinema, 1988.
Meserve, *Casualties of War,* Columbia, 1989.
Jim, *We're No Angels,* Paramount, 1989.
Terry Noonan, *State of Grace,* Orion, 1991.

Also appeared as narrator, *Dear America,* 1987.

FILM WORK

(Director) *The Indian Runner* (also see below), MGM-Pathe, 1991.

TELEVISON APPEARANCES; MOVIES

Concrete Cowboys, CBS, 1979.
Don Fremont, *The Killing of Randy Webster,* CBS, 1981.

Also appeared in *Hellinger's Law,* 1981.

TELEVISION APPEARANCES; SERIES

(Television debut) *Barnaby Jones,* CBS, 1979.

WRITINGS:

The Indian Runner (screenplay), MGM-Pathe, 1991.

OTHER SOURCES:

PERIODICALS

American Film, August, 1991, p. 18.
Interview, September, 1991, p. 94.
New York Times, September 15, 1991, p. H13.
People, February 11, 1985, p. 137; September 24, 1990, p 53.
Playboy, November, 1991, p. 30.
Premiere, October, 1991, p. 60.*

* * *

PETERS, Bernadette 1948-

PERSONAL: Born Bernadette Lazzara, February 28, 1948, in Jamaica, NY; daughter of Peter (a truck driver) and Marguerite (a homemaker; maiden name, Maltese) Lazzara. *Education:* Attended Quintana School for Young Professionals, New York City; studied acting with David Le Grant, tap dancing with Oliver McCool III, and singing with Jim Gregory.

ADDRESSES: Agent—Richard Grant and Associates, 8500 Wilshire Blvd., Suite 250, Beverly Hills, CA 90211.

CAREER: Actress. Performed in concert in Edmonton, Alberta, 1961; nightclub entertainer, beginning in the 1970s.

MEMBER: Actors' Equity Association, American Federation of Television and Radio Artists, Screen Actors Guild.

AWARDS, HONORS: Drama Desk Award, outstanding performance, 1968, for *Dames at Sea; Theatre World* Award, 1968, for *George M!;* Antoinette Perry Award nomination, best supporting actress in a musical play, 1971, for *On the Town;* Antoinette Perry Award nomination, best actress in a Broadway musical, 1974, for *Mack and Mabel;* Emmy Award nomination, outstanding continuing or single performance by a supporting actress in a variety or music program, 1977, for *The Muppet Show;* Best of Las Vegas Award, 1980; Golden Globe Award, best film actress in a musical/comedy, 1981, for *Pennies from Heaven;* Antoinette Perry Award nomination, best actress in a musical, 1984, for *Sunday in the Park with George;* Antoinette Perry Award, best actress in a musical, and Drama Desk Award, best actress in a musical, both 1986, for *Song and Dance;* Distinguished Performance Award, Drama League of New York, 1986; Hasty Pudding Woman of the Year Award, 1987; Drama Desk Award nomination, 1987.

CREDITS:

STAGE APPEARANCES

Tessie, *The Most Happy Fella,* New York City Center Theatre, New York City, 1959.
Cinderella, *The Penny Friend,* Stage 73 Theatre, New York City, 1966-67.
(Broadway debut) Understudy, *The Girl in the Freudian Slip,* Booth Theatre, New York City, 1967.
Bettina, *Johnny No-trump,* Cort Theatre, New York City, 1967.
Alice, *Curley McDimple,* Wheeler Theatre, New York City, 1967-68.
Josie Cohan, *George M!* (also see below), Palace Theatre, New York City, 1968.
Ruby, *Dames at Sea,* Bouwerie Lane Theatre, New York City, 1968-69.
Gelsomina, *La Strada,* Lunt-Fontanne Theatre, New York City, 1969.
Consuelo, *Nevertheless They Laugh,* Lambs Club Theatre, New York City, 1971.
Hildy, *On the Town,* Imperial Theatre, New York City, 1971-72.
Dorine, *Tartuffe,* Philadelphia Drama Guild Theatre, Philadelphia, PA, 1972-73.
Mabel Normand, *Mack and Mabel,* Majestic Theatre, New York City, 1974.
Sally, *Sally and Marsha,* Manhattan Theatre Club/Downstage, New York City, 1982.
Dot, *Sunday in the Park with George* (also see below), Playwrights Horizons, New York City, 1983, then Booth Theatre, 1984-85.
Emma, *Song and Dance,* Royale Theatre, New York City, 1985-86.
Witch, *Into the Woods* (also see below), Martin Beck Theatre, New York City, 1987-89.

Also appeared as Alice Burton, *This Is Google,* 1962; and Jenny, *Riverwind,* 1966.

MAJOR TOURS

Gypsy, midwestern U.S. cities, 1961-62.
Carolotta Monti, *W. C.,* U.S. cities, 1971.

FILM APPEARANCES

Allison, *Ace Eli and Rodger of the Skies,* Twentieth Century-Fox, 1973.
Warden's secretary, *The Longest Yard,* Paramount, 1974.
Vilma Kaplan, *Silent Movie,* Twentieth Century-Fox, 1976.
Dee, *Vigilante Force,* United Artists, 1976.
Melody, *W. C. Fields and Me,* Universal, 1976.
Marie, *The Jerk,* Universal, 1979.
Aqua, *Heartbeeps,* Universal, 1981.
Eileen, *Pennies from Heaven,* Metro-Goldwyn-Mayer, 1981.
Rutanya Wallace, *Tulips,* Avco Embassy, 1981.
Lily, *Annie,* Columbia, 1982.
Eleanor, *Slaves of New York,* Tri-Star, 1989.
Lou Ann McGuinn, *Pink Cadillac,* Warner Brothers, 1989.
Muse, *Alice,* Orion, 1990.
Marie d'Agoult, *Impromptu,* Hemdale, 1991.

TELEVISION APPEARANCES; SPECIALS

Josie Cohan, *George M!* (adaptation of the Broadway musical), NBC, 1970.
Bing Crosby—Cooling It (variety special), NBC, 1970.
Lady Larken, *Once upon a Mattress,* CBS, 1972.
Burt and the Girls, NBC, 1973.
Bing Crosby—Cooling It (variety special), CBS, 1973.
Josie Cohan, *George M!* (variety special), CBS, 1976.
Bing Crosby's White Christmas, CBS, 1976.
Ringmaster, *Circus of the Stars,* CBS, 1977.
Bob Hope's All-Star Comedy Tribute to Vaudeville, NBC, 1977.
Uncle Tim Wants You, CBS, 1977.
The Beatles Forever, NBC, 1977.
Mac Davis's Christmas Odyssey: 2010, NBC, 1978.
Perry Como's Springtime Special, ABC, 1979.
Ringmaster, *Circus of the Stars,* CBS, 1979.
Musical Comedy Tonight, PBS, 1979.

Sally, *Bob Hope in the Star Makers,* NBC, 1980.
Baryshnikov in Hollywood, CBS, 1982.
Bob Hope's All-Star Birthday at Annapolis, NBC, 1982.
Texaco Star Theatre: Opening Night, NBC, 1982.
George Burns and Other Sex Symbols, NBC, 1982.
Bob Hope's Pink Panther Thanksgiving Gala, NBC, 1982.
George Burns Celebrates Eighty Years in Show Business, NBC, 1983.
The 38th Annual Tony Awards, CBS, 1984.
Bob Hope's Happy Birthday Homecoming, NBC, 1985.
The Night of 100 Stars II, ABC, 1985.
The 40th Annual Tony Awards, CBS, 1986.
Dot and Marie, *Sunday in the Park with George,* Showtime, 1986.
Happy Birthday Hollywood, ABC, 1987.
The Music Makers: An ASCAP Celebration of American Music at Wolf Trap, PBS, 1987.
The 41st Annual Tony Awards, CBS, 1987.
The 59th Annual Academy Awards Presentation, ABC, 1987.
A Star-Spangled Celebration, ABC, 1987.
Evening at Pops, PBS, 1987.
Ruby Lee Carter, *Diana Ross . . .Red Hot Rhythm and Blues,* ABC, 1987.
The 42nd Annual Tony Awards, CBS, 1988.
The Kennedy Center Honors: A Celebration of the Performing Arts, CBS, 1989.
A Broadway Christmas, Showtime, 1990.
The 44th Annual Tony Awards, CBS, 1990.
The 33rd Annual Grammy Awards, CBS, 1991.

Also appeared on *Bob Hope's Women I Love—Beautiful but Funny,* 1982.

TELEVISION APPEARANCES; EPISODIC

"We Interrupt This Season," *NBC Experiment in Television,* NBC, 1967.
Carol Burnett Show, CBS, 1969 and 1974.
"Lost Paradise," *Theatre in America,* PBS, 1971.
"Love and the Hoodwinked Honey," *Love, American Style,* ABC, 1973.
"The Double Date," *Maude,* CBS, 1975.
"Gloria Suspects Mike," *All in the Family,* CBS, 1975.
"In Again, Out Again," *McCoy,* NBC, 1976.
"The Day New York Turned Blue," *McCloud,* NBC, 1976.
Host, *Saturday Night Live,* NBC, 1981.
"Sleeping Beauty," *Faerie Tale Theater,* Showtime, 1983.
"Trevor Farrell," *An American Portrait,* CBS, 1984.
Tammy Faye Bakker, "Fall from Grace," *Sunday Night at the Movies,* NBC, 1990.
Witch, "Into the Woods," *American Playhouse,* PBS, 1991.

Appeared as a child on *Horn & Hardart Children's Hour, Juvenile Jury,* and *Name That Tune;* appeared as host, *Rich, Thin, and Beautiful;* also appeared on *The Muppet Show,* 1977, *They Said It with Music, Lonely Man, House of Numbers, Ten Seconds to Hell,* and *Warriors Five.*

OTHER TELEVISION APPEARANCES

Doris, *The Owl and the Pussycat* (pilot), NBC, 1975.
Charlotte (Charley) Drake, *All's Fair* (series), CBS, 1976-77.
Trudy Engels, *The Islander* (pilot), CBS, 1978.
Genevieve Seltzer, *The Martian Chronicles* (miniseries), NBC, 1980.
Marie Rothenberg, *David* (movie), ABC, 1988.
Jane Murray, *The Last Best Year of My Life* (movie), ABC, 1990.

RECORDINGS:

ALBUMS

Bernadette Peters, MCA, 1980.
Now Playing, MCA, 1981.
Sondheim: Sunday in the Park with George, RCA, 1985.

Also recorded *A Collector's Sondheim,* 1985, and *Bernadette Peters in "Song and Dance": The Songs,* 1986.

OTHER SOURCES:

PERIODICALS

People Weekly, March 29, 1982, p. 70.*

*   *   *

PETTY, Lori

PERSONAL: Born in Tennessee; daughter of a Pentecostal minister.

CAREER: Actress.

CREDITS:

FILM APPEARANCES

Lila, *Cadillac Man,* Orion, 1990.
Tyler, *Point Break,* Twentieth Century-Fox, 1991.
Kit Keller, *A League of Their Own,* Columbia, 1992.

TELEVISION APPEARANCES; MOVIES

Willie, *Bates Motel,* NBC, 1987.
Cassie, *Perry Mason: The Case of the Musical Murder* (also known as *Perry Mason: The Case of the Final Curtain*), NBC, 1989.

TELEVISION APPEARANCES; PILOTS

Kate Phoenix, *San Berdoo,* ABC, 1989.

TELEVISION APPEARANCES; EPISODIC

Jo Lanier, *The Line,* NBC, 1987.
Jeannie Pardonales, "Monster Manor," *Police Story,* ABC, 1988.
Cricket, *The Thorns,* ABC, 1988.
Suzanne Dunne, *Booker,* Fox, 1989.*

* * *

PITT, Brad 1964(?)-

PERSONAL: Born c. 1964, in Oklahoma; son of an owner of a trucking company. *Education:* Studied journalism at University of Missouri until 1987; studied acting with Roy London.

ADDRESSES: Office—10100 Santa Monica Blvd., No. 1600, Los Angeles, CA 90067. *Manager*—Cynthia Pett, The Brillstein Company, 9200 Sunset Blvd., Suite 428, Los Angeles, CA 90069.

CAREER: Actor.

CREDITS:

FILM APPEARANCES

Dwight Ingalls, *Cutting Class,* Gower Street, 1989.
Happy Together, Borde Releasing, 1989.
Joe Maloney, *Across the Tracks* (also known as *Nowhere to Run*), Rosenbloom Entertainment, 1990.
Contact, Chanticleer, 1991.
J. D., *Thelma and Louise,* Metro-Goldwyn-Mayer/Pathe, 1991.
The Favor, Orion, 1992.
Johnny, *Johnny Suede,* Miramax, 1992.
Cool World, Paramount, 1992.

TELEVISION APPEARANCES; MOVIES

The Image, HBO, 1990.
Billy Canton, *Too Young to Die?,* NBC, 1990.

TELEVISION APPEARANCES; SERIES

Walker Lovejoy, *Glory Days* (also known as *The Kids Are All Right*), Fox, 1990.

TELEVISION APPEARANCES; EPISODIC

Two-fisted Tales, Fox, 1992.

Also appeared on episodes of *Dallas,* CBS, and *Another World,* NBC.

POLONSKY, Abraham 1910- (Emmett Hogarth, a joint pseudonym)

PERSONAL: Full name, Abraham Lincoln Polonsky; born December 5, 1910, in New York, NY; son of Henry and Rebecca (Rosoff) Polonsky; married Sylvia Marrow, 1937; children: Susan, Henry Victor. *Education:* City College of New York (now of the City University of New York), B.A., 1932; Columbia University, LL.B., 1935. *Religion:* Jewish.

ADDRESSES: Agent—Gersh Agency, 250 North Canon Dr., Beverly Hills, CA 90210.

CAREER: Writer and director. City College of New York (now City College of the City University of New York), New York City, instructor in English, 1932-42; admitted to the bar, 1935; worked as a lawyer with a Manhattan firm, 1930s; gave technical advice to radio personality Gertrude Berg (*The Goldbergs*), 1930s, which led to writing for radio; blacklisted, 1951-66. *Military service:* U.S. Office of Strategic Services, 1943-45, served in European theater.

AWARDS, HONORS: Academy Award nomination, best original screenplay, 1947, for *Body and Soul.*

CREDITS:

FILM DIRECTOR

(With Don Weis) *Force of Evil* (also see below), Metro-Goldwyn-Mayer (MGM), 1948.
Tell Them Willie Boy Is Here (also see below), Universal, 1969.
Romance of a Horse Thief, Allied Artists, 1971.

WRITINGS:

SCREENPLAYS

(With Frank Butler and Helen Deutsch) *Golden Earrings* (based on the novel by Yolanda Foldes), Paramount, 1947.
Body and Soul (also known as *An Affair of the Heart*), United Artists, 1947.
(With Ira Wolfert) *Force of Evil* (based on Wolfert's novel *Tucker's People*), MGM, 1948.
(With Vera Caspary) *I Can Get It for You Wholesale* (also known as *Only the Best;* based on the novel by Jerome Weidman), Twentieth Century-Fox, 1951.
(With Howard Rodman and Harry Kleiner) *Madigan* (based on Richard Dougherty's novel *The Commissioner*), Universal, 1968.
Tell Them Willie Boy Is Here (based on Harry Lawton's novel *Willie Boy . . . A Desert Manhunt*), Universal, 1969.
Avalanche Express (based on the novel by Colin Forbes) Twentieth Century-Fox, 1979.

(With Wendell Mayes) *Monsignor* (based on the novel by Jack Alain Leger), Twentieth Century-Fox, 1982.

NOVELS

(With Mitchell A. Wilson under joint pseudonym Emmett Hogarth) *The Goose Is Cooked,* Simon & Schuster, 1940.
The Enemy Sea, Little, Brown, 1943.
The World Above, Little, Brown, 1951.
A Season of Fear, Cameron Associates, 1956.
Zenia's Way, Lippincott, 1980.

OTHER

Author of essays, short stories, and scripts for radio and television.

OTHER SOURCES:

BOOKS

Contemporary Authors, Volume 104, Gale, 1982.
Dictionary of Literary Biography, Volume 26: *American Screenwriters,* Gale, 1984.*

* * *

PRICE, Frank 1930-

PERSONAL: Born May 17, 1930, in Decatur, IL; son of William F. and Winifred A. (Moran) Price; married Katherine Huggins, May 15, 1965; children: Stephen, David, Roy, Frank. *Education:* Attended Michigan State University, 1949-50.

ADDRESSES: Office—Price Entertainment Inc., 10202 West Washington Blvd., Culver City, CA 90232.

CAREER: Motion picture and television executive. Columbia Broadcasting System (CBS-TV), New York City, story editor and writer, 1951-53; Columbia Pictures, Hollywood, CA, story editor and writer, 1953-57; National Broadcasting Company (NBC-TV), Hollywood, CA, story editor, 1957-58; ZIV-TV, Hollywood, CA, producer and writer, 1958; Universal Television, Universal City, CA, producer and writer, 1959-64, vice president, 1964-71, senior vice president, 1971-73, executive vice president in charge of production, 1973-74, president, 1974-78, vice president of MCA, Inc., 1976-78; Columbia Pictures Productions, Burbank, CA, president, 1978-79; Columbia Pictures, Burbank, chairman, member of board of executives and chief executive officer, c. 1979-84; Universal, Universal City, chairman of motion picture group, president of Universal Pictures, and vice president of MCA, Inc., 1984-86; Price Entertainment Inc., Culver City, CA, founder, chairman, and chief executive officer, 1987-90, integrated into Columbia Pictures, 1990; Columbia Pictures, Culver City, chairman and member of board of directors, 1990-91; Price Entertainment Inc., chairman and chief executive officer, 1991—. *Military service:* U.S. Navy, 1948-49.

MEMBER: Writers Guild of America, West.

CREDITS:

TELEVISION EXECUTIVE PRODUCER; MOVIES

Split Second to an Epitaph, NBC, 1968.
San Francisco International, NBC, 1970.
Alias Smith and Jones, ABC, 1971.

TELEVISION PRODUCER; MOVIES

The Doomsday Flight, NBC, 1966.
The City, ABC, 1971.
I Love a Mystery, NBC, 1973.

TELEVISION EXECUTIVE PRODUCER; SERIES

The Virginian, NBC, 1963-65 and 1969-70.
(And creator) *Convoy,* NBC, 1965.
Ironside, NBC, 1967-68.
It Takes a Thief, ABC, 1968-69.

TELEVISION PRODUCER; SERIES

The Tall Man, NBC, 1961-62.

FILM PRODUCER

Gladiator, Columbia, 1992.

Shared responsibility for productions of *Kramer vs. Kramer,* Columbia, 1979, *Stripes,* Columbia, 1981, *Tootsie,* Columbia, 1982, *Gandhi,* Columbia, 1982, *Ghostbusters,* Columbia, 1984, *Out of Africa,* Universal, 1985, *Back to the Future,* Universal, 1985, and *Boyz 'n the Hood,* Columbia, 1991.

* * *

PUTTNAM, David 1941-

PERSONAL: Full name, David Terence Puttnam; born February 25, 1941, in Southgate, England; son of Leonard Arthur (a photographer) and Marie Beatrix (a homemaker) Puttnam; married Patricia Mary Jones, 1961; children: Sasha, Debbie. *Education:* Minchenden Grammar School, London. *Avocational interests:* Watching cricket, going to movies.

ADDRESSES: Office—Enigma Productions, 13/15 Queen's Gate Place Mews, London SW7 5BG, England.

CAREER: Film producer. Worked for an advertising agency, 1958-66, and as a photographers' agent, 1966-68; Enigma Productions, London, England, founder and producer, 1968—. National Film and Television School, governor, 1974—, chairman, 1988—; National Film Finance Corp., director, 1980-85; Anglia Television Group, director, 1982—; Bristol University, visiting professor of film, 1986—; Columbia Pictures, chairman and chief executive officer, 1986-87; ITEL International (television distribution agency), chairman, 1988—; Survival Anglia, director, 1988—; served on Cinema Films Council and governing council of the British Academy of Film and Television Arts. Council for the Protection of Rural England, president, 1985—; Tate Gallery, trustee, 1986—.

MEMBER: Royal Geographic Society (fellow), Royal Photographic Society (fellow), Royal Society of Arts (fellow), Marylebone Cricket Club.

AWARDS, HONORS: Jury Award, Cannes Film Festival, 1977, for *The Duellists;* Academy Award nomination (with Alan Marshall), best picture, 1978, for *Midnight Express;* Academy Award, best picture, 1981, for *Chariots of Fire;* Michael Balcon Award, British Academy of Film and Television Arts, 1981, for outstanding contribution to British film industry; Academy Award nomination, best picture, 1984, for *The Killing Fields;* Academy Award nomination, best picture, and Palme d'Or, Cannes Film Festival, both (with Fernando Ghia) 1986, for *The Mission;* decorated Chevalier dans l'Ordre des Arts et des Lettres, France, 1986, promoted to Officier, 1991; Eastman Second Century Award, Eastman Board of Governors, 1988, for "ongoing contributions to the development of young talent in the movie business"; Emmy Award, outstanding drama/comedy special and miniseries, 1991, for *The Josephine Baker Story;* Award for Cablecasting Excellence (ACE) nomination, best movie or miniseries, 1992, for *Without Warning: The James Brady Story;* decorated Commander of the Order of the British Empire; LL.D., Bristol University, 1983, and University of Leeds, 1992; Litt.D., Leicester University, 1986; fellow, Manchester Polytechnic, 1989; honorary fellow, Chartered Society of Designers.

CREDITS:

FILM PRODUCER

Melody (also known as *S.W.A.L.K.*), Levitt-Pickman, 1971.
(With Sanford Lieberson) *The Pied Piper,* Paramount, 1972.
(With Lieberson) *That'll Be the Day* (also see below), EMI, 1974.
(With Lieberson; and music producer and arranger with Dave Edmunds) *Stardust* (sequel to *That'll Be the Day*), Columbia, 1974.
(With Roy Baird) *Lisztomania,* Warner Brothers, 1975.
The Duellists, Paramount, 1977.
(With Alan Marshall) *Midnight Express,* Columbia, 1978.
(With Gerald Ayres) *Foxes,* United Artists, 1980.
Chariots of Fire, Twentieth Century-Fox, 1981.
Local Hero, Warner Brothers, 1983.
The Killing Fields, Warner Brothers, 1984.
(With Stuart Craig) *Cal,* Warner Brothers, 1985.
(With Fernando Ghia) *The Mission,* Warner Brothers, 1986.
(With Catherine Wyler) *Memphis Belle,* Warner Brothers, 1990.
Meeting Venus, Warner Brothers, 1991.

FILM PRODUCER, WITH OTHERS; DOCUMENTARIES

Swastika, Black Inc., 1973.
Brother, Can You Spare a Dime?, Dimension Pictures, 1974.
James Dean, the First American Teenager, Visual Programme Systems (Great Britain), 1975.

Also coproducer of *Double-Headed Eagle.*

FILM EXECUTIVE PRODUCER

Mahler, New Line Cinema, 1973.
The Last Days of Man on Earth, New World, 1973.
Bugsy Malone, Paramount, 1976.
Secrets, Samuel Goldwyn, 1982.
Kipperbang (also known in England as *P'Tang, Yang, Kipperbang*), Twentieth Century-Fox, 1982.
Experience Preferred but Not Essential, Samuel Goldwyn, 1982.
Those Glory Glory Days, Twentieth Century-Fox, 1983.
Sharma and Beyond, Cinecom, 1983.
Red Monarch, Enigma, 1983.
Winter Flight, Cinecom, 1984.
Forever Young, Twentieth Century-Fox, 1984.
Mr. Love, Warner Brothers, 1985.
The Frog Prince, Warner Brothers, 1985.
Defence of the Realm, Warner Brothers, 1985.
Arthur's Hallowed Ground, Cinecom, 1985.
Knights and Emeralds, Warner Brothers, 1986.

TELEVISION EXECUTIVE PRODUCER

The Josephine Baker Story (movie), HBO, 1991.
Without Warning: The James Baker Story (movie), HBO, 1991.
"A Dangerous Man: Lawrence after Arabia," *Great Performances* (episodic), PBS, 1992.

WRITINGS:

(With Derrik Mercer) *Rural England: Our Countryside at the Crossroads,* photographs by Derry Brabbs, Macdonald, 1988.

Contributor to *The Third Age of Broadcasting,* edited by Brian Wenham, Faber, 1982. Contributor of articles and reviews to *New Statesman & Society.*

OTHER SOURCES:

BOOKS

Kipps, Charles, *Out of Focus: Power, Pride, and Prejudice—David Puttnam in Hollywood,* Morrow, 1989.
Yule, Andrew, *Fast Fade: David Puttnam, Columbia Pictures, and the Battle for Hollywood,* Delacorte, 1988.

PERIODICALS

American Film, November, 1984, p. 14.
Films and Filming, March, 1983, p. 7.
Newsweek, May 20, 1985, p. 84.
Observer (London), March 17, 1985, p. 19; August 30, 1987, p. 9.
People, November 16, 1987, p. 125.
Time, May 1, 1989, p. 62.
Vanity Fair, April, 1988, p. 96.
Variety, May 18, 1988, p. 7.
Wall Street Journal, February 20, 1987, p. 1.

* * *

PUZO, Mario 1920-

PERSONAL: Born October 14, 1920, in New York, NY; son of Antonio (a railroad trackman) and Maria (Le Conti) Puzo; married Erika Lina Broske, 1946; children: Anthony, Joey, Dorothy, Virginia, Eugene. *Education:* Attended New School for Social Research and Columbia University. *Avocational interests:* Gambling, tennis, Italian cuisine, dieting.

ADDRESSES: *Contact*—Bert Fields, Greenberg, Glusker, Fields, Claman & Machtinger, Los Angeles, CA.

CAREER: Writer. Worked variously as a messenger with New York Central Railroad, New York City, public relations administrator with U.S. Air Force in Europe, administrative assistant with U.S. Civil Service, New York City, and editor-writer with Magazine Management. *Military service:* U.S. Army Air Forces, World War II, served in Germany; became corporal.

AWARDS, HONORS: All with Francis Ford Coppola: Academy Award, best screenplay based on material from another medium, Screen Award, Writers Guild of America, West, Inc., best screenplay adapted from another medium, both 1972, and Golden Globe Award, best screenplay, 1973, all for *The Godfather;* Academy Award, best screenplay adapted from another medium, and Screen Award, Writers Guild of America, West, Inc., best screenplay adapted from another medium, both 1974, for *The Godfather, Part II;* Golden Globe Award nomination, best screenplay, 1990, for *The Godfather Part III.*

CREDITS:

TELEVISION APPEARANCES; SPECIALS

The Godfather Family: A Look Inside, HBO, 1990.

WRITINGS:

SCREENPLAYS

(With Francis Ford Coppola) *The Godfather* (based on Puzo's novel of the same title; also see below), Paramount, 1972.
(With Coppola) *The Godfather, Part II* (based on Puzo's novel *The Godfather*), Paramount, 1974.
(With George Fox) *Earthquake,* Universal, 1974.
(With David Newman, Leslie Newman, and Robert Benton) *Superman* (based on a story by Puzo, from the comic strip created by Jerry Siegel and Joel Shuster), Warner Brothers, 1978.
(With D. Newman and L. Newman) *Superman II* (based on a story by Puzo, from characters created by Siegel and Shuster), Warner Brothers, 1980.
(With Coppola) *The Godfather Part III,* Paramount, 1990.

NOVELS

The Dark Arena, Random House, 1955, revised, Bantam, 1985.
The Fortunate Pilgrim, Atheneum, 1964.
The Godfather (Literary Guild and Book-of-the-Month Club selections), Putnam, 1969.
Fools Die (Book-of-the-Month Club selection), Putnam, 1978.
The Sicilian, Linden Press/Simon & Schuster, 1984.
The Fourth K, Random House, 1990.

OTHER

The Runaway Summer of Davie Shaw (juvenile), illustrated by Stewart Sherwood, Platt & Munk, 1966.
The "Godfather" Papers and Other Confessions, Putnam, 1972.
Inside Las Vegas (nonfiction), photographs by Michael Abramson, Susan Fowler-Gallagher, and John Launois, Grosset, 1977.

Creator of stories for the movies *A Time to Die,* by John Goff, Matt Cimber, and William Russell, Almi, 1983, and *The Cotton Club* (with William Kennedy and Coppola), by Kennedy and Coppola, Orion, 1984. Contributor to books, including *The Immigrant Experience: The Anguish of Becoming an American,* edited by Thomas C. Wheeler, Dial, 1971. Contributor of articles, reviews, and stories to *American Vanguard, New York, Redbook, Holiday, New York Times Magazine,* and other publications.

ADAPTATIONS: The Sicilian was adapted for the screen by Steve Shagan and directed by Michael Cimino for

Twentieth Century-Fox, 1987; *The Fortunate Pilgrim* was adapted for television and broadcast as *Mario Puzo's the Fortunate Pilgrim* by NBC, 1988.

OTHER SOURCES:

BOOKS

Contemporary Authors New Revision Series, Volume 4, Gale, 1981.
Contemporary Literary Criticism, Gale, Volume 1, 1973, Volume 2, 1974, Volume 6, 1976, Volume 36, 1986.
Dictionary of Literary Biography, Volume 6: *American Novelists since World War II, Second Series,* Gale, 1981.
Green, Rose B., *The Italian-American Novel,* Fairleigh Dickinson University Press, 1974.
Madden, David, editor, *Rediscoveries,* Crown, 1972.
Major Twentieth-Century Writers, Gale, 1991.*

* * *

PYNE, Daniel 1955-

PERSONAL: Full name Daniel John Pyne; born June 29, 1955, in Oak Park, IL; son of Charles Joseph (a sculptor) and Barbara Louise (Petersen) Pyne; married Joan Elizabeth Cashel (a musician), August 30, 1986; children: Katie. *Education:* Stanford University, B.A., economics, 1976; University of California, Los Angeles, M.F.A., theater arts, 1982.

ADDRESSES: Office—Universal Studios, 100 Universal City Plaza, Universal City, CA 91608. *Agent*—Bauer Benedek Agency, P.O. Box 5514, Beverly Hills, CA 90209.

CAREER: Screenwriter and producer. *Menlo-Atherton Recorder,* Menlo Park, CA, sports editor, 1976; Maxwell Arnold Agency, San Francisco, CA, copywriter, 1977-78.

CREDITS:

TELEVISION WORK; SERIES

Supervising producer and creator, *Hard Copy* (also see below), CBS, 1987.
Executive producer and creator, *The Street,* syndicated, 1988.
Executive producer, *The Antagonists* (also see below), CBS, 1991.

WRITINGS:

FOR TELEVISION

Story editor, *Matt Houston* (series), ABC, 1982-83.
(And executive story editor) *Miami Vice* (series), NBC, beginning in 1984.
(Coauthor) *Hard Copy* (pilot), CBS, 1987.
(With John Mankiewicz and Charles Grant Craig) *The Return of Desperado* (movie), NBC, 1988.
The Antagonists (series), CBS, 1991.

SCREENPLAYS

Pacific Heights, Twentieth Century-Fox, 1990.
(With Lem Dobbs) *The Hard Way,* Universal, 1991.
(With Jeffrey Price and Peter Seaman) *Doc Hollywood,* Warner Brothers, 1991.

Also wrote screenplay for *Red Heat.*

OTHER SOURCES:

PERIODICALS

New York Times, March 3, 1991.*

R

RAGNI, Gerome 1942-1991

PERSONAL: Born September 11, 1942, in Pittsburgh, PA (one source says Canada); died of cancer, July 10, 1991, in New York, NY; son of Lawrence and Stephanie (Williams) Ragni; married wife, Stephanie, May 18, 1963; children: Eric. *Education:* Attended Georgetown University and Catholic University of America; studied acting with Philip Burton.

CAREER: Actor and writer.

AWARDS, HONORS: Barter Theatre Award, outstanding actor, 1963; *Variety* Poll of New York Drama Critics Award, best lyricist (with James Rado), 1968, and Antoinette Perry Award nomination, best musical play (with Rado and Galt MacDermot), 1969, both for *Hair;* Broadway cast album of *Hair* received Grammy Award, musical cast show—best album, 1968, Gold Record, original cast album, Recording Industry Association of America, 1969, and was named best-selling original cast album, National Association of Recording Merchandisers, 1969, 1970, and 1971; Grammy Award, record of the year, and Gold Record, both 1969, for "Aquarius/Let the Sun Shine In."

CREDITS:

STAGE APPEARANCES

War, Village South Theatre, New York City, 1963.
Hamlet, Lunt-Fontanne Theatre, New York City, 1964.
Hang Down Your Head and Die, Mayfair Theatre, New York City, 1964.
Tom, *The Knack,* New Theatre of Brooklyn, New York City, 1964.
Viet Rock, Martinique Theatre, New York City, 1966.
Berger, *Hair* (also see below), Anspacher Theatre, New York City, 1967, then Biltmore Theatre, New York City, and national touring company, U.S. cities, both 1968.

Made stage debut as Father Corr, *Shadow and Substance,* Washington, DC, 1954; also appeared at Village Gate nightclub, New York City, 1974.

FILM APPEARANCES

Hamlet, Warner Brothers, 1964.
Lions Love, Raab, 1969.

RECORDINGS:

ALBUMS

Hair (also see below), RCA, 1968.
Dude, the Highway Life (also see below), Columbia, 1972.

WRITINGS:

BOOK AND LYRICS FOR STAGE MUSICALS

(With James Rado) *Hair: A Tribal Love-Rock Musical* (two-act; music by Galt MacDermot; includes songs "Aquarius," "Hair," "Easy to Be Hard," "Where Do I Go?," "Good Morning Starshine," "Flesh Failures [Let the Sun Shine In]"), first produced at New York Shakespeare Festival Theatre, New York City, 1967, revised version first produced at Biltmore Theatre, New York City, 1968, published by Pocket Books, 1969.
Dude, the Highway Life (music by MacDermot), produced at Broadway Theatre, New York City, 1972.
(With Rado) *Jack Sound and His Dog Star Blowing His Final Trumpet on the Day of Doom* (music by Steve Margoshes), produced at Ensemble Studio Theatre, New York City, 1977.

Also collaborated with Rado and MacDermot on musical *Sun.*

ADAPTATIONS: Hair was adapted for film by Michael Weller and released by United Artists, 1979.

OBITUARIES AND OTHER SOURCES:

BOOKS

Contemporary Authors, Volume 105, Gale, 1982, pp. 396-99.

PERIODICALS

Los Angeles Times, July 15, 1991, p. A22.
New York Times, July 13, 1991, p. 9.*

* * *

RAIMI, Sam 1959-

PERSONAL: Full name, Samuel M. Raimi; born October 23, 1959, in Royal Oak, MI; son of Leonard Ronald (a merchant) and Celia Barbara (a merchant; maiden name, Abrams) Raimi. *Education:* Attended Michigan State University, 1977-79. *Politics:* Independent. *Religion:* Jewish.

ADDRESSES: Office—Renaissance Motion Pictures, 195 West Nine Mile Rd., Ferndale, MI 48220. *Agent*—InterTalent, 9200 Sunset Blvd., Penthouse 25, Los Angeles, CA 90069.

CAREER: Director, screenwriter, and actor. Vice president and cofounder of Renaissance Motion Pictures, Ferndale, MI, 1979—.

MEMBER: Michigan State University Society for Creative Filmmaking (founder, served as president, 1978-79).

AWARDS, HONORS: Best horror film, Knokke'heist Film Festival (Belgium), 1982, best horror film and best special effects, Sitges Film Festival (Spain), 1982, first prize of critics and first prize of public, Paris Festival of Science Fiction, Fantasy, and Horror, 1983, and best horror film of the year, *Fangoria* Magazine, 1983, all for *The Evil Dead;* best director award, 1986, for *Crimewave.*

CREDITS:

FILM WORK

Director, *The Evil Dead* (also see below), New Line Cinema, 1983.
Director, *Crimewave* (also known as *The XYZ Murders* and *Broken Hearts and Noses;* also see below), Embassy, 1985.
Director and executive producer, *Evil Dead Two: Dead by Dawn* (also see below), Rosebud Releasing, 1987.
Director, *Darkman* (also see below), Universal, 1990.

Also served as executive producer of *Easy Wheels,* 1989.

FILM APPEARANCES

Drive-in Security, *Spies Like Us,* Warner Brothers, 1985.
Cult leader, *Thou Shalt Not Kill. . . Except,* Filmworld, 1987.
Parade reporter, *Maniac Cop,* Shapiro Glickenhaus, 1988.
Snickering gunman, *Miller's Crossing,* Twentieth Century-Fox, 1990.

Also appeared as Randy, *Intruder,* 1989.

WRITINGS:

SCREENPLAYS

The Evil Dead, New Line Cinema, 1983.
(With Joel and Ethan Coen) *Crimewave,* Embassy, 1985.
(With Scott Spiegel) *Evil Dead Two: Dead by Dawn,* Rosebud Releasing, 1987.
(With Chuck Pfarrer, Ivan Raimi, Daniel Goldin, and Joshua Goldin) *Darkman* (based on a story by Sam Raimi), Universal, 1990.

Also the author or coauthor of unpublished and unproduced screenplays, including *The Hudsucker Proxy* and *We Saps Three,* both 1984, *Women on Wheels,* 1985, and *Witches,* 1986.

ADAPTATIONS: Characters from *Darkman* have been adapted for comic books.

OTHER SOURCES:

BOOKS

Contemporary Authors, Volume 123, Gale, 1988, p. 319.

PERIODICALS

Premiere, August, 1990, p. 46.*

* * *

RAMIS, Harold 1944-

PERSONAL: Full name, Harold Allen Ramis; born November 21, 1944, in Chicago, IL; son of Nathan and Ruth (Cokee) Ramis; married Anne Jean Plotkin, July 2, 1967 (marriage ended); married Erica Mann, May 7, 1989; children: Violet Isadora, Julian Arthur. *Education:* Washington University, B.A., 1966.

ADDRESSES: Office—Ocean Pictures, c/o Sony Studios, 10202 West Washington Blvd., Culver City, CA 90232. *Agent*—Jack Rapke, Creative Artists Agency, 9830 Wilshire Blvd., Beverly Hills, CA 90212.

CAREER: Writer, actor, director, and producer. *Playboy,* associate editor, 1968-70.

MEMBER: American Federation of Television and Radio Artists, Writers Guild of America, Directors Guild of America, Screen Actors Guild, Academy of Motion Picture Arts and Sciences.

AWARDS, HONORS: Academy of Canadian Television and Radio Artists (ACTRA) Award, best writer—variety (with others), 1978; distinguished alumni award, Washington University, 1988.

CREDITS:

FILM APPEARANCES

Russell Ziskey, *Stripes* (also see below), Columbia, 1981.
Voice of Zeke, *Heavy Metal,* Columbia, 1981.
Dr. Egon Spengler, *Ghostbusters* (also see below), Columbia, 1984.
Steven Buchner, *Baby Boom,* Metro-Goldwyn-Mayer, 1987.
Alan Appleby as an adult, *Stealing Home,* Warner Brothers, 1988.
Dr. Egon Spengler, *Ghostbusters II* (also see below), Columbia, 1989.

FILM WORK

Director, *Caddyshack* (also see below), Orion, 1980.
Director, *National Lampoon's Vacation,* Warner Brothers, 1983.
Executive producer, *Back to School* (also see below), Orion, 1986.
Director, *Club Paradise* (also see below), Warner Brothers, 1986.
Executive producer, *Armed and Dangerous* (also see below), Columbia, 1986.

STAGE APPEARANCES

The National Lampoon Show (also see below), New Palladium, New York City, 1975.

Appeared in various revues at Second City Theatre, Chicago, IL, 1969-73.

TELEVISION APPEARANCES; SERIES

Second City Television (also see below), syndicated, 1976-78.

TELEVISION APPEARANCES; SPECIALS

The Rodney Dangerfield Show: I Can't Take It No More (also see below), ABC, 1983.
Richard Lewis I'm in Pain Concert, Showtime, 1985.
Second City Twenty-fifth Anniversary Special, HBO, 1985.
Comic Relief, HBO, 1986.
Will Rogers: Look Back in Laughter (also see below), HBO, 1987.
Time Warner Presents the Earth Day Special, ABC, 1990.

TELEVISION WORK; SPECIALS

Producer, *Rodney Dangerfield Special: It's Not Easy Bein' Me* (also see below), ABC, 1980.
Executive producer, *Will Rogers: Look Back in Laughter,* HBO, 1987.

WRITINGS:

SCREENPLAYS

(With Douglas Kenney and Chris Miller) *National Lampoon's Animal House,* Universal, 1978.
(With Dan Goldberg, Len Blum, and Janice Allen) *Meatballs,* Paramount, 1979.
(With Kenney and Brian Doyle-Murray) *Caddyshack,* Orion, 1980.
(With Goldberg and Blum) *Stripes,* Columbia, 1981.
(With Dan Aykroyd) *Ghostbusters,* Columbia, 1984.
(With Peter Torokvei, Steven Kampmann, and Will Porter) *Back to School* (based on a story by Rodney Dangerfield, Greg Fields, and Dennis Snee), Orion, 1986.
(With Doyle-Murray) *Club Paradise* (based on a story by Miller, Ed Roboto, Tom Leopold, and David Standish), Warner Brothers, 1986.
(With Torokvei) *Armed and Dangerous* (based on a story by Ramis, Brian Grazer, and James Keach), Columbia, 1986.
(With Torokvei) *Caddyshack II,* Warner Brothers, 1988.
(With Aykroyd) *Ghostbusters II,* Columbia, 1989.

FOR TELEVISION; WITH OTHERS

Second City Television (series), syndicated, 1976-78.
Delta House (pilot), ABC, 1979.
The Rodney Dangerfield Special: It's Not Easy Bein' Me, ABC, 1980.
The Rodney Dangerfield Show: I Can't Take It No More (special), ABC, 1983.

FOR STAGE

(With John Belushi, Brian Doyle-Murray, Bill Murray, and Gilda Radner) *The National Lampoon Show,* produced at New Palladium, New York City, 1975.

Also coauthor of revues for Second City Theatre, Chicago, IL, 1970-73.

OTHER

Author with Rodney Dangerfield of story "Rover Dangerfield" (also see below); writer for *National Lampoon Radio Show,* 1974-75; contributor to periodicals, including *Premiere.*

ADAPTATIONS: Characters created by Ramis and Aykroyd in *Ghostbusters* and *Ghostbusters II* were adapted for animated television series *The Real Ghostbusters,* ABC, 1986-88, and *Slimer! and the Real Ghostbusters,* ABC, 1988—; "Rover Dangerfield" was adapted for film and released by Warner Brothers, 1991.

OTHER SOURCES:

BOOKS

Contemporary Authors, Volume 128, Gale, 1990, pp. 332-35.

* * *

RAMSEY, Logan 1921-

PERSONAL: Full name, Logan Carlisle Ramsey, Jr.; born March 21, 1921, in Long Beach, CA; son of Logan Carlisle (a navy officer) and Harriet Lillian (Kilmartin) Ramsey; married Anne Mobley (an actress), June 26, 1954. *Education:* St. Joseph's College, B.S., 1943; studied acting with Jasper Deeter at Hedgerow Theatre Repertory Company, 1940-44. *Avocational Interests:* Painting.

ADDRESSES: Office—12923 Killion St., Van Nuys, CA 91401.

CAREER: Actor and director. Previously employed as an advertising copywriter. *Military service:* U.S. Navy, 1942, served in European and Pacific theaters of operations; became lieutenant.

MEMBER: Actors' Equity Association, American Federation of Television and Radio Artists, Screen Actors Guild, Actors Studio.

AWARDS, HONORS: Clarence Derwent Award, 1951, for *The High Ground.*

CREDITS:

FILM APPEARANCES

Television director, *A Face in the Crowd,* Warner Brothers, 1957.
George Hale, *The Hoodlum Priest,* United Artists (UA), 1961.
Something Wild, UA, 1961.
Doc, *Banning,* Universal, 1967.
Officer Faye Lapid, *Head,* Columbia, 1968.
Mr. Simmons, *Childish Things,* Filmworld, 1969.
Detective Jelinek, *Pendulum,* Columbia, 1969.
Walter Clapp, *The Reivers,* National General, 1969.
La Follette, *The Traveling Executioner,* Metro-Goldwyn-Mayer, 1970.
Babe Duggers, *Jump,* Cannon, 1971.
Scott, *The Sporting Club,* Avco Embassy, 1971.
Detective West, *What's the Matter with Helen?,* UA, 1971.
Glass Houses, Columbia, 1972.
Uncle Albert, *Outside In* (also known as *Red, White, and Busted*), Robbins International, 1972.
Doctor, *Some Call It Loving,* CineGlobe, 1973.
John Witter, *Walking Tall,* Cinerama, 1973.
Dentist, *Busting,* UA, 1974.
John Witter, *Walking Tall, Part II,* American International, 1975.
Deputy coroner, *Cornbread, Earl and Me,* American International, 1975.
Commissioner, *Farewell, My Lovely,* Avco Embassy, 1975.
Coley, *Treasure of Matecumbe,* Buena Vista, 1976.
John Witter, *Final Chapter—Walking Tall,* American International, 1977.
Edmund Oberlin, *Mean Dog Blues,* American International, 1978.
Luther Quince, *Any Which Way You Can,* Warner Brothers, 1980.
Mayor Neville, *Joysticks* (also known as *Video Madness*), Jensen Farley, 1983.
George, *Say Yes,* Cinetel, 1986.
Jim Bob Collins, *Pass the Ammo,* New Century-Vista, 1988.
Man in shelter, *Scrooged,* Paramount, 1988.
Xavier Rhodes, gravedigger, *Dr. Hackenstein,* Vista Street, 1988.
Top Drone, *Meet the Hollowheads,* Moviestore, 1989.
General Brehon Somervell, *Fat Man and Little Boy,* Paramount, 1989.

Also appeared in *Fury on Wheels,* 1971.

TELEVISION APPEARANCES; MOVIES

Holmes, *The Devil and Miss Sarah,* ABC, 1971.
Walter Beal, *Beg, Borrow . . . or Steal,* ABC, 1973.
Raymond Bleisch, *The Law,* NBC, 1974.
Thurston Carson, *Attack on Terror: The FBI Versus the Ku Klux Klan,* CBS, 1975.
Riley, *The Last Day,* NBC, 1975.
Dr. Emil Schaeffer, *Testimony of Two Men,* syndicated, 1977.
J. Edgar Hoover, *Blind Ambition,* CBS, 1979.
Captain Sweeney, *Damien: The Leper Priest,* NBC, 1980.
Leonard Gray, *The Ladies,* NBC, 1987.

TELEVISION APPEARANCES; SERIES

Warden Wilbur Poindexter, *On the Rocks,* ABC, 1975-76.

TELEVISION APPEARANCES; PILOTS

Toby Loomis, *The Rookies,* ABC, 1972.
Wilson, *Letters from Three Lovers,* ABC, 1973.
Dale, *Conspiracy of Terror,* NBC, 1975.
J. T. Dashwood, *Little Women,* NBC, 1978.
Flannagan, *Lassie: The New Beginning,* ABC, 1978.
Museum curator, *The Monkey Mission,* NBC, 1981.

OTHER TELEVISION APPEARANCES

Christy, "The Devil's Disciple," *Hallmark Hall of Fame* (special), NBC, 1955.

Andy, "The Joke and the Valley," *Hallmark Hall of Fame* (special), NBC, 1961.

D. L. Lewis, *Roots: The Next Generations* (miniseries), ABC, 1979.

Congressman Ike LaCouture, *The Winds of War* (miniseries), 1983.

Len Kunkle, *The Best Times* (special), NBC, 1985.

Appeared on episodes of *Edge of Night, Route 66,* and *The Defenders,* all CBS, and *Naked City,* ABC.

STAGE APPEARANCES

(Broadway debut) Christy, *The Devil's Disciple,* City Center Theatre, then Royale Theatre, both New York City, 1950.

Willy Pentridge, *The High Ground,* 48th Street Theatre, New York City, 1951.

Lionel, *In the Summer House,* Playhouse Theatre, New York City, 1953.

Second God, *The Good Woman of Setzuan,* Phoenix Theatre, New York City, 1956.

George Scudder, *Sweet Bird of Youth,* Martin Beck Theatre, New York City, 1959.

Argan, *'Toinette,* Theatre Marquee, New York City, 1961.

Schnozz, *Marathon 33,* American National Theatre and Academy, New York City, 1963.

Tavern keeper, *My Kinsman, Major Molineux,* American Place Theatre, New York City, 1964.

The Last Days of Lincoln, Theatre de Lys, New York City, 1965.

Willy Kane, *The Great Indoors,* Eugene O'Neill Theatre, New York City, 1966.

A Meeting by the River, Cleveland Playhouse, Cleveland, OH, 1971-72.

Wild Air, Los Angeles Actors Theatre, Los Angeles, CA, 1979-80.

Made stage debut as Bardolph in *Henry IV, Part 1* with the Hedgerow Theatre Repertory Company; also appeared as Christy, *The Devil's Disciple,* Valere, *The Physician in Spite of Himself,* Eben, *Family Portrait,* witch doctor, *The Emperor Jones,* Malcolm, *Macbeth,* and in *Arms and the Man,* all with the Hedgerow Theatre Company, 1940-43; appeared in productions for the South Coast Repertory Theatre, Costa Mesa, CA, 1979-80; also appeared as Wolf, *Liliom,* the tycoon, *Midnight at Eight,* and the Egyptian, *Daughters of Atreus.*

STAGE WORK

Director, *The Seagulls of 1933,* Sherman Oaks Playhouse, Los Angeles, CA, 1975.*

RAPF, Matthew 1920-1991

OBITUARY NOTICE—See index for *CTFT* sketch: Born October 22, 1920, in New York, NY; died December 11, 1991, in Malibu, CA. Screenwriter and producer. Beginning his career as a screenwriter with Metro-Goldwyn-Mayer (MGM), Columbia, and Eagle-Lion after World War II, Rapf joined MGM as an associate producer in the late 1940s. There he worked on such films as *Half a Hero, Big Leaguer,* and *Desperate Search.* He was later employed as a producer and executive producer of television programs for Universal and Columbia Pictures TV. His best known television series included *Kojak, Slattery's People, Ben Casey,* and *The Loretta Young Show.*

OBITUARIES AND OTHER SOURCES:

BOOKS

International Motion Picture Almanac, Quigley, 1991, p. 262.

PERIODICALS

Variety, December 16, 1991, p. 74.

* * *

RASULALA, Thalmus 1939-1991 (Jack Crowder)

OBITUARY NOTICE—See index for *CTFT* sketch: Born Jack Crowder, November 15, 1939, in Miami, FL; died of a heart attack due to complications from leukemia, October 9, 1991, in Albuquerque, NM. Actor. In a career that spanned three decades, Rasulala appeared on stage, in films, and on numerous television shows. His films credits include roles in *Blacula, The Last Hard Men, Fun with Dick and Jane,* and, in 1991, *New Jack City.* Rasulala appeared as Omoro in the acclaimed 1977 television miniseries *Roots,* and in the series *What's Happening* and *One Life to Live.* He appeared in dozens of television episodes for such programs as *All in the Family* and *Scarecrow and Mrs. King,* and in television movies, including *The Autobiography of Miss Jane Pittman* and *The Preppie Murder.* He has also performed under the name Jack Crowder.

OBITUARIES AND OTHER SOURCES:

PERIODICALS

Variety, October 14, 1991, pp. 257-58.

* * *

REASONER, Harry 1923-1991

OBITUARY NOTICE—See index for *CTFT* sketch: Born April 17, 1923, in Dakota City, IA; died of cardiopulmonary arrest, August 6 (one source says 7), 1991, in Norwalk, CT. Broadcast journalist and author. Reasoner is remembered for his warm, personal style and credibility in the field of broadcast news as well as for his quality writing. During thirty-five years in network television, he spent twenty-seven with the Columbia Broadcasting System (CBS). Reasoner's early career consisted of stints as a newspaper writer, publicity director, and radio and television reporter. After he joined CBS in 1956, his duties included field reporting, White House correspondence, news writing, and anchoring. In 1958 Reasoner covered school desegregation efforts in Little Rock, Arkansas, a piece of reporting that he recalled in his memoir, *Before the Colors Fade,* as his best. Ten years later he and Mike Wallace became the original correspondents for CBS's long-running news magazine *60 Minutes.* In 1970 Reasoner left the network to become an evening news anchor for ABC; he returned to CBS and *60 Minutes* in 1979, where he continued to work full time until May of 1991. He won several awards for television news, including four Emmy Awards and a George Foster Peabody Award. He was the author of a novel, *Tell Me About Women,* and a compilation of essays titled *The Reasoner Report.*

OBITUARIES AND OTHER SOURCES:

BOOKS

Who's Who in the East, 24th edition, Marquis, 1991.

PERIODICALS

Chicago Tribune, August 7, 1991, section 3, p. 11.
Hollywood Reporter, August 8, 1991, p. 11; August 27, 1991, p. 3.
Los Angeles Times, August 7, 1991, pp. A1 and A16.
New York Times, August 7, 1991, p. D21.
Times (London), August 13, 1991, p. 14.
Variety, August 12, 1991, p. 55.
Washington Post, August 7, 1991, p. D7.

* * *

REMICK, Lee 1935-1991

OBITUARY NOTICE—See index for *CTFT* sketch: Full name, Lee Ann Remick; born December 14, 1935, in Boston (some sources say Quincy), MA; died of cancer, July 2, 1991, in Los Angeles, CA. Actress. Remick originally planned a career in ballet, but at age sixteen she joined a summer stock company in Hyannis, Massachusetts, beginning an acting career that would last nearly forty years. She debuted on Broadway in 1953, portraying a teenager in *Be Your Age,* and by 1966 had earned an Antoinette Perry Award nomination for her role in *Wait Until Dark.* Remick's wholesome attractiveness and emotional depth helped her gain numerous film roles in the late 1950s and early 1960s, and critics praised her performances in such movies as *Anatomy of a Murder, Wild River,* and *Days of Wine and Roses.* As she grew older and was offered fewer leading roles in films, Remick turned to television as the medium to display her talents. She appeared in a number of mini-series, including *Jennie, Ike, Haywire,* and *The Women's Room,* as well as in numerous television movies, such as *Around the World in Eighty Days* and *Bridge to Silence.* She continued to perform despite suffering from kidney and lung cancer later in her life. Among her last appearances was in a 1990 production of *Love Letters* at Beverly Hills's Canon Theater.

OBITUARIES AND OTHER SOURCES:

BOOKS

Who's Who of American Women, 17th edition, Marquis, 1991, p. 820.

PERIODICALS

Variety, July 8, 1991, pp. 62-63.

* * *

REVILL, Clive 1930-

PERSONAL: Born April 18, 1930, in Wellington, New Zealand; son of Malet Barford and Eleanor May (Neel) Revill; married Valerie Nelson. *Education:* Attended Rongotai College; Victoria University, Wellington, New Zealand; and Old Vic School, 1950-52. *Avocational interests:* Golf, driving, and flying.

CAREER: Actor.

CREDITS:

STAGE APPEARANCES

(Broadway debut) Sam Weller, *Mr. Pickwick,* Plymouth Theatre, New York City, 1952.
(London debut) Pearson, *Listen to the Wind,* Arts Theatre, 1955.
Trinculo, *The Tempest,* Drury Lane Theatre, London, 1957.
Ratty, *Toad of Toad Hall,* Drury Lane Theatre, 1957.
Bob-Le-Hotu, *Irma La Douce,* Lyric Theatre, London, 1958-1960, then Plymouth Theatre, 1960-61.
Ko-Ko, *The Mikado,* Sadler's Wells Theatre, London, 1962.
Fagin, *Oliver!,* Imperial Theatre, New York City, 1963.
Jean-Paul Marat, *The Marat/Sade,* Royal Shakespeare Company (RSC), Aldwych Theatre, London, 1964.
Barabas, *The Jew of Malta,* RSC, Aldwych Theatre, 1964.

Sheridan Whiteside, *Sherry,* Alvin Theatre, New York City, 1967.
The General, *The Unknown Soldier and His Wife,* Chichester Festival, c. 1968-c. 1969.
Caliban, *The Tempest,* Chichester Festival, c. 1968-c. 1969.
Mr. Antrobus, *The Skin of Our Teeth,* Chichester Festival, c. 1968-c. 1969.
A Who's Who of Flapland, Royal Court Theatre, London, and Theatre Upstairs, London, 1969.
Max Beerbohm, *The Incomparable Max,* Royale Theatre, New York City, 1971.
Moriarty, *Sherlock Holmes,* Broadhurst Theatre, New York City, 1975.
Clare Quilty, *Lolita,* Brooks Atkinson Theatre, New York City, 1981.

Appeared in productions with the Ipswich Repertory Theatre Company, 1953-55; and the Shakespeare Memorial Theatre Company, Stratford-on-Avon, England, 1956-c. 1958, including *Cymbeline, Hamlet, Julius Caesar, King John, Love's Labour's Lost, Measure for Measure, The Merchant of Venice,* and *The Tempest.*

MAJOR TOURS

Major-General Stanley, *Pirates of Penzance,* U.S. cities, 1981-c. 1982.
William Cartwright/Your Chairman, *Drood!* (also known as *The Mystery of Edwin Drood*), U.S. cities, 1988.

FILM APPEARANCES

Reach for the Sky, J. Arthur Rank, 1957.
Fourth Earl, *The Headless Ghost,* American International, 1959.
Andrews, *Bunny Lake Is Missing,* Columbia, 1965.
Dr. Menken, *A Fine Madness,* Warner Bros., 1966.
Inspector "Manny" McGinnis, *Kaleidoscope,* Warner Bros., 1966.
McWhirter/Sheik Abu Tahir, *Modesty Blaise,* Twentieth Century-Fox, 1966.
Frank Wheatly, *The Double Man,* Warner Bros., 1967.
Serapkin, *Fathom,* Twentieth Century-Fox, 1967.
Joseph, *The High Commissioner* (also known as *Nobody Runs Forever*), Cinerama, 1968.
Charles, *Italian Secret Service,* Cineriz, 1968.
Vucovich, *The Shoes of the Fisherman,* Metro-Goldwyn-Mayer, 1968.
Cesare Sado, *The Assassination Bureau,* Paramount, 1969.
Rogozhin, *The Private Life of Sherlock Holmes,* United Artists, 1970.
George, *The Buttercup Chain,* Columbia, 1971.
Alexander Lynch-Gibbon, *A Severed Head,* Columbia, 1971.
Carlo Carlucci, *Avanti!,* United Artists, 1972.
The Drunk, *Escape to the Sun,* Cinevision, 1972.
Dr. Chris Barrett, *The Legend of Hell House,* Twentieth Century-Fox, 1973.
Alf Chestermann, *The Black Windmill,* Universal, 1974.
The Businessman, *The Little Prince,* Paramount, 1974.
Ballad Singer, *Galileo,* American Film Theatre, 1975.
Quon, *One of Our Dinosaurs Is Missing,* Buena Vista, 1975.
Billy Baker, *Matilda,* American International, 1978.
Voice of Emperor, *The Empire Strikes Back,* Twentieth Century-Fox, 1980.
Garcia, *Zorro, the Gay Blade,* Twentieth Century-Fox, 1981.
Voice of Kickback, *The Transformers* (animated), DEG, 1986.
Prime Minister, *The Emperor's New Clothes,* Cannon, 1987.
King Mezzer, *Rumpelstiltskin,* Cannon, 1987.
C.H.U.D. II: Bud the C.H.U.D., Vestron, 1989.
Money Matthew, *Mack the Knife,* 21st Century, 1990.
Let Him Have It, Fine Line Features, 1991.

Also appeared as Hammond in *Boulevard du Rhum,* 1971; Bay of Algiers in *Ghost in the Noonday Sun,* 1973; and John Fennel in *Licking Hitler,* 1977. Appeared in *Once Upon a Tractor.*

TELEVISION APPEARANCES; MINI-SERIES

Finlay Perkin, *Centennial,* NBC, 1978-79.
Lord Loudoun, *George Washington,* CBS, 1984.

TELEVISION APPEARANCES; MOVIES

Dundas Slater, *The Great Houdini,* ABC, 1976.
Victor De Salle, *She's Dressed to Kill,* NBC, 1979.
Mr. Dussel, *The Diary of Anne Frank,* NBC, 1980.
Charlie Chaplin, *Moviola: The Scarlet O'Hara War,* NBC, 1980.
Tea Bags, *Joe Dancer: The Monkey Mission,* NBC, 1981.
Raul, *Samson and Delilah,* ABC, 1984.
Vincent Faunce, *A Masterpiece of a Murder,* NBC, 1986.
Jake Spanner, Private Eye, USA, 1989.

TELEVISION APPEARANCES; SPECIALS

Coachman, *Pinocchio,* CBS, 1976.
John Wellington Wells, *The Sorcerer* (part of "Compleat Gilbert and Sullivan" series), PBS, 1985.
Prime Minister, *The Emperor's New Clothes,* Showtime, 1985.
Sylvia Fine Kaye's Musical Comedy Tonight III (The Spark and the Glue), PBS, 1985.
Voice, *The Butter Battle Book* (animated), TNT, 1989.

TELEVISION APPEARANCES; SERIES

Vector, Dirk's Evil Wizard, *Wizards and Warriors,* CBS, 1983.
Voice, *Dragon's Lair* (animated), ABC, 1984-85.

Voice, *Turbo-Teen* (animated), 1984-85.
Voice of Galeo, *Snorks* (animated), 1984-86.
Voice, *Pound Puppies* (animated), ABC, 1986-88.
Frost, *Mama's Boy,* NBC, 1987-88.

TELEVISION APPEARANCES; PILOTS

E. P. Woodhouse, Allison's Assistant, *Winner Take All,* CBS, 1977.
Erik Clawson, *Death Ray 2000,* NBC, 1981.
Dr. Carey, *13 Thirteenth Avenue,* CBS, 1983.
Prime Minister Weyback, *Royal Match,* CBS, 1985.

OTHER TELEVISION APPEARANCES

Also appeared in *Barn Pow, Ben Franklin in Paris, A Bit of Vision, Candida, Chicken Soup with Barley, Columbo, Faerie Tale Theatre, Feather and Father, Hopcroft in Europe, A Man Called Sloane, Marya, Mill Hill, Murder She Wrote, The New Avengers, Nobody's Perfect, The Piano Player, Platonov, The Sorcerer, A Sprig of Broome, Volpone,* and *Zapp.**

* * *

REYNOLDS, Bill
See REYNOLDS, William

* * *

REYNOLDS, William 1910-
(Bill Reynolds, William H. Reynolds)

PERSONAL: Full name William Henry Reynolds; born June 14, 1910, in Elmira, NY. *Education:* Graduated from Princeton University.

ADDRESSES: Agent—Gersh Agency, 250 North Canon Dr., Beverly Hills, CA 90210.

CAREER: Editor and producer. Fox Film Corporation, swing gang laborer, beginning 1934; Paramount, assistant editor, 1936-37, editor, 1937-42; Twentieth Century-Fox, editor, 1947-62; free-lance editor, 1962—. *Military service:* Served 1942-46.

MEMBER: Motion Picture Academy of Arts and Sciences, American Cinema Editors.

AWARDS, HONORS: Academy Award nomination, best film editing, 1961, for *Fanny;* Academy Award, best film editing, 1965, for *The Sound of Music;* Academy Award nominations, best film editing, 1966, for *The Sand Pebbles,* 1969, for *Hello, Dolly!,* and 1972, for *The Godfather;* Academy Award, best film editing, 1973, for *The Sting;* Academy Award nomination, best film editing, 1977, for *The Turning Point;* named one of three top film editors in a *Film Comment* poll of film editors.

CREDITS:

FILM ASSISTANT EDITOR

The Farmer Takes a Wife, Twentieth Century-Fox, 1935.
The Gay Deception, Twentieth Century-Fox, 1935.
Big Brown Eyes, Paramount, 1936.
Her Master's Voice, Paramount, 1936.
Palm Springs (also known as *Palm Springs Affair*), Paramount, 1936.
Spendthrift, Paramount, 1936.
John Meade's Woman, Paramount, 1937.
Honeymoon in Bali, (also known as *My Love for Yours*), Paramount, 1939.
A Night at Earl Carroll's, Paramount, 1940.
Typhoon, Paramount, 1940.

FILM EDITOR, EXCEPT WHERE INDICATED

(With Otho Lovering) *52nd Street,* United Artists (UA), 1937.
(With Lovering) *Algiers,* UA, 1938.
So Ends Our Night, UA, 1941.
Moontide, Twentieth Century-Fox, 1942.
Carnival in Costa Rica, Twentieth Century-Fox, 1947.
Give My Regards to Broadway, Twentieth Century-Fox, 1948.
The Street with No Name, Twentieth Century-Fox, 1948.
You Were Meant for Me, Twentieth Century-Fox, 1948.
Come to the Stable, Twentieth Century-Fox, 1949.
Mother Is a Freshman (also known as *Mother Knows Best*), Twentieth Century-Fox, 1949.
Halls of Montezuma, Twentieth Century-Fox, 1951.
The Day the Earth Stood Still, Twentieth Century-Fox, 1951.
The Frogmen, Twentieth Century-Fox, 1951.
Take Care of My Little Girl, Twentieth Century-Fox, 1951.
The Outcasts of Poker Flat, Twentieth Century-Fox, 1952.
Red Skies of Montana (also known as *Smoke Jumpers*), Twentieth Century-Fox, 1952.
Beneath the 12-Mile Reef, Twentieth Century-Fox, 1953.
(Under name William H. Reynolds) *Dangerous Crossing,* Twentieth Century-Fox, 1953.
The Kid from Left Field, Twentieth Century-Fox, 1953.
Desiree, Twentieth Century-Fox, 1954.
Three Coins in the Fountain, Twentieth Century-Fox, 1954.
Daddy Long Legs, Twentieth Century-Fox, 1955.
Good Morning, Miss Dove, Twentieth Century-Fox, 1955.
Love Is a Many-Splendored Thing, Twentieth Century-Fox, 1955.
Bus Stop (also known as *The Wrong Kind of Girl*), Twentieth Century-Fox, 1956.
Carousel, Twentieth Century-Fox, 1956.
Producer with Richard Widmark, *Time Limit,* UA, 1957.

In Love and War, Twentieth Century-Fox, 1958.
Beloved Infidel, Twentieth Century-Fox, 1959.
Blue Denim (also known as *Blue Jeans*), Twentieth Century-Fox, 1959.
Compulsion, Twentieth Century-Fox, 1959.
Wild River, Twentieth Century-Fox, 1960.
Tender Is the Night, Twentieth Century-Fox, 1961.
(Under name William H. Reynolds) *Fanny,* Warner Brothers, 1961.
(With Gene Milford, Eda Warren, and Folmar Blangsted) *Taras Bulba,* UA, 1962.
Kings of the Sun, UA, 1963.
Ensign Pulver, Warner Brothers, 1964.
The Sound of Music, Twentieth Century-Fox, 1965.
Our Man Flint, Twentieth Century-Fox, 1966.
The Sand Pebbles, Twentieth Century-Fox, 1966.
Star! (also known as *Those Were the Happy Times*), Twentieth Century-Fox, 1968.
Hello, Dolly!, Twentieth Century-Fox, 1969.
The Great White Hope, Twentieth Century-Fox, 1970.
(Under name William H. Reynolds) *What's the Matter with Helen?,* UA, 1971.
(With Peter Zinner) *The Godfather,* Paramount, 1972.
Two People, Universal, 1973.
The Sting, Universal, 1973.
The Great Waldo Pepper, Universal, 1975.
(With Danford Greene) *The Master Gunfighter,* Billy Jack, 1975.
The Seven-Percent Solution, Universal, 1977.
The Turning Point, Twentieth Century-Fox, 1977.
(Under name Bill Reynolds) *Old Boyfriends,* Avco Embassy, 1979.
A Little Romance, Orion, 1979.
(With Lisa Fruchtman, Gerald Greenberg, and Tom Rolf; and post-production executive) *Heaven's Gate,* UA, 1980.
Nijinsky, Paramount, 1980.
(Under name William H. Reynolds) *Making Love,* Twentieth Century-Fox, 1982.
Author! Author!, Twentieth Century-Fox, 1982.
Yellowbeard, Orion, 1983.
(With Raja Gosnell) *The Lonely Guy,* Universal, 1984.
The Little Drummer Girl, Warner Brothers, 1984.
(With Herve De Luze) *Pirates,* Cannon, 1986.
Dancers, Cannon, 1987.
(With Richard A. Cirincione and Stephen A. Rotter) *Ishtar,* Columbia, 1987.
A New Life, Paramount, 1988.
Rooftops, New Visions, 1989.
Taking Care of Business (also known as *Filofax*), Hollywood/Buena Vista, 1990.
Newsies, Buena Vista, 1992.*

REYNOLDS, William H.
See REYNOLDS, William

* * *

RICHARDS, Martin 1932-

PERSONAL: Born Morton Richard Klein, March 11, 1932; son of Sidney (a stockbroker) and Shirley (Mandel) Klein; married Mary Lea Johnson (a producer), August 11, 1978. *Education:* Attended New York University.

ADDRESSES: Office—c/o Producer Circle Company, 1350 Avenue of the Americas, New York, NY 10019; and 9200 Sunset Blvd., Los Angeles, CA 90069.

CAREER: Producer. Casting director for major motion pictures, 1968-75; with wife, Mary Lea Johnson, formed Producer Circle Company in 1975 to produce works for theatre and film. As a child, appeared on Broadway in *Mexican Hayride* and *West Side Story.* Performed in various nightclubs, on television in *Arthur Godfrey's Talent Scouts* and *Chance of a Lifetime;* sang with the Paul Whiteman Orchestra; recorded for ASCOT and Capitol Records.

MEMBER: League of New York Theatres and Producers, Academy of Motion Picture Arts and Sciences.

AWARDS, HONORS: Antoinette Perry Award nomination (with Joseph Harris and Ira Bernstein), best Broadway musical, 1978, for *On the Twentieth Century;* Antoinette Perry Award (with others), best Broadway musical, producer, 1979, for *Sweeney Todd: The Demon Barber of Fleet Street;* Antoinette Perry Award nomination (with others), best play, 1982, for *Crimes of the Heart;* Antoinette Perry Award (with others), best musical, 1984, for *La Cage Aux Folles;* Antoinette Perry Award nomination (with others), best musical, 1985, for *Grind;* Antoinette Perry Award nomination (with others), best musical, 1989, for *Grand Hotel: The Musical;* Antoinette Perry Award (with others), best musical, 1991, for *The Will Rogers Follies.* Also recipient of various other awards including New York Drama Critics Award.

CREDITS:

STAGE PRODUCER

(With others) *Chicago,* Forty-Sixth Street Theatre, New York City, 1975-78.
(With others) *The Norman Conquests,* Morosco Theatre, New York City, 1975-76.
(With others) *Rockabye Hamlet,* Minskoff Theatre, New York City, 1976.
(With others) *On the Twentieth Century,* St. James Theatre, New York City, 1978, then Fisher Theatre, De-

troit, MI, 1979, later Orpheum Theatre, San Francisco, CA, 1979.
(With others) *Sweeney Todd: The Demon Barber of Fleet Street,* Uris Theatre, New York City, 1979-80.
(With others) *Goodbye Fidel,* New Ambassador Theatre, New York City, 1980.
(With others) *Crimes of the Heart,* Manhattan Theatre Club, New York City, 1980, then John Golden Theatre, New York City, 1981-82.
(With Mary Lea Johnson and Francine LeFrak) *March of the Falsettos,* Playwrights Horizons Theatre, New York City, 1981, then Westside Arts/Cheryl Crawford Theatre, New York City, 1981-82.
(With others) *A Doll's Life,* Mark Hellinger Theatre, New York City, 1982.
(With others) *La Cage Aux Folles,* Palace Theatre, New York City, 1983-87.
(With others) *Mayor,* Latin Quarter Theatre, New York City, 1985, then Top of the Gate Theatre, New York City, 1985-86.
(With others) *Grind,* Mark Hellinger Theatre, 1985.
(With the Schubert Organization) *Roza,* Royale Theatre, New York City, 1987.
(With others) *Grand Hotel: The Musical,* Martin Beck Theatre, New York City, 1989.
(With others) *The Will Rogers Follies,* Palace Theatre, 1991—.

Also producer of *Dylan,* New York City, 1972.

FILM PRODUCER

(With John Lauricella) *Some of My Best Friends Are . . .* (also known as *The Bar*), American International, 1971.
(With Stanley O'Toole) *The Boys from Brazil,* Twentieth Century-Fox, 1978.
The Shining, Warner Brothers, 1980.
(With Tom Fiorello) *Fort Apache, the Bronx,* Twentieth Century-Fox, 1981.*

* * *

RITTER, John 1948-

PERSONAL: Full name, Johnathan Southworth Ritter; born September 17, 1948, in Burbank, CA; son of Tex (a country and western singer) and Dorothy Fay (an actress; maiden name, Southworth) Ritter; married Nancy Karen Morgan (an actress), October 16, 1977; children: Jason, Tyler, Carly. *Education:* University of Southern California, B.A., theater arts, 1971; studied with Stella Adler and Nina Foch; spent four years at Harvey Lembeck Comedy Workshop; also studied at Mary Carver Studio.

ADDRESSES: Office—c/o Robert Myman, 11777 San Vicente Blvd., No. 880, Los Angeles, CA 90049. *Agent*—Nicole David, Triad Artists, 10100 Santa Monica Blvd., 16th Floor, Los Angeles, CA 90067.

CAREER: Actor. Partner, with Robert Myman, of Adam Productions, 1984—.

MEMBER: Actors Equity Association, Screen Actors Guild, American Federation of Television and Radio Artists, United Cerebral Palsy Association (member of board of directors).

AWARDS, HONORS: Honored with a star on the Hollywood Walk of Fame, the 1768th, next to his father's; Emmy Award nominations, best actor in a comedy series, 1977 and 1980, Emmy Award, best actor in a comedy series, 1984, and Golden Globe Award, best actor in a television comedy series, Hollywood Foreign Press Association, 1984, all for *Three's Company;* Los Angeles Area Emmy Award, best co-host, 1986, for *Superfest: A Celebration of Ability;* Emmy Award nomination, best actor in a comedy series, 1987, and People's Choice Award, best male performer in a new television program, Proctor & Gamble Productions, 1988, both for *Hooperman.*

CREDITS:

TELEVISION APPEARANCES; SERIES

Reverend Matthew Fordwicke, *The Waltons,* CBS, 1972-76.
Jack Tripper, *Three's Company,* ABC, 1977-84.
Jack Tripper, *Three's a Crowd* (also known as *Three's Company, Too*), ABC, 1984-85.
Harry Hooperman, *Hooperman,* ABC, 1987–89.

TELEVISION APPEARANCES; PILOTS

What's Up, America? (also known as *What's Up?*), NBC, 1971.
Minister, *Evil Roy Slade,* NBC, 1972.
Ben Sikes, *Bachelor at Law,* CBS, 1973.
Host, *Completely Off the Wall,* ABC, 1979.

TELEVISION APPEARANCES; MOVIES

Walter Wingate, *The Night That Panicked America,* ABC, 1975.
Paul Stallings, *Leave Yesterday Behind,* ABC, 1978.
Bubba Newman, *The Comeback Kid,* ABC, 1980.
Robert Christenberry, *In Love with an Older Woman,* CBS, 1982.
Tom McPherson, *Pray TV,* ABC, 1982.
Alan O'Black, *Sunset Limousine,* CBS, 1983.
Danny Loeb, *Love Thy Neighbor,* ABC, 1984.
Alex Schuster, *Letting Go,* ABC, 1985.
Judge Harold Benton, *A Smoky Mountain Christmas,* ABC, 1986.
Frank Coleman, *Unnatural Causes,* NBC, 1986.
Voice, *Flight of the Dragons,* ABC, 1986.

Phil Reed, *The Last Fling,* ABC, 1987.
David Royce, *Prison for Children,* CBS, 1987.
Tricks of the Trade, CBS, 1988.
Barney Rusher, *My Brother's Wife* (also known as *The Middle Ages*), ABC, 1989.
L. Frank Baum, *Dreamer of Oz: The L. Frank Baum Story,* NBC, 1990.

Also appeared as Dr. Paul Saunders, *The Summer My Father Grew Up,* 1991.

TELEVISION APPEARANCES; SPECIALS

General Electric's All-Star Anniversary, ABC, 1978.
The Goldie Hawn Special, CBS, 1978.
Marty, *Ringo,* NBC, 1978.
That Thing on ABC, ABC, 1978.
How to Survive the Seventies and Maybe Even Bump into Happiness, CBS, 1978.
The Celebrity Football Classic, NBC, 1979.
Co-host, *Echoes of the Sixties,* NBC, 1979.
Host, *John Ritter: Being of Sound Mind and Body,* ABC, 1980.
Host, *The Singing Cowboys Ride Again,* syndicated, 1982.
The Fantastic Miss Piggy Show, ABC, 1982.
Host, *Life's Most Embarrassing Moments,* ABC, 1983.
The Bob Hope Special: Bob Hope's Super Birthday Special, NBC, 1984.
Host, *The Secret World of the Very Young,* CBS, 1984.
Memories Then and Now, CBS, 1988.
Host, *ABC Presents a Royal Gala,* ABC, 1988.
Host, *United Cerebral Palsy's Starathon,* syndicated, 1988-91.
The 15th Annual People's Choice Awards, CBS, 1989.
The Valvoline National Driving Test, CBS, 1989.
Stand-Up Comics Take a Stand!, Family Channel, 1989 and 1990.
Host, *The American Red Cross Emergency Test,* ABC, 1990.
Host, *A Celebration of Country,* ABC, 1991.
A User's Guide to Planet Earth: The American Environment Test, ABC, 1991.

Also appeared in numerous other special programs, including as host, *Weekend with the Stars Telethon for Cerebral Palsy,* 1978-80; *All-Star Party for Lucille Ball,* 1984; *Donald Duck's 50th Birthday,* 1984; *The 21st Annual Academy of Country Music Awards,* 1986; *The 38th Annual Emmy Awards,* 1986; host, *Disney's Living Seas,* 1986; host, *Teenage America—Glory Years,* 1986; host, *Superfest: A Celebration of Ability,* 1986-88; presenter, *The 13th Annual People's Choice Awards,* 1987; *Welcome Home,* 1987; *Superstars and Their Moms,* 1987; *The Special Olympics Opening Ceremonies,* 1987; *It's Howdy Doody Time: A 40-Year Celebration,* 1987; and *Happy Birthday, Hollywood!,* 1987.

TELEVISION APPEARANCES; EPISODIC

(Television debut) *Dan August,* ABC, 1971.
"Two Doves and Mr. Heron," *Hawaii Five-O,* CBS, 1972.
Medical Center, CBS, 1973.
"Deal Me Out," *M*A*S*H,* CBS, 1973.
"Deliver Us Some Evil," *Kojak,* CBS, 1974.
"Sorry, Wrong Mother," *The Bob Newhart Show,* CBS, 1974.
"The Hostages," *Starsky and Hutch,* ABC, c. 1975.
"Landslide," *Movin' On,* NBC, 1975.
"Hardball," *Mannix,* CBS, 1975.
"Who's Happy Now?," *Theater in America,* PBS, 1975.
"Chain of Command," *Petrocelli,* NBC, 1975.
"The Price of Terror," *Barnaby Jones,* CBS, 1975.
"Murder by Proxy," *Streets of San Francisco,* ABC, 1975.
"Ted's Wedding," *The Mary Tyler Moore Show,* CBS, 1975.
The Rookies, ABC, 1975.
Doc, CBS, 1976.
"How to Land a Man," *Rhoda,* CBS, 1976.
Phyllis, CBS, 1976.
"Dealer's Choice—Blackmail," *Hawaii Five-O,* CBS, 1977.
Loves Me, Loves Me Not, CBS, 1977.
"Phyllis's Career Change," *Phyllis,* CBS, 1977.
"Oh, Dale," *The Love Boat,* ABC, 1977.
Jack Tripper, "The Party," *The Ropers,* ABC, 1979.
The Associates, ABC, 1980.
"Little Miseries," *Insight,* syndicated, 1981.
"The Emperor's Fortune," *The Love Boat,* ABC, 1983.
Pryor's Place, CBS, 1984.
"Lucy Makes a Hit with John Ritter," *Life with Lucy,* ABC, 1986.
Mr. Loud, "Mickey's 60th Birthday Special," *The Magical World of Disney,* NBC, 1989.
"Disney-MGM Studios Theme Park Grand Opening," *The Magical World of Disney,* NBC, 1989.
Ben Hanscom, "Stephen King's *It,*" *ABC Novel for Television,* ABC, 1990.
Patrick Serreau, *Anything But Love* (also see below), ABC, 1991-92.

TELEVISION EXECUTIVE PRODUCER

(With others) *Anything But Love* (series), ABC, 1989-92.
(With others) *Have Faith,* ABC, 1989.
(With others) *Poochinski* (pilot), NBC, 1990.

FILM APPEARANCES

Roger, *The Barefoot Executive,* Buena Vista, 1971.
Wendell, *Scandalous John,* Buena Vista, 1971.
Rider, *The Other,* Twentieth Century-Fox, 1972.
Hart, *The Stone Killer,* Columbia, 1973.
Franklin Frank, *Nickelodeon,* Columbia, 1976.

Paul, *Breakfast in Bed,* William Haugse Productions, 1978.
Chet Roosevelt, *Americathon,* United Artists (UA), 1979.
Steve Nichols, *Hero at Large,* Metro-Goldwyn-Mayer (MGM), 1980.
Devil, *Wholly Moses!,* Columbia, 1980.
Charles Rutledge, *They All Laughed,* Twentieth Century-Fox/UA, 1981.
Bob Wilson, *Real Men,* MGM/UA, 1987.
Zach Hutton, *Skin Deep,* Twentieth Century-Fox, 1989.
Ben Healy, *Problem Child,* Universal, 1990.
Ben Healy, *Problem Child 2,* Universal, 1991.
Garry Lejeune, *Noises Off,* Touchstone/Amblin Entertainment, 1992.
Roy Knable, *Stay Tuned,* Warner Bros., 1992.

STAGE APPEARANCES

Cafeteria Style Lunch and *Momsie and the Midnight Bride* (double bill), Center Theatre Group, New Theatre for Now, c. 1970.
A Meeting by the River, Center Theatre Group, New Theatre for Now, c. 1971.
Desire under the Elms, Berkshire Theatre Festival, Kennedy Center for the Performing Arts, Washington, DC, c. 1974.
Battle of Angels, Westport Country Playhouse, Westport, CT, then Fallmouth Theatre, Fallmouth, MA, later Cape Playhouse, Dennis, MA, 1981.
Tom Bryce, *The Unvarnished Truth,* Ahmanson Theater, Los Angeles, c. 1985.
A Place to Stay, Westport Country Playhouse, then Cape Playhouse, 1985.
Love Letters, Canon Theatre, Beverly Hills, CA, 1990.

Made stage debut at Edinburgh Festival, Edinburgh, Scotland, 1968; appeared in *The Glass Menagerie,* Totem Pole Playhouse, Maryland; *Butterflies Are Free,* Totem Pole Playhouse; *As You Like It,* First Los Angeles Free Shakespeare Festival; *The Tempest,* a Shakespeare Society production; *Nevada,* Mark Taper Forum Laboratory, Los Angeles; and *Feiffer's People.*

* * *

RIVERS, Joan 1933(?)-

PERSONAL: Born Joan Alexandra Molinsky, June 8, 1933 (some sources say 1935, 1937, or 1939) in Brooklyn, NY; daughter of Meyer C. (a doctor) and Beatrice (Grushman) Molinsky; married Jimmy Sanger, 1957 (marriage annulled, 1958); married Edgar Rosenberg (a writer and producer), July 15, 1965 (died August 14, 1987); children: Melissa. *Education:* Attended Connecticut College for Women; Barnard College, NY, B.A. (English and anthropology), 1954 (some sources say 1958). *Avocational interests:* Antiques.

ADDRESSES: Manager—Dorothy Melvin, DTM Management, 145 South Fairfax Ave., Suite 201 B, Los Angeles, CA 90036.

CAREER: Comedian and actress. Worked in the publicity department of Lord and Taylor, and as a fashion coordinator for Bond Clothing Stores before beginning entertainment career; member of From the Second City comedy tour group, 1961-62. Cystic Fibrosis Society, national chairman, 1982—; benefit performer for AIDS, 1984.

MEMBER: Phi Beta Kappa.

AWARDS, HONORS: Georgie Award, Best Comedienne of 1975, American Guild of Variety Artists; Las Vegas Comedienne of the Year Awards, 1976 and 1977; Cleo awards, best performance in a television commercial, 1976 and 1982; Jimmy Award for Best Comedian, 1981; Woman of the Year, Hadassah, 1983; Woman of the Year, Harvard Hasty Pudding Society, 1984. Received nightclub performer of the year award, New York Friars Club.

CREDITS:

TELEVISION APPEARANCES; SERIES

Host, *That Show Starring Joan Rivers,* NBC, 1968.
Regular guest host, *The Tonight Show,* NBC, 1971-86.
Host, *The Late Show* (also known as *The Late Show Starring Joan Rivers*), Fox, 1986-87.
The Hollywood Squares (also known as *The New Hollywood Squares*), syndicated, beginning 1987.
The Joan Rivers Show, syndicated, 1989—.

TELEVISION APPEARANCES; SPECIALS

Celebrity Challenge of the Sexes 4, CBS, 1979.
Circus of the Stars, CBS, 1980.
Lily—Sold Out, CBS, 1981.
Joan Rivers: Can We Talk?, six episodes, BBC, 1986.
WrestleMania 2, Showtime, 1986.
NBC's 60th Anniversary Celebration, NBC, 1986.
Kraft Salutes the George Burns 90th Birthday Special, CBS, 1986.
The Barbara Walters Special, ABC, 1986.
The 38th Annual Emmy Awards, NBC, 1986.
Caesar's 20th Birthday Celebration, Showtime, 1987.
The 39th Annual Emmy Awards, Fox, 1987.
Pee-wee's Playhouse Christmas Special, CBS, 1988.
NBC News Report on America: Stressed to Kill, NBC, 1988.
Macy's Thanksgiving Day Parade, NBC, 1989.
Second Annual Valvoline National Driving Test, CBS, 1990.
Night of 100 Stars III, NBC, 1990.
Happy Birthday, Bugs: 50 Looney Years, CBS, 1990.

Comic Relief IV, HBO, 1990.
The 44th Annual Tony Awards, CBS, 1990.
The 11th Annual ACE Awards (also known as *The Golden ACE Awards*), 1990.
The Very Best of the Ed Sullivan Show, CBS, 1991.
The 18th Annual Daytime Emmy Awards, CBS, 1991.
Host, *Showtime Comedy Club All-Stars V,* Showtime, 1991.
As herself, *Public Enemy Number 2,* Showtime, 1991.

TELEVISION APPEARANCES; EPISODIC

Appeared as guest host on *Saturday Night Live,* NBC.

OTHER TELEVISION APPEARANCES

Reporter, *Comedy News II* (pilot), ABC, 1973.
The Real Trivial Pursuit, ABC, 1985.
Square One TV, PBS, 1987.
The World of Jewish Humor, PBS, 1990.
Irma Summers, *How to Murder a Millionaire* (movie; also known as *The Beverly Hills Get Rich Quick Murders, Bad Times in Beverly Hills, Your Money or Your Wife,* and *The Couch Potato Murders*), CBS, 1990.

Also appeared in *The Shape of Things,* 1973.

TELEVISION WORK

Creator, *Husbands, Wives and Lovers* (series; also see below), CBS, 1978.

FILM APPEARANCES

Joan, *The Swimmer,* Columbia, 1968.
Second nurse, *Rabbit Test* (also see below), Avco Embassy, 1978.
As herself, *Uncle Scam,* New World Pictures of Philadelphia, 1981.
The Muppets Take Manhattan, Tri-Star, 1984.
U.S. President, *Les Patterson Saves the World,* Hoyts, 1987.
Voice of Dot Matrix, *Spaceballs,* Metro-Goldwyn-Mayer/United Artists, 1987.

FILM WORK

Director, *Rabbit Test* (also see below), Avco Embassy, 1978.

STAGE APPEARANCES

(Broadway debut) Jill Fairchild, *Fun City* (also see below), Morosco Theatre, New York City, 1972.
Kate, *Broadway Bound,* Broadhurst Theatre, New York City, between 1986 and 1988.

RECORDINGS:

ALBUMS

Joan Rivers Presents Mr. Phyllis and Other Funny Stories, Warner Brothers, 1965.
What Becomes a Semi-legend Most, Geffen Records, 1983.

WRITINGS:

(Coauthor) *Fun City* (play), first produced at Morosco Theatre, New York City, 1972.
Having a Baby Can Be a Scream, Hawthorn, 1975.
(With Jay Redack) *Rabbit Test* (screenplay), Avco Embassy, 1978.
The Life and Hard Times of Heidi Abromowitz, Delacorte, 1984.
(With Richard Meryman) *Enter Talking* (autobiography), Delacorte, 1986.

Nationally syndicated columnist for the *Chicago Tribune,* 1973-76.

TELEVISION SCRIPTS

(With Agnes Gallin) *The Girl Most Likely To . . .* (movie; adapted from Rivers's story), ABC, 1973.
(With Hal Dresner), *Husbands and Wives* (pilot for series *Husbands, Wives and Lovers*), CBS, 1977.

Also wrote for *Candid Camera,* CBS; collaborated with Michael McWhinney for portions of the *Ed Sullivan* show; wrote for entertainers Phyllis Diller and Zsa Zsa Gabor.

ADAPTATIONS: The Life and Hard Times of Heidi Abromowitz was the subject of a television special broadcast by Showtime, 1985.

OTHER SOURCES:

PERIODICALS

People, May 26, 1986, pp. 30-35; February 19, 1990, pp. 67-69.
Time, April 11, 1983, pp. 85-86.*

* * *

RODDENBERRY, Gene 1921-1991

OBITUARY NOTICE—See index for *CTFT* sketch: Full name, Eugene Wesley Roddenberry; born August 19, 1921, in El Paso, TX; died of a heart attack, October 24, 1991, in Santa Monica, CA. Film and television executive, screenwriter, and author. Roddenberry is remembered as the creator of the 1960s space-age science fiction television series *Star Trek,* which inspired motion pictures, a sequel series, and devoted fans known as Trekkies. Roddenberry's career in television began after he served as a pilot in

World War II—earning a Distinguished Flying Cross—and worked for a commercial airline. From 1953 to 1962 he wrote scripts for such programs as *Goodyear Theater, Dragnet,* and *Naked City,* winning an Emmy Award for the 1950s western series *Have Gun, Will Travel.* It was with *Star Trek,* however, that Roddenberry received substantial critical acclaim, including a Hugo Award. He stressed characterization in the series and predicted that the future held the promise of harmonious relationships throughout the universe. The premiere episode aired in 1966, and although new shows were produced for only three seasons, reruns have been broadcast on more than two hundred television stations throughout America and in nearly fifty countries. This continuing popularity led to spin-offs, and when the first *Star Trek* motion picture was filmed in 1979, Roddenberry served as producer and became the executive consultant for the next three films. He was also the executive producer of the television sequel series, *Star Trek: The Next Generation,* which began in 1987. Roddenberry's books include *The Making of "Star Trek," Star Trek: The Motion Picture,* and *The Making of "Star Trek: The Motion Picture."*

OBITUARIES AND OTHER SOURCES:

BOOKS

Who's Who in America, 46th edition, Marquis, 1990.

PERIODICALS

Chicago Tribune, October 25, 1991, section 1, p. 10; October 27, 1991, section 2, p. 10.
Los Angeles Times, October 25, 1991, p. A3; October 26, 1991, p. F1.
New York Times, October 25, 1991, p. B5; October 26, 1991, p. 26.
Star Trek, October-November, 1989, pp. 3-9.
Variety, October 28, 1991, p. 62.
Washington Post, October 25, 1991, p. C4.

* * *

ROIZMAN, Owen 1936-

PERSONAL: Born September 22, 1936, in Brooklyn, NY; son of Sol Roizman (a cinematographer); married Mona Lindholm, December 6, 1964; children: Eric. *Education:* Gettysburg College, B.A., mathematics, 1958.

ADDRESSES: Agent—Murray Neidorf, Perry & Neidorf, 9720 Wilshire Blvd., Third Floor, Beverly Hills, CA 90212.

CAREER: Cinematographer. Director of television commercials.

MEMBER: American Society of Cinematographers, Academy of Motion Picture Arts and Sciences.

AWARDS, HONORS: Academy Award nomination, best cinematography, 1971, for *The French Connection;* Emmy Award nomination, best cinematography in special entertainment programming, 1972, for *Singer Presents Liza with a "Z";* Academy Award nominations, best cinematography, 1973 (with Billy Williams), for *The Exorcist,* 1976, for *Network,* and 1982, for *Tootsie.*

CREDITS:

FILM CINEMATOGRAPHER

The French Connection, Twentieth Century-Fox, 1971.
The Gang That Couldn't Shoot Straight, Metro-Goldwyn-Mayer (MGM), 1971.
The Heartbreak Kid, Twentieth Century-Fox, 1972.
Play It Again, Sam, Paramount, 1972.
(With Billy Williams) *The Exorcist,* Warner Brothers, 1973.
The Taking of Pelham One, Two, Three, United Artists (UA), 1974.
The Stepford Wives, Columbia, 1975.
Three Days of the Condor, Paramount, 1975.
Independence, Twentieth Century-Fox, 1976.
Network, MGM/UA, 1976.
The Return of a Man Called Horse, UA, 1976.
Sergeant Pepper's Lonely Hearts Club Band, Universal, 1978.
Straight Time, Warner Brothers, 1978.
The Electric Horseman, Universal, 1979.
The Black Marble, Avco Embassy, 1980.
Absence of Malice, Columbia, 1981.
True Confessions, UA, 1981.
Taps, Twentieth Century-Fox, 1981.
Tootsie, Columbia, 1982.
Vision Quest, Warner Brothers, 1985.
I Love You to Death, Tri-Star, 1990.
Havana (also see below), Universal, 1990.
Grand Canyon, Twentieth Century-Fox, 1991.
The Addams Family, Paramount, 1991.

Also cinematographer for unreleased film *Stop,* Warner Brothers, 1970.

FILM APPEARANCES

Santos, *Havana,* Universal, 1990.

TELEVISION CINEMATOGRAPHER

Singer Presents Liza with a "Z" (special), NBC, 1972.

OTHER SOURCES:

PERIODICALS

American Cinematographer, April, 1977; October, 1979; April, 1982; April, 1990; November, 1991.
Film Comment, April, 1984, p. 32.

ROSE, Reginald 1920-

PERSONAL: Born December 10, 1920, in New York, NY; son of William (a lawyer) and Alice (Obendorfer) Rose; married Barbara Langbart, September 5, 1943 (marriage ended); married Ellen McLaughlin, July 6, 1963; children: (first marriage) Jonathan, Richard, Andrew and Steven (twins); (second marriage) Thomas, Christopher. *Education:* Attended City College (now of the City University of New York), 1937-38.

ADDRESSES: Office—Defender Productions, c/o David W. Katz & Co., East 40th St., New York, NY 10016. *Agent*—Preferred Artists, 16633 Ventura Blvd., Suite 1421, Encino, CA 91436.

CAREER: Screenwriter and playwright. Warner Brothers, clerk and publicity writer, then advertising copywriter, early 1950s; president of Defender Productions, Inc., 1961—, Reginald Rose Foundation, 1963—, and Ellrose Equities. *Military service:* U.S. Army, Quartermaster corps, 1942-46; became first lieutenant.

MEMBER: Dramatists Guild, Authors League of America, Writers Guild of America (East).

AWARDS, HONORS: Writers Guild of America award and Emmy Award, best written dramatic material, both 1954, for "Twelve Angry Men" (television play), *Studio One;* Emmy Award nomination, best teleplay writing—one hour or more, 1956, for "Tragedy in a Temporary Town," *Alcoa Hour-Goodyear Theater;* Academy Award nominations, best picture (with Henry Fonda) and best screenplay based on material from another medium, and Edgar Allan Poe Award, best motion picture screenplay, Mystery Writers of America, all 1957, for *Twelve Angry Men* (film); citation, Berlin Film Festival, 1958; Laurel Award, Writers Guild of America, 1958; Emmy Award nomination, outstanding writing achievement—drama special, 1960, for "The Sacco-Vanzetti Story," *Sunday Showcase;* Writers Guild of America award, Edgar Allan Poe Award, best motion picture screenplay, and Emmy Award, outstanding writing achievement—drama series, all 1962, for *The Defenders;* Emmy Award (with Robert Thom), outstanding writing achievement—drama series, 1963, for "The Madman," *The Defenders;* Emmy Award nomination, outstanding writing—drama special, 1968, for "Dear Friends," *CBS Playhouse;* Laurel Award, Writers Guild of America, 1987; Emmy Award nomination, outstanding writing—mini-series, 1987, for *Escape from Sobibor.*

CREDITS:

FILM PRODUCER

(With Henry Fonda) *Twelve Angry Men* (also see below), United Artists, 1957.

WRITINGS:

TELEVISION

"The Bus to Nowhere," *Out There,* CBS, 1951.
"Twelve Angry Men" (also see below), *Studio One,* CBS, 1954.
"Thunder on Sycamore Street," *Studio One,* CBS, 1954.
"The Remarkable Incident at Carson Corners," *Studio One,* CBS, 1954.
"Dino" (also see below), *Studio One,* CBS, 1954.
"The Death and Life of Larry Benson," *Studio One,* CBS, 1954.
"The Expendable House," *Philco Television Playhouse-Goodyear Theater,* NBC, 1955.
"The Incredible World of Horace Ford," *Studio One,* CBS, 1955.
"Crime in the Streets" (also see below), *Elgin Hour,* ABC, 1955.
"Tragedy in a Temporary Town," *Alcoa Hour-Goodyear Theater,* NBC, 1956.
"The Defender" (pilot for series *The Defenders;* also see below), *Studio One,* CBS, 1957.
"A Quiet Game of Cards," *Playhouse 90,* CBS, 1959.
"A Marriage of Strangers," *Playhouse 90,* CBS, 1959.
"The Cruel Day," *Playhouse 90,* CBS, 1959.
"The Sacco-Vanzetti Story" (also see below), *Sunday Showcase,* NBC, 1960.
(With others, and creator) *The Defenders* (series), CBS, 1961-65.
"Dear Friends," *CBS Playhouse,* CBS, 1968.
(And creator) *The Zoo Gang* (series), NBC, 1975.
The Four of Us (pilot), ABC, 1977.
Studs Lonigan (mini-series), NBC, 1979.
The Rules of Marriage (movie), CBS, 1982.
(With Rita Mae Brown) *My Two Loves* (movie), ABC, 1986.
Escape from Sobibor (mini-series), CBS, 1987.

Also author of television play *Black Monday.* Contributor of scripts to *Philco Television Playhouse, Kraft Television Playhouse,* and *The Twilight Zone.*

PLAYS

Black Monday, produced at Vandam Theatre, New York City, 1962.
Twelve Angry Men, produced at Queen's Playhouse, London, England, 1964.
The Porcelain Year, produced at Locust Street Theatre, Philadelphia, PA, then Shubert Theatre, New Haven, CT, both 1965.
Dear Friends, produced in Edinburgh, Scotland, 1968, produced at Lakewood Little Theatre, Cleveland, OH, 1969.
This Agony, This Triumph (based on "The Sacco-Vanzetti Story"), produced in California, 1972.

Also author of *Baxter!,* 1973.

SCREENPLAYS

Crime in the Streets, Allied Artists, 1956.
Twelve Angry Men, United Artists (UA), 1957.
Dino, Allied Artists, 1957.
Man of the West (based on the novel *The Border Jumpers* by Will C. Brown), UA, 1958.
The Man in the Net (based on the novel *Man in the Net* by Patrick Quentin), UA, 1958.
Baxter!, National General, 1972.
The Wild Geese (based on the novel of the same title by Daniel Carney), Allied Artists, 1978.
Somebody Killed Her Husband, Columbia, 1978.
The Sea Wolves (based on the novel *The Boarding Party* by James Leasor), Paramount, 1981.
(With Brian Clark) *Whose Life Is It Anyway?,* Metro-Goldwyn-Mayer (MGM)/UA, 1981.
The Final Option (based on the novel *The Tiptoe Boys* by George Markstein; also known as *Who Dares Wins*), MGM/UA, 1983.
Wild Geese II (based on the novel *The Square Circle* by Carney), Universal, 1985.

OTHER

Six Television Plays, Simon & Schuster, 1957.
The Thomas Book, Harcourt, 1972.

OTHER SOURCES:

BOOKS

Contemporary Authors, Volume 73, Gale, 1979, pp. 538-539.

PERIODICALS

AB Bookman's Weekly, October 17, 1977.
Christian Science Monitor, December 4, 1967.
Newark Evening New, December 3, 1967.
New York Herald Tribune, June 1, 1960.
New York Times, August 6, 1977.
New York World Telegram and Sun, September 2, 1961.*

* * *

ROSENBERG, Stuart 1927-

PERSONAL: Born August 11, 1927, in Brooklyn, NY; son of David and Sara (Kaminsky) Rosenberg; married Margot Pohoryles, August 4, 1950; children: Benjamin. *Education:* New York University, B.A., 1949; three years of graduate study.

ADDRESSES: Agent—William Morris Agency, 151 South El Camino Drive, Beverly Hills, CA 90212.

CAREER: Director and producer. *Military service:* U.S. Naval Reserve, 1945-47.

MEMBER: Directors Guild.

AWARDS, HONORS: Directors Guild of America award nominations, 1962, 1963, 1964, 1964; Emmy Award, outstanding directorial achievement in drama, 1963, and Emmy Award nomination, outstanding directorial achievement in drama, 1964, both for *The Defenders.*

CREDITS:

FILM DIRECTOR

(With Burt Balaban) *Murder, Inc.,* Twentieth Century-Fox, 1960.
Question 7, Louis de Rochemont Associates, 1961.
Cool Hand Luke, Warner Brothers, 1967.
The April Fools, National General, 1969.
Move, Twentieth Century-Fox, 1970.
WUSA, Paramount, 1970.
Pocket Money, National General, 1972.
(And producer) *The Laughing Policeman* (released in England as *An Investigation of Murder*), Twentieth Century-Fox, 1973.
The Drowning Pool, Warner Brothers, 1975.
Voyage of the Damned, Avco Embassy, 1976.
The Amityville Horror, American International, 1979.
Love and Bullets, Associated Film Distribution, 1979.
Brubaker, Twentieth Century-Fox, 1980.
The Pope of Greenwich Village, Metro-Goldwyn-Mayer/United Artists, 1984.
(Under pseudonym Alan Smithee) *Let's Get Harry,* Tri-Star, 1987.
My Heroes Have Always Been Cowboys (also known as *Home Grown*), Samuel Goldwyn, 1991.

TELEVISION DIRECTOR; EPISODIC

The Big Story, NBC, between 1949 and 1957.
Decoy, syndicated, 1957.
Naked City, ABC, between 1958 and 1963.
The Untouchables, ABC, between 1959 and 1963.
Rawhide, CBS, between 1959 and 1966.
Bus Stop, ABC, between 1961 and 1962.
The Defenders, CBS, between 1961 and 1965.
Ben Casey, ABC, between 1961 and 1966.
The Bob Hope Chrysler Theater, NBC, between 1963 and 1967.
Run for Your Life, NBC, between 1965 and 1968.
The Name of the Game, NBC, between 1968 and 1972.

Also director for episodes of *Espionage, Alfred Hitchcock Presents,* and *The Twilight Zone.*

OTHER TELEVISION WORK

Producer, *Head of the Family* (pilot for *The Dick Van Dyke Show*), CBS, 1960.
Director, *Fame Is the Name of the Game* (pilot for *The Name of the Game*), NBC, 1966.

Also director of *Asylum for a Spy,* 1967.

* * *

ROSQUI, Tom 1928-

PERSONAL: Full name, Thomas Francis Rosqui; born June 12, 1928, in Oakland, CA; son of Anthony (a traffic manager) and Sally (a salesperson; maiden name, Jardin) Rosqui; married Erica Fishman (an actress), August 18, 1963. *Education:* Sacramento City College, A.A., 1948; University of the Pacific, B.A., 1951.

CAREER: Actor. *Military service:* U.S. Navy, 1952-54.

MEMBER: Screen Actors Guild, Actors' Equity Association, Delta Psi Omega, Omega Phi Alpha.

CREDITS:

STAGE APPEARANCES

(Stage debut) Caterer's man, *The Cocktail Party,* Curran Theatre, San Francisco, CA, 1951, then Peter Quilpe, Biltmore Theatre, Los Angeles, CA, 1951.
Salarino, *The Merchant of Venice,* Club Theatre, New York City, 1955.
Michael, *The Fourposter,* Red Barn Theatre, Westboro, MA, 1955.
Elgin, *The Country Girl,* Red Barn Theatre, 1955.
Uncle, *The Golddiggers,* Red Barn Theatre, 1955.
Witch boy, *The Dark of the Moon,* Red Barn Theatre, 1955.
Steve Stackhouse, *Separate Rooms,* Red Barn Theatre, 1955.
Slater, *The Moon is Blue,* Red Barn Theatre, 1955.
Husband, *Meet the Wife,* Red Barn Theatre, 1955.
Freddie, *Getting Gertie's Garter,* Red Barn Theatre, 1955.
Chesney, *Charlie's Aunt,* Red Barn Theatre, 1955.
Husband, *Apron Strings,* Red Barn Theatre, 1955.
Psychiatrist, *Champagne Complex,* Red Barn Theatre, 1955.
Jose, *Cradle Snatchers,* Red Barn Theatre, 1955.
Levinson, *East Lynne,* Red Barn Theatre, 1955.
Billings, *The Happiest Day of Your Life,* Red Barn Theatre, 1955.
Jake, *Sailor Beware,* Red Barn Theatre, 1955.
Johnny, *Lullaby,* Studio Theatre, Washington DC, 1956.
Prescott, *Wake Up, Darling,* White Barn Theatre, Irwin, PA, 1956.
Serensky, *Anastasia,* White Barn Theatre, 1956.
Ferelli, *The Fifth Season,* White Barn Theatre, 1956.
Bo Decker, *Bus Stop,* White Barn Theatre, 1956.
Heathcliffe, *Wuthering Heights,* White Barn Theatre, 1956.
Lefty McShane, *The Hot Corner,* White Barn Theatre, 1956.
Glenn Griffin, *The Desperate Hours,* White Barn Theatre, 1956.
Harris, *Tea and Sympathy,* White Barn Theatre, 1956.
Jay, *A Roomful of Roses,* White Barn Theatre, 1956.
Solid Gold Cadillac, White Barn Theatre, 1956.
The Seven Year Itch, White Barn Theatre, 1956.
Callahan, *Detective Story,* Fred Miller Theatre, Milwaukee, WI, 1957.
Michael, *Jenny Kissed Me,* Fred Miller Theatre, 1957.
Tom, *The Glass Menagerie,* Fred Miller Theatre, 1957.
Sanders, *Harvey,* Fred Miller Theatre, 1957.
Pugh, *Clutterbuck,* Fred Miller Theatre, 1957.
Segius, *Arms and the Man,* Fred Miller Theatre, 1957.
Jay, *A Roomful of Roses,* Fred Miller Theatre, 1957.
Jarvis, *Member of the Wedding,* Fred Miller Theatre, 1957.
Nicky, *Bell, Book, and Candle,* Fred Miller Theatre, 1957.
Michael, *The Fourposter,* Red Barn Theatre, Saugatuck, MI, 1957.
Bud, *Anniversary Waltz,* Red Barn Theatre, Saugatuck, 1957.
Uncle Ben, *The Little Foxes,* Red Barn Theatre, Saugatuck, 1957.
The Count, *Candlelight,* Red Barn Theatre, Saugatuck, 1957.
Gil, *Janus,* Red Barn Theatre, Saugatuck, 1957.
Carl, *Bus Stop,* Red Barn Theatre, Saugatuck, 1957.
Stanley Kowalski, *Streetcar Named Desire,* Red Barn Theatre, Saugatuck, 1957.
Don Juan, *Don Juan in Hell,* Red Barn Theatre, Saugatuck, 1957.
Johnny, *Roberta,* Red Barn Theatre, Saugatuck, 1957.
Peg o' My Heart, Red Barn Theatre, Saugatuck, 1957.
Write Me a Murder, Red Barn Theatre, Saugatuck, 1957.
Paul, *A Gift of Fury,* The Actor's Workshop, San Francisco, CA, 1958.
Hicky, *The Iceman Cometh,* The Actor's Workshop, 1958.
Biff, *Death of a Salesman,* The Actor's Workshop, 1958.
Cleante, *The Miser,* The Actor's Workshop, 1958.
Harry, *Prometheus Found,* The Actor's Workshop, 1958.
Dr. Bonfant, *The Waltz of the Toreadors,* The Actor's Workshop, 1958.
Oedipus, *The Infernal Machine,* The Actor's Workshop, 1958.
Dr. Sugar, *Suddenly, Last Summer,* The Actor's Workshop, 1958.

The Messenger, *Cock-a-Doodle-Dandy,* The Actor's Workshop, 1958.
Clov, *The Endgame,* The Actor's Workshop, 1958.
Judge Hawthorn, *The Crucible,* The Actor's Workshop, 1958.
Muscari, *The Busy Martyr,* The Actor's Workshop, 1959.
George Dillon, *Epitaph for George Dillon,* The Actor's Workshop, 1959.
Dick Dudgeon, *The Devil's Disciple,* The Actor's Workshop, 1960.
Christian Melrose, *Saint's Day,* The Actor's Workshop, 1960.
Eugene d'Ettouville, *The Rocks Cried Out,* The Actor's Workshop, 1960.
Jerry, *The Zoo Story,* The Actor's Workshop, 1961.
Edgar, *King Lear,* The Actor's Workshop, 1961.
John Tarleton, *Misalliance,* The Actor's Workshop, 1961.
Edmund, *King Lear,* The Actor's Workshop, 1961.
Musgrave, *Sergeant Musgrave's Dance,* The Actor's Workshop, 1961.
Title role, *Becket,* The Actor's Workshop, 1961.
Douglas, *Henry IV, Part 1,* The Actor's Workshop, 1961.
Two for the Seesaw, Tunn Theatre, Redwood City, CA, 1962.
Malvolio, *Twelfth Night,* The Actor's Workshop, 1962.
Tom, *The Glass Menagerie,* The Actor's Workshop, 1963.
Jack, *Telegraph Hill,* The Actor's Workshop, 1963.
The Inquisitor, *Galileo,* The Actor's Workshop, 1963.
Theobald, *The Underpants,* The Actor's Workshop, 1963.
Sir Politick, *Volpone,* The Actor's Workshop, 1963.
Lord of the Inn, *The Taming of the Shrew,* The Actor's Workshop, 1963.
Aston, *The Caretaker,* The Actor's Workshop, 1963.
Ashuwa, *The Caucasion Chalk Circle,* The Actor's Workshop, 1963.
Dangerfield, *The Ginger Man,* The Actor's Workshop, 1963, then 1964.
Shannon, *Night of the Iguana,* The Actor's Workshop, 1963, then 1964.
Prometheus, *The Birds,* The Actor's Workshop, 1963, then 1964.
Uncle Vanya, The Actor's Workshop, 1965.
(Broadway debut) Citizen Barere, *Danton's Death,* Lincoln Center Repertory Company, Vivian Beaumont Theatre, New York City, 1965.
The Country Wife, Vivian Beaumont Theatre, 1965.
Frantz, *The Condemned of Altoona,* Vivian Beaumont Theatre, 1966.
Limping man, *The Caucasion Chalk Circle,* Vivian Beaumont Theatre, 1966.
Neighbor, *The Alchemist,* Vivian Beaumont Theatre, 1966.
Victor, *Yerma,* Vivian Beaumont Theatre, 1966.
Vitek, *The East Wind,* Vivian Beaumont Theatre, 1967.
He, "Wandering," Henry James, "Stars and Stripes," Man, "Skywriting," Mr. Wilson, "Tour," He, "Camera Obscura," and Jebbie, "Rats," *Collision Course* (eleven-bill), Cafe Au Go-Go, New York City, 1968.
Tom Jason, *Brotherhood,* St. Mark's Playhouse, New York City, 1970.
Sergeant Match, *What the Butler Saw,* McAlpin Rooftop Theatre, New York City, 1970.
Saul, *L.A. under Siege,* Studio Arena Theatre, Buffalo, NY, 1970.
Capt. Paul Barret, *Defender of the Faith,* Plymouth Theatre, New York City, 1970.
Harry, "Eli, the Fanaticon," *Unlikely Heroes: 3 Phillip Roth Stories,* Plymouth Theatre, 1971.
Lucky, *Waiting for Godot,* Sheridan Square Playhouse, New York City, 1971.
William Herndon, *The Lincoln Mask,* Plymouth Theatre, 1972.
Steve Hubbel, *A Streetcar Named Desire,* Vivian Beaumont Theatre, 1973.
The Vienna Notes, Center Theatre Group, Mark Taper Forum, Los Angeles, 1979.
Jesse/Bush, *The American Clock: A Mural for the Theatre,* Mark Taper Forum, 1983.
Driving around the House, South Coast Repertory Theatre, Costa Mesa, CA, 1986.
Tartuffe, Los Angeles Theatre Center, Los Angeles, CA, 1987.
Fire marshall, *Sarcophagus,* Los Angeles Theatre Center, 1988.
The Geography of Luck, Los Angeles Theatre Center, 1990.

Also appeared as Christy, *The Playboy of the Western World,* 1957; Canon, *Shadow and Substance,* 1957; and Jean-Paul Marat, *Marat/Sade,* 1966.

FILM APPEARANCES

Bettor, *Days of Wine and Roses,* Warner Brothers, 1962.
Henry, *The Crazy Quilt,* Farallon, 1966.
Madigan, Universal, 1968.
Private detective, *The Thomas Crown Affair,* United Artists, 1968.
Defense Attorney Keller, *The Pursuit of Happiness,* Columbia, 1971.
Rocco Lampone, *The Godfather, Part II,* Paramount, 1974.
Jason Morgan, *The Great Texas Dynamite Chase,* New World Pictures, 1976.
General Sampson, *MacArthur,* Universal, 1977.
Chief Gill, *Defense Play,* Trans World, 1988.
Norman, *Guilty by Suspicion,* Warner Brothers, 1991.

Also appeared as second patrolman, *Heroes,* 1977, and Hunter, *Airport 77,* 1977.

TELEVISION APPEARANCES; MOVIES

Detective Phelan, *The Connection,* ABC, 1973.
Father, *The Migrants,* CBS, 1974.
Fletcher, *Dead Man on the Run,* ABC, 1975.
The New, Original Wonder Woman, ABC, 1975.
Edwin Knopf, *F. Scott Fitzgerald in Hollywood,* ABC, 1976.
Amos Eran, *Raid on Entebbe,* NBC, 1977.
Sergeant John Guffy, *Lady of the House,* NBC, 1978.
Police commander, *Act of Violence,* CBS, 1979.
Tom Burham, *The Night the City Screamed,* ABC, 1980.
Barney French, *Memorial Day,* CBS, 1983.

TELEVISION APPEARANCES; SERIES

Jason Maxwell, *All My Children,* ABC, 1972.

TELEVISION APPEARANCES; EPISODIC

"The Office Party," *Kraft Television Theatre,* NBC, 1954.
"The Counsel," *Kraft Television Theatre,* NBC, 1955.
Lineup, CBS, 1960.
Voice of Edward Weston, "How Young I Was," and "The Strongest Way of Seeing," *U.S.A.—Photography,* National Educational Television, 1966.
Phil, "A Party for Divorce," *NT Television Theatre,* National Educational Television, 1967.
Unemployed man, "A Memory of Two Mondays," *Great Performances,* PBS, 1974.
Fred, *Zero Intelligence,* ABC, 1976.*

* * *

ROSS, Edward
See BRAZZI, Rossano

* * *

RUDIN, Scott 1958-

PERSONAL: Born July 14, 1958, in New York, NY.

CAREER: Producer. Worked as a production assistant on Broadway; later became a casting director in film. Twentieth-Century Fox, producer, beginning 1984, executive vice-president of production, president of production, 1986-87.

AWARDS, HONORS: Emmy Award nomination, outstanding drama special—prime time, 1983, for *Little Gloria . . . Happy at Last;* Emmy Award, outstanding children's program—prime time, and nomination, outstanding children's entertainment special—daytime, both 1983, for *He Makes Me Feel Like Dancin'.*

CREDITS:

FILM PRODUCER, EXCEPT AS INDICATED

(With Edgar J. Scherick) *I'm Dancing As Fast As I Can,* Paramount, 1982.
(With Scherick and David A. Nicksay) *Mrs. Soffel,* Metro-Goldwyn-Mayer/United Artists (MGM/UA), 1984.
(With Scherick) *Reckless,* MGM/UA, 1984.
(With William Sackheim) *Pacific Heights,* Twentieth Century-Fox, 1990.
Executive producer, *Flatliners,* Columbia, 1990.
Regarding Henry, Paramount, 1991.
Little Man Tate, Orion, 1991.
The Addams Family, Paramount, 1991.
Executive producer, *Sister Act,* Touchstone, 1992.

FILM CASTING DIRECTOR

King of the Gypsies, Paramount, 1978.
The Wanderers, Orion, 1979.
Last Embrace, UA, 1979.
Simon, Warner Brothers, 1980.
Hide in Plain Sight, UA, 1980.
Resurrection, Universal, 1980.

TELEVISION EXECUTIVE PRODUCER, EXCEPT AS INDICATED

Producer, *Revenge of the Stepford Wives* (movie), NBC, 1980.
(With Scherick) *Little Gloria . . . Happy at Last* (movie), NBC, 1982.
(With Scherick) *He Makes Me Feel Like Dancin'* (documentary special), NBC, 1983.

THEATRE WORK

Production assistant, *Equus,* Plymouth Theatre, New York City, beginning 1974.*

* * *

RULE, Elton H. 1917-1990

PERSONAL: Born in 1917 in Stockton, CA; died of cancer, May 5, 1990, in Beverly Hills, CA; married Betty Louise Bender; children: Cindy Rule Dunne, Christie, James. *Education:* Attended Sacramento College.

CAREER: Broadcasting executive. Worked at KROY-Radio, Sacramento, CA, beginning in 1938; KLAC-TV, Los Angeles, CA, advertising salesperson, after World War II; American Broadcasting Company, New York City, 1952-84, general sales manager of KECA-TV (became KABC-TV) in Los Angeles, 1953-60, general manager of KABC-TV, 1960-68, vice president of KABC-TV, 1961-68, president of ABC-TV Network, 1968-70, group vice president of ABC Inc., 1969-72, president of ABC division, 1970-72, president and chief operating officer of ABC Inc., 1972-83, member of executive committee of ABC Inc., 1972-84, vice chairman of ABC Inc., 1983-84; Academy of Television Arts and Sciences Foundation, president, 1989-90. Institute of Sports Medicine and Athletic Trauma, Lenox Hill Hospital, member of advisory board, beginning in 1973; University of California, Los Angeles, School of Medicine, member of board of visitors, beginning in 1980; Rule/Starger Productions, cofounder, c. 1987; associated with Paradigm Entertainment (production firm), late 1980s; R. P. Cos. (investment firm), chairman. *Military service:* U.S. Army, Infantry, served during World War II in Pacific Ocean theater.

MEMBER: California Broadcasters Association (president, 1966-67).

AWARDS, HONORS: Gold Medal Award, International Radio and Television Society, 1975; award for outstanding achievement in business management, University of Southern California School of Business Administration, 1978; Governor's Award, Academy of Television Arts and Sciences, 1981; Distinguished Achievement Award, Pacific Pioneer Broadcasters, 1984; Distinguished Service Award, National Association of Broadcasters, 1984.

CREDITS:

TELEVISION APPEARANCES; SPECIALS

The Television Academy Hall of Fame, FOX, 1987.

OBITUARIES AND OTHER SOURCES:

PERIODICALS

Forbes, July 19, 1982, p. 66.
Variety, May 9, 1990, p. 92.*

* * *

RUSSELL, Shirley 1935-

PERSONAL: Born Shirley Ann Kingdon in 1935 in London, England; married Ken Russell (a film director), 1957 (divorced, 1979); children: Alex, James, Victoria, Xavier, Toby. *Education:* Attended Royal College of Art, London.

CAREER: Costume designer.

AWARDS, HONORS: British Academy of Film and Television Arts Award, film—costume design, 1979, for *Yanks;* Academy Award nominations, costume design, 1979, for *Agatha,* and 1981, for *Reds.*

CREDITS:

FILM COSTUME DESIGNER

Women in Love, United Artists (UA), 1969.
The Boy Friend, Metro-Goldwyn-Mayer (MGM), 1971.
The Music Lovers, UA, 1971.
The Devils, Warner Brothers, 1971.
Savage Messiah, MGM, 1972.
Mahler, Visual Programme Systems, 1974.
The Little Prince, Paramount, 1974.
Tommy, Columbia, 1975.
Lisztomania, Warner Brothers, 1975.
Valentino, UA, 1977.
(And production designer) *Agatha,* Warner Brothers, 1979.
Cuba, UA, 1979.
Yanks, Universal, 1979.
Reds, Paramount, 1981.
Lady Chatterley's Lover, Prodis, 1981.
The Return of the Soldier, Twentieth Century-Fox, 1983.
Wagner, Alan Landsburg, 1983.
The Razor's Edge, Columbia, 1984.
(With John Mollo) *Greystoke: The Legend of Tarzan, Lord of the Apes,* Warner Brothers, 1985.
The Bride, Columbia, 1985.
(And production designer) *Blood Red Roses,* Other Cinema, 1986.
Hope and Glory, Columbia, 1987.

Also costume designer for *French Dressing,* 1963, *Billion Dollar Brain,* 1967, *Inserts,* 1975, and *News from Nowhere,* 1977.

TELEVISION COSTUME DESIGNER

Costume designer for *Clouds of Glory,* 1978.

WRITINGS:

Contributor to periodicals, including *Cinema* and *Films and Filming.**

* * *

RUSSELL, Theresa 1957-

PERSONAL: Born Theresa Paup, 1957, in San Diego, CA; married Nicolas Roeg (a director), 1986; children: Stratten Jack, Maxim. *Education:* Attended high school in Burbank, CA; studied acting at Lee Strasberg Institute.

CAREER: Actress.

MEMBER: Screen Actors Guild.

AWARDS, HONORS: National Association of Theatre Owners (NATO) Award, star of tomorrow, 1986.

CREDITS:

FILM APPEARANCES

Cecilia Brady, *The Last Tycoon,* Paramount, 1976.
Jenny Mercer, *Straight Time,* Warner Brothers, 1978.
Tracy, *Eureka,* United Artists, 1983.
Sophie, *The Razor's Edge,* Columbia, 1984.
The actress, *Insignificance,* Island Alive, 1985.
King Zog, "Un ballo in maschera," *Aria,* Virgin Vision, 1987.
Catharine, *Black Widow,* Twentieth Century-Fox, 1987.
Linda Henry, *Track 29,* Island, 1988.
Jenny Hudson, *Physical Evidence,* Columbia, 1989.
Lottie Mason, *Impulse,* Warner Brothers, 1990.
Liz, *Whore,* Trimark Pictures, 1991.
Gabriela, *Kafka,* Miramax, 1992.
Marie Davenport, *Cold Heaven,* Hemdale, 1992.

Appeared as Milena Flaherty, *Bad Timing: A Sensual Obsession,* 1980; also appeared in *Smoke.*

TELEVISION APPEARANCES; MINI-SERIES

Maureen Dean, *Blind Ambition,* CBS, 1979.

OTHER SOURCES:

PERIODICALS

American Film, April, 1989, p. 34.
Interview, November 5, 1985, p. 70.*

S

SAGEBRECHT, Marianne 1945-

PERSONAL: Born in 1945 in Starnberg, Germany.

ADDRESSES: *Contact*—Michael Donaldson, Dern & Donaldson, 1901 Avenue of the Stars, Suite 400, Los Angeles, CA 90067.

CAREER: Actress. Manager of a cabaret revue; creator of the touring revue *Opera Curiosa,* 1977.

CREDITS:

FILM APPEARANCES

Irrsee (also known as *Sea of Errors*), Friederike Pezold, 1984.
Marianne, *Sugarbaby,* Kino International, 1985.
Fraulein Hermann, *Crazy Boys,* Bischoff and Co., 1987.
Jasmin Munchgstettner, *Out of Rosenheim,* Futura-Filmverlag der Autoren, 1987, released as *Bagdad Cafe,* Island, 1988.
Magda, *Moon Over Parador,* Universal, 1988.
Rosalie Greenspace, *Rosalie Goes Shopping,* Weltvertrieb des Autoren, 1989.
Susan, *The War of the Roses,* Twentieth Century-Fox, 1989.
Martha, *Martha und Ich* (also known as *Martha and I*), SACIS, 1990.

Also appeared in *The Swing.*

* * *

SALOMON, Mikael 1945-

PERSONAL: Born February 24, 1945, in Copenhagen, Denmark; immigrated to United States, 1986; son of George and Eva Salomon.

ADDRESSES: *Agent*—Sanford-Skouras & Gross, 1015 Gailey Ave., No. 301, Los Angeles, CA 90024.

CAREER: Cinematographer and visual effects creator. Began career in Europe; director of commercials; has worked on more than fifty films.

MEMBER: American Society of Cinematographers.

AWARDS, HONORS: Danish Film Critics award, 1983, for *Hearts Are Trump;* Danish Academy Award, 1984, for *The Flying Devils; Mejor Fotografia* (Spanish award), 1986, for *Barndommens gade;* ACE Award, National Cable Television Association, 1987, for *The Man Who Broke One Thousand Chains;* American Society of Cinematographers Award nomination, best cinematography—theatrical feature, and Academy Award nomination, cinematography, both 1989, for *The Abyss;* Academy Award nomination for visual effects, 1991, for *Backdraft.*

CREDITS:

FILM CINEMATOGRAPHER, EXCEPT AS NOTED

The Dreamers (also known as *Fantasterne* and *The Phantasts*), Saga, 1967.
Me and My Kid Brother (released as *Mig og min lillebror og Boelle,* 1970), Saga, 1974.
Welcome to the Club, Columbia, 1971.
Private Party (released as *Et doegn med Ilse,* 1971), Crone, 1976.
Why? (released as *Hvorfor goer De det?,* 1971), Palladium, 1977.
The Hottest Show in Town (released as *Min soesters boern, naar De er vaerst,* 1971), Saga, 1978.
Bedside Freeway (released as *Rektor paa sengekanten,* 1972), Palladium, 1977.
(Additional photography) *Zero Population Growth,* Sagittarius, 1972.

Three from Haparanda (also known as *De tre fraan Haparanda*), Sveriges Radio, 1973.
The Five (also known as *De fem*), Panorama, 1974.
Five on the Run (also known as *De fern paa flugt*), Panorama, 1975.
Kun Sandheden (also known as *Nothing but the Truth*), ASA, 1975.
The Owlfarm Brothers (also known as *Broedrene paa Uglegaarden*), ASA, 1975.
Violets Are Blue (released as *Violer er blaa,* 1975), ASA, 1980.
Hearts Are Trump (released as *Hjerter er Trumf,* 1975), ASA, 1983.
Magic in Town (also known as *Min soesters boern i byen*), Saga, 1976.
Cop (released as *Stroemer,* 1976), Metronome, 1982.
Pas paa ryggen, Professor! (also known as *Watch Your Back, Professor!*), Ulf Pilgaard, 1977.
(With Torbjoern Andersson) *Elvis! Elvis!,* Moviemakers/Swedish Film Institute/Sandrews, 1977.
Around the World, Svensk Filmindustri, 1978.
Behind Closed Doors, Closed Door Productions, 1979.
Threesome, Group One Films, 1979.
Tumult (also known as *Sonja 16 aar*), Athena, 1979.
The Baron (released as *Slaegten,* 1979), Panorama, 1984.
Tell It Like It Is, Boys, ASA, 1981.
Tintomare, Columbia, 1981.
The Marksman (also known as *Skytten*), Steen Herdel, 1983.
The Flying Devils (also known as *De flyvende djaevle*), Metronome, 1984.
Once a Cop . . . (also known as *Engang Stroemer . . .*), DR, 1985.
Barndommens gade (also known as *Street of My Childhood* and *Early Spring*), Metronome, 1986.
The Wolf at the Door (also known as *Oviri*), Manson, 1986.
Peter von Scholten, Warner Brothers/Metronome, 1987.
Zelly and Me, Columbia, 1988.
Stealing Heaven, New World, 1988.
Torch Song Trilogy, New Line Cinema, 1988.
The Abyss, Twentieth Century-Fox, 1989.
Always, Universal, 1989.
(And Gyrosphere operator) *Arachnophobia,* Buena Vista, 1990.
(And second unit visual effects photographer) *Backdraft,* Universal, 1991.
Far and Away, Universal, 1992.

Also cinematographer for *Motorvejdpaa Sengekanten,* 1972; performed aerial photography for *Time Out,* 1987.

TELEVISION CINEMATOGRAPHER

The Man Who Broke One Thousand Chains, HBO, 1987.

OTHER SOURCES:

PERIODICALS

American Cinematographer, May, 1991.
Cinefex, November, 1991.
Hollywood Reporter Craft Series: Cinematographers, February 19, 1991, pp. S-14-15.

* * *

SAMPSON, Bill
See ERMAN, John

* * *

SARANDON, Susan 1946-

PERSONAL: Full name, Susan Abigail Sarandon; born October 4, 1946, in New York, NY (one source says Edison, NJ); daughter of Phillip Leslie (a nightclub singer, television producer, and advertising executive) and Lenora Marie (Criscione) Tomalin (one source says Tomaling); married Chris Sarandon (an actor), September 16, 1967 (divorced, 1979); companion of Tim Robbins (an actor), 1988—; children: (with film director Franco Amurri) Eva Maria Livia Amurri, (with Robbins) one son. *Education:* Catholic University of America, B.A., drama and English, 1968.

ADDRESSES: Agent—Martha Luttrell, International Creative Management, 8899 Beverly Blvd., Los Angeles, CA 90048.

CAREER: Actress. Worked variously as a secretary, switchboard operator, house cleaner, and model; formed improvisational theatre group with Richard Dreyfuss, Peter Boyle, Andre Gregory, and other actors, in the 1980s.

MEMBER: Actors' Equity Association, Screen Actors Guild, American Federation of Television and Radio Artists, Academy of Motion Picture Arts and Sciences, National Organization of Women, Amnesty International, American Civil Liberties Union, Performing Artists for Nuclear Disarmament, Madre.

AWARDS, HONORS: Academy Award nomination, best actress, and Genie Award, best foreign actress, both 1981, for *Atlantic City;* named best actress, Venice Film Festival, 1982, for *Tempest;* Academy Award nomination, best actress, Golden Globe Award nomination, best actress in a drama, and British Academy of Film and Television Arts Award nomination, best actress in a leading role, all 1992, all for *Thelma and Louise.*

CREDITS:

FILM APPEARANCES

Melissa Compton, *Joe,* Cannon, 1970.
Sarah, *Lovin' Molly,* Columbia, 1974.
Peggy Grant, *The Front Page,* Universal, 1974.
Mary Beth, *The Great Waldo Pepper,* Universal, 1975.
Janet Weiss, *The Rocky Horror Picture Show,* Twentieth Century-Fox, 1975.
Chloe, *Dragonfly* (also known as *One Summer Love*), American International Pictures, 1976.
Catherine Douglas, *The Other Side of Midnight,* Twentieth Century-Fox, 1977.
Checkered Flag or Crash, Universal, 1978.
Ginny, *The Great Smokey Roadblock* (also known as *The Last of the Cowboys;* also see below), Dimension, 1978.
Rose, *King of the Gypsies,* Paramount, 1978.
Hattie, *Pretty Baby,* Warner Brothers, 1978.
Madeleine Ross, *Something Short of Paradise,* American International Pictures, 1979.
Sally, *Atlantic City,* Paramount, 1980.
Stephanie, *Loving Couples,* Twentieth Century-Fox, 1980.
Aretha, *Tempest,* Columbia, 1982.
Sarah Roberts, *The Hunger,* Metro-Goldwyn-Mayer (MGM)/United Artists (UA), 1983.
Emily, *The Buddy System,* Twentieth Century-Fox, 1984.
Judith Singer, *Compromising Positions,* Paramount, 1985.
Jane Spofford, *The Witches of Eastwick,* Warner Brothers, 1987.
Annie Savoy, *Bull Durham,* Orion, 1988.
Da Grande, Titanus, 1988.
Sandra Boon, *Sweet Heart's Dance,* Tri-Star, 1988.
Melanie Bruwer, *A Dry White Season,* MGM/UA, 1989.
Erik the Viking, Orion, 1989.
Christine Starkey, *The January Man,* MGM/UA, 1989.
Narrator, *The Monkey People* (documentary; originally released with different narrator as *Le Peuple singe*), Revcom, 1989.
Narrator, *Through the Wire* (documentary), Original Cinema, 1990.
Nora Baker, *White Palace,* Universal, 1990.
Louise Sawyer, *Thelma and Louise,* MGM/Pathe, 1991.
Ann, *Light Sleeper,* New Line Cinema, 1992.

Other appearances include *Lady Liberty,* 1972, C. C. Wainwright, *Crash,* 1976, *In Our Hands,* 1984, as Tawna Titan, *Bob Roberts,* 1992, and *Walk Away Madden.*

FILM WORK

Coproducer, *The Great Smokey Roadblock* (also known as *The Last of the Cowboys*), Dimension, 1978.

STAGE APPEARANCES

Interpreter/Tricia Nixon, *An Evening with Richard Nixon and. . . ,* Sam S. Shubert Theatre, New York City, 1972.
Maude Mix, *A Coupla White Chicks Sittin' around Talkin',* Astor Place Theatre, New York City, 1980-81.
Marjorie, *Extremities,* Westside Arts Center, New York City, 1982-83.

Also appeared in *A Stroll in the Air, Albert's Bridge,* and *Private Ear, Public Eye.*

TELEVISION APPEARANCES; MOVIES

Allie Calhoun, *F. Scott Fitzgerald and "The Last of the Belles,"* ABC, 1974.
Colonel Margaret Ann Jessup, *Women of Valor,* CBS, 1986.

Also appeared in *The Haunting of Rosalind,* 1973, and *The Satan Murders,* 1974.

TELEVISION APPEARANCES; MINISERIES

Livilla, *A.D.,* NBC, 1985.
Edda Ciano, *Mussolini: The Decline and Fall of Il Duce* (also known as *Mussolini and I*), HBO, 1985.

TELEVISION APPEARANCES; SPECIALS

Deborah Reed, *Lives of Benjamin Franklin: The Whirlwind,* CBS, 1974.
Host, *Your Water, Your Life* (documentary), PBS, 1988.
Host, *Postpartum: Beyond the Blues* (documentary; also known as *Postpartum: The Birth of the Blues* and *Signature*), Lifetime, 1989.
Comic Relief Four, HBO, 1990.
Living in America (interview), VH-1, 1990.
Narrator, *Primates: The Almost Human Animals* (documentary), The Disney Channel, 1991.
The Sixty-third Annual Academy Awards, ABC, 1991.
A User's Guide to Planet Earth: The American Environment Test (educational documentary), ABC, 1991.

TELEVISION APPEARANCES; SERIES

Patrice Kahlam, *A World Apart,* ABC, 1970-71.
Sarah Fairbanks, *Search for Tomorrow,* CBS, 1972-73.

TELEVISION APPEARANCES; EPISODIC

"The Rimers of Eldritch," *Playhouse New York,* PBS, 1972.
Calcucci's Department, CBS, 1973.
Eileen, "June Moon," *Theater in America,* PBS, 1974.
Owen Marshall, Counsellor at Law, 1981.
Helene Shaw, "Sense of Humor: Who Am I This Time," *American Playhouse,* PBS, 1982.

Beauty, "Beauty and the Beast," *Faerie Tale Theater,* Showtime, 1984.
"Dolores Huerta," *An American Portrait,* CBS, 1986.
"He'll See You Now," *Oxbridge Blues,* Arts and Entertainment, 1986.

RECORDINGS:

ALBUMS

The Rocky Horror Picture Show (original motion picture cast), Rhino, 1976, reissued, 1989, released as *The Rocky Horror Picture Show: Fifteenth Anniversary Box Set* (contains all recorded cast versions of the show, including motion picture and stage), 1990.

OTHER SOURCES:

BOOKS

Celebrity Register 1990, Simon & Schuster, 1990, p. 375.
Contemporary Newsmakers 1986 Cumulation, Gale, 1986, 345-47.

PERIODICALS

American Film, May, 1983, p. 30; May, 1991, p. 22.
Harper's Bazaar, July, 1983, p. 72; August, 1988, p. 122.
Interview, June, 1991, p. 104.
Mother Jones, February/March, 1989, p. 30.
New York Times, January 14, 1983.
Playboy, May, 1989, p. 63.
Premiere, May, 1988.
Rolling Stone, February 9, 1989, p. 39.
Time, December 17, 1984, p. 82.*

* * *

SARDE, Philippe 1945-

PERSONAL: Born June 21, 1945, in Neuilly-sur-Seine, France. *Education:* Attended the Paris Conservatory; studied with Noel Gallon.

ADDRESSES: *Agent*—Creative Artists Agency, 9830 Wilshire Blvd., Beverly Hills, CA 90212.

CAREER: Composer.

AWARDS, HONORS: Academy Award nomination, best original score, 1980, for *Tess;* Genie Award nomination, best music score, 1986, for *Joshua Then and Now.*

CREDITS:

FILM WORK

Music adaptation, *Des Enfants gates* (also see below), 1977, released in the U.S. as *Spoiled Children,* Corinth, 1977.
Music adaptation and song performer ("Like a Bird on the Wing"), *Loulou* (also see below), Gaumont, 1979.
Music adaptation (based on an eighteenth-century melody), *The Innocent* (also known as *Les Innocents;* also see below), Union Generale Cinematographique (UGC), c. 1987.
Music arranger of title theme and music adaptation, *Lost Angels* (also see below), Orion, 1989.
Music arranger, *Eve of Destruction* (also known as *L'Ange de la destruction;* also see below), Orion, 1991.

Also music arranger, *Un Dimanche a la compagne,* 1984.

WRITINGS:

FILM SCORES, EXCEPT WHERE INDICATED

Les Choses de la vie, 1970, released in the U.S. as *The Things of Life,* Columbia, 1970.
Le Chat, 1971, released in the U.S. as *The Cat,* Joseph Green, 1975.
Max et les ferrailleurs, CFDC, 1971.
Cesar and Rosalie (also known as *Cesar et Rosalie*), Cinema 5, 1972.
Le Fils (also known as *The Son*), Imperia Films, 1972.
Charlie et ses deux nenettes (also known as *Charlie and His Two Birds*), Societe Nouvelle, 1973.
Les Corps celestes (also known as *Heavenly Bodies*), Societe Nouvelle de Cinema, 1973.
La Grande Bouffe (originally released as *La grande abbuffata;* also known as *Blow-Out, The Big Feast, The Great Feed,* and *The Grande Bouffe*), ABCKO, 1973.
Le Train (released in the U.S. as *The Train*), Fox-Lira, 1973.
L'Horloger de Saint Paul, 1974, released in the U.S. as *The Clockmaker of St. Paul* (also known as *The Clockmaker*), Joseph Green, 1974.
Lancelot du Lac (also known as *Le Graal*), 1974, released in the U.S. as *Lancelot of the Lake* (also known as *The Grail*), CFDC-New Yorker Films, 1975.
Le Mariage a la mode (also known as *Marriage a la mode*), Societe Nouvelle de Cinema, 1974.
Les Seins de glace (also known as *Icy Breasts*), Fox-Lira, 1974.
Souvenirs d'en France (also known as *Inside Memories of France*), AMLF, 1974.
Touche pas a la femme blanche!, 1974, released in the U.S. as *Don't Touch White Women!,* CFDC, 1974.
La Valise (also known as *The Suitcase*), Gaumont, 1974.
Vincent, Francois, Paul . . . et l'autres, 1974, released in the U.S. as *Vincent, Francois, Paul and the Others,* Joseph Green, 1974.
Un Divorce heureux, UGC, 1975, released in the U.S. as *A Happy Divorce,* CFDC, 1975.
Histoire d'O (also known as *The Story of O*), Canon, 1975.
Un Sac de billes (also known as *A Bag of Marbles*), AMLF, 1975.
Barocco, Films La Boetie, c. 1976.

(And music and lyrics with Jean-Roger Cousimon) *Le Juge et l'assassin,* 1976, released in the U.S. as *The Judge and the Assassin,* Libra, 1979.

Le Juge Fayard dit le sheriff (also known as *Judge Fayard Called the Sheriff*), Gala Film, c. 1976.

Liza (also known as *La Cagna*), CRDC-Pathe-Sirus-Oceanic, 1976.

Le Locataire, 1976, released in the U.S. as *The Tenant,* Paramount, 1976.

Mado, Joseph Green, 1976.

Marie poupee (also known as *Marie the Doll*), Parafrance, 1976.

La Race des "seigneurs" (released in the U.S. as *The "Elite" Group*), Films La Boetie, 1976.

Sept morts par ordonnance (also known as *Seven Deaths by Prescription*), AMLF, 1976.

L'Ultima Donna (also known as *La Derniere Femme*), 1976, released in the U.S. as *The Last Woman,* Columbia, 1976.

Comme la lune (also known as *As the Moon*), Exportation Francaise Cinematographique, 1977.

Le Crabe Tambour, 1977, released in the U.S. by Interama, 1984.

Des Enfants gates, 1977, released in the U.S. as *Spoiled Children,* Corinth, 1977.

Le Diable, probablement, 1977, released in the U.S. as *The Devil, Probably,* Gaumont, 1977.

Un Moment d'egarement (also known as *A Summer Affair*), Roissy Films, 1977.

Mort d'un pourri (also known as *Morte di un operatore;* released in the U.S. as *Death of a Corrupt Man*), Adel, 1977.

Un Taxi mauve (released in the U.S. as *The Purple Taxi*), Davis Films, 1977.

La Vie devant soi, 1977, released in the U.S. as *Madame Rosa,* Warner Brothers-Columbia-New Line, 1977.

La Clef sur la porte (one source says *La Cle sur la porte;* released in the U.S. as *The Key Is in the Door*), Cineproduction, 1978.

Une Histoire simple, AMLF, 1978, released in the U.S. as *A Simple Story,* Quartet, 1979.

Ils sont fous ces sorciers, Lira, 1978.

Passe-montagne (released in the U.S. as *Mountain Pass*), Pari Films, 1978.

Reve de singe (also known as *Ciao maschio*), Gaumont, 1978, released in the U.S. as *Bye Bye Monkey,* Fida.

Les Soeurs Bronte, 1978, released in the U.S. as *The Bronte Sisters,* Gaumont, 1979.

Le Sucre (released in the U.S. as *The Sugar*), Gaumont, 1978.

The Adolescent (originally released as *L'Adolescente;* also known as *The Adolescent Girl*), Parafrance, c. 1979.

Chiedo asilo, 1979, released in the U.S. as *My Asylum,* Gaumont, 1979.

Flic ou voyou (released in the U.S. as *Cop or Hood*), Gaumont, 1979.

Song, *Loulou,* Gaumont, 1979.

Tess, Columbia, c. 1979.

Le Toubib (released in the U.S. as *The Medic*), Adel, 1979.

La Femme flic (also known as *The Woman Cop*), AMLF, 1980.

Un Mauvais Fils, Sara/Antenne-2, 1980.

Les Ailes de la colombe (also known as *Wings of the Dove*), Gaumont, 1981.

Beau pere, New Line, 1981.

Cher inconnue, 1981, released in the U.S. as *I Sent a Letter to My Love,* Atlantic, 1981.

Le Choix des armes, 1981, released in the U.S. as *Choice of Arms,* Parafrance, 1983.

Coup de torchon (released in the U.S. as *Clean Slate*), Parafrance, 1981.

Ghost Story, Universal, 1981.

La Guerre du feu, 1981, released in the U.S. as *The Quest for Fire,* Twentieth Century-Fox, 1982.

Storie di ordinaria follia, 1981, released in the U.S. as *Tales of Ordinary Madness,* Fred Baker, 1983.

Le Choc (also known as *The Shock*), UGC, 1982.

Hotel des Ameriques (also known as *Hotel of the Americas*), Parafrance, 1982.

Que les gros salaires levent le doight!!! (also known as *Will the High Salaried Workers Please Raise Their Hands!*), Parafrance, 1982.

L'Ami de Vincent (also known as *A Friend of Vincent*), AMLF, 1983.

Attention! Une femme peut en cacher une autre, 1983, released in the U.S. as *My Other Husband,* Triumph, 1985.

L'Etoile du nord, United Artists, c. 1983.

Garcon!, Sara/Renn Productions, 1983, released in the U.S. by AMLF, 1985.

J'ai epouse une ombre (released in the U.S. as *I Married a Shadow*), AMLF, 1983.

Lovesick, Warner Brothers, 1983.

Premiers desirs, AMLF, 1983.

Stella, Fox-Hachette, 1983.

The Story of Piera (also known as *Storia di Piera*) UGC, 1983.

L'Ete prochain (also known as *Next Summer*), Parafrance, 1984.

Fort Saganne, AAA, 1984.

La Garce, Sara, 1984.

Joyeuses paques, Sara, 1984.

La Pirate (also known as *The Pirate*), AMLF, 1984.

Ca n'arrive qu'a moi, Sara-Films A2, c. 1985.

Le Cowboy, A.S. Productions, 1985.

(With music of Ludwig van Beethoven and Amadeus Mozart) *Harem,* UGC, 1985.

L'Homme aus yeux d'argent, AAA-Revcom, 1985.

Hors la loi, Sara-Cerito, 1985.
Joshua Then and Now, Twentieth Century-Fox, 1985.
Rendezvous, Spectrafilm, 1985.
La Tentation d'Isabelle, MK2, 1985.
Cours prive (also known as *Private Classes*), Sara-CDF, 1986.
Devil in the Flesh, J.C. Williamson Film Management-World Film Alliance, c. 1986.
(And music and lyrics with Pierre Perret) *L'Etat de grace* (also known as *State of Grace*), AAA, 1986.
Everytime We Say Goodbye, Tri-Star, 1986.
The Manhattan Project (also known as *Manhattan Project: The Deadly Game*), Twentieth Century-Fox, 1986.
Mon beau-frere a tue ma soeur (also known as *My Brother-In-Law Has Killed My Sister*), World Marketing, c. 1986.
Pirates, Cannon, 1986.
La Puritaine (also known as *The Prude*), MK2, 1986.
Scene of the Crime (also known as *Le Lieu du crime*), Kino International, 1986.
(And music and lyrics with Caroline Huppert) *Sincerely Charlotte* (also known as *Signe Charlotte*), New Line, 1986.
Comedy! (also known as *Comedie!*), Sara-CDF, 1987.
De guerre lasse, Sara-CDF, c. 1987.
Les Deux Crocodiles (also known as *Two Crocodiles*), Sara-CDF, 1987.
Ennemis intimes (also known as *Intimate Enemies*), AAA, 1987.
L'Ete dernier a Tanger (also known as *Last Summer in Tangiers*), AAA, 1987.
Funny Boy, Jupiter Communications, 1987.
The Innocent (also known as *Les Innocents*), UGC, c. 1987.
Les Mois d'avril sont meurtriers (also known as *April Is a Deadly Month*), Sara-CDF, 1987.
Noyade interdite (also known as *Widow's Walk*), Bac, 1987.
Poker, Sara-CDF, 1987.
A Few Days with Me (also known as *Quelques jours avec moi*), Galaxy International, 1988.
La Couleur du vent, Bac, 1988.
La Maison assassinee, Gaumont, 1988.
La Maison de jade, AAA, 1988.
Mangeclous, AAA, 1988.
L'Ours, AMLF, 1988.
La Travestie, AAA, 1988.
The Bear, Tri-Star, 1989.
Chambre a part (also known as *Separate Bedrooms*), UGC/Flach Films, 1989.
L'Invite surprise (also known as *The Surprise Guest* and *The Surprise Invitation*), Gaumont, 1989.
Lost Angels, Orion, 1989.
Music Box, Tri-Star, 1989.
Reunion, Films Ariadne, 1989.
Winter of '54: Father Pierre (also known as *Hiver 54, l'abbe Pierre, Hiver 54, Abbe Pierre, Winter 54,* and *L'Abbe Pierre*), Circle Releasing Corporation, 1989.
La Baule les pins, UGC, 1990, released in the U.S. as *C'est la vie,* Samuel Goldwyn, 1990.
Faux et usage de faux (also known as *Forgery and the Use of Forgeries*), UGC, 1990.
La Fille des collines (also known as *La figlia delle colline* and *The Hill Girl*), UGC, 1990.
Lord of the Flies, Columbia, 1990.
Lung Ta: Riders on the Wind (also known as *Lung Ta: Les Cavaliers du vent, Lung Ta: Forgotten Tibet, Les Cavaliers du vent,* and *Riders on the Wind*), Zeitgeist Films, 1990.
Le Petit Criminel (also known as *The Little Gangster* and *Little Criminal*), AMLF, 1990.
Eve of Destruction (also known as *L'Ange de la destruction*), Orion, 1991.
Jalousie (also known as *Jealousy*), Bac, 1991.
J'embrasse pas (also known as *I Don't Kiss*), Bac, 1991.
Pour Sacha (also known as *For Sacha*), UGC, 1991.
La Tribu (also known as *The Tribe*), AAA, 1991.

Also composer for *La Liberte en croupe,* 1970; *Sortie de secours,* 1970; *Le Droit a aimer* (released in the U.S. as *The Right to Love*), 1972; *Dorothea,* 1974; *La Cage,* 1975; *Deux hommes dans la ville,* 1975; *Folle a tuer,* 1975; *Les Galettes de Pont Aven,* 1975; *Pas de problemes,* 1975; *Adieu poulet,* 1976; *On aura tout vu!* (also known as *The Bottom Line*), 1976; *Violette et Francois* (released in the U.S. as *Violette and Francois*), 1977; *Es-ce bien raisonnable?,* 1980; and *Il faut tuer Birgitt Haas* (released in the U.S. as *Birgitt Haas Must Be Killed*), 1981.*

* * *

SAVANT, Doug

PERSONAL: Born in Burbank, CA. *Education:* Attended University of California, Los Angeles.

ADDRESSES: *Agent*—J. Michael Bloom, 9200 Sunset Blvd., Suite 710, Los Angeles, CA 90069.

CAREER: Actor.

MEMBER: Screen Actors Guild.

CREDITS:

FILM APPEARANCES

Boy, *Secret Admirer,* Orion, 1985.
Brad, *Teen Wolf,* Atlantic Releasing, 1985.
Tim Hainey, *Trick or Treat,* De Laurentiis Entertainment Group, 1986.
Ashby, *The Hanoi Hilton,* Cannon, 1987.

Mike McGill, *Masquerade,* Metro-Goldwyn-Mayer/United Artists, 1988.
Eric Kinsley, *Paint It Black,* Vestron, 1989.
Attila, *Red Surf,* Arrowhead, 1990.

Also appeared in *Shaking the Tree,* 1990.

TELEVISION APPEARANCES; MOVIES

The Knife and Gun Club, ABC, 1990.
Jeff Colburn, *Aftermath: A Test of Love,* CBS, 1991.

TELEVISION APPEARANCES; SERIES

Appeared as Mack Mackenzie, *Knots Landing,* CBS; also appeared in *Best Times.*

TELEVISION APPEARANCES; EPISODIC

Appeared on episodes of *Cagney and Lacey,* CBS, and *Hotel,* ABC.

STAGE APPEARANCES

Appeared in a community theater production of *Hello Dolly!**

*   *   *

SAWYER, Diane 1945-

PERSONAL: Born December 22, 1945, in Glasgow, KY; daughter of E. P. (a county judge) and Jean W. (an elementary school teacher; maiden name, Dunagan) Sawyer; married Mike Nichols (a producer and director), April 29, 1988. *Education:* Wellesley College, B.A., 1967; attended University of Louisville Law School. *Avocational interests:* Reading (especially nineteenth-century novels), watching films, singing.

ADDRESSES: Office—1965 Broadway, New York, NY 10023.

CAREER: Broadcast journalist. WLKY-TV, Louisville, KY, weather reporter and general reporter, 1967-70; assistant to White House Deputy Press Secretary Jerry Warren, assistant to White House Press Secretary Ron Ziegler, and assistant to President Richard M. Nixon, Washington, DC, 1970-74; researcher for Nixon's memoirs, San Clemente, CA, 1974-78; CBS-News, New York City, general assignment reporter and State Department correspondent, 1978-81.

MEMBER: Council on Foreign Relations.

AWARDS, HONORS: Selected America's Young Woman of the Year (also known as America's Junior Miss), 1963; Emmy Award nominations, news and documentary program segment, 1979, for "Hostages—300 Days," and interview segment, 1981, for "Richard Nixon," both *CBS Morning News;* Emmy Award nomination, interview segment, 1983, for "Admiral Rickover," *60 Minutes;* Matrix Award, New York chapter of Women in Communications, 1984; Emmy Award nominations, interview segments, 1986, for "Dancing on Her Grave," and 1987, for "The City of Garbage—Sister Emanuelle," both *60 Minutes;* Peabody Award for public service, 1989; Emmy Award nominations, investigative journalism segment, for "The Second Battlefield," interview segment, for "Katherine the Great," and coverage of a continuing news story, for "Murder in Beverly Hills," all 1991, *PrimeTime Live.*

CREDITS:

TELEVISION APPEARANCES; SERIES

Co-anchor, *CBS Morning News,* CBS, 1981-84.
Correspondent, *60 Minutes,* CBS, 1984-89.
Co-anchor, *PrimeTime Live,* ABC, 1989—.

TELEVISION APPEARANCES; SPECIALS

David Letterman's Second Annual Holiday Film Festival, NBC, 1986.
48 Hours on Crack Street, CBS, 1986.
The Soviet Union—Seven Days in May, CBS, 1987.
The Television Academy Hall of Fame, FOX, 1990.
Edward R. Murrow: This Reporter, PBS, 1990.

TELEVISION APPEARANCES; EPISODIC

Occasional correspondent for *The American Parade,* 1984, and *Walter Cronkite's Universe.*

OTHER SOURCES:

BOOKS

Contemporary Authors, Volume 115, Gale, 1985.

PERIODICALS

Harper's Bazaar, November, 1984, p. 232.
Interview, September, 1984, p. 100.
Life, August, 1989, p. 72.
New York Times, September 30, 1981.
People, November 5, 1984, p. 78.*

*   *   *

SCHAFER, Natalie 1900-1991

OBITUARY NOTICE—See index for *CTFT* sketch: Born November 5, 1900, in Red Bank, NJ (some sources say New York, NY); died of cancer, April 10, 1991, in Beverly Hills, CA. Actress. Schafer was best known for her role as Lovey Howell in the CBS television comedy series *Gilligan's Island,* which originally aired from 1964 to 1967 and is still in syndication. She revived that character in three reunion episodes in 1978, 1979, and 1981. Among her stage credits are supporting roles in the Broadway productions *Lady in the Dark, Susan and God,* and *The Doughgirls.* Schafer made her film debut in the mid-1940s, appearing with Lana Turner in *Marriage Is a Private Affair;* she again worked with Turner in the film *Keep Your Powder Dry* in 1945 and in the short-lived television series *The Survivors* from 1969 to 1970. Popular as a character actress, Schafer often portrayed wealthy socialites. Her other credits include appearances in the films *Wonder Man, The Snake Pit, Secret Beyond the Door, The Day of the Locust, Beverly Hills Brats,* and *Forever, Darling,* and guest roles in television sitcoms and drama series, including *I Love Lucy, Route 66, 77 Sunset Strip, The Brady Bunch,* and *The Beverly Hillbillies.* She performed for the last time in 1990, appearing in the cable film *I'm Dangerous Tonight.* Schafer was also author of an episode for the television series *The Love Boat.*

OBITUARIES AND OTHER SOURCES:

BOOKS

International Motion Picture Almanac, edited by Richard Gertner, Quigley, 1991, p. 284.

PERIODICALS

Hollywood Reporter, April 12, 1991, pp. 3, 70.
Variety, April 15, 1991, p. 218.

* * *

SCHICKEL, Richard 1933-

PERSONAL: Full name, Richard Warren Schickel; born February 10, 1933, in Milwaukee, WI; son of Edward John and Helen (Hendricks) Schickel; married Julia Carroll Whedon, March 11, 1960 (divorced); married Carol Rubinstein, December 27, 1985 (deceased); children: (first marriage) Erika, Jessica. *Education:* University of Wisconsin, B.S., 1956, graduate study, 1956-57.

ADDRESSES: Home—Los Angeles, CA. *Office—Time,* Rockefeller Center, New York, NY 10020; Legal Productions, 1551 South Robertson, Los Angeles, CA 90036. *Agent*—Don Congdon Associates, 156 Fifth Ave., New York, NY 10010.

CAREER: Sports Illustrated, New York City, reporter, 1956-57; *Look,* New York City, senior editor, 1957-60; *Show,* New York City, senior editor, 1960-62, book columnist, 1963-64; NBC-TV, book critic for *Sunday,* 1963-64; Rockefeller Brothers Fund, New York City, consultant, 1965; *Life,* New York City, film reviewer, 1965-72; *Time,* New York City, film reviewer, 1972—. Lecturer in art history, Yale University, 1972 and 1976.

MEMBER: National Society of Film Critics, Writers Guild of America, Directors Guild of America, New York Film Critics.

AWARDS, HONORS: New Republic Young Writer Award, 1959; Guggenheim fellowship, 1964-65; Emmy Award nomination, documentary program achievement, 1973, for *The Men Who Made the Movies;* Emmy Award nomination, outstanding program achievement, 1976, for *Life Goes to the Movies: The Big Event;* British Film Institute Book Award, 1985, and Theatre Library Association Award, 1987, both for *D. W. Griffith: An American Life;* Emmy Award nomination, outstanding informational special, 1987, for *Minnelli on Minnelli: Liza Remembers Vincente.*

CREDITS:

TELEVISION PRODUCER; SPECIALS

Hollywood: You Must Remember This (also see below), PBS, 1972.

(And director) *The Men Who Made the Movies* (eight parts; also see below), PBS, 1973.

Life Goes to the Movies: The Big Event (also see below), NBC, 1976.

The Making of "Star Wars" (also see below), ABC, 1976.

(And director) *Into the Morning: Willa Cather's America* (also see below), PBS, 1978.

(And director) *Funny Business* (also see below), CBS, 1978.

(And director) *The Horror Show* (also see below), CBS, 1979.

SPFX: The Making of "The Empire Strikes Back" (also see below), CBS, 1980.

(And director) *James Cagney: That Yankee Doodle Dandy* (also see below), PBS, 1981.

From Star Wars to Jedi: The Making of a Saga (also see below), CBS, 1983.

(And director) *Minnelli on Minnelli: Liza Remembers Vincente,* PBS, 1987.

Cary Grant: A Celebration (also see below), ABC, 1988.

(And director) *Gary Cooper: American Life, American Legend* (also see below), TNT, 1989.

(And director) *Myrna Loy: So Nice to Come Home To* (also see below), TNT, 1990.

(And director) *Barbara Stanwyck: Fire and Desire* (also see below), TNT, 1991.

Segment producer of "Akira Kurosawa," *The 62nd Annual Academy Awards Presentation,* 1990; "Myrna Loy and Zanuck/Brown Tribute Films," *The 63rd Annual Academy Awards Presentation,* 1991; and "Satyajit Ray," *The 64th Annual Academy Awards Presentation,* 1992.

WRITINGS:

BOOKS

The World of Carnegie Hall, Messner, 1960.
The Stars, Dial, 1962.
Movies: The History of an Art and an Institution, Basic Books, 1964.
The Gentle Knight (juvenile), Abelard, 1964.
(With Lena Horne) *Lena,* Doubleday, 1965.
The World of Goya, Time-Life, 1968.
(Editor with John Simon) *Film 67/68,* Simon & Schuster, 1968.
The Disney Version: The Life, Times, Art, and Commerce of Walt Disney, Simon & Schuster, 1972, revised edition, Touchstone, 1985.
His Pictures in the Papers, Charterhouse, 1973.
Harold Lloyd: The Shape of Laughter, New York Graphic Society, 1974.
(With Bob Willoughby) *The Platinum Years,* Random House, 1974.
The Men Who Made the Movies, Atheneum, 1975.
The World of Tennis, Random House, 1975.
(With Douglas Fairbanks, Jr.) *The Fairbanks Album,* New York Graphic Society, 1976.
Another I, Another You: A Love Story for the Once Married, Harper, 1978.
Singled Out, Viking, 1981.
Cary Grant: A Celebration, Little, Brown, 1983.
D. W. Griffith: An American Life, Simon & Schuster, 1984.
Intimate Strangers: The Culture of Celebrity, Doubleday, 1985.
James Cagney: A Celebration, Little, Brown, 1985.
(With Michael Walsh) *Carnegie Hall: The First One Hundred Years,* Abrams, 1987.
Schickel on Film, Morrow, 1989.
(With Sid Avery) *Hollywood at Home,* Crown, 1990.
Marlon Brando: A Life in Our Times, Atheneum, 1991.
Double Indemnity, British Film Institute, 1992.

Also author of *Second Sight: Notes on Some Movies,* 1972, and *Striking Poses,* 1987.

TELEVISION SCRIPTS; SPECIALS, EXCEPT AS NOTED

The Film Generation, PBS, 1969.
The Movie-Crazy Years, PBS, 1971.
Hollywood: You Must Remember This, PBS, 1972.
The Men Who Made the Movies (eight parts), PBS, 1973.
Life Goes to the Movies: The Big Event, NBC, 1976.
The Making of "Star Wars," ABC, 1976.
The Coral Jungle (series), syndicated, 1976.
Into the Morning: Willa Cather's America, PBS, 1978.
Funny Business, CBS, 1978.
The Horror Show, CBS, 1979.
SPFX: The Making of "The Empire Strikes Back," CBS, 1980.
James Cagney: That Yankee Doodle Dandy, PBS, 1981.
From Star Wars to Jedi: The Making of a Saga, CBS, 1983.
Cary Grant: A Celebration, ABC, 1988.
Gary Cooper: American Life, American Legend, TNT, 1989.
Myrna Loy: So Nice to Come Home To, TNT, 1990.
Barbara Stanwyck: Fire and Desire, TNT, 1991.

Also writer for *Happy Anniversary 007—25 Years of James Bond,* 1987.

* * *

SCHULTZ, Michael A. 1938-

PERSONAL: Born November 10, 1938, in Milwaukee, WI; son of Leo and Katherine Frances (Leslie) Schultz; married Gloria Lauren Jones. *Education:* Marquette University, B.F.A (theater).

ADDRESSES: Office—P.O. Box 1940, Santa Monica, CA 90406. *Agent*—Shapiro & Lobell, 111 West 40th Street, New York, NY 10018.

CAREER: Director and producer of theatre, film, and television productions.

AWARDS, HONORS: Obie Award, *Village Voice,* best direction, 1968, for *Song of the Lusitanian Bogey;* Antoinette Perry Award nomination, best director of a dramatic play, and Drama Desk Award, outstanding director, both 1969, both for *Does a Tiger Wear a Necktie?;* inductee, Black Filmmakers Hall of Fame, 1991; Lifetime Achievement Award, Miami International Coproduction Film Conference, 1992. Honorary Ph.D., Emerson University, 1984.

Schultz also received the Christopher Award for *Ceremonies in Dark Old Men.*

CREDITS:

STAGE APPEARANCES

Francesco, "Benito Cereno," *The Old Glory* (also see below), American Place Theatre, New York City, 1964, then Theatre De Lys, New York City, 1965.

STAGE DIRECTOR, EXCEPT WHERE INDICATED

Stage manager, *The Old Glory,* American Place Theatre, 1964, then Theatre De Lys, both New York City, 1965.
Stage manager, *Command Performance,* Maidman Playhouse, 1966.
Waiting for Godot, McCarter Theatre, Princeton, NJ, 1966.

Lighting Director, *Daddy Goodness,* Negro Ensemble Company, St. Mark's Playhouse, New York City, 1968.

Song of the Lusitanian Bogey, Negro Ensemble Company, St. Mark's Playhouse, then London, England, both 1968.

Kongi's Harvest, Negro Ensemble Company, St. Mark's Playhouse, 1968.

God is a (Guess What?), Negro Ensemble Company, St. Mark's Playhouse, 1968-69.

Does a Tiger Wear a Necktie?, Eugene O'Neill Memorial Theatre, Waterford, CT, then Belasco Theatre, New York City, both 1969.

The Reckoning, St. Mark's Playhouse, 1969.

Every Night When the Sun Goes Down, Eugene O'Neill Memorial Theatre, 1969.

The Dream on Monkey Mountain, Eugene O'Neill Memorial Theatre, 1969, then Mark Taper Forum Theatre, 1970, later St. Mark's Playhouse, 1971.

Operation Sidewinder, Vivian Beaumont Theatre, New York City, then Mark Taper Forum Theatre, Los Angeles, both 1970.

Sambo, Mobile Theatre (travelling outdoor performances throughout New York City), 1970.

Woyzeck, St. Mark's Playhouse, 1970.

The Three Sisters, Westport Country Playhouse, Westport, CT, 1973.

Thoughts, Westport Country Playhouse, then Theatre De Lys, both 1973.

The Poison Tree, Westport Country Playhouse, 1973.

The Cherry Orchard, Anspacher Theatre, New York City, 1973.

What the Winesellers Buy, Mark Taper Forum Theatre, then Vivian Beaumont Theatre, later New Theatre for Now, Los Angeles, all 1974.

Mulebone, Helen Hayes Public Theatre at Lincoln Center, New York City, 1991.

FILM DIRECTOR

Together for Days (also known as *Black Cream*), Olas, 1972.

Honeybaby, Honeybaby, Kelly/Jordan, 1974.

Cooley High, American International, 1975.

Car Wash, Universal, 1976.

Greased Lightning, Warner Brothers, 1977.

Which Way is Up?, Universal, 1977.

Sgt. Pepper's Lonely Hearts Club Band, Universal, 1978.

Scavenger Hunt, Twentieth Century-Fox, 1979.

Carbon Copy, Avco Embassy, 1981.

Bustin' Loose, Universal, 1983.

The Last Dragon, Tri-Star, 1985.

(And producer; with Doug McHenry) *Krush Groove,* Warner Bros., 1985.

(And producer; with George Jackson) *Disorderlies,* Warner Bros., 1987.

Livin' Large, Samuel Goldwyn/Night Life, 1991.

TELEVISION DIRECTOR

Toma (series), ABC, 1973.

Movin' On (series), NBC, 1974.

The Rockford Files (series), NBC, 1974.

Change at 125th Street (pilot), CBS, 1974.

Baretta (series), ABC, 1975.

Starsky & Hutch (series), ABC, c. 1977.

(And producer) *Earth, Wind and Fire in Concert* (special), HBO, 1982.

Benny's Place (movie), ABC, 1982.

The Jerk, Too (pilot), NBC, 1984.

Timestalkers (movie), CBS, 1986.

The Spirit (movie), ABC, 1987.

Rock 'n' Roll Mom (movie; segment of *Disney Sunday Movie*), ABC, 1988.

Tarzan in Manhattan (movie), CBS, 1989.

Jury Duty: The Comedy (movie), ABC, 1990.

Hammer, Slammer, and Slade (pilot), ABC, 1990.

Dayo, NBC, 1992.

Also director of *To Be Young, Gifted, and Black,* 1972, *Carbon Copy,* 1981, and *For Us the Living,* 1983. Director of documentary, *Fade Out—The Erosion of Black Images in the Media,* and *Ceremonies in Dark Old Men.*

* * *

SCIORRA, Annabella

PERSONAL: Born near Hartford, CT; daughter of a veterinarian.

ADDRESSES: Agent—International Creative Management, 8899 Beverly Blvd., Los Angeles, CA 90048.

CAREER: Actress.

MEMBER: Screen Actors Guild.

CREDITS:

FILM APPEARANCES

Donna, *True Love,* Metro-Goldwyn-Mayer/United Artists, 1989.

Heather Peck, *Internal Affairs,* Paramount, 1990.

Donna, *Cadillac Man,* Orion, 1990.

Carol, *Reversal of Fortune,* Warner Brothers, 1990.

Susan, *The Hard Way,* Universal, 1991.

Angela Tucci, *Jungle Fever,* Universal, 1991.

Claire Bartel, *The Hand That Rocks the Cradle,* Buena Vista, 1991.

TELEVISION APPEARANCES; MOVIES

Octavia, *Mario Puzo's The Fortunate Pilgrim* (also known as *Mamma Lucia*), NBC, 1988.

TELEVISION APPEARANCES; EPISODIC

Nicole, "Prison Stories: Women on the Inside," *HBO Showcase,* 1991.

OTHER SOURCES:

PERIODICALS

Interview, April, 1991, pp. 119, 128.
Premiere, October, 1991, p. 59.*

* * *

SCOTT, Martha 1914(?)-

PERSONAL: Full name, Martha Ellen Scott; born September 22, 1914 (some sources list 1916), in Jamesport, MO; daughter of Walter (a farmer and maintenance engineer) and Letha (McKinley) Scott; married Carleton W. Alsop (a radio and film producer), September 16, 1940 (marriage dissolved, July 23, 1946); married Mel Powell (a composer, pianist, and educator), 1946; children: (first marriage) one son; (second marriage) two daughters. *Education:* University of Michigan, B.A., 1934.

ADDRESSES: Agent—Bresler, Wolf, Cota, Livingston, 190 North Canon Dr., Beverly Hills, CA 90210. *Contact*—14054 Chandler Blvd., Van Nuys, CA 91401.

CAREER: Actor and producer. Began career as actor in eastern U.S. regional theaters; performer in radio programs, 1936-38; acted in stock productions in Michigan and Massachusetts in the 1930s; organized and served as a director of the Plumstead Playhouse production company, 1969.

MEMBER: Actors Equity Association, American Federation of Television and Radio Artists, Screen Actors Guild.

AWARDS, HONORS: Academy Award nomination, best actress, 1940, for *Our Town.*

CREDITS:

STAGE APPEARANCES

Cordelia, *King Lear,* Globe Theatre, World's Fair, Chicago, IL, 1934.
Bianca, *The Taming of the Shrew,* Globe Theatre, 1934.
Hermia, *A Midsummer Night's Dream,* Globe Theatre, 1934.
Celia, *As You Like It,* Globe Theatre, 1934.
Witch, *Macbeth,* Globe Theatre, 1934.
Hero, *Much Ado about Nothing,* Globe Theatre, 1934.
(Broadway debut) Emily Webb, *Our Town,* Henry Miller Theatre, New York City, 1938, then City Center, New York City, 1944.
Seventh Heaven, Bucks County Playhouse, New Hope, PA, 1939.
Girl, *Foreigners,* Belasco Theatre, New York City, 1939.
Mara Sutro, *The Willow and I,* Windsor Theatre, New York City, 1942.
Katherine Rogers, *Soldier's Wife,* John Golden Theatre, New York City, 1944.
Sally Middleton, *The Voice of the Turtle,* Morosco Theatre, New York City, 1945.
Connie Frazier, *It Takes Two,* Biltmore Theatre, New York City, 1947.
Margaret Clitherow, *Design for a Stained Glass Window,* Mansfield Theatre, New York City, 1950.
Nancy Willard, *Gramercy Ghost,* Morosco Theatre, 1951.
Sylvia, *The Number,* Biltmore, 1951.
Ellen Turner, *The Male Animal* (also see below), City Center, 1952, then Music Box, New York City, 1952.
Ma Pennypacker, *The Remarkable Mr. Pennypacker,* Coronet Theatre, Los Angeles, CA, 1953.
Mary Reece, *Cloud Seven,* John Golden Theatre, 1958.
Lucy Greer, *A Distant Bell,* Eugene O'Neill Theatre, New York City, 1960.
Nina, *The Tumbler,* Helen Hayes Theatre, New York City, 1960.
Fanny Lowe, *The Forty-ninth Cousin,* Ambassador Theatre, New York City, 1960-61.
Lillian Hudson, *Future Perfect,* Cape Playhouse, Dennis, MA, 1961.
Mattie Martin, *Open Book,* Pasadena Playhouse, Los Angeles, CA, 1963.
Edith Lambert, *Never Too Late,* Playhouse, New York City, 1964.
Nettie Cleary, *The Subject Was Roses* (also see below), Royale Theatre, New York City, 1965.
Mrs. Antrobus, *The Skin of Our Teeth,* Eisenhower Theatre, John F. Kennedy Center, Washington, DC, 1975, then Mark Hellinger Theatre, New York City, 1975.
Rebecca Nurse, *The Crucible,* Belasco Theatre, New York City, 1991-92.

Acted in various summer theatre productions, including such roles as Elizabeth Barrett in *The Barretts of Wimpole Street,* 1947, and Stella Hallam in *Another Language,* 1950; also appeared in a production of *Please Do Not Disturb* at the Locust Valley Playhouse in New York.

STAGE WORK; PRODUCER

(With Plumstead Playhouse) *Our Town,* ANTA Theatre, New York City, 1969.
(With Joel Spector and Bernard Wiesen) *First Monday in October,* Majestic Theatre, New York City, 1978.

Also theatre producer with Henry Fonda and Alfred De Liagre at the Kennedy Center, 1968.

MAJOR TOURS

Ellen Turner, *The Male Animal,* U.S. cities, 1953.

Toured in summer stock productions as Mary in *The Complaisant Lover,* 1962, and as Pamela Pew-Pickett in *Tchin-Tchin,* 1963. Toured with production of *The Subject Was Roses.*

RADIO APPEARANCES

Pepper Young's Family, NBC, 1937.
The Career of Alice Blair, Mutual, 1937-38.
John's Other Wife, NBC, 1937-38.

Debuted on radio as a "ten buck scream" on a ghost story with Orson Welles, on CBS.

FILM APPEARANCES

(Film debut) Emily Webb, *Our Town,* United Artists (UA), 1940.
Jane Peyton Howard, *The Howards of Virginia* (released in England as *Tree of Liberty*), Columbia, 1940.
Ella Bishop, *Cheers for Miss Bishop,* UA, 1941.
Hope Morris Spence, *One Foot in Heaven,* Warner Brothers, 1941.
Marta Keller, *They Dare Not Love,* Columbia, 1941.
Janie Prescott, *Hi Diddle Diddle* (also known as *Diamonds and Crime* and *Try and Find It*), UA, 1943.
Catherine Allen, *In Old Oklahoma* (also known as *War of the Wildcats*), Republic, 1943.
Stage Door Canteen, UA, 1943.
Olivia, *So Well Remembered,* RKO Radio Pictures (RKO), 1947.
Georgia Wilson, *Strange Bargain,* RKO, 1949.
Mother Reed, *When I Grow Up,* Eagle-Lion, 1951.
Eleanor Hilliard, *The Desperate Hours,* Paramount, 1955.
Yochabel, *The Ten Commandments,* Paramount, 1956.
Lottie Graham, *Eighteen and Anxious* (also known as *No Greater Sin*), Republic, 1957.
Mrs. Webster, *Sayonara,* Warner Brothers, 1957.
Miriam, *Ben Hur,* Metro-Goldwyn-Mayer, 1959.
Voice of Mrs. Arable, *Charlotte's Web* (animated film), Paramount, 1973.
Sister Beatrice, *Airport 1975,* Universal, 1974.
Adelaide, *The Turning Point,* Twentieth Century-Fox, 1977.
Virginia Camalier, *Doin' Time on Planet Earth,* Cannon, 1989.

FILM WORK; PRODUCER

(With Paul Heller) *First Monday in October,* Paramount, 1981.

TELEVISION APPEARANCES; EPISODIC

Lights Out, NBC, 1946, 1949-52.
Teller of Tales, CBS, 1950-51, NBC, 1951.
The Web, CBS, 1950-54.
Ben Hecht's Tales of the City, CBS, 1953.
Revlon Mirror Theater, NBC, 1953, CBS, 1953.
Omnibus, CBS, 1955.
"Give and Take," *Robert Montgomery Presents,* NBC, 1957.
"A Trip to Paradise," *Playhouse Ninety,* CBS, 1959.
Kit Tyler, pilot episode, *You're Only Young Twice,* CBS, 1960.
"The Wooden Dish," *Play of the Week,* WNTA, 1961.
Route Sixty-six (series), CBS, 1962.
The Nurses (series), CBS, 1963.
Greatest Show on Earth, ABC, 1963.
"Two Faces of Treason," *Dupont Show of the Month,* NBC, 1963.
Cimmarron Strip (series), CBS, 1967.
The F.B.I. (series), ABC, 1967.
Ironside (series), NBC, 1969.
Paris 7000 (series), ABC, 1970.
Longstreet (series), ABC, 1971.
"Lemonade," *Hollywood Television Theatre,* PBS, 1971.
The Delphi Bureau (series), ABC, 1972.
Murder in the First Person Singular, ABC, 1972.
Suzy's mother, pilot episode, *My Wife Next Door,* NBC, 1975.
Betty Robbins, pilot episode, *A Girl's Life,* ABC, 1989.

Also appeared in episodes of *Lux Video Theatre, Murder She Wrote,* CBS, *Hotel,* ABC, and *Columbo,* NBC.

TELEVISION APPEARANCES; SERIES, EXCEPT WHERE NOTED

Host/narrator (with Mel Brandt), *Modern Romances* (serial), NBC, 1954-58.
Martha Hartley, *The Bob Newhart Show,* CBS, 1972-78.
Helen Elgin, *The Bionic Woman,* ABC, 1976-77, NBC, 1977-78.
Mrs. Shepard, *Dallas,* NBC, 1978-91.
Sarah Randall, *The Word* (mini-series), CBS, 1978.
Elizabeth Gorey, *Married: The First Year,* CBS, 1979.
Penelope, *Beulah Land* (mini-series), NBC, 1980.
Margaret Millington, *Secrets of Midland Heights,* CBS, 1980-81.

TELEVISION APPEARANCES; MOVIES

Mrs. Stone, *The Devil's Daughter,* ABC, 1973.
Mrs. Reynolds, *Thursday's Game,* ABC, 1974.
Mother Michael, *The Abduction of Saint Anne,* ABC, 1975.
Miss McDonald, *Medical Story,* NBC, 1975.
Mrs. Farrell/Aunt Louisa, *Charleston,* NBC, 1979.
Hilda Wollman, *Father Figure,* CBS, 1980.

Gram Walsh, *Adam,* NBC, 1983.
Martina Shelburne, *Summer Girl,* CBS, 1983.
Gram Walsh, *Adam: His Song Continues,* NBC, 1986.
Genger, *Love and Betrayal* (also known as *Throwaway Wives*), CBS, 1989.
Sarah, *Daughter of the Streets,* ABC, 1990.

TELEVISION APPEARANCES; SPECIALS

"William Holden: The Golden Boy," *Crazy about the Movies,* Cinemax, 1989.

Played Mummsie in *The Legendary Curse of the Hope Diamond,* 1975.

OTHER SOURCES:

PERIODICALS

Life, December, 1984, p. 9.*

* * *

SEAGAL, Steven 1952-

PERSONAL: Born in 1952; married Kelly LeBrock (an actress and model). *Education:* Studied martial arts under masters in Japan.

ADDRESSES: *Agent*—Todd Smith, Creative Artists Agency, 9830 Wilshire Blvd., Beverly Hills, CA 90212. *Publicity*—Paul Bloch, Rogers and Cowan, 122 East Forty-second St., New York, NY 10168.

CAREER: Actor, writer, producer, and martial arts expert. Earned black belt in numerous martial arts disciplines, including karate and aikido; became first non-Asian to open a martial arts academy in Japan; worked as fight scene choreographer for motion pictures; worked in international security and personal protection; opened Aikido Ten Shin Dojo, a martial arts academy in Los Angeles, CA.

MEMBER: Screen Actors Guild.

CREDITS:

FILM APPEARANCES

(Film debut) Nico Toscani, *Above the Law* (also see below), Warner Brothers, 1988.
Mason Storm, *Hard to Kill* (also see below), Warner Brothers, 1990.
John Hatcher, *Marked for Death* (also known as *Screwface;* also see below), Twentieth Century-Fox, 1990.
Gino Felino, *Out for Justice* (also known as *The Price of Our Blood* and *The Night;* also see below), Warner Brothers, 1991.

FILM WORK; PRODUCER

(With Andrew Davis) *Above the Law* (based on story by Seagal and Davis; also see below), Warner Brothers, 1988.
(With Michael Grais and Mark Victor) *Marked for Death* (also see below), Twentieth Century-Fox, 1990.
(With Arnold Kopelson) *Out for Justice,* Warner Brothers, 1991.

FILM WORK; MARTIAL ARTS CHOREOGRAPHER/ COORDINATOR

The Challenge, Rank Film Distributors, 1982.
Above the Law, Warner Brothers, 1988.
Hard to Kill, Warner Brothers, 1990.
Marked for Death, Twentieth Century-Fox, 1990.

TELEVISION APPEARANCES

Naked Hollywood (also known as *A&E Premieres*), Arts and Entertainment, 1991.
Guest host, *Saturday Night Live,* NBC, 1991.

OTHER SOURCES:

PERIODICALS

Gentleman's Quarterly, March, 1991, p. 231.
People, November 19, 1990, p. 163.*

* * *

SEAGULL, Barbara
See HERSHEY, Barbara

* * *

SEINFELD, Jerry 1954(?)-

PERSONAL: Born c. 1954 in Brooklyn, NY; son of Kalman (in business) and Betty Seinfeld. *Education:* Graduated with degree in communications from Queens College, 1976.

CAREER: Comedian, actor, and screenwriter.

AWARDS, HONORS: American Comedy Award, funniest male comedy club stand-up, 1988; Emmy Award nomination, outstanding writing in a comedy series, 1991, and American Comedy Award, funniest actor in a television series, 1992, both for *Seinfeld.*

CREDITS:

TELEVISION APPEARANCES; SERIES

Title role, *Seinfeld* (also known as *The Seinfeld Chronicles;* also see below), NBC, 1989.

TELEVISION APPEARANCES; SPECIALS

Tonight Show Starring Johnny Carson 19th Anniversary Special, NBC, 1981.
Tonight Show Starring Johnny Carson 24th Anniversary Special, NBC, 1986.
Disneyland's Summer Vacation Party, NBC, 1986.
"Rodney Dangerfield—It's Not Easy Bein' Me," *On Location,* HBO, 1986.
"Jerry Seinfeld—Stand-Up Confidential," *On Location* (also see below), HBO, 1987.
An All-Star Celebration: The '88 Vote, ABC, 1988.
Late Night With David Letterman Seventh Anniversary Show, NBC, 1989.
"Montreal International Comedy Festival," *HBO Comedy Hour,* HBO, 1989.
Second Annual Valvoline National Driving Test, CBS, 1990.
Night of 100 Stars, III (also see below), NBC, 1990.
Funny Business with Charlie Chase, The Nashville Network, 1990.
The 4th Annual American Comedy Awards, ABC, 1990.
42nd Annual Primetime Emmy Awards Presentation, Fox, 1990.
Spy Magazine Presents How to Be Famous, NBC, 1990.
The Second Annual Aspen Comedy Festival, Showtime, 1990.
The 43rd Annual Primetime Emmy Awards Presentation, Fox, 1991.
Today at 40, NBC, 1992.

TELEVISION WORK

Creator with Larry David, *Seinfeld* (series; also known as *The Seinfeld Chronicles;* also see below), NBC, 1989.

STAGE APPEARANCES

Night of 100 Stars III, Radio City Music Hall, New York City, 1990.

WRITINGS:

FOR TELEVISION

"Jerry Seinfeld—Stand-up Confidential," *On Location* (special), 1987.
Seinfeld (series; also known as *The Seinfeld Chronicles*), NBC, 1989.

OTHER SOURCES:

PERIODICALS

New York Times, September 29, 1991, pp. H33-34.*

SEMEL, Terry 1943-

PERSONAL: Born February 24, 1943, in New York, NY; son of Ben and Mildred (Wenig) Semel; married Jane Bovingdon, August 24, 1977; children: Eric Scott, Courtenay Jane, Lily Bovingdon. *Education:* Long Island University, B.S., 1964; City College of the City University of New York, M.B.A., 1967.

ADDRESSES: Office—Warner Brothers, Inc., 4000 Warner Blvd., Burbank, CA 91522.

CAREER: Motion picture executive. Certified public accountant for an accounting firm, 1965-66; Warner Brothers, Inc., business manager in New York City, Cleveland, OH, and Los Angeles, CA, 1966-71; CBS Cinema Center Films, Studio City, CA, domestic sales manager, 1970-72; Walt Disney's Buena Vista, Burbank, CA, vice-president and general manager, 1972-75; W. B. Distribution Corp., Burbank, president, 1975-78; Warner Brothers, Inc., Burbank, chief operating officer, 1979—, executive vice-president, 1979-80, president, 1980—. Revlon, Inc., member of board of directors.

AWARDS, HONORS: Named Pioneer of the Year, Foundation of Motion Picture Pioneers.*

* * *

SHEEN, Charlie 1965-

PERSONAL: Original name, Carlos Irwin Estevez; born September 3, 1965, in New York City (some sources say Los Angeles, CA); son of Ramon (an actor; professionally known as Martin Sheen) and Janet Estevez; brother of Emilio Estevez. *Education:* Attended University of Kansas. *Avocational interests:* Sports, music.

ADDRESSES: Agent—William Morris Agency, 151 El Camino, Beverly Hills, CA 90212.

CAREER: Actor.

MEMBER: Screen Actors Guild.

AWARDS, HONORS: Discovery of the Year Award, Hollywood Women's Press Club, 1987.

CREDITS:

FILM APPEARANCES

Matt Eckert, *Red Dawn,* Metro-Goldwyn-Mayer/United Artists, 1984.
Bo Richards, *The Boys Next Door,* New World-Republic Entertainment International, 1985.
Garth Volbeck, *Ferris Bueller's Day Off,* Paramount, 1986.
Cappie Roew, *Lucas,* Twentieth Century-Fox, 1986.
Chris Taylor, *Platoon,* Orion, 1986.

City Burger manager, *Wisdom,* Twentieth Century-Fox, 1986.
The Wraith/Jake Kesey, *The Wraith,* New Century-Vista, 1986.
Bud Fox, *Wall Street,* Twentieth Century-Fox, 1987.
Ted Varrick, *No Man's Land,* Orion, 1987.
Paul Tracy, *Three for the Road,* New Century-Vista, 1987.
Hap Felsch, *Eight Men Out,* Orion, 1988.
Dick Brewer, *Young Guns,* Twentieth Century-Fox, 1988.
Rickie Vaughn, *Major League,* Paramount, 1989.
Narrator, *Tale of Two Sisters,* Vista Street Entertainment, 1989.
Beverly Hills Brats, Taurus Entertainment, 1989.
Peter, *Courage Mountain,* Triumph, 1990.
Lieutenant Dale Hawkins, *Navy SEALS,* Orion, 1990.
Carl Taylor, *Men at Work,* Triumph, 1990.
David Ackerman, *The Rookie,* Warner Brothers, 1990.
Franklin Bean, Jr., *Cadence* (also known as *Stockade* and *Count a Lonely Cadence*), New Line Cinema/Republic, 1990.
Bob, *Backtrack* (also known as *Catchfire* and *A Time to Die*), Live Entertainment, 1990.
Topper Harley/Rhett Butler/Superman, *Hot Shots!* Twentieth Century-Fox, 1991.

Made film debut in *Grizzly II: The Predator,* 1984; appeared as the thief in *Never on Tuesday,* 1989, in *Johnny Utah,* and as an extra in *Apocalypse Now.*

FILM WORK

Producer and director, *R.P.G. II* (short film).

TELEVISION APPEARANCES; MOVIES

Ken Cruze, *Silence of the Heart,* CBS, 1984.
Man shaving, *Out of the Darkness,* CBS, 1985.
Backtrack, Showtime, 1992.

Made television debut as an extra, *The Execution of Private Slovik,* CBS, c. 1974; also appeared in *Jack London's California,* ABC.

OTHER TELEVISION APPEARANCES

All-Star Tribute to Kareem Abdul-Jabbar (special), NBC, 1989.

Also appeared on an episode of *Amazing Stories.*

WRITINGS:

Author of *R.P.G. II* (short film) and *A Piece of My Mind* (poems).

OTHER SOURCES:

PERIODICALS

Interview, February, 1987, p. 35.
People, March 9, 1987.
Playboy, September, 1990, p. 116.*

*   *   *

SHEINBERG, Sidney 1935-

PERSONAL: Full name, Sidney Jay Sheinberg; born January 14, 1935, in Corpus Christi, TX; son of Harry and Tillie (Grossman) Sheinberg; married Lorraine Gottfried, August 19, 1956; children: Jonathan J., William David. *Education:* Columbia University, A.B., 1955, LL.B., 1958.

ADDRESSES: Office—MCA, Inc., 100 Universal City Plaza, Universal City, CA, 91608.

CAREER: Executive. University of California, Los Angeles, associate in law, 1958-59; MCA, Inc., Universal City, CA, member of staff, 1959-69, corporate executive vice-president, 1969-73, president of television division, 1971-74, corporate president and chief operating officer, 1973—.

MEMBER: Association of Motion Picture and Television Producers (chair of board of directors).*

*   *   *

SHERIDAN, Jamey 1951-

PERSONAL: Born July 12, 1951, in Pasadena, CA; son of Marvin Daniel (an actor and stuntman) and Josephine Suzanne (Hayes) Sheridan. *Education:* University of California, Santa Barbara, B.A., 1976. *Avocational interests:* Writing, reading fiction.

ADDRESSES: Agent—Mary Sames, Sames & Rollnick Associates, Ltd., 250 West 57th St., New York, NY 10107.

CAREER: Actor.

MEMBER: Actors Equity Association, Screen Actors Guild, American Federation of Television and Radio Artists.

AWARDS, HONORS: Antoinette Perry Award nomination, best actor in a featured dramatic role, 1987, for *All My Sons.*

CREDITS:

FILM APPEARANCES

New York officer, *Jumpin' Jack Flash,* Twentieth Century-Fox, 1986.
Porter, *The House on Carroll Street,* Orion, 1988.
Moss, *Distant Thunder,* Paramount, 1988.
Joe, *Stanley and Iris,* Metro-Goldwyn-Mayer/United Artists, 1990.

Mugger, *Quick Change,* Warner Brothers, 1990.
Tim Weaver, *Talent for the Game,* Paramount, 1991.
Michael O'Fallon, *All I Want for Christmas* (also known as *Home for Christmas* and *Home for the Holidays*), Paramount, 1991.
Nick, *A Stranger Among Us,* Hollywood Pictures, 1992.

TELEVISION APPEARANCES; SERIES

Jack Shannon, *Shannon's Deal,* NBC, 1990.

TELEVISION APPEARANCES; EPISODIC

(Television debut) George Wayne, "Mystery at Fire Island," *CBS Mystery Theatre,* CBS, 1980.
Frankie Raimendo, *The Doctors,* NBC, 1981.
LaBecque, *Another World,* NBC, 1984.
Webb Ettlee, *St. Elsewhere,* NBC, 1984.
Spenser for Hire, ABC, 1986.
Private Eye, NBC, 1987.
Brother Ted, "A Mother's Courage: The Mary Thomas Story" (also known as "The Long Shot"), *The Magical World of Disney,* NBC, 1989.

Also appeared as a guest star on *The Equalizer,* CBS.

OTHER TELEVISION APPEARANCES

Detective Bo Davis, *One Police Plaza* (movie), CBS, 1986.
Jack Shannon, *Shannon's Deal* (pilot), NBC, 1989.
Horn, *Murder in High Places* (movie; also known as *Out of Season*), NBC, 1991.

STAGE APPEARANCES

(Stage debut) Hoss, *Tooth of Crime,* Williamstown Theatre Festival (second company), Williamstown, MA, 1978.
(Off-Broadway debut) Spud, *Just a Little Bit Less Than Normal,* Manhattan Theatre Club, New York City, 1979.
Chris, *The Arbor,* Manhattan Theatre Club, 1979.
Private Wars, and Gately, *Lone Star* (double bill), Center Stage Theatre Mainstage, Baltimore, MD, 1979.
Bilton, *Major Barbara,* Circle in the Square, New York City, 1980.
Mike Morgan, *One Wedding, Two Rooms, Three Friends,* Manhattan Theatre Club, 1980.
Sandy, *The Man Who Came to Dinner,* Circle in the Square, 1980.
Hoagy, *Hoagy, Bix, and Wolfgang Beethoven Bunkhaus,* Indiana Repertory Theatre, Indianapolis, 1980.
Paul, *Loose Ends,* Alliance Theatre Company, Atlanta, GA, 1981.
Deathtrap, Pennsylvania Stage Company, Allentown, 1981.
Joe Mackin's voice, *The Singular Life of Albert Nobbs,* Manhattan Theatre Club, 1982.
Bernardo and Fortinbras, *Hamlet,* New York Shakespeare Festival, Public/Anspacher Theatre, New York City, 1982.
Homesteaders, Capitol Repertory Company, Albany, NY, 1982.
Macduff, *Macbeth,* Ark Theatre Company, 1983.
Marcus Antonius, *Julius Caesar,* Alliance Theatre Company, 1983.
Sergeant Toomey, *Biloxi Blues,* Neil Simon Theatre, New York City, 1985.
Chris Keller, *All My Sons,* John Golden Theatre, New York City, 1987.
James Tyrone, Jr., *Long Day's Journey into Night,* Neil Simon Theatre, 1988.
Bartender, *Ah, Wilderness!,* Neil Simon Theatre, 1988.

Also appeared as James Tyrone in *Moon for the Misbegotten* and as Lysander in *A Midsummer Night's Dream,* Williamstown Theatre Festival; appeared with the National Shakespeare Festival, Old Globe Theatre, San Diego, CA, 1976.

OTHER SOURCES:

PERIODICALS

American Film, April, 1991, p. 49.
Premiere, April, 1991, p. 47.

* * *

SHERIDAN, Nicollette 1963-

PERSONAL: Born November 21, 1963, in Worthing, Sussex, England; immigrated to Los Angeles, CA, c. 1973; daughter of Sally Savalas; married Harry Hamlin (an actor), September 7, 1991. *Avocational interests:* Traveling, painting, reading, motorcycle riding, horseback riding, skiing.

CAREER: Actress and model. Worked for Elite Modeling Agency, New York City.

CREDITS:

TELEVISION APPEARANCES; SERIES

Taryn Blake, *Paper Dolls,* ABC, 1984.
Paige Matheson, *Knots Landing,* CBS, beginning in 1986.

TELEVISION APPEARANCES; MOVIES

Banda Drake, *Dark Mansions,* ABC, 1985.
Hattie Stubbs, *Agatha Christie's "Dead Man's Folly,"* CBS, 1986.
Lucky Santangelo, *Jackie Collins' "Lucky/Chances,"* NBC, 1990.
Adrienne Erickson, *Deceptions,* Showtime, 1990.

TELEVISION APPEARANCES; EPISODIC

"Murder on the Rocks," *Scene of the Crime,* NBC, 1985.

OTHER TELEVISION APPEARANCES

CBS All-American Thanksgiving Day Parade, CBS, 1987.
Battle of the Network Stars (special), ABC, 1988.
The 43rd Annual Primetime Emmy Awards Presentation, Fox, 1991.

FILM APPEARANCES

The Sure Thing, *The Sure Thing,* Embassy, 1985.*

* * *

SHERMAN, Dick
See SHERMAN, Richard M.

* * *

SHERMAN, Richard M. 1928-
(Dick Sherman)

PERSONAL: Full name, Richard Morton Sherman; born June 12, 1928, in New York, NY; son of Al and Rosa (Dancis) Sherman; married Ursula Gluck, July 6, 1957; children: Linda Sue, Gregory Vincent, Victoria Lynn. *Education:* Attended University of Southern California, 1945; Bard College, B.A., 1949.

ADDRESSES: Contact—c/o Sherbro Music Company, 9030 Harratt St., #2, Los Angeles, CA 90069.

CAREER: Composer, lyricist, and screenwriter. Walt Disney Productions, Burbank, CA, songwriter and composer, 1960-71; free-lance songwriter and composer, 1971—. *Military service:* U.S. Army, 1953-55.

MEMBER: Academy of Motion Picture Arts and Sciences, Broadcast Music, Inc., National Academy of Recording Arts and Sciences, Composers and Lyricists Guild, Writers Guild of America.

AWARDS, HONORS: All with brother, Robert B. Sherman—Academy Award, best score, and Grammy Award, best score, both 1964, for *Mary Poppins;* Academy Award, best song, 1964, for "Chim Chim Cheree," from *Mary Poppins;* Christopher Medal, 1965; Academy Award nomination, best song, 1968, for "Chitty Chitty Bang Bang," from *Chitty Chitty Bang Bang;* Academy Award nomination, best song score, 1971, for *Bedknobs and Broomsticks;* Academy Award nomination, best song, 1971, for "The Age of Not Believing," from *Bedknobs and Broomsticks;* Academy Award nomination, best song score, and Moscow Film Festival First Prize, best song score, both 1973, for *Tom Sawyer;* Academy Award nomination, best song score, 1977, for *The Slipper and the Rose;* Academy Award nomination, best song, 1977, for "The Slipper and the Rose Waltz," from *The Slipper and the Rose;* Academy Award nomination, best song, 1978, for "When You're Loved," from *The Magic of Lassie;* one diamond, four platinum, and sixteen gold records between 1965 and 1983; star on Hollywood Walk of Fame.

RECORDINGS:

Has recorded the comedy album *Smash Flops.*

WRITINGS:

FILM MUSIC AND LYRICS, EXCEPT WHERE INDICATED; WITH ROBERT B. SHERMAN

The Absent-Minded Professor, Buena Vista, 1961.
The Parent Trap, Buena Vista, 1961.
Big Red, Buena Vista, 1962.
Bon Voyage, Buena Vista, 1962.
Moon Pilot, Buena Vista, 1962.
Miracle of the White Stallions (also known as *The Flight of the White Stallions*), Buena Vista, 1963.
Summer Magic, Buena Vista, 1963.
The Sword in the Stone (animated), Buena Vista, 1963.
Mary Poppins (includes song "Chim Chim Cheree"), Buena Vista, 1964.
Those Calloways, Buena Vista, 1964.
The Monkey's Uncle, Buena Vista, 1965.
That Darn Cat, Buena Vista, 1965.
Follow Me, Boys!, Buena Vista, 1966.
The Happiest Millionaire, Buena Vista, 1967.
The Jungle Book (animated), Buena Vista, 1967.
Chitty Chitty Bang Bang (includes song "Chitty Chitty Bang Bang"), United Artists (UA), 1968.
The One and Only Genuine Original Family Band, Buena Vista, 1968.
(And with Terry Gilkyson, Floyd Huddleston, and Al Rinker) *The Aristocats* (animated), Buena Vista, 1970.
Bedknobs and Broomsticks (includes song "The Age of Not Believing"), Buena Vista, 1971.
Snoopy, Come Home! (animated), National General, 1972.
Charlotte's Web (animated), Paramount, 1973.
Tom Sawyer (based on *The Adventures of Tom Sawyer* by Mark Twain; also see below), UA, 1973.
Huckleberry Finn (based on *The Adventures of Huckleberry Finn* by Twain; also see below), UA, 1974.
Music, *The Slipper and the Rose* (also known as *The Story of Cinderella;* includes song "The Slipper and the Rose Waltz"; also see below), Universal, 1976.
The Magic of Lassie (includes song "When You're Loved"; also see below), International Picture Show, 1978.

Also composer of music and lyrics for *Winnie the Pooh,* 1965, *The Castaways, Legend of Lobo, Merlin Jones,* and *Symposium of Popular Songs.*

SCREENPLAYS; WITH ROBERT B. SHERMAN

Tom Sawyer, UA, 1973.
Huckleberry Finn, UA, 1974.
(And with Bryan Forbes) *The Slipper and the Rose,* Universal, 1976.
(And with Jean Holloway) *The Magic of Lassie,* International Picture Show, 1978.

Also author of *Little Nemo* and *Magic Journeys.*

TELEVISION MUSIC; SERIES; WITH ROBERT B. SHERMAN

Walt Disney's Wonderful World of Color, NBC, beginning in 1961.

Also composer for *Bell Telephone Hour,* NBC, *Welcome to Pooh Corner,* and *The Enchanted Musical Playhouse.*

STAGE MUSIC AND LYRICS

(With Robert B. Sherman) *Over Here!,* produced at Shubert Theatre, New York City, 1974.
(With Milton Larsen) *New Faces of 1980,* produced at Bonfils Theatre, Denver, CO, c. 1980.

OTHER MUSIC

(Under name Dick Sherman) Song, "What's Your Sad Story?," *Nightmare,* UA, 1956.

Composer, with Robert B. Sherman, of "It's a Small World" (theme song of Disneyland and Walt Disney World) and of several popular songs between 1950 and 1960, including "Tall Paul," "Pineapple Princess," and "You're Sixteen."

OTHER SOURCES:

BOOKS

Contemporary Authors, Volume 107, Gale, 1983, p. 469.*

* * *

SHERMAN, Robert B. 1925-

PERSONAL: Full name, Robert Bernard Sherman; born December 19, 1925, in New York, NY; son of Al and Rosa (Dancis) Sherman; married Joyce Ruth Sasner, September 27, 1953; children: Laurie Shane, Jeffrey Craig, Andrea Tracy, Robert Jason. *Education:* Attended University of California, Los Angeles, 1943; Bard College, B.A., 1949.

ADDRESSES: *Office*—c/o Mike Conner Office, 9030 Harratt St., Los Angeles, CA 90069.

CAREER: Composer, lyricist, and screenwriter. Freelance songwriter, 1952-60; Music World Corp., president, beginning in 1958; Walt Disney Productions, Burbank, CA, songwriter and composer, 1960-c. 1968; United Artists, Beverly Hills, CA, composer and lyricist, beginning in 1969; Musi-Classics, Inc., vice-president; free-lance composer. *Military service:* U.S. Army, 1943-45, served in infantry in Europe; received Purple Heart.

MEMBER: Academy of Motion Picture Arts and Sciences, American Federation of Television and Radio Artists, National Academy of Recording Arts and Sciences, Composers and Lyricists Guild (member of executive board), Writers Guild of America, Dramatists Guild, Authors League.

AWARDS, HONORS: With brother, Richard M. Sherman—Academy Award, best score, and Grammy Award, best score, both 1964, for *Mary Poppins;* Academy Award, best song, 1964, for "Chim Chim Cheree," from *Mary Poppins;* Christopher Medal, 1965; Academy Award nomination, best song, 1968, for "Chitty Chitty Bang Bang," from *Chitty Chitty Bang Bang;* Academy Award nomination, best song score, 1971, for *Bedknobs and Broomsticks;* Academy Award nomination, best song, 1971, for "The Age of Not Believing," from *Bedknobs and Broomsticks;* Academy Award nomination, best song score, and Moscow Film Festival First Prize, best song score, both 1973, for *Tom Sawyer;* Academy Award nomination, best song score, 1977, for *The Slipper and the Rose;* Academy Award nomination, best song, 1977, for "The Slipper and the Rose Waltz," from *The Slipper and the Rose;* Academy Award nomination, best song, 1978, for "When You're Loved," from *The Magic of Lassie;* one diamond, four platinum, and sixteen gold records between 1965 and 1983; star on Hollywood Walk of Fame.

Other awards—Christopher Medal, 1974; B.M.I. Pioneer Award, 1977; Golden Cassette awards, 1983, for *Mary Poppins, The Jungle Book,* and *Bedknobs and Broomsticks;* Mouscar Award, Disney Studios.

CREDITS:

TELEVISION WORK

Co-producer, *Goldilocks* (special), NBC, 1970.

STAGE WORK

Co-producer of *Victory Canteen* (also see below), 1971.

WRITINGS:

FILM MUSIC AND LYRICS, EXCEPT WHERE INDICATED; WITH RICHARD M. SHERMAN

The Absent-Minded Professor, Buena Vista, 1961.
The Parent Trap, Buena Vista, 1961.
Big Red, Buena Vista, 1962.
Bon Voyage, Buena Vista, 1962.
Moon Pilot, Buena Vista, 1962.

Miracle of the White Stallions (also known as *The Flight of the White Stallions*), Buena Vista, 1963.
Summer Magic, Buena Vista, 1963.
The Sword in the Stone (animated), Buena Vista, 1963.
Mary Poppins (includes song "Chim Chim Cheree"), Buena Vista, 1964.
Those Calloways, Buena Vista, 1964.
The Monkey's Uncle, Buena Vista, 1965.
That Darn Cat, Buena Vista, 1965.
Follow Me, Boys!, Buena Vista, 1966.
The Happiest Millionaire, Buena Vista, 1967.
The Jungle Book (animated), Buena Vista, 1967.
Chitty Chitty Bang Bang (includes song "Chitty Chitty Bang Bang"), United Artists (UA), 1968.
The One and Only Genuine Original Family Band, Buena Vista, 1968.
(And with Terry Gilkyson, Floyd Huddleston, and Al Rinker) *The Aristocats* (animated), Buena Vista, 1970.
Bedknobs and Broomsticks (includes song "The Age of Not Believing"), Buena Vista, 1971.
Snoopy, Come Home! (animated), National General, 1972.
Charlotte's Web (animated), Paramount, 1973.
Tom Sawyer (based on *The Adventures of Tom Sawyer* by Mark Twain; also see below), UA, 1973.
Huckleberry Finn (based on *The Adventures of Huckleberry Finn* by Twain; also see below), UA, 1974.
Music, *The Slipper and the Rose* (also known as *The Story of Cinderella;* includes song "The Slipper and the Rose Waltz"; also see below), Universal, 1976.
The Magic of Lassie (includes song "When You're Loved"; also see below), International Picture Show, 1978.

Also composer of music and lyrics for *Winnie the Pooh,* 1965, *The Castaways, Legend of Lobo, Merlin Jones,* and *Symposium of Popular Songs.*

SCREENPLAYS; WITH RICHARD M. SHERMAN

Tom Sawyer, UA, 1973.
Huckleberry Finn, UA, 1974.
(And with Bryan Forbes) *The Slipper and the Rose,* Universal, 1976.
(And with Jean Holloway) *The Magic of Lassie,* International Picture Show, 1978.

Also author of *Little Nemo* and *Magic Journeys.*

TELEVISION MUSIC; SERIES; WITH RICHARD M. SHERMAN

Walt Disney's Wonderful World of Color, NBC, beginning in 1961.

Also composer for *Bell Telephone Hour,* NBC, *Welcome to Pooh Corner,* and *The Enchanted Musical Playhouse.*

STAGE MUSIC

(With Richard M. Sherman) Music and lyrics, *Over Here!,* produced at Shubert Theatre, New York City, 1974.

Also composer of music and lyrics for *Victory Canteen,* 1971.

OTHER MUSIC

Composer, with Richard M. Sherman, of "It's a Small World" (theme song of Disneyland and Walt Disney World) and of several popular songs between 1950 and 1960, including "Tall Paul," "Pineapple Princess," and "You're Sixteen."

OTHER SOURCES:

BOOKS

Contemporary Authors, Volume 108, Gale, 1983, p. 451.*

* * *

SHIPP, John Wesley

ADDRESSES: Agent—J. Michael Bloom Agency, 233 Park Ave. S., 10th Floor, New York, NY 10017.

CAREER: Actor.

AWARDS, HONORS: Emmy Award, best supporting actor in a daytime drama series, 1985, for *As the World Turns;* Emmy Award, best guest performance in a daytime drama series, 1986, for *Santa Barbara.*

CREDITS:

TELEVISION APPEARANCES; SERIES

Kelly Nelson, *The Guiding Light,* CBS, 1980-84.
Doug Cummings, *As the World Turns,* CBS, 1985.
Barry Allen, *The Flash,* CBS, 1990.

OTHER TELEVISION APPEARANCES

Callahan, *Summer Fantasy* (movie), NBC, 1984.
Santa Barbara (episodic), NBC, 1986.
Voice of Spex, *The Danger Team* (animated special), ABC, 1991.
Dennis Becker, *Baby of the Bride* (movie), CBS, 1991.

FILM APPEARANCES

Barney Bux, *The Neverending Story II: The Next Chapter,* Warner Brothers, 1990.

STAGE APPEARANCES

Greg, *Vera, with Kate,* Wonderhorse Theatre, 1980.
Josh, *Sit Down and Eat before Our Love Gets Cold,* West Side Y Arts Center, 1985.
Jake, *Safe Sex,* Lyceum Theatre, New York City, 1987.

Rick, *Stopping the Desert,* 45th Street Theatre, New York City, 1987.
Cat on a Hot Tin Roof, Walnut Street Theatre, Philadelphia, PA, 1987.
Mario Pagnutti, *Tamara,* Park Avenue Armory, 1987.

RECORDINGS:

ALBUMS

Recorded *Images,* which includes Shipp's rendition of "On the Inside," the theme song for the series *Prisoner: Cellblock H.**

* * *

SHORE, Howard

ADDRESSES: Agent—Triad Artists Agency, 10100 Santa Monica Blvd., 16th Floor, Los Angeles, CA 90067.

CAREER: Composer, music director and producer, and conductor. Began career as musical director for *Saturday Night Live.*

AWARDS, HONORS: Genie Award nomination for best music score, 1980, for *The Brood;* Genie Award for best music score, 1989, for *Dead Ringers;* British Academy of Film and Television Arts Award nomination, best original film music, 1992, for *The Silence of the Lambs.*

CREDITS:

STAGE WORK; MUSIC PRODUCER

Gilda Radner, Live from New York, Winter Garden Theatre, New York City, 1979.

FILM WORK

Conductor, *Dead Ringers* (also see below), Twentieth Century-Fox, 1988.
Music supervisor, *Postcards from the Edge* (also see below), Columbia, 1991.
Conductor, *A Kiss before Dying* (also see below), Universal, 1991.

Also music producer, *Belizaire the Cajun,* 1985.

TELEVISION WORK; MUSIC DIRECTOR

Coca-Cola Presents Live: The Hard Rock (also known as *Live: The Hard Rock*), NBC, 1988.

WRITINGS:

FILM MUSIC

I Miss You, Hugs and Kisses, Astral, 1978.
The Brood (also known as *Chromosome*), New World Pictures, 1979.
Scanners, Avco Embassy, 1981.
Silkwood, Rank, 1983.
Videodrome, Universal, 1983.
Places in the Heart, Tri-Star, 1984.
After Hours, Geffen-Warner Brothers, 1985.
Fire with Fire, Paramount, 1986.
The Fly, Twentieth Century-Fox, 1986.
Nadine, Tri-Star, 1987.
Heaven, Island Pictures, 1987.
Big, Twentieth Century-Fox, 1988.
Dead Ringers, Twentieth Century-Fox, 1988.
Moving, Warner Brothers, 1988.
Signs of Life (also known as *One for Sorrow, Two for Joy*), Avenue Entertainment, 1989.
She-Devil, Orion, 1990.
An Innocent Man, Buena Vista, 1990.
Quick Change, Warner Brothers, 1991.
Postcards from the Edge, Columbia, 1991.
Naked Lunch, Twentieth Century-Fox, 1991.
The Silence of the Lambs, Orion, 1991.
A Kiss before Dying, Universal, 1991.
Prelude to a Kiss, Twentieth Century-Fox, 1992.

TELEVISION MUSIC; SPECIALS

Steve Martin's Best Show Ever, NBC, 1981.
The New Show, NBC, 1984.
Big Shots in America, NBC, 1985.*

* * *

SHORT, Roger, Jr.
See EYEN, Tom

* * *

SHUE, Elisabeth 1964(?)-

PERSONAL: Born c. 1964, in Wilmington, DE; daughter of James (a lawyer and real estate developer) and Anne (a bank executive; maiden name, Wells) Shue. *Education:* Attended Wellesley College, 1981-83, and Harvard University, 1985-86.

ADDRESSES: Office—76 South Orange Ave., South Orange, NJ 07079.

CAREER: Actress.

CREDITS:

FILM APPEARANCES

Ali, *The Karate Kid,* Columbia, 1984.
Jane Chase, *Link,* Cannon, 1986.
Chris Parker, *Adventures in Babysitting,* Buena Vista, 1987.
Jordan Mooney, *Cocktail,* Buena Vista, 1988.
Jennifer, *Back to the Future Part II,* Universal, 1989.
Jennifer, *Back to the Future Part III,* Universal, 1990.

Lori Craven, *Soapdish,* Paramount, 1991.
Adele Horner, *The Marrying Man,* Buena Vista, 1991.

TELEVISION APPEARANCES; EPISODIC

Kathy Shelton, "Double Switch" (also known as "Switching Places"), *The Disney Sunday Movie,* ABC, 1987.
Alice Adams, "Hale the Hero," *General Motors Playwrights Theatre,* Arts and Entertainment, 1992.

OTHER TELEVISION APPEARANCES

Jackie Sarnac, *Call to Glory* (series; also known as *Air Force*), ABC, 1984-85.

STAGE APPEARANCES

(Broadway debut) Donna Silliman, *Some Americans Abroad,* Vivian Beaumont Theatre, New York City, 1990.*

* * *

SIEGEL, Don 1912-1991

OBITUARY NOTICE—See index for *CTFT* sketch: Born October 26, 1912, in Chicago, IL; died after a long illness, April 20, 1991, in Nipoma, CA. Director, producer, and actor. Siegel was best known for his action and "B" films, most notably *Dirty Harry,* starring Clint Eastwood, and the original version of *Invasion of the Body Snatchers.* Among the actors he directed for film were John Wayne in *The Shootist,* Mickey Rooney in *Baby Face Nelson,* Richard Widmark in *Madigan,* Ronald Reagan in *The Killers,* Walter Matthau in *Charley Varrick,* and Charles Bronson in *Telefon.* Siegel directed Eastwood in four other films, including *Two Mules for Sister Sarah* and *Escape from Alcatraz.* He also served as producer of *Dirty Harry, The Killers, Escape from Alcatraz,* and *Charley Varrick,* among others. Siegel made cameo appearances in several films, including *Play Misty for Me,* directed by Eastwood, the 1978 remake of *Invasion of the Body Snatchers,* and *Into the Night,* his last work in film. He appeared in several of his own films as well. Siegel produced the ABC television series *The Legend of Jesse James* during the mid-1960s and directed the NBC television movies *The Hanged Man* in 1964 and *The Stranger on the Run,* starring Henry Fonda, in 1967. Before his directing debut in 1945, Siegel was responsible for developing the Warner Brothers montage department. He had been writing his memoirs for several years at the time of his death.

OBITUARIES AND OTHER SOURCES:

PERIODICALS

Hollywood Reporter, April 23, 1991, pp. 3, 58.
Variety, April 29, 1991, pp. 109-110.

SIEGEL-TABORI, Kristoffer
See TABORI, Kristoffer

* * *

SINBAD 1956-

PERSONAL: Full name, David Adkins Sinbad; born November 18, 1956, in Benton Harbor, MI; married, wife's name, Meredith; children: Paige, Royce. *Education:* Attended University of Denver.

ADDRESSES: Agent—Agency for the Performing Arts, 9000 Sunset Blvd., No. 1200, Los Angeles, CA 90069. *Publicist*—Bridget Hahn, Jo-Ann Geffen Public Relations, 3151 Cahuenga Blvd. West, No. 235, Los Angeles, CA 90068.

CAREER: Comedian and actor. Appears in nightclubs; toured with Miami Sound Machine, Smokey Robinson, Kool and the Gang, The Pointer Sisters, B. B. King, the Commodores, Anita Baker, and Luther Vandross; performs in children's theatres. *Military service:* U.S. Air Force.

MEMBER: Screen Actors Guild.

AWARDS, HONORS: Comedy finalist on *Star Search.*

CREDITS:

TELEVISION APPEARANCES; SERIES

Brian Lightfoot, *The Redd Foxx Show,* ABC, 1986.
Co-host, *Keep On Cruisin',* CBS, 1987.
Host, *It's Showtime at the Apollo,* syndicated, beginning in 1987.
Walter Oakes, *A Different World,* NBC, 1987-91.

TELEVISION APPEARANCES; EPISODIC

"Take No Prisoners: Robert Townsend and His Partners in Crime II," *HBO Comedy Hour,* HBO, 1988.
Super Bloopers and New Practical Jokes, NBC, 1990.
"Sinbad: Brain Damaged" (also see below), *HBO Comedy Hour,* HBO, 1991.

Also appeared on episodes of other programs, including *Late Show,* 1988; *The Cosby Show,* NBC; *Star Search,* syndicated; *Today,* NBC; and *The Hollywood Squares.*

TELEVISION APPEARANCES; SPECIALS

Stand-Up Comics Take a Stand!, Family Channel, 1989.
The Third Annual Soul Train Music Awards, syndicated, 1989.
The Sixteenth Annual Black Filmmakers Hall of Fame, syndicated, 1989.
Motown Thirty: What's Goin' On!, CBS, 1990.
A Laugh, a Tear, syndicated, 1990.
America's All-Star Tribute to Oprah Winfrey, ABC, 1990.

The Twenty-second Annual NAACP Image Awards, NBC, 1990.
Sinbad and Friends All the Way Live . . .Almost (also see below), ABC, 1991.
The Seventeenth Annual People's Choice Awards, CBS, 1991.
Muhammad Ali's Fiftieth Birthday Celebration, ABC, 1992.
The Twenty-fourth Annual NAACP Image Awards, NBC, 1992.
Sinbad & Friends All the Way Live . . . Almost (also see below), ABC, 1992.

OTHER TELEVISION APPEARANCES

Himself, *Club Med* (movie), ABC, 1986.

TELEVISION WORK; EPISODIC

Executive producer, "Sinbad: Brain Damaged," *HBO Comedy Hour,* HBO, 1991.

TELEVISION WORK; SPECIALS

Executive producer, *Sinbad and Friends All the Way Live . . .Almost* (also see below), ABC, 1991.

FILM APPEARANCES

Andre Krimm, *Necessary Roughness,* Paramount, 1991.

Also appeared as a stand-up comic, *That's Adequate,* 1989.

RECORDINGS:

ALBUMS

Albums include *Brain Damaged.*

WRITINGS:

TELEVISION SPECIALS

Sinbad and Friends All the Way Live . . .Almost, ABC, 1991.*

* * *

SISKEL, Gene 1946-

PERSONAL: Full name Eugene Kal Siskel; born January 26, 1946, in Chicago, IL; son of Nathan W. and Ida (Kalis) Siskel; married Marlene Iglitzen, 1980; children: Kate Adi, Callie Gray. *Education:* Yale University, B.A., 1967.

ADDRESSES: *Office—Chicago Tribune,* 435 North Michigan Ave., Chicago, IL, 60611.

CAREER: Film critic. *Chicago Tribune,* Chicago, IL, film critic, 1969—; WBBM-TV, Chicago, film critic, 1974—; Public Broadcasting Service, Washington, DC, co-host of weekly television show, *Sneak Previews,* 1978-82; WTTW-TV, host of Nightwatch Station, 1979-80; co-host of syndicated weekly television show *At the Movies,* 1982-86, and *Siskel and Ebert and the Movies,* 1986—; CBS, New York City, film critic, 1990—.

MEMBER: National Academy of Television Arts and Sciences, CORO Foundation (fellow, 1968), Yale Club, Sigma Delta Chi.

AWARDS, HONORS: Emmy Award nominations for outstanding informational series, 1984 and 1985, for *At the Movies;* Emmy Award nominations for outstanding informational series, 1987, 1988, and 1991, for *Siskel and Ebert and the Movies;* Clio Award, 1988, for *Siskel and Ebert and the Movies.*

CREDITS:

TELEVISION APPEARANCES; SPECIALS

Siskel & Ebert: The Future of the Movies with Steven Spielberg, George Lucas, and Martin Scorsese, syndicated, 1990.
Siskel & Ebert: If We Picked the Winners, syndicated, 1990.
The Siskel & Ebert Special, syndicated, 1990.

WRITINGS:

Contributor to periodicals, including *Playboy, Saturday Review,* and *Variety.*

OTHER SOURCES:

PERIODICALS

Architectural Digest, October, 1989, p. 256.
Ms., June, 1981.
Newsweek, April 11, 1983.
People, August 20, 1984, p. 61.
Playboy, June, 1984, p. 129; February, 1991, p. 51.*

* * *

SKOLIMOWSKI, Jerzy 1938-

PERSONAL: Full name, Jerzy Yurek Skolimowski; born May 5, 1938, in Lodz (some sources say Warsaw), Poland; emigrated from Poland, 1967; son of Stanislau (an architect) and Maria (Postnikoff) Skolimowski; married Joanna Szczerbic; children: two sons. *Education:* Warsaw University, diploma in literature and history, 1959; graduated from State Superior Film School, Lodz, Poland, 1964.

ADDRESSES: *Office*—c/o Film Polski, ul. Mazowiecka 6/8, 00-048 Warsaw, Poland. *Agent*—Leading Artists

Inc., 445 North Bedford Dr., Penthouse, Beverly Hills, CA 90212.

CAREER: Director, writer, and actor.

MEMBER: Directors Guild of America.

AWARDS, HONORS: Grand Prize, International Festival of Sports Films (Budapest, Hungary), 1962, for *Boxing;* award from Film Critics Club of Polish Journalists' Association, 1966, for *Identification Marks: None;* award from Federation Internationale de la Presse Cinematographique, Mannheim Film Festival, and Grand Prix, Arnheim, both 1966, for *Walkover;* Grand Prize, Bergamo Film Festival, 1966, and Special Award of Jury, Valladolid Festival, both for *Barrier;* Golden Bear for best film, Berlin Film Festival, 1967, for *Le Depart;* named Director of the Year, *International Film Guide,* 1970; Special Jury Grand Prize, Cannes International Film Festival, 1978, for *The Shout;* award for best screenplay, Cannes International Film Festival, and British Film Award, both 1982, for *Moonlighting;* Special Jury Prize, Venice Film Festival, 1985, for *The Lightship.*

CREDITS:

FILM WORK; DIRECTOR, EXCEPT AS NOTED

(And producer, art director, and editor) *Rysopis* (title means *Identification Marks;* released in the U.S. as *Identification Marks: None,* New Yorker, 1969; also see below), Film Polski, 1964.

(And co-editor) *Walkower* (released in the U.S. as *Walkover,* New Yorker, 1969; also see below), Film Polski, 1965.

Bariera (released in the U.S. as *Barrier;* also see below), Film Polski, 1966.

Le Depart (title means *The Start;* also see below), Elisabeth Films, 1967.

(And co-art director) *Rece do gory* (title means *Hands Up;* also see below), Film Polski, 1967.

Director of one episode (and art director) *Dialog 20-40-60* (anthology; also see below), Filmstudio Barrandov (Czechoslovakia), 1968.

The Adventures of Gerard (also see below), United Artists (UA), 1970.

Deep End (also see below), Paramount, 1970.

King, Queen, Knave, Avco Embassy, 1972.

The Shout (also see below), Films, Inc., 1978.

(And producer with Mark Shivas) *Moonlighting* (also see below), Universal, 1982.

(And producer) *Success Is the Best Revenge* (also see below), Gaumont, 1984.

The Lightship (released in the U.S. as *The Lightship,* CBS-Castle Hill, 1986), CBS/Warner Brothers, 1985.

Torrents of Spring (also see below), Millimeter, c. 1990.

Director of other films, including *Lady Frankenstein,* 1976; *Wrzask* (title means *The Scream;* also see below), 1978; *Fucha* (also see below), 1982; and *Ferdydurke* (also see below), 1991. Also director of short films, including *Oko wykol, Hamles,* and *Erotyk,* all 1960; and *Boks* (title means *Boxing*), *Piednadze albo zycie,* and *Akt,* all 1961 (also see below for all short films).

FILM APPEARANCES

Niewinni czarodzieji (title means *Innocent Sorcerers;* also see below), [Poland], 1960.

Andrzej Leszczyc, *Rysopis* (title means *Identification Marks;* released in the U.S. as *Identification Marks: None,* New Yorker, 1969; also see below), Film Polski, 1964.

Andrzej Leszczyc, *Walkower* (released in the U.S. as *Walkover,* New Yorker, 1969; also see below), Film Polski, 1965.

Andrzej Leszczyc, *Rece do gory* (title means *Hands Up;* also see below), Film Polski, 1967.

Boss, *Moonlighting,* Universal, 1982.

Hoffmann, *Circle of Deceit* (also known as *False Witness*), UA Classics, 1982.

Colonel Chaiko, *White Nights,* Columbia, 1985.

Doc, *Big Shots,* Twentieth Century-Fox, 1987.

Victor Victorovich, *Torrents of Spring,* Millimeter, c. 1990.

Also appeared in *Boks* (title means *Boxing*), 1961.

WRITINGS:

SCREENPLAYS

(With Jerzy Andrzejewski) *Niewinni czarodzieji* (title means *Innocent Sorcerers*), [Poland], 1960.

(With Roman Polanski and Jakub Goldberg) *Noz w wodzie* (released in the U.S. as *Knife in the Water,* Kanawha Films, 1963), Film Polski, 1962, translation by Boleslaw Sulik published in *Polanski: Three Film Scripts; Knife in the Water, Repulsion, Cul-de-sac,* Harper, 1975, published as *Knife in the Water, Repulsion, and Cul-de-sac: Three Films by Roman Polanski,* Lorrimer, 1975.

Rysopis (title means *Identification Marks;* released in the U.S. as *Identification Marks: None,* New Yorker, 1969), Film Polski, 1964.

Walkower (released in the U.S. as *Walkover,* New Yorker, 1969), Film Polski, 1965.

Bariera (released in the U.S. as *Barrier*), Film Polski, 1966.

Rece do gory (title means *Hands Up*), Film Polski, 1967.

(With Andrzej Kostenko) *Le Depart* (title means *The Start*), Elisabeth Films, 1967, translation published as *Der Start,* Verlag Filmkritik (Frankfurt, Germany), 1968.

Writer of one episode, *Dialog 20-40-60* (anthology), Filmstudio Barrandov (Czechoslovakia), 1968.

(With H. A. L. Craig, Henry Lester, and Gene Gutowski) *The Adventures of Gerard* (based on short stories by Arthur Conan Doyle), UA, 1970.

(With Jerzy Gruza and Boleslaw Sulik) *Deep End*, Paramount, 1970.

Poslizg (title means *Slip-Up*), [Poland], 1972.

(With Michael Austin) *The Shout* (based on a short story by Robert Graves), Films, Inc., 1978.

(With Boleslaw Sulik, Barry Vince, and Danuta Witold Stok) *Moonlighting*, Universal, 1982.

(With Michael Lyndon) *Success Is the Best Revenge*, Gaumont, 1984.

(With Arcangelo Bonaccorso) *Torrents of Spring* (based on the novel by Ivan Turgenev), Millimeter, c. 1990.

Screenwriter of other films, including *Wrzask* (title means *The Scream*), 1978; *Fucha*, 1982; and *Ferdydurke*, 1991. Also screenwriter of film shorts, including *Oko wykol*, *Hamles*, and *Erotyk*, all 1960; and *Boks* (title means *Boxing*), *Piednadze albo zycie*, and *Akt*, all 1961.

TELEVISION PLAYS

Author of the television play *Przy Jaciel* (title means *A Friend*).

OTHER

Gdzies blisko siebie (poems; title means *Somewhere Close to Oneself*), Slask (Katowice, Poland), 1958.

Siekiera i niebo (poems; title means *Hatchet and the Sky*), Czytelnik (Warsaw, Poland), 1959.

Also author of *Ktos sie utopil* (one-act play; title means *Somebody Got Drowned*), 1961, and of short stories. Author of *Moje rundy* (poem; title means *My Rounds*), published in *Nowa kultura*, 1957.

OTHER SOURCES:

BOOKS

Borin, Fabrizio, *Jerzy Skolimowski*, Florence, 1987.

Contemporary Authors, Volume 128, Gale, 1990, pp. 386-390.

Contemporary Literary Criticism, Volume 20, Gale, 1982, pp. 347-356.

PERIODICALS

American Film, December, 1986.

Film Comment, fall, 1968; November/December, 1982.

Films and Filming, December, 1968.

People, November 18, 1985.

Sight and Sound, summer, 1968.*

SLOCOMBE, Douglas 1913-

PERSONAL: Born February 10, 1913, in London, England. *Education:* Attended school in Paris, France.

ADDRESSES: *Agent*—London Management, 235/241 Regent St., London W1R 7AG, England.

CAREER: Cinematographer. Worked variously in England as a journalist and feature writer, as a photojournalist for *Life* and *Paris-Match*, at Ealing Studios, and for the Ministry of Information.

AWARDS, HONORS: British Academy Award, 1964, for *The Servant;* Academy Award nomination, best cinematography, 1972, for *Travels with My Aunt;* British Academy Award, 1974, for *The Great Gatsby;* Academy Award nomination, best cinematography, and British Academy Award, both 1977, both for *Julia;* Academy Award nomination, best cinematography, 1981, for *Raiders of the Lost Ark*.

CREDITS:

FILM WORK; CINEMATOGRAPHER, EXCEPT WHERE INDICATED

(With Wilkie Cooper) *The Big Blockade*, Ealing, 1942.

(With Ernest Palmer) *For Those in Peril*, Ealing, 1944.

The Girl on the Canal (also known as *Painted Boats*), Ealing, 1947.

The Loves of Joanna Godden, General Films Distributors, 1947.

Another Shore, Ealing, 1948.

(With Jack Parker) *The Captive Heart*, Ealing, 1948.

It Always Rains on Sunday, Eagle Lion, 1949.

Kind Hearts and Coronets, General Films Distributors, 1949.

Saraband (also known as *Saraband for Dead Lovers*), Eagle Lion, 1949.

Cage of Gold, Ealing, 1950.

Dance Hall, General Films Distributors, 1950.

(With J. Seaholme) *Hue and Cry*, General Films Distributors, 1950.

A Run for Your Money, Universal, 1950.

The Lavender Hill Mob, Universal, 1951.

Crash of Silence (also known as *Mandy*), General Films Distributors, 1952.

His Excellency, Ealing, 1952.

The Man in the White Suit, J. Arthur Rank/Universal, 1952.

The Titfield Thunderbolt, Universal, 1953.

Lease of Life, General Films Distributors, 1954.

The Love Lottery, General Films Distributors, 1954.

The Light Touch (also known as *Touch and Go*), Universal, 1955.

Decision against Time (also known as *The Man in the Sky*), Metro-Goldwyn-Mayer (MGM), 1957.

Panic in the Parlour (also known as *Sailor Beware!*), Distributors Corp. of America, 1957.
The Smallest Show on Earth (also known as *Big Time Operators*), Times Films, 1957.
All at Sea (also known as *Barnacle Bill*), MGM, 1958.
Davy, MGM, 1958.
Tread Softly Stranger, Bentley, 1959.
The Boy Who Stole a Million, British Lion, 1960.
Circus of Horrors, American International, 1960.
The Mark, Twentieth Century-Fox, 1961.
Scream of Fear (also known as *Taste of Fear*), Columbia, 1961.
Freud (also known as *The Secret Passion*), Universal, 1962.
The L-Shaped Room, Columbia, 1962.
Wonderful to Be Young! (also known as *The Young Ones*), Paramount, 1962.
Guns at Batasi, Twentieth Century-Fox, 1964.
The Servant, Landau, 1964.
The Third Secret, Twentieth Century-Fox, 1964.
A High Wind in Jamaica, Twentieth Century-Fox, 1965.
The Blue Max, Twentieth Century-Fox, 1966.
Promise Her Anything, Paramount, 1966.
Fathom, Twentieth Century-Fox, 1967.
The Fearless Vampire Killers; or, Pardon Me but Your Teeth Are in My Neck (also known as *Dance of the Vampires*), MGM, 1967.
Robbery, Embassy, 1967.
Boom!, Universal, 1968.
The Lion in Winter, Avco Embassy, 1968.
The Italian Job, Paramount, 1969.
The Buttercup Chain, Columbia, 1971.
Murphy's War, Paramount, 1971.
The Music Lovers, United Artists (UA), 1971.
Travels with My Aunt, MGM, 1972.
Jesus Christ, Superstar, Universal, 1973.
The Destructors (also known as *The Marseilles Contract*), American International, 1974.
The Great Gatsby, Paramount, 1974.
Hedda, Brut, 1975.
The Maids, American Film Theatre, 1975.
Rollerball, UA, 1975.
That Lucky Touch, Allied Artists, 1975.
The Bawdy Adventures of Tom Jones, Universal, 1976.
Nasty Habits, Brut, 1976.
The Sailor Who Fell from Grace with the Sea, Avco Embassy, 1976.
Julia, Twentieth Century-Fox, 1977.
Additional sequences, *Close Encounters of the Third Kind,* Columbia, 1977.
Caravans, Universal, 1978.
Lost and Found, Columbia, 1979.
The Lady Vanishes, J. Arthur Rank/Group I, 1980.
Nijinsky, Paramount, 1980.
(With Paul Beeson) *Raiders of the Lost Ark,* Paramount, 1981.
Never Say Never Again, Warner Brothers, 1983.
The Pirates of Penzance, Universal, 1983.
Indiana Jones and the Temple of Doom, Paramount, 1984.
Water, J. Arthur Rank, 1985.
Lady Jane, Paramount, 1986.
(With Beeson and Robert Stevens) *Indiana Jones and the Last Crusade,* Paramount, 1989.

FILM WORK; PHOTOGRAPHER

Made debut as photographer for *Lights out in Europe* (documentary). Also worked as director of photography for *Dead of the Night,* 1945, *Ludwig II,* 1954, and *Heaven and Earth,* 1956.

TELEVISION WORK

Photography, *Love among the Ruins* (movie), ABC, 1975.

Also worked on *The Corn Is Green,* 1979.

OTHER SOURCES:

PERIODICALS

American Cinematographer, May, 1978.*

*   *   *

SNELL, Peter 1941-

PERSONAL: Born November 17, 1941.

ADDRESSES: Office—British Lion Film Productions, Ltd., Pinewood Studios, Pinewood Rd., Iver, Bucks SL0 0NH England.

CAREER: Producer. British Lion Film Productions, head of production and managing director, 1973-75; affiliated with Robert Stigwood group, 1975-78; Britannic Film and Television, chief executive, 1985-86; British Lion Film Productions, owner and chief executive, 1988—.

CREDITS:

FILM PRODUCER

The Winter's Tale, Warner Brothers, 1968.
(With Trevor Wallace) *Subterfuge,* COM, 1969.
(With Joseph Shaftel) *Goodbye Gemini,* Cinerama, 1970.
Julius Caesar, COM/American International, 1970.
Antony and Cleopatra, J. Arthur Rank, 1973.
The Wicker Man, Warner Brothers, 1974.
Hennessy, American International, 1975.
Bear Island, Columbia, 1980.
Lady Jane, Paramount, 1986.
A Prayer for the Dying, Samuel Goldwyn, 1987.

Also producer of *Some May Live, A Month in the Country,* and *Carnaby 68.*

FILM EXECUTIVE PRODUCER

Mother Lode, Agamemnon, 1982.
Squaring the Circle, Metromedia, 1983.
Turtle Diary, Samuel Goldwyn, 1985.

TELEVISION WORK; MOVIES

Producer, with Burt Nodella, *The Hostage Tower,* CBS, 1980.
Executive producer, *A Man for All Seasons,* TNT, 1988.
Producer, *Tears in the Rain,* Showtime, 1988.
Executive producer, *Treasure Island,* TNT, 1990.
Executive producer, *Crucifer of Blood,* TNT, 1991.*

* * *

SNIPES, Wesley 1963(?)-

PERSONAL: Born c. 1963, in Bronx, NY. *Education:* Attended High School for the Performing Arts, New York City; studied acting at State University of New York College at Purchase; trained as a dancer and singer.

ADDRESSES: Manager—c/o Dolores Robinson Management, 335 North Maple Dr., Suite 250, Beverly Hills, CA 90210.

CAREER: Actor. Worked installing telephones before beginning acting career.

MEMBER: Screen Actors Guild.

AWARDS, HONORS: Image Award for best dramatic actor.

CREDITS:

FILM APPEARANCES

Roland Jenkins, *Streets of Gold,* Twentieth Century-Fox, 1986.
Trumaine, *Wildcats,* Warner Brothers, 1986.
Willy Mays Hays, *Major League,* Paramount, 1989.
Shadow Henderson, *Mo' Better Blues,* Universal, 1990.
Thomas Flannigan, *King of New York,* New Line, 1990.
Nino Brown, *New Jack City,* Warner Brothers, 1991.
Flipper Purify, *Jungle Fever,* Universal, 1991.
Sidney Deane, *White Men Can't Jump,* Twentieth Century-Fox, 1992.
John Cutter, *Passenger 57,* Warner Brothers, 1992.
Raymond Hill, *The Waterdance,* JBW Productions, 1992.

Also appeared as Warren in *The Waterdance,* 1992.

TELEVISION APPEARANCES; SPECIALS

Sergeant Bookman, *Vietnam War Story,* HBO, 1988.
Patrolman Lou Barton, *H.E.L.P.* (also known as *911*), ABC, 1990.

STAGE APPEARANCES

L. B., *The Boys of Winter,* Biltmore Theatre, New York City, 1985.
Sister Boom Boom and Richard Pabich, *Execution of Justice,* Virginia Theatre, New York City, 1986.

Also appeared as Puck in *A Midsummer Night's Dream.*

RECORDINGS:

VIDEOS

Appeared in the music video *Bad,* with Michael Jackson, 1987.

OTHER SOURCES:

PERIODICALS

Hollywood Reporter, March 23, 1992, pp. S12-S13, S21.
New York Times, March 27, 1991, p. B6.
Premiere, July, 1991, p. 78-79.*

* * *

SOMMER, Josef 1934-

PERSONAL: Full name, Maximilian Josef Sommer; born June 26, 1934 in Greifswald, Germany; son of Clemons (a professor) and Elisebeth Sommer; children: Maria. *Education:* Carnegie-Mellon University, B.F.A., 1957; also studied at the American Shakespeare Festival in Stratford, CT, 1962-64.

CAREER: Actor. *Military service:* U.S. Army, 1958-60.

AWARDS, HONORS: Fulbright grant to study professional theatre in Germany, 1960-61; Obie Award, 1982, for *Lydie Breeze.*

CREDITS:

STAGE APPEARANCES

(Debut) Bodo, *Watch on the Rhine,* Carolina Playmakers, Chapel Hill, NC, 1943.
Lord Ross, *Richard II,* American Shakespeare Festival, Stratford, CT, 1962.
Sir Richard Vernon, *Henry IV, Part I,* American Shakespeare Festival, Stratford, CT, 1962.
Lord Rivers, *Richard III,* American Shakespeare Festival, Stratford, CT, 1964.
Antonio, *Much Ado about Nothing,* American Shakespeare Festival, Stratford, CT, 1964.
First Player, *Hamlet,* American Shakespeare Festival, Stratford, CT, 1964.
Cominius, *Coriolanus,* American Shakespeare Festival, Stratford, CT, 1965.
Lord Capulet, *Romeo and Juliet,* American Shakespeare Festival, Stratford, CT, 1965.

Duke of Albany, *King Lear,* American Shakespeare Festival, Stratford, CT, 1965.
King Henry IV, *Falstaff (Henry IV, Part II),* American Shakespeare Festival, Stratford, CT, 1966.
Fourth Tempter, *Murder in the Cathedral,* American Shakespeare Festival, Stratford, CT, 1966.
Title role, *Julius Caesar,* American Shakespeare Festival, Stratford, CT, 1966.
Tartuffe, Seattle Repertory Theatre, Seattle Center, Seattle, WA, between 1966 and 1967.
Malvolio, *Twelfth Night,* San Diego National Shakespeare Festival, Old Globe Theatre, 1967.
Captain E. Dumain, *All's Well That Ends Well,* San Diego National Shakespeare Festival, Old Globe Theatre, 1967.
John of Gaunt, *Richard II,* American Shakespeare Festival, Stratford, CT, 1968.
Captain, *Androcles and the Lion,* American Shakespeare Festival, Stratford, CT, 1968.
Don Adriano de Armado, *Love's Labour's Lost,* American Shakespeare Festival, Stratford, CT, 1968.
George, *Who's Afraid of Virginia Woolf,* Seattle Repertory Theatre Company tour, Bergen Norway International Theatre Festival, 1969.
All's Well That Ends Well, American Shakespeare Festival, Stratford, CT, 1970.
(Broadway debut) Brabantio and understudy for Iago, *Othello,* American Shakespeare Festival, Anta Theatre, New York City, 1970-71.
Defense, *The Trial of the Catonsville Nine,* Good Shepherd Faith Church, New York City, 1971, then Lyceum Theatre, New York City, 1971.
Dr. Karl Yaeger, *Children! Children!,* Ritz Theatre, New York City, 1972.
Nikolai Skrobotov, *Enemies,* Repertory Theater of Lincoln Center, Vivian Beaumont Theater, New York City, 1972.
Antonio, *The Merchant of Venice,* Repertory Theater of Lincoln Center, Vivian Beaumont Theater, 1973.
Schmidt, *Full Circle,* Anta Theatre, 1973.
Arnold J. Pilger, *Who's Who in Hell,* Lunt-Fontanne Theatre, New York City, 1974.
Richard III, Long Wharf Theatre, New Haven, CT, 1974-75.
William, *The Dog Ran Away,* Ensemble Studio Theatre, New York City, 1975.
The Government Inspector, Hartman Theatre Company, Stamford, CT, 1975-76.
Interviewer, *The Shadow Box,* Morosco Theatre, New York City, 1977.
The Archbishop's Ceiling, John F. Kennedy Center for the Performing Arts, Washington, DC, 1976-77.
Alphabetical Order, Long Wharf Theatre, New Haven, CT, 1976-77.
Spokesong, Long Wharf Theatre, 1978.
Alan, *Drinks before Dinner,* Public/Newman Theater, New York City, 1978.
Summerfolk, Long Wharf Theatre, between 1978 and 1979.
Francis, Frank's grandfather, *Spokesong or The Common Wheel,* Circle in the Square, New York City, 1979.
Clifton A. Feddington, *The 1940's Radio Hour,* St. James Theatre, New York City, 1979-80.
Dr. Michael Emerson, *Whose Life Is It Anyway?,* Royale Theatre, New York City, 1980.
George, *The Lady And The Clarinet,* Center Theatre Group/Mark Taper Forum, Los Angeles, CA, 1980.
Joshua Hickman, *Lydie Breeze,* American Place Theatre, New York City, 1982.
Martin Engel, *Black Angel,* Circle Repertory Theatre, New York City, 1982-83.
George, *The Lady And The Clarinet,* Lucille Lortel Theatre, New York City, 1983.
Victor Marsden, *Love Letters on Blue Paper,* Hudson Guild Theatre, New York City, 1984.
Bullie's House, Long Wharf Theatre, 1985.
Leopold, *Largo Desolato,* New York Shakespeare Festival, Public/Newman Theater, 1986.
Audrey Botvinnik, *A Walk in the Woods,* Yale Repertory Theatre, New Haven, CT, 1987.
Love Letters, Promenade Theatre, New York City, 1989.
Polonius, *Hamlet,* New York Shakespeare Festival, Public/Anspacher Theater, 1990.

Appeared in various productions for the Seattle Repertory Theatre, 1966-67, 1967-68, 1968-69, 1969-70, and 1971-72; American Shakespeare Festival, Stratford, CT, 1970-71, 1972; American Shakespeare Theatre, Stratford, CT, 1976; American Conservatory Theatre, San Francisco, CA, 1970-71; Hartford Stage Company, Hartford, CT, 1975-76; McCarter Theatre Company, Princeton, NJ, 1975-76.

FILM APPEARANCES

Rothko, *Dirty Harry,* Malpaso/Warner Brothers, 1971.
Peter Russell, *Man on a Swing,* Paramount, 1974.
(Under name M. Josef Sommer) Committee Chairman, *The Front,* Columbia, 1976.
Larry Butler, *Close Encounters of the Third Kind,* Columbia, 1977.
Dr. Dienhart, *Oliver's Story,* Paramount, 1978.
McAdam, *Absence of Malice,* Columbia, 1981.
State Department Official, *Reds,* Paramount, 1981.
Roy Lefcourt, *Rollover,* Warner Brothers, 1981.
Adrian Pruitt, *Hanky-Panky,* Columbia, 1982.
Narrator, *Sophie's Choice,* Universal, 1982.
George Bynum, *Still of the Night,* Metro-Goldwyn-Mayer/United Artists, 1982.
Sam Taylor, *Independence Day,* Warner Brothers, 1983.

Max Richter, *Silkwood,* Twentieth Century-Fox, 1983.
Whitman, *Iceman,* Universal, 1984.
Dr. Jeffrey Stewart, *D.A.R.Y.L.,* Paramount, 1985.
Barney Taber, *Target,* Warner Brothers, 1985.
Deputy Commissioner Schaeffer, *Witness,* Paramount, 1985.
Lt. Walt Koznicki, *The Rosary Murders,* New Line, 1987.
Lt. Lannon, *Dracula's Widow,* DEG, 1988.
Judge Fenwick, *Chances Are,* Tri-Star, 1989.
Waldo Winchester, *Bloodhounds of Broadway,* Columbia, 1989.
Father, *Forced March,* Shapiro Glickenhaus, 1990.
Priest, *Shadows and Fog,* Orion, 1992.

Also appeared as Jack Ockham, *Saigon—Year of the Cat,* 1983.

TELEVISION APPEARANCES; MOVIES

Henry Mills, *Too Far to Go,* NBC, 1979.
Mr. Parker, *Doctor Franken,* NBC, 1980.
Dr. Martin Grossman, *The Henderson Monster,* CBS, 1980.
George Barton, *Agatha Christie's "Sparkling Cyanide,"* CBS, 1983.
Rafferty, *Brotherly Love,* CBS, 1985.
James Angelton, *Yuri Nosenko, KGB,* HBO, 1986.
Gerald Ford, *The Betty Ford Story,* ABC, 1987.
General Winder, *Special Friendship,* CBS, 1987.
Jack Finley, *Money, Power, Murder* (also known as *Dead Air*), CBS, 1989.
Esterman, *Bionic Showdown: The Six Million Dollar Man and the Bionic Woman* (also known as *Return of the Six Million Dollar Man and the Bionic Woman II*), CBS, 1989.
Al Duffield, *Bridge to Silence,* CBS, 1989.
Martin Ransil, *When Will I Be Loved?,* NBC, 1990.
Franklin D. Roosevelt, *The Kennedys of Massachusetts* (also known as *The Fitzgeralds and the Kennedys*), ABC, 1990.
Stewart Merriman, *Before the Storm* (also known as *Spy Games, Under Cover, Undercover,* and *The Company*), ABC, 1991.
Joseph Kennedy, *A Woman Named Jackie* (also known as *A Woman Called Jackie*), NBC, 1991.

Also appeared as Jim Neal, *The Execution of Raymond Graham,* 1985.

TELEVISION APPEARANCES; EPISODIC

Doc, "The Wide Net," *American Playhouse,* PBS, 1987.
Polonius, "Hamlet," *Great Performances,* PBS, 1990.

OTHER TELEVISION APPEARANCES

Narrator, *Fires of the Mind* (also known as *The Infinite Voyage*), PBS, 1988.
Dr. Sam Garrison, *Hothouse* (also known as *The Clinic*), ABC, 1988.

Also made the following appearances: Nikolai Skrobotov, *Enemies,* 1974; Varnum, *Valley Forge,* 1975; *The Adams Chronicles,* 1976; Nathaniel Hawthorne, host and narrator, *The Scarlet Letter,* 1979; *Morning Becomes Electra,* and *Saigon.**

* * *

SPAULDING, Douglas
See BRADBURY, Ray

* * *

SPIELBERG, Steven 1947-

PERSONAL: Born December 18, 1947, in Cincinnati, OH; son of Arnold (an electrical engineer) and Leah (a concert pianist; maiden name, Posner) Spielberg; married Amy Irving (an actress), November 27, 1985 (divorced, 1989); married Kate Capshaw (an actress), October 12, 1991; children: (first marriage) Max Samuel; (second marriage) Sasha. *Education:* California State College (now University), Long Beach, B.A., 1970. *Avocational interests:* Audio-visual gimmicks, custard pies, skeet shooting.

ADDRESSES: Office—Amblin' Entertainment, 100 Universal Plaza #477, Universal City, CA 91608. *Agent*—Creative Artists Agency, 9830 Wilshire Blvd., Beverly Hills, CA 90212.

CAREER: Director, producer, and screenwriter. Won film contest at age thirteen with the war movie *Escape to Nowhere;* made numerous films in college; made short film, *Amblin',* which earned him the position of director on television series and films; formed Amblin' Entertainment production company, 1986, named after his short film of the same name.

MEMBER: Directors Guild of America, Screenwriters Guild of America.

AWARDS, HONORS: Academy Award nomination, best director, 1977, for *Close Encounters of the Third Kind;* Academy Award nomination, best director, 1981, for *Raiders of the Lost Ark;* Academy Award nominations for best picture and best director, both 1982, both for *E.T. the Extra-Terrestrial;* National Alliance of Theater Owners' producer of the year and director of the year awards, 1982; Hasty Pudding man of the year award, Hasty Pudding Theatricals, 1983; Academy Award nomination for best picture, outstanding directorial achievement award for feature films, Directors Guild of America, and Golden

Globe film director's award, all 1985, all for *The Color Purple;* Emmy Award nomination, best director of a drama series, 1985-86, for "The Mission" (episode of *Amazing Stories* series); Irving G. Thalberg Award, Academy of Motion Picture Arts and Sciences, 1986, for consistent high quality in filmmaking; academy fellow and film award, both from British Academy of Film and Television Arts, both 1986; honorary doctorate in creative arts, Brandeis University, 1986; Emmy Award, outstanding animated program, 1990, for *Tiny Toon Adventures: The Looney Beginning.*

CREDITS:

FILM DIRECTOR

The Sugarland Express (also see below), Universal, 1974.
Jaws, Universal, 1975.
Close Encounters of the Third Kind (also see below), Columbia, 1977.
1941, Universal, 1979.
Raiders of the Lost Ark, Paramount, 1981.
E.T. the Extra-Terrestrial (also see below), Universal, 1982.
Twilight Zone—The Movie (director of "Kick the Can" segment; also see below), Warner Brothers, 1983.
Indiana Jones and the Temple of Doom, Paramount, 1984.
The Color Purple (also see below), Warner Brothers, 1985.
Empire of the Sun (also see below), Warner Brothers, 1987.
Always (also see below), Universal, 1989.
Indiana Jones and the Last Crusade, Paramount, 1989.
Hook, TriStar, 1991.

Directed first professional film *Amblin,'* 1969. Also assisted director Kevin Reynolds in the production of Reynolds's 1985 film *Fandango,* starring Kevin Costner.

FILM EXECUTIVE PRODUCER

I Wanna Hold Your Hand, Universal, 1978.
Used Cars, Columbia, 1980.
Continental Divide, Universal, 1981.
Gremlins, Warner Brothers, 1984.
Young Sherlock Holmes, Paramount, 1985.
Back to the Future, Universal, 1985.
The Goonies (also see below), Warner Brothers, 1985.
An American Tail, Universal, 1986.
The Money Pit, Universal, 1986.
Inner Space, Warner Brothers, 1987.
Batteries Not Included, Universal, 1987.
Who Framed Roger Rabbit?, Buena Vista, 1988.
The Land before Time (also known as *The Land before Time Began*), Universal, 1988.
Back to the Future II, Universal, 1989.
Dad, Universal, 1989.
Tummy Trouble (Roger Rabbit animated short), Buena Vista, 1989.
Arachnophobia, Hollywood, 1990.
Back to the Future III, Universal, 1990.
Gremlins 2: The New Batch, Warner Brothers, 1990.
Roller Coaster Rabbit (Roger Rabbit animated short), Buena Vista, 1990.

FILM PRODUCER

(With Kathleen Kennedy) *E.T. the Extra-Terrestrial,* Universal, 1982.
(With Frank Marshall) *Poltergeist* (also see below), Metro-Goldwyn-Mayer (MGM)/United Artists (UA), 1982.
(With John Landis) *Twilight Zone—The Movie,* Warner Brothers, 1983.
(With Kennedy, Marshall, Quincy Jones, Jon Peters, and Peter Gubers) *The Color Purple,* Warner Brothers, 1985.
(With Kennedy and Marshall) *Empire of the Sun,* Warner Brothers, 1987.
(With Kennedy and Marshall) *Always,* Universal, 1989.
Joe Versus the Volcano, Warner Brothers, 1990.
An American Tail: Fievel Goes West, Universal, 1991.

FILM APPEARANCES

Cook County clerk, *The Blues Brothers,* Universal, 1983.
Listen Up (also known as *Listen Up: The Lives of Quincy Jones*), Warner Brothers, 1990

Also appeared in *Chambre 666,* 1982.

TELEVISION DIRECTOR; MOVIES

Duel, Universal TV, 1971.
Something Evil, CBS, 1972.
Savage, Universal TV, 1973.

TELEVISION DIRECTOR; PILOTS

Night Gallery (director of second story), NBC, 1969.

TELEVISION DIRECTOR; EPISODIC

"Murder by the Book," *Columbo,* NBC, 1971.

TELEVISION DIRECTOR; SERIES

Night Gallery, NBC, 1971-72 (sixty-minute episodes), 1972-73 (thirty-minute episodes).
Owen Marshall: Counselor at Law, ABC, 1971-74.
The Psychiatrist, NBC, 1971.
Amazing Stories (also known as *Steven Spielberg's Amazing Stories;* anthology series; also see below), NBC, 1985-87.

TELEVISION EXECUTIVE PRODUCER; PILOTS

Tiny Toon Adventures: The Looney Beginning (pilot), CBS, 1990.

TELEVISION EXECUTIVE PRODUCER; SERIES

Amazing Stories (also see below), NBC, 1985-87.
Tiny Toon Adventures (also known as *Tiny Toons* and *Tiny Tunes*), syndicated, 1990.

TELEVISION APPEARANCES; SPECIALS

Funny, You Don't Look Two Hundred, ABC, 1987.
The Fifty-ninth Annual Academy Awards, ABC, 1987.
Premiere: Inside the Summer Blockbusters, Fox, 1989.
Siskel & Ebert: The Future of the Movies with Steven Spielberg, George Lucas, and Martin Scorcese, syndicated, 1990.
The Muppets Celebrate Jim Henson, CBS, 1990.
The Eighteenth Annual American Film Institute Life Achievement Award: A Salute to Sir David Lean, ABC, 1990.
The Sixty-second Annual Academy Awards Presentation, ABC, 1990.
The Movie Awards, CBS, 1991.

Also appeared in the television special *Roger Rabbit and the Secrets of Toontown,* 1988.

OTHER TELEVISION APPEARANCES

Something Evil (movie), CBS, 1972.
China Odyssey: Empire of the Sun (documentary), CBS, 1987.
Martin Scorcese Directs (documentary), PBS, 1990.

WRITINGS:

SCREENPLAYS

Close Encounters of the Third Kind (also see below), Columbia, 1977.
(With Michael Grais and Mark Victor) *Poltergeist,* MGM/UA, 1982.

FILM STORY IDEAS

Ace Eli and Rodger of the Skies, Twentieth Century-Fox, 1973.
(With Hal Barwood and Matthew Robbins) *The Sugarland Express,* Universal, 1974.
The Goonies, Warner Brothers, 1985.

TELEVISION STORY IDEAS

Creator of *Amazing Stories* and of story ideas for two of its episodes, "The Mission" and "The Wedding Ring," NBC, 1985-87.

OTHER

Co-author, with Patrick Mann, of book adaptation of *Close Encounters of the Third Kind.*

OTHER SOURCES:

BOOKS

Contemporary Authors, Volume 77-80, Gale, 1979.
Mott, Donald R. and Cheryl McAllister Saunders, *Steven Spielberg,* Twayne, 1986.

PERIODICALS

American Film, June, 1988, pp. 12, 14-16.
New York Times, January 10, 1988, pp. 21, 30.
Times (London), March 11, 1990, pp. 1, 6.

* * *

STEIGER, Rod 1925-

PERSONAL: Full name, Rodney Stephen Steiger; born April 14, 1925, in Westhampton, Long Island, NY; son of Frederick (an entertainer) and Lorraine (an entertainer; maiden name, Driver) Steiger; married Sally Gracie (an actress), 1952 (divorced, 1958); married Claire Bloom (an actress), September 19, 1959 (divorced); married Sherry Nelson, April, 1973 (divorced, 1979); married Paula Ellis; children: (second marriage) Anna Justine. *Education:* Studied acting at New School for Social Research, 1946-47; studied at American Theatre Wing, Dramatic Workshop, and at Actors Studio, New York City. *Avocational interests:* Swimming, tennis, painting, composing music, writing poetry, collecting modern art.

ADDRESSES: Agent—c/o Martin Baum, Creative Artists Agency, 1888 Century Park East, 14th Floor, Los Angeles, CA 90067.

CAREER: Actor. Veteran's Administration, Office of Dependents and Beneficiaries, office assistant, c. 1945. Member of Civil Service Little Theatre Group, 1945. *Military service:* U.S. Naval Reserve, 1942-45.

MEMBER: Screen Actors Guild, Metropolitan Museum of Art, life member.

AWARDS, HONORS: Sylvania Award, one of five best dramatic television performers of the year, 1953, for *Marty* and *You are There;* Academy Award nomination, best supporting actor, 1954, for *On the Waterfront;* Academy Award nomination, best actor, 1965, Berlin Film Festival Award, best actor, 1964, and British Film Academy Award, best foreign actor in a leading role, 1966, all for *The Pawnbroker;* Emmy Award, best actor, 1958, for "The Lonely Wizard," *Schlitz Playhouse;* Emmy nomination, outstanding single performance by an actor in a lead role, 1964, for *Bob Hope Presents the Chrysler Theatre;* Academy Award, best performance by an actor in a leading role, 1967, New York Film Critics Award, best actor, 1967, British Film Academy Award, best foreign actor in a leading role, 1967, and Golden Globe Award, best actor, 1968, all for *In the Heat of the Night;* Genie Award nomination, best performance by a foreign actor, 1980, for *Jack London's Klondike Fever;* Genie Award nomination, best performance by a foreign actor, 1981, for *The Lucky Star;* Montreal World Film Festival Award, best actor, 1981, for *The Chosen.*

CREDITS:

STAGE APPEARANCES

Detective, *Night Music,* Equity Library Theatre, New York City, 1951.
Bandit, *Rashomon,* Music Box Theatre, New York City, 1959.
Harry Davis, *A Short Happy Life,* Moore Theatre, Seattle, WA, then Harford Theatre, Los Angeles, 1961.
Actor-manager, Father Mapple, Captain Ahab, *Moby Dick,* New York City, 1962.
Voice of Poseidon, *The Trojan Women,* Circle in the Square, New York City, 1963.

Also performed in *Seagulls Over Sorento,* 1953, and *An Enemy of the People,* 1953; performed in the Actor's Studio touring production of *The Trial of Mary Dugan.*

FILM APPEARANCES

Frank, *Teresa,* Metro-Goldwyn-Mayer (MGM), 1951.
Charley Malloy, *On the Waterfront,* Columbia, 1954.
Stanley Hoff, *The Big Knife,* United Artists (UA), 1955.
Major Alla Guillion, *The Court-Martial of Billy Mitchell* (also known as *One-Man Mutiny*), Warner Brothers, 1955.
Jud Fry, *Oklahoma,* Magna Theatres, 1955.
Nick Benko, *The Harder They Fall,* Columbia, 1956.
Vasquez, *Back from Eternity,* RKO, 1956.
Pinky, *Jubal,* Columbia, 1956.
O'Meara, *Run of the Arrow,* Universal, 1957.
Paul Hochen, *The Unholy Wife,* Universal, 1957.
Carl Schaffner, *Across the Bridge,* Rank, 1957.
Paul Hoplin, *Cry Terror,* MGM, 1958.
Title role, *Al Capone,* Allied Artists, 1959.
Paul Mason, *Seven Thieves,* Twentieth Century-Fox, 1960.
Dr. Edmund McNally, *The Mark,* Twentieth Century-Fox, 1960.
Frank Morgan, *World in My Pocket* (originally released as *Vendredi 13 heures, Pas de mentalite, Il mondo nella mia tasca, Einem freitag um halb zwolf;* also known as *On Friday at Eleven*), MGM, 1960.
Detective Sergeant Koleski, *Thirteen West Street* (also known as *The Tiger Among Us*), Columbia, 1961.
Destroyer Commander, *The Longest Day,* Twentieth Century-Fox, 1962.
Tiptoes, *Convicts Four* (also known as *Reprieve*), Allied Artists, 1962.
City councilman, *Hands Over the City* (originally released as *La Mani Sulla Cite,* 1962) Galatea Films, 1963.
Sol Nazerman, *The Pawnbroker,* Allied Artists/Landau/American International, 1964.
Leo, *The Time of Indifference* (originally released as *Gli indifferenti, Les Deux rivales*), Continental Distributing, 1965.
Victor Komarovsky, *Doctor Zhivago,* MGM, 1965.
Mr. Joyboy, *The Loved One,* MGM, 1965.
Bill Gillespie, *In the Heat of the Night,* UA, 1967.
The General, *The Girl and the General,* MGM, 1967.
Christopher Gill, *No Way to Treat a Lady,* Paramount, 1968.
Pope John XIII, *And There Came a Man,* Brandon, 1968.
Master Sergeant Albert Callan, *The Sergeant,* Warner Bros., 1968.
Carl, *The Illustrated Man,* Warner Bros., 1969.
Steve Howard, *Three Into Two Won't Go,* Universal, 1969.
Napoleon Bonaparte, *Waterloo,* Paramount, 1970.
Harold Ryan, *Happy Birthday, Wanda June,* Columbia, 1971.
Juan Miranda, *Duck! You Sucker* (originally released as *Giu la testa;* also known as *Fist Full of Dynamite*), UA, 1972.
Laban Feather, *The Lolly-Madonna Wars* (also known as *Lolly-Madonna XXX*), MGM, 1973.
Benito Mussolini, *The Last Days of Mussolini* (originally released as *Mussolini: Ultimo Atto;* also known as *The Last Four Days*), Paramount, 1974.
Gene Giannini, *Re: Lucky Luciano* (originally released as *A proposito Luciano*), Avco Embassy, 1975.
Title role, *Hennessy,* American International, 1975.
W. C. Fields, *W. C. Fields and Me,* Universal, 1976.
General Webster, *Breakthrough* (also known as *Sergeant Steiner*), Maverick, 1978.
Senator Andrew Madison, *F.I.S.T.,* UA, 1978.
Louis, *Dirty Hands* (originally released as *Les innocents aux mains sales,* 1975), New Line, 1978.
Father Delaney, *The Amityville Horror,* American International, 1979.
Soapy Smith, *Jack London's Klondike Fever* (also known as *Klondike Fever*), CFI Investments, 1979.
Joe Bomposa, *Love and Bullets,* Associated Film Distribution, 1979.
Colonel Gluck, *The Lucky Star,* Tele Metropole Internationale, 1980.
Benito Mussolini, *Lion of the Desert* (also known as *Omar Mukhtar*), United Film Distributors, 1980.
U.S. Marshall Bill Tilghman, *Cattle Annie and Little Britches,* Universal, 1981.
Reb Saunders, *The Chosen,* Twentieth Century-Fox, 1982.
Lieutenant McGreavy, *The Naked Face,* Cannon, 1985.

Dr. Philip Lloyd, *The Kindred,* F/M Entertainment, 1987.
Pa, *American Gothic,* Vidmark, 1987.
Jason Hannibal, *Feel the Heat* (also known as *Catch the Heat*), Trans World, 1987.
Mayor Eamon Flynn, *The January Man,* MGM/UA, 1988.
Reverend Kahl, *Ballad of the Sad Cafe,* Angelika Films, 1991.
Charlie D'Amico, *Men of Respect,* Columbia, 1991.
Ben Kallin, *Guilty as Charged,* IRS Releasing, 1992.

Appeared as Colonel Webster, *Teil Steiner: Das eiserne Kreuz 2,* 1979; Martin, *That Summer of White Roses,* 1989; Judge Prescott, *Twist of Fate,* 1989. Also starred in *The Tiger among Us,* 1961, *Gli Eroi,* 1972, *The Heroes,* 1975, Charlie, *Wolf Lake,* 1979, *The Magic Mountain,* 1982, *Portrait of a Hitman,* 1984, *Tennessee Waltz,* 1989, *Sauf votre respect,* 1989, *Exiles,* 1989, and appeared in *The Player,* 1992. Also starred in *A Question of Life.*

TELEVISION APPEARANCES; EPISODIC

"Raymond Schindler, Case One," *Goodyear Television Playhouse,* NBC, 1952.
Marty Poletti, "Marty," *Goodyear Television Playhouse,* NBC, 1953, reaired on *The Golden Age of Television,* PBS, 1981.
Andrei Vishinsky, "Rudolph Hess," *You Are There,* CBS, 1953.
Charles Steinmetz, "The Lonely Wizard," *Schlitz Playhouse of Stars,* CBS, 1957.
Sheriff, "A Town Has Turned to Dust," *Playhouse 90,* CBS, 1958.
The Twelfth Annual People's Choice Awards, CBS, 1986.
Guest appearance, *Reflections on the Silver Screen With Professor Richard Brown,* AMC, 1990.
Miracle on 44th Street, A Portrait of the Actors Studio (documentary; part of the *American Masters* series), PBS, 1991.

Steiger appeared in over 250 live television dramas from 1948-1953 on *Kraft Television Theatre,* NBC, *Philco Television Playhouse,* NBC, and *Bob Hope Presents the Chrysler Theater,* NBC; appeared on *Danger* and *Sure as Fate,* both CBS; appeared in the role of Radio operator, *My Brother's Keeper,* 1953. Also appeared in *The Movie Maker,* 1967, *Der Zauberberg,* 1982, *I Love Liberty,* 1982, and *Hello, Actor's Theatre,* 1985.

TELEVISION APPEARANCES; MOVIES

Pontius Pilate, *Jesus of Nazareth* (mini-series), NBC, 1977.
Robert E. Peary, *Cook and Peary: The Race to the Pole,* CBS, 1983.
Oliver Easterne, *Hollywood Wives* (mini-series), ABC, 1985.
Mordechai Samuels, *Sword of Gideon,* HBO, 1986.
Silas Slaten, *Desperado: Avalanche at Devil's Ridge,* NBC, 1988.
Sir Harry Oakes, *Passion and Paradise* (mini-series), ABC, 1989.
Gordon Kahl, *In the Line of Duty: Manhunt in the Dakotas* (also known as *The Twilight Murders*), NBC, 1991.

WRITINGS:

Author of the screenplay *In Time of War,* sold to United Artists.

OTHER SOURCES:

PERIODICALS

American Film, January-February, 1982, pp. 36-39.
New Yorker, October 28, 1961.*

* * *

STRASSER, Robin 1945-

PERSONAL: Born May 7, 1945, in New York, NY; daughter of Martin and Anne Strasser; married Laurence Luckinbill (an actor), c. 1965 (divorced); married Richard Hogan (a television executive), 1983 (divorced, 1985); children: (first marriage) Nicholas, Benjamin. *Education:* Graduated from High School for the Performing Arts, New York City, 1962; studied drama at Yale University for one year.

ADDRESSES: Agent—STE Representation, 9301 Wilshire Blvd., Suite 312, Beverly Hills, CA 90210.

CAREER: Actress. Apprentice at New York Shakespeare Festival and Williamstown Summer Theatre; American Conservatory Theatre, New York City, founding member of repertory company.

AWARDS, HONORS: Emmy Award nominations, outstanding actress in a daytime drama series, 1981, 1983, and 1984, and Emmy Award, outstanding actress in a daytime drama series, 1982, all for *One Life to Live.*

CREDITS:

TELEVISION APPEARANCES; SERIES

Rachel Davis Cory, *Another World,* NBC, 1967-71 and 1972.
Dr. Christina Karras, *All My Children,* ABC, 1976-79.
Dianne Kirkwood, *Knots Landing,* CBS, 1979.
Dorian Lord Callison, *One Life to Live,* ABC, 1979-87.

Also appeared in *The Secret Storm,* CBS.

TELEVISION APPEARANCES; MOVIES

Nancy Donovan, *Glitz,* NBC, 1988.
Elizabeth Stern, *Baby M,* ABC, 1988.
Felice Richmond, *Blind Faith,* NBC, 1990.
Jewel Carmen, *White Hot: The Mysterious Murder of Thelma Todd* (also known as *Hot Toddy*), NBC, 1991.

TELEVISION APPEARANCES; EPISODIC

Appeared in episodes of *Murder-Impossible* and *Coach.*

OTHER TELEVISION APPEARANCES

Appeared in *The Child Is Mine.*

FILM APPEARANCES

Barbara, *The Bride* (also known as *The House That Cried Murder*), Unisphere, 1973.

STAGE APPEARANCES

Linda Kingsley, *The Impossible Years,* Playhouse Theatre, New York City, 1965-67.
Nancy Stoddard, *The Country Girl,* New York City Center Theatre, 1966.
Penelope, *A Meeting by the River,* Edison Theatre, New York City, 1972.
Cross Country, New Theatre for Now, New York City, 1974-75, then Mark Taper Forum, Los Angeles, CA, 1975-76.
Diamonds in the Rough, New Theatre for Now, 1975-76.
Jennie Malone, *Chapter Two,* Imperial Theatre, New York City, 1977-79, then Eugene O'Neill Theatre, New York City, 1979.
Margarita, *Loving Reno,* New York Theatre Studio, New York City, 1983.

Made Broadway debut in *The Irregular Verb to Love,* 1963. Also appeared in *The Shadow Box.*

STAGE WORK

Producer (with Andrew Harris), *The Life of Galileo,* Havemeyer Laboratory, Columbia University, New York City, 1978.

OTHER SOURCES:

PERIODICALS

People Weekly, May 23, 1988, p. 55.*

* * *

SUBOTSKY, Milt
See Subotsky, Milton

SUBOTSKY, Milton 1921-1991
(Milt Subotsky)

PERSONAL: Born September 27, 1921, in New York, NY; died of heart disease, June 27, 1991, in London, England; married, wife's name, Fiona; children: two sons. *Education:* Attended Brooklyn Technical High School and Cooper Union College of Engineering.

CAREER: Producer and writer. Wrote, directed, and edited documentary and educational films; wrote and produced live television programs, 1941; affiliated with television film series *Junior Science,* 1954; founded Amicus Productions Ltd., c. 1962, and Sword and Sorcery Productions, 1975. Worked on a syndicated newspaper column with Billy Rose after World War II. *Wartime service:* Wrote technical training films and edited Signal Corps films and camp newspaper during World War II.

CREDITS:

FILM PRODUCER; WITH MAX J. ROSENBERG

(And music director) *Rock, Rock, Rock!* (also see below), Distributor Corp. of America, 1956.
Jamboree (also known as *Disc Jockey Jamboree*), Warner Bros., 1957.
The Last Mile (also see below), United Artists (UA), 1959.
Dr. Terror's House of Horrors (also see below), Regal Films, 1965.
Dr. Who and the Daleks (also see below), Regal Films, 1965.
The Skull (also see below), Paramount, 1965.
Daleks—Invasion Earth 2150 A.D. (also known as *Invasion Earth 2150 A.D.;* sequel to *Dr. Who and the Daleks;* also see below), British Lion, 1966.
The Psychopath, Paramount, 1966.
The Deadly Bees, Paramount, 1967.
The Terrornauts, Embassy, 1967.
They Came from Beyond Space (also see below), Embassy, 1967.
The Birthday Party, Continental, 1968.
Danger Route, UA, 1968.
Torture Garden, Columbia, 1968.
Thank You All Very Much (released in England as *A Touch of Love*), Columbia, 1969.
The Mind of Mr. Soames, Columbia, 1970.
Scream and Scream Again, American International, 1970.
The House That Dripped Blood, Amicus, 1971.
I, Monster (also see below), Cannon, 1971.
Asylum (also known as *House of Crazies*), Cinerama, 1972.
Tales from the Crypt (also see below), Cinerama, 1972.
What Became of Jack and Jill? (also known as *Romeo and Juliet, 1971—A Gentle Tale of Sex, Violence, Corruption and Murder*), Twentieth Century-Fox, 1972.
And Now the Screaming Starts, Cinerama, 1973.

The Vault of Horror (also known as *Tales from the Crypt II;* also see below), Cinerama, 1973.
The Beast Must Die, Cinerama, 1974.
From Beyond the Grave (also known as *The Creature from beyond the Grave* and *Creatures*), Warner Bros., 1974.
Madhouse, American International, 1974.

FILM PRODUCER

Just for Fun (also see below), Columbia, 1963.
(With Andrew Donally) *Dominique,* Subotsky, 1978.
The Monster Club, ITC, 1981.
Stephen King's "Cat's Eye," Metro-Goldwyn-Mayer (MGM)/UA, 1985.
(With Martha Schumacher) *Maximum Overdrive,* DeLaurentiis Entertainment Group, 1986.

Also coproducer and codirector of *The World of Abbott and Costello,* 1965.

TELEVISION PRODUCER

(With Andrew Donally) *The Martian Chronicles* (miniseries), NBC, 1980.
(With David Thomas) *Stephen King's "Sometimes They Come Back"* (movie), CBS, 1991.

WRITINGS:

FILM SCRIPTS

(And music and lyrics with others) *Rock, Rock, Rock!* (based on a story by Subotsky and Phyllis Coe), Distributor Corp. of America, 1956.
(With John Rawlins and Jeffrey Lynn) *Lost Lagoon,* UA, 1958.
(With Seton I. Miller) *The Last Mile* (based on the play of the same title by John Wexley), UA, 1959.
(Author of original story only) *Horror Hotel* (also known as *The City of the Dead*), Trans-Lux, 1960.
(And songs, some with Norrie Paramor) *Ring-a-Ding Rhythm* (also known as *It's Trad, Dad!*), Columbia, 1962.
Just for Fun, Columbia, 1963.
Dr. Terror's House of Horrors, Regal Films, 1965.
Dr. Who and the Daleks (based on the BBC television series *Dr. Who*), Regal Films, 1965.
The Skull (based on Robert Bloch's story "The Skull of the Marquis de Sade"), Paramount, 1965.
Daleks—Invasion Earth 2150 A.D. (also known as *Invasion Earth 2150 A.D.;* sequel to *Dr. Who and the Daleks*), British Lion, 1966.
They Came from Beyond Space (based on Joseph Millard's novel *The Gods Hate Kansas*), Embassy, 1967.
I, Monster, Cannon, 1971.
Tales from the Crypt (based on the stories "Tales from the Crypt" and "The Vault of Horror" by Al Feldstein, Johnny Craig, and William Gaines), Cinerama, 1972.
The Vault of Horror (also known as *Tales from the Crypt II;* based on writings by Feldstein and Gaines), Cinerama, 1973.
At the Earth's Core (based on the novel of the same title by Edgar Rice Burroughs), American International, 1976.

TELEVISION SCRIPTS

(Under name Milt Subotsky) *Quizzing the News* (series), ABC, 1948-49.

Also contributed scripts to *Lights Out, Danger, Suspense, The Clock, Mr. I. Magination,* and *The Golden Treasury of Classic Fairy Tales.*

OTHER

Author of a book, *The Golden Treasury of Classic Fairy Tales,* and coeditor of a science fiction anthology.

ADAPTATIONS: Dr. Terror's House of Horrors was novelized by John Burke.

OBITUARIES AND OTHER SOURCES:

PERIODICALS

Variety, July 8, 1991, p. 63.*

T

TABORI, Kristoffer 1955(?)-
(Kristoffer Siegel-Tabori)

PERSONAL: Born Christopher Donald Siegel, August 4, c. 1955, in Malibu, CA; son of Don Siegel (a film director) and Viveca Lindfors (an actress); stepson of George Tabori (a playwright). *Education:* Attended High School for the Performing Arts, New York City; studied acting with Ada Mather, Diana Maddox, George Tabori, and Viveca Lindfors; studied dance with Gui Andrisano, voice with Joseph Scott and Bob Harrison, and acrobatics with Vincent Gugleotti.

ADDRESSES: Office—172 East 95th St., New York, NY 10028.

CAREER: Actor. Arena Stage, Washington, DC, member of company, 1976-77 and 1977-78; South Coast Repertory, Costa Mesa, CA, member of company, 1980-81; National Shakespeare Festival, San Diego, CA, member of company, 1981.

MEMBER: Actors' Equity Association, Screen Actors Guild, American Federation of Radio and Television Artists.

AWARDS, HONORS: Theatre World Award, 1970, for *How Much, How Much?*

CREDITS:

STAGE APPEARANCES

Balthassar, *The Merchant of Venice,* Berkshire Theatre Festival, Stockbridge, MA, 1966.

Waiting for Godot, Berkshire Theatre Festival, 1966.

The Threepenny Opera, Berkshire Theatre Festival, 1966.

A Funny Thing Happened on the Way to the Forum, Berkshire Theatre Festival, 1966.

Three Boards and a Passion, Royal Alexandra Theatre, Toronto, Ontario, Canada, 1966.

Jose, *The Guns of Carrar,* American National Theatre Academy (ANTA), Theatre de Lys, New York City, 1968.

Arthur, *A Cry of Players,* Vivian Beaumont Theatre, New York City, 1968-69.

Player queen and second grave digger, *Hamlet,* American Shakespeare Festival (ASF) Theatre, Stratford, CT, 1969.

Tyler Bishop, *The Penny Wars,* Royale Theatre, New York City, 1969.

The boy Davy, *Henry V,* ASF, ANTA Theatre, New York City, 1969.

Joe Morris, *Dream of a Blacklisted Actor,* ANTA, Theatre de Lys, 1969.

Charley Gordon, *How Much, How Much?,* Provincetown Playhouse, New York City, 1970.

Romeo, *Romeo and Juliet,* Studio Arena Theatre, Buffalo, NY, 1972.

Prince Hal, *Henry IV, Part I,* Mark Taper Forum, Los Angeles, CA, 1972.

Orlando, *As You Like It,* Los Angeles Shakespeare Festival, Pilgrimage Theatre, Los Angeles, 1973.

The Rose Tattoo, Walnut Street Playhouse, Philadelphia, PA, 1973.

Leeds, *The Wager,* Manhattan Theatre Club, New York City, 1974, then Eastside Playhouse, New York City, 1974-75.

Title role, *Hamlet,* Theatre Venture '75, Beverly, MA, 1975.

Dennis Wicksteed, *Habeas Corpus,* Martin Beck Theatre, New York City, 1975-76.

St. Joan, Long Wharf Theatre, New Haven, CT, 1976-77.

Spud, *Scribes,* Phoenix Theatre, New York City, 1977.

An Evening with Viveca Lindfors and Kristoffer Tabori, Manhattan Theatre Club, 1980.

Inspector Jogot, *The Trouble with Europe,* Marymount Manhattan Theatre, New York City, 1980.

Robert, *Boy Meets Girl,* South Coast Repertory Theatre, Costa Mesa, CA, 1981.
Cantorial, Stamford Center for the Arts, Stamford, CT, 1984.
Stuart Thorne, *The Common Pursuit,* Promenade Theatre, New York City, 1986-87.

Also appeared in *Macbeth,* Los Angeles, CA, 1983; as Thisbe, *A Midsummer Night's Dream,* Young Men's Hebrew Association, New York City; and in *Little Emil and the Detectives.*

FILM APPEARANCES

Boy scout, *John and Mary,* Twentieth Century-Fox, 1969.
Oliver's boyfriend, *The Sidelong Glances of a Pigeon Kicker* (also known as *Pigeons*), Metro-Goldwyn-Mayer/Pathe, 1970.
Phil Fuller, *Making It,* Twentieth Century-Fox, 1971.
Dirty Harry, Warner Brothers, 1971.
Danny, *Journey through Rosebud,* Cinerama, 1972.
Charlie, *Girlfriends,* Warner Brothers, 1978.

Also appeared in *Sweet Charity,* 1959, and in *Weddings and Babies.*

TELEVISION APPEARANCES; MOVIES

David Carlyle, *Family Flight,* ABC, 1972.
Allan Campbell, *Truman Capote's "The Glass House,"* CBS, 1972.
Steve Glynn, *Terror on the Beach,* CBS, 1973.
John Savage, *Brave New World,* NBC, 1980.
Michael Stein, *Arthur Hailey's "Strong Medicine,"* syndicated, 1986.
Chester Brundage, *King of the Olympics: The Lives and Loves of Avery Brundage,* syndicated, 1988.
In the Arms of a Killer, NBC, 1992.

TELEVISION APPEARANCES; EPISODIC

Jonathan, "Neither Are We Enemies," *Hallmark Hall of Fame,* NBC, 1970.
Bert, "A Memory of Two Mondays," *N.E.T. Playhouse,* PBS, 1971.
"The One-Eyed Mule's Time Has Come," *Nichols,* NBC, 1971.
Medical Center, CBS, 1972.
"A Lesson in Loving," *Owen Marshall, Counselor at Law,* ABC, 1973.
"The Friends of Danny Beecher," *Toma,* ABC, 1974.
"The Faith of Childish Things," *Marcus Welby, M.D.,* ABC, 1974.
"Walk a Tightrope," *The Rookies,* ABC, 1974.
"Flashpoint," *Cannon,* CBS, 1974.
"The Lady's Not for Burning," *Hollywood Television Theater,* PBS, 1974.
"The Orchid Killer," *Barnaby Jones,* CBS, 1975.
"Most Likely to Succeed," *Streets of San Francisco,* ABC, 1976.
"Wolf Pack Killer," *Most Wanted,* ABC, 1976.
"The Class Hustler," *What Really Happened to the Class of '65?,* NBC, 1977.
"The Story of the Ten Commandments," *Greatest Heroes of the Bible,* NBC, 1979.
"Only Rock 'n' Roll Will Never Die," *Rockford Files,* NBC, 1979.
Trapper John, M.D., CBS, 1979.
"Rappaccini's Daughter," *American Short Story,* PBS, 1980.
"Terror at the Academy," *T. J. Hooker,* ABC, 1982.
"Life, Death, and Vinnie Duncan," *Trapper John, M.D.,* CBS, 1983.
Small and Frye, CBS, 1983.
"Send in the Clowns," *Trapper John, M.D.,* CBS, 1984.
"Taking a Chance on Love," *Facts of Life,* NBC, 1984.
"Baja 1,000," *The Fall Guy,* ABC, 1984.
"We're Off to Kill the Wizard," *Murder, She Wrote,* CBS, 1984.
"Sing a Song of Murder," *Murder, She Wrote,* CBS, 1985.
"Her Pilgrim Soul," *Twilight Zone,* CBS, 1985.
"Wax Poetic," *Blacke's Magic,* NBC, 1986.
"Crime of Passion," *Hunter,* NBC, 1986.
"Under Siege," *Tour of Duty,* CBS, 1988.
Jerry Hyland, "Once in a Lifetime," *Great Performances,* PBS, 1988.
Sir Henry Baskerville, "The Return of Sherlock Holmes, Series 2," *Mystery!,* PBS, 1988.

Also appeared in *The Young Lawyers.*

TELEVISION APPEARANCES; PILOTS

Harry, *Behind the Lines,* ABC, 1980.
Dr. Maxwell Carson, *The Chicago Story* (also see below), NBC, 1981.
Bruce Wines, *Braker,* ABC, 1985.
Scott Diamond, *Home* (also known as *The Costigans*), ABC, 1987.

OTHER TELEVISION APPEARANCES

Ben Cady, *QB VII* (mini-series), ABC, 1974.
Benny Bache, *Benjamin Franklin: The Statesman* (special), CBS, 1975.
Al Blackman, *Seventh Avenue* (mini-series), NBC, 1977.
Luke Gray as an adult, *Black Beauty* (mini-series), NBC, 1978.
Dr. Maxwell Carson, *Chicago Story* (series), NBC, 1982.

TELEVISION WORK

(Under name Kristoffer Siegel-Tabori) Director, "Perfect Date," *ABC Afterschool Special,* ABC, 1990.*

TALLY, Ted 1952-

PERSONAL: Born April 9, 1952, in Winston-Salem, NC; son of David K. (a school administrator) and Dorothy E. (a teacher; maiden name, Spears) Tally; married Melinda Kahn (an art gallery director), December 11, 1977. *Education:* Yale University, B.A., 1974, M.F.A., 1977.

ADDRESSES: Agent—Arlene Donovan/Patty Detroit, International Creative Management, 40 West Fifty-seventh St., New York, NY 10019.

CAREER: Playwright and screenwriter. Instructor at playwriting seminar at Yale University, 1977-79; master artist in residence at Atlantic Center for the Arts, 1983.

MEMBER: Writers Guild of America, Dramatists Guild, Playwrights Horizons (member of artistic board), Academy of Motion Picture Arts and Sciences.

AWARDS, HONORS: Kazan Award and Theron Rockwell Field Prize, both from Yale University, both 1977, for *Terra Nova;* Columbia Broadcasting System Foundation playwriting fellowship from Yale University, 1977; award from Los Angeles newspaper *Drama-Logue,* 1979, for *Terra Nova;* New York State Creative Artists Public Service Grant, 1980; John Gassner Award, New York Outer Critics Circle, 1981, for *Coming Attractions;* National Endowment for the Arts grant in playwriting, 1983-84; Obie Award, playwriting, *Village Voice,* 1984, for *Terra Nova;* Guggenheim fellow, 1985-86; Christopher Award, 1988, for *The Father Clements Story;* Academy Award, best adapted screenplay, Writers Guild Award, Chicago Film Critics Award, Saturn Award, Golden Globe Award, and British Academy Award nominations, best screenplay, all 1991, all for *The Silence of the Lambs.*

WRITINGS:

STAGE PLAYS

Terra Nova (also see below), first produced at Yale Repertory Theatre, New Haven, CT, 1977, then American Place Theatre, New York City, 1984, published by Doubleday, 1981.

Hooters (also see below), first produced at Playwrights Horizons, 1978, later at Hudson Guild Theatre, New York City, 1982, published by Dramatists Play Service, 1978.

Coming Attractions, first produced at Playwrights Horizons, Mainstage Theatre, New York City, 1980-81, published by Samuel French, 1982.

Silver Linings (collection of revue sketches; first produced as individual pieces in numerous separate revues), published by Dramatists Play Service, 1983.

Little Footsteps, first produced at Playwrights Horizons, 1986, published by Doubleday, 1986.

(Contributor of sketch, with others) *Urban Blight,* produced at Manhattan Theatre Club, New York City, 1988.

"The Gettysburg Sound Bite," part of *Festival of One Act Comedies,* produced at Judith Anderson Theatre, New York City, 1989.

Contributor to anthologies, including *Plays from Playwrights Horizons,* 1987.

SCREENPLAYS FOR FILMS

(With Alvin Sargent) *White Palace* (based on the novel by Glenn Savan), Universal, 1990.

The Silence of the Lambs (based on the novel by Thomas Harris), Orion, 1991.

SCREENPLAYS FOR TELEVISION

Hooters, Playboy Channel, 1983.
(With John Bruce) *Terra Nova,* BBC, 1984.
(Contributor) *The Comedy Zone,* CBS, 1984.
(With Arthur Heinemann) *The Father Clements Story,* NBC, 1987.

OTHER SOURCES:

BOOKS

Contemporary Authors, Volume 124, Gale, 1988, pp. 437-42.

Contemporary Literary Criticism, Volume 42, Gale, 1987, pp. 365-68.

* * *

TARTIKOFF, Brandon 1949-

PERSONAL: Born January 13, 1949, in Freeport, Long Island, NY; son of Jordon (a clothing manufacturer) and Enid (a cruise company employee) Tartikoff; married Lilly Samuels (a former dancer with the New York City Ballet), 1982; children: Calla Lianne. *Education:* Yale University, B.A. (with honors), English, 1970.

ADDRESSES: Office—Paramount Pictures Corporation, 5555 Melrose Ave., Los Angeles, CA 90038-3197.

CAREER: Television network and film executive. WYNH-TV (ABC-TV affiliate station), New Haven, CT, director of advertising and promotion, 1971-73; WLS-TV (ABC-TV affiliate), Chicago, IL, director of advertising and promotion, 1973-76; ABC-TV, New York City, director of dramatic programs, 1976-77; NBC-TV Entertainment, Burbank, CA, director of comedy programs, 1977-78, vice-president of programs, 1978-80, president, 1980-90, chairman, 1990-91; Paramount Pictures, Los Angeles, CA, chairman, 1991—.

MEMBER: Hollywood Radio and Television Society (former president).

AWARDS, HONORS: Named one of ten outstanding Americans, United States Jaycees, 1981; Tree of Life Award, Jewish National Foundation, 1986; Broadcaster of the Year, Television, Radio, and Advertising Club of Philadelphia, 1986; Gordon Grand fellow, Yale University, 1988, for distinguished service in the world of industry, business and finance.

CREDITS:

TELEVISION WORK; SERIES

Creator, *House Party with Steve Doocy* (also known as *The Open House Show*), syndicated, 1990.

TELEVISION APPEARANCES; SPECIALS

Bob Hope Buys NBC?, NBC, 1985.
America Talks Back, NBC, 1986.
NBC Investigates Bob Hope, NBC, 1987.
NBC Presents the AFI Comedy Special (also known as *The AFI Comedy Special* and *The American Film Institute Comedy Special*), NBC, 1987.
The Television Academy Hall of Fame (also known as *The 4th Annual Television Academy Hall of Fame*), Fox, 1987.
Inside "Family Ties": Behind the Scenes of a Hit, PBS, 1988.

SIDELIGHTS: During his years at NBC, Brandon Tartikoff brought the network from a number three rating up to a number one rating by introducing such new shows as *Cheers, The Cosby Show, Hill Street Blues, St. Elsewhere, The Golden Girls, Family Ties, Miami Vice,* and *L.A. Law.*

OTHER SOURCES:

BOOKS

Contemporary Newsmakers, Volume 2, Gale, 1985.

PERIODICALS

Newsweek, May 16, 1983.
People, November 12, 1984.
Rolling Stone, October 22, 1987.*

* * *

TAVOULARIS, Dean 1932-

PERSONAL: Born in 1932.

ADDRESSES: *Agent*—The Gersh Agency Inc., 250 North Canon Dr., Suite 202, Beverly Hills, CA 90210.

CAREER: Production designer and art director.

MEMBER: International Alliance of Theatrical Stage Employees.

AWARDS, HONORS: Academy Award for art direction—set decoration, 1974, for *The Godfather, Part II;* Academy Award nomination for art direction—set decoration, 1978, for *The Brink's Job;* Academy Award nomination for art direction—set decoration, 1979, for *Apocalypse Now;* Academy Award nomination for best achievement in art direction, 1988, for *Tucker: The Man and His Dream;* Academy Award nomination for best achievement in art direction, 1990, for *The Godfather, Part III.*

CREDITS:

FILM ART DIRECTOR

Inside Daisy Clover, Warner Brothers, 1965.
Bonnie and Clyde, Warner Brothers, 1967.
Candy, Cinerama, 1968.
Petulia, Warner Brothers, 1968.
A Man in Love, Cinecom, 1987.

FILM PRODUCTION DESIGNER

Little Big Man, National General, 1970.
Zabriskie Point, Metro-Goldwyn-Mayer, 1970.
The Godfather, Paramount, 1972.
The Conversation, Paramount, 1974.
The Godfather, Part II, Paramount, 1974.
Farewell, My Lovely, Avco Embassy, 1975.
The Brink's Job, Universal, 1978.
Apocalypse Now, United Artists, 1979.
The Escape Artist, Orion-Warner Brothers, 1982.
(With Eugene Lee) *Hammett,* Warner Brothers, 1982.
One from the Heart, Columbia, 1982.
The Outsiders, Warner Brothers, 1983.
Rumble Fish, Zoetrope Universal, 1983.
Peggy Sue Got Married, Tri-Star, 1986.
Gardens of Stone, Tri-Star, 1987.
Tucker: The Man and His Dream, Paramount, 1988.
"Life without Zoe," *New York Stories,* Buena Vista, 1989.
The Godfather, Part III, Paramount, 1990.
Final Analysis, Warner Brothers, 1992.

OTHER FILM WORK

Visual consultant, *Heat,* New Century-Vista, 1987.

TELEVISION APPEARANCES; SPECIALS

Hearts of Darkness: A Filmmaker's Apocalypse, Showtime, 1991.

OTHER SOURCES:

PERIODICALS

Esquire, June, 1989, p. 88.
Theatre Crafts, August-September, 1988, p. 32.*

TAYLOR, Robert U. 1941-

PERSONAL: Full name, Robert Umholtz Taylor; born July 21, 1941, in Lexington, VA; son of John (a chemist; executive vice president of Viscose Corp.) and Helen (Dold) Taylor; married Jane Shure, June, 1963 (divorced, 1965); married Margaret Karagias, July 31, 1971. *Education:* Attended University of Pennsylvania, and Pennsylvania Academy of the Fine Arts; studied set design under Donald Oenslager and Charles Elson at Yale Drama School.

ADDRESSES: Contact—c/o United Scenic Artists, Local 829, AFL-CIO, 575 Eighth Ave., New York, NY, 10018.

CAREER: Setting, lighting, and costume designer. Peterborough Players, Peterborough, NH, set and costume designer, 1964; Westchester Theatre, Westchester, NY, set and costume designer, 1964. Colonnades Theatre Lab, New York City, cofounder. Hunter College of the City University of New York, New York City, instructor; Princeton University, Princeton, NJ, instructor.

MEMBER: United Scenic Artists (Local 829).

AWARDS, HONORS: Drama Desk Award, set design, 1972, for *The Beggar's Opera;* Obie Award, set design, 1975, for *Polly.*

CREDITS:

STAGE WORK; SET DESIGNER

Hansel and Gretel, New Haven Opera Society, New Haven, CT, 1965.
Under Milk Wood, Guthrie Experimental Theatre, Minneapolis, MN, 1966.
(And costume designer) *Bacchae,* Yale School of Drama, New Haven, 1966.
Enrico IV, Yale Repertory Theatre, New Haven, CT, 1967.
We Bombed in New Haven, Yale Repertory Theatre, 1967.
The Bench, Gramercy Arts Theatre, New York City, 1968.
(And costume designer) *The Balcony,* Loeb Experimental Theatre, Harvard University, Cambridge, MA, 1968.
(And costume designer) *Troilus and Cressida,* Loeb Experimental Theatre, 1968.
The Judas Applause, Chelsea Theatre Center, Brooklyn Academy of Music, New York City, 1969.
A Streetcar Named Desire, City Island Theatre, New York City, 1969.
But Most of Us Cry in Movies, La Mama E.T.C., New York City, 1970.
The Nest, Mercury Theatre, New York City, 1970.
Ardele, Playhouse in the Park, Cincinnati, OH, 1970.
More War in Store, Old Reliable Theatre, New York City, 1970.
Touch, Village Arena Theatre, New York City, 1970.
Coocooshay, Public Theatre, New York City, 1970.
Istanboul, Actors' Playhouse, New York City, 1971.
(And lighting designer) *Catch 22,* John Drew Theatre, East Hampton, Long Island, NY, 1971.
Unlikely Heroes, Plymouth Theatre, New York City, 1971.
The Beggar's Opera, Chelsea Theatre Center, 1972.
Saved, Cherry Lane Theatre, New York City, 1972.
We Bombed in New Haven, Circle in the Square, New York City, 1972.
Lady Day: A Musical Tragedy, Chelsea Theatre Center, 1972.
The Foursome, Arena Stage Theatre, Washington, DC, 1972.
(And visuals designer) *In the Matter of J. Robert Oppenheimer,* Goodman Memorial Theatre, Chicago, IL, 1972.
A Look at the Fifties, Arena Stage Theatre, 1973.
Enemies, Arena Stage Theatre, 1973.
Raisin, Arena Stage Theatre, 1973, then 46th Street Theatre, New York City, 1973.
Sisters of Mercy, Shaw Festival, Niagara-on-the-Lake, Ontario, Canada, 1973.
The Seagull, McCarter Theatre, Princeton, NJ, 1973.
The Entertainer, McCarter Theatre, 1973.
The Daughter-in-Law, McCarter Theatre, 1974.
You Never Can Tell, McCarter Theatre, 1974.
Fashion, McAlpin Theatre, New York City, 1974.
Polly, Chelsea Theatre Center, 1975.
Beyond the Horizon, McCarter Theatre, 1975.
'Tis Pity She's a Whore, McCarter Theatre, 1975.
Mother Courage and Her Children, McCarter Theatre, 1975.
Kingdom of Earth, McCarter Theatre, 1975.
Romeo and Juliet, McCarter Theatre, 1975.
Lamppost Reunion, Little Theatre, New York City, 1975.
Boccaccio, Edison Theatre, New York City, 1975.
Second Wind, Colonnades Theatre Lab, New York City, 1975.
A Month in the Country, Colonnades Theatre Lab, 1975.
Reflections, Colonnades Theatre Lab, 1975.
Happy End, Martin Beck Theatre, New York City, 1977, then Chelsea Theatre Center, 1977.
The Ballroom in St. Patrick's Cathedral, Colonnades Theatre Lab, 1978.
Moliere in Spite of Himself, Colonnades Theatre Lab, 1978.
(With Marjorie Kellogg) *Showdown at the Adobe Motel,* Hartman Theatre Company, Stamford, CT, 1981.
(With Kellogg) *Moliere in Spite of Himself,* Hartman Theatre Company, 1981.
(With Kellogg) *Merton of the Movies,* Hartman Theatre Company, 1981.

(With Kellogg) *Semmelweiss,* Hartman Theatre Company, 1981.
Happy Sunset, Inc., Greek Theatre of New York, New York City, 1982.

Also designed sets for Playhouse in the Park, Cincinnati, OH, 1971. Taylor has shown paintings in three one-man shows, and his work is hung in six U.S. galleries. He has also acted as a design consultant to architects and advertising agencies.*

* * *

TERRY, Thomas
See TERRY-THOMAS

* * *

TERRY-THOMAS 1911-1990
(Thomas Terry, Terry Thomas)

PERSONAL: Born Thomas Terry Hoar Stevens, July 14, 1911, in Finchley, London, England; died of Parkinson's disease, January 8, 1990, in Godalming, Surrey, England; son of Ernest Frederick (a business executive) and Ellen Elizabeth (Hoar) Stevens; married Ida Patlanskey (a dancer), 1938 (divorced, 1962); married Belinda Cunningham, c. 1963; children: (second marriage) Tiger, Cushan. *Education:* Attended Ardingley College, Sussex. *Avocational interests:* Horseback riding, water skiing, cricket, hunting, photography.

CAREER: Actor, comedian, and writer. Worked variously as a clerk, meat salesman, band organizer and leader, and dancer; toured vaudeville, impersonating singers Al Jolson and Paul Robeson; worked as an extra and bit player in motion pictures, beginning in 1935; performed in cabarets and music halls, beginning in late 1930s; performed in nightclubs, including the Palladium, London, 1946, and the Waldorf Astoria Hotel, New York City, 1951. *Military service:* Royal British Army, released in 1946, served in signal corps; became sergeant; received four military service medals.

CREDITS:

FILM APPEARANCES

Extra, *It's Love Again,* Gaumont, 1936.
Terry, *A Date with a Dream,* Grand National, 1948.
Announcer, *Helter Skelter,* General Film Distributors, 1949.
Freddy Forrester, *Melody Club,* Eros, 1949.
The Lucky Mascot (also known as *The Brass Monkey*), Allied Artists, 1951.
Major Hitchcock, *Private's Progress,* British Lion, 1956.
Boughtflower, *The Green Man,* Distributors Corporation of America, 1957.
Bertrand Welch, *Lucky Jim,* Kingsley International, 1957.
(As Terry Thomas) Alfred Green, *Brothers in Law,* BC, 1957.
Romney, *Blue Murder at St. Trinian's,* British Lion, 1958.
Policeman, *Happy Is the Bride,* Kassler, 1958.
Ivan, *Tom Thumb,* Metro-Goldwyn-Mayer (MGM), 1958.
Lord Mayley, *Your Past Is Showing* (also known as *The Naked Truth*), J. Arthur Rank, 1958.
Major Hitchcock, *I'm All Right, Jack,* British Lion, 1959.
Billy Gordon, *Too Many Crooks,* Lopert, 1959.
Major Albert Rayne, *Make Mine Mink,* Continental, 1960.
Cadogen de Vere Carlton-Browne, *Man in a Cocked Hat* (also known as *Carlton-Browne of the F.O.*), Show, 1960.
Raymond Delauney, *School for Scoundrels,* Continental Distributing, 1960.
Reggie Blake, *His and Hers,* Eros, 1961.
Professor Bruce, *Bachelor Flat,* Twentieth Century-Fox, 1962.
J. Barker-Rynde, *Kill or Cure,* MGM, 1962.
Archibald Bannister, *A Matter of Who,* MGM, 1962.
Lieutenant "Piggy" Wigg, *Operation Snatch,* Continental Distributing, 1962.
Ludwig, *The Wonderful World of the Brothers Grimm,* MGM, 1962.
Spender, *The Mouse on the Moon,* United Artists (UA), 1963.
J. Algernon Hawthorne, *It's a Mad, Mad, Mad, Mad World,* UA, 1963.
Charles, *How to Murder Your Wife,* UA, 1965.
(As Terry Thomas) Major Foskett, *You Must Be Joking!,* Columbia, 1965.
Assistant mortician, *Strange Bedfellows,* Universal, 1965.
Sir Percival Ware-Armitage, *Those Magnificent Men in Their Flying Machines; Or How I Flew from London to Paris in 25 Hours and 11 Minutes* (also known as *Those Magnificent Men in Their Flying Machines*), Twentieth Century-Fox, 1965.
El Caid, *Bang, Bang, You're Dead* (also known as *Our Man in Marrakesh* and *Marrakesh*), American International, 1966.
First Tailor: Brigadier, *The Daydreamer,* Embassy, 1966.
Freddie Munster, *Munster, Go Home,* Universal, 1966.
Scoutmaster, *The Sandwich Man,* J. Arthur Rank, 1966.
Godfrey Deane, *The Wild Affair,* Goldstone, 1966.
Constable, *The Karate Killers,* MGM, 1967.
Lord Aldric and James, *Kiss the Girls and Make Them Die,* Columbia, 1967.
Sten Martin, *The Perils of Pauline,* Universal, 1967.

(As Terry Thomas) Captain Sir Harry Washington-Smythe, *Those Fantastic Flying Fools* (also known as *Jules Verne's Rocket to the Moon* and *Blast-Off*), American International, 1967.
Technical advisor, *A Guide for the Married Man,* Twentieth Century-Fox, 1967.
Minister of Finance, *Danger: Diabolik,* Paramount, 1968.
H. William Homer, *Don't Raise the Bridge, Lower the River,* Columbia, 1968.
Gilbert Tilly, *How Sweet it Is,* National General Pictures, 1968.
Ladislau Walichek, *Where Were You When the Lights Went Out?,* MGM, 1968.
Hotel manager, the General, and the Duke, *Arabella,* Universal, 1969.
Reginald, *Don't Look Now* (also known as *Don't Look Now . . . We're Being Shot At*), Buena Vista, 1969.
Sir Cuthbert Ware-Armitage, *Those Daring Young Men in Their Jaunty Jalopies* (also known as *Monte Carlo or Bust!*), Paramount, 1969.
Charles Goodwyn, *2000 Years Later,* Warner Brothers/Seven Arts, 1969.
Albert, *Twelve Plus One,* Cofci/Cef, 1970.
Captain, *Le Mur de l'Atlantique* (also known as *The Atlantic Wall*), Societe Nouvelle de Cinema, 1970.
Dr. Longstreet, *The Abominable Dr. Phibes,* American International, 1971.
Lombardo, *Dr. Phibes Rises Again,* American International, 1972.
Gli Eroi (also known as *Les Heros* and *Heroes*), Cineriz, 1972.
Voice of Sir Hiss, *Robin Hood* (animated), Buena Vista, 1973.
Critchit, "The Neat Job," *The Vault of Horror* (also known as *Tales from the Crypt II*), Cinerama, 1973.
Spanish Fly, EMI, 1975.
Max Nugget, *Side by Side,* GTO, 1975.
Voice of the Bull, *The Mysterious House of Dr. C.,* Samuel Bronston, 1976.
(As Terry Thomas) Mr. Square, *The Bawdy Adventures of Tom Jones,* Universal, 1976.
Prison Governor, *The Last Remake of Beau Geste,* Universal, 1977.
Dr. Mortimer, *The Hound of the Baskervilles* (released in the U.S. by Atlantic, 1980), Hemdale Releasing Corporation, 1978.
(As Terry Thomas) *See No Evil,* National Film Board of Canada, 1988.

Also appeared in a bit part in *For Freedom,* General Film Distributors, 1940; appeared in *Seven Times Seven,* 1973; *Who Stole the Shah's Jewels?,* 1974; *The Tempest,* 1979; and *Thirteen.* Appeared as Terry Thomas in *Arthur!! Arthur?,* 1970.

TELEVISION APPEARANCES; SERIES

Howdy, ABC, 1970.

Starred on *How Do You View?,* 1951-52, and *Strictly T-T,* 1956.

TELEVISION APPEARANCES; EPISODIC

(American television debut) "Who Killed Julian Buck?," *Burke's Law,* ABC, 1963.
Showtime (variety show), CBS, 1968.

Also appeared on the *Ed Sullivan Show,* and on the British programs *My Wildest Dream* and *What's My Line?*

OTHER TELEVISION APPEARANCES

Bird in Hand (special), BBC-TV, 1955.
Everybody's Got a System (special), ABC, 1965.
Tour of Monaco (special), ABC, 1968.
Gordon Elliot, *I Love a Mystery* (pilot), NBC, 1973.

Made television debut in 1948. Also appeared on other British and U.S. programs.

STAGE APPEARANCES

Ensemble, *Piccadilly Hayride* (revue), Prince of Wales Theatre, London, 1946-47.

Appeared in *Humpty Dumpty,* 1954, *Room for Two,* 1955, and *Large as Life,* 1958. Also appeared on stage under the name Thomas Terry.

MAJOR TOURS

Dick Whittington, South African cities, 1953.

RADIO APPEARANCES

Friends to Tea, BBC, 1938.

Appeared on his own radio series *To Town with Terry,* 1948-49, and *Top of the Town,* 1951-52.

WRITINGS:

Filling the Gap, M. Parrish, 1959.

Wrote numerous skits for performance in cabarets and music halls, and on radio and television.

OBITUARIES AND OTHER SOURCES:

BOOKS

Contemporary Authors, Volume 130, Gale, 1990, p. 438.

PERIODICALS

Daily News (London), January 9, 1990, p. 11.
Los Angeles Times, January 9, 1990.
New York Times, January 9, 1990.
Variety, January 17, 1990, p. 22.
Washington Post, January 9, 1990.*

THOMAS, Marlo 1938-

PERSONAL: Full name, Margaret Julia Thomas; born November 21, 1938, in Detroit, MI; daughter of Danny (an actor and comedian) and Rose Marie (Cassanti) Thomas; married Phil Donahue (a television talk-show host and author), May 22, 1980. *Education:* Attended the University of Southern California.

ADDRESSES: Agent—Michael Ovitz, Creative Artists Agency, 9830 Wilshire Blvd., Beverly Hills, CA 90212.

CAREER: Actress, producer, and writer.

MEMBER: Ms. Foundation, National Women's Political Caucus.

AWARDS, HONORS: Golden Globe Award, best television actress, 1967, and Emmy Award nominations, outstanding continued performance by a lead actress in a comedy series, 1967, 1968, 1969, and 1970, all for *That Girl;* Emmy Award, outstanding children's special, 1973, and George Foster Peabody Broadcasting Award, television, 1974, for *Marlo Thomas and Friends in Free to Be . . . You and Me;* Emmy Award, best performer in a children's program, 1981, for *The Body Human: Facts for Girls;* Emmy Award, outstanding lead actress in a special, 1985, for *Nobody's Child;* Emmy Award, outstanding children's program, 1988, for *Free to Be . . . a Family.*

CREDITS:

TELEVISION APPEARANCES; SERIES

Stella Barnes, *The Joey Bishop Show,* NBC, 1961-62.
Ann Marie, *That Girl,* ABC, 1966-71.

TELEVISION APPEARANCES; EPISODIC

The Body Human: Facts for Girls, CBS, 1980.

Appeared in *Zane Grey Theater* (also known as *Dick Powell's Zane Grey Theater*), CBS; *Dobie Gillis,* CBS; and *Thriller,* NBC.

TELEVISION APPEARANCES; SPECIALS

The girl, *Marlo Thomas in Acts of Love—and Other Comedies,* ABC, 1973.
Host, *Marlo Thomas and Friends in Free to Be . . . You and Me* (based on Thomas's book of the same title; also see below), ABC, 1974.
A Tribute to "Mr. Television," Milton Berle, NBC, 1978.
Love, Sex . . . and Marriage (also see below), ABC, 1983.
Marie Balter, *Nobody's Child,* CBS, 1986.
The Fortieth Annual Tony Awards, CBS, 1986.
The Thirty-ninth Annual Emmy Awards, FOX, 1987.
The Forty-first Annual Emmy Awards, FOX, 1989.
Night of One Hundred Stars III, NBC, 1990.
Fifth Annual Better World Society Awards Dinner, TBS, 1990.
The Meaning of Life, CBS, 1991.
The Forty-third Annual Emmy Awards, FOX, 1991.
Host, *Funny Women of Television: A Museum of Television and Radio Tribute,* NBC, 1991.
The Barbara Walters Special, ABC, 1992.

TELEVISION APPEARANCES; MOVIES

Mary Bailey Hatch, *It Happened One Christmas* (also see below), ABC, 1977.
Title role, *The Lost Honor of Kathryn Beck* (also see below), CBS, 1984.
Tess Lynd, *Consenting Adult,* ABC, 1985.
Lucille "Sis" Levin, *Held Hostage: The Sis and Jerry Levin Story* (also known as *Forgotten: The Sis and Jerry Levin Story* and *Beirut*), ABC, 1991.

TELEVISION WORK; EXECUTIVE PRODUCER

Love, Sex . . . and Marriage (special), ABC, 1983.
The Lost Honor of Kathryn Beck (movie), CBS, 1984.
Leap of Faith (movie), CBS, 1988.
Free to Be . . . a Family (special; based on Thomas's book of the same title; also see below), ABC, 1988.
CBS Summer Playhouse (pilot), CBS, 1988.
Taken Away (movie; also known as *Torn Apart* and *Give Me My Child*), CBS, 1989.
Wish You Were Here (series), CBS, 1990.

TELEVISION WORK; PRODUCER

(With Carole Hart) *Marlo Thomas and Friends in Free to Be . . . You and Me* (special; also see below), ABC, 1974.
(With Hart) *It Happened One Christmas* (movie), ABC, 1977.

FILM APPEARANCES

Title role, *Jenny* (also known as *And Jenny Makes Three*), Cinerama, 1969.
Sally Cramer, *Thieves,* Paramount, 1977.
Reva Prosky, *In the Spirit,* Castle Hill, 1991.

Also appeared in *The Cricket of the Hearth,* 1968.

STAGE APPEARANCES

(Broadway debut) Sally Cramer, *Thieves,* Broadhurst Theatre, 1974.
Herself, *V.I.P. Night on Broadway,* Shubert Theatre, New York City, 1979.
Barbara Kahn, *Social Security,* Ethel Barrymore Theatre, New York City, 1986.

Also appeared in a London production of *Barefoot in the Park.*

RECORDINGS:

ALBUMS

Free to Be. . . You and Me (also see below), Arista, 1973.
Free to Be . . . a Family (also see below), A & M, 1988.

WRITINGS:

(Editor with Carole Hart, Letty Cottin Pogrebin, and Mary Rodgers; author of introduction) *Free to Be . . . You and Me,* McGraw-Hill, 1974.
(Editor) *Free to Be. . . a Family: A Book about All Kinds of Belonging,* Bantam, 1987.

OTHER SOURCES:

PERIODICALS

Harper's Bazaar, October, 1980, p. 171.
Ladies Home Journal, November, 1980, p. 80; May, 1981, p. 138.
McCall's, March, 1986, p. 10.
New York Times, March 11, 1973.*

* * *

THOMAS, Terry
See TERRY-THOMAS

* * *

THOMASON, Harry 1940(?)-

PERSONAL: Born c. 1940, in Hampton, AR; married Judy Crump (divorced); married Linda Bloodworth (a television and film writer and producer), 1983; children: (first marriage) Stacy. *Education:* Received B.A. in physical education, speech and drama from Southern Arkansas University. *Avocational interests:* Football; amateur pilot.

ADDRESSES: Office—Mozark Productions, c/o Columbia Pictures Television, Columbia Plaza E., Burbank, CA 91505. *Agent*—Dan Richland, Richland, Wunsch, & Hohman, 9220 Sunset Blvd., Suite 311, Los Angeles, CA 90069.

CAREER: Television and film producer and director; coowner (with wife Linda Bloodworth-Thomason) of Mozark Productions.

AWARDS, HONORS: Christopher Award, 1980, for *A Shining Season;* People's Choice Award, 1982, for *The Blue and the Gray;* Emmy Award nominations, outstanding comedy series, 1988, 1989, and 1990, and Emmy Award nomination, outstanding directing in a comedy series, 1989, all for *Designing Women.*

CREDITS:

TELEVISION EXECUTIVE PRODUCER WITH LINDA BLOODWORTH-THOMASON; SERIES

Lime Street, ABC, 1985.
(And director) *Designing Women,* CBS, 1986-89.
(And director) *Evening Shade,* CBS, 1990-91.

TELEVISION PRODUCER

A Shining Season (movie), CBS, 1979.
To Find My Son (movie), CBS, 1980.
(With Charles B. Fitzsimons) *Riker* (series), CBS, 1981.
(And supervising producer; with Lee Majors, Harker Wade, Larry Brody, and Robert Janes) *The Fall Guy* (series; also see below), ABC, 1981-84.
(With Hugh Benson) *The Blue and the Gray* (mini-series), CBS, 1982.
(With Lee Majors) *How Do I Kill a Thief—Let Me Count the Ways* (pilot), ABC, 1982.

OTHER TELEVISION WORK

Executive producer, *London and Davis in New York* (pilot), CBS, 1984.
Executive producer (with wife Linda Bloodworth-Thomason) and director, *The Designing Women Special: Their Finest Hour* (special), CBS, 1990.
Director, *Evening Shade* (premiere), CBS, 1990.

FILM WORK

Producer and director, *Encounter with the Unknown,* Libert Films, 1973.
Producer and director, *So Sad about Gloria,* Libert Films, 1973.

Also director of *The Great Lester Boggs,* 1975, and producer of *The Hard Hats.*

WRITINGS:

TELEPLAYS

Coauthor of *Tiger Eyes,* based on Judy Blume's book of the same title, with Blume. Author of several episodes of *The Fall Guy,* ABC.

OTHER SOURCES:

PERIODICALS

New York Times, March 3, 1991, pp. 29-30.

* * *

THURMAN, Uma 1970-

PERSONAL: Full name Uma Karuna Thurman; born 1970, in Boston, MA; daughter of Robert (a professor of religion) and Nena (a model and psychotherapist; maiden name, von Schlebrugge) Thurman.

CAREER: Actress and model.

CREDITS:

FILM APPEARANCES

Laura, *Kiss Daddy Good Night,* Beast of Eden, 1987.
Georgia Elkans, *Johnny Be Good,* Orion, 1988.
Cecile de Volanges, *Dangerous Liaisons,* Warner Brothers, 1988.
Venus/Rose, *The Adventures of Baron Munchausen,* Columbia/Tri-Star, 1989.
Daphne McBain, *Where the Heart Is,* Buena Vista, 1990.
June Miller, *Henry and June,* Universal, 1990.
Diana, *Final Analysis,* Warner Brothers, 1992.

TELEVISION APPEARANCES; MOVIES

Maid Marian, *Robin Hood* (also known as *The Adventures of Robin Hood*), Fox, 1991.

SIDELIGHTS: "Uma" is the name of a Hindu goddess.

OTHER SOURCES:

PERIODICALS

American Film, September, 1990, pp. 22-27, 46-48.
Interview, July, 1987, pp. 72-73.
People, February 6, 1989, pp. 118-119.*

* * *

TICOTIN, Rachel 1958-

PERSONAL: Surname is pronounced "*tick*-oh-tin"; born November 1, 1958, in New York, NY; daughter of Abe (a used car salesman) and Iris (an educator; maiden name, Torres) Ticotin. *Education:* Attended Professional Children's School.

ADDRESSES: Agent—c/o International Creative Management, 8899 Beverly Blvd., Los Angeles, CA 90048.

CAREER: Actress. Member of dance company headed by Tina Ramirez; danced with Ballet Hispanico in New York; also worked with choreographers Alvin Ailey, Geoffrey Holder, Donald McKayle, and Anna Sokolow.

CREDITS:

FILM APPEARANCES

Gypsy dancer, *King of the Gypsies,* Paramount, 1978.
Isabella, *Fort Apache, the Bronx,* Twentieth Century-Fox, 1981.
Rachel, *Critical Condition,* Paramount, 1987.
Melina, *Total Recall,* Tri-Star, 1990.
Kim Brandon, *FX2—The Deadly Art of Illusion,* Orion, 1991.
Grace, *One Good Cop,* Buena Vista, 1991.

FILM WORK

Production assistant, *The Wanderers,* Orion, 1979.
Production assistant, *Dressed to Kill,* Filmways, 1980.
Production assistant, *Raging Bull,* United Artists, 1980.
Dance assistant, *Four Friends* (also known as *Georgia's Friends*), Twentieth Century-Fox, 1981.

TELEVISION APPEARANCES; MOVIES

Rachel Martin, *Love, Mary,* CBS, 1985.
Victoria Garcia, *Rockabye,* CBS, 1986.
Raquel Santos, *When the Bough Breaks,* NBC, 1986.
Sonia, *Spies, Lies, and Naked Thighs,* CBS, 1988.
Astrid, *Keep the Change,* TNT, 1992.

TELEVISION APPEARANCES; SERIES

Corporal Grace Pavlik, *For Love and Honor,* NBC, 1983-84.
Teresa Storm, *Ohara,* ABC, 1987-88.

TELEVISION APPEARANCES; EPISODIC

Elena, "Ancient Eyes," *Stingray,* NBC, 1986.
Iris Martinez, "Esperanza," *Prison Stories: Women on the Inside,* HBO, 1991.

STAGE APPEARANCES

Princess, *The King and I,* City Center Theatre, New York City, 1968.
The Butterfingers Angel, Mary and Joseph, Herod the Nut, and the Slaughter of Twelve Hit Carols in a Pear Tree, Syracuse Stage Theatre, Syracuse, NY, c. 1979.
Chile Girl, *The Sun Always Shines for the Cool,* BMC Production Company, 78th Street Theatre Lab, 1979.
The Lesson, Union Square Theatre, New York City, c. 1981.

OTHER SOURCES:

PERIODICALS

New York Times, February 27, 1981.
TV Guide, October 15, 1983, p. 10.*

* * *

TOMITA, Tamlyn

PERSONAL: Born in Okinawa. *Education:* Attended University of California, Los Angeles; studied acting with Lynette Katselas, voice with Carl Jones and Casey Rankin, and ballet at Stanley Holden Dance Center.

ADDRESSES: Agent—Artist's Group Ltd., 1930 Century Park W., Suite 403, Los Angeles, CA 90067. *Publicist*—

Carol Gettko, Guttman & Pam Ltd., 8500 Wilshire Blvd., No. 801, Beverly Hills, CA 90211.

CAREER: Actress.

MEMBER: Asian Pacific Alliance for Creative Equality (APACE; founding member), The Anataeus Project (charter member).

AWARDS, HONORS: Drama-Logue Award, best actress performance, 1991, for *The Winter Crane.*

CREDITS:

FILM APPEARANCES

Kumiko, *The Karate Kid Part II,* Columbia, 1986.
Lily Kawamura, *Come See the Paradise,* Twentieth Century-Fox, 1990.

Also appeared as Lan, *Vietnam, Texas,* 1990; and in *Hawaiian Dream,* 1988.

TELEVISION APPEARANCES; EPISODIC

Tour of Duty, CBS, 1987.
"To Heal a Nation," *General Electric Theater,* NBC, 1988.
Miyeko Matsuda, "Hiroshima Maiden," *WonderWorks,* PBS, 1988.

OTHER TELEVISION APPEARANCES

Sally, *Hiroshima: Out of the Ashes* (movie), NBC, 1990.

Also appeared as Ming Li in *Santa Barbara* (series), NBC.

STAGE APPEARANCES

The Winter Crane, Fountain Theatre, Los Angeles, CA, 1991.
Don Juan: A Meditation, Mark Taper Forum, Los Angeles, CA, 1991.
Nagasaki Dust, Philadelphia Theatre Company, Plays and Player's Theatre, Philadelphia, PA, 1992.

OTHER SOURCES:

PERIODICALS

American Film, January, 1991, p. 48.
Connoisseur, January, 1991, p. 96.
Interview, December, 1990, p. 44.

* * *

TOWNSEND, Sue 1946-

PERSONAL: Born April 2, 1946, in Leicester, England. *Education:* Attended secondary school in England. *Politics:* Socialist. *Religion:* Atheist.

ADDRESSES: Agent—Giles Gordon, 43 Doughty St., London, England.

CAREER: Writer. Worked for British Broadcasting Corp. (BBC); worked variously as a garage attendant, salesperson, and factory worker. Trained community worker.

MEMBER: Leicester Phoenix Playwrights Association.

AWARDS, HONORS: Thames Television bursary, 1980, for *Womberang; The Adrian Mole Diaries* was chosen one of American Library Association's Best Books for Young Adults, 1986.

WRITINGS:

STAGE PLAYS

Womberang (one-act; also see below), produced at Leicester Haymarket Theatre, Leicester, England, 1979, then Soho Polytechnic Theatre, London, 1980.
The Ghost of Daniel Lambert, first produced at Phoenix Arts Centre, Leicester, and Leicester Haymarket Theatre, 1981.
Dayroom, first produced at Croydon Warehouse Theatre, Croyden, England, 1981.
Captain Christmas and the Evil Adults, first produced at Phoenix Arts Centre, 1982.
Bazaar and Rummage (also see below), first produced at Royal Court Theatre/ Upstairs, London, 1982.
Are You Sitting Comfortably?, first produced at Croydon Warehouse Theatre, 1983.
Groping for Words (two-act; also see below), first produced at Croydon Warehouse Theatre, 1983.
Bazaar and Rummage; Groping for Words; Womberang: Three Plays, published by Methuen, c. 1984.
The Great Celestial Cow, first produced at Leicester Haymarket Theatre, then Royal Court Theatre, London, both 1984, published by Methuen, 1984.
The Secret Diary of Adrian Mole Aged 13 3/4: The Play (two-act; also see below), music and lyrics by Ken Howard and Alan Blaikley, first produced at Phoenix Theatre, then Wyndham's Theatre, London, both 1984, published by Methuen, 1985.

Also author of *Ear, Nose, and Throat,* c. 1988, and *Disneyland It Ain't,* 1990.

TELEVISION PLAYS

Bazaar and Rummage, BBC, 1983.
The Secret Diary of A. Mole (series; also see below), Thames TV, beginning in 1986, syndicated in the United States, 1987.
The Growing Pains of Adrian Mole (series; also see below), syndicated, 1988.

Contributor to the series *Revolting Women,* BBC, 1981.

RADIO PLAYS

The Secret Diary of A. Mole (series), BBC-Radio 4, beginning in 1982.

(With Carole Hayman) *The Refuge* (series), BBC-Radio 4, 1987.

BOOKS

The Secret Diary of Adrian Mole Aged 13 3/4 (young adult), illustrated by Caroline Holden, Methuen, 1982.
The Growing Pains of Adrian Mole (young adult), Methuen, 1984.
The Adrian Mole Diaries: A Novel (contains *The Secret Diary of Adrian Mole Aged 13 3/4* and *The Growing Pains of Adrian Mole*), Methuen, 1985.
The Secret Diary of Adrian Mole Aged 13 3/4 Songbook, Methuen, 1985.
Rebuilding Coventry: A Tale of Two Cities (novel), Methuen, 1988.

OTHER

Columnist, *Woman's Realm,* 1983-85. Contributor of stories and plays to periodicals, including *Times, New Statesman,* and *Airport.*

ADAPTATIONS: *The Secret Diary of Adrian Mole Aged 13 3/4* has been adapted into an audiocassette, Talking Tape, 1983, and a computer game, Mosaic, 1985; *The Growing Pains of Adrian Mole* has been adapted into an audiocassette, EMI Records/Listen for Pleasure, 1985, and a computer game, Mosaic, 1987.

OTHER SOURCES:

BOOKS

Contemporary Authors, Volume 127, Gale, 1989, p. 456.
Something about the Author, Volume 55, Gale, 1989, p. 158.*

* * *

TRUMBULL, Douglas 1942-

PERSONAL: Born, 1942, in Los Angeles, CA. *Education:* Studied architecture at El Camino College, Torrence, CA.

ADDRESSES: *Office*—Showscan Film Corp., 3939 Landmark St., Culver City, CA 90232-2315.

CAREER: Special effects technician, director, and writer. Graphic Films, Los Angeles, CA, educational and technical filmmaker, c. 1960; Future General Corporation, founder, 1974. Inventor of Showscan film process, 1983. President of Berkshire Motion Pictures.

AWARDS, HONORS: Academy Award nomination (with others), best special visual effects, 1977, for *Close Encounters of the Third Kind;* Academy Award nomination (with others), best special visual effects, 1979, for *Star Trek: The Motion Picture;* Academy Award nomination (with Richard Yuricich and David Dryer), best special visual effects, 1982, for *Blade Runner.*

CREDITS:

FILM SPECIAL EFFECTS DIRECTOR, EXCEPT WHERE INDICATED

(With Augie Lohman) *Candy,* Cinerama, 1968.
(With Stanley Kubrick and others) *2001: A Space Odyssey,* Metro-Goldwyn-Mayer, 1968.
The Andromeda Strain, Universal, 1971.
(With others, and director) *Silent Running,* Universal, 1972.
(With others) *Close Encounters of the Third Kind,* Columbia, 1977.
(With others) *Star Trek: The Motion Picture,* Paramount, 1979.
(With Richard Yuricich and David Dryer) *Blade Runner,* Warner Brothers, 1982.
Producer and director, *Brainstorm,* United Artists, 1983.

Also special effects director and director of the short *To the Moon and Beyond,* 1964.

TELEVISION WORK; SERIES

Executive producer (with Jerry Zeitman and Robert Kline), *The Starlost,* syndicated, 1973.

TELEVISION WORK; EPISODIC

Special effects director, "The Borrowers," *Hallmark Hall of Fame,* NBC, 1973.

WRITINGS:

Contributor to periodicals, including *Action, American Cinematographer, Cahiers du Cinema* (Paris), *Cinefantastique, Ecran Fantastique* (Paris), *Film Comment, Filmmaker's Newsletter, Films Illustrated* (London), *Sight and Sound* (London), *Starburst* (London), and *Take One.*

OTHER SOURCES:

BOOKS

International Dictionary of Film and Filmmakers, Volume 4: *Writers and Production Artists,* St. James Press, 1987.

PERIODICALS

American Cinematographer, February, 1979.
American Film, January, 1979; May, 1984, p. 49.
Cinefex, April, 1982.
Inc., May, 1984, p. 35.
Omni, December, 1985, p. 41.
People, February 15, 1982, p. 38.
Show, July 23, 1970.
Technology Review, February, 1982, p. 60.

Variety, June 14, 1989, p. 35.*

* * *

TRYON, Thomas 1926-1991

OBITUARY NOTICE—See index for *CTFT* sketch: Born January 14, 1926, in Hartford (some sources say Wethersfield), CT; died of cancer, September 4, 1991, in Los Angeles, CA. Actor and writer. Tryon began his acting career after serving in the Navy during World War II. He first appeared on Broadway in the musical *Wish You Were Here* and acted in live television dramas before his Hollywood debut in a series of Walt Disney television movies. Tryon's other film credits include *The Story of Ruth, The Longest Day, I Married a Monster from Outer Space, In Harm's Way,* and *The Cardinal,* in which his portrayal of the title character earned him a Golden Globe nomination. Tryon switched to writing in the early 1970s, beginning with *The Other,* a best-selling suspense novel, which he adapted and executive produced for film. Tryon's writings include *Harvest Home,* adapted for television, *Lady, Crowned Heads, All That Glitters: Five Novellas, The Night of the Moonbow,* and *The Wings of the Morning,* the first book in a three-volume historical set. Scheduled for future publication is the second book in the series, *By the Rivers of Babylon.*

OBITUARIES AND OTHER SOURCES:

PERIODICALS

Variety, September 9, 1991, p. 102.

* * *

TSYPIN, George 1954-

PERSONAL: Surname pronounced "*Sip*-pen"; born, 1954, in the U.S.S.R. (now Commonwealth of Independent States); immigrated to United States, 1979; son of a painter and an actress; married; children: one daughter. *Education:* Institute of Architecture, Moscow, B.F.A., 1977; New York University, M.F.A., theatre design, 1984.

CAREER: Set designer. Worked as urban planner in the Soviet Union, and for Haines Lundberg Waehler (an architectural firm) in New York City. "George Tsypin: All That Is Solid Melts into the Air," an exhibit of large-scale sculpture based on Tsypin's set designs, was displayed in an environment of his own creation at the Twining Gallery in New York City, 1991.

AWARDS, HONORS: International Competition: Free and Spontaneous View on Contemporary Theatre for New Generations, 1978; All Soviet Competition of Diploma First Prize, 1979; De Menil fellowship, 1983; Seidman Award for Excellency in Design, 1986; Helen Hayes Award nomination, 1987; Obie Award for sustained excellence in set design, 1990.

CREDITS:

STAGE SET DESIGNER

The Power and the Glory, Philadelphia Drama Guild, Philadelphia, PA, 1984.

Jesse's Land, American Jewish Theatre, New York City, 1984.

The Count of Monte Cristo, American National Theatre, Eisenhower Theatre, John F. Kennedy Center for the Performing Arts, New York City, 1985.

A Seagull, American National Theatre, Eisenhower Theatre, John F. Kennedy Center for the Performing Arts, 1985.

The Balcony, American Repertory Theatre, Cambridge, MA, 1986.

Idiot's Delight, American National Theatre, John F. Kennedy Center for the Performing Arts, 1986.

Suor Angelica, Opera Company of Philadelphia, Philadelphia, PA, 1986.

Ajax, American National Theatre, John F. Kennedy Center for the Performing Arts, 1986.

Measure for Measure, Arena Stage Theatre, Washington, DC, 1986.

Galileo, Goodman Theatre, Chicago, IL, 1986.

Death in Venice, Opera Company of Philadelphia, 1986.

Zangezi: A Supersaga in Twenty Planes, Museum of Contemporary Art, Los Angeles, CA, then Brooklyn Academy of Music, New York City, 1986.

The Bob Hope War Zone Special, Terrace Theatre, John F. Kennedy Center for the Performing Arts, 1986.

Don Giovanni, PepsiCo Summerfare, 1987.

Leon and Lena (and lenz), Guthrie Theatre, Minneapolis, MN, 1987, and on tour with *Frankenstein—Playing with Fire.*

Electrification of the Soviet Union, Glyndebourne Opera Festival, Glyndebourne, England, 1988.

Landscape of the Body, Goodman Theatre, 1988.

Tannhauser, Chicago Lyric Opera, Chicago, IL, 1988.

Nothing Sacred, American Conservatory Theatre, San Francisco, CA, 1989.

The Misanthrope, La Jolla Playhouse, La Jolla, CA, then Goodman Theatre, 1989.

Cymbeline, New York Shakespeare Festival, Public/Newman Theatre, New York City, 1989.

The Screens, Guthrie Theatre, 1989.

Henry IV, Part I and Part II, New York Shakespeare Festival, 1991.

The Death of Klinghoffer, Brooklyn Academy of Music, 1991, and later on tour in Lyons, France, and in San Francisco and Los Angeles.

Mr. Jelly Lord, Mark Taper Forum, 1991.

Designed sets for the Portland Stage Company, Portland, ME, 1985-86; the Arena Stage, Washington, DC, 1986-87 and 1989-90; the Guthrie Theatre, 1987-88 and 1989-90; and the American Conservatory Theatre, 1989-90.

FILM PRODUCTION DESIGNER

The Cabinet of Dr. Ramirez, Capital Entertainment, 1991.

TELEVISION SET DESIGNER; SPECIALS

Don Giovanni, ORF National TV, Maison de la Culture, 1990.

TELEVISION SET DESIGNER; EPISODIC

"Peter Sellars Directs Don Giovanni," *Great Performances,* PBS, 1991.

TELEVISION APPEARANCES; SPECIALS

Destination Mozart: A Night at the Opera with Peter Sellars, PBS, 1990.

OTHER SOURCES:

PERIODICALS

American Theatre, December, 1990, pp. 22-29, 63-64.
Theatre Crafts, February, 1991, pp. 35-38, 52-54.*

* * *

TURMAN, Lawrence 1926-

PERSONAL: Born November 28, 1926, in Los Angeles, CA. *Education:* Attended University of California, Los Angeles.

ADDRESSES: *Office*—21336 Pacific Coast Highway, Malibu, CA 90265.

CAREER: Producer. Worked in the textile business; employed by Kurt Frings Agency until 1960; Millar-Turman Productions, cofounder, 1960.

AWARDS, HONORS: Academy Award nomination, best picture, 1967, for *The Graduate.*

CREDITS:

FILM WORK; PRODUCER, EXCEPT WHERE INDICATED

(With Stuart Millar) *The Young Doctors,* United Artists (UA), 1961.
(With S. Millar) *I Could Go On Singing,* UA, 1963.
(With S. Millar) *The Best Man,* UA, 1964.
The Flim-Flam Man (also known as *One Born Every Minute*), Twentieth Century-Fox, 1967.
The Graduate, Embassy, 1967.
The Great White Hope, Twentieth Century-Fox, 1970.
And director, *The Marriage of a Young Stockbroker,* Twentieth Century-Fox, 1971.
(With David Foster) *The Drowning Pool,* Warner Bros., 1975.
Executive producer, *The Nickel Ride,* Twentieth Century-Fox, 1975.
(With D. Foster) *Heroes,* Universal, 1977.
First Love, Paramount, 1977.
Walk Proud (also known as *Gang*), Universal, 1979.
(With D. Foster) *Caveman,* UA, 1981.
(With D. Foster) *The Thing,* Universal, 1982.
And director with D. Foster, *Second Thoughts,* Universal, 1983.
(With D. Foster) *Mass Appeal,* Universal, 1984.
(With D. Foster) *The Mean Season,* Orion, 1985.
(With D. Foster) *Running Scared,* Metro-Goldwyn-Mayer/UA, 1986.
(With D. Foster) *Short Circuit,* Tri-Star, 1986.
(With D. Foster and Gary Foster) *Short Circuit 2,* Tri-Star, 1988.
(With D. Foster and John Turman) *Full Moon in Blue Water,* Trans World, 1988.
(With D. Foster) *Gleaming the Cube,* Twentieth Century-Fox, 1988.

Also produced *Pretty Poison.*

TELEVISION WORK; MOVIES; EXECUTIVE PRODUCER

She Lives, ABC, 1973.
Unwed Father, ABC, 1974.
Get Christie Love! (pilot; also see below), ABC, 1974.
The Morning After, ABC, 1974.
(With D. Foster) *The Gift of Life,* CBS, 1982.
(With D. Foster) *Between Two Brothers,* CBS, 1982.
(With D. Foster) *News at Eleven,* CBS, 1986.
Jesse (also known as *Desert Nurse*), CBS, 1988.

OTHER TELEVISION WORK

Executive producer (with David L. Wolper), *Get Christie Love!* (series), ABC, 1974-75.*

* * *

TURNER, Janine 1963(?)-

PERSONAL: Born December 6, c. 1963, in Lincoln, NE; daughter of Turner (an airline pilot) and Janice Gauntt.

ADDRESSES: *Contact*—c/o *Northern Exposure,* CBS Television, Los Angeles, CA 90036.

CAREER: Actress. Wilhelmina Agency, New York City, model.

AWARDS, HONORS: Golden Globe Award nomination, best actress in a drama, Hollywood Foreign Press Association, 1992, for *Northern Exposure.*

CREDITS:

TELEVISION APPEARANCES; SERIES

Janie-Claire Willow, *Behind the Screen,* CBS, 1981-82.
Laura Templeton, *General Hospital,* ABC, 1982.
Maggie O'Connell, *Northern Exposure,* CBS, 1990—.

TELEVISION APPEARANCES; EPISODIC

Happy Days, ABC, 1983.
"Words and Music," *Boone,* NBC, 1983.
"The Good, the Bad, and the Priceless," *The Master,* NBC, 1984.
"Bone Crunch," *Mickey Spillane's Mike Hammer,* CBS, 1984.
"KITTnapp," *Knight Rider,* NBC, 1985.

Made television debut in an episode of *Dallas,* 1980.

TELEVISION APPEARANCES; SPECIALS

The 43rd Annual Primetime Emmy Awards, Fox, 1991.
Grand marshal, *The Cotton Bowl Parade,* CBS, 1991.

FILM APPEARANCES

Young Doctors in Love, Twentieth Century-Fox, 1982.
Brooke Delamo, *Knights of the City,* New World, 1985.
Shevaun, *Tai-Pan,* de Laurentiis Entertainment Group, 1986.
Linda Aikman, *Monkey Shines: An Experiment in Fear,* Orion, 1988.
Nancy Beth Marmillion, *Steel Magnolias,* Tri-Star, 1989.
Cheryl, *The Ambulance* (also known as *Into Thin Air*), Triumph Releasing, 1990.

OTHER SOURCES:

PERIODICALS

People Weekly, May 13, 1991, pp. 55-56.

* * *

TYZACK, Margaret 1931-

PERSONAL: Born September 9, 1931; daughter of Thomas Edward and Doris (Moseley) Tyzack; married Alan Stephenson, 1958; children: one son. *Education:* Attended St. Angela's Ursuline Convent, Forest Gate, London; trained for the stage at the Royal Academy of Dramatic Art.

ADDRESSES: Agent—c/o Representation Joyce Edwards, 275 Kennington Road, London SE11 6BY, England.

CAREER: Actress.

AWARDS, HONORS: Gilbert Prize for Comedy; British Academy of Film and Television Arts Award, television—best actress, 1969, for *The First Churchills;* Order of the British Empire, 1970; Emmy Award nomination, outstanding continued performance by an actress in a leading role in a drama or comedy limited episodes, 1973, for *Masterpiece Theatre;* Laurence Olivier Award, Actress of the Year—Revival, Society of West End Theatre, 1981, for *Who's Afraid of Virginia Woolf?;* Antoinette Perry Award nomination, outstanding performance by a featured actress in a play, 1983, for *All's Well That Ends Well;* Variety Club of Great Britain Award for Best Stage Actress, 1987, and Antoinette Perry Award, best performance by a featured actress in a play, 1990, both for *Lettice and Lovage.*

CREDITS:

STAGE APPEARANCES

Bystander, *Pygmalion,* Chesterfield Civic Theatre, Chesterfield, England, 1951.
Mag Keegan, *Progress to the Park,* Royal Court Theatre, London, 1959.
Miss Frost, *The Ginger Man* (also see below), Royal Court Theatre, 1959.
Vassilissa, *The Lower Depths,* Royal Shakespeare Company (RSC), Arts Theatre Club, London, 1962.
Miss Frost, *The Ginger Man,* Pembroke Theatre, Croydon, England, 1963.
Jacqueline Harrison, *Find Your Way Home,* Open Space Theatre, London, 1970.
Queen Elizabeth, *Vivat! Vivat Regina!,* Piccadilly Theatre, London, 1971.
Volumnia, *Coriolanus* (also see below) RSC, Stratford-on-Avon, England, 1972.
Portia, *Julius Caesar* (also see below) RSC, Stratford-on-Avon, 1972.
Tamora, *Titus Andronicus,* RSC, Stratford-on-Avon, 1972.
Portia, *Julius Caesar,* RSC, Aldwych Theatre, London, 1973.
Volumnia, *Coriolanus,* RSC, Aldwych Theatre, 1973.
Maria Lvovna, *Summerfolk,* RSC, Aldwych Theatre, 1974, then Brooklyn Academy of Music, New York City, 1975.
Milly, *People Are Living There,* Royal Exchange Theatre, Manchester, England, 1979.
Martha, *Who's Afraid of Virginia Woolf?,* National Theatre, London, 1981.
Countess of Rossillon, *All's Well That Ends Well* (also see below), RSC, Barbican Theatre, London, then Martin Beck Theatre, New York City, 1983.
Sybil Birling, *An Inspector Calls,* Greenwich Theatre, London, 1983-84.
Mornings at Seven, Westminster Theatre, London, 1984.

Rose, *Tom and Viv,* Royal Court Theatre, London, 1985, then Public Theatre, LuEsther Hall, New York City, 1985.

Night Must Fall, Greenwich Theatre, 1986-87.

Lotte Schoen, *Lettice and Lovage,* Globe Theatre, London, 1987, then Ethel Barrymore Theatre, New York City, 1990.

Also appeared as Lady MacBeth in *Macbeth,* Nottingham, England, 1962; as Madame Ranevsky in *The Cherry Orchard,* Exeter, England, then on tour, 1969; as Countess of Rossillon in *All's Well That Ends Well,* Mrs. Alving in *Ghosts,* and Queen Margaret in *Richard III,* all Stratford, Ontario, 1977.

FILM APPEARANCES

Night Sister, *Behind the Mask,* GW Films, 1958.

Room 43 (released in England as *Passport to Shame*), Cory, 1959.

Hilda, *Highway to Battle,* Paramount, 1961.

Elizabeth Gee, *Ring of Spies* (released in England as *Ring of Treason*), British Lion, 1964.

Almoner, *The Whisperers,* United Artists/Lopert, 1967.

Elena, *2001: A Space Odyssey,* Metro-Goldwyn-Mayer, 1968.

Sister Bennett, *Thank You All Very Much* (released in England as *A Touch of Love*), Columbia, 1969.

Conspirator Rubinstein, *A Clockwork Orange,* Warner Brothers, 1971.

Nurse Adams, *The Legacy* (also known as *The Legacy of Maggie Walsh*), Universal, 1979.

Annie Morgan, *Quartermass Conclusion,* Euston, 1980.

Pink Lady, *Mr. Love,* Warner Brothers/Goldcrest, 1986.

Madame Lambert, *Prick up Your Ears,* Samuel Goldwyn, 1987.

Also appeared as Lady Emmeline in *The Wars,* 1983, and as Dowager Countess in *The King's Whore,* 1990.

TELEVISION APPEARANCES; SERIES

Winnifred, *The Forsyte Saga,* PBS, 1969-70.

Antonia, *I Claudius* (originally appeared as a thirteen-hour BBC series), *Masterpiece Theater,* PBS, 1978.

Also appeared in *Cousin Bette,* c. 1970-72, as Queen Anne in *The First Churchills,* 1971, in *Quartermass,* 1979, and in *A Winter's Tale.*

TELEVISION APPEARANCES; MOVIES

Queen Elizabeth, *Charles & Diana: A Royal Love Story,* ABC, 1982.

Madame de Guidice, *The Corsican Brothers,* CBS, 1985.

TELEVISION APPEARANCES; EPISODIC

Clothilde Bradbury-Scott ("Nemesis"), "Agatha Christie's Miss Marple, Series III," *Mystery!,* PBS, 1987.

Helen Seymour, *The Young Indiana Jones Chronicles,* ABC, 1992.

U-V

UHRY, Alfred 1936-

PERSONAL: Born December 3, 1936, in Atlanta, GA; son of Ralph K. (a furniture designer and artist) and Alene (a social worker; maiden name, Fox) Uhry; married Joanna Kellogg (a teacher), June 13, 1959; children: Emily Uhry Rhea, Elizabeth Uhry MacCurrach, Kate, Nell. *Education:* Brown University, B.A., 1958.

ADDRESSES: *Agent*—Flora Roberts Agency, 157 West 57th St., Penthouse A, New York, NY 10019.

CAREER: Playwright, lyricist, and librettist. Worked with composer Frank Loesser, 1960-63; Calhoun High School (private school), New York City, instructor in English and drama, until 1980; New York University, New York City, instructor in lyric writing, 1985-88; Goodspeed Opera House, East Haddam, CT, librettist, 1980-84; worked on comedy scripts for television; Dramatists Play Service, board member.

MEMBER: Academy of Motion Picture Arts and Sciences, Dramatists Guild (chairman of Dramatists Guild Foundation).

AWARDS, HONORS: Drama Desk Award nomination, 1975, and Antoinette Perry Award nomination, best book of a Broadway musical, 1976, both for *The Robber Bridegroom;* Drama Desk Award nomination and Pulitzer Prize, drama, both 1987, and Los Angeles Drama Critics Circle award, writing, 1989, all for *Driving Miss Daisy* (play); Academy Award and Writers Guild of America Award, both for best screenplay adaptation, 1989, for *Driving Miss Daisy.*

CREDITS:

FILM WORK

Associate producer, *Driving Miss Daisy* (also see below), Warner Bros., 1989.

WRITINGS:

Driving Miss Daisy (play), produced at Playwrights Horizons Theatre, New York City, 1987, produced at Henry Fonda Theatre, Los Angeles, 1989, published by Theatre Communications Group, 1988.

MUSICAL PLAYS

Lyrics (book by Terrence McNally; music by Robert Waldman), *Here's Where I Belong* (based on John Steinbeck's novel *East of Eden*), produced at Billy Rose Theatre, New York City, 1968.

Book and lyrics (music by Waldman), *The Robber Bridegroom* (two-act; based on Eudora Welty's novella of the same title), produced at St. Clement's Church, New York City, 1974, produced at Harkness Theatre, New York City, 1975, produced at Biltmore Theatre, New York City, 1976, published by Drama Book Specialists, 1978.

Chapeau (based on a French farce, *An Italian Straw Hat*), produced at Saratoga Performing Arts Center, Saratoga Springs, NY, 1977.

Lyrics (book by Conn Fleming; music by Waldman), *Swing,* produced at Playhouse Theatre, Wilmington, DE, 1980, produced at John F. Kennedy Center for the Performing Arts, Washington, DC, 1980.

(Adapter) George M. Cohan, *Little Johnny Jones* (two-act), produced at Alvin Theatre, New York City, 1982.

(Adapter) Laurence Schwab, B. G. DeSylva, and others, *Follow Thru,* produced at Goodspeed Opera House, East Haddam, CT, 1984-85.

Book (with John Weidman) and lyrics (music by Waldman), *America's Sweetheart* (based on John Kobler's book of the same title), produced by Hartford Stage Company, Hartford, CT, 1985.

Adapted musical comedies for revivals, including *Funny Face.*

SCREENPLAYS

(With Amy Jones, Perry Howze, and Randy Howze) *Mystic Pizza* (based on a story by Jones), Metro-Goldwyn-Mayer, 1988.
Driving Miss Daisy (adapted from his play of the same title), Warner Bros., 1989.

Also author of screenplay *Rich in Love,* Metro-Goldwyn-Mayer.

OTHER SOURCES:

BOOKS

Contemporary Authors, Volume 133, Gale, 1991, pp. 404-07.
Contemporary Literary Criticism, Volume 55, Gale, 1989, pp. 264-67.

PERIODICALS

New York Times, June 4, 1989.
People, May 23, 1988, p. 85.

* * *

VANCE-STRAKER, Marilyn

CAREER: Costume designer.

AWARDS, HONORS: Academy Award nomination, best achievement in costume design, 1987, for *The Untouchables.*

CREDITS:

FILM COSTUME DESIGNER, EXCEPT WHERE INDICATED

Fast Times at Ridgemont High, Universal, 1982.
48 Hours, Paramount, 1982.
Jeckyll and Hyde . . . Together Again, Paramount, 1982.
Streets of Fire, Universal/RKO Radio Pictures, 1984.
(With Winnie Brown and Ronald I. Caplan) *The Wild Life,* Universal, 1984.
Romancing the Stone, Twentieth-Century Fox, 1984.
Weird Science, Universal, 1985.
The Breakfast Club, Universal, 1985.
Ferris Bueller's Day Off, Paramount, 1986.
Jo Jo Dancer, Your Life Is Calling, Columbia, 1986.
Pretty in Pink, Paramount, 1986.
Visual consultant, *The Wraith,* New Century/Vista, 1986.
Predator, Twentieth-Century Fox, 1987.
Some Kind of Wonderful, Paramount, 1987.
The Untouchables, Paramount, 1987.
Throw Momma from the Train, Orion, 1987.
Cross My Heart, Universal, 1987.
Die Hard, Twentieth-Century Fox, 1988.
The Great Outdoors, Universal, 1988.
Action Jackson, Lorimar, 1988.
Road House, Metro-Goldwyn-Mayer (MGM)/United Artists (UA), 1989.
Uncle Buck, Universal, 1989.
The Package, Orion, 1989.
Little Monsters, MGM/UA, 1989.
Pretty Woman, Buena Vista, 1990.
The Last of the Finest (also known as *Street Legal* and *GBTI: Blue Heat*), Orion, 1990.
Executive producer and wardrobe consultant, *The First Power,* Orion, 1990.
The Adventures of Ford Fairlane (also known as *Ford Fairlane*), Twentieth-Century Fox, 1990.
Die Hard 2 (also known as *Die Harder*), Twentieth-Century Fox, 1990.
Predator 2, Twentieth-Century Fox, 1990.
The Rocketeer, Buena Vista, 1991.
Ricochet, Warner Brothers, 1991.
The Last Boy Scout, Warner Brothers, 1991.
Hudson Hawk, Tri-Star, 1991.*

* * *

VANOFF, Nick 1930(?)-1991

PERSONAL: Born c. 1930, in Macedonia, Greece; died of cardiac arrest, March 20, 1991, in Los Angeles, CA; son of Fima Vanoff; married wife, Felisa; children: Nicholas, Flavio. *Education:* Studied directing with Theodore Komisarjevsky in New York.

CAREER: Producer and director. Worked previously as a dancer with the Charles Weidman Dance Theatre and as a principal dancer with the New York City Center Opera Company; danced on Broadway in *Kiss Me, Kate;* appeared on television and in nightclubs; worked as a cue-card holder for *The Perry Como Show,* becoming associate producer. Partner in Yongestreet Productions, packagers of *Hee Haw* and other television specials and series. Founding director, with wife Felisa, of the Foundation for the Joffrey Ballet; served on the board of directors of the Center Theatre Group. Co-owner of Sunset-Gower Studios (formerly Columbia Studios). *Military service:* U.S. Marines.

AWARDS, HONORS: Emmy Award nominations, outstanding variety series, 1965 and 1966, both for *The Hollywood Palace;* Emmy Award, outstanding variety musical series, and Emmy Award nomination, outstanding new series, both 1972, both for *The Julie Andrews Hour;* Directors Guild Award nomination, 1974; Emmy Award nomination (with George Stevens, Jr.), outstanding program achievement—special events, 1980, for *The Kennedy Center Honors: A Celebration of the Performing Arts;* Emmy

Award nominations (with Stevens), outstanding variety, music or comedy program, 1982 and 1990, for *The Kennedy Center Honors: A Celebration of the Performing Arts;* Emmy Awards (with Stevens), outstanding variety, music or comedy program, 1984 and 1986, for *The Kennedy Center Honors: A Celebration of the Performing Arts;* Emmy Award (with Stevens), outstanding special events, 1989, for *The Kennedy Center Honors: A Celebration of the Performing Arts;* Antoinette Perry Award, best musical, 1990, for *City of Angels;* named 1990 Showman of the Year, Publicists Guild.

CREDITS:

TELEVISION PRODUCER; SERIES

(With William O. Harbach) *Tonight!,* NBC, 1954-57.
(With Ray Charles) *The Kraft Music Hall,* NBC, 1958-62.
(With Del Jack) *The King Family Show,* ABC, 1965-66, 1969.
(With Harbach) *The Julie Andrews Hour,* ABC, 1972-73.
The Sonny and Cher Show, CBS, 1976-77.
The Big Show, NBC, 1980.

Also producer of *Night Life.*

TELEVISION PRODUCER; SPECIALS

Just Polly and Me, CBS, 1960.
The Bing Crosby Christmas Show, ABC, 1962.
(And director) *The Bing Crosby Show,* NBC, 1963, then CBS, 1964.
(With Harbach) *Bing Crosby and Carol Burnett—Together Again for the First Time,* NBC, 1969.
(And director) *The Perry Como Christmas Show,* CBS, 1974.
(And director) *The Perry Como Sunshine Show,* CBS, 1974.
(And director) *Perry Como's Summer of '74,* CBS, 1974.
(With George Stevens, Jr.) *The Kennedy Center Honors: A Celebration of the Performing Arts,* CBS, 1978-80, 1982, 1984-86, 1988, and 1990.
Merry Christmas . . .with Love, Julie, syndicated, 1979.
Julie Andrews: The Sound of Christmas, ABC, 1987.
Jackie Mason on Broadway (adaptation of play *The World According to Me;* also see below), HBO, 1988.
(With Stevens; and executive producer) *The Kennedy Center Honors: A Celebration of the Performing Arts,* CBS, 1989.

TELEVISION EXECUTIVE PRODUCER; SERIES

The Hollywood Palace, ABC, 1964-70.
(With Harbach) *The Milton Berle Show,* ABC, 1966-67.
The Don Knotts Show, NBC, 1970-71.
(With Gary Smith and Dwight Hemion) *On Stage America,* syndicated, 1984.

TELEVISION EXECUTIVE PRODUCER; SPECIALS

The Don Adams Special: Hooray for Hollywood, CBS, 1970.
(With Harbach) *Swing Out, Sweet Land,* NBC, 1976.
(With Stevens) *The Kennedy Center Honors: A Celebration of the Performing Arts,* CBS, 1987.

TELEVISION EXECUTIVE PRODUCER; PILOTS

Camp Grizzly, ABC, 1980.

STAGE PRODUCER

(With Arthur Cantor) *By George,* Lyceum Theatre, New York City, 1967.
The World According to Me, Brooks Atkinson Theatre, New York City, 1986-1988, reopened, 1988.
(With Roger Berlind) *City of Angels* (musical), Virginia Theatre, New York City, 1989.

FILM WORK

Executive producer, *White Dog* (also known as *Trained to Kill*), Paramount, 1982.
Producer, *Eleni,* Warner Brothers, 1985.

OBITUARIES AND OTHER SOURCES:

PERIODICALS

Hollywood Reporter, March 22, 1991.
New York Times, March 22, 1991.
Variety, March 25, 1991.*

* * *

van RUNKLE, Theadora

CAREER: Costume designer. Worked previously as a commercial artist; made film debut as a sketch artist for Dorothy Jeakins on *Hawaii.*

AWARDS, HONORS: Academy Award nomination, best costume design, 1967, and Golden Tiberius, Italian design industry, both for *Bonnie and Clyde;* Academy Award nomination, best costume design, 1974, for *The Godfather, Part II;* Golden Crown Award, Millinery Institute of America, for *Mame;* Emmy Award, best costume design—series, 1983, for "Dungeon of Death," *Wizards and Warriors;* Academy Award nomination, best costume design, 1986, for *Peggy Sue Got Married.*

CREDITS:

FILM COSTUME DESIGNER

Bonnie and Clyde, Warner Brothers, 1967.
Bullitt, Warner Brothers, 1968.
I Love You, Alice B. Toklas! (also known as *Kiss My Butterfly*), Warner Brothers, 1968.

(With Ron Postal and Alan Levine) *The Thomas Crown Affair* (also known as *Thomas Crown and Company* and *The Crown Caper*), United Artists (UA), 1968.
The Arrangement, Warner Brothers, 1969.
(With Enrico Sabbatini) *A Place for Lovers,* Metro-Goldwyn-Mayer, 1969.
(With Allen Levine and Joanne Haas) *The Reivers,* National General, 1969.
Johnny Got His Gun, Cinemation, 1971.
Ace Eli and Rodger of the Skies, Twentieth Century-Fox, 1973.
Kid Blue, Twentieth Century-Fox, 1973.
Mame, Warner Brothers, 1974.
The Godfather, Part II, Paramount, 1974.
Nickelodeon, Columbia, 1976.
New York, New York, UA, 1977.
Same Time, Next Year, Universal, 1978.
(With Richard Bruno) *Heaven Can Wait,* Paramount, 1978.
The Jerk, Universal, 1979.
(With Madeline Graneto) *Heartbeeps,* Universal, 1981.
S.O.B., Paramount, 1981.
The Best Little Whorehouse in Texas, Universal, 1982.
(With Ron Heilman and Linda M. Henrikson) *Rhinestone,* Twentieth Century-Fox, 1984.
Peggy Sue Got Married, Tri-Star, 1986.
Native Son, Cinecom, 1986.
Everybody's All American (also known as *When I Fall in Love*), Warner Brothers, 1988.
Troop Beverly Hills (also known as *Be Prepared*), Weintraub Entertainment Group/Columbia, 1989.
Stella, Buena Vista, 1990.
The Butcher's Wife, Paramount, 1991.

Also costume designer for *Myra Breckinridge,* 1970, and *Wildfire,* 1988.

TELEVISION COSTUME DESIGNER; EPISODIC

"Dungeon of Death," *Wizards and Warriors,* CBS, 1983.

WRITINGS:

Contributor to magazines, including *Cinema.**

W

WALLACE, Mike 1918-
(Myron Wallace)

PERSONAL: Born Myron Leon Wallace, May 9, 1918, in Brookline, MA; son of Frank (an insurance broker) and Zina (Sharfman) Wallace; married Norma Kaphan, August 27, 1940 (divorced, 1948); married Buff Cobb (an actress), 1949 (divorced, 1955); married Lorraine Perrigord (an artist), August 21, 1955 (divorced, 1985); married Mary Yates, June 28, 1986; children: Peter (deceased); Christopher, Anthony, Pauline (stepchildren). *Education:* University of Michigan, A.B., 1939. *Religion:* Jewish. *Avocational interests:* Current affairs, reading, tennis.

ADDRESSES: Office—CBS News, Columbia Broadcasting System, 524 West 57th St., New York, NY 10019.

CAREER: Interviewer, reporter, and writer. WOOD-WASH Radio, Grand Rapids, MI, newscaster, announcer, and writer, 1939-40; WXYZ-Radio, Detroit, MI, newscaster, narrator, and announcer, 1940-41; worked as a free-lancer for radio stations in Chicago, IL; *Chicago Sun-Times,* Chicago, reporter for "Air Edition," 1941-43 and 1946-48; host of several radio and television programs and narrated documentaries, 1952-56; WABD-TV, New York City, news anchor, during mid-1950s; CBS News, staff correspondent, 1963—, coeditor of *60 Minutes,* 1968—. U.S. State Department cultural exchange delegation concerning television to the Soviet Union (now the Commonwealth of Independent States), chair, 1958. *Military service:* U.S. Naval Reserve, 1943-46; submarine force communications officer, later in charge of radio entertainment; served in Pacific theater; became lieutenant junior grade.

MEMBER: American Federation of Television and Radio Artists, Academy of Television Arts and Sciences (executive vice-president, 1960-61), Sigma Delta Chi (fellow).

AWARDS, HONORS: Boston Headliners Award, 1957; Robert E. Sherwood Award, 1957; Golden Globe Award, Hollywood Foreign Press Association, best television show, 1958; George Foster Peabody Broadcasting Awards, University of Georgia, 1963 and 1971; Emmy Award nomination, individual achievement in coverage of special events, 1968, for "Coverage of the Democratic Convention and Surrounding Events," *CBS News Special Reports and Special Broadcasts;* Emmy Award nomination, individual achievement in regularly scheduled news programs, 1970, for "Interviews with Meadlo and Medina," *CBS Evening News with Walter Cronkite;* Carr Van Anda Award, Ohio University, 1977; Thomas Hart Benton Award, Kansas City Art Institute Board of Governors, 1978; Emmy Award nomination (with Harry Moses), 1981, for "Jean Seberg," *The Mike Wallace Profiles;* inducted into the Academy of Television Arts and Sciences' Hall of Fame, 1991.

All for *60 Minutes:* Emmy Award nomination (with Harry Reasoner), individual achievement in cultural documentary and magazine-type program or series, 1969; Emmy Award nominations, individual achievement in regularly scheduled magazine-type programming, 1970, and 1973 for "Dita Beard Interview"; Emmy Awards, individual achievement in regularly scheduled magazine-type programming, 1971 and 1972; Alfred I. du Pont-Columbia University Award in Broadcast Journalism, Columbia University, outstanding reporting, 1972 and 1983; Emmy Awards, regularly scheduled magazine-type programming, 1973, for "The Selling of Colonel Herbert," and 1973, for work as a correspondent in the series; Emmy Award nomination (with Don Hewitt and Harry Moses), achievement for regularly scheduled magazine-type programs, 1974, for "Local News and the Rating War"; Emmy Award nomination, television news broadcaster, 1974; Emmy Awards, programs and program segments,

1979 (with David Lowe, Jr.), for "Misha," 1980 (with Nancy Lea), for "Bette Davis," 1980 (with Lowe), for "Here's . . . Johnny!," 1981 (with Allan Maraynes), for "Killer Wheels," 1981 (with Marion F. Goldin), for "The Last Mafioso" (story about Jimmy Fratianno), and 1981 (with Barry Lando), for "Wanted" (Terpil/Korkala Interview); Emmy Award nominations, programs and program segments, 1980 (with Lando), for "The Iran File," and 1980 (with Maraynes), for "Scientology: The Clearwater Conspiracy"; Emmy Award nomination (with Lando), coverage of a continuing news story, 1982, for "Honor Thy Children"; Emmy Award nomination (with Grace Diekhaus), background/analysis of a single current story, 1982, for "Martina"; Emmy Award nomination, investigative journalism, 1982 (with William H. Willson), for "Small Town"; Emmy Awards, investigative journalism, 1982 (with Ira Rosen), for "The Nazi Connection," and 1987 (with Lowell Bergman), for "The McMartin Preschool"; Emmy Award nominations, interview/interviewer, 1982 (with Lando), for "Jacob Timerman," 1983 (with Rosen), for "Man of Honor," and 1988 (with Rosen), for "Day for FBI"; Emmy Award nomination (with Hewitt, Philip Scheffler, and Charles Lewis), 1987, for "First Jersey Securities"; Emmy Award (with Jim Jackson), interview/interviewer, 1988, for "Arthur Miller."

CREDITS:

TELEVISION APPEARANCES; NEWSMAGAZINE TELECASTS

Correspondent, *60 Minutes,* CBS, 1968—.

TELEVISION APPEARANCES; OTHER NEWS TELECASTS

Anchor, *The CBS Morning News,* CBS, c. 1963-66.
Host, "The National Driver's Test," *CBS News Special,* CBS, 1965.
Correspondent, *CBS Evening News with Walter Cronkite,* CBS, c. 1970.
Host and narrator, *The Mike Wallace Profiles* (pilot; also see below), CBS, 1981.
"Uncounted Enemy: A Vietnam Deception," *CBS Reports,* CBS, 1982.
Special correspondent, *Campaign '86: Election Night,* CBS, 1986.
Reporter, *Campaign '88: Election Night,* CBS, 1988.
The Politics of Privacy (panel discussion), PBS, 1988.
Ethics in America (panel discussion), PBS, 1989.
CBS News Special: Lucy, CBS, 1989.
America's Toughest Assignment: Solving the Education Crisis (documentary), CBS, 1990.
Eyes on the Prize II (documentary), PBS, 1990.
Mike Wallace: Then and Now, A CBS News Special (also see below), CBS, 1990.
Soldiers of Music: Rostropovich Returns to Russia (documentary), PBS, 1991.

Also appeared as an interviewer on *Nightbeat,* WABD, New York City, 1956-57.

TELEVISION APPEARANCES; HOST OF QUIZ AND GAME SHOWS, EXCEPT AS NOTED

(As Myron Wallace) *Majority Rules,* ABC, 1949-50.
Guess Again, CBS, 1951.
Panelist, *The Name's the Same,* ABC, between 1951 and 1955.
I'll Buy That, CBS, 1953.
What's in a Word, CBS (one source says ABC), 1954.
The Big Surprise (also known as *The $100,000 Big Surprise*), NBC, 1956-57.
Who Pays (originally titled *Who's the Boss,* 1954), NBC, 1959.

TELEVISION APPEARANCES; HOST OF OTHER SERIES

(With Buff Cobb), *All around the Town* (interview show), CBS, 1951-52.
(With Cobb), *Mike and Buff* (variety show; originally titled *Two Sleepy People*), CBS, c. 1951-53.
Adventure (educational series for children), CBS, 1953.
The Mike Wallace Interview, ABC, c. 1957-58.
(With Joyce Davidson), *P.M. East-P.M. West* (talk show), syndicated, 1961-62.
Biography (documentary series), syndicated, c. 1961-64.

TELEVISION APPEARANCES; DRAMATIC ROLES

(As Myron Wallace; television debut) Lt. Anthony Kidd, *Stand By for Crime* (series), ABC, 1949.
Suspense, CBS, 1953.
"For the Defense," *Studio One,* CBS, 1955.
"The Changing Ways of Love," *The Seven Lively Arts,* CBS, 1957.

OTHER TELEVISION APPEARANCES

Night of 100 Stars III, NBC, 1990.
The Television Academy Hall of Fame, Fox, 1990.

RADIO APPEARANCES; EPISODIC

Narrated episodes of radio series, including *The Lone Ranger* and *The Green Hornet.* Appeared on daytime serials, including *Ma Perkins* and *The Guiding Light.*

STAGE APPEARANCES

Appeared in Broadway production of *Reclining Figure,* 1954.

STAGE WORK

Coproducer, *Debut,* Theatre-by-the Sea, Matunuck, RI, 1955.

WRITINGS:

TELEVISION

(With Harry Moses) *The Mike Wallace Profiles* (pilot), CBS, 1981.
Mike Wallace: Then and Now, A CBS News Special, CBS, 1990.

OTHER

Mike Wallace Asks, Simon & Schuster, 1958.
(With Gary Paul Gates) *Close Encounters* (memoirs), Morrow, 1984.

Author of column, "Mike Wallace Asks," *New York Post,* 1957-58.

* * *

WALLACE, Myron
See WALLACE, Mike

* * *

WALSTON, Ray 1918(?)-

PERSONAL: Born November 2, 1918, in New Orleans, LA (some sources say November 2, 1924, in Laurel, MS); son of Harry Norman (a lumber man) and Mittie (Kimball) Walston; married Ruth Calvert, November 3, 1943; children: Katherine Ann. *Education:* Graduated from high school in New Orleans. *Avocational interests:* Polo, riding, shooting, bicycling, photography, chess, and cooking.

CAREER: Actor.

MEMBER: American Federation of Radio and Television Artists, Screen Actors Guild, Actors Equity Association, The Lambs, The Players, Magic Club.

AWARDS, HONORS: Clarence Derwent Award, best supporting actor, and *Variety* New York Critics Poll Award, both 1949, both for *Summer and Smoke;* Antoinette Perry Award, best actor in a musical, 1956, for *Damn Yankees.*

CREDITS:

STAGE APPEARANCES

(Stage debut) Buddy, *High Tor,* Community Players Theatre, Houston, TX, 1938.
Hadrian, *You Touched Me,* Cleveland Play House, Cleveland, OH, 1943.
(Broadway debut) Osric, *Hamlet,* Columbus Circle Theatre, New York City, 1945.
Schwartz, *The Front Page,* Royale Theatre, New York City, 1946.
Mississip', *Kiss Them for Me,* Clinton Playhouse, Clinton, CT, 1947.
Sam Phelps, *Three Indelicate Ladies,* Shubert Theatre, New Haven, CT, 1947, later Wilbur Theatre, Boston, MA, 1947.
The Survivors, Playhouse, New York City, 1948.
Mr. Kramer, *Summer and Smoke,* Music Box Theatre, New York City, 1948.
Ratliff, *Richard III,* Booth Theatre, New York City, 1949.
Rodla, *Mrs. Gibbon's Boys,* Music Box Theatre, 1949.
Telephone Man, *The Rat Race,* Ethel Barrymore Theatre, New York City, 1949.
(London debut) Luther Billis, *South Pacific,* Drury Lane Theatre, 1951.
Mac, *Me and Juliet,* Majestic Theatre, New York City, 1953.
Captain Jonas, *House of Flowers,* Alvin Theatre, New York City, 1954.
Applegate, *Damn Yankees,* 46th St. Theatre, New York City, 1955.
Michael Haney, *Who Was That Lady I Saw You With?,* Martin Beck Theatre, New York City, 1958.
Eddie, *Agatha Sue, I Love You,* Henry Miller's Theatre, New York City, 1966.
The Rivals, Philadelphia Drama Guild, Philadelphia, PA, 1972.
Lutz, *The Student Prince,* Academy of Music, Philadelphia, PA, 1973.
A Gala Tribute to Joshua Logan, Imperial Theatre, New York City, 1975.
Last Meeting of the Knights of the White Magnolia, Cleveland Play House, 1976.

Also guest artist, Philadelphia Drama Guild, Philadelphia, PA, 1971-72, and Cleveland Play House, Cleveland, OH, 1975-78.

MAJOR TOURS

Luther Billis, *South Pacific,* U.S. cities, 1950.
Applegate, *Damn Yankees,* U.S cities, 1955-56.
Steward, *The Canterbury Tales,* U.S. cities, 1969-70.

FILM APPEARANCES

Lt. "Mac" McCann, *Kiss Them for Me,* Twentieth Century-Fox, 1957.
Applegate, *Damn Yankees,* Warner Bros., 1958.
Luther Billis, *South Pacific,* Twentieth Century-Fox, 1958.
Phil Stanley, *Say One for Me,* Twentieth Century-Fox, 1959.
Mr. Dobisch, *The Apartment,* United Artists (UA), 1960.
Cob O'Brien, *Portrait in Black,* Universal, 1960.
Leo Sullivan, *Tall Story,* Warner Bros., 1960.

Iggy, *Convicts Four,* Allied Artists, 1962.
Mr. Quimby, *Who's Minding the Store?,* Paramount, 1963.
Wylie Driberg, *Wives and Lovers,* Paramount, 1963.
Orville J. Spooner, *Kiss Me, Stupid,* Claude/Lopert, 1964.
Stuart Clancy, *Caprice,* Twentieth Century-Fox, 1967.
Mad Jack Duncan, *Paint Your Wagon,* Paramount, 1969.
J.J. Singleton, *The Sting,* Universal, 1973.
Mr. Whiney, *Silver Streak,* Twentieth Century-Fox, 1976.
Senator Sturges, *The Happy Hooker Goes to Washington,* Cannon, 1977.
Poopdeck Pappy, *Popeye,* Paramount, 1980.
Kore, *Galaxy of Terror,* New World Cinema, 1981.
Mr. Hand, *Fast Times at Ridgemont High,* Universal, 1982.
Walter Tatum, *O'Hara's Wife,* Davis-Panzer, 1983.
Chauncey, *Private School,* Universal, 1983.
Vendor, *Johnny Dangerously,* Twentieth Century-Fox, 1984.
Burton Timmer, *Rad,* Tri-Star, 1986.
1st Judge, *From the Hip,* DEG, 1987.
Gramps, *O.C. and Stiggs,* Metro-Goldwyn-Mayer/UA, 1987.
Charles MacLeod, *Blood Relations,* Miramax, 1988.
1st Patient, *Paramedics,* Vestron, 1988.
A Man of Passion, Golden Sun, 1989.
Gramps, *Saturday the 14th Strikes Back,* Concorde, 1989.
Pops, *Ski Patrol,* Triumph, 1990.
Dr. Mnesyne, *Popcorn,* Studio Three Film Corporation, 1991.
Candy, *Of Mice and Men,* Metro-Goldwyn-Mayer, 1992.

TELEVISION APPEARANCES; MOVIES

The Killers, CBS, 1959.
Eddie Eppes, *For Love or Money,* CBS, 1984.
Johnny Kent, *Amos,* CBS, 1985.
Mr. Harmon, *Ask Max,* ABC, 1986.
Wendell Paulson, *Crash Course,* NBC, 1988.
Horace Groot, *Red River,* CBS, 1988.
Cappy Connors, *Class Cruise,* NBC, 1989.
Bob Augustine, *I Know My First Name Is Steven,* NBC, 1989.
Prison librarian, *Angel of Death,* CBS, 1990.
Corkscrew, *Fine Gold,* syndicated, 1990.
Monsignor McCutchen, *Pink Lightning,* Fox, 1991.
Mr. Wurtz, *One Special Victory,* NBC, 1991.

Also appeared as Thaddeus in *The Fall of the House of Usher,* 1982.

TELEVISION APPEARANCES; SERIES

Uncle Martin O'Hara, *My Favorite Martian,* CBS, 1963-66.
Reese Vernon, *Oh Madeline,* ABC, 1983-84.

TELEVISION APPEARANCES; EPISODIC

(Television debut) *Suspense,* CBS, 1950.
Playhouse 90, CBS, 1956-60.
Bob Richards, "Stop Susan Williams," *Cliffhangers,* NBC, 1979.

Also appeared in "Uncle Harry," *Play of the Week,* 1950; and on the programs *Studio One,* CBS, *You Are There,* CBS, *Producer's Showcase,* NBC, *The Ed Sullivan Show,* CBS, *The Perry Como Show,* NBC, and *The Arthur Godfrey Show.*

TELEVISION APPEARANCES; SPECIALS

Dave Corween, "There Shall Be No Night," *Hallmark Hall of Fame,* NBC, 1957.
Voice of Matt, *Runaway Ralph* (animated), ABC, 1988.
Voice of Matt, *Ralph S. Mouse* (animated), ABC, 1991.

TELEVISION APPEARANCES; PILOTS

Harry Burns, *Harry's Business,* NBC, 1961.
The Stranger, *Satan's Waitin',* CBS, 1964.
Professor Stoneman, *Danny and the Mermaid,* CBS, 1978.
Frank Anders, *Institute for Revenge,* NBC, 1979.
Michael, *The Kid with the Broken Halo,* NBC, 1982.
Abner Litto, *This Girl for Hire,* CBS, 1983.
Diesel, *The Jerk, Too,* NBC, 1984.
Ed, *Hurricane Sam,* CBS, 1990.*

* * *

WALTERS, Thorley 1913-1991

PERSONAL: Born May 12, 1913, in Teingrace, Devonshire, England; died July 6, 1991, in London, England; son of Prebendary Thomas Collins (a priest) and Mary Francis (Swinstead) Walters. *Education:* Attended Monkton Combe School; studied drama at Old Vic School. *Avocational interests:* Swimming, surf riding, photography.

CAREER: Actor. Member of acting companies at Old Vic Theatre, 1933-35, and Manchester Repertory Theatre, 1935-36; served as a director of the Royal General Theatrical Fund.

CREDITS:

STAGE APPEARANCES

(Stage debut) *The Admirable Bashville,* Old Vic Theatre, London, 1933.
Gentle Rain, Vaudeville Theatre, London, 1936.
Do You Remember, Vaudeville Theatre, 1936.
Edward Davis, *Mary Goes to See,* Haymarket Theatre, London, 1938.
Philip Hamilton, *High Fever,* Arts Theatre Club, London, 1938.

George Perrey, *Cottage to Let,* Wyndham's Theatre, London, 1940.
Lieutenant Fisher, *Escort,* Lyric Theatre, London, 1942.
Jerry Seymour and, later, David Naughton, *Claudia,* St. Martin's Theatre, London, 1942.
Tim Garrett, *Under the Counter,* Phoenix Theatre, London, 1945.
(Broadway debut) Tim Garrett, *Under the Counter,* Shubert Theatre, New York City, 1947.
Jimmy Denham, *Her Excellency,* Hippodrome Theatre, London, 1949.
Peter Lynton, *Gay's the Word,* Saville Theatre, London, 1951.
Over the Moon (revue), Piccadilly Theatre, London, 1953.
Johann Schneider, *The Roses Are Real,* Gaiety Theatre, Dublin, Ireland, 1963, and Vaudeville Theatre, 1964.
Title role, *Mr. Pim Passes By,* Hampstead Theatre Club, London, 1968.

Also appeared as Abbe Vignali, *St. Helena,* Daly's Theatre.

MAJOR TOURS

Tim Garrett, *Under the Counter,* Australian and New Zealand cities, 1948-49.

Also toured as Tom, *Think of a Number,* 1937; Peter Lynton, *Gay's the Word,* 1950; and in revue *Bits and Pieces,* 1954.

FILM APPEARANCES

Once in a New Moon, Twentieth Century-Fox, 1935.
Von Raugwitz, *Among Human Wolves* (also known as *Secret Journey*), Anglo-American, 1940.
Frazier, *Design for Murder* (also known as *Trunk Crime*), World, 1940.
Ronnie, *It Happened to One Man* (also known as *Gentleman of Venture*), RKO Radio Pictures, 1941.
Channing, *They Were Sisters,* Universal, 1945.
Andrew, *The Gay Intruders* (also known as *Medal for the General*), Anglo-American, 1946.
Stefan Ravenne, *Waltz Time,* Anglo-American, 1946.
Salesman, *Josephine and Men,* British Lion, 1955.
Chadwick, *You Can't Escape,* Associated British Films/Pathe, 1955.
Captain Bootle, *Private's Progress,* British Lion, 1956.
Preston, *Rotten to the Core,* Cinema V, 1956.
Raymond Courtney, *Who Done It?,* J. Arthur Rank, 1956.
Photographer, *The Birthday Present,* British Lion, 1957.
Jimmy, *A Novel Affair* (also known as *The Passionate Stranger*), Continental, 1957.
Charles, *Second Fiddle,* British Lion, 1957.
Major, *Blue Murder at St. Trinian's,* British Lion, 1958.
Jim, *Happy Is the Bride,* Kassler, 1958.
Smith, *A Lady Mislaid,* Associated British Films/Pathe, 1958.
Trevor, *The Truth about Women,* Continental Distributing, 1958.
Brown, *Don't Panic Chaps!,* Columbia, 1959.
Colonel Edmonds, *French Mistress,* British Lion, 1960.
Colonel Bellingham, *Man in a Cocked Hat* (also known as *Carlton-Browne of the F.O.*), Show, 1960.
Lieutenant Commander Cummings, *Invasion Quartet,* Metro-Goldwyn-Mayer (MGM), 1961.
Cedric Ackenthorpe, *Murder She Said* (also known as *Meet Miss Marple*), MGM, 1961.
Lieutenant Jerome Robertson, *Petticoat Pirates,* Warner Bros./Pathe, 1961.
Butters, *The Pure Hell of St. Trinian's,* Continental Distributing, 1961.
Mr. Prince, *The Risk* (also known as *Suspect*), Kingsley International, 1961.
Colonel Arkwright, *Two-Way Stretch,* International-Show Corporation of America, 1961.
Lattimer, *The Phantom of the Opera,* Universal, 1962.
Dr. Watson, *Sherlock Holmes and the Deadly Necklace* (also known as *Sherlock Holmes und das Halsband des Todes* and *Valley of Fear*), Screen Gems, 1962.
Tranquilax executive, *Heavens Above!,* British Lion/Romulus/Janus, 1963.
Edgar Otis, *The Earth Dies Screaming,* Twentieth Century-Fox, 1964.
Commander Winters, *Ring of Spies* (also known as *Ring of Treason*), British Lion, 1964.
Dr. Hertz, *Frankenstein Created Woman,* Twentieth Century-Fox, 1965.
Colonel, *Joey Boy,* British Lion, 1965.
Ludwig, *Dracula—Prince of Darkness,* Twentieth Century-Fox, 1966.
Vicar, *The Family Way,* Warner Bros., 1966.
Martin Roth, *The Psychopath,* Paramount, 1966.
Lawyer Patience, *The Wrong Box,* Columbia, 1966.
Inspector Frisch, *Frankenstein Must Be Destroyed!,* Warner Bros., 1969.
General Jowett, *The Last Shot You Hear,* Twentieth Century-Fox, 1969.
Staff officer in ballroom, *Oh! What a Lovely War,* Paramount, 1969.
Sir John Forrester, *Twisted Nerve,* National General, 1969.
Colleague, *Bartleby,* British Lion, 1970.
Bellamy, *The Man Who Haunted Himself,* Levitt-Pickman, 1970.
Hubbard, *Sophie's Place* (also known as *Crooks and Coronets*), Warner Bros./Seven Arts, 1970.
Manager of Carlton Hotel, *There's A Girl in My Soup,* Columbia, 1970.
Magistrate, *Trog,* Warner Bros., 1970.

Forbush, Sr., *Cry of the Penguins* (also known as *Mr. Forbush and the Penguins*), British Lion, 1972.
Burgermeister, *Vampire Circus,* Twentieth Century-Fox, 1972.
Major Finn, *Young Winston,* Columbia, 1972.
Dr. Watson, *The Adventures of Sherlock Holmes' Smarter Brother,* Twentieth Century-Fox, 1975.
Dr. Edward Norfolk, *The People That Time Forgot,* American International, 1977.
Hugh Culpepper-Brown, *The Wildcats of St. Trinian's,* Wildcat, 1980.
Major John Sholto, *The Sign of Four,* Mapleton, 1983.
Ned Quilley, *The Little Drummer Girl,* Warner Bros., 1984.

Also appeared in *Sherlock Holmes and the Silver Blaze,* 1977, and *In the Secret State.*

TELEVISION APPEARANCES; EPISODIC

"Cousin Bette," *Masterpiece Theatre,* PBS, 1972.
Doughty Strove, "Paradise Postponed," *Masterpiece Theatre,* PBS, 1986.
Mr. Dick, "David Copperfield," *Masterpiece Theatre,* PBS, 1988.
"A Murder of Quality," *Masterpiece Theatre,* PBS, 1991.

TELEVISION APPEARANCES; MINI-SERIES

Prince of Wales, *Jennie: Lady Randolph Churchill,* PBS, 1975.
Tinker, Tailor, Soldier, Spy, PBS, 1980.

OTHER TELEVISION APPEARANCES

Dr. Ledworth, *Death in Small Doses* (special), ABC, 1973.

Also appeared in series *A. P. Herbert's Misleading Cases,* 1967, and *The Edwardians;* and movie *The Richest Man in the World;* appeared in *Ring Once for Death, The Duchess of Duke Street, After the Party, Spider's Web, The Man on the Screen, Henry V,* and *Malice Aforethought.*

OBITUARIES AND OTHER SOURCES:

PERIODICALS

Variety, July 15, 1991.*

*   *   *

WARNER, Julie

PERSONAL: Education: Brown University, graduate in theater arts, 1987.

ADDRESSES: Agent—Susan Smith and Associates, 121 North San Vicente Blvd., Beverly Hills, CA 90211.

CAREER: Actress.

CREDITS:

FILM APPEARANCES

Wrangler, *Winterhawk,* Howco International, 1975.
One of Joe's women, *Flatliners,* Columbia, 1990.
Lou, *Doc Hollywood,* Warner Brothers, 1991.

TELEVISION APPEARANCES; EPISODIC

Appeared on episodes of *21 Jump Street,* Fox, *Carol and Company,* NBC, *The Outsiders,* Fox, and *Star Trek: The Next Generation,* syndicated.

OTHER TELEVISION APPEARANCES

Jennie Slade, *Stolen: One Husband* (movie; also known as *I Want Him Back*), CBS, 1990.

Also appeared as the girlfriend of Andrew Dice Clay on an HBO special.

OTHER SOURCES:

PERIODICALS

New York Times, August 11, 1991, p. 10H.
People Weekly, August 19, 1991, p. 47.*

*   *   *

WARNER, Malcolm-Jamal 1970-

PERSONAL: Born August 18, 1970, in Jersey City, NJ; son of Pamela Warner (son's business manager). *Education:* Professional Children's School, Manhattan, NY, graduated with honors. *Avocational interests:* Music.

ADDRESSES: Agent—Artists First, 8230 Beverly Blvd., No. 23, Los Angeles, CA 90048.

CAREER: Actor. Began career at age nine; appeared in commercials for Walt Disney World; director of music videos, including one for New Edition. Spokesperson for Smoke Free Generation and honorary youth chairperson for the National Parent Teacher Association (PTA). Active in anti-drug campaign for teenagers.

MEMBER: Screen Actors Guild, Osmond Foundation's Miracle Network (national chairman).

AWARDS, HONORS: NAACP Image Award, best performance by an actor in a comedy, and Emmy Award nomination, 1986, both for *The Cosby Show.*

CREDITS:

TELEVISION APPEARANCES; SERIES

Theodore Huxtable, *The Cosby Show* (also see below), NBC, 1984-92.

TELEVISION APPEARANCES; MOVIES

Joey, *The Father Clements Story,* NBC, 1987.

TELEVISION APPEARANCES; EPISODIC

"Stop the Presses," *Matt Houston,* 1982.
"A Nation Divided," *Call to Glory,* ABC, 1984.
"The Network," *Matlock,* NBC, 1987.
Ben Sweet, *Tour of Duty,* CBS, 1992.

Also appeared as host of *Saturday Night Live,* NBC, and *Friday Night Videos,* NBC.

TELEVISION APPEARANCES; SPECIALS

Andy Williams and the NBC Kids Search for Santa, NBC, 1985.
NBC's 60th Anniversary Celebration, NBC, 1986.
Super Bloopers and New Practical Jokes, NBC, 1988.
The 20th Annual NAACP Image Awards, NBC, 1988.
Battle of the Network Stars XIX, ABC, 1988.
National Basketball Players Association Awards, syndicated, 1989.
Bill Cosby Salutes Alvin Ailey, NBC, 1989.
Best Catches, CBS, 1989.
Host, *Smithsonian Institution: America's Time Machine,* syndicated, 1989.
Cullen Sturgis, *Mother's Day,* CBN, 1989.
Time Warner Presents the Earth Day Special, ABC, 1990.
The Stellar Gospel Music Awards, syndicated, 1990.
The Greatest Practical Jokes of All Time, NBC, 1990.
Big Bird's Birthday; or, Let Me Eat Cake, PBS, 1991.
The 5th Annual American Comedy Awards, ABC, 1991.
Panelist, *Summit for the '90s,* TBS, 1991.
Host, *Cool Moves—Teens Together,* PBS, 1991.
Goodwill ambassador, *Children's Miracle Network Television,* syndicated, 1991.

Also appeared in *Motown Returns to the Apollo, Macy's Thanksgiving Day Parade,* and *Fast Copy,* all 1985; as host, *Disneyland's Summer Vacation Party,* and as Charlie Curtis, *A Desperate Exit,* both 1986; appeared in *Walt Disney World Celebrity Circus, A Star-Spangled Celebration, Comic Relief II,* and *The 19th Annual NAACP Image Awards,* all 1987; and in *Straight Out of Brooklyn,* 1991.

TELEVISION APPEARANCES; PILOTS

Friday Night Surprise, NBC, 1988.

TELEVISION WORK; EPISODIC

Director of one episode, *The Cosby Show,* NBC, c. 1990.

TELEVISION WORK; SPECIALS

Worked as co-producer of four specials for young people.

STAGE APPEARANCES

Frankie, *Three Ways Home,* Astor Place Theatre, New York City, 1988.

RECORDINGS:

VIDEOS

Appeared in *Show Off! A Kid's Guide to Being Cool,* 1986; hosted *Home Alone: A Kid's Guide to Playing It Safe on Your Own,* a video that contains warnings to youngsters about possible dangers at home and at play; and hosted a series of reading motivation videos for children.

WRITINGS:

Theo and Me: Growing Up Okay, Dutton, 1988.

OTHER SOURCES:

PERIODICALS

Daily News (New York), February 16, 1986, p. 3.
New York Post, April 15, 1987, p. 70.*

* * *

WATERS, John 1946-

PERSONAL: Born April 22, 1946, in Baltimore, MD; son of John (in fire-protection equipment business) and Pat Waters. *Education:* Attended University of Baltimore, 1965, and New York University, 1966. *Avocational interests:* Attending trials, teaching in jail.

ADDRESSES: Agent— Bill Block, Inter Talent, 131 South Rodeo Dr., Suite 300, Beverly Hills, CA 90212.

CAREER: Producer, director, cinematographer, screenwriter, actor, and journalist. Worked in book stores; teacher of English and film at Patuxent Institution, a psychiatric prison in Maryland, 1983-86. Lecturer at comedy clubs and colleges.

AWARDS, HONORS: Co-recipient of Charlie Comedy Award for special contribution to art of comedy, Association of Comedy Artists, 1987; "John Waters Days" have been proclaimed by the governor of Maryland and the mayor of Baltimore.

CREDITS:

FILM DIRECTOR

(And producer, cinematographer, and editor) *Mondo Trasho* (also see below), New Line Cinema, 1969.
(And producer) *Multiple Maniacs,* New Line Cinema, 1970.
(And producer, cinematographer, and editor) *Pink Flamingos* (also see below), New Line Cinema, 1972.

(And producer and cinematographer) *Female Trouble* (also see below), New Line Cinema, 1974.
(And producer) *Desperate Living* (also see below), New Line Cinema, 1977.
(And producer) *Polyester* (also see below), New Line Cinema, 1981.
(And producer with Rachel Talalay and Stanley F. Buchthal) *Hairspray* (also see below), New Line Cinema, 1988.
Cry-Baby (also see below), Universal, 1990.

Also director of short films (also see below) *Hag in a Black Leather Jacket,* 1964, *Roman Candles,* 1966-67, *Eat Your Makeup,* 1968, and *The Diane Linkletter Story,* 1970.

FILM APPEARANCES

Used car salesman, *Something Wild,* Orion, 1986.
Dr. Fredrickson, *Hairspray,* New Line Cinema, 1988.
First robber, *Homer & Eddie,* Skouras, 1989.

WRITINGS:

SCREENPLAYS

Mondo Trasho, New Line Cinema, 1969.
Pink Flamingos, New Line Cinema, 1972.
Female Trouble, New Line Cinema, 1974.
Desperate Living, New Line Cinema, 1977.
Polyester, New Line Cinema, 1981.
Hairspray, New Line Cinema, 1988.
Cry-Baby, Universal, 1990.

Also author of screenplays for *Hag in a Black Leather Jacket,* 1964, *Roman Candles,* 1966-67, *Eat Your Makeup,* 1968, and *The Diane Linkletter Story,* 1970.

OTHER

Shock Value: A Tasteful Book about Bad Taste (autobiography), Dell, 1981.
Crackpot: The Obsessions of John Waters (essays), Macmillan, 1986.
Trash Trio: Three Screenplays (contains *Pink Flamingos, Desperate Living,* and *Flamingos Forever* [unproduced]), Vintage Books, 1988.

Also contributor to periodicals, including *Rolling Stone, Vogue, Vanity Fair, American Film, Film Comment, New York Times Book Review,* and *British Vogue.*

OTHER SOURCES:

BOOKS

Contemporary Authors, Volume 130, Gale, 1990.
Newsmakers 88, Gale, 1989.
Waters, John, *Shock Value: A Tasteful Book about Bad Taste,* Dell, 1981.

PERIODICALS

American Film, April, 1990, pp. 33-37.
Daily News Magazine, February 14, 1988, p. 26.
Fangoria, August, 1982, pp. 36-39.
Interview, December 1986, p. 208; February 1990, p. 92.
New Statesman & Society, July 13, 1990, p. 33.
New York Times, February 21, 1988, pp. 23, 37.
New York Times Magazine, April 7, 1991, p. 34.
Rolling Stone, May 17, 1990, p. 30.
Theatre Crafts, May, 1990, p. 42.

* * *

WATERSTON, Sam 1940-

PERSONAL: Full name, Samuel Atkinson Waterston; born November 15, 1940, in Cambridge, MA; son of George Chychele (a teacher and director) and Alice Tucker (a painter; maiden name, Atkinson) Waterston; married Barbara Rutledge Johns (a photographer and writer), 1964 (marriage ended); married Lynn Louisa Woodruff (a model), January 26, 1976; children: (first marriage) James S.; (second marriage) Graham C., Elisabeth P., Katherine B. *Education:* Attended Groton Academy; studied at Sorbonne, University of Paris, 1960-61; Yale University, B.A., 1962; studied with John Berry at American Actors Workshop in Paris, and with Frank Corsaro and Herbert Berghoff in New York City. *Avocational interests:* Skiing, sailing, tennis.

ADDRESSES: Agent—Agency for the Performing Arts, Inc., 9000 Sunset Blvd., Suite 315, Los Angeles, CA 90069.

CAREER: Actor.

MEMBER: Actors Equity Association, Screen Actors Guild, American Federation of Television and Radio Artists.

AWARDS, HONORS: Obie Award, performance, *Village Voice,* Drama Desk Award, outstanding performance, and Drama Critics Circle Award, all 1972, for *Much Ado about Nothing;* Emmy Award nomination, best supporting actor in a drama, 1973, for *The Glass Menagerie;* Academy Award nomination, best actor, British Academy of Film and Television Arts, and Golden Globe Award nomination, both 1981, for "Oppenheimer"; Academy Award nomination, best actor, 1984, for *The Killing Fields;* Golden Globe Award nomination, best actor in a drama, 1992, for *I'll Fly Away.*

CREDITS:

TELEVISION APPEARANCES; SERIES

Professor Quentin E. Deverill, *Q.E.D.,* CBS, 1982.
Forrest Bedford, *I'll Fly Away,* NBC, 1991—.

TELEVISION APPEARANCES; MOVIES

Tom, *The Glass Menagerie,* ABC, 1973.
Michael Elliott, *Reflections of Murder,* ABC, 1974.
Benedick, *Much Ado about Nothing,* CBS, 1974.
C. D. Bryan, *Friendly Fire,* ABC, 1979.
David Bentells, *Games Mother Never Taught You,* CBS, 1982.
Doc Kearns, *Dempsey,* CBS, 1983.
Paul Wilcox, *In Defense of Kids,* CBS, 1983.
Bernie Wallace, *Love Lives On,* ABC, 1985.
Paul Broadbent, *Finnegan Begin Again,* HBO, 1985.
Commander Allard Renslow, *The Fifth Missile* (also known as *The Gold Crew*), NBC, 1986.
Abraham Lincoln, *Gore Vidal's Lincoln,* NBC, 1988.
William L. Shirer, *The Nightmare Years,* TNT, 1989.
Andrew Stuart, *Lantern Hill* (also known as *Jane of Lantern Hill*), Disney, 1990.

Also appeared in *Diabolique,* 1975, and *The Shell Seekers.*

TELEVISION APPEARANCES; EPISODIC

(Television debut) *Camera Three,* CBS, 1964.
J. Robert Oppenheimer, "Oppenheimer," BBC, 1978, then broadcast as an episode of *American Playhouse,* PBS, 1982.
Amazing Stories, NBC, 1985.
Travis Coles, "The Room Upstairs," *Hallmark Hall of Fame,* CBS, 1987.
John Honeyman, "Walk in the Woods" (also see below), *American Playhouse,* PBS, 1989.

Also appeared in episodes of *N.Y.P.D.,* ABC; *Hawk,* ABC; and *Dr. Kildare.*

TELEVISION APPEARANCES; SPECIALS

The Good Lieutenant, PBS, 1967.
Liberty Weekend, ABC, 1986.
The 40th Annual Tony Awards, CBS, 1986.
Host, *Generation at Risk,* PBS, 1987.
Abraham Lincoln and Justice Louis Brandeis, *The Blessings of Liberty,* ABC, 1987.
The 42nd Annual Tony Awards, CBS, 1988.
Narrator, *The American Experience,* PBS, 1988.
Terrorist on Trial: The United States of America vs. Salim Ajami, PBS, 1988.
Night of 100 Stars III (also see below), NBC, 1990.
Voice of Abraham Lincoln, *The Civil War,* PBS, 1990.

Also appeared in other specials, including *Robert Lowell,* 1966, and *My Mother's House,* PBS.

FILM APPEARANCES

(Film debut) Andy, *The Plastic Dome of Norma Jean,* Compton, 1966.
Oliver, *Fitzwilly* (also known as *Fitzwilly Strikes Back*), United Artists (UA), 1967.
Desmond, *Generation* (also known as *A Time for Giving*), Avco Embassy, 1969.
Taylor, *Three,* UA, 1969.
The cameraman, *Cover Me Babe,* Twentieth Century-Fox, 1970.
Alex, *Who Killed Mary What'ser Name?* (also known as *Death of a Hooker*), Cannon, 1971.
James, *Savages,* Angelika, 1972.
Nick Carraway, *The Great Gatsby,* Paramount, 1974.
Cecil Colson, *Rancho Deluxe,* UA, 1975.
Philip Le Clerq, *Dandy, the All American Girl* (also known as *Sweet Revenge*), Metro-Goldwyn-Mayer (MGM)/UA, 1976.
Graham, *Journey into Fear* (also known as *Burn Out*), Sterling Gold, 1976.
Lieutenant Peter Willis, *Capricorn One,* Warner Bros., 1978.
Mike, *Interiors,* UA, 1978.
White Bull, *Eagle's Wing,* Rank, 1979.
William McClusky, *Sweet William,* World Northal, 1980.
Frank Canton, *Heaven's Gate,* UA, 1980.
Cutter, *Hopscotch,* Avco Embassy, 1980.
Sydney Schanberg, *The Killing Fields,* Warner Bros., 1984.
Cal Morse, *Warning Sign,* Twentieth Century-Fox, 1985.
Gerry Morrison, *Flagrant Desir* (also known as *A Certain Desire*), Hemdale, 1986.
Harry Crandall, *Just between Friends,* Orion, 1986.
David, *Hannah and Her Sisters,* Orion, 1986.
Mr. Jones, *The Devil's Paradise,* Overview, 1987.
Peter, *September,* Orion, 1987.
Swimming to Cambodia, Cinecom, 1987.
Ben, *Crimes and Misdemeanors,* Orion, 1989.
Woody, *Welcome Home,* Columbia/Rank, 1989.
Matthew Trant, *The Man in the Moon,* MGM/Pathe, 1991.

Also appeared in *Mahoney's Estate,* 1970; as Jack Edwards, *Mindwalk,* 1990; and in *A Captive in the Land,* 1991; *Coup de Foudre; The French Revolution;* and *The Teddy Bear Habit.*

STAGE APPEARANCES

Estragon, *Waiting for Godot,* Clifton Playhouse, Clifton, CT, 1962.
Jonathan Rosepettle, *Oh, Dad, Poor Dad, Mama's Hung You in the Closet and I'm Feeling So Bad* (also see below), Morosco Theatre, New York City, 1963.
Wessy, *Thistle in My Bed,* Grammercy Arts Theatre, New York City, 1963.
Silvius, *As You Like It,* New York Shakespeare Festival (NYSF), New York City, 1963.

Colin, *The Knack* (also see below), New Theatre, New York City, 1964.

Woodfin, *Fitz* (double bill with *Biscuit*), Circle in the Square, New York City, 1966.

Eh?, Playhouse in the Park, Cincinnati, OH, 1966.

Understudy, *First One Asleep, Whistle,* Belasco Theatre, New York City, 1966.

Kent, *La Turista,* American Place Theatre/St. Clement's Church, New York City, 1967.

Aburbio, *Posterity for Sale,* American Place Theatre/St. Clement's Church, 1967.

Robert, *Halfway Up the Tree,* Brooks Atkinson Theatre, New York City, 1967.

Aslan, *Ergo,* NYSF, Public/Anspacher Theatre, New York City, 1968.

Jim, *Red Cross,* and Jack Argue, *Muzeeka* (double bill), Provincetown Playhouse, New York City, 1968.

Prince Hal, *Henry IV, Part I,* NYSF, Delacorte Theatre, New York City, 1968.

Prince Hal, *Henry IV, Part II,* NYSF, Delacorte Theatre, 1968.

Rosencrantz and Guildenstern Are Dead, Williamstown Theatre Festival, Williamstown, MA, 1969.

Operation Sidewinder, Williamstown Theatre Festival, 1969.

Gary Rogers, *Spitting Image,* Theatre de Lys, New York City, 1969.

John Grass, *Indians,* Brooks Atkinson Theatre, 1969-70.

Phanocles, *The Brass Butterfly,* Chelsea Theatre Center, Brooklyn Academy of Music, Brooklyn, NY, 1970.

Aaron, *And I Met a Man,* Lincoln Square Theatre, New York City, 1970.

Simon Bliss, *Hay Fever,* Helen Hayes Theatre, New York City, 1970.

Thomas Lewis, *The Trial of the Catonsville Nine,* Good Shepherd-Faith Church, then Lyceum Theatre, New York City, 1971.

Cloten, *The Tale of Cymbeline,* NYSF, Delacorte Theatre, 1972.

Mosca, *Volpone,* Center Theatre Group, Mark Taper Forum, Los Angeles, CA, 1972.

Oliver, *A Meeting by the River,* Center Theatre Group, Mark Taper Forum, then Edison Theatre, New York City, 1972.

Laertes, *Hamlet,* NYSF, Delacorte Theatre, 1972.

Benedick, *Much Ado about Nothing,* NYSF, Delacorte Theatre, 1972, then Winter Garden Theatre, New York City, 1972-73.

Prospero, *The Tempest,* NYSF, Public/Mitzi E. Newhouse Theatre, New York City, 1974.

Torvald Helmer, *A Doll's House,* NYSF, Vivian Beaumont Theatre, New York City, 1975.

Title role, *Hamlet,* NYSF, Delacorte Theatre, 1975, then Vivian Beaumont Theatre, 1975-76.

Narrator, *King David,* Church of Our Savior, New York City, 1976.

Vicentio, *Measure for Measure,* NYSF, Delacorte Theatre, 1976.

Chez nous, Manhattan Theatre Club, New York City, 1977.

Vladimir, *Waiting for Godot,* BAM/Lepercq Space, New York City, 1978.

Oliver, *Lunch Hour,* Ethel Barrymore Theatre, New York City, 1980-81.

Joshua Hickman, *Gardenia,* Manhattan Theatre Club/Downstage, 1982.

Enemies, Williamstown Theatre Festival, 1982.

Alexander Vershinin, *Three Sisters,* Manhattan Theatre Club/Downstage, 1982-83.

Traveler in the Dark, American Repertory Theatre, Cambridge, MA, 1983-84.

David, *Benefactors,* Brooks Atkinson Theatre, 1985-86.

John Honeyman, *A Walk in the Woods,* Booth Theatre, New York City, 1988.

Night of 100 Stars III, Radio City Music Hall, New York City, 1990.

Made stage debut as Page in *Antigone.* Also appeared in *The Paisley Convertible,* New York City, 1966; in *Uncle Vanya,* San Diego, CA, 1979; and as the bill collector, *A Streetcar Named Desire,* Group Twenty Theatre, Wellesley, MA.

MAJOR TOURS

Jonathan, *Oh, Dad, Poor Dad, Mama's Hung You in the Closet and I'm Feeling So Bad,* U.S. cities, 1963.

Colin, *The Knack,* U.S. cities, 1966.*

* * *

WATSON, Susan 1938-

PERSONAL: Full name, Susan Elizabeth Watson; born December 17, 1938, in Tulsa, OK; daughter of Robert J. (a geologist and geophysicist) and Gretchen (Warren) Watson; married Roger LePage (an actor), October 30, 1959 (marriage ended, 1963); married Norton W. Wright (a producer), February 16, 1964; children: one son. *Education:* Studied dancing with Suzanne Aker in Tulsa, OK, 1954-57, and with Hanya Holm in New York City, 1955; attended Juilliard School of Music, 1957-58; studied dancing with Peter Gennaro in New York City, 1958-62; studied acting with Uta Hagen at HB Studio in New York City, 1959-62; studied singing with Tony Franco, 1961, and Karen Gustafson, 1962, both in New York City. *Avocational interests:* Water sports, diving, skiing, traveling.

ADDRESSES: Agent—International Famous Agency, 1301 Avenue of the Americas, New York, NY 10019.

CAREER: Actress, singer, and dancer.

AWARDS, HONORS: Tulsa Philharmonic Youth Concert Award, 1955; Tulsa Opera Dance Scholarship, 1956; Antoinette Perry Award nomination, best supporting actress in a musical, 1966, for *A Joyful Noise.*

CREDITS:

STAGE APPEARANCES

(Stage debut) Baby Betsy, *By the Beautiful Sea,* Starlight Theatre, Kansas City, MO, 1957.
Silk Stockings, Toronto Music Tent, Toronto, Ontario, Canada, 1958.
Happy Hunting, Toronto Music Tent, 1958.
Velma and understudy for the role of Maria, *West Side Story,* Her Majesty's Theatre, London, 1958.
Girl, *The Fantasticks* (also see below), Minor Latham Theatre, New York City, 1959.
Ensemble, *Lend an Ear* (revue), Renata Theatre, 1959.
Ensemble, *Follies of 1910* (revue), Carnegie Playhouse, 1960.
(Broadway debut) Kim MacAfee, *Bye Bye Birdie,* Martin Beck Theatre, New York City, 1960.
Lili, *Carnival!* (also see below), Imperial Theatre, New York City, 1961.
Lili, *Carnival!* (also see below), St. Louis Municipal Opera, St. Louis, MO, 1963.
Louisa, *Gypsy,* St. Louis Municipal Opera, 1963.
Janine Nicolet, *Ben Franklin in Paris,* Lunt-Fontanne Theatre, New York City, 1964.
Carrie Pipperidge, *Carousel,* New York State Theatre, New York City, 1965.
Laurey, *Oklahoma!,* New York City Center, New York City, 1965.
Amy Spettigue, *Where's Charley?,* New York City Center, 1966.
Jenny Lee, *A Joyful Noise,* Mark Hellinger Theatre, New York City, 1966.
Angel, *Celebration,* Ambassador Theatre, New York City, 1969.
Cynthia Mason, *Beggar on Horseback,* Vivian Beaumont Theatre, New York City, 1970.
Title role, *No, No, Nanette,* Forty-sixth Street Theatre, New York City, 1971.
Fran Kubelik, *Promises, Promises,* Meadow Brook Theatre, Cedar Grove, NJ, 1972, then Milwaukee Melody Top, Milwaukee, WI, 1973.
Funny Face, Studio Arena, Buffalo, NY, 1973, then Ford's Theatre, Washington, DC, 1974.
Viola, *Twelfth Night,* Washington Shakespeare Festival, Sylvan Theatre, 1974.
Cecily, *The Importance of Being Earnest,* Washington Shakespeare Festival, Sylvan Theatre, 1974.
Julia, *The Rivals,* Roundabout Theatre Stage One, New York City, 1974.
Female lecturer, *The Bone Room,* Portfolio Studio, New York City, 1975.
Tintypes, South Coast Repertory, Mainstage, Costa Mesa, CA, 1982.
Amalia Balash, *She Loves Me,* California Music Theatre, Pasadena, c. 1988.

Appeared in the title role in productions of *Gigi* at Paper Mill Playhouse, Milburn, NJ, Poinciana Playhouse, Palm Beach, FL, and Westport Country Theatre, Westport, CT; appeared as Marian, *Music Man,* Paper Mill Playhouse.

MAJOR TOURS

Lili, *Carnival!,* U.S. cities, 1961.

TELEVISION APPEARANCES; EPISODIC

American Musical Theatre, CBS, 1962.
The Dobie Gillis Show, CBS, 1963.
Bell Telephone Hour, NBC, 1964.
"Rodgers and Hart Revisited," *Studio 2,* CBS, 1964.
Sesame Street, PBS, 1970.
The David Frost Show, syndicated, 1971.

Also appeared in "Jerome Kern and the Princess," *Studio 2,* CBS.

TELEVISION APPEARANCES; PILOTS

Jennie Brown, *Maggie Brown* (also known as *Trader Brown*), CBS, 1963.

TELEVISION APPEARANCES; SPECIALS

Luisa, "The Fantasticks," *Hallmark Hall of Fame,* NBC, 1964.
Peggy, *The Front Page,* ABC, 1970.

TELEVISION APPEARANCES; MOVIES

His Mistress, NBC, 1984.
Louise Abbruzzese, *The Betty Ford Story,* ABC, 1987.
Convicted: A Mother's Story, NBC, 1987.

FILM APPEARANCES

Doctor Faustus, Columbia, 1967.*

* * *

WAYANS, Damon 1961(?)-

PERSONAL: Born c. 1961, in New York, NY.

ADDRESSES: *Agent*—Jeff Krask, Triad, 10100 Santa Monica Blvd., 16th floor, Los Angeles, CA 90067.

CAREER: Actor and comedian. Has performed as a stand-up comedian in nightclubs in New York City.

AWARDS, HONORS: Emmy Award nominations, outstanding writing in a variety or music program, 1990 and 1991, and outstanding individual performance in a variety or music program, 1991, all for *In Living Color.*

CREDITS:

TELEVISION APPEARANCES; SERIES

Saturday Night Live, NBC, 1985-86.
In Living Color (also see below), Fox, 1990—.

TELEVISION APPEARANCES; SPECIALS

"Take No Prisoners: Robert Townsend and His Partners in Crime II," *HBO Comedy Hour,* HBO, 1988.
"The Mutiny Has Just Begun: Robert Townsend and His Partners in Crime III," *HBO Comedy Hour,* HBO, 1989.
MTV's 1990 Video Music Awards, MTV, 1990.
Motown 30: What's Goin' On!, CBS, 1990.
American Music Awards, ABC, 1991.
"Damon Wayans: The Last Stand?," *HBO Comedy Hour* (also see below), HBO, 1991.

TELEVISION APPEARANCES; EPISODIC

One Night Stand, HBO, 1989.

TELEVISION WORK

Executive producer, "Damon Wayans: The Last Stand?," *HBO Comedy Hour,* HBO, 1991.

FILM WORK

Executive producer, *Mo' Money* (also see below), Columbia, 1992.

FILM APPEARANCES

Banana man, *Beverly Hills Cop,* Paramount, 1984.
Second bodyguard and Willie, *Hollywood Shuffle,* Samuel Goldwyn, 1987.
Jerry, *Roxanne,* Columbia, 1987.
T-Bone, *Colors,* Orion, 1988.
Leonard, *I'm Gonna Git You Sucka,* Metro-Goldwyn-Mayer/United Artists, 1988.
Percy, *Punchline,* Columbia, 1988.
Zeebo, *Earth Girls Are Easy,* Vestron, 1989.
Voice of Eddy, *Look Who's Talking Too,* Tri-Star, 1990.
Jimmy Dix, *The Last Boy Scout,* Warner Brothers, 1991.
Johnny, *Mo' Money* (also see below), Columbia, 1992.

WRITINGS:

TELEVISION SERIES

(With others) *In Living Color,* Fox, 1990—.

FILM SCREENPLAYS

Mo' Money, Columbia, 1992.*

WAYANS, Keenen Ivory 1958(?)-

PERSONAL: Born c. 1958, in Harlem, NY; son of Howell (a retail manager) and Elvira Wayans. *Education:* Attended Tuskegee Institute.

ADDRESSES: Contact—Fox Television Center (KTTV), 5746 Sunset Blvd., Hollywood, CA 90028.

CAREER: Actor, director, screenwriter, and producer. Began career as a stand-up comedian, working at comedy clubs in New York City and Los Angeles, CA.

MEMBER: Screen Actors Guild, Directors Guild of America, Screen Writers Guild.

AWARDS, HONORS: Emmy Award for outstanding variety, music, or comedy program, and Emmy Award nomination for outstanding writing in a variety or music program, both 1990, both for *In Living Color;* Emmy Award nominations for outstanding writing in a variety or music program and for outstanding individual performance in a variety or music program, both 1991, both for *In Living Color.*

CREDITS:

TELEVISION APPEARANCES; SERIES

Recruit Duke Johnson, *For Love and Honor,* NBC, 1983-84.
In Living Color (also see below), Fox, 1990—.

TELEVISION APPEARANCES; SPECIALS

Motown Thirty: What's Goin' On!, CBS, 1990.
MTV's 1990 Video Music Awards, MTV, 1990.
A Laugh, a Tear (comedy), syndicated, 1990.
Story of a People: The Black Road to Hollywood, syndicated, 1991.
Comic Relief V, HBO, 1991.
A Comedy Salute to Michael Jordan (also known as *Los Angeles and Chicago Salute to Michael Jordan*), NBC, 1991.
The Fifth Annual American Comedy Awards, ABC, 1991.
The American Music Awards, ABC, 1991.
A Party for Richard Pryor, CBS, 1991.

OTHER TELEVISION APPEARANCES

Ray Brewster, *Irene* (pilot), NBC, 1981.

Appeared as a guest on *A Different World,* NBC, *Benson,* ABC, and *Cheers,* NBC.

TELEVISION WORK; SERIES

Executive producer and creator, *In Living Color* (also see below), Fox, 1990—.

OTHER TELEVISION WORK

Producer (with Robert Townsend), *Robert Townsend and His Partners in Crime* (comedy special; also see below), HBO, 1987.

Executive producer, *Hammer, Slammer, and Slade* (comedy pilot; also see below), ABC, 1990.

FILM APPEARANCES

Comic, *Star 80,* Ladd Company/Warner Brothers, 1983.

Donald/Jerry Curl, *Hollywood Shuffle* (also see below), Samuel Goldwyn, 1987.

Raw (also see below), Paramount, 1987.

Jack Spade, *I'm Gonna Git You Sucka* (also see below), Metro-Goldwyn-Mayer (MGM)/United Artists (UA), 1988.

FILM WORK

Co-producer, *Raw* (also see below), Paramount, 1987.

Director, *I'm Gonna Git You Sucka* (also see below), MGM/UA, 1988.

WRITINGS:

FOR TELEVISION

(With Townsend) *Robert Townsend and His Partners in Crime* (comedy special), HBO, 1987.

In Living Color (series), Fox, 1990—.

Hammer, Slammer, and Slade (pilot), ABC, 1990.

SCREENPLAYS, EXCEPT WHERE INDICATED

(With Townsend) *Hollywood Shuffle,* Samuel Goldwyn, 1987.

(With Eddie Murphy and Townsend), *Raw* (sketch portions), Paramount, 1987.

I'm Gonna Git You Sucka, MGM/UA, 1988.

(With Townsend) *The Five Heartbeats,* Twentieth Century-Fox, 1991.

OTHER SOURCES:

PERIODICALS

Hollywood Reporter, January 25, 1989.

New York, October 8, 1990, p. 28-35.*

* * *

WEAVER, Sigourney 1949-

PERSONAL: Given name, Susan Alexandra Weaver; born October 8, 1949, in New York, NY; daughter of Sylvester L. Weaver (a television executive) and Elizabeth Inglis (an actress); married James Simpson (a director), 1984; children: Charlotte. *Education:* Attended Sarah Lawrence College; Stanford University, B.A., English, 1971; Yale University, M.A., drama, 1974.

ADDRESSES: Agent—Sam Cohn, International Creative Management, 40 West 57th St., New York, NY 10019.

CAREER: Actress. Member of various theatre groups in California in the early 1970s; performer in cabarets and television commercials; producer for Goat Cay Productions, beginning c. 1988.

MEMBER: Actors Equity Association, Screen Actors Guild.

AWARDS, HONORS: Academy Award nomination, best supporting actress, 1984, for *Ghostbusters;* Antoinette Perry Award nomination, outstanding featured actress in a play, 1985, for *Hurlyburly;* Academy Award nomination, best actress, 1986, for *Aliens;* NATO Award, star of the year, 1986; Golden Apple Award, star of the year, 1988; Academy Award nomination, best actress, 1988, and Golden Globe Award, best actress, 1989, both for *Gorillas in the Mist;* Academy Award nomination, best supporting actress, 1988, and Golden Globe Award, best supporting actress, 1989, both for *Working Girl;* Drama Desk Award nomination (with Christopher Durang), for *Das Lusitania Songspiel.*

CREDITS:

STAGE APPEARANCES

Watergate Classics, Yale Repertory Theatre, New Haven, CT, 1973.

Initiate, *The Frogs,* Yale Repertory Theatre, 1974.

Understudy for role of Marie-Louise Durham, *The Constant Wife,* Shubert Theatre, New York City, 1975.

Lidia, *Titanic,* Direct Theatre, New York City, then produced in a double bill with *Das Lusitania Songspiel* (also see below), Van Dam Theatre, New York City, both 1976.

Das Lusitania Songspiel (also see below), first produced in a double bill with *Titanic,* Van Dam Theatre, then Direct Theatre, both 1976.

Gemini, Playwrights Horizons, New York City, 1976.

Freydis, *Marco Polo Sings a Solo,* Public/Newman Theatre, New York City, 1977.

Annabella, *Conjuring an Event,* American Place Theatre, New York City, 1978.

A Flea in Her Ear, Hartford Stage Company, John W. Huntington Theatre, Hartford, CT, 1978.

New Jerusalem, New York Shakespeare Festival (NYSF), Public/Other Stage Theatre, New York City, 1979.

Elizabeth Caulder, *Lone Star,* Travel Light Theatre, Chicago, IL, 1980.

Das Lusitania Songspiel (also see below), Chelsea Theatre Center, New York City, 1980.

As You Like It, Dallas Shakespeare Festival, Dallas, TX, 1981.
Prudence, *Beyond Therapy,* Marymount Manhattan Theatre, New York City, 1981.
Old Times, Williamstown Theatre Festival, Williamstown, MA, c. 1981.
Darlene, *Hurlyburly,* Goodman Theatre, Chicago, then Promenade Theatre, New York City, later Ethel Barrymore Theatre, New York City, all 1984.
The Marriage of Bette and Boo, NYSF, Public Theatre, 1985.
Portia, *The Merchant of Venice,* The Classic Stage Company, New York City, 1986-87.

Other appearances include summer stock productions of *A Streetcar Named Desire* and *You Can't Take It with You,* Southbury, CT, c. 1965; Jenny, *Darryl and Carol and Kenny and Jenny* (also known as *Better Dead Than Sorry*), c. 1971; *A Streetcar Named Desire,* 1986; understudy, *Captain Brassbound's Conversation; The Nature and Purpose of the Universe;* and *Naked Lunch* (also see below).

FILM APPEARANCES

Alvy's date outside theatre, *Annie Hall,* United Artists, 1977.
Ripley, *Alien,* Twentieth Century-Fox, 1979.
Tony Sokolow, *Eyewitness* (also known as *The Janitor*), Twentieth Century-Fox, 1981.
Jill Bryant, *The Year of Living Dangerously,* Metro-Goldwyn-Mayer, 1982.
Mrs. De Voto, *Deal of the Century,* Warner Bros., 1983.
Dana Barrett, *Ghostbusters,* Columbia, 1984.
Jessica Fitzgerald, *Une femme ou deux* (also known as *One Woman or Two*), Orion Classics, 1985.
Ripley, *Aliens,* Twentieth Century-Fox, 1986.
Dr. Lauren Slaughter, *Half Moon Street* (also known as *Escort Girl*), Twentieth Century-Fox, 1986.
Dian Fossey, *Gorillas in the Mist,* Universal, 1988.
Katherine Parker, *Working Girl,* Twentieth Century-Fox, 1988.
Dana Barrett, *Ghostbusters II,* Columbia, 1989.
Helmut Newton: Frames from the Edge (documentary), RM Associates/Cine Classic, 1989.
Ripley, *Alien 3* (also see below), Twentieth Century-Fox, 1992.

Also appeared in *Madman,* 1976.

FILM WORK

Co-producer, *Alien 3,* Twentieth Century-Fox, 1992.

TELEVISION APPEARANCES; EPISODIC

"Clement Clark Moore," *An American Portrait,* CBS, 1985.
Guest host, *Saturday Night Live,* NBC, 1986.
Hollywood Insider, USA, 1988.
Narrator, "The Peachboy," *We All Have Tales,* Showtime, 1991.

TELEVISION APPEARANCES; SERIES

The Best of Families, PBS, 1977.

Also appeared as Avis Ryan in *Somerset,* NBC, in the mid-1970s.

TELEVISION APPEARANCES; SPECIALS

Fifty-ninth Annual Academy Awards Presentation, ABC, 1987.
The Making of "Gorillas in the Mist," syndicated, 1988.
"Twilight of the Gorilla," *Mutual of Omaha's Spirit of Adventure,* ABC, 1988.
The Third Annual Hollywood Insider Academy Awards Special, USA, 1989.
Our Common Future, Arts and Entertainment, 1989.
Premiere: Inside the Summer Blockbusters, Fox, 1989.
American Tribute to Vaclav Havel and a Celebration of Democracy in Czechoslovakia, PBS, 1990.

OTHER TELEVISION APPEARANCES

Appeared in *The Sorrows of Gin,* c. 1979.

WRITINGS:

PLAYS

(With Christopher Durang) *Das Lusitania Songspiel* (based on theatre songs of Bertolt Brecht), first produced in a double bill with *Titanic* at Van Dam Theatre, New York City, 1976.

Also author, with Christopher Durang, of *Naked Lunch.*

OTHER SOURCES:

BOOKS

Newsmakers, 1988 Cumulation, Gale, 1989, p. 466.

PERIODICALS

American Film, October, 1983, p. 32.
Esquire, July, 1984, p. 73.
Film Comment, December, 1986, p. 18; July/August, 1986, p. 4.
Interview, July, 1988, p. 34.
New York Times, December 21, 1986.
Premiere, October, 1988, pp. 43-48.
Time, July 28, 1986, p. 60.*

* * *

WEINSTEIN, Paula H. 1945-

PERSONAL: Born November 19, 1945, in New York, NY; daughter of Isadore Meyerson and Hannah (a producer; maiden name, Dorner) Weinstein. *Education:* Attended Columbia University. *Politics:* Democrat. *Religion:* Jewish.

ADDRESSES: Office—24016 Malibu Rd., Malibu, CA 90265; and c/o Columbia Pictures Industries, Columbia Plaza, Burbank, CA 91505.

CAREER: Producer and studio executive. Theatrical agent with William Morris Agency, Beverly Hills, CA, and International Creative Management, Los Angeles, CA, 1973-76; Warner Bros., Burbank, CA, vice president for production, 1976-78; Twentieth Century-Fox, Los Angeles, 1978-80, began as vice-president for production, became vice president for worldwide production; Ladd Co., partner and vice president for production, 1980-81; United Artists Corp., president in motion picture division, 1981-82; independent producer, affiliated with Columbia Pictures, Burbank, 1983—; consultant to Columbia Pictures, beginning in 1987; executive consultant to Metro-Goldwyn-Mayer.

CREDITS:

FILM WORK

Producer (with Gareth Wigan), *American Flyers,* Warner Brothers, 1985.

Executive producer, *Illegally Yours* (also known as *Double Duty*), Metro-Goldwyn-Mayer (MGM)/United Artists (UA), 1988.

Producer, *A Dry White Season,* MGM/UA, 1989.

Producer (with Mark Rosenberg and Bill Finnegan), *The Fabulous Baker Boys,* Twentieth Century-Fox, 1989.

TELEVISION WORK; EPISODIC

Executive producer, "Bejewelled," *The Magical World of Disney,* Disney Channel, 1991.

OTHER TELEVISION WORK

Producer, *Unauthorized Biography: Jane Fonda* (special), syndicated, 1988.

Executive producer, *The Rose and the Jackal* (movie), TNT, 1990.*

* * *

WERTENBAKER, Timberlake

CAREER: Writer. Worked as a journalist in New York, NY, and as a teacher in Greece in the late 1970s before beginning career as a playwright; Arts Council Resident Writer for Shared Experience Theatre Company, 1983; Thames Television Resident Writer at the Royal Court Theatre, London, 1985.

AWARDS, HONORS: All-London Playwrights' Award for *The Third;* Arts Council of Great Britain bursary, 1983; Most Promising Playwright Award, *Plays and Players* magazine, 1985, for *The Grace of Mary Traverse;* Olivier Award, best play, 1988, Antoinette Perry Award nomination, best play, 1991, and New York Drama Critics Circle Award, all for *Our Country's Good;* Olivier Award nomination, best play, and Susan Smith Blackburn Prize, 1992, for *Three Birds Alighting on a Field;* Mrs. Giles Whiting Award for general body of work.

WRITINGS:

PLAYS

This Is No Place for Tallulah Bankhead, produced in London, 1978.

The Third, produced in London, 1980.

Second Sentence, produced in Brighton, England, 1980.

Case to Answer, produced in London, 1980, then Ithaca, New York, 1981.

Breaking Through, produced in London, 1980.

New Anatomies, produced by Women's Theatre Group, I.C.A. Theatre, London, 1980.

Inside Out, produced in Stoke-on-Trent, England, 1982.

Home Leave, produced in Ipswich, Suffolk, England, 1982.

(Translator) Marivaux, *False Admissions* (also see below), produced in London, 1983.

(Translator) Marivaux, "False Admissions" and "Successful Strategies," *Successful Strategies* (double bill), produced at Lyric Studio Theatre, London, 1983.

Abel's Sister, produced at Theatre Upstairs, London, 1984, then in New York City, 1985.

The Grace of Mary Traverse, produced at Royal Court Theatre, London, then in New York City, both 1985, published by Faber, 1985.

(Translator) Jean Anouilh, *Leocadia* (radio play), broadcast in 1985, published in Anouilh's *Five Plays,* Methuen, 1987.

(Adapter and translator) Ariane Mnouchkine, *Mephisto,* produced by Royal Shakespeare Company (RSC), Barbican Theatre, London, 1986.

Our Country's Good, produced at Royal Court Theatre, 1988, then by the Center Theatre Group, Mark Taper Forum, Los Angeles, CA, 1989, later at Nederlander Theatre, New York City, 1991.

The Love of the Nightingale, produced by RSC, 1989, then produced by L.A. Theatre Works, Santa Monica, CA, 1990, published in *The Love of the Nightingale* [and] *The Grace of Mary Traverse,* Faber, 1990.

Three Birds Alighting on a Field, produced in England, c. 1992.

Also translator of Maurice Maeterlink's *Pelleas and Melisande* and Federico Garcia Lorca's *The House of Bernarda Alba.*

SCREENPLAYS

The Children, Film Four International, 1990.

Also author of *Do Not Disturb.*

OTHER SOURCES:

BOOKS

Contemporary Dramatists, 4th edition, St. James Press, 1988, pp. 553-55.

PERIODICALS

New York Times, February 28, 1992, p. C2.*

* * *

WHEATON, Wil 1972(?)-

PERSONAL: Born c. 1972, in California.

ADDRESSES: Agent—Michael Gruber, William Morris Agency, 151 El Camino, Beverly Hills, CA 90212.

CAREER: Actor.

MEMBER: Screen Actors Guild.

CREDITS:

FILM APPEARANCES

Voice of Martin, *The Secret of NIMH,* Metro-Goldwyn-Mayer/United Artists, 1982.
Jeff Radcliffe, *Hambone and Hillie,* New World Pictures, 1984.
Tim, *The Buddy System,* Twentieth Century-Fox, 1984.
Louis's friend, *The Last Starfighter,* Universal, 1984.
Gordie Lachance, *Stand by Me,* Columbia, 1986.
Zachary Hayes, *The Curse* (also known as *The Farm*), Trans World, 1987.
Joey Trotta, *Toy Soldiers,* Tri-Star, 1991.
Kipp Gibbs, *December,* IRS Media, 1991.

TELEVISION APPEARANCES; SERIES

Wesley "Wes" Crusher, *Star Trek: The Next Generation,* syndicated, 1987—.

TELEVISION APPEARANCES; MOVIES

Donald Branch at age eight, *A Long Way Home,* ABC, 1981.
Clyde, *The Defiant Ones,* ABC, 1986.

TELEVISION APPEARANCES; PILOTS

Mitchell, *Long Time Gone,* ABC, 1986.
Billy Milton, *The Man Who Fell to Earth,* ABC, 1987.

Also appeared in CBS's *13 Thirteenth Avenue.*

TELEVISION APPEARANCES; SPECIALS

The Billy Crystal Comedy Hour, NBC, 1982.
Amos Cotter, "The Shooting," *CBS Afternoon Playhouse,* CBS, 1982.
Erich Weiss, title role, "Young Harry Houdini," *Disney Sunday Movie,* ABC, 1987.
Drug Free Kids: A Parent's Guide, PBS, 1988.
The Hollywood Christmas Parade, syndicated, 1988, 1989.
Nick Karpinsky, "My Dad Can't Be Crazy . . . (Can He?)," *ABC Afterschool Special,* ABC, 1989.

TELEVISION APPEARANCES; EPISODIC

Appeared in episodes of *St. Elsewhere, Family Ties,* and *Highway to Heaven.**

* * *

WHITLOCK, Albert 1915-
(Albert J. Whitlock)

PERSONAL: Born in 1915, in London, England; married; children: two.

CAREER: Special effects technician. Disney Studios, Hollywood, CA, special effects technician, 1954-61; free-lance designer, 1961-63; Universal International Films, North Hollywood, CA, designer of special effects, beginning in 1963.

AWARDS, HONORS: Academy Award nomination, best visual effects, 1967, for *Tobruk;* Emmy Award nomination, outstanding achievement in any area of creative technical crafts, 1970, for special photographic effects in *Vanished;* Academy Award (with Frank Brendel and Glen Robinson), special achievement in visual effects, 1974, for *Earthquake;* Academy Award (with Robinson), special achievement in visual effects, 1975, for *The Hindenburg;* Emmy Award (with others), outstanding special visual effects, 1985, for *A. D.*

CREDITS:

FILM SPECIAL EFFECTS TECHNICIAN, EXCEPT WHERE INDICATED

The Man Who Knew Too Much, Paramount, 1956.
Greyfriars Bobby, Buena Vista, 1961.
Captain Newman, M.D., Universal, 1963.
I'd Rather Be Rich, Universal, 1964.
Island of the Blue Dolphins, Universal, 1964.
Mirage, Universal, 1965.
Shenandoah, Universal, 1965.
That Funny Feeling, Universal, 1965.
The War Lord, Universal, 1965.
(With Farciot Edouart and John Burke) *Ship of Fools,* Columbia, 1965.
Beau Geste, Universal, 1966.

Blindfold, Universal, 1966.
Munster, Go Home, Universal, 1966.
Tobruk, Universal, 1966.
The Rare Breed, Universal, 1966.
King's Pirate, Universal, 1967.
The Reluctant Astronaut, Universal, 1967.
Rough Night in Jericho, Universal, 1967.
Thoroughly Modern Millie, Universal, 1967.
The War Wagon, Universal, 1967.
Counterpoint, Universal, 1967.
The Ballad of Josie, Universal, 1968.
Hellfighters, Universal, 1968.
In Enemy Country, Universal, 1968.
P. J., Universal, 1968.
The Shakiest Gun in the West, Universal, 1968.
Colossus: The Forbin Project (also known as *Colossus 1980* and *The Forbin Project*), Universal, 1969.
The Learning Tree (also known as *Learn, Baby, Learn*), Warner Brothers, 1969.
Topaz, Universal, 1969.
Skullduggery, Universal, 1970.
Catch-22, Filmways, 1970.
(With Leslie Hillman, Wally Veevers, and Whitney McMahon) *Diamonds Are Forever,* United Artists (UA), 1971.
Mattes, *The Andromeda Strain,* Universal, 1971.
One More Train to Rob, Universal, 1971.
(Under name Albert J. Whitlock) *Raid on Rommel,* Universal, 1971.
Matte work supervisor, *Slaughterhouse-Five,* Universal, 1972.
Frenzy, Universal, 1972.
(With Jim White) *The Day of the Dolphin,* Avco Embassy, 1973.
Showdown, Universal, 1973.
(With Bob Warner) *The Sting,* Universal, 1973.
(With Frank Brendel, Jack McMasters, and Glen Robinson) *Earthquake,* Universal, 1974.
Funny Lady, Columbia, 1975.
(With Robinson) *The Hindenburg,* Universal, 1975.
Matte artist, *The Man Who Would Be King,* Columbia, 1975.
Day of the Locust, Paramount, 1975.
Two-Minute Warning, Universal, 1976.
(With Brendel) *Family Plot,* Universal, 1976.
W. C. Fields and Me, Universal, 1976.
Bound for Glory, UA, 1976.
(Under name Albert J. Whitlock; with Van der Veer, Chuck Gaspar, Wayne Edgar, and others) *Exorcist II: The Heretic,* Warner Brothers, 1977.
Rollercoaster, Universal, 1977.
Airport '77, Universal, 1977.
The Last Remake of Beau Geste, Universal, 1977.
MacArthur the Rebel General, Universal, 1977.
The Sentinel, Universal, 1977.
(Under name Albert J. Whitlock) *High Anxiety* (also see below), Twentieth Century-Fox, 1977.
The Car, Universal, 1977.
(With Al Griswold) *The Wiz,* Universal, 1978.
(With Curtis Dickson) *I Wanna Hold Your Hand,* Universal, 1978.
The Prisoner of Zenda, Universal, 1979.
Dracula, Universal, 1979.
Cheech and Chong's Next Movie (also known as *High Encounters of the Ultimate Kind*), Universal, 1980.
In God We Trust (also known as *Gimme That Prime Time Religion*), Universal, 1980.
The Blues Brothers, Universal, 1980.
The Island, Universal, 1980.
(With Stan Winston) *Heartbeeps,* Universal, 1981.
Ghost Story, Universal, 1981.
(Under name Albert J. Whitlock) *History of the World, Part I,* Twentieth Century-Fox, 1981.
Cat People, Universal/RKO Radio Pictures, 1982.
The Best Little Whorehouse in Texas, Universal, 1982.
Missing, Universal, 1982.
(With Roy Arbogast, Leroy Routly, and Michael A. Clifford) *The Thing,* Universal, 1982.
(With Syd Dutton and Melbourne Arnold) *Psycho II,* Universal, 1983.
(Under name Albert J. Whitlock) *The Wicked Lady,* Metro-Goldwyn-Mayer (MGM)/UA, 1983.
The Sting II, Universal, 1983.
(Under name Albert J. Whitlock) *Greystoke: The Legend of Tarzan, Lord of the Apes,* Warner Brothers, 1984.
(Under name Albert J. Whitlock) *The Lonely Guy,* Universal, 1984.
Special matte consultant, *Clue,* Paramount, 1985.
Red Sonja, MGM/UA, 1985.
Dune, Universal, 1985.
Coming to America (also known as *Quest, The Zamunda*), Paramount, 1988.
Millennium, Twentieth Century-Fox, 1989.
The Neverending Story II: The Next Chapter, Warner Brothers, 1990.
(Under name Albert J. Whitlock) *Stephen King's Graveyard Shift,* Paramount, 1990.

FILM SPECIAL EFFECTS DESIGNER

The Birds, Universal, 1963.
Marnie, Universal, 1964.
Torn Curtain, Universal, 1966.

FILM APPEARANCES

(Under name Albert J. Whitlock) Arthur Brisbane, *High Anxiety,* Twentieth Century-Fox, 1977.

TELEVISION SPECIAL EFFECTS TECHNICIAN; MOVIES

Once upon a Dead Man, NBC, 1971.
O'Hara, United States Treasury: Operation Cobra, CBS, 1971.
The Harness, NBC, 1971.
The Hound of the Baskervilles, ABC, 1972.
Short Walk to Daylight, ABC, 1972.
Deliver Us from Evil, ABC, 1973.
The Questor Tapes, NBC, 1974.
A Cry in the Wilderness, ABC, 1974.
Killdozer, ABC, 1974.
It Happened One Christmas, ABC, 1977.
Masada, ABC, 1981.
Female Artillery, ABC, 1983.
A. D., NBC, 1985.

TELEVISION SPECIAL EFFECTS TECHNICIAN; MINI-SERIES

Vanished, NBC, 1970.

OTHER SOURCES:

PERIODICALS

American Cinematographer, January, 1986.*

* * *

WHITLOCK, Albert J.
See WHITLOCK, Albert

* * *

WHITTON, Margaret 1950-
(Peggy Whitton)

PERSONAL: Born November 30, 1950, in Philadelphia, PA (some sources say Baltimore, MD); daughter of James Richmond (a military officer) and Margaret Eleanora (a nurse; maiden name, Brown) Whitton; married Bill Russell (a cabinet maker), c. 1970 (divorced, 1978). *Education:* Attended Northeast High School, Fort Lauderdale, FL. *Avocational interests:* Baseball.

ADDRESSES: Agent—Triad Artists, Inc., 10100 Santa Monica Blvd., No. 1600, Los Angeles, CA 90067.

CAREER: Actress. Worked variously as a bicycle messenger, cab driver, and dog walker.

MEMBER: Screen Actors Guild, American Federation of Television and Radio Artists, Actors Equity Association.

CREDITS:

FILM APPEARANCES

(Film debut) Jacki Steinberg, *Love Child*, Warner Brothers, 1982.
Molly, *9 1/2 Weeks*, Metro-Goldwyn-Mayer (MGM)/United Artists (UA), 1986.
Darla, *The Best of Times*, Universal, 1986.
Katrina, *Ironweed*, Tri-Star, 1987.
Vera Prescott, *The Secret of My Success*, Universal, 1987.
Rachel Phelps, *Major League*, Paramount, 1989.
Holly Stevenson, *Little Monsters*, MGM/UA, 1989.

Also appeared as the first lady in the segment "Success Wanters," *National Lampoon Goes to the Movies*, 1982.

TELEVISION APPEARANCES; EPISODIC

Claire Hart, *Search for Tomorrow*, CBS, 1974.
Michele Hogarth, "None So Blind," *Kojak* (also known as *The ABC Saturday Mystery*), ABC, 1990.

Also appeared as the mother in "Motherlove," *Film Boston*, PBS.

OTHER TELEVISION APPEARANCES

Barbara Donnelly, *Hometown* (series), CBS, 1985.
Louisa Phillips, *A Fine Romance* (series), ABC, 1989.
TGIF Comedy Preview (special), ABC, 1991.
Naomi, *The Summer My Father Grew Up* (movie), NBC, 1991.
Genny, *Good and Evil* (series), ABC, 1991.

STAGE APPEARANCES

(Off-Broadway debut; under name Peggy Whitton) Sylvia, *Nourish the Beast*, Cherry Lane Theatre, New York City, 1973, then under the title *Baba Goya*, American Place Theatre, New York City, 1973.
Stella Hallam, *Another Language*, Equity Library Theatre, New York City, 1975.
The Tempest, Indiana Repertory Theatre, Indianapolis, 1976-77.
Hamlet, Folger Theatre Group, Washington, DC, 1977-78.
Nessa Vox, *The Art of Dining*, Public/Newman Theatre, New York City, 1979.
Nina, *Chinchilla*, Marymount Manhattan Theatre, New York City, 1979.
Bianca, *Othello*, New York Shakespeare Festival (NYSF), Delacorte Theatre/Central Park, New York City, 1979.
Dede Walker, *One Tiger to a Hill*, Manhattan Theatre Club/Upstage, New York City, 1980.
Romeo and Juliet, Folger Theatre Group, 1980-81.
Lady Percy, *Henry IV, Part I*, NYSF, Delacorte Theatre, 1981.
Charlotte, *Don Juan*, NYSF, Delacorte Theatre/Central Park, 1982.
Title role, *Camille*, Tyrone Guthrie Theatre, Minneapolis, MN, 1982.

Jane, *Steaming,* Brooks Atkinson Theatre, New York City, 1982-83.
Time and the Conways, Huntington Theatre Company, Boston, MA, 1982-83.
Miss Simmons, Stella, and member of the ensemble, *My Uncle Sam,* NYSF, Public Theatre/Other Stage, New York City, 1983.
Mindy, *Aunt Dan and Lemon,* Public Theatre/Martinson Hall, New York City, 1986.
Drunk woman, hitcher's mother, and South American woman passenger, *Ice Cream* [with] *Hot Fudge* (double bill), Public/Newman Theatre, 1990.

Also appeared in *Arthur* and *The Wager.* Toured as Lucy Seward, *Dracula,* U.S. cities, 1978-79; and as Corinna Stroller, *The House of Blue Leaves,* eastern U.S. cities. Member of Yale Repertory Theatre, New Haven, CT, 1976-77.

OTHER SOURCES:

PERIODICALS

People Weekly, June 1, 1987, p. 92.*

* * *

WHITTON, Peggy
See WHITTON, Margaret

* * *

WILKINSON, Colm 1944-

PERSONAL: Born June 5, 1944, in Dublin, Ireland; son of Thomas Wilkinson (a masonry and asphalt contractor); married Deirdre Murphy (a television production assistant), 1970; children: Aaron, Judith, Simon, Sarah.

CAREER: Actor and singer. Member of Royal Shakespeare Company, London. Worked in the family contracting business; singer with Witnesses, an Irish pop music band.

AWARDS, HONORS: Laurence Olivier Award nomination, best actor, 1985, Helen Hayes Award, Outer Critics Circle Award, *Theatre World* Award, Antoinette Perry Award nomination, best actor in a musical, and Drama Desk Award nomination, best actor, 1987, all for *Les Miserables;* Dora Mavor Moore Award, outstanding performance by a male actor in a revue or musical, 1989, for *Phantom of the Opera.*

CREDITS:

STAGE APPEARANCES

Jean Valjean, *Les Miserables* (also see below), Royal Shakespeare Theatre, London, 1985-86, then Radio City Music Hall, New York City, 1987, later Broadway Theatre, New York City, 1987-88.
Title role, *Phantom of the Opera* (also see below), Sydmonton, England, 1985, then Pantages Theatre, Toronto, Ontario, 1989-92.

Appeared as Judas, *Jesus Christ Superstar* (also see below), Dublin, Ireland, 1972, then London, 1974; appeared in the concert *Stage Heroes* (also see below); also appeared in *Rock Nativity, Adam and Eve, Fire Angel,* and *Voices.*

MAJOR TOURS

Played Judas, *Jesus Christ Superstar,* British national tour; appeared in the concert tour *Tim Rice and Friends,* Hong Kong, London, and Los Angeles, CA; also appeared in *One Man Show,* an international concert tour.

TELEVISION APPEARANCES; SPECIALS

The Kennedy Center Honors: A Celebration of the Performing Arts, CBS, 1986.
The 41st Annual Tony Awards, CBS, 1987.
A Broadway Christmas, Showtime, 1990.

RECORDINGS:

ALBUMS

Has appeared on soundtrack recordings of *Les Miserables,* 1987, *Highlights from "Jekyll and Hyde,"* 1990, and *Evita;* also released *Stage Heroes,* and several other solo albums.

OTHER SOURCES:

PERIODICALS

New York Times, March 19, 1987.
People Weekly, March 30, 1987.*

* * *

WILLIAMS, John 1932-
(John T. Williams, Johnny Williams)

PERSONAL: Full name, John Towner Williams; born February 8, 1932, in Flushing, NY; son of John, Sr. (a percussionist) and Esther Williams; married Barbara, c. 1956 (died, 1974); married Samantha Winslow (a photographer and interior decorator), 1980; children: (first marriage) Jennifer, Mark, Joe. *Education:* North Hollywood High School, diploma, 1950; attended University of California at Los Angeles, before 1952, and Juilliard School of Music, c. 1955; studied privately with Mario Castelnuovo-Tedesco (composition) and Rosina Lhevinne (piano). *Avocational interests:* Playing chamber music, tennis, golf.

ADDRESSES: Office—Boston Pops Orchestra, 301 Massachusetts Ave., Boston, MA 02115. *Agent*—Michael

Gorfaine, Gorfaine/Schwartz Agency, 3301 Barham Blvd., Suite 201, Los Angeles, CA 90068.

CAREER: Composer and conductor. Pianist for Columbia and Twentieth Century-Fox, beginning in 1956; Boston Pops Orchestra, conductor and music director, 1980—, conductor of Boston Pops Esplanade Orchestra. Worked as jazz pianist; guest conductor with orchestras including Cleveland Orchestra, Denver Symphony, Indianapolis Symphony, London Symphony Orchestra, Los Angeles Philharmonic, Montreal Orchestra, Philadelphia Orchestra, and Toronto Orchestra. *Military service:* U.S. Air Force, 1952-54.

AWARDS, HONORS: Grammy Award nomination, soundtrack album—score, motion picture, or television, 1961, for *Checkmate;* Emmy Award nominations, outstanding achievement in original music for television, 1962 and 1963, both for *Alcoa Premiere;* Academy Award nomination, best scoring of music—adaptation or treatment, 1967, for *Valley of the Dolls;* Emmy Award, music composition, 1968, for *Heidi;* Academy Award nomination, best original score for a motion picture—not a musical, 1969, for *The Reivers;* Academy Award nomination, best score of a musical picture—original or adaptation, 1969, for *Goodbye Mr. Chips.*

Emmy Award, music composition, 1971, for *Jane Eyre;* Academy Award, best adaptation and/or original song score, 1971, for *Fiddler on the Roof;* Academy Award nominations, best original dramatic score, 1972, for *The Poseidon Adventure* and *Images;* Academy Award nomination, best original dramatic score, 1973, for *Cinderella Liberty;* Academy Award nomination, best song (with Paul Williams), 1973, for "(You're So) Nice to Be Around," *Cinderella Liberty;* Academy Award nomination, best original song score and/or adaptation, 1973, for *Tom Sawyer;* Academy Award nomination, best original dramatic score, 1974, for *The Towering Inferno;* Academy Award, best original score, Grammy Award, best original score for a motion picture or television special, and Golden Globe Award, best original film score, all 1975, for *Jaws;* Grammy Award nomination, best instrumental arrangement (with Henry Mancini, Herb Spencer, and Al Woodbury), 1976, for "The Disaster Movie Suite"; Academy Award, best original score, Grammy awards, best original score for a motion picture or television special and best pop instrumental, and Golden Globe Award, best original film score, all 1977, for *Star Wars* (film score); Grammy Award nomination, album of the year, 1977, for *Star Wars* (album); Grammy Award, best instrumental composition, 1977, for main title from *Star Wars;* Grammy Award, best original score for a motion picture or television special, Grammy Award nomination, best pop instrumental, and Academy Award nomination, best original score, 1977, all for *Close Encounters of the Third Kind;* Grammy Award, best instrumental composition, 1977, for theme from *Close Encounters of the Third Kind;* Grammy Award, best original score for a motion picture or television special, and Academy Award nomination, best original score, both 1978, for *Superman;* Grammy Award, best instrumental composition, and Grammy Award nomination, best pop instrumental, both 1978, for main title theme from *Superman.*

Grammy awards, best original score for a motion picture or television special and best instrumental composition, and Academy Award nomination, best original score, all 1980, for *The Empire Strikes Back;* Grammy Award nominations, best instrumental composition and best pop instrumental, both 1980, for "Yoda's Theme," *The Empire Strikes Back;* Grammy Award nomination, best instrumental composition, 1980, for "The Imperial March (Darth Vader's Theme)," *The Empire Strikes Back;* Grammy Award, best original score for a motion picture or television special, and Academy Award nomination, best score, both 1981, for *Raiders of the Lost Ark;* Academy Award, best original score, Grammy awards, best pop instrumental and best original score for a motion picture or television special, and Golden Globe Award, best original film score, all 1982, for *E.T. The Extra-Terrestrial;* Grammy awards, best instrumental arrangement and best instrumental composition, both 1982, for "Flying," *E.T. The Extra-Terrestrial;* Grammy Award nomination, best pop instrumental, 1982, for "Adventure on Earth"; Academy Award nomination, best original song (with Alan Bergman and Marilyn Bergman), 1982, for "If We Were in Love," *Yes, Giorgio;* Academy Award nomination, best original score, and Grammy Award nomination, best original score for a motion picture or television special, both 1983, for *Return of the Jedi;* Academy Award nominations, best original score, 1984, for *Indiana Jones and the Temple of Doom* and *The River;* Grammy Award, best instrumental composition, 1984, for "Olympic Fanfare and Theme," *The Official XXIIIrd Olympiad at Los Angeles;* Grammy Award nomination, best recording for children (with Dudley Moore and Boston Pops Orchestra), 1985, for *Prokofiev—Peter and the Wolf;* Academy Award nomination, best original score, and Grammy Award nomination, best original instrumental background score for motion picture or television, both 1987, for *The Witches of Eastwick;* British Academy Award, Academy Award nomination, best original score, and Grammy Award nomination, best original instrumental background score for motion picture or television, all 1987, for *Empire of the Sun;* Grammy Award nomination, best instrumental composition, 1988, for "The Olympic Spirit," *1988 Summer Olympic Games;* Academy Award nomination, best original score, and Golden Globe Award nomination, both 1988, for *The Accidental Tourist;* Academy Award nomination, best original score, and Golden

Globe Award nomination, both 1989, for *Born on the Fourth of July;* Academy Award nomination, best original score, and Grammy Award nomination, best original instrumental background score, both 1989, for *Indiana Jones and the Last Crusade;* Academy Award nomination, best original score, 1990, for *Home Alone;* Academy Award nomination, best original song (with Leslie Bricusse), 1990, for "Somewhere in My Memory," *Home Alone;* Academy Award nomination, best original score, 1991, for *JFK;* Academy Award nomination, best original song (with Bricusse), 1991, for "When You're Alone," *Hook;* honorary degrees from institutions including Anselm College, Berklee College of Music, Boston University, New England Conservatory of Music, Northeastern University, Providence College, Tufts University, University of Massachusetts—Boston, University of South Carolina, and University of Southern California; several gold and platinum record awards from Recording Industry Association of America.

CREDITS:

TELEVISION APPEARANCES; SERIES

(With Boston Pops Orchestra) *Evening at Pops,* PBS, 1980—.

TELEVISION APPEARANCES; SPECIALS

Pavarotti and Friends, ABC, 1982.
(With Boston Pops Orchestra) *A Christmas at Pops,* PBS, 1986.
Liberty Weekend, ABC, 1986.
The Special Olympics Opening Ceremonies, ABC, 1987.
(With Boston Pops Orchestra) *Blue Cross and Blue Shield Presents Season's Greetings, An Evening with John Williams and the Boston Pops Orchestra,* NBC, 1988.
Bernstein at Seventy, PBS, 1989.
(With Boston Pops Orchestra) *Christmas at Pops,* PBS, 1990.
(With Boston Pops Orchestra) *Songs of Freedom,* PBS, 1992.

Also appeared in *Kennedy Center Honors: A Celebration of the Performing Arts,* 1984.

TELEVISION MUSIC DIRECTOR

48th Annual Academy Awards Presentation, ABC, 1976.

FILM MUSIC DIRECTOR

(Under name Johnny Williams) *Not with My Wife, You Don't* (also see below), Warner Bros., 1966.
(And music arranger) *Fiddler on the Roof,* United Artists (UA), 1971.
Tom Sawyer (also see below), UA, 1973.
The Deer Hunter, Warner Bros., 1978.
The Witches of Eastwick (also see below), Warner Bros., 1987.

OTHER FILM WORK

Pianist, *South Pacific,* Twentieth Century-Fox, 1958.
Music arranger, *Some Like It Hot,* UA, 1959.
Music arranger, *The Apartment,* UA, 1960.
Pianist, *West Side Story,* UA, 1961.
Pianist, *The Monster Club,* ITC, 1981.
Title music performer, *Beyond the Limit* (also known as *The Honorary Consul*), Paramount, 1983.
Music performer, *Emma's War* (also see below), Curzon, 1986.

Also performed "Raiders March" for *Best Defense,* 1984.

RECORDINGS:

ALBUMS; FILM AND TELEVISION SOUNDTRACKS

(Under name Johnny Williams) *Checkmate,* Columbia, 1961.
Jane Eyre, Silva Screen, 1971.
Earthquake, Varese Sarabande, 1974.
The Eiger Sanction, Varese Sarabande, 1975.
Jaws, MCA, 1975.
Close Encounters of the Third Kind, Arista, 1977.
(With London Symphony Orchestra) *Star Wars,* Twentieth Century Records, 1977.
(With London Symphony Orchestra) *The Fury,* Varese Sarabande, 1978.
Jaws II, Varese Sarabande, 1978.
Superman, Warner Bros., 1978.
(With London Symphony Orchestra) *Dracula,* Varese Sarabande, 1979.
1941, Bay Cities, 1980.
The Empire Strikes Back, RSO, 1980.
Raiders of the Lost Ark, Polydor, 1981.
E.T. The Extra-Terrestrial, MCA, 1982.
Return of the Jedi, Polygram/RSO, 1983.
Indiana Jones and the Temple of Doom, Polydor, 1984.
The River, Varese Sarabande, 1985.
SpaceCamp, RCA, 1986.
Empire of the Sun, Warner Bros., 1987.
The Witches of Eastwick, Warner Bros., 1987.
The Accidental Tourist, Warner Bros., 1989.
Born on the Fourth of July, MCA, 1989.
Always, MCA, 1990.
Home Alone, CBS, 1990.
Presumed Innocent, Varese Sarabande, 1990.
Stanley and Iris, Varese Sarabande, 1990.

Also recorded *The Empire Strikes Back,* 1980, and *Indiana Jones and the Last Crusade.*

ALBUMS; WITH THE BOSTON POPS ORCHESTRA

Pops in Space, Phillips, 1981.

(With Dudley Moore) *Prokofiev—Peter and the Wolf,* Phillips, 1985.
Music of the Night, Sony Classical, 1990.

Also recorded numerous other albums, including *Pops on the March,* 1981; *We Wish You a Merry Christmas,* 1981; *Pops around the World (Digital Overtures),* 1982; *That's Entertainment (Pops on Broadway),* 1982; *Boston Pops on Stage,* 1984; *Holst: The Planets,* 1989; *Pops Britannia,* 1989; *I Love a Parade* and *The Spielberg/Williams Collaboration,* both Sony Classical; *Aisle Seat; Pops out of This World; America, the Dream Goes On;* and *With a Song in My Heart,* with Jessye Norman.

OTHER

The Official Music of the XXIIIrd Olympiad Los Angeles 1984 (includes "Olympic Fanfare and Theme"), Warner Bros., 1984.

Arranger, with Henry Mancini, Herb Spencer, and Al Woodbury, of "The Disaster Movie Suite," RCA, 1976. Recorded the song "Adventure on Earth." Affiliated with six albums with Andre Previn; jazz pianist on two albums by Shelly Manne for Capitol.

WRITINGS:

FILM SCORES; EXCEPT WHERE NOTED

Daddy-O (also known as *Out on Probation*), American International, 1959.
(Under name Johnny Williams) *Because They're Young,* Columbia, 1960.
(Under name Johnny Williams) *The Secret Ways,* Universal, 1961.
(Under name Johnny Williams) *Bachelor Flat,* Twentieth Century-Fox, 1962.
(Under name Johnny Williams) *Diamond Head,* Columbia, 1962.
(Under name Johnny Williams) *Gidget Goes to Rome,* Columbia, 1963.
(Under name Johnny Williams) *John Goldfarb, Please Come Home,* Twentieth Century-Fox, 1964.
(Under name Johnny Williams) *The Killers* (also known as *Ernest Hemingway's The Killers*), Universal, 1964.
(Under name Johnny Williams) *None but the Brave,* Warner Bros., 1965.
(Under name Johnny Williams) *The Rare Breed,* Universal, 1966.
(Under name Johnny Williams) *How to Steal a Million,* Twentieth Century-Fox, 1966.
(Under name Johnny Williams) *The Plainsman,* Universal, 1966.
(Under name Johnny Williams) *Not with My Wife, You Don't* (includes songs "A Big Beautiful Ball" and "My Inamorata," with Johnny Mercer), Warner Bros., 1966.
(Under name Johnny Williams) *Penelope* (includes songs "The Sun Is Gray," with Gale Garnett, and "Penelope," with Leslie Bricusse), Metro-Goldwyn-Mayer (MGM), 1966.
(Under name Johnny Williams) *A Guide for the Married Man* (includes song "A Guide for the Married Man," with Bricusse), Twentieth Century-Fox, 1967.
(Under name Johnny Williams) *Fitzwilly* (also known as *Fitzwilly Strikes Back*), UA, 1967.
(Under name Johnny Williams) *Valley of the Dolls,* Twentieth Century-Fox, 1967.
(Under name Johnny Williams) *Sergeant Ryker* (expanded version of television movie *The Case against Paul Ryker* [also see below]), Universal, 1968.
Daddy's Gone A-Hunting, National General, 1969.
Goodbye Mr. Chips, MGM, 1969.
(Under name Johnny Williams) *The Reivers,* National General, 1969.
(Under name Johnny Williams) *Story of a Woman* (also known as *Storia di una donna;* includes song "Uno di Qua, L'Altra di La," with A. Amurri), Universal, 1970.
Jane Eyre, British Lion, 1971.
The Cowboys, Warner Bros., 1972.
Images, Columbia, 1972.
Pete 'n' Tillie, Universal, 1972.
The Poseidon Adventure, Twentieth Century-Fox, 1972.
The Man Who Loved Cat Dancing, MGM, 1973.
The Paper Chase, Twentieth Century-Fox, 1973.
Cinderella Liberty (includes song "[You're So] Nice to Be Around," with lyrics by Paul Williams), Twentieth Century-Fox, 1973.
The Long Goodbye (includes song "The Long Goodbye," with Mercer), UA, 1973.
(Adapter) Richard M. Sherman and Robert B. Sherman, *Tom Sawyer,* UA, 1973.
Conrack, Twentieth Century-Fox, 1974.
The Sugarland Express, Universal, 1974.
Earthquake, Universal, 1974.
The Towering Inferno, Twentieth Century-Fox/Warner Bros., 1974.
The Eiger Sanction, Universal, 1975.
Jaws, Universal, 1975.
Family Plot, Universal, 1976.
The Missouri Breaks, UA, 1976.
Midway (also known as *The Battle of Midway*), Universal, 1976.
Black Sunday, Paramount, 1977.
(Under name John T. Williams) *Star Wars* (includes "Yoda's Theme" and "The Imperial March [Darth Vader's Theme]"), Twentieth Century-Fox, 1977.
Close Encounters of the Third Kind, Columbia, 1977.
Raggedy Ann and Andy, Twentieth Century-Fox, 1977.
The Fury, Twentieth Century-Fox, 1978.

Jaws II, Universal, 1978.
Superman (includes song "Can You Read My Mind," with Bricusse), Warner Bros., 1978.
Meteor, American International, 1979.
Quintet, Twentieth Century-Fox, 1979.
Dracula, Universal, 1979.
1941, Universal, 1979.
The Empire Strikes Back, Twentieth Century-Fox, 1980.
Raiders of the Lost Ark, Paramount, 1981.
Heartbeeps, Universal, 1981.
Monsignor, Twentieth Century-Fox, 1982.
E.T. The Extra-Terrestrial (includes "Flying"), Universal, 1982.
Yes, Giorgio (includes song "If We Were in Love," with Alan Bergman and Marilyn Bergman), MGM/UA, 1982.
Return of the Jedi, Twentieth Century-Fox, 1983.
(With Ken Thorne) *Superman III,* Warner Bros., 1983.
Shark theme, *Jaws 3-D,* Universal, 1983.
Indiana Jones and the Temple of Doom, Paramount, 1984.
The River, Universal, 1984.
Emma's War, Curzon, 1986.
SpaceCamp, Twentieth Century-Fox, 1986.
The Witches of Eastwick (includes "Balloon Sequence" and "Devil's Dance"), Warner Bros., 1987.
Empire of the Sun, Warner Bros., 1987.
(With Michael Small) *Jaws: The Revenge,* Universal, 1987.
(With Alexander Courage) *Superman IV: The Quest for Peace,* Warner Bros., 1987.
(Contributor of music) *The Secret of My Success,* Universal, 1987.
The Accidental Tourist, Warner Bros., 1988.
Always, Universal, 1989.
Born on the Fourth of July, Universal, 1989.
Indiana Jones and the Last Crusade, Paramount, 1989.
Stanley and Iris, MGM/UA, 1990.
Presumed Innocent, Warner Bros., 1990.
Home Alone (includes song "Somewhere in My Memory," with lyrics by Bricusse), Twentieth Century-Fox, 1990.
JFK, Warner Bros., 1991.
Hook (includes songs "When You're Alone," with lyrics by Bricusse, "We Don't Wanna Grow Up," and "Pick 'em Up"), TriStar, 1991.
Far and Away, Universal, 1992.

Also contributed to *Garden of Cucumbers,* Mirisch Corp.

TELEVISION THEMES; SERIES

(Under name Johnny Williams; with Pete Rugolo and Morton Stevens) *Checkmate,* CBS, 1960-62.
(Under name Johnny Williams) *Alcoa Premiere,* ABC, 1961-63.
Wide Country, NBC, 1962-63.
Lost in Space, CBS, 1965-68.
The Time Tunnel, ABC, 1966-67.
Amazing Stories, NBC, 1985.

Also composer of theme music for *Bachelor Father.*

MUSIC FOR TELEVISION MOVIES

(Under name Johnny Williams) Score, "The Case against Paul Ryker," *Kraft Suspense Theater,* NBC, 1963.
Score, *Heidi* (includes song "A Place of My Own," with Rod McKuen), NBC, 1968.
"Wicket's Theme," *The Ewok Adventure,* ABC, 1984.

MUSIC FOR TELEVISION SPECIALS

(Under name Johnny Williams) Score, "Jane Eyre" (includes "Reunion"), *Hallmark Hall of Fame,* NBC, 1971.
"America, the Dream Goes On," *I Love Liberty,* ABC, 1982.
"We're Lookin' Good!," *The Special Olympics Opening Ceremonies,* ABC, 1987.
"The Olympic Spirit," *1988 Summer Olympic Games,* NBC, 1988.
1988 Winter Olympic Games, ABC, 1988.
Parade of athletes theme music, *Victory and Valor: A Special Olympics All-Star Celebration,* ABC, 1991.
"Scherzo for Today," *Today at Forty,* NBC, 1992.

OTHER MUSIC FOR TELEVISION

(Under name Johnny Williams) *The Cowboys* (series), ABC, 1974.

Composer of "Mission Theme," NBC News, 1985; composer for *Playhouse 90* (series), CBS; and *Once upon a Savage Night.*

OTHER COMPOSITIONS

"Olympic Fanfare and Theme," *The Official XXIIIrd Olympiad at Los Angeles,* Warner Bros., 1984.

Also composer of "Jubilee 350 Fanfare for the Boston Pops," 1980; "Liberty Fanfare," 1987; clarinet concerto, 1991; "With a Song in My Heart" and "Swing, Swing, Swing" (with Jessye Norman); "Essay for Strings"; two symphonies; and concertos for violin and flute.

ADAPTATIONS: Williams's music for *Superman* was adapted by Ken Thorne for *Superman II,* Warner Bros., 1980.

OTHER SOURCES:

PERIODICALS

Down Beat, March, 1981, pp. 20-22 and 64.
People, June 23, 1980, pp. 47-48 and 51-52.
Stereo Review, December, 1980, p. 74.

WILLIAMS, John T.
See WILLIAMS, John

* * *

WILLIAMS, Johnny
See WILLIAMS, John

* * *

WILLIAMS, Robin 1951-

PERSONAL: Born July 21, 1951 (some sources say 1952), in Chicago, IL; son of Robert W. (an auto executive) and Laurie Williams; married Valerie Velardi, June 4, 1978 (divorced, c. 1988); married Marsha Garces, April 30, 1989; children: (first marriage) Zachary; (second marriage) Zelda, Cody. *Education:* Attended Claremont Men's College and College of Marin; studied speech and drama at The Juilliard School, 1973-76.

ADDRESSES: Office— P.O. Box 480909, Los Angeles, CA 90048. *Agent*—Creative Artists Agency, 9830 Wilshire Blvd., Beverly Hills, CA 90212.

CAREER: Actor and comedian. Has worked as a street mime in New York City, at an organic ice cream parlor in Mill Valley, CA, and as a bartender in San Francisco, CA. Member of the Committee, an improvisational comedy troupe, in San Francisco. Member of comedy workshops in San Francisco and Hollywood, CA, in the 1970s.

AWARDS, HONORS: Golden Apple Award (also known as Discovery of the Year Award), Hollywood Women's Press Club, 1978; Emmy Award nomination, outstanding lead actor in a comedy series, 1978, Golden Globe Award, best actor in a television comedy series, 1979, and People's Choice Award, best male performer in a new television program, 1979, all for *Mork and Mindy;* Grammy Award, best comedy recording, 1979, for *Reality. . . What a Concept;* Grammy Award nomination, best new artist, 1979; Grammy Award nomination, best comedy recording, 1983, for *Throbbing Python of Love;* Emmy Award, outstanding individual performance in a variety or music program, 1987, for *A Carol Burnett Special: Carol, Carl, Whoopi, and Robin;* American Comedy Award, funniest male performer in a television special, 1987; Grammy Award, best comedy recording, 1987, for *A Night at the Met;* American Comedy awards, funniest male performer of the year, 1987 and 1988; Academy Award nomination, best performance by an actor in a leading role, 1987, Golden Globe Award, best actor in a musical or comedy, 1988, and American Comedy Award, funniest actor in a motion picture, 1988, all for *Good Morning, Vietnam* (film); American Comedy awards, best male stand-up comic, 1987, 1988, and 1989; Grammy Award, best comedy recording, 1988, for *Good Morning, Vietnam* (recording); Emmy Award, outstanding individual performance in a variety or music program, 1988, for *ABC Presents a Royal Gala;* American Comedy Award, funniest male performer in television special, 1988, for *Comic Relief II;* Grammy Award, best children's recording, 1988, for *Pecos Bill;* Hasty Pudding Man of the Year, Hasty Pudding Theatricals, 1989; Academy Award nomination, best performance by an actor in a leading role, 1989, and Golden Globe Award nomination, best actor, both for *Dead Poets Society;* American Comedy Award, funniest male performer in a television special, 1990, for *Comic Relief III;* Academy Award nomination, best performance by an actor in a leading role, and Golden Globe Award, best actor in a musical or comedy, both 1992, for *The Fisher King;* ACE Award, National Cable Television Association, for *Comic Relief.*

CREDITS:

STAGE APPEARANCES

V.I.P. Night on Broadway, Shubert Theatre, New York City, 1979.
Night of 100 Stars, Radio City Music Hall, New York City, 1982.
Estragon, *Waiting for Godot,* Lincoln Center, Mitzi E. Newhouse Theatre, New York City, 1988.
Voice, *The Acting Company,* John F. Kennedy Center for the Performing Arts, Terrace Theatre, Washington, DC, c. 1989.

Also appeared in a stand-up comedy routine, Metropolitan Opera House, New York City, 1986. Appeared at clubs in San Francisco, CA, in the 1970s, including Holy City Zoo, Intersection, Great American Music Hall, and the Boardinghouse; appeared regularly as a stand-up comedian at the Comedy Store, Los Angeles, CA, 1976-77; also appeared at other Los Angeles clubs, including Improvisation, Off the Wall, and the Ice House.

TELEVISION APPEARANCES; SERIES

The Richard Pryor Show, NBC, 1977.
Mork, *Mork and Mindy* (also see below), ABC, 1978-82.
Voice of Mork, *Mork and Mindy* (animated), ABC, 1982-83.

TELEVISION APPEARANCES; EPISODIC

America 2Night (also known as *Fernwood 2-Night*), syndicated, 1978.
Mork, *Happy Days,* ABC, 1978 and 1979.
Out of the Blue, ABC, 1979.
"The Tale of the Frog Prince," *Faerie Tale Theatre,* Showtime, 1982.

Pryor's Place, CBS, 1984.
"Just for Laughs," *Short Stories,* Arts and Entertainment, 1987.
Robert Kline Time, USA, 1988.
Narrator, "The Fool and the Flying Ship," *We All Have Tales,* Showtime, 1991.
"Naked Hollywood" (documentary), *A & E Premieres,* Arts and Entertainment, 1991.

Also has appeared on *Saturday Night Live,* NBC, *Ninety Minutes Live,* and *The Alan Hamel Show.*

TELEVISION APPEARANCES; SPECIALS

Laugh-In, NBC, 1977-78.
Battle of the Network Stars, ABC, 1978.
Host, *E.T. and Friends—Magical Movie Visitors* (documentary), CBS, 1982.
I Love Liberty, ABC, 1982.
An Evening with Robin Williams (also see below), HBO, 1983.
Richard Lewis I'm in Pain Concert, Showtime, 1985.
Host, *Comic Relief,* HBO, 1986.
Comic Relief: Backstage Pass (documentary), HBO, 1986.
Barbra Streisand: One Voice, HBO, 1986.
Robin Williams: An Evening at the Met (also see below), HBO, 1986.
The Young Comedians All-Star Reunion, HBO, 1986.
Co-host, *Fifty-eighth Annual Academy Awards Presentation,* ABC, 1986.
A Carol Burnett Special: Carol, Carl, Whoopi, and Robin, ABC, 1987.
Host, *Will Rogers: Look Back in Laughter* (also known as *Will Rogers: An American Hero*), HBO, 1987.
Superstars and Their Moms, ABC, 1987.
Comic Relief II, HBO, 1987.
Tommy Wilhelm, "Seize the Day," *Great Performances,* PBS, 1987.
Jonathan Winters: On the Ledge, Showtime, 1987.
Jonathan Winters Special, Showtime, 1988.
ABC Presents a Royal Gala, ABC, 1988.
An All-Star Celebration: The '88 Vote, ABC, 1988.
"An All-Star Toast to the Improv" (also known as "An All-Star Salute to the Improv"), *HBO Comedy Hour,* HBO, 1988.
Sixtieth Annual Academy Awards Presentation, ABC, 1988.
The Comedy Store Fifteenth Year Class Reunion (also known as *Comedy Store Reunion*), NBC, 1988.
Free to be . . . a Family, ABC, 1988.
Host, *Comic Relief III,* HBO, 1989.
The Barbara Walters Special, ABC, 1989.
The Prince's Trust Gala, TBS, 1989.
Saturday Night Live Fifteenth Anniversary, NBC, 1989.
Host, *Comic Relief IV,* HBO, 1990.
An Evening with Bette, Cher, Goldie, Meryl, Olivia, Lily, and Robin, ABC, 1990.
Time Warner Presents the Earth Day Special (also see below), ABC, 1990.
"The Walt Disney Company Presents the American Teacher Awards," *The Magical World of Disney,* The Disney Channel, 1990.
The Dream Is Alive: The Twentieth Anniversary Celebration of Walt Disney World, CBS, 1991.
Entertainers '91: The Top Twenty of the Year, ABC, 1991.
Talking with David Frost, PBS, 1991.
Dame Edna's Hollywood, NBC, 1992.
Host, *Comic Relief V,* HBO, 1992.

Also appeared in *Robin Williams: Off the Wall,* HBO, *Robin Williams Live,* 1985, and *The Great American Laugh Off.*

TELEVISION WORK; EPISODIC

Director, *Mork and Mindy,* ABC, 1978.

FILM APPEARANCES

Title role, *Popeye,* Paramount, 1980.
T. S. Garp, *The World According to Garp,* Warner Bros., 1982.
Donald Quinelle, *The Survivors,* Columbia, 1983.
Vladimir Ivanoff, *Moscow on the Hudson,* Columbia, 1984.
Jack Dundee, *The Best of Times,* Universal, 1986.
Jack Moniker, *Club Paradise,* Warner Bros., 1986.
Adrian Cronauer, *Good Morning, Vietnam* (also see below), Buena Vista, 1987.
Narrator, *Dear America* (also known as *Dear America: Letters Home from Vietnam*), Taurus Entertainment Company, 1987.
King of the Moon, *The Adventures of Baron Munchausen,* Columbia/Tri-Star, 1989.
John Keating, *Dead Poets Society,* Buena Vista, 1989.
Joey O'Brien, *Cadillac Man,* Orion, 1990.
Dr. Malcolm Sayer, *Awakenings,* Columbia, 1990.
Dr. Cozy Carlisle, *Dead Again,* Paramount, 1991.
Parry, *The Fisher King,* Tri-Star, 1991.
Peter Banning/Peter Pan, *Hook,* Tri-Star, 1991.
Voice of Batty Koda, *Fern Gully . . . the Last Rainforest* (animated), Twentieth Century-Fox, 1992.

Also appeared in *Can I Do It . . . Till I Need Glasses?,* 1977 (one source says 1979), and *The Last Laugh.*

RECORDINGS:

COMEDY ALBUMS

Reality . . . What a Concept, Casablanca, 1979.
Throbbing Python of Love, Casablanca/Polygram, c. 1983.
A Night at the Met, Columbia-CBS, 1987.

Also has recorded *Good Morning, Vietnam,* c. 1987.

VIDEOS

Narrator, *Pecos Bill* (animated; also see below), Sony, c. 1988.

Also appeared in *Comedy Tonight,* 1977, *Catch a Rising Star's Tenth Anniversary,* 1983, *Robin! Tour de Face!,* 1987, *Reunion—Tenth Annual Young Comedians,* 1987, and *Video Yesterbloop.*

TAPED READINGS

Pecos Bill, Rabbit Ears Books, 1988.

WRITINGS:

TELEVISION SPECIALS

An Evening with Robin Williams, HBO, 1983.
Robin Williams: An Evening at the Met, HBO, 1986.

Also contributor of material to *Time Warner Presents the Earth Day Special,* ABC, 1990.

OTHER SOURCES:

BOOKS

Newsmakers, 1988 Cumulation, Gale, 1989, pp. 483-86.

PERIODICALS

Esquire, June, 1988, p. 114; June, 1989, p. 108.
Interview, August, 1986, p. 38.
Newsweek, July 7, 1986, p. 52.
New York Times, April 15, 1984; May 28, 1989.
People, September 13, 1982, p. 92; February 22, 1988, p. 78.
Premiere, January, 1988, pp. 39-41.
Rolling Stone, February 22, 1988, p. 28; February 21, 1991, p. 22.

* * *

WILLIAMS, Sammy 1948-

PERSONAL: Full name, Samuel Joseph William; born November 13, 1948, in Trenton, NJ; son of Joseph (a factory worker) and Nona (a hospital attendant) Williams. *Education:* Rider College, Trenton, NJ; John Tucci School of Dance; studied with artists Jo Jo Smith and Wally Harper and at Luigi's, New York City. *Avocational interests:* Bicycling, ice-skating, swimming, cooking, gardening.

ADDRESSES: Agent—The Lantz Office, Suite 2500, 888 Seventh Avenue, New York, NY 10106.

CAREER: Actor and dancer. Appeared in television advertisements, including commercials for Tropicana Orange Juice, 1973, and promotions for performances of the Broadway production *A Chorus Line.* Worked previously for the New Jersey Department of Transportation.

MEMBER: Actor's Equity Association, American Federation of Television and Radio Artists, Screen Actors Guild.

AWARDS, HONORS: Antoinette Perry Award, best actor in a featured role in a Broadway musical, and Obie Award, *Village Voice,* both 1976, both for *A Chorus Line.*

CREDITS:

STAGE APPEARANCES

Jerome, *South Pacific,* Music Circus Theatre, Lamberton, NJ, 1960.
Swing dancer, *The Happy Time,* Ahmanson Theatre, Los Angeles, then Broadway Theatre, New York City, 1967-68.
Paul, *A Chorus Line,* Newman Theatre, New York City, 1975, then Schubert Theatre, New York City, 1975, then Curran Theatre, San Francisco, CA, 1975-78, later Shubert Theatre, Los Angeles, CA, 1976.

MAJOR TOURS

Hello, Dolly!, U.S. cities, 1969.
Dancer, *Applause,* Palace Theatre, 1970-72, then U.S. cities, 1972-73.
Chorus, *Seesaw,* U.S. cities, 1974.
Chorus, *No, No, Nanette,* Guber theater circuit, 1974.
Paul, *A Chorus Line,* U.S. cities, c. 1979-85.

FILM APPEARANCES

Harold Gorman, *God Told Me To* (also known as *Demon*), New World, 1976.

TELEVISION APPEARANCES

Ed Sullivan Theatre, CBS, 1968.
Fred Astaire Special, NBC, 1973.

Also appeared on *The Twenty-third Annual Tony Awards Presentation,* CBS, 1970.

RECORDINGS:

ALBUMS

Williams performed on the original-cast recordings of *The Happy Time, Applause,* and *A Chorus Line.*

OTHER SOURCES:

BOOKS

Notable Names in the American Theatre, James T. White & Co., 1976, p. 1228.*

WILSON, August 1945-

PERSONAL: Born in 1945, in Pittsburgh, PA; son of August (a baker) and Daisy (a cleaning woman) Wilson; married second wife, Judy Oliver (a social worker); children: (first marriage) Sakina Ansari.

ADDRESSES: Contact—Emily Kretschmer (assistant), 1290 Grand Ave., Suite 105, St. Paul, MN 55105; c/o John Breglio, 1285 Avenue of the Americas, New York, NY 10019; c/o New American Library, 1633 Broadway, New York, NY 10019.

CAREER: Writer. Worked as founder and director of Black Horizons Theatre Company in Pittsburgh, PA, beginning in 1968; scriptwriter for Science Museum of Minnesota, 1978-80.

AWARDS, HONORS: Award for best play of 1984-85 from New York Drama Critics' Circle, 1985, Antoinette Perry Award nomination, 1985, and Whiting Writers' Award from the Whiting Foundation, 1986, all for *Ma Rainey's Black Bottom;* Outstanding Play Award from American Theatre Critics, 1986, Drama Desk Award for Outstanding New Play of 1986-87, award for best play of 1986-87 from New York Drama Critics' Circle, Pulitzer Prize for drama, 1987, Antoinette Perry Award for best play, 1987, and award for best Broadway play from Outer Critics Circle, 1987, all for *Fences;* John Gasner Award for best American playwright from Outer Critics Circle, 1987; named Artist of the Year by *Chicago Tribune,* 1987; award for best play of 1987-88 from New York Drama Critics' Circle, and Antoinette Perry Award nomination, 1988, both for *Joe Turner's Come and Gone;* named to list of Literary Lions by New York Public Library, 1988; Drama Desk Award for Outstanding New Play of 1989-90, award for best play of 1988-90 from New York Drama Critics' Circle, Pulitzer Prize for drama, 1990, Antoinette Perry Award nomination, 1990, and Outstanding Play Award from American Theatre Critics, all for *The Piano Lesson;* Antoinette Perry Award nomination, best play, 1992, and American Theatre Critics' Association Award, both for *Two Trains Running.* Also recipient of Bush and Guggenheim Foundation fellowships.

CREDITS:

TELEVISION APPEARANCES

MacNeil/Lehrer Newshour, 1987.
Bill Moyers' World of Ideas, PBS, 1988.
The Forty-third Annual Tony Awards (special) CBS, 1989.
Story of a People: Expressions in Black, syndicated, 1991.

WRITINGS:

PLAYS

Jitney (two-act), first produced in Pittsburgh, PA, at the Allegheny Repertory Theatre, 1982.
Ma Rainey's Black Bottom, first produced in New Haven, CT, at the Yale Repertory Theatre, 1984, produced on Broadway at the Cort Theatre, 1984, published by New American Library, 1985.
Fences, first produced at the Yale Repertory Theatre, 1985, produced on Broadway at the 46th Street Theatre, 1987, published by New American Library, 1988.
Joe Turner's Come and Gone, first produced at the Yale Repertory Theatre, 1986, produced on Broadway, 1988, published by New American Library, 1988.
The Piano Lesson, first produced at the Yale Repertory Theatre, 1987, produced on Broadway at the Walter Kerr Theatre, 1990.
Two Trains Running, first produced at the Yale Repertory Theatre, 1990, then at the John F. Kennedy Center for the Performing Arts, Washington, DC, 1991.

Also author of *Black Bart and the Sacred Hills,* 1981; *The Mill Hand's Lunch Bucket,* 1983; and *Fullerton Street;* contributor to *Urban Blight.*

OTHER

Author of the book for a stage musical about jazz musician Jelly Roll Morton; poetry anthologized in *The Poetry of Blackamerica,* Adoff. Contributor to periodicals, including *Black Lines* and *Connection.*

OTHER SOURCES:

BOOKS

Contemporary Literary Criticism, Gale, Volume 39, 1986, Volume 50, 1988, Volume 63, 1991.
Major Twentieth-Century Writers, Gale, 1991.

PERIODICALS

Chicago Tribune, February 9, 1986, section, 13, pp. 12-13.
Christian Science Monitor, October 16, 1984, pp. 29-30.
Ebony, November, 1987, pp. 68, 70, 72, 74.
Esquire, April, 1989, pp. 116, 118, 120, 122-127.
Essence, August, 1987, pp. 51, 111, 113.
New York Newsday, April 20, 1987.
New York Times, March 15, 1987; March 27, 1988, pp. 1, 34.

WIMMER, Brian 1960(?)-

PERSONAL: Born c. 1960, in Provo, UT. *Education:* Attended Brigham Young University; studied at Actors Repertory Theatre, New York City.

ADDRESSES: *Agent*—Inter-Talent, 131 South Rodeo Dr., Suite 300, Beverly Hills, CA 90212.

CAREER: Actor. Worked as a model, a film production assistant at Sundance Institute, and at a ski resort.

MEMBER: Screen Actors Guild.

CREDITS:

TELEVISION APPEARANCES; SERIES

Boonie Lanier, *China Beach,* ABC, 1988-90.

TELEVISION APPEARANCES; MOVIES

Denzil Ray, *What Price Victory* (also known as *Hail Alma Mater* and *The Price of Victory*), ABC, 1988.
Frank Hughes, *Dangerous Pursuit* (also known as *Fast Lane*), USA, 1990.
Alex Dante, *The World's Oldest Living Bridesmaid,* CBS, 1990.
Honor Thy Mother, CBS, 1992.

Also appeared in *True Confessions.*

TELEVISION APPEARANCES; SPECIALS

Host from Coconut Grove, *Dick Clark's New Year's Rockin' Eve,* ABC, 1988.
Battle of the Network Stars XIX, ABC, 1988.
Host and narrator, *The Extreme Edge,* ABC, 1992.

FILM APPEARANCES

Footloose, Paramount, 1984.
Do-gooder, *A Nightmare on Elm Street, Part II: Freddy's Revenge,* New Line, 1985.
Trent, *Less Than Zero,* Twentieth Century-Fox, 1987.
Cage, *Under the Boardwalk,* New World, 1988.
Willie Husband, *Late for Dinner* (also known as *Freezer*), Columbia, 1991.

RECORDINGS:

VIDEOS

Appeared in the Beach Boys music video *Getcha Back.**

* * *

WINKLER, Irwin 1931-

PERSONAL: Born May, 28, 1931, in New York, NY; son of Sol and Anna Winkler. *Education:* New York University, B.A., 1955.

ADDRESSES: *Office*—Winkler Films, 10125 West Washington Blvd., Culver City, CA 90230.

CAREER: Producer and director of motion pictures. William Morris Agency, New York City, messenger, secretary, projectionist, and agent, 1955-62; formed theatrical talent agency with Robert Chartoff, 1962; Chartoff-Winkler Productions, Los Angeles, CA, cofounder, 1966, president, 1966—; Winkler Films, Culver City, CA, owner, 1982—. *Military service:* U.S. Army, 1951-53.

MEMBER: Director's Guild of America.

AWARDS, HONORS: Jury Prize, Cannes Film Festival, 1970, for *The Strawberry Statement;* Academy Award, best picture, and Los Angeles Film Critics Award, best picture, both 1976, both for *Rocky;* Academy Award nomination, best picture, and Los Angeles Film Critics Award, best picture, both 1980, both for *Raging Bull;* Academy Award nomination, best picture, 1983, for *The Right Stuff;* named Commander d'Artes et de Lettres, French Minister of Culture, 1985; Academy Award nomination, best picture, 1990, for *Goodfellas.*

CREDITS:

FILM PRODUCER; WITH ROBERT CHARTOFF

The Split, Metro-Goldwyn-Mayer (MGM), 1968.
(And with Sydney Pollack) *They Shoot Horses, Don't They?,* ABC-Cinerama, 1969.
Leo the Last, United Artists (UA), 1970.
The Strawberry Statement, MGM, 1970.
Believe in Me, MGM, 1971.
The Gang That Couldn't Shoot Straight, MGM, 1971.
(And with Louis John Carlino) *The Mechanic,* UA, 1972.
The New Centurions, Columbia, 1972.
Thumb Tripping, Avco Embassy, 1972.
Up the Sandbox, National General, 1972.
Busting, UA, 1974.
The Gambler, Paramount, 1974.
*S*P*Y*S*,* Twentieth Century-Fox, 1974.
Breakout, 1975.
Peeper, Twentieth Century-Fox, 1975.
Nickelodeon, Columbia, 1976.
Rocky, UA, 1976.
New York, New York, UA, 1977.
Valentino, UA, 1977.
Uncle Joe Shannon, UA, 1978.
Rocky II, UA, 1979.
Raging Bull, UA, 1980.
True Confessions, UA, 1981.
Author! Author!, Twentieth Century-Fox, 1982.
Rocky III, UA, 1982.
The Right Stuff, Warner Bros., 1983.
Rocky IV, MGM-UA, 1985.
Rocky V, UA, 1990.

FILM PRODUCER

(With Judd Bernard) *Double Trouble,* MGM, 1967.
(With Bernard) *Blue,* Paramount, 1968.
Revolution, Warner Bros., 1985.
Round Midnight, Warner Bros., 1986.
Betrayed, MGM-UA, 1988.
Music Box, Tri-Star, 1989.
Goodfellas, Warner Bros., 1990.

FILM DIRECTOR

Guilty by Suspicion (also see below), Warner Bros., 1991.

TELEVISION APPEARANCES; SPECIALS

"Martin Scorsese Directs," *American Masters,* PBS, 1990.

WRITINGS:

Guilty by Suspicion (screenplay), Warner Bros., 1991.

OTHER SOURCES:

PERIODICALS

American Premiere, May/June, 1991, pp. 4-8.*

* * *

WOLFE, Ian 1896-1992

OBITUARY NOTICE—See index for *CTFT* sketch: Born November 4, 1896, in Canton, IL; died January 23, 1992, in Los Angeles, CA. Actor. Wolfe is remembered as a character actor who began his career in the theater with *The Claw* in 1919 and went on to appear in more than 160 films. His first movie, in 1934, was *The Barretts of Wimpole Street;* he most recently played Forger in the 1990 release, *Dick Tracy.* In between, he appeared in a wide variety of films—ranging from action adventures, to dramas, to comedies, to romances, to mysteries—including *Mutiny on the Bounty, Rebel without a Cause, Invisible Man's Revenge, Up the Academy, Witness for the Prosecution, Reds, Romeo and Juliet,* and *THX 1138.* Wolfe also played guest roles on several television shows, including *The Andy Griffith Show, Bonanza, The Twilight Zone, Star Trek, Cheers,* and *Amazing Stories.* His television movie credits include ABC's *Devil's Daughter* and *Mae West,* and *James A. Michener's "Dynasty"* and *LBJ: The Early Years,* both for NBC.

OBITUARIES AND OTHER SOURCES:

PERIODICALS

Variety, February 3, 1992, pp. 93-94.

WONG, B. D. 1962-

PERSONAL: Born October 24, 1962, in San Francisco, CA. *Education:* Studied acting with Don Hotton and voice with Tony McDowell.

ADDRESSES: Agent—Agency for the Performing Arts, 888 Seventh Ave., New York, NY 10019.

CAREER: Actor.

MEMBER: Actors Equity Association, Screen Actors Guild, American Federation of Television and Radio Artists, Asian Pacific Alliance for Greater Equality (founder), ART (New York; member of board of directors).

AWARDS, HONORS: Antoinette Perry Award and Drama Desk Award, both for best featured actor, Clarence Derwent Award, Outer Critics Circle Award, and Theatre World Award, all 1988, for *M. Butterfly.*

CREDITS:

STAGE APPEARANCES

Androcles and the Lion, Town Hall, New York City, 1982.
Song Liling, *M. Butterfly,* Eugene O'Neill Theatre, New York City, 1988.
Ariel, *The Tempest,* Roundabout Theatre, New York City, 1989.

Also appeared in *See Below Middle Sea,* Taper Too; *Gifts of the Magi,* Coast Playhouse, Los Angeles, CA; *Mail,* Pasadena Playhouse, Pasadena, CA; *A Chorus Line;* and West Coast Company production of *La Cage Aux Folles.*

FILM APPEARANCES

Boy on the street, *The Karate Kid II,* Columbia, 1986.
Jimmy Chiu, *Family Business,* Tri-Star, 1989.
Edward, *The Freshman,* Tri-Star, 1990.
James Lew, *Mystery Date,* Orion, 1991.
Howard Weinstein, *Father of the Bride,* Buena Vista, 1991.

Also appeared in *The Lounge People* (unreleased), and *No Big Deal.*

TELEVISION APPEARANCES

Appeared in the movies *Goodnight Sweet Wife: A Murder in Boston* and *Crash Course,* and on episodes of *Shannon's Deal, Baltimore, Double Switch, Sweet Surrender, Shell Game, Hard Copy,* and *Blacke's Magic.*

OTHER SOURCES:

PERIODICALS

Gentlemen's Quarterly, May, 1989, p. 83.
Movieline, summer, 1991.
New York Times, March 25, 1988.

Premiere, December, 1991, p. 54.
San Francisco Focus, December, 1990.

* * *

WOOD, Peter 1927(?)-

PERSONAL: Full name, Peter Lawrence Wood; born October 8, 1927 (one source cites 1928), in Colyton, Devonshire, England; son of Frank and Lucy Eleanor (Meeson) Wood. *Education:* Attended Downing College, Cambridge. *Avocational interests:* Swimming, sailing, and travelling.

ADDRESSES: Office—National Theatre, Waterloo Rd., London S.E.1, England. *Contact*—11 Warwick Ave, London W.9, England.

CAREER: Director for theatre and television. Gained early experience working on amateur productions; spent three years as assistant stage manager and understudy in *Seagulls over Sorento;* director for Worthing Repertory Theatre; resident director for Oxford Playhouse, 1955-56, and for Arts Theatre, London, 1956-57; associate director of National Theatre, 1978—. *Military service:* Served in Royal Air Force, 1946-48.

AWARDS, HONORS: Evening Standard Award, 1958, for *The Iceman Cometh;* Arts Council grant, 1958; Emmy Award nomination, outstanding directorial achievement in drama, 1971, for "Hamlet," on *Hallmark Hall of Fame;* Antionette Perry Award nomination, best director of a Broadway play, 1975, for *Travesties.*

CREDITS:

STAGE WORK; DIRECTOR

(Directorial debut) *The Moment of Truth,* Arts Theatre Club, Cambridge, England, 1954.
The Bald Prima Donna [and] *The New Tenant* (double bill), Arts Theatre Club, London, England, 1956.
No Laughing Matter, Arts Theatre Club, London, 1957.
The Iceman Cometh, Arts Theatre Club, London, 1958, then Winter Garden Theatre, London, 1958.
The Birthday Party, Lyric Theatre, London, 1958.
Mary Stuart, Old Vic Company, Edinburgh Festival, Edinburgh, Scotland, 1958, then Old Vic Theatre, London, 1958.
Who's Your Father, Cambridge Theatre, Cambridge, 1958.
As You Like It, Shakespeare Festival, Stratford, Ontario, Canada, 1959.
Five Finger Exercise, Comedy Theatre, London, 1959.
The Winter's Tale, Shakespeare Memorial Theatre, Stratford-on-Avon, England, 1961.
The Devils, Aldwych Theatre, London, 1961.
Hamlet, Shakespeare Memorial Theatre, 1961.
The Private Ear and the Public Eye, Globe Theatre, London, 1962, then (U.S. debut) Morosco Theatre, New York City, 1963.
The Beggar's Opera, Aldwych Theatre, 1963.
The Master Builder, National Theatre Company, Old Vic Theatre, 1964.
Carving a Statue, Haymarket Theatre, London, 1964.
Poor Richard, Helen Hayes Theatre, New York City, 1964.
(Codirector) *History Cycle,* Royal Shakespeare Company, 1964.
Love for Love, National Theatre Company, Old Vic Theatre, 1965, later performed in Moscow, USSR (now the Commonwealth of Independent States).
Incident at Vichy, Phoenix Theatre, London, 1966.
The Prime of Miss Jean Brodie, Wyndham's Theatre, London, 1966.
Love for Love, Expo 1967, Montreal and Toronto, Canada, 1967, then National Theatre, 1985.
White Liars and Black Comedy, Lyric Theatre, 1967.
Design for Living, Center Theatre Group, Ahmanson Theatre, Los Angeles, CA, 1971.
Jumpers, National Theatre Company, Old Vic Theatre, 1972, then Kennedy Center, Washington DC, 1974, then Billy Rose Theatre, New York City, 1974, later Aldwych Theatre, 1985.
Dear Love (also see below), Comedy Theatre, 1973.
Travesties, Aldwych Theatre, 1974, then Ethel Barrymore Theatre, New York City, 1975.
Macbeth, Center Theatre Group, Ahmanson Theatre, 1975, then Staatsoper Theatre, Vienna, 1982.
Long Day's Journey into Night, Center Theatre Group, Ahmanson Theatre, 1977.
She Stoops to Conquer, Burgtheater, Vienna, Austria, 1978.
The Guardsman, National Theater, London, 1978.
The Double Dealer (also see below), National Theater, 1978.
Night and Day, Phoenix Theatre, 1978, then ANTA Theatre, New York City, 1979.
Undiscovered Country, National Theatre, 1979.
The Provok'd Wife, National Theatre, 1980.
Don Giovanni, Covent Garden, London, 1981.
On the Razzle (also see below), National Theatre, 1981.
Windy City, Victoria Palace Theatre, London, 1982.
The Real Thing, Strand Theatre, London, 1982.
The Rivals, National Theatre, 1983.
Orion, King's Theatre, Edinburgh, 1984.
Rough Crossing, National Theatre, 1984.
The American Clock, National Theatre, 1986.
Dalliance, National Theatre, 1986.
The Threepenny Opera, National Theatre, 1986.
Wildfire, Phoenix Theatre, 1986.
Otello, Staatsoper Theatre, 1987.

Hapgood, Aldwych Theatre, 1988.
Les Liaisons dangereuses, Center Theatre Group, Ahmanson Theatre, 1989.
The Beaux Stratagem, National Theatre Company, Lyttelton Theatre, 1989.
The School for Scandal, National Theatre Company, Olivier Theatre, London, 1990.

Also directed *Rosencrantz and Guildenstern Are Dead,* 1971, *Betrayal,* Vienna, 1978, *Il Seraglio,* Glyndebourne, 1980, 1988, and *The Silver King,* Chichester, England, 1990. Directed the operas *The Mother of Us All,* Santa Fe, New Mexico, 1976, *Cosi fan tutte,* Santa Fe, 1977, and *Orione,* Santa Fe, 1983.

MAJOR TOURS

Director, *Loot,* English Cities, 1965.

FILM WORK; DIRECTOR

In Search of Gregory, Universal, 1970.

TELEVISION WORK; DIRECTOR

"Hamlet," *Hallmark Hall of Fame,* NBC, 1970.
Long Day's Journey into Night (based upon an Old Vic Theatre production; also see below), ABC, 1973.

Also directed *Shakespeare,* episode I, 1976, *Dear Love,* 1976, *Flint,* 1977, *The Double Dealer,* 1980, *On the Razzle,* 1986, and *The Dog It Was That Died,* 1988.

RECORDINGS:

Has directed for both Caedmon Records and RCA.

WRITINGS:

(With Michael Blake) *Long Day's Journey into Night* (television adaption of Eugene O'Neill's play), ABC, 1973.

OTHER SOURCES:

PERIODICALS

Times (London), April 22, 1990, p. E7.*

* * *

WORTH, Irene 1916-

PERSONAL: Born June 23, 1916, in Nebraska; daughter of a superintendent of schools. *Education:* University of California, Los Angeles, B.Ed., 1937; studied with Elsie Fogarty, London, 1944-45. *Avocational interests:* Music, painting, sculpture, architecture, education.

ADDRESSES: Agent—Sam Cohn, International Creative Management, 40 West 57th St., 6th Floor, New York, NY 10019.

CAREER: Actress. Member of Shakespeare Festival of Canada, Stratford, Ontario, 1953 and 1970, Royal Shakespeare Company, 1962-64, and Old Vic Repertory Company. Worked with International Company for Theatre Research, Paris and Iran, 1971. Also worked as a schoolteacher.

MEMBER: Royal National Theatre of Great Britain.

AWARDS, HONORS: National Television Award, *Daily Mail* (London), 1953, for *The Lady from the Sea;* British Television Award, best actress, 1953, for *The Lake;* British Academy Award, best actress in a leading role, British Academy of Film and Television Arts, 1958, for *Orders to Kill;* Page One Award, New York Newspaper Guild, and Antoinette Perry Award nomination, best dramatic actress, both 1960, for *Toys in the Attic;* Antoinette Perry Award, best dramatic actress, 1965, for *Tiny Alice;* London *Evening Standard* Award, 1966, for *Suite in Three Keys;* award from Variety Club of Great Britain, 1967, for *Heartbreak House;* Whitbread Anglo-American Award, outstanding actress, 1967; Worth was appointed Commander of the Most Excellent Order of the British Empire by Queen Elizabeth II, 1975; Antoinette Perry Award, best dramatic actress, and Jefferson Award, both 1976, for *Sweet Bird of Youth;* Drama Desk Award, best actress in a play, and Antoinette Perry Award nomination, best actress in a Broadway play, both 1977, for *The Cherry Orchard;* inducted into New York Theatre Hall of Fame, 1979; D.Arts, Tufts University, 1980; Obie Award, performance, *Village Voice,* 1982, for *The Chalk Garden;* D.F.A., Queens College of the City University of New York, 1986; Obie Award, sustained achievement in the theatre, 1989; Emmy Award nomination, outstanding supporting actress in a mini-series or special, 1989, for "The Shell Seekers," *Hallmark Hall of Fame;* Mayn's Award of Honor for Art and Culture, 1990; Drama Desk Award, featured actress in a play, and Antoinette Perry Award, best dramatic actress, both 1991, for *Lost in Yonkers.*

CREDITS:

STAGE APPEARANCES

(Stage debut) Cecily Hardin, *The Two Mrs. Carrolls,* Booth Theatre, New York City, 1943.
(London debut) Elsie, *The Time of Your Life,* Lyric Theatre, Hammersmith, England, 1946.
Miss Phillipa Form, *This Way to the Tomb!,* Mercury Theatre, London, 1946.
Annabelle Jones, *Love Goes to Press,* Embassy Theatre, then Duchess Theatre, both London, 1946.
Donna Pascuala, *Drake's Drum,* Embassy Theatre, 1946.
Ilona Szabo, *The Play's the Thing* (also see below), Lyric Theatre, then St. James's Theatre, London, 1947.
Title role, *Iris,* Q Theatre, London, 1947.

Olivia Brown, *Love in Idleness,* Q Theatre, 1948.

Mary Dalton, *Native Son,* Bolton's Theatre, London, 1948.

Title role, *Lucrece,* Bolton's Theatre, 1948.

Eileen Perry, *Edward, My Son,* His Majesty's Theatre, 1948.

Lady Fortrose, *Home Is Tomorrow* (also see below), Cambridge Theatre, London, 1948.

Olivia Raines, *Champagne for Delilah,* New Theatre, London, 1949.

Celia Coplestone, *The Cocktail Party* (also see below), Edinburgh Festival, Edinburgh, Scotland, 1949, then Henry Miller's Theatre, New York City, 1950, later New Theatre, London, 1950.

Desdemona, *Othello* (also see below), Old Vic Theatre, London, 1951.

Helena, *A Midsummer Night's Dream* (also see below), Old Vic Theatre, 1951.

Catherine de Vausselles, *The Other Heart* (also see below), Old Vic Theatre, 1952.

Portia, *The Merchant of Venice* (also see below), Old Vic Theatre, 1953.

Lady Macbeth, *Macbeth* (also see below), Old Vic Company, London, 1953.

Helena, *All's Well That Ends Well* (also see below), Stratford Shakespeare Festival, Stratford, Ontario, 1953.

Queen Margaret, *Richard III,* Stratford Shakespeare Festival, 1953.

Frances Farrar, *A Day by the Sea,* Haymarket Theatre, London, 1953.

Argia, *The Queen and the Rebels* (also see below), Midland Theatre, Coventry, England, then Haymarket Theatre, 1955.

Alcestis, *A Life in the Sun,* Edinburgh Festival, 1955.

Marcella, *Hotel Paradiso,* Winter Garden Theatre, New York City, 1956.

Title role, *Mary Stuart,* Phoenix Theatre, New York City, 1957, then Edinburgh Festival, later Old Vic Theatre, 1958.

Sara Callifer, *The Potting Shed,* Globe Theatre, London, 1958.

Rosalind, *As You Like It,* Stratford Shakespeare Festival, 1959.

Albertine Prine, *Toys in the Attic,* Hudson Theatre, New York City, 1960.

Marquise de Merteuil, *The Art of Seduction,* Royal Shakespeare Company (RSC), Aldwych Theatre, London, 1962.

Goneril, *King Lear* (also see below), RSC, Stratford-upon-Avon, England, 1962, then Aldwych Theatre, 1962, later New York State Theatre, New York City, 1964.

Dr. Mathilde von Zahnd, *The Physicists* (also see below), Aldwych Theatre, 1963.

Clodia Pulcher, *The Ides of March,* Haymarket Theatre, 1963.

Miss Alice, *Tiny Alice,* Billy Rose Theatre, New York City, 1964, then Aldwych Theatre, 1970.

Hilde Latymer, "A Song at Twilight," Anne Hilgay, "Shadows of the Evening," and Anna-Mary Conklin, "Come into the Garden Maud," *Suite in Three Keys,* Queen's Theatre, London, 1966.

Io, *Prometheus Bound,* Yale University, New Haven, CT, 1967.

Hesione Hushabye, *Heartbreak House,* Chichester Festival, Chichester, England, then Lyric Theatre, 1967.

Jocasta, *Oedipus* (also see below), Old Vic Theatre, 1968.

Title role, *Hedda Gabler,* Stratford Theatre, Stratford, Ontario, 1970.

Dora Lang, *Notes on a Love Affair,* Globe Theatre, London, 1972.

Madame Arkadina, *The Seagull,* Chichester Festival, 1973, and Greenwich Theatre, London, c. 1973.

Gertrude, *Hamlet,* Greenwich Theatre, 1974.

Mrs. Alving, *Ghosts,* Greenwich Theatre, 1974.

Sweet Bird of Youth, Festival Theatre at Barat College, Lake Forest IL, and Brooklyn Academy of Music, Brooklyn, NY, 1975.

Princess Kosmonopolis, *Sweet Bird of Youth,* Harkness Theatre, New York City, 1975-76.

Lyobiv Andreyevna, *The Cherry Orchard,* New York Shakespeare Festival (NYSF), Vivian Beaumont Theatre, New York City, 1977.

Winnie, *Happy Days,* NYSF, Public/Newman Theatre, New York City, 1979.

Letters of Love and Affection (solo reading), Roundabout Theatre/Stage One, New York City, 1979.

Elizabeth, *The Lady from Dubuque,* Morosco Theatre, New York City, 1980.

Miss Ella Rentheim, *John Gabriel Borkman,* Circle in the Square, New York City, 1980-81.

Miss Madrigal, *The Chalk Garden,* Roundabout Theatre/Stage One, 1982.

L'Olimpiade, Edinburgh Festival, 1982.

Isabel Hastings Hoyt, *The Golden Age,* Jack Lawrence Theatre, New York City, 1984.

Volumnia, *Coriolanus,* National Theatre, 1984, then NYSF, Public/Anspacher Theatre, 1988-89.

The Bay at Nice, National Theatre, London, 1986.

You Never Can Tell, Haymarket Theatre, 1987.

Lost in Yonkers, Richard Rodgers Theatre, New York City, c.1991.

Also appeared as Lina, *Misalliance,* Lake Forest, IL, 1976; as Kate, *Old Times,* Lake Forest, 1977; in *After the Season,* Lake Forest, 1978; and in *The Physicists,* Washington, DC, 1983. Gives solo recitals and dramatic readings.

MAJOR TOURS

(Stage debut) Fenella, *Escape Me Never,* U.K. cities, 1942.
Ilona Szabo, *The Play's the Thing,* U.K. cities, 1946.
Return Journey, U.K. cities, 1947.
Lady Fortrose, *Home Is Tomorrow,* U.K. cities, 1948.
Desdemona, *Othello,* Old Vic Company, South African cities, 1952.
Catherine de Vausselles, *The Other Heart,* Old Vic Company, South African cities, 1952.
Helena, *A Midsummer Night's Dream,* Old Vic Company, South African cities, 1952.
Lady Macbeth, *Macbeth,* Old Vic Company, South African cities, 1952.
Goneril, *King Lear,* Royal Shakespeare Company, world tour, 1964.
Men and Women of Shakespeare, U.S. universities and South American cities, 1966-67.

FILM APPEARANCES

Lina Linari, *One Night with You,* Universal, 1948.
Miss Jackson, *Secret People,* Lippert, 1952.
Leonie, *Orders to Kill,* United Motion Picture, 1958.
Francoise De Gue, *The Scapegoat,* Metro-Goldwyn-Mayer (MGM), 1959.
Queen Elizabeth, *Seven Seas to Calais* (also known as *Il Dominatore dei Sette Mari*), MGM, 1963.
Goneril, *King Lear,* Altura, 1971.
The Queen Mother, *Nicholas and Alexandra,* Columbia, 1971.
Madeleine's mother, *Rich Kids,* United Artists, 1979.
Mrs. Sokolow, *Eyewitness* (also known as *The Janitor*), Twentieth Century-Fox, 1981.
Helga ten Dorp, *Deathtrap,* Warner Bros., 1982.
Ida Sabol, *Fast Forward,* Columbia, 1985.

TELEVISION APPEARANCES; SPECIALS

Hazel Crawford, *Myself a Stranger,* BBC, 1949.
Leslie, *Counsel's Opinion,* BBC, 1949.
Title role, *Antigone,* BBC, 1949.
Title role, *The Duchess of Malfi,* BBC, 1949.
Dawn, Day, and Night, BBC, 1951.
Anne, *William's Other Anne,* BBC, 1953.
Stella, *The Lake,* BBC, 1953.
Ellida Wangel, *The Lady from the Sea,* BBC, 1953.
Title role, *Candida,* BBC, 1955.
Nurse Wayland, *The Sacred Flame,* BBC, 1955.
Mrs. Moon, *Mr. Kettle and Mrs. Moon,* ATV, 1957.
Mrs. Gunhild Borkman, *John Gabriel Borkman,* ATV, 1958.
Inez, *Other People's Houses,* ATV, 1960.
Rachel Verney, *The Offshore Island,* CBC, 1961.
White lady, *Stray Cats and Empty Bottles,* BBC, 1964.
Rose Fish, *Variations on a Theme,* ITV, 1966.
Mrs. Railton-Bell, *Separate Tables,* HBO, 1983.
The 45th Annual Tony Awards, CBS, 1991.

Also appeared in *The American,* 1950; as Clytemnesta, *Prince Orestes,* 1959; as Jocasta, *Oedipus,* 1960; and as Miss Collins, *Portrait of a Madonna,* BBC.

TELEVISION APPEARANCES; MOVIES

Ruth Friedlander, *Forbidden,* HBO, 1985.

Also appeared in *The Displaced Person,* 1977.

TELEVISION APPEARANCES; EPISODIC

Patty Benedict, "The Big Knife," *American Playhouse,* PBS, 1988.
Dolly Keeling, "The Shell Seekers," *Hallmark Hall of Fame,* ABC, 1989.

Also appeared on *Girl Talk,* ABC; and in "The Poems of Edith Sitwell," *Camera Three,* CBS.

RADIO APPEARANCES

Appeared in British radio productions as Lady Fortrose, *Home Is Tomorrow,* 1949; Celia, *The Cocktail Party,* 1951; Cleopatra, *Goddess and God,* 1953; Anna Petrovna, *Ivanov,* 1954; title role, *Major Barbara,* 1954; Helena, *All's Well That Ends Well,* 1954; Argia, *The Queen and the Rebels,* 1954; Karen Selby, *The Flashing Stream,* 1955; Laurencia, *Fuente Ovejuna,* 1955; the Marquise, *A Door Must Be Kept Open or Shut,* 1955; Charlotte, *The Golden Bowl,* 1955; Isabella Andreini, *The Great Desire I Had,* 1955; Mrs. Porella, *Man, Beast, and Virtue,* 1957; Lady Godiva, *Scandal at Coventry,* 1958; Baroness Munster, *The Europeans,* 1958; Portia, *The Merchant of Venice,* 1958; Rebecca West, *Rosmersholm,* 1958; Dr. Mathilda Von Zahnd, *The Physicists,* 1963; Lucile, *Duel of Angels,* 1964; and Eve, *The Tree.* Also appeared on *London Forum,* 1954; *What Goes On,* 1956; *This Is Britain,* 1956; and *Woman's Hour: Guest of the Week,* 1963.

OTHER SOURCES:

PERIODICALS

New York Times, February 5, 1976.
Times (London), July 1, 1990.

* * *

WRIGHT, Robert C. 1943-

PERSONAL: Full name, Robert Charles Wright; born April 23, 1943, in Rockville Center (one source says Hempstead), NY; son of an engineer and a schoolteacher; married Suzanne Werner, August 26, 1967; children: Kate, Christopher, Maggie. *Education:* College of the Holy Cross, B.A., history, 1965; University of Virginia,

LL.B., 1968. *Avocational interests:* Swimming, boating, playing tennis.

ADDRESSES: Office—National Broadcasting Company, 30 Rockefeller Plaza, New York, NY 10112.

CAREER: Business executive. Admitted to the Bar of New York State, 1968, Bar of Virginia State, 1968, Bar of Massachusetts State, 1970, and Bar of New Jersey State, 1971. General Electric Company, lawyer in plastics division, 1969-70; law secretary to U.S. District Court Chief Judge Lawrence A. Whipple, Jr., New Jersey, beginning in 1970; lawyer in private practice in Newark, NJ; General Electric Company, Pittsfield, MA, associated with plastics division, 1973-80, became manager of strategic planning, then general manager of engineering plastics operation, and later general sales manager for nationwide plastics division, 1976; Cox Cable Communications, Atlanta, GA, president, 1980-83; General Electric Company, vice-president and general manager of housewares and electronics division, 1983-84; General Electric Financial Services Inc., Stamford, CT, president and chief executive officer, 1984-86; National Broadcasting Company (NBC), New York City, president and chief executive officer, 1986—, also chairman. *Military service:* U.S. Army reserve infantry; became lieutenant.*

* * *

WRIGHT, Teresa 1918-

PERSONAL: Full name, Muriel Teresa Wright; born October 27, 1918, in New York, NY; daughter of Arthur (an insurance agent) and Martha (Espy) Wright; married Niven Busch (a story editor), 1942 (divorced); married Robert Woodruff Anderson (divorced); married Carlos Pierre (marriage ended); remarried Robert Woodruff Anderson. *Education:* Attended Columbia High School, Maplewood, NJ; studied acting at Wharf Theatre, Provincetown, MA, 1937-38.

CAREER: Actress. Performed with Tanworth Barnstormers, Tanworth, NH, 1939, Hartford Stage Company, Hartford, CT, 1970-71, and Long Wharf Theatre, New Haven, CT, 1971-72; Cleveland Playhouse, Cleveland, OH, guest artist, 1978-79.

AWARDS, HONORS: Academy Award nomination, best supporting actress, 1941, for *The Little Foxes;* Academy Award nomination, best actress, 1942, for *The Pride of the Yankees;* Academy Award, best supporting actress, 1942, for *Mrs. Miniver;* Emmy Award nomination, best actress in a single performance, 1957, for "The Miracle Worker," *Playhouse 90;* Emmy Award nomination, outstanding actress in a single performance, 1960, for "The Margaret Bourke-White Story," *Sunday Showcase;* Drama Desk Special Award (with Nancy Marchand, Maureen O'Sullivan, and Elizabeth Wilson), outstanding ensemble performance, 1979; Emmy Award nomination, outstanding guest actress in a drama series, 1989, for *Dolphin Cove.*

CREDITS:

STAGE APPEARANCES

Understudy for Emily, *Our Town* (also see below), Henry Miller's Theatre, New York City, 1938.

Blossom Trexel, *Susan and God,* Wharf Theatre, Provincetown, MA, 1938.

Mary Skinner, *Life with Father,* Empire Theatre, New York City, 1939-41.

Linnea Ecklund, *Salt of the Earth,* Shubert Theatre, New Haven, CT, 1952.

Bell, Book, and Candle, Sombrero Playhouse, Phoenix, AZ, 1953.

Lizzy Curry, *The Rainmaker,* La Jolla Playhouse, La Jolla, CA, 1954.

Cora Flood, *The Dark at the Top of the Stairs,* Music Box Theatre, New York City, 1957.

Alice, *I Never Sang for My Father,* Longacre Theatre, New York City, 1968.

Mary Hallen, *Who's Happy Now?,* Village South Theatre, New York City, 1969.

A Passage to E. M. Forster (concert reading), Theatre de Lys, New York City, 1970.

Mary Tyrone, *Long Day's Journey into Night,* Hartford Stage Company Theatre, Hartford, CT, 1971.

Death of a Salesman, Philadelphia Drama Guild, Philadelphia, PA, 1973-74.

Linda Loman, *Death of a Salesman,* Walnut Theatre, Philadelphia, 1974, then Circle in the Square, New York City, 1975.

The Soldier's Tale and *The Knight of the Burning Pestle* (double bill), Long Wharf Theatre, New Haven, CT, 1974-75.

Lily Miller, *Ah, Wilderness!,* Circle in the Square, 1975.

Suite in Two Keys, Arlington Park Theatre, Arlington Heights, IL, 1976-77.

The Master Builder, Eisenhower Theatre, Washington, DC, 1977.

All the Way Home, Hartford Stage Company Theatre, 1977-78.

Threads, Cleveland Playhouse, Cleveland, OH, 1978-79.

Cora Swanson, *Morning's at Seven,* Lyceum Theatre, New York City, 1980-81, then Center Theatre Group, Ahmanson Theatre, Los Angeles, CA, 1981-82.

Emily, *Wings,* Old Globe Theatre, San Diego, CA, 1983.

All's Well That Ends Well, Folger Shakespeare Theatre, Washington, DC, 1987-88.

Also appeared as the daughter, *The Vinegar Tree,* 1938; in *The King's Maid,* Boston, MA, 1941; as Georgia Elgin, *The Country Girl,* Vancouver, British Columbia, 1953; in *The Heiress,* Palm Springs, CA, 1954; and in *You Can't Take It with You.*

MAJOR TOURS

Rebecca, then Emily, *Our Town,* eastern U.S. cities, 1938-39.
The little girl, *What a Life,* U.S. cities, 1939.
Pheasant, *White Oaks,* U.S. cities, 1939.
Mary McKellaway, *Mary, Mary,* U.S. cities, 1962.
Pamela Pew-Picket, *Tchin-Tchin,* U.S. cities, 1963.
Katherine Butler Hathaway, *The Locksmith,* U.S. cities, 1965.
Beatrice, *The Effect of Gamma Rays on Man-in-the-Moon Marigolds,* U.S. cities, 1972-73.

FILM APPEARANCES

Alexandra Giddens, *The Little Foxes,* RKO Radio Pictures, 1941.
Carol Beldon, *Mrs. Miniver,* Metro-Goldwyn-Mayer (MGM), 1942.
Eleanor Gehrig, *The Pride of the Yankees,* RKO Radio Pictures, 1942.
Young Charlie, *Shadow of a Doubt,* Universal, 1943.
Isabel Drury, *Casanova Brown,* RKO Pictures, 1944.
Peggy Stephenson, *The Best Years of Our Lives,* RKO Pictures, 1946.
Millicent Hopkins, *The Imperfect Lady,* Paramount, 1947.
Thorley Callum, *Pursued,* Warner Bros., 1947.
Kate Farrell, *The Trouble with Women,* Paramount, 1947.
Lark Ingoldsby, *Enchantment,* RKO Radio Pictures, 1948.
Ellen, *The Capture,* RKO Radio Pictures, 1950.
Ellen, *The Men* (also known as *Battle Stripe*), United Artists (UA), 1950.
Julia Lawrence, *California Conquest,* Columbia, 1952.
Edna Miller, *Something to Live For,* Paramount, 1952.
Laurie Osborne, *The Steel Trap,* Twentieth Century-Fox, 1952.
Annie Jones, *The Actress,* MGM, 1953.
Ellen Braden, *Count the Hours* (also known as *Every Minute Counts*), RKO Radio Pictures, 1953.
Grace Bridges, *Track of the Cat,* Warner Bros., 1954.
Ruth Simmons, *The Search for Bridey Murphy,* Paramount, 1956.
Mary Saunders, *Escapade in Japan,* Universal/RKO Radio Pictures, 1957.
Elizabeth Grant, *The Restless Years* (also known as *The Wonderful Years*), Universal, 1958.
Santha Dixon, *Hail, Hero!,* National General, 1969.
Mrs. Spencer, *The Happy Ending,* UA, 1969.
May, *Roseland,* Cinema Shares International, 1977.
Laura Roberts, *Somewhere in Time,* Universal, 1980.
Grandmother, *The Good Mother,* Buena Vista, 1988.

TELEVISION APPEARANCES; EPISODIC

"The Sound of Waves Breaking," *Lux Video Theater,* CBS, 1952.
"And Never Come Back," *Robert Montgomery Presents Your Lucky Strike Theater,* NBC, 1952.
"Dress in the Window," *Schlitz Playhouse of Stars,* CBS, 1952.
"Alicia," *Hollywood Opening Night,* NBC, 1952.
"And Suddenly You Knew," *Ford Television Theater,* NBC, 1953.
"The Happiest Day," *Ford Television Theater,* NBC, 1954.
"The End of Paul Dane," *U.S. Steel Hour,* ABC, 1954.
"The Long Goodbye," *Climax,* CBS, 1954.
Henry Fonda Presents the Star and the Story, syndicated, 1955.
"Stars Don't Shine," *Ford Television Theater,* NBC, 1955.
"The Good Sisters," *Four Star Playhouse,* CBS, 1955.
"Love Is Eternal," *General Electric Theater,* CBS, 1955.
"Her Crowning Glory," *Rheingold Theater,* NBC, 1955.
"Driftwood," *Elgin Hour,* ABC, 1955.
"Red Gulch," *U.S. Steel Hour,* ABC, 1955.
"Intolerable Portrait," *Your Play Time,* NBC, 1955.
"My Uncle O'Moore," *Loretta Young Show,* NBC, 1955.
"The Enchanted Cottage," *Lux Video Theater,* NBC, 1955.
"Lady in the Wind," *Ford Television Theater,* NBC, 1955.
Judith, "The Devil's Disciple," *Hallmark Hall of Fame,* NBC, 1955.
"Undertow," *Alcoa Hour,* NBC, 1955.
Doris Walker, "Miracle on 34th Street," *Twentieth Century-Fox Hour,* CBS, 1955.
"Number Five Checked Out," *Screen Directors Playhouse,* NBC, 1956.
"Once to Every Woman," *Four Star Playhouse,* CBS, 1956.
Title role, "The Louella Parsons Story," *Climax,* CBS, 1956.
"The Secret Place," *Star Stage,* NBC, 1956.
"The Lonely Ones," *Rheingold Theater,* NBC, 1956.
"The Faithful Heart," *Studio '57,* syndicated, 1956.
"Witness to Condemn," *Schlitz Playhouse of Stars,* CBS, 1956.
"Child of the Regiment," *Twentieth Century-Fox Hour,* CBS, 1956.
Annie Sullivan, "The Miracle Worker," *Playhouse 90,* CBS, 1957.
"Sister Louise Goes to Town," *Schlitz Playhouse of Stars,* CBS, 1957.
"Edge of Innocence," *Playhouse 90,* CBS, 1957.

"Trap for a Stranger," *U.S. Steel Hour,* CBS, 1959.
"The Hours Before Dawn," *U.S. Steel Hour,* CBS, 1959.
"Pit of Silence," *Adventures in Paradise,* ABC, 1959.
"The Margaret Bourke-White Story," *Sunday Showcase,* NBC, 1960.
"Shadow of a Soldier," *Our American Heritage,* NBC, 1960.
Margit Brandt, "Intermezzo," *Theater '62,* NBC, 1961.
"The Big Laugh," *U.S. Steel Hour,* CBS, 1962.
"Big Deal in Laredo," *DuPont Show of the Month,* NBC, 1962.
"Three Wives Too Many," *Alfred Hitchcock Hour,* CBS, 1964.
"My Son, My Son," *Bonanza,* NBC, 1964.
"The Pill Man," *The Defenders,* CBS, 1964.
"Lonely Place," *Alfred Hitchcock Hour,* NBC, 1964.
"The Prosecutor," *The Defenders,* CBS, 1965.
"Yesterday's Vengeance," *Lancer,* CBS, 1969.
"Appalachian Autumn," *CBS Playhouse,* CBS, 1969.
"The Camerons Are a Special Clan," *Owen Marshall, Counselor at Law,* ABC, 1973.
"Murder on the 13th Floor," *Hawkins,* CBS, 1974.
"Terror in the Night," *Wide World of Mystery,* ABC, 1976.
Grandpa Goes to Washington, NBC, 1978.
"The Golden Honeymoon," *American Short Story,* PBS, 1980.
"The Christmas Presence," *The Love Boat,* ABC, 1982.
The Guiding Light, CBS, 1986.
"The Firebird," *Morning Star/Evening Star,* CBS, 1986.
Alice Blair, "A Rose for Alice," *Morning Star/Evening Star,* CBS, 1986.
Sophia Jane, "The Fig Tree," *WonderWorks,* PBS, 1987.
"Mr. Penroy's Vacation," *Murder, She Wrote,* CBS, 1988.
Dolphin Cove, CBS, 1989.
Myra Holcombe, "Lethal Innocence" (also known as "Vermont/Cambodia Story"), *American Playhouse,* PBS, 1991.

Also appeared on *The Kate Smith Show.*

OTHER TELEVISION APPEARANCES

Eleanor Hilliard, *The Desperate Hours* (special), ABC, 1967.
Alice Graves, *Crawlspace* (movie), CBS, 1972.
Edith Reynolds, *The Elevator* (movie), ABC, 1974.
Alice Cutler, *Flood* (movie), NBC, 1976.
Mae Driscoll, *Bill: On His Own* (movie), CBS, 1983.
Mothers by Daughters (special), PBS, 1985.
Helene Berman, *Perry Mason: The Case of the Desperate Deception* (movie; also known as *The Case of the Paris Paradox*), NBC, 1990.*

Y-Z

YESTON, Maury 1945-

PERSONAL: Born October (one source says December) 23, 1945, in Jersey City, NJ; son of David (in business) and Frances (in business; maiden name, Haar) Yeston; married Anne Sheedy (a flutist), November 13, 1982; children: Jake, Max. *Education:* Yale University, B.A., 1967, Ph.D., 1974; Clare College, Cambridge University, M.A., 1972 (one source says 1969); trained for the stage with the BMI Musical Theatre workshop and Lehman Engel.

ADDRESSES: Agent—Flora Roberts, 157 West 57th St., New York, NY 10019.

CAREER: Composer and lyricist. Yale University, New Haven, CT, associate professor in department of music, 1974-82, director of undergraduate studies in music, 1976-82; BMI Musical Theatre Workshop, teacher, beginning in 1982.

MEMBER: Dramatists Guild, Society of Music Theory, American Musicological Society.

AWARDS, HONORS: Antoinette Perry Award, best score of a musical, Grammy Award nomination (with Michael Berniker), best cast show album, and Drama Desk Award, best score of a musical, all 1982, all for *Nine;* BMI Award, 1982; Antoinette Perry Award nomination (with George Forrest and Robert Wright), best original musical score, 1990, for *Grand Hotel.*

CREDITS:

TELEVISION APPEARANCES; EPISODIC

"You're the Top: The Cole Porter Story," *American Masters,* PBS, 1990.

RECORDINGS:

Has recorded "Goya: A Life in Song," 1989.

WRITINGS:

STAGE MUSIC

Title song and incidental music, *Cloud Nine,* Theatre de Lys, New York City, 1981.

Music and lyrics, *Nine,* produced at Forty-Sixth Street Theatre, 1982, libretto published as *Nine: The Musical,* Doubleday, 1983.

Music and lyrics, *One Two Three Four Five,* Manhattan Theatre Club, City Center Stage II, New York City, 1987.

Additional music and lyrics, *Grand Hotel,* Martin Beck Theatre, New York City, 1989.

ORCHESTRAL COMPOSITIONS

Composer of "Movement for Cello and Orchestra," first performed in 1967.

OTHER

The Stratification of Musical Rhythm, Yale University Press, 1976.

(Editor) *Readings in Schenker Analysis and Other Approaches,* Yale University Press, 1977.*

* * *

ZEA, Kristi 1948-

PERSONAL: Born in New York City, 1948. *Education:* Attended the High School of Music and Art, New York City; Columbia University, New York City, B.A.

ADDRESSES: Agent—Boaty Boatwright, c/o International Creative Management, 40 West 57th St., New York, NY 10019.

CAREER: Costume and production designer. Worked as a stylist for a commercial photographer before becoming a free-lance commercial stylist and art director; over a fifteen year span worked as consultant, costume designer, production designer, associate producer, and director for numerous movies, plays, and television programs.

MEMBER: United Scenic Artists, Directors Guild of America, Phi Beta Kappa.

CREDITS:

FILM COSTUME DESIGNER

Fame, United Artists, 1980.
Endless Love, Universal, 1981.
Shoot the Moon, Metro-Goldwyn-Mayer, 1982.
Lovesick, Warner Brothers, 1983.
Terms of Endearment, Paramount, 1983.
Beat Street, Orion, 1984.
Best Defense, Paramount, 1984.
Birdy, Tri-Star, 1984.
Unfaithfully Yours, Twentieth Century-Fox, 1984.
Silverado, Columbia, 1985.
Dead End Kids, Ikon-Mabou Mines, 1986.

FILM PRODUCTION DESIGNER

Married to the Mob, Orion, 1988.
Miss Firecracker, Corsair, 1989.
"Life Lessons," *New York Stories* (triple-feature; also contains "Life without Zoe," and "Oedipus Wrecks"), Buena Vista, 1989.
Goodfellas, Warner Brothers, 1990.
The Silence of the Lambs, Orion, 1991.
The Super, Twentieth Century-Fox, 1991.

OTHER FILM WORK

Costume designer for Diane Keaton, *The Little Drummer Girl,* Warner Brothers, 1984.
Associate producer, *Lucas,* Twentieth Century-Fox, 1986.
New York art director, *Angel Heart,* Tri-Star, 1987.

TELEVISION WORK; MOVIES

Costume designer, *For Ladies Only* (movie), NBC, 1981.

TELEVISION WORK; EPISODIC

Director, "A Domestic Dilemma," *Women & Men 2* (also known as *Women & Men: In Love There Are No Rules*), HBO, 1991.

STAGE COSTUME DESIGNER

The Balcony, American Repertory Theatre, Cambridge, MA, 1985.

OTHER SOURCES:

PERIODICALS

Cine Fantastique, February, 1992.
New York, July 15, 1991.
New York Times, August 18, 1991
Premiere, September, 1991, pp. 44-45.
Theatre Crafts, April, 1989, pp. 58-67.

* * *

ZIEFF, Howard 1943-

PERSONAL: Born in 1943, in Los Angeles, CA.

ADDRESSES: *Agent*—Mike Marcus, Creative Artists Agency, 9830 Wilshire Blvd., Beverly Hills, CA 90212.

CAREER: Director. Worked as a newsreel photographer for a television station in Los Angeles, CA; still and advertising photographer in New York City.

AWARDS, HONORS: Advertising awards for television commercial photography.

CREDITS:

FILM DIRECTOR

Slither, Metro-Goldwyn-Mayer (MGM), 1973.
Hearts of the West (also known as *Hollywood Cowboy*), MGM/United Artists, 1975.
House Calls, Universal, 1978.
The Main Event, Warner Brothers, 1979.
Private Benjamin, Warner Brothers, 1980.
Unfaithfully Yours, Twentieth Century-Fox, 1984.
The Dream Team, Universal, 1989.
My Girl, Columbia, 1991.

TELEVISION DIRECTOR; SERIES

House Calls, CBS, 1979.
Private Benjamin, CBS, 1981.

OTHER SOURCES:

PERIODICALS

Film Comment, April, 1984, pg. 57.*

* * *

ZIMMER, Hans 1958(?)-

PERSONAL: Born c. 1958, in Frankfurt, Germany.

ADDRESSES: *Agent*—Gorfaine-Schwartz Agency, 3301 Barham Blvd., Suite 201, Los Angeles, CA 90068.

CAREER: Composer and musician. Member of musical group The Buggles, late 1970s.

AWARDS, HONORS: Academy Award nomination, best achievement in music, original score, 1988, for *Rain Man;* British Academy of Film and Television Arts Award nomination, best original film music, 1992, for *Thelma and Louise.*

CREDITS:

FILM WORK

Music producer, *The Last Emperor,* Columbia, 1987.

WRITINGS:

FILM SCORES

(With Stanley Myers) *Moonlighting,* Universal, 1982.
(With Myers) *Success Is the Best Revenge,* Gaumont, 1984.
Terminal Exposure (also known as *Double Exposure*), Omega, 1987.
(With Myers) *The Wind,* Omega, 1987.
(With Myers) *The Zero Boys,* Omega, 1987.
(With Myers) *Taffin,* Metro-Goldwyn-Mayer/United Artists (MGM/UA), 1988.
Wonderland (also known as *The Fruit Machine*), Vestron, 1988.
(With Myers) *The Nature of the Beast,* Film Four International, 1988.
(With Luis Bonfa) *Prisoner of Rio,* Multi Media/Samba, 1988.
Burning Secret, Vestron, 1988.
(With Myers) *Paperhouse,* Vestron, 1988.
Rain Man, MGM/UA, 1988.
A World Apart, Atlantic, 1988.
Paperhouse, Vestron, 1988.
Black Rain, Paramount, 1989.
Diamond Skulls, Film Four/British Screen, 1989.
Driving Miss Daisy, Warner Brothers, 1989.
Twister, Greycat Films, 1989.
Bird on a Wire, Universal, 1990.
Chicago Joe and the Showgirl, New Line Cinema, 1990.
Days of Thunder, Paramount, 1990.
Fools of Fortune, New Line Cinema, 1990.
Green Card, Buena Vista, 1990.
The Neverending Story II: The Next Chapter, Warner Brothers, 1990.
Pacific Heights, Twentieth Century-Fox, 1990.
Backdraft, Universal, 1991.
Regarding Henry, Paramount, 1991.
Thelma and Louise, MGM/Pathe, 1991.
Radio Flyer, Columbia, 1991.
The Power of One, Warner Bros., 1992.
A League of Their Own, Columbia, 1992.

Also wrote music for *Arcadia,* 1988.

TELEVISION MUSIC

Wild Horses (movie), CBS, 1985.
First Born (movie), Arts and Entertainment, 1989.
To the Moon, Alice (special), Showtime, 1990.
Millennium: Tribal Wisdom and the Modern World (mini-series), PBS, 1992.

OTHER SOURCES:

PERIODICALS

Premiere, May, 1991, p. 46.*

* * *

ZINNEMANN, Tim

PERSONAL: Born in Los Angeles, CA; son of Fred Zinnemann (a director). *Education:* Attended Columbia University.

CAREER: Producer. Began career as a film editor; has also worked as an assistant director.

AWARDS, HONORS: Emmy Award nomination, outstanding drama or comedy special, 1979, for *The Jericho Mile.*

CREDITS:

FILM PRODUCER, EXCEPT WHERE INDICATED

(With Stanley Beck) *Straight Time,* Warner Bros., 1978.
The Long Riders, United Artists, 1980.
A Small Circle of Friends, United Artists, 1980.
Tex, Buena Vista, 1982.
Impulse, Twentieth Century-Fox, 1984.
Executive producer, *Crossroads,* Columbia, 1986.
(With George Linder) *The Running Man,* Tri-Star, 1987.
Executive producer, *Pet Sematary,* Paramount, 1989.

FILM ASSISTANT DIRECTOR

The Great White Hope, Twentieth Century-Fox, 1970.
Carnal Knowledge, Avco Embassy, 1971.
(And associate producer) *The Cowboys,* Warner Bros., 1972.
The King of Marvin Gardens, Columbia, 1972.
Cinderella Liberty, Twentieth Century-Fox, 1973.
(And associate producer) *Smile,* United Artists, 1975.
The Day of the Locust, Paramount, 1975.
(And unit production manager) *Farewell, My Lovely,* Avco Embassy, 1975.

TELEVISION WORK; MOVIES

Producer, *The Jericho Mile,* ABC, 1979.*

Cumulative Index

To provide continuity with *Who's Who in the Theatre,* this index interfiles references to *Who's Who in the Theatre,* 1st-17th Editions, and *Who Was Who in the Theatre* (Gale, 1978) with references to *Contemporary Theatre, Film, and Television,* Volumes 1-10.

References in the index are identified as follows:

CTFT and volume number—*Contemporary Theatre, Film, and Television,* Volumes 1-10
WWT and edition number—*Who's Who in the Theatre,* 1st-17th Editions
WWasWT—*Who Was Who in the Theatre*

C

D

E

F

G

H

I

J

L

Cumulative Index

M

N

O

P

Q

R

S

T

U

V

W

Cumulative Index